McGraw-Hill
Modern
Scientists
and
Engineers

Volume 1 A-G

McGraw-Hill Book Company

New York
St. Louis
San Francisco

Auckland	London	New Delhi	Singapore
Bogotá	Madrid	Panama	Sydney
Hamburg	Mexico	Paris	Tokyo
Johannesburg	Montreal	São Paulo	Toronto

McGraw-Hill
Modern Scientists and Engineers

Volume 1 A-G

Library of Congress Cataloging in Publication Data

McGraw-Hill modern scientists and engineers.

    Edition of 1966-1968 published under title:
McGraw-Hill modern men of science.
    Includes indexes.
    1. Scientists—Biography. 2. Engineers—Biography.
I. McGraw-Hill Book Company. II. McGraw-Hill modern
men of science.
Q141.M15 1980   509'.22   79-24383
ISBN 0-07-045266-0

Contents of Volume 1

A solid star indicates an autobiography. An open star indicates
a biography approved by the subject but written by someone else.
No star indicates that the subject has not reviewed the biography.

Preface

THE MCGRAW-HILL MODERN SCIENTISTS AND ENGINEERS is a revised and expanded edition of the *McGraw-Hill Modern Men of Science* (vol. 1, 1966; vol. 2, 1968). These volumes were acclaimed as a ". . . compendium of contemporary scientific biographies [which] furnishes a fine and, in some respects, unique reference source. . . ." *(Booklist). Science Books* highly recommended them for "Readers who desire authoritative, meaningful accounts of scientific achievement. . . ." This new edition continues in the spirit of the original volumes, fulfilling the objective ". . . to present extended biographical data on contemporary leaders of science [and engineering] around the world in a form possessing reference value for the librarian and educational value for the student."

The technical literature reports on discoveries and developments without consideration of the researchers themselves. Professional directories and other reference works generally provide little more than conventional biographical chronologies. The unique collection of in-depth, authoritative biographies in the three volumes of *Modern Scientists and Engineers* gives a meaningful account of individual achievements by revealing the workings of the scientific mind in dealing with problems and finding solutions. Through these detailed accounts of personal experience the reader is able to better understand the complexities of modern science and engineering and is brought closer to the world of the scientific community.

Building on the original publication, this edition reflects the vast proliferation of scientific and technological advances since the 1960s. Three hundred of the 1140 biographies are new. As before, the individuals were selected by the editors from recipients of major awards and prizes given by the leading societies, organizations, and institutions of the world. The scope is international and extends in time from the leaders of the 1920s to the 1978 Nobel Prize winners. We regret that space limitations prevented us from inviting many outstanding men and women to participate in this work, and we would like to express our appreciation to those who did.

To ensure accuracy and authority, each person, to the extent possible, was asked to write about his or her own work. Nearly a thousand kindly agreed to do so, and these autobiographical entries are designated by a solid star in the heading of the article. The remaining articles were prepared by qualified specialists, that is, associates, relatives, or professionals with the expertise to understand and interpret the subject's work. These articles were reviewed and corrected by the subject, whenever possible, and are designated by an open star in the heading. Some of the subjects (usually deceased) were not able to review the material; in such cases, the Consulting Editors acted as referees. These articles can be identified by the absence of a star. In addition, all of the biographies originally published in *Modern Men of Science* were updated either by the subject, if living, or by the editors.

Science is a cooperative enterprise that relies on collaboration and the exchange of information. Many of the individuals in this work have cooperated with or influenced each other as they endeavored to succeed in their investigations. To guide the reader in following these interactions, the articles contain cross-references to related articles in the three volumes. These are set in small capitals for emphasis.

Although *Modern Scientists and Engineers* can be used independently, it is useful as a biographical supplement to the *McGraw-Hill Encyclopedia of Science and Technology* (4th ed., 1977). Conversely, the Encyclopedia provides comprehensive coverage of the specialized disciplines discussed in the biographies. Therefore, at the end of an article, reference may be made to subjects in the Encyclopedia for "background" information.

Access to the material is simplified by a table of contents in each volume and by the two-part index in volume 3. The first part is a field index grouping articles according to the biographee's area of interest. A name may appear under more than one field if there is more than one area of activity. All names are listed under general categories (such as biology, chemistry, physics, or engineering); some names are repeated for specialized areas (such as zoology, analytical chemistry, theoretical physics, or civil engineering). The second part, an analytical index, directs the reader to every mention of a person or subject in the volumes.

We would like to express our appreciation to the following contributors, to whom we are indebted: Prof. E. N. da C. Andrade (for the article on Sir Edward Appleton); Lt. Col. Cortland P. Auser; William R. Bauer (Jerome R. Vinograd); Douglas W. Bowden, Jr.; Maj. Ray L. Bowers; Charles K. Bradsher (Charles R. Hauser); Peter Castro; Dr. Charles J. Cazeau; Dr. Charles V. Clemency; Dr. Rita H. Cornforth (John W. Cornforth); Dr. Richard E. Cover; Sir Gavin de Beer (Sir Julian Huxley); Prof. Maurice Ewing (Merle A. Tuve); Prof. Walter Feit (Richard D. Brauer); George Foley (Sidney Farber); Scott E. Forbush (Julius Bartels); Edgar N. Gilbert (Harry Nyquist); Dr. Victor Goertzel (Linus Pauling); Dr. Leon B. Gortler; Anne Greenberg; Marvin A. Gross; Dr. Hyman Guthwin; Raymond F. Halloran; Dr. Joseph H. Hamilton; Dr. Margaret K. Harlow (Harry F. Harlow); Prof. James B. Hendrickson (R. B. Woodward); Arvid Herzenberg (George J. Schulz); Prof. Antony Hewish (Sir Martin Ryle); Harold G. Kastan; C. Glen King (Paul Gyorgy); Dr. John S. King; Diederik E. Kuenen (Philip H. Kuenen); Daniel N. Lapedes; Thomas G. Lawrence; Richard Lefler; Prof. I. R. Lehman; Dr. Norman L. Levin; Alan D. Levy; Warren K. Lewis, Jr., and Rosalind H. Williams (Warren K. Lewis); Moses R. Lipeles; Robert A. Lufburrow; Wallace Manheimer; Dr. Vincent E. McKelvey (Donald F. Hewett); H. P. Mlejnek (John H. Argyris); Dr. James E. Mulvaney (Carl S. Marvel); Dr. Jytte Muus (Gertrude E. Perlmann); Dr. Thomas F. Nealon, Jr., and Mrs. Lovell Thompson (John H. Gibbon, Jr.); Herbert A. Nestler; Anne M. Newman; Matthew Notkins; Prof. Frank Press (Hugo Benioff); G. Alan Robison (Earl W. Sutherland); Herb Rosen (John S. Foster, Jr.); Maj. John H. Scrivner, Jr.; Claudio Segre (Emilio Segre); Dorothy Sheffield (George B. Dantzig); Lavonne O. Tarleton; Marie Tharp (Bruce C. Heezen); Prof. John G. Trump (Robert Jemison Van de Graaff); Dr. Tien-tzou Tsong (Erwin W. Mueller); G. J. van den Berg (Cornelis Gorter, Jr.); Prof. Hao Wang (Kurt Gödel); Robert Weinberger; Dr. Harold Weinstock; Harvey Weiss; Dr. Glenn Wiggins (Edmund M. Walker); Bob D. Wilder; Prof. L. Wilke (Karl Ziegler); Bernard Witkop (Percy L. Julian); Marvin Yelles; Dr. David D. Zink; and Morris Ziskind.

Finally, we gratefully acknowledge the contribution of Dr. Jay E. Greene, Editor in Chief of vol. 1 of the original *Modern Men of Science*.

Sybil P. Parker
Editor in Chief

McGraw-Hill
Modern Scientists and Engineers

Volume 1 A-G

ABELSON, PHILIP HAUGE
★ American geochemist

Born Apr. 27, 1913, Tacoma, WA, U.S.A.

Abelson made contributions to the fields of nuclear physics, chemistry, microbiology, organic geochemistry, and to studies of the origin of life. He also wrote many items on science policy.

As a graduate student in 1939 at the Radiation Laboratory, University of California, Berkeley, Abelson was the first American scientist to identify products of uranium fission. These included three radioactive isotopes of antimony, six of tellurium, and four of iodine. In 1940 Abelson's attention focused on some work that E. M. McMillan had done the previous year on neutron irradiation of thin layers containing uranium. McMillan had found that most of the fission products escaped from the layer, but that a nonrecoiling 2.3-day beta emitter remained. Emilio Segrè had postulated that the activity followed the chemistry of the ordinary rare earths and that the substance was not a transuranic. An alternative explanation occurred to Abelson. He felt that the activity was due to element 93, but that instead of being an ekarhenium, element 93 was a member of a new rare-earth series. Pointing out that cerium could exist in two valence states, Abelson thought that the easiest way to demonstrate the existence of element 93 might be by its response to oxidizing and reducing agents. He conducted some experiments at the department of terrestrial magnetism of the Carnegie Institution of Washington with encouraging but not clear-cut results. The intensities there did not permit use of thin-foil technique. *See* MCMILLAN, EDWIN MATTISON.

Abelson went to Berkeley and discussed his ideas with McMillan. The two scientists then collaborated in the discovery of element 93 (neptunium). McMillan prepared and irradiated some of his thin-layer material. Within a day Abelson demonstrated that the 2.3-day activity could exist in at least two valence states. In the reduced state the fluoride was precipitated with a cerium carrier. However, in the presence of fluoride and bromate in acid solution, the activity remained in solution while fission-product rare earths precipitated. Abelson also learned that element 93 is more readily reduced than uranium. Thus he was able to show by repeated precipitations that the 2.3-day activity is the daughter of a 23-minute uranium activity. The total duration of the research plus preparation of a letter to the editor of the *Physical Review* was 5 days.

In 1940 nuclear physicists were already talking of the possibility of nuclear reactors and atomic weapons. There was uncertainty whether a chain reaction could be established using natural uranium. Uranium enriched in ^{235}U seemed the key to many possibilities; partial enrichment of ^{235}U would guarantee a successful chain reaction. One application advocated by Ross Gunn of the Naval Research Laboratory was as a source of power for submarines.

The prospects for large-scale isotope separation were dim. At that time only microgram quantities of uranium had been fractionated. Few uranium chemicals were available. Abelson devised a method for large-scale synthesis of UF_6 from UF_4 and produced the first 100 kilograms of the substance. He discovered that the uranium isotopes could be partially separated by liquid thermal diffusion. The process was conducted in an annular space with cold wall at 70°C and hot wall at 286°C, with columns 14 meters long. In a single column a maximum enrichment from 0.7 percent ^{235}U to 1.4 percent ^{235}U was obtained. By mid-1943 more than 100 kilograms of partially fractionated ^{235}U had been obtained, by far the largest amount of fractionated uranium available at that time. A small pilot plant at the Naval Research Laboratory, then a larger pilot plant at the Philadelphia Naval Base,

and finally a 2100-column plant at Oak Ridge, TN, were built. The partially enriched uranium (0.85 percent ^{235}U) was used as feed for the electromagnetic separation plant, which in turn produced the ^{235}U employed in one of the first atomic bombs.

After World War II Abelson led a small group that prepared a feasibility report (dated Mar. 28, 1946) on the atomic submarine. The group showed that a nuclear reactor, shielding, and associated propulsion equipment could be substituted for the then conventional equipment and that a very useful submarine might result. Among the advantages cited for an atomic submarine was long range at high speed under water. The report also stated that "this fast submarine will serve as an ideal carrier and launcher of rocketed atomic bombs."

In 1946 Abelson began a new scientific career in biophysics. The new venture was a consequence of discussions involving M. A. Tuve, then recently appointed director of the department of terrestrial magnetism of the Carnegie Institution of Washington. Abelson and Tuve concluded that one of the great future frontiers lay in the application of physical methods and theory to biological problems. Subsequently, Abelson was appointed chairperson of a biophysics section, which soon included four physicists and a biologist. The group exploited opportunities created by availability of radioactive tracers, notably ^{14}C. Using tagged glucose and other tagged compounds, including amino acids and CO_2, and employing the technique of isotopic competition, Abelson outlined many of the pathways of the biosynthesis of amino acids in microorganisms. See TUVE, MERLE ANTONY.

In 1953 Abelson became director of the Geophysical Laboratory of the Carnegie Institution of Washington and embarked on still another career as one of the nation's pioneers in organic geochemistry. Among his discoveries was the identification of original amino acids preserved in fossils, especially shells. He found alanine, glutamic acid, glycine, leucine, and valine in many old fossils. Subsequently, with T. C. Hoering and Patrick Parker, Abelson isolated fatty acids in old rocks, including some more than a billion years old. In the late 1960s Abelson also elucidated some of the mechanisms involved in the conversion of biological ma-

terials into natural gas and petroleum. An important step is incorporation of amino acids into humic acid and kerogen. Abelson also contributed to the study of the origin of life. He pointed out in 1966 that most model experiments, such as that of S. L. Miller and H. C. Urey, employ assumptions not consonant with the realities of geochemistry. Abelson advanced evidence to support the hypothesis that the Earth's primitive atmosphere consisted largely of CO, N_2, and H_2. Solar irradiation of this mixture produced HCN, which polymerized in the primitive ocean, giving rise to amino acids. Abelson further pointed out that the nature of the environment limited the number of compounds available for life, which began in a thin rather than a thick soup. See UREY, HAROLD CLAYTON.

In 1962, in addition to his work at the Carnegie Institution, Abelson accepted the editorship of *Science,* America's leading scientific weekly. In more than 300 editorials and scores of lectures, he treated many aspects of the interaction of science and public policy. He joined J. S. Huxley in the view that humankind now has the power to control its destiny. Abelson felt that at least some scientists should attempt to build bridges between science and society and that such efforts might be the most significant which responsible scientists could engage in during the foreseeable future. See HUXLEY, SIR JULIAN (SORELL).

Abelson entered what is now Washington State University in 1930 and received a B.S. in chemistry in 1933 and an M.S. in physics 2 years later. He then entered the University of California at Berkeley, working with Lawrence and the cyclotron in the Radiation Laboratory. After receiving the Ph.D. in physics in 1939, Abelson became associated with the department of terrestrial magnetism of the Carnegie Institution of Washington. Except for wartime work at the Naval Research Laboratory, he remained with the institution, serving as its president from 1971 to 1978. For his wartime service Abelson was given in 1945 the Navy's highest civilian recognition, the Distinguished Civilian Service Medal. He also received the Modern Medicine Award (1967), Mellon Institute Award from Carnegie-Mellon University (1970), Joseph Priestley Award from Dickinson College (1973), Kalinga Prize from UNESCO (1973), and Scientific Achievement Award of the

American Medical Association (1974). He was elected to the National Academy of Sciences in 1959.

For background information *see* BACTERIAL METABOLISM; BIOSPHERE, GEOCHEMISTRY OF; FISSION NUCLEAR; ISOTOPE; ISOTOPE (STABLE) SEPARATION; REACTOR, SHIP PROPULSION in the McGraw-Hill Encyclopedia of Science and Technology. ∎

ABRAHAM, EDWARD PENLEY
★ British biochemist

***Born** June 10, 1913, Southampton, Hampshire, England*

At the outbreak of World War II Abraham held a Rockefeller Fellowship in Stockholm. He returned to his homeland, and Howard Florey offered him a place in the Sir William Dunn School of Pathology, Oxford. This led to his work on penicillin and later to the discovery of cephalosporin C. See FLOREY OF ADELAIDE, BARON (HOWARD WALTER FLOREY).

In the spring of 1940 a study of penicillin that had been initiated by Florey and E. B. Chain and undertaken with N. G. Heatley reached a highly promising stage. Abraham joined with Chain in attempts to isolate penicillin. By 1941 they had prepared material which could be used in clinical trials, and had also discovered a penicillin-destroying enzyme, penicillinase, which appeared to be partly responsible for penicillin resistance. Subsequently, they collaborated with Sir Robert Robinson, Wilson Baker, J. W. Cornforth, and others of the Dyson Perrins Laboratory, Oxford, and became part of an extensive Anglo-American cooperative effort to determine the structure of penicillin and to produce it synthetically. The work in Oxford led to the characterization of some of the key degradation products of penicillin and to a proposal by Abraham, Chain, and Baker in 1943 of a β-lactam structure for the penicillin molecule. This structure was finally established by x-ray crystallographic analysis by Dorothy Hodgkin and Barbara Low in 1945. *See* CHAIN, ERNST BORIS; CORNFORTH, SIR JOHN (WARCUP); HODGKIN, DOROTHY CROWFOOT; ROBINSON, SIR ROBERT.

After the war Abraham undertook a study of other antibiotics and became interested in biologically active peptides with unusual and unstable chemical groups. He was joined by Guy Newton, who came as a D.Phil. student and remained a close and highly valued collaborator until his premature death in 1969. They isolated the antibacterial peptide, bacitracin, and showed that it contained a labile thiazoline ring. Bacitracin had chemotherapeutic properties, but its toxicity to the kidney precluded its widespread use in medicine.

The interest in unstable peptides and the wartime work on penicillin bore further fruit in 1953 with the discovery of the first cephalosporin. In 1945 Giuseppi Brotzu had isolated a species of *Cephalosporium* from a sewage out-fall at Cagliari, Sardinia, and had shown that it produced material with activity against a variety of bacteria. He believed that his crude product showed promise of being clinically useful, but was unable to carry his observations further and failed to interest Italian pharmaceutical companies. Thus, in 1948, he sent a culture of his *Cephalosporium* to Oxford.

Early studies in the Sir William Dunn School of Pathology showed that Brotzu's fungus produced an antibiotic which was soluble in organic solvents and was active against only a few species of bacteria. Abraham concluded that this could not be the substance observed in Sardinia and found that culture fluids of the *Cephalosporium* contained a second antibiotic which was hydrophilic, had a broad range of activity, and behaved in some respects like a labile peptide. With Newton, he purified this substance and showed that it was a new type of penicillin with a δ-linked D-α-aminoadipyl side chain. The new penicillin (I), named

penicillin N, was undoubtedly responsible for the activity seen by Brotzu. Under the

(I)

American name Synnematin, it underwent small clinical trials and was reported to be more effective than chloramphenicol in the treatment of typhoid fever, but it was never produced on a commercial scale.

During an academic chemical study of penicillin N in 1953, Abraham and Newton discovered a third antibiotic which would not have been detected in a conventional screening program. The new substance, cephalosporin C, was the first of the cephalosporins. It had been concentrated during the purification of penicillin N, but was more stable than the latter in acid solutions. Preliminary experiments showed that cephalosporin C was of potential medical interest, beause it resembled penicillin N in some of its properties but was resistant to hydrolysis by penicillinase. At that time penicillinase-producing staphylococci that were highly resistant to penicillin had become prevalent, and there was an acute need for an antibiotic which had the low toxicity of penicillin but retained its activity in the presence of the enzyme.

Helped by a supply of material from an antibiotics research station of the Medical Research Council, Abraham and Newton made a detailed study of the chemistry of cephalosporin C and in 1959 proposed the β-lactam structure (II), which was

(II)

later confirmed by Hodgkin and E. N. Maslen in an x-ray crystallographic analysis. In addition, they showed, with C. W. Hale, that the acetoxy group in the molecule could be readily replaced by other groups to yield cephalosporins with different ranges of activity. Reasoning by analogy, they thought it likely that ceph-

alosporins which would have a much higher activity than cephalosporin C against some bacteria, but would retain a resistance to penicillinase, would be obtained by exchanging the α-aminoadipyl side chain of cephalosporin C for less polar side chains. With Bronwen Loder, they showed that this was so by obtaining the nucleus of the molecule, 7-aminocephalosporanic, in very small yield and attaching the nucleus to different N-acyl groups. The subsequent finding in the Lilly Research Laboratories of a method for producing the nucleus in high yield led to production of very large numbers of cephalosporins by pharmaceutical companies and to the introduction of a succession of cephalosporins into medicine.

After the war the British government founded a National Research Development Corporation whose object was to foster the development of research in the national interest. Patents derived from the work at Oxford on the cephalosporins were assigned to the corporation and earned substantial royalties, since the world sales of these antibiotics climbed in 15 years to more than $1,000,000,000 (U.S.) per annum. Abraham and Newton were able to set up charitable trust funds into which part of the royalties could be diverted for the support of medical, biological, and chemical research.

Abraham graduated with first-class honors from the Queen's College in the school of natural sciences at Oxford in 1936. He received the M.A. and Ph.D. from Oxford in 1941. He became a fellow of Lincoln College, Oxford, in 1948 and professor of chemical pathology in 1964. Elected a fellow of the Royal Society in 1958, Abraham was awarded the society's Royal Medal and became a commander in the Order of the British Empire in 1973. He received the Scheel Medal of the Swedish Academy of Pharmaceutical Sciences and the Chemical Society Award in Medicinal Chemistry (both in 1975). He became an honorary fellow of the Queen's College (1973), Linacre College (1976), and Lady Margaret Hall (1978), Oxford.

Abraham wrote *Biochemistry of Some Peptide and Steroid Antibiotics* (1957) and *Biosynthesis and Enzymic Hydrolysis of Penicillins and Cephalosporins* (1974).

For background information *see* ANTIBOTIC; BACITRACIN; PENICILLIN in the McGraw-Hill Encyclopedia of Science and Technology. ∎

ADAMS, LEASON HEBERLING
★ American geophysicist

Born Jan. 16, 1887, Cherryvale, KS, U.S.A.
Died Aug. 20, 1969, Silver Spring, MD, U.S.A.

In the course of researches on the properties of various materials when exposed to very high pressures, Adams reached the conclusion that precise measurements of the elastic properties of ordinary rocks and rock-forming minerals could be made to yield information, more definite than ever before, on the nature of the Earth's interior. He devised experimental methods for carrying out the necessary measurements and showed how to apply the results to illuminate certain geophysical problems relating to the deeper parts of the Earth. For this achievement, and for other contributions in the field of Earth sciences, he was awarded in 1950 the William Bowie Medal of the American Geophysical Union.

In the late 19th century it was generally believed that the Earth consisted of a relatively thin crust floating on a molten interior. Gradually, however, scientists recognized that this was far too simple a picture of the Earth as a whole. It became evident that with more definite information about the interior, important conclusions could be drawn concerning not only the nature of the interior but the origin and early history of the globe as well. Adams concluded that a key for solving these mysteries would be discovered through a knowledge of the elastic properties of

typical rocks under high pressure. The observations of seismologists had given abundant results on wave velocities at various depths below the surface. These wave velocities depended on the elastic constants of the materials, and measurements of elastic properties—especially bulk modulus and rigidity—could be combined with seismological results to furnish a probe to solve some of the mysteries of the Earth's interior. The difficulty was that in those early days no one had ever succeeded in finding a method for making reliable measurements of the elastic constants of common rocks.

In 1919, while engaged in developing techniques for high-pressure measurements at the Geophysical Laboratory of the Carnegie Institution of Washington, Adams turned his attention to elastic constants. The principal difficulty in determining the elasticity of ordinary rocks was their slight but almost universal porosity, which prevented the application of conventional methods. Adams found a practicable method for solving the problem. This consisted of making a cylinder of the rock, enclosing it in a hermetically sealed thin metal jacket, and subjecting it to high pressure while immersed in a mobile liquid within a pressure vessel. The piston displacement required to generate the given pressure provided a measure of the volume change of the rock and hence of its bulk modules. Adams also showed how the bulk modules alone could be used to determine wave velocities with useful precision.

The first important result of these measurements, obtained by applying some well-known mathematical procedures, was the positive conclusion that the high central density necessary to account for the density of the Earth as a whole could not be produced by the compression of ordinary silicate rocks but must be due to an intrinsically heavy material, such as the nickel-iron of metallic meteorites. Even more important was the discovery that, of all the well-known rock types, only two, dunite and eclogite (a garnet-jadeite rock), have elastic properties that can yield the high wave velocities found by the Albanian seismologist A. Mohorovičić to exist at relatively shallow depths. On various grounds, the first of these two choices is generally preferred, and the striking conclusion is that the whole Earth, except for a nickel-iron core and a thin crust, consists entirely of four chemical elements (iron, magnesium, silicon, and oxygen), the crust

being composed of ordinary rock types, with possibly a thin layer of eclogite rock between the crust and the underlying mantle.

These measurements also had a direct bearing on the differentiation of the Earth into a chemically complex crust and a chemically simple mantle. The Earth and other planets are generally believed to have been formed by the compaction of a primeval dust cloud. This, by the effect of the slight, but important, universal radioactive heating, would eventually become molten and then, by well-known crystallization laws, would produce just such a dunite mantle as is indicated by the elasticity measurements. Not all geophysicists agree with this deduction, but there has been no other simple explanation of the formation of the Earth's crust.

During World War I Adams assisted in the production of optical glass, which had not previously been manufactured in the United States. Together with associates, he invented a method of annealing glass that is particularly advantageous for large blocks. The new procedure was successfully applied in the fabrication of the 200-inch (5.08-meter) mirror for the Mount Palomar telescope. For this work he was given the Longstroth Medal of the Franklin Institute. In World War II he was chief of Division One (ballistics) of the Office of Scientific Research and Development.

A product of the farm belt, Adams spent his early boyhood in central Illinois. He attended a one-room country school, later entering the University of Illinois at 15, and graduating in 1906 with a B.S. in chemical engineering. After serving first as an industrial chemist and then as a physical chemist in the newly formed Technologic Branch of the U.S. Geological Survey, he went in 1910 to the Geophysical Laboratory of the Carnegie Institution of Washington, where he was named director in 1937 and from which he retired in 1952. Thereafter he continued active in research, first as consultant to the director of the National Bureau of Standards and then, from 1958 to 1965, as visiting professor of geophysics (later professor in residence) at the University of California at Los Angeles. He was elected to the National Academy of Sciences in 1943.

For background information *see* EARTH, INTERIOR OF; GEOPHYSICS; HIGH-PRESSURE PHENOMENA in the McGraw-Hill Encyclopedia of Science and Technology. ∎

ADAMS, ROGER
★ American chemist

Born Jan. 2, 1889, Boston, MA, U.S.A.
Died July 6, 1971, Urbana, IL, U.S.A.

While investigating hydrogenation of various unsaturated organic compounds, Adams prepared in a very easy way a noble-metal catalyst that enabled reactions to take place more readily at low temperatures and pressures than had previously been possible with either noble-metal or base-metal catalysts. Now known as the Adams catalyst, this has proved to be of great utility and to be the most satisfactory catalyst for hydrogenation of many types of organic molecules. Not until 40 years after the discovery were other catalysts described that were purported to have activities comparable to or superior to those of the Adams catalyst.

In 1816 the British chemist Humphry Davy was the first to note the catalytic action of platinum. During the next decade the German chemist Johann Wolfgang Döbereiner noted that the catalytic effect was enhanced if the platinum was powdered, that is, was made into what is now called platinum sponge. Catalysis is the most satisfactory method for effectively combining hydrogen with an unsaturated compound. Base-metal catalysts, such as nickel or cobalt, were first used for this purpose by the French chemist Paul Sabatier in 1897.

Although scientists had demonstrated that platinum and palladium were the most active catalysts for hydrogenations at low temperatures and pressures, no easy

method had been discovered for preparing very active palladium and platinum catalysts and no method was known for preparing with certainty in successive experiments platinum or palladium catalysts of uniform activity. Adams prepared platinum and palladium dioxides by fusing chloroplatinic acid or palladium chloride with sodium nitrate. The resulting metal dioxides were isolated by cooling the melt and digesting with water. When he added a small charge of the brown metal oxide to the solution of the unsaturated compound and treated with hydrogen, the oxide was promptly reduced, and a suspension of the black finely divided metal resulted. The metal then catalyzed the hydrogenation of the organic compound. The convenience in preparation and the great effectiveness of the Adams catalyst under mild conditions has been widely recognized.

Adams made extensive studies on the elucidation of structure of many naturally occurring compounds. In 1925, in collaboration with Ralph L. Shriner at the University of Illinois, he investigated the composition of chaulmoogra oil, a mixture of fatty-acid glycerides once used to treat leprosy. Adams established the structure of hydrocarpic and chaulmoogric acids obtained by saponification of the oil and demonstrated the presence in each of a cyclopentene ring. Following this work, he synthesized many analogous acids that, in the form of esters, exhibited physiological action similar to chaulmoogra oil.

Adams determined the structure of gossypol, the toxic yellow pigment of cottonseed, the presence of which restricted for many years the general utilization of cottonseed oil and meal until a cheap and convenient method for its destruction was discovered.

Adams's studies clarifying the structure of the narcotic principle of marijuana demonstrated also that the test commonly used at the time by the Federal Bureau of Narcotics for detection of marijuana was actually indicating merely the presence of an innocuous companion product. Methods for synthesizing analogous substances with similar narcotic properties were developed, and a variety of interesting products was realized.

Researches also were directed to the toxic alkaloids that cause cattle poisoning and that are commonly found in plants on Texas ranches. These compounds occur especially in various species of *Senecio, Crotalaria, Trichodesma,* and *Heliotropium.*

Among Adams's many other investigations were the synthesis of local anesthetics, studies on anthraquinones, organic arsenic compounds, and the synthesis and reactions of a new class of compounds with exceptionally high reactivity, quinone mono- and diimides. In addition, while serving as a major in the Chemical Warfare Service during World War I, he synthesized phenarsazine chloride, a sternutatory substance, better known as Adamsite.

Adams also investigated extensively steric hindrance due to restricted rotation about a single bond as found in substituted biphenyls, diphenylbenzenes, phenylpyrrols, bipyrryls, arylolefins, and arylamines. He demonstrated that substitution in the ortho positions to the bond between the rings was effective in hindering rotation and that the ortho substituents could be arranged in sequence of effectiveness. For example, in the biphenyl series the relative stability of several compounds was studied by measuring the rate of conversion of an optically active form of the substance into its racemic modification. The effectiveness of the groups to slow up the rate of racemization falls into the following order with the bromine atoms showing the greatest effect:

$$Br>CH_3>Cl>NO_2>CO_2H>OCH_3>F$$

The youngest of four children, Adams was educated at Harvard University, receiving his A.B. in 1909, his A.M. in 1910, and his Ph.D. in chemistry in 1912. Afterward he went to the University of Berlin and the Kaiser Wilhelm Institute in Dahlem for further study, returning to Harvard in 1913 as an instructor in organic chemistry. In 1916 he became an assistant professor at the University of Illinois; he was appointed professor there in 1919 and chairperson of the department of chemistry and chemical engineering in 1926. In 1954 he became a research professor and in 1957 professor emeritus.

Among Adams's many awards were the Davy Medal of the Royal Society of London (1945); the A. W. Hofmann Medal of the German Chemical Society (1953); the W. H. Nichols (1927), the Willard Gibbs (1936), the T. W. Richards (1944), and the Priestley (1946) medals of the American Chemical Society; the Franklin Medal of the Franklin Institute of the State of Pennsylvania (1960); the Gold Medal of the American Institute of Chemists; and the National Medal of Science (1964). He was elected to the National Academy of Sciences in 1929.

Adams's achievements as member of the National Defense Research Committee during 1941–46 resulted in his being awarded the U.S. Medal for Merit and his appointment as Honorary Commander of the British Empire (C.B.E.). He always took an active part in the activities of the American Chemical Society, serving on many committees, as president in 1935, and as chairperson of the board of directors from 1944 to 1950. He was president of the American Association for the Advancement of Science in 1950.

Adams was coauthor of *Laboratory Experiments in Organic Chemistry* (6th ed. 1970), editor in chief of *Organic Reactions* for 20 years, and editor of two volumes of *Organic Syntheses*.

For background information *see* HYDROGENATION; ORGANIC CHEMISTRY; PLATINUM in the McGraw-Hill Encyclopedia of Science and Technology. ∎

AGNEW, HAROLD MELVIN
★ American physicist

Born Mar. 28, 1921, Denver, CO, U.S.A.

After the *Enola Gay* was airborne on its way to Hiroshima on Aug. 6, 1945, the final assembly of the nuclear weapon aboard took place. The weapon used at Nagasaki, however, was fully assembled before it left Tinian. Had there been an accident on takeoff, it is conceivable that all of the installations, aircraft, and personnel on the north end of the island would have been lost. Agnew flew on the Hiroshima mission and was present during the Nagasaki takeoff. He later engaged in activities related to the United States weapons development program. Since those first days concerted effort has been directed to guaranteeing that the nation's nuclear weapons will be used only when properly authorized and will not produce a nuclear yield if they are involved in an accident. For his contribution to the development of nuclear weapons and for his success in working with the armed services to assure the maximum safety and effectiveness of atomic weapons systems, Agnew received the U.S. Atomic Energy Commission's Ernest O. Lawrence Award in 1966.

In 1942 Agnew joined the Metallurgical Laboratory of the U.S. Army's Manhattan Engineer District at the University of Chicago. He worked with Enrico Fermi and Herbert Anderson and was with them at Stagg Field when the first nuclear reaction went critical on December 2. When it was decided that weapon design would take place at Los Alamos, Agnew and his wife moved there in 1943. He became involved in measuring needed basic nuclear cross sections in a group with John Manley, Bernard Waldman, and Heinz Barshall. However, the field of applied nuclear physics proved more interesting to him, and he became involved in a program with Luis Alvarez to measure the yield of the Hiroshima weapon. This experiment, conducted over Hiroshima at the time of the explosion, proved successful. In 1946 Agnew returned to the University of Chicago to obtain his doctorate, but went back to Los Alamos in 1949. There he collaborated with Richard Taschek and Arthur Hemmendinger in measuring the light-particle reaction cross sections necessary to develop the thermonuclear weapons. *See* FERMI, ENRICO.

These studies led directly into weapon design work. It became apparent that the scientific developments were outpacing the military concepts and plans for utilizing them. Agnew became involved in helping the military establishment anticipate future developments by the Atomic Energy Commission. With the development of new weapon delivery systems and United States membership in NATO, new problems of command and control arose. AEC Commissioner James T. Ramey, then staff director of the Joint Committee on Atomic Energy of the U.S. Congress, and Senator Clinton P. Anderson of New Mexico called upon Agnew to join them in studying these problems. As a result of their work, systems were conceived and developed which allowed the government to have better command and control over its nuclear stockpile without inhibiting rapid utilization by the military.

Agnew majored in chemistry at the University of Denver, obtaining an A.B. in 1942. He received an M.S. in 1948 and a Ph.D. in physics under Fermi from the University of Chicago in 1949. He worked at Los Alamos from 1943 to 1946 and again from 1949 except for a period in 1961–64, when he served as scientific adviser to the Supreme Allied Commander in Europe. In September 1970 he became director of the Los Alamos Scientific Laboratory. As the first senator from Los Alamos County, Agnew served in the New Mexico State Senate from 1955 to 1961. Among his memberships on many government panels and committees, he served on the U.S. Air Force Scientific Advisory Board (1957–68), U.S. Army Scientific Advisory Panel (chair, 1964–70), President's Scientific Advisory Committee–Aircraft Panel (1965–72), and the General Advisory Committee–U.S. Arms Control and Disarmament Agency (chair, 1974–78). Agnew was a member of the National Academy of Engineering and a fellow of the American Physical Society and of the American Association for the Advancement of Science. In 1971 he received the NASA Public Service Award for his dedicated service as a member of the Aerospace Safety Advisory Panel which contributed significantly to the success of the Apollo program.

For background information *see* ATOMIC BOMB; NUCLEAR REACTION in the McGraw-Hill Encyclopedia of Science and Technology. ∎

AIGRAIN, PIERRE RAOUL ROGER
★ French physicist

Born Sept. 28, 1924, Poitiers, Vienne, France

After the discovery of minority carrier injection in semiconductors by William Shockley, John Bardeen, and W.H. Brattain in 1948, Aigrain studied various connected phenomena related to the simultaneous presence of electrons and holes in semiconductors. This led him in sequence from a study of the photoelectromagnetic (PEM) phenomena, to injection electroluminescence and its use as a spectroscopic tool in solid-state physics and its application to semiconductor lasers, to the problem of electromagnetic-wave propagation in semiconductors showing a Hall effect. *See* BARDEEN, JOHN; BRATTAIN, WALTER HOUSER; SHOCKLEY, WILLIAM.

Bardeen and his coworkers had shown that minority carriers could be injected in semiconductors either through *pn* junctions as in transistors or through light. It was thus important to understand the mechanisms of recombination of these minority carriers with those already present in the semiconductors. This study could be pursued in two main directions, one relatively global in which the time necessary for a carrier to disappear was studied without detailed reference to the mechanisms for its recombination, and one more analytic in which emphasis was put on the physical mechanisms for recombination and the detection of the corresponding energy.

Pursuing the second line, Aigrain showed that this energy can in some cases appear in the form of light. The study of the emitted spectrum can give information on the energy level in semiconductors of comparable accuracy and detail as that obtained in gases through optical spectroscopy. The same line was being pursued at the same time by W. Haynes and later by many others. In 1958 Aigrain proposed at the Brussels Conference on Semiconductors that this light emission in semiconductors can take the form of stimulated emission, thus opening the possibility for the construction of semiconductor lasers.

The other line of study had first led Aigrain to study the photoelectromagnetic phenomenon discovered some 25 years earlier by Kikoin and Noskov, but the explanation of which could not be given accurately before the discovery of minority-carrier motion. In this phenomenon a plate of semiconductor illuminated with a magnetic field parallel to the surface is the seat of a voltage perpendicular to the magnetic field. The study of this voltage, which is due to the separation by the magnetic field of unlike charges diffusing perpendicularly to the surface

where they have been produced, can lead to a large amount of detailed information on recombination mechanisms in semiconductors. The PEM effect can also be used for practical purposes, for example, light detectors. There are some connected phenomena, such as the photomagnetomechanical effect (appearance of a torque due to light in certain geometries) or the photoparamagnetic effect (increased apparent paramagnetism of an illuminated semiconductor). Further experimental studies in other laboratories of this last phenomenon apparently indicated unexpectedly large diffusion lengths for injected carriers. Although these phenomena were later explained on the basis of trapping of charged carriers, reflection about these effects led Aigrain to consider possible long-lived excitation in semiconductors placed in a magnetic field. He was thus led to reconsider the problem of the century-old Hall effect. When the electric field is rotating around the magnetic field, the Hall effect behaves as a nonreciprocal reactance. This opens the way to propagation of circularly polarized electromagnetic waves, even of low frequencies. Aigrain dubbed these waves helicons, and they were later discovered both in semiconductors and in metals. Through their interactions with various other excitations (magnons, phonons, and so forth), helicons have become a powerful tool for the study of solids.

Aigrain started his career as a French naval officer; he spent 3 years at the Carnegie Institute of Technology in Pittsburgh, where he obtained a D.Sc. in 1948. He obtained a D.Sc. from the University of Paris in 1950 and taught at the University of Lille from 1952 to 1954. In 1954 he became a professor at the University of Paris, and served also as director general of higher education from 1965 to 1968. He was science director of the Defense Research Directorate of the French Ministry of Defense during 1961–65. In 1961 he was elected a foreign member of the American Academy of Arts and Sciences. He was also a member of the French Physical Society. He was appointed general delegate to the Recherche Scientifique et Technique in 1968.

Aigrain was coauthor of two books on semiconductor physics, *Les Semi-conducteurs*(1958) and *Electronic Processes in Solids*(1962).

For background information *see* PHO-

TOEMISSION; SEMICONDUCTOR in the McGraw-Hill Encyclopedia of Science and Technology. ∎

ALBERT, ABRAHAM ADRIAN
★ American mathematician

Born *Nov. 9, 1905, Chicago, IL, U.S.A.*
Died *June 7, 1972, Chicago, IL, U.S.A.*

In 1905 L. E. Dickson defined a class of algebras called cyclic algebras. These are a special case of what are now called crossed product algebras, and which are defined as follows: Let F be any field and Z be a normal algebraic extension field of degree (that is, dimension) n over F. Then the Galois group G of Z over F consists of n distinct automorphisms, $z \rightarrow z^\rho$ of Z, leaving F fixed. Consider a set $g = \{a_{\rho,\sigma}\}$, of nonzero elements $a_{\rho,\sigma}$ in Z, which are given for every pair ρ,σ of automorphisms in G. Embed Z in a space A which is the vector space direct sum of n copies Zy_ρ of Z and so has dimension n^2 over F. Make A into an algebra by defining products by the formula below for

$$(zy_\rho)(wy_\sigma) = [(z \cdot w^\rho)a_{\rho,\sigma}]y_{\rho,\sigma}$$

every z and w of Z and all ρ,σ in G. The condition on g which results from $(y_\rho y_\sigma)y_\tau = y_\rho(y_\sigma y_\tau)$ for all ρ,σ,τ in G, implies that A is associative. In this case A is called a crossed product over its center F. When G is a cyclic group and ρ generates G, one can take $y_\sigma = y^i$ for every $\sigma = \rho^i$, and y^n is in F. Then A is a cyclic algebra.

The main problem in the theory of associative algebras is the determination of all division algebras. Every associative division algebra A has dimension n^2 over the field F which is its center. Then n is called the degree of A, and is actually the degree of a maximal subfield of F. All division algebras of degree $n = 1, 2, 3$ have been known to be cyclic since 1921. In his 1928 Ph.D. dissertation Albert showed that all division algebras of degree four are crossed products. In 1932 he proved the existence of noncyclic division algebras of degree four.

Albert and others developed a theory of direct products of simple associative algebras. As a consequence of these results and some properties of cyclic fields and of associative algebras over a p-adic field, it was shown by Helmut Hasse, Richard Brauer, Emmy Noether, and Albert that every division algebra whose center is an algebraic number field is a cyclic algebra.

The multiplication algebra of a pure Riemann matrix is an associative division algebra over an algebraic number field with certain special properties. Albert determined the precise structure of these algebras in 1934, and also proved the existence of a pure Riemann matrix whose multiplication algebra is any such algebra, and whose elements are all algebraic numbers. He was awarded the Cole Prize of the American Mathematical Society for this work in 1939.

In 1941 Albert began his major study of the structure of nonassociative algebras. He produced the general structure theory of Jordan algebras, and later gave a construction of exceptional Jordan division algebras. He also constructed the major classes of finite nonassociative division algebras. This work provided most of the known classes of finite nondesarguesian projective division ring planes.

A merchant's son, Albert majored in mathematics at the University of Chicago, receiving his B.S in 1926, his M.S. in 1927, and his Ph.D. in 1928. He held a National Research Council Fellowship at Princeton in 1928–29, taught at Columbia from 1929 to 1931, and returned to Chicago in 1931. He became a full professor in 1941, chairperson of the department from 1958 to 1962, and dean of the Division of the Physical Sciences in 1962. He was appointed E. H. Moore Distinguished Service Professor in 1960. He was elected to the National Academy of Sciences in 1943.

Albert wrote *Modern Higher Algebra* (1937), *Structure of Algebras* (1939), *Introduction to Algebraic Theories* (1941), *College Algebra* (1946), *Solid Analytic Geometry* (1949), *Fundamental Concepts of Higher Algebra* (1956), *An Introduction to Finite Projective Planes,* with Reuben Sandler (1968), and *Tensor Products of Quaternion Algebras* (1972).

For background information *see* AL-GEBRA in the McGraw-Hill Encyclopedia of Science and Technology. ■

ALDER, KURT
German chemist

***

Born *July 10, 1902, Königshutte, Germany (now Chorzów, Poland)*
Died *June 20, 1958, Cologne, Germany*

Alder, along with the German chemist Otto Diels, was responsible for the elucidation and development of the diene synthesis, now commonly called the Diels-Alder reaction. For this work the two were awarded the Nobel Prize in chemistry in 1950. *See* DIELS, OTTO PAUL HERMANN.

The diene synthesis involves condensation of a conjugated olefin, the diene, with an activated double bond, the dienophile, to form a cyclic product. Isolated instances of such condensations were reported as early as 1893, but Diels and Alder were the first to recognize the versatility of the reaction, and in a series of papers beginning in 1928 they demonstrated its remarkably broad scope.

Alder and his coworkers carried out a systematic study of the reactivity of a large number of dienes and dienophiles, many of which they synthesized for the first time. They also established the structure and stereochemistry of all new Diels-Alder adducts. This work provided a firm foundation for all later investigations. Alder was particularly interested in bridged-ring systems, which were formed when cyclic dienes were used. In his early work Alder determined the structure and the mode of formation of the polymers of cyclopentadiene. Later he demonstrated the ease with which members of the camphor and norcamphor family, natural products containing bridged-ring systems, could be synthesized.

The Diels-Alder reaction has been invaluable in producing thousands of organic compounds whose syntheses would have been otherwise impossible or at best very difficult. It has been used in the production of insecticides, dyes, drying and lubricating oils, and pharmaceuticals. Its uses are constantly being extended, and its full potential has yet to be realized.

In addition to his work on the diene synthesis, Alder conducted research in problems of autoxidation and polymerization. He also worked on the preparation and composition of synthetic rubber.

Alder studied chemistry at the University of Berlin and then went to the University of Kiel, where he took his doctorate in 1926 under the direction of Diels. In 1930 he was appointed reader, and in 1934 professor of chemistry, at the University of Kiel, remaining there until 1936. He then worked in the research laboratories of I. G. Farben Industrie at Leverkusen until 1940, when be became professor of chemistry and director of the Chemistry Institute at the University of Cologne. He was named dean of the philosophical faculty at Cologne in 1949.

For background information *see* DIELS-ALDER REACTION in the McGraw-Hill Encyclopedia of Science and Technology. ■

ALEXOPOULOS, CONSTANTINE JOHN
★ American mycologist

***

Born *Mar. 17, 1907, Chicago, IL, U.S.A.*

Alexopoulos became interested in the plasmodial slime molds (Myxomycetes), on which subject he became a specialist, when he was preparing for his doctoral examination in 1932. His interest in these organisms was further stimulated when, during World War II, he observed many species in the Amazon River valley of Brazil. He began studying the Myxomycetes seriously in 1948, when he became associated with E. S. Beneke at Michigan State University, and started collecting them in Beneke's company throughout Michigan and in Jamaica, W.I., where they discovered an undescribed species.

While teaching mycology at Michigan State, Alexopoulos became painfully aware of the need for a textbook suitable for beginning mycology courses, and he wrote *Introductory Mycology* (1952). In collaboration with Beneke, he also wrote *Laboratory Manual for Introductory Mycology,* to accompany the textbook.

Alexopoulos continued his floristic studies of Myxomycetes in Greece as a senior Fulbright research scholar at the National University of Athens (1954–55), adding 50 or more species to the known myxomycete "flora" of that country. While in Greece, he received an offer from the University of Iowa to head its department of botany, which he accepted with alacrity because he welcomed the opportunity to become associated with George W. Martin, then the world's foremost authority on the taxonomy of the Myxomycetes, and to have access to the Macbride-Martin Myxomycete Collection, one of the finest in the world. In Iowa he became interested in the labora-

tory cultivation of Myxomycetes, the majority of which had not been grown in artificial culture from spore to spore, and his research was crowned with success when he grew two species of Myxomycetes which had never before been induced to complete their life cycles on artificial media. In so doing, he discovered that there are three distinct types of plasmodia (the plasmodium is the assimilative stage of the slime molds) in this group of organisms instead of just one, as had been thought up to that time and, more important, that the plasmodial type was directly correlated with major taxonomic myxomycete groups and was, therefore, of considerable systematic and phylogenetic significance; he used this subject as the theme of his presidential address to the Mycological Society of America, published in 1960. This work increased his interest in attempting to elucidate the life history pattern of the Myxomycetes, and he directed the doctoral research of O. R. Collins, who obtained proof of the existence of heterothallism (sexual reproduction through different mating types) in this group by means of single-spore cultures and rigid analysis of clonal crosses (these results were published by Collins in 1961).

About this time, Alexopoulos decided that he did not wish to make administration his career, and he left Iowa to become professor of botany at the University of Texas at Austin in 1962. The fact that much of Texas has a subtropical climate influenced his decision, for he wanted to investigate the myxomycete flora of that area and compare it with that of the Neotropics. In Texas he also had free access to the famous electron microscope laboratory of the Plant Research Institute (later the Cell Research Institute); by that time it had become evident to him that only ultrastructural studies could solve some important life history problems of the Myxomycetes to which his laboratory culture studies had led him. Foremost of these unsolved problems was the exact location of meiosis (reduction division) in the myxomycete life cycle—a very controversial subject—which was elucidated by Henry Aldrich, one of Alexopoulos's graduate students, in his Ph.D. dissertation in 1966.

Another important piece of research that came out of his laboratory at that time was the doctoral dissertation of George C. Carroll, on ascosporogenesis

in the Ascomycetes, a group of fungi in which Alexopoulos had been interested for 20 years; both he and his students, at Michigan State and at Iowa, had made important contributions to this subject. In 1966 the researches of Aldrich and Carroll were published under the sole authorship of the students, for Alexopoulos did not agree with the common practice of student-professor authorship of dissertations. While continuing his research on the laboratory cultivation of Myxomycetes, Alexopoulos became aware of the influence of the environment on the morphology of the sporophores, which is the basis of myxomycete classification, and he became a crusader for the experimental approach to the taxonomy of the Myxomycetes, which he used as the theme of the 19th Annual Lecture to the Mycological Society of America, which he delivered in 1968 and published in 1969. At the same time, he continued his floristic studies with a number of forays into tropical lands (Honduras, many of the Caribbean islands, and Hawaii). In collaboration with José Sáenz R. of the University of Costa Rica, he added to the knowledge of the distribution of tropical Myxomycetes and later described a number of previously unknown species, but only after testing the validity of their taxonomic characters under different environmental conditions. He established and expanded the University of Texas Myxomycete Collection (UTMC), probably the best publicly supported collection of these organisms in the Southern states.

The son of Greek parents who had emigrated to the United States, Alexopoulos was taken to Greece at the age of 6. He received his early education in private and public schools in Athens and Piraeus. Returning with his family to the United States 6 years later, he finished his secondary school education and enrolled at the University of Illinois at Urbana in the College of Agriculture, earning a B.S. degree with honors in 1927. A recipient of the College of Agriculture Scholarship (1927), he earned the M.S. degree in horticulture (cytology) and, with the aid of a graduate fellowship, the Ph.D. degree in botany (mycology) in 1932. He taught mycology at the University of Illinois until 1935, when he accepted a position at Kent State University in Ohio. He served as director of the Phytopathological Laboratory of the Institute of Chemistry and Agriculture "Nicholaos Canellopoulos" in

Piraeus in 1938, on leave of absence from Kent State, and published a paper on some fungi from Greece, as well as on antifungal antibiosis by Actinomycetes, a subject he had pursued with some success at Kent State. During World War II he worked as a field technician in the Amazon River valley of Brazil for the United States government's Rubber Development Corporation (1942–43) and then joined the Greece Mission of the United Nations Relief and Rehabilitation Administration (1943–47), serving as agricultural rehabilitation officer and later as deputy director of the Division of Agriculture and Fisheries. He returned to the United States from Greece in 1947 to join the faculty of Michigan State University as mycologist. He spent his sabbatical leave (1954–55) as a senior Fulbright research scholar at the National University of Athens, returned to Michigan State for a year, and in 1956 became professor and head of the department of botany at the University of Iowa at Iowa City. In 1962 he became a professor at the University of Texas at Austin, and professor emeritus in 1977. Alexopoulos served as president of the Mycological Society of America in 1959, of the Botanical Society of America in 1963, and of the International Mycological Association in 1971–77. In 1967 he was awarded the Botanical Society of America Certificate of Merit. He was elected a fellow of the American Academy of Arts and Sciences in 1976 and corresponding member of the Academy of Athens in 1977.

The eminently successful second edition of *Introductory Mycology* was published in 1962, and was translated into five languages. The third edition, prepared with the collaboration of Charles W. Mims, a former student, was in press in 1979. Alexopoulos coauthored *Algae and Fungi*, with H. C. Bold (1967); *The Biology of the Myxomycetes,* with W. D. Gray (1968); *The Myxomycetes: A World Monograph,* with G. W. Martin (1969); and the *Morphology of Plants and Fungi* (publication pending), with H. C. Bold and Theodore Delevoryas. He also wrote over 80 articles on fungi and Myxomycetes for professional journals and contributed articles to several encyclopedias, including the McGraw-Hill Encyclopedia of Science and Technology and the Encyclopaedia Britannica.

For background information *see* MYXOMYCETES in the McGraw-Hill Encyclopedia of Science and Technology. ∎

ALFVÉN, HANNES OLOF GÖSTA
☆ Swedish physicist

Born May 30, 1908, Norrkoeping, Sweden

Alfvén pioneered in developing the field of magnetohydrodynamics (MHD), the study of the motion of an electrically conducting fluid interacting with magnetic fields, and, in particular, the subject of plasma physics, the branch of MHD in which the fluid under study is a highly ionized gas consisting of nearly equal numbers of positive and negative charged particles. He was chiefly concerned with plasmas in stars, in the geomagnetic field, and in interplanetary and interstellar space, but his theories were basic to the study of laboratory plasmas encountered in the development of controlled thermonuclear fusion. For his contributions, he shared the 1970 Nobel Prize in physics with L. Néel. *See* NÉEL, LOUIS EUGÈNE FÉLIX.

Alfvén showed that under suitable conditions the magnetic field lines are "frozen" into the plasma, so that when a plasma moves, the magnetic field moves along with it. The conditions for this to be true are that the magnetic Reynolds number be much greater than unity, and the plasma be dense enough that the mean free path of the electrons is smaller than the size of the plasma. These conditions are often, but not always, satisfied in the large-scale plasmas encountered in geophysics and astrophysics.

In 1942 Alfvén pointed out that the outward transfer of angular momentum in the plasma from which the solar system was formed would tend to equalize the angular velocity at all distances from the center. This would explain why nearly all of the momentum in the solar system is concentrated in the planets rather than the Sun. (In 1943 Alfvén also used the rigidity property to explain why the sunspot material does not sink under its own weight, even though it is denser than the material surrounding it.)

Because the plasma is essentially glued to the magnetic field lines, the latter behave like stretched elastic strings. In 1942 Alfvén showed that a plasma can transmit transverse hydromagnetic waves, now known as Alfvén waves, which can be thought of as vibrations propagated along these strings. This analogy can also be used to calculate the velocity of the waves. For several years Alfvén's discovery was generally dismissed because of a widespread misconception that electromagnetic waves could not propagate in a conducting medium, and because it did not seem possible to experimentally verify the existence of such waves. However, Alfvén's waves were later observed in liquid metals by S. O. Lundquist (1949) and M. B. Lehnert (1954), working in Alfvén's laboratory, and were first demonstrated in plasmas in 1959. They have been used to explain micropulsations of the geomagnetic field and the close relation between magnetic disturbances at widely separated points on the Earth's surface which are linked by magnetic field lines. Many kinds of plasma waves have been found in addition to the pure transverse waves introduced by Alfvén, and this has led to the study of the dispersive properties of plasmas.

Alfvén also developed a perturbative theory describing the motion of a charged particle in electric and magnetic fields. In this theory, the particle is regarded as moving on a circular path about a "guiding center" which is itself in motion. The theory is applicable to gradually varying magnetic fields, that is, those in which the distance over which the magnetic field changes appreciably is much larger than the radius of the circular path. Alfvén showed that in these fields the circular path expands or contracts in such a way that the magnetic flux included in the path is approximately constant. For a nonrelativistic particle, this means that the particle's magnetic moment is also approximately constant. Alfvén also obtained the equations governing the drifting motion of the guiding center. The guiding-center approximation is consistent with the concept of frozen-in field lines since, to a first approximation, the guiding center moves along, and with, the field lines.

In 1939 Alfvén applied this approximation to the study of magnetic storms and auroras. He pointed out that particles in the Earth's magnetic field should bounce back and forth along the field lines, being reflected by increasing magnetic fields. The concept of magnetic mirrors later became one of the fundamental approaches to confining plasmas for controlled thermonuclear fusion. Alfvén also introduced the concept of a ring current formed by the trapped particles.

Many of Alfvén's ideas were initially ignored or rejected, only to be used many years later, often without awareness of their originator. However, in the 1950s, experimental research on confining extremely hot plasmas in order to achieve thermonuclear fusion revealed that these plasmas displayed numerous instabilities which could not be described by the mathematically rigorous theories. But the magnetohydrodynamic theories previously developed by Alfvén could account for many of these instabilities and were used by physicists to discover how the worst of them could be avoided. Alfvén's theories were also able to explain many of the observations made by spacecraft, such as the Van Allen belts, and they came to be so widely used by space physicists that Alfvén himself began to warn against their unwarranted application. He stressed that when electrostatic double layers are produced in low-density plasmas, the frozen-in picture is not valid and that its use without observing this limitation easily leads to erroneous conclusions.

In the late 1950s Alfvén returned to work on the problem of the origin of the solar system. It is generally agreed that this involved a process in which a magnetized plasma condensed into small solid grains and the grains accreted into successively larger bodies. Alfvén suggested that the small asteroids, comets, and meteoroids could represent a much earlier stage in the accretion process than the larger planets and satellites, and he therefore advocated spacecraft voyages to asteroids and comets to gain information about this process that might not be available elsewhere. In 1973 he suggested that the process might be continuing in the accretion of comets from meteors, an idea which was again contrary to generally accepted views. Alfvén also developed an idea proposed by Oskar Klein

that the universe should be symmetric in the sense that there should be equal quantities of matter and antimatter. This cosmology is in conflict with the generally accepted "big bang" cosmology.

Alfvén obtained his Ph.D. from the University of Uppsala in 1934 and then became a researcher at the Nobel Institute for Physics in Stockholm. He became a professor at the Royal Institute of Technology in Stockholm in 1940 and a professor at the University of California at San Diego in 1967. He was a member of the Swedish Academy of Sciences and the Swedish Academy of Engineering Sciences and was a foreign associate of the U.S. National Academy of Sciences and other academies. He was awarded the Gold Medal of the Royal Astronomical Society (1967) and the Lomonosov Gold Medal of the Soviet Academy of Sciences (1971). He was a member of the Swedish Science Advisory Council and served as president of the Pugwash Conference on Science and World Affairs. He warned against the dangers associated with nuclear energy and nuclear bombs.

Alfvén often published his original work in relatively inaccessible journals, because he always had serious trouble with the peer review system. He collected much of his early work in the book *Cosmical Electrodynamics* (1950). He also wrote *On the Origin of the Solar System* (1954), *Cosmical Electrodynamics: Fundamental Principles,* with C. G. Fälthammar (1963), *Worlds-Antiworlds: Antimatter in Cosmology* (1966), *Structure and Evolutionary History of the Solar System,* with G. Arrhenius (1975), and a number of nontechnical books.

For background information *see* ASTEROID; COMET; COSMOGONY; COSMOLOGY; MAGNETOHYDRODYNAMICS; MAGNETOSPHERE; PLASMA PHYSICS; SOLAR WIND; SUN; WAVES AND INSTABILITIES IN PLASMAS in the McGraw-Hill Encyclopedia of Science and Technology. ∎

ALLER, LAWRENCE HUGH
★ American astronomer

Born Sept. 24, 1913, Tacoma, WA, U.S.A.

The chemical compositions of the stars may offer important clues to their history and to nuclear processes occurring within their interiors, and may even shed light on the evolution of the Galaxy. Following application of the Saha ionization theory

in the 1920s and recognition of special excitation mechanisms, it became obvious that most of the differences between the spectra of stars could be explained by differences in their temperatures and atmospheric pressures. Attempts were made to explain in this way even stars whose spectra were rich in heavy metals (those of spectral class S), but the explanation failed for the cool carbon stars. As late as 1945 distinguished astrophysicists asserted that differences in the chemical composition of the stars did not exist.

Quantitative studies of the spectra of hot stars with broad bright lines (Wolf-Rayet stars) convinced Aller that well-known differences in their spectra could be explained only as arising from actual chemical composition differences. The elements involved—helium, carbon, nitrogen, and oxygen—included those characteristic of the carbon-nitrogen energy generation cycle. Later, in collaboration with Joseph W. Chamberlain, Aller undertook a quantitative spectroscopic analysis of two so-called subdwarf stars. Superficially their spectra resembled those of stars with surface temperatures of the order of 8000–9000 K with prominent hydrogen lines and weak metal lines. The character of the metallic line spectrum indicated a temperature more nearly comparable with that of the Sun, 5700 K, a conclusion subsequently verified by color measurements of these stars. The stars were metal-deficient; later, more detailed studies by J. L. Greenstein and Aller showed the metal-hydrogen ratio to

be about 0.01 that of the Sun. Presumably, these very ancient stars were formed when the metal-hydrogen ratio was very much smaller in the Galaxy than it is now. *See* GREENSTEIN, JESSE LEONARD.

High-temperature stars recently formed from the interstellar medium were studied by Aller, who pioneered in applying model atmosphere methods to the star Gamma Pegasi (1949). In 1955 Aller, Gunther Elste, and Jun Jugaku applied improved theories of hydrogen line broadening and allowed for the effects of variation of temperature and density throughout the radiating layers upon the observed spectral lines in order to derive stellar chemical compositions.

In the late 1950s Leo Goldberg, Edith Müller, and Aller undertook a comprehensive spectrochemical analysis of the Sun. Further refinements were developed by J. E. Ross and Aller. In their method of spectrum synthesis, elemental abundances were established by theoretically reproducing small sections of the real spectrum. Aller, Ross, and others applied this method to the determination of abundances of a number of metals in the Sun and to a Magellanic Cloud supergiant star.

At Harvard in 1937 D. H. Menzel initiated a theoretical study of physical processes in gaseous nebulae, attempting to establish quantitative interpretations of observable spectroscopic features in terms of electron temperature, density, radiation field, and chemical composition. Aller undertook a prominent role in these investigations and supplemented theoretical insights with spectroscopic observations. After he left Harvard, he continued this work at the McDonald, Mount Wilson, and Lick observatories. In 1949 Aller, C. W. Ufford, and J. H. Van Vleck noted that the relative intensities of the 3726- and 3729-angstrom (372.6- and 372.9-nanometer) "forbidden" lines of ionized oxygen are sensitive indicators of the densities of gaseous nebulae. *See* MENZEL, DONALD HOWARD; VAN VLECK, JOHN HASBROUCK.

Accurate spectrophotometric measurements are important to theoretical interpretations of stars and gaseous nebulae. In 1953 Aller and W. Liller were among those who pioneered in photoelectric spectrophotometry of gaseous nebulae. In the 1960s, at Lick Observatory, M. F. Walker and Aller used the Lallemand electronographic camera to measure extremely weak spectral lines that lie below the practical limit of conventional photo-

graphic spectroscopy. Later, Aller applied the Robinson-Wampler image tube scanner to measure both faint and strong lines in a large number of gaseous nebulae. This wealth of observational material, much of it secured and assessed in collaboration with Stanley J. Czyzak, illustrated the great range in density concentration, excitation, structure, and chemical composition in the so-called planetary nebulae, which surround certain stars in advanced evolutionary stages. Lindsay Smith and Aller carried out extensive studies of the spectra of these residual stars, which appear to be objects on the verge of becoming white dwarfs. In particular, the spectra of many of these stars show OVI λ3811,38 lines, noted by Aller in 1946 in the spectrum of the central star of NGC 246.

Additional studies involved the interstellar medium, the material from which stars are formed. In 1958 Liller and Aller applied photoelectric spectrophotometric measurements to ascertain the chemical composition of the Orion Nebula.

In the late 1930s N. U. Mayall and Aller measured the rotation of the Triangulum Galaxy M 33 and determined its mass. Aller found (1942) that the ionized hydrogen HII regions exhibited an excitation that depended on the distance from the nucleus. Studies of the chemical compositions of such nebulosities in external galaxies have received much attention. Photoelectric spectrophotometric measurements of the Tarantula Nebula (30 Doradus) in the Large Magellanic Cloud by D. J. Faulkner and Aller in 1960 showed helium to be deficient in this object as compared with the Galaxy, a result later confirmed by Peimbert. Extensive studies of HII regions in Magellanic Clouds by Aller and his coworkers demonstrated (in harmony with results of other workers) deficiencies of N, O, Ne, and other elements as compared with the Galaxy.

Additional researches by Aller and his associates concerned calculations of atomic line strengths, stellar spectral energy distributions, spectra of A-type stars of peculiar composition, "combination" variables believed to be stars near the end of their evolution, nova-type stars, notably Eta Carinae and RR Telescopii, the solar corona, and the nature of particles in the zodiacal light.

Aller was taken out of school at the age of 15 to serve his father's chimerical ambitions to find gold. He was rescued from

a poverty-stricken life in a mining camp by his elder sister, Jane Kegg, and D. H. Menzel, later director of Harvard Observatory. Although Aller had not finished high school, Menzel arranged for him to enter the University of California as a special student. He was transferred to regular status after a semester, and received his A.B. in 1936. In 1943 Aller took his Ph.D. in astronomy at Harvard University, where he was a junior fellow in the Society of Fellows during 1939–42 and instructor in physics in 1942–43. He was assistant professor of astronomy at Indiana University from 1945 to 1948. In 1948 he went to the University of Michigan as associate professor and became full professor in 1954. He served as visiting professor at the Australian National University and at the University of Toronto before going to the University of California at Los Angeles in 1962. Aller was visiting professor at the universities of Sydney, Tasmania, and Queensland and at the Raman Institute (Bangalore), and was research associate at Hale Observatories and at Radiophysics, Commonwealth Scientific and Industrial Research Organization (Sydney). He was elected to the American Academy of Arts and Sciences in 1961 and to the National Academy of Sciences in 1962.

Aller wrote *Nebulae,* with L. Goldberg (1943; 2d ed., by Aller, 1971), and *Astrophysics* (2 vols., 1953–54; 2d ed. of vol. 1, 1962), *Gaseous Nebulae* (1956), and *Abundance of Elements* (1961).

For background information *see* ASTRONOMICAL SPECTROSCOPY; NEBULA; STAR in the McGraw-Hill Encyclopedia of Science and Technology. ■

ALVAREZ, LUIS WALTER
★ American physicist

Born June 13, 1911, San Francisco, CA, U.S.A.

In the early 1960s a "population explosion" occurred in the list of elementary particles. This rapid increase from some 30 known particles to more than 100 was primarily the result of the teaming of the liquid hydrogen bubble chamber and the proton synchrotron. Alvarez was the leader in building a series of ever larger liquid-hydrogen bubble chambers, together with the necessary new types of measuring devices and the data analysis systems required to "extract the physics" from the raw bubble-chamber film. For this achievement, he was awarded the Nobel Prize for physics in 1968.

In 1952 Donald Glaser demonstrated the first bubble chamber, showing cosmic-ray tracks in a small glass bulb containing ether. Several groups of physicists started immediately to develop the bubble chamber into a practical tool for use in high-energy physics. The Alvarez group was the first to observe tracks in liquid hydrogen, in 1954. Thereafter they built increasingly larger hydrogen chambers, each of which was in turn the world's largest. (Donald Gow and Paul Hernandez played important roles in this program.) For almost 5 years after its completion in early 1959, the 72-inch (1.83-meter) chamber was the largest; eventually it was surpassed by the 80-inch (2.03-meter) Brookhaven chamber. *See* GLASER, DONALD ARTHUR.

Concurrently, Alvarez recognized that the measurement techniques then used to analyze cloud-chamber pictures were too slow by a factor of 100 to cope with the flood of photographs that would come from his planned large chambers. The basic parameters of the proposed semiautomatic measuring machines were tabulated by Alvarez in 1955; their first embodiment appeared a year later in the "Franckenstein" of Hugh Bradner and Jack Franck. This machine, and others that followed its design philosophy, became the basis for the modern standard measurement technique. As Alvarez suggested in 1955, the final link in the new

data reduction technique involved high-speed electronic computer analysis of the "Franckenstein" output data. Many members of his group played important roles in this new project, in particular Frank Solmitz, Lynn Stevenson, and Arthur Rosenfeld.

The computer programs made it possible to observe particles with lifetimes of the order of 10^{-22} second; older techniques cut off at lifetimes less than 10^{-12} second. In 1960 Alvarez and his collaborators announced the discovery of the first three very short-lived strange particles. Members of the Alvarez group subsequently found about half of the known short-lived particles, or resonances, as they are commonly called. Almost all the new particles were found in liquid-hydrogen bubble chambers, using Franckenstein-like devices and geometry and kinematics computer programs of the type introduced into physics by the Alvarez group.

Prior to his involvement in bubble-chamber physics, Alvarez had been active in nuclear physics and cosmic-ray research. Either alone or with a single collaborator, he discovered the east-west effect in cosmic rays, the radioactivity of tritium, the isotopic stability of ^{3}He, K-electron capture, the long-range alpha particles accompanying fission, and several short-lived isotopes; he also made the first measurement of the magnetic moment of the neutron, the first nonradioactive observation of an artificially created isotope, the analysis of the spectrum of ^{198}Hg, the first time-of-flight neutron spectrometer, and the first acceleration of heavy ions in a cyclotron. His published suggestion concerning charge-exchange acceleration led directly and quickly to the tandem Van de Graaff generator. From 1945 through 1947 he led a group that built the first proton linear accelerator. In 1956 he and his associates discovered the unexpected phenomenon of fusion catalysis by mu mesons.

Alvarez attended the University of Chicago (B.S., 1932; M.S., 1934; Ph.D., 1936) and in 1938 joined the faculty of the University of California at Berkeley. Active in microwave radar research in World War II, he was the author of a dozen government-owned patents in the radar field. His inventions included ground-controlled approach (with Lawrence Johnston), the "eagle system" for blind bombing, microwave beacons, and many linear antenna arrays. At Los Ala-

mos, he suggested the technique used to detonate the implosion weapon. He flew as scientific observer at Alamogordo and Hiroshima. In 1965 he suggested that cosmic rays could be used to search the Second Pyramid at Giza for unknown chambers. He then led a joint Egyptian-American team effort which finally concluded that the pyramid was quite solid. His scientific and engineering achievements were recognized by four honorary degrees, the Collier Trophy of the National Aeronautical Society (1946), U.S. Medal for Merit (1947), John Scott Medal given by the Philadelphia Board of Directors of City Trusts (1953), Einstein Medal of the Strauss Foundation (1961), Pioneer Award of the American Institute of Electrical and Electronic Engineers (1963), National Medal of Science (1964), and Michelson Award of Case-Western Reserve University (1965). He was named California Scientist of the Year in 1960. President of the American Physical Society in 1969, Alvarez was a member of the National Academy of Sciences and the National Academy of Engineering. His activities outside the world of physics included being a director of several corporations, including the Hewlett-Packard Company, and the founder and chairman of the board of two optical companies.

For background information *see* BUBBLE CHAMBER; ELEMENTARY PARTICLE; PARTICLE ACCELERATOR; STRANGE PARTICLES in the McGraw-Hill Encyclopedia of Science and Technology. ■

AMBARTSUMIAN, VICTOR AMAZASPOVICH

☆ Soviet (Armenian) astrophysicist

***Born** Sept. 18, 1908, Tiflis, Georgia, Russia*

While studying stellar associations and stellar evolution, Ambartsumian arrived at a theory of cosmogony based on the process of rarefaction rather than condensation. This theory accounts for a number of celestial phenomena that cannot be adequately explained by any other currently accepted cosmological model.

About 1924 the English astronomer and physicist A. S. Eddington suggested that the enormous densities of white dwarf stars (approaching 6×10^4 grams per cubic centimeter) were due to the presence of degenerate matter, a gas in which the electrons and ionized nuclei of

atoms, under the influence of extreme pressures, are tightly packed to produce very high densities. During the 1930s the Soviet physicist L. D. Landau predicted that immensely dense bodies would be found concealed within the interiors of some of the more massive stars. In 1934 the American astronomers Fritz Zwicky and Walter Baade posited the existence of neutron stars—celestial bodies in which the internal pressure was so great that the atoms were completely stripped of their electrons and the nuclei compressed to densities approximating 5×10^{10} grams per cubic centimeter. The theory of neutron stars was later worked out by the American physicist J. R. Oppenheimer and the Canadian physicist G. M. Volkoff. Thus by World War II the concept of extremely dense celestial bodies was well established. *See* BAADE, WALTER; LANDAU, LEV DAVYDOVICH; OPPENHEIMER, J. ROBERT.

In the late 1940s Ambartsumian began to investigate a long-standing question concerning the direction of evolution of cosmic bodies: did such bodies evolve toward condensation or toward rarefaction and disintegration of their substance? In 1947 he showed that the Galaxy contained young stars forming two types of groups: O associations and T associations. He showed that these associations were unstable; subsequent observations demonstrated that certain of them were in fact breaking up. Short-term groups of the Trapezium system type were shown to be made up of especially young stars.

From this it followed that stars arise in groups as a result of the disintegrations of very massive bodies, which Ambartsumian called protostars. The disintegration of a protostar might result in some of its material being changed into diffuse matter. This explained why groups of young stars were densely immersed in gaseous mist. Observation confirmed this process of disintegration. Ambartsumian rejected, however, the idea that the density of a protostar might equal that of a neutron star.

Ambartsumian later turned to the phenomena of radio galaxies. In a series of articles begun in 1955, he showed that the current theory, which held such a galaxy to be the result of the collision of two ordinary galaxies, was incorrect. He considered that radio galaxies arose from ordinary galaxies as a result of enormous explosions in their nuclei.

In the 1950s Ambartsumian was occupied with the consequences of his theory of galactic nuclei, which gained a series of unexpected confirmations after 1960. He concluded that the various characteristics of galaxies resulted from the continued activity of the galactic nuclei over long periods of time. He considered it evident that this activity conditioned the existence of supermassive bodies in galaxies.

Ambartsumian applied the idea of a transition from a dense state to one less dense in the extragalactic province. He maintained that the filaments of cosmic gas connecting many multiple galaxies are the last connections between bodies that were spewed forth by the same protogalaxy. He further contended that the variable dwarf stars found in stellar associations have retained remnants of hypermatter within their cores, since observations have revealed that their irregular fluctuations of brightness are caused by occasional surface emissions.

In addition to his work in cosmogony, Ambartsumian made major contributions to the study of stellar associations, particularly in relation to type O and type T stars. He also developed the theory of radial equilibrium of planetary nebulae, demonstrated the role of ultraviolet radiation and the radiation of lines of the Lyman series, and explained the physical composition of the shells of meteorites.

Ambartsumian studied at Leningrad University and Pulkovo Observatory. He became a lecturer and research worker at Leningrad University in 1931, leaving in 1944 to become a professor of astrophys-

ics at Erevan University. In 1945 he was made director of the Biurakan Observatory in the Armenian S.S.R. In 1947 he became president of the Armenian Academy of Sciences. He became a member of the U.S.S.R. Academy of Sciences in 1953. He served as president of the International Astronomical Union (1961–64) and the International Council of Scientific Unions (1968–72). He was awarded the Gold Medal of the Royal Astronomical Society of Great Britain (1960), the Catherine Wolfe Bruce Medal of the Astronomical Society of the Pacific (1960), and the Lomonosov Gold Medal of the U.S.S.R. Academy of Sciences (1973). He also received the Order of Lenin (four times), the Order of the Red Banner of Labor (1945, 1956), and the Stalin Prize (1946, 1950), and was named Hero of Socialist Labor (1968). He was elected a foreign associate of several academies, including the American Academy of Arts and Sciences (1958), U.S. National Academy of Science (1959), and the Royal Society of London (1969).

Ambartsumian wrote *Theoretical Astrophysics* (1958).

For background information *see* COSMOGONY; GALAXY; STAR in the McGraw-Hill Encyclopedia of Science and Technology. ∎

AMES, BRUCE N.
★ American biochemist and geneticist

Born Dec. 16, 1928, New York, NY, U.S.A.

In 1964, while studying mutations which altered control mechanisms for gene expression in bacteria, Ames started thinking about whether the mutation rate in humans would be increased by their exposure to the many new chemicals in the modern world. This led him over the next 10 years to develop a sophisticated but simple test for detecting environmental mutagens (see illustration).

Ames and his colleagues then showed that about 90 percent of the organic chemicals causing cancer in people or animals could be detected as mutagens in his test system. This work lent strong support to the somatic mutation theory of cancer and provided a simple and rapid method that is being used by thousands of laboratories and industries for identifying the many environmental mutagens (and presumptive carcinogens), both human-caused and natural. This work started a revolution in genetic toxicology. Ames received many awards for this and other scientific work, including the first research award of the Federation of American Societies for Experimental Biology.

The first stage of the development of the test was the identification of a small set of histidine-requiring mutants in *Salmonella* bacteria that were particularly sensitive in detecting a variety of known mutagens in a back mutation test. P. E. Hartman and Ames had made thousands of histidine mutants in the course of their classic studies on the regulation of the histidine operon. During this early work Ames and H. J. Whitfield, Jr., made an extremely important advance in mutagenesis theory in the identification of the acridine half-mustards as the first class of effective frameshift mutagens in bacteria. These mutagens contained a flat aromatic ring system that could have a stacking interaction with deoxyribonucleic acid (DNA). This led him to add to his test system several tester strains containing mutants revertible by different frameshift mutagens; he later showed that each of these had a characteristic long repetitive sequence in the DNA at the site of the histidine mutation. This work later led Ames to the recognition that certain active forms of carcinogens were frameshift mutagens having the same type of structural attributes.

Over the years Ames improved the test system in a variety of ways, many of these making use of the sophisticated advances in molecular biology that came out of

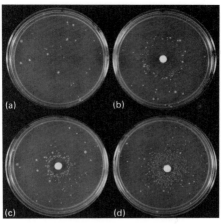

Test for environmental mutagen. Each petri plate contains tester strain TA98, and plates *c* and *d* also contain a rat liver microsomal activation system. Mutagens were applied to filter-paper disks, which were then placed in the center of plates *b-d*. *(a)* Control plate, showing spontaneous revertants. In the other plates, mutagen induced revertant colonies (circle around disk) were produced by *(b)* the Japanese food additive furylfuramide (AF-2), *(c)* the carcinogen aflatoxin B_1, and *(d)* 2-aminofluorene. *(From B. N. Ames, J. McCann, and E. Yamasaki, Methods for detecting carcinogens and mutagens with the Salmonella/mammalian-microsome mutagenicity test, Mutation Research, 31:347, 1975)*

basic research with the enteric bacteria. A major advance in detecting carcinogens came with the addition of a liver homogenate to the test system as a first approximation of mammalian metabolism.

A study by Ames and Joyce McCann on the validation of the *Salmonella* test involved 300 chemicals that had been examined in animal cancer tests. This validation showed the power of the test, and their finding that about 90 percent of carcinogens were detected as mutagens was subsequently confirmed in several other validations in other laboratories.

Many important environmental chemicals with very widespread human exposure were discovered by using Ames's test, and Ames was involved with two of these: hair dyes and the flame retardant *tris*-(2,3-dibromopropyl) phosphate.

Ames made a number of important discoveries in molecular biology in addition to his work in genetic toxicology. These included his pioneering studies on the regulation of the histidine operon and the discovery of the role of the transfer ribonucleic acid tRNA[his] in the regulation. His paper with R. G. Martin on sucrose gradient centrifugation for determining the molecular weight of proteins in com-

plex mixtures was one of the most cited papers in the scientific literature (*Journal of Biological Chemistry*, 236:1372–1379, 1961).

Ames was brought up in New York City, where he graduated from the Bronx High School of Science in 1946. He received his B.A. in biochemistry from Cornell University in 1950 and his Ph.D. in biology from the California Institute of Technology in 1953. He spent 15 years at the National Institutes of Health, mainly in the National Institute of Arthritis and Metabolic Diseases. He joined the biochemistry department at the University of California at Berkeley as a full professor in 1968. Ames received the Eli Lilly Award of the American Chemical Society in 1964, and was elected to the National Academy of Sciences in 1972. In 1960 he married Dr. Giovanna Ferro-Luzzi (also on the faculty at Berkeley). In 1961 they spent their sabbatical in the laboratories of F. H. C. Crick in Cambridge, England, and F. Jacob in Paris. *See* CRICK, FRANCIS HARRY COMPTON; JACOB, FRANÇOIS.

For background information *see* BACTERIAL GENETICS; CANCER (BIOLOGY); MOLECULAR BIOLOGY; MUTATION; ONCOLOGY in the McGraw-Hill Encyclopedia of Science and Technology. ∎

AMMANN, OTHMAR HERMANN

American engineer

Born *Mar. 29, 1879, Schaffhausen, Switzerland*
Died *Sept. 22, 1965, Rye, NY, U.S.A.*

As engineer and designer, Ammann was responsible for the planning and construction of the George Washington Bridge, the Lincoln Tunnel, the Triborough and Bronx-Whitestone bridges, and the Verrazano-Narrows Bridge, all in New York City. For his engineering achievements he received the National Medal of Science in 1964.

A 1902 graduate in civil engineering of the Swiss Federal Polytechnic Institute, Ammann went to the United States in 1904 and was employed on the construction of steel railway bridges. In 1905 he joined the Pennsylvania Steel Company and worked on the Queensboro Bridge in New York City. From 1912 to 1923 he was chief assistant to the consulting engineer Gustav Lindenthal, helping to design and construct the Hell Gate Bridge in

New York City and the Ohio River Bridge at Sciotoville, OH.

In 1923 Ammann established his own consulting office and began designing a bridge he proposed to build across the Hudson River, connecting upper Manhattan and New Jersey. The Port of New York Authority in 1924 agreed to undertake and finance this project (later called the George Washington Bridge), and Ammann was made first chief bridge engineer. Completed in 1931, the bridge (spanning 3500 feet, or 1050 meters, a record at the time) embodied several departures in design. In so massive a suspension bridge, Ammann believed he could safely omit the customary stiffening trusses at the level of the roadway that serve to minimize sideways vibration, since the bridge's own weight would keep it steady. This economy extended to the design of the towers, whose original plans called for concrete, steel, and stone construction. By substituting an openwork steel design, Ammann also effected an esthetic advance.

From 1930 to 1937 Ammann held the post of chief engineer of the New York Port Authority, and was its director of engineering from 1937 to 1939. In this capacity he directed the planning and construction of the Triborough Bridge, the Bronx-Whitestone Bridge, and the 8216-foot (2465-meter) Lincoln Tunnel under the Hudson River. He also served as a member of the board of engineers of the Golden Gate Bridge, which was opened in 1937.

Ammann returned to private consultation in 1939, and for the next several years he designed bridges (including the Yorktown Bridge) and highways in New York and New Jersey. In 1946 he entered into partnership with Charles S. Whitney, an engineer engaged in the design of bridges and specialized structures. The firm of Ammann and Whitney designed and supervised construction of the Throgs Neck Bridge in New York City, the Dulles International Airport in Washington, DC, and three buildings for New York City's Lincoln Center for the Performing Arts. Ammann drew up plans for the Verrazano-Narrows Bridge, spanning New York harbor from Brooklyn to Staten Island. This bridge, opened in 1965, is the longest and heaviest suspension bridge in the world.

Ammann recognized the importance of esthetics in bridge construction and designed his structures for the optimum combination of simplicity, engineering perfection, and beauty.

For background information *see* BRIDGE in the McGraw-Hill Encyclopedia of Science and Technology. ∎

ANDERS, EDWARD
★ American cosmochemist

Born June 21, 1926, Libau, Latvia

Anders is known for his studies of meteorites and lunar rocks, aimed at reconstructing the early history of the solar system. He and his associates solved several major problems in this area and made significant contributions to others: origin of diamonds and organic matter in meteorites; chemical processes in the solar nebula; composition of the planets; presolar matter in meteorites; and relations between meteorites and asteroids.

Anders began his work on meteorites in 1959 by questioning the established view that meteorites came from lunar-sized bodies (diameters of 1500–2000 kilometers) rather than from asteroids (10–300 kilometers). With M. E. Lipschutz, he showed that meteoritic diamonds, previously cited as evidence for large bodies with high internal pressures, actually had formed by high-speed impacts, such as that which made the Arizona Meteor Crater. With R. A. Fish and G. G. Goles, he showed that large bodies were not necessary for melting and gravitational phase separations, provided a transient heat source had been present, such as the extinct radionuclide ^{26}Al. (Evidence for extinct ^{26}Al in meteorites was obtained in 1974.)

In 1964 Anders wrote an influential review on the origin of meteorites, attempting to synthesize all available information on the subject. It marked the beginning of a long-term effort (mainly with John W. Larimer) to explain the chemical composition of meteorites and planets. The picture that emerged over the next decade was that meteorites were original condensates from the solar nebula (as first suggested by H. C. Urey and John A. Wood), but modified by four fractionation processes that enriched or depleted whole groups of elements. With R. Ganapathy, J. W. Morgan, and T. Owen, Anders extended this concept to the Earth, Moon, and Mars and showed that their chemical compositions could be derived from the abundances of only four index elements: iron, uranium, potassium, and thallium. *See* UREY, HAROLD CLAYTON.

Parallel with these efforts, Anders tried to account for the organic matter found in carbonaceous chondrites, the most primitive meteorites. With R. Hayatsu and M. H. Studier, he showed between 1965 and 1977 that essentially all organic compounds seen in meteorites could be produced in the solar nebula from CO, H_2, and NH_3 in the presence of meteoritic dust as a catalyst, under the conditions already inferred from the inorganic chemistry of meteorites. This process—a variant of the industrial Fischer-Tropsch synthesis—also seemed able to account for most interstellar molecules.

In the early 1960s Anders and his pathologist colleague, F. W. Fitch, were the principal opponents of the vigorously promoted claim that the organic compounds in meteorites were the products of extraterrestrial life. They showed that the alleged microfossils in carbonaceous chondrites ("organized elements") actually were airborne contaminants, such as fly ash or pollen grains. The most spectacular example turned out to be a ragweed pollen grain that had been distorted into a bizarre, unfamiliar shape by histological staining.

Starting with the *Apollo 11* mission in 1969, Anders and his coworkers (notably, Morgan, Ganapathy, J. C. Laul, U. Krähenbühl, J. Hertogen, and M. J. Janssens) took part in the study of lunar samples. By neutron activation analysis for various rare elements, they established the Moon's extraordinary depletion in volatile and noble metals and the history of its bombardment by meteorites. For the past 3.5×10^9 years, the Moon was bombarded mainly by micrometeorites of primitive composition—presumably dust of disintegrating comets. Previous to that, it was bombarded mainly by larger bodies (diameters to 100 km) of more varied, fractionated composition—presumably late building blocks of the planets.

Later, Anders and his group (R. S. Lewis, B. Srinivasan, and L. Alaerts) studied primordial noble gases in primitive meteorites. By developing novel mineral separation techniques, they made major progress in unraveling the complex tangle of isotopically distinct noble gas components. One of these components is presolar, and apparently resides in dust grains ejected from red giant stars. Another, still controversial, component may represent decay products of a volatile superheavy element (of atomic number 113–115?) that perhaps once existed in meteorites.

Anders fled his native Latvia during World War II and began his higher education at the University of Munich in 1946. Barred for 2 years from immigration to the United States on the grounds that this would be "prejudicial to the interests of the United States," he finally entered in 1949 and resumed his education at Columbia University (A.M., 1951; Ph.D., 1954; Medal for Excellence, 1966), where he was strongly influenced by his research sponsor, the radiochemist J. M. Miller. After a year as instructor in chemistry at the University of Illinois, he joined the University of Chicago in 1955, holding joint appointments in the chemistry department and the Enrico Fermi Institute. In 1973 he was appointed Horace B. Horton Professor of Physical Sciences. His honors included the Newcomb Cleveland Prize (American Association for the Advancement of Science, 1959), the J. Lawrence Smith Medal (National Academy of Sciences, 1971), and the Frederick C. Leonard Medal (Meteoritical Society, 1974). Anders was elected to the American Academy of Arts and Sciences (1973), the National Academy of Sciences (1974), and the Royal Astronomical Society (1974).

For background information *see* COSMOGONY; METEORITE; SUPERTRANSURANICS in the McGraw-Hill Encyclopedia of Science and Technology. ∎

ANDERSON, CHARLES ALFRED
★ American geologist

Born June 6, 1902, Bloomington, CA, U.S.A.

Anderson was introduced to the problems of volcanic rocks in 1928, when he studied a cinder cone and its associated lava flows east of Lassen Peak in northern California. Throughout his professional career volcanic rocks were a major interest, with emphasis on field studies leading to the preparation of geologic maps illustrating the sequence of events, followed by microscopic and chemical studies of the rocks.

The basaltic lava flows east of Lassen Peak contain scattered broken crystals and fragments of quartz, SiO_2, whereas no quartz is present in the fine crystal matrix of the lava, but bright green olivine crystals, $(Mg, Fe)_2SiO_4$, are conspicuous. Olivine is an orthosilicate and can crystallize only from lava that is deficient in SiO_2, so the quartz cannot be in equilibrium with the olivine; the association, together with the absence of quartz in the olivine-bearing matrix, indicates that the quartz is foreign and must have been picked up by the molten lava as it rose in the volcanic vent. Later studies by Anders in the Clear Lake area north of San Francisco revealed foreign quartz in other olivine basaltic flows, as well as the reverse relationship of scattered olivine crystals in rhyolitic obsidian, which has a high SiO_2 content; the magnesian-rich olivine is obviously not in equilibrium with the obsidian and is another example of the mixing of foreign material in rising molten lava.

West of Lassen Peak, extensive bouldery plains are striking features of the landscape, and in 1929 Anderson made a study of the volcanic rocks exposed in the canyons cut into the plains. He found that mudflows originating from old volcanoes to the east were responsible for the spreading out of thick accumulations of unsorted angular lava fragments in a matrix of volcanic ash. As the fine ash was washed out of the matrix, the boulders lagged behind and were concentrated on the surface. The concept of mudflows for the origin of these kinds of volcanic deposits has been widely accepted. In 1930 Anderson studied the decomposition of lava fragments immersed in hot springs near Lassen Peak, and he found fragments with an unaltered core grading outward to a soft powdery exterior. The progressive leaching of the iron, aluminum, magnesium, calcium, sodium, and potassium from the fragments leaves a residue of high silica content, similar to altered rocks found in some ore deposits.

Spectacular obsidian flows, about 1000 years old, in the Medicine Lake Highland in northeastern California attracted Anderson's attention in 1932, and his detailed geologic mapping proved that one of the flows began with the eruption of dacite, continued with the simultaneous eruption of rhyolitic obsidian mixed with the dacite, and ended with the eruption solely of rhyolitic obsidian. A single lava flow composed of two dissimilar rock types is rare, and the preservation of the flow top and margins is so clear at Medicine Lake as to leave no doubt that this is a composite flow, an interpretation that has been helpful in understanding older but similar composite flows. Anderson then prepared a geologic map of the entire Medicine Lake Highland, which documents a complex volcanic history starting with the building of a broad-shield volcano and culminating in the central collapse to form an oval-shaped caldera. New volcanic vents formed along the caldera margins, erupting a series of lava flows that buried the caldera walls. The obsidian flows 1000 years of age mark the final episode of the volcanic history.

In 1939 Anderson joined C. W. Merriam in the mapping of the Roberts Mountains in central Nevada, which documented the existence of a low-angle thrust fault in which Ordovician lava flows and tuffs, black shales, and bedded cherts were thrust eastward over limestones of Ordovician and Devonian age. Subsequent geologic studies have demonstrated that the Roberts thrust is an impressive and widespread tectonic feature in central Nevada, marking the close of an important orogenic disturbance. The mapping of the Tertiary volcanic rocks in the Roberts Mountains revealed that they were erupted on an erosion surface that existed prior to the normal faulting that displaced the thrust plate and lava flows. Chemical studies showed that these central Nevada lavas have a high potassium content, unlike the lava in California and Oregon, but similar to many of the lavas in Utah and New Mexico.

The Scripps Institution of Oceanography sponsored a scientific cruise to the Gulf of California in 1940, and Anderson was invited to participate in land surveys on some of the islands in the gulf, as well as in selected areas in Sonora and Baja California. Volcanic rocks are important elements in land geology, and sufficient evidence was gathered to indicate that the Gulf of California originated in early Pliocene time and that the dislocation along the western margin of the gulf coincided in part with a chain of older volcanic vents. Only one island represents a volcanic cone built on the gulf floor.

During World War II Anderson joined the U.S. Geological Survey and made an intensive study of the copper deposit at Bagdad, AZ. The geologic mapping revealed that the copper deposit is localized in a central stock of granodiorite porphyry at the intersection of two dike swarms. Structural disturbances produced a number of intersecting fractures in this stock, which served as a sponge for rising, hot, mineralizing solutions to react with the granodiorite porphyry. Some of the calcium, sodium, and magnesium was removed, and potassium, sulfur, and copper were added to form new K-feldspar, pyrite, and chalcopyrite.

After the war Anderson was involved in a long-term study of Precambrian volcanic rocks in central Arizona. He and his associates, S. C. Creasey, P. M. Blacet, and M. H. Krieger, were successful in recognizing original textures and structures in the old volcanic rocks, and by patient geologic mapping they were able to portray the distribution of the diverse volcanic rocks and to determine their sequence. The rocks have been metamorphosed by the addition of 5–6 percent (by volume) of water during a period of increased heat flow and crustal deformation about 1,700,000,000 years ago. Chemical studies show that migration of sodium and potassium was important during metamorphism, indicating that recrystallization in part took place in an open system. The unraveling of the folded and faulted structure of these old volcanic rocks is of value for mineral exploration in the area, since the known ore deposits can now be related to particular segments of the volcanic sequence and to particular structural environments.

Anderson received his A.B. from Pomona College in 1924 and his Ph.D. from the University of California, Berkeley, in 1928. He taught geology at the University of California until 1942, when he joined the U.S. Geological Survey. He was chief of the Mineral Deposits Branch from 1953 to 1958 and chief geologist of the Survey from 1959 to 1964. He was elected to the American Academy of Arts and Sciences in 1956 and to the National Academy of Sciences in 1957.

Anderson wrote *The Tuscan Formation of Northern California* (1933), *Volcanoes of the Medicine Lake Highland, California* (1941), and articles on his studies in Nevada, the Gulf of California, and Arizona.

For background information *see* LAVA; VOLCANO; VOLCANOLOGY in the McGraw-Hill Encyclopedia of Science and Technology. ∎

ANDERSON, EDGAR SHANNON
★ American botanist

> **Born** Nov. 9, 1897, Forestville, NY, U.S.A.
> **Died** June 18, 1969, St. Louis, MO, U.S.A.

Anderson was among those who brought the techniques and concepts of cytology and genetics to problems of classification and phylogeny. In 1936 he demonstrated that the semi-isolated local populations of the common blue irises of eastern North America are independent evolutionary units, each differentiating in its own way. From a variety of evidence he established the hypothesis that *Iris versicolor* is a hybrid between two older American species that doubled its chromosome number and is fertile and true-bleeding. With cytological and taxonomic colleagues, he monographed the tradescantias native to the United States, incidentally discovering *Tradescantia palu-*

dosa, widely useful in cytological and radiation laboratories.

With the genus *Apocynum* he made progeny tests of the rare putative hybrid between two common American species and demonstrated that the chief effect of hybridization in this group is to increase variability in the parental species. This led ultimately to his introduction of the term "introgressive hybridization" to denote the gradual infiltration of the germ plasm of one species into that of another as a consequence of hybridization and repeated backcrossing. In its shortened form, "introgression," this term is now commonly used, and Anderson became most widely known for his short monograph on introgression (1949) and for his studies of the importance of hybridization in evolution.

As a corollary to these studies, Anderson in 1939 analyzed character recombination in the second generation of a semifertile cross between two very dissimilar species of flowering tobacco. He measured the recombinations actually achieved and demonstrated that they were a fraction of those possible without such hindrances as linkage and the multiple effects of single factors. He showed that the total effect of linkage was greater than had been realized and that in such hybrids all the multiple factor characters that went into the cross together tended to be partially associated in the progeny.

This led Anderson to an interest in other wide crosses, and when P. C. Man-

gelsdorf and R. G. Reeves demonstrated in 1939 that *Zea mays* could be hybridized with *Tripsacum,* he joined H. C. Cutler in studying the latter genus. *See* MANGELS-DORF, PAUL CHRISTOPH.

Anderson discovered that the prevailing classifications of maize were artificial and that a natural classification might be possible but could only be worked toward as a goal. With his students, he began the study of the total variation pattern of maize, ancient and modern, concentrating on neglected features such as the male inflorescence. The innumerable cultivated varieties of *Z. mays* were found to be roughly divisible into natural regional groups (about 200 in the New World).

Anderson and his students assisted in the study and monographing of them under a committee set up by the National Academy of Sciences–National Research Council. Through these studies he became interested in the importance of studying cultivated plants and weeds by a fusion of herbarium, cytological, and experimental-plot techniques.

In his attempts to study evolution in natural populations by measuring and analyzing their variation patterns, Anderson worked out a series of semigraphical techniques for dealing with such problems. The most generally adaptable of these techniques, pictorialized scatter diagrams, have been widely used.

The son of a professor of dairy husbandry, Anderson majored in horticulture and botany at Michigan State University, receiving his B.S. in 1918. His graduate training was under E. M. East at the Bussey Institution of Harvard University, where he earned an M.S. in 1920 and an Sc.D. in 1922. From 1931 to 1935 he was arborist to the Arnold Arboretum of Harvard University, and lecturer in botany at Harvard University. From 1922 to 1931, and again after 1935, he held joint appointments in the Henry Shaw School of Botany of Washington University and at the Missouri Botanical Garden, both in St. Louis. Anderson was elected to the National Academy of Sciences in 1954.

Anderson wrote *Introgressive Hybridization* (1949) and *Plants, Man and Life* (1952; rev. ed. 1967).

For background information *see* BREEDING, PLANT; CYTOLOGY; SPECIES POPULATION in the McGraw-Hill Encyclopedia of Science and Technology. ∎

ANDERSON, PHILIP WARREN
★ American physicist

Born *Dec. 13, 1923, Indianapolis, IN, U.S.A.*

For his contributions to the field of condensed matter physics, Anderson received the American Physical Society's O. E. Buckley Prize in 1964, the Dannie Heineman Prize of the Göttingen Academy of Sciences in 1975, the Nobel Prize (jointly with N. F. Mott and J. H. Van Vleck) in 1977, and the Guthrie Medal of the Institute of Physics (London) in 1978. *See* MOTT, SIR NEVILL (FRANCIS); VAN VLECK, JOHN HASBROUCK.

In the spectroscopy of gases, the line spectra are broadened when the gas density is high. To explain the breadths in terms of intermolecular interactions, or even better to learn about molecular interactions from the breadths, Anderson, building on the simpler theories of H. A. Lorentz, Foley, and others, developed a more general methodology for such problems, useful in the whole range from microwave through infrared and optical spectroscopy; and he calculated some of the first quantitative results for line breadths from known molecular interactions. The methods are still being used.

Anderson's attention was next focused on insulating magnetic materials such as ferrites and antiferromagnetic oxides. The problem was to discover what caused the alignment of atomic magnetic moments and spins and the particular arrangements observed. Building on H. A. Kramers's

old concept of "superexchange," he explored mechanisms for the interactions. Plausible assumptions about the interactions explained the spin patterns and the Curie-Néel points observed. Later, he tied in this theory (following the work of others) with modern crystal field theory, the theory of the behavior of isolated magnetic ions in insulators, and made a start toward a quantitative as well as qualitative theory of the exchange interactions responsible for this kind of magnetism. Anderson worked, too, on a number of other magnetic problems, notably the antiferromagnetic ground state and spin waves, where his contribution foreshadowed some of the methodology of modern many-body theory; and the localized state in metals (following J. Friedel), an idea important in the theory of magnetic alloys and closely related to more general problems of why iron and other transition metals are magnetic.

Following from this work, he studied the so-called Kondo effect involving anomalies in the scattering of very-low-energy free electrons by magnetic impurities, and gave the first qualitative solution of the problem of the state at low temperatures. This was one of the earliest applications or renormalization group techniques to solid-state and statistical mechanics problems. The work on magnetic impurities was cited by the Nobel Committee.

In the early 1950s line shapes and breadths in the various fields of magnetic resonance spectroscopy were opening up. Nicolaas Bloembergen, E. M. Purcell, and R. V. Pound had pioneered many fruitful ideas in nuclear resonance, and Van Vleck had done the same for electronic resonance, but again a quantitative mathematical understanding was needed to help in learning about atomic motions and interactions from the observed spectrum. Ferromagnetic resonance was even more a closed book from this point of view. Anderson contributed a mathematical methodology for attacking the problems of "exchange narrowing" and "motional narrowing" and relating them to atomic motion and exchange. He also undertook various studies of interactions and mechanisms. In ferromagnetic resonance, collaborative work with H. Suhl and others pioneered the ideas of imperfection broadening and spin-wave pumping, which clarified the field.

When the first theory explaining the ancient puzzle of superconductivity appeared in 1957—the BSC theory of John Bardeen, L. N. Cooper, and J. R. Schrieffer—basic problems of principle remained. Anderson was among the first to elucidate these questions and generalize the Bardeen-Cooper-Schrieffer methodology.

Anderson contributed to the solutions of a number of problems in the field of superconductivity. For example, the effects of imperfections on superconductivity are puzzlingly small in some cases, large in others. His "Theory of Dirty Superconductors" and related work introduced concepts and methodology that made this an accessible problem.

Again, the interactions that cause superconductivity are those between electrons and lattice vibrations that are fundamental to many other metallic properties, such as resistance; Bardeen, Cooper, and Schrieffer made no quantitative progress in calculating superconductivity from interactions, or vice versa. A combined theoretical and experimental attack on this problem, involving Anderson and others, led to remarkably detailed confirmation of the basic theory, as well as to ways of obtaining detailed information about metals more easily from superconductivity than from any other source. Essentially, this work led to an entirely new kind of spectroscopy—that of the electron-phonon interaction via tunneling spectroscopy in solids.

With Pierre Morel, a student and coworker in this endeavor, Anderson discussed in 1960 the physical properties of an anisotropic version of the BCS theory which they predicted might occur in the mass-3 isotope of liquid helium. This phenomenon was discovered by Osheroff and coworkers in 1972, and rather surprisingly one of the phases observed follows the earliest theory very well. With William F. Brinkman, Anderson explained, using a form of many-body technique known as spin fluctuation theory, the presence and properties of this phase, and contributed to the present rather complete understanding of these complex materials in many ways. The strongly anisotropic phase is now known as the ABM (Anderson-Brinkman-Morel) phase.

The nature of superconductivity is most clearly exhibited when the phenomenon breaks down, that is, when the superconductor shows resistance, or in a weak link such as a Josephson junction. Anderson worked in this area both theoretically and experimentally with the goal of demonstrating graphically that superconductivity involves coherent matter waves in the way lasers involve coherent light waves.

In the course of collaborative studies with G. Feher of line width effects of impurities in silicon, Anderson conceived in 1956–58 the concept of localization: the sudden failure of the process of quantum transport (such as spin diffusion or electronic conduction) when the randomness of the potential is sufficiently great. This idea was taken up by Mott, was extended (especially by use of the idea of the mobility edge), and after many years has become accepted as the keystone of what theoretical understanding scientists have of quantum transport in amorphous irregular, or random, systems, at least when these are metallically conducting or insulating. Other theoretical concepts relating to random systems (spin glass, tunneling centers in glass, attractive centers) occupied Anderson during later years. This work was cited for the Heineman Prize and the Nobel Prize.

The son and grandson of Midwestern science professors, Anderson majored in electronic physics at Harvard, receiving a B.S. summa cum laude in 1943. After doing antenna engineering at the Naval Research Laboratory in 1943–45, he returned to Harvard to do a thesis on pressure broadening with J. H. Van Vleck (M.A. 1947; Ph.D. 1949).

Thereafter Anderson was associated with the Bell Telephone Laboratories, serving in 1958–60 as chairperson of the theoretical physics department. In 1967 he was made a permanent "visiting" professor at Cambridge University, spending half of each year there until 1975; he then became Joseph Henry Professor (part-time) at Princeton University, and held the rank of consulting director at Bell Telephone Laboratories. He was a member of the National Academy of Sciences. Anderson wrote *Concepts in Solids* (1963).

For background information *see* MAGNETISM; SOLID-STATE PHYSICS; SPECTROSCOPY; SUPERCONDUCTIVITY in the McGraw-Hill Encyclopedia of Science and Technology. ∎

ANDRADE, EDWARD NEVILLE DA COSTA
★ English physicist

Born Dec. 27, 1887, London, England
Died June 6, 1971, London, England

Andrade's researches in physics were concerned with the mechanical properties of matter in the solid and liquid states. A

law concerning the creep of metals and a law governing the variation of the viscosity of liquids with temperature are particularly associated with his name. In his first papers on the flow of metals under large stresses, Andrade emphasized the advantage of measuring the movement under conditions of constant stress rather than under the then prevalent conditions of constant load, which means continuously increasing stress. A device now in general use for the maintenance of constant stress is the Andrade-Chalmers bar, an improvement on the one first used by Andrade. In these early papers he established the existence of a transient flow with strain proportional to $t^{1/3}$ (Andrade's law) and of a quasi-viscous flow with strain proportional to t for a variety of metals, including solid mercury. He also showed that the very different behavior of the different metals at atmospheric temperature was determined by the relation of this temperature to the melting point. This work, carried out at University College, London, before World War I, was the foundation of the study of metallic creep as a precise science. It was interrupted by a year at Heidelberg devoted to work on the electrical properties of flames.

In 1913 Andrade went to work with Ernest Rutherford at Manchester. They carried out the first measurements of the wavelength of the gamma rays from radium, which had an important bearing on the question of radioactive isotopes. The outbreak of World War I in 1914 cut short Andrade's collaboration with the

founder of the modern theory of the atom.

After the war, having no opportunity to work on atomic themes, Andrade turned his attention to the viscosity of liquids. In 1930 he put forward a simple formula, usually known by his name, expressing the variations of viscosity with temperature, and a more precise version of the formula, which has been shown to represent experimental results very accurately. With student collaborators he worked out an experimental method, depending upon the damping of oscillations of a suspended sphere containing the liquid, for measuring the viscosity of liquid metals, which, being monomolecular, are the simplest form of liquid. Andrade was able to determine the viscosity of many metals in liquid form over a range of temperature with this method. The viscosity at melting point was found to obey a simple law. The effect of an electric field on the viscosity of normal, nonconducting liquids was established for the first time by the use of alternating fields, since there is no effect for nonpolar liquids, but a very small increase of viscosity proportional to the square of the field with polar liquids. Very large effects recorded by previous workers were shown to be spurious.

Andrade also took up work on single crystals of metals, which he had prepared accidentally before World War I. With Robert Roscoe he elaborated a method, which has since been widely used, of preparing single-crystal rods of metals of low melting point. Later, with Cyril Henderson, Andrade developed a method for metals of high melting point. The deformation of single-crystal rods of metals of hexagonal and face-centered cubic structure under stress was investigated in detail, and the differences of behavior were explained in terms of crystal structure. With single crystals of gold and silver, the phenomenon known as "easy glide" was discovered and elaborated.

A variety of problems in the field of sound were also solved during the period between the wars, including that of the remarkable behavior of particles in Kundt's tube. The behavior of the sensitive flame was analyzed and explained.

After World War II Andrade devised the method of studying the flow of polycrystalline metals under simple shear stress. With the appropriate apparatus this method has great advantages over the usual procedure of measuring the increase of strain under tension. The mechanical conditions are simpler; the sense of the

stress can be reversed at will; and the visible surface of the metal remains plane and of constant area, so that the behavior of the crystal grains accessible to microscopic or x-ray examination is typical of those throughout the metal. Andrade, in collaboration with K. H. Jolliffe, carried out a detailed investigation of the flow of the typical face-centered cubic metal lead by this method, which resulted in the discovery of new types of flow. In particular, they found a deformation strictly proportional to $t^{1/2}$, which takes place at small strains before the $t^{1/3}$ regime is established. Also, at large shear strains, exceeding 30 percent, they found a non-Newtonian viscous behavior, the rate of flow at constant stress being constant and the same for forward or reversed direction of stress. At lower strains, before the grain structure of the metal is thoroughly broken up, the behavior under forward and reversed stress is quite different and very informative. With D. A. Aboav, Andrade investigated the flow of the typical hexagonal metal cadmium under simple shear, which showed differences of behavior from lead, explicable in terms of the crystal structure. In general, the complicated flow behavior of polycrystalline metals under the simple conditions of stressing in question could be explained in terms of intragranular behavior and grain boundary adjustment and migration. With Aboav he also investigated grain growth in metals, with results that threw new light on the problems.

Andrade became an authority in certain areas of the history of science, in particular the work of Newton, Hooke, and their contemporaries, as well as the early days of the Royal Society. From its inception he was chairman of the Royal Society committee dealing with the publication of Newton's letters.

Andrade's scientific career was not without its difficulties. The period of World War I, much of which he spent at the front, broke off his work with Rutherford. It was not until his appointment as Quain Professor of Physics in the University of London in 1928 that he had facilities for experimental research, and those very exiguous. Until the outbreak of war again in 1939, he built up a research school in which, with very simple apparatus, the work on viscosity, metal single crystals, and sound problems was carried out. During World War II, when he was employed in government work, his laboratory was destroyed by bombs. With it

went all his notes, a collection of valuable books, and manuscript letters from great figures in the world of science, including Lord Rutherford, Sir James Frazer, Sir Charles Sherrington, Charles Barkla, and Svante Arrhenius, with whom he was on terms of intimate friendship until the latter's death in 1927. After the war, then, there was nothing left of Andrade's laboratory but one or two bare rooms and some sand, with which he carried out, in collaboration with J. W. Fox, research on the mechanism of dilatancy. In 1950 Andrade was appointed director in the Royal Institution of Great Britain and director of the Davy Faraday Research Laboratory, posts from which he resigned in 1952. The work on the flow of metals under simple shear and on grain growth was carried out at the Imperial College of Science, where he became senior research fellow. Andrade was elected a fellow of the Royal Society in 1935 and later received the society's Hughes Medal. He was elected Membre Correspondant de l'Académie des Sciences, Institut de France, in 1950 and was awarded many honors in France. He was Chevalier Légion d'Honneur, Membre d'Honneur of the Société Française de Physique, and recipient of the Grande Médaille Osmond and the Holweck Prize.

His contact with Rutherford inspired Andrade to write *The Structure of the Atom* (1923; rev. 3d ed. 1927), which was for a time the standard work on the subject. For the general reader he wrote *The Mechanism of Nature* (1930), translated into six foreign languages. Andrade was the author of other popular works on aspects of physics; of books on Newton, Rutherford, and the Royal Society; and of accounts of Doppler and his work, and of Benjamin Franklin's life in London.

For background information *see* CREEP OF MATERIALS; METAL, MECHANICAL PROPERTIES OF; SINGLE CRYSTAL; VISCOSITY OF LIQUIDS in the McGraw-Hill Encyclopedia of Science and Technology. ∎

ANDREWES, CHRISTOPHER HOWARD
★ British virologist

Born June 7, 1896, London, England

Andrewes's lifelong interest in natural history—birds, insects, and plants—greatly influenced his approach to viruses,

the main subject of study throughout his career. He was fortunate in beginning a life of work in medical research at a time when viruses were first becoming the object of serious interest to laboratory workers. He was thus working throughout a period of tremendous advances in this field. Although he worked at different times with many viruses infecting animals, including those causing tumors, his main contributions were in three areas: influenza, common colds, and virus classification.

In 1933, working with Wilson Smith and P. P. Laidlaw, Andrewes first transmitted the virus of human influenza to an experimental animal, the ferret, and thus laid the foundations of present knowledge of this virus infection. He continued to study it for many years. In 1947 it became clear to him that the antigenic changes which the virus periodically underwent needed to be studied on a worldwide basis. The World Health Organization (WHO) was readily persuaded to take an interest, and Andrewes, rather to his surprise and dismay, found himself in charge of a World Influenza Center, with an associated network of influenza laboratories throughout the world. The chief function of the center was to collect and compare influenza viruses from different countries; it soon seemed that new variants, when they appeared, tended to spread rapidly around the world, displacing older ones. This knowledge was a matter of importance for manufacture of flu vaccines, because vaccines against out-of-date strains

were of little or no use against new ones, and early information concerning changes in the antigenic composition of the virus was greatly valued. Later, networks of reference centers for viruses of other kinds were set up by WHO, and these networks followed the pattern originally laid down for influenza study.

The other most troublesome infection of temperate climes is the common cold. By 1946 almost all the important viruses affecting humans, other than colds, had been transmitted to animals or cultivated in fertile hens' eggs, so Andrewes undertook the formidable task of trying to do something about colds. No other approach being possible, it was necessary to use volunteers to test for the presence of virus in materials under unvestigation, by putting drops up the nose and waiting to see whether a cold developed. The Medical Research Council supported Andrewes by setting up a common cold research unit at Salisbury. Here volunteers came, two dozen or so at a time, every fortnight, prepared to be given common colds in the cause of science; mostly they enjoyed the experience. The primary objective was to find a way to make a common cold virus accessible to quantitative study in the laboratory. But whereas an attack of influenza had yielded results 14 days after the opening shot of the campaign, it took 14 years before a similar success attended work on the common cold. Attempts to infect animals or to grow the virus in eggs were unsuccessful, so in 1952 Andrewes concentrated the attack, in which a number of colleagues were concerned, on attempts to grow the virus in tissue culture. A glimmering of success came in the following year, but it was not until 1960 that David Tyrrell and colleagues, working in the Salisbury laboratory, found a way of regularly growing cold viruses—now known as rhinoviruses—in culture. Unfortunately it later appeared that there are so many serological types of these rhinoviruses that specific prophylaxis may not be easily achieved.

In 1949 Andrewes and Dorothy Horstmann, who was visiting from Yale, showed that some viruses were readily inactivated by ether while others were not. When ether sensitivity and size were taken together, the first indications of a rational classification of viruses began to appear. A classification of viruses published about that time seemed to An-

drewes to be on wholly wrong lines, laying too much stress on the symptoms produced and neglecting more fundamental characteristics. He contacted the International Committee for the Nomenclature of Bacteria, which then set up a subcommittee, with Andrewes as its head, to deal with viruses. At the first meeting in Rio de Janeiro in 1950, at subsequent international congresses in Rome, Stockholm, Montreal, and Moscow, and by means of correspondence and questionnaires, the matter was bit by bit hammered out. Most virologists were long apathetic, but finally much interest was engendered and the acquisition of new facts, particularly about virus morphology, led to general agreement as to the basis on which virus classification should proceed.

Andrewes studied medicine at St. Bartholomew's Hospital in London, qualifying in 1921. He then spent a few years combining clinical medicine and laboratory work: two of them, 1923–25, were at the Hospital of the Rockefeller Institute in New York.

In 1927 Andrewes opted for a laboratory career and joined the staff of the National Institute for Medical Research at Hampstead, moving with it later to Mill Hill. He remained at the institute for 34 years, until his retirement in 1961, becoming head of the Division of Bacteriology and Virus Research in 1940 and deputy director of the institute in 1952. Andrewes was elected a fellow of the Royal Society in 1939 and knighted in 1961; he was elected a foreign associate of the U.S. National Academy of Sciences in 1964.

Before retiring he had accumulated an enormous mass of records about viruses, and this was distilled into a textbook, *Viruses of Vertebrates* (1964; 3d ed., with H. G. Pereira, 1972), which brought together, on a taxonomic basis, the viruses affecting humans and other vertebrates. He also wrote *Viral and Bacterial Zoonoses* with J. R. Walton (1977). Other books, *The Common Cold* (1965), *The Natural History of Viruses* (1967), *The Lives of Wasps and Bees* (1969), *Viruses and Cancer* (1970), and *In Pursuit of the Common Cold* (1973), were less technical, being directed to lay as well as medical readers.

For background information *see* ANIMAL VIRUS; COLD, COMMON; INFLUENZA in the McGraw-Hill Encyclopedia of Science and Technology. ∎

ANFINSEN, CHRISTIAN BOEHMER
★ American biochemist

Born *Mar. 26, 1916, Monessen, PA, U.S.A.*

Anfinsen began his studies on the amino acid sequences, biosynthesis, and three-dimensional structures of proteins in 1948, focusing on what may be called the evolutionary design of proteins. His work helped establish that the so-called primary structure of proteins—that is, the amino acid sequence—contains all the information necessary to determine the complex and unique three-dimensional structure that characterizes each protein molecule in living cells. For his work on the three-dimensional structure and function of ribonuclease and the phenomenon of spontaneous folding of protein chains, Anfinsen received the Nobel Prize in chemistry in 1972.

During 1954–55, as a recipient of the Rockefeller Public Service Award, Anfinsen worked in the laboratories of Kai Linderstrøm-Lang at the Carlsberg Laboratory in Copenhagen. His work in this stimulating environment led him to appreciate the potential of research on proteins as organic chemicals, stripped of their classical mystique as large, amorphous macromolecules. He wrote, with Robert Redfield, a review article on the relationships between protein structure and function that strongly influenced his later research activities. The attitudes developed during this period—that proteins are like other organic molecules, only larger and more complex—led directly to the studies on the spontaneous folding of polypeptide chains.

Although Anfinsen's work was mainly of a purely biochemical nature, its implications may be more important in evolutionary theory. The information content of living cells appears to be encoded exclusively in the linear arrangement of nucleotides within the enormously large strands of deoxyribonucleic acid (DNA) molecules that constitute the genetic material of the cell nucleus and of certain other cellular organelles. This information is translated, through the mechanisms of protein biosynthesis, into linear polypeptide chains. Three-dimensional structure first appears when these linear polypeptides undergo a transition that converts them into the highly coiled and folded form that characterizes the enzymes, hormones, and structural proteins of living cells. At the same time these biologically inert polypeptides assume their characteristic biological function.

Biological function, therefore, may be thought of as a series of problems in the geometry of protein molecules, in which amino acid residues that may be quite distant from one another in a linear sense are brought into close proximity to create an "active center" that facilitates the performance of a unique biological function. Thus, at the molecular level, the process of evolution may be envisioned as the "selection" of protein molecules possessing amino acid sequences determined by the nucleotide sequences of the particular portions of DNA that code for them and that can fold into three-dimensional forms compatible with the function in question. Anfinsen's experimental studies make it possible to predict that computer programs can be devised which will permit the computation of protein geometry without the laborious application of crystallographic analysis so elegantly applied by M. F. Perutz, J. C. Kendrew, D. C. Phillips, and their colleagues. *See* KENDREW, JOHN COWDERY; PERUTZ, MAX FERDINAND.

Anfinsen and his colleagues showed that a variety of native proteins, particularly those containing rigid, covalent cross linkages in the form of disulfide bonds, could be converted by reduction of these bonds in denaturing solvents into random linear chains. These randomized protein chains, after purification and exposure to oxidizing conditions at neutrality, were found to reform the same disulfide bonds and to assume three-dimensional conformations indistinguishable from the original native protein.

The son of a Norwegian engineer, Anfinsen received a B.A. from Swarthmore College in 1937. He studied organic chemistry at the University of Pennsylvania (M.S., 1939) and, after a year of fellowship at the Carlsberg Laboratory in 1939–40, studied in the department of biological chemistry at Harvard Medical School, receiving his Ph.D. in 1943. He left Harvard Medical School in 1950 to become chief of the Laboratory of Cellular Physiology and Metabolism in the National Heart Institute of the National Institutes of Health. He returned to Harvard Medical School as professor of biological chemistry in 1962–63, then went to the National Institute of Arthritis and Metabolic Diseases in 1963 as chief of the Laboratory of Chemical Biology. In addition to his research activities, Anfinsen served as director of the Research Associate Program at the National Institutes of Health and as a member of the board of governors of the Weizmann Institute of Science in Rehovoth, Israel. From 1973 onward, his research was concerned with the isolation of human interferon and with attempts to characterize this antiviral material. He was elected to the American Academy of Arts and Sciences in 1958, to the National Academy of Sciences in 1963, and to the Royal Danish Academy in 1964. He was the recipient of seven honorary degrees.

Anfinsen wrote *The Molecular Basis of Evolution* (1959).

For background information *see* MOLECULAR BIOLOGY; PROTEIN in the McGraw-Hill Encyclopedia of Science and Technology. ∎

APKER, LEROY
★ American experimental physicist

Born *June 11, 1915, Rochester, NY, U.S.A.*

Studies of photoelectric emission of electrons from semiconductors by Apker and his colleague, E. A. Taft, led to the discovery of a new process called exciton-induced photoemission in potassium iodide crystals. In this phenomenon, energy first was absorbed from a beam of ultraviolet radiation by the ions of the entire crystal. Subsequently, in a secondary process, it was concentrated with surprisingly high efficiency onto a relatively small number of electrons localized in defects called color centers. For contributions to the understanding of energy transfer in crystals, Apker received the Buckley Prize of the American Physical Society in 1955.

In the early 1930s R. H. Fowler and L. A. DuBridge showed that the quantum theory of electrons in solids substantially explained the previously puzzling behavior of photoemission from metals. E. U. Condon in 1938 pointed out that photoelectrons from semiconductors should behave in a markedly different way. R. A. Millikan had suspected something like this as long ago as 1916, when he was verifying Einstein's photoelectric equation, but theoretical background for further exploration and understanding was lacking at that time. *See* CONDON, EDWARD UHLER.

In 1948 at the General Electric Research Laboratory in Schenectady, Apker, Taft, and J. E. Dickey completed experiments that clearly showed the effect discussed 10 years before by Condon. They concluded that the fastest photoelectrons from a semiconductor such as germanium or tellurium were much slower than those from a metal like platinum that had the same work function—the latter being the quantity that determines the behavior of the thermionic electron emission and the contact potential. Useful conclusions could be drawn about the electronic structure of the semiconductors by making these photoelectric measurements. An important factor here was that process of energy transfer was relatively simple. In a typical case, an electron in the semiconductor first absorbed the entire energy of a photon in the beam of incident ultraviolet radiation. Then it escaped as a photoelectron through the barrier at the semiconductor surface.

At the time that this work was being done, an intriguing group of ionic crystals had been very little explored by photoelectric methods. These were the alkali halides, such as potassium iodide. It is possible for some of the negative iodine ions to be missing in this crystal structure and for the vacant places to be filled with electrons. Such defects, color centers, absorb visible and ultraviolet radiation, coloring the crystal in a range of photon energies for which it is normally quite transparent. It was well known that ab-

sorption of visible radiation could set the trapped electrons free inside the crystal, producing photoconductivity. In contrast, there had been very little work on photoemission, and it appeared that this would be an interesting area to examine. It turned out that visible and near-ultraviolet radiation not only produced photoconductivity but also produced photoemission. The latter was similar to that from the more usual metals and semiconductors.

Farther in the ultraviolet, however, a very different kind of photoemission was discovered. In this region of the spectrum, the potassium iodide crystal itself has a very sharp, intense absorption line, which is due to the formation of electrically neutral entities called excitons. These excitons transferred energy with remarkably high efficiency to the electrons in the color centers, the excited electrons being ejected from the crystal as exciton-induced photoemission. In later work, it became clear that this is a relatively common phenomenon in other ionic crystals, such as barium oxide.

A student of L. A. DuBridge, Apker attended the University of Rochester, receiving an A.B. in 1937 and a Ph.D. in physics in 1941. In that year he joined the staff of the General Electric Research Laboratory in Schenectady, NY.

For background information *see* COLOR CENTERS; PHOTOEMISSION; SEMICONDUCTOR in the McGraw-Hill Encyclopedia of Science and Technology. ∎

APPLETON, SIR EDWARD (VICTOR)
English physicist

Born Sept. 6, 1892, Bradford, Yorkshire, England
Died Apr. 21, 1965, Edinburgh, Scotland

Appleton's fame is founded on his demonstration of the existence of the ionosphere and on his detailed investigations of its structure, distribution, and variations. This work had a profound theoretical and practical importance: theoretical, as bearing on the ionization produced by solar photons and particles in the tenuous upper atmosphere and its wide influence on the physics of near space; practical, as concerning the reflection, and so the transmission, of radar waves. For "his work on the physical properties of the upper atmosphere and especially for his

discovery of the ionospheric region called the Appleton layer," Appleton received the Nobel Prize in physics in 1947.

An electrified layer in the upper atmosphere had been postulated independently by Oliver Heaviside and A. E. Kennelly in 1902, both of whom pointed out that the reflection of electromagnetic waves by such a layer would account for the transmission of wireless signals from England· to Newfoundland effected by Guglielmo Marconi. Such transmission could have taken place only if the waves had followed the curvature of the Earth's surface. There was, however, no other indication of the existence of such a layer, let alone of its nature or height.

During World War I, Appleton, as a temporary officer dealing with radio, became familiar with the use of thermionic valves, then a novelty, with which relatively powerful transmitters and receivers could be built, and was confronted with the problem of fading signals. After the war he conceived the notion of interference between waves reflected from an ionized layer in the upper atmosphere and the direct waves traveling along the Earth's surface. Working with transmitter and receiver about 70 miles (112 kilometers) apart, he showed, with the assistance of M. A. F. Barnett, that slow frequency modulation in the transmitter produced a series of maxima and minima in the received signal. The number of beats produced by a given change of frequency gave a direct estimate of the height of the reflecting layer above the ground, which

came out to be about 90 kilometers. This result was confirmed by determining the angle made by the reflected beam with the horizontal, given by comparing the simultaneous signal variations received with a loop aerial and with a vertical antenna. In this manner the existence of an ionized reflecting layer was first established.

The degree of reflection depends upon the frequency of the waves and the density of ionization. Appleton found that this reflection varied with the time of day, due, as subsequently demonstrated, to the varying intensity of the ionizing solar radiation. In particular, before dawn the reduction of ionization by recombination allowed the Kennelly-Heaviside layer, or E layer as it is now called, to be penetrated by the incident radiation. He established that reflection then took place at an upper layer of intense ionization, which he termed the F layer: it is now generally known as the Appleton layer. The lower boundary of this layer he found to be about 230 kilometers above the Earth.

Appleton then proceeded to investigate in detail the structure and properties of the layers, a task on which he was engaged for the rest of his life. He employed the method of vertical sounding and made extensive use of the pulse method devised by G. Breit and M. A. Tuve in 1925, observing by cathode-ray registration the echo effect from short-duration signals. With the cooperation of G. Builder, he established a new effect of prime importance: the Earth's magnetic field made the ionosphere a doubly refracting medium, which he showed to be theoretically deducible if the effective charged particles were free electrons. This leads to a doubling of the echoes. From a general theory of the propagation of radio waves in an ionized medium under the influence of a magnetic field, he deduced a relation between the electron density and the critical penetration frequency, which enabled him to find the maximum electron density for any layer and to investigate experimentally how this depended upon the time of day, the season of the year, the sunspot cycle, and, in general, any event, including eclipses, that governed the rate of emission of the solar photons producing the ionization. In this way the solar control of the ionosphere was demonstrated in great detail. *See* BREIT, GREGORY; TUVE, MERLE ANTONY.

Appleton established many details of the structure of the ionosphere, such as a weakly ionized D layer below the E layer and the resolution of the Appleton layer into two strata under certain conditions. He studied the world morphology of the F2 layer, demonstrating the marked geomagnetic control of the ionization and, with his collaborators, showing that lunar tidal oscillations could be detected in the D, E, and F layers. In his last years he devoted much attention to storms in the ionosphere and the perturbations produced by electric currents flowing in it. He took an active part in international investigations of the upper atmosphere, including the Second International Polar Year, 1932–33, and the International Geophysical Year, 1957–58.

At St. John's College, Cambridge, which he entered in 1911, Appleton had a brilliant career, interrupted by his military service in World War I. Upon his return to Cambridge, he began his work on the ionosphere and so distinguished himself that, in 1924, at the age of 32, he was appointed Wheatstone Professor of Physics at the University of London. There he carried out much of his fundamental work. In 1936 he returned to Cambridge as Jacksonian Professor of Natural Philosophy, a distinguished post in which his predecessor had been C. T. R. Wilson. At the outbreak of World War II he was appointed Secretary of the Department of Scientific and Industrial Research, an important administrative post in which he was largely responsible for the government's attitude toward research. In 1949 he was made principal and vice-chancellor of the University of Edinburgh, which offices he held at the time of his death. He was knighted in 1941.

For background information *see* IONOSPHERE in the McGraw-Hill Encyclopedia of Science and Technology. ∎

ARBER, WERNER
☆ Swiss molecular biologist

***Born** June 3, 1929, Gränichen, Switzerland*

Arber and his associates carried out investigations which enabled them to determine the molecular mechanism of host-controlled restriction-modification of bacterial viruses and which led to the discovery of restriction enzymes. For this work, Arber shared the 1978 Nobel Prize in medicine or physiology with H. O. Smith and P. Nathans. *See* NATHANS, PETER; SMITH, HAMILTON.

The phenomenon of host-induced variation, which later came to be known as host-controlled restriction-modification, was first observed in the early 1950s. It was found that bacteriophages grown in one strain of bacteria are often able to grow only poorly in a second strain (restriction). However, the few phage particles which survive and emerge from the second strain are able to grow normally upon reinfection of the second strain (modification), but now grow poorly in the first strain.

In 1960 Arber began a study of the molecular basis of this phenomenon with D. Dussoix. In 1962 Arber and Dussoix found that host-controlled modification involved changes in the bacteriophage deoxyribonucleic acid (DNA), and that host-controlled restriction involved the breakdown of this DNA. Although the DNA breakdown prevented phage infection, certain phage genes were found to survive in abortively infected bacteria. When the same pairs of bacterial strains were used in conjugation experiments, the same restriction and modification effects were revealed to act on the cellular DNA. Hence the ability to modify or break down DNA was a property of the host bacteria, which could act on foreign bacterial DNA as well as on virus DNA. This was confirmed in 1966 by W. B. Wood, working in Arber's laboratory, by the isolation and characterization of bacterial mutants defective in restriction and modification.

From these observations, Arber and his

colleagues developed a model explaining restriction and modification. According to this model, certain bacterial strains contain a restriction enzyme or endonuclease which cleaves a DNA molecule upon recognition of specific nucleotide sequences in the DNA. In order to protect their own DNA, these same strains also contain a strain-specific modification enzyme that recognizes the same nucleotide sequences and methylates them, thereby preventing their cleavage by the restriction enzyme. When unprotected bacteriophages infect these strains, the phage DNA is destroyed by the restriction enzyme, except for a small fraction which is methylated by the modificaton enzyme before the restriction enzyme can act on it. The modified phages can then grow normally upon reinfection of the second strain.

This model was confirmed by a number of investigations. U. Kühnlein and Arber isolated phages which had undergone mutations at recognition sites, and which were then unaffected by restriction or modification enzymes. Further studies of phage mutants by Kühnlein, Arber, and J. Smith demonstrated a direct correlation between DNA methylation and host-controlled modification. Kühnlein, S. Linn, and Arber proceeded to isolate a modification DNA methylase from *Escherichia coli* strain B. However, the most important confirmation of the model came in 1968, when Linn and Arber partially purified and determined the activity of a restriction enzyme from *E. coli* strain B, and M. Meselson and R. Yuan similarly purified and characterized a restriction enzyme from *E. coli* strain K.

The discovery of restriction enzymes raised the possibility of using these substances to prepare DNA fragments appropriate to determining the nucleotide sequences of DNA, and to study its genetic organization and perhaps manipulate it in the test tube. However, the restriction enzymes discovered by Linn and Arber and by Meselson and Yuan belonged to a class, later named type I, which recognize a specific DNA nucleotide sequence but cleave the DNA at random locations, far removed from the recognition site. Such enzymes could not be used to study and manipulate gene structure. It remained for Smith and his colleagues to isolate the first of the type II restriction enzymes, which both recognize and cleave a specific site, and for Nathans and his colleagues to use those enzymes to study the structure of DNA, leading to a revolution in molecular

genetics and molecular biology. But these achievements were made possible by the understanding of host-controlled restriction-modification gained by Arber and his associates.

Arber graduated from the Eidgenössiche Technische Hochschule (Federal Institute of Technology) in Zurich in 1953, and received his doctorate from the University of Geneva in 1958. In 1958–59 he was a research associate in medical microbiology at the University of Southern California. In 1960 he joined the faculty of the University of Geneva, where he became extraordinary professor of molecular genetics in 1965. In 1970 he became ordinary professor of molecular biology at the University of Basel.

For background information *see* BACTERIOPHAGE; DEOXYRIBONUCLEIC ACID (DNA); GENETIC MAPPING in the McGraw-Hill Encyclopedia of Science and Technology. ∎

ARGYRIS, JOHN H.
☆ British and Greek scientist in applied
mechanics and structural engineering

Born Aug. 19, 1913, Volos, Greece

The development of a computer-oriented method of structural analysis was initiated in 1953, when Argyris formulated the matrix theory of structures by using a concise and novel matrix notation. Though computers in the early 1950s were by no means perfect and sophisticated tools, it was already clear to Argyris

that electronic digital computers would revolutionize the whole approach to theory and practice in engineering. The only question was how to utilize the computer in an intelligent and efficient manner. A great deal of effort was required in engineering theory and mathematical as well as physical methods in order to devise techniques which would produce successful results and also remain within a specified budget. Argyris accomplished this in 1954 with the dual formulation of the matrix force and displacement methods—now collectively known as the finite-element methods (FEM)—in the form of pioneering papers which were later compiled as a book, *Energy Theorems and Structural Analysis* (1960; 4th ed., 1970). This book is still in use as an introduction to the field of matrix or finite-element methods. T. von Kármán described the original series of articles as a revolutionary beginning of a new era. After this event Argyris was in the front line of FEM research and the application of FEM to all fields of applied mechanics. *See* VON KÁRMÁN, THEODORE.

Interestingly, Argyris started his scientific career in the classical static analysis of structures. His joint publication with P. C. Dunne, "The General Theory of Conical and Cylindrical Tubes under Torsion and Bending," constituted both a pinnacle and an end of a period in the analytical theory of aircraft structures.

After the introduction of the matrix methods in structural analysis, the matrix force method was the first to be developed to a highly sophisticated level for the analysis of aircraft and other complex structures. This was partly because of the limited capacity of computers at that time. One of the highlights of the new method was an ingenious device for the efficient simulation of cutouts and modifications on the computers.

Modern Fuselage Analysis and the Elastic Aircraft, a book published jointly with S. Kelsey in 1963, is still remembered by Argyris's older collaborators as a pinnacle of sophistication and generality in the field of fuselage analysis. It continues to be used in the United States and Europe for conventional fuselages. When this book appeared, the moment of decision between the force approach and the displacement approach had come. New technologies for lightweight, high-strength aircraft and the advent of the space age brought about a total revolution in structural design. The force method was seen to be burdened with deficiencies which at the time were difficult, if not impossible, to overcome. On the other hand, Argyris had clearly foreseen that the displacement method (subsequently named by others the direct stiffness method), if properly applied, held great promise for meeting those difficulties. It was simpler, more general, and better suited to programming on modern computers, especially in the nonlinear domain of large displacements and nonelastic material properties. This moment marked the beginning of an explosive development which was finally crowned by the creation of large-scale finite-element systems and a general industrial application of the matrix methods.

In the modern Institute for Statics and Dynamics of Aerospace Structures (University of Stuttgart), which was shaped and equipped by Argyris, the first large-scale finite-element programming systems (ASKA and its predecessors) were realized.

The pioneering paper "Continua and Discontinua" (1966), constituting the Opening Address to the International Conference on Matrix Methods, confirmed the leading position that Argyris held in the realization of his basic concepts and witnessed the intensive development toward defining necessary finite elements and deriving their respective stiffness matrices. One of the basic characteristic features in this development is the natural formulation of the matrix displacement and stiffness method. This has provided a most significant interpretation of the elastic and inelastic behavior of an element, from both the physical and mathematical points of view. It not only yields concise and elegant matrix expressions for the elements, especially for simplex elements, but leads in an effortless manner to understanding of the nonlinear effects associated with large displacements. As late as 1974, this original idea led to a fundamental new development, the natural factor formulation of the structural stiffness matrix, which was published with O. E. Brönlund as coauthor. "Continua and Discontinua" also marks the initiation of a future line of development which includes the study of displacements, plasticity and large strains, dynamic effects, optimization, and thermoelastic problems.

Of course, the name of Argyris is also associated with the definition of numerous types of finite elements, such as the TUBA family of plate elements and its generalization to shells, namely SHEBA. Both families of elements overcome in a natural and elegant way the considerable difficulties encountered in dividing plates, and especially shells, into discrete elements. SHEBA is (as of early 1979) the only fully compatible shell element for shells of arbitrary curvature. Since 1968, the year of its publication, it has been used with considerable success in various practical problems.

The idea of finite elements may also be extended to other fields of applied mechanics. "Finite Elements in Time and Space" (1968) and "The Incompressible Lubrication Problem" (1968) are instances of contributions by Argyris and his collaborators. They were followed by various investigations in potential flow and other two- and three-dimensional flows using finite elements.

In the design of the Olympic Stadium roof in Munich in 1972, there appeared considerable deficiencies in the methods available for the calculation of prestressed cable networks. It was mainly Argyris's contribution which helped to close this gap and added so much to the knowledge of nonlinear structural analysis. "Large Deflection Analysis of Prestressed Networks" (1972) opened a fruitful period in a wide field of civil engineering analysis which now encompasses, at the Stuttgart Institute, items that are as varied as complex shells, prestressed concrete pressure vessels, and suspension bridges. The work on static analysis and shape-finding of the suspension roofs was followed by investigations of their dynamic behavior. These led to a number of publications, such as "Nonlinear Oscillations Using the Finite-Element Technique" (1973), which develops a family of conditionally stable algorithms for the economical computation of large nonlinear as well as linear systems.

Linear analysis of large structures is today a matter of routine, and to a great extent this is due to the original contributions of Argyris. More recent developments have extended the use of standard matrix procedures to problems of large deformations in solid mechanics. "Large Natural Strains and Some Difficulties Due to Nonlinearity and Incompressibility in Finite Elements" (1974) solves in an elegant manner the complex task of combining large strains and large displacements. Also remarkable is the new definition of commutable large rotations in space, in the paper "On Large Displacement–Small Strain Analysis of Structures with Rotational Degrees of Freedom" (1978), which allows an elegant analysis of beams and shells under large displacements. Equally enticing is the adaptation of the natural formulation to inelastic large deformations, in "Incremental Formulation in Nonlinear Mechanics and Large Strain Elasto-Plasticity" (1978).

Argyris was the offspring of an old Byzantine family which produced statesmen, poets, and scientists (such as Constantine Carathéodory). He studied civil engineering at the Technical University of Athens from 1931 to 1934 and earned his engineering degree (Dipl.Ing.) in 1936 at the Technical University of Munich. Subsequently, he became a research assistant with G. Worch, and then from 1937 to 1939 he was senior structural and project engineer with Gollnow, a large steel construction firm in Stettin. He proceeded to the Technical Universities of Berlin and Zurich in order to extend his studies in the fields of aeronautics, mechanics, mathematics, and physics. In 1943 he joined the research department of the Royal Aeronautical Society and led the structure and flutter division. In 1949 he became reader in aeronautical structures at the Imperial College of Science and Technology in London, and in 1955 he was appointed to a newly created chair of aeronautical structures of the University of London—the only one of its kind in the Commonwealth. In 1957 he received the D.Sc. (engineering) from the University of London. In 1959, while retaining his chair at London, he assumed three positions at the University of Stuttgart: professor of aerospace sciences, director of the Institute for Statics and Dynamics, and director of the Computing Center. He initiated and maintained the faculty of aerospace science at the University of Stuttgart. Argyris became a member of various committees and councils. He was elected a fellow of the Royal Aeronautical Society, London (1955), of the American Institute of Aeronautics and Astronautics (1967), and of the Academy of Athens (1973). His awards included the George Taylor Prize (Gold Medal) and the Silver Medal of the Royal Aeronautical Society, London (both 1971), and the Von Kármán Medal of the American Society of Civil Engineers (1975).

In addition to the books mentioned above, Argyris wrote *Stressing of Conical Tubes (Wing Stress Manual),* with P. C. Dunne (1949–50), *Structural Analysis,* with Dunne (1952), *Recent Advances in*

Matrix Methods of Structural Analysis (1964), and *An Elementary Introduction into Structural Mechanics,* with H.-P. Mlejnek (1979). He published over 230 papers.

For background information *see* FUSE-LAGE; MATRIX THEORY; STRUCTURAL ANALYSIS in the McGraw-Hill Encyclopedia of Science and Technology. ■

ARNETT, EDWARD McCOLLIN
★ American chemist

Born Sept. 25, 1922, Philadelphia, PA, U.S.A.

The fundamental factors which influence the reactivity of organic compounds are their structures, the presence of catalysts, the conditions of temperature and pressure, and the solvent medium in which the reaction occurs. A considerable part of Arnett's research contribution was devoted to clarifying the role of solvents in organic chemistry.

Proton transfer is the most general reaction in organic chemistry. Through the protonation of bases, or the deprotonation of acids, neutral molecules are converted into ions which are often much more reactive than their uncharged precursors. Arnett and his coworkers devoted a number of years to devising means for the quantitative comparison of an enormous range of acidic and basic molecules in terms of their abilities to transfer protons to basic solutions or from acidic ones. In their hands, reaction calo-

rimetry became a particularly powerful tool for studying the thermochemistry of proton transfer for many classes of organic compounds.

During the early 1970s several new techniques were developed for measuring proton transfer equilibria in the gas phase. In some cases, the relative acid or base strengths of important organic compounds were drastically different in the gas phase from the strengths of the compounds in solution. Obviously the factor which had to be responsible for the difference was the interaction between the solvent molecules and the molecules and ions engaged in the equilibrium. Arnett and his colleagues developed rigorous thermochemical treatments for isolating the solvation energies for many such reactions, thereby solving a number of classical problems of physical organic chemistry. In most of these cases, anomalous orders of reactivity could be traced to previously unexpected solvation effects on the ions in the reaction. Again, intensive previous studies of solution thermodynamics were of great value for understanding the new results for solvation energies. For a number of years, a series of spectroscopic and thermodynamic measurements of hydrogen bonding and ion complexing had been made in Arnett's laboratory. Also, a number of papers were published dealing with the unusual interactions of hydrophobic molecules and ions with water. These studies laid a solid groundwork for interpreting solvation phenomena. The unexpected breakthrough in gas-phase physics, combined with Arnett's results in water and strongly acidic and basic systems, was able to answer questions which had puzzled chemists for nearly a century. The results also point the way to possible means for greatly extending the range of organic chemistry in solution.

The possibility of such an extension becomes apparent when it is realized that the effects of changes in molecular structure are often enormously greater in the gas phase than they are in solution. Thus, the role of solvent is often to provide a great damping or leveling effect on reactivity. Once the factors which produce this attenuation effect are identified, it may be possible to release a considerable part of the inherent variations in reactivity which are presently suppressed by the presence of solvent. A first step in this direction was taken by Arnett and J. F. Wolf, who were able to demonstrate a factor of nearly a trillion in the ability of

methyl groups to stabilize sulfonium and phosphonium ions compared with equivalent ammonium ions. Here, the main difference was shown to be in differing tendencies to distribute positive charge from the ions to the solvent.

Later the Arnett group studied the effect of molecular structure on the stabilities of carbonium ions, some of the fundamental intermediates of organic chemistry. Here again, enormous energetic differences equivalent to those found in the gas phase may be demonstrated in solution and, again, the lack of hydrogen bonding is probably the leading factor.

The development of large digital computers for storage and retrieval of chemical information provides new opportunities for handling the growth of the chemical literature. Realizing this opportunity, Arnett organized the Pittsburgh Chemical Information Center in 1966 as a large-scale research project for investigating how computer-searching of the literature could be implemented for the benefit of research chemists. The interdisciplinary effort involved library scientists and sociologists in addition to chemists and computer specialists. Over a thousand chemists in American and British academic and industrial organizations participated in the experiment.

Arnett also became involved in the study of optically active interfacial systems. Biological membranes are composed of optically active molecules, and their stereochemistry undoubtedly plays an important role in biological specificity. However, remarkably little is known about the aggregation of optically active surfactants at interfaces. The Arnett group succeeded in showing that stereochemical configuration can play a significant role in the packing of lipid molecules at interfaces and, furthermore, that stereospecificity can be affected by the acidity of the adjacent aqueous phase. This promises to be an active area of research for a few years.

Arnett was raised in the Quaker community of Philadelphia. His father was a physician with associations at Drexel University, the University of Pennsylvania Medical School, and the Episcopal Hospital. His mother was active in the peace movement and in the promotion of women's rights and justice for minority groups. Arnett attended the Germantown Friends School and the University of Pennsylvania, receiving his Ph.D. in 1943. He worked at the Max Levy Company in Philadelphia for 4 years and then taught at Western Maryland College. He moved to Harvard University, where he did postdoctoral research with Paul Bartlett. In 1957 he was appointed assistant professor of chemistry at the University of Pittsburgh, and professor in 1964. He was a visiting professor at the universities of Illinois, Colorado, New Hampshire, Canterbury, and Harvard. He served on the Petroleum Research Fund Advisory Board and the Committee on Chemical Information of the National Research Council. In 1976 he received the Pittsburgh Award, and in 1977 the James Flack Norris Award of the American Chemical Society.

Arnett coauthored *Computer-Based Chemical Information,* with A. Kent (1973).

For background information *see* CARBONIUM ION; ORGANIC REACTION MECHANISM; STEREOCHEMISTRY; THERMOCHEMISTRY in the McGraw-Hill Encyclopedia of Science and Technology. ■

ARNON, DANIEL ISRAEL
★ American biochemist

Born Nov. 14, 1910, Warsaw, Poland

Arnon's early research was mainly concerned with inorganic metabolism of plants, especially with the role of inorganic micronutrients (trace elements). His main contributions in this area were the discovery of vanadium as an essential micronutrient for the growth of algae and the discovery (with P. R. Stout) of molybdenum as an essential micronutrient for

the growth of higher plants and algae. His interest in the function of micronutrients in plant metabolism led him eventually to shift his main research activity to photosynthesis, especially the biochemistry of its photochemical phase.

Arnon began his work on the premise that the biochemistry of energy conversion in photosynthesis, like the biochemistry of fermentation in an earlier period, would be elucidated only when the process was removed from the functional and structural complexity of whole cells. He chose to investigate photosynthesis by isolated chloroplasts, the chlorophyll-containing organelles of plant cells. R. Hill had shown in 1937 that, upon illumination, isolated chloroplasts produced oxygen but were incapable of assimilating carbon dioxide or generating a strong reductant, needed for carbon dioxide assimilation. Later work by other investigators led to the conclusion that isolated chloroplasts also lacked the capacity to form adenosinetriphosphate (ATP), a compound known to serve as an energy carrier in all living cells and needed specifically for carbon dioxide assimilation. It appeared therefore that, contrary to earlier theories, photosynthesis could not be confined to chloroplasts.

In 1954, using different methods, Arnon (with F. R. Whatley and M. B. Allen) obtained with isolated spinach choloroplasts an assimilation of carbon dioxide to the level of carbohydrates (including starch) with a simultaneous evolution of oxygen, at physiological temperatures and with no energy supply except visible light. Carbon dioxide assimilation by chloroplasts was accompanied by the discovery of photosynthetic phosphorylation or photophosphorylation. This discovery revealed a new process for the formation of ATP. In photophosphorylation the chlorophyll-containing particles of photosynthetic cells convert solar energy into the pyrophosphate-bond energy of ATP independently of carbon dioxide assimilation. Photophosphorylation differs from the well-known processes of ATP formation in fermentation and respiration in that it does not consume any energy-rich chemical substrate (the only "substrate" consumed is light quanta).

The experiments with isolated chloroplasts unveiled a new major site of ATP formation in nature. Chloroplasts and, as soon became clear from the work of others, all photosynthetic membranes have the capacity to utilize the electromagnetic

energy of sunlight for the formation of ATP by the process of photophosphorylation. In the early type of photophosphorylation, later renamed cyclic photophosphorylation, the only product formed was ATP. In 1957 Arnon and his associates discovered a second type of photophosphorylation, named noncyclic photophosphorylation, in which ATP formation was stoichiometrically coupled with oxygen production and formation of a strong reductant, nicotinamide adenine dinucleotide phosphate (NADP), the hydrogen carrier in living cells. Noncyclic photophosphorylation accounted, aside from oxygen evolution, for all the reduced NADP and part of the ATP—two substances known to be required for the assimilation of carbon dioxide. The additional ATP needed for carbon dioxide assimilation had to come from cyclic photophosphorylation. Jointly, cyclic and noncyclic photophosphorylation constituted the "light phase" of photosynthesis that generates the assimilatory power (made up of ATP and reduced NADP) that is required for carbon dioxide assimilation by reactions independent of light. Arnon (with A. V. Trebst and H. Y. Tsujimoto) substantiated the validity of this view of photosynthesis by experimentally separating its light and dark phases in isolated choloroplasts. First, chloroplasts were allowed to form ATP and reduced NADP in the light and in the absence of carbon dioxide. Next, radioactive carbon dioxide was added in the dark and was found to be converted to carbohydrates at the expense of the ATP and reduced NADP formed previously in the light.

The concept that emerged from this work was that cyclic and noncyclic photophosphorylation represent the conversion of solar energy into the main forms of biochemical energy, ATP and reducing power, that first enter the biosphere via photosynthesis. Photosynthetic cells conserve and store the energy of the photochemically generated ATP and reducing power through the biosynthesis of organic compounds. When these are later degraded by fermentation and respiration, ATP and reducing power are regenerated for general use in cellular metabolism.

In 1962 Arnon (with K. Tagawa) found that illuminated chloroplasts did not reduce NADP directly but first reduced an iron-containing protein, present in all photosynthetic cells and in certain anaerobic bacteria and now called ferredoxin. They crystallized ferredoxin and found that it had an oxidation-reduction potential about 100 millivolts more electronegative than NADP and was therefore the most electronegative electron carrier known in cellular physiology. Ferredoxins from different organisms were at least partly interchangeable in catalyzing NADP reduction by illuminated chloroplasts. In further experiments (with M. Shin) the "photoreduction" of NADP was resolved into three reactions: (*a*) a photochemical reduction of ferredoxin, followed by two dark reactions; (*b*) a reduction of a flavoprotein enzyme by reduced ferredoxin; and (*c*) a reduction of NADP by the reduced flavoprotein. The flavoprotein enzyme native to chloroplasts was crystallized and named ferredoxin-NADP reductase.

Photoreduced ferredoxin thus emerged as the most electronegative, chemically characterized substance that had been isolated from the photosynthetic apparatus. The recognition of the importance of ferredoxin in the energy conversion reactions of photosynthesis was greatly enhanced when Arnon (with Tagawa, Tsujimoto and B. D. McSwain) found that, apart from NADP reduction, ferredoxin was also involved in the formation of ATP and in the evolution of oxygen. Ferredoxin acts as a catalyst of cyclic photophosphorylation; in noncyclic photophosphorylation the photoreduction of ferredoxin is coupled with a stoichiometric formation of ATP and evolution of oxygen. Thus it became clear that oxygen evolution and photophosphorylation are the key events in the conversion of radiant energy into chemical energy by chloroplasts that are coupled with the photoreduction of ferredoxin.

In later research Arnon (with B. B. Buchanan, M. C. W. Evans, and R. Bachofen) uncovered a new, direct role of ferredoxin in the assimilation of carbon dioxide. They found in photosynthetic bacteria two enzyme systems that can use directly, without mediation by NADP, the strongly electronegative potential of ferredoxin for reductive incorporation of carbon dioxide: pyruvate synthase, which uses reduced ferredoxin to form pyruvate from acetyl coenzyme A (CoA) and carbon dioxide, and α-ketoglutarate synthase, which uses reduced ferredoxin to form α-ketoglutarate from succinyl CoA and carbon dioxide. The two ferredoxin-dependent carboxylation reactions, together with two other known carboxylation reactions, phosphopyruvate carbox-

ylase and isocitric dehydrogenase, form a new cyclic pathway for carbon dioxide assimilation in photosynthetic bacteria. One complete turn of the cycle incorporates four molecules of carbon dioxide and results in the synthesis of oxalacetate. Oxalacetate may then be further metabolized through the cycle to provide intermediates with two to six carbons for the synthesis of amino acids, lipids, and other cell constituents. The new cycle, named the reductive carboxylic acid cycle, appears especially well adapted to the synthesis of lipids and amino acids, which are the main products of bacterial photosynthesis.

Arnon's later research elucidated the interrelations between cyclic and noncyclic photophosphorylation in chloroplasts and led to the discovery of a regulatory mechanism for cyclic photophosphorylation. His research also concerned the role of different forms of ferredoxin and other iron-sulfur proteins in photosynthetic electron transport and photophosphorylation and in biological nitrogen fixation.

Arnon received his B.S. in 1932 and his Ph.D. in 1936 at the University of California, Berkeley, where D. R. Hoagland aroused his interest in plant biochemistry and strongly influenced his choice of a scientific career. Arnon joined the staff of the University of California in 1936 and remained there continuously, except for military service during World War II. He was appointed professor of cell physiology and research biochemist at the University of California, Berkeley, where he also served as the founding chairperson of the department of cell physiology (1961–78) and biochemist in the Agricultural Experiment Station (1958–78). He was a Guggenheim fellow twice: in the Molteno Institute and department of biochemistry at Cambridge University, England, in 1947–48, and in the Hopkins Marine Station of Stanford University in 1962–63. He was a Fulbright research fellow at the Max Planck Institut für Zellphysiologie in Berlin-Dahlem in 1955–56. He was elected to the Academie d'Agriculture de France in 1955, the U.S. National Academy of Sciences in 1961, the American Academy of Arts and Sciences in 1962, the Royal Swedish Academy of Sciences in 1969, and the Deutsche Akademie der Naturforscher Leopoldina in 1974; he became an honorary member of the Spanish Biochemical Society in 1975. Among his honors are the Newcomb Cleveland Prize of the American Association for the Ad-

vancement of Science in 1940, the Charles F. Kettering Award for research in photosynthesis in 1963, the Stephen Hales Prize of the American Society of Plant Physiologists in 1966, and the National Medal of Science in 1973.

For background information *see* BACTERIAL PHOTOSYNTHESIS; CHLOROPHYLL; PLANT METABOLISM; PHOTOSYNTHESIS in the McGraw-Hill Encyclopedia of Science and Technology. ■

ASTWOOD, EDWIN BENNETT
★ American physician

Born Dec. 29, 1909, Bermuda
Died Feb. 17, 1976, Hamilton, Bermuda

Astwood probably became best known for his elucidation of the mechanism whereby certain chemical compounds lead to enlargement of the thyroid. Experiments in rats (1942–43) indicated that the compounds interfere with the synthesis of the thyroid hormone, and that goiter is due to a compensatory oversecretion of thyrotropin from the pituitary. The compounds (thiourea and thiouracil) were given to patients with overactive thyroids, and eventually a workable treatment for hyperthyroidism was developed. Later more effective compounds were found.

One of the most telling arguments that these compounds act in this way was the finding that treatment with thyroid hormone prevents or reverses a goiter. Patients with thyroid enlargement without hyperthyroidism were treated with thyroid hormone, and in many of them the thyroid enlargement regressed. The concept that goiter is, in most instances, a compensatory adaptation to thyroid deficiency gradually gained acceptance over the years, and operations upon simple or nodular goiter for cosmetic or cancerophobic reasons declined.

Astwood's earliest work was concerned with the effects of sex hormones on the development of the mammary gland in the rat. This led to an interest in the rat's estrous cycle and its control by the follicle-stimulating and luteinizing hormones of the pituitary. His experiments showed clearly that neither of these hormones can account for the function of the corpora lutea. A third gonadotropin, labeled luteotropin, was characterized for this species and was subsequently identified with prolactin—the substance responsible for the secretion of crop milk in the pigeon and for the initiation of lactation in most mammals. Later work also showed that the corpora lutea of other species are controlled in quite other ways. It was further found that the extended functioning of the corpora lutea during pregnancy in the rat is sustained by a hormone secreted by the placenta.

Studies on luteotropin led to work on corticotropin (ACTH). As early as 1942, Astwood had prepared crude extracts which were more potent than the described protein hormone. The hormone was found to be readily destroyed in fresh pituitary tissue, so the glands were dried in acetone and then extracted with glacial acetic acid. In 1951 oxidized cellulose was used as an ion-exchange medium for purification, and a product was obtained which was 100 times as active as the originally described protein. This preparation had wide clinical application, and was used by others to elucidate the structure of further purified hormone.

Astwood received his B.S. at Washington Missionary College in 1929 and his M.D. and C.M. at McGill University Medical School in 1934. At McGill he gained his first interest in endocrinology from serving as a laboratory helper under J. B. Collip and, later, from discussion with J. S. L. Browne while Astwood was an intern at the Royal Victoria Hospital, Montreal (1934–35). At the Johns Hopkins Hospital in 1935–37, he had the opportunity to work with rats, and it was there that experimental experience was first gained. His research work was furthered by a Rockefeller Foundation fel-

lowship to the biology department of Harvard University, under F. L. Hisaw. This stimulating experience led to his Ph.D. in 1939 and a thesis on the control of the function of the corpus luteum of the rat. After a return to Johns Hopkins Hospital as an associate obstetrician in 1939, he set up a laboratory for the study of reproduction. In 1940 he was appointed to the department of medicine at the Peter Bent Brigham Hospital, and was given research laboratories in the department of pharmacology at Harvard Medical School.

Astwood moved in 1945 to the New England Medical Center Hospitals and Tufts University, where he had much improved laboratory and clinical facilities. Studies on human thyroid function, using the new iodine-131, were initiated, several pituitary factors were purified, studies were carried out on the substances causing mobilization of fat from the adipose depots, and, in association with numerous young researchers, he was involved with work on the endocrine systems. He became professor of medicine at Tufts University School of Medicine, senior physician at the New England Medical Center Hospitals, and director of the Endocrine Service and Clinical Research Ward of these hospitals.

Astwood received a number of honors, including the Ciba Award of the Endocrine Society in 1944, the Cameron Prize of the University of Edinburgh in 1948, the Philips Medal of the American College of Physicians in 1949, the Borden Award of the Association of the American Medical Colleges in 1952, the Lasker Award of the American Public Health Association in 1954, and the Koch Award of the Endocrine Society in 1967. He was elected to the National Academy of Sciences in 1957. In 1967 he was given an honorary D.Sc. by the University of Chicago.

For background information *see* ENDOCRINE MECHANISMS; HORMONE in the McGraw-Hill Encyclopedia of Science and Technology. ∎

ATIYAH, MICHAEL FRANCIS
★ British mathematician

Born Apr. 22, 1929, London, England

Atiyah's most important contributions to mathematics concerned the creation of K theory and the discovery of many of its

important applications to geometry and analysis.

Most of Atiyah's work in developing K theory was done in collaboration with F. Hirzebruch. In 1956 Hirzebruch proved what came to be known as the Riemann-Roch-Hirzebruch theorem, a generalization of the Riemann-Roch theorem from the case of a compact Riemann surface to the case of a projective algebraic manifold. This theorem was further generalized by A. Grothendieck in the course of his systematic reworking of the entire field of algebraic geometry. In carrying out this generalization, Grothendieck introduced a contravariant functor which, to each algebraic manifold X, associated a ring constructed with the aid of isomorphism classes of algebraic vector bundles over X. In 1959 Atiyah and Hirzebruch suggested doing the same thing for a compact topological space X, and for complex vector bundles over X. Thus, for every compact topological space X they defined a ring $K(X)$ in a geometrically natural way, from which is derived the name K theory.

Starting with $K(X)$, and making use of the periodicity theorem of R. Bott, Atiyah and Hirzebruch were able to construct an exact sequence which was analogous to the exact sequence of cohomology, and which, in fact, satisfied all the axioms of the cohomology theory of S. Eilenberg and N. Steenrod except the axiom of dimension. The resulting theory was christened extraordinary cohomology, and its importance was quickly made evident by the applications in algebraic topology and other fields discovered by Atiyah and Hirzebruch. Among these were the proof of Riemann-Roch theorems for differentiable manifolds, and nonimmersion and nonembedding theorems for projective spaces. Other mathematicians also discovered important applications. For example, in 1962 J. F. Adams used K theory to resolve a long-standing classical problem, that of determining the maximum number of fields of linearly independent vectors on the n-dimensional sphere.

However, perhaps the most far-reaching application of K theory was the index theorem, proven by Atiyah and I. Singer in 1963: Let X be an n-dimensional compact differentiable manifold of class C^∞ in without boundary, and let d be an elliptic differential operator on X. This operator is a linear mapping from $\Gamma(E)$ to $\Gamma(F)$, where E and F are complex vector bundles of class

C^∞ over X, and $\Gamma(E)$ and $\Gamma(F)$ are linear spaces over the complex field consisting of C^∞ cross sections of E and F respectively. The dimensions of the kernel and cokernel of this mapping, dim Ker d and dim CoKer d, are known to be finite, and the analytic index $\text{ind}_a (d)$ is defined to be the integer dim Ker d − dim CoKer d. This index is invariant under continuous deformations of d, and I. M. Gelfand had conjectured in 1960 that one should therefore be able to calculate it from purely topological invariants of X and d. This was the task that Atiyah and Singer succeeded in carrying out. Using K theory, they were able to define a topological index $\text{ind}_t (d)$. The Atiyah-Singer index theorem states that the analytic index $\text{ind}_a (d)$ equals the topological index $\text{ind}_t (d)$. It thus establishes a bridge between two vast fields of mathematics: the analysis of partial differential equations on the one hand and algebraic topology on the other. *See* GELFAND, IZRAIL MOISEEVICH.

Atiyah and Singer also proved a generalized form of the index theorem, involving a sequence of elliptic differential operators forming an elliptic complex. From this result they showed that the Riemann-Roch-Hirzebruch theorem is valid not only for projective algebraic manifolds but also for arbitrary compact complex manifolds. In 1964 Atiyah and Bott extended the index theorem to compact manifolds with boundary, and in 1968 Atiyah and Singer obtained another generalization for the case where a compact Lie group operates on manifolds, vector bundles, and elliptic operators in a reasonable way. This generalization is closely related to the Lefschetz fixed-point theorem. Indeed, Atiyah and Bott were able to extend the Lefschetz fixed-point theorem to include the case of elliptic complexes.

Atiyah's father was a public official and the author of several books concerned with the Arab world, and his younger brother was a professor and scholar of law. Atiyah received his B.A. (1952) and Ph.D. (1955) from Trinity College, Cambridge. He remained at Cambridge as research fellow (1954–58) and university lecturer (1958–61) before going to Oxford, where he was reader in mathematics (1961–63) and Savilian Professor of Geometry (1963–69).

From 1969 to 1972 Atiyah was professor of mathematics at the Institute for Advanced Study in Princeton. In 1973 he returned to Oxford as Royal Society Research Professor at the Mathematical Institute. He was awarded the Fields Medal of the International Congress of Mathematicians (1966) and the Royal Medal of the Royal Society (1968). He was elected a fellow of the Royal Society (1962) and a foreign member of a number of academies, including the American Academy of Arts and Sciences (1969) and the U.S. National Academy of Sciences.

Atiyah wrote *K-Theory* (1967), *Introduction to Commutative Algebra*, with I. G. MacDonald (1969), and *Elliptic Operators and Compact Groups* (1974).

For background information *see* DIFFERENTIAL EQUATION; TOPOLOGY in the McGraw-Hill Encyclopedia of Science and Technology. ∎

AUERBACH, CHARLOTTE
★ British geneticist

Born May 14, 1899, Crefeld, Germany

Auerbach has been called the mother of chemical mutagenesis. She herself did not think she merited this title. It is true that she was the first to discover a highly effective chemical mutagen, mustard gas (sulfur mustard). But this was due to the fact that pharmacologists in the University of Edinburgh had a hunch that mustard gas, because of its pharmacological similarity to x-rays, might be mutagenic, and asked her to test this on *Drosophila*. The result was spectacular beyond expectation, but the credit goes to those who suggested the test, not to Auerbach who carried it out by a routine procedure. Moreover, other chemical mutagens were discovered simultaneously or nearly so in Germany, Switzerland, and the Soviet Union. Nor had Auerbach a hand in the successful search for other chemical mutagens that went on for decades after this, and is still going on. She felt rightly that without chemical knowledge she could act only as a technician in this type of work, testing hypotheses that had been made by chemists.

What Auerbach herself considered her main merit was the study of mutagenesis in depth, which she carried on until her retirement. By that time, similar studies had long been taken up in other laboratories, often through former collaborators of hers. Her method of work was very thorough, very honest, and very critical. She was not given to generalizations, but went slowly from observation to conclusion to further observation, proceeding step by step until the results led to a definite conclusion or at least to a hypothesis that agreed with all the results but could not be fully proved with the means at her disposal. It gave her great satisfaction to find how many of these hypotheses were later shown to have been correct. She had a strong, almost passionate, dislike of the facile acceptance and generalization of plausible but unproved and untestable hypotheses that so often penetrate whole areas of research and block new ideas. In fact, quite a few of her more important findings arose from experiments that were started to test such a dubious hypothesis and ended up by not only disproving it but revealing new problems and new means of dealing with them.

The discovery of the double helix, while coming to Auerbach as to all geneticists as a tremendous revelation, brought in its wake a consequence for mutation research which distressed her profoundly. For many years after this discovery, it was fashionable to explain all mutational phenomena in terms of chemical changes in deoxyribonucleic acid (DNA), and the whole of mutation research appeared in danger of becoming a branch of nucleic acid chemistry. Throughout these years, Auerbach strove hard to keep alive the knowledge that mutagenesis is a biological process of many steps, of which a chemical change in DNA is only the first, although an indispensable one. She was delighted when the discovery of enzymes for DNA replication and repair at last led the way back from the test tube to the living cell.

Auerbach's first analysis of chemical mutagenesis was carried out on *Drosophila,* using mustard gas and nitrogen mustard. The results promptly revealed the main peculiarities of chemical mutagens and defined areas of research that were explored by her and others to the end of her career. The main areas were: the relation between chromosome breakage and gene mutation; the delayed action of chemical mutagens as opposed to the immediate effects of x-rays; and the tendency of chemicals to produce the so-called replicating instabilities, that is, unstable genes that not only continue over many cell cycles to throw off the same mutation but also can replicate in the unstable state. Using fission yeast, her collaborators studied this last phenomenon in greater detail, but its mechanism was not elucidated. At the time of her retirement, Auerbach had come to suspect that the final explanation might be found by research on insertion sequences. Fission yeast was also used in her laboratory for studying the way in which one-strand lesions in DNA are changed into two-strand mutations. These experiments led to the hypothesis of heteroduplex repair several years before its reality was proved in molecular studies. During a stay in Oak Ridge, TN, in the United States, Auerbach herself had switched from *Drosophila* to *Neurospora.* She used it first for showing that spontaneous mutations can occur in the absence of DNA replication, a conclusion that subsequently was confirmed by J. W. Drake. The main program of the work with fungi carried out for many years by her, her students, and collaborators was the analysis of mutagen specificity, that is, the selective action of certain mutagens on certain genes. This was one of the phenomena for which nucleic acid chemistry offered a plausible but unproved explanation. Auerbach's results showed that, in one of the textbook examples of mutagen specificity, the whole of the striking phenomenon arose during secondary steps in mutagenesis: repair or expression. This was the beginning of studies concerning metabolic and physiological influences on mutagenesis carried out by her colleague and successor B. J. Kilbey.

The latest development in mutation research, its application to the detection of environmental mutagens, tended to shock Auerbach through its pragmatism that, unavoidably, leads to violation of the strictly scientific principles that meant so much to her. Yet she felt it her duty to participate in these endeavors, and she did this by acting as a member of a government committee, by accepting the honorary presidency of the second international congress on environmental mutagen research, and of the United Kingdom society on the same subject, and by acting as a sponsor and adviser of a European Economic Community program on mutagen testing carried out in Edinburgh.

Auerbach came from a German-Jewish family which, on her father's side, had had two generations of scientists. Her grandfather had been an anatomist, discoverer of Auerbach's plexus in the human intestine; her father was a chemist, and one of her uncles a physicist. She came to Edinburgh in 1933 as a victim of nazism, obtained her Ph.D. at the Institute of Animal Genetics (1935), and remained there for the remainder of her career, with several sabbatical interruptions spent in the United States and Japan. She had the good fortune to be introduced to mutation research by H. J. Muller, who spent the year before World War II in her institute. The University of Edinburgh awarded her a D.Sc. (1947) and later a personal chair (1967). She was honored with the Keith Medal of the Royal Society of Edinburgh (1947), the Darwin Medal of the Royal Society of London (1977), awards of the environmental mutagen societies of the United States (1972) and Europe (1974), and honorary degrees from the universities of Leiden, Cambridge, and Dublin. She was elected an honorary member of the Genetical Society of Japan (1966) and the Danish Academy of Sciences (1968), and a foreign associate of the U.S. National Academy of Sciences (1970). She loved teaching and was very interested in the task of popularizing science. *See* MULLER, HERMANN JOSEPH.

In addition to two textbooks, *Mutation Methods,* (1962) and *Mutation Research* (1976), Auerbach wrote two popular books, *Genetics in the Atomic Age* (1956, 1965) and *The Science of Genetics* (1962, 1969), both of which were translated into many languages.

For background information *see* GENETICS; MUTATION in the McGraw-Hill Encyclopedia of Science and Technology. ∎

AUGER, PIERRE VICTOR
★ French physicist

Born May 14, 1899, Paris, France

From the outset of his work in 1922 Auger interested himself in the cloud chamber method discovered by C. T. R. Wilson and applied it to studying the photoelectric effect produced by x-rays on gas atoms. The Wilson method provided him with the most direct means of obtaining detailed information on the photoelectrons produced, since their trajectories could be followed as soon as they left the atom that had absorbed the quantum of radiation. Auger aimed to simplify the phenomenon and to obtain the photoelectric effect on a single category of atoms, rather than on all those of the mixture of air and water vapor used hitherto. He filled the chamber with hydrogen, which has a very low x-ray absorption coefficient, and a small proportion of highly absorbent and chemically neutral heavy gases, such as krypton and xenon.

While providing information on the directions in which the photoelectrons were emitted, this method revealed the effect of the radiations emitted by the positive ion left behind after the departure of the electron. Thus, if the photons of fluorescence (that is, the characteristic x-rays emitted by atoms ionized in their inner, or K and L, layers) were reabsorbed in the gas of the chamber, they should show up in the form of short electron trajectories.

Auger was able to observe some instances of this reabsorption in the gas, but usually found that the expected electron trajectory started from the same point as the electron trajectory attributable to the first photoelectron, that is, the two tracks started from the positive ion itself. The common source of the tracks meant that an internal conversion of the photon of fluorescence had to be taking place when it became reabsorbed among the electrons of the very ion from which it had sprung. Such reabsorption would diminish the fluorescence correspondingly, since the photon was not emitted outside, a fact that could be checked by global methods.

Numerous experiments enabled Auger to show that the phenomenon is a general one and amounts, in fact, to "nonradiating" transitions among the electrons of atoms ionized in depth; the fall of peripheral electrons toward the free places in the inner levels is directly accompanied by the emission of electrons that carry away the liberated energy in kinetic form. This phenomenon was named the Auger effect, and the corresponding electrons Auger electrons. The ionization of the positive remainder increases with each repetition of the effect. N. Perrin later proved that certain heavy atoms can, by a series of Auger effects, attain a positive charge as high as 28 elementary charges. The effect thus discovered is similar to the internal conversion of gamma rays and Klein and Rosseland's collisions of the second kind.

Shortly after James Chadwick's discovery of neutrons in polonium-beryllium source radiations, Auger established their energy spectrum, and was able to demonstrate the existence of a group forming a continuous band of low energies. He explained the emission of such neutrons as a peculiar mechanism of disintegration of the beryllium nucleus by alpha particles without the latter being captured. *See* CHADWICK, SIR JAMES.

Much of Auger's work was devoted to cosmic rays. He was able to reveal the tracks of penetrating corpuscles in a double expansion chamber before and after their passage through half a meter of lead. The nonelectronic nature of these particles thus became a certainty (1935), and was finally demonstrated in 1938 when C. D. Anderson discovered the muon.

Auger next studied the cosmic showers in the form of photoelectron cascades and sought the existence of very-high-energy particles by looking for the very extensive showers which they ought to produce in passing through the atmosphere. By means of high-speed-resolution coincidence-counting equipment (10^{-6} second in 1938), built with the help of Roland Maze, Auger demonstrated the existence of enormous atmospheric showers, which he called "grandes gerbes" and which are also known as extensive air showers or extensive Auger showers (EAS). The great size of these showers, which contain tens of millions of electrons and photons spread over areas of thousands of square meters, enabled Auger to attribute energies exceeding 10^{15} electronvolts to the initial particle from which these showers originate. Later estimates raised the figure to 10^{20} electronvolts, giving the extensive Auger showers the highest known energy of any natural phenomenon. It is a billion times that which the most powerful proton accelerator can attain. How corpuscular radiations with this amount of energy are created in the universe is still an unsolved problem of cosmic physics, though partial explanations have been suggested by various physicists, in particular, Enrico Fermi. *See* FERMI, ENRICO.

Auger studied at the Ecole Normale Supérieure and the Faculty of Sciences at the University of Paris, where he obtained his doctorate in 1926. He remained associated with the university throughout his career, becoming a full professor in 1937. His research work was carried out first at Jean Perrin's laboratory there and then at the Ecole Normale Supérieure. He played an important role in the establishment of both French and international scientific research bodies. After taking part during World War II in the work of the Anglo-Canadian Atomic Energy Research group in Montreal, he returned to France in 1945 to help found the Commissariat a l'Energie Atomique. In 1952, as director of the Department of Sciences at UNESCO, he was responsible for setting up the European Nuclear Research Organization (CERN). After organizing the Centre National d'Etudes Spatiales (National Space Study Center) in France, he spent the years from 1960 to 1964 in bringing about the establishment of the European Space Research Organization (ESRO), of which he became director-general in 1962.

Auger wrote works on cosmic rays; a book of scientific philosophy, *L'homme Microscopique;* and *Main Trends in Scientific Research,* prepared for the United Nations and UNESCO (1961).

For background information *see* AUGER EFFECT; CLOUD CHAMBER; COSMIC RAYS in the McGraw-Hill Encyclopedia of Science and Technology. ∎

AVERY, OSWALD THEODORE
American physician and biologist
___

Born *Oct. 21, 1887, Halifax, Nova Scotia, Canada*
Died *Feb. 20, 1955, Nashville, TN, U.S.A.*

While investigating the transformation of one strain of pneumococcus (the bacterium causing pneumonia) into another, Avery discovered that the substance responsible for the hereditary alteration of the cell is deoxyribonucleic acid (DNA). This established the specificity of DNA in biological reactions, and ultimately served as the initial rung in the ladder of genetic studies further extended by the work of such Nobel laureates as G. W. Beadle, Arthur Kornberg, Severo Ochoa, and M. H. F. Wilkins. *See* BEADLE, GEORGE WELLS; KORNBERG, ARTHUR; OCHOA, SEVERO; WILKINS, MAURICE HUGH FREDERICK.

In 1928 Frederick Griffith, a British pathologist, reported that when he inoculated mice with a mixture of a harmless strain of living pneumococci and the killed remains of a virulent strain, the mice died from an infection with live organisms of the virulent variety. He further reported that subsequent generations of the bacteria retained the new-found virulence. Since it was logical to assume that the dead organisms had not come to life, Griffith theorized that something in their bodies had transformed the living harmless strain into an infectious one. At first his report was viewed with skepticism by many authorities, including Avery, who believed strongly in immunological specificity. However, Avery asked an assistant, Martin H. Dawson, to try to duplicate Griffith's experiments. Dawson not only did so but in 1931, working at Columbia University with Richard H. P. Sia, succeeded in causing killed pneumococci to transform living organisms in laboratory glassware instead of in mice. A year later James L. Alloway, a member of Avery's group at the Rockefeller Institute, succeeded in using a cellfree extract rather than whole dead cells as the transforming agent, indicating that the agent involved is a chemical substance.

These results caused Avery to enter the investigation personally. He decided that the best approach would be to separate from capsulated pneumococci a soluble fraction capable of bringing about the change in culture. Working at the Rockefeller Institute in New York City, first with C. M. MacLeod and later with Maclyn McCarty, Avery grew large quantities of the virulent type III capsulated pneumococcus. From these cultures Avery extracted the chemical constituents of the organisms and tested the transforming power of each fraction. By 1944 he had arrived at a practically pure substance that could transfer to noncapsulated variants and their subsequent generations the hereditary property to produce the capsular polysaccharide of the strain used for preparation of the extract. This fraction proved to be identical with one of the nucleic acids, DNA. See MCCARTY, MACLYN; MACLEOD, COLIN MUNRO.

However, Avery felt that at this point he could still not be certain that the active agent is the DNA in the fraction or a small amount of protein contaminant. To verify the result, first McCarty and then Moses Kunitz prepared a quantity of DNase, an enzyme that would destroy the DNA without affecting any protein that was present. When upon treatment with the DNase the fraction lost its transforming power, Avery and his coworkers

had demonstrated that DNA is the effective agent in inducing an inheritable change in a living organism. This finding provided the impetus for a major change in the thinking of geneticists. While the nucleic acids had previously been thought of as biologically inert substances, the work of later reseachers, notably Alfred E. Mirsky, demonstrated that DNA is present in all animal organisms and, hence, that a similarity exists in the mechanism of heredity among all animal species, from the smallest bacterium to the largest mammal.

Avery's lifelong work with pneumococci began in 1913 in collaboration with A. Raymond Dochez. The two investigated the types of pneumococci present in pneumonic patients and in carriers. This investigation, which was to exert a great deal of influence on the evolution of medical microbiology, had as one result the discovery of specific soluble substances of pneumococcus origin in the blood and urine during lobar pneumonia.

Among his other studies was that of the role played by the capsular polysaccharides in determining the immunological specificity and virulence of pneumococci. This investigation permitted the development of sensitive and specific diagnostic procedures: serological typing and a skin test for the demonstration of a circulating antibody. More important, it proved that virulence and immunity can be analyzed apart from the parasite as a whole in terms of some highly specialized cellular component—in the case of pneumococci, the polysaccharide capsule.

The son of a clergyman, Avery moved to New York City with his family in 1887. He received his A.B. from Colgate University in 1900 and his M.D. from the College of Physicians and Surgeons of Columbia University in 1904. After serving as an assistant to a New York City physician for several months, he decided that he found little pleasure in the practice of medicine. He became interested in the pathogenesis of infectious diseases and, with the aid of a research fund, began a study of the phagocytic index in respiratory disease. Avery obtained a permanent position in the Hoagland Laboratory in Brooklyn in 1906 and remained there until 1913. In that year he joined the Rockefeller Institute Hospital as a bacteriologist, remaining at the Institute for 43 years before retiring to Nashville, TN, in 1947. Among the honors and awards he

received were the John Phillips Memorial Award of the American College of Physicians in 1932, the Copley Medal of the Royal Society of London in 1945, and the Kober Medal of the Association of American Physicians in 1947. Avery was elected to the National Academy of Sciences in 1933, and was made a foreign member of the Royal Society of London in 1944.

For background information see BACTERIOLOGY, MEDICAL; DEOXYRIBONUCLEIC ACID (DNA); PNEUMOCOCCUS; TRANSFORMATION, BACTERIAL in the McGraw-Hill Encyclopedia of Science and Technology. ∎

AXELROD, JULIUS
☆ American pharmacologist

Born May 30, 1912, New York, NY, U.S.A.

For his description of the metabolic pathway for the catecholamine neurotransmitters noradrenaline and adrenaline, identification and isolation of the enzymes involved, and determination of the effect of drugs upon the uptake and release of these amines, Axelrod shared the 1970 Nobel Prize in medicine or physiology with Ulf von Euler and Bernard Katz. See KATZ, SIR BERNARD.

Axelrod's interest in pharmacology and drug metabolism began with analgesic drugs and was furthered by his association with Bernard D. Brodie. In the early

1950s he did research on amphetamines and on compounds which are related structurally to catecholamines. As a result of this work, Axelrod discovered the enzymes that metabolize drugs in the body. Because of this background, when Axelrod joined the National Institute of Mental Health in 1955, he selected the metabolism of noradrenaline and adrenaline as a research project. He succeeded in elucidating the metabolic transformation of these two catecholamines, and discovered and isolated catechol-O-methyltransferase (COMT), the enzyme that produces O-methylation of catecholamines. COMT acts on the amines mainly outside the neuron. Axelrod and his coworkers found other methyl transferases that were involved in biogenic amine metabolism.

Shortly after the work on O-methylation, the availability of tritiated noradrenaline and adrenaline (that is, the compounds contained tritium for labeling purposes) made possible a study of the distribution of adrenaline in animal tissues. This research was furthered when two members of Axelrod's group, H. Weil-Malherbe and L. G. Whitby, developed methods for measuring noradrenaline, adrenaline, and their O-methylated metabolites in tissues. The studies showed that tissues heavily supplied with sympathetic nerves, such as the heart, spleen, and pineal gland took up the tritiated amines in a physiologically active form and that the amines circulating in the tissues were taken up and retained by the sympathetic nerve endings. The experimental data also indicated that there were several mechanisms by which noradrenaline released from nerve terminals was inactivated. Of these mechanisms, the major one was its reuptake by the sympathetic nerves.

Axelrod and his group demonstrated the effect of drugs on the sympathetic nerves by determining the rate at which tritiated adrenaline was taken up and released from tissues. Drugs such as cocaine and amphetamine blocked the uptake of noradrenaline into nerves, while reserpine caused a release of the neurotransmitter.

The study of the fate of noradrenaline in the brain was made possible by J. Glowinski's technique of bypassing the blood-brain barrier by injecting tritiated noradrenaline into the brain through the lateral ventricle. The results indicated that the tritiated amine mixed with the noradrenaline in the brain and remained there protected from metabolism for long periods of time. The presence of the labeled catecholamine in the brain enabled Axelrod and his group to study the effects of psychoactive drugs on noradrenaline. Antidepressant drugs appeared to make more noradrenaline available in the brain. The rate of turnover or utilization of noradrenaline in the brain was also investigated. The fastest rate occurred in the hypothalamus and the slowest in the cerebellum. Subsequent work indicated that the rate was also affected by stress, sleep, and changes in temperature.

Studies into the synthesis of adrenaline established that phenyl N-methyl transferase, an enzyme found mainly in the adrenal medulla and to a smaller extent in the brain, catalyzes the last step in the synthesis of catecholamines. As a result of these and other experiments, it appeared that regulation of catecholamine synthesis in the body is under hormonal and neural regulation. Adrenocorticotropic hormone (ACTH) and nerve activity were shown to influence the activity of the enzymes needed for biosynthesis of catecholamines. The biosynthesis of these amines is precisely controlled by the nervous system. In the adrenal gland continued stimulation of the splanchnic nerve increases the release of catecholamines. There was also evidence by other investigators of a feedback mechanism in that noradrenaline regulates its own synthesis.

Experiments with the pineal gland by Axelrod and his colleagues showed that noradrenaline released by the sympathetic nerve fibers increases the synthesis of new N-acetyl transferase molecules, which are essential in the control of the hormone melantonin by the adrenergic nervous system.

Axelrod also studied the role of certain lipids in membrane structure and function and how biological signals pass through cell membranes.

Axelrod received his B.S. from the College of the City of New York in 1933, his M.S. from New York University in 1941, and his Ph.D. from George Washington University in 1955. He worked at the Laboratory of Industrial Hygiene (1935–46) and then at the New York University Research Service (1946–49), where he began his association with Brodie; their collaborative work was later carried on at the National Heart Institute in Bethesda, MD (1949–55). In 1955 Axelrod joined the staff of the National Institute of Mental Health, subsequently becoming chief of the section of pharmacology of the Laboratory of Clinical Sciences. He published many research papers on his studies. In addition to the Nobel Prize, he was honored with the Distinguished Service Award of the Association for Research in Nervous and Mental Disorders (1965) and the Albert Einstein Award of Yeshiva University (1971), among others. He was elected a member of the National Academy of Sciences (1971) and the American Association for the Advancement of Science, and a fellow of the American Academy of Arts and Sciences.

For background information *see* NEUROPHYSIOLOGY in the McGraw-Hill Encyclopedia of Science and Technology. ■

BAADE, WALTER
American astronomer

Born *Mar. 24, 1893, Schröttinghausen, Westphalia, Germany*
Died *June 25, 1960, Göttingen, Westphalia, Germany*

While trying to resolve the bright stars in the nucleus of the Andromeda Nebula, Baade formulated the concept of stellar populations. He later applied this concept to the results of photometric measurements of classic cepheid variables to increase the distance scale of the universe by a factor of 2.

In 1912 the period-luminosity relationship for variable stars in the Small Magellanic Cloud was discovered by Henrietta Swan Leavitt of the Harvard College Observatory. The variable stars were of the short-period RR Lyrae type, but Ejnar Hertzsprung of the Leiden Observatory in the Netherlands showed that these were similar to the long-period classical cepheid variables of the Delta Cephei type, and in 1913 he made the first attempt to correlate the relationship in absolute magnitude. This correlation was successfully achieved by Harlow Shapley of the Mount Wilson Observatory in 1914, and it served as the basis for his model of the Milky Way Galaxy, which was announced 4 years later. During the interim, Shapley noticed that the Hertzsprung-Russell (H-R) diagram for stars in globular clusters differed drastically from the H-R diagram for stars in the neighborhood of the Sun and in galactic clus-

ters. However, this observation was largely disregarded after he announced it in 1915. The period-luminosity relationship, as calibrated by Shapley, was used by Edwin P. Hubble of the Mount Wilson Observatory to assign a distance of about 900,000 light-years (8.51×10^{18} kilometers), later reduced to about 750,000 light-years (7.1×10^{18} kilometers), to the Andromeda Nebula in 1929. All other extragalactic distances were then based on the distance to the Andromeda Nebula. *See* SHAPLEY, HARLOW.

Although Hubble had resolved the spiral arms of the Andromeda Nebula into stars in 1923, all subsequent attempts to resolve the nucleus had failed. In 1944, while working at the Mount Wilson Observatory, Baade decided to use the 100-inch (2.54-meter) Hooker telescope to try to resolve the nucleus of the Andromeda Nebula into its component stars. He believed that he had an excellent chance to succeed, for the sky was free of artificial light because of the wartime blackout of the nearby cities of Los Angeles and Pasadena. Since the brightest stars in the spiral arms of the nebula are blue supergiants of high surface temperature, Baade chose to use blue-sensitive plates. However, the nucleus remained unresolved. Then, although it was unlikely that a red star could be detected when the far brighter blue stars had failed to appear on earlier plates, he tried a red-sensitive plate. To his amazement, not only did the nucleus of the nebula resolve into individual stars but so did the previously unresolved companion elliptical nebulae M 32 and NGC 205. Baade realized that whereas the brightest stars in the arms of spiral galaxies are blue, the brightest stars in the nuclei of such galaxies and in elliptical galaxies are red. Furthermore, he found that while these red stars are brighter than the red giants observed in the Sun's region of the Milky Way, they are similar to those seen in globular clusters.

From these findings, Baade reached the conclusion that there must be two distinct classes of stellar populations, which he designated population I and population II. Population I includes younger stars, the brightest of which are the blue-white supergiants associated with interstellar gas and dust; population I stars are found in the arms of spiral galaxies and in galactic clusters. Population II includes older stars, the brightest of which are the red

B

are the red supergiants that are not associated with interstellar gas and dust; population II stars are found in the nuclei of spiral galaxies, in elliptical galaxies, and in globular clusters. Although later work indicated that there are more than two stellar populations and that Baade's conclusions were too general, his contribution played a significant role in developing the theory of stellar evolution.

The concept of stellar populations led Baade to revise the scale of extragalactic distances. When the 200-inch (5.08-meter) Hale telescope at the Mount Palomar Observatory became operational in 1948, Baade used it to continue his investigations. Since the telescope could photograph objects down to an apparent magnitude of 22.4 in a 30-minute exposure, Baade expected plates of the nucleus of the Andromeda Nebula to show RR Lyrae variables, which at maximum brightness should have had an apparent magnitude of 22.4. However, only the brightest population II stars appeared on the plate. Baade realized that since the absolute magnitude of the RR Lyrae stars produced the wrong apparent magnitude when substituted into the equation relating absolute magnitude, distance, and apparent magnitude, the distance assumed for the Andromeda Nebula must be incorrect. He finally obtained satisfactory agreement between distance and magnitude by assuming that there are two period-luminosity curves for variable stars instead of one. One curve gave the relationship for the type I variables, such as RR Lyrae, of population I, and the other the relationship for the type II variables, such as Delta Cephei, of population II. The absolute magnitude of the population I variables, Baade found, is 1.5 magnitudes less than that of the population II variables of the same period. Thus, in 1952, Baade announced that, based on the fact that a decrease in magnitude of 1.5 is equivalent to an increase in distance by a factor of two, the Andromeda Nebula was 1.5×10^6 light-years (1.42×10^{19} kilometers) distant. Since all other extragalactic distances were based on the calculated distance of the Andromeda Nebula, this had the effect of doubling the distance to all extragalactic objects. Not only was Baade's work confirmed by a number of observers, but later evidence showed that the correction factor is probably closer to three than to two. By doubling the size of the universe, Baade

helped to reconcile a number of contradictions resulting from the previous scale—such as the time interval required to account for the velocity of the external galaxies and the radioactive determination of the Earth's age—to the evolutionary model of the universe.

Among Baade's many other accomplishments was the discovery of two unique asteroids. In 1924 he located Hidalgo, whose aphelion is farther from the Sun than that of any other asteroid, and in 1949 he discovered Icarus, whose perihelion is closer to the Sun than that of any other asteroid. He also identified a distorted galaxy in Cygnus, called Cygnus A, which was the first discrete radio source to be discovered, in 1953.

Baade attended the universities of Münster and Göttingen, receiving his Ph.D. from the latter in 1919. In that year he became an assistant at the Hamburg Observatory, and in 1927 he was appointed an astronomer there. Beginning in 1920, he served simultaneously as a Privatdozent at the University of Hamburg. In 1931 Baade left both posts to join the Mount Wilson Observatory as an astronomer, and in 1948 he also became an astronomer at the Mount Palomar Observatory. He retired from these positions in 1958. He returned to the University of Göttingen in 1959 as Gauss Professor, serving in that capacity until his death. Baade was awarded the Gold Medal of the Royal Astronomical Society of Great Britain and the Bruce Medal of the Astronomical Society of the Pacific.

For background information *see* COSMOGONY; GALAXY, EXTERNAL; NEBULA; RADIO ASTRONOMY; STAR in the McGraw-Hill Encyclopedia of Science and Technology. ∎

BABCOCK, HORACE W.
★ American astronomer

Born Sept. 13, 1912, Pasadena, CA, U.S.A.

As early as 1934 Babcock recognized that although polarization of radiation from astronomical objects had been largely neglected, it had the potential for yielding much information about magnetic phenomena. His subsequent research was largely concerned with magnetic fields of stars and of the Sun. For the Mount Wilson 2.5-meter telescope with

its high-dispersion spectrograph, he provided in 1946 a differential analyzer for circular polarization with the aim of investigating sharp-line stars. The hope was to detect coherent magnetic fields in these stars through the Zeeman effect in their spectra—the magnetic splitting of spectrum lines into characteristically polarized components. He expected that hotter, main-sequence stars, known to rotate much more rapidly than the Sun, might well possess far stronger general magnetic fields, sufficient to bring the Zeeman effect within the range of measurability, notwithstanding the weakness of the radiation. The earliest tests resulted in the discovery of a magnetic field of about 1500 gauss in the A0p star 78 Virginis. (The Earth's field is 0.6 gauss.) This was soon followed by the discovery of a regularly reversing magnetic field in the peculiar A-type star HD 125248.

The search for other magnetic stars was carried forward largely with the 5-meter Hale Telescope at Palomar Mountain. By 1966 the existence of magnetic fields was confirmed in 130 stars. Most were in the range between a few hundred gauss and 5000 gauss, but Babcock found that the A0p star HD 215441 possessed an exceptionally strong magnetic field of about 34,000 gauss. Practically all stellar magnetic fields vary; a few always show the same magnetic polarity, but the great majority reverse their polarity from time to time. Many were found to show periodic reversals. Some magnetic variables have

periods as short as 4 days, others as long as 2350 days. Most of the magnetic stars were known to be peculiar in the sense that their spectra show abnormally strong (and variable) lines of such elements as chromium, strontium, silicon, europium, and other rare-earth elements. An outstanding example of a group of magnetic variables is the star 53 Camelopardalis, which displays magnetic variations between +3700 and −5100 gauss during a period of 8.03 days, with synchronously alternating strong lines of the chromium group and of the rare-earth group of elements.

It is now generally held that all magnetic variables are periodic and that they can be represented by the rigid rotator model described by D. W. N. Stibbs and A. J. Deutsch. In this model, the magnetic dipole axis is highly inclined to the rotational axis of the star (and may be eccentric as well); the abundance of certain chemical elements is enhanced as a function of magnetic polarity and magnetic latitude, so that the zones or patches on the stellar surface present to the observer a periodically changing pattern of magnetic field strength and spectrum peculiarity as the star rotates. A variety of physical processes have been proposed to account for the zonal concentration of chemical elements, but with no clear success.

The observations of stellar magnetism stimulated the development, by other investigators, of the theory of magnetohydrodynamics in the context of astrophysics. The magnetic fields are probably primeval, having condensed with the gas from the interstellar medium when the star was formed. Magnetic fields are important in modifying activity in the convective layers of stars and in generating flares. Around rotating stars, the magnetic field is vital in coupling the star to the circumstellar ionized medium; such coupling results in the transfer of angular momentum, slowing the rotation of the star and accelerating the surrounding ionized medium or plasma. Especially in view of the ubiquity of stellar magnetism, this concept is important in an early stage of formation of planetary systems, as it explains the distribution of angular momentum in the system before condensation of the medium into solid bodies orbiting the star; it forms much of the basis for the opinion that a great many stars besides the Sun probably have planetary systems.

From 1952 to 1958 Babcock collaborated with his father, Harold D. Babcock, in the invention and use of the solar magnetograph, a system for measuring and recording the strength, polarity, and distribution of magnetic fields (as well as velocity fields) over the surface of the Sun. Primary innovations included an electrooptic birefringent crystal used with a powerful grating spectrograph and an ac amplifier with synchronous demodulation, as well as techniques for scanning the Sun's image and conformally mapping the data. The instrument recorded fields as weak as a small fraction of a gauss. It provided a wealth of new data on the systematics of the Sun's surface features and resulted in the discovery of weak magnetic fields near the Sun's poles of rotation (the elusive general field) and of the reversal of the Sun's polar fields that is linked with the 22-year sunspot cycle.

In 1961 Babcock advanced a theory of the Sun's magnetic cycle based on T. G. Cowling's idea of subsurface amplification of the magnetic field by differential rotation. Involving a systematic pattern of twisted flux ropes in the outer convection zone, the model accounted for active regions, for Spörer's law of sunspot distribution, for the reversal of the Sun's polar magnetic fields, and for a number of related phenomena. The observations and the theory forced acceptance of the concept of severing and reconnection of lines of force, with a resultant outflow (solar wind) of tenuous plasma from the Sun.

Between 1949 and 1963 Babcock improved the technology for the ruling of diffraction gratings, so necessary for the advancement of astrophysics. Innovations included the cylindrical monorail and a simplified method of interferometric control of groove spacing. With the ruling engines of the Mount Wilson Observatory, more than 100 original gratings of the highest quality and large size were produced. About 60 gratings were provided to other observatories or laboratories, and many others were put to use in spectrographs of the Mount Wilson and Palomar Observatories.

Other advances in the field of instrumentation included an exposure meter for astronomical spectrographs with subtraction of dark noise of the photomultiplier (1949), an automatic guider (star tracker) of general utility (1948), field equipment for the continuous measurement and recording of astronomical seeing (1963),

and a Morse code translator based on the binary number system (1944). A template spectrometer for the measurement of stellar magnetic fields and radial velocities in real time was built in 1955.

In 1963 Babcock began guiding the establishment and construction, for the Carnegie Institution of Washington, of the Las Campanas Observatory in Chile with its 1-meter Swope Telescope and 2.5-meter Du Pont Telescope. The project was initiated with a survey to determine the best location for an observatory in the Southern Hemisphere. The innovative Du Pont Telescope was designed by the staff of the Hale Observatories; it provided excellent instrumental performance at a site unsurpassed for the quality of its natural observing conditions.

Babcock was strongly influenced by association with his father and other members of the group at the Mount Wilson Observatory. He received a B.S. in physics and engineering at the California Institute of Technology in 1934 and a Ph.D. from the University of California in 1938. His thesis was based upon observations he made at the Lick Observatory on the rotation of the spiral galaxy in Andromeda (M 31), showing that high angular velocity prevails in the outer reaches of that galaxy and that its mass is about 10^{11} suns. After experience at the Yerkes and McDonald observatories, he engaged in wartime research at the Massachusetts Institute of Technology and the California Institute of Technology. This work involved indicator circuits for airborne radar and the development of launching and aiming systems for aircraft ordnance rockets. He joined the staff of the Mount Wilson Observatory in 1946 and became director of the Mount Wilson and Palomar Observatories (later the Hale Observatories) in 1964. He was elected to the National Academy of Sciences in 1954. Among the awards he received were the Draper Medal of the National Academy of Sciences (1957), the Bruce Medal of the Astronomical Society of the Pacific, and the Eddington Medal and the Gold Medal of the Royal Astronomical Society (London).

Most of Babcock's scientific publications appear in the *Astrophysical Journal* and other journals.

For background information *see* ASTRONOMICAL SPECTROSCOPY; STAR; SUN; ZEEMAN EFFECT in the McGraw-Hill Encyclopedia of Science and Technology. ∎

BADGER, RICHARD McLEAN

★ American physical chemist and
molecular spectroscopist

Born May 4, 1896, Elgin, IL, U.S.A.
Died Nov. 26, 1974, Altadena, CA,
U.S.A.

Badger worked in several fields of physical chemistry, though his predominant scientific interest over many years was the application of spectroscopy to the solution of chemical problems. These included particularly the structures of polyatomic molecules, both the very small and the very large, especially the proteins and simpler related substances; the problem of hydrogen bonding; and the relation of potential constants to internuclear distances. While Badger was a graduate student, his interest was directed toward spectroscopy through his association with Richard C. Tolman and with Paul S. Epstein. Tolman was engaged in one of the earliest attempts to calculate thermodynamic properties of simple molecules by the application of quantum statistical mechanics, then in a very elementary state, and was using internuclear distances roughly estimated from gas kinetic data. At Tolman's suggestion, Badger became involved in checking the calculations and saw the possibility of improvement by the use of the spectroscopic moments of inertia, just then becoming available. Shortly thereafter he became aware of the possibilities which infrared spectroscopy offers to the chemist through a lecture presentation by Epstein of the remarkable high-resolution work being done at the University of Michigan.

For very practical reasons Badger's first experimental work in spectroscopy was in the far infrared. Diffraction gratings were very difficult to obtain, but coarse gratings suitable for the long-wave regions could be made with the relatively primitive facilities available. These made possible the discovery of the pure rotation spectrum of ammonia, the first rotation spectrum of a polyatomic molecule to be interpreted. This work confirmed the symmetrical pyramidal structure of ammonia and cleared up a former misinterpretation of the 10-micrometer band, then so interesting as the first example of inversion doubling. At this time the development of new photographic sensitizers was making the near infrared available for convenient investigation, and Badger turned his attention in this direction. He continued work on ammonia with R. Mecke in Bonn, but unfortunately theory was not yet developed for the interpretation of vibration-rotation bands of symmetrical rotors with degenerate vibrations. However, a number of papers followed on overtone and combination bands of simple polyatomic molecules that directed attention to the great variability of the OH group frequency, most puzzling until correlated with the hydrogen bonding tendency of this group. This subject proved to be a continuing interest and was the basis for 17 papers directly or indirectly bearing on the subject of hydrogen bonding. Badger was also struck by regularities in the potential constants of simple molecules. He formulated an empirical rule, commonly known as Badger's rule, that expresses a periodic relation between the distance and force constant of diatomic molecules. This systematization of experimental data resulted in disclosing several errors in the literature. The rule is less accurate for polyatomic molecules, but has frequently been used to estimate distances in the absence of precise data.

World War II diverted Badger's research activities to other fields, including a side interest in the physical chemistry of high polymers and ultimately in proteins and related substances, which were the subject of later spectroscopic studies. The war interval was not without compensation, since the important advances in techniques and instrumentation enormously facilitated infrared spectroscopy. With his student co-workers, Badger investigated the spectra of a series of simple polyatomic molecules with interesting structural problems. In particular, nitrous acid offered an unusual case of the double minimum problem and ozone presented a dilemma of long standing. A reasonable interpretation of the infrared spectrum had seemed impossible, until the discovery by M. Kent Wilson and Badger of a new band attributable to the v_1 symmetrical stretch. This resolved the difficulty and established spectroscopically the obtuse angled model for the ozone molecule.

Badger's secondary education began in Brisbane, Australia, and continued at the Elgin Academy, in Illinois. His college career, begun at the Junior College of the Elgin Academy and continued at Northwestern University, was interrupted by World War I. He finally received his B.S. (1921) and Ph.D. (1924) from the California Institute of Technology. He remained there, with some interruptions, and was active in teaching and research until his retirement as emeritus in 1966. In 1928–29 Badger was Rockefeller International fellow at the universities of Göttingen and Bonn, and in 1931 he was lecturer at the University of California, Berkeley. During World War II he was engaged in work for the Army Air Force, the National Defense Research Committee, the Manhattan District, the Office of Scientific Research and Development, and the Office of Naval Research. He was elected a member of the National Academy of Sciences in 1952 and a fellow of the American Academy of Arts and Sciences in 1961. He was John Simon Guggenheim Memorial fellow in 1960–61. In 1961 he received the Manufacturing Chemists Association Medal for excellence in college teaching in chemistry.

Badger wrote or coauthored 85 publications in scientific journals.

For background information *see* BOND ANGLE AND DISTANCE; HYDROGEN BOND; MOLECULAR STRUCTURE AND SPECTRA; SPECTROSCOPY in the McGraw-Hill Encyclopedia of Science and Technology. ∎

BAGNOLD, RALPH ALGER

★ British physicist

Born Apr. 3, 1896, Devonport, England

Bagnold's interest in the physical mechanisms responsible for the natural transport of granular material by wind and by water was aroused by accident. While in the Royal Engineers, he was posted to Egypt in 1926 and happened to join a small group of young officers whose hobby was to explore the possibilities of cross-country travel in light cars. The special techniques Bagnold developed not only made very long, entirely self-contained journeys possible but also enabled hitherto impenetrable fields of sand dunes to be crossed. For his subsequent explorations of the then largely unknown remote areas of the Libyan Desert, he was awarded the Founder's Gold Medal of the Royal Geographical Society in 1933.

During these journeys Bagnold became fascinated by the geometrical order and regular behavior of the great desert dunes, which posed many problems. Why, for instance, does sand accumulate into discrete dunes instead of scattering as does fine dust? Why, during even a violent sand storm, does the sand cloud extend no more than a meter or so above ground? What kind of force maintains the upward dispersion of the sand cloud against that of gravity? How is the mass rate of sand movement related to the wind strength? Bagnold retired from the army in 1935 to devote himself to a scientific study of these problems. Experiments in a homemade wind tunnel of his own design yielded answers to all the above questions and to many others. The results were published in 1941 in *The Physics of Blown Sand and Desert Dunes,* which remains the standard textbook on the subject. The underlying principles soon began to be applied successfully to the

protection of the Arabian oil fields from sand engulfment.

In 1938, at the joint instigation of the Institution of Civil Engineers and the French Department des Ponts et Chaussées, Bagnold turned his attention to the problem of the dislodgement by breaking waves of the great concrete blocks used in the construction of seawalls and breakwaters. By installing a piezo cell in a model concrete wall at the end of a wave tank at Imperial College, London, he quickly showed from oscillograph records that the impact of a concave wavefront against a plane wall could create high instantaneous pressures which, if distributed over a whole water-filled interstice, could give forces sufficient to dislodge a block. The results suggested how the probability of such an event could be minimized.

On the outbreak of war in 1939 Bagnold was recalled to the Army. By the accident of a convoy collision at sea he again found himself in Egypt. Owing to his almost unique knowledge of the great waterless interior desert and of how to travel in it, he was entrusted by General Wavell with the urgent raising and command of a special force, the Long Range Desert Group. This, the first and most lastingly successful of the many so-called private armies created during the war, operated for both raiding and reconnaissance throughout interior Libya.

Bagnold was elected a fellow of the Royal Society of London in 1944. On his return to England he at first undertook an experimental investigation of sand movement by waves, with reference to beach formation and change, sponsored by the Combined Operations Directorate. Convinced, as a physicist, that the natural mechanism of granular transport by one fluid, water, must obey the same underlying laws as that of transport by another fluid, air, he became interested in a comparative study of the two transport phenomena. It was apparent that many of the differences were attributable to the great disparity in the density ratio, about 2000:1 for sand and air and 2.6: 1 for sand and water. It also became apparent that all attempts to find a rational quantitative explanation of the transport mechanism along the kinematic lines traditional to hydraulic engineers must inevitably be self-defeating, for by ignoring the excess density of the solids the essential condition on which the whole phenomenon must depend was removed from consideration.

Adopting a new and more rational approach, Bagnold regarded the flowing fluid, air or water, as a transporting machine, dependent on the rates of kinetic energy supply and of transport work done against friction. This led at once to the concept that the transport rate of solids by immersed weight is primarily related to stream power, both quantities having the same dimensions of an energy rate. By a simple homemade experiment he showed that the sustained shearing of a dispersion of granular solids causes, by the creation of transverse components of grain momentum by collision, elastic or otherwise, a normal grain stress tending to further dispersion. The ratio of the applied shear stress to the normal dispersive stress appeared as a dynamic friction coefficient of the same order as the limiting static contact coefficient. Thus the immersed weight of an unsuspended bedload of saltating grains is simply proportional to the fluid shear stress directly applied to the saltation.

In 1958 Bagnold visited Washington, DC, as a consultant to the U.S. Geological Survey on the invitation of Luna B. Leopold. This resulted in a lasting cooperation in an effort to understand the transport of sediments by rivers. At Bagnold's instigation a number of critical experiments were carried out which removed much of the previous confusion and uncertainty on the subject.

Son of a colonel in the Royal Engineers, Bagnold received a regular commission in that corps in March 1915 and was immediately posted to a field unit in Belgium, where he served till the end of World War I. He took an honors degree in engineering at Cambridge University in 1921. He retired from the British army in 1935, having served in Egypt, India, and China. He was recalled in 1939, serving in the Middle East until released in 1944. He was awarded the G. K. Warren Prize by the U.S. National Academy of Sciences in 1969, the Penrose Medal by the Geological Society of America in 1970, the Wollaston Medal by the Geological Society of London in 1971, and the Sorby Medal by the International Association of Sedimentologists in 1978.

For background information *see* DESERT EROSION FEATURES; FLUID-FLOW PROPERTIES; NEAR-SHORE PROCESSES; STREAM TRANSPORT AND DEPOSITION; WAVE MOTION IN FLUIDS in the McGraw-Hill Encyclopedia of Science and Technology. ∎

BAILAR, JOHN CHRISTIAN, JR.
★ American chemist

Born May 27, 1904, Golden, CO, U.S.A.

In 1933 Bailar conceived the idea that optically active inorganic complex ions might undergo reactions accompanied by optical inversions. With his students, he discovered several reactions of this type and elucidated their mechanism. He also studied the phenomenon of stereospecificity in inorganic complexes and, with E. J. Corey, explained the cause of this phenomenon.

In a long series of papers (1893–1916), Alfred Werner demonstrated that properly substituted octahedral metal amines can exist in geometrically and optically isomeric forms. He also showed that geometrical isomers can be transformed into each other. Paul Walden observed in 1895 that certain organic reactions proceed, under some conditions, with retention of configuration but, under other conditions, with inversion—that is, one optical isomer can be converted into the other. Trained in both organic and inorganic chemistry, Bailar believed that both branches of the science were subject to the same laws and that phenomena exhibited by organic substances might well be observed in the behavior of inorganic substances as well. Subsequent studies showed that the relationship between organic and inorganic structures was not as simple as he had originally supposed, but his guiding principle was sound and led him to search for a "Walden inversion" in the reactions of cobalt complexes. His original goal of using the reactions of in-organic compounds to elucidate the behavior of simpler organic compounds was not achieved because the mechanism of the reactions of tetrahedral organic structures and octahedral inorganic complexes are not sufficiently similar for direct comparison. But his discovery of optical inversion in the inorganic reactions stimulated research that opened up the field of inorganic reaction mechanisms.

Stereospecificity in inorganic complexes has been known since the early part of this century, but no adequate explanation for it was offered until Corey and Bailar postulated that most five-membered chelate rings are puckered rather than flat and that such a ring, if it bears a substituent group, achieves the greatest stability (with respect to the remainder of the molecule) when the substituent group occupies an "equatorial" position on the ring. This theory is in accord with the quantitative measurements that have been made, and has been generally accepted. Bailar's work on stereospecificity led to the discovery of partial asymmetric synthesis of octahedral complexes and to methods of determining the relative configurations of organic molecules.

In 1965, at the request of the U.S. Department of Agriculture, Bailar undertook a series of studies on the selective hydrogenation of soybean methyl ester. He and his students developed both homogeneous and heterogeneous catalysts that catalyze the reduction of some, but not all, of the double bonds in this ester, and then extended the work to other polyolefinic substances. He also carried out studies on reactions of coordination compounds in the solid state.

Bailar's father was a professor of chemistry and began his son's education in chemistry at an early age. Bailar majored in chemistry at the University of Colorado, where he received his B.A. in 1924 and M.A. (specializing in inorganic chemistry) in 1925. The University of Michigan awarded him a Ph.D. in organic chemistry in 1928. During the years at Michigan, he became interested in the phenomena of isomerism and molecular rearrangements. This interest persisted after he assumed a position as instructor in inorganic chemistry at the University of Illinois in 1928, and he soon found that his organic training and interests could be easily transferred to inorganic chemistry. He became professor of chemistry at Illinois in 1943. During World War II he served as an official investigator for the National Defense Research Committee and did research on smoke screens and poisonous gases. In 1964 he was awarded the Priestley Medal of the American Chemical Society, in 1965 the Frank P. Dwyer Medal of the Chemical Society of New South Wales, in 1966 the Alfred Werner Gold Medal of the Swiss Chemical Society, and in 1978 the Heyrovský Medal of the Czechoslovak Academy of Sciences. He formally retired in 1968, but continued to carry on research and lecturing.

Bailar was editor in chief of volume 4 of *Inorganic Syntheses* and of the monograph *The Chemistry of Coordination Compounds* (1956). He coauthored textbooks in general chemistry with B S. Hopkins, with T. Moeller and J. Kleinberg (1965), and with Moeller and others (1978).

For background information *see* OPTICAL ACTIVITY; STEREOCHEMISTRY in the McGraw-Hill Encyclopedia of Science and Technology. ■

BAKER, ALAN
★ British mathematician

Born Aug. 19, 1939, London, England

The study of transcendental numbers, springing from diverse sources in the 19th century, has now grown into a fertile and extensive theory enriching widespread branches of mathematics. Baker contributed much to this development; in particular, in 1966 he obtained a result on linear forms in the logarithms of algebraic numbers that provided the key to the resolution of a wide variety of diophantine problems. He was awarded the Fields Medal for his work at the International Congress of Mathematicians held in Nice in 1970.

The researches had their origin in the famous seventh problem, which D. Hilbert raised at the International Congress held in Paris in 1900. Hilbert pointed out that much difficulty still attached to questions relating to irrationality and transcendence—notwithstanding the admirable works of C. Hermite (1873) and F. Lindemann (1882) which had furnished proofs of the transcendence of e and π, and thereby a solution to the ancient Greek problem concerning the squaring of the circle. By way of illustration, he proposed the problem of establishing the transcendence of $2^{\sqrt{2}}$ or, more generally, that of α^β, where α is algebraic and β is an algebraic irrational. He believed that a solution probably lay further in the future than a proof of the Riemann hypothesis or Fermat's last theorem, but, should a solution be found, it would certainly lead to valuable new methods and insights. A special case of Hilbert's problem had been posed by L. Euler more than a century before, but no apparent progress had been made toward its solution.

The problem was solved independently by A. O. Gelfond and T. Schneider in 1934; the solution derived from some surprising studies on integral integer-valued functions by which Gelfond had succeeded earlier in establishing the transcendence of e^π. The next year, Gelfond refined his techniques and thereby obtained a positive lower bound for a linear form in two logarithms. It was natural to conjecture that an analogous result would hold for arbitrarily many logarithms, and indeed it was soon realized that such a result would have important consequences. But for about 30 years the problem of extension seemed resistant to attack. It was solved by Baker in 1966; and the techniques devised for its solution—in particular, an algorithm for the construction and extrapolation of functions of several complex variables—form the basis of the principal effective methods in number theory known to date.

One of the main applications relates to the theory of diophantine equations. Mathematicians have been interested since antiquity in questions concerning the determination of the totality of inte-

gers having certain prescribed properties, for instance, the totality of integers x, y satisfying $f(x,y) = 0$, where f denotes a polynomial with integer coefficients; and numerous techniques have been employed through the centuries to resolve many problems in this field. The early work tended to be of an ad hoc character, the arguments involved being specifically related to the particular numerical example under consideration, but the trend in recent times has been toward the development of general coherent theories. Especially noteworthy in this connection were the works of A. Thue (1909) and C. L. Siegel (1929) which completely settled the question as to when the equation $f(x,y) = 0$ has only finitely many solutions. But the method of Thue and Siegel was not effective and did not lead to a determination of the totality of solutions. In fact, it did not even provide an algorithm for deciding when such an equation is soluble, which is a special case of another of Hilbert's famous list of problems, namely, his tenth.

In 1967 Baker applied his results on linear forms in logarithms to give the first effective theorems in this context. In particular, he obtained explicit upper bounds for all solutions of Thue's equation $F(x,y) = m$, where F denotes a binary irreducible form; of Mordell's equation $y^2 = x^3 + k$ (1968); and of the hyperelliptic equation $y^2 = f(x)$ (1969). And, in collaboration with J. Coates, he gave an algorithm for determining all the integer points on any algebraic curve of genus 1 (1970). Subsequently, Baker and others strengthened the basic theory of linear forms in logarithms; a striking new series of results on exponential diophantine equations was the direct outcome of this development. Quite remarkable, for instance, was the demonstration by R. Tijdeman (1976) that the Catalan equation $x^m - y^n = 1$ has only finitely many solutions in integers x, y, m, n, all of which can be effectively bounded. In general, the bounds furnished by the theory are large, typically of the order of 10 raised to the 10^{500} power or more; nevertheless, it was shown that they suffice in simple cases to enable one to compute the complete list of solutions.

Baker's theory has found many other applications. It has been used, for example, to solve some classical problems raised in the *Disquisitiones Arithmeticae* (1801) of K. F. Gauss; it has yielded the first effective improvement on Liouville's

inequality of 1844, concerning the approximation of algebraic numbers by rationals; and it has been instrumental in solving some outstanding problems in the p-adic theory of numbers. In fact, it has generated several very active areas of research, notably in the realm of elliptic and Abelian functions, and with regard to properties of arithmetical sequences, and that research continues to flourish.

Baker studied at University College, London, from 1958 to 1961, and then at Trinity College, Cambridge, where he was elected a fellow in 1964. In London and in Cambridge there were strong schools of number theory, the one in Cambridge led by H. Davenport, and they undoubtedly had a considerable influence on his choice of field of research. Baker taught for several years in Cambridge and was appointed to a personal professorship of pure mathematics in the university in 1974; he also lectured widely elsewhere, especially in the United States. He was elected a fellow of the Royal Society of London in 1973.

Baker wrote *Transcendental Number Theory* (1975), formerly an Adams Prize essay. He also edited, with D. W. Masser, *Transcendence Theory: Advances and Applications* (1977).

For background information *see* NUMBER THEORY in the McGraw-Hill Encyclopedia of Science and Technology. ∎

BAKER, JOHN FLEETWOOD (BARON BAKER OF WINDRUSH)

★ English structural engineer and educator

Born Mar. 19, 1901, Wallasey, Cheshire, England

Baker made two major contributions. First, he enunciated a fundamentally new branch of structural theory and developed from it a rational method of designing steel-framed structures which was adopted worldwide. As an offshoot of this work, he was responsible for the design of all the successful air raid shelters used in Britain and for the protection of industrial production during World War II. Second, as professor of civil engineering at Bristol University and then for 25 years as professor of mechanical sciences and head of the department of engineering at the University of Cambridge, he made considerable contributions to engineering education and research. J. G. Crowther, in *Fifty Years with Science* (1970), said: "Baker's

engineering department in Cambridge became the largest in the University and he tirelessly insisted that it should accordingly receive appropriate consideration. No one has done more to raise the intellectual status of engineering in England. Forty years ago his conception of the equality of engineering with mathematics and physics was rare."

Baker's intention on leaving Cambridge in 1923 was to enter industry as a chemical engineer, but there were no jobs. In desperation, after 6 months' unemployment, he accepted an Air Ministry post. This was a fateful move, as he was put to work on a structural problem and was later transferred to the Royal Airship Works to work on the design of the R101 airship. In 1928 Baker moved to the steel industry and began his major work. The constructional steel industry, threatened by the growing popularity of reinforced concrete, set up the Steel Structures Research Committee in the hope that it would produce a more economical design method for steel structures than the rule-of-thumb method in common use. Baker was technical officer to this committee and built up a team which carried out the first successful tests of steel-framed buildings. From the data collected, a rational design method was produced by 1936 and was described in the three reports of the committee and in the first volume (1954) of Baker's book *The Steel Skeleton*. The method, based on elastic theory, was a failure since it was unacceptable to designers in industry because of its supposed complexity.

Baker could not believe that the steel structure, dependent as it was on an irrational design method, had reached its zenith in 1936. By now professor of civil engineering at Bristol University, he began a new investigation of the behavior of steel structures when loaded beyond the working, or elastic, range until they collapsed as mechanisms by the formation of plastic hinges. This was interrupted by the war in 1939, when Baker became a scientific adviser to the Air Raid Precautions Department of the Ministry of Home Security. However, he soon realized that his 3-year study of collapse had provided the key to make the aircraft factories, then being erected, almost invulnerable to structural failure due to bomb attack. He set up a design and development section for this work, but the first assignment of the group was to redesign the air raid shelters for the protection of the civilian population, using the principles of continuity and ductility which he enunciated, since enemy bombing had shown that the prewar designs were unsatisfactory. An entirely new form of shelter (the Morrison) was designed by Baker for use inside a dwelling house—more than 1,250,000 shelters were issued to householders. He had great difficulty in persuading the ministry bureaucrats to accept his shelter designs and his team's later efforts when it turned to its real work of protecting industrial production. These experiences were described in his book *Enterprise versus Bureaucracy* (1978).

In 1943 Baker moved to Cambridge to become professor of mechanical sciences and head of the department of engineering. Engineering had been taught at Cambridge since 1783, and for 40 years or more the department had been the largest in the university, responsible for the teaching of 10 percent of all undergraduates. However, between the two world wars teaching had been accomplished at the expense of research. Baker was determined that the Cambridge department should continue to be a great teaching school, but he considered that this would be possible only if it were also an outstanding research institution. With the war over, he collected funds, persuaded the university to establish many new professorships and other posts, to which he had no difficulty appointing distinguished colleagues, and to allow him to build spacious well-equipped laboratories. The department grew and throve in every way: one measure of its success was that between 1948 and 1965 no less than 21 members of its staff left Cambridge to become professors and take charge of engineering departments in other universities.

In addition to the fascinating work of building up the department, Baker participated in other university administration, and in work outside the university; for example, he served on the University Grants Committee (1953–63), the Council of the Institution of Civil Engineers, (1947–56, 1958–63, 1964–66, vice-president 1968–70), and as a consultant to the British Admiralty (1948–63). He also built up a research team to continue the work begun in Bristol.

By 1956 the team had revolutionized the design of steel structures, developing a fundamentally new branch of structural theory based on the mechanisms of collapse of rigidly jointed frames. A design method—the plastic method—was then deduced which proved to be simple to apply and led to savings of steel of the order of 25 percent. The team had to convince industry of the validity of their work by designing, for trusting clients a dozen or more important buildings. This done, the use of the method spread throughout the world until almost all steel buildings, certainly all single-story structures, characterized by the ubiquitous rigidly jointed pitch-roofed portal frame were designed plastically. This work was described in the second volume (1956) of *The Steel Skeleton*.

Baker attended school at Rossall and took an engineering degree at Cambridge in 1923. He was appointed professor of civil engineering at Bristol University in 1933, staying there until his move to Cambridge in 1943. He retired from Cambridge in 1968. He received many honors: For his war work, in 1941 he was appointed an officer of the Order of the British Empire, in 1961 he became a knight bachelor, and in the New Year's Honours List of 1977 he was created life peer. He was elected a fellow of Clare College, Cambridge (1943), of the Royal Society (1956), and of the Fellowship of Engineering (1976). He was awarded the Telford Gold Medal (1932), the Howard Quinquennial Medal (1937), and the Ewing Medal (1952) of the Institution of Civil Engineers; the Institution Gold Medal of the Institution of Structural Engineers (1953); The Royal Medal of the Royal Society (1970); and the Brooker Medal of the Welding Institute (1977).

Baker's other books were *Differential Equations of Engineering Science* (1929),

Analysis of Engineering Structures (1936; 4th ed. 1968), and *Plastic Design of Frames* (vol. 1, 1969).

For background information *see* BUILD-INGS; STRUCTURAL ANALYSIS in the McGraw-Hill Encyclopedia of Science and Technology. ■

BAKER, WILLIAM OLIVER
★ American chemist

Born *July 15, 1915, Chestertown, MD, U.S.A.*

In studies with C. P. Smyth at Princeton stimulated by the theories of molecular dipoles of P. J. W. Debye, Baker began a new phase in solid-state science. He showed that the rotation of molecules in crystals reduced the entropy of fusion to a ratio of about 2 and drastically raised the melting point and reduced the liquid range of a variety of compounds. This explained, among other things, the belief in organic chemistry that highly symmetrical molecules, such as tertiary butyl compounds, camphor, and many others, would have high melting points and would sublime readily. This work was extended to solid solution formation by symmetrical structures, in which case both thermal and dielectric studies of polar components, such as mixtures of tertiary butyl chloride in carbon tetrachloride, yielded new insight into eutectics and other multiphase crystallizations. It was also applied to the aliphatic chain systems, such as cetyl alcohol and stearic and palmitic esters, whose unsuspected mobility in the solid state (around the long-chain axis) explained curious plastic properties as well as thermodynamic properties of these components of natural waxes and other biological substances. *See* DEBYE, PETER JOSEPH WILLIAM; SMYTH, CHARLES PHELPS.

In 1939 Baker joined the research program at Bell Telephone Laboratories devoted to a basic understanding of the chemistry and physics of high polymers, which then promised to provide major mechanical and insulating materials for use in the fields of electronics and telecommunications. Working to this end, he studied a variety of simple polyamides and polyesters based on the syntheses of W. H. Carothers. By x-ray, dielectric, dynamical, and chemical studies, he discovered the thermal conditioning of microcrystalline plastics through which all present processes for assuring fiber, film, and bulk rigidity and tenacity are derived. Principles were developed for determining the structural quality in the solid state not only of the linear condensation polymers, but also of natural systems such as regenerated cellulose. The x-ray linewidth techniques that Baker found to express lateral ordering of parallel chains were widely applied in manufacturing control of such commercial processes as rayon tire cords and nylon extrusions.

During World War II Baker's principal tasks were the preparation of strong and stable polymer dielectric radiators for the earliest shipborne radar and the application of new principles of polymer science to the national synthetic rubber program. The latter work resulted in a rapid optical method for the control of the composition of synthetic rubber and discovery of a new kind of molecule still widely used in controlling the critical processing and viscoelasticity of rubbery systems. Instead of having the typical chainlike molecules of most synthetic polymers, these new molecules were globular or loose molecular networks. Discovery of these molecules, called microgels, the largest discrete synthetic molecules known, stimulated development of modern light-scattering techniques for molecular weight determination as based on the work of Albert Einstein and Debye.

In the postwar period Baker broadened his particular interest in the structure of molecular solids into what was to become known as materials science. With his coworkers he found that the new microcrystalline polymers, such as polyethylene, could be made with such control of average chain length, structure, and crystallinity that rather massive structural functions could be achieved, for example, the replacement for lead in heavy communications and power cables. This caused a great advance in the economy of cable production and usage. The scientific base studies revealed that, under multiaxial stressing, microcrystalline polymers—now extensively used in all sorts of containers, films, tubings, plumbing, and so forth—were subject to destructive cracking, especially in the presence of certain common liquids, unless the molecular weight was adjusted specifically to minimize this mechanical effect. Such chemical controls are now used worldwide to assure the quality of modern polymers.

In another phase of his contribution to the development of materials science, Baker collaborated with W. P. Mason and J. H. Heiss in the application of high-frequency piezoelectric transducers to the study of the viscoelastic properties of macromolecular solids, liquids, and solutions. By simultaneous use of compressional and shear waves over a wide range of frequencies extending into hundreds of megahertz, the general pattern of elasticity and flow of many model structures was revealed. The first work on shear relaxations in dilute solutions of polymers indicated the processes of chain configuration and chain entanglement as causes of the vital technical qualities of flexibility and resilience in fibers and plastics. *See* MASON, WARREN PERRY.

Baker's work on electrical properties of molecular solids continued over several decades. He discovered the large temperature-induced direct-current conductivity of polyamides, which also was analyzed in association with the remarkable dielectric properties of these analogs of natural polypeptides. The unsuspected electronic, as well as quasi-ionic, conductivity in hydrogen-bonded organic systems was subsequently extended, in collaboration with F. H. Winslow, in a wide range of densely cross-linked polymers composed of carbon, hydrogen, and oxygen. Using the techniques of solid-state electronics, including electron paramagnetic resonance and the Hall effect, Baker found that by chemical variation of the proportions of carbon and hydrogen in highly conjugated, densely cross-linked polymers (polydivinyl benzene and so on), it was possible to create a continuous transition between paramagnetic but insulating solids and highly semiconducting systems of rather low charge mobility but high carrier concentration. This led eventually to a highly refractory form of pyrolytic-type graphite, forming a system called polymer carbons. Studies of the chemistry of these transformations and of these highly cross-bonded structures led to an interesting by-product—the realization that a particular shape of polymer network would be maintained macroscopically even during the intense energy absorption of hydrogen and oxygen dissociation during very high temperature exposure. Hence, in 1954–55, when Baker chaired the National Research Council Subgroup on Synthetic Materials for Missile Nosecones and Satellite Heat Shields, the use of an organic ablating structure was proposed. Such composite, netted polymers were subsequently developed in a number of Federal contract laboratories, and were the basis for most reentry protection systems of intercontinental missiles and Earth satellites, including all of the known crewed satellite recoveries. An earlier application of Baker's interest in cross-linking of polymers was the invention of the first polyester casting and laminating resins which contain little or no residual unsaturation. These were "cured" by the peroxide-catalyzed or other radical-catalyzed catalysis associated with the abstraction of hydrogens from the main polymer chain, especially from methylene groups on the alpha carbons relative to the ester linkages.

Beginning in 1955, Baker was responsible for the research programs of Bell Telephone Laboratories. During this period his associates created Earth satellite communications, the microwave maser, the optical laser, and the superconducting solenoid, among other physical facilities for modern science and electronic communications. In his department extensive discoveries were made of principles for organizing and programming high-speed digital computers, which were based on the solid-state diodes and transistors earlier produced in the physical sciences research of Bell Laboratories. Hence, Baker's interests turned to the broader fields of telecommunications and information processing, which benefit from the various facilities derived from materials science and the chemistry and physics of solids. In 1973 Baker became president of Bell Laboratories.

Baker also worked for the Federal science offices, serving as an original member of the President's Science Advisory Committee and as chairperson of the initial panels on scientific and technical information and on materials research and development. First to chair the National Science Information Council, he also was a member of the National Science Board from 1960 to 1966. From 1959 to 1977, under five administrations, he served as a member of the President's Foreign Intelligence Advisory Board. In 1976 he became consultant to the National Security Agency, having served as a member of its Scientific Advisory Board from 1960.

Baker received his B.S. (1935) from Washington College and his Ph.D. (1938) from Princeton University, as well as numerous honorary degrees. In 1963 he received the Perkin Medal, an international award for applied chemistry. He received the Priestley Medal (1966), the Parsons Award (1976), and the Gibbs Medal (1978), all from the American Chemical Society. He also received the American Institute of Chemists (AIC) Honor Scroll in 1962, the AIC Gold Medal in 1975, the Edgar Marburg Award in 1967, the American Society for Testing and Materials Award to Executives in 1967, the Industrial Research Institute Medal in 1970, the Frederik Philips Award in 1972, the *Industrial Research* Man-of-the-Year Award in 1973, the Sigma Xi Procter Prize in 1973, Princeton University's James Madison Medal in 1975, the Mellon Institute Award in 1975, the Society of Research Administrators Award for Distinguished Contributions to Research Administration in 1976, the Fahrney Medal of the Franklin Institute in 1977, and the Von Hippel Award of the Materials Research Society in 1978. Baker was elected to the Directors of Industrial Research in 1956, the National Academy of Sciences in 1961, the American Philosophical Society in 1963, the American Academy of Arts and Sciences in 1965, the Institute of Medicine in 1972, and the National Academy of Engineering in 1975. He became an honorary member of the Chemists' Club (New York) in 1974, and a fellow of the Franklin Institute in 1977.

Author of more than 80 scientific and technical papers, Baker served on the editorial advisory boards of the *Journal of Polymer Science, Chemical and Engineering News,* and *Carbon.* He contributed to 21 books and obtained 13 patents.

For background information *see* POLYESTER RESINS; POLYMERIZATION in the McGraw-Hill Encyclopedia of Science and Technology. ∎

BALL, ERIC GLENDINNING
★ American biochemist

Born July 12, 1904, Coventry, England

Lacking funds to undertake graduate training in physical chemistry, Ball accepted a position in 1926 as a research assistant in the department of physiological chemistry at the University of Pennsylvania. Fascinated by the opportunities afforded by this rapidly growing area of investigation and encouraged by D. Wright Wilson, head of the department, he entered graduate school there and embarked upon a career in biochemistry. After he completed his Ph.D. work, his earlier interest in physical chemistry led him to seek postdoctoral work with W. Mansfield Clark at the Johns Hopkins Medical School. There, first as a National Research Council fellow and then, as a staff member, he carried out investigations on the oxidation-reduction potentials of a number of biological systems. This led to an interest in the mechanisms of biological oxidations and the enzymes related to these processes. *See* CLARK, WILLIAM MANSFIELD.

In 1937–38 Ball spent a year as a Guggenheim fellow in the laboratories of Otto Warburg at the Kaiser Wilhelm Institut für Zellphysiologie in Berlin-Dahlem. There he purified xanthine oxidase and showed that it contained flavin adenine dinucleotide. He also estimated the oxidation-reduction potentials of the cytochromes and deduced that the order of reaction within the cell of these components must be *a, c, b.* His work on xanthine oxidase won for him the Eli Lilly Award in biochemistry in 1940. In the fall of that year he became a member of the department of biological chemistry at the Harvard Medical School. During the war years he carried on investigations first on the mustard gases and then on the malarial parasite. The team of researchers under his supervision achieved the first cultivation of the malarial parasite in culture. At war's end he returned to studies in the field of biological oxidations and intermediary metabolism. Working with his students, he conducted investigations leading to the recognition of cytochrome c' and b_5, the high content of phospholipids in the electron transmitter system, and other discoveries.

In 1958 Ball's attention was directed to adipose tissue, brown and white. White adipose tissue had long been regarded as relatively inert metabolically and was looked upon mainly as a storehouse for fat. Work in a number of laboratories indicated that this was a misconception, at least for certain species, and that various metabolic processes in this tissue could be made to proceed apace when stimulated by the addition of certain hormones. For example, the addition of minute amounts of insulin to adipose tissue in test-tube experiments resulted in a marked acceleration of glucose uptake with its conversion primarily to fat. Consideration of the known events that occur in this lipogenic event led Ball and his students to devise a simple manometric procedure to measure the carbon dioxide evolved and in turn to study the action of insulin. The procedure was also useful for the assay of minute quantities of insulin and of substances that mimic or inhibit the action of insulin. He and his students also elucidated the quantitative details of the enzymatic processes by which glucose is converted to fat in adipose tissue. This led to the recognition of a new pathway for the production of reduced triphosphopyridine nucleotide, a coenzyme essential for fat synthesis.

During these studies on adipose tissue a new role for insulin as an antilipolytic agent was found. This new function of insulin has been ascribed to its ability to suppress the formation of cyclic 3′,5′-adenosinemonophosphate. This compound, first described by E. W. Sutherland and his coworkers as important in the control of cellular glycogen mobilization, has now been recognized as a key substance in the control of a number of other metabolic processes. Various investigators showed

that the rate of cyclic adenosinemonophosphate formation is increased by a number of hormones. Insulin now appears to be able to exert a counterbalancing effect upon this action of these hormones, besides regulating glucose uptake by certain tissues. *See* SUTHERLAND, EARL WILBUR, JR.

Brown adipose tissue is a special type found most abundantly in hibernators and in newborn fur-bearing animals. Its color is largely due to its high content of cytochromes, and it is capable of unusually high rates of oxygen consumption. Work in Ball's laboratory and in other laboratories suggested that this tissue serves as a furnace to supply heat to the animal during arousal from hibernation or at times of excessive heat loss, for example, during cold exposure or before fur has developed.

Long interested in marine biology and the comparative biochemistry of marine forms, Ball spent his summers at the Marine Biological Laboratory at Woods Hole, MA, and served as a member of the corporation of this institute and of the Bermuda Biological Station. He became a member of the national advisory board for the operation of the *Alpha-Helix,* the oceangoing vessel for biological studies operated by the Scripps Institution of Oceanography at La Jolla.

Upon retiring from Harvard, Ball took up year-round residence in his enlarged summer home in Woods Hole. This permitted the establishment of a laboratory at the Marine Biology Laboratory, where he resumed his investigations into the comparative biochemistry of marine organisms on a full-time basis. Freed from academic administrative duties, he once again experienced the joy of performing experiments with his own hands and had the time to write a small book entitled *Energy Metabolism* (1973).

Son of an Episcopal minister, Ball was born in England, but received nearly all of his education in the United States. He received a B.S. in 1925, M.A. in 1926, and D.Sc. (honorary) in 1949 from Haverford College in Pennsylvania, a Ph.D. in 1930 from the University of Pennsylvania, and an M.A. (honorary) in 1942 from Harvard University. After a year as National Research Council fellow at John Hopkins Medical School, he became a staff member there in 1930. He moved to Harvard in 1940, where be became associate professor in 1942 and full professor in 1946. In 1952 he was appointed chairperson of the Divi-

sion of Medical Sciences, a part of the Faculty of Arts and Sciences established in 1908 to train Ph.D. candidates in the medical school. In 1971 he retired from Harvard with the title of Edward S. Wood Professor of Biological Chemistry Emeritus. Ball was awarded the Cruzeiro du Sol by the Brazilian government in 1945 and the Certificate of Merit by the United States government in 1948. He was elected a member of the American Academy of Arts and Sciences in 1945 and of the National Academy of Sciences in 1948.

For background information *see* ADENYLIC ACID, CYCLIC; ADIPOSE TISSUE; BIOLOGICAL OXIDATION; ENERGY METABOLISM; INSULIN in the McGraw-Hill Encyclopedia of Science and Technology. ∎

BALTIMORE, DAVID
☆ American virologist

Born Mar. 7, 1938, New York City, NY, U.S.A.

For his studies establishing the mechanism by which ribonucleic acid (RNA) tumor viruses reproduce in animal cells and the relationship of the virus in the cell to cancer, Baltimore shared the Nobel Prize in medicine or physiology in 1975 with Renato Dulbecco and Howard Temin. Temin had independently made the same discovery concerning the mechanism of the RNA tumor virus. *See* DULBECCO, RENATO; TEMIN, HOWARD M..

As a graduate student in Richard Franklin's laboratory at the Rockefeller University, Baltimore began to work with picornaviruses, a nontumor group of RNA virus that includes mengovirus and poliovirus, to find out how the RNA virus could multiply in the cell without the intervention of deoxyribonucleic acid (DNA). In the early 1950s F. H. C. Crick and J. Watson established the structure of DNA and the mechanism by which it operates as the cell's genetic factory. In this scheme there appeared to be no explanation for the invasive RNA virus's ability to duplicate itself or to so affect the cell's genetic apparatus that transformation into a tumor cell occurred. Baltimore continued the work with poliovirus as a postdoctoral fellow in Dulbecco's laboratory at the Salk Institute and later in his own laboratory at the Massachusetts Institute of Technology (MIT). From their studies on poliovirus and those conducted at other laboratories on other RNA viruses, he and his associates found that there are many genetic systems operating in viruses. *See* CRICK, FRANCIS HARRY COMPTON; WATSON, JAMES DEWEY.

Baltimore and his group worked with another RNA virus, vesicular stomatitis virus (VSV). They found that VSV-infected cells had as many as nine RNAs compared with the four types found in poliovirus-infected cells. They showed that the VSV messenger RNAs were complementary to the base sequence of the RNA in the VSV infecting particle. Since there was no evidence that the infected cell had an enzyme to transcribe the virion RNA, Baltimore reasoned that the enzyme, RNA polymerase, had to come into the cell with the infecting virus particle. Further work with VSV and later with Newcastle virus demonstrated existence of the enzyme.

Baltimore then decided to concentrate on retroviruses—the group name for RNA tumor viruses—and to look for either an RNA or DNA polymerase in the infected cells. If a DNA polymerase could be found, the question of how such RNA viruses multiply in cells could be answered. He and his group were able to demonstrate a ribonuclease-sensitive DNA polymerase activity first in Rauscher virus and then in Rous sarcoma virus. DNA polymerase in the RNA virus was called a reverse transcriptase because it showed that the flow of genetic information did not have to go from DNA to RNA but could flow from RNA to DNA. Baltimore continued the study of reverse transcriptase, ultimately showing that it can make an infective copy of viral RNA. He also developed methods for studying in cell culture how leukemia viruses can cause leukemic cells to develop. Because the leukemic cells he was studying are related to antibody-forming cells, his interests subsequently turned to the study of development of cells of the immune system.

Baltimore received a bachelor's degree from Swarthmore College in 1960 and a Ph.D. from MIT in 1964. He then worked at the Salk Institute until 1968, when he returned to MIT. He became an associate professor there in 1968 and a professor in 1972. Baltimore married a colleague and collaborator, Alice Huang. In addition to the Nobel Prize, Baltimore received many honors, including the Eli Lilly Award in 1971 and a lifetime research professorship from the American Cancer Society in 1973.

For background information *see* ANIMAL VIRUS; LYSOGENY; TRANSCRIPTASE, REVERSE in the McGraw-Hill Encyclopedia of Science and Technology. ∎

BARDEEN, JOHN
★ American physicist

Born May 23, 1908, Madison, WI, U.S.A.

For their work leading to the invention of the transistor, Bardeen, William Shockley, and W. H. Brattain were awarded the Nobel Prize in physics in 1956. For the development of the theory of superconductivity, often called the BCS theory (from the initials of the developers), Bardeen, L. N. Cooper, and J. R. Schrieffer shared the 1972 Nobel Prize in physics. Bardeen was the first to win two Nobel prizes in the same field. *See* BRATTAIN, WALTER HOUSER; COOPER, LEON N.; SCHRIEFFER, JOHN ROBERT; SHOCKLEY, WILLIAM.

For many years after its discovery by H. Kamerlingh Onnes in 1911, superconductivity was one of the outstanding puzzles of physics. It was not until 1957 that an adequate explanation was given by Bardeen and his associates. The theory that they proposed, together with its subsequent developments, not only accounted successfully for the major aspects of superconductivity but was used to predict new phenomena and thus gave a great stimulus to the field.

Prior to the development of the Bardeen-Cooper-Schrieffer theory, much had been learned about the properties of superconductors, and the general lines along which an explanation might be found on the basis of quantum theory was fairly well established. At very low temperatures, a few degrees above absolute zero, many metals and alloys become superconducting, losing all trace of resistance to flow of electricity. In 1933 W. Meissner discovered another property that is perhaps even more basic: a magnetic field is excluded from the interior of a superconducting body. The state with the magnetic flux excluded is the unique and stable state in the presence of a magnetic field; the currents that flow near the surface to shield the interior from the magnetic field have no tendency to decay. Shortly thereafter, Fritz and Heinz London proposed a phenomenological theory to account for both vanishing resistance and the Meissner effect. Fritz London suggested that an explanation might follow from quantum theory, normally applied only on the atomic scale. He suggested that a superconductor behaves like a single large quantum system and that "the long-range order of the average momentum is to be considered one of the fundamental properties of the superconducting state." He predicted that the magnetic flux threading a superconducting ring or cylinder is quantized to integral multiples of a basic unit, and this was subsequently observed. *See* LONDON, HEINZ.

Bardeen first became interested in superconductivity in the mid-1930s, and was strongly influenced by London's ideas. A little later he made an unsuccessful attempt to develop a theory. This work was interrupted in 1941, when he went into military work. After the war he took a position at the Bell Telephone Laboratories and became interested in semiconductors. Work done there led to the invention of the transistor. It was not until 1950 that he resumed work on superconductivity, following the experimental discovery of the isotope effect by a group at Rutgers University and by E. Maxwell. They found that the critical temperature below which the metal becomes superconducting depends on isotopic mass.

If mass is important, the motion of the atoms or ions that make up the metal must be involved, and this suggested that superconductivity depended somehow on the interaction between the electrons and the vibrational motion of atoms. Independently of knowledge of the isotope effect, H. Fröhlich also attempted to develop a theory of superconductivity on this basis. These early attempts (about 1950–51) ran into difficulties that were not overcome until 1957.

Bardeen and his associates found that the key to understanding superconductivity is a pairing interaction between the electrons resulting from an effective attraction induced by the interaction between electrons and atomic vibrations. The superconducting ground state is made up of configurations in which the states of the individual electrons are occupied in pairs of opposite spin and momentum, such that if in any configuration one of the states is occupied, the other is also. If there is current flow, the total momentum of each pair is different from zero but is exactly the same for all pairs. It is this that gives the long-range order of the momentum distribution suggested by Fritz London. Random scattering of individual electrons does not change the common momentum of the pairs, so that a current once started will persist indefinitely unless subjected to a force, such as an electric field, which acts on all or a large fraction of the pairs at the same time.

The theory was developed to account quantitatively for many properties of superconductors in terms of a few measurable parameters. Experiments carried out by a number of people demonstrated the quantum aspects of superconductors in striking ways, in most cases following theoretical predictions. Perhaps the most striking predictions are those of B. D. Josephson. Known as the Josephson effects, they led to the development of very sensitive detecting devices for currents, voltages, and magnetic fields, and also to computer components which promise to be much faster and use far less power than those based on semiconductors.

A similar pairing interaction occurs between the particles (neutrons and protons) in nuclei. Mathematical methods developed to explain superconductivity in metals were applied successfully to account for various features of nuclear structure. The methods were also used in the theory of elementary particles.

Bardeen received B.S. and M.S. degrees in electrical engineering from the University of Wisconsin in 1928 and 1929, respectively, and a Ph.D. in mathematical physics from Princeton University in 1936. Prior to his graduate studies at Princeton, he worked for several years with the Gulf Research and Development Corporation as a geophysicist. Subsequently, he was a postdoctoral fellow at Harvard University, assistant professor of physics at the University of Minnesota, a physicist at the U.S. Naval Ordnance Laboratory during World War II, and research physicist at the Bell Telephone Laboratories. In 1951 he became professor of physics and electrical engineering at the University of Illinois and, in 1975, emeritus professor. Bardeen's main research interests were in the theory of solid-state and low-temperature physics, with emphasis on semiconductors and superconductivity. He was elected to the National Academy of Sciences in 1954, and received many other honors.

For background information *see* SEMICONDUCTOR; SUPERCONDUCTIVITY; TRANSISTOR in the McGraw-Hill Encyclopedia of Science and Technology. ∎

BARKER, HORACE ALBERT
★ American biochemist

Born Nov. 29, 1907, Oakland, CA, U.S.A.

Most of Barker's research was on the degradation of organic compounds by anaerobic bacteria and the chemistry of these fermentations. His interest in bacterial metabolism was first stimulated by C. B. van Niel and A. J. Kluyver. At that time knowledge of the pathway of carbohydrate degradation by the glycolytic path and tricarboxylic acid (TCA) cycle was developing rapidly, but little was known about the chemistry of most bacterial fermentations. Barker's first significant contribution to this area resulted from studies of the bacterial formation of methane. He developed methods for the isolation of methane-producing bacteria and obtained purified cultures of several species. One of the cultures was shown to couple the oxidation of ethanol to acetic acid with the reduction of carbon dioxide to methane, thus apparently confirming the hypothesis of van Niel that all biological methane is formed by carbon dioxide reduction. T. C. Stadtman and Barker later showed that methane is also formed from carbon dioxide in the fermentations of propionate and butyrate, whereas in fermentations of acetate and methanol, methane is derived entirely from the methyl group of these substrates. Their observations led to the proposal of a more general theory of the chemistry of methane formation. *See* KLUYVER, ALBERT JAN; VAN NIEL, CORNELIS BERNARDUS.

During studies of the methane fermentation of ethanol by enrichment cultures, a massive anaerobic conversion of ethanol to butyric acid and caproic acid was observed. *Clostridium kluyveri,* the bacterium responsible for the synthesis of these volatile fatty acids, was isolated and was shown by Barker, M. D. Kamen, and B. T. Bornstein to convert ethanol and acetate to C_4 and C_6 fatty acids by the successive condensation of C_2 units. Subsequent studies by E. R. Stadtman and

Barker demonstrated that these reactions can occur in cell-free enzyme preparations. Acetylphosphate, a product of ethanol oxidation, was shown to be reversibly reduced to butyrate. Since none of the previously considered C_4 intermediates in butyrate synthesis was active in this system, it was postulated, and later demonstrated, that the true intermediates are linked to F. Lipmann's coenzyme A. A very active phosphotransacetylase was discovered in *C. kluyveri* extracts. This enzyme, which catalyzes a reversible transfer of acetyl groups between phosphate and coenzyme A, was later used by E. R. Stadtman to demonstrate enzymatic synthesis of acetyl coenzyme A. *See* KAMEN, MARTIN D.; LIPMANN, FRITZ ALBERT.

Clostridium kluyveri was also used to investigate the synthesis of amino acids from C_2 compounds and carbon dioxide. About 25% of the carbon in the cell materials is derived from carbon dioxide, and the remainder from C_2 substrates. By the use of ^{14}C-labeled acetate or carbon dioxide, Neil Tomlinson and Barker showed that C_3 amino acids (alanine, serine) are formed by a C_2-C_1 condensation, and the C_4 amino acid (aspartic) by a C_3-C_1 condensation, with the carboxyl groups being derived from carbon dioxide. The origin of the carbon atoms of glutamate was inconsistent with its formation via the usual TCA cycle reactions. Later enzymatic studies by G. Gottschalk and Barker proved that glutamate is synthesized from oxalacetate and acetyl coenzyme A via the TCA cycle reaction, but the enzyme that forms citrate is unusual in the stereospecificity of the reaction it catalyzes.

Barker and his associates carried out a series of investigations of the anaerobic decomposition of amino acids, purines, and related compounds by soil bacteria isolated after enrichment in media containing single nitrogenous substrates. Several species so obtained were highly specialized with respect to the compounds fermented. Thus, one species fermented glycine preferentially, another used alanine, serine, or threonine, a third decomposed uric acid and other purines, and a fourth attacked glutamate with special facility. The sequence of chemical reactions and the specialized enzymatic systems in some of these bacteria were studied. The path of glutamate fermentation by *C. tetanomorphum* was shown to involve the formation of several branched chain compounds. The key reaction is the reversible conversion of glutamate to 3-methylaspartate by glutamate mutase. This reaction was found to require a new, light-sensitive cofactor that was isolated and identified as a coenzyme form of pseudovitamin B_{12}.

H. Weissbach, J. I. Toohey, and Barker subsequently isolated the analogous vitamin B_{12} coenzyme from *C. tetanomorphum* and other anaerobic bacteria. Toohey and Barker showed that the coenzyme is present in the livers of humans and animals. Weissbach and others established that the corrinoid coenzymes contain an adenine nucleoside moiety not present in vitamin B_{12}; this was later shown by P. G. Lenhert and D. C. Hodgkin to be a 5'-deoxyadenosyl group attached to the cobalt atom of the vitamin by a novel cobalt-carbon bond. These developments stimulated interest in the biochemical role of corrinoid compounds. R. L. Blakley and Barker found that the vitamin B_{12} coenzyme was required for the enzymatic conversion of ribonucleotides to deoxyribonucleotides by the ribonucleotide reductase of *Lactobacillus leichmannii*. *See* HODGKIN, DOROTHY CROWFOOT.

While investigating the metabolism of anaerobic bacteria, Barker and his associates found that acetic acid synthesis from carbon dioxide is a rather common process. This was first observed by use of $^{14}CO_2$ in *C. thermoaceticum,* which couples the oxidation of glucose to acetate and carbon dioxide with the reduction of carbon dioxide to acetate. A similar process was later observed in fermentations of purines and of glycine.

Barker and his associates investigated the pathway of lysine degradation by clostridia. They demonstrated that this pathway involves three novel enzymatic reactions: the reversible transfer of amino groups between carbon atoms 2 and 3 and between carbon atoms 5 and 6 of the six-carbon chain of lysine, and at a later stage, the reversible conversion of 3-keto-5-aminohexanoate and acetyl coenzyme A to 3-aminobutyryl·CoA and acetoacetate. A similar β-keto acid cleavage reaction was also shown to occur during the degradation of β-lysine by an aerobic bacterium.

In collaboration with M. Doudoroff, W. Z. Hassid, and N. O. Kaplan, Barker participated in the first demonstration of enzymic sucrose synthesis from fructose and glucose-1-phosphate by sucrose phosphorylase from *Pseudomonas saccharophila*. The enzyme was shown to function as a glucosyl-transferring agent using phosphate, fructose, and certain other sugars as glucosyl acceptors. This study substantially broadened the concept of enzymatic group transfer.

The son of a public school administrator, Barker studied at Stanford University and the University of Chicago, receiving both his A.B. (1929) and his Ph.D. in chemistry (1933) at Stanford. He spent 2 years as a postdoctoral fellow at the Hopkins Marine Station with T. Skogsberg and C. B. van Niel, and a year at the Technical University in Delft, Netherlands, with A. J. Kluyver. He later studied with F. Lipmann at Massachusetts General Hospital and with A. Kornberg at the National Institutes of Health.

Barker joined the staff of the department of plant nutrition, University of California, as a soil microbiologist in 1936, transferred to the department of plant biochemistry in 1950, and to the biochemistry department in 1959; he became emeritus in 1975. He was honored with the Sugar Research Award with M. Doudoroff and W. Z. Hassid (1945), the Neuberg Medal (1959), the Borden Award in Nutrition (1962), the California Museum of Science and Industry Award (1966), the Gowland Hopkins Medal (1967), and the National Medal of Science (1968). He was elected to the National Academy of Sciences in 1953.

Barker wrote some 225 papers and the book *Bacterial Fermentations* (1957).

For background information *see* BACTERIAL COENZYME; BACTERIAL ENZYME; BACTERIAL METABOLISM; FERMENTATION; METHANOGENESIS, BACTERIAL; VITAMIN B_{12} in the McGraw-Hill Encyclopedia of Science and Technology. ∎

BARR, MURRAY LLEWELLYN
★ Canadian anatomist

Born June 20, 1908, near Belmont, Ontario, Canada

While studying the effects of prolonged activity on the structure of nerve cells, Barr and a graduate student, Ewart G. Bertram, noticed in 1949 that nuclei of nerve cells of female cats contained a mass of chromatin that was lacking in male cats. Subsequent studies by Barr and his colleagues showed that this sex difference was generally present in tissues of most representatives of the mammalian class, including humans. The chromatin mass in question came to be called the sex chromatin or Barr body, and it formed the basis of tests that were developed for the study of patients with developmental defects of the reproductive system. Sections prepared from small skin biopsy specimens were used in the first instance. This technique was subsequently replaced by the simple buccal smear test, which consisted of the inspection of cells obtained by rubbing the lining of the mouth for the presence or absence of sex chromatin.

This work by Barr and his colleagues coincided with technical advances which permitted the study of the chromosome complement in mammalian cells. J. H. Tjio and A. Levan (1954) were able to show that the correct chromosome number for humans was 46, rather than 48, as had been believed for many years. S. Ohno (1959) and others demonstrated the source of the sex chromatin by showing that one X chromosome of the female (XX) was strongly condensed or heteropycnotic, constituting the sex chromatin, whereas the second X chromosome of the female and the X chromosome of the male (XY) were attenuated or euchromatic and invisible in resting nuclei. Even before chromosome analysis (karyotyping) became an established procedure, use of the sex chromatin test indicated that certain abnormalities of sex development were due to errors of the sex chromosome complex. For example, Lawson Wilkins and colleagues (1954) found that sex chromatin was lacking in females with Turner's syndrome, and E. R. Plunkett and Barr (1956) found that sex chromatin

was present in males with Klinefelter's syndrome.

For a number of years, the buccal smear test and karyotyping were companion techniques, the sex chromatin test being used in surveys of large populations or for individual patients to select those for whom a chromosome analysis should be carried out. As the work progressed in Barr's laboratory and elsewhere, patients with enlarged sex chromosome complexes were discovered. Regardless of the number of X chromosomes, only one was attenuated and genetically active, whereas all other X chromosomes present were condensed and genetically inactive, each appearing as a mass of sex chromatin. The usefulness of the sex chromatin test therefore lay in the basic rule that the number of sex chromatin masses was one less than the number of X chromosomes. The combined use of the two techniques revealed the following sex chromosome abnormalities, among others. In females, the XO (X nothing) error is the cause of Turner's syndrome, characterized by shortness of stature and sterility. Other females have an excess of X chromosomes (three or four); they seldom have significant physical defects, although there is an increased incidence of mental retardation. Various intersexual sex chromosome complexes are responsible for Klinefelter's syndrome in males, characterized by sterility and an increased risk of mental retardation. The complex is usually XXY, but it may be XXYY, XXXY, or XXXXY. Chromosome analysis also revealed structural abnormalities of the X or Y chromosome, which may result in errors of development. Although the sex chromatin test played an important role in the development of human cytogenetics, it was used less frequently as proficiency in karyotyping improved.

A farmer's son of Northern Irish extraction, Barr received the B.A. (1930), M.D. (1933), and M.Sc. (1938) from the University of Western Ontario. Aside from a 6-year interruption during World War II, when he served as a medical officer (wing commander) with the Royal Canadian Air Force, Barr spent his entire career at the University of Western Ontario, where he became head of the department of anatomy. Numerous awards in recognition of his research included the Flavelle Medal of the Royal Society of Canada (1959), an award by the Joseph P. Kennedy, Jr., Foundation (1962), and the Gairdner Award of Merit (1963). Barr

became a fellow of the Royal Society of London in 1972.

For background information *see* CHRO-MOSOME; HUMAN GENETICS; MENTAL DEFICIENCY in the McGraw-Hill Encyclopedia of Science and Technology. ∎

BARSCHALL, HENRY HERMAN
★ American nuclear physicist

Born Apr. 29, 1915, Berlin, Germany

Following the discovery of the neutron by James Chadwick in 1932, Enrico Fermi and his coworkers found that this particle had many surprising properties. In particular, neutrons slowed down in hydrogenous materials produced new types of nuclei and new elements, including transuranic elements, a finding that resulted in the discovery of nuclear fission. Whereas Fermi studied primarily the properties of slow neutrons, Barschall's research concerned the behavior of the primary fast neutrons produced in nuclear reactions (that is, neutrons that had not been slowed down). This work led to the first recognition of the importance of the spin-orbit force in the interaction of neutrons with nuclei, to the development of the optical model of the nucleus, and to the introduction of the idea of preequilibrium processes in nuclear reactions. Barschall's work was recognized by the award of the first T. W. Bonner Prize by the American Physical Society (1965) and by his election to the National Academy of Sciences (1972). *See* CHADWICK, SIR JAMES; FERMI, ENRICO.

Early in 1939 Niels Bohr brought the news of the discovery of fission to Princeton. Immediately, experiments were begun to study this phenomenon. Barschall, who was then a student at Princeton, participated in the first measurement of the total energy release in fission and in investigations into the probability of fission induced by fast neutrons in thorium and uranium. His measurements of the interaction of fast neutrons with helium led, in collaboration with John Wheeler, to the conclusion that the spin-orbit interaction was much larger in nuclear processes than in atomic processes—a conclusion that is the basis of the shell model of the nucleus. During World War II Barschall participated, under the auspices of the Manhattan Project, in measurements of neutron interactions, and he determined the intensity of the shock wave from the first nuclear weapon test. Beginning in 1946 Barschall and his students at the University of Wisconsin studied resonances for fast neutrons, a process investigated earlier by Fermi for slow neutrons and explained by Niels Bohr in terms of the compound nucleus hypothesis. Barschall found that such resonances played an important role for fast neutrons also but that the predictions of the compound nucleus model were inconsistent with the observed energy dependence of the interaction probability. These measurements were interpreted by H. Feshbach and V. F. Weisskopf in terms of the optical model of the nucleus. According to this model, neutrons often pass through a nucleus without being absorbed and without forming a compound system. Barschall's study of fast neutron resonances furthermore showed that some resonances produce minima in the interaction probability, rather than the maxima originally observed by Fermi. These minima in the energy dependence affect neutron shielding in that neutrons of particular energies may pass through some materials without obstruction. Later measurements of the energy distribution of neutrons emitted from highly excited nuclei contradicted the previously used model, according to which neutrons evaporate in a manner analogous to the evaporation from a hot liquid. This work was another result that was inconsistent with the hypothesis that all nuclear reactions proceed through a compound nucleus. *See* BOHR, NIELS HENRIK DAVID; FESHBACH, HERMAN; WEISSKOPF, VICTOR FREDERICK; WHEELER, JOHN ARCHIBALD.

In 1971 Barschall became interested in the use of fast neutrons for the treatment of malignant disease. He participated in the development of suitable neutron sources and in experiments related to neutron dosimetry and the biological effects of neutrons. The development of neutron sources for radiotherapy was also applicable to the development of facilities for testing materials for fusion reactors. In addition, he measured fast neutron cross sections of importance to materials problems in fusion reactors.

Barschall went to the United States in 1937 and became a graduate student at Princeton University, where he received a Ph.D. in physics in 1940. He then taught a year at Princeton and 2 years at the University of Kansas. After becoming an American citizen in 1943, he went to the Los Alamos Laboratory. In 1946 he joined the faculty of the University of Wisconsin, where he chaired the physics department on several occasions and became John Bascom Professor in 1973. He took an active interest in the publication of physics journals and served as associate editor or member of the editorial board of several. In 1972 he became editor of the nuclear physics section of the *Physical Review* of the American Physical Society. He served on committees of the National Research Council, of the American Institute of Physics, and of the American Physical Society and was the second chairperson of the Division of Nuclear Physics of the American Physical Society.

For background information *see* NEUTRON; NEUTRON CROSS SECTION; NUCLEAR REACTION; SCATTERING EXPERIMENTS, NUCLEAR in the McGraw-Hill Encyclopedia of Science and Technology. ∎

BARSKI, GEORGES
★ French biologist

Born *July 9, 1909, Warsaw, Poland*

Early in his career Barski became interested in the interaction between different animal cells as well as different microorganisms and viruses in laboratory cultures. This was a fundamental influence on his choice of research subjects, and constituted the foundation of his scientific philosophy.

At the Pasteur Institute in Paris, Barski studied the interaction between animal cells and tuberculosis bacilli in laboratory

cultures and proved that, when phagocytized by some cells, especially of the lymphoid series, the microorganisms were to some extent protected against the action of streptomycin introduced into the medium. This favored the development of substrains of streptomycin-resistant bacilli.

In another series of investigations, Barski studied specific characteristics of lesions in cells exposed to different antibiotics or viruses or both. A new kind of code for the recognition and evaluation of many virus infections was thus elaborated. In an extension of this work, he explored the action of numerous antibiotics, especially of the aureomycin and chloromycetin families.

From the time of its foundation in 1958, Barski's laboratory at the Gustave-Roussy Cancer Institute in Villejuif, France, was involved in long-term cultures of cells of mice, humans, and other species, focusing in particular on their so-called spontaneous malignant transformation. Barski became involved in a comparative study of sister clones of common origin showing very high (N1) or very low (N2) malignant properties. These characteristics were accompanied by distinct differences in the chromosomal aspect of the two selected cell lines, the NI strain showing mitosis with predominantly 40–50 "normal-looking" chromosomes with usually one extralong marker, and the N2 strain showing mitosis with chiefly 70–80 chromosomes with 10 or more easily recognizable metacentric markers.

The question Barski tried to answer by appropriate experiments concerned the possible transfer, from one of the cells to the other, of some properties, particularly the property of producing or, perhaps, suppressing tumor growth.

When both types of cells were placed together in mixed cultures, it was observed that a new type of cell, obviously accumulating in its nuclei chromosomes originating from both the high and the low cancer cells, was created. Barski called these cells somatic hybrids, and much to his excitement, he was able to observe that they were not at all ephemeral, but were relatively stable formations able to maintain their essential mixed characteristics for years. On the basis of these experiments, which were repeated in his laboratory and later by other investigators, a new hypothesis was formulated which seemed, at first, to be perfectly heretical and which was generally accepted only some years after the first of Barski's papers on the subject were published in 1960–61. According to this hypothesis, the somatic cells of upper Metazoa could, in certain circumstances, fuse and "copulate" in a sense, like gametes or bacteria, and form new cells that have hybrid nuclei. These nuclei—laboratory-made biological units obtained by deliberate somatic cell fusion—in turn have the capability of multiplying. After some technical difficulties, essentially concerned with the problem of selection and isolation of hybrid cell clones from the mixed-cell population, were surmounted, the new hybridization procedure opened new avenues in many areas of experimental cell biology, cancer research, virology, and genetics. The hope arose that sexual crossing, the conventional method for analysis of heredity since the memorable works of Mendel, could be replaced or at least supplemented considerably by the procedure of crossing of somatic cells in a laboratory environment, this procedure providing a rate of replication close to that of bacteria, that is, a growth rate at least a thousand times more rapid than that occurring in the same organisms by the time sexual maturity is reached.

Concerning the problem of the transfer of malignant properties between cells of high and low malignancy cultivated together, no definite conclusion could be reached at that time as to whether the tumor-producing capacity was transferred by a mysterious "cancer factor" acting as a support of the malignancy, or whether, as shown by some investigations, the malignancy is the result of chromosomal loss occurring after the hybridization. Further progress in the analysis of malignancy by cell hybridization was achieved by experimentation with somatic hybrids obtained by the fusion of cells from different species. Some interesting results were obtained that showed that the tumor-producing capacity of the malignant parental cell line could be expressed in such a heterospecific hybrid, but the fundamental question was still unanswered.

Important work was accomplished by Barski and his group in studying the C-type viruses in mice. He developed the concept of the genetic variability responsible for the pathological and epidemiological complexity of their expression either as "innocent bystanders" or as highly pathogenic agents. Some substrains of these viruses remained fully infectious though nonpathogenic when introduced into newborn animals. They could be used safely as live vaccines. In some cases, it was observed that these kinds of nonpathogenic virus substrains were capable, when inoculated into newborn animals, to provide very effective protection against the highly pathogenic virus variants. This protection was of the substitution rather than of the interferon type.

In later work Barski and his group investigated cell-mediated immune reactions in animal hosts bearing originally syngeneic tumors. They demonstrated in laboratory tests of confrontation of peritoneal lymphoid cells with target tumor cells in several host-tumor systems that, after the initial specific antitumor immune reaction, the situation changed radically when the tumor size surpassed nearly one-twentieth of the weight of the animal: the specific antitumor immunity lowered considerably. However, excision of the tumor reactivated this reaction.

Barski completed his studies in Warsaw, graduating (Ph.D.,1946) from the Faculty of Natural Sciences and Mathematics, Department of Microbiology. After World War II, having lost his family in Poland, he emigrated to France (1945) and entered (1947) the Pasteur Institute, Virus Division, in Paris. In 1947 he was admitted as *attaché de recherche* at the French National Center of Scientific Research (CNRS). In 1963 he was appointed research director of CNRS. In 1958 he organized the Tissue Culture and Virus Laboratory at the Gustave-Roussy National Cancer Institute at Villejuif; he also served as director of the laboratory. He spent a year (1965–66) at the Sloan-Kettering Cancer Institute in New York as a recipient of the Alfred P. Sloan Foundation Award (1965). Barski was also awarded the prize of the French Academy of Sciences (1963), the New York Academy Cressy Morrisson Award (1963), the annual prize of the Jean-Louis Camus Foundation for Cancer Research (1971), the Griffuel International Prize for Cancer Research (1973), and the Paul Ehrlich Prize (1976).

For background information *see* CANCER (BIOLOGY); CYTOCHEMISTRY; GENETICS, SOMATIC CELL; PHAGOCYTOSIS in the McGraw-Hill Encyclopedia of Science and Technology. ∎

BARTELS, JULIUS
German geophysicist

Born Aug. 17, 1899, Magdeburg, Germany
Died Mar. 6, 1964, Göttingen, Germany

Early in his career Bartels recognized that adequate description and interpretation of the causes of temporal variations in geophysical phenomena required the application of sound statistical analysis. He was the first to discern clearly that statistical tests of significance for apparently systematic variations would be seriously modified unless procedures were devised to take account of the autocorrection present in the deviations from average variations in most geophysical variables. Thus he developed rigorous statistical procedures especially suited to the needs of geophysics. Not only did he describe these techniques in publications for the use of other investigators, but he also applied them fruitfully to many problems in geomagnetism and aeronomy.

Bartels's investigations led to a clear discrimination between the geomagnetic variations arising from wave and particle radiation from the Sun. He developed measures for the solar-wave radiation, based on the diurnal variations of the horizontal component of the geomagnetic field at the Equator; these have the highest correlations yet found between any geophysical variable and sunspots. He also derived indices for the effects of solar-particle radiation on geomagnetic variations. One of them provided, from geomagnetic data, a sensitive measure for the influx of solar particles into the auroral region. The widely used planetary indices, K_p, were prepared through his efforts for each 3-hour interval since 1932.

Bartels applied his statistical methods to provide a sound description and understanding of the periodic effects of the Moon's gravitational influence on atmospheric tides and the consequent influence on geomagnetic and ionospheric variations. His techniques provided the means of clearly discriminating among random, periodic, and quasi-periodic variations that had often been confused previously. These variations he used to investigate the 27-day variations in geomagnetic activity associated with the solar period of rotation. He found that the phases of the waves from consecutive groups of several 27-day intervals were unrelated, which indicated the decay of particle radiation from one group of sunspots and the subsequent emission from another active group of sunspots appearing elsewhere on the Sun. These waves were designated as quasi-persistent.

Bartels even found 27-day variations in magnetic activity for some intervals with no visible spots on the Sun. From this effect he postulated the existence of active M regions capable of emitting particle radiation. The M regions were later shown by astronomers at Mount Wilson Observatory to be the same regions where sunspots subsequently developed. From a sequence of 10,000 daily values of geomagnetic activity, he showed that there was not a single 27-day interval having all its days either magnetically quiet or magnetically disturbed. This demonstrated

that the solar surface was never everywhere active or everywhere quiet.

Bartels received his Ph.D. from the University of Göttingen in 1923. For the next 4 years he worked with the famous geomagnetician Adolph Schmidt, at the same time lecturing in geophysics at the University of Berlin. From 1927 to 1941 he was professor of meteorology and physics and head of the Meteorological Institute at the Forstliche Hochschule in Eberswalde, and from 1941 to 1945 professor of geophysics at the University of Berlin. In 1945 he became professor of geophysics and director of the Geophysical Institute at Göttingen. He was also, from 1956, director of the Max Planck Institute for Aeronomy at Lindau. In 1964 he was awarded the Bowie Medal of the American Geophysical Union.

Bartels wrote *Geomagnetism,* with Sydney Chapman (2 vols., 1940).

For background information *see* GEO-MAGNETISM in the McGraw-Hill Encyclopedia of Science and Technology. ■

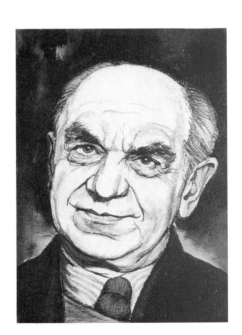

BARTLETT, SIR FREDERIC (CHARLES)

★ British experimental psychologist

Born Oct. 20, 1886, Stow-on-the-Wold, England
Died Sept. 30, 1969, Cambridge, England

The experimental psychological study of memory was initiated by Hermann Ebbinghaus in 1885. He used lists of non-

sense syllables, each member of which could be regarded as equivalent in difficulty to any other member. The lists had to be learned or partially learned under prescribed conditions and then recalled by the learner after a given lapse of time in varied orders with or without prompting. This model treated memory as a kind of receptacle or storehouse, into which whatever was memorized disappeared for a time, to be recovered later with more or less accuracy. It became the accepted model for the great bulk of psychological experiments on recall. After taking part in, and directing, many investigations in this conventional form, Bartlett became convinced that the results threw little light upon how remembering takes place in the course of everyday behavior. In this case, the material which is recalled has only rarely been given careful or prolonged preliminary study, and the recall itself is prompted by immediate environmental demands and is carried out to answer the challenges of these demands.

Accordingly, Bartlett set to work to devise experiments for the investigation of remembering as distinct, though not entirely different, from the more conventional sense of "the memory." Preliminary experiments on perception demonstrated that what is perceived at any moment is partially determined by earlier experiences, though these are rarely specifically reinstated. Then Bartlett embarked upon a large series of experiments on remembering as an event of everyday occurrence. He used material consisting of short connected stories of a familiar form, of descriptive prose, of arguments, and of pictures. His observers read, heard, or looked at this material, but were never required to "learn it by heart." At determined and recorded intervals later, the observers were asked to "remember" what they had read, heard, or seen, or were given conditions by the experimenter such that the material could be used to help or hinder their response. It soon became apparent that as the "remembered" material was made use of from interval to interval, and particularly as it was passed on from person to person within a group, it was in constant and often radical process of change. Especially where groups of socially related members were involved, the recorded versions approached or assumed forms of accepted conventions. Bartlett was therefore led to a study of the social determining factors in remembering. He himself made field studies in Africa, and he obtained many results from students in other countries.

The theories of remembering to which all these experiments led treated recall as a thoroughly active process. What is claimed to be reinstated is in constant but ordered change, and is organized, coded, and controlled by its relation to current demands on behavior. These ordered changes were clarified, and the likelihood of their occurrence considered.

This work on remembering was begun before World War I. When the war came, Bartlett's attention was officially diverted to investigations of skills as a consequence of his appointment to organize and develop psychological studies on the selection of naval ratings and officers enlisted for antisubmarine work. After the war the remembering experiments and their analysis were completed and published. The British Medical Research Council of which he then became a member, was interested in various personnel problems as they affected the military services, and Bartlett was appointed a member of the personnel committees, first of the Royal Air Force and then of the navy and army. When World War II broke out, he became the leader of a research group, mainly working at Cambridge University, whose concern was to develop new methods for the study of human skills, particularly of those involved in flying and the ground control of flight. In prescribing and proving these methods, leading parts were also played by Kenneth Craik, a most brilliant student whose death by accident closely following the war was an irreparable loss, and by G. C. Drew, who became professor of psychology in the University of London.

Bartlett's investigations into remembering had led him to the view that human thinking processes were a further development in the same directions, but relatively free from temporal and spatial control. The work on skill had convinced him that the achievements of bodily skills were precursors, on a more elementary level, of the processes which lead from perception, through remembering, to thinking proper. It further appeared that, by utilizing the methods which had been successfully explored in the investigation of bodily skills, more objectively based information could be obtained about the conditions and nature of the higher-level skills of thinking.

Bartlett's experimental work was thus along three main lines, regarded as closely related: the leading characteristics of remembering, those of bodily skills, and the nature and conditions of the thinking processes.

Bartlett graduated from the University of London and from St. John's College, Cambridge, of which he became a fellow. He was made a Commander of the Order of the British Empire in 1932 and was knighted in 1941, both mainly for his work for the Royal Air Force and the Admiralty. A fellow of the Royal Society of London, he was elected a foreign member of the Philosophical Society of Philadelphia, the U.S. National Academy of Sciences, and the American Academy of Arts and Sciences as well as the psychological societies of France, Italy, Belgium, Sweden, Spain, Switzerland, and Turkey. He was awarded the Baly Medal of the Royal College of Physicians, the Huxley Medal of the Royal Anthropological Society, a Royal Medal of the Royal Society, the Longacre Award of the Aero Medical Association, and the Gold Medal of the International Academy of Aviation and Space Medicine.

Bartlett's best-known books are *Remembering: An Experimental and Social Study* (1932), *The Mind at Work and Play* (1951), and *Thinking: An Experimental and Social Study* (1956).

For background information *see* MEMORY; VERBAL LEARNING in the McGraw-Hill Encyclopedia of Science and Technology. ∎

BARTLETT, NEIL
★ British chemist

Born *Sept. 15, 1932, Newcastle-upon-Tyne, England*

While investigating the fluorides of the platinum metals, Bartlett in 1962 prepared the first chemical compound of a noble gas. The noble gases were discovered by Lord Rayleigh and by Sir William Ramsey and his coworkers in the 1890s. The first noble gas to be discovered, and the most abundant, argon, was quickly subjected to intensive chemical and physical examination and found to be chemically inert. Henri Moissan, the first to prepare fluorine, attempted to prepare an argon fluoride in 1895, and his failure impressed him and his friend Ramsey with the inertness of the gas. Several perceptive chemists pointed to the greater likelihood of the heavier (and much rarer) gases krypton and xenon entering into chemical combination. L. C. Pauling, in particular, suggested in 1933 that xenon and krypton fluorides should be preparable, and in the same year an abortive attempt was made to prepare a xenon fluoride. The failure to sustain claims to noble gas compounds, together with the inability of experienced investigators to carry out the most favorable syntheses, contributed to an acceptance of the complete inertness of the gases, but it was probably not the most important contributing factor. Undoubtedly, the popularity of the simple electronic theories of valence, which emphasize the special stability of the noble gas configurations, had a major influence. The scarcity of the most favorable gas, xenon, and the instability of radon, which should be the most chemically active gas, were also contributing factors. *See* PAULING, LINUS CARL.

Bartlett started his independent research with the intention of defining more clearly the factors which limit the oxidation states of the elements. The noble metals, in particular, attracted his interest because of the promise of a greater range of oxidation states. Investigation of these elements also promised to be of value in his concern to define more clearly the relationship of the ligand geometry of molecules and crystals to the valence electron configurations of the central atom. The synthetic work, which involved fluorides and oxyfluorides, was therefore accompanied by structural studies. This combination was to prove vital to the discoveries which followed.

The compound of prime importance in the discovery of xenon chemistry was investigated initially in the belief that it would prove to be an oxyfluoride of 6-valent platinum. The compound was first observed as a sublimable red solid produced when platinum or platinum compounds were treated with fluorine in glass apparatus at moderate temperatures. The red solid was marked by great chemical reactivity, and it proved necessary to develop special techniques to analyze it. In 1961 Bartlett, with D. H. Lohmann, established the empirical formula as PtO_2F_6. Extensive chemical and physical characterization clearly indicated the compound to be a salt, dioxygenyl hexafluoroplatinate, $O_2^+[PtF_6]^-$. This was the first example known to represent either of the ions. It was particularly remarkable for its oxidized oxygen cation. This formulation implied that the molecular fluoride, platinum hexafluoride, which had been reported by Bernard Weinstock and J. G. Malm in 1958, should be capable of oxidizing molecular oxygen. This proved to be so, the two gases combining spontaneously at ordinary temperatures and pressures, as shown in reaction (1).

$$O_2(g) + PtF_6(g) \rightarrow O_2^+[PtF_6]^-(s) \quad (1)$$

Although the salt formulation had seemed appropriate early in the research, it posed the difficulty that, in order for oxidation of molecular oxygen to proceed spontaneously, the enthalpy for reaction (2) was required to be more exothermic

$$\Delta H(PtF_6(g) + e \rightarrow PtF_6^-(g)) \quad (2)$$

than -160 kilocalories (-669 kilojoules) per mole (that is, approximately twice the value for atomic fluorine or atomic chlorine). The proof of the salt formulation, therefore, pointed to platinum hexafluoride as the most powerfully oxidizing molecular species recognized so far. Bartlett noted that the ionization potentials of the heavier noble gases (xenon, 12.2 electronvolts; radon, 10.5 electronvolts) were as low as, or lower than, molecular oxygen (12.2 electronvolts), and hence he concluded that these gases should also be oxidizable. In his investigations in 1962 xenon gas proved to be as easy to oxidize as molecular oxygen. The orange-yellow solid formed in the spontaneous gas-gas reaction was designated xenon hexafluoroplatinate, $Xe^+[PtF_6]^-$. The work on xenon hexafluoroplatinate stimulated investigation of the other noble gases in a number of laboratories, and compounds of krypton, xenon, and radon were thus well characterized chemically and physically. Major consequences of the discovery of the chemical activity of the heavier noble gases were the development of a greater awareness of the limitations of simple valence theory and the focusing of attention on the nature of bonding in these and related compounds.

In later work Bartlett and his group exploited the noble gas fluorides and other powerful oxidizers, such as the transition-metal hexafluorides, and O_2^+ salts, to prepare a variety of species with novel oxidation states. Thus they were able to prepare the first quinquevalent gold compounds (containing the AuF_6^- ion) and the first salts containing perfluoroaromatic cations ($C_6F_6^+$ and $C_{10}F_8^+$). They prepared new first-stage graphite salts, of high electrical conductivity, which they were able to closely define structurally and establish as true salts of formula $C_8^+MF_6^-$ (the intercalated MF_6^- species being AsF_6^- or OsF_6^- or IrF_6^-). Moreover, Bartlett and his group prepared the first example of a layer-form boron nitride of a graphite salt. The boron nitride salt $((BN)_4SO_3F)$ is an electrical conductor, whereas boron nitride is an insulator.

Bartlett was an undergraduate and graduate student at King's College, Newcastle-upon-Tyne, from 1951 to 1957; his Ph.D. work was done with P. L. Robinson. He was senior chemistry master at the Duke's School, Alnwick, for a year, and in 1958 moved to the University of British Columbia, where he served on the faculty for 8 years. In 1966 he was appointed a professor of chemistry at Princeton University, and he served as professor of chemistry at the University of California at Berkeley, beginning in 1969. Among the honors awarded Bartlett were the 1962 Corday-Morgan Medal and Prize of the Chemical Society of Great Britain, the 1965 Research Corporation Award (United States), the 1965 E. W. R. Steacie Prize (Canada), the 1971 Dannie Heineman Prize of the Göttingen Academy, and the 1976 Robert A. Welch Award of the Robert A. Welch Foundation, Texas. He was elected to the Deutsche Akademie der Naturforscher Leopoldina, Halle, in 1969, the Royal Society of London in 1973, and the American Academy of Arts and Sciences and the Akademie der Wissenschaften in Göttingen in 1977.

For background information *see* INERT GASES; VALENCE in the McGraw-Hill Encyclopedia of Science and Technology. ■

BARTLETT, PAUL DOUGHTY
★ American chemist

***Born** Aug. 14, 1907, Ann Arbor, MI, U.S.A.*

O f the stages in which organic chemistry developed, the early 19th century saw the evolution of the art of isolating and analyzing pure organic compounds; in the latter part of the 19th century molecular structures and arrangements in space were deduced. By the 1930s it was possible to establish electronic fine structures and the molecular mechanisms involved in chemical change. Throughout his career Bartlett sought the principles and particulars of many kinds of mechanisms involved in the reactions of organic compounds. For his achievements in this field he received the American Chemical Society's Award in Pure Chemistry in 1938, Roger Adams Award and Willard Gibbs Medal, both in 1963, the National Medal of Science in 1968, and the Linus Pauling and Nichols medals in 1975–76.

As a first result of general applicability Bartlett showed experimentally, with D. S. Tarbell in 1936, that halogenation of the double bond is a two-step process. In the same period he showed that the kinetics of the Wagner-Meerwein rearrangement was consistent only with catalyzed ionization as the rate-controlling step. He was the first to show (in 1939 with L. H. Knox) the value, for the study of reaction mechanisms, of the unreactive bridgehead halides (I), which can neither react with the usual umbrellalike inversion nor yield normal coplanar carbonium ions like that of tertiary butyl (II). Triptycene was first

(I)

(II)

synthesized as part of this program (M. J. Ryan and S. G. Cohen). With R. Wistar, Bartlett proved that, contrary to the textbooks of the time, diazonium ions (which are electron-seeking) and not diazohydroxides are the species responsible for coupling to azo dyes, acting on the electron-rich amines or phenoxide ions. *See* TARBELL, DEAN STANLEY.

With A. Schneider, Barlett synthesized tri-tertiary-butyl carbinol, the most crowded simple molecule yet made at the time, and began a long-term study of the peculiar properties of highly branched molecules, including steric acceleration of the ionization process.

In 1943 Bartlett's group at Harvard University began to publish on polymerization. The fate of initiating fragments in polystyrene was traced (Cohen) for the first time, the peculiar kinetics of the polymerization of allyl esters was accounted for (R. Altschul), induced decomposition of benzoyl peroxide was provided with its now accepted explanation (K. Nozaki), some absolute rate constants in the rapid polymerization of vinyl acetate were accurately measured (C. G. Swain and H. Kwart), and the nature of the action of some one-, two-, and three-stage polymerization inhibitors was worked out (Kwart, G. S. Hammond, and D. Trifan). Bartlett's interest in free radicals continued in later studies of the general process of concerted decomposition of peresters and azo compounds into three fragments

and of the thermal generation of free radicals by styrene alone (R. R. Hiatt) or with molecular iodine (Trifan and A. Factor). Pairs of free radicals generated at very low temperatures were characterized by their singlet or triplet spin states, their lifetimes, and their stereochemistry (J. M. McBride, 1967). Some useful new initiators of chain reactions resulted from the perester studies.

In 1944 Bartlett, F. E. Condon, and Schneider discovered the extremely rapid interconversion between carbonium ions and branched paraffins by hydride transfer and showed that this reaction was the missing link in understanding the industrial reaction of paraffin alkylation as an ionic sequence. In 1956 Bartlett and J. D. McCollum showed that the long-lived triphenylcarbonium ion captured hydride ions from secondary alcohols, as ketones were known to do from alkoxide ions.

Research for the National Defense Research Committee during World War II led to recognition of the roles of the sulfur and nitrogen atoms of mustard-gas-like compounds as neighboring groups in displacement reactions in the sense elucidated by S. Winstein for halogen atoms (Swain and S. D. Ross). In an excursion outside the realm of mechanism, Bartlett's group made 725 compounds for testing as tropical-insect repellents during this period.

Interest in bicyclic compounds led to an explanation of the endo-exo rearrangement in dicyclopentadiene derivatives (Schneider) and to the first long-lived carbonium ion demonstrably intermediate in molecular rearrangements by direct physical methods of observation (E. R. Webster, C. E. Dills, and H. G. Richey, Jr.).

The formation of carbonium ions by the π-route was demonstrated by systematic variation of the structures of unsaturated compounds undergoing ring closure. Bartlett and his coworkers were the first to treat the interconversion of the molecular forms of elemental sulfur as a problem in reaction mechanisms of ring compounds (G. Meguerian, E. F. Cox, and R. E. Davis). They showed that the less stable S_6 undergoes polymerization by traces of sulfide or sulfite ions to linear polysulfur, which in turn depolymerizes to the stable rings of S_8 [Eq. (1)] (G. Lohaus, C. Weis, and Davis).

In an early demonstration of a role of metal clusters in organic reaction mechanisms, Bartlett showed, with S. Friedman

(1)

and M. Stiles, that the tetrameric secondary and tertiary organolithium compounds in ether had the power (unlike Grignard reagents, but like transition-metal complexes) to bring about insertion of ethylene between the carbon and the metal.

By simultaneous use of kinetics, different kinds of spectroscopy, and chemical isolation, many aspects of the chemistry of free radicals were explored. It was shown (with R. E. Pincock) that the 9-decalyl free radical, most stable in the trans conformation, could be generated from a suitable precursor in the cis form and captured on its way to the trans by such a powerful scavenger as oxygen under 500 atmospheres (50 megapascals) pressure. With the new initiator azocumene, it was demonstrated, with S. F. Nelsen, that the cumyl radical dimerizes not only to the stable bicumyl but reversibly to a less stable quinoid isomer [Eq. (2)].

(2)

It was later shown by W. T. Nauta and coworkers that the classical hexaphenylethane, from which the first recognized free radical was formed, has a structure of this type. With T. G. Traylor, using doubly labeled O_2 of molecular weight 36, Bartlett showed the generality of a chain-termination mechanism in autoxidation reactions, in which two peroxy radicals form a short-lived tetroxide whose middle two oxygen atoms split out, leaving a radical pair capable of combining in part to a termination product [Eq. (3)]. The equi-

$$2 \overset{|}{\underset{|}{+}} OO\cdot \;\rightleftharpoons\; \overset{|}{\underset{|}{+}} O{\sim}_O{\sim}^O{\sim}O \overset{|}{\underset{|}{+}}$$

$$\downarrow -70$$

$$\overset{|}{\underset{|}{+}} O{-}O \overset{|}{\underset{|}{+}} \;\leftarrow\; 2 \overset{|}{\underset{|}{+}} O\cdot + O_2 \quad (3)$$

$$\overset{|}{\underset{|}{+}} OO\cdot + \cdot O \overset{|}{\underset{|}{+}} \;\overset{<-30}{\rightleftharpoons}\; \overset{|}{\underset{|}{+}} O{\sim}_O{\sim}^O \overset{|}{\underset{|}{+}}$$

libria and rates involved in this process were studied by electron-spin resonance (with G. Guaraldi), and examples of the linear trioxide so identified were prepared in crystalline form (with M. Lahav).

Another family of unstable oxidation intermediates was demonstrated in the reaction of elementary oxygen with diphenylcarbene, which yields the trappable Criegee carbonyl oxide $(C_6H_5)_2COO$.

In a comprehensive program of research on cycloaddition, Bartlett and his coworkers established the conditions under which stepwise reaction via biradicals competes with the concerted process allowed under the orbital symmetry rules for 2 + 4 but forbidden for 2 + 2 cycloadditions. The stepwise mechanism, which is always allowed, is general for 2 + 2 cases and is favored in 2 + 4 addition in many cases with some well-defined structural characteristics. Photosensitized cycloadditions provided a model of the behavior of triplet molecules as intermediates.

The discovery, with A. P. Schaap, that singlet excited oxygen adds to the carbon-carbon double bond without loss of configuration, and hence by a concerted mechanism, launched a series of mechanistic studies of photosensitized oxidation. With N. Shimizu, Bartlett discovered that α-diketones such as biacetyl photosensitize the oxidation of olefins by free oxygen to epoxides (one O atom in a three-membered ring) more generally and more efficiently than do the commonly used sensitizers leading to dioxygen addition. The epoxide oxygen was shown (with J. Becherer) to come from the O_2 molecule and not from the diketone.

Bartlett also gave attention to a number of self-contained mechanistic problems not part of the larger programs mentioned. Among them were the chemistry of α- and β-lactones, the control of ster-

eochemistry in the carbonylation of carbonium ions, the chemistry of phosphite ozonides, a luminescent reaction of sulfuranes, and the unusual mechanism of conversion of the cyclopentadiene-dichloroketene adduct into tropolone.

Bartlett attended the Indianapolis public schools and Amherst College. He received his Ph.D. from Harvard in 1931. He was a National Research fellow at the Rockefeller Institute in 1931–32 and an instructor at the University of Minnesota in 1932–34 before joining the Harvard faculty.

In 1948 he became Erving Professor of Chemistry at Harvard (emeritus in 1975). In 1974 he became Robert A. Welch Professor at Texas Christian University, Fort Worth. He was elected to the American Academy of Arts and Sciences in 1946, the National Academy of Sciences in 1947, and the American Philosophical Society in 1978. He was also an honorary member of the British, Swiss, and Japanese chemical societies.

In addition to publishing about 220 papers in chemical journals, and chapters in four books, Bartlett wrote *Nonclassical Ions* (1965).

For background information *see* ORGANIC CHEMISTRY in the McGraw-Hill Encyclopedia of Science and Technology. ∎

BARTON, DEREK HAROLD RICHARD
☆ British chemist

Born Sept. 8, 1918, Gravesend, Kent, England

Noting the difference in the rates of reaction of steroid and triterpenoid isomers in which the functional group was placed in similar environments, Barton in 1949 conceived the explanation that different spatial orientations of these functional groups were involved. This explanation was proved to be correct and led to the beginning of the field of conformational analysis in organic chemistry. For pioneering this work he received the first Roger Adams Award of the American Chemical Society in 1959, the Davy Medal of the Royal Society of London in 1961, and the Nobel Prize in 1969.

By 1947 O. Hassel in Norway had demonstrated by electron diffraction studies that cyclohexane (I) and its derivatives exist mainly as chair-shaped molecules. The attached hydrogen atoms, or

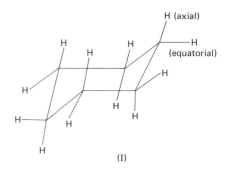

functional groups, can adopt either an equatorial position pointing away from the center or a shielded position parallel to the axis of the ring. Barton realized that in complex systems where the conformation was fixed, the reactivity of a group would depend on whether it was attached in an axial or equatorial position. *See* HASSEL, ODD.

To confirm his ideas Barton made extensive studies in the steroid and terpene fields. He found important correlations between chemical reactivity and preferred conformation, thus enabling much stereochemical information to be interpreted rationally.

By 1956 Barton had extended his studies to a wide variety of natural products, including some phenolic materials. At this time he made a further important observation. The structure of "Pummerer's ketone" had been proposed as (II) in the reaction shown. This was disputed on mechanistic grounds, the coupling of radicals from the *p*-cresol precursor being expected, instead, to give pattern (III).

(II)

(III)

The latter proved to be correct. Barton quickly realized the biosynthetic importance of such oxidative coupling of phenols. On surveying naturally occurring compounds, he concluded that the structures of many phenols and alkaloids could be explained and predicted. He employed two methods of verification to test his hypothesis. In the first, the synthesis of natural products, such as usnic acid and galanthamine from simple precursors, was accomplished in the laboratory. In the second, plants were fed with the postulated intermediates that were radioactively labeled. The theory is of particular value in understanding the biosynthesis of many complex alkaloids. Subsequently Barton elucidated the biosynthesis of diverse classes of compounds, including erythrina, morphine, indole, and Amaryllidaceae alkaloids. This enabled concise and useful biomimetic syntheses to be undertaken.

An interest in radical reactions having been aroused, Barton turned his attention, concurrently with the study of oxidative coupling, to the development of new radical reactions, initially with the object of preparing oxy radicals. Possible photochemical routes were studied. During some related work he noticed that systems containing dienones were rapidly isomerized. He then made a detailed study on various natural products containing the dienone moiety in which the complex transformations undergone by santonin during photolysis were unraveled.

On conformational grounds, Barton predicted that if a hydrogen atom in the same molecule was spatially oriented in the vicinity of the generated oxy radical, abstraction of that hydrogen atom intramolecularly would be preferred. This prediction was substantiated, and culminated in 1959 in the synthesis, by a simple route, of the naturally occurring hormone aldosterone. The work was carried out at the Research Institute for Medicine and Chemistry, Cambridge, MA. Barton made important contributions to the chemistry of penicillins and their interconversion into the clinically important cephalosporins. Much important synthetic work on tetracycline antibiotics was also carried out.

Besides the discoveries mentioned above, Barton made important contributions to the pyrolysis of organic chlorides (1945–52) and the development and applications of carbanion autoxidations (after 1960), both processes being important industrially. He also determined the constitutions and stereochemistry of many complicated natural products, especially in the terpenoid field, and carried out pioneering work on the relationship of molecular rotation to structure in complex organic molecules. Steroids including lanosterol, ergosterol, and vitamin D were studied in detail. Biosynthetic pathways were elucidated and synthetic work was undertaken. Barton's diverse accomplishments included the study of organofluoride, seleninic, and sulfur compounds. The unique chemistry of the nitrogen-sulfur bond, selective fluorination of natural products, and a study of extrusion reactions are a few examples of his work.

Barton received his B.Sc. in 1940 and his Ph.D. in 1942 at Imperial College, London. After a few years in government and industrial research, he returned to Imperial College in 1945, first as an assistant lecturer and then as an I.C.I. Research Fellow (1946–49). For the year 1949–50 he was a visiting lecturer at Harvard University, during which time the concept of conformational analysis was born. Returning to England, he obtained the position of reader at Birkbeck College, London, being elected to a chair in chemistry in 1953. In 1955 he was appointed Regius Professor of Chemistry at Glasgow University. In 1957 he returned to Imperial College as professor of organic chemistry and remained in that position until 1978, when he retired to assume the position of director at L'Institut de Chimie des Substances Naturelles in France. He gained his D.Sc. (London) in

1949 and was elected to the fellowship of the Royal Society in 1954. After 1949 Barton had close connections with American chemistry and spent a portion of each year in the United States.

For background information *see* CONFORMATIONAL ANALYSIS in the McGraw-Hill Encyclopedia of Science and Technology. ∎

BASOLO, FRED
★ American chemist

***Born** Feb. 11, 1920, Coello, IL, U.S.A.*

Long interested in the preparation and reactions of coordination compounds of the transitional metals, Basolo turned to the problem of how these reactions take place after he joined the chemistry faculty at Northwestern University in 1946. Physical organic chemists had made important contributions to the understanding of reaction mechanisms of organic compounds, but little had been done with inorganic compounds. Basolo initiated a research program designed to study in detail the kinetics and stereochemistry of ligand substitution reactions of cobalt(III) complexes. His experience with these compounds allowed him and his coworkers to make rapid progress with the details of how such reactions proceed. They found that, except for the hydroxide ion, the rates of reaction did not depend on the reagent reacting with the cobalt complex. However, the rates of reaction did accelerate markedly with an increase in size of the nonleaving groups attached to cobalt. These results were interpreted as involving the initial slow breaking of the bond between cobalt and the leaving group, followed by a rapid addition of the entering group. This type of mechanism has withstood the test of time for cobalt complexes, and it is also largely applicable to other metal systems in which six groups are attached to the metal center.

Platinum(II) complexes have only four groups attached to platinum, and there was reason to expect these complexes to react by a mechanism different from that occurring in metals with six attached groups. The experiments of Basolo and his coworkers were the first to establish this difference in behavior. The rates of reaction of platinum(II) complexes depend on the entering reagent, and the rates diminish as the size of the nonleaving groups on the platinum increases. This behavior requires that the entering group attack the metal and cause the breaking of the bond between the metal and the leaving group. Such a reaction path depends on the nature of the entering group, and the rate decreases as the other groups on the metal become bulky and make it difficult for the group to enter. These investigations on substitution reactions of metal complexes containing six and four groups, respectively, largely provided the foundation for the elucidation of the reaction processes of such systems in solution. During the 1960s and 1970s these types of studies continued in laboratories around the world, and extended to much more complicated metal complexes such as some of the large metal proteins.

Basolo and his research group also pioneered in the application of mechanistic concepts to the syntheses of new metal complexes, as well as to the syntheses of known compounds by new methods. This approach was most successful, and it came to play a significant role in synthetic inorganic chemistry. For example, Basolo and his students were able to employ such a mechanistic approach in preparing the first metal thiocyanato (M-SCN) and isothiocyanato (M-NCS) isomers. These are pairs of compounds in which the metals and the groups attached to them are the same, except that the thiocyanate ion (NCS^-) in one compound is attached to the metal through the sulfur atom, and in the other member of the pair it is attached through the nitrogen. There are now many other examples of such linkage isomers, and much has been learned about

the various factors that play an important role in the stability of these isomers.

Other types of compounds that were studied in Basolo's laboratory are the metal carbonyls or transition-metal organometallic compounds. His early work provided data, still in use, on the rates of carbon monoxide exchange with some of the simpler metal carbonyls. His work was also the first to suggest that insertion reactions in these compounds may in fact proceed by ligand migration. Compounds of this type continued to be investigated in many different laboratories as possible catalysts for certain important commercial processes, for example, coal gasification.

During the 1970s Basolo turned his attention to the study of synthetic oxygen carriers. The best-known oxygen carrier is hemoglobin, which interacts with oxygen to form oxyhemoglobin and which supports most of animal life. Coordination chemists have known since the late 1930s that certain synthetic cobalt complexes are also able to add and release oxygen rapidly. However, all of the cobalt-oxygen compounds that had been obtained were of the type containing two cobalt atoms for each oxygen. They were thus different from hemoglobin, in which each iron molecule is attached to an oxygen molecule. Fortunately, Basolo and his students were able to obtain several compounds containing one oxygen molecule attached to one cobalt molecule, and thus they were able to investigate compounds more closely related to the natural proteins. They also discovered the first example of a synthetic manganese porphyrin which carries oxygen, and they contributed to studies of oxygen carriers of iron complexes at low temperature and on rigid surfaces.

The son of Italian immigrant parents, Basolo spent his childhood in a small coal mining community in southern Illinois. He received his B.Ed. in chemistry at Southern Illinois Normal in 1940 and his Ph.D. in inorganic chemistry at the University of Illinois in 1943. After spending 3 years as a research chemist at the Rohm and Haas Chemical Company in Philadelphia, he joined the faculty at Northwestern University in 1946 as an instructor. He became a full professor in 1959, and chaired the chemistry department in 1969–72. He also chaired the Inorganic Division of the American Chemical Society (ACS) in 1970, the board of trustees of the Gordon Research Conferences in 1976, and the Chemistry Section of the

American Association for the Advancement of Science in 1979. For his fundamental investigations on the mechanisms of substitution reactions and syntheses of metal complexes, Basolo received the ACS Awards for Research in Inorganic Chemistry (1964) and for Distinguished Service in Inorganic Chemistry (1975). He was elected to the National Academy of Sciences in 1979.

Basolo wrote *Mechanisms of Inorganic Reactions,* with R. G. Pearson (1958; 2d ed. 1967) and *Coordination Chemistry,* with R. C. Johnson (1964). *See* JOHNSON, R. C.; PEARSON, RALPH G.

For background information *see* COORDINATION CHEMISTRY; ORGANOMETALLIC COMPOUND; TRANSITION ELEMENTS in the McGraw-Hill Encyclopedia of Science and Technology. ∎

BASOV, NICOLAI GENNEDIYEVICH
Soviet physicist

Born 1922

While studying the interactions between incident electromagnetic waves and matter, Basov conceived of a method for amplifying the original waves by having atoms or molecules release identical waves, in phase, at a multiplying rate. This method led to the invention by C. H. Townes of the maser, a device for microwave amplification by the stimulated emission of radiation. Subsequently, amplification of visible radiation, the laser, was achieved. The new field known as quantum electronics—electronics with quantum mechanics having a key role—quickly grew out of these achievements. For his fundamental studies in this area, Basov received the 1964 Nobel Prize in physics, which he shared with his co-worker A. M. Prochorov and with Townes of the United States. *See* PROCHOROV, ALEKSANDR MIKHAILOVICH; TOWNES, CHARLES HARD.

In 1917 Einstein conducted a thermodynamic study of the nature of the interaction between electromagnetic radiation and atoms or molecules. Previously, similar analyses had indicated that amplification could never be produced by such interactions without violating the second law of thermodynamics. This law states that a process in which the entropy, the degree of disorder, of an isolated system decreases could not occur. However, Einstein followed thermodynamic reasoning further and derived a relationship governing the rate of change of electromagnetic radiation confined in a region where it interacts with a group of molecules. The first two terms of his equation represented the known processes of absorption and spontaneous energy release. Einstein discovered that the third and last term represented an unknown type of emission from an upper energy state produced by the mere presence of the radiation intensity. This was called stimulated emission.

For equilibrium at any positive temperature T, Boltzmann's law, expressed in the equation below, relates the probabili-

$$N_B = N_A e - \frac{(E_B - E_A)}{kT}$$

ties N_A and N_B of electrons in the quantum states A and B. Here $E_B - E_A$ is the energy difference between the states under consideration, and the state B is a higher energy state than A; k is Boltzmann's constant; and T is the absolute temperature. This law requires $N_B < N_A$ at any positive absolute temperature. Einstein's discovery showed that if $N_B > N_A$, the rate of change of radiation in the system would always be positive. Thus the incident radiation would become amplified. The condition $N_B > N_A$ was termed population inversion and became known as a condition of negative temperature, since in Boltzmann's law it may be obtained by assuming a negative absolute temperature.

Basov reasoned that population inversion was a practical means for amplification of electromagnetic radiation. He realized that, in order to make an assembly of molecules or atoms amplify, the equilibrium of the electrons within the energy levels must be disturbed. The probability of finding electrons in higher energy levels must be greater than that of finding them in the lower levels. He further reasoned that the crucial requirement was to produce positive feedback of the incoming waves to force the electrons to the higher level by some type of resonant circuit. It was also necessary to ensure that the gain in energy by the stimulated transition from the higher to the lower level was greater than the circuit losses. If these conditions were satisfied, Basov indicated, then a mass of a certain type could be assembled that would be sensitive to incoming waves. Electrons within the mass would be excited into a higher energy level, producing a population inversion, or the so-called condition of negative temperature. The electrons would simultaneously fall back into the original levels, releasing waves identical to those that first entered.

A successful device was first produced in 1954 at Columbia University by Townes, who found a way to assemble ammonia molecules in a resonant chamber, such that when a radio wave at 24,000 megahertz, in the radar or microwave region, encountered the chamber, additional waves of that frequency were produced by the ammonia molecules. This produced a cascade effect in the chamber, resulting in an enormous amplification of the original wave and a confirmation of Basov's predictions. In July 1960 T. H. Maiman announced the construction of a device employing the maser principle for light waves. It consisted of a long crystal of synthetic ruby enclosed in a spiral flashtube of xenon. Flashes of light from the xenon excited the electrons in the crystal and produced a population inversion. When these electrons dropped back to their ground state, they emitted a form of visible radiation never seen before. The light wavelengths, all of the same frequency, were precisely in step—a condition known as temporal and spatial coherency. The extraordinary properties of coherent light were quickly put to a wide variety of tasks, including delicate surgical operations where burning is needed, measurements, and precise signaling. In practice the maser and laser stimulated emission may be obtained from the lowest radio frequencies to the ultraviolet region. *See* MAIMAN, THEODORE HAROLD.

Basov joined the Lebedev Institute, Moscow, in 1948 as a laboratory assistant. This was 2 years before he graduated from the Moscow Engineering and Physics Institute. In 1958 he became a deputy director of the Lebedev Institute. He became a member of the Communist party in 1951 and received the Lenin Prize in 1959 for the work described above. The degree of doctor of physical-mathematical sciences, more advanced than the American Ph.D., was earned in 1957. He was elected a corresponding member of the Soviet Academy of Sciences in 1962, one step lower than academician.

For background information *see* ELECTROMAGNETIC RADIATION; LASER; MASER in the McGraw-Hill Encyclopedia of Science and Technology. ∎

BATCHELOR, GEORGE KEITH
★ British applied mathematician

***Born** Mar. 8, 1920, Melbourne, Australia*

The needs of World War II drew Batchelor into research connected with the design and operation of aircraft immediately after he received a degree in mathematics and physics at the University of Melbourne in 1940. His work on a variety of aerodynamical problems at the Aeronautical Research Laboratory in Melbourne during the war years led to his sustained interest in fluid mechanics, which dominated his later research. He became interested in particular in the turbulent motion of fluids, which at that time represented the major unsolved problem in fluid dynamics. In 1945 he went to Cambridge, England, as a research student to work on turbulent flow under the supervision of Sir Geoffrey Taylor, who remained an inspiring influence for the subsequent 30 years. The pioneering studies of Taylor in the 1930s had shown what conceptual and mathematical framework was needed for the description of turbulence, and other work by Taylor, together with the penetrating contribution of A. N. Kolmogoroff in 1941, indicated some universal features of the small-scale components of the motion. Batchelor was one of the first to recognize the value of Kolmogoroff's theory, and much of his research on turbulence during 1945–53 was devoted to extensions of the work of these two men and its application to a variety of physical problems involving turbulence. *See* TAYLOR, SIR GEOFFREY (INGRAM).

Many of Batchelor's later papers on turbulence concerned diffusion and dispersion of some nonuniform property of the fluid (such as the concentration of material which is suspended or dissolved in the fluid, temperature, or magnetic field strength in a highly conducting fluid) in turbulent flow. He realized that there is a significant difference between problems in which material is being diffused relative to a fixed point and those in which different portions of the fluid are diffusing relative to one another. The former type involves only the statistics of a typical marked element of the fluid which originates at the fixed point. For example, the average concentration of smoke at positions downwind of a chimney or fire can be calculated if one knows the statistical properties of the path of a typical smoke-bearing element of fluid which has passed near the source of smoke. This brings in the properties of wind turbulence, which are known to be dominated by proximity to a boundary and to depend on distance from it in a simple way. Batchelor was able to account for several features of the observed concentrations, including the strange tendency for a smoke-bearing element to migrate upward at a constant average velocity (indicating an accelerating character of the diffusion, which arises from the continually increasing size of the relevant eddies).

The more difficult concept of relative diffusion of marked fluid elements involves the joint probability distribution of the velocities of different elements, and there are interesting connections with the tendency for material lines and surfaces (that is, those which coincide always with the same fluid particles) continually to increase in size in a turbulent flow. The way in which the linear dimensions of a cloud of marked fluid increases, on the average, can be analyzed, provided the cloud is small enough for the relative diffusion to be dominated by those small eddies of the turbulence to which the Kolmogoroff local-equilibrium theory applies. One of the results agreed with an inference from observations in the atmosphere made many years ago, namely, that the cloud width increases with time to the power 3/2; but, in general, experimental information about relative diffusion was lacking. Another related piece of work was concerned with the spatial distribution of some quantity such as temperature or dissolved salt which is being convected by a turbulent motion and diffused by molecular transfer. By devising a suitable model of the way in which neighboring level surfaces of concentration are being extended and brought closer together (on the average), Batchelor was able to determine the functional form of the small-scale end of the spectrum of concentration.

Early in the 1960s Batchelor set aside research on turbulence and turned to the writing of a large textbook on fluid dynamics for students which would incorporate, at an introductory level, the important advances which had been made in the understanding of fluid-flow systems during the previous 30 or 40 years. He found this educational task to be absorbing and rewarding, and in some ways more exacting than the writing of a research monograph. At the completion of this book, he sought a new field of research which was at once unconventional and promising. His choice was the mechanics of two-component mixtures, which involves rheology as well as fluid mechanics and is of considerable interest in chemical and mechanical engineering and in colloid science. When one component is in the form of small particles suspended in the second (fluid) component, the task is usually to characterize this mixture as an equivalent continuous medium with new rheological properties. The first contribution to this kind of problem was made by Albert Einstein in 1906, when he calculated the effective viscosity of a dilute suspension of small rigid spherical particles. In Einstein's calculation, the spheres are assumed to be so far apart that the fluid motion near one of them is independent of the presence of the others. By devising new methods to allow for the effect of interactions between the particles, Batchelor was able to extend the results to larger particle concentrations. The positions of particles in a fluid suspension are normally random, and probability theory methods have proved to be as relevant in this new field as they were in Batchelor's earlier studies of turbulence. Similar considerations of the mutual interaction of particles were applied in calculations of the rheological properties of a suspension of parallel rodlike particles, which give a distinctive nonisotropic structure to the medium; of the average speed of particles in a cloud falling through fluid under gravity; and of the coefficient of diffusion of very small particles due to their Brownian motion.

Batchelor's interest in fluid mechanics and its many fields of application led him to see the value of a journal which would bring together papers on the analytical and the experimental and applied aspects of the subject, and in 1956 he founded the *Journal of Fluid Mechanics*. He remained senior editor, and saw more than 90 volumes published by the Cambridge University Press. He took an active part in the establishment in 1959 of the department of applied mathematics and theoretical physics at the University of Cambridge, and was appointed its first head. The form of the department reflected his belief that theoreticians in different branches of physical science and engineering can profit by close association with one another. He helped to launch a new series of informal specialized research seminars in Europe in 1964, and chaired the European Mechanics Committee which organized these Euromech Colloquia. Batchelor believed that through such constructive activities, motivated by the simple urge to create something which improves the existing situation, he made a contribution to science which was perhaps as valuable as his research.

For his early work on turbulence, Batchelor was elected a fellow of Trinity College in 1947. He was appointed to a lectureship at the University of Cambridge in 1948, and remained at Cambridge thereafter. He was elected a fellow of the Royal Society in 1957, a foreign honorary member of the American Academy of Arts and Sciences in 1959, a member of the Royal Society of Uppsala in 1972, and a foreign member of the Polish Academy of Sciences in 1975. In 1964 he was appointed to the newly established professorship of applied mathematics at the University of Cambridge. He held honorary doctorates of science from the University of Grenoble (1959) and the Technical University of Denmark (1974).

Batchelor wrote *The Theory of Homogeneous Turbulence* (1953) and *An Introduction to Fluid Dynamics* (1967), and he edited *Surveys in Mechanics* (1956) and *The Scientific Papers of G. I. Taylor* (vol. 1, 1958; vol. 2, 1960; vol. 3, 1963; vol. 4, 1971).

For background information *see* FLUID DYNAMICS; FLUID MECHANICS; FLUID-FLOW PRINCIPLES; FLUID-FLOW PROPERTIES; TURBULENT FLOW in the McGraw-Hill Encyclopedia of Science and Technology. ∎

BATES, SIR DAVID (ROBERT)
★ Irish theoretical physicist

Born November 1916, Omagh, Northern Ireland, United Kingdom

In 1937 Bates began research under H. S. W. Massey at Queen's University, Belfast. He was given the task of calculating the rate at which electrons recombine radiatively with atomic oxygen ions and of applying the results to the terrestrial ionosphere (where, until the results were obtained, the process was widely misbelieved to be important). This master's degree project greatly influenced Bates's scientific life, arousing in him a lasting interest in atomic and molecular physics and its applications to, in particular, natural phenomena.

After World War II Bates was appointed to the staff of University College, London, where Massey was then Goldsmid Professor of Mathematics. The two resumed the search for the solution to the enigma posed by the extremely high recombination rate observed in the ionosphere. They first considered the mutual neutralization of positive and negative ions, because at the time geomagneticians wrongly supposed that the lunar geomagnetic variations could be explained only if ions, though undetected by radio probes, far outnumber electrons in the E layer, comprising ionized air occurring at 100–120 kilometers above the Earth. By considering the processes leading to the formation and destruction of the ions, they showed that negative ions are rare (contrary to the supposition of geomagneticians) and, consequently, mutual neutralization is unimportant. After examining and eliminating other possibilities, they postulated in 1947 that dissociative recombination, in which an electron combines with a molecular ion to give neutral products of dissociation, is rapid and is the process operative in the E layer; and they further postulated that this process is indirectly responsible for the loss of the atomic ions, which are certainly produced, these being first converted into molecular ions by charge-transfer collisions with molecules. They pointed out that the gas density in the F layer (the region of the atmosphere between 140 and 300 kilometers) is so low that charge transfer is the rate-limiting step which explains why an attachment law is simulated. Bates later noted the probable importance of ion-molecule reactions in the ionosphere. The correctness of the proposed general scheme has been firmly established.

The proposal that dissociative recombination is rapid was originally put forward rather hesitantly, because at the time such processes were erroneously regarded as occurring through the weak coupling between the nuclear and electronic motions. It was not until 1950 that Bates, visiting the United States, envisaged how dissociative recombination occurs and derived the basic formula for the rate coefficient.

During the course of this visit Bates collaborated with another European scientist, M. Nicolet, in the pioneering study of the effect of hydrogen on the photochemistry of an oxygen atmosphere. The study provided an explanation of the presence of the rotational-vibrational bands of hydroxyl in the nightglow. He also collaborated with L. Spitzer, Jr., in the pioneering study of the formation and destruction of CH and CH⁺ radicals in the interstellar medium. This later led him to give a semiclassical formulation of the process of radiative association. *See* SPITZER, LYMAN, JR.

Of the papers on atomic physics which Bates wrote while at University College, the most frequently cited is the one with his first research student, Agnete Damgaard, entitled "On the Calculation of the Absolute Strengths of Spectral Lines." The object was primarily to meet a pressing need of astrophysicists. Bates and Damgaard recognized that high accuracy could be achieved by representing the initial and final wave functions by the Coulomb functions corresponding to the observed term values, the divergence at the origin being avoided by a suitable truncation. They presented the results in a set of easily used tables covering most spectral lines of interest.

In 1951 Bates was appointed to the chair of applied mathematics at Queen's University, Belfast. To avoid duplication of research effort, Massey and he agreed that the strong London group would concentrate on electron collisions and the embryo Belfast group (shortly to be strengthened by A. Dalgarno, B. L. Moiseiwitsch, and A. L. Stewart) would concentrate on heavy-particle collisions.

The nonorthogonality of the initial and final wave functions in the charge-transfer problem makes the standard application of first-order perturbation theory unsatisfactory in that the calculated cross section is improperly dependent on the interaction potential adopted. Bates recognized this and showed how the difficulty might be avoided. In 1958 he also noticed that the perturbed stationary state (PSS) approximation, which N. F. Mott had introduced in 1931 for treating collisions between atomic systems, does not reduce to the Born approximation in the high-velocity limit as it should. With R. McCarroll he showed that the original version of the PSS approximation has two unrelated major defects and modified the approximation appropriately. In a well-known paper he and D. A. Williams drew attention to the remarkable extent to which the cross sections for slow collisions between atomic systems may be influenced by degeneracies in the united atom limit. The discovery has had widespread repercussions; for example, it is an essential element in the explanation of the Everhard effect. *See* MOTT, SIR NEVILL (FRANCIS).

Bates and A. R. Holt developed the powerful semiclassical (or eikonal) approximation for the treatment of inelastic collisions in 1966. He and D. S. F. Crothers devised a method of overcoming the difficulties which arise in this approximation if the classical trajectories associated with the various states of importance in a collision process differ significantly.

After the revival of interest in classical collision theory brought about by the work of M. Gryzinski, Bates and his associates took up the subject. They confirmed that even should the necessary conditions for the validity of classical mechanics not be met, the error introduced by using them may not be as serious as the error caused by the more drastic physical approximations which may be needed to make a quantal calculation feasible. For example, in the case of charge transfer between heavy atoms and light nuclei, Bates and R. A. Mapleton on modifying an old classical approximation due to L. H. Thomas obtained better results than any yet obtained by a quantal treatment. Again, in the case of ionization of complex atoms by electron impact, Bates using the classical binary collision approximation and correcting for the finite mean free path of the projectile electron within the atom obtained, with little labor, cross sections at least as accurate as those obtained by any quantal calculations which are yet practicable even with the aid of fast modern computers.

With A. E. Kingston and R. W. P. McWhirter, Bates gave the theory of, and did extensive calculations on, collisional-radiative recombination, the interlinked set of processes, dominant in dense plasmas, in which the energy of the recombining electron is carried away either by a colliding free electron or by emitted radiation. He and Kingston later proved that the relaxation times associated with the electronic and ionic temperatures are much shorter than the relaxation time associated with the plasma density. This is of considerable importance because it means that the two temperatures are not

independent variables—they are determined by the plasma density and the boundary conditions.

Bates and his associates also devoted much effort to investigating electron-ion and ion-ion recombination in an ambient gas. Taking the latter case, he, R. J. Moffett, and M. R. Flannery devised a quasi-equilibrium statistical theory giving essentially exactly the low-density limit to the rate coefficient for the Thomson three-body process. Bates showed in 1975 that the simple formula which P. Langevin derived in 1903 for the rate coefficient in the high-density region is correct, even though as had long been realized his neglect of diffusion is completely unjustified: thus the rate-limiting process is drift along the fixed field, not diffusion down a predetermined concentration gradient (rather the concentration gradient adjusts itself to give the required rate). With I. Mendaš he conducted computer-simulated experiments from the low to the high gas density limits. Specific cognizance was taken of binary recombination, the rate coefficient for which was discovered to depend on the gas density.

In 1978 Bates completed the much needed formulation of the transition-state theory for ion-molecule reactions. This entailed making allowance for the polarization attraction, for the existence of a long-lived collision complex, and for the absence of activation energy (for which it does not suffice simply to put the activation energy equal to zero.)

Bates was educated at the Royal Belfast Academical Institution, Queen's University, Belfast, and University College, London. In the period 1939–45 he was engaged on scientific work for the Admiralty. He was lecturer and then reader at University College in the period 1945–51 and thereafter held a chair at Queen's University, Belfast. He was elected a member of the Royal Irish Academy in 1952 (vice-president, 1976–77), fellow of the Royal Society in 1955, and honorary foreign member of the American Academy of Arts and Sciences in 1974. The compilation *Atomic Processes and Applications* (P. G. Burke and B. L. Moiseiwitsch, eds.) was published in 1976 in honor of his sixtieth birthday. He was awarded the Hughes Medal of the Royal Society in 1970, the Chree Medal of the Institute of Physics in 1973, and the Gold Medal of the Royal Astronomical Society in 1977; and was knighted in 1978. He edited *The Planet Earth, Quan-*

tum Theory, and *Atomic and Molecular Processes* and was editor in chief of *Planetary and Space Science* and is coeditor (with I. Estermann until 1973, with B. Bederson thereafter) of *Advances in Atomic and Molecular Physics.*

For background information *see* AERONOMY; AIRGLOW; ATOMIC PHYSICS; SCATTERING EXPERIMENTS, ATOMIC AND MOLECULAR in the McGraw-Hill Encyclopedia of Science and Technology. ∎

BATES, LESLIE FLEETWOOD
★ British physicist

Born Mar. 7, 1897, Kingswood, Bristol, England
Died Jan. 20, 1978, Nottingham, England

Either by accident or design, some scientists are moved at an early age to take a main and an abiding interest in a particular branch of a great subject. When Bates had barely turned 17, he found himself, almost by accident, acting as a student assistant in a minor research in magnetism at the University of Bristol. World War I interrupted his academic career, and for some 4 years he served as a commissioned radiographer with the British army in India before returning to Bristol to do research on magnetism in earnest. There he came under the influence of A. P. Chattock and collaborated with him in the first of a series of measurements of the gyromagnetic ratio, which started with the direct determination for iron and nickel and eventually culminated in Willie Sucksmith's brilliant determination of the ratios for many paramagnetic ions. These measurements were most opportune, for they almost coincided with the publication of papers on the inner quantum number and the Landé *g* factor.

Bates spent a 2-year interlude, 1922–24, in the Cavendish Laboratory, Cambridge, working under the supervision of Ernest Rutherford on a series of experiments in radioactivity. These included the determination of the ranges of alpha particles in the rare gases, later used by others in cloud chamber work. Bates was then appointed to the staff of University College, London. He regarded the Cambridge interlude as very valuable to him—for did not the great Rutherford himself say that it did nobody any harm to follow another branch of experimental work for a time? It was nevertheless only an important break in the orderly development of his magnetic work, to which he soon returned.

In London Bates became interested in the properties of manganese and its alloys. In those days pure manganese was a rarity, and he made his material by electrolyzing manganese into mercury and then boiling off the mercury in a vacuum. With such starting material he made several manganese compounds and, in particular, investigated the unusual electrical, magnetic, and thermal properties of MnAs. This material is still of considerable magnetic interest, and the original measurements have value after half a century. The method of preparing a pure metal by electrolysis into mercury was also used to prepare chromium, which was found to exhibit a small magnetic change, in the region of 40°C, of interest in the study of antiferromagnetism.

When, in 1936, Bates was appointed Lancashire-Spencer Professor in University College, Nottingham, he continued to study the electrical and magnetic properties of metals in dilute concentrations in mercury—in particular, iron, nickel, and cobalt. Some remarkable properties of nickel amalgams were thus discovered. It was unfortunate that these experiments were curtailed by the outbreak of World War II, as otherwise the production of iron particles for compressed powder magnets might have been started earlier.

Wartime work for the Interservices Research Bureau brought Bates into contact with special uses of permanent magnet materials. He devised methods for the measurement of their energy of magnetization relationships and measured the change in electrical resistivity caused by the application of magnetic fields either longitudinal or transverse to the axis of a specimen when carrying an electric current. The resistivity of every modern high-coercivity alloy so investigated always decreased on the application of a magnetic field in marked contrast to the behavior, for example, of cobalt, where a longitudinal field produced an increase and a transverse field produced a decrease in resistivity.

A keen interest in hysteresis phenomena caused Bates to start a series of direct measurements of the very small heat changes which accompany step-by-step changes of magnetization in ferromagnetic materials in low and moderate magnetic fields. His object was to obtain information concerning the magnetization processes which actually take place. In such experiments the temperature changes are of the order of 10^{-6} °C, and usually reversible and irreversible changes are superimposed. It was found that by using special techniques and highly sensitive apparatus the reversible changes could be measured separately. From the Leeds school came another, indirect method of measurement: the temperature of a specimen was changed quickly by some 2°C or so, and the accompanying change in magnetization was recorded. A theory of E. C. Stoner and Philip Rhodes showed a means of allowing for heat changes due solely to changes in spontaneous magnetization. Hence, experiment and theory could be successfully compared over higher-field regions where the magnetization process was probably that of domain vector rotations whose heat changes could be calculated from a knowledge of anisotropy constants. But in very low fields where vector rotation is very unlikely to be a principal magnetization process, several different processes are likely to occur simultaneously. A graphical method of examination of a wealth of experimental data was developed by Bates and A. J. Pacey, and this permitted consideration of the data in the light of a number of modern theories of coercivity for soft magnetic materials. It was found that each coercivity formula could be separated into two parts. One of these, denoted by β, was temperature-dependent, so that information concerning it might be derived from the magnetothermal measurements. In the case of nickel, it emerged that within certain field ranges $\beta = \gamma$ = the energy per unit area of a domain wall. *See* STONER, EDMUND CLIFTON.

The need for detailed knowledge of magnetization processes engendered a keen interest in their possible visualization by powder, electron microscope, and polarized light techniques. Consequently, in Nottingham new colloids with new techniques and methods of surface preparation of materials were developed. Emphasis was always placed on quantitative aspects of domain study. Numerical data were found for well-known closure domain systems—for example, for the echelon pattern discovered by D. H. Martin, for spike and tube systems, and for domains of reverse magnetization. The techniques were successfully applied to permanent magnet materials and to many ferrites.

Attempts were made to correlate domain powder patterns with corresponding magnetothermal measurements. Using a single-crystal specimen of silicon-iron, it was shown that in a state of technical saturation small spikes and domains of reverse magnetization gave rise to thermal changes which were indistinguishable from those due to vector rotations. In fact, the Bitter figure studies and the magnetothermal measurements provided evidence that very dissimilar domain structures often have essentially the same energy values. Many of the results of these researches were reviewed in the Guthrie Lecture which was delivered at the Nottingham International Conference on Magnetism, 1964.

Postwar developments in atomic energy produced a happy collaboration with Harwell in measuring the electric, magnetic, and thermal properties of pure uranium and thorium and their alloys with metals such as Nd, Ce, Pd, Nb, Zr, and Mo. This resulted in the collection of data which formed a basis for informed discussion of the valency behaviors and the electron band configurations of these metals.

Bates held strongly that a university instructor should be actively associated with the administration, teaching, and the general conduct of university affairs. He was for considerable periods a member of the governing bodies of the institutions he served. He was for many years a member of council of the Physical Society and president in 1950–52. He was actively concerned with the Association of University Teachers (England and Wales) and was president in 1937–38. He was awarded the Holweck Prize of the English and French Physical Societies in 1949, was elected a fellow of the Royal Society of London in 1950, and was created Commander of the Order of the British Empire in 1966 for work in civil defense.

Bates wrote *Modern Magnetism* (1939; 4th ed. reprint 1963).

For background information *see* HYSTERESIS, MAGNETIC; MAGNETIZATION; MANGANESE COMPOUND in the McGraw-Hill Encyclopedia of Science and Technology. ∎

BATES, ROGER GORDON
★ American chemist

Born May 20, 1912, Cummington, MA, U.S.A.

In a study of the properties of ionic solutions extending over many years, Bates developed improved techniques of high precision for the study of acid-base behavior, collected data of primary quality for numerous systems in aqueous and nonaqueous media, and elaborated a pH scale that formed the basis of an international standard for the measurement of this quantity. For his achievements, he received the American Chemical Society's Fisher Award in Analytical Chemistry in 1969.

Prior to the 1930s most data on solutions of electrolytes were subject to the uncertainties of semiprecise reference electrodes and the indeterminate liquid-junction potentials associated with their use. In graduate study and later as a postdoctoral research associate in the laboratory of H. S. Harned at Yale, Bates developed an interest in this problem and skills in the application of cells without liquid junction and the use of hydrogen electrodes, the primary reference for electrochemical measurements of ions in solution. At the National Bureau of Standards (NBS), where he spent the major portion of his scientific career, Bates carried out a long-range program to generate primary reference data for strong and weak electrolytes in aqueous, nonaqueous, and mixed solvents. In so doing, he devised new variations in electrochemical methodology.

About the time Bates arrived at NBS, the need for a precisely defined standard pH scale was being felt, especially in medical research and in the clinical laboratory. It was evident that pH should be related as directly as possible to the hydrogen electrode and to ionic activities and that liquid-junction potentials should be avoided. Nevertheless, theory was no guide in assigning numerical values to the activities of any ionic species. Recognizing that a standard pH scale must, for this reason, have a conventional or arbitrary basis, Bates embarked on a comparative study of reasonable conventions for its definition. He showed that standard pH values for reference solutions could be obtained, with an uncertainty no greater than ±0.01 unit, from measurements of cells without liquid junction, provided the ionic strength did not exceed 0.1. This approach led to the establishment of the NBS activity scale of pH, defined in terms of primary reference buffer solutions selected for their internal consistency. He then showed that the methods used to standardize pH in aqueous media could also be extended to other solvents, and similar scales for alcohol-water mixtures and for heavy water were set up.

It was not long, however, before a demand for reference solutions with a pH assigned to ±0.001 unit arose. To meet this need, it was necessary to select a single convention rather than the mean of several conventions, on which the earlier scales were based. Bates accomplished this important step in collaboration with E. A. Guggenheim of the United Kingdom and within the framework of the International Union of Pure and Applied Chemistry. The resulting standard was adopted, sometimes with slight modifica-

tion, by the major industrialized nations. For the first time, pH measurements in all countries of the world were placed on a common basis, and accurate comparisons were possible.

During the early 1970s, at the University of Florida, Bates's studies of pH and nonaqueous solvents took a new direction, with an experimental program elucidating the role of ion-solvent interactions in accounting for the effect of changes of solvent on acid-base equilibria. By this time, scales of ionic activity had acquired a new significance, following the development during the 1960s of a new breed of electrodes selective for a variety of ions other than the hydrogen ion. Like the pH glass electrode, these ion-selective electrodes responded to ionic activity and required standard reference solutions for their calibration. Bates showed that extension of the pH convention to concentrated solutions, in which ion-selective electrodes were often used, was not a suitable expedient. Instead, he and R. A. Robinson put forth a new method which ascribed specific differences among ionic activities to the different degrees of hydration of each ionic species. This approach was successful, and reference solutions for the precise standardization of several different types of ion-selective electrodes were established.

Born on a Massachusetts farm, Bates received the B.S. degree from the University of Massachusetts in 1934 and the Ph.D. from Duke University in 1937. Two years of postdoctoral research as Sterling fellow at Yale University were followed by an appointment to the staff of NBS in Washington. His career there spanned 30 years; he served first as research chemist and later as chief of the Electrochemical Analysis Section. He spent a year (1953–54) as a visiting scientist at the University of Zurich, and in 1962 studied for a shorter period in Paris and Oxford. In 1969 he became professor of chemistry at the University of Florida. Bates received the highest award of the U.S. Department of Commerce, the Gold Medal for Exceptional Service, in 1957. His contributions to solution chemistry and electroanalysis brought him the Hillebrand Award of the Chemical Society of Washington in 1956 and the American Chemical Society Award in Analytical Chemistry in 1969. He was highly involved in international standardization activities in the field of chemistry, and during 1953–59 and 1971–79 chaired the

Commission on Electroanalytical Chemistry of the International Union of Pure and Applied Chemistry.

Bates wrote *Electrometric pH Determination* (1954) and *Determination of pH: Theory and Practice* (1964; rev. ed. 1973).

For background information *see* ANALYTICAL CHEMISTRY; ELECTROCHEMISTRY; PH in the McGraw-Hill Encyclopedia of Science and Technology. ∎

BATTERSBY, ALAN RUSHTON
★ British organic chemist

Born Mar. 4, 1925, Leigh, Lancashire, England

From an early enthusiasm for the rich chemistry of natural substances, Battersby became fascinated by the problem of how these often complex molecules were biosynthesized. With carbon-14 becoming available in Europe early in the 1950s (and later tritium), it was possible to discover, often in precise detail, the many steps involved, for example, in the natural pathway to morphine. This first work on higher plants led to the elucidation of pathways in bacteria, algae, and mammals.

The initial experiments were on the biosynthesis of morphine in the opium poppy. Chemical arguments and structural relations allowed the selection of likely substances known to be available in living things (amino acids and their relatives) which could possibly act as biochemical precursors of morphine. But the tests of these relationships required syntheses of the possible precursors in a form specifically labeled with carbon-14 at one or more known sites. The next hurdle was to find out how to introduce these labeled molecules into the biosynthetic "machinery" of the plants, and a range of effective methods was developed. Precursors which were incorporated in these ways into morphine made it radioactive. By controlled chemical degradation, it was then possible to show the sites of labeling in the morphine molecule. Gradually these experiments pinpointed a set of substances which stood as markers on the biosynthetic pathway. Then a similar combination of synthesis, incorporation experiments, and degradation allowed Battersby and his colleagues to probe forward and backward on the pathway from each marker until the complete sequence was uncovered.

This powerful approach was strengthened still further by developing multiple labeling methods and by testing stereochemical relations between precursor and final product. For many of the biosynthetic pathways, key representatives of the intermediates which had been discovered by the labeling experiments were isolated in pure form from the living system. A considerable number of biosynthetic sequences in higher plants were thus mapped out over the 1954–68 period, including that producing colchicine, the agent which arrests cell division, and those leading to the medicinally important indole alkaloids.

From 1968, the efforts of Battersby and his group turned to studies of enzyme-mediated reactions and to work on the biosynthesis of the pigments of life. The former effort aimed to establish a network of stereochemical relationships for the action of families of enzymes. Thus, he wanted to know whether all enzymes which decarboxylate α-amino acids, or which oxidize amines, work in the same stereochemical sense. The decarboxylases have turned out to be stereochemically uniform, but not the amine oxidases; the latter are responsible in part for control of the levels of highly active amines in brain, liver, and plasma.

What have been called the pigments of life comprise chlorophylls, heme, cytochromes, and vitamin B_{12}; they are involved in much of the fundamental chemistry of life on this planet. It was known by the late 1960s that the first three groups of pigments are all biosynthesized from the same parent macrocycle, uroporphyrinogen-III, and later vitamin B_{12} was also shown to have the same parent. The key importance of uroporphyrinogen-III thus stood out. Remarkably, its structure was an unexpected one which had arisen because living systems had developed, over evolutionary time, some way of switching the expected chemistry. Progress here depended on labeling with the stable isotope, carbon-13, combined with nuclear magnetic resonance spectroscopy. It was a crucial decision to work in this way, for not only was it possible to determine complex labeling patterns without degradation, but this approach also allowed C-C bond-making and bond-breaking processes to be probed.

Heme was the first target, and the carbon-13 approach led to an understanding of the nature of the single rearrangement step which produces uroporphyrinogen-III; chickens, bacteria, and algae were all shown to biosynthesize uroporphyrinogen-III in exactly the same way. Further synthetic work and enzymic experiments proved that the single rearrangement occurs after straightforward head-to-tail assembly of the four identical primary building blocks.

For vitamin B_{12}, vast numbers of pathways were possible, so it was essential to gain clues by detecting intermediates. Eventually, in collaboration with Soviet microbiologists, two intermediates were isolated, and they were shown to be partially C-methylated macrocyles (isobacteriochlorins). Excitingly, one of the two was found to be identical with the metal-free form of the prosthetic group of sulfite reductase enzymes which had been isolated earlier in the United States and was of partially known structure. This evolutionary and biosynthetic link between vitamin B_{12} and the sulfite-reducing enzymes illustrated once again what had been shown by the earlier studies to be a characteristic feature of nature's synthetic work, namely, that complex substances are often built by molding and modifying the available clay.

After graduating from the University of Manchester (M.Sc., 1946), Battersby moved to the University of St. Andrews (Ph.D., 1949) for his first academic appointment. He studied at the Rockefeller Institute, New York (1950), and at the University of Illinois (1951) before moving in 1954 to the University of Bristol (D.Sc., 1962). From 1962 to 1969 he was professor of organic chemistry at the University of Liverpool, and then he assumed a chair at Cambridge in 1969 (Sc.D., 1975). Mostly with coauthors, he had written about 250 papers as of early 1979. He was elected a fellow of the Royal Society in 1966, and was awarded their Davy Medal in 1977. From the Chemical Society he received the Corday-Morgan (1959), Tilden (1963), Hügo Müller (1972), Flintoff (1975), and Natural Products (1979) medals. The University of Zurich awarded him the Paul Karrer Medal (1977). He received honorary doctorates from St. Andrews and the Rockefeller University in 1977.

For background information *see* BIOCHEMISTRY; BIOLOGICAL SPECIFICITY; TRACER, RADIOACTIVE in the McGraw-Hill Encyclopedia of Science and Technology. ∎

BEACH, FRANK AMBROSE

★ American psychobiologist

Born Apr. 13, 1911, Emporia, KS, U.S.A.

As a graduate student in experimental psychology, Beach was profoundly influenced by Karl S. Lashley and was led to concentrate in the area of physiological psychology. His doctoral research concerned brain function and instinctive behavior in mammals. Contemporary theory held that learning depended upon the cerebral cortex, whereas instinctive (unlearned) behavior was mediated by lower brain centers. Beach's initial experiments showed that the innately organized pat-

tern of maternal behavior in primiparous rats was disorganized following removal of large amounts of the neocortex. Courtship and mating in males of the same species were reduced or abolished by this type of brain injury. Apparently, those parts of the central nervous system already known to mediate learning were also involved in unlearned behavior patterns.

Investigations of brain mechanisms and sexual behavior led Beach next to questions concerning the role of gonadal hormones—their involvement in mating activities and their relationship to the central nervous system. Systematic studies of various species of rodents demonstrated a clear-cut sexual dimorphism with respect to the involvement of the cerebral cortex and hormones from the sex glands. The mating activities of females appeared to be relatively independent of higher nervous centers and fairly directly controlled by ovarian secretions, whereas analogous behavior in males was powerfully influenced by the cortex and to a limited degree independent of testicular hormone.

Extension of these investigations to include more highly evolved species of mammals resulted in formulation of a working hypothesis describing the possible course of evolutionary changes in the physiological mechanisms controlling sexual life. Beach theorized that in the course of evolution of higher mammals (culminating in the Primates, including humans) there occurred a progressive increase in the extent to which mechanisms within the neocortex shaped and directed sexual activities, and a concomitant decrease in the importance of ovarian and testicular chemical products.

This hypothesis helped to explain a number of differences between the characteristics of sexual behavior as it was manifested at different levels in the mammalian scale. For example, the fact that individual learning and experience seem to make a much more pronounced contribution to the sexual psychology of Primates than to that of rodents and carnivores was tentatively related to the proportionately greater dependence of Primates upon cortical mechanisms. This same evolutionary shift in balance accounted for the apparent reduction in the degree to which Primate sexual expression depends upon gonadal hormones.

Continuation of the experimental program involved studies of more and more

vertebrate species in an attempt to elucidate the importance of three major groups of factors affecting sexual activity. These were the central nervous system, the endocrine system, and the individual's previous experience and learning. Beach aimed to develop a broadly comparative theory that would take into account species' differences as reflections of past evolutionary change, and at the same time would illuminate general laws or principles which are applicable to the vertebrate class.

Beach majored in education at Kansas State Teacher College at Emporia, where he received his B.S. in 1933 and his M.S. in psychology in 1934. He took his Ph.D. in psychology at the University of Chicago in 1940. From 1936 to 1942 he was assistant curator in the department of experimental biology at the American Museum of Natural History, New York, and from 1942 to 1946 curator and chair of the department of animal behavior. He was professor (1946–52) and Sterling Professor (1952–58) of psychology at Yale University. In 1958 he became professor of psychology at the University of California at Berkeley, and eventually Faculty Research Lecturer. Beach received the Warren Medal of the Society of Experimental Psychologists in 1951 and the Distinguished Scientific Contribution Award of the American Psychological Association in 1958. He was elected to the National Academy of Sciences in 1949 and to the American Philosophical Society in 1961.

For background information *see* INSTINCTIVE BEHAVIOR; PSYCHOLOGY, PHYSIOLOGICAL AND EXPERIMENTAL in the McGraw-Hill Encyclopedia of Science and Technology. ∎

BEADLE, GEORGE WELLS

☆ American geneticist

Born Oct. 22, 1903, Wahoo, NE, U.S.A.

Working with the biochemist E. L. Tatum, Beadle demonstrated that in hereditary transmission a single gene was responsible for the development of a single enzyme and that the smallest details of the species' biochemical reactions were governed by particular genes. By putting modern genetics on a chemical basis, he was in part responsible for the development of the new field of biochemical genetics. For their work in proving that genes affect heredity by controlling cell chemistry, Beadle and Tatum were jointly awarded the 1958 Nobel Prize in medicine or physiology. Joshua Lederberg, a former student of Tatum's, shared this Nobel Prize for his related work on the genetic mechanism of bacteria. *See* LEDERBERG, JOSHUA; TATUM, EDWARD LAWRIE.

Long before the experiments in which Beadle participated, it was known that hereditary characters are transmitted from parents to offspring by means of special elements in the ovum and spermatozoon, called genes. The resulting organism receives from each parent certain characteristics that are determined by this genetic material. The cells that together constitute the organism will each contain a full set of gene characteristics of the species.

The characteristics transmitted from generation to generation by the genes represent a bewildering multiplicity of variation in function and structure. Until the efforts of Beadle and Tatum, who demonstrated the possibility of chemical analysis of such structures, it was impossible to trace straightforward lines that could serve as a background for an experimental study.

In the early 1900s Thomas Hunt Morgan studied mutant characters in *Drosophila melanogaster* and confirmed the theory of linkage in genetics—the tendency for genes close together on a chromosome to be transmitted together. Later, Calvin B. Bridges supported this linkage theory by demonstrating that the aberrant behavior

of sex-linked genes in *Drosophila* is paralleled by the same aberrant behavior of the chromosomes that determine sex.

Up to this time, researchers had been concerned mostly with the mechanisms by which genes and chromosomes are transmitted. Sir Archibald Garrod, however, was one of the earliest to investigate the nature of the genes. He studied congenital diseases, which he called "inborn errors of metabolism," and in particular the disease of alkaptonuria, characterized by the excretion of homogentisic acid in urine, which makes the urine turn dark on exposure to air. Garrod theorized that this heritable disorder was the result of the lack of a "ferment" (now called enzyme) which catalyzes the normal action and that the lack is caused by a defect in a single recessive gene. In 1923 he wrote: "We may further conceive that the splitting of the benzene ring of homogentisic acid in normal metabolism is the work of a special enzyme, that in congenital alkaptonuria this enzyme is wanting." Although Garrod's theory made little impression on scientists at the time, it was the unrecognized beginning of biochemical genetics.

Beadle, working with the biologist Boris Ephrussi in 1935, advanced a hypothesis like that of Garrod, namely, that genes concerned with eye-pigment formation in *Drosophila* were in immediate control of chemical reactions via specific enzymes. These investigations led directly to Beadle's subsequent research with Tatum.

At that time there were approximately 26 separate eye-color genes known in *Drosophila*. Making a series of transplants of mutant eyes into wild-type hosts, Beadle tried to discover the influence of "diffusible substances," in the host, on transplanted eyes. Specifically, would cinnabar eyes (a bright red eye color like vermilion but differentiated by a second chromosome recessive gene) and vermilion eyes when transplanted into wild-type larvae become wild-type or maintain their initial characters? The result was that the transplanted eyes were wild-type. In a similar experiment these researchers discovered that the vermilion mutant gene blocks one reaction and the cinnabar mutant gene interrupts a second. A vermilion eye in a cinnabar host makes pigment because it can, in its own tissues, convert the vermilion substance into cinnabar substance and pigment. In it, the second type of reaction is not blocked. This scheme involves the following concepts: (1) a se-

quence of two gene-regulated chemical reactions, one gene identified with each; (2) the accumulation of intermediates prior to blocked reactions; and (3) the ability of the mutant blocked in the first reaction to make use of an intermediate accumulated as a result of a genetic interruption of the second reaction. Beadle, in his Nobel Prize acceptance speech, stated: "What was later called the one-gene–one-enzyme concept was clearly in our minds at this time, although, as I remember, we did not so designate it."

The traditional tools of the geneticists had been corn and fruit flies. However, seeking a simple organism for his work with Tatum, Beadle remembered a lecture he had heard by B. O. Dodge on the red bread mold, *Neurospora crassa*. This simple organism has many advantages for the scientist over either corn or *Drosophila*. It has a shorter generation time and produces many more progeny. It is grown easily in a culture medium containing sugar, salts, and the vitamin biotin. For their experiments, it was decided to produce mutations using x-rays, since Beadle believed that the best way to study the mystery of the chromosomes was to find some mutation that affected the chemical behavior of an organism. By producing a large number of such mutations and by means of an analysis of the material, Beadle and Tatum succeeded in demonstrating that the body substances are synthesized in the individual cell step by step in long chains of chemical reactions, and that genes control these processes by individually regulating definite steps in the chains.

Neurospora mates and reproduces sexually and can also grow asexually; thus, large quantities can be produced from a single spore. Asexual spores were irradiated, then crossed with a strain of the opposite mating type, and the spores thus formed by sexual reproduction were laid out on a sheet of agar jelly containing the minimum nutrients. From this batch some sprouted and grew normally, showing no effect of the x-rays; some had received too much radiation and were dead; and a few sprouted but failed to grow. In an attempt to determine what was lacking in this latter batch, 1000 spore cultures were fed special diets containing vitamins, amino acids, and other growth-stimulating chemicals.

The 299th culture showed that the addition of vitamin B_6, pyridoxine, was sufficient to restore the ailing strain to proper growth. When that strain was mated with the parental strain, the defect was transmitted to the next nonirradiated generation in the expected mendelian manner: four mutant and four nonmutant spores in each spore sac, proving the involvement of a single mutated gene. Beadle and Tatum pointed out that radiation had damaged a specific gene that had been responsible for producing an enzyme essential for the production of vitamin B_6 out of the simple nutrients. Later trials with other affected genes produced strains requiring other dietary supplements for proper growth. Beadle compared this need on the part of *Neurospora* to the diabetic's need for insulin when it is not manufactured by the body.

Following their initial success, Beadle and Tatum continued their studies and traced the defects they had created in the *Neurospora* to interference with intermediate metabolism in the formation of amino acids and vitamins. Their work was credited with solving some of the basic riddles of heredity and opening new vistas in cancer research. Their methods were utilized during World War II in the manufacture of penicillin, also a mold product, resulting in a fourfold increase in production at a critical period. Beadle's work has also had great value for scientists who have sought to control genetic diseases by chemical treatment. For example, phenylketonuria (PKU), a heritable ailment that results in feeble-mindedness, is caused by inability to convert phenylalanine into the amino acid tyrosine. When detected soon after birth, PKU can be controlled by reducing the amount of phenylalanine in the diet.

After Beadle retired from academic administration in 1968, he returned to additional studies of the origin of *Zea mays*, Indian corn, which R. A. Emerson and he had concluded was derived from the Mexican plant called teosinte assigned by early plant taxonomists to the genus *Euchaena*, species *mexicana*. This conclusion was not accepted by Paul C. Mangelsdorf and associates, who later had postulated that modern corn was derived from a wild *Zea* much like the oldest archeological specimens of primitive corn found in a dry cave in the Tehuacan Valley of Mexico and carbon-13-dated as having grown some 7000 years before the present. For many reasons Beadle did not accept this origin and subsequently spent the major portion of his research efforts reexamining an

array of evidence judged to support the Emerson view that modern corn was selected from teosinte by Indians of Mexico beginning perhaps 10,000–20,000 years ago. *See* MANGELSDORF, PAUL CHRISTOPH.

Beadle received his B.Sc. and M.Sc. at the College of Agriculture of the University of Nebraska in 1926 and his Ph.D. in genetics at Cornell University in 1931. He was a National Research Council fellow and then instructor at the California Institute of Technology from 1931 to 1935. After a year in Paris he was an assistant professor of genetics at Harvard (1936–37), professor of biology at Stanford (1937–46), and professor of biology and chairperson of the Division of Biology at the California Institute of Technology (1946–61). In 1961 he became president of the University of Chicago, retiring in 1968. He was elected to the National Academy of Sciences in 1944.

Beadle wrote *An Introduction to Genetics,* with A. H. Sturtevant (1939), *Genetics and Modern Biology* (1963), and *The Language of Life: An Introduction to Genetics,* with his wife, Muriel B. Beadle.

For background information *see* GENETICS in the McGraw-Hill Encyclopedia of Science and Technology. ■

BEAMS, JESSE WAKEFIELD
★ American physicist

Born Dec. 25, 1898, Belle Plaine, KS, U.S.A.
Died July 23, 1977, Charlottesville, VA, U.S.A.

Beams started his research with an investigation of the initial stages of the electrical breakdown in gases and, principally, the initiation of the electric spark in air. He soon found that in order to proceed properly, methods with much-higher-time resolving-power capability had to be developed for observing the light emitted, as well as the potential and current in the initial stages of the breakdown. For measuring the potential and current during the breakdown, he developed transmission line techniques, but later employed the cathode-ray oscillograph. For observing the light emitted in the breakdown, he improved and modified the Kerr cell light shutter, previously used by G. Abraham and A. N. Lemoine and by Lord Rayleigh,

until it could be made to open and close in less than 10^{-9} second at any desired time. He modified and stabilized the air-supported, air-driven turbine of Henriot and Huguenard, and used it to spin a high-speed rotating mirror, with which optical phenomena occurring in less than 10^{-9} second could be observed. With these devices it was possible to photograph the light emitted in the initial stages of the electrical spark in gases at various pressures and in a high vacuum. In some cases it was possible to measure the propagation of luminosity in the discharge, as well as the first appearance of the various spectral lines in the discharge. With the same techniques he found that the time lag in the fluorescence in some substances was very small ($\sim 10^{-8}$ second).

In the mid-1920s many physicists believed that the light quantum had a finite length of at least 3 meters. In collaboration with E. O. Lawrence, Beams used the Kerr cell and rotating mirror techniques to show that if the light quantum had a finite length, it was less than about 10 centimeters. They showed that photoelectrons were emitted from a metal surface in less than 10^{-9} second after the light quanta struck the surface—that is, any time lag in the photoelectric effect was less than 10^{-9} second. Later these phenomena became understandable from the new quantum mechanics and the Heisenberg indetermination principle. *See* LAWRENCE, ERNEST ORLANDO.

Soon after returning to the University of Virginia from Yale, Beams became in-

terested in the production and use of high-energy particles, and in collaboration with his colleague L. B. Snoddy and students W. T. Ham and H. Trotter he developed a new type of linear particle accelerator. The ions were accelerated down a long tube by an electrical field, which was made to move with the same speed of the ions, like a surfboard riding an ocean wave. Both ions and electrons with energies in excess of 10^6 electronvolts were produced, but the work was terminated by the approach of World War II.

In the late 1920s Beams became interested in the physical properties of some of the proteins which T. Svedberg had recently shown to consist of very large molecules by means of his ultracentrifuge. Most of these large-molecular-weight substances existed in dilute solutions and were mixed with many other substances. Calculations indicated that a centrifuge mounted on the air-supported, air-driven turbine previously developed for spinning the rotating mirror should be able to purify all of these substances. However, Beams found that in many cases even though the centrifugal field was greater than 10^6 times gravity, true molecular sedimentation did not occur because of convection currents induced by thermal gradients on the centrifuge. Fortunately, however, even in these high centrifugal fields, the substances studied were not deactivated or harmed in any observable way. The thermal gradients in the centrifuge were traced to the effect of air friction on the rotor, which in 1934 led Beams and his student E. G. Pickels to develop the first centrifuge which spun in a high vacuum (10^{-6} torr; 133 micronewtons per square meter). In this ultracentrifuge the residual air pressure surrounding the rotor was so low that air friction was negligible and true molecular sedimentation was obtained. Many of the substances of importance in biology, medicine, and chemistry have been purified and characterized by ultracentrifuges based upon this original prototypal vacuum-type ultracentrifuge. By adapting the vacuum-type ultracentrifuge to the separation of gases and vapors, Beams and his students A. V. Masket and C. Skarstrom obtained in 1935 the first separation of isotopes by centrifuging. Soon after the discovery of uranium fission, Beams, Snoddy, and their students employed the centrifuge for the successful separation of the uranium isotopes.

With F. T. Holmes, Beams magneti-

cally suspended and spun a small steel rod inside a sealed vacuum chamber. Immediately following World War II, this magnetic suspension method of freely supporting and spinning ferromagnetic bodies was further developed and stabilized by Beams's group at the University of Virginia, and it became the essential element in his magnetically suspended vacuum-type ultracentrifuge. There are two principal centrifuge methods for determining the molecular weights of substances in solution. In the first method the rate of sedimentation is measured, and in the second method the density gradient across the centrifuge cell is determined after equilibrium between sedimentation and diffusion has been obtained. This second, or equilibrium, method is much more reliable, but it requires the centrifuge rotor to be free of fluctuation in speed and temperature variations to a much greater extent than in the first method. The magnetically suspended vacuum-type ultracentrifuge solved these problems and became an ideal equilibrium ultracentrifuge. In collaboration with D. W. Kupke and his students, Beams was able to determine the molecular weights of a large number of substances, including many proteins and heavy viruses, with an absolute precision of between 1 and 0.1 percent over the molecular weight range from 10^2 to 10^8.

In order to determine the absolute value of the molecular weight of a substance by centrifuging, it is necessary to know its partial specific volume. Also, the partial specific volume itself is of importance in characterizing a molecule. Unfortunately, standard methods of measuring the partial specific volume require more of the pure material than is usually available in the case of most of the interesting, biologically important compounds. Beams solved this problem by devising the magnetic densitometer, with which the partial specific volumes are routinely determined with a precision of 0.1 percent, and the solution densities are determined to 1 part in 10^5 with less than 1 percent solutions 0.3 milliliter in volume. With this precision interesting variations in partial specific volume were found with changes in pH and with pressure.

The magnetically suspended centrifuge provides an excellent method of testing the tensile strengths of materials, because the clamps on the test specimen, which may produce stress concentrations, are

eliminated. With this method, in collaboration with his students, Beams discovered that very thin films of metals become much stronger than the bulk material. They were able to measure the absolute value of the adhesion between the film and the rotor. Furthermore, they measured the tensile strength of a number of fine fibers and so-called iron whiskers from room temperature down to liquid helium temperature with increased reliability. In some of these experiments the rotor speed exceeded 1,500,000 revolutions per second and produced centrifugal fields over 10^9 times gravity. The almost negligible friction in the magnetically suspended rotor in a high vacuum enabled Beams and his students to measure with increased precision the pressure of light, the angular momentum of light, and the gravitational constant G in the Newton gravitational relation below.

$$F = G \frac{m_1 m_2}{d^2}$$

Born on a farm in Kansas, Beams received an A.B. from Fairmount College (now Wichita State University) in 1921, an M.S. in mathematics from the University of Wisconsin in 1922, and a Ph.D. in physics from the University of Virginia in 1925. He was an instructor in physics and mathematics at the present Auburn University in 1922–23. He held a National Research Council Fellowship at Virginia in 1925–26 and at Yale in 1926–27, after which he was an instructor at Yale during 1927–28. He then returned to the University of Virginia, where he served as associate professor, professor, department chairperson, and Smith Professor of Physics. He served as president of the American Physical Society, vice-president of the American Philosophical Society, and vice-president and chair of Section B of the American Association for the Advancement of Science. He was elected to the National Academy of Sciences in 1943 and the American Academy of Arts and Sciences in 1949. Beams received the Potts Medal in 1942, the Thomas Jefferson Award in 1955, the John Scott Award in 1956, and the Lewis Award in 1958 for his work with ultracentrifuges. During World War II he served as a principal investigator with the Office of Scientific Research and Development and did research on isotope separation, military weapons, and ramjets. He later served on several government committees, including the General Advisory Committee of the Atomic Energy Commission.

For background information *see* Centrifugation; Isotope (stable) separation; Quantum mechanics; Spark, electric; Ultracentrifuge in the McGraw-Hill Encyclopedia of Science and Technology. ∎

BÉKÉSY, GEORG VON
☆ American physicist

***Born** June 3, 1889, Budapest, Hungary*
***Died** June 13, 1972, Honolulu, HI, U.S.A.*

While performing research in physiological acoustics, Békésy determined the physical events that occur in all strategically important points within the transmission system of the ear. His discoveries resulted in the development of refined diagnostic procedures and treatments for diseases of the ear. In recognition of his achievements in the study of the hearing processes, particularly for his discoveries concerning the mechanics of the inner ear, Békésy was awarded the 1961 Nobel Prize for physiology or medicine, the first physicist to receive this honor.

The first study of the hearing processes was made by the German physicist and physiologist H. L. F. von Helmholtz, who in 1857 proposed the resonance theory of hearing. According to this theory, the transverse fibers of the basilar membrane in the cochlea of the inner ear acted as tuned resonators. Each of these fibers was tuned to a particular frequency, and when a sound of a given frequency reached the

ear it caused a particular fiber to vibrate. Subsequent theories of hearing differed in the manner in which the basilar membrane vibrated when a sound wave struck the eardrum. One variation relied on the generation of standing waves and another on traveling waves. A third variation, called the telephone theory, was proposed by the English physiologist William Rutherford in 1886. This theory assumed that the entire cochlear partition moved as a whole.

In 1923, while working at the Research Laboratory of the Hungarian Telephone System, Békésy began his researches in physiological acoustics. His initial studies concerned themselves with the eardrum. He was subsequently led to the intuitive conclusion that the basilar membrane would exhibit traveling waves when one section of it was put into motion by an alternating pressure. Focusing his attention on the elasticity and friction of the basilar membrane, for the next 2 decades he measured and mapped vibration amplitudes and phases for sinusoidal forces applied to the stapes footplate, and determined the physical constants responsible for the vibration patterns. When he had completed these observations and made measurements of such variables of elasticity as the volume elasticity of the cochlear partition, he constructed a mechanical model of the cochlea. The model, whose vibratory behavior was identical to that of the cochlear partition, was made of a rubber membrane stretched over a metal frame. By varying the thickness of the membrane, and thus its volume elasticity, and pressing a pointed object into it, Békésy found he could produce deformation patterns that corresponded to those predicted by the four theories proposed for the vibration of the basilar membrane. He then realized that he could decide which of the theories represented the function of the inner ear by further measurements of the volume elasticity of the cochlear partition. These measurements confirmed that vibrations of the eardrum transmitted to the fluid of the cochlea set up traveling waves in the basilar membrane.

Békésy then proceeded to build an enlarged model of the cochlea. This consisted of a water-filled plastic tube and a membrane 30 centimeters long. This device, which exhibited traveling waves of the same type as those seen in the human ear, had a usable frequency range of two

octaves. After some experimentation with this apparatus, Békésy decided to add a nerve supply. The use of a frog skin for this purpose had earlier proved to be impractical. However, he found that by placing his forearm against the model he could sense the vibrations as they traveled along the membrane. He discovered in this way that although the waves traveled the length of the 30-centimeter membrane with almost unchanged amplitude, his arm sensed the vibration in only a 2- to 3-centimeter-long section of the membrane. He further found that when the frequency of the stimulus was increased, the section of sensed vibration moved toward the end of the model that represented the stapes footplate, while the section moved in the opposite direction when the frequency was decreased. Hence, he realized, the cochlea acts as a neuromechanical frequency analyzer.

In addition to his theoretical studies of the hearing processes, Békésy also developed a new type of audiometer. Announced in 1946, the patient-operated instrument has applications other than the testing of the hearing function. For example, it can be used to detect the change in the light sensitivity of the eye during adaptation to darkness.

The son of a diplomat, Békésy studied chemistry at the University of Berne in Switzerland. He then attended the University of Budapest in Hungary, receiving his Ph.D. in physics in 1923. In that year he joined the Research Laboratory of the Hungarian Telephone System, which was operated by the post office. He remained there until 1946. During that period he spent 1 year, during 1926 and 1927, at the Central Laboratory of the Siemens and Halske A. G. in Berlin, Germany. He was a professor of experimental physics at the University of Budapest from 1939 to 1946. In the latter year he went to Sweden, where he became associated with the Karolinska Institute in Stockholm. Although he emigrated to the United States in 1947, Békésy continued his association with the institute until 1952. He became a research assistant at the Psychoacoustic Laboratory of Harvard University in 1947, and in 1949 he was appointed senior research fellow in psychophysics there. He was elected to the National Academy of Sciences in 1956.

Békésy wrote *Experiments in Hearing* (English translation, 1960) and *Sensory Inhibition* (1967).

For background information *see* AUDI-OMETRY; EAR (VERTEBRATE); HEARING (HUMAN) in the McGraw-Hill Encyclopedia of Science and Technology. ■

BELLMAN, RICHARD
☆ American mathematician

Born Aug. 26, 1920, New York, NY, U.S.A.

Bellman's study of multistage decision processes led him to put forth the theory of dynamic programming, which provided a new approach for dealing with deterministic processes, such as the calculus of variations, and afforded a basis for the consideration of stochastic processes, such as Markovian decision processes, and adaptive processes. In particular, the theory led to work on initial value problems.

The problems arising from the control of systems led Bellman to investigations in which he used the calculus of variations and dynamic programming. His monograph on the subject (1958) was translated into Russian and was influential in the Soviet Union. Bellman's work on control theory was a natural outgrowth of his dissertation on stability theory at Princeton.

Bellman used invariant embedding in an innovative approach to mathematical physics and to many aspects of mathematical analysis, replacing two-point boundary value problems with initial value problems and thereby achieving a more

direct calculation of the solution and greatly simplifying the analysis. In his early work in this area, he applied the method to problems of radiative transfer.

Among other theories in Bellman's mathematical work were time lag processes, branching processes, and differential and integral inequalities.

Beginning about 1950, Bellman became interested in the capabilities of digital computers. On the one hand, he was drawn to a study of numerical algorithms and simulation; many of his investigations in this area were concerned with dynamic programming. On the other hand, he developed a continuing interest in artificial intelligence and, sometimes in collaboration with others, published numerous works on the subject.

Bellman's work was marked by a concern for the application of mathematics to other fields. For example, applications of mathematics to engineering and economics could be found in his theory of dynamic programming and in his invariant embedding approach. Applications to mathematical physics occurred in his work on radiative transfer, and his work on simulation was relevant to the business world. There were many implications in the field of medicine: he proposed mathematical models applicable to pharmacokinetics, cardiology, radiation dosimetry, scan-rescan processes, neurophysiology, and simulation in psychiatry.

Later work in mathematical physics was related to electromagnetic theory and optics, and the use of computers and simulation in psychiatry and medical interviewing was also investigated.

Bellman and John Wilkinson carried out studies on the application of mathematics to the social sciences during a period of several years, and Bellman dealt, in addition, with the general question of the interaction between mathematics and society. His interest in education, in particular, in the teaching of mathematics, prompted the publication of textbooks on the subject. With E. Stanley Lee, he turned to the energy issue, investigating in turn, coal gasification and nuclear, solar, tidal, and geothermal energy.

Bellman received his B.A. at Brooklyn College in 1941, his M.A. at the University of Wisconsin in 1943, and his Ph.D. at Princeton University in 1946. He was assistant professor of mathematics at Princeton (1946–48) and associate professor at Stanford University (1948–52).

From 1953 to 1965 he was employed by the RAND Corporation in Santa Monica, CA, and then became professor of mathematics, electrical engineering, and medicine at the University of Southern California. Bellman was awarded the first Norbert Weiner Prize in applied mathematics by the American Mathematical Society and the Society for Industrial and Applied Mathematics (1970), the first Dickson Prize by Carnegie-Mellon University (1970), and the John von Neumann Theory Award by the Institute of Management Sciences and the Operations Research Society of America (1976). He was a fellow of the American Academy of Arts and Sciences and a member of the National Academy of Engineering (1977).

The author of 30 books and 7 monographs, Bellman also published more than 600 research papers. He served as editor of two journals, *Journal of Mathematical Analysis and Applications* and *Mathematical Biosciences,* and of the series "Mathematics in Science and Engineering." ■

BELOZERSKY, ANDREI NIKOLAEVITCH
★ Soviet biochemist and molecular biologist

Born Aug. 29, 1905, Tashkent, Russia
Died Jan. 2, 1973, Moscow, U.S.S.R.

The main fields of Belozersky's research were nucleic acids and nucleoproteins of higher and lower plants, including the bacteria. He started his research in the early 1930s. At that time nucleic acids were considered to be no more than one of the numerous groups of substances of biological origin. No one could then anticipate that nucleic acids, according to their biological importance, could stand on a level with such important and highly specific components of living matter as proteins. It was even considered that the animal organisms had their own peculiar thymonucleic acid or, as it is called today, deoxyribonucleic acid (DNA), and that the plant organisms had their own yeast nucleic acid or, in modern terminology, ribonucleic acid (RNA). As far back as 1924 R. Feulgen and H. Rossenbeck with the aid of the cytochemical reaction, which they had worked out, demonstrated the presence of DNA in the nuclei of plant cells. At that time, however, the literature contained no authentic data on the isolation and identification of DNA from plants.

The first cycle of Belozersky's work was devoted to the proof of the presence of DNA in higher plants. In a number of researches the presence of DNA was proved by the thymine-pyrimidine base, so typical for DNA, found in plant nucleoproteins. In 1936 DNA was first isolated in the pure state and identified by studying the products of its hydrolysis. These experiments finally established the unity of the chemical structure of nuclear material of the plant and the animal cells. RNA was always found together with DNA. Therefore it was evident that DNA and RNA are always present in higher plants.

In the next cycle of Belozersky's research it was necessary to establish the presence and the type of nucleic acids in microorganisms, the representatives of the "lower" realm of living organisms, and particularly in bacteria. The very first analysis, performed in 1939–41, showed that nucleic acids of both types (DNA and RNA) are always present in bacteria. In conjunction with the earlier data on higher plants, these researches established the universal distribution of both types of nucleic acids in plants of different phylogenetic groups.

This research showed, furthermore, that bacteria deserve special attention because the content of the nucleic acids in the bacterial cell is particularly high: over 20 percent of the dry weight of the bacteria. The large amount led, as far back as the late 1930s, to the conclusion that this weight factor is probably connected with a higher biological activity of the bacterial cell, intensive reproduction, and wonderful adaptability to the environment. In 1941 the weight changes of nucleic acids during bacterial cell development were studied, and it was concluded that there is a great variability in the amount of nucleic acids depending on the age of the bacterial culture. Thus, a correlation between the age and the biological activity of the cell and the age and the amount of nucleic acids in the cell was established.

Belozersky was the first to establish the presence of nonbasic proteins in the nucleoproteins of the nucleus (1936). Thus he modified the then existing conception that only basic proteins of the histone and protamine types were present in the nucleoproteins of the nucleus. While the work of E. and E. Stedmann and later that of A. E. Mirsky established the presence of higher (nonbasic) proteins together with histones in animal nucleoproteins of the nucleus, there was no direct experimental data concerning histones in plants. Belozersky and G. T. Abelev filled in that gap. They isolated a histone from a "structural" nucleoprotein of the wheat embryo and identified and analyzed it. That research demonstrated the unity of general principles of organization of the nuclear apparatus of animals and higher plants.

Although repeated attempts to isolate histone were not successful, Belozersky assumed that bacterial chromatin generally has no histones and contains only higher proteins. This assumption was later confirmed and is now considered one of the most important differences between bacterial chromosomes, in which the greater part of DNA is not covered with protein, and those of higher organisms with a typical nucleus, in which the DNA threads are bound with histones throughout their length. Simultaneously, the existence of different types of bonds between the proteins and the nucleic acids in nucleoproteins was established, and it was shown that the interrelation between the proteins and the nucleic acids may change during the ontogenesis.

The situation radically changed in the early 1950s when Erwin Chargaff developed new methods for nucleic acid analysis and the specificity of these biologically important compounds was shown. In this connection Belozersky's laboratory had studied for many years the nucleotide composition of DNA and RNA in higher plants, fungi, algae, actinomycetes, and bacteria and also in vertebrate and invertebrate animals. That vast experimental material led to the important conclusion that DNA of the whole organic world, of all representatives of higher and lower forms, is in the main composed of only four deoxynucleotides. Thus the DNA macromolecule of every organism is built to the same pattern and to the same nucleotide ratio; these principles, established in the early 1950s and known as the Chargaff rules, underlie the DNA structure. The DNA of different phylogenetic groups of organisms is undoubtedly of taxonomic importance. A comparative study of DNA and RNA nucleotide composition in a large group of bacteria established a positive correlation between the composition of DNA and a certain fraction of RNA in the cell (A. S. Spirin and Belozersky, 1957). Already in 1957 this fact predicted the existence of messenger RNA, which was later (1961) isolated in several laboratories. *See* CHARGAFF, ERWIN.

A series of studies was devoted to the exchange of polyphosphates—a special group of phosphorus compounds, polymers of phosphoric acid, which apparently play an important role in the activity of some lower organisms and are the sources of energy and phosphorus in various biosynthetic processes. New data were obtained on the formation of polyphosphates in lower organisms and also on their interrelation with other biologically active compounds. As to polyphosphates, research was conducted on the chemical nature of the volutin cell inclusion, typical for some microorganisms. According to Belozersky, the base of volutin is a complex consisting of polyphosphates and RNA.

In the late 1940s Belozersky investigated antibiotics. In collaboration with T. S. Paskina, Belozersky was the first to study the amino acid composition of gramicidin S.

Belozersky completed his undergraduate studies at Tashkent University in 1927; from 1927 to 1930 he stayed on doing postgraduate work. In 1930 he was appointed assistant in the plant biochemistry department of Moscow University; he became associate professor in 1932, full professor in 1947, and head of the department in 1960. In 1965 Belozersky set up and headed a research laboratory of organic biochemistry. In 1958 he was elected corresponding member and in 1962 full member of the Academy of Sciences of the U.S.S.R.

For background information *see* BACTERIAL CELL CHEMISTRY; CELL NUCLEUS; DEOXYRIBONUCLEIC ACID (DNA); NUCLEIC ACID; NUCLEOPROTEIN in the McGraw-Hill Encyclopedia of Science and Technology. ■

BENACERRAF, BARUJ
★ American immunologist

Born Oct. 29, 1920. Caracas, Venezula

Benacerraf was responsible for a major contribution to modern immunology, the discovery of specific immune-response (Ir) genes that control specific immune responses to thymus-dependent antigens.

The first Ir gene identified was the one determining the response of guinea pigs to a polypeptide composed only of lysine residues. (The antigens most commonly used for experiments on Ir genes are synthetic polypeptides of limited structural diversity.) Benacerraf found that strain 2 guinea pigs carry a gene that enables them to mount an immune response against this antigen, whereas strain 13 guinea pigs do not. The reverse is true for a gene controlling responses to a polypeptide of glutamic acid and tyrosine residues. After these early studies, many investigators, including Benacerraf, identified at least 30 Ir genes in the mouse, guinea pig, rat, and rhesus monkey, and probably humans. The genes are dominant, and they determine both cellular and humoral immune responses.

By using standard genetic techniques, researchers prepared a detailed map of the major histocompatibility complex (MHC) on chromosome 17 of the mouse. Benacerraf and H. O. McDevitt found that the Ir genes are located within this gene complex in the so-called I region. The total number of Ir genes is unknown, but the chromosomal segment containing them is long enough to carry many genes.

Another important observation of Benacerraf was that all responses specified by Ir genes involve activities of T lymphocytes. Two major classes of lymphocytes participate in immune responses. The B (for bone marrow–derived) cells are the precursors of the antibody-secreting cells and are thus responsible for humoral immunity. The T cells are the effectors of cellular immunity, and they may act directly to destroy foreign antigens, including transplanted organs. In addition, they may regulate antibody production by either helping or suppressing B cell activities. Production of antibodies against some antigens does not require the cooperation of helper T cells, but production of antibodies against other antigens does. Only the production of antibodies requiring helper T cells is affected by Ir genes.

Several lines of evidence indicated that the Ir gene products are also important in controlling interactions between cells of the immune system. Benacerraf and D. H. Katz showed that the T and B lymphocytes of mice cannot cooperate unless they both carry identical genes located in the MHC and, specifically, in that portion of the MHC containing the Ir genes. They proposed that genes in the I region code for T cell products needed for interaction with B cells and also code for the corresponding sites on the B cell membrane. Genes which are needed for the interaction of T cells and macrophages are also located in the histocompatibility gene complex.

The implications of the research on Ir genes are not just theoretical; these studies may also contribute to a better understanding of human disease. A number of investigators showed associations between certain human diseases and specific histocompatability antigens. Most of the diseases involve defective or inappropriate immune responses, and many are thought to be of autoimmune origin; that is, they may be caused by an attack of the immune system on the body's own tissues. Among these conditions are ankylosing spondylitis, Reiter's disease, psoriasis, Graves' disease, multiple sclerosis, and ragweed hayfever.

Although human Ir genes have not been as thoroughly studied and mapped as those of the mouse, they are also known to be closely linked to histocompatability antigens. Thus, many investigators believe that the association between diseases and histocompatibility antigens may actually represent an association between the disease and Ir genes. The presence or absence of genes controlling the capacity to make immune responses could obviously have much to do with disease susceptibility.

Benacerraf, who lived in France until 1940, received his *bachelor ès lettres* in Paris in 1940, his B.S. at Columbia University in 1942, and his M.D. from the Medical College of Virginia in 1945. He was a research fellow in the department of microbiology at the College of Physicians and Surgeons, Columbia University, from 1948 to 1950, and then returned to France for 6 years as *chargé de recherches* at the Centre National de la Recherche Scientifique in Paris. He returned to the United States in 1956 as professor of pathology at New York University School of Medicine, and in 1968 went to the National Institutes of Health, Bethesda, MD, as chief of the Laboratory of Immunology at the National Institute of Allergy and Infectious Diseases. In 1970 he became Fabyan Professor of Comparative Pathology and chairperson of the department of pathology at Harvard Medical School. Benacerraf was elected a member of the American Academy of Arts and Sciences and of the National Academy of Sciences. He received the Rabbi Shai Shacknai Lectureship and Prize in Immunology and Cancer Research from the Hebrew University of Jerusalem in 1974, and the T. Duckett Jones Memorial Award of the Helen Hay Whitney Foundation in 1976, and he gave the R. E. Dyer Lecture at the National Institutes of Health in 1969. He was president of the American Association of Immunologists (1973–74), president of the Federation of American Societies for Experimental Biology (1974–75), and vice-president of the International Union of Immunological Societies (1977).

Benacerraf was coeditor, with D. H. Katz, of *Immunological Tolerance: Mechanisms and Potential Therapeutic Applications* (1974), and he was author of *Immunogenetics and Immunodeficiency* (1975) and, with E. R. Unanue, *Immunology,* 1979, a textbook.

For background information *see* IMMUNOLOGY; IMMUNOLOGY, CELLULAR in the McGraw-Hill Encyclopedia of Science and Technology. ∎

BENEDICT, MANSON

★ American engineer

Born Oct. 9, 1907, Lake Linden, MI, U.S.A.

Benedict's work in applied chemistry and chemical and nuclear engineering evolved from the solid grounding in physical chemistry that he received as a student of Louis J. Gillespie and James A. Beattie at the Massachusetts Institute of Technology (MIT). From 1932 to 1935 he collaborated with Beattie on use of the nitrogen gas thermometer for measurements on the thermodynamic temperature scale. From 1935 to 1937 as a National Research fellow in the laboratory of P. W. Bridgman at Harvard, he measured the pressure-volume-temperature properties of nitrogen and argon at high pressures. This led to appointment as research associate in geophysics at Harvard, where he made some of the first measurements of thermodynamic properties of aqueous solutions above the critical temperature of water.

Benedict's first industrial position was with the M. W. Kellogg Company, where he coordinated a research program with MIT and the California Institute of Technology aimed at understanding the properties of hydrocarbon mixtures needed for design of distillation equipment at high pressures. He used experimental results obtained at the two schools and his own laboratory to develop the Benedict-Webb-Rubin equation of state. This was the first equation to represent the thermodynamic properties of gas and liquid mixtures at supercritical pressures with sufficient accuracy for engineering design. Benedict and his associates used this equation to prepare widely used charts for predicting liquid-vapor equilibria in hydrocarbon mixtures.

In the early 1940s Benedict made measurements on liquid-vapor equilibria in systems for separating toluene from naphtha by azeotropic or extractive distillation and developed the theory of these distillation processes. This work brought him to the attention of Percival C. Keith, who as vice-president for engineering at Kellogg had been asked by the Office of Scientific Research and Development to investigate the feasibility of the gaseous diffusion process for separating uranium-235 from natural uranium. Favorable assessment of the process by Keith and Benedict led to a decision by the Manhattan Project to build the K-25 gaseous diffusion plant at Oak Ridge, TN. Benedict was in charge of process development for the plant, devised design procedures, set process specifications, and assisted in plant startup in 1944–46.

Although this isotope separation project was only indirectly related to nuclear engineering, it brought Benedict in touch with Edward Teller. In 1947 Teller persuaded the new Atomic Energy Commission (AEC) to form a Reactor Safeguard Committee and invited Benedict to become its chemical engineering member. The knowledge of nuclear reactor technology which Benedict thus acquired qualified him to accept appointment as MIT's first professor of nuclear engineering. *See* TELLER, EDWARD.

Before he could take up residence at MIT, Benedict was asked by the AEC to organize and head an Office of Operations Analysis, to develop procedures for optimizing the expansion in plutonium and uranium-235 production capacity then contemplated by the AEC. While serving the AEC in Washington, in 1951–52, Benedict introduced the price scale for uranium enriched in U-235 based on the concept of separative work now universally used for charging for uranium enrichment services.

At MIT from 1952 to 1957, Benedict and Thomas H. Pigford organized a new nuclear engineering curriculum and wrote the book *Nuclear Chemical Engineering* (1957), the first text on the chemical technology of the nuclear fuel cycle. Rapid growth of student enrollment in nuclear engineering at MIT led to formation of a nuclear engineering department, with Benedict as its first head. During most of this period Benedict was a member of the General Advisory Committee of the AEC.

Benedict's interest in science was kindled by his father, C. Harry Benedict, chief metallurgist for Calumet and Hecla Consolidated Copper Company in Lake Linden, MI. He majored in chemistry at Cornell University and MIT, receiving a Ph.D. from the latter in 1935. He did experimental research in high-pressure thermodynamics at Harvard until 1937. He was with the M. W. Kellogg Company and Kellex Corporation from 1938 to 1946. From 1946 to 1951 he was director of process development for Hydrocarbon Research, Inc. He was in charge of operations analysis for the AEC in 1951. In 1951 he became professor of nuclear engineering at MIT and in 1958 head of the nuclear engineering department, serving until 1971. He was appointed to the General Advisory Committee of the AEC by President Dwight D. Eisenhower in 1958, and was its chairperson from 1962 to 1964. He was elected to the National Academy of Sciences (1956) and the National Academy of Engineering.

For background information *see* DISTILLATION; ISOTOPE (STABLE) SEPARATION; NUCLEAR ENGINEERING; URANIUM in the McGraw-Hill Encyclopedia of Science and Technology. ∎

BENIOFF, HUGO

☆ American geophysicist

Born Sept. 14, 1899, Los Angeles, CA, U.S.A.

Died Feb. 29, 1968, Mendocino, CA, U.S.A.

For his contributions to the study of earthquakes, and particularly to instrumental seismology, Benioff received the

Arthur L. Day Medal of the Geological Society of America in 1957 and the William Bowie Medal of the American Geophysical Union in 1965.

Benioff developed a family of seismological instruments of novel mechanical and electronic design. In the 1930s he built a variable reluctance seismograph that, with minor modifications, was selected for use in the worldwide standard seismograph network. It formed the basis of the detection system recommended by the Geneva Conference of Experts for the detection of nuclear tests. It has made possible the precise determination of travel-time curves, the extension of the magnitude scale to teleseismic events, and the worldwide availability of first motion data to recover source mechanism. Benioff's strain seismograph, also developed in the 1930s, can monitor propagating mantle surface waves, free oscillations of the Earth, and secular strain variations. Besides seismographs, Benioff developed a version of the mercury tiltmeter, sensitive microbarographs, magnetovariagraphs, electronic pianos and string instruments, underwater sound transducers, oscillographs, and galvanometers.

In the area of geophysical theory, Benioff was the first to suggest that the response spectrum was the important parameter to consider in antiseismic design. He demonstrated that the geographic distribution of aftershocks was related to the dimension of the primary fault. He proposed that the distribution of epicenters

could be used as evidence for the fault origin of oceanic deeps. His method of using the magnitude-energy relationship to deduce the seismic release of strain has been widely adopted. Using this procedure, he was able to show that rate earthquakes reveal a global pattern of strain accumulation and release. He also showed that the strain rebound characteristics derived from sequences of earthquakes could be used to separate the crust and upper mantle into zones having different mechanical properties. With these data and the geographical and depth distribution of earthquake foci, Benioff was able to characterize tectonic activity of continental margins and deep-sea trenches in a novel, yet mechanically significant, way.

Intrigued by the source mechanism of earthquakes, Benioff tried to deduce source dimensions from strain-energy considerations. He applied laboratory results on the form of creep strain to explain the source of aftershock energy. He showed how the direction of fault progression should lead to an asymmetrical radiation pattern of seismic waves. He proposed that although shallow earthquakes can be explained satisfactorily by the elastic rebound theory, certain deep earthquakes appear to involve volume collapse.

Long mantle waves were first analyzed and properly interpreted on records provided by Benioff. It is the standing-wave interference pattern of these world-circling waves that gives rise to the free oscillations of the Earth. Benioff's suggestion that instrumental developments made it feasible to detect free oscillations stimulated theorists at the Weizmann Institute to find methods of predicting the periods of free oscillations for real Earth models. Experimental teams at the California Institute of Technology, Columbia University, and the University of California at Los Angeles subsequently found oscillations in one of the most elegant experiments in geophysics.

Benioff was educated at Pomona College (B.A., 1921) and the California Institute of Technology (Ph.D., 1935). He worked as an assistant at the Mount Wilson Observatory summers from 1917 to 1921, then served as assistant physicist with the Seismological Laboratory of the Carnegie Institution of Washington in Pasadena from 1924 to 1937. In 1937 he joined the faculty at the California Institute of Technology, where he was professor of seis-

mology from 1950 to 1964. He was elected to the National Academy of Sciences in 1953.

For background information *see* EARTH-QUAKE; SEISMOGRAPH; SEISMOLOGY in the McGraw-Hill Encyclopedia of Science and Technology. ∎

BENZER, SEYMOUR
★ American biologist

***Born** Oct. 15, 1921, New York, NY, U.S.A.*

A signal achievement in genetics was the demonstration that genes are ordered in a one-dimensional array in chromosomes. Classically, genes were regarded as the "atoms" of heredity, acting as indivisible units when parts of chromosomes undergo recombination. Benzer's work showed that a single functional gene can be split into hundreds of smaller recombining elements. Furthermore, these elements are themselves arranged in a strictly linear array. This splitting of the gene and unraveling of its internal structure forced a reexamination of classical concepts of the elementary units of heredity.

Benzer began his career as a physicist, receiving his Ph.D. at Purdue University in 1947. As a graduate student, he worked under the direction of Karl Lark-Horovitz in a group developing germanium semiconductor devices for application to radar. Out of this work came a number of discoveries concerning solid-state diodes, *pn* junctions, and photodiodes that helped set the stage for the development of the transistor. On reading Erwin Schrödinger's book, *What Is Life?* (1945), however, he was captivated by the possibilities of applying physical concepts to biological problems and of using viruses as model systems for gene replication. Taking a leave of absence from Purdue to learn biology, he spent a year at Oak Ridge National Laboratory, a summer with Cornelius van Niel at Pacific Grove, 2 years with Max Delbrück at the California Institute of Technology, and 1 year at the Pasteur Institute in Paris, where he was associated with André Lwoff, Jacques Monod, and François Jacob. He returned to Purdue in 1952 and undertook work with phage T4, a virus that infects bacteria and makes a hundred copies of itself in about 20 minutes. *See* DELBRÜCK, MAX; JACOB, FRANÇOIS; LWOFF, ANDRÉ; MONOD, JACQUES; VAN NIEL, CORNELIS BERNARDUS.

At that time Alfred Hershey had just shown that the part of the phage that carries its hereditary information is its deoxyribonucleic acid (DNA). Shortly thereafter, J. D. Watson and F. H. C. Crick announced their discovery of the molecular structure of DNA. Their conception of a gene was a certain length of the (double-stranded) coil of DNA, comprising perhaps a thousand paired nucleotides, the specific sequence of nucleotides containing the information to determine, say, the amino acid sequence of a particular enzyme. This concept suggested that a gene should be topologically linear, should have well-defined beginning and end points, and should be divisible into many smaller parts. However, to demonstrate this experimentally was very difficult. The problem was that as two points of a chromosome are closer together, the probability of a chance event that splits the structure between those points is less. In ordinary organisms popular in genetics, such as the fruit fly, *Drosophila,* the probability of observing a split between two points within a single gene is extremely small. *See* CRICK, FRANCIS HARRY COMPTON; HERSHEY, ALFRED DAY; WATSON, JAMES DEWEY.

The key was discovered in 1954, when Benzer found that a certain type of mutant of phage T4, the *r*II mutant, was unable to multiply on a certain host strain of bacteria, whereas the normal phage T4 could multiply. Thus, if a cross was made

between two *r*II mutants, each having a mutation at a different site in the length of DNA constituting the *r*II gene, it would be easy to detect any progeny in which a recombination event had occurred such that two nonmutated portions of the gene (each contributed by one of the mutants) were joined to form a normal gene. If even one such progeny particle arose in as many as 10^8 offspring from the cross, it could be detected by its activity on the selective bacterial strain. A calculation showed that this easily was enough sensitivity to permit the detection of recombination between two mutants even if their respective mutations were located only one nucleotide apart in the DNA. Thus, by using this system, the gene could be split into its ultimate parts.

By isolating thousands of *r*II mutants and crossing them in appropriate combinations, it was possible to construct a detailed map of the region of the chromosome of phage T4 that controlled the *r*II function. This was greatly facilitated by the discovery of mutants in which segments of the structure had apparently been deleted (the ends being rejoined so that the DNA remained continuous). Given two such mutants in which the deleted portions overlapped, it was impossible to generate a normal gene by recombination of the two. Conversely, if recombination was obtained when two mutants were mated, it could be concluded that their mutations did not overlap. If the topology of the gene is really linear, crosses between various such mutants should give results compatible with a map in which each deletion is represented as a segment in a one-dimensional jigsaw puzzle. That result was found for hundreds of deletion mutants, confirming the topological prediction from the Watson-Crick model.

Thus, the hereditary structure needed by the phage to multiply on the selective bacterial strain consists of many parts distinguishable by mutation and recombination. Is this region to be thought of as one gene (because it controls one characteristic) or as hundreds of genes? Although a mutation at any one of the sites leads to the same observed physiological defect, this effect may be due to blocks in a series of separate functions that combine to give a particular end result. To define a functional unit, a test known in genetics as the cis-trans comparison was applied to the *r*II mutants. That test showed that the *r*II region could be divided into two func-

tional segments; each segment could function independently, regardless of what defect might be contained in the other. The term cistron was coined to denote such a functional unit. Each of the cistrons had sharp boundaries, as expected from the DNA structure. Some years later, Benzer and his student Sewell Champe showed that if the space between the two cistrons is deleted, thus joining the remaining segments, the two formerly independent units became functionally joined. This outcome implied that the normal structure contains elements to indicate the end of one cistron and the start of the next.

By mapping the locations at which point mutations arose, it was shown that there are enormous differences in spontaneous mutability at various sites, as might be expected from different local sequences of nucleotides. Working with Ernst Freese, Benzer showed that specific chemical substances—for example, 5-bromouracil, which enters DNA in place of thymine—induce mutations specifically at certain points and that those points are different from the ones at which spontaneous mutations most frequently occur. This finding suggested the feasibility of understanding the genetic map in chemical terms. In order to better understand the molecular basis of mutation, Benzer spent the year 1957–58 at the Cavendish Laboratory of the University of Cambridge, England, working on nucleic acid and protein structure with Crick, Sydney Brenner, and Vernon Ingram.

Returning once more to Purdue, Benzer and Champe extended the studies involving nucleotide base analogs to work with 5-fluorouracil, which enters messenger ribonucleic acid (mRNA), thereby causing errors not in the hereditary information of the genes, but in the transcribed information which determines the phenotype. They showed that it was possible thus to reverse certain mutant defects in an individual without altering its inheritance. This kind of study made it possible to obtain information concerning the identity of the nucleotides at the various points in the genetic structure. They also found that certain mutations in phage could be reversed by suppressor mutations of the host bacterium. Further analysis showed that the mechanism at play in certain suppressors was an actual modification of the genetic code. A code word that constituted nonsense when read according to the code of one bacterium became meaningful when read by the code of a suppressor strain. They speculated that the suppressor mutation operated by altering one of the elements of the cell's machinery for translating mRNA into amino acid sequences. The prime candidates were transfer RNA (tRNA) and the amino acid–activating enzymes, which act together in the translation process.

Investigation revealed that these substances were indeed subject to genetic modification, showing considerable differences in properties from one species to another. Collaborating with Bernard Weisblum, Robert Holley, and Gunther von Ehrenstein, Benzer showed that for a given amino acid there could be several versions of tRNA, each responding to a different mRNA code word. This demonstration established a physical basis for degeneracy in the genetic code. It also showed, as Crick had predicted years before, that once an amino acid is attached to tRNA, it is the RNA and not the amino acid that determines the specificity for incorporation of the amino acid into protein. This was also shown in another way, in collaboration with F. Chapeville, F. Lipmann, Weisblum, von Ehrenstein, and W. Ray, by attaching an amino acid A to its normal tRNA and then changing it, while still attached, to another amino acid B. When transferred into protein, amino acid B went into the position where A normally belonged. *See* LIPMANN, FRITZ ALBERT.

Inspired partly by the possibility of applying the new knowledge of molecular biology to problems of brain function and partly by curiosity as to the genetic control of behavior, Benzer turned his attention to behavioral biology. He spent the years 1965–67 at the California Institute of Technology working in Roger Sperry's psychobiology laboratory and remained at Caltech as professor of biology to investigate the behavior of the fruit fly, *Drosophila.*

Reasoning that the development and structure of the nervous system must be largely dictated by information contained in the genes, Benzer took the approach of altering relevant genes one at a time to produce perturbations in specific macromolecules affecting behavior. *Drosophila* seemed a good organism for such studies because methods were available for inducing mutations at a high rate, and the already extensive knowledge of its biology and genetics could be drawn upon in

tackling problems of behavior. The fact that many flies of a given genotype could be produced would make it possible to carry out behavioral measurements on an entire population and thus obtain instant results of a statistical significance that would ordinarily require many repeated measurements on an individual.

Initially, there was an exploration of whole-organism behavior and the possibilities of producing changes by single-gene mutations. The principle of countercurrent distribution, ordinarily used for separating molecules with different partition coefficients, was adapted to the separation of behavioral mutants from normal flies. It was found that mutants affecting a wide variety of behaviors, including visual responses, locomotor activity, sexual courtship, and circadian rhythm, could indeed be isolated. For example, R. Konopka and Benzer induced gene changes to produce arrhythmic flies, and also ones whose biological clock was based on a 19-hour or 28-hour period instead of the normal, approximately 24-hour period. Such mutants showed clearly that the period of the biological clock is endogenous to the organism and is not dependent on external (sidereal) factors.

Benzer and his students D. Ready and T. Hansen studied the formation of the neurocrystalline array of photoreceptors in the *Drosophila* eye. Using mosaics, they showed that the eight photoreceptors of one ommatidium do not necessarily originate from a single parent cell. Rather, the assembly of photoreceptors and pigment cells into the array occurs irrespective of their ancestry. This result stood in contrast to the strict lineage relationships of neuronal specificity observed in some other organisms, and indicated that both mechanisms exist and must be considered in the development of any neural network.

An important step in characterizing a behavioral mutant is to identify its focus, that is, the organ or tissue which is responsible for the behavioral change. Y. Hotta and Benzer applied the technique of mosaic fate mapping to the localization of the foci of various behavioral mutants, providing an incisive method for identifying the relevant structures. To do this more precisely required the development of markers for the nervous system that could be genetically linked to behavioral mutations. D. Kankel and J. Hall in Benzer's laboratory developed such a chemical technique using a null allele for the

acid phosphatase gene, which made it possible to locate the parts of the normal nervous system on the fate map. The foci for various mutants could thus be related to specific neural structures. Mosaic mapping was also applied by Hotta, Benzer, and Hall to the dissection of the complex behavior of sexual courtship, which involves a sequence of fixed action patterns programmed by the genes. In this way they identified the parts of the animal that must be male or female in order to provoke or perform particular steps in the sequence.

Drosophila was also excellent material for neurophysiological investigations. Benzer's students L. Jan and Y.-N. Jan showed that the segmental muscles of the body wall of the *Drosophila* larva could be easily penetrated by microelectrodes. They were thus able to study the properties of the neuromuscular junction in detail and to identify abnormalities in synaptic transmission of certain mutants. In temperature-sensitive paralytic mutants that function normally at ordinary temperatures but become paralyzed when the temperature is raised, the gene can be used as a switch to turn behavior on and off. Thus mutants that have characteristics which would ordinarily be lethal can be maintained in a viable condition if they are raised at permissive temperatures. A mutational block anywhere in the pathway from nerve excitability to muscle contraction can cause paralysis. Benzer and his colleagues O. Siddiqi, the Jans, C. Wu, and B. Ganetzky showed that various temperature-sensitive mutants have quite different characteristics. In some, nerve conduction is blocked at high temperature, and in others, synaptic transmission becomes defective.

The demonstration by W. Quinn, W. Harris, and Benzer that *Drosophila* is capable of associative learning opened up the possibility of neurogenetic analysis of learning. The first mutants deficient in this process were isolated in Benzer's laboratory by D. Byers, who also found that the dunce mutant lacks one of the two major cyclic nucleotide phosphodiesterases that are present in normal flies. This suggested a possible beginning to the identification of some of the biochemical steps involved in memory formation by knocking out genes corresponding to the individual steps.

Benzer received his B.A. in 1942 from Brooklyn College and his M.S. in 1943 and Ph.D. in physics in 1947 at Purdue

University, where he was an assistant professor in 1947–48. He was a biophysicist at the Oak Ridge National Laboratory in 1948–49, a research fellow in biophysics at the California Institute of Technology in 1949–51, and a Fulbright research scholar at the Pasteur Institute in Paris in 1951–52. Returning to Purdue, he was assistant professor of biophysics in 1952–53, and associate professor in 1953–58, spending the year 1957–58 as a National Science Foundation senior research fellow at the MRC Laboratory for Molecular Biology at Cambridge University. Returning again to Purdue, he was a professor in 1958–61 and Stuart Distinguished Professor of Biology from 1961. In 1965 he moved to Caltech, becoming a professor in 1967 and James G. Boswell Professor of Neuroscience in 1975. He received the Ricketts Award from the University of Chicago in 1961, the Gairdner Foundation Award in Toronto in 1964, the Lasker Award in 1971, the T. Duckett Jones Award of the Helen Hay Whitney Foundation and the Prix Mayer of the French Academy of Sciences in 1975, the Louisa Gross Horwitz Prize of Columbia University in 1976, the Harvey Prize of the Technion in Israel and the Warren Triennial Prize of the Massachusetts General Hospital in 1977, and the Dickson Prize of Carnegie-Mellon University in 1978. He was elected to the American Academy of Arts and Sciences in 1959, to the National Academy of Sciences in 1961, and to the American Philosophical Society in 1962, and he became a foreign member of the Royal Society of London in 1976. He held honorary D.Sc. degrees from Purdue, Columbia, Yale, and Brandeis Universities, and from the City University of New York.

For background information *see* GENE; GENETIC MAPPING; MOLECULAR BIOLOGY; MUTATION; NUCLEIC ACID in the McGraw-Hill Encyclopedia of Science and Technology. ∎

BERANEK, LEO L.

★ American communications engineer

Born Sept. 15, 1914, Solon, IA, U.S.A.

In November 1940 Beranek was appointed director of the Electro-Acoustics Laboratory at Harvard. The assignment was to improve voice communication at the high noise levels of all types of mili-

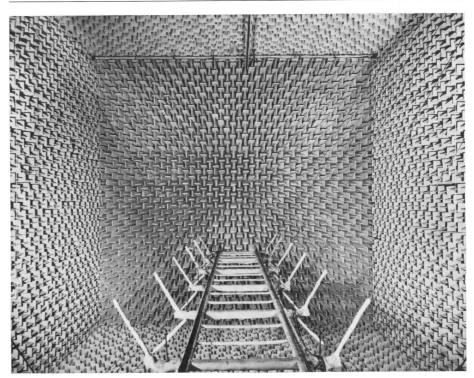

Fig. 1. The first anechoic chamber in the United States, built at Harvard University in 1943.

tary vehicles and the rarefied atmosphere of unpressurized high-altitude military aircraft. New microphones, earphones, ear cushions, amplifiers, and oxygen masks were developed to exclude noise and to enhance the intelligibility of spoken words in combat. In addition, lightweight, effective materials and structures for lining aircraft cabins were developed, which are commonly used in today's commercial aircraft.

During this period Beranek designed America's first large echo-free quiet space in which to test audio and sound equipment and the hearing acuity of human beings (Fig. 1). The interior of this "anechoic" (without echo) room at Harvard had a floor of 38 × 50 feet (11.6 × 15.2 meters) and a height of 38 feet (11.6 meters). It was lined with 19,000 wedges, with an 8 × 8 inch (20 × 20 centimeter) base and 58-inch (1.47-meter) length, made of rigid glass-fiber board. This construction absorbed about 99.9 percent of sound energy incident on it between 70 and 10,000 hertz. Thousands of such anechoic rooms ranging in size from cubes of 6 feet (1.8 meters) to 60 feet (18 meters) have been built, many also designed to provide echo-free test space for radio-frequency waves.

In the late 1940s Beranek devised a procedure for rating noises in terms of their effect on the ability of two persons to converse at stated voice levels and distances. Called the speech interference level, this rating procedure became a major tool for specifying acceptable noise levels in aircraft and other vehicles. This concept was then extended by Beranek to noise levels in rooms, where he showed that comfort is related to both the speech interference level and the overall loudness level of room noise. These noise criteria are used widely for specifying acceptable background noise in offices, studios, conference rooms, auditoriums, and work spaces.

In 1947–48 at MIT, Beranek supervised the graduate theses of dozens of students; performed research in acoustics and noise control, resulting in over 130 technical and scientific papers; and assumed leadership in the development of international standards on noise criteria and acoustical measurements.

In 1948 R. H. Bolt and Robert B. Newman of the Massachusetts Institute of Technology (MIT) joined Beranek to form the Cambridge, MA, firm of Bolt Beranek and Newman, consultants in computer applications, acoustics, and noise control. The firm now has offices in three cities and employs over 800 persons. Beranek was its first president and held that position until 1969.

In 1950–51 Beranek designed the world's largest muffler, 400 feet (122 meters) long and 30 × 40 feet (9 × 12 meters) in cross section, to silence the ear-splitting noise of the National Aeronautics and Space Administration's new supersonic wind tunnel in Cleveland, OH. (Fig. 2). This structure consisted of three parts: a set of Helmholz sound-absorbing resonators, surrounding the existing 200-foot-long (61-meter) airflow diffuser, which attenuated noises in the 5–11-hertz range of tones; a second set of resonators in a 100-foot-long (30-meter) section for attenuating the 11–20-hertz range of tones; and a set of six parallel ducts, each 15 × 15 feet (4.6 × 4.6 meters) square and 100 feet (30 meters) long fitted with 6-inch-thick (15-centimeter) rigid glass-fiber board, spaced 2 feet (0.6 meter) from the outer walls for attenuating the remaining tones. This advanced design led to the construction of noise control structures for hundreds of jet engine test cells at factories, airports, and military airbases throughout the world.

In the late 1950s Beranek served as acoustical consultant to the Port Authority of New York and New Jersey, where he worked with others to establish exte-

Fig. 2. The world's largest muffler, on the supersonic wind tunnel at the NASA Lewis Laboratory in Cleveland.

rior noise-level specifications for commercial jet aircraft. Their recommendations were responsible for the addition of engine exhaust mufflers and the design of new jet engines which permitted the successful introduction of the new jet-propelled aircraft into the nation's commercial airports.

Beranek and his firm served as acoustical consultants for Lincoln Center's Philharmonic Hall. The firm's "final design," modeled primarily after Symphony Hall in Boston and presented in 1969, was scrapped by the Lincoln Center Building Committee because it seated only 2400 persons. Its considerably different replacement design, which was executed, received adverse criticism from many musicians and music critics. In 1975 the interior of Philharmonic Hall (Avery Fisher Hall) was demolished and a new interior substituted which closely resembles the 1969 design.

In 1969 the Federal Communications Commission granted Boston Broadcasters, Inc. (BBI) the right to operate a television station on channel 5 in Boston. Beranek switched from acoustics to broadcasting and became BBI's first president and chief executive officer. Dedicated to extensive local news and public

affairs programming, the station, which began broadcasting on Mar. 19, 1972, earned a large number of national and regional television awards for outstanding achievement in presenting high-quality artistic, entertaining, educational, informational, and public service programming.

Beranek received a B.A. degree in physics and mathematics from Cornell College (Iowa) in 1936. In 1940 he received a D.Sc. degree from Harvard University after completing a research thesis on the acoustical behavior of porous materials. He was an assistant professor at Harvard University from 1941 to 1946 and associate professor at MIT from 1947 to 1958. Thereafter he was a lecturer at MIT. His honors included: honorary doctorates from Cornell College (1946), Worcester Polytechnical Institute (1971), and Suffolk University (1979); U.S. Presidential Certificate of Merit for meritorious contributions during World War II (1948); Silver Medal from the Society of French Language Acousticians (1966); Gold Medals from the Audio Engineering Society (1971) and the Acoustical Society of America (1975); and Abe Lincoln Television Award of the Southern Baptist Convention (1975). He was elected a member of the American Academy of Arts and Sciences (1952) and the National Academy of Engineering (1966). Active in public service in his later years, Beranek served as an officer in numerous civic and media-related organizations.

Beranek wrote *Acoustic Measurements* (1949), *Acoustics* (1954), *Noise Reduction* (1960), *Music, Acoustics and Architecture* (1962), and *Noise and Vibration Control* (1971).

For background information *see* ANE-CHOIC CHAMBER; ARCHITECTURAL ACOUSTICS; NOISE CONTROL in the McGraw-Hill Encyclopedia of Science and Technology. ■

BERG, PAUL
★ American biochemist

***Born** June 30, 1926, New York, NY, U.S.A.*

In the course of studies on the mechanism of acetyl coenzyme A (acetyl CoA) synthesis in certain microbial cells, Berg, while still a research fellow in Arthur Kornberg's laboratory, discovered a new mechanism for activating carboxyl groups with adenosinetriphosphate (ATP). This type of reaction was subsequently shown to be the prototype for a variety of reactions involving acyl group activation, particularly the activation of amino acids for protein biosynthesis. It was during the investigation of amino acid activation that Berg and his associates recognized the existence of discrete enzymes and ribonucleic acid (RNA) molecules specific for

activating each amino acid for protein assembly. For these contributions Berg received the Eli Lilly Prize in 1959 and the California Scientist of the Year Award in 1963. *See* KORNBERG, ARTHUR.

After receiving the Ph.D. in biochemistry at Western Reserve University in 1952 for studies on the metabolism of one-carbon compounds and the synthesis of the labile-methyl group of methionine, Berg traveled to Copenhagen for a year's study in H. Kalckar's laboratory. There, with W. K. Joklik, he discovered a new enzyme involved in nucleoside polyphosphate metabolism; this enzyme, nucleoside diphosphokinase, is a transphosphorylase which forms nucleoside triphosphates from the corresponding diphosphates. As is now recognized, this is a key enzyme in forming the nucleoside triphosphate precursors for RNA and deoxyribonucleic acid (DNA) biosynthesis.

In 1953 Berg joined Kornberg's new department of microbiology at Washington University in St. Louis. There his experiments led to the deduction that acetyl CoA formation proceeds via an enzyme-bound intermediate, an acetyl adenylate, formed in the reaction of ATP, acetic acid, and the enzyme protein. This enzyme-bound acyl adenylate reacts with the sulfhydryl group of coenzyme A to form acetyl CoA, thereby regenerating the free enzyme. Work in other laboratories has now established the existence of the predicted enzyme-acyl-adenylate complex and shown that this type of mechanism is the first step in the metabolic utilization of the higher fatty acids as well.

In 1955 during the studies of fatty acid activation, Berg showed that there are enzymes which catalyze the same partial reaction with the amino acids, that is, the formation of enzyme-amino acyl adenylates. During his search for the naturally occurring amino acyl acceptor, he independently discovered the existence of RNA molecules to which the activated amino acids become esterfied. Such amino acyl RNAs were later proved to be an integral component of the machinery for translation of genetic messages into protein molecules; the amino acyl RNAs interact specifically with the nucleic acid triplets which code for each amino acid.

Berg's work helped clarify how the specificity of amino acyl RNA synthesis is achieved. Studies in his laboratory established that a single enzyme protein activates each amino acid and then transfers

In 1962 Berg's laboratory announced the isolation of an enzyme which synthesizes RNA from nucleoside triphosphates and uses DNA to direct the order of assembly of the RNA nucleotides. In a series of investigations over the next few years, strong emphasis was placed on clarifying the way that DNA directs RNA synthesis and the way the enzymically synthesized RNA directs protein formation. These studies provided a firm foundation on which to mount an attack on the problem of how these two processes might be regulated.

During 1964–67 Berg and his colleagues demonstrated that genetically altered transfer RNA (tRNA) molecules can cause misreading of the genetic code. Studies with such altered RNAs provided important insights into the specificity of amino acyl tRNA synthesis and utilization in protein biosynthesis.

From 1968 onward, Berg's researches dealt with the molecular biology of viral oncogenesis, focusing principally on the organization and genetic functioning of a tumor virus (SV40) chromosome. He and his students developed methods for dissecting, reconstructing, and mapping small chromosomes, and were pioneers in recombinant DNA research. Berg was a leader in the public policy debate regarding the benefits and risks of recombinant DNA experimentation and in the formulation of means for ensuring safe practices in this research frontier.

Berg completed his undergraduate training in biochemistry at Pennsylvania State University (B.S., 1948) after military service in 1943–46. After receiving his Ph.D. from Western Reserve University in 1952, he spent 2 years in postdoctoral training as a U.S. Public Health Service fellow, first at the Institute of Cytophysiology in Copenhagen and later the activated amino acyl group to a specific attachment site on a special class of RNA molecules. Because the accuracy with which each amino acid is attached to its corresponding RNA is crucial for ensuring correct translation of genetic information, Berg's laboratory concentrated on the problem of the structure and the specificity of both the individual enzymes and RNA species. Later, in collaboration with Charles Yanofsky's laboratory, it was established that mutations which affect the specificity of the amino acid activation process can alter the accuracy of translation of the genetic message. *See* YANOFSKY, CHARLES.

at Washington University in St. Louis. He remained in the microbiology department at Washington University during 1954–59 as a scholar in cancer research and then as assistant and associate professor of microbiology. In 1959 Berg was awarded the Eli Lilly Prize in biochemistry and moved to Stanford University, where he became professor of biochemistry. In 1963 he was designated California Scientist of the Year, and 3 years later he was elected to both the American Academy of Arts and Sciences and the National Academy of Sciences. Between 1969 and 1972 Berg was designated a distinguished alumnus of Pennsylvania State University, was rewarded twice for his teaching at Stanford University with the Kaiser Award, and received the V. D. Mattia Prize of the Roche Institute for Molecular Biology. In 1973 the Salk Institute appointed Berg as a nonresident fellow. In 1974 he was elected to the U.S. Institute of Medicine, and during 1975 he served as president of the American Society of Biological Chemists. Yale University and the University of Rochester awarded Berg honorary doctorates in 1978.

For background information *see* EN-ZYME; LIPID METABOLISM; NUCLEIC ACID; PROTEIN in the McGraw-Hill Encyclopedia of Science and Technology. ∎

BERKNER, LLOYD VIEL
★ American physicist and engineer

Born Feb. 1, 1905, Milwaukee, WI, U.S.A.

Died June 4, 1967, Washington, DC, U.S.A.

During the early years of long-distance radio transmission, it was not clear why radio waves of short wavelength travel almost unattenuated for very long distances around the Earth. By the early 1920s the theories of O. Heaviside and A. E. Kennelly, calling for an ionized layer some 100 kilometers (about 60 miles) above the Earth, had been shown to account for the transmission of very long wavelengths. But these theories could not explain the even better performance of the shorter radio wavelengths.

Berkner became interested in these phenomena as a high school student at Sleepy Eye, MN. Using an amateur radio station, in 1923 he established records in relaying messages by short-wave radio between the East Coast and Hawaii. After

graduating from the University of Minnesota in 1927, he continued his studies of high-frequency radio transmission in the Antarctic on the first Byrd Antarctic Expedition in 1928–30. There he showed that high-frequency waves from antipodal points change their direction of travel following the night hemisphere preferentially. Upon his return to the United States, he continued his studies in physics at the George Washington University.

Following the work of G. Breit and M. A. Tuve, who showed that short radio pulses are discretely reflected from the ionized regions above, Berkner, working at the Carnegie Institution of Washington, devised the first instrument to map the height, distribution, and ionic density of the ionized layers of the outer atmosphere, or the ionosphere. Thousands of these complex instruments, known as ionosondes, are now employed over the Earth to describe the three major ionized layers—the E, F_1, and F_2—and their variation with time. Employing this method in Washington, Peru, Australia, and Alaska, Berkner showed how these layers varied diurnally, seasonally, and geographically; their critical dependence on sunspot activity; and their disruption by magnetic storms and solar chromospheric eruptions. Out of this work of Berkner (and related work of others) emerged not only the complete explanation of the propagation of high-frequency radio waves, but also the daily prediction service of the National Bureau of Standards, which forecasts high-frequency

radio performance at varying distances. *See* BREIT, GREGORY; TUVE, MERLE ANTONY.

Because the ionized layers showed an interrelationship with meteorology of the Earth's outer atmosphere, Berkner became interested in the origin and development of the atmosphere as early as 1935. Success in obtaining relevant measurements and scientific data required space vehicles, and this necessity resulted in his interest and leadership in space activities. The need for worldwide measurements of the Earth on an organized basis led to his proposal in 1950 for the International Geophysical Year (IGY), the most comprehensive study of the Earth ever undertaken. This study was organized under the International Council of Scientific Unions, of which Berkner became president during the IGY, 1957–59. He also coordinated international planning for scientific research in space during the period in which the first spacecraft were launched by the Soviet Union and the United States.

Berkner's interest in the atmospheres of the planets led to the formulation in 1963 with L. C. Marshall of a general theory of the origin and historical development of the atmospheres of the inner planets. This theory shows that on the Earth oxygen has appeared in significant quantities only in the last one-eighth of its history. The appearance of oxygen in significant concentrations is dependent wholly on the presence of primitive photosynthetic life over sufficient areas. The rise of oxygenic pressures and the advance of evolution toward more complex organic forms constitute an intimately related interaction. More advanced and widespread photosynthetic life produces the atmospheric oxygen required for further evolution of even more advanced forms of organisms, and so on. Only a planet of just the right size and temperature regime can ever acquire an oxygenic atmosphere, and with it the more advanced forms of life.

In engineering, Berkner's initial work with electromagnetic pulses put him in the forefront of development of aircraft radar and navigation devices. As a naval aviator from 1926 (rising to the grade of rear admiral, USNR), he took charge of all engineering of electronics for naval aircraft during World War II. Subsequently, under Vannevar Bush he organized the Research and Development Board of the Department of Defense (now Directorate of Defense Research and Engineering).

Later, acting directly under Secretary of State Dean Acheson, Berkner organized the military program under NATO and, following his extensive study, the Science Office of the Department of State in 1950. He was active in the studies establishing the Distant Early Warning System, and he was also one of the codiscoverers in 1951 of ionospheric scattering propagation.

Berkner received a B.S. in electrical engineering from the University of Minnesota in 1927. After his return from the Byrd Expedition in 1930, he joined the National Bureau of Standards in Washington, moving in 1933 to the Carnegie Institution, where he remained until 1951. In that year he became president of Associated Universities, Inc., and in 1960 he was named president and later chairman of the board of trustees of the Southwest Center for Advanced Studies in Dallas. In addition to numerous government decorations and honorary degrees, Berkner received the John A. Fleming Medal and the William Bowie Medal of the American Geophysical Union, the Cleveland Abbe Award of the American Meteorological Society, and the Public Service Medal of the National Aeronautics and Space Administration. He was elected to the National Academy of Sciences in 1948 and to the American Academy of Arts and Sciences in 1956.

The author of more than 100 scientific and engineering papers, Berkner wrote, among other books, *Rockets and Satellites* (1958), *Science in Space* (1961), and *The Scientific Age* (1964).

For background information *see* ATMOSPHERE, EVOLUTION OF; IONOSPHERE; RADIO-WAVE PROPAGATION in the McGraw-Hill Encyclopedia of Science and Technology. ■

BERNAL, JOHN DESMOND
☆ British physicist

Born May 10, 1901, Nenagh, Ireland
Died Sept. 15, 1971, London, England

One of the pioneer investigators in x-ray crystallography, Bernal contributed to the discipline both by his own investigations and by the guidance given to his students. He developed a very powerful, simple graphic method, based on the concept of the reciprocal lattice, for the indexing of crystal planes. He also put forward a theory of the structure of water and, later,

proposed a model of the structure of liquids in general.

X-ray diffraction studies began about 1912 with the investigations of Max von Laue. Hearing of his efforts, William Henry Bragg and his son, William Lawrence Bragg, worked out the mathematical details involved in the investigation and derived the equation that bears their name. About 1921 the German crystallographer Paul P. Ewald proposed the concept of the reciprocal lattice to facilitate visualization of the crystal lattice which Bernal independently developed. *See* BRAGG, SIR (WILLIAM) LAWRENCE.

About 1926, while conducting research at the Davy-Faraday Laboratory of the Royal Institution under the direction of William Henry Bragg, Bernal undertook the preparation of a chart for indexing x-ray diffraction photographs from single crystals. Now known as the Bernal chart, it included two sets of curves, from which could be read the radial and axial cylindrical coordinates of the point in reciprocal space that corresponded to any particular x-ray reflection. The two coordinates were ζ, the distance of any reciprocal-lattice point from the equatorial plane, and ξ, the distance of the point from the axis of rotation. To construct his chart, Bernal worked out ζ and ξ for all positions on a cylindrical film. By drawing on a transparent surface two sets of curves through the positions that he had calculated, Bernal created a tool that necessitated only placing a rotation photograph on the chart and reading off the ζ and ξ coordinates for every spot on the film,

thus saving many tedious hours of calculation.

In 1933 Bernal and R. H. Fowler published the results of their study of the structure of water and ionic solutions. The x-ray patterns they discussed suggested that water retains in part a hydrogen-bonded structure similar to that of ice. They pointed out that, as temperature increases, more and more of these bonds are ruptured. The oxygen molecules may then arrange themselves in a manner approximating more and more closely the closest packing in spheres. There would be a significant increase in density for such a packing compared with the open packing of the completely hydrogen-bonded structure of ice. They suggested that this might explain the increase in density of water as its temperature increases from 0 to 4°C.

Bernal investigated many areas of crystallography. With Dorothy Crowfoot (later Crowfoot Hodgkin), he investigated liquid crystals and made significant contributions to the crystallography of the mesomorphic state. During 1932–34 Bernal, Crowfoot, and I. Fankuchen collaborated on a crystallographic analysis of sterols and discovered the common structure of their nucleus. During the 1930s, also, Bernal realized that use might be made of a particular property of proteins, namely, that many of them form crystals. He took the first x-ray photograph of a protein crystal, pepsin, in 1934; later he joined with Fankuchen, Max F. Perutz, and Crowfoot to take the first x-ray diffraction photographs of crystals of hemoglobin, chymotrypsin, and insulin. *See* HODGKIN, DOROTHY CROWFOOT; PERUTZ, MAX FERDINAND.

In 1935 Bernal studied the structure of tobacco mosaic virus solutions. This virus was shown to be a nucleoprotein, whose structure was finally solved by his pupil, Rosalind Franklin, as were several other viruses of a crystalline nature by A. Klug and his coworkers.

During the late 1950s Bernal attempted to make a model of a liquid structure that would give a better approximation to the distribution function than does the hard-sphere model. He began by assuming that a liquid consists essentially of a set of molecules similarly—but never identically—placed with respect to one another. He also restricted himself to the simplest case of spherical molecules and assumed that liquids are essentially homogeneous. He built a number of physical models and found that in each the molecules tended to show fivefold symmetry, which was unusual in that crystals do not exhibit such a symmetry. To check his results and eliminate the human factor involved in building the physical models, Bernal used a computer at the University of London (employing a program devised by his son, M. J. M. Bernal) to produce a mathematical model. The computer produced a dense but random distribution of points (representing molecules) with the one condition that there be a minimum distance between them. This equidistance model, in which each molecule is surrounded by a limited number of others at equal distances, corresponds to the structure of a model with rigid molecules without attractive forces. Although not yet commonly accepted, Bernal's model may lead to a rigorous theory of the liquid state. Bernal also directed a team of workers investigating the structure of proteins, liquids, viruses, magnetic materials, and corrosion products. This latter work, in conjunction with J. W. Jeffery and H. F. W. Taylor, was directed to solving the structure of portland cement and related materials. Bernal had been for many years very interested in the origin of life, especially chemical evolution, and developed an explanation of biogenesis, published in his book *Origin of Life* (1967).

Bernal was educated in England, studying at Stonyhurst College, Bedford School, and Emmanuel College, Cambridge (M.A., 1922). After performing crystallographic research at the Davy-Faraday Laboratory from 1923 to 1927, he became a lecturer in structural crystallography at Cambridge. He retained the post until 1934, when he was named assistant director of research in crystallography. In 1938 Bernal left Cambridge to become a professor of physics at Birkbeck College, University of London. During World War II he worked for the Ministry of Home Security on protection against bomb damage, and he was later adviser to the Air Ministry and scientific adviser to the Chief of Combined Operations. In 1963 he was named professor of crystallography at Birkbeck. Among his prizes and awards was the Royal Medal of the Royal Society (1945), of which he had become a fellow in 1937.

Bernal wrote several books of social significance, such as *The Social Function of Science* (1939), the concepts of which were expanded in *Science of Science* (1964), and

World without War (1958). His technical works included *The Physical Basis of Life* (1951) and *Science and Industry in the Nineteenth Century* (1953; 2d ed. 1970).

For background information *see* LIQUID; WATER; X-RAY CRYSTALLOGRAPHY; X-RAY DIFFRACTION in the McGraw-Hill Encyclopedia of Science and Technology. ∎

BERNER, ROBERT ARBUCKLE
★ American geochemist, sedimentologist, and oceanographer

Born Nov. 25, 1935, Erie, PA, U.S.A.

Berner's principal scientific achievement was in the application of physical chemistry and mathematical modeling to the study of sediments and sedimentary processes. For his contributions to mineralogical-geochemical studies of sediments, he received the Mineralogical Association of America Award in 1971.

Berner's studies of modern sediments began in 1959, when he was a graduate student in geology at Harvard University. While conducting a standard sedimentological survey of some tidal flat sediments of Cape Cod, he became fascinated by their color (brown at the top, black in the middle, and light gray at depth) and their odor (H_2S). Earlier workers had suggested that the black color was due to "iron sulfide" of uncertain composition. From laboratory studies conducted at Harvard, Berner was able to show that the blackening material was a mixture of disordered forms of two new substances, te-

tragonal FeS (subsequently named mackinawite) and cubic Fe_3S_4 (subsequently named greigite). He later found that these minerals were thermodynamically unstable relative to pyrite in marine sediments, and he therefore attributed the loss of black color with depth to their transformation to pyrite. Also at this time, he developed an electrode technique for measuring the concentration of dissolved H_2S in sediments, and from such measurements he was able to show that the measured oxidation potential of most anoxic sediments is controlled by electron transfer between sulfide and polysulfide ions. During his graduate work, he was introduced to the importance of studying interstitial water chemistry by Raymond Siever, and to the application of physical chemistry to sedimentological problems by Robert M. Garrels, both of Harvard.

After receiving the Ph.D. from Harvard in 1962, Berner conducted further studies of sulfur in anoxic sediments that led him in 1964 to construct a theoretical model to explain the depth distribution of dissolved sulfate in anoxic sediments in terms of molecular diffusion, burial, and bacterial sulfate reduction. This type of modeling, thereafter much used and called diagenetic modeling, was virtually unprecedented at the time. Later (1971, 1975, 1976) he continued this work, developing more generalized models applicable to any sedimentary substance. In 1978 he was occupied with writing a book on diagenetic modeling.

During 1964–74 Berner also conducted studies of calcium carbonate in modern sediments. He was able to show (1965) that large portions of the oceans are undersaturated with respect to $CaCO_3$, and that the disappearance of $CaCO_3$ at great depth in deep-sea sediments is largely a kinetic phenomenon and is not due, simply, to undersaturation of the deep oceans with respect to $CaCO_3$. Later, in 1972 and 1974, together with John W. Morse, he showed that highly nonlinear dissolution kinetics measured in the laboratory could be called upon to explain this disappearance.

In 1969 Berner, continuing his studies of iron minerals, published a paper in which he showed that many red beds (sediments colored red by the mineral hematite) could form thermodynamically during burial from the dehydration of yellow-brown goethite (the chief pigment of most soils and sands). This meant that red beds did not necessarily form from originally red material and that, as a result, several paleoclimatic theories based on an original red color were probably in error.

In 1971 Berner published a book entitled *Principles of Chemical Sedimentology* in which he attempted to show how the study of sediments could be approached in terms of the basic principles of physical chemistry, especially through the application of chemical kinetics.

From 1971 to 1978 Berner was occupied with developing more general models for diagenetic processes and the acquisition of data to test them. The distribution and rates of formation or consumption of ammonia, phosphate, sulfate, and methane in anoxic sediments of Long Island Sound, off the New York and Connecticut coasts, were studied in collaboration with several graduate students and research associates of the Friends of Anoxic Mud (FOAM) group. During this period, in other research, Berner discovered that major removal of phosphate from seawater may take place by adsorption on hydrothermally produced iron oxides in the ridge portions of the deep sea, and that much more of the calcium carbonate sedimenting to the deep-sea floor is present as shells of aragonitic pteropods (swimming snails) than was formerly realized. He also turned his interests to the study of weathering in soils and applied a new technique, x-ray photoelectron spectroscopy, to the testing of theories for the weathering of feldspar minerals. With his colleagues, Berner was able to directly demonstrate that feldspar dissolution during weathering does not proceed by the formation of a protective surface layer of clay, as previously believed. From this work, and some theoretical considerations, Berner subsequently predicted that mineral dissolution in general, under earth surface conditions, is limited by the rate of detachment of ions or atoms from crystal surfaces and not by their transport through solution.

Berner obtained his B.S. (1957) and M.S. (1958) from the University of Michigan, both in geology. He received the Ph.D. degree in geology from Harvard University in 1962. After spending a year as a Sverdrup postdoctoral fellow at the Scripps Institution of Oceanography, he accepted the post of assistant professor, and later associate professor, in the department of geophysical sciences at the University of Chicago (1963–65). In 1965 he joined the faculty of the department of geology and geophysics of Yale

University, where he was promoted to full professor in 1971. From 1968 to 1972 he was an Alfred P. Sloan fellow in the physical sciences at Yale, and in 1972 a Guggenheim fellow at the Swiss Federal Institute for Water Pollution Research. He was a councilor of the Geochemical Society (1976–79) and a member of the U.S. National Committee for Geochemistry (1978–81).

Besides his 1971 book, Berner wrote over 70 research papers in the fields of geochemistry, sedimentology, and oceanography. He became an associate editor of the *American Journal of Science* in 1968.

For background information *see* MARINE GEOLOGY; RED BEDS; SEDIMENTATION in the McGraw-Hill Encyclopedia of Science and Technology. ∎

BERS, LIPMAN
★ American mathematician

Born May 22, 1914, Riga, Latvia

Most of Bers's mathematical work concerned the interrelations between two fields of mathematical analysis: complex function theory and elliptic partial differential equations.

The simplest elliptic equation is the classical Laplace equation (1). Its theory is identical with the theory of analytic functions of a complex variable (2), that is, of functions representable by power series (3). The theory of a general linear second-

$$u_{xx} + u_{yy} = 0 \qquad (1)$$

$$z = x + \sqrt{-1}y \qquad (2)$$

$$\sum_0^\infty a_n(z - z_0)^n \qquad (3)$$

order partial differential equation in the plane can be reduced to the study of so-called pseudoanalytic functions. The theory of these functions (developed by Bers and, along somewhat different lines, by I. N. Vekua), parallels many essential features of classical function theory.

A typical result reads as follows: For every equation of the type considered, there exist two sequences of particular solutions $\varphi_0, \varphi_2, \ldots, \Psi_0, \Psi_1, \ldots$, analogous to the real and imaginary parts of z^n, such that every solution $\Phi(x,y)$ defined near $z = 0$ may be written as series (4),

$$\sum_0^\infty (\alpha_n\varphi_n + \beta_n\psi_n) \qquad (4)$$

which is both convergent and asymptotic. The latter statement means that the difference between Φ and the sum of the first N terms of the series is of the order $|z|^{N+1}$. Similar particular solutions exist for any other point z_0; they are linear combinations of the functions φ_j, Ψ_j.

Pseudoanalytic functions are also used in studying nonlinear elliptic equations, in particular the equation describing the two-dimensional flow of a gas at subsonic speeds. These applications provided the original motivation for the theory. In studying the equation of a gas flow and similar nonlinear equations, one also uses another, much older, generalization of analytic functions: quasiconformal mappings. These are solutions of a certain elliptic equation (Beltrami's equation), which may be described as the Laplace equation on a curved surface.

Quasiconformal mappings have now been applied to classical function theory. This approach was pioneered by O. Teichmüller and developed by L. V. Ahlfors, Bers, and others. Here is an example of such an application.

An algebraic curve is the set of pairs of complex numbers (z,w) satisfying an irreducible polynomial equation $P(z,w) = 0$. To every algebraic curve there belongs a nonnegative integer g, the genus of the curve. If $g = 0$, the curve can be represented parametrically by rational functions. For instance, the circle (5) admits the parametric representation (6). If $g = 1$, the curve can be parametrized by ellip-

$$z^2 + w^2 = 1 \qquad (5)$$

$$z = \frac{1 - t^2}{1 + t^2}$$
$$w = \frac{2t}{1 + t^2} \qquad (6)$$

tic functions. The construction of a parametric representation by single-valued meromorphic functions for curves of any genus was one of the major achievements of 19th-century mathematics. Using quasiconformal mappings, Bers proved that it is possible to uniformize simultaneously all algebraic curves of genus $g > 1$. More precisely, there exist, for every fixed $g > 1$, $5g - 5$ analytic functions $\varphi_1(s_1, \ldots, s_{3g-3}, t), \ldots, \varphi_{5g-5}(s_1, \ldots, s_{3g-3}, t)$ of $3g - 2$ complex variables with the following properties: If C is an algebraic curve of genus g, then there exist $3g - 3$ numbers $s_1, \ldots, s_{3g-3}$ and two rational functions p_1, p_2 of $5g - 5$ variables such that formulas (7) are a parametric

$$z = p_1 [\psi_1 \psi_1 , \ldots , s_{3g-3}, t), \ldots ,$$
$$\varphi_{5g-5}(s_1, \ldots , s_{3g-3}, t)]$$

$$w = p_2 [\varphi_1 (s_1, \ldots , s_{3g-3}, t), \ldots , \quad (7)$$
$$\varphi_{5g-5}(s_1, \ldots , s_{3g-3}, t)]$$

representation of C. Here $s_1, \ldots , s_{3g-3}$ are fixed and t varies over a certain domain. Conversely, if $s_1, \ldots , s_{5g-5}$ are chosen arbitrarily within a certain domain, and p_1, p_2 are any two rational functions, the above formulas define an alegbraic curve of genus at most g. This result belongs to the theory of moduli, a field which is now under active investigation by many mathematicians.

Bers received his Dr.Rer.Nat. at the University of Prague, Czechoslovakia, in 1938. He went to the United States in 1940 and participated in the wartime research and training program in applied mathematics at Brown University. After teaching at Syracuse University and spending 2 years at the Institute for Advanced Study, he went to New York University, where he taught for 14 years. He became professor of mathematics at Columbia University in 1964 and Davies Professor of Mathematics in 1973. He served as president of the American Mathematical Society from 1975 to 1977. He was elected to the American Academy of Arts and Sciences (1961) and the National Academy of Sciences (1964).

Bers wrote *Mathematical Aspects of Subsonic and Transonic Gas Dynamics* (1958), *Partial Differential Equations,* with F. John and M. Schechter (1967), and *Calculus* (1969; 2d ed., with F. Karal, 1976).

For background information *see* DIFFERENTIAL EQUATION in the McGraw-Hill Encyclopedia of Science and Technology. ∎

BERSON, JEROME ABRAHAM
★ American chemist

Born May 10, 1924, Sanford, FL, U.S.A.

Although quantum mechanics provides, in principle, a theoretical framework for describing chemical reactions, in practice, its predictions are often imprecise. Most organic molecules (compounds of carbon) contain many atoms and many chemical bonds. Therefore, several competing reaction pathways with nearly equal energy barriers are accessible, and the essence of the problem of chemical reactivity is the prediction of the fine structure of the reaction energy surface. Berson's laboratory

elucidated the detailed mechanisms of complex reaction pathways in systems chosen to test quantum-mechanical theories of molecular structure and reactivity. For this work, he received the American Chemical Society's James Flack Norris Award in physical organic chemistry in 1978.

In 1965 R. B. Woodward and R. Hoffmann put forward a most fruitful scheme for predicting concerted reactions, that is, reactions in which the atoms of the chemical bonds being formed and broken remain connected throughout. They classified reactions as either allowed (energetically favorable) or forbidden (energetically unfavorable) according to the wave-mechanical phase relationships of the reacting orbitals (orbital symmetry). The scheme was uniquely attractive because of its success in correlating the results of a few puzzling experiments then available, but it was also uniquely vulnerable because it predicted a whole range of new phenomena that had not yet been discovered. Berson and his coworkers devised and synthesized test molecules for which the preexisting theories and the orbital symmetry scheme made conflicting predictions of chemical behavior. The tests thus were risky in the sense that the theories were placed in competition. In several crucial cases, the predictions of the orbital symmetry scheme were confirmed. A few examples follow. *See* HOFFMANN, ROALD; WOODWARD, ROBERT BURNS.

Orbital symmetry manifests itself with special clarity by its control of the stereochemical course of certain unimolecular

rearrangements. In these reactions, which require no outside agency other than thermal activation, the original connections between atoms are broken, and new arrangements of bonds are established within the reacting molecules. Earlier concepts of how these processes take place suggested that the new bond to the migrant carbon atom in a so-called 1,3-sigmatropic rearrangement should be formed on the same side that the old one previously occupied. In fact, however, Berson and George L. Nelson observed in 1967 that, in a specially constructed test molecule, every time this rearrangement occurred, the migrant carbon turned a complete somersault and attached the new bond to the opposite face. This startling behavior had no explanation in conventional terms but was exactly that predicted by orbital symmetry.

Many chemical reactions are made difficult by steric hindrance, that is, by the mutual repulsion of atoms which cannot simultaneously occupy the same space. In 1969 Berson and Stephen S. Olin devised a set of molecules in which the reactions allowed by orbital symmetry would be opposed by steric hindrance. Again, the idea was to test the strength of orbital symmetry by pitting this factor against a countervailing influence. The reactions involved the thermal decomposition of a six-membered ring into fragments; the dominance of the orbital symmetry influence was revealed once again by the stereochemistry of the products.

The cyclopropane molecule consists of a ring of three carbon atoms, each bearing two hydrogen atoms. If a hydrogen on each of two carbons is replaced by another atom or group, two different 1,2-disubstituted cyclopropanes can be formed. One of them has the substituent cis and the other trans, that is, either on the same or on the opposite sides of the plane of the carbon atoms. It had been known for some time that such stereoisomers could be interconverted by heat. In fact, this very simple reaction has been the most intensely studied of all thermal unimolecular rearrangements. The major question about the mechanism is whether the reaction takes place by individual rotation of one substituted carbon or by synchronous rotation of a substituted and an unsubstituted carbon. The synchronous double rotation had been predicted by an extension of orbital symmetry theory, but several searches had failed to detect the process. However, in 1975 Berson and Larry

D. Pedersen showed that the synchronous double rotation is the major pathway in the stereomutation when the two substituents are the simplest possible ones, deuterium atoms, and with Barry K. Carpenter, they also found the process to be a dominant feature of the stereomutation of 1-phenyl-2-deuteriocyclopropane.

The son of immigrant parents, Berson attended the City College of New York and received the B.S. degree in 1944. He worked briefly at Hoffmann-LaRoche, Inc., in Nutley, NJ, before entering the armed forces. After overseas service in the China-Burma-India theater, he returned to the study of chemistry in 1946, when he undertook graduate work at Columbia University. He received the M.A. in 1947 and the Ph.D. in 1949, carrying out his research under the guidance of W. E. Doering. After a year at Harvard University as a National Research Council postdoctoral fellow in Woodward's laboratory, he held academic appointments at the universities of Southern California (1950–63) and Wisconsin (1963–69) before moving to Yale University in 1969. He chaired the department of chemistry at Yale from 1971 to 1974. He was elected to the National Academy of Sciences in 1970.

For background information *see* MOLECULAR STRUCTURE AND SPECTRA; ORGANIC REACTION MECHANISM; STEREOCHEMISTRY in the McGraw-Hill Encyclopedia of Science and Technology. ∎

BESICOVITCH, ABRAM SAMOILOVITCH

★ British mathematician

Born Jan. 24, 1891, Berdiansk, U.S.S.R

Died Nov. 2, 1970, Cambridge, England

Besicovitch started work in probabilities. In a sequence of trials, each trial results in appearance or nonappearance of the same event, with probabilities p_n and $q_n = (1 - p)$ at the nth trial. Instead of the usual integral expressing the limit of the probability for the number of appearance to be included in a large interval, he gave an asymptotic expression for each particular value of the number.

In early work on the Riemann integrability of functions, a plane set of segments of length greater than 1, of all directions, of Jordan outer plane measure zero was constructed. The existence of such a set

being a fundamental point of set theory led also to a solution of the Kakeya problem, which attracted great interest among mathematicians for a decade about 1920. The problem is on the lower bound of the area of a domain that is swept over by a segment of length 1 that turns continuously through 360°. The answer is that the lower bound is 0.

Among problems on integrability, Besicovitch was concerned with the existence of the integral (1) in the Cauchy-

$$\int_0^\pi \frac{f(x+t) - f(x-t)}{t} dt \qquad (1)$$

Lebesgue sense, for $f(x) \in L$ for almost all x. Its existence marks a deep structural property of real functions and in particular of linear point sets. The existence had been proved by complicated methods, and a direct proof by methods of sets of points was desirable. He gave it first for functions of the class L^2 and then generalized to the class L.

In the early days of the development of the theory of almost periodic functions created by H. Bohr, Besicovitch worked on various generalizations of almost periodicity and on their extent. He showed that none of the generalizations was wide enough for the Riesz-Fischer theorem to hold, a theorem without which no natural correspondence between almost periodic functions and the general trigonometric series existed. By introducing B^p almost periodic functions ($p \geq 1$) this gap was filled up. Later, in a joint paper with H.

Bohr, the study of almost periodicity in terms of "functional spaces" was carried out. The basic space A is one of trigonometric polynomials in $-\infty < x < +\infty$. Various distances between points of the space (functions) are introduced, as in Eqs. (2). Convergence in the sense of each

$$D_u\{f,g\} = u.b \mid f(x) - g(x) \mid$$

$$D_{S^p}\{f,g\} = u.b \left\{ \int_x^{x+1} \mid f(t) - g(t) \mid^p dt \right\}^{1/p}$$

$$D_{B^p}\{f,g\} = \overline{M} \left\{ \mid f(x) - g(x) \mid^p \right\}^{1/p} \qquad (2)$$

distance is defined naturally, and the closure of A in the sense of each of the distances is defined as the set of all limit points of A in the sense of each distance. The main results are that for various distances the corresponding closures represent various classes of almost periodicity, introduced before, and there is a general result that for each class an approximating sequence can be given by Fejer-Bochner polynomials.

For almost periodic functions of a complex variable Besicovitch gave conditions for the Parseval theorem to hold beyond the strip of boundedness of the function. He also carried out a study under which the Parseval theorem holds for functions representable by a convergent Dirichlet series. Other work on complex variables included a study of conditions for a function to be analytic, their behavior in the neighborhood of nonisolated singularities, and conditions for the existence of mean values of analytic functions in a strip. For integral functions of order < 1, he gave densities of r for which Littlewood-Wiman inequalities hold.

The problem on the forms of equilibrium of a uniform fluid mass had previously been reduced to the existence of the maximum of the Newton potential. The existence of the absolute maximum had been known, and Besicovitch proved that a relative maximum does not exist.

In the general theory of functions of a real variable Besicovitch's work on differentiation included the first construction of a continuous function that does not admit either a two-sided derivative or a one-sided one at any point, which thus completed the Weierstrass problem. He also solved a number of general problems on differentiation of functions of one or more variables and also differentiation of additive functions and in particular of integrals, with the development of appropriate general covering principles.

Study of general point sets on the background of the measure formed a considerable part of Besicovitch's work on real variables. Two general classes of sets, regular sets and irregular ones, are defined. The two classes are totally distinct. The regular ones have at almost all points the density equal to 1. Also at almost all points they have a tangent, and they differ from a finite set of rectifiable arcs only by a subset of arbitrarily small measure. The irregular sets have no tangent, the lower density is different from the upper one and is $\leq \frac{3}{4}$ (a strong conjecture is that it is $\leq \frac{1}{2}$), and the projection on almost all directions is 0. The result obtained is that the most general set consists of a regular component and an irregular one, which really completes the subject.

Similarly Besicovitch studied linearly measurable sets of lines. A fundamental result is that the plane measure of a regular set is always infinite and of an irregular one is 0. The importance of this result is seen if one remembers difficulties connected with the construction of the set wanted for the Kakeya problem, a very particular case of an irregular set. For simple curves of h-dimensional measure, he established the distribution of one-sided densities along the curve.

Besicovitch's study of surfaces started with the definition of area. The dominant definition of the area of a skew surface (Lebesgue-Frechet definition) was shown by him to be inadequate (a finite area having a positive three-dimensional measure, the existence of a solid, which is a topological sphere, with volume as large as desired and area of surface as small as desired). The problems solved with this definition had to be redone, and defining the area as the Hausdorff two-dimensional measure, he proved the existence of the minimum area subtending a given contour.

In the theory of numbers Besicovitch studied some sequences of integers. He proved that the sequence of squares is normal and also that under some restrictions the theorem known as the $a + \beta$ theorem was true.

Besicovitch received his first degree from the University of St. Petersburg in 1912. He taught at the universities of Perm and St. Petersburg from 1914 until 1925, when he emigrated from the Soviet Union. In England he taught at the University of Liverpool. From 1927 to 1950 he was Cayley Lecturer in Mathematics at Cambridge University; from 1950 until his retirement in 1958 he was Rouse Ball Professor of Mathematics there. He was awarded the Royal Society's Sylvester Medal in 1952.

Besicovitch wrote *Almost Periodic Functions* (1932).

For background information *see* DIFFERENTIATION; INTEGRATION; PARTIAL DIFFERENTIATION; PROBABILITY in the McGraw-Hill Encyclopedia of Science and Technology. ■

BEST, CHARLES HERBERT
★ Canadian physiologist and medical researcher

Born Feb. 27, 1899, West Pembroke, ME, U.S.A.

Died Mar. 31, 1978, Toronto, Ontario, Canada

At 22, Best joined F. G. Banting in a partnership that soon resulted in the discovery of insulin. It has been estimated that between 20,000,000 and 30,000,000 diabetics would not be alive today had it not been for their discovery. Besides its clinical importance, insulin has proved to be one of the greatest tools ever provided for medical investigators. It has opened doors in many branches of the biological sciences.

Both Banting and Best were interested in diabetes for personal reasons. Before receiving his B.A. in 1921 at the University of Toronto, Best had already decided to take his M.A. and extend the work on sugars that had engaged his attention as a fellow in physiology during his final undergraduate year. About the same time, Banting, while practicing medicine in London, Ontario, had formulated a hypothesis that was vital to the initiation of the work. He approached J. J. R. Macleod, head of the department of physiology at the University of Toronto, to obtain permission to explore his idea at his alma mater. Macleod, extremely skeptical, felt Banting needed to work with someone trained in essential physiological and biochemical methods if any advance in knowledge was to be achieved. Knowing that Best had such training, Macleod finally gave permission for them to work in his department during the summer while he was abroad and the rest of the staff were on holiday. There was no question of remuneration.

The two enthusiasts began their collaboration on May 17, 1921. During the hot summer months they worked day and night in the deserted department. They first prepared a neutral or faintly acid extract of the degenerated pancreas glands of laboratory dogs. This was accomplished by ligation of the pancreatic ducts for 10 weeks, when the degenerated glands were removed and extracted with ice-cold Ringer's solution. The extract, kept at a low temperature, was then injected intravenously or subcutaneously into the moribund depancreatized dogs. The invariable result was marked reduction of the percentage of sugar in the blood and of the amount of sugar excreted in the urine. Banting and Best found that rectal injections were not effective; that the extent and duration of the reduction of sugar varied directly with the amount of extract injected; that pancreatic juice destroyed the active principle of the extract; that the reducing action was not a dilution phenomenon, since (1) hemoglobin estimations before and after administration of the extract were identical, (2) injections of large quantities of saline did not affect blood sugar, and (3) similar quantities of extracts of other tissues did not cause reduction of blood sugar; that extract made by 0.1 percent acid was effectual in lowering the blood sugar; that the presence of extract enabled a diabetic animal to retain a much greater percentage of injected sugar than it would otherwise; and that extract prepared in neutral saline and kept in cold storage retained its potency for at least 7 days. Boiled extract had no effect on the reduction of blood sugar.

On Nov. 14, 1921, Banting and Best

presented their findings for the first time before the members of the medical faculty at a meeting of the University of Toronto Physiological Society. Later they presented their findings to the Academy of Medicine of Toronto. The first insulin was administered to a diabetic patient in the Toronto General Hospital on Jan. 11, 1922, and during the next 6 weeks seven patients were treated and observed. The observations furnished material for the initial clinical publication, which appeared in the Canadian Medical Association Journal in March 1922, and which verified that the findings in diabetic dogs were completely confirmed in human diabetics.

In addition to achieving many important advances in the study of insulin and diabetes, Best introduced the first anticoagulant for the prevention of thrombosis; discovered a new enzyme, histaminase, which destroys histamine; found a new vitamin, choline, which prevents damage to the liver; initiated in 1939 the Canadian Serum Project to provide human serum for military use during World War II; and, as director of the Royal Canadian Navy's Medical Research Division, collaborated with colleagues in making many practical contributions to the war effort.

A doctor's son, Best entered the University of Toronto in 1916. He soon enlisted in the field artillery, returning to the university at the end of World War I. He received his B.A. in 1921, M.A. in 1922, M.B. in 1925, and M.D. in 1932. He was with Connaught Laboratories as director of the insulin division from 1922 to 1925, assistant director of the laboratories from 1925 to 1931, associate director from 1931 to 1941, and honorary consultant after 1941. When the Ontario legislature established the Banting and Best Department of Medical Research at the University of Toronto, Best served there as research associate from 1923 to 1941 and as director following Banting's death in 1941. He was also assistant professor of physiological hygiene in the University of Toronto from 1926 to 1928; in 1929 he became professor of physiology and head of the department. The recipient of numerous honorary degrees and scientific prizes, he was elected a foreign associate of the U.S. National Academy of Sciences in 1950.

With Norman B. Taylor, Best wrote three physiology texts: *The Physiological Basis of Medical Practice* (7th ed. 1961; 9th ed., revised by J. R. Brobeck, 1973); *The Human Body* (4th ed. 1963); and *The Living Body* (4th ed. 1958). *The Selected Papers of Charles H. Best* was published by the University of Toronto Press in 1963.

For background information *see* DIABETES; INSULIN in the McGraw-Hill Encyclopedia of Science and Technology. ∎

BETHE, HANS ALBRECHT
★ American physicist

Born July 2, 1906, Strasbourg, France (then Germany)

Bethe's best-known achievement is his theory of energy production in the stars. Published in 1938, this propounds a theoretical description of deuteron fusion and the carbon cycle as mechanisms to explain how the rate of energy production in the interior of the Sun is sufficient to offset energy losses from its surface. Moreover, he was almost unique among contemporary physicists for the breadth of his contributions to physics, which ranged from the fundamental particles of nuclear physics to ballistic missiles. In 1967 Bethe received the Nobel Prize in physics for contributions to the theory of nuclear reaction and for his theory of energy production in stars.

In 1935–37 Bethe and two collaborators wrote a comprehensive treatise on the subject of nuclear physics, which was then in its infancy. This work remained the standard text for young nuclear physicists for at least 15 years. In it, Bethe clarified the theory of nuclear forces, the structure of nuclei, and the theory of nuclear reactions. During World War II he applied this knowledge as leader of the Theoretical Division of the Los Alamos Scientific Laboratory, which designed the first atomic bomb. After the war he continued to work on nuclear energy, but mainly on its application for the peaceful production of power. Beginning in 1973, he wrote and spoke extensively on the need to use nuclear energy to replace the world's dwindling resources of oil. On the more fundamental side, he explored the particles that are responsible for nuclear forces. In later years he was mainly interested in the connection between the nuclear forces and the structure of actual nuclei.

Bethe worked extensively on the collision of charged particles with atoms. He developed the quantum theory of this process, which he used to predict the distance a fast particle can penetrate through matter. This is important for the design of experiments in nuclear physics and of shields to protect persons from harmful nuclear radiations. He also calculated the radiation emitted from fast electrons.

Unlike most physicists who work on nuclear or atomic problems, Bethe was also interested in classical physics. During the war he worked on the theory of shock waves, and this experience was very useful to him in his work on the atom bomb and later on the effects of atomic weapons. He also made contributions to the design of the heat shield for ballistic missiles when they reenter the atmosphere.

When Bethe developed his theory of energy production in the stars in 1938, A. S. Eddington and others had made extensive contributions to an understanding of the probable physical conditions in the interiors of stars. From a knowledge of the mass, radius, and luminosity (amount of energy emitted per second) of a star, detailed information about temperature variations and pressure gradients, as well as a good deal of information about its internal physics, was formulated. Because of the enormous temperature postulated for the Sun's interior, it was considered likely that nuclear energy must be the source that sustains solar radiation. Physicists were at a loss, however, to explain the system of nuclear reactions that would account for the rate of energy production by the Sun consistent with astrophysical observations.

Accepting the astronomers' calculation of 2×10^7°C for the central temperature of the Sun, Bethe found a series of thermonuclear reactions that could proceed with sufficient intensity to support solar radiation. Because of the high temperature in the interior of the Sun, the reactant nuclei possess the high kinetic energy necessary to penetrate each other, each reaction requiring only the collision of two bodies. He carefully examined all possible nuclear reactions, both those observed in experiments performed with the cyclotron and others that were merely postulated theoretically, and divided these into two groups. In one were the reactions in which only protons were consumed, and in the other those in which other light nuclei were also consumed. Astrophysical evidence had shown that protons are enormously more abundant in stars than other nuclei. Some elements, like Li, Be, and B, are extremely rare in stars. Bethe therefore argued that reactions consuming these rare nuclei should be excluded because they could not supply the energy for billions of years as required. Only protons (and perhaps helium nuclei) are abundant enough to supply energy throughout the long life of a star, and among these only protons can penetrate sufficiently easily into other nuclei to develop energy at a sufficient rate. He found only two nuclear reactions that fulfilled all requirements: deuteron fusion and the carbon cycle. Of these, only the carbon cycle will produce energy fast enough to explain the energy production in the more brilliant stars like Sirius.

Bethe found that the nucleus ^{12}C is unique. Not only does it react with protons at a sufficient rate to explain the energy production in the Sun and other stars, but also it undergoes a cycle of reactions that terminates in the final stage with the formation of a new ^{12}C. The carbon nucleus thus serves as a catalytic agent that is regenerated in the cycle. In fact, the final result of the cycle is equivalent to the fusion of four protons into a nucleus of helium and the release of energy, in terms of the mass energy equivalence law, resulting in a 1 percent difference of mass.

In the carbon cycle, the first transformation occurs when a proton enters the nucleus of a ^{12}C. Under the conditions prevailing in the Sun, this happens on the average of about once in 40,000 years. The product is radioactive ^{13}N and the simultaneous emission of a gamma photon. This radiation reaches the surface, Bethe reasoned, not by a straight route but by a complicated zigzag path during which it is constantly being absorbed by other atoms

and reemitted in new directions and ultimately at a much lower frequency. It is this slow escape of radiation, which Bethe estimated to require 10^6 years, that maintains the high interior temperature of the Sun which in turn, maintains the thermonuclear reactions. About 10 minutes after it is formed, the ^{13}N spontaneously decays with the emission of a positron and becomes the stable isotope ^{13}C. Approximately 7,000 years later, the second thermonuclear reaction occurs; the carbon nucleus captures a proton and becomes stable ^{14}N, which emits a gamma ray. The next stage, about 10^6 years later, is a thermonuclear reaction with the penetration of a third proton into ^{14}N to produce the isotope ^{15}O; this is unstable and decays to ^{15}N with the emission of a positron. The final stage, about 20 years later, is still another thermonuclear reaction, in which a fourth proton is captured by ^{15}N and the product splits into two parts, ^4He and ^{12}C.

Bethe's synthesis of a helium nucleus by the carbon cycle was simultaneously and independently suggested by C. F. von Weizsacker in Germany, but he did not investigate whether this process had the correct rate for the Sun and other stars. At the same time, Bethe and C. L. Critchfield accomplished the calculations for a proton-proton sequence that involved the direct building of the helium nucleus from hydrogen and that fitted the observed facts equally well. The rate at which the competitive cycles proceed is extremely sensitive to temperature, so that the selection of a mechanism depends upon the internal temperature of the star. For stars with interior temperatures greater than the Sun's, the carbon cycle appears to predominate; for cooler bodies with interior temperatures in the region of 10^7 degrees, deuteron fusion is the more important synthesis. Both cycles have the widest possible acceptance among astrophysicists for explaining the relation between solar energy and its lifetime of radiation.

In 1970 Bethe returned to astrophysical problems. With several collaborators, he calculated the distribution of matter in neutron stars, the new type of stars which had been discovered in 1968 in the form of pulsars. This work showed that the maximum possible mass for a neutron star was somewhat under twice the mass of the Sun.

In 1978, again with several collaborators, Bethe investigated the behavior of

matter in a collapsing giant star. This collapse, which is due to gravitation, gives rise to the supernova phenomenon in which a star emits tremendous amounts of light and its material is scattered over the Galaxy. Bethe and collaborators found that the initial collapse leads to densities at the center of the star which are much greater than the density in nuclei, whereas previous investigators had thought that the density would stay well under nuclear density. The new findings are believed to be important for the supernovae explosion.

The son of a university professor, Bethe studied at the University of Frankfurt and took his doctorate at the University of Munich under A. J. W. Sommerfeld in 1928. He taught theoretical physics at various German universities until 1933, and for the next 2 years at the universities of Manchester and Bristol. In 1935 he joined the faculty of Cornell University. Among many honors, he received the Draper Medal of the National Academy of Sciences in 1947 and the Eddington Medal of the Royal Astronomical Society in 1963, both for his work on the stars; the U.S. Medal of Merit in 1946 for his work on the atomic bomb; and the Enrico Fermi Award of the U.S. Atomic Energy Commission in 1961 for his general work in nuclear physics and atomic energy. He was elected to the National Academy of Sciences in 1944.

Bethe wrote *Elementary Nuclear Theory* (1947; 2d ed., with P. Morrison, 1956), *Quantum Mechanics of One- and Two-Electron Atoms,* with E. E. Salpeter (1957), *Splitting of Terms in Crystals* (1958), and *Intermediate Quantum Mechanics* (1964). His main work was published in more than 250 papers in scientific journals.

For background information *see* CARBON-NITROGEN CYCLE; NUCLEAR PHYSICS; PROTON-PROTON CHAIN; SUN in the McGraw-Hill Encyclopedia of Science and Technology. ■

BIERMANN, LUDWIG FRANZ BENEDIKT
★ German astrophysicist

***Born** Mar.13, 1907, Hamm, Westphalia, Germany*

The general success of A. S. Eddington's theory of stellar structure led to a widespread impression that the temperature gradient valid for radiative transport of

energy was an adequate approximation also in case of thermal instability, that is, if this gradient exceeded the adiabatic value. After 1930 it became increasingly probable that in many stars the nuclear processes producing the energy radiated away are highly concentrated in the central regions, which therefore should be thermally unstable. The value of the actual temperature gradient in such a region was determined in 1932 by Biermann, then a graduate student at Göttingen; he showed that a minute excess above the adiabatic gradient was sufficient for having all the energy carried by turbulent convection, such that the adiabatic temperature gradient was a good approximation to the actual gradient. This proof used Prandtl mixing length theory; analogous results using slightly different formulations of the transport equation were obtained in 1934 by T. G. Cowling and again in 1938 by E. Öpik. Cowling proposed also the first stellar model with an adiabatic central convective zone, the point source model of 1934. During the subsequent years the possibilities of more general stellar models were discussed between Biermann and Cowling, and in 1938 Biermann showed that solar-type stars should possess a rather large outer convective zone. This model fulfilled the standard surface boundary conditions, using the best values of the surface layer's opacity then available, which were soon confirmed after the discovery of the negative hydrogen ion by R. Wildt. *See* ÖPIK, ERNST JULIUS.

In 1942 Biermann proposed a sunspot model, based on the assumption of an inhibition of the convective energy transport underneath the sunspots by their magnetic fields; these fields are regarded as the basic feature of a sunspot, a model which has remained under active discussion to the present day. In 1946 the highly nonthermal state of the outermost parts of the Sun's atmosphere and similar stars was traced back to the production, in the outer parts of the above-mentioned convective layer, of progressive waves carrying energy outward. The result was arrived at independently by M. Schwarzschild in 1948.

Bright comets show, in addition to the often more conspicuous curved dust tails, a straight and long gas tail consisting of molecular ions, that is to say, of a plasma. These tails show much more structure and variability than dust tails do; the displacement in time of individual structures permits derivation of velocities and accelerations. Whereas the accelerations acting upon the dust particles, which make up the curved tails, can easily be explained by the pressure of solar light, those acting on the plasma tails are many times larger than the ones which could be ascribed to the absorption and reemission of solar light. In 1951 Biermann proposed to ascribe the acceleration of the plasma tails to an until then unknown component of the Sun's corpuscular radiation, which, from the observed properties of the cometary plasma tails, had to be present at all times and had to be emitted by the Sun in all directions, whereas the component's density could be very low in view of very small densities observed in the cometary gas tails. The transfer of momentum was linked to the well-known properties of interpenetrating plasmas; this transfer of momentum was known to be particularly effective if magnetic fields were embedded in them, as was believed by some authors even then, a point elaborated by H. Alfvén in 1957. *See* ALFVÉN, HANNES OLOF GÖSTA.

An observational argument in favor of Biermann's hypothesis was C. Hoffmeister's discovery in 1943 of an approximately linear relationship between the deviation of the axis of such tails from the antisolar direction which, as Biermann showed, was a natural consequence of his hypothesis, if the velocity of the solar plasma flowing through interplanetary space was somewhere between the speed of sound in the solar corona and the speeds ascribed to the nonstationary clouds of solar plasma causing geomagnetic storms. In 1958 E. Parker showed that the existence of the new quasistationary and omni-directional component of the Sun's corpuscular radiation, which he termed the solar wind, could be regarded as a natural consequence of the dynamical state of the solar corona. The values of the density in the new corpuscular component proposed in 1951 were later found to be seriously on the high side, because of similar errors in the then current values for the density in the plasma clouds causing big magnetic storms, and of similar errors in the interpretation of the zodiacal light's polarization, whereas other, later observations and arguments led to considerably lower densities. These contradictions persisted until the first in-place measurements over sufficiently long periods of time were made from space vehicles in 1962; they confirmed the existence of a component of the Sun's corpuscular radiation present at all times for the neighborhood of the ecliptic and also the presence of magnetic fields embedded in them, which couple the cometary plasma to the solar wind plasma. At about the same time it became gradually clear why the arguments which had led to the higher values originally proposed were in error. The presence of the solar wind outside of the ecliptic plane was confirmed by measurements of the interplanetary scintillation in the radio frequencies, but the largest amount of observational data on the solar wind outside of the ecliptic still consists of the observations of cometary plasma tails. *See* PARKER, EUGENE NEWMAN.

Biermann was educated at the universities of Hannover, München, Freiburg, and Göttingen (Ph.D., 1932). He worked subsequently at the universities of Edinburgh (1933–34), Jena (1934–37), and Berlin-Babelsberg (1937–45), and lectured at the universities of Berlin (1938–45), Hamburg (1945–48), Göttingen (1948–58), and München, where he was appointed Honorarprofessor in 1959. In 1947 he joined the Max Planck Institut für Physik in Göttingen, which in 1958 was transferred to München as the Max Planck Institut für Physik und Astrophysik; he became director of the Institut für Astrophysik. He received the Copernicus Prize (1943), the Bruce Gold Medal of the Astronomical Society of the Pacific (1967), the Emil Wiechert Medal of the German Geophysical Society (1973), and the Gold Medal of the Royal Astronomical Society (1974). He was elected to a number of academies and societies, including the Bavarian Academy of Sciences (1961), and to the U.S. National Academy of Sciences (1976) as a foreign associate.

Biermann wrote *Dynamics of Interplanetary Material,* which formed part 2 of *Cosmic Gas Dynamics* (M. S. Uberoi, ed., 1973).

For background information *see* COMET; STAR; STELLAR EVOLUTION; SUN in the McGraw-Hill Encyclopedia of Science and Technology. ∎

BIGELEISEN, JACOB
★ American chemist

Born May 2, 1919, Paterson, NJ, U.S.A.

Bigeleisen founded the modern school of isotope chemistry. His researches, both experimental and theoretical, established the fundamental bases for the differences in the chemical behavior of isotopes. As a result, scientists have been able to predict and develop new processes for the separation of isotopes. For this work he received the U.S. Atomic Energy Commission's E. O. Lawrence Award in 1964. The utilization of the differences in chemical behavior of isotopes has opened up new areas in chemical physics, geochemistry, molecular biology, and chemical kinetics. For his work on isotope effects in chemical kinetics, Bigeleisen received the American Chemical Society's Award for

Nuclear Application in Chemistry in 1958.

Isotopes were discovered early in the 20th century by the study of natural radioactive decay of heavy elements. For a long time it was assumed that isotopes were truly indistinguishable chemically. A major change came when Harold Urey discovered deuterium, and large differences were found between the chemical properties of protium and deuterium. Small but definite differences were found for the heavy elements. *See* UREY, HAROLD CLAYTON.

Early in World War II Bigeleisen became associated with Urey on problems connected with isotope separation. Late in 1943 he began to ponder two questions:(1) How large could the differences in chemical properties of the isotopes of a given element be?(2) How did these isotope effects depend on the chemical properties and structure of a molecule? Early in 1944 he and Maria Goeppert Mayer found a very simple solution to this question for gases at equilibrium. They discovered that it was possible to explain all the differences in chemical properties of isotopes in gases at equilibrium by considering the vibrations of atoms in a molecule. According to Heisenberg's uncertainty principle, it is impossible to specify simultaneously the exact position and velocity of a particle. This makes it impossible to confine an atom to a precise position in a molecule. As a result of this motion, an atom in a molecule possesses vibrational energy even at absolute zero. Since the vibrational energy is proportional to the frequency of motion, and since light atoms oscillate with higher frequencies than heavy atoms, it is easier to dissociate a molecule containing a light isotope than a heavy isotope of an element. From this principle, the heavy isotope of an element favors the chemical species in which it is most strongly bound chemically. The differences in chemical properties of isotopes of an element, from one compound to another, are a direct measure of the change in chemical bonding of this element from compound to compound. The answer to Bigeleisen's question—how large can these isotopic differences be—was established on a quantitative scale. At the bottom of the scale, with no difference, was the free atom; at the top were those chemical compounds for which the bonding is strongest. For instance, for isotopes of hydrogen, the largest effects were found in

water, and no effects occurred in hydrogen atoms. Generally, the differences decreased with temperature. This is the basis of the oxygen isotope paleothermometer. *See* MAYER, MARIA GOEPPERT.

The ability of an isotope to measure changes in chemical bonding makes it a valuable tool for the study of molecular forces, the changes in molecular forces as molecules react, and the study of interactions of various types of bonding with one another. With this approach Bigeleisen was able to develop the theory of how isotopes differ in their rates of chemical reaction. From measured differences in rates of isotopic reactions, it is now possible for scientists to learn about the paths that molecules follow when they react and to learn about the associated energy changes. Such investigations by the isotopic and other methods are now at the forefront of chemical research.

Later Bigeleisen extended the theory of isotopic behavior to the liquid and solid states. Guided by the theory he had developed for isotopic behavior in liquids, he investigated experimentally the question of how the properties of a liquid depend on the mass distribution in a molecule. At Los Alamos, in 1955, Bigeleisen and E. C. Kerr showed that HT behaved differently from an isotopic molecule with the same total mass, D_2. Subsequent experiments at Brookhaven demonstrated differences between two types of nitrous oxide with ^{15}N; in another investigation, the various deuterated ethylenes were studied. The investigation of the effect of molecular mass distribution on the properties of a liquid revealed that the motion of a molecule is different in a liquid or solid from that in a gas, where the translation and rotation of the molecule are independent of one another. Both are independent of the vibrations of the atoms within the molecule. In the liquid or solid, all of these motions become coupled with one another. The experiments confirmed the theory. A new field for investigation had been opened.

The son of immigrant parents, Bigeleisen majored in chemistry at New York University (B.A., 1939). After graduation he started research with Otto Redlich at the State College of Washington (M.S., 1941). He went on to work with Gilbert N. Lewis, the dean of American physical chemists, at the University of California, Berkeley (Ph.D., 1943). During World War II he worked on isotope separation for the Manhattan District at Columbia

University. After the war he was a fellow at the Enrico Fermi Institute, Unversity of Chicago (1946–48). In 1948 he joined the newly formed Brookhaven National Laboratory. In addition, Bigeleisen was visiting professor at Cornell University in 1953. He was a National Science Foundation senior fellow and visiting professor at Eigden Technical Hochschule, in Switzerland, in 1962–63. He was the Gilbert N. Lewis Lecturer in 1963. Bigeleisen was elected a fellow of the American Physical Society, the American Chemical Society, and the American Association for the Advancement of Science, and a member of the National Academy of Sciences (1966).

For background information *see* ISO-TOPE in the McGraw-Hill Encyclopedia of Science and Technology. ∎

BIOT, MAURICE ANTHONY
★ American engineer, physicist, and applied mathematician

Born May 25, 1905, Antwerp, Belgium

The work and original contributions which distinguish Biot's career cover an unusually broad range of science and technology, including applied mechanics, sound, heat, thermodynamics, aeronautics, geophysics, and electromagnetism. The level of his work ranged from the highly theoretical and mathematical to practical applications and patented inventions.

Biot's pioneering work in the 1930s on the response of structures to transient disturbances led to the key concept of the response spectrum as a universally applied tool in the design of earthquake-proof structures and in many other problems. During the same period he published his first papers on a new approach to the nonlinear theory of elasticity which accounted for the effect of initial stress.

Aeronautical problems and fluid mechanics were the object of most of Biot's efforts during the 1940s. He developed the three-dimensional aerodynamic theory of oscillating airfoils, as well as new methods of vibration analysis based on matrix theory and generalized coordinates. These led to design procedures widely applied to complex aircraft structures in order to prevent catastrophic flutter. He also patented an electrical analog flutter predictor based on a simple circuit design which simulated aerodynamic forces. After World War II he continued work on nonstationary aerodynamics and aeroelasticity, including studies of the divergence instability of thin supersonic wings and the first evaluation of the transonic drag of an accelerated body.

In the 1950s Biot's work was concerned primarily with problems of solid mechanics, porous media, thermodynamics, and heat transfer. He developed a new approach to the thermodynamics of irreversible processes by introducing a generalized form of free energy as a key potential. The formulation was associated with new variational principles and Lagrangian-type equations. With the introduction of internal coordinates, the results provided the thermodynamic foundation of a completely general theory of anisotropic viscoelasticity and thermoelasticity. As a by-product of this work, Biot developed a new approach to heat transfer, based on generalized coordinates and a Lagrangian systems analysis, which proved to have remarkable accuracy and avoided some of the physical inconsistencies of traditional methods. He gave a systematic presentation of this work in a monograph published in 1970, indicating its applicability to many other problems, such as those of aquifers or neutron diffusion in nuclear reactor design.

Biot's interest in the mechanics of porous media dated back to 1940, when he published a fundamental paper on soil mechanics and consolidation. He returned to the subject in the 1950s in the more general context of rock mechanics, in connection with problems in the oil industry. On the basis of his earlier work in thermodynamics, he published a large number of papers which provided a completely general and systematic theory of porous solids containing a viscous fluid. He showed that three types of acoustic waves exist in such media.

For a short period in the mid-1950s Biot became involved with rocket radio-guidance problems and the question of disturbance from ground reflections. To evaluate this effect, he developed an original theory for the reflection of electromagnetic and acoustic waves from a rough surface, showing that the effect of the roughness can be replaced by a smooth boundary condition. At the same time, in collaboration with I. Tolstoy, he introduced an approach to pulse-generated transient waves based on a continuous spectrum of normal coordinates. The combination of the two methods provided the only practical solution of some important problems.

In a series of papers starting in 1957, Biot extended his earlier work on the mechanics of initially stressed solids, developing a mathematical theory of folding instability of stratified viscous and viscoelastic solids. He verified the results in the laboratory and used them with considerable success to explain the dominant features of geological structures. The results were also found to be consistent with the geological time scale. In particular, he brought to light the phenomenon of internal buckling of a confined anisotropic or stratified medium under compressive stress, and provided a quantitative analysis. He applied the theory with the same success to problems of gravity instability and salt dome formation. In a 1965 monograph he presented a systematic treatment of the mechanics of initially stressed continua. On the basis of these developments in the theory of stratified media, Biot derived a new approach to the analysis of engineering structures which involved multilayered plates and composite materials. He brought out the characteristic stress-distribution features of strongly anisotropic materials, which are significant from an engineering standpoint.

In the 1970s Biot's formulation of his variational principle of virtual dissipation in the thermodynamics of irreversible processes, along with his new approach to open systems, represented a contribution which was fundamental and far-reaching. The variational principle led to a synthesis of classical mechanics and irreversible thermodynamics. At the same time, he originated new concepts in the thermodynamics of open systems which eliminated the traditional difficulties inherent in J. W. Gibbs's classical theory. As a consequence, he derived a new chemical thermodynamics, leading to the concept of the intrinsic heat of reaction, which provided an improved measure of the true chemical energy, as well as new expressions for the affinity and heat of reaction. He applied these new theories to obtain field equations directly in systems in which deformations are coupled to thermomolecular diffusion and chemical reactions. From this basis, he also developed further the theory of porous media, including heat and mass transport with phase changes and adsorption effects.

Biot graduated from Louvain University with a bachelor in philosophy degree (1927), and he received the degrees of mining engineer (1929), electrical engineer (1930), and doctor of science (1931) from that university. He received a Ph.D. at the California Institute of Technology in 1932. He held teaching positions at Harvard (1934–35), Louvain (1935–37), Columbia (1937–45), and Brown (1946–50) universities. During World War II, as a lieutenant commander in the U.S. Navy, he headed the structural dynamics section of the Bureau of Aeronautics (1943–45).

Biot wrote *Mathematical Methods in Engineering,* with T. von Kármán (1940), *Mechanics of Incremental Deformations* (1965), and *Variational Principles in Heat Transfer* (1970).

For background information *see* AERO-ELASTICITY; FLUID, NON-NEWTONIAN; SOIL MECHANICS; STRESS AND STRAIN; THERMODYNAMICS, CHEMICAL in the McGraw-Hill Encyclopedia of Science and Technology. ∎

BIRCH, ARTHUR JOHN
★ Australian chemist

Born Aug. 3, 1915, Sydney, Australia

A graduate of the University of Sydney, Birch went to Oxford in 1938 to work with Sir Robert Robinson. In 1941, as a war researcher, he was asked to attempt the synthesis of cortical hormone analogs. Since those based on the hexoestrol nucleus proved to have estrogenic female hormone activity, he attempted to simplify instead

the nucleus of the natural hormones to make total synthesis easier. The six-membered rings of the steroid nucleus suggested the appropriateness of benzenoid starting materials, which would, however, need to be only partially hydrogenated. Catalytic methods then known led only to complete hydrogenation. Birch evolved the method that became known as the Birch reduction, which involved the use of alkali metals and alcohols in liquid ammonia to cause addition of only two atoms of hydrogen to a benzene ring. This method led eventually in 1948 to the total synthesis of the first biologically active analog of the male sex hormones—19-nortestosterone. This hormone was the first totally synthetic sex hormone of the nonaromatic type, although it lacked the 19-methyl group of the natural series, later synthesized by others. The male series was chosen because of the simplicity of the group (hydroxyl) producing this type of biological activity. Later workers employing essentially the same process added the known activating groups for progestational activity and produced 19-norsteroid analogs, which proved to be effective as oral contraceptives. Virtually all substances used as contraceptive pills belong to this series and are made by using the Birch reduction.

The reduction method proved to have a much wider use, and in synthetic chemistry has almost displaced the previous methods using high-pressure catalytic hydrogenation of aromatic rings. The method also proved to have a very useful and predictable outcome in controlling the spatial

configurations of molecules to which it leads.

In synthetic work Birch was much more interested in devising methods, rather than in using them to solve individual synthetic problems. The steroid work, for example, led to the first recognition of polyphosphoric acid as a cyclizing agent, and to various methods of introducing angular methyl groups. These include the methylanilinomethylene blocking group, the copper-catalyzed conjugate addition of Grignard reagents, and the addition of carbenes. The last method is still probably the best way to introduce the missing 19-methyl group into the estrone series, now readily available by total synthesis.

In 1952, on appointment to a chair in Sydney, Birch was faced with the problem of what research could be done. In those days, shortage of equipment, few students beyond the master's degree level, no research funds, and great distances from sources of supply placed serious limits on research. He abandoned the steroid syntheses and turned therefore to the one advantage Australia possessed: natural products. This new interest was partly due to work in the laboratory of Lord Todd in Cambridge (1949–52). A general program, involving the accumulation of small pieces of information in the form of natural product structures which could be combined in the form of biosynthetic theories, was commenced. Avoiding alkaloids, which were then the favorite topic in biosynthesis, Birch put forward the biogenetic "polyketide hypothesis." This drew on two bases: a knowledge through personal acquaintance with J. W. Cornforth and G. J. Popjak of the importance of acetyl coenzyme A (acetate) in the biosynthesis of steroids and fats, and an accidental observation of one natural product structure: campnospermonol. This structure contains an obvious oleic acid unit, and the simple question then asked was: if this comes from acetate, does the rest of the molecule also arise in this way? Comparative anatomy of structures showed that cyclizations of acetate-derived polyketide chains could explain many structures which were hitherto apparently unrelated: about 3000 examples were subsequently described. *See* CORNFORTH, SIR JOHN (WARCUP); TODD OF TRUMPINGTON, BARON (ALEXANDER ROBERTUS TODD).

The theory immediately reduced a jumble of apparently unrelated structures to order. Examples include the anthocyanin pigments of flowers and the tetracycline antibiotics. Ancillary hypotheses were needed, some concerned with loss of oxygen, and some with the introduction of other units such as methyl and terpene groups. In this connection, Birch suggested for the first time the biochemical process of *C*-methylation from methionine. From 1952 to 1967, first in Sydney and then in Manchester, complete biochemical support in many examples was provided for all of these theories by means of radiocarbon precursors. In 1958 this work also provided the first experimental proof of the predicted concerted carbonium ion cyclizations of terpenes to cyclic diterpenes, using gibberellic and rosenonolactone. Several other biosynthetic hypotheses, all put forward on the grounds that nature works by processes recognizable to the chemist, despite the admitted importance of enzymes, were shown to be correct. The program also led to the determination of the structure of many natural products, some by biogenetic methods.

On the grounds that further progress in these areas depended on enzyme chemistry, in which he was not interested, Birch returned to synthetic chemistry. He believed that organic chemists had unduly neglected organometallic chemistry as an organic tool, particularly in relation to stoichiometric, as distinct from catalytic, aspects. After about 1965 he examined organometallic compounds of transition metals as tools in organic synthesis, principally using rhodium (homogeneous hydrogenation) and iron complexes. The iron complexes were shown to lead quantitatively to stereospecific reactions of various kinds, including the sensitization of purely carbon systems to nucleophilic reagents.

Birch was also interested and active in scientific organizations, government, industry (as a consultant), and scientific education. He served as treasurer of the Australian Academy of Science, president of the Royal Australian Chemical Institute, and chairperson of the Australian Government Independent Inquiry into the Commonwealth Scientific and Industrial Organization. He organized a major scientific exhibition for the Australia 75 — Festival of Science and Art. He received a number of scientific awards in Australia, Belgium, Czechoslovakia, the United Kingdom, and the United States, including the Davy Medal of the Royal Society. He was a fellow of the Australian Academy of Science and the Royal Society, and a full foreign member of the Academy of Science of the U.S.S.R.

For background information *see* ADRENAL CORTEX STEROID; ORGANOMETALLIC COMPOUNDS; STEROID in the McGraw-Hill Encyclopedia of Science and Technology. ■

BIRCH, FRANCIS
★ American geophysicist

Born Aug. 22, 1903, Washington, DC, U.S.A.

After graduating from Harvard with a degree in electrical engineering, and working for 2 years for the New York Telephone Company, Birch decided to shift to the study of physics. An American Field Service Fellowship enabled him to spend 2 years at the University of Strasbourg (1926–28), where he acquired a taste for research in the laboratory of Pierre Weiss and, as a junior author, wrote several papers on magnetism. Returning to Harvard as a graduate student in physics, he began an apprenticeship in P. W. Bridgman's high-pressure laboratory and completed his thesis, on the electrical resistance and critical point of mercury, in 1932. With some qualifications in physical measurements, but none in geology, he was invited to undertake a study of the physical properties of geological materials; this became a lifelong task. *See* BRIDGMAN, PERCY WILLIAMS.

The initial geophysical studies were suggested by Reginald A. Daly, who had long realized the inadequacy of existing data on the physical properties of rocks. Notably scanty was information on systematic relationships among properties such as density, elastic-wave velocities, and composition, at various combinations of pressure and temperature. In addition to his valuable guidance, Daly contributed a collection of representative igneous rocks for experimental use which was subsequently used by investigators at Harvard and elsewhere.

Most of Birch's work was concerned with elasticity, phase relations, thermal properties and heat flow, and the composition of the Earth's interior. Besides his own measurements and those of his assistants and students, he drew upon Bridgman's great accumulation of high-pressure data and upon observations on extreme pressure resulting from wartime research with explosives. The theory of finite strain, given a correct formulation in 1937 by F. D. Murnaghan, provided a framework that could be used for evaluating the effect of pressure on elastic properties, and thus for analyzing the rise of seismic velocities with depth in the Earth. Results were published in 1939 and, after revisions of seismic velocities by H. Jeffreys and K. E. Bullen, again in 1952. The principal conclusions of the 1952 paper, which included a review of pertinent thermodynamic data, were as follows: between depths of 900 and 2900 kilometers (the lower mantle) the Earth is uniform in composition and phase, with elastic properties not found for any (then) known silicate oxides but comparable with those of certain close-packed oxides; between about 200 and 900 kilometers the rise of seismic velocities is higher than can be attributed to compression of a single phase, again signaling a transition to high-pressure phases. *See* MURNAGHAN, FRANCIS DOMINIC.

Other suggestions concerned the Earth's core: crystalline iron was proposed for the inner core, in accord with a 1940 paper, and the outer liquid core was thought to require light alloying elements in addition to the predominant iron. Most of these ideas were later confirmed: high-pressure silicates were synthesized, discontinuities of seismic structure were detected in the transition zone, and various correlations of discontinuities with phase changes were suggested. The solidity of the inner core was confirmed in 1971 by A. M. Dziewonski and F. Gilbert, with the discovery of certain modes of vibration of the Earth which could not exist if the inner core were liquid. The measurements with explosively generated high pressures showed phase changes for nearly all the silicates studied, and placed important limits on the densities to be expected at the highest terrestrial pressures.

Of Birch's studies, the first, on thermal problems, with Harry Clark, introduced a semblance of order in measurements of the thermal conductivity of rocks. The next step was to combine conductivities with thermal gradients for the estimation of heat flow; in the 1930s there were no determinations of heat flow based on samples and temperatures taken from a common mass of rock. Measurements in England (A. E. Benfield) and South Africa (E. C. Bullard), designed to remedy this situation, were undertaken approximately simultaneously. Opportunities for the measurement of temperature and sampling for conductivity were scarce, a circumstance which led to interest in tunnels under substantial cover as well as the more directly useful vertical borings. A thorough study, with extensive sampling and corrections for the evolution of surface topography, was made on the Adams Tunnel through the Front Range in Colorado in 1947. In the 1960s it became feasible to drill a few vertical holes solely for heat-flow determinations, as well as to open older exploration holes for this purpose. A major program, directed mainly by Robert F. Roy, produced about 130 new determinations in the United States, and demonstrated a remarkable dependence of heat flow upon local, bedrock radioactivity, which permitted a tentative separation between near-surface heat generation and heat produced at greater depths.

Birch attended public schools in Washington, DC, and entered Harvard University in 1920, receiving his bachelor's degree in 1924. After spending 2 years at the University of Strasbourg, he returned to Harvard, where he was appointed research associate in geophysics in 1933. He moved up the academic ladder, becoming Sturgis-Hooper Professor of Geology in 1949 and emeritus professor in 1974. He was on leave of absence from Harvard during 1942–45, first as a staff member of the Radiation Laboratory at the Massachusetts Institute of Technology, and then as an officer in the U.S. Naval Reserve in the Bureau of Ships in Washington and at Los Alamos, NM.

Birch was awarded the Legion of Merit in 1945. He received the Day Medal (1950) and the Penrose Medal (1969) of the Geological Society of America, the Bowie Medal of the American Geophysical Union (1960), the National Medal of Science (1968), the Vetlesen Prize of Columbia University (1969; shared with Sir Edward Bullard), an honorary degree from the University of Chicago (1970), and the Gold Medal of the Royal Astronomical Society (1973). He was elected to the American Academy of Arts and Sciences (1942), the National Academy of Sciences (1950), and the American Philosophical Society (1955). He became an honorary member of the Geological Society of London in 1967, and an associate of the Royal Astronomical Society in 1973. He was elected a fellow of the American Physical Society and the Geological Society of America (president, 1964), and a member of the Seismological Society of America.

Birch published about 100 papers, many in collaboration with assistants, students, and research fellows. He was editor of the *Handbook of Physical Constants,* published by the Geological Society of America in 1942. This was the first attempt at a comprehensive, critical collection of physical data for rocks, combining the efforts of 19 compilers. It provided a starting point for much subsequent work, and a revision, edited by S. P. Clark, was published in 1966.

For background information *see* GEOPHYSICS; HIGH-PRESSURE PHENOMENA in the McGraw-Hill Encyclopedia of Science and Technology. ∎

BIRD, ROBERT BYRON

★ American chemical engineer and educator

Born Feb. 5, 1924, Bryan, TX, U.S.A.

Bird's contributions were in the field of transport phenomena, including both the understanding of the molecular mechanisms of, and the solving of problems in, fluid dynamics, heat transfer, and mass transfer. The four books he coauthored provided interpretation and sytematization of this material for use by engineers and scientists.

Bird's introduction to transport phenomena began with his doctoral work, with J. O. Hirschfelder at the University of Wisconsin, on the calculation of trans-

port properties of gases from intermolecular forces, and continued with his postdoctoral research, with J. de Boer at the University of Amsterdam, on quantum effects in gases at low temperatures. This phase of his career culminated in the publication of a treatise, *Molecular Theory of Gases and Liquids,* by Hirschfelder, C. F. Curtiss, and Bird (1954), which brought together information on transport properties (viscosity, thermal conductivity, and diffusivity), equations of state, and intermolecular forces. *See* HIRSCHFELDER, JOSEPH OAKLAND.

A summer at the Du Pont Experimental Station convinced Bird of the need for developing a textbook which would help engineers and scientists to understand and use the equations of change of transport phenomena (the differential equations for conservation of mass, momentum, and energy as applied to multicomponent fluids). After several years of research devoted to non-Newtonian fluid mechanics, non-Newtonian heat transfer, viscous dissipation heat effects, and multicomponent diffusion, work was begun on a book that went through 21 printings in 18 years and was translated into Spanish, Italian, Czech, and Russian—*Transport Phenomena,* by Bird, W. E. Stewart, and E. N. Lightfoot (1960).

From about 1958 onward Bird specialized in research on transport phenomena in polymeric liquids; these fluids cannot be described by the equations of classical fluid dynamics (that is, the Navier-Stokes equations) since they do not have linear stress–rate-of-strain relations. This work

covered two main areas: (1) the development of constitutive equations (that is, expressions for the stress tensor), and (2) experimental and theoretical studies of rheological behavior and fluid dynamics problems. The second area included flow in annuli, flow around spheres, performance of rolling-ball and falling-cylinder viscometers, viscous heating in cone-and-plate viscometers, percolation through porous media, squeeze-film lubrication, secondary flows in disk-cylinder systems, elongational flows, and converging flows. The long-range objective of this work was to develop methods of solving polymeric fluid dynamic problems utilizing fragmentary data on rheological properties obtained from viscometric and other experiments. About 1968 Bird, along with A. S. Lodge, J. D. Ferry, J. L. Schrag, and M. W. Johnson, Jr., helped to found the Rheology Research Center at the University of Wisconsin.

After 1968 Bird turned his attention to the kinetic theory of polymer solutions in order to investigate the connection between macromolecular structure and rheological properties. During this period two lengthy research publications appeared: the first (with H. R. Warner and D. C. Evans) summarized and extended the kinetic theory of solutions in which the polymer solute molecules are modeled as elastic or rigid dumbbells; the second (with Curtiss and O. Hassager) established a new phase-space statistical-mechanical theory for polymer solutions which then provided the basis for further theoretical developments and detailed calculations. These two decades of research on continuum and molecular theories of polymer rheology were concluded with the publication of a two-volume monograph, *Dynamics of Polymeric Liquids,* vol. 1: *Fluid Dynamics,* by Bird, R. C. Armstrong, and Hassager (1977); and vol. 2: *Kinetic Theory,* by Bird, Hassager, Armstrong, and Curtiss (1977). These volumes presented both continuum and molecular viewpoints and also emphasized the interrelation between the two kinds of theories; the preparation of the two volumes was influenced in part by consultation, seminars, and short courses at the Union Carbide Company.

Bird simultaneously pursued a second major interest, namely, applied linguistics. Because of his research and teaching activities in the Netherlands, he became interested in the teaching of the Dutch language. This activity resulted in the publication of a graded and annotated series of short stories, essays, and poems by Dutch authors, *Een Goed Begin—A Contemporary Dutch Reader,* by Bird and W. Z. Shetter (1963, 1971). Then he turned his attention to the problems facing the scientist or engineer who wishes to translate technical material from Japanese to English. He first made an extensive study of the frequency of occurrence of *kanji* (Chinese characters) in technical Japanese writings; then, with this information at hand, he coauthored the first scientific Japanese reader, *Comprehending Technical Japanese,* by E. E. Daub, Bird, and N. Inoue (1975).

The son of a civil engineer, Bird received his B.S. in chemical engineering at the University of Illinois in 1947 and his Ph.D. in chemistry at the University of Wisconsin in 1950. After postdoctoral experience at the Instituut voor Theoretische Physica in Amsterdam (1950–51) and the Theoretical Chemistry Institute at the University of Wisconsin (1951–52), he joined the chemistry faculty at Cornell University. In 1953, after a summer at the Du Pont Experimental Station, he returned to the University of Wisconsin to join the chemical engineering department, where he became full professor in 1957; he chaired the department in 1964–68, and was named Burgess Professor in 1968 and then Vilas Research Professor in 1972. He was a Fulbright visiting professor and Guggenheim scholar at the Technische Hogeschool in Delft (1958) and a Fulbright lecturer at Kyoto and Nagoya universities in Japan (1962–63). He received honorary doctor of engineering degrees from Lehigh University (1972), Washington University (1973), and the Technische Hogeschool in Delft (1977). For his achievements in the field of transport phenomena, he received the William H. Walker (1962), Professional Progress (1965), and Warren K. Lewis (1974) awards of the American Institute of Chemical Engineers; the Bingham Medal (1974) of the Society of Rheology; and the Curtis McGraw (1959) and Westinghouse (1960) awards of the American Society of Engineering Education. Bird was elected to the National Academy of Engineering in 1969. He was elected a fellow of the American Physical Society in 1970 and a fellow of the American Institute of Chemical Engineers in 1972; he chaired the Wisconsin Section of the American Chemical Society in 1967, and was vice-president of the University of Wisconsin Chapter of Sigma Xi in 1959–60. He served on the editorial advisory boards of a number of journals.

For background information *see* FLUID, NON-NEWTONIAN; HEAT TRANSFER; RHEOLOGY; VISCOSITY OF GASES; VISCOSITY OF LIQUIDS in the McGraw-Hill Encyclopedia of Science and Technology. ■

BJERKNES, JACOB AALL BONNEVIE
★ American meteorologist

Born Nov. 2, 1897, Stockholm, Sweden
Died July 7, 1975, Los Angeles, CA, U.S.A.

While working in the storm-warning service in Bergen, Norway, in 1918, Bjerknes noticed that new, growing cyclones (centers of low pressure) frequently originated from a wave on a preexisting atmospheric front over the Atlantic, the nascent cyclone center being formed at the apex of a warm tongue of air intruding into cold air territory. From this initial finding the typical life cycle of cyclones was formulated and used in weather forecasting in all middle- and high-latitude locations.

The concept of atmospheric fronts was known before 1918, particularly as the "cold front" forming the forward edge of invading cold air. But the frontal wave with a "warm front" ahead of the apex and a "cold front" following it became a new feature on well-analyzed weather maps. As a consequence, young cyclones analyzed to have frontal-wave structure and great contrast in temperature between the air masses on either side of the front could be predicted to intensify; as a corollary, less intensification and eventual loss of kinetic energy could be expected in older cyclones within which the wave shape had been replaced by a vortex structure with cold core.

Intensification of cyclones is due to formation of new kinetic energy or advective concentration of existing kinetic energy into the volume occupied by the cyclone, or both. The latter process could not be investigated until systematic upper-air observations became available, but the former process was, in 1918, assumed by Bjerknes to convert potential energy into kinetic in the young wave cyclones at a rate sufficient to explain their early growth. J. Holmboe and others later confirmed this qualitative theory through a treatment of hydrodynamical models that simulated atmospheric fronts on the rotating Earth. Such models actually fostered unstable, growing waves whose lengths were of the order 1000–3000 kilometers observed in the atmosphere.

The theoretical picture of the mechanism of growing cyclones was largely developed through the study of weather maps at the bottom of the atmosphere before the three-dimensional picture of the same phenomena could be analyzed with data from networks of radiosonde balloons. Once the daily mapping of the upper troposphere and the lower stratosphere started during World War II, waves aloft were seen to be coupled with the moving frontal waves below, but also longer waves were discovered that move very slowly or even remain stationary for long periods. Important theoretical innovations followed this breakthrough in observation technique. Bjerknes's contribution, made in collaboration with Holmboe, was to define the concept of the "level of nondivergence." That level is located roughly at the altitude where atmospheric pressure is half that at the ground. At that level, the absolute vorticity of air parcels is quasi-conservative, and the field of that quantity can be predicted approximately from initial conditions by advective methods. From that idea John von Neumann and C.-G. A. Rossby developed the scheme of day-by-day prediction by electronic computers of the flow at the level of nondivergence that has become the basis of modern weather forecasting. *See* ROSSBY, CARL-GUSTAF ARVID; VON NEUMANN, JOHN.

Bjerknes thereafter confined his research to the phenomena that could not be very well handled by electronic computers, such as the isentropic up and down gliding of the air next to atmospheric fronts, the effect of sharp anticyclonic curvature of upper-air currents leading to deepening of the downwind trough, and so forth, all of which belong in the thinking of the forecaster who is to translate the electronic output into real weather predictions. Increasingly he turned his attention also to the processes of large-scale ocean-atmosphere interaction, which are important for their influence on the long trends of weather changes.

Grandson of mathematics professor C. A. Bjerknes (1825–1903) and son of physics professor V. F. K. Bjerknes (1862–1951), Jacob Bjerknes received his university training in Oslo, Norway, leading to a Ph.D. in 1924. His father's work, in hydrodynamics applied to the atmosphere, inspired him to seek a meteorological career. He entered the weather forecasting service in Bergen, Norway, in 1918, and became professor of meteorology in Bergen in 1931. He served upon invitation a year at the Swiss, and twice for half a year at the British, meteorological offices. Unable to return to Norway after a lecture trip in the United States in 1940, he was appointed to the first professorship in meteorology at the University of California at Los Angeles. He became a United States citizen in 1946. Elected to the National Academy of Sciences in 1947, Bjerknes was awarded the Bowie Medal of the American Geophysical Union in 1945, the Rossby Medal of the American Meteorological Society in 1960, and the National Medal of Science in 1966.

For background information *see* CYCLONE; FRONT; OCEAN-ATMOSPHERE RELATIONS; WEATHER FORECASTING AND PREDICTION in the McGraw-Hill Encyclopedia of Science and Technology. ∎

BLACK, HAROLD STEPHEN
★ American electrical engineer

Born *Apr. 14, 1898, Leominster, MA, U.S.A.*

Black was 29 when he invented the negative feedback amplifier, which some consider the Bell Telephone Laboratories'

greatest electronic contribution during its first 35 momentous years. In 1958 Mervin J. Kelly, then president of Bell Telephone Laboratories, wrote: "Although many of Black's inventions have made great impact, that of the negative feedback amplifier is indeed the most outstanding. It easily ranks coordinate with De Forest's invention of the audion as one of the two inventions of broadest scope and significance in electronics and communications of the past 50 years." For this achievement and for his successful development of the negative feedback principle, Black received many honors, including the 1952 Research Corporation Award.

Early in his career Black was assigned the task of reducing amplifier distortion so that a large number of multichannel amplifiers could be hooked up in tandem to carry telephone calls over longer distances. The job required an amplifier vastly superior to any then existing. Many other researchers before Black were aware of this need. Their only approach, however, and indeed Black's first approach, was to try to improve the tube characteristic. Electron tube research groups vigorously pursued this course in an attempt to provide an adequately linear input-output characteristic, but to no avail.

In the course of his work, Black attended a talk by Charles P. Steinmetz and came away impressed with the Steinmetz method of getting down to fundamentals. He applied the same method to his own problem and came up with a restatement

of his goal: to remove distortion from the amplifier output. Before that he had attempted to obtain amplification without distortion by specifying unrealistically superior vacuum tubes and other amplifier parts. He now turned to an acceptance of imperfect amplifier parts, regarded the output as composed of what was wanted plus what was not wanted, looked upon anything not wanted as distortion, and asked himself how to isolate and then annihilate this distortion.

Black immediately observed that by reducing the output to the same amplitude as the input and subtracting one from the other he would be left with distortion only, which could then be amplified in a separate tube and used to cancel out distortion in the original amplifier output. This feedback-feedforward system was set up in 1923 to demonstrate that unwanted output distortion could be either reduced or suppressed. While this demonstration circuit did not use negative feedback, it did prove that a complete and better solution was theoretically possible.

For more than 3 years Black struggled with his problem, using approaches too complex for satisfactory application. He was searching for an innovation that would simplify the circuit and perfect its operation. Finally, a mathematical analysis convinced him that, merely by utilizing negative feedback to insert a part of the output signal into the input in negative phase, he could obtain virtually any desired reduction in distortion products at the expense of a sacrifice in amplification.

This final mathematical analysis was conceived in a flash as Black was crossing the Hudson River on the Lackawanna ferryboat en route from home to the Bell laboratories. He wrote the equations that led to the solution on the back of his newspaper. Despite immediate recognition of its importance and prompt experimental verification, years of additional work were required before his application of negative feedback found widespread commercial use.

The application of Black's principle of negative feedback was not limited to telecommunications. Many industrial and military applications of amplifiers would not be possible without its use. Many new weapon systems, such as radar-directed bombing and radar-controlled missiles, depend on negative feedback for their success. The entire field of industrial control mechanisms and the development of servomechanisms theory and its applica-

tions are extensions of Black's principle of feedback and are generally recognized as such. In psychology and physiology this principle also sheds light on the nature of the mechanisms that control the operations of animals, including humans—that is, on how the brain and senses operate.

Upon completion of his training in electrical engineering at Worcester Polytechnic Institute, Black in 1921 joined the research organization of the Bell System, where he remained until 1963. In 1963 he became principal research scientist with General Precision Inc., working as a consultant on advanced communications and guidance feedback techniques pertaining to aerospace interests.

Black wrote *Modulation Theory* (1953).

For background information *see* AMPLITUDE MODULATION; FREQUENCY MODULATION; PULSE MODULATION in the McGraw-Hill Encyclopedia of Science and Technology. ∎

BLACKETT, PATRICK MAYNARD STUART

☆ British physicist

Born Nov. 18, 1897, London, England
Died July 13, 1974, London, England

At the suggestion of Ernest Rutherford, Blackett built an improved version of the Wilson cloud chamber. Utilizing this and subsequent instruments, he was able to photograph the tracks of a nuclear disintegration and the tracks of a cosmic-ray shower for the first time. For these

achievements he was awarded the Nobel Prize in physics in 1948.

The cloud chamber method for tracking atomic and subatomic particles was developed by C. T. R. Wilson in 1911. Wilson was able to produce a sudden expansion in a chamber containing air saturated with water vapor. When this occurred, the air became super-saturated and the vapor condensed out on any small ionized particles in the chamber. This condensation mechanism is identical to that which gives rise to cloud formation in the atmosphere. As an ionizing particle moved through the chamber, it left a track of condensed vapor affording visible evidence of its path. Photographs taken at random were used to record the tracks. These sometimes showed branching of a particular track, which often proved to be an indication of a nuclear collision.

Early works by Rutherford on the dynamics of single collisions of subatomic particles using scintillation methods had failed to produce quantitative results, although he believed he had changed nitrogen into oxygen by the bombardment of nitrogen with alpha particles. In fact, he could not determine what actually happened during the collision between an alpha particle and a nitrogen nucleus, although fast protons were observed being emitted. There were two distinct possibilities. One was that the alpha particle could have left the nucleus as a free particle after the collision. In this case a cloud chamber would show a forked track, the three emergent tracks being due to the alpha particle, the ejected proton, and the recoil nucleus. The other possibility was that the alpha particle might be captured. Such a process would be indicated by the observation of only two emergent tracks, those of the emitted proton and of the recoil nucleus.

In 1925 Blackett used an improved cloud chamber capable of taking a photograph every 15 seconds to study the forked tracks due to collisions of alpha particles with nitrogen atoms. The photographs of these collisions showed only two emergent particles. By applying the principles of conservation of charge and mass, Blackett deduced that in addition to the proton the other emergent particle must be a heavy isotope of oxygen ($^8O_{17}$). This work gave the first photographic representation and detailed knowledge of a typical nuclear transformation process.

Later, in collaboration with G. P. S. Occhialini, Blackett began to study the energetic particles found in cosmic rays. The major problem in observing tracks of these particles had been that cloud chamber photographs were taken in a completely random fashion, and only 2 to 5 percent of these photographs showed cosmic-ray tracks. Blackett and Occhialini devised a method by which cosmic rays could take their own picture. They placed Geiger counters both above and below a vertical cloud chamber so that any ray passing through the two counters would also pass through the chamber. A coincidence circuit, that is, one that emits a pulse only when a particle passes through both counters within a very short time interval, was used to actuate the expansion of the chamber. The expansion was made so rapid that the ions produced by a ray had not had time to diffuse much before the expansion was complete. This method of a Geiger counter-controlled chamber yielded a set of cosmic-ray tracks on 80 percent of the photographs taken.

By the latter part of 1932, Blackett and Occhialini had accumulated 700 photographs of cosmic rays. Many of these photographs showed groups of associated rays, a phenomenon named a cosmic-ray shower. It was determined that about half the particles in a shower were positively charged, while the remaining particles were found to be negatively charged. In addition, the mass of each positive particle was approximately that of the positron, the elementary particle discovered earlier that year by C. D. Anderson. The rough equality of numbers of positive and negative particles, along with the knowledge that positrons do not occur naturally on Earth, led Blackett and Occhialini to the conclusion that the positrons and electrons were created together in collision processes initiated by high-energy cosmic rays. Still later, while working with Occhialini and James Chadwick, Blackett found that electron-positron pairs were also produced when high-energy gamma rays were absorbed by heavy atoms. The creation of an electron-positron pair, as a result of the disintegration of an energetic but massless gamma ray, was found to be in agreement with Einstein's mass-energy conversion relation. *See* CHADWICK, SIR JAMES.

In later years Blackett engaged in studies of rock magnetism. His aim was to trace back to the beginning of geological time both the history of the Earth's magnetic field and the motion of the continental land masses relative to each other

and to the geographical poles. For his work in paleomagnetism, as well as for his earlier studies of cosmic-ray showers and heavy mesons, he was awarded the Royal Society's Copley Medal in 1956.

From 1914 to 1919 Blackett served as an officer in the Royal Navy. After World War I he entered Magdalene College of Cambridge University, receiving his B.A. in 1921 and his M.A. in 1923. As a fellow of King's College he continued his research at the Cavendish Laboratory until 1933, when he was appointed professor of physics at Birkbeck College, University of London. From 1937 to 1953 he was Langworthy Professor of Physics at the University of Manchester. During World War II Blackett headed an operations research group engaged in radar and anti-U-boat work. In 1953 he became head of the physics department at the Imperial College of Science and Technology, London. He retired in 1963 but continued as professor of physics there. In 1965 he was elected president of the Royal Society of London.

Blackett wrote *Rayons Cosmiques* (1934), *Military and Political Consequences of Atomic Energy* (1948), *Lectures on Rock Magnetism* (1956), *Atomic Weapons and East-West Relations* (1956), and *Studies of War* (1962).

For background information *see* CLOUD CHAMBER; COSMIC RAYS; NUCLEAR REACTION; POSITRON in the McGraw-Hill Encyclopedia of Science and Technology. ∎

BLALOCK, ALFRED
American physician

Born Apr. 5, 1899, Culloden, GA, U.S.A.

Died Sept. 15, 1964, Baltimore, MD, U.S.A.

In 1944 Blalock, together with Helen Taussig, developed and performed an operation to relieve the circulatory distress of a "blue baby." Although this first patient died within a year, later patients survived, and the operative procedure became accepted. For his contribution to the blue baby operation, and to other aspects of pediatric surgery, Blalock received the 1948 Passano Foundation Award and the 1954 Lasker Award of the American Public Health Association. *See* TAUSSIG, HELEN BROOKE.

Blalock's work, which eventually led to

the blue baby operation, began in a quite unrelated manner: he was seeking to determine whether any relationship existed between high blood pressure and hardening of the arteries. In order to investigate this, he performed operations on dogs, diverting systemic blood vessels into their lungs in order to increase their pulmonary blood pressure. These operations were inconclusive with respect to Blalock's main investigation, but he did note that the dogs who had been operated on were in exceptionally fine health.

In 1941 Blalock was at Johns Hopkins, where he encountered Taussig. The latter had seen many blue babies and had developed a theory that due to a congenital vascular malformation the pulmonary circulation of affected infants was unable to provide sufficient oxygenated blood to their bodies, hence the blue color. Taussig had heard of Blalock's dog operations and felt that a similar procedure might be successfully employed in blue babies.

Eventually, in 1944, Blalock and Taussig performed their first blue baby operation: the patient, a female infant, was born with a defect in the large artery supplying blood to her lungs. So little blood was able to pass to her lungs that her oxygen intake was dangerously curtailed. When Blalock operated, he severed one of the arteries carrying blood to the body from the lungs. One end of this artery he pulled around and fastened to a slit in the opposite lung artery. One of the patient's lungs was then deliberately collapsed, blood thus being forced into the opposite

pulmonary artery. With this shunt from the general circulation to that of one lung, enough oxygen was gathered to supply the entire body. This first patient died 9 months later, but other patients survived the procedure and went on to lead normal lives—which would otherwise have been impossible.

In addition to his development of the blue baby operation, Blalock is known for his extensive contributions to knowledge of surgical shock. He demonstrated that loss of blood was responsible for shock and instituted the use of plasma or whole-blood transfusions to compensate for the loss.

Blalock received his B.A. from the University of Georgia in 1918 and his M.D. at the Johns Hopkins University in 1922. After an internship and residency at the Johns Hopkins Hospital, he joined the faculty of the Vanderbilt University School of Medicine, becoming professor of surgery there in 1938. In 1941 he returned to Johns Hopkins as professor of surgery and director of the department of surgery at the Medical School and as surgeon-in-chief of the Johns Hopkins Hospital. He retired from these posts in 1964, shortly before his death. Blalock was elected to the National Academy of Sciences in 1945.

For background information *see* CARDIOVASCULAR SYSTEM DISORDERS in the McGraw-Hill Encyclopedia of Science and Technology. ■

BLEANEY, BREBIS
★ British physicist

Born *June 6, 1915, London, England*

Bleaney began his research in physics in 1937 in the Clarendon Laboratory, Oxford, under the guidance of F. E. Simon. Bleaney's measurements of the thermal and magnetic properties of potassium chromium alum suggested that the then current vapor pressure scale of liquid helium was in error near 1 K. In 1939 Simon, who had already criticized this scale on thermodynamic grounds, led the calculation of a fresh scale, which was verified by measurements of Bleaney and R. A. Hull, using the susceptibility of paramagnetic salts as an intermediate standard thermometer.

In January 1940 Bleaney became the youngest member of a group working for the British Admiralty in the Clarendon

Laboratory on centimeter waves. In collaboration with J. H. E. Griffiths, Bleaney successfully built small klystrons to oscillate at 3 centimeters' wavelength. About 200 reflex klystrons were supplied to act as local oscillators in experimental radar systems at this wavelength in 1941–42. A reflex klystron of novel design for 1.25 centimeters' wavelength (which later became the 2K50 tube) was then developed with D. Roaf. Measurements on the inversion spectrum of ammonia, NH_3, at wavelengths between 1 and 2 cm were begun as a fundamental study of pressure broadening; with R. P. Penrose, Bleaney analyzed the rotational structure of the inversion band in 1945–46. This work, the first application of wartime microwave techniques to high-resolution spectroscopy, initiated a fertile field of investigation in microwave gas spectroscopy.

The discovery in 1945 of ferromagnetic resonance by Griffiths and the realization that level splittings of order 0.1 cm^{-1} in paramagnetic salts (such as the chromium alums) could be measured by centimeter wave spectroscopy led to a rapid development of electron spin resonance in the Clarendon Laboratory. Detailed and extensive measurements by D. M. S. Bagguley showed the power of this method of investigation and the need for measurements to be carried out at low temperatures to avoid broadening through spin-lattice relaxation. A simple cavity spectrometer, operating down to 14 K, was designed by Bleaney and Penrose in 1946–47, and it revealed the temperature dependence of the splitting of the spin

quartet ground states of the chromium alums. Hyperfine structure in a diluted copper salt was discovered by Penrose during a visit to the Kamerlingh Onnes Laboratory, Leiden, in 1949. In the following years detailed experimental studies of hyperfine structure were made by Bleaney and a number of collaborators in salts of the iron (3d), the lanthanide (4f), and the actinide (5f) groups. During this period the importance of covalent effects and of ligand hyperfine structure, particularly in the palladium (4d) and platinum (5d) groups, was demonstrated by the parallel work of J. Owen and Griffiths. At the same time the theory of the magnetic resonance spectrum, based on the earlier work of J. H. Van Vleck, was worked out in the Clarendon Laboratory by M. H. L. Pryce, A. Abragam, K. W. H. Stevens, R. J. Elliott, and others. Most of the basic features of the theory, including the use of an "effective spin" Hamiltonian, resulted from this work, and day-by-day collaboration between theoreticians and experimentalists ensured particularly rapid progress. *See* VAN VLECK, JOHN HASBROUCK.

Paramagnetic substances form the "working fluid" in the method of magnetic cooling for obtaining temperatures well below 1 K. Much of the work in electron spin resonance was directed toward finding the best "coolants" and providing exact data on paramagnetic salts of interest in low-temperature physics. The determination of spin-spin interactions from the resonance spectrum of "pairs" of ions in semidilute salts was initiated in 1953, and this has become an invaluable tool in the study of exchange interaction. Measurements of hyperfine structure, during which the correct values of a number of nuclear spins were established, proved particularly valuable in furthering work on oriented nuclei. Methods of producing spatially oriented nuclei, which could be detected through the anisotropy in their radioactive emissions (particularly gamma rays) had been discussed by N. Kurti and Simon in the 1930s. Following the arrival of H. Halban in Oxford in 1946, as well as the rapid development of the low-temperature school in Oxford after World War II, preparations were made for specific experiments on nuclear orientation. At a meeting in Simon's office to discuss the best type of experiment, Bleaney suggested that the local anisotropy of a paramagnetic ion due to interaction with its ligand field could be used as the mechanism producing orientation. This simplified the experimental problem, since adiabatic demagnetization of a suitable paramagnetic salt to zero field should be sufficient, eliminating the need (in the Gorter-Rose method) for an external field to define an orientation axis (in fact, such a field often acts in competition with the internal fields). The first successful nuclear orientation experiment, based on this suggestion, was carried out in 1951, and the method has since been extensively exploited. In later work Bleaney explored the correlation between hyperfine structures in salts and metals of the rare-earth group and examined the importance of ligand field effects in intermetallic lanthanide compounds.

From 1973, Bleaney was interested in enhanced nuclear magnetism in lanthanide compounds with singlet electronic ground states. This was investigated by using nuclear magnetic resonance, together with F. N. H. Robinson and M. R. Wells, and by means of experiments involving enhanced nuclear cooling and nuclear orientation, in collaboration with the group led by N. J. Stone.

Bleaney went to Westminster City School, London, and then to Oxford University, where he took his B.A. in physics in 1937 and his D.Phil. in 1939. He was lecturer in physics at Oxford from 1945 to 1957. In 1957 he was appointed Dr. Lee's Professor of Experimental Philosophy and head of the Clarendon Laboratory, Oxford, in succession to Sir Francis Simon. On resigning this position in 1977, Bleaney became Warren Research Fellow of the Royal Society, and received the title of emeritus professor. He was elected a fellow of the Royal Society in 1950, and was awarded the Charles Vernon Prize of the Physical Society of London in 1952 and the Hughes Medal of the Royal Society in 1962. In 1974 he was elected a corresponding member (and in 1978 *associé étrangé*) of the Académie des Sciences (Institut de France), and in 1978 a foreign honorary member of the American Academy of Arts and Sciences.

Bleaney wrote *Electricity and Magnetism,* with his wife Betty Bleaney (1957; 2d ed. 1965; 3d ed. 1976), and *Electron Paramagnetic Resonance,* with A. Abragam (1970; French transl. 1971; Russian transl. 1972).

For background information *see* KLYSTRON; PARAMAGNETISM in the McGraw-Hill Encyclopedia of Science and Technology. ∎

BLINKS, LAWRENCE ROGERS
★ American botanist

***Born** Apr. 22, 1900, Michigan City, IN, U.S.A.*

Blinks contributed to plant physiology through the study of the simplest plants, the algae, his interest in them being aroused by his teacher at Harvard, W. J. V. Osterhout. They went to Bermuda in 1923, working on the giant-celled marine alga *Valonia,* and Blinks continued to utilize this genus and other coenocytes throughout his career.

Blinks's first experiments dealt with the electrical conductance of protoplasm—a measure of the ease with which ions enter or leave the cell. It had long been appreciated that living cells interpose a considerable resistance to current flow, but Blinks was the first to assign a value to it. This ranged from about 10,000 ohms per square centimeter of cell surface in *Valonia* to 100,000 ohms per square centimeter in the fresh-water plant *Nitella.* Considering the extremely thin structures involved (the plasma and vacuolar membranes), this was the resistance to be expected from an oily rather than an aqueous layer.

One of the most important of Blinks's early findings was on the action potential of *Nitella.* When a low stimulating potential is applied to the cells, such an action can be initiated and will then pass at about 1 centimeter per second down the cell. As the cell's potential falls toward zero, so does its electrical resistance. Both then recover in 10–15 seconds. Such fall of re-

sistance was later found in the squid axon by K. S. Cole. *See* COLE, KENNETH STEWART.

The resistance of large algal cells had to be measured with direct current, since even at 1000 hertz the impedance had much lower values. This fall is due to the high capacitance of the membranes, spread as they are in single or double uninterrupted layers. The capacitance was found to be about 1 microfarad per square centimeter of cell surface—a value also displayed by many other living cells. In addition to the static capacitance to be expected of a thin, oily layer, there appeared to be a polarization capacitance also, dependent on frequency of measurement and probably due to the differential mobility of ions (such as K^+ and Cl^-) in the membrane.

There occurs in Bermuda another large algal cell, the sea-bottle, which floats in sea water. Its sap, unlike that of *Valonia,* displays no accumulation (even partial exclusion) of potassium. Blinks recognized it as the genus *Halicystis* (now regarded as the sexual generation of *Derbesia*), and he spent many years on its study, both in Bermuda and in California. Curiously enough, the California species accumulates potassium fairly well. Yet both plants display almost the same potential (emf) across the protoplasm: about 70–80 millivolts. Furthermore, the vacuole can be perfused with sea water, so that there is no solute gradient across the protoplasm as a whole; yet the potential remains almost unchanged. These factors necessarily threw the emphasis on gradients within the cytoplasm and on asymmetrical properties of the membrane systems. Substitution of various anions (such as nitrate, sulfate, acetate, formate, lactate, and glutamate) for the chloride of sea water caused a very large change of potential, reversing the negative emf to some 40 millivolts positive (sign of sap). This was due to the much lower mobility of these anions in the outer surface of the protoplasm; on the other hand, a substitution of such anions in the vacuole (by perfusion) produced a much smaller effect. It could hence be postulated that there was a rather large potential across the outer (plasma) membrane, and a much smaller one across the vacuolar membrane (tonoplast), because of the presence of indiffusible anions (organic acids, amino acids, proteins, and others) in the cytoplasm and a negligible concentration of them in the sea water or sap. The observed potential was the algebraic sum of the larger plasma and the smaller tonoplast potentials. If either of the membranes was altered, the potential could be increased, decreased, or reversed.

One of the simplest ways to alter one membrane (probably the plasma membrane) was by exposure of *Halicystis* to dilute ammonia or other weak bases: at a certain threshold value the potential reversed, in a sigmoid time course. The reverse in potential seemed to have been caused by the entrance of the undissociated weak base, since the effect was increased by higher pH and decreased by lower. Light also favored such emf reversal, since photosynthesis increased the pH (due to CO_2 utilization). Curiously, however, the potential often increased before falling and reversing, as if the first effect of light were an increased acidity. This unexpected result demanded independent measurement, which was supplied by glass electrodes in direct contact with the cells or other algal tissues. On illumination the pH was indeed often found to decrease before it rose in the expected fashion—the first evidence of an initial "acid gush," identified by Robert Emerson as caused by CO_2 evolution.

Influenced by this electrical measurement, Blinks developed an electrode measurement for oxygen based on the polarographic method. Instead of dropping mercury, however, in 1938 Blinks and R. K. Skow applied a polarized platinum electrode directly to the tissue. The diffusion distance was reduced to a minimum, and the responses to light were extremely rapid; the method also directly indicated rates rather than absolute amounts. It showed many previously unsuspected parts of the photosynthetic induction period, such as an "oxygen gush" immediately after an anoxic period. The speed of the response was utilized by Blinks and F. T. Haxo in 1949 to study photosynthetic action spectra of a large number of marine algae. Although green and brown algae showed good correspondence between absorption spectra and photosynthetic activity (indicating the participation of most pigments), red algae showed remarkable deviations, with very high efficiency in green light (absorbed by the accessory pigment phycoerythrin) but much lower activity in red or blue light. Since red or blue light is absorbed by chlorophyll, the function of this important pigment was thrown into considerable question.

The electrode method also was the first to indicate chromatic transients—changes in the steady-state photosynthetic rate when the wavelength of light is suddenly changed (for example, from red to green). Both of these effects found their explanation shortly afterward when Emerson discovered photosynthetic enhancement—an increased efficiency resulting from light absorption by two pigment systems: chlorophyll *a* and accessory pigments, such as carotenoids, phycobilins, or other chlorophylls.

In 1966 Blinks introduced the Australian alga *Boergesenia* into physiological study. It resembles *Valonia* in many respects, but its normal potential is larger and can be reversed readily by a variety of agents. Light is especially effective upon its potential.

Blink's subsequent research concerned oscillatory potentials induced in *Halicystis* by exposures to increased potassium or decreased magnesium in sea water.

Blinks graduated cum laude from Harvard in 1923. He received his M.A. in 1925 and his Ph.D. in general physiology in 1926, also from Harvard. After 7 years on the staff of the Rockefeller Institute for Medical Research, in 1933 he was appointed associate professor of plant physiology at Stanford University, being promoted to professor of biology in 1936. He was director of Stanford's Hopkins Marine Station from 1943 to 1965. He became professor emeritus in 1965, and was then appointed professor of biology at the new Santa Cruz campus of the University of California; he retired in 1972. He was elected to the American Academy of Arts and Sciences in 1949 and to the National Academy of Sciences in 1955.

For background information *see* AL-GAE; CELL MEMBRANES; CELL-SURFACE IONIZATION; PHOTOSYNTHESIS; PHYS-IOLOGICAL ACTION SPECTRA in the McGraw-Hill Encyclopedia of Science and Technology. ∎

BLOCH, FELIX
★ American physicist

***Born* Oct. 23, 1905, Zurich, Switzerland**

Through the combination of electromagnetic and nuclear phenomena, Bloch discovered a method of studying the magnetism of atomic nuclei in normal matter. It permitted measurements of very high precision and became a valuable tool for research in physics and chemistry. Independently and simultaneously, the same discovery was made by E. M. Purcell, with whom Bloch shared the Nobel Prize for physics in 1952. *See* PURCELL, EDWARD MILLS.

Bloch's interest in nuclear magnetism derived from Otto Stern's 1933 experiments on molecular beams, which showed that the magnetic moment of the proton was almost three times as large as expected and indicated that the neutron attached to it in the deuteron also possessed a magnetic moment. In 1936 Bloch pointed out that this property could be used to produce polarized neutron beams by passing them through magnetized iron. The verification of this effect, and the use of a radio technique previously applied to atomic beams, led him in 1939 to the first accurate measurement of the magnetic properties of the neutron. *See* STERN, OTTO.

Following his work on radar during World War II, Bloch realized in 1945 that the use of radio techniques was not restricted to beams of particles but could be developed into a purely electromagnetic method applicable to normal substances. Under suitably chosen conditions, it proved possible to reorient the magnetic moments of the nuclei in such a way that their resultant moment underwent a precessional variation around the direction of the constant magnetic field to which they were exposed. Bloch achieved this with a radio transmitter in resonance with the precession frequency character-

istic of the nucleus under investigation, so that he dealt with nuclear magnetic resonance. The novelty of his method lay in the fact that the variation of the resultant moment produced (according to Faraday's principle of electromagnetic induction) a voltage in a coil surrounding the sample. This nuclear induction was detected in a radio receiver. The signals, thus recorded, conveyed a great variety of information.

In the first place, the signals revealed the magnetic moment of individual nuclei as well as their angular momentum, both of which were significant for the knowledge of nuclear structure. In the second place, the frequency of the signal from a given nucleus—for example, that of hydrogen in water—depended on the external magnetic field strength and thus led to the construction of reliable and very sensitive magnetometers, used in geophysical studies, among others. A third important property of the signals arose from the fact that they were often markedly influenced by the environment in which the observed nuclei were located, so that they supplied new data about the constitution of solids, liquids, and gases. In many cases, such data were established to be intimately connected with the chemical constitution of molecules and so resulted in a powerful new method of analytical chemistry, and of biology as well. Besides several other interesting features that appeared under various circumstances, it was found that the precession frequencies observed from chemically indistinguishable isotopes—that is, from nuclei with different structure of the same element—were widely separated from each other and hence furnished a convenient indicator for isotope analysis.

Planning originally to become an engineer, Bloch entered the Swiss Federal Institute of Technology in Zurich. After a year, he switched to physics, and later went to the University of Leipzig, where he received his Ph.D. in 1928 with a thesis on metallic conduction recognized to be basis for the modern theory of solids. After postdoctoral work in several European countries, he held a teaching position in Leipzig but left Germany upon Hitler's ascent to power in 1933. In the following year he joined Stanford University, later becoming Max H. Stein Professor of Physics; he retired in 1971. He became a United States citizen in 1939. During World War II he worked for the Manhattan District and at the Radio Research Laboratory of Harvard University. In

1954 and 1955 he served as the first director general of the European Commission for Nuclear Research (CERN) in Geneva, and in 1965 as president of the American Physical Society. He was elected to the National Academy of Sciences in 1948.

For background information *see* MAGNETIC MOMENT; MOLECULAR BEAMS; NUCLEAR MOMENTS in the McGraw-Hill Encyclopedia of Science and Technology. ∎

BLOCH, HERMAN S.
★ American chemist

Born June 15, 1912, Chicago, IL, U.S.A.

The period 1936–77, during which Bloch was engaged in industrial catalytic research, was one of revolutionary changes in the huge petroleum refining industry—changes in which the use of heat and pressure to effect chemical modification was supplanted by a host of specialized catalytic processes. The research group at Universal Oil Products Company (now UOP, Inc.), of which Bloch was a member, originated many of these processes, and Bloch himself was a significant contributor to them. Much of his research has centered on correlating knowledge of reaction mechanisms, of the kinetics of competitive reactions, and of the thermodynamic limitations of the systems involved, to define the types of catalyst and the operating conditions required for the

selective production of the desired products.

Thus Bloch's early work with his collaborator Charles L. Thomas on the cracking of pure hydrocarbons with synthetic heterogeneous catalysts of the silica-alumina type disclosed the close parallelism of the behavior of these heterogeneous acidic composites at high temperatures to the behavior of strong liquid acids or Friedel-Crafts salts at temperatures several hudred degrees lower. The reactions induced by the metal oxide composites were essentially the acid-catalyzed reactions of carbonium ions, and included hydride transfer as a key reaction which could be rate-limiting (as in the case of paraffin cracking) or determinative of the product type (unsaturated at normal cracking temperatures, saturated at somewhat lower temperatures). Later, Bloch elucidated the mechanism by which unsaturated hydrocarbons in the presence of strong acid catalysts are converted in part to cycloparaffins and in part to cyclic polyolefins which form strong complexes with the catalyst—the well-known acid sludge. This mechanism involved polymerization, cyclization, and hydride transfer, all acid-catalyzed.

With the discovery by his colleague Louis Schmerling that the alkylation of isoparaffins by olefins in the presence of acid catalysts was a chain reaction, it became apparent to Bloch and his coworkers that the isomerization of *n*-paraffins by strong acid catalysts of the Friedel-Crafts type must also be a chain reaction in which both the chain-initiating step and one of the chain-propagating steps were abstraction of secondary hydride ions from the *n*-paraffin. The earliest paraffin isomerization catalysts were Friedel-Crafts salts such as aluminum chloride, but these were short-lived because of the formation of catalyst sludge. After the introduction of platinum-containing acidic catalysts for naphtha reforming, of which the first was the Platforming catalyst invented by Bloch's associate Vladimir Haensel, catalysts of the same type but of enhanced acidity supplanted the Friedel-Crafts catalysts for paraffin isomerization. These catalysts were long-lived, but operated at higher temperatures than the Friedel-Crafts catalysts, limiting the per-pass yield of isoparaffins because the equilibrium amount of isoparaffins varies inversely with the temperature. *See* HAENSEL, VLADIMIR.

In order to permit the platinum-containing duofunctional catalyst to operate at lower temperatures, Bloch and his co-workers developed a new generation of such catalysts in which the degree of acidity approached that of Friedel-Crafts catalysts, permitting operation at temperatures comparable with those used with the latter. These new catalysts, which are used in the presence of hydrogen, are very long-lived and provide near-equilibrium isoparaffin yields in a desirable low-temperature range. The strong acidity permits secondary hydride abstraction (the rate-limiting step) at these relatively low temperatures.

The catalyst and process which Bloch and his coworkers developed for the selective dehydrogenation of *n*-paraffins to *n*-olefins were an excellent example of the control of competitive reactions by the judicious choice of catalyst components. Based on a platinum-alumina composite, which had been found to dehydrogenate paraffins at a very fast rate, this catalyst was modified to include an alkalizer in an amount which effectively suppressed acid-catalyzed reactions without unduly diminishing the dehydrogenation rate; and an attenuator which reduced the cyclicizing tendency of platinum by over 80 percent, while it simultaneously diminished the electrophilic character of the platinum so that it showed virtually no selectivity for adsorption of olefins as compared with paraffins. The inclusion of these catalyst modifiers, and the selection of reaction conditions compatible with the properties of the catalyst, so strongly suppressed the side reactions of cyclization, isomerization, cracking, and polymerization that dehydrogenation of paraffins to monoolefins was the single major surviving reaction, even at near-equilibrium conversions. The *n*-olefins produced by this process have been widely used as intermediates for the production of biodegradable detergents of the alkylbenzene sulfonate type.

The successful development of catalysts for the control of automotive emissions serves as a further illustration of the design of catalysts to operate effectively under peculiarly demanding conditions. In this service, catalysts must effect high conversions (of the order of 90 percent) of reactants present in low concentrations, under conditions of high throughput, and must be able to become operative at relatively low temperatures while maintaining their activity for long periods of time which include intervals of very-

high-temperature use (approximately 1000°C) and exposure to a variety of catalyst poisons. The catalysts which Bloch and his coworkers developed met all these requirements by use of a high-surface-area, high-porosity alumina base chemically stabilized to resist phase change induced by high temperatures, noble metal blends (such as platinum and palladium) which combined the temperature stability of one component with the poison resistance of the other, and methods of positioning the noble metals on the support to provide an optimum combination of activity and poison resistance. Such catalysts were in successful commercial use in the late 1970s.

The son of immigrant parents, Bloch received his B.S. (1933) and Ph.D. (1936) degrees from the University of Chicago, where he held the Gustavus F. Swift Research Fellowship. He joined the staff of Universal Oil Products Company in 1936 as a research chemist, and after a succession of promotions became director of catalysis research, a position he held until his retirement in 1977. He served as chairperson of the board of directors of the American Chemical Society for 5 years (1973–77), and was elected to the National Academy of Sciences in 1975. For his research, which resulted in 270 U.S. patents, he received the Eugene J. Houdry Award in Applied Catalysis from the Catalysis Society (1971), the E. V. Murphree Award in Industrial and Engineering Chemistry from the American Chemical Society (1974), and the Richard J. Kokes Memorial Award from the Johns Hopkins University (1975).

For background information *see* CATALYSIS; FRIEDEL-CRAFTS REACTION; ORGANIC REACTION MECHANISM; THERMODYNAMICS, CHEMICAL in the McGraw-Hill Encyclopedia of Science and Technology. ∎

BLOCH, KONRAD EMIL
★ American biochemist

***Born** Jan. 21, 1912, Neisse, Germany*

In the course of metabolic studies with isotopic tracers beginning in 1941, Bloch, in collaboration with D. Rittenberg, demonstrated that acetic acid is a major precursor of cholesterol in animal tissues. This observation permitted him to trace the numerous transformations of fat and carbohydrate metabolites to cholesterol.

For this contribution he was awarded the Nobel Prize in medicine or physiology in 1964, sharing it with Feodor Lynen. *See* LYNEN, FEODOR.

In 1932 Harold Urey of Columbia University had discovered heavy hydrogen (deuterium) and devised methods for producing the isotope in large quantities. Soon thereafter the heavy isotopes of carbon (^{13}C), nitrogen (^{15}N), and oxygen (^{18}O) also became available. R. Schoenheimer and Rittenberg at Columbia recognized the unique usefulness of isotopic tracers for metabolic studies and developed a methodology that laid the basis for the many achievements of modern biochemistry, including the elucidation of cholesterol biosynthesis. *See* UREY, HAROLD CLAYTON.

Cholesterol, a waxlike substance with the elementary composition $C_{27}H_{40}O$, is found in all animal cells. It contains a fused tetracyclic (perhydrophenanthreme) ring system to which an eight-carbon aliphatic side chain is attached. After it had been shown that the two-carbon compound acetic acid contributes to the biological synthesis of cholesterol, Bloch set out to determine in what manner acetic acid molecules combine to form first medium-sized units and then the larger precursor molecules of cholesterol. Animals were given isotopic acetic acid, and the isotopic tracer was located in the various portions of the cholesterol molecules found in the tissues. From the pattern in which isotopic hydrogen and carbon were distributed in cholesterol, Bloch made the following

predictions: (1) In the first stages, three molecules of acetic acid combine to form a branched five-carbon or isopentenyl intermediate. (2) Six of the isopentenyl units are linked together to form the acyclic thirty-carbon compound squalene. (3) Squalene cyclizes and undergoes various molecular rearrangements to form lanosterol, a tetracyclic substance closely related to cholesterol. Between 1946 and 1958, Bloch's laboratory, Lynen and his collaborators in Munich, and J. W. Cornforth and G. Popják in England provided the experimental basis for the postulated sequence: acetic acid → isopentenyl unit → squalene → lanosterol → cholesterol. The hypothetical isopentenyl unit was identified as isopentenylpyrophosphate, and it proved to be a key intermediate in the biosynthesis not only of cholesterol but also of numerous other natural products, including the terpenes, carotenes, and rubber. In Bloch's estimates, the overall conversion of acetic acid to cholesterol requires 30 to 35 steps. *See* CORNFORTH, SIR JOHN (WARCUP).

Cholesterol is vital for the functioning of animal cells. One of its functions is to supply the chemically related bile acids, compounds that aid in fat absorption. Cholesterol is also the parent substance for the various vertebrate steroid hormones (cortisone and the sex hormones). Some of these relationships were demonstrated by Bloch in 1942 and 1945. Cholesterol also seems to serve in all animal cells in the additional and more general role of stabilizing the various membrane structures which envelop the cell plasma.

In later years the biological origin of unsaturated fatty acids was one of Bloch's main interests. In animal tissues and in many microorganisms, long-chain fatty acids are synthesized by the repeated addition of malonyl conenzyme A (CoA) units to acetyl CoA. This process leads to the formation of the saturated compounds palmitic and stearic acids. As Bloch showed, enzyme systems from animal tissues and from yeast then introduce double bonds into the saturated acids to form the corresponding olefins (oleic and palmitoleic acids). These reactions require molecular oxygen and therefore do not occur in anaerobic organisms. The so-called essential fatty acids, that is, those containing two or more double bonds per molecule, are formed by similar oxygen-requiring reactions.

Bloch studied chemistry at the Technische Hochschule, Munich, between 1930 and 1934. After a brief stay in a Swiss research institute, he emigrated to the United States in 1936 and entered Columbia University as a graduate student. He received his Ph.D. in 1938 and remained at Columbia until 1946. He then became a member of the biochemistry department of the University of Chicago, and in 1954 joined Harvard University as Higgins Professor of Biochemistry. In 1964 he received the Fritzsche Award of the American Chemical Society. He was elected to the American Academy of Arts and Sciences in 1955 and the National Academy of Sciences in 1956.

For background information *see* CHOLESTEROL; TRACER, RADIOACTIVE in the McGraw-Hill Encyclopedia of Science and Technology. ∎

BLOEMBERGEN, NICOLAAS
★ American physicist

Born Mar. 11, 1920, Dordrecht, Netherlands

While studying the effects of magnetic resonance in crystals at low temperature, Bloembergen conceived the method of three-level and multilevel pumping to energize masers. Solid-state multilevel masers are used as extremely sensitive low-noise receivers in radio telescopes, in radar tracking stations, and in the ground-based receivers of the Telstar satellite communication system, which provides a microwave link between continents. Optical masers or lasers are also energized by multilevel pumping, and have found widespread use as highly directional, highly monochromatic, powerful sources of light. For his discovery Bloembergen was awarded the American Physical Society's Buckley Prize in 1958. He also shared with C. H. Townes the Morris Liebman Award of the Institute of Radio Engineers in 1959. *See* TOWNES, CHARLES HARD.

The practical importance of achieving a medium with an inverted population that could serve as an amplifier or oscillator (or both) for electromagnetic radiation was realized independently by Townes at Columbia University and N. G. Basov and A. M. Prochorov at the Academy of Sciences in Moscow. They separated a beam of ammonia molecules. The molecules in the upper state of a pair of energy levels, called an inversion doublet, were focused in a microwave cavity. Stimulated emission of radiation produced a coherent microwave oscillator or atomic clock with a frequency determined by the separation of the inversion doublet. For this achievement they were awarded the 1964 Nobel Prize in physics. Townes aptly called the new device a maser, an acronym for microwave amplification by stimulated emission of radiation. *See* BASOV, NICOLAI GENNEDIYEVICH; PROCHOROV, ALEKSANDR MIKHAILOVICH.

While the beam device was useful as a frequency standard, its power level was extremely low due to the relatively small number of molecules available in a beam in high vacuum. It also lacked the characteristics of tunability and broad-band amplification desirable in a low-noise amplifier. Bloembergen looked for ways to upset the thermal population of energy levels in a solid on a continuous basis. He reasoned that if the thermal equilibrium of the spin levels of paramagnetic ions in a crystal at low temperature could be inverted, the magnetic resonances absorption could be changed into a powerful emission. Furthermore, the magnetic resonances are rather broad and can be tuned by the application of an external magnetic field. Populations of spin levels could be changed on a continuous basis by the application of powerful pump fields. This had been demonstrated by Bloembergen in his thesis experiments on nuclear magnetic relaxation carried out in 1947 at Harvard University with E. M. Purcell and R. V. Pound. A powerful pump field at the frequency ν would tend to equalize the population of a pair of energy levels separated by $h\nu$. The absorption and stimulated emission at this frequency would be balanced. *See* POUND, ROBERT VIVIAN; PURCELL, EDWARD MILLS.

Bloembergen then considered the case where this pair of energy levels was not adjacent, but where an intermediate level C existed between the levels whose populations had been equalized by the pump. If C has the same population as the two levels connected by the pump, nothing useful will result. If level C has a higher population, then inversion will occur between C and the lowest level. If C has a lower population, inversion occurs between the highest level and C. Therefore negative absorption or stimulated emission may generally be expected to occur at one smaller frequency or another, if sufficiently strong pumping power is applied between nonadjacent energy levels. This principle proved to be correct. In essence it is similar to that of a heat engine. The pump serves as a hot thermal reservoir; the crystal lattice serves as a cold reservoir. Just as in a thermodynamic Carnot cycle, useful energy can be extracted in the form of stimulated electromagnetic radiation. A coherent oscillator or amplifier results.

In 1956 Bloembergen published directions for the construction of a continuously operating solid-state maser. A crystal containing certain magnetic ions of the iron group and the rare-earth group of the periodic system would be placed in a microwave circuit in a helium dewar between the poles of an external magnet. The magnitude and orientation of this field would be adjusted so that the spacing between two nonadjacent levels would correspond to a pump field supplied by an external source. A weak signal at a lower frequency, such as might be received by a radio telescope, would also be fed into the microwave cavity containing the crystal. If the stimulated emission was larger than the small eddy-current losses in the walls of the microwave circuit, a low-noise microwave amplifier would result. Bloembergen and coworkers achieved maser operation in 1957 at 21-centimeter wavelength, which is of interest in radio astronomy because it corresponds to the radiation from galactic and extragalactic atomic hydrogen.

In the meantime the correctness of Bloembergen's reasoning was proved by various other groups working in different wavelengths. Because of its importance for long-range microwave communication via artificial satellites, H. E. D. Scovil at the Bell Telephone Laboratories built in 1956 the first multilevel maser, using gadolinium ethyl sulfate, one of the salts proposed by Bloembergen. The principle of pumping in a multilevel energy system is also basic to the operation of all optical masers or lasers. Technical improvements were subsequently made by many people. Broad-band traveling-wave masers were developed. Ruby, which is a crystal of sapphire (Al_2O_3) containing chromium ions as an impurity, proved to be an excellent maser crystal. Ruby is an excellent material for both a microwave maser and an optical laser. Different sets of energy levels of the chromium ion are involved for operation at the widely different frequencies.

Beginning in 1961, Bloembergen used many types of lasers developed by others to study the properties of matter at very high optical intensities available in laser beams. At these high intensities, the classical laws of optics are considerably modified. Bloembergen and his associates formulated and established many of the laws of nonlinear optics. He also made significant contributions to the related field of nonlinear spectroscopy, including Doppler-free two-photon absorption spectroscopy, laser-induced electric breakdown, and unimolecular dissociation of polyatomic molecules by infrared laser pulses.

Bloembergen received his B.A. and M.A. in physics in 1941 and 1943, respectively, from the University of Utrecht. The German occupation forces closed the university in 1943, and Bloembergen taught himself quantum mechanics by reading H. A. Kramers's book on this subject by the light of an oil lamp during the "hunger winter" of 1944. In 1946 he went to Harvard University, where he did research for his thesis with E. M. Purcell. He obtained a Ph.D. degree in physics in 1948 at the University of Leiden, where he was a research associate. From 1949 to 1951 he was a junior fellow in the Society of Fellows at Harvard. In 1951 he became an associate professor and in 1957 Gordon McKay Professor of Applied Physics at Harvard. In 1974 he also became Rumford Professor of Physics at Harvard. He served as a visiting professor at the University of Paris, and the University of California, Berkeley, and as Lorentz Professor at the University of Leiden.

Bloembergen received the Stuart Ballantine Medal of the Franklin Institute in 1961. He was one of the recipients of the National Medal of Science in 1974 for his "pioneering applications of magnetic resonance to the study of condensed matter and for subsequent scientific investigations and inventions concerning the interaction of matter with coherent radiation." In 1978 he was awarded the Lorentz Gold Medal by the Royal Dutch Academy of Sciences in Amsterdam. Bloembergen was elected a member of the National Academy of Sciences in 1960. He was also a foreign correspondent of the Royal Dutch Academy of Sciences and the Indian Academy of Science in Bangalore.

Bloembergen wrote *Nuclear Magnetic Relaxations* (1948; 2d ed. 1961) and *Nonlinear Optics* (1965) and published over 200 papers in scientific journals.

For background information *see* LASER; MASER in the McGraw-Hill Encyclopedia of Science and Technology. ∎

BLUMBERG, BARUCH SAMUEL
★ American physician

Born July 28, 1925, New York, NY, U.S.A.

In 1976 Blumberg (along with D. Carleton Gajdusek) was awarded the Nobel Prize in physiology or medicine for discoveries concerning new mechanisms for the origin and dissemination of infectious diseases, a recognition of his work on the hepatitis virus. *See* GAJDUSEK, D. CARLETON.

Blumberg's undergraduate and graduate training was in physics and mathematics. After his service in the Navy during World War II, his interest in problems related more directly to humans led to his completing medical school at the College of Physicians and Surgeons of Columbia University and then spending 4 years of clinical training at Bellevue and Presbyterian hospitals in New York City. His Ph.D. thesis at Oxford University was related to a problem in the physical chemistry of the hyaluronic acid protein macromolecule, a major constituent of the ground substance found in connective tissue, synovial fluid, and other biological materials.

While in medical school, Blumberg had worked in a hospital in a mining community in Surinam (then Dutch Guiana) in northern South America. He conducted disease surveys among the indigenous and migrant populations of this largely undeveloped country, and was struck by the large differences in responses to disease and infection, primarily relating to agents associated with filariasis (elephantiasis) and malaria, among the different ethnic groups inhabiting the country. This concern with the question of why some people get sick and others do not—that is, a study of factors related to health as well as those which result in illness—guided much of his later research.

While at Oxford, Blumberg was influenced by the zoological and genetic thinking then prevalent in that institution and in Great Britain. In 1956 he began an investigation of inherited biochemical and immunological variation in humans which might bear on differences in susceptibility to disease. He utilized recently introduced techniques for the separation of blood proteins, for example, the starch gel electrophoresis method of the British scientist O. Smithies and the double diffusion in agar gel technique developed by O. Ouchterlony in Sweden. Using these methods, it was possible to distinguish many more serum protein entities than had been identified with previously available techniques.

During the next few years Blumberg made a series of field trips to different parts of the world to search for undiscovered variants of blood and to determine the distribution of the genes which controlled the presence or absence of variants. Most of the systems studied were polymorphic traits. The then current theory (derived from the genetic interpretation of Darwinism) held that the frequency of the several genes controlling the system was affected by different selective forces operating in the environment. Hence, studies were made on populations living in very different circumstances, among them, the Yoruba and Fulani of Nigeria, Basques of northern Spain, Greeks, Italians, American whites and blacks, Athabaskan Indians, Eskimos and Aleuts of Alaska, Algonkian-speaking Indians of Labrador and Quebec (the Naskapi, Montagnais, Micmacs), Indians of the southwestern United States, Mexico, and South America (Pima, San Carlos Apache, Cashinahua), Micronesians from the Marshall Islands, Japanese and Chinese, Indians from Madras and its environs in India, and Filipinos from Cebu. During this period Blumberg acquired an interest in anthropology, in part because, in many remote places, the only other visitors were anthropologists. In later years, when he moved to Philadelphia, he became a member of the department of anthropology at the University of Pennsylvania, a position he enjoyed immensely. Beginning in 1967, he taught courses in medical anthropology. About 10 years later, a major program in biomedical anthropology was developed at the University of Pennsylvania, and he continued to take an active role in teaching and directing the program.

By 1963 it had become obvious that there were a number of inherited serum proteins that were polymorphic. The existence of multiple forms of proteins implied that patients who required transfusion would be likely to receive blood containing serum proteins which they themselves had not inherited. On the basis of this presumption, Blumberg and his colleague, the British medical scientist A. C. Allison, reasoned that some patients who received many blood transfusions could raise specific antibodies against constituents of serum. Using the technique of double diffusion in agar gel, which can detect precipitating antibodies, they began a systematic search of the sera of transfused patients, testing them against panels of sera from normal individuals and patients. Soon they found the serum of a patient with an intractable anemia which defined a complex system of inherited antigenic specificities on the serum low-density lipoproteins. Encouraged by this finding, a fulfillment of the experimental prediction, Blumberg, along with H. J. Alter and S. Visnich, continued the search for additional precipitating antibodies. They found an antibody in the serum of a transfused thalassemia patient from New York with characteristics different from those of the previously discovered lipoprotein antiserum. It was different in appearance, shape, and staining, and it reacted with only a single serum in the panel of 24 against which it was tested—the serum of an Australian aborigine.

What was the cause of this unusual reaction between a New York patient and an aborigine from Australia? A survey for the presence of the antigen in several populations showed that although it was very rare in normal people, it was quite common in patients with leukemia. It was also common in populations living in tropical places; for example, it occurred in 6 percent of the population in the Philippines, 15 percent in Taiwan, and 6 percent in West Africa. The hypothesis was made that since Australia antigen was rare in normal people but common in leukemia, there could be a factor, possibly inherited, which made individuals susceptible on the one hand to the development of leukemia and on the other to the persistent presence of Australia antigen in their blood. A corollary of this hypothesis was that groups of people who had a high risk of developing leukemia would also have a high frequency of Australia antigen. One such group comprises patients with Down's syndrome—mental retardation associated with trisomy of chromosome 21. Institutionalized patients with Down's syndrome were tested, and the prediction was fulfilled. About one-third of the patients carried the Australia antigen. Thus, not only was weight given to the predictive powers of the hypothesis, but it was now possible to study individuals close to the Philadelphia laboratory rather than distant aborigines or leukemia patients.

It was found that the presence of Australia antigen was persistent. If a Down's syndrome patient had the antigen at one point in time, on subsequent testing the trait was always present. If the antigen was absent on first testing, it was absent on subsequent testing. An exception was discovered: A patient who initially did not have the antigen was found on a subsequent testing to be positive. He was admitted to the hospital for observation, and it was noted that between the negative and positive tests he had developed a form of anicteric (without jaundice) inflammation of the liver—hepatitis.

On the basis of this and similar observations, Blumberg and his colleagues tested the hypothesis that Australia antigen was associated with viral hepatitis. When this was found to be so, they hypothesized that the antigen was on the virus that caused viral hepatitis. A series of observations, including visualization, with the electron microscope, of virus particles in the blood of carriers of the virus antigen, bore out this hypothesis.

Subsequently, more sensitive tests of hepatitis B virus—the virus identified by the reaction—were developed. Within a few years these tests were nearly universally applied to the testing of blood donors to detect occult carriers of hepatitis virus. As a consequence, posttransfusion hepatitis due to hepatitis B decreased markedly.

A few years after the hepatitis virus was identified, the virus related to hepatitis A was visualized and characterized. In addition, another class of viruses, so-called non-A, non-B virus, which is similar to hepatitis B, was detected, although not fully identified. A vaccine for hepatitis B was developed by Blumberg and his colleague I. Millman and was in the process of animal and human testing in 1978. If proved safe and effective, the vaccine might find wide use in preventative programs in parts of the world, particularly Asia and Africa, where hepatitis is very common and is a major contributor to mortality and morbidity.

What may prove to be the most far-reaching results of Blumberg's work is the body of data which indicates that chronic infection with hepatitis B virus may be necessary for the development of primary cancer of the liver. This carcinoma is the most common form of cancer in males in some parts of sub-Saharan Africa, in southern Asia, and Oceania. These regions correspond to the high-frequency areas for hepatitis B carriers. Scientists in Japan and China showed that carriers of the hepatitis B virus are much more likely to develop liver cancer than uninfected people are. If this hypothesis is supported, it implies that primary cancer of the liver can be prevented by the control of infection with hepatitis B virus; and the vaccine introduced by Blumberg and Millman, and other public health measures, may be effective in doing this.

The studies of Blumberg and his colleagues were particularly broad and encompassed many scientific disciplines. Entomological studies showed that the virus may be carried by mosquitoes and bedbugs. There is a curious relation of the virus to the sex of its hosts. Male humans are more likely to become carriers of the

virus, and females are more likely to develop antibody to the surface antigen after infection. There also appears to be a relationship between the response of parents to hepatitis B infection and the sex of their offspring. There have also been behavioral studies on the social and psychological problems caused by the identification of occult hepatitis carriers who, in some cases, were stigmatized by this biological characteristic.

Blumberg received the B.S. degree from Union College (Schenectady, NY) in 1946. He spent the academic year 1946–47 as a graduate student at Columbia University, in the department of physics and mathematics. He completed his studies for the M.D. degree at the College of Physicians and Surgeons of Columbia University in 1951 and earned the Ph.D. in biochemistry in 1957 at Oxford University in England. Blumberg received the Albion O. Bernstein, M.D., Award of the Medical Society of the State of New York (1969); the Eppinger Prize of the University of Freiburg (1973); the Passano Award (1974); the Modern Medicine Distinguished Achievement Award, the Gairdner Foundation International Award, the Karl Landsteiner Memorial Award (all in 1975); and the Richard and Hinda Rosenthal Foundation Award (1977). He was an honorary fellow of Balliol College, Oxford, and he received an honorary degree from the University of Paris, as well as from several American institutions.

For background information *see* HEPATITIS in the McGraw-Hill Encyclopedia of Science and Technology. ∎

BOCHNER, SALOMON
★ American mathematician

***Born** Aug. 20, 1899, Cracow, Poland (then Austria-Hungary)*

In 1969–70, when observing Bochner's seventieth birthday with a Jubilee Volume, former students described his research interests as probability theory, harmonic analysis, complex manifolds, complex variables, complex and almost periodic functions, and Fourier analysis. Furthermore, he wrote books and articles (*The Role of Mathematics in the Rise of Science*, 1966; *Eclosion and Synthesis*, 1969; articles in *Dictionary of the History of Ideas*, 1973) on the role of the concepts of space, infinity, real numbers, functions, and continuity in major junctures and upheavals in the rise of West-

ern mathematics, such as the decline of Greek mathematics in its own phase, the sudden emergence of analysis in the late Renaissance, and a subtle but very tangible change of style in mathematics in the transition from the 18th to the 19th century.

All undulatory phenomena in science and technology lead paradigmatically to the same kind of mathematical functions which until the early 20th century were usually of the same periodic kind shown in expression (1), the integer exponents

$$f(x) \sim \sum_m c_m e^{imx} \qquad (1)$$

$\{m\}$ representing frequencies. But in the 20th century there suddenly arose in various contexts the need of functions in which the frequencies are not commensurate. Harald Bohr created one such class of functions, termed almost-periodic, with expansions shown in expression (2), in which the $\{\lambda_n\}$ can be any real

$$f(x) \sim \sum_{n=0}^{\infty} c_m e^{i\lambda_n x} \qquad (2)$$

numbers whatsoever. To "sum" such an expansion means to construct finite sums of the form of expression (2) which approximate to the values of $f(x)$. Bohr's summation procedure was quite complicated, but Bochner soon suggested to him a much simpler one, the so-called Bochner-Fejèr process, and it was this that brought them together in 1924.

Bochner also gave a characterization of the Bohr functions by a certain topological compactness property, and John von Neumann used it to extend almost-periodicity from euclidean space to general

groups. In 1932 came the "Bochner integral," which is the Lebesgue integral for functions whose values are not numbers but elements of a Banach space. Bochner soon introduced a corresponding generalization for Bohr functions, his "abstract" almost-periodic functions; they have been applied by Luigi Amerio in Italy, and are being studied intensively by S. Zaidman in Canada. In 1961 Bochner introduced almost-automorphic functions, which are more general than Bohr functions, and a doctoral study of them by William A. Veech launched Veech on his distinguished career in topological dynamics. *See* VON NEUMANN, JOHN.

Bochner's theorem on positive-definite functions states that a continuous complex-valued function $\varphi(\alpha)$ is representable as Fourier-Stieltjes integral (3), with $dF \geq 0$ if and only if for any finitely many points $\alpha_1, \ldots, \alpha_n$, and complex constants $c_1, \ldots, c_n$ relation (4) holds. This

$$\varphi(\alpha) = \int_{-\infty}^{\infty} e^{i\alpha x}\, dF(x) \qquad (3)$$

$$\sum_{p,q=1}^{n} c_p \bar{c}_q \varphi(\alpha_p - \alpha_q) \geq 0 \qquad (4)$$

criterion has several applications in the theory of probability; it is also usable for the derivation of the spectral representation of a self-adjoint operator in Hilbert space; and it has been generalized and applied to functions on topological group spaces.

Bochner was a precursor in the theory of the so-called Schwartz distributions in that he introduced generalized Fourier transforms for functions that do not grow faster at infinity than a power of x. Also, he was the first to introduce, in 1936, the much studied process of spherical summability of multiple Fourier series; and by a nonobvious construction he showed that Riemann's classical localization property in one dimension does not have the "expected" analog in two dimensions.

In the field of several complex variables Bochner's achievements were as follows. (1) In 1943 he used the "Bochner-Martinelli kernel" to prove Hartogs's key theorem that for a bounded domain with connected boundary a holomorphic function on the boundary has a continuation into the entire interior of the domain. Reese Harvey, Blaine Lawson, and John Polking have been promoting the theory in remarkably original studies. (2) In 1938 he proved that the envelope of holomorphy of a tube is again a tube, the basis of the

envelope tube being the convex closure of the basis of the original tube. (3) He created, for real and complex manifolds, the topic of "curvature and Betti numbers" (there is a book under this title by K. Yano and S. Bochner, 1953); and Kunihiko Kodaira fully acknowledged his indebtedness to the "Bochner method" involved for obtaining his acclaimed "vanishing theorem." (4) There is a "Bochner-(Deane) Montgomery theorem" (1946) that on a compact complex manifold the Lie group of holomorphic automorphism is a complex Lie group. (5) The book (with W. T. Martin) *Several Complex Variables* (1948) had a fifth printing in 1967.

In probability theory, in 1946, Bochner constructed, analyzed, and introduced the Fourier transform of a rather general type of stochastic process, randomizing not point functions but additive set functions, obtaining not only Wiener's differential space but other homogenous processes in this way (*Harmonic Analysis and the Theory of Probability,* 1956).

Finally, in 1977 it became generally known that Zorn's lemma of 1933 had been fully published and applied by Bochner in 1926.

After attending high school in Berlin, Bochner studied mathematics at the University of Berlin, terminating with a Ph.D. in 1921. In 1924–26 he studied, partly as a fellow of the International Education Board, with Harold Bohr in Copenhagen and with G. H. Hardy and J. E. Littlewood in Oxford and Cambridge. In 1926–33 he was lecturer at the University of Munich, where he wrote his first book on Fourier integrals. In 1933 he joined the mathematics department of Princeton University and in 1951 became Henry Burchardt Fine Professor there.

In 1968 he was made Edgar Odell Lovett Professor at Rice University, for many years heading the mathematics department. A member of the National Academy of Sciences (1950), in January 1979 he was a recipient of the Leroy P. Steele Prize of the American Mathematical Society.

Bochner also wrote *Fourier Transforms* (1949) and *Fourier Integrals* (1959), his most quoted publication because of the theorem on positive-definite functions.

For background information *see* ANALYSIS OF VARIANCE; FOURIER SERIES AND INTEGRALS; INTEGRAL TRANSFORM in the McGraw-Hill Encyclopedia of Science and Technology. ■

BOGOLUBOV, NIKOLAI NIKOLAEVICH
★ Soviet theoretical physicist and mathematician

Born Aug. 21, 1909, Gorki, Soviet Union

Bogolubov started his scientific career in Kiev as the pupil of a distinguished Soviet mathematician, N. Krylov. He had written his first scientific paper, concerning a problem of the calculus of variation, in 1924 at the age of 14.

Bogolubov's early investigations of direct methods for solving extremum problems gained wide recognition. In 1928 he participated in the famous international meeting in Bologna, and one of his works was awarded the prize of the Academy of Sciences of Bologna. During this period he developed a new approach to the theory of uniform (almost periodic) functions.

In later years Bogolubov was involved not only in scientific research, which he continued without interruption, but also with the organization of science and with teaching. In 1947 he was elected a corresponding member of the U.S.S.R. Academy of Sciences, and in 1953 he became academician. Bogolubov was subsequently a member of the presidium and the director of the Section of Mathematics of the academy.

In 1964 Bogolubov became director of the Joint Institute for Nuclear Research, an international center of socialist countries for fundamental research located in Dubna.

Bogolubov's scientific work covered a wide range of problems in theoretical physics. He was one of the formulators, together with Krylov, of the theory of nonlinear oscillations (1932). In a number of papers he devised a rigorous mathematical foundation for the use of asymptotic methods in nonlinear mechanics. These methods made it possible to obtain solutions not only in the first approximation in some small parameter but also in the higher orders, and they were applied to the analysis of both periodic and quasiperiodic oscillation processes.

Bogolubov's methods for the qualitative solution of the nonlinear mechanics equations, which led him to a new construction of the invariant measure, were of great significance, not only for nonlinear mechanics but also for the general theory of dynamic systems. These methods have become classical.

Bogolubov studied the problem of formation of the Markov stochastic processes and found that it was possible to use Markov methods for large scales of time. He introduced a concept about the hierarchy of the relaxation time in statistical mechanics which had a decisive influence on the subsequent development of the statistical theory of irreversible processes.

To solve problems concerning the statistical mechanics of classical systems, Bogolubov proposed methods using distribution functions and generating functionals which made it possible to calculate the thermodynamic functions in terms of molecular properties of matter.

A distribution function system that was used for the analysis of nonequilibrium processes led Bogolubov to a general method of constructing kinetic equations for interacting particle systems on the basis of the general premises of statistical mechanics. The solution of kinetic equations suggested by Bogolubov was based on a generalization of his asymptotic methods of nonlinear mechanics.

This method proved highly effective in the solution of problems in ferromagnetism. Bogolubov studied the problem of the degeneration of nonideal gases and showed that weakly nonideal Bose gas may exist in a degenerate state, in which case it will be superfluid, whereas an ideal gas does not possess this property. In this way, a theoretical model was evolved for the phenomenon of superfluidity. Bogolubov brought out the dominant role of the interaction of correlated pairs of parti-

cles with opposite momenta. He showed that the same type of excitation also occurred in superconductors, in which a decisive part is played by the interaction of electrons with lattice oscillations. Overcoming considerable mathematical difficulties, Bogolubov constructed a consistent microscopic theory of superfluidity and showed that superconductivity can be considered to be a superfluidity of the electron gas.

During the 1950s Bogolubov produced a series of papers dealing with quantum field theory in which he introduced, in an original manner, the methods used earlier in statistical physics. He built a theory, not by means of the traditional Hamiltonian formalism but on the basis of explicitly formulated fundamental physical requirements, the most important of which was the condition of causality.

Of great significance in the development of modern theory was Bogolubov's rigorous proof of dispersion relations, which gained wide use in particle physics. Dispersion relations for the transition amplitude between two states are a direct consequence of causality in the behavior of the system, and they provide a means for testing basic principles of field theory. With great imagination and with the aid of powerful mathematical tools, Bogolubov constructed, for the first time, an axiomatic physical theory that changed the thinking on the subject among physicists.

One of Bogolubov's major achievements was his proof of the "edge of the wedge" theorem, which was thereafter called Bogolubov's theorem. It found nontrivial applications in modern theoretical physics and mathematics.

In the study of quark models, Bogolubov suggested a number of simple explanations for the observed regularities in the framework of such models. He also suggested that the methods of analysis of self-similar solutions, which were used in classical gas hydrodynamics, be applied to the description of deep inelastic processes of particle interactions. He was then led to the concept of self-similar asymptotics in quantum field theory. Concerning the problem of the nature of nuclear matter, Bogolubov evolved a new approach and proposed (1958) a superfluid model of nuclei which became fundamental to the modern theory of nuclei.

The wide range of Bogolubov's scientific interests, his profound ideas, and the powerful mathematical methods which he developed, together with his extraordi-

nary ability as a teacher, had a considerable influence on contemporary theoretical physicists. His pupils carried out research in scientific centers of the Soviet Union and other countries. He authored about 200 papers, and his 15 monographs were published in a variety of languages.

Bogolubov was an influential figure in national science and social policy. He was a deputy of the Supreme Council of the U.S.S.R. and an active participant in the Paguosh Movement, which aimed to promote science in a peaceful world.

Bogolubov received the highest awards from the Soviet Union for his outstanding achievements in science. He was made a Hero of Socialist Labor and was awarded the Lenin and State prizes. Respected by the international scientific community, Bogolubov was elected an honorary member of the scientific academies of Bulgaria, the German Democratic Republic, Poland, and Heidelberg, of the National Academy of Sciences of the United States, and of the American Academy of Arts and Sciences in Boston. He received the Helmholtz Gold Medal of the Academy of Sciences of the German Democratic Republic, the Max Planck Gold Medal of the Physical Society of the Federal Republic of Germany, the Benjamin Franklin Medal, the Dannie Heineman Prize, and many others.

Bogolubov's major monographs translated into English include *Introduction to Non-Linear Mechanics* (1943), *On Some Statistical Methods in Mathematical Physics* (1945), *Lectures on Quantum Statistics* (1949), *Introduction to the Quantum Field Theory* (1958), *Problems of Dispersion Relations* (1958), and *A New Method in the Theory of Superconductivity* (1958).

For background information *see* BOSE-EINSTEIN STATISTICS; CALCULUS OF VARIATIONS; DISPERSION RELATIONS; HELIUM, LIQUID; QUANTUM FIELD THEORY; QUARKS; STATISTICAL MECHANICS; STOCHASTIC PROCESS; SUPERCONDUCTIVITY in the McGraw-Hill Encyclopedia of Science and Technology. ∎

BOHR, AAGE
☆ Danish physicist

Born June 19, 1922, Copenhagen, Denmark

While attempting to explain why in certain instances calculations of the quadrupole moment of the nucleus based on the

nuclear shell model are very much smaller than the observed value, Bohr in collaboration with Ben R. Mottelson proposed the collective or unified model of the nucleus. In their model Bohr and Mottelson retained the essential features of the nuclear shell model, but also brought out the analogy between the surface of the nucleus and that of a liquid drop. Thus, the collective model reconciled the nuclear shell model with its predecessor, the liquid drop model. For this work Bohr shared the 1975 Nobel Prize in physics with Mottelson and L. J. Rainwater. *See* MOTTELSON, BEN R.; RAINWATER, LEO JAMES.

In 1936 the Danish physicist Niels Bohr advanced the liquid drop theory of the nucleus. On this basis the fission of uranium discovered a few years later could be understood in terms of the analogy between an unstable atomic nucleus and a rupturing water drop. In the liquid drop model the form of the nucleus is determined by a balance between Coulomb repulsive forces between like charges (protons) and inward-directed forces of surface tension. In 1949 J. Hans D. Jensen, working in Germany with O. Haxel and H. E. Suess, and Maria Goeppert Mayer, working independently in the United States, advanced the shell model of the nucleus. In their model the nucleus, like the electron shells of the atom, displays all the properties of a quantum-mechanical system of particles. *See* BOHR, NIELS HENRIK DAVID; JENSEN, J. HANS D.; MAYER, MARIA GOEPPERT.

About 1950, working at the University of Copenhagen and at Columbia University in New York, Aage Bohr began to study those phenomena that did not seem to fit the nuclear shell model, whose validity had been generally established, to determine in what way the model could be refined. The calculation of the quadrupole moments of nuclei of odd mass number on the basis of the nuclear shell model involved the assumption that the nuclear core, consisting of all the nucleons except the odd one, was spherical. Bohr made the assumption—first proposed by Rainwater—that the odd nucleon, regardless of whether it was a neutron or a proton, would distort the core. This distortion, Bohr realized, would make an additional contribution to the quadrupole moment.

Based on this assumption, Bohr and Mottelson developed the collective model of the nucleus, which they announced in 1952. The fundamental postulate of the model is that, because of the collective action of the nucleons, the surface of the nucleus behaves like that of a liquid drop. The deformation caused by the odd nucleon moves across the surface of the nuclear core in the form of waves, which are equivalent to surface oscillations and rotations. Near closed shells, the nuclear equilibrium shape is spherical and the models of excitation correspond to vibrations about equilibrium in addition to the single particle excitations of the shell model. When the shells are partially filled, the nucleus may acquire a permanent distortion, usually of spheroidal shape. For such deformed nuclei, the low energy modes of excitation involve a new degree of freedom corresponding to rotational motion. Although the nucleus does not rotate like a rigid structure, the resulting spectrum of states could be treated by quantum-mechanical methods previously developed for the study of molecules. As a result, Bohr and Mottelson were able to calculate the energies and other properties of nuclear states for the various values of the rotational quantum number. The results thus derived were found to be in excellent agreement with the empirical evidence.

Although his principal investigations dealt with the structure of the nucleus and with its rotational states, Bohr made contributions to other areas of physics. Among these were his researches in superconductivity, in which he attempted to explain the stability of permanent currents, and his studies of elementary particles.

One of four sons of Niels Bohr, Aage Bohr studied at the University of Copenhagan (M.Sc., 1946; Dr.Phil., 1954). He became a research assistant at the Institute of Theoretical Physics in Copenhagen in 1946, and served as director of the institute from 1962 to 1970. In 1975 he was appointed director of Nordita, in Copenhagen. Bohr was named professor of physics at the University of Copenhagen in 1956. In 1944–45 he worked at the Los Alamos Scientific Laboratory, where the atomic bomb was developed. He was a member of the Institute for Advanced Study at Princeton, NJ, in 1949, and he engaged in research at Columbia University in New York City in 1949–50. Bohr was awarded the Dannie Heineman Prize of the American Physical Society (1960), the Pius XI Medal (1963), the Atoms for Peace Award of the Ford Motor Company Fund (1969), the Rutherford Medal of the Institute of Physics (1972), and the Wetherill Medal of the Franklin Institute (1974). He was elected a foreign member of the American Academy of Arts and Sciences (1965) and the National Academy of Sciences (1971).

Bohr wrote *Collective and Individual-Particle Aspects of Nuclear Structure,* with B. R. Mottelson (1953; 2d ed., paper, 1957), and *Nuclear Structure,* also with Mottelson (vol. 1, 1969; vol. 2, 1975; vol. 3 to be published).

For background information *see* ATOMIC STRUCTURE AND SPECTRA; NUCLEAR STRUCTURE in the McGraw-Hill Encyclopedia of Science and Technology. ∎

BOHR, NIELS HENRIK DAVID
Danish physicist

Born Oct. 7, 1885, Copenhagen, Denmark
Died Nov. 18, 1962, Copenhagen, Denmark

While studying atomic structure and radiation, Bohr applied quantum theory to the Rutherford atomic model and developed in 1913 the first consistent theory to explain the arrangement and motion of the electrons in the outer atom. Using his theory, Bohr was able to account quantitatively for the spectrum and atomic structure of hydrogen. The theory was also able to account for variations in properties of the elements and for the main

features of the x-ray and optical spectra shown by all the elements. For his achievements in the study of structure and radiations of atoms, Bohr was awarded the Nobel Prize in physics in 1922.

By the beginning of the 20th century, the classical theory of electrodynamics, which assumed continuous emission and adsorption of energy, was found inadequate to explain many phenomena, particularly those connected with electromagnetic radiation. In an attempt to overcome this inadequacy, the German physicist Max Planck, while studying blackbody radiation in 1900, made the fundamental assumption that a system of oscillating electrical particles emits and absorbs energy discontinuously, in quanta, such that the energy of the quantum, E, is proportional to the frequency of the radiation, ν as shown in Eq. (1), where h is Planck's con-

$$E = h\nu \qquad (1)$$

stant. This new theory was used by Albert Einstein in 1905 in the field of specific heats to explain the deviations from the law of Dulong and Petit. Einstein also recognized how physical phenomena like the photoelectric effect may depend directly on individual quantum effects; he concluded that any radiation process involves the emission or absorption of individual light quanta, or photons, which have energy and momentum.

The failure of the theories of classical physics to account for atomic phenomena was emphasized by developments in knowledge of the structure of atoms. The scattering of alpha rays in passing through thin metal sheets led the British physicist Ernest Rutherford in 1911 to propose a theory for the structure of the atom in which electrons revolve in closed orbit around a positively charged nucleus. But the Rutherford atomic model contained inherent defects according to classical physics. Since the orbital electrons are charged bodies moving in the electrostatic field of the nucleus, they should continuously emit radiation. The electrons would thus lose kinetic energy and gradually spiral into the nucleus. In addition, the hydrogen spectrum should have been a broad band from the red end of the spectrum to the violet. Experimental evidence showed, however, that the hydrogen atom is stable and has a line spectrum.

In 1913 Bohr reasoned that Rutherford's atomic model could be saved by applying the new quantum theory. Since it was the assumption from classical physics of the continuous emission of radiation that was causing the difficulties, Bohr assumed that if radiation were emitted discontinuously in quanta, it was reasonable to suppose that there were certain stable orbits in which electrons could move without loss of energy and that radiation would be emitted only when an electron moved from one such stable orbit into another. He formalized his reasoning into two revolutionary assumptions. One of these was that an atomic system is stable (that is, exists without radiating energy) only when in a definite series of allowed energy states. Further, every change in the energy of the atom is associated with a process in which the atom passes completely from one allowed state to another. The other assumption was that when such a transition between stationary states occurs with the emission or absorption of electromagnetic light waves, the amount of energy emitted or absorbed each time shall equal $h\nu$. Denoting the energy of the atom before and after the emission of radiation by E_1 and E_2, relation (2) may be

$$h\nu = E_1 - E_2 \quad \text{or} \quad \nu = \frac{E_1}{h} - \frac{E_2}{h} \qquad (2)$$

written. Thus, the radiation is of a single frequency, that is, it is monochromatic.

With these assumptions, it was possible to account for the fact that the spectra of the elements consist of sharp lines rather than continuous bands. Since radiation is emitted only in quanta and only when an electron jumps from one allowed state to another, the frequency of the radiation emitted would depend only upon the difference in kinetic energies of the electron in the two states. Since the allowed states are fixed, so too are the kinetic energies in those states. Thus each line in the atomic spectra of the elements corresponds to an electronic transition between two such states. In this way Bohr was able to account quantitatively for the atomic spectrum of hydrogen, giving a quantum number N, which had the values 1, 2, 3, and so on, to the allowed states and showing that the jump of an electron from the second to the first state would give one particular spectral line, the jump from the third to the second another unique spectral line, and so on. During the 1920s the apparent contradiction invoked by the behavior of the electrons in Bohr's atomic model was resolved by two discoveries. The French physicist Louis Victor de Broglie showed that the electron was not only a particle but also a waveform. He then showed (1924) how consideration of a standing waveform for an electron in a Bohr atom would explain the mysterious quantization rule for the electron and permit it to circle the nucleus without radiating. A year later the Austrian physicist Erwin Schrödinger developed his mathematical formulation of de Broglie's hypothesis, and the theory of the standing waves was seen to be verified. *See* BROGLIE, PRINCE LOUIS DE.

Bohr did not abandon classical mechanics in his theory; in fact, he assumed that the motion in the allowed states could be described by its use. Quantum theory was essential to describe the transitions between these states. Moreover, while radiation could not be described on the basis of classical electrodynamics, Bohr felt that there was a far-reaching correspondence between transitions from one stationary state to another and the various harmonic components of motion. He felt that this correspondence was of such a nature that his theory of spectra was a rational generalization of the classical theory of radiation. This reasoning led to a secondary but great contribution—his "correspondence principle," stating that at sufficiently low frequencies the laws of quantum theory converge toward and become identical with the laws of classical electrodynamics.

Thus Bohr was able to correlate four different theories of radiation and atomic structure: classical electrodynamics; empirical knowledge of the spectra based on the work of J. J. Balmer, W. Ritz, and J. R. Rydberg; Rutherford's atomic model; and Planck's quantum theory of heat radiation. By 1916 other theorists, starting with the German physicist Arnold Sommerfeld, began to associate themselves with the Bohr theory, and the further development of nuclear physics was shaped by the Bohr atom. Although Bohr originally conceived of the atom as having a shell-like structure in which the electrons moved in circular paths about the nucleus, this was later modified into the Bohr-Sommerfeld model of the atom in which the electrons travel in elliptical orbits.

Bohr received his doctorate at the University of Copenhagen in 1911. He then studied at Cambridge under J. J. Thomson and spent a year teaching at the University of Manchester, where he worked with Rutherford on atomic structure. Returning to the University of Copenhagen, Bohr published in 1913 his remarkable series of papers on the spectrum and atomic structure of hydrogen. The Copenhagen Institute of Theoretical Physics was established through his influence in 1920 and became one of the leading intellectual centers of Europe. Bohr served as its director and also as president of the Royal Danish Academy of Science. In 1939 Bohr laid the broad foundations of a "liquid droplet" theory of nuclear phenomena, showing an analogy in the fission of uranium between an unstable atomic nucleus and a rupturing water drop. Again, a bold theory of Bohr's led to much fruitful research toward an understanding of the atom. During World War II he fled from Denmark to England and then to the United States, where he worked on the Manhattan Project. It was Bohr who predicted that uranium-235 was the isotope that would undergo fission and be suitable for the atomic weapon. He was an advocate of international atomic control, and he won the first Atoms for Peace Award in 1957.

Bohr wrote *The Theory of Spectra and Atomic Constitution* (1922).

For background information *see* ATOMIC STRUCTURE AND SPECTRA in the McGraw-Hill Encyclopedia of Science and Technology. ∎

BOLTON, ELMER KEISER
☆ American chemist and research director

Born June 23, 1886, Philadelphia, PA, U.S.A.

Died July 30, 1968, Wilmington, DE, U.S.A.

During a long association with the chemistry and manufacture of organic compounds, Bolton contributed in leadership and direction to three historic undertakings: the establishment of a domestic synthetic dyestuff industry; the research that led to the first general-purpose synthetic rubber to be developed either in the United States or abroad; and the phase of the program of fundamental studies in polymerization phenomena that led to the discovery of nylon and other long-chain molecular structures of major importance. He was director of what is now the Central Research Department of E. I. du Pont de Nemours and Company from 1930 until his retirement in 1951.

Bolton began his career in industrial organic research in 1915, about the time the Du Pont Company decided to undertake the manufacture of synthetic dyes, for which America was largely dependent upon Germany, and had established the Organic Chemicals Department. The following year, with the supply situation becoming more critical, Bolton was placed in charge of a group of chemists learning, in the laboratory, the complex dye-manufacturing processes that had been developed abroad. Beginning with a small group making intermediates from benzol—with

which Du Pont had experience in explosives—the new project grew swiftly into a large unit of several hundred research workers. By 1926 sufficient progress had been made in developing the new industry to enable Du Pont to plan an extension of activities in new areas of organic chemistry.

Bolton proposed that work be undertaken on synthetic rubber. Many years of research by European chemists had failed to produce a satisfactory substitute for the natural latex, but Bolton's management was ready to accept the "long chance" for success offered by his proposal. Recognizing in J. A. Nieuwland's process for making divinylacetylene from three molecules of acetylene a possible path to the ultimate goal, Bolton suggested a modification that produced monovinylacetylene—a compound made by the union of two molecules of acetylene. Treatment of the monovinylacetylene with hydrochloric acid resulted in a previously unknown material, which was called chloroprene. Research chemists assigned to the rubber problem soon determined that chloroprene could be converted into a rubberlike material superior to natural rubber in certain respects.

Beginning in 1928, Bolton was charged with the responsibility of selecting and directing research on promising developments stemming from the fundamental studies carried out by a group of organic chemists under the supervision of Wallace H. Carothers. The efforts of the Carothers group was directed to the condensation of aliphatic amino acids and of aliphatic dibasic acids and aliphatic diamines under conditions that favored long-chain molecules. After establishing a broad knowledge of this class of long-chain molecules, Carothers was encouraged by Bolton to initiate a project aiming at the synthesis of molecules that might have interest as a new textile fiber. The polyamide eventually born of this effort was nylon.

Bolton majored in chemistry at Bucknell University, where he received his A.B. degree in 1908. At Harvard he received his M.A. and Ph.D. degrees and in 1913 was awarded its Sheldon Fellowship, with a reappointment in 1914, under which he engaged in postdoctoral research at the Kaiser Wilhelm Institut für Chemie in Berlin-Dahlem. There, in the laboratory of Professor Richard Willstätter, he isolated and established the chemical constitution of the pigments of geraniums, scarlet sage, and dark-red chrysanthemums. In 1941 Bolton received the Chemical Industry Medal, awarded annually by the American Section of the Society of Chemical Industry; in 1945, its Perkin Medal; and in 1954, the Willard Gibbs Medal, awarded by the Chicago Section of the American Chemical Society. He was elected to the National Academy of Sciences in 1946.

For background information *see* DYE; NYLON; POLYMERIZATION in the McGraw-Hill Encyclopedia of Science and Technology. ∎

BOMBIERI, ENRICO
☆ Italian mathematician

Born Nov. 26, 1940, Milan, Italy

Bombieri has done important work in many fields of mathematics, including number theory, univalent functions, several complex variables, partial differential equations, and algebraic geometry. Only a few of his most important results will be discussed here.

In the field of number theory, Bombieri has played a major role in improving the method of the large sieve, previously developed by J. V. Linnik and A. Rényi; he used this method to obtain a basic result concerning the distribution of prime numbers among arithmetic progressions, now known as Bombieri's mean value theorem. Let $\pi(x;q,a)$ be the number of primes $p \leq x$ such that p is in the arithmetic progression $a, a+q, a+2q, a+3q, \ldots$. If the integers a and q have a common

divisor greater than 1, then there is at most one such prime. On the other hand, P. G. L. Dirichlet proved that if the greatest common divisor of a and q, denoted (a,q), equals 1, then there are infinitely many such primes. The prime number theorem for arithmetic progressions asserts, in addition, that if $(a,q) = 1$, then $\pi(x;q,a)$ is approximately $\pi(x)/\phi(q)$, where $\pi(x)$ is the total number of primes $p \leq x$, and $\phi(q)$ is the number of integers a, $1 \leq a \leq q$, such that $(a,q) = 1$. The prime numbers are thus distributed rather evenly among the arithmetic progressions in which they can lie. However, this result has been proved only for fairly small values of q, and it is often important to know something about the size of the error $E(x;q,a)$, defined by Eq. (1), for large val-

$$E(x;q,a) = \pi(x;q,a) - \pi(x)/\phi(q) \quad (1)$$

ues of q. Bombieri's mean value theorem asserts that $E(x;q,a)$ is small on the average. Specifically, it states that for any positive constant A there exist positive constants B and C such that inequality (2) is

$$\sum_{q \leq Q} \max_{\substack{a \\ (a,q)=1}} \left| E(x;q,a) \right| < Cx(\log x)^{-A} \quad (2)$$

satisfied, provided that $Q < x^{1/2}(\log x)^{-B}$.

This theorem gives rise to a general method for treating problems that could previously be solved only by highly complicated techniques or by the assumption of the unproved extended Riemann hypothesis, such as I. M. Vinogradov's theorem (1937) that every sufficiently large odd integer is the sum of three primes, Linnik's theorem (1961) that every sufficiently large integer is the sum of a prime and two squares, and J. Chen's result (1966) that every sufficiently large even integer is the sum of a prime and an integer with at most two prime factors. Although the twin prime hypothesis (that there are infinitely many pairs of primes which differ by 2) and the Goldbach conjecture (that every even integer greater than 2 is the sum of two primes) remain unproved, Bombieri's mean value theorem has enabled closer approaches to be made to both these conjectures. In 1974 Bombieri invented a new asymptotic sieve which raised the possibility of coming still closer to Goldbach's conjecture.

Another area in which Bombieri has made major contributions is the study of minimal surfaces, that is, surfaces of least area spanning a prescribed boundary. He helped prove the existence of singular points for an important class of such sur-

faces. E. De Giorgi and others had shown that n-dimensional minimal surfaces in R^{n+1} (the euclidean space of $n+1$ dimensions) which are locally the boundaries of sets have no interior singular points for $1 \leq n \leq 6$. However, in 1969 Bombieri, De Giorgi, and E. Giusti constructed a seven-dimensional minimal surface of this type in R^8 which contains an essential singular point; it then follows that such singularities exist for all $n \leq 7$. The character of the problem thus changes at dimension 7.

In the same work, a function $f : R^8 \to R$ was constructed whose graph in R^9 is a minimal surface which is not a hyperplane. In contrast, in 1968 J. Simons, extending the work of S. Bernstein and others, had shown that, if $f : R^n \to R$, with $n \leq 7$, has a graph which is a minimal surface, then this graph must be a hyperplane. The two results furnished an example of a class of nonlinear elliptic partial differential equations, the minimal surface equations satisfied by the fs, whose solution sets change drastically with increasing dimension.

Bombieri, in collaboration with De Giorgi, Giusti, and M. Miranda, obtained analytic estimates for functions f defining minimal surfaces, and for functions u defined on the minimal surfaces and satisfying partial differential equations defined there. Such estimates are important for understanding the structure of the space of solutions of the minimal surface equation in a fixed dimension. In 1969–70 S. Lang and Bombieri collaborated on applying similar estimates to problems in transcendental number theory. As an outgrowth of this work, Bombieri in 1970 proved a theorem concerning algebraic values of meromorphic functions of several complex variables.

Another important result of Bombieri is his proof of the local validity of Bieberbach's conjecture. Let S denote the family of functions of the form $f(z) = z + a_2z^2 + a_3z^3 + \ldots$ which are holomorphic and univalent on the unit disk $|z| \leq 1$. Bieberbach's conjecture states that, if $f(z)$ is in S, then the real part of a_n, denoted $\mathrm{Re}\, a_n$, is equal to or less than n. The conjecture has been proved for $2 \leq n \leq 6$ and for various subfamilies of S. In 1965 P. R. Garabedian and M. Schiffer proved that, for even ns, $n - \mathrm{Re}\, a_n$ is nonnegative if $2 - \mathrm{Re}\, a_2$ is sufficiently small. In 1967 Bombieri extended the local validity of Bieberbach's conjecture to all integers n. Specifically, he proved inequalities (3) and (4), where the limit inferior is taken over all functions of the family S.

$$\liminf_{a_2 \to 2} \frac{n - \operatorname{Re} a_n}{2 - \operatorname{Re} a_2} > 0 \text{ for } n \text{ even} \quad (3)$$

$$\liminf_{a_3 \to 3} \frac{n - \operatorname{Re} a_n}{3 - \operatorname{Re} a_3} > 0 \text{ for } n \text{ odd} \quad (4)$$

Bombieri received his degree in mathematics from the University of Milan in 1963. He was appointed to the chair of analysis at the University of Caligari in 1965 and to the chair of analysis at the University of Pisa in 1966. In 1974 he was appointed to the chair of mathematics at the Scuola Normale Superiore in Pisa, and in 1977 he became professor of mathematics at the Institute for Advanced Study in Princeton. In 1974 he received the Fields Medal of the International Congress of Mathematicians, and in 1976 the Feltrinelli Prize from the Accademia Nazionale dei Lincei (Italy). He was elected an honorary member of the London Mathematical Society in 1978.

For background information *see* COMPLEX NUMBERS AND COMPLEX VARIABLES; DIFFERENTIAL EQUATION; NUMBER. THEORY in the McGraw-Hill Encyclopedia of Science and Technology. ∎

BONNER, JAMES FREDERICK
★ American biologist

Born Sept. 1, 1910, Ansley, U.S.A.

Bonner's work was concerned with the mechanism by means of which a single cell, the fertilized egg, gives rise to an adult creature made up of many different kinds of cells. This process is known as development. All cells contain the directions for cell life written in the deoxyribonucleic acid (DNA) of their chromosomes. These directions include specification of how to make the many kinds of protein enzyme molecules by means of which the cell converts available building blocks into substances suitable for making more cells. To make enzyme molecules, the DNA prints off ribonucleic acid (RNA) copies of itself — messenger RNA molecules; these messenger RNA molecules are decoded by ribosomes, also made by the DNA; as a ribosome decodes the messenger RNA molecule, it uses the information to assemble a specific kind of enzyme molecule.

This picture of cell life provided by molecular biology applies to all cells of all organisms. But the bodies of higher life forms, such as people or pea plants, possess different kinds of cells. For example, some cells make hemoglobin while others do not. The new approach to differentiation is based upon the fact that all the cells in the body of a higher organism have exactly the same amount and kind of DNA, that is, the same genetic information. When a single cell, the fertilized egg, divides into two cells, each of these receives a complete set of the genetic DNA. In the course of embryonic development, however, the cells of the embryo soon become different from one another. Some produce hemoglobin, some muscle enzymes, some liver enzymes, and so on. The genetic information for making hemoglobin, for example, is in all cells, but it is used in only those few cells that are to be the red blood cells. In all the other cells, the genetic information for making hemoglobin is turned off or repressed. To find out what causes development and differentiation to take place, it is necessary to find out what is in the cell that determines which particular units of the genetic information—which particular genes will be active and make their characteristic messenger RNA and which will be repressed or inactive.

Bonner's approach to the study of development was first to find out how to isolate chromosomes and cause them to make their messenger RNA in the test tube. It proved easy to isolate chromosomes, and such purified chromosomes made RNA, provided they were given the RNA building blocks. If ribosomes that had been freed of messenger RNA were added to the system, as well as the 20 amino acids (the building blocks of enzyme molecules), enzyme molecules were made. Bonner and his coworker, Ru-Chih Huang, showed that the repressed genes were those complexed with and covered by a histone protein. When the histone was removed from the chromosome, the genes previously repressed were derepressed. Whether histones are the only kind of repressor is not yet known.

Bonner accomplished the dissociation of DNA from histone by the use of high concentrations of salt. This worked nicely but not selectively, derepressing all repressed genes. In the living cell derepression is selective; one or a few genes may be turned on or off without influencing others. Bonner and his associates found that certain kinds of small molecules were able to turn the activity of particular genes off or on. These small molecules included the hormones. A hormone on arrival at its target organ turns on an individual or whole set of genes, causing the production of characteristic enzyme molecules not previously produced by those cells. This is dramatically exemplified by the case of arousal from dormancy, studied by Bonner and Dorothy Tuan. The buds of freshly harvested potatoes do not grow; they are said to be dormant. The chromosomes of the cells of the dormant bud are almost completely repressed and therefore cannot make any messenger RNA. Bonner found that dormancy could be ended at any time by supplying the bud with a particular hormone, gibberellic acid, or a synthetic substitute, ethylenechlorohydrin. Treatment with a minute amount of one of these materials caused the buds to grow. The chemical caused a substantial proportion of the genetic complement to be derepressed and to become active in RNA making. Many hormones work in this way, and Bonner sought to describe in molecular detail the way in which hormone-and histone-DNA complex interact to cause derepression.

It was shown by Bonner and Keiji Marushige in 1971 and by others, including Joel Gottesfeld in 1974 and later years, that a small fraction of the genetic apparatus of the mammalian genome, such as the liver genome, is solubilized much more rapidly than is the rest by nucleic acids degrading enzymes, such as deoxyribonuclease (DNase) II. This rapidly attacked portion of the chromosome turned out to be the expressed portion, that is, the portion which is transcribed by RNA polymerase and which yields nuclear

RNA and therefore messenger RNA. By this methodology it became possible to separate the expressed portion from the nonexpressed portion of the genome and to discover the differences between them. The expressed portion, which constitutes 5 to 10 or at most 20 percent (in brain) of the total DNA of the genetic apparatus, is complexed with histones, as is the nonexpressed portion. The histones of the expressed portion do not stabilize DNA against melting and, in general, do not interact with DNA with the same rigor as the histones of the nonexpressed portion. It was subsequently found by Bonner and colleagues that acetylation of the N-terminal peptides of the histones of the expressed portions cause the histones to release the DNA, make it transcribable by RNA polymerase and, hence, become expressed. The molecules which cause the histone acetylase, a chromosomal enzyme, to transfer acetyl groups to the specific histones which cover the DNA sequences to be expressed in a particular cell type have not yet been identified. Bonner, together with other workers in this field, studied this matter by isolating particular individual DNA fragments containing expressed DNA sequences, isolating them by recombinant DNA technology, reconstituting them with histones to form nonexpressed fragments of the genome or mini-chromosomes, and then trying to find out what materials in the nucleus cause expressed portions to become expressed by means of acetylation.

Bonner's studies grew out of his earlier interest in the study of ribosomes. In the early 1950s it became apparent that the synthesis of enzyme molecules was due to some kind of entity within the cell, an entity larger than enzyme molecules but smaller than the mitochondria. Bonner and Paul Ts'o isolated this entity in 1955. They found that the particles involved were what are now known as ribosomes and that they were made of equal amounts of RNA and protein. Bonner next tried to find out where the RNA of ribosomes came from. It turned out that the RNA of ribosomes was made in the nucleus, and this led to the study of how RNA was made. This is turn led logically to the discovery in 1960 of chromosomal RNA synthesis, the process now known as DNA-dependent RNA synthesis. The ribosomal study was built upon earlier studies by Bonner and his colleagues on how to separate the different kinds of particles inside cells from one another. They

had developed methods for the isolation of mitochondria from plant cells, and in 1951 had shown that the mitochondria thus isolated not only carried out all of the respiratory oxidations but also conducted the process, now known as oxidative phosphorylation, by means of which the energy liberated in respiration was conserved and made available to all processes requiring energy.

Both Bonner's parents were chemists. Like his five brothers and one sister, Bonner majored in chemistry at the University of Utah, receiving his A.B. in 1931. As an undergraduate he became interested in biology through the influence of Theodosius Dobzhansky. At the California Institute of Technology, where he received his Ph.D. in biology in 1934, he worked with T. H. Morgan, A. H. Sturtevant, K. V. Thimann, H. E. Dolk, and F. W. Went, among others. After study abroad in Holland and Switzerland, he joined the staff of Caltech in 1935. He was elected to the National Academy of Sciences in 1950. *See* DOBZHANSKY, THEODOSIUS; STURTEVANT, ALFRED HENRY; THIMANN, KENNETH VIVIAN; WENT, FRITS WARMOLT.

Bonner wrote *Plant Biochemistry* (1950); *Principles of Plant Physiology*, with A. W. Galston (1952); *The Next 100 Years*, with Harrison Brown and John Weir (1957); *The Nucleohistones*, with Paul Ts'o (1954); *The Molecular Biology of Development* (1965); *The Next 90 Years*, with Brown (1967); *Plant Biochemistry Mark II*, with Joseph Varner (1965); *Plant Biochemistry Mark III*, with Varner (1977); and *The Next 80 Years*, with Brown (1977).

For background information *see* CHROMOSOME THEORY OF HEREDITY; DEOXYRIBONUCLEIC ACID (DNA); DORMANCY; MITOCHONDRIA; RIBONUCLEIC ACID (RNA); RIBOSOMES in the McGraw-Hill Encyclopedia of Science and Technology. ■

BORN, MAX
★ British theoretical physicist

> ***Born*** *Dec. 11, 1882, Breslau, Silesia, Prussia*
> ***Died*** *Jan. 5, 1970, Göttingen, West Germany*

In the course of a long scientific career, Born made significant contributions to many branches of theoretical physics. He

played a central role in the development of quantum mechanics, which is the basis of modern atomic and nuclear physics. For this work he was awarded the Nobel Prize in physics in 1954.

The discovery of quantum mechanics was made at Göttingen, Germany, where Born was appointed professor of physics in 1921. With his assistants, first Wolfgang Pauli, then Werner Heisenberg, he started on a program to investigate how far the quantum theory of the atom by Niels Bohr and Arnold Sommerfeld was valid for more complicated systems; Heisenberg and he showed that it did not account for the line spectrum of the helium atom. They endeavored then to develop a new atomic mechanics. The first success was due to Heisenberg, who introduced a perfectly new way of dealing with physical quantities. He gave Born his paper to be sent in for publication. Born saw at once its fundamental importance and discovered soon that Heisenberg's formalism was identical with the matrix calculus well known to mathematicians. He formulated for the first time the famous matrix relation $qp - pq = ih/2\pi$ between a coordinate q of a particle and its conjugate momentum p (h being Planck's constant). As Heisenberg was on holiday, Born enlisted the help of P. Jordan, one of his senior pupils, and developed with him the quantum mechanics of the motion of a particle in one dimension. After his return to Göttingen, Heisenberg joined with Born and Jordan in the generalization of this work to three-dimensional problems. A complete quantitative expla-

nation was obtained for the positions and intensities of atomic spectral lines and for other phenomena that had mystified physicists for 20 years. Starting also from Heisenberg's paper, P. A. M. Dirac in Cambridge, England, developed the theory independently. *See* BOHR, NIELS HENRIK DAVID; DIRAC, PAUL ADRIEN MAURICE; PAULI, WOLFGANG.

Meanwhile, in Zurich, Erwin Schrödinger had followed a quite different trend of thoughts initiated by Louis de Broglie, on wave mechanics, leading to the same results. The essential equivalence of Schrödinger's method and that which had been discovered in Göttingen was, however, soon demonstrated by Schrödinger himself. Born was quick to accept and assimilate Schrödinger's contribution and showed how it could be applied to determine the intensity and angular distribution of a beam of particles that had been scattered by an atomic target. The importance of this application eventually transcended that of the theory of the bound states of atomic systems, on which the explanation of spectral lines was based. *See* BROGLIE, PRINCE LOUIS DE.

In spite of the success of the mathematical theories in accounting for experimental data, the actual meaning of quantum mechanics was still obscure. Perhaps Born's most striking contribution to the subject was the physical interpretation that he supplied. In the mathematical formalism, the state of an atomic system is represented by an abstract vector with an arbitrary and usually infinite number of components. Born showed that each component can be regarded as an amplitude, the square of which is the probability that an experimental measurement on an atomic system will yield a particular result. This statistical interpretation carried with it the implication that atomic phenomena are not deterministic: the result of an individual experiment cannot be predicted with certainty, though the probability of obtaining a given result can be computed, by the use of Born's prescription. The waves determined by Schrödinger's wave mechanics were proved to have no more than a statistical significance and, even so, only in relation to a particular type of ideal measurement. Schrödinger objected strongly to this interpretation, and so, for different reasons, did Max Planck, Albert Einstein, and Louis de Broglie. But, in spite of the eminence of those few who opposed it, the concept of the indeterministic

nature of atomic phenomena has been generally accepted. Niels Bohr, as well as Born, eventually played an important part in gaining acceptance of this revolution in scientific thought. But the most important influence was undoubtedly the wealth of applications that followed, in which experimental work invariably confirmed Born's interpretation. Born took part in some of these applications himself: his work with J. R. Oppenheimer on the quantum mechanics of molecules and his book with Kun Huang on the quantum mechanics of crystal lattices are well-known examples. *See* OPPENHEIMER, J. ROBERT.

This latter book is the last summarizing of another part of Born's life work, *The Dynamical Theory of Crystal Lattices*. His first book had the same title in German (*Dynamik der Kristallgitter*, 1915) but was still based on classical mechanics. He followed the subject of lattice dynamics through his whole life with many collaborators and pupils. It can be regarded as the theoretical base of the modern theory of the solid state.

Born also worked in other subjects, for example, stability of elastic systems, thermodynamics, and statistical mechanics of condensed gases and liquids. He suggested a new type of symmetry in physical systems, called principle of reciprocity, which was successfully used in the theory of elementary particles.

Born's father was professor of anatomy at the University of Breslau; he did fundamental research in embryology and the theory of evolution, and first recognized the corpus luteum as the organ that produced the sex hormones—a discovery that led to modern research on fertility. Born's mother, who came from a Silesian industrial family, died when he was quite young; his father died during his last year at school. Born attended a gymnasium in Breslau, then studied at the universities of Breslau, Heidelberg, Zurich, and finally Göttingen, where the great mathematicians David Hilbert, Hermann Minkowski, and Felix Klein were his teachers. After graduating as Ph.D., he visited Cambridge. In 1908 he returned to Göttingen, first as Minkowski's assistant and then as a lecturer. There, in 1913, he married Hedwig Ehrenberg. In 1915 he was appointed to a professorship in Berlin to relieve Planck in teaching; but World War I had begun, and Born was soon in military service, fortunately in an artillery research establishment where he had time to spare for continuing work in theoret-

ical physics. He cemented a friendship with Einstein during this period. After the war he went from Berlin to Frankfurt for 2 years, where he did some experimental work. Then he obtained the professorship in Göttingen, where the foundations of quantum mechanics were developed. Many famous theoretical physicists came to work in Göttingen during this period. Along with many Jewish refugees, Born left Germany when Hitler came to power. After 3 years in Cambridge and a visit to India, he was appointed to the Tait Chair at the University of Edinburgh, where he remained for 17 years until his retirement in 1953. He then settled at Bad Pyrmont, a picturesque spa not far from Göttingen. He consistently condemned the warlike uses of modern scientific knowledge. He was elected a foreign associate of the U.S. National Academy of Sciences in 1955.

Born published many papers and books, of which *Atomic Physics* (1935; 7th ed. 1962) became most popular; his Waynflete Lectures, under the title *Natural Philosophy of Cause and Chance* (1949), give a semipopular account of several of his scientific and philosophical interests. A textbook of optics in German (1933) evolved from one of his lecture courses; a modernized version in English, *Principles of Optics*, was written in collaboration with E. Wolf (1959; 5th ed. 1975). Two volumes of *Selected Papers* were published (1963) by the Academy of Göttingen. During his retirement Born wrote many articles and some books on the problem of the responsibility of scientists arising from the use of nuclear energy in war and peace.

For background information *see* QUANTUM MECHANICS in the McGraw-Hill Encyclopedia of Science and Technology. ∎

BOTHE, WALTHER
German physicist

Born Jan. 9, 1891, Oranienburg, Germany
Died Aug. 2, 1957, Heidelberg, Germany

While studying the scattering of light on practically free electrons, Bothe devised a technique for the simultaneous detection of the scattered quantum and the recoil electron. This "coincidence method" became the foundation for subsequent investigations by physicists of nuclear reactions and cosmic radiation. For this achievement Bothe received, jointly with Max Born, the Nobel Prize for physics in 1954. *See* BORN, MAX.

In 1924 Niels Bohr, H. A. Kramers, and J. C. Slater published a paper dealing with the wave-particle duality of light. To account for this duality in terms of the then accepted theories of optics, they proposed that the laws of conservation of energy and momentum might not be valid on the atomic level; the laws would be statistically satisfied only on a macroscopic scale, not for a single emission of light. Bothe accepted the challenge of devising an experiment to confirm or deny this hypothesis. The experiment was to be designed to answer the question of whether it was a scatter quantum and a recoil electron that were simultaneously emitted in the recoil process or whether there was a chance relationship between the two. *See* BOHR, NIELS HENRIK DAVID.

Bothe's coworker was Hans Geiger, who had just developed a counter for detecting not only heavy particles but also electrons. This so-called needle counter could respond to light quanta of energies sufficiently high to release electrons within the counter. The experimental arrangement consisted of two needle counters that were bombarded by a beam of x-rays. The recoil process occurred in one counter, and this was recorded. The scattered quanta had to penetrate the other counter, actuating it by scattering, with much lower probability, another electron. At this time the readings of both

counters were recorded side by side on a moving paper chart and the occurrence of any temporal coincidences between the pointer readings noted. Such coincidences could arise only from two particles emitted in the same recoil process or from a particle that had passed through both needle counters at a high velocity. Bothe and Geiger found that periodic coincidences were occurring; the strict validity of the law of conservation of energy was therefore upheld even on an atomic scale. When the experiment was repeated with radiothorium as a source of impinging gamma radiation instead of the x-rays, the same results were obtained.

Bothe's coincidence method was quickly applied to the field of cosmic radiation. Coincidences caused by cosmic radiation were seen in unscreened counters and when absorbing layers of variable thickness were applied around the counters. These experiments led in 1929 to the conclusion that cosmic radiation does not consist primarily of powerful gamma rays but of material particles with an energy of at least 10^9 electronvolts. Following this, coincidence arrangements were used with increasing numbers of counters combined with cloud chambers, ionization chambers, and scintillation counters. Instead of using photographic recording, the method used electronic circuits and mechanical counters.

Another important area in which the coincidence method was applied was that of nuclear reactions. For example, Bothe and others found it was possible to determine whether two or more gamma quanta generated in a nuclear reaction came from the same unstable nucleus. If this were so, they would be given off practically simultaneously; if, however, they were formed during conversion of separate nuclei, they would be emitted alternatively. The solution of this problem was necessary to measure reaction energies and determine nuclear mass. Analogous problems in natural and artificial radioactivity were tackled experimentally in this manner.

Bothe studied physics at the University of Berlin, where he was a student of Max Planck. From 1913 to 1930, except for military service during World War I, he worked at the Physikalisch-Technische Reichanstalt in Berlin. In 1930 he became professor of physics and director of the Institute of Physics at the University of Giessen. He moved to the University of Heidelberg in 1932, becoming in 1934 director of the Institute of Physics at the

Max Planck Institute for Medical Research in Heidelberg.

For background information *see* PARTICLE DETECTOR in the McGraw-Hill Encyclopedia of Science and Technology. ∎

BOUDART, MICHEL
★ American chemist and chemical engineer

Born June 18, 1924, Brussels, Belgium

Interested in heterogeneous catalysis since engineering college days, Boudart became converted to a lifelong study of the subject by Sir Hugh Taylor, with whom he worked in Princeton as a chemistry pre- and postdoctoral student. He designed and made systematic studies of the physical characterization of catalytic materials and the kinetics of catalytic reactions. *See* TAYLOR, SIR HUGH (STOTT).

In 1955 and 1956 Boudart, then on the Princeton faculty, worked during two summers in the Linden, N.J., laboratories of Esso Research and Engineering Company, where he and Larry Spenadel succeeded in defining the state of aggregation of platinum metal in the reforming catalysts used in petroleum refining. This work was the beginning of a long line of investigations by Boudart and his students dealing with the preparation, characterization, and catalytic activity of small metal particles contained in porous nonmetallic supports such as silica, alumina, zeolites, or carbon.

In their 1960 paper Spenadel and Bou-

dart reported that platinum in reforming catalysts was present as very small clusters or rafts with almost all of the metallic atoms exposed. This view is now universally accepted. The next step was to study the rate of a reaction on such clusters, to express it as a turnover frequency N (the number of molecules transformed per catalytic site per second), and to determine the effect on N of platinum cluster size. The work was started in 1961 at the University of California at Berkeley and completed in 1966 at Stanford, with the decisive help of John E. Benson. The first problem was to improve the method of Spenadel and Boudart for obtaining a reliable count of the number of surface platinum atoms. The count could then be used to express reaction rate per surface atom, that is, to obtain turnover frequency N. The conclusion was that N for the hydrogenation of cyclopropane to propane decreased by a factor of 2 when the size of the metal particles varied from 1 to 100 nanometers. The reason why this finding attracted considerable attention was Boudart's recognition that what mattered was not the twofold change but the fact that the change was trivially small. It was concluded that the reaction was facile or structure-insensitive. Several such reactions were subsequently discovered. More than 10 years later, the Stanford work was repeated at Northwestern University. The new results obtained on different catalysts agreed with the old ones. Moreover, excellent agreement with the new and old work was reported by researchers at Berkeley who used single crystals of platinum as catalysts.

The demonstrated reproducibility of catalytic data in different laboratories with samples of a given metal in the form of small or large crystals changed totally accepted views about heterogeneous catalysis, which until the early 1960s was still largely regarded as an industrial art with jealously guarded proprietary recipes. Reactions for which this reproducibility could not be observed were called structure-sensitive. In a later attempt at discriminating such reactions from structure-insensitive ones, Boudart noted in 1976 that the two classes of reactions catalyzed by metals might be ascribed to the need, or lack of it, respectively, of a cluster or ensemble of surface sites in the rate-determining process. If only one or two surface atoms are required per catalytic site, the reaction rate varies very little with particle size or crystallographic orienta-

tion, does not change much when a group VIII metal (such as nickel) is alloyed with a group Ib metal (such as copper), and is not too strikingly different from one group VIII metal to another. Reactions in this class include those where C-H or H-H bonds are made or broken. By contrast, if the catalytic site contains an ensemble of adjacent atoms, the reaction rates change typically by an order of magnitude with particle size or crystallographic orientation, can change by several orders of magnitude upon alloying between an active and an inactive metal, and can differ by many orders of magnitude among group VIII metals. Reactions of this second class include those where the bonds in $N{\equiv}N$, $C{=}O$, and $C{-}C$ are made or broken. The implications and applications of this classification are important not only in heterogeneous catalysis but in homogeneous catalysis as well.

Born in Brussels and raised in a family that respected the applications of science more than science itself and in a school that stressed the classics at the expense of science and mathematics, Boudart received his 5-year engineering degree in 1947 from the University of Louvain. The same year, he sailed to the United States and went to Princeton University, where he stayed for 14 years as a graduate student in chemistry (Ph.D., 1950), research assistant and associate, assistant to the director of Project SQUID, and assistant and associate professor of chemical engineering. In 1961 he moved to the University of California at Berkeley, where he was professor of chemical engineering until 1964. Then he became a professor of chemical engineering and chemistry at Stanford University, where he directed his laboratory for the study of adsorption and catalysis. He received the Richard H. Wilhelm Award in Chemical Reaction Engineering of the American Institute of Chemical Engineers (1974) and the Kendall Award in Surface and Colloid Chemistry of the American Chemical Society (1977). Boudart was elected to the National Academy of Sciences in 1975 and to the National Academy of Engineering in 1979.

Boudart wrote *Kinetics of Chemical Processes* (1968).

For background information *see* ADSORPTION; CATALYSIS; KINETIC METHODS OF ANALYSIS; REFORMING IN PETROLEUM REFINING in the McGraw-Hill Encyclopedia of Science and Technology. ∎

BOVET, DANIEL
☆ Italian pharmacologist

Born Mar. 23, 1907, Neuchâtel, Switzerland

While conducting research in therapeutic chemistry, Bovet observed organic compounds that proved effective as muscle relaxants (used to supplement light general anesthesia during surgery) and antihistamines (useful in alleviating the effects of allergies). In recognition of his discoveries relating to synthetic compounds that inhibit the action of certain body substances, and especially their action on the vascular system and the skeletal muscles, Bovet was awarded the 1957 Nobel Prize for medicine or physiology.

The alkaloid curare has long been used by South American aborigines as a dart poison. While it has no effect on the central nervous system, curare causes complete relaxation of the muscles, and death may ensue as the result of respiratory failure. In the mid-18th century, the French geographer Charles La Condamine brought samples of the poison to Europe. The structure of one of the physiologically active principles of curare, *d*-tubocurarine, was identified in 1935, and years later a chemically pure alkaloid was introduced as an adjuvant to anesthesia.

Following the first observations by Griffith and Cullen concerning the muscle relaxant properties of curare in surgery, Bovet worked to develop a synthetic curare. He proceeded to synthesize molecules chemically related to the chosen models and to prepare relatively simple derivatives with analogous properties. In this way, Bovet synthesized more than 400 compounds that simulated the effects of the natural product in varying degrees. One of these compounds, succinylcholine, came closest to duplicating the activity of curare, and clinical tests showed it to be an effective substitute. This made it possible to use succinylcholine as a muscle relaxant whose effective dosages could be determined with precision. By its use, the surgeon is able to produce complete muscle relaxation with only light anesthesia, thus avoiding some detrimental effects of deep anesthesia.

Prior to beginning his work with curare, Bovet had developed the first antihistaminic compound. Histamine, which is found in all body tissues, was believed to be the causative agent in producing allergy symptoms. Every body tissue reacts to histamine in some way, and excessive amounts intensify reactions to the point where discomfort sets in. When introduced by means other than adsorption through the intestine, histamine is extremely toxic, indicating that it is undoubtedly present in the body in a nontoxic combination, probably with a protein.

Bovet realized that relief from allergy symptoms would probably require a mechanism that could interfere with the production of free histamine from this combined form. In collaboration with A. M. Staub, he considered the similarities among histamine, adrenaline, and acetylcholine. He then began to investigate substances that demonstrated a specific antagonism for histamine, comparable to that shown by sympatholitics and parasympatholitics for adrenaline and acetylcholine, respectively. In 1937 he succeeded in producing the first antihistamine, thymoxydiethylamine, which was too toxic to be used clinically. However, thymoxydiethylamine served as the basis for the derivation of almost all subsequent antihistamines. Thus, Bovet's research led to the development in the 1950s of new antihistaminic drugs, which have proved to be of use in relieving the symptoms associated with such allergies as hay fever, hives, and poison oak.

Bovet's earliest work was concerned with the development of the sulfa drugs. Soon after its discovery in 1935, the orange-red dye sulfamyldiaminobenzene was found to have chemotherapeutic properties by the German biochemist Gerhard Domagk. Since this dye was found to be effective against streptococci in the human body but ineffective when added to laboratory cultures, Bovet theorized that the complex organic dye was broken down in the body to simpler compounds that worked against the streptococci. He therefore proceeded to reduce it to its component compounds. One of these, sulfanilamide, proved to be effective against streptococci both in the body and in cultures. With this evidence to support his premise, Bovet began to synthesize derivatives of sulfanilamide in an effort to discover even more therapeutic compounds. He found that the majority of the superior derivatives had the common feature of a complex organic group in the place of a hydrogen atom in the sulfonamide group, SO_2NH_2. Although this finding led to the preparation of numerous derivatives, only a few had both the high antibacterial activity and the low toxicity to human beings to permit their use in chemotherapy. Sulfanilamide and its derivatives are of value in combatting many types of bacterial infection. Unfortunately, most of the sulfa drugs are only sparingly soluble in water. For this reason they tend to deposit in the kidneys and interfere with the excretory function. This has been overcome in part, however, by having the patient increase his water intake to aid in the solution of the sulfa drugs and speed their elimination from the kidneys. *See* DOMAGK, GERHARD.

In addition to his chemotherapeutic work with the sulfa drugs, Bovet studied the ataraxics, or tranquilizers, and the oxytocii, substances that resemble oxytocin (hormone regulating uterine contraction during childbirth) in activity.

The son of a professor of pedagogy, Bovet studied at the University of Geneva, receiving the "license" (a degree intermediate between the baccalaureate and the doctorate) in 1927 and a D.Sc. in zoology and comparative anatomy in 1929. He accepted a position as assistant in the Laboratory of Therapeutic Chemistry at the Pasteur Institute in Paris in that year, and was appointed director in 1936. He left this post in 1947 to become chief of the Laboratory of Therapeutic Chemistry at the Instituto Superiore di Sanità in Rome. In 1964 he became professor of pharmacology at the University of Sassari, and in 1971 professor of psychobiology at the University of Rome. From 1969 to 1975 he was also director of the Laboratory of Psychobiology and Psychopharmacology at the Consiglio Nazionale delle Richerche in Rome. He was elected a member of the Accademia Nazionale dei XL (1949), the Accademia Nazionale dei Lincei (1958), the American Academy of Arts and Sciences (1960), and the Royal Society of London (1962).

Bovet was the author or coauthor of several books, among them *Curare and Curarelike Agents*, with F. Bovet-Nitti and G. R. Marini-Betolò (1959), and *Controlling Drugs*, with R. H. Blum and J. Moore (1974).

For background information *see* ANTIHISTAMINES; PHARMACOGNOSY; SULFA DRUGS in the McGraw-Hill Encyclopedia of Science and Technology. ∎

BOWEN, EDMUND JOHN
★ British chemist

***Born** Apr. 29, 1898, Worcester, England*

Bowen's experimental work ranged over the field of photochemistry, fluorescence, and chemiluminescence. For his work on the elucidation of photochemical reactions, and for his study of fluorescence and phosphorescence in relation to the molecular processes concerned, he was awarded the Davy Medal of the Royal Society of London in 1963.

At the time of World War I (in which Bowen served as a gunner officer) photochemistry was just beginning to assimilate the concepts of the arly quantum theory. Bowen's first researches were determinations of quantum yields, particularly of the photodecompositions of the oxides of chlorine. These measurements were extended to certain photochanges in crystals and to carbonyl compounds in solution. The photochemical oxidations of acetaldehyde in the vapor and solution were shown to be chain reactions depending on the square root of the light intensity, changing to a direct dependence in presence of inhibitors. Quantum yields of light emission during the oxidation of phosphorus vapor under various conditions were examined.

In 1936 Bowen developed the fluorescent quantum counter, in which ultraviolet or visible light, as from a fluorescent solution, is collected on a fluorescent screen with filter, and the fluorescence emitted from this measured with a photocell. With the advent of sensitive photomultipliers, this method has been utilized by a number of investigators for the determination of absolute fluorescence yields of solutions. Bowen used it to obtain values for the fluorescent yields of solutions of aromatic hydrocarbons. These measurements were accompanied by determinations of photooxidation and photodimerization in the same systems in order to elucidate the mechanisms of reaction and the relation between the alternatives of reemission, reaction, or energy degradation of electronically excited molecules.

The reversible quenching effect of dissolved oxygen on the fluorescence of a number of solutions was discovered in 1939, and it was later shown that such quenching occurs with almost unit efficiency at every molecular encounter. Collisional concentration quenching was shown to be nearly as efficient; both processes are closely diffusion-controlled. Studies were also made of the effect of temperature on fluorescence yields, and it was found that solvent viscosity affected yields even when collisional quenching was absent. For these measurements an apparatus was devised in an attempt to minimize the numerous sources of error associated with determinations of absolute fluorescence yields.

After the hypothesis of singlet-singlet electronic energy transfer between molecules had been put forward by Förster, there was a period when some workers attributed the effect to reabsorption by the second substance of fluorescence emitted by the first. Bowen gave the first incontrovertible refutation of this view by quantitative measurements on a system where the first (absorbing) substance had a low fluorescence yield and the second a high one (1953). Transfer of energy via fluorescence could not lead to a final high yield, yet a high yield was in fact found.

Son of a primary school headmaster, Bowen won a scholarship to Balliol College, Oxford, coming into residence in 1915–16, then returning after war service to take the degrees of M. A. in 1922 and D.Sc. in 1947. He was elected a fellow of University College, Oxford, in 1922, and worked in the Balliol and Trinity laboratories transferring to the newly built Physical Chemistry Laboratory in 1940 and later becoming Aldrichian Praelector in Chemistry. He was elected to the Royal Society of London in 1935.

Bowen wrote *The Chemical Aspects of Light* (2d ed. 1946) and *The Fluorescence of Solutions,* with F. Wokes (1953). He edited *Recent Progress in Photobiology* (1965) and *Luminescence in Chemistry* (1968).

For background information *see* CHEMILUMINESCENCE; FLUORESCENCE; PHOTOCHEMISTRY in the McGraw-Hill Encyclopedia of Science and Technology. ■

BOWEN, IRA SPRAGUE
☆ American astrophysicist

Born Dec. 21, 1898, Seneca Falls, NY, U.S.A.
Died Feb. 6, 1973, Altadena, CA, U.S.A.

While studying the spectra of planetary nebulae, Bowen identified and explained the strong green emission lines, previously attributed to some element not known on the Earth, as emanating from ionized nitrogen and oxygen under the influence of low pressures that could not be reproduced in terrestrial laboratories. The explanation of these "forbidden" lines (in contrast to the "permitted" lines observed in the laboratory) led to major advances in the spectroscopic study of celestial bodies, particularly the nebulae.

The strongest lines in the spectra of planetary nebulae are certain green lines, which were first observed by the English astronomer William Huggins during the 1860s. These long resisted identification and were incorrectly attributed either to a hypothetical element, nebulium, not known on the Earth or to complicated atomic spectra possessing a large number of lines in the optical region. By the early 20th century, however, knowledge of the periodic table had increased to the point where it became doubtful if an element such as nebulium could exist, and the suspicion grew that the nebular spectral lines might emanate from a gas of exceedingly low density.

By this time, also, the mechanism of the production of spectral lines was well established. A spectral line arises when an electron in an atom jumps from one energy level to another. The jumps, or transitions, that are easy to accomplish and normally result in strong lines are called "permitted," while those that are more difficult to accomplish and normally result in weak lines are called "forbidden." By a spectral analysis it is possible to deduce the energy levels between which the jumps occur.

Bowen suggested that the strong green "nebulium" lines of planetary nebulae might result from forbidden transitions from metastable states. An atom in an excited state may return to a lower energy level either by radiating energy or by losing it in a collision with another atom. Bowen reasoned that if the atoms were at a metastable energy level in which they remained in an excited state for an extended period, and if the average time between collisions was short, then practically all of the atoms would lose their energy by the collision process instead of by radiation. He assumed that this was the case in terrestrial laboratories, where the average time between collisions under the

most rarefied conditions was about 10^{-3} second, so that no spectral lines of a wavelength indicative of a jump between the metastable and ground (lowest energy) levels could be observed. However, since the average time between collisions of atoms in planetary nebulae was estimated to be between 10^{-4} and 10^{-5} second, Bowen reasoned that the radiative process of energy loss might be predominant, giving rise to observable spectral lines.

In 1927 Bowen's calculations revealed that the wavelengths of three of the spectral lines attributed to nebulium coincided with those that would be expected from highly improbable transitions within the lowest energy levels of doubly ionized oxygen, O III. As shown in the accompanying diagram, where B and C represent

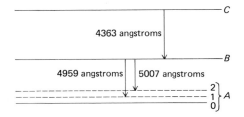

metastable energy levels, transitions between B and A_1 and between B and A_2 produce spectral lines with wavelengths of 4959 and 5007 angstroms (495.9 and 500.7 nanometers), respectively, which correspond to the wavelengths of a pair of intense, green nebular spectral lines. Also, a transition from C to B produces a spectral line with a wavelength of 4363 angstroms (436.3 nanometers), the wavelength of another nebular line. By comparing his calculated wavelengths of forbidden transitions with observed, but unidentified, wavelengths in nebular spectra, Bowen found that the most conspicuous lines were due to forbidden transitions of singly and doubly ionized oxygen, O II and O III, and singly ionized nitrogen, N II. Bowen's discovery led to the identification of other spectral lines, particularly in the solar corona where they had been attributed to another hypothetical element, coronium. This in turn led to advances in the study of the chemical composition, temperature, and density of the Sun and other bodies.

In 1938 Bowen devised the "image slicer," an instrument for increasing the efficiency of a slit spectrograph. In objective prism spectroscopy a prism is placed in front of the telescope lens to separate the light of different wavelengths. A

number of different images are thus formed, each of which is a picture of the celestial body in a particular wavelength of a particular element. However, images of nearly the same color, such as the 4959- and 5007-angstrom radiations of O III, overlap to a great extent. The slit spectrograph eliminates this difficulty but has the disadvantage of wasting a large part of the light at the slit. In Bowen's image slicer the light falls on a system of mirrors before reaching the spectrograph slit. The mirrors slice the original image into a series of strips and align them end to end along the slit. This produces a series of narrow spectra, decreasing the time required to prepare a total spectrogram of a large body. Bowen also contributed to the study of cosmic rays.

Bowen majored in physics at Oberlin College, receiving his A.B. in 1919. He did graduate work at the University of Chicago and at the California Institute of Technology, where he received his Ph.D. in physics in 1926 and remained as a member of the faculty, becoming a full professor in 1931. In 1946 he was appointed director of the Mount Wilson Observatory and in 1948 director of the combined Mount Wilson and Palomar observatories. He retired from this position in 1964, remaining a distinguished service staff member. Among other awards, Bowen received the Draper Medal of the National Academy of Sciences in 1942, the Rumford Medal of the American Academy of Arts and Sciences in 1948, the Bruce Medal of the Astronomical Society of the Pacific in 1957, and the Gold Medal of the Royal Astronomical Society in 1966. He was elected to the National Academy of Sciences in 1936.

For background information *see* AS-TRONOMICAL SPECTROSCOPY; NEBULA, GASEOUS in the McGraw-Hill Encyclopedia of Science and Technology. ∎

BOWEN, NORMAN LEVI
American geologist

Born *June 21, 1887, Kingston, Ontario, Canada*
Died *Sept. 11, 1956, Washington, DC, U.S.A.*

During his investigations of phase equilibria among silicate systems, Bowen discovered the significance of the reaction principle in petrogenesis. The experimental studies that led to his hypothesis,

which has been called the most important contribution to petrology in the 20th century, established Bowen as one of the outstanding pioneers in experimental petrology.

The importance of experimental laboratory studies in geology was at one time questioned by many workers, who believed that field observation alone—using the Earth as their laboratory—was sufficient. Furthermore, the findings of laboratory phase-equilibrium studies were considered suspect, because equilibrium is rarely attained in nature.

Bowen, however, strongly believed in the desirability of laboratory studies as an adjunct to geological field observations. He felt that the only practical method for studying the physical chemistry of geological processes was to determine what occurred under equilibrium conditions. Then, he thought, the investigator could evaluate the factors that led to the failure to attain equilibrium in nature and estimate the magnitude and direction of the effects of these deviations from equilibrium. Bowen conceived of this relationship as one in which the laboratory studies could provide a chemical basis for hypotheses on origins and the associated field studies could modify these as required by observation to provide an explanation of the mechanism of petrogenesis.

Bowen became interested in the physical chemical approach to geology as an undergraduate. His investigations of liquidus-solidus relations, both in his

graduate work and in his early years as a researcher, laid the groundwork for his most important study: phase equilibria among silicates. These studies, from 1910 to 1917, led him to formulate his theory on reaction processes in magmas during the process of cooling.

In 1921, working at the Geophysical Laboratory of the Carnegie Institution of Washington, Bowen began to study the problem of diffusion against gravity of a heavy liquid into a lighter liquid using diopside (a silicate of calcium and magnesium commonly having a variable ferrous silicate content) and plagioclase (soda-lime silicates) melts; then he studied the extent of diffusion by measuring the refractive index of the glass across the contact plane of the solidified melts.

Bowen fused the results of his earlier work on phase equilibria among silicates with the results of his studies of diffusion to produce his paper "The Reaction Principle in Petrology" (1922). In the paper he showed the relative unimportance of the eutectic relation when compared with the reaction relation between liquid and crystal phases. He demonstrated that the crystallization and differentiation of the rocks of an igneous sequence were controlled by a continuous and discontinuous reaction series, which he was able to define. Bowen then showed how this accounted for H. Rosenbusch's normal order of crystallization, an empirically derived rule for which no one had previously been able to find a theoretical basis.

Bowen also made a number of other contributions of fundamental importance to petrology. Among these were the succession of mineral assemblages that will be formed at successively higher temperatures in the metamorphism of impure carbonate rocks, the reactions in silicates of ferrous iron, and the importance of the residua system in petrogenesis. Equally significant is the legacy of his experimental philosophies and techniques, which have been of importance in developing ceramic technology.

The youngest son of a British immigrant, Bowen entered the Faculty of Arts at Queen's University in Kingston, receiving his A.M., with university medals in chemistry and mineralogy, in 1907. He then entered the Faculty of Applied Science at the university and received his B.Sc. in mineralogy and geology in 1909. The Massachusetts Institute of Technology awarded him his Ph.D. in 1912. Although he had been doing summer field work (for the Ontario Bureau of Mines from 1907 to 1909 and for the Geological Survey of Canada in 1910) prior to receiving his doctorate, Bowen decided to concentrate on experimental laboratory studies; he therefore joined the Carnegie Institution of Washington as an assistant petrologist in 1912. In 1919 he left the institution to become professor of geology at Queen's University, but returned the following year. He left the institution again in 1937 to accept the chair of Charles L. Hutchinson Distinguished Service Professor of Petrology at the University of Chicago. Bowen was named head of the geology department in 1945, but left the university in 1947 to return to the Carnegie Institution as a petrologist. He retired in 1952. Among the awards he received were the Bigsby Medal (1931) and the Wollaston Medal (1950) of the Geological Society of London, the Penrose Medal (1941) of the Geological Society of America, the Miller Medal (1943) of the Royal Society of Canada, and the Roebling Medal (1950) of the Mineralogical Society of America. Bowen was elected president of the Mineralogical Society of America in 1937 and of the Geological Society of America in 1946. He was elected to the National Academy of Sciences in 1935 and to foreign membership in the Royal Society of London in 1949.

Bowen wrote *The Evolution of the Igneous Rocks* (1928; 2d ed. 1956; paper 1956).

For background information *see* FUSED-SALT PHASE EQUILIBRIA; PETROLOGY; SILICATE PHASE EQUILIBRIA in the McGraw-Hill Encyclopedia of Science and Technology. ∎

BOYD, WILLIAM CLOUSER
★ American immunochemist

Born Mar. 4, 1903, Dearborn, MO, U.S.A.

In 1945 Boyd conceived the idea that if some plant proteins could have species specificity for animal erythrocytes, as shown by Karl Landsteiner, then some plants might have individual, or blood group, specificity. Tested that same day, the idea proved to be correct, and the first plant tested, the common lima bean, proved to be specific for human blood group antigen A. His report, coupled with a similar report by K. O. Renkonen in Finland, led to the testing in various laboratories of thousands of plant specificities. The name proposed for these substances by Boyd, lectins, was incorporated into English and other languages.

This discovery provided an inexpensive and ready source of substances with various blood group specificities. Discoveries by Boyd and other workers soon provided reagents for the diagnosis of secretors and nonsecretors and for the separation of persons of blood groups A and AB into the subgroups A_1 and A_2 and A_1B and A_2B. These new methods became standard.

In addition to its practical application, however, Boyd's discovery had great theoretical significance, for it opened up an almost unlimited source of substances imitating very closely the specificity and behavior of antibodies. Chemical study of these substances, purified, enabled immunochemists to draw conclusions as to the chemical natures of the specifically reactive groups in lectins and ultimately in antibodies. Thus Boyd and S. Matsubara determined the amino acid composition of the portion of the lima bean lectin that combines specifically with the blood group A antigen. Boyd and H. M. Bhatia determined the number of specifically reactive A sites on a human group A erythrocyte and found a much higher value (over 10,000,000) than had been previously estimated.

Boyd's techniques were extremely simple. Seeds of various plants were ground in a mill and extracted with saline (0.9 percent sodium chloride solution). This

extract was reacted with suspensions in saline of human red blood cells of various blood groups. The reactions were read in test tubes after centrifuging, without the use of a microscope. In later work he coupled the lectins with radioactive iodine (^{131}I) and determined the amount combining with red cells by radioactive counting. Still later he used lectins coupled with colored dyes, reading the reaction in a photoelectric colorimeter. By this method he discovered a potent and specific anti-A agglutinin in the expressed body fluids of the land snail *Otala (Helix) lactea.*

Boyd's discovery had wide application, and extracts of plants prepared according to his methods were sold by a number of commercial supply houses. Many investigators confirmed and extended Boyd's results, and discovered other blood group specificities in plant extracts. Anti-M and anti-N lectins were discovered, and like most of the longer-known lectins, became available commercially.

Boyd was brought up on a farm in Missouri. He received B.A. and M.A. degrees from Harvard University (1925 and 1926). While he was a teaching fellow at Boston University Medical School, he performed research leading to his Ph.D. in 1930. During World War II Boyd worked in the Harvard Plasma Fractionation Laboratory (a high-priority paramilitary project) at Harvard Medical School. He worked as a civilian for the U.S. Navy in Cairo, Egypt, in 1949–50. In 1948 he became professor of immunochemistry at Boston University and, in 1969, professor emeritus. He was visiting professor of biochemistry and nutrition at the University of Puerto Rico in 1970–71 and research associate in 1973 at the University of California at San Diego.

Boyd was awarded a Guggenheim Fellowship in 1935, and studied the blood groups in Ireland, Wales, the Soviet Union, Egypt, and Spain (the Basques). On a later Guggenheim (1937) he studied the Bedouin in the Syrian Desert and worked in Egypt. As a Fulbright fellow in 1952, he studied the Pakistanis. Boyd traveled to Turkey, Greece, North Africa, Brazil, Israel, India, Japan, and elsewhere in the course of his scientific research, and became conversant with eight languages. He became a member of the American Association for the Advancement of Science, the American Association of Immunologists, the American As-

sociation of Physical Anthropologists, the American Society of Human Genetics, Sigma Xi, the Boston Mycological Club, the American Academy of Arts and Sciences, and the New York Academy of Science, and he was a fellow of the Science Fiction Writers of America and an honorary member of the British Association of Immunologists.

In addition to publishing about 300 papers in various scientific journals, Boyd wrote *Blood Grouping Technic,* with Fritz Schiff (1942), *Fundamentals of Immunology* (1943; 4th ed. 1966), *Genetics and the Races of Man* (1950), *Biochemistry and Human Metabolism,* with B. S. Walker and I. Asimov (1952; 3d ed. 1957), *Races and People,* with Asimov (1955), and *Introduction to Immunochemical Specificity* (1962).

For background information *see* BLOOD GROUPS; SEROLOGY in the McGraw-Hill Encyclopedia of Science and Technology. ∎

BRACHET, JEAN LOUIS AUGUSTE
★ Belgian biologist

Born Mar. 19, 1909, Etterbeek, Belgium

Brachet first became interested in the biochemical role of the cell nucleus when he was 18 years old. A lecture on cytology given by his teacher Pol Gérard aroused his interest; experiments carried out long before were described in detail to illustrate the fact that cells deprived of their

nuclei could survive for hours, or even days, and maintain many of their former activities. This initial impetus guided Brachet's choice of study toward a then little explored subject: nucleic acids and their distribution in the nucleus and cytoplasm of living cells.

At that time the key words deoxyribonucleic acid (DNA) and ribonucleic acid (RNA) were still unknown; the terms in use were "animal" and "plant" nucleic acids. Indeed, though evidence was scanty, it was thought that DNA occurred only in animal cells and RNA only in plant cells. Biochemical studies of nucleic acid synthesis in developing sea urchin eggs led Brachet in 1933 to the conclusion that the multiplication of nuclei and DNA synthesis were intimately linked. He was also able to show that the cytoplasm of these eggs contained large amounts of the "plant" nucleic acid. He thus provided for the first time clear evidence that RNA might well be a constituent of animal, as well as plant, cells. However, few scientists were ready to accept such evidence. But Brachet's personal conviction led him to elaborate a simple cytochemical technique to determine the intracellular localization of RNA. The method was based on the acidic nature of nucleic acids, which causes them to combine readily with basic dyes; the basophilia of the cells, therefore, seemed likely to be due to the presence of nucleic acids. Simple staining, however, was not adequate to distinguish between the two types of nucleic acid. To achieve this, a method had to be found which could selectively eliminate one or the other of the acids from the cell. A specific test for RNA was found when Brachet succeeded in eliminating RNA by enzymatic degradation, by treating killed cells with ribonuclease. After a pretreatment of this kind, RNA-containing structures were no longer found to stain with basic dyes. It thus became possible to determine accurately the distribution of RNA in the cell by comparing normal and ribonuclease-treated, stained cells. This method for the cytochemical detection of RNA became classic and was used by numerous investigators.

An extensive study of RNA distribution was carried out by Brachet in the late 1930s and led to the conclusion that RNA is present in the nucleus and the cytoplasm of all cells, both animal and plant. An attempt to correlate the RNA content of the cytoplasm and the biochemical properties of the cells brought out an important feature: Brachet—at the same time as T. O. Caspersson in Stockholm—was struck by the fact that the cells "rich" in RNA are always those which actively synthesize proteins. Such a correlation between RNA content and protein synthesis was not easily accepted by biochemists, although Brachet had shown in 1941 that biochemical analyses of the RNA content of various tissues agree with the inferences drawn from the cytochemical tests.

Despite the difficulties of war conditions (Brachet's laboratory was closed, and he spent several months in prison as a hostage), he managed to continue research. He and his colleagues R. Jeener and H. Chantrenne showed that the relationship between RNA content and protein synthesis still holds at the subcellular level; the theory that the microsomes (the particles which contain most of the cytoplasmic RNA) must be important agents in protein synthesis could be shown by indirect experiments. The direct demonstration of this now well-established fact could not be given by his Brussels group, because the necessary radioactive isotopes and equipment were not available in Belgium during the years after the war.

In view of technical and financial difficulties, Brachet went back to problems of a more biological nature: the biochemical mechanisms of cell differentiation during embryonic development, and the biochemical role of the cell nucleus. His experiments on frog eggs showed that substances which destroy RNA (the enzyme ribonuclease, for instance) or inhibit its synthesis (actinomycin) block the development of the embryos—demonstrating that ordered RNA and protein synthesis is an absolute requirement for morphogenesis. The biochemical functions of the cell nucleus were analyzed in unicellular organisms (amebas, the giant unicellular alga *Acetabularia*, sea urchin eggs); it is easy to separate these cells, mechanically, into two parts, nucleate and anucleate. It then becomes possible to compare the biochemical activities of the two kinds of fragments. The results obtained, in the case of animal organisms, were clear: removal of the nucleus does not immediately abolish protein synthesis, but it ultimately results in the disappearance of cytoplasmic RNA. These early experiments, in 1955, agreed perfectly with the later accepted view that cytoplasmic RNA

is first synthesized in the nucleus and then transferred to the cytoplasm. A more complex situation was encountered in the case of the alga *Acetabularia,* in which both RNA and protein synthesis continue for several weeks in the absence of the nucleus. The reasons for this paradox were made clear by later work of Brachet and his colleagues: The chloroplasts (which bear chlorophyll, necessary for photosynthesis) contain DNA, and they can replicate and produce RNA in the absence of the nucleus. Therefore, net DNA, RNA, and protein syntheses are still possible in anucleate fragments of the alga. The composition and the possible functions of cytoplasmic DNA, both in eggs and in *Acetabularia,* continued to be one of the main subjects of research in Brachet's laboratory.

In later years Brachet divided his time between the department of molecular biology at the University of Brussels and the Laboratorio di Embriologia Molecolare in Naples. His main research interests were the induction of meiosis in amphibian eggs with hormones and the role of the polyamines in sea urchin eggs.

Son of a distinguished experimental embryologist, Brachet graduated from the medical school of the University of Brussels in 1934, and became a professor in the faculty of sciences of the university in 1938. In 1964 he was also appointed director of the Group on Molecular Embryology at the International Laboratory of Genetics and Biophysics, Naples. In 1976 he became professor emeritus at the university. A recipient of the Francqui (Belgium), Mayer (France), and Heineken (Netherlands) prizes, Brachet was elected a foreign member of the American Academy of Sciences (1959), the U.S. National Academy of Sciences (1965), the Royal Society of London (1966), the Académie des Science de Paris (1974), and the Accademia Nazionale dei Lincei (Italy, 1978).

Brachet wrote *Embryologie chimique* (1944), *Chemical Embryology* (1950), *Biochemical Cytology* (1957), *The Biochemistry of Development* (1960), and *Introduction to Molecular Biology* (1974). With A. E. Mirsky he edited *The Cell* (6 vols., 1964).

For background information *see* CELL (BIOLOGY); CELL NUCLEUS; DEOXYRIBONUCLEIC ACID (DNA); NUCLEIC ACID; RIBONUCLEIC ACID (RNA) in the McGraw-Hill Encyclopedia of Science and Technology. ∎

BRAGG, SIR (WILLIAM) LAWRENCE
★ British physicist

Born Mar. 31, 1890, Adelaide, South Australia
Died July 1, 1971, London, England

In collaboration with his father, William Henry Bragg, Bragg developed the x-ray analysis of the arrangement of atoms in crystalline structures. This analysis made it possible to study the architecture of matter, to understand the way in which its structure arises from the nature of interatomic forces, and to explain the physical properties of matter in terms of atomic arrangement. For their work they were jointly awarded the Nobel Prize for physics in 1915.

In 1912 M. von Laue in Germany published his famous discovery of the diffraction of x-rays by the regularly arranged atoms in a crystal. At that time W. H. Bragg believed that x-rays were not waves but neutral particles radiating from the x-ray tube. He was led to this belief by his experiments on the ionization of a gas by x-rays, which he correctly interpreted as being produced by cathode rays excited in individual atoms by the x-ray bombardment. In the summer holiday of 1912 father and son often discussed possible explanations of Laue's results as due to particles shooting down avenues in the crystal. But when the younger Bragg returned to Cambridge, where he was a student, and studied Laue's paper intensively, he was soon convinced on the one hand that his results could only be explained in terms of waves, and on the other hand that certain complex features in the distribution of the diffracted spots were not due to the characteristics of the x-rays, as Laue had supposed, but to the character of the crystalline arrangement. This idea resulted in Bragg's analyzing a few simple crystals, starting with rock salt, and showing that x-rays are specularly reflected from crystal planes.

The elder Bragg based his experimental work on this last discovery, and constructed the x-ray spectrometer and found the spectra of a number of elements. He was at first mainly interested in x-rays, but it soon became evident that the spectrometer was a far more powerful means of analyzing crystals than the Laue photograph. It was at this point that father and son joined forces and together founded the new science of x-ray crystallography.

After World War I, W. H. Bragg founded a school of x-ray crystallography at the Royal Institution in London, and W. L. Bragg created one in his physics department in Manchester. These two schools trained almost all the first generation of x-ray crystallographers.

Just after the war W. L. Bragg put forward the idea of "atomic radii." Although in its original form it had a wrong datum line, this conception helped very greatly in analysis. Then with his researchers he developed quantitative methods of measurement, comparing the incident and diffracted beams ("absolute measurements"). This development had a profound influence and made it possible to determine structures with many uncertain variables or "parameters." They used the silicates as experimental material and were led to a much deeper understanding of minerals in general. He had also a team under A. J. Bradley investigating alloys, and with E. S. Williams and C. Sykes developed the theory of the "order-disorder" phenomenon. Concurrently, his father in London started and developed the analysis of organic bodies.

W. L. Bragg tried consistently to improve x-ray analysis as a tool, and this led to his interest in the analysis of biological molecules containing many thousands of atoms, which was so spectacularly achieved by M. F. Perutz and J. C. Kendrew in the Medical Research Council unit that grew up in the Cavendish Laboratory, and by D. Phillips in Bragg's laboratory in London. *See* KENDREW, JOHN COWDERY; PERUTZ, MAX FERDINAND.

Apart from research, Bragg's main interest was in lecturing and teaching. He was fascinated by the problems of popular lecturing and talks to young people, and reached tens of thousands in this way.

W. L. Bragg got his first degree in mathematics at Adelaide University, where his father was professor of physics, and then entered Trinity College, Cambridge. In World War I he had the assignment of starting sound ranging (locating enemy guns by sound) for the British Army in France and Belgium. He was professor of physics at Manchester (1919–37), director of the National Physical Laboratory (1937–38), Cavendish Professor at Cambridge (1938–53), and, after 1954, director of the Royal Institution.

Bragg wrote *X-rays and Crystal Structure,* with W. H. Bragg (1915), *The Crystalline State* (1934), *Electricity* (1936), *Atomic Structure of Minerals* (1937), and *Crystal Structures of Minerals,* with G. F. Claringbull (1965).

For background information *see* X-RAY CRYSTALLOGRAPHY; X-RAY DIFFRACTION in the McGraw-Hill Encyclopedia of Science and Technology. ■

BRAMBELL, FRANCIS WILLIAM ROGERS

★ British zoologist

Born Feb. 25, 1901, Sandycove, County Dublin, Ireland
Died June 6, 1970, Bangor, Caernarvonshire, Wales

Studying the transference of protein molecules in mammals from the circulation of the mother to that of the offspring, Brambell and his associates showed that in the rabbit the transference occurred during gestation by way of the uterine cavity and the fetal yolk sac, not across the placenta as had been supposed. Transmission was shown to be a selective process in that gamma globulins are transmitted more readily than other serum proteins, irrespective of molecular size, and those of some species more readily than those of others. For this achievement Brambell in 1964 was awarded a Royal Medal of the Royal Society of London.

In 1892 Paul Ehrlich showed that, in mice, maternal circulating antibodies were transmitted to the young both while they were still in the uterus and after birth by way of the mammary secretions. It was later found that young mammals are equipped with passive immunity transferred to them from their mothers before they develop an active immunity of their own. This occurs before birth in rabbits, guinea pigs, and humans, and immediately after birth in domestic ungulates; rats, mice, dogs, and cats acquire it both before and after birth. It was assumed that transmission before birth was by way of the placenta.

In the 1930s Brambell was studying the estrous cycles and reproduction of various mammals in the wild state. This led to an extensive study of prenatal mortality in wild rabbits, when these animals were of economic importance in World War II. Trying to find the cause of this mortality, he found that maternal serum proteins were present normally in the contents of the embryonic yolk sac. This caused him to suspect that the antibody globulins might be transferred by this route. He and his associates demonstrated that this was so by the use of globulins, labeled by their biological activity, or by radioisotopes, together with experimental surgery of the gravid uterus and fetus. This approach made possible precise comparisons of the rates of transmission of various serum proteins and led to the discovery of the selective nature of the process, those protein molecules that were not transmitted to the fetal circulation being degraded by the fetal cells.

The investigation was extended to transmission in rats and mice, particularly to that which occurs after birth by way of the mother's milk and the intestine of the

young animal. Again the transmission was found to be selective; moreover, some gamma globulins interfered with the transmission of others. To account for these results, Brambell suggested that the globulins were absorbed into the cells by pinocytosis and that the molecules that were to be transmitted to the circulation became attached to specific receptors in the cells, the unattached molecules being degraded. Results from many other laboratories later confirmed the route of transmission in rabbits, the selective nature of the transmission, and, by electron microscopy, the pinocytotic absorption.

Brambell's researches threw light on the method of transmission of large molecules across biological membranes and on the selective attachment of proteins to cells, as well as on the processes by which the young animal acquired its immunity from the mother. They bore not only on problems concerning the resistance of the infant to infections but also on hemolytic diseases of the newborn caused by transmission of maternal antibodies that react with antigens of the young that the mother lacks.

Educated at Trinity College, Dublin, where he received a B.A. in 1922, and Ph.D. in 1924, Brambell worked subsequently at University College, London, graduating D.Sc. in 1927, and at King's College, London. He was appointed professor of zoology in the University College of North Wales, Bangor, of the University of Wales, in 1930.

Brambell wrote *The Development of Sex in Vertebrates* (1930), *Antibodies and Embryos,* with W. A. Hemmings and M. Henderson (1951), and *The Transmission of Passive Immunity from Mother to Young* (1970).

For background information *see* IMMUNITY in the McGraw-Hill Encyclopedia of Science and Technology. ∎

BRATTAIN, WALTER HOUSER
☆ American physicist

Born Feb. 10, 1902, Amoy, China

While trying to understand the surface properties of semiconductors, Brattain, in cooperation with John Bardeen, demonstrated amplification in a germanium wafer. This experiment led to the invention of the first transistor—the point-contact transistor. For this achievement Brattain received the 1956 Nobel Prize in physics jointly

with Bardeen and William Shockley, his associates at the Bell Telephone Laboratories. *See* BARDEEN, JOHN; SHOCKLEY, WILLIAM.

Scientific understanding of semiconductors began with the application of quantum mechanics to the theory of solids in the 1930s. Particularly important was Sir Alan Wilson's work describing conduction in terms of excess electrons and holes. In semiconductors, electric current flow can be greatly increased when imperfections are present in the crystal's electronic structure. These imperfections can be of two types: excess electrons freed from the valence bonds of the crystal or places known as "holes" from which electrons are missing in the bonds. By adding the proper impurities to the semiconductor crystal, one can obtain crystals with either excess electrons (*n*-type) or with holes (*p*-type).

On the basis of the Mott-Schottky theories of rectification, Shockley believed that he could make a semiconductor amplify electrical signals by modulating the flow of electrons inside the material with an external electric field. Failure to obtain amplification and other unexplained experimental results led Bardeen to suggest that the electric field was prevented from entering the semiconductor by a layer of electrons trapped on its surface.

To test this theory, Brattain directed light on *n*-type germanium and found that this produced a change in potential between the germanium and a metal electrode near its surface (contact potential).

The extra holes and electrons produced by the light changed the surface charge and consequently the surface potential of the germanium. These experiments were then tried with liquids between the metal electrode and the germanium, and R. B. Gibney and Brattain found that if the liquid was an electrolyte the surface potential of the germanium could be changed by the electrical bias between the electrode and the germanium. This was recognized as Shockley's field effect.

Bardeen suggested to Brattain a geometrical arrangement to use the electrolytic field effect to make an amplifier. They first used a block of *p*-type silicon on which a thin *n*-type surface layer had been produced by oxidation. A point contact surrounded by, but insulated from, a drop of electrolyte was made to be the layer. A large-area low-resistance contact was made to the base of the block. They found they could control the magnitude of the current from the base to the point by applying a potential to the electrolyte. Current amplification at very low frequencies was then achieved.

The silicon was next replaced with *n*-type germanium, and power amplification was obtained still only at low frequencies. The lack of any response at higher frequencies, they reasoned, was due to the electrolyte. They therefore decided to replace the electrolyte with a layer of evaporated gold on top of an anodic oxide film formed on the germanium. When this experiment was tried, a new effect, now known as transistor action, was observed. In the process the oxide film had been washed off, and the gold film was in contact with the germanium surface.

Brattain and Bardeen found that current flowing in the forward direction from the gold contact influenced current flowing in the reverse direction in a neighboring point contact in such a way as to produce amplification. This suggested that holes were flowing from the gold contact biased in the forward direction to the other contact biased in the reverse direction with respect to the base contact.

Experiments were continued, and on Dec. 23, 1947, a speech amplifier giving a power amplification of 18 or more, with good quality and good frequency response, was demonstrated. The first transistor was essentially a small wafer of germanium onto one surface of which two gold contacts were made, side by side and very close together. On the opposite surface of the wafer, an ohmic third contact was made. Later the gold contacts were replaced with bronze points cut like a chisel.

The descendant of a pioneer family, Brattain spent his early life on his parents' cattle ranch in Washington. He majored in physics and mathematics at Whitman College, where he received his B.S. in 1924. Two years later he received his M.A. from the University of Oregon and in 1929 his Ph.D. from the University of Minnesota. After completing graduate studies, he worked for the radio section of the National Bureau of Standards in Washington, DC, for a year. During World War II he was associated with the National Defense Research Committee at Columbia University, where he worked on magnetic detection of submarines. Having joined the staff of Bell Telephone Laboratories in 1929 as a research physicist, he held that position until his retirement in 1967. From 1962 to 1972 he spent varying amounts of time teaching courses at Whitman. In 1965 David Frasco, a chemistry professor at Whitman, and Brattain began research on phospholipid bilayers as a model for the surface of living cells. From 1967 to 1975 this research was sponsored by Battelle Northwest Laboratories, Richland, WA, during which time Donald R. Kalkwarf joined the team. This work was then continued at Whitman College.

In additon to the Nobel Prize, Brattain was awarded jointly with Bardeen the Stuart Ballantine Medal of the Franklin Institute (1952) and the John Scott Medal (1955). He also received a number of honorary degrees. He was elected to the National Academy of Sciences in 1959 and to the American Academy of Arts and Sciences in 1956.

For background information *see* SEMI-CONDUCTOR; TRANSISTOR in the McGraw-Hill Encyclopedia of Science and Technology. ∎

BRAUER, RICHARD
American mathematician

Born *Feb. 10, 1901, Berlin, Germany*
Died *Apr. 17, 1977, Boston, MA, U.S.A.*

Brauer's early mathematical interests centered on the theory of representations of groups and the structure of algebras. The intimate connection between these two subjects had recently been recog-

nized due, at least in part, to some joint work of his with E. Noether, in which they exhibited the close relationship between splitting fields and maximal subfields of a simple algebra.

In two later papers Brauer introduced what is now known as the Brauer group of a field. Consider the set of all isomorphism classes of central simple algebras over a field F. The product of two such algebras is defined by the tensor product over F, and two such algebras are said to be equivalent if they have isomorphic division ring components. The set of all equivalence classes forms the Brauer group $B(F)$ of F. Brauer studied $B(F)$ by using what are now known as Brauer factor sets. He showed that much can be learned about the structure of central division algebras over F from the study of $B(F)$ and its relationship to the groups $B(K)$, as K ranges over extension fields of F.

The main problem in the theory of simple algebras is to describe all the division algebras with a given center F, or more modestly, to describe $B(F)$. If F is algebraically closed, then trivially $B(F) = 1$. Already in 1878 G. F. Frobenius had shown that $B(R)$ is of order 2 if R is the field of real numbers or, equivalently, that the system of the Hamiltonian quaternions is the only central division algebra over R. In 1905, J. H. M. Wedderburn had shown that $B(F) = 1$ when F is finite. By the 1920s attention was beginning to be focused on the much deeper problem

of describing central simple algebras over algebraic number fields.

A central simple algebra A over a field F is cyclic if A contains a subfield K with $[A{:}F] = [K{:}F]^2$, such that K is a Galois extension of F with a cyclic Galois group. This concept was first introduced by L. E. Dickson in 1923. He conjectured that every central simple algebra over an algebraic number field is cyclic. In 1931 a joint paper by Brauer, H. Hasse, and Noether, proved Dickson's conjecture. The paper also contains the description of a complete set of numerical invariants which characterize a central division algebra over a number field. This theorem is the climax of a long development in the theory of algebras which began with the work of Wedderburn in the United States and I. Schur in Germany before World War I.

Brauer's first paper on the representations of finite groups over finite fields appeared in 1935. The main result asserts that the number of absolutely irreducible representations of a finite group G over a field of characteristic p is equal to the number of p'-classes of G. Brauer also showed that an absolutely irreducible representation is determined by its trace function. This work was the beginning of a lifelong interest in what he called the theory of modular representations of finite groups. (It should perhaps more accurately be termed the theory of representations over local domains and their residue class fields.)

During the next 40 years Brauer wrote more than 50 papers on the theory of modular representations and its applications to the structure of finite simple groups. In this work he found it necessary to prove some new results in the theory of characters, and in particular discovered his theorem on the characterization of characters: (I) Let θ be a class function defined on a group G such that θ_H is a generalized character for every elementary subgroup H of G. Then θ is a generalized character of G. (II) Every generalized character of G is of the form

$$\sum_H a_H \alpha_H^G$$

where H ranges over the elementary subgroups of G, each α_H is a generalized character of H, and each a_H is an integer. Immediate consequences of this result are that Artin L-series are meromorphic and the field of gth roots of unity is a splitting field of a group of order g.

During the late 1940s Brauer had observed that some very simple properties of involutions (elements of order 2 in a group) can be used to derive some surprisingly strong results concerning the structure of groups of even order. In his unpublished thesis, K. A. Fowler used such results to give a characterization of the groups $SL_2(2^n)$ in terms of involutions. In 1955 Brauer and Fowler published a joint paper on groups of even order. The results and point of view of this paper have turned out to be the key to much of the subsequent development of the theory of finite simple groups of even order. One result asserts that if H is a finite group which contains an involution in its center, then there are only a finite number of finite simple groups in which the centralizer of an involution is isomorphic to H. The problem of classifying simple groups in terms of the structure of the centralizer of an involution has become known as Brauer's program. This approach has proved to be extremely fruitful and, when combined with other points of view, is now rapidly bringing the classification of finite simple groups within reach.

Brauer received his Ph.D. from the University of Berlin in 1926. He was appointed privatdozent in 1927 at the University of Königsberg. When the Nazis came to power in 1933, he emigrated to the United States and spent 1933–34 at the University of Kentucky and 1934–35 at the Institute for Advanced Study as H. Weyl's assistant. In 1935 Brauer joined the faculty at the University of Toronto. In 1948 he was appointed a professor at the University of Michigan, and in 1952 he accepted a chair at Harvard, where he stayed until his retirement in 1971. Brauer was elected to the National Academy of Sciences in 1954. He was president of the American Mathematical Society in 1959–60. In 1963 he was appointed an honorary member of the London Mathematical Society. In 1971 he was awarded the National Medal for Scientific Merit. He received honorary degrees from the University of Waterloo in 1968, the University of Chicago in 1969, the University of Notre Dame in 1974, and Brandeis University in 1975.

For background information *see* ALGEBRA, ABSTRACT; ALGEBRA, LINEAR; GROUP THEORY; RING THEORY in the McGraw-Hill Encyclopedia of Science and Technology. ∎

BRAUMAN, JOHN I.
★ American chemist

***Born** Sept. 7, 1937, Pittsburgh, PA, U.S.A.*

For his work in exploring and understanding reactions of negative ions in the gas phase, Brauman received the American Chemical Society Award in Pure Chemistry in 1973 and the Harrison Howe Award in 1976.

Having studied acidities of weak organic acids in solution while he was a graduate student, Brauman was aware of the influence of solvation on stabilities of ions. In 1968, with the recent development of ion cyclotron resonance (ICR) mass spectrometry, he realized that it would be possible to measure conveniently the position of equilibria for simple ionic reactions: AH + B⁻ ⇌ A⁻ + BH. Using the ICR method, he and his student Larry Blair determined that the order of acidities of aliphatic alcohols in the gas phase was *tert*-butyl alcohol > isopropyl alcohol > ethyl alcohol > methyl alcohol > water, an order exactly reversed from that in protic solvents. This work had a great impact on the thinking of chemists, many of whom had previously assumed, in the absence of any definite information, that solution acidities always reflected molecular properties rather than a mix of intrinsic and solvation effects.

The work on alcohols was extended to a variety of other molecules, giving rise to further interesting observations, among which was that toluene, a hydrocarbon, was a stronger acid than water in the gas phase. Studies of this sort ultimately culminated in an extensive enterprise in many laboratories, in which scales of gas-phase acidities were determined, placing ionic equilibria in a solvent-free environment on a firm basis.

The major qualitative features to come out of this work were: (1) in general, larger ions (both positive and negative) tend to be relatively more stable than smaller ions, and (2) hydrogen bonding to oxygen and nitrogen acids and bases plays a major role in determining their properties in solution.

In another important aspect of ionic thermochemistry, Brauman and his students used the ICR detection method to study photodetachment of electrons from gas-phase negative ions. In this experiment (A⁻ + $h\nu$ → A + e^-), the minimum energy required to remove an electron could be determined and related to the electron affinity of the corresponding neutral species. Using this technique, Brauman was able to measure the electron-binding energy in a wide variety of negative ions; electron affinities of an extensive number of polyatomic radicals became known for the first time. Brauman was also able to work out a theory of threshold shapes which predicted how the probability of removing an electron varies with the energy of the photon which produces electron ejection.

Finally, Brauman studied the kinetics of thermal ion-molecule reactions and showed how rates of slow reactions can be explained. His models for these reactions involved collision complexes which can dissociate back to reactants or go on to products. Because the barriers to proceed to products lie below the energies of the reactants, these reactions have the unusual property of proceeding more slowly as the energy or temperature is raised.

In addition to gas-phase ion chemistry, Brauman was also involved in studies of organic and organometallic reaction mechanisms, solution carbanion chemistry, and Rayleigh light scattering.

Brauman did his undergraduate work in chemistry at the Massachusetts Institute of Technology (B.S., 1959) and his graduate work at the University of California at Berkeley (Ph.D., 1963), where he was a National Science Foundation (NSF) fellow. He spent 9 months at the University of California at Los Angeles as an NSF postdoctoral fellow and then joined the faculty at Stanford as assistant professor of chemistry in 1963. He became associate professor in 1969 and professor in 1972. He was elected to the National Academy of Sciences in 1976.

For background information *see* CYCLOTRON RESONANCE EXPERIMENTS; THERMOCHEMISTRY in the McGraw-Hill Encyclopedia of Science and Technology. ∎

BRAUN, ARMIN CHARLES JOHN
★ American plant biologist

Born Sept. 5, 1911, Milwaukee, WI, U.S.A.

Using plant tumor cells as an experimental model, Braun defined in physiological and biochemical terms the reason why such cell types grow autonomously and thus fail to respond to the morphogenetic restraints that govern so precisely the growth of all normal cells within an organism. He also determined the nature of the heritable cellular change that leads to the autonomous growth of a plant tumor cell. The significance of this work lies in the fact that the dynamics of these relatively simple plant tumor systems are now rather well understood and may, therefore, serve as useful models for the elucidation of certain principles that underlie tumorous growth generally. For his contributions Braun received the Newcomb Cleveland Award of the American Association for the Advancement of Science in 1949.

The striking similarities that exist between plant and animal tumor cells were recognized early in the 20th century by Erwin F. Smith of the U.S. Department of Agriculture, and by C. O. Jensen, a Danish pathologist who, because of his pioneering studies in the transplantation of animal tumors, is generally regarded as the father of modern experimental cancer research. It was not, however, until 1941 that Philip R. White, in collaboration with Braun, demonstrated unequivocally, with the use of tissue culture methods, that the plant tumor cell, like the animal cancer cell, is a persistently altered cell that reproduces true to type, and that a host contains no adequate control mechanism against the growth of such a cell. Thus plant tumor cells possess the essential biological characteristics upon which all other diagnostic features of tumorous diseases of animals ultimately depend.

Since the tumor problem is, in essence, a dynamic problem of abnormal and autonomous cell growth and division, Braun attempted to characterize the cellular changes that result in a capacity for autonomous growth of a plant tumor cell. He found that during the transition from a normal cell to a rapidly growing, fully autonomous tumor cell a series of quite distinct but well-defined biosynthetic systems, which represent the entire area of metabolism concerned with cell growth and division, become progressively and persistently activated. The degree of activation of those biosynthetic systems within a cell determines the rate at which the tumor cell grows. Included among the biosynthetic systems shown to be persistently unblocked in the plant tumor cell are those that produce two hormones, one of which is concerned with cell enlargement and chromosomal deoxyribonucleic acid (DNA) replication, while the other acts synergistically with the first to trigger cell division. These two substances remove all the arrest points that are present in the normal cell division cycle and that regulate the growth of normal cells. Since these two growth-regulating substances are persistently synthesized by plant tumor cells, they maintain the pattern of synthesis concerned with growth and division in those cells. In addition, a number of biosynthetic systems, the products of which are required for the production of the nucleic acids, the specialized mitotic proteins, and other substances that are needed specifically for cell growth and division, are functional in the

tumor cells. Normal resting cells do not produce the essential growth-regulating substances. Thus, the capacity for autonomous growth of the plant tumor cell finds its explanation in the fact that the tumor cells have acquired the capacity to produce all of the essential growth-regulating substances and metabolites that their normal counterparts require for growth and division but cannot make.

Braun demonstrated further that the essential biosynthetic systems shown to be activated during the transformation of a normal cell to a tumor cell can again be repressed under certain special experimental conditions, and thus a complete recovery from the tumorous state can be achieved. This finding is significant because it demonstrates that the nuclei of the normal and tumor cells are genetically equivalent, and thus the tumorous state in the biological system studied depends on a change in the expression, rather than on a change in the integrity, of the genetic information that is present in a cell. Whether the normal phenotype or the tumor phenotype is expressed is thus determined by how the genetic information present in a totipotential genome is regulated in a cell.

That results obtained with plant tumor cells may have broader biological implications was suggested by findings that the cancerous state of cells from a broad spectrum of tumors found in frogs, newts, mice, rats, and hamsters, as well as certain cancers of humans, is reversible. The finding that the cancerous state is not necessarily irreversibly fixed in a cell, as was believed for so many years, not only provides insight into the nature of cancer as a biological phenomenon but opens, in principle at least, entirely new avenues of approach for the control of certain cancers. Insights obtained with the use of plant tumors as they relate generally to the tumor problem were discussed in detail in Braun's book *The Story of Cancer: On Its Nature, Causes, and Control* (1977).

A teacher's son, Braun majored in plant pathology and microbiology at the University of Wisconsin, where he received his B.S. in 1934 and his Ph.D. in 1938. He pursued predoctoral studies in several European scientific institutions in 1937. He joined the Rockefeller Institute as a fellow in 1938. Except for the period 1943–46, when he served as a captain in the U.S. Army, he remained at the Rockefeller Institute (now the Rockefeller University), reaching the rank of professor and member in 1959. He was elected to the National Academy of Sciences in 1960 and to the American Academy of Arts and Sciences in 1966.

For background information *see* CANCER (BIOLOGY); ONCOLOGY; TUMOR in the McGraw-Hill Encyclopedia of Science and Technology.

BRAUNSTEIN, ALEKSANDR EVSEYEVICH

★ Soviet biochemist

Born May 26, 1902, Kharkov, Russia

In 1937 Braunstein discovered, in collaboration with Maria G. Kritzman, the enzymatic interconversion, in muscle and other types of cells, of amino and keto acids by way of intermolecular transfer of the amino group. This process is now called transamination. In 1945 E. E. Snell in the United States, as well as other investigators, demonstrated the involvement of vitamin B_6, in the form of pyridoxal phosphate (PLP), in biological transamination and in the decarboxylation of amino acids. Braunstein then started extensive investigations on the functions of vitamin B_6 in intermediary nitrogen metabolism. He and his associates demonstrated several previously unknown coenzyme functions of PLP in the metabolism of tryptophan and of sulfur-containing and hydroxy amino acids. They detected some new enzymatic steps in amino acid catabolism, including the formation of alanine from tryptophan via

kynurenine and of glycine via aldol decondensation of threonine and its homologs. A general theory of the mechanism of PLP-dependent enzymatic reactions of amino acids, together with a classification of these reactions, was proposed by Braunstein and M. M. Shemyakin in 1952–53. Similar ideas were independently developed by Snell and coworkers. From 1960 onward Braunstein was engaged with a group of enzymologists, organic chemists, and physicists in systematic investigations of the molecular structure, catalytic mechanism, and selective inhibition of aminotransferases and other PLP-dependent enzymes. He and his coworkers were active in two major achievements: the complete elucidation of the primary structure of aspartate aminotransferase and of its three-dimensional structure by x-ray diffraction. *See* SHEMYAKIN, MIKHAIL MIKHAILOVICH; SNELL, ESMOND EMERSON.

Although the enzymatic transfer of hydrogen and of phosphate groups had been demonstrated earlier, it was the work of Braunstein on transamination that attracted general attention to the fundamental significance of various types of group transfer reactions in intermediary metabolism and in enzyme catalysis. In many cases, a specific group of the enzyme protein or of a coenzyme acts as the intermediate carrier of a substrate fragment; this is exemplified by the acceptor function of PLP in amino group transfer. The transamination reaction is frequently quoted in textbooks as a prototype of group transfer.

Braunstein's early work indicated the almost ubiquitous occurrence of transamination reactions in living cells, the participation of an extensive range of substrates, and the predominant role of glutamic acid among these. It was shown that the coupling of transamination with reversible deamination of glutamate and with other specific enzymatic transformations of glutamic and aspartic acids results in carrier-linked reaction sequences of major importance for the assimilation of ammonia nitrogen into amino acids, and for conversion of the amino acids to secondary and excretory metabolites of nitrogen (such as purine and pyrimidine nucleotides, ammonia, urea, and uric acid). In particular, it was demonstrated that one of the main pathways for the biosynthesis of many amino acids involves indirect reductive amination of keto acids by the joint action of aminotransferases and

glutamate dehydrogenase (or alanine dehydrogenase in some species of microorganisms and higher plants). Reversal of this reaction sequence provides one of several alternative transamination-dependent paths for the indirect oxidative deamination of amino acids. These experimental findings and Braunstein's generalizations concerning the fundamental role of transamination as an essential link in the assimilation and dissimilation of nitrogen, and in the integration and reciprocal control of intermediary nitrogen metabolism and cell respiration, were largely confirmed later with the advent of refined analytical methods. The work was extended by many other investigators.

Braunstein's second, and closely related, major field of research was the problem of enzymatic pyridoxal catalysis. Here the Braunstein-Snell theory was amply validated and gained general acceptance. This theory was one of the first successful applications of modern physical organic chemistry to the interpretation of an extensive group of important biochemical reactions.

The investigations of Braunstein and his associates laid the basis for solution of various physiological and medical problems of practical importance. These relate to animal and human nutrition, to the mode of action of certain antibiotics and drugs, and to the pathogeny, diagnosis, and treatment of metabolic disorders and other diseases. Thus, for example, the assay of aminotransferase activity in the blood of patients proved of considerable value for the differential diagnosis of cardiac, hepatic, and other diseases. Braunstein's work on PLP enzymes contributed to elucidation of the nature of disturbances of tryptophan metabolism in B_6-deficient animals, and of the role of such disturbances (depression of nicotinic acid formation via kynurenine) in the pathogenesis of pellagra. It also provided a rationale for the detection and treatment of B_6 deficiency associated with normal and toxemic pregnancy. Later researches conducted in his laboratory were important in clarifying the biochemical mechanisms of action of several antibiotics and antimetabolites, including cycloserine, its derivatives, and different amino acid analogs. On this basis, rational principles were developed by R. M. Khomutov and others for the design of new selective inhibitors of PLP enzymes.

The chemical and biological aspects of transamination and other pyridoxal-catalyzed reactions and their key role in the metabolism of nitrogen and sulfur were surveyed by Braunstein in a number of review papers published in English or French, as well as in lectures delivered at international conferences and congresses. Beginning in the 1940s, he was actively involved in planning and organizing biochemical research, as a member and officer of various national and international scientific councils, learned committees, and editorial boards.

Son of a professor of ophthalmology, Braunstein graduated from the State Medical Institute in Kharkov in 1925 and moved to Moscow. After 3 years of postgraduate studies in V. A. Engelhardt's group at the A. Bakh Institute of Biochemistry, he served until 1936 as senior investigator in several research institutes, working on problems of glycolytic and respiratory phosphorylation and on the metabolic detoxication of aromatic compounds. He received the degrees of M.D. in 1928 and D.Biol.Sci. in 1938, and achieved the grade of professor in biochemistry in 1939. He successively became head of laboratories on intermediary nitrogen metabolism in the All-Union Institute of Experimental Medicine in 1936 and in the Institute of Biological and Medical Chemistry in 1944. In 1961 he moved to the Institute of Physico-Chemical Biology (now the Institute of Molecular Biology) of the Academy of Sciences of the U.S.S.R. as head of a laboratory working on the chemical basis of biological catalysis. Braunstein was elected to full membership of the Academy of Medical Sciences in 1945 and of the Academy of Sciences of the U.S.S.R. in 1964. He received honorary doctorates from several universities, and was elected honorary member of several foreign scientific societies and academies, including the American Society of Biological Chemists and the American Academy of Arts and Sciences, both in 1961. In 1974 he was elected a foreign associate of the National Academy of Sciences. Braunstein was the recipient of numerous awards and honors, including a prize of the Mendeleyev Chemical Society (1939), a U.S.S.R. State Prize for achievements in the medical sciences, with M. G. Kritzman (1941), the Labor Red Banner Order (twice), the Lenin Order and "Sickle and Hammer" Golden Star (1972), and tributary to the honorary title "Hero of Socialist Labor."

Braunstein wrote *Biochemistry of Amino Acid Metabolism,* in Russian (1949), and the chapters "Pyridoxal Phosphate" in vol. 2 (2d ed. 1960) and "Amino Group Transfer" in vol. 9 (3d ed. 1973) of *The Enzymes.* He was editor and coauthor of *Enzymes* (1964), vol. 2 of the series *Fundamentals of Molecular Biology,* in Russian.

For background information *see* AMINO ACIDS; ENZYME; TRANSAMINATION; VITAMIN B$_6$ in the McGraw-Hill Encyclopedia of Science and Technology. ∎

BREIT, GREGORY
★ American physicist and engineer

Born July 14, 1899, Nikolayev, Russia

Breit specialized in many areas of research, including quantum theory, quantum electrodynamics, hyperfine structure, radio ionosphere, radio communications, and resonance theory of nuclear reactions and forces between nucleons.

The White House news release on the occasion of Breit's being awarded one of the National Science medals for 1967 said: "Many years before the atomic bomb and the nuclear reactor focused the world's attention on nuclear physics Professor Breit was at work at this frontier. His leadership was responsible for the first proton accelerator (atom smasher) in this country, and for important aspects of knowledge which made possible the wartime Manhattan Project. He has also contributed significantly to ordnance development during World War II and to our understanding of the ionosphere." His citation for the medal itself read: "For pioneering contributions to the theoretical understanding of nuclear structure and particle dynamics, for highly significant work in atomic and ionospheric physics, and for the inspiration he has given to several generations of American physicists."

In 1945 Breit was made a fellow of the Institute of Radio Engineers (now the Institute of Electrical and Electronic Engineers) "for pioneering in the experimental probing of the ionosphere, and for having initiated at an early date the pulse method of probing by reflection which is the basis of modern radar."

In a citation in 1954, upon the conferring of the honorary degree of doctor of science by the University of Wisconsin, Breit was described as "a ground breaker extraordinary in many sectors of experimental and theoretical physics." He was also cited as an early inquirer into a method which "ultimately led to the perfection of radar; brilliant collaborator in the development of the Breit-Wigner theory of nuclear resonances; far-sighted pioneer in the Manhattan Atomic Project; unflagging toiler in the basic research which flowered in the invention of the betatron."

In 1964 Breit received the Franklin Medal of the Franklin Institute of Philadelphia "for his more than forty-five years of research in physics, during which he pioneered in fields of increasing importance to our knowledge of nuclear structures, and especially for his theoretical analyses of the results of scattering experiments, which have given us an understanding of the quantitative features of nuclear forces."

Breit's World War II service included degaussing for the Naval Ordnance Laboratory; organization and research on technological and military applications of uranium fission for the Uranium Committee of the National Defense Research Committee, renamed Section S of the Office of Scientific Research and Development, with headquarters at the National Bureau of Standards; participation in the initial organization of the Metallurgical Laboratory at Chicago; research on the proximity fuse at the Applied Physics Laboratory of the Johns Hopkins University and related projects at the Ballistic Research Laboratory at Aberdeen Proving Ground.

During the war Breit was instrumental in getting work started on the original atom bomb project. Scientists in the early years of this work used the term "fast fission," and Breit, who was at the Metallurgical Laboratory in Chicago, had the unique code name "Coordinator of Rapid Rupture."

While working at the Washington Navy Yard on the problem of defense against magnetic mines, Breit invented a device called a magnetic extrapolator which cut down from a month to a single day the time required for two men to make a complete study of a large ship. The device was in service for some years during and after the war but has since been replaced by digital computers. At the time, however, when German magnetic mines were interfering with Atlantic shipping, it furnished answers in the quickest way.

Breit has been credited by Edward Teller as one of the key men who helped prove that the hydrogen bomb would not ignite the atmosphere or the ocean in an uncontrolled reaction. He was called on to review the calculations before the first tests of the H-bomb in 1952. These calculations were carried on at the Los Alamos Scientific Laboratory, and also partly at the Sloane Physics Laboratory at Yale University. *See* TELLER, EDWARD.

As chairperson of a subcommittee of the Reference Committee on Publications, Breit was concerned with withholding from open publication such papers on nuclear disintegration and related subjects as could be of use to a possible enemy in developing sources of nuclear energy such as "atomic reactors" and A-bombs. Publication in scientific journals through voluntary patriotic action by authors and editors was delayed with the advice of the committee until the critical period was over.

Breit studied at the School of Emperor Alexander in Nikolayev from 1909 to 1915, at which time he emigrated to the United States. He became a citizen in 1918 through the naturalization of his father. He attended the Johns Hopkins University, where he was awarded Hopkins scholarships (1916–17, 1917–18) and a university fellowship (1919–1920). He earned three degrees there (A.B., 1918; M.A., 1920; Ph.D., 1921) as well as an honorary degree in 1976. He was a National Research fellow during 1921–23, first at the University of Leyden, then at Harvard. He began his teaching career as an assistant professor of physics at the University of Minnesota (1923–24). Then he accepted a post as mathematical physicist in the department of terrestrial

magnetism of the Carnegie Institution of Washington, serving there until 1929 but taking time out in 1928 for several months at the Technische Hochschule in Zurich, Switzerland. In 1926 at Carnegie he initiated experiments in nuclear physics and developed with colleagues the multi-section high-voltage accelerating tube.

Breit was professor of physics at New York University from 1929 to 1934 and at the University of Wisconsin from 1934 to 1947. During this period he also served as research associate at the Carnegie Institution of Washington (1922–44) and was a visitor at the Institute for Advanced Study at Princeton, NJ (1935–36). From 1939 until 1945 he was on leave from the University of Wisconsin, working on various war projects. He joined the faculty at Yale University in 1947 and in 1958 was named the first Donner Professor at that institution.

Breit reached the mandatory retirement age at Yale in 1968 and accepted a position as Distinguished Service Professor at the State University of New York at Buffalo beginning with the fall term in 1968. He served in this position through the academic year 1975–76, then carried on research as an emeritus thereafter. He was elected a member of the National Academy of Sciences in 1939.

For background information *see* ATOMIC BOMB in the McGraw-Hill Encyclopedia of Science and Technology. ∎

BREMER, FRÉDÉRIC
★ Belgian physiologist

Born June 28, 1892, Arlon, Belgium

After an initial period during which he studied spinal and cerebellar physiology, Bremer devoted himself mainly to the physiology of the cerebral cortex, together with the subcortical and commissural structures involved in its activities. His name is associated with an important development in the investigation of the neurophysiological mechanisms which condition the sleep and waking states of the mammalian brain. In 1935 he showed that the interruption, by a transsection of the rostral brainstem, of the flow of nervous impulses ascending toward the forebrain produces in the latter a functional condition which has many analogies with natural sleep and the sleeplike state produced by barbiturate drugs. The electro-

physiological and pharmacological analyses of these two hypnoid states led him to the conclusion that the sleeplike condition which characterizes the residual activity of the forebrain when it is separated from the rest of the neuraxis by a mesencephalic transsection is due to the lack of a continuous energizing influence exerted normally on its nerve nets by the impact of indispensable afferent impulses. Sections of the spinal cord immediately below the medulla showed that this energizing influence is maintained in the intact, complete encephalon.

Bremer's experiments, which provided neurophysiologists with the now classical preparations of the "cerveau isolé" and the "encéphale isolé," introduced the two concepts of a "cortical tonus" and of its critical reduction by the "deafferentation" of the forebrain. The fundamental significance of the two concepts was not affected when H. W. Magoun and Giuseppe Moruzzi demonstrated in 1949 that the ascending activating impulses which the mesencephalic section blocks are essentially those which are emitted by a portion of the brainstem neuronal network known as the reticular formation. The concepts survived, also, the discovery in 1959 by Moruzzi and his associates of an antagonistic hypnogenetic influence exerted on the arousal system by a nervous structure more caudally located in the brainstem core. *See* MORUZZI, GIUSEPPE.

In the course of his study of the sleep processes, Bremer was led to analyze the

various components of the elementary responses evoked in the cortical receiving areas by synchronous volleys of sensory impulses. He showed that the presence of the late oscillatory component of these evoked potentials is of critical importance for perceptual awareness, a fact which was later confirmed by the microphysiological recording of the discharges of neuronal units. In 1952 he made, with Terzuolo, a significant contribution to the knowledge of the reciprocal relation which exists between the cortical mantle and the ascending reticular formation. He described the process by which the cerebral cortex is able to promote its own arousal by a corticoreticular control mechanism. The analysis he and his associates made of the processes involved in arousal disclosed the powerful facilitatory effect exerted on the operations of the cortical receiving areas and of their thalamic relay nuclei by the direct or indirect stimulation of the reticular formation. Later such reticulocortical sensory dynamogenesis proved to be especially important for the visual area responses and to be associated there with the the activity of oculomotor structures.

The theoretical interpretation of the electroencephalographic method discovered by H. Berger was promoted by Bremer's analysis of elementary responses. It also benefited from two other aspects of his research: first, his methodical analysis of the "spontaneous" oscillatory potentials of the brain cortex (the "brain waves"), which Bremer, on the basis of his spinal cord studies with V. Bonnet, attributed very early to synchronized synaptic potentials of the cortical nerve cells; and second, by his contribution to the elucidation of the various mechanisms of this bioelectrical synchronization.

The son of a teacher of Latin and Greek, Bremer received his M.D. from the University of Brussels in 1919. He studied neurology with Pierre Marie in Paris and physiology with W. B. Cannon in Boston, then did research in H. W. Cushing's laboratory in Boston and in C. S. Sherrington's laboratory in Oxford. After a period as instructor of physiology, he was, from 1932 until his retirement in 1962, professor and head of the department of physiopathology at the University of Brussels Medical School. The recipient of honorary degrees from the universities of Aix-Marseille, Montpellier, Strasbourg, and Utrecht, Bremer was elected a foreign member of the American Academy of Arts and Sciences in 1958.

Besides monographs on the cerebellum and muscle tone, Bremer wrote *L'Activité electrique du cortex cérébral* (1938) and *Some Problems in Neurophysiology* (1953), the texts of lectures delivered at the universities of Paris and London.

For background information *see* NERVOUS SYSTEM (VERTEBRATE); RETICULAR FORMATION (VERTEBRATE BRAIN); SLEEP AND DREAMING, PSYCHOPHYSIOLOGY OF in the McGraw-Hill Encyclopedia of Science and Technology. ∎

BRESLOW, RONALD
★ American chemist

Born Mar. 14, 1931, Rahway, NJ, U.S.A.

Breslow's main activity was the synthesis of new molecules whose properties were expected to be of interest, and the study of how chemical and biochemical reactions occur. This work led him to the synthesis of the most fundamental compound which shows the special stability known as aromaticity, and to the postulation and demonstration of the opposite property, antiaromaticity, in some other compounds. He also synthesized a number of simple molecules which perform reactions similar to those catalyzed by the complicated natural catalysts, the enzymes. In the area of elucidating how reactions occur, his most important contribution was the discovery of the chemical pathway by which vitamin B_1, thiamine, performs its biological functions.

For a century it has been known that the molecule benzene, C_6H_6, is unusually stable. Advances in the application of the theory of quantum mechanics to chemical problems made it clear that the special stability of benzene was due to the presence of six electrons which could move around the benzene ring. The theory predicted that molecules would be specially stable if they had 2, 6, 10, 14, etc., such electrons. Breslow realized that the most fundamental system, with two mobile electrons, would be the cyclopropenyl cation, $C_3H_3^+$ (I), the simplest aromatic system. No such molecule was known, and new methods had to be invented to prepare it. Breslow and his students developed such methods to prepare compounds related to the cyclopropenyl cation, and finally in 1967 they prepared the compound itself. It indeed proved to have special stability, and was the fundamental aromatic unit. This work led to a burst of activity in other laboratories to prepare and characterize other new aromatic compounds; thousands of papers were published in this field.

Compounds were predicted to have special stability with 2, 6, 10, etc., mobile electrons, but the theory was ambiguous with respect to other numbers, such as four mobile electrons. Breslow's approach to this was experimental. He prepared species such as the cyclopropenyl anion (II) and the cyclopentadienyl cation (III) with four mobile electrons in the ring and found that these were unusually unstable. For this reason he proposed that such molecules be described as antiaromatic. This finding helped to clarify the relationship between structure and properties of organic compounds and to stimulate the development of new theoretical techniques which adequately account for the findings.

Such work involves an extension of natural chemistry, since substances are prepared which are quite different from any chemical compounds found in the natural world. Chemistry is also concerned with the transformations of molecules, which are called chemical reactions. The most significant natural chemical reactions occur in living organisms, the biochemical reactions catalyzed by enzymes. Thus Breslow and his coworkers were also concerned with trying to imitate and extend the reactions catalyzed by enzymes, by using not the large protein enzymes but instead smaller chemical catalysts. The goal here is twofold: to understand how enzymes work in biochemical reactions and to develop new chemical reactions which perform useful transformations.

The attainment of the first goal is illustrated by Breslow's work with thiamine. It was known that the very complicated molecule thiamine pyrophosphate (IV) acts as a very special catalyst (a coenzyme) in some enzyme reactions which are central to life, but it was not known how the molecule works or even which section of the molecule plays the key role. Breslow studied a model reaction in which thiamine pyrophosphate performs the same function as in its biochemical reactions but without the enzyme. Because the enzyme is absent, the reaction is thousands of times slower than the enzymatic process. Breslow tried smaller pieces of the thiamine pyrophosphate molecule and found that some of them still worked in the model reaction. By this process he zeroed in on the key section of the molecule and discovered that one part of the thiamine pyrophosphate had unexpected reactivity (V). This discovery led him to deduce the detailed mechanism by which vitamin B_1 plays its biochemical role. This suggestion was completely confirmed, and the function of thiamine pyrophosphate is no longer a mystery.

Enzyme model systems can also be used to develop new chemical reactions. By considering what was known about the biochemical reactions by which steroid hormones are produced in living systems, Breslow realized that a very simple chemical reaction might be able to imitate some of the highly selective biochemical reactions performed by enzymes. This idea led to a new style of chemical synthesis, in which transformations which had been possible only in living organisms could be imitated in the laboratory. One result was an improved method for preparing cortisone, a steroid used in treating arthritis and inflammation.

A physician's son, Breslow majored in chemistry at Harvard University, where he received his A.B. in 1952 and his Ph.D. in 1955. After a year at Cambridge University in England, he went to Columbia University, where he became professor of chemistry in 1962 and S. L. Mitchill Professor of Chemistry in 1967. He received the American Chemical Society Award in Pure Chemistry and the National Fresenius Award (1966), the Mark van Doren Medal and the Baekeland Medal (1969), the Harrison Howe Award (1974), the Remsen Award (1977), and

the Roussel Prize (1978). He was elected to the National Academy of Sciences in 1966 and served as chairperson of its Division of Chemistry from 1974 to 1977.

Breslow wrote *Organic Reaction Mechanisms* (1966; 2d ed. 1969).

For background information *see* AROMATIC HYDROCARBON; ENZYME; ORGANIC CHEMICAL SYNTHESIS in the McGraw-Hill Encyclopedia of Science and Technology. ■

BREWER, LEO
★ American chemist

Born June 13, 1919, St. Louis, MO, U.S.A.

Work with the Manhattan District (atomic bomb) Project during World War II stimulated Brewer's interest in the chemical behavior of high-temperature systems. Thereafter he engaged in a long series of investigations aiming to establish the general principles of high-temperature behavior and to develop new materials and methods for research in high-temperature systems. For his achievements in this field, Brewer received the U.S. Atomic Energy Commission's E. O. Lawrence Memorial Award in 1961.

In the early 1940s the chemical properties of metallic plutonium were unknown. While engaged on the Manhattan Project at Berkeley, CA, Brewer and a group consisting of L. A. Bromley, N. L. Lofgren, and P. W. Gilles were assigned the tasks of predicting the possible range of

high-temperature chemical behavior of plutonium metal; of developing refractory materials capable of containing molten plutonium without excessive contamination, even if the worst prediction should be true; and finally of developing a microanalytical procedure for the determination of oxygen.

The first of these tasks led to a fundamental examination of the principles of high-temperature behavior of all the elements, which resulted in a series of papers describing the high-temperature behavior of metals, oxides, halides, and many other compounds. The second task led to the development of the refractory sulfides of cerium, thorium, and uranium, which were fabricated into forms capable of containing the most electropositive metals. The third task led to a theory of solvents for vacuum-fusion analysis of metals and to the development of a micro method of analysis of electropositive metals using a molten-platinum bath.

The examination of high-temperature data indicated that the commonly accepted values for the enthalpy of carbon gas and the dissociation energy of N_2 were probably too low. Following the war, Brewer, with Gilles and F. A. Jenkins, undertook the study of the vapor pressure of graphite and demonstrated a much higher enthalpy of carbon gas. Also, a flame study by Brewer, A. G. Gaydon, and N. Thomas demonstrated a high dissociation energy for N_2. These experiments stimulated a large number of confirming experiments that clearly established the high values for both atomic carbon and nitrogen. *See* GAYDON, ALFRED GORDON.

The wartime study also uncovered abnormalities in vapor-pressure data that indicated polymerization in high-temperature vapors. With Lofgren, Brewer undertook a study of cuprous chloride and demonstrated that cuprous chloride vapor contained mainly Cu_3Cl_3. This led to a general theory predicting that saturated high-temperature vapors would be complex mixtures of species and that the complexity would increase with increasing temperature. These predictions were later confirmed by high-temperature workers for many systems. Brewer's interest in halide vapors continued with work on molybdenum oxychloride with N. Hultgren, spectroscopic studies of gaseous monohalides by M. D. Shetlar and D. W. Green, and extensive reviews, with G. R. Somayajulu and E. Brackett, of the thermodynamics of halide vapors. Interest in the kinetics of high-temperature vaporization processes, initiated by the graphite vapor-pressure work, led to work with K. Moztfeldt on Na_2CO_3 and with J. S. Kane on phosphorus that characterized some features of kinetic barriers to vaporization and resulted in generalizations about the occurrence and consequences of low vaporization and condensation coefficients.

With H. Haraldsen, D. L. Sawyer, D. H. Templeton, C. H. Dauben, and O. H. Krikorian, Brewer continued work on refractories with pioneering studies of the refractory silicides and borides and consideration of the nature of their chemical bonding. The importance of oxides in high-temperature systems had led Brewer to theoretical and experimental work with A. W. Searcy, D. F. Mastick, R. K. Edwards, F. Greene, P. Zavitsanos, G. R. B. Elliott, J. L. Margrave, R. F. Porter, S. Trajmar, G. M. Rosenblatt, R. M. Walsh, R. H. Hague, D. W. Green, and H. L. Johansen that characterized the high-temperature thermodynamics of oxides.

Along with the previous spectroscopic studies of halide and oxide gases, a substantial spectroscopic study of gases in equilibrium with graphite was carried out with L. K. Templeton, J. G. Phillips, Krikorian, W. T. Hicks, J. L. Engelke, and L. Hagan. The spectroscopic studies then branched into two directions. First, C. G. James, E. R. Worden, R. G. Brewer, F. E. Stafford, R. A. Berg, J. Link, A. Chutjian, P. T. Cunningham, and S.-G. Chang carried out studies designed to fix thermodynamic data of gases by way of radiative-lifetime determinations. These studies uncovered unexpected dissociative processes in the excitation of iodine vapor which were finally clarified by the work of J. B. Tellinghuisen. Second, the isolation-matrix technique pioneered by G. Pimentel was used to characterize high-temperature gases. Studies by C. B. Meyer, G. D. Brabson, B. A. King, D. Solan, D. D. Jensen, J. L. Wang, C.-A. Chang, W. W. Duley, and L. Andrews dealt with the condensation reactions of high-temperature species upon cooling to liquid hydrogen temperature with matrix gases, and the resulting spectra.

The previous interest in the nature of the chemical bonding of refractory solids and the extensive spectroscopic studies of high-temperature gases converged in the use of the correlation of electronic and crystal structures by N. Engel to predict structures and thermodynamic properties of metals and intermetallic phases. Thus the enthalpies of fusion and sublimination of the lanthanide metals were used to predict the electronic levels of the gaseous lanthanides, which in turn were used to predict properties of the actinide metals. The improved understanding of the relationship between the spectroscopic properties of the atoms and the structures and stability of the solid metals led to a number of practical applications. For example, it was possible to predict the structures and compositions of the phases of most of the 2,000,000,000 multicomponent phase diagrams of the transition metals. The generalized Lewis acid base theory as applied to transition metals in the context of the Engel correlation predicted very strong interactions between the transition metals on the left-hand side of the periodic table which have vacant d-electron orbits with the platinum group metals which have nonbonding d-electron pairs. Brewer, together with G. Stowe, P. Riessenfeldt, and P. R. Wengert, was able to confirm the expectations of the theory with the demonstration of an excess partial molal Gibbs energy of solution of zirconium of the order of $-100,000$ calorie (-4.184×10^5 joule) per gram-atom. This interest in metals was applied to a critical evaluation and compilation of ternary phase diagrams with S.-G. Chang. A subsequent application was the use by Brewer and R. H. Lamoreaux of the bonding models that were developed to calculate the thermodynamic properties and complete phase diagrams of a hundred of the binary phase diagrams of molybdenum with the elements ranging from hydrogen to lawrencium.

Brewer received his B.S. at the California Institute of Technology in 1940 and his Ph.D. at the University of California, Berkeley, in 1943. After wartime work with the Manhattan District Project at Berkeley, he joined the faculty there in 1946, becoming professor of physical chemistry in 1955. He served as head of the Inorganic Materials Research Division of the Lawrence Berkeley Laboratory from 1961 to 1975. He was elected to membership in the National Academy of Sciences in 1959.

For background information *see* REFRACTORY; THERMOCHEMISTRY; THERMODYNAMIC PROCESSES in the McGraw-Hill Encyclopedia of Science and Technology. ∎

BRIDGMAN, PERCY WILLIAMS
American physicist

Born Apr. 21, 1882, Cambridge, MA, U.S.A.
Died Aug. 20, 1961, Randolph, NH, U.S.A.

A leakproof seal that Bridgman devised for his high-pressure apparatus enabled him to attain very high pressures and to study their effects on the physical properties of matter. Bridgman's original measurements included many discoveries in the fields of polymorphic transitions of substances, high-pressure effects on both ordinary and heavy water, the viscosity of fluids, and the elastic properties of solid bodies. For his achievements in the design and construction of high-pressure apparatus and in the formulation of techniques basic to the continued investigation of high-pressure physics, Bridgman was awarded the 1946 Nobel Prize in physics.

The origin of high-pressure physics can be traced to the middle of the 18th century when the English physicist John Canton demonstrated that water was measurably compressible. Although subsequent high-pressure research was limited by the difficulty in preparing suitable apparatus, the French physicists L. P. Cailletet and E. H. Amagat made significant contributions during the second half of the 19th century. Amagat developed a special technique for ensuring an effective seal which permitted him to obtain pressures of 3000 atmospheres (304 megapascals). However, the assumption that Amagat's pressure limit of 3000 atmospheres could not be exceeded due to leakages developing in the hydrostatic assembly caused interest in the branch of physics to decline.

In 1905, while working toward his doctorate at Harvard University, Bridgman began to study certain optical phenomena under the influence of pressure. When an explosion damaged part of the equipment, he tried to find a use for the pressure assembly. To this end he developed a sealing device that enabled him to exceed Amagat's limit by ever-increasing factors. The fundamental principle of his apparatus lay in the method by which the piston was packed. The basic hydrostatic equipment is a piston forced into a cylindrical hole in a steel block and made to exert a compressive strength upon a liquid. To prevent the liquid from leaking past the piston, Bridgman designed a packing assembly consisting of a ring of hardened steel, a cup-shaped washer of soft steel, a packing of soft rubber, and a mushroom-shaped, heat-treated steel device that he inserted between the liquid and the piston. The essential feature of this arrangement was that the stem of the mushroom did not reach entirely through the steel ring but remained unsupported. This method has been described as the principle of the unsupported area. In practice, the entire effort of the piston was transmitted to the mushroom through the packing. Since the total area of the packing was less than the total area of the piston by an amount equal to the area of the stem, the pressure in the packing was greater, by a fixed percent, than the pressure exerted by the piston in the liquid. The result was a system protected against leakage at any pressure range and effective for any modification of design.

Although greater emphasis had been given to the study of temperature effects on the properties of matter, Bridgman realized that pressure was as important an independent variable as temperature. To demonstrate his assumptions, Bridgman had to develop experimental techniques suited to ascending pressure ranges, to make full and accurate descriptions of the magnitude of these pressures, and to locate transition points in the behavior of substances that could be used as indications of applied pressures. The problem that first presented itself, with regard to technique, was the extension of the range;

the second problem was to find what could be done with the new pressures.

Proceeding on the assumption that the limits of a pressure range were set by the strength of the containing vessel, Bridgman made an intensive investigation of materials. His first apparatus was a cylinder of one-piece construction of the best heat-treated alloy steel. At a pressure of 12,000 atmospheres (1216 megapascals), Bridgman studied nearly all the ordinary physical properties of substances and was able, in some instances, to reach 20,000 atmospheres (2027 megapascals), for brief periods of time.

Bridgman's next step toward a higher pressure range was to combine the best materials with special methods of construction. He equipped the pressure cylinder with an external support and increased the compressive strength of the piston through the use of tungsten carbide or carboloy. With this technique, Bridgman was able to perform routine experiments up to 30,000 atmospheres (3040 megapascals), to introduce electrically insulated leads into the apparatus, and to repeat practically all the former experiments at this new range. By reducing test volumes, Bridgman was later able to extend the pressure range to 50,000 atmospheres (5066 megapascals).

A number of techniques now being available to Bridgman, he attempted another extension of the pressure range. By utilizing tungsten carbide construction for the cylinder and immersing the pressure vessel in a fluid, which in turn was subject to a pressure of 30,000 atmospheres, a new pressure range of 100,000 atmospheres (10,133 megapascals) was readily sustained. At this range, Bridgman discovered that the pressures were no longer truly hydrostatic, and he had to devise novel departures from his earlier techniques to measure electrical resistance, compressibility, and shearing strength of elements, alloys, and compounds. He was able to extend this range to 425,000 atmospheres (12,666 megapascals) in a limited number of cases.

Employing a modification of Bridgman's apparatus to obtain 100,000 atmospheres, in 1955 engineers of the General Electric Company successfully synthesized industrial-grade diamonds from graphite. Among the numerous results that Bridgman achieved were the identification of seven different modifications of ice as well as two new forms of phosphorus: a

stable black phosphorus and an unstable form. Bridgman's work is of direct application to geophysics, crystallography, and other branches of science and technology. It is of theoretical importance in the investigation of the effects of high pressure on the outer structure of the atom.

A reporter's son, Bridgman attended Harvard University, receiving his A.B. in 1904, his M.A. in 1905, and his Ph.D. in physics in 1908. He immediately joined the faculty at Harvard, becoming an instructor in 1910, an assistant professor in 1919, and professor of mathematics and natural philosophy in 1926. He retired in 1954.

Bridgman wrote a number of books, among them *The Logic of Modern Physics* (1927), *The Physics of High Pressure* (1931), and *The Nature of Physical Theory* (1936).

For background information *see* HIGH-PRESSURE PHENOMENA; HIGH-PRESSURE PROCESSES in the McGraw-Hill Encyclopedia of Science and Technology. ■

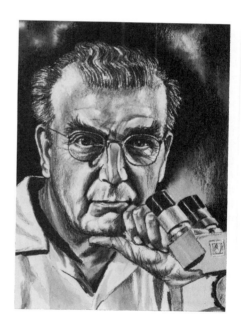

BRINK, ROYAL ALEXANDER
★ American geneticist

***Born** Sept. 16, 1897, Woodstock, Ontario, Canada*

Brink's major research dealt with a directed form of heritable change that he encountered in maize and named paramutation in 1958. He observed that the level of action of an *R* gene, which conditions anthocyanin formation in seed and plant, invariably was reduced following passage through a heterozygote with a stippled allele. The altered form of *R* was gametically transmissible, though it reverted partially toward the standard level when it was made homozygous. The stippled factor was not altered in the heterozygote with *R*. The *R* allele sensitive to this unusual kind of heritable change was said to be paramutable, and the stippled factor was described as paramutagenic. Counterparts of paramutation in maize had been reported earlier by Bateson and Pellew in the garden pea, by Lilienfeld in *Malva,* and by Renner in *Oenothera,* but these examples of the phenomenon were less favorable for study than the *R* case.

In cooperation with his graduate students and other associates, Brink showed that paramutation involves chromosome components that, unlike conventional genes, are extremely labile under certain conditions and can be heritably altered in particular ways at will. Biological interest in this phenomenon rests on the fact that the observed changes in level of gene action reflect the operation of elements in the chromosome. *R*-locus dependence of the *R* phenotype was proved in a test which showed that a paramutant *R* and a distinctively marked normal *R* persisted in their respective states in a common cytoplasm. The first *R* allele whose paramutability was studied conditioned pigment formation in both seed and plant. It was observed that sensitivity to paramutation was unaltered when this factor mutated to colorless plant, but was abolished by mutation to colorless seed. Evidently paramutability rests on an *R*-locus component intimately associated with seed pigmentation.

Three lines of evidence, all indirect, led Brink to conclude that paramutation occurs in vegetative cells. First, it was shown that conjugation at meiosis of a paramutable and a paramutagenic allele is not a condition of paramutation. Second, it was observed that following the application of pollen carrying a highly sensitive *R* allele to the silks of a plant heterozygous for a paramutagenic and a nonparamutagenic factor, the resulting seeds carrying the paramutagenic factor form significantly less pigment than the other class. Third, it was demonstrated by testing separately the pollen formed in different tassel branches that plants in which paramutation is occurring are mosaics for level of potential *R* action. Thus, paramutation

may proceed at different rates in different cell lineages within the individual plant. The various states of *R* in pollen from a given tassel are assumed to reflect the sum of the paragenetic changes that have occurred between fertilization and plant maturity in the respective cell lineages entering the tassel.

Seed color phenotypes based on a paramutable *R* factor of given origin can be obtained in a range from self-color, in single dose, to near-colorless. These different levels of *R* pigmenting potential can be generated by passing *R* through heterozygotes carrying appropriately chosen paramutagenic alleles. The level of action of an *R* factor initially in an intermediate state can be raised by maintaining the factor heterozygous with a colorless allele, or it can be reduced by passing the factor through a heterozygote with the stippled, or other strongly paramutagenic, gene.

The continuous variation in level of *R* action that may be induced by these breeding procedures suggests that the chromosomal basis of paramutability is a repressor segment adjacent to the *R* gene consisting of repeating units whose numbers may be altered. The degree of repression of *R* action is assumed to be a function of the multiplicity of the units making up the repressor segment. If many units are present, *R* action is only weakly expressed, and vice versa. According to this hypothesis, paramutation consists in a change in the number of units within the repressor segment. Such changes may be visualized as occurring during somatic mitosis as a result of misreplication of the postulated repeating units.

Paramutation rests primarily on the metastability of paramutable *R* alleles, and it is not the result of a property conferred by a paramutagenic partner in a heterozygote. The level of action of a paramutable *R* of stock culture origin rises significantly in successive generations of hemizygotes, that is, in plants lacking an *R* partner. This fact shows that paramutagenic factors do not instigate paramutation; they act as adjuvants of the process, which can also occur in their absence. Studies showed that the treatment of seed with alkylating agents, such as diethyl sulfate, regularly promotes heritable derepression of a paramutated *R* allele. This regular increase in level of *R* action is understandable on the assumption that the alkylating agent causes loss of material from the repressor segment either by direct deletion or through an effect on the

chromosome replication process that leads indirectly to the loss of repressor units.

Born and reared on a dairy farm, Brink received his early education in a rural primary school and the Woodstock Collegiate Institute. He received a B.S.A. from the Ontario Agricultural College in 1919. Following a year as chemist with Western Canada Flour Mills, Winnipeg, he entered the University of Illinois and was awarded an M.S. in 1921. He continued graduate study in genetics with E. M. East at Harvard University, where he received a D.Sc. in 1923. Brink was appointed to the staff of the department of genetics at the University of Wisconsin in 1922, and spent his entire professional career there. He was chairperson of the department of genetics from 1939 to 1951. Brink was elected to the National Academy of Sciences in 1947 and to the American Academy of Arts and Sciences in 1960.

Managing editor of *Genetics* (1952–57), Brink also edited *Heritage from Mendel* (1965), the proceedings of the Mendel Centennial Symposium sponsored by the Genetics Society of America.

For background information *see* ALLELE; CHROMOSOME; GENE ACTION in the McGraw-Hill Encyclopedia of Science and Technology. ■

BRODE, ROBERT BIGHAM
★ American physicist

Born June 12, 1900, Walla Walla, WA U.S.A.

Brode showed in his first research publication (1925) that molecules, such as nitrogen and carbon monoxide or methane and argon, with similar arrangements of their external electrons have very similar cross sections for the collision of slow electrons. His later observations on mercury, cadmium, and zinc were interesting in their marked similarity and in the magnitude of the cross sections. Cadmium was the largest and mercury the smallest. This is the inverse of the order of their ionization potentials. Similar results were obtained by Brode for the alkali atoms. The very large cross sections that were found could have been expected from the low ionization potentials. For electrons with about 2 volts' energy, cesium, the atom with the lowest ionization potential, has a cross section that is 110 times the cross section of helium, the atom with the highest ionization potential. The alkali atoms have resonance peaks in their cross sections for energies near their excitation potentials. While the magnitude of the cross section is qualitatively explained by the binding forces on the external electrons, the quantitative theoretical handling of the problem requires, even for the alkali atoms, involved wave-mechanical treatment that is only now possible with modern computers. The results of these computations are in satisfactory agreement with Brode's observations. The survival quality of Brode's work is indicated in a 1966 survey that describes his paper as one of the most used references in the field of collisions of charged particles.

In 1935 Brode spent a year in research with P. M. S. Blackett at Birkbeck College, London, working on counter-controlled cloud chambers. Returning to Berkeley, he developed cloud chamber techniques to give quantitative measurements of the specific ionization and momentum of high-energy cosmic-ray electrons. The application of this technique in 1938, with D. Corson, confirmed the theoretical prediction for increasing specific ionization with the increasing energy for electrons with a relativistic mass above about four times the rest mass. This property of all high-energy charged masses has been important in distinguishing between protons and mesons with very high energy. After the war Brode resumed his measurements of momentum, specific ionization, and range of cosmic-ray me-

sons. From a large number of measurements he obtained a value for the rest mass of the mu meson of 210 ± 5 times the electron's rest mass. The excess of positive mu mesons and the related east-west asymmetry at sea level and at mountain stations to 12,000 feet (3700 meters) were studied. Observations of cosmic-radiation particles were made in a cloud chamber combined with the field of a permanent magnet and flown in a B-29 at 30,000 feet (9100 meters). As a part of the International Geophysical Year program, Brode established neutron monitor stations at Berkeley, Honolulu, and Elsworth (Antarctic). *See* BLACKETT, PATRICK MAYNARD STUART.

During World War II, Brode was unit supervisor for research and development in the Johns Hopkins Applied Physics Laboratory, where the proximity fuse was developed. Later he was group leader for fusing in the Ordnance Division of the Los Alamos Atomic Laboratory. He was given the Presidential Certificate of Merit for these activities.

The development of the National Science Foundation into its position as a leader and supporter of American science has required the services of many scientists. Brode served as a member and chairperson of the Physics Advisory Panel, as a member of the University Science Development Panel, and as associate director for research in 1958–59. He was elected a member of the council or governing board of the American Physical Society, the American Association of Physics Teachers, and the American Institute of Physics. He served as vice-president for Section B and president of the Pacific Division of the American Association for the Advancement of Science.

With his background of 4 years of research and study abroad and his service on selection panels for Rhodes, National Research Council, Atomic Energy, National Science Foundation, and Fulbright awards, Brode was well prepared for his appointment to the Board of Foreign Scholarships by President John F. Kennedy. In the organization of international conferences and commissions, he served as a United States delegate to two General Assembly meetings of the International Council of Scientific Unions and as vice-president during 1954–60 of the International Union of Pure and Applied Physics.

Brode was active in the University of California Academic Senate, where he

served on many committees; he was chairperson of the Berkeley Division, the statewide Academic Council, the Budget Committee, and the Educational Policy Committee. He was a leader in the "oath controversy" between the faculty and the regents of the University of California, and worked for the restoration of academic freedom through the American Association of University Professors. He served in that organization on Committee A (Academic Freedom), on the council, and as vice-president.

Brode received his B.Sc. from Whitman College in 1921. In 1924 he received the first Ph.D. in physics awarded by the California Institute of Technology. The next 3 years were spent in postdoctoral research at Oxford as a Rhodes scholar, at Göttingen as an International Educational Board fellow, and at Princeton as a National Research Council fellow. In 1927 he was appointed assistant professor of physics at the University of California, Berkeley, becoming an associate professor in 1930 and full professor in 1932. He retired in 1967. Brode was elected in 1949 to the National Academy of Sciences, of which his identical twin, the chemist Wallace Brode, also became a member. In 1960 he was elected a fellow of the American Academy of Arts and Sciences. He received honorary degrees from Whitman College (1954) and the University of California, Berkeley (1970). *See* BRODE, WALLACE REED.

For background information *see* CLOUD CHAMBER; COSMIC RAYS; SCATTERING EXPERIMENTS, ATOMIC AND MOLECULAR in the McGraw-Hill Encyclopedia of Science and Technology. ∎

BRODE, WALLACE REED
★ American chemist and spectroscopist

Born *June 12, 1900, Walla Walla, WA, U.S.A.*
Died *Aug. 10, 1974, Washington, DC, U.S.A.*

Much of what is known of the influence of substituents on the absorption spectra of azo dyes is mainly due to Brode. Of the more than 200 technical papers published by him, about half are concerned with azo dyes. In his studies on color and constitution, Brode demonstrated substituent effects on resonance-dye structures in the induction of coplanarity, conjugation of resonant centers, and the partial or total

inhibition of coplanarity of chromophoric-coupled resonant structures. Much of the monoazo study was broadened to include polyazo compounds and the effects induced by coplanar conjugation of disazo and polyazo compounds.

While much of Brode's earlier work in dyes involved the azo series, subsequent studies covered many classes of dyes, including phthalein and sulfonphthalein, anthraquinone, indigo, thioindigo, and natural dyestuffs. His extension of the observed phototropic effects in interconversion of *cis-* and *trans-*azo compounds to the *cis-* and *trans-*indigo and thioindigo series provided some of the best available examples of what he termed the "chameleon" effect, in which dyestuffs changed color to conform to the color of the light to which they were irradiated. The solutions of thioindigo and its derivatives change to red when exposed to red light and to blue when exposed to blue light—proof of the configuration being assigned through bridged rings which were specific to only one configuration.

As a by-product of his early work on the measurement of absorption spectra and optical rotation of the compounds he was studying, Brode had to design and build many of the essential instruments, including automatic recording spectrophotometers and spectropolarimeters. His development of the techniques and establishment of a laboratory for spectrophotometric and spectrographic studies led to his pioneering in the creation in the

early 1930s of one of the first courses in chemical spectroscopy and to his writing the textbook *Chemical Spectroscopy* (1939; 2d ed. 1943). The combination of his training as a synthetic organic and dye chemist and as a designer and builder of optical instruments led to his chairing the first committee on absorption spectra of the American Society for Testing Materials and to his honorary membership on the committee on emission spectra. From 1950 to 1960 he edited the *Journal of the Optical Society of America*. He was elected president of the Optical Society in 1961 and served on the board of governors of the American Institute of Physics in 1958 and from 1960 to 1963.

Although he was active in optics, Brode considered his principal career to have been that of a synthetic organic chemist. His major technical papers are mostly concerned with organic synthesis. He was one of five students of Roger Adams chosen to present papers at a symposium to honor that leader of American organic chemistry on his retirement in 1954. In this lecture Brode surveyed his own research studies, including the work initiated with Adams and continued in later years by Brode on the adsorption of asymmetric dyes on optically active fibers and the mechanism of dyeing of fibers. This work showed that asymmetric dyes are not preferentially adsorbed. Other researchers, however, had found to the contrary, and Brode had repeated some of these dissenting experiments but was unable to confirm them. The question was not fully settled until some 30 years later when Bradley, Brindley, and Easty in England repeated the Adams-Brode experiments and fully confirmed their validity. *See* ADAMS, ROGER.

The broad experience which Brode developed in the field of dyestuffs and color description led to some interesting related diversions in his contributions to science and education. He contributed extensively to the American Association for the Advancement of Science program in the elementary grades in experimental work involving color descriptions and dye reactions. With his wife, he collected American Indian artifacts and art work and developed a personal acquaintance with many Indian leaders. In particular, he studied the synthetic and natural dyes used by the Indians in the production of woven rugs and provided some helpful advice. Using samples from his extensive

Indian rug collection, he gave popular lectures on the dyes used by the American Indians.

Widely known, but not always credited as to source, are the teaching models which Brode and his associates developed for organic chemistry. These "molecular models" sets, developed in the early 1930s, were designed as a low-price aide for individual students, and the laboratory manual prepared for use with these models was reprinted in several editions. These models have wooden pegs for single bonds, coil springs for double bonds, and brightly colored balls for atoms (yellow for hydrogen, black for carbon, and red for oxygen); they are designed on an inch-to-angstrom scale. Many research groups acquire the sets in quantity to study stereoisomerism, ring strain, and configuration problems.

Brode's father was a professor of zoology. An older brother became a professor of biology. Wallace Brode was one of a set of triplets; all three pursued scientific careers, Wallace and his identical twin, the physicist Robert Brode, achieving election to the National Academy of Sciences. Wallace Brode did his undergraduate work at Whitman College (B.S., 1921) and received his graduate degrees at the University of Illinois (M.S., 1922; Ph.D., 1925). He did postdoctoral work on a Guggenheim Fellowship at Leipzig, Zurich, and Liverpool. From 1928 to 1948 he taught at Ohio State University, then served as associate director of the National Bureau of Standards from 1948 to 1958. During World War II he was head of the Paris Liaison Office of the Office of Scientific Research and Development, receiving for this service the Presidential Certificate of Merit. He headed the Science Department of the Navy Laboratory at Inyokern (China Lake) and served on the advisory boards of a number of defense and atomic energy activities. As science adviser to the Secretary of State from 1958 to 1960, he established the science office in the Department of State and the scientific attaché program in United States embassies in the major scientific nations. He wrote extensively on international science, national science policy, and the scientific work force in the United States and other nations and served as a member of the Scientific Manpower Commission. In addition to honorary degrees and honorary memberships in a number of scientific societies, Brode received the Priestley

Medal of the American Chemical Society, the Department of Commerce Exceptional Service Award, and the Distinguished Spectroscopist Award of the Society of Applied Spectroscopy. He was elected to the National Academy of Sciences in 1954. *See* BRODE, ROBERT BIGHAM.

Brode published more than 200 technical and survey articles in American and foreign scientific journals. In addition to his text, *Chemical Spectroscopy,* he coedited the manual *Laboratory Outlines and Notebook for Organic Chemistry* (1949), served as editor of *Science in Progress* (series 12–16, 1962–66), and contributed chapters to many standard reference texts.

For background information *see* DYE; ORGANIC CHEMICAL SYNTHESIS; SPECTROSCOPY in the McGraw-Hill Encyclopedia of Science and Technology. ∎

BROGLIE, PRINCE LOUIS DE
★ French physicist

Born Aug. 15, 1892, Dieppe, Seine-Inférieure, France

In 1905 Albert Einstein, in his theory of light quanta, affirmed the coexistence in light of waves and particles (today called photons) and drew from this the explanation of the photoelectric effect. During the following years he developed this idea in a series of works that are today too often forgotten. Having long meditated on Einstein's conceptions and on all the quantum phenomena then known, de Broglie, in some notes published in the proceedings of the Paris Academy of Sciences in 1923 and then in his doctoral thesis in 1924, extended the idea of the coexistence of waves and particles to all the particles of microphysics, particularly to electrons. The concept that guided him then was that these particles are very small regions of very high concentrations of energy in the interior of the wave transporting them.

The existence of the wave associated with the particle in this new "wave mechanics" was soon confirmed by the success of the theoretical work of Erwin Schrödinger and by the experimental discovery by C. J. Davisson and Germer, then by G. P. Thomson, of the phenomenon of electron diffraction. Preserving his initial idea, de Broglie, in an article published in the *Journal de Physique* in May 1927, developed his mode of envisaging the coexistence of waves and particles in the form of a "theory of double solution." At the Solvay Conference, which met at Brussels in October 1927, the interpretation of the new mechanics upheld by Max Born, Niels Bohr, and their students and linked to Bohr's conception of "complementarity" was opposed to de Broglie's. Called upon at that time to uphold his teachings, de Broglie expounded at length the interpretation that, despite the important objections raised by Einstein and Schrödinger, was adopted by the majority of theoretical physicists. *See* BOHR, NIELS HENRIK DAVID; BORN, MAX; THOMSON, SIR GEORGE (PAGET).

For 15 years de Broglie reviewed his ideas on the theory of the double solution and considerably developed them. Only his three principal hypotheses will be stated here.

1. The real wave (or wave v) is a physical process that evolves in space and time according to the equations of propagation well known in wave mechanics. As for the particle, it is a sort of small object, the seat of a very great concentration of energy, which is constantly located in its wave and which is displaced according to a law specified below. The wave ψ usually employed in quantum mechanics is a fictitious wave connected to the real wave v by the formula $\psi = Cv$, where C is a normalization constant so that the quantity $|\psi|^2$ can give in absolute value the probability of the particle's presence in the element of volume. The single fact of granting that the particle is constantly located in its own wave makes it possible to remove completely the very serious objections that can be made to the present interpretation.

2. If the motion of the particle is not subject to the perturbations discussed in hypothesis 3 below, this motion will be constantly defined by the "guiding law" stated as follows: "If the wave v is written in the form $v = \alpha\ (x,y,z,t)\ \exp\ [(\hbar i)\ \varphi(x,y,z,t)]$ where α and φ are real, the quantity of motion of the particle is equal at every point of its trajectory to the gradient of the function φ at that point and at that instant." It is easily proved that this guiding law can also be stated this way: "The particle moves in its wave in such fashion that its internal vibration remains constantly in phase with the wave that carries it." When one accepts the guiding law, one can perceive the reason why the quantity $|\psi|^2$ gives at each point and at each instant the probability of the particle's presence. But a more rigorous demonstration of this deduction requires the introduction of a supplementary hypothesis:

3. The particle is constantly in energetic contact with a hidden medium that it is natural to identify with the "subquantum medium," the existence of which was suggested in 1954 by Bohm and Vigier in an article in the *Physical Review.* As a result of the continual perturbations that its permanent contact with the subquantum medium imposes upon it, the particle must be animated by a kind of Brownian movement which constantly causes it to leap from one trajectory defined by the guidance formula to another, as in a hydrodynamic flow one molecule of a hot fluid passes constantly from one streamline to another. It is the incessant skipping of the particle in its wave that permits a better proof of the statistical significance of the quantity.

But then one is almost necessarily led to believe that the subquantum medium constitutes a kind of hidden thermostat with which the particle is constantly in contact. On this basis, de Broglie was led to formulate a "hidden thermodynamics of particles," which, when better developed, seems to him bound to play a great role in the future progress of quantum physics.

De Broglie became convinced that the interpretation of wave mechanics based on the principles just stated will make possible an understanding of the true physical significance of the formalisms presently employed in quantum mechancis and an explanation of their success. The physical realities hidden behind the formalisms will finally be perceived and, undoubtedly, new explanations and predictions will be obtained. The present situation, then, seems analogous to that which existed at the time when classical thermodynamics constituted a rigorous formalism permitting exact predictions but resting on admittedly arbitrary, a priori principles. It is the statistical interpretation of thermodynamics, due principally to L. E. Boltzmann and J. W. Gibbs, which made it possible to understand the true nature of entropy and finally to predict or explain new phenomena.

At the Univerity of Paris, de Broglie received his *Licencié ès lettres* (1910), *Licencié ès sciences* (1913), and *Docteur ès sciences* (1924). He was professor of theoretical physics at the University of Paris from 1932 to 1962. Winner of the Nobel Prize for physics (1929), he was elected to the French Academy in 1944, to the Royal Society of London in 1953, to the U.S. National Academy of Sciences in 1948, and to the American Academy of Arts and Sciences in 1958.

De Broglie wrote *Matter and Light: The New Physics* (English transl. 1939), *New Perspectives in Physics* (English transl. 1962), *The Current Interpretation of Wave Mechanics: A Critical Study* (English transl. 1964), *La thermodynamique de la particule isolée* (1964), and *Certitudes et incertitudes de la science* (1966). He edited *Wave Mechanics and Molecular Bilogy* (1966).

For background information *see* DE BROGLIE WAVELENGTH; QUANTUM MECHANICS; QUANTUM THEORY, NONRELATIVISTIC in the McGraw-Hill Encylcopedia of Science and Technology. ■

BRONK, DETLEV WULF
American biophysicist

Born *Aug. 13, 1897, New York, NY, U.S.A.*

Died *Nov. 17, 1975, New York, NY, U.S.A.*

After assuming the presidency of the Rockefeller Institute for Medical Research (now Rockefeller University) in 1953, Bronk guided its evolution into a unique center for graduate study in the United States and one of the finest graduate schools in the world. During his administration the institute's university foundations were laid and its educational policies developed.

In 1901 John D. Rockefeller endowed the institute in New York City as a pioneering grant-giving agency. By 1903 a decision was made to conduct research, and the institute was modeled on the European laboratories presided over by such notables as Robert Koch, Louis Pasteur, and Ivan Pavlov. After World War II the trustees of the institute decided that university and medical school laboratories had begun to undertake research that had once been in the exclusive domain of the Rockefeller. As a result, the institute no longer securely held the position of innovator that had accounted to a large degree for its eminence. A committee was organized to chart the course of the institute, and from this group emerged a plan to utilize the institute's facilities for training talented young investigators and for working more intimately with universities.

Bronk was then asked to accept the post of president and chief executive officer of the institute, combining two formerly separate positions, and to guide the reorganization. He decided to undertake the task, for he believed the new position provided an unusual opportunity to devote much of his time to research while developing a unique international institution for the furtherance of science. In 1954 the institute's original charter was amended to make it a graduate university, and it became part of the University of the State of New York with the authority to grant the degrees of Ph.D. and Sc.D. At this time the name was shortened to

the Rockefeller Institute to reflect its broadened purposes.

Among the many ways in which the institute differed from conventional graduate schools were that it had no undergraduate college, it had a faculty-to-student ratio of 2:1, and there was no fixed program of study. Under Bronk's direction a graduate fellow was expected to choose his or her own curriculum by selecting a combination of courses, tutorials, and independent readings followed by self-directed study and research. Complete academic freedom was the keynote of Bronk's plan. At the Rockefeller a student could work for weeks, or even months, with a particular investigator and then withdraw without penalty to work with another if the student so chose.

The success of Bronk's leadership is borne out by the statistics of the first decade of the new program. Of the more than 200 appointments to fellowships, 73 received their degrees and 118 were still studying at the Rockefeller. As a result of the achievements during this period, in the spring of 1965 the institution was renamed the Rockefeller University to reflect the changes and the new direction that had been taken under Bronk.

Bronk's administrative abilities benefited a number of academic institutions. While at Swarthmore College he helped to organize the honors program for undergraduates. Later he was the first director of the Johnson Research Foundation of Medical Physics at the University of Pennsylvania. Bronk also served as president of the Johns Hopkins University, where he tried to bridge the gap between undergraduate and graduate study, emphasizing the progress of the individual student. During World War II he served as coordinator of research in the U.S. Army Air Corps Air Surgeon's Office, where he was concerned with the physiological aspects of high-altitude flight.

As a researcher, Bronk worked in the areas of both biophysics and physiology. He studied the nature of sensation, body movement control, the chemical excitation of nerves and nerve impulses, and the electrochemical methods of measuring oxygen consumption in nerve fibers.

Bronk received his A.B. (1920) from Swarthmore College, and his M.S. (1922) and Ph.D. in physics and physiology (1926) from the University of Michigan. After serving as an instructor at the University of Pennsylvania and the University of Michigan, he joined the faculty at Swarthmore in 1924, becoming professor of zoology and dean of men in 1927. Two years later he accepted a position as professor of biophysics and director of the Johnson Research Foundation at the University of Pennsylvania. In 1949 he resigned these positions to become president of Johns Hopkins, where he remained until joining the Rockefeller Institute.

Bronk was the chairperson of the National Research Council from 1946 to 1950 and the president of the National Academy of Sciences–National Research Council from 1950 to 1962. Among the many honors he received were the Priestley Award (1956), the Franklin Medal of the Franklin Institute (1961), the Presidential Medal of Freedom (1964), the Public Welfare Medal of the National Academy of Sciences (1964), and the National Medal of Science (1968). ∎

BROQUIST, HARRY P.
★ American chemist

Born Jan. 23, 1919, Chicago, IL, U.S.A.

Lysine (I), α-ε-diaminohexanoic acid, is one of the eight essential or indispensable amino acids that people must have in their diets to sustain life. They either meet their nutritional need for lysine by consumption of animal-derived foods where lysine is present in ample amounts or by judicious consumption of a variety of

$$
\begin{array}{l}
\text{H}_2\text{NCH}\text{---COOH} \\
\quad | \\
\quad \text{CH}_2 \\
\quad | \\
\quad \text{CH}_2 \\
\quad | \\
\quad \text{CH}_2 \\
\quad | \\
\quad \text{CH}_2 \\
\quad | \\
\quad \text{NH}_2 \qquad \text{(I)}
\end{array}
$$

plant foods where lysine is present in varying amounts. But the penultimate source of lysine is from plants, and much of Broquist's research concerned the mechanism of biosynthesis of this amino acid by certain lower plants and ultimately led to the complete elucidation of the aminoadipic acid pathway of lysine biosynthesis. This research has important nutritional overtones, for it suggested a means for the economical production of lysine for use as a protein supplement in those foodstuffs poor in lysine.

Not only is lysine used in all living cells for the synthesis of protein, but because of its specific chemical nature, it is uniquely endowed to participate in specific intracellular processes and transformations of great biochemical importance. Studies in Broquist's laboratory at Vanderbilt University led to the discovery that lysine participates in the biosynthesis of carnitine (II). Carnitine is a biocatalyst

$$
(\text{CH}_3)_3 \overset{\oplus}{\text{N}}\text{CH}_2\text{CHCH}_2\text{COOH} \qquad \text{(II)}
$$
$$
\qquad\qquad\quad | \\
\qquad\qquad \text{OH}
$$

essential for fatty acid oxidation, a complex process wherein cells ultimately obtain much of their energy. Thus this research links lysine and protein metabolism with lipid and energy metabolism.

Because lysine level is poor in many of the common cereal grain foodstuffs consumed in large parts of the world by humans, there has long been considerable interest in developing methods for the economical production of lysine, so that it might be readily available as a protein supplement for such foodstuffs. Broquist discovered that common yeasts such as those used in the baking and brewing industries had the capacity to produce large amounts of lysine when grown with α-aminoadipic or its immediate precursor, α-ketoadipic acid. Animal feeding trials demonstrated that such high-lysine yeasts could meet the requirement of test ani-

mals for lysine. Economical synthesis of these adipic acid derivatives by either chemical or biological means, followed by conversion to lysine by yeast fermentation, thus permits an attractive method for the production of a high-quality protein supplement for animal or human consumption.

As can be appreciated from the chemical structure of aminoadipic acid (III), its

$$
\begin{array}{l}
\text{H}_2\text{NCH}\text{---COOH} \\
\quad | \\
\quad \text{CH}_2 \\
\quad | \\
\quad \text{CH}_2 \\
\quad | \\
\quad \text{CH}_2\text{COOH} \qquad \text{(III)}
\end{array}
$$

conversion to lysine involves reductive amination of carbon-6 to a primary amine. The precise biochemical nature of these events was elucidated and led to the discovery of a new amino acid, saccharopine (IV), which was involved in this process.

$$
\begin{array}{l}
\text{H}_2\text{NCH}\text{---COOH} \\
\quad\quad | \\
\quad\quad \text{CH}_2 \\
\quad\quad | \\
\quad\quad \text{CH}_2 \\
\quad\quad | \\
\quad\quad \text{CH}_2 \\
\quad\quad | \\
\text{COOH}\;\;\text{CH}_2 \\
\quad | \qquad | \\
\text{CH}\text{---NH} \\
\quad | \\
\text{CH}_2 \\
\quad | \\
\text{CH}_2\text{COOH} \qquad \text{(IV)}
\end{array}
$$

Saccharopine can be viewed as a molecule in which the ε-N atom of lysine is shared with the α-amino group of glutamic acid. Indeed, saccharopine was shown to be derived by reduction of a product formed from the condensation of α-aminoadipic semialdehyde with glutamic acid.

Although these studies of lysine biosynthesis were carried out exclusively with either yeast or bread mold *Neurospora crassa*, subsequent research from other laboratories demonstrated that higher animals degrade lysine arising from the breakdown of tissue proteins to α-ketoadipic acid by a reverse of the process that fungi use for synthesizing lysine from ketoadipic acid. Ketoadipic acid then is subsequently broken down in animals to small molecules that can be readily oxidized. Thus studies of lysine biosynthesis in fungi indirectly contributed to a knowledge of lysine catabolism in humans.

In recent years a form of lysine in which the ϵ-amino group is completely methylated has been found in animal tissues and urine. From structural considerations Broquist and his collaborators conceived the idea that trimethyllysine (V) may be a

$$\overset{\oplus}{(CH_3)_3}NCH_2CH_2CH_2CH_2CHNH_2COOH \qquad (V)$$

precursor of carnitine, as mechanisms are known in bacteria wherein lysine can be degraded to a 4-C compound plus a 2-C compound. Thus if trimethyllysine could be converted to N-trimethylaminobutyric acid, this compound has long been known to be the immediate precursor of carnitine. Hence a link between lysine metabolism and carnitine biosynthesis could be visualized.

In support of this hypothesis Broquist found, for example, that when the fungus *N. crassa* was grown with lysine in which either carbon 1 or carbon 6 was labeled with ^{14}C, carnitine biosynthesized by the fungus was radioactive only with $6\text{-}^{14}C$ lysine as the substrate. Detailed isotopic studies together with enzymatic evidence from this and other laboratories led to the complete elucidation of the pathway of carnitine biosynthesis from lysine. It had long been known that the penultimate source of the N-methyl groups of carnitine was methionine. Hence carnitine is formed in the body from two essential amino acids, lysine and methionine. From a nutritional point of view this relationship is reminiscent of the tryptophan-niacin precursor-product relationship in which higher animals can synthesize the vitamin niacin if an adequate amount of tryptophan is in the diet. Indeed, current research in certain areas of the world where protein malnutrition (and lysine deficiency) is prevalent indicates that serum carnitine levels are low. Thus a nutritional application of the research that has been described is that it points the way to the production of a high lysine yeast to complement cereal grain proteins, and also to serve in providing a critical precursor for carnitine biosynthesis.

Broquist's contributions to lysine research were recognized by their inclusion in prestigious national and international symposia and in publications in quality journals. In 1969 he was the recipient of the Borden Award for Nutritional Research, given by the American Institute of Nutrition.

Broquist received his Ph.D. in biochemistry at the University of Wisconsin in 1949, during a period in which training and interest in nutritional biochemistry were emphasized. He retained this interest through the years with appointments in a Nutrition and Physiology Research Section, Lederle Laboratories Inc. (1949–58), in the College of Agriculture, University of Illinois (1958–69), and in the School of Medicine, Vanderbilt University, where he became a member of the faculty in 1969.

For background information *see* AMINO ACIDS; LYSINE; PROTEIN METABOLISM in the McGraw-Hill Encyclopedia of Science and Technology. ∎

BROUWER, DIRK
★ American astronomer

Born *Sept. 1, 1902, Rotterdam, Netherlands*
Died *Jan. 31, 1966, New Haven, CT, U.S.A.*

Brouwer's principal scientific contributions were in the field of dynamical astronomy or celestial mechanics, a subject that, according to Laplace, is "a great problem of mechanics, the arbitrary data of which are the elements of the celestial movements. Its solution depends both on the accuracy of observations and on the perfection of analysis." Brouwer's activity was mostly in the direction of perfecting the methods of analysis and adapting them to changing conditions. In addition, his active interest in the observational aspects of celestial mechanics was shown by his contributions to photographic astrometry. For his contributions to celestial mechanics Brouwer received the Gold Medal of the Royal Astronomical Society in 1955.

An important branch of dynamical astronomy is planetary theory. A general planetary theory is a solution of the differential equations of motion of a planet in which the attractions by the Sun and the various principal planets are taken into account. If the planetary attractions were ignored, the body would move in a fixed ellipse in accordance with Kepler's laws. A planetary theory gives expressions as functions of the time for the deviations of the actual motion from the motion in a fixed ellipse. Although the equations of motion are simplest in rectangular coordinates, no satisfactory method for obtaining the perturbations in rectangular coordinates existed until Brouwer (1944) solved the problem and thereby created a new method for constructing general planetary theories.

All conventional forms of planetary theory have the drawback that the time is present in the coefficients of periodic terms. Such a theory may represent the motion of a planet satisfactorily for a number of centuries, but it fails to yield information on the character of the orbital changes over periods of, say, millions of years. The theory of secular variations, first developed by Lagrange, overcomes this drawback at the cost of ignoring the periodic effects. Several such solutions have been made at various times. An extensive solution was made by Brouwer and A. J. J. van Woerkom (1950). From such a solution the long-term changes in the orbits of asteroids may be calculated. In this way the Japanese astronomer Hirayama succeeded in establishing the existence of six families of asteroids, the members of which have so nearly identical secular elements that the common origin of the members of a family from a parent body cannot be questioned. Brouwer refined Hirayama's work and showed the existence of additional groups of asteroids that also exhibit similarities in their secular elements. Somewhat related was his earlier study (1947) of the secular variations of Encke's Comet and its relationship with the Taurid group of meteors.

The rapid development of high-speed calculating machines after 1945 benefited the entire field of celestial mechanics. The method of numerical integration was applied with increasing success to the study of orbits. An early major undertaking was that by W. J. Eckert, Brouwer, and G. M. Clemence (1951), which by numerical integration provided accurate orbits of the five outer planets for the years 1653 to 2060. *See* CLEMENCE, GERALD MAURICE.

Other contributions in related fields were a method of orbit correction by Eckert and Brouwer (1937) that has been generally adopted throughout the world, and a study (1937) of the rounding error affecting numerical integration. The latter yielded the result that the error in the position in the orbit increases statistically as the 3/2 power of the number of integration steps; the errors in the elements that determine the size, shape, and orientation of the orbit increase as the 1/2 power of the number of steps.

Among the most puzzling problems of astronomy was that posed by the gaps in the distribution of the thousands of small planets between the orbits of Mars and Jupiter; Brouwer explained these satisfactorily in 1963. He also showed that the fluctuations in the rate of rotation of the Earth are of a statistical character that would be produced by random disturbances, and he proposed the name "ephemeris time," which has been adopted throughout the world for the measure of time that is free from such effects. In 1959 he solved the problem of the effect of the oblateness of the Earth on the motions of artificial satellites. This solution, of great practical value as well as theoretical interest, is completely general and immediately applicable to any satellite.

In addition to his contributions to celestial mechanics, Brouwer successfully tackled several knotty problems in astrometry, which may be called the accurate mapping of the stars and derivation of their motions. As director of the Yale Observatory after 1941, he gave vigorous support to its traditional activity in this field and devised important new techniques and programs. With the financial assistance of the Ford Foundation he caused to be constructed a double 20-inch (50.8-centimeter) astrographic telescope installed at the Yale-Columbia Southern Observatory in the province of San Juan, Argentina, which is operated in cooperation with the University of Cuyo, a national university of Argentina. With this telescope the astrometric program initiated at the Lick Observatory for the northern hemisphere will be extended to cover the entire sky.

Son of a civil service employee in the city of Rotterdam, Brouwer studied mathematics and astronomy in the University of Leiden, where he specialized in celestial mechanics under Willem de Sitter and received the Ph.D. degree in 1927. In September 1927 he went to the United States on an International Education Board Fellowship for postdoctoral study at the University of California, Berkeley, and Yale University. In 1928 he became research assistant to E. W. Brown at Yale. He remained at Yale, becoming in 1941 a professor, chairman of the department of astronomy, and director of the observatory. In 1944 he was named Munson Professor of Natural Philosophy and Astronomy. He was elected to the National Academy of Sciences in 1951.

Brouwer wrote *Methods of Celestial Mechanics,* with G. M. Clemence (1961).

For background information *see* CELESTIAL MECHANICS; EPHEMERIS TIME in the McGraw-Hill Encyclopedia of Science and Technology. ∎

BROWN, DONALD DAVID
★ American developmental biologist
***Born** Dec. 30, 1931, Cincinnati, OH, U.S.A.*

Soon after entering medical school at the University of Chicago, Brown became interested in biochemical research. He obtained his M.D. in 1956, but spent most of his medical school days studying the

mechanism of bacteriophage invasion. Phage research introduced him to biochemical genetics, and he decided even then that he would apply this new genetics to the study of embryonic development.

Following internship, Brown studied the metabolism of histidine at the National Institutes of Mental Health for 2 years. Having gained valuable biochemical experience, he then spent a year at the Pasteur Institute (1959–60) with J. Monod. At that time Monod and F. Jacob were developing their important ideas on bacterial control mechanisms. During that year these French workers proposed that circulating repressors control gene action and showed that messenger ribonucleic acid (mRNA) is the direct gene product. *See* JACOB, FRANÇOIS; MONOD, JACQUES.

Brown returned to the United States in 1960 prepared to use these new ideas and methods for the study of embryonic development. The department of embryology of the Carnegie Institution of Washington had an international reputation for its morphological studies of human embryonic development and for experimental embryology. Brown arrived there as a postdoctoral student in fall of 1960, and became the first staff member (1962) at Carnegie to be oriented to biochemical and genetic research.

In order to study gene function in development, Brown reasoned that direct gene products must be isolated and characterized. Prior to that time, biochemical studies had been concerned with changes in proteins during development. Brown turned toward the synthesis of RNA molecules as direct indicators of gene activity. He selected frog embryos because of the large amounts of embryonic material suited for chemical analysis. He first characterized various kinds of RNAs known to be synthesized in large amounts by cells. These included the three kinds of ribosomal RNA (28S, 18S, and 5S) and transfer RNAs. Embryos and growing oocytes were found to synthesize these various RNAs at differing rates that depend on the stage of the cell's development. In his first studies he used the leopard frog (*Rana pipiens*), but in 1963 he changed to the South African clawed toad (*Xenopus*) because of a newly discovered genetic defect, the anucleolate mutant. Brown and J. B. Gurdon showed that mutant embryos were unable to synthesize 28S and 18S ribosomal RNA (rRNA).

This discovery confirmed that the nucleolus is the site of rRNA synthesis, and it led to the detection, and the first isolation and characterization, of genes—the rRNA genes. The first purification of these genes was accomplished in 1966 by H. Wallace and M. Birnstiel. Brown's research, along with that of Birnstiel and J. Gall, helped to characterize the rRNA genes in *Xenopus*.

In 1968 Brown and I. B. Dawid found that during oogenesis the genes for rRNA are amplified about a thousandfold in the ovarian germ cell (oocyte). These extra genes then produce huge quantities of ribosomes that are found in the mature egg. Brown then considered the question of whether amplification of specific genes is a general method for cell specialization. In 1972 Y. Suzuki, L. P. Gage, and Brown showed that the gene for fibroin, the principal protein of silk, was not changed in silk gland cells, where the gene was expressed. Thus amplification could not account for the immense production of silk by these glands.

Convinced that most genes must be controlled by other kinds of molecules in cells, Brown turned his full attention to the isolation and characterization of genes of known function.

In 1971 Brown isolated the genes for 5S rRNA from *Xenopus*. This was the second gene of known function to be isolated. Five different genes for 5S RNA from two species of *Xenopus* were isolated and completely sequenced by Brown and his colleagues. More is known about these simple genes than about any other eukaryotic gene. They remained the primary focus of Brown's work. The goal of this research was to reproduce in the test tube the exact conditions that control the expression of these genes in the living cell.

Brown's only contact with science and medicine as a child was through his father, a physician. He entered Dartmouth College in 1949 as a premedical major and left after 3 years to attend medical school at the University of Chicago, from which he graduated in 1956 with an M.D. and an M.S. in biochemistry. Following 1 year of internship in New Orleans and 2 years in the Public Health Service at the National Institutes of Health in Bethesda, MD, he trained for 1 year at the Pasteur Institute as a special fellow of the National Cancer Institute. All the research in his chosen specialty of developmental biology was carried out in the department of embryol-

ogy of the Carnegie Institution of Washington in Baltimore, of which he became director. Among his awards was the U.S. Steel Award for research in molecular biology (1973), the V. D. Mattia Award of the Roche Institute (1976), and the Boris Pregel Award in Biology of the New York Academy of Sciences (1977). He was elected to the National Academy of Sciences in 1973, and received an honorary D.Sci. and Distinguished Alumni Award from the University of Chicago in 1976.

For background information *see* EMBRYOLOGY, EXPERIMENTAL; GENE ACTION; RIBONUCLEIC ACID (RNA) in the McGraw-Hill Encyclopedia of Science and Technology. ∎

BROWN, GEORGE HAROLD
★ American electrical engineer

Born Oct. 14, 1908, North Milwaukee, WI, U.S.A.

In the course of his thesis work and subsequently in industry, Brown produced a body of theory and analytical deductions, supported by many experimental results, that became the basis for practices in the design of antennas for radio broadcasting.

In 1934 vertical radiators were just coming into use, and they failed to perform in accordance with the generally accepted theory. In a series of mathematical analyses, measurements on models, and confirming field tests, Brown, an engineer with Radio Corporation of America, dem-

onstrated that the departure from theory was due to nonsinusoidal distribution of current on the antenna and that the error was particularly large for antennas of nonuniform cross section, such as the guyed cantilever type then in vogue. Further field experiments with top loading by means of "top hats" confirmed this and led to the now universal use of uniform cross-section towers. The full results of this work were published in April 1935 in the *Proceedings of the Institute of Radio Engineers* and immediately became the standard reference in this field.

In the January 1937 issue of the same journal, Brown published his now-famous paper "Directional Antennas." Explaining the method of calculating directional patterns, and including illustrations of a large number of standard patterns, this paper, along with his earlier papers, found its way into the notebooks of every station engineer and most consultants. A whole generation of broadcast engineers learned about directional arrays from this paper, and most of the directional arrays thereafter were probably calculated from it.

In 1936 Brown conceived the turnstile antenna for FM radio and television broadcasting long before television had become a commercial service. The turnstile antenna is now the standard unit for commercial television broadcasting.

Continuing his investigations in 1937 and 1938, Brown derived the now-classic generalized equation that solved a variety of problems such as the flow of heat in materials heated by radio-frequency power, the voltages on guy-wire insulators of transmitting towers, and the performance of wave antennas.

In 1938 Brown turned his attention to television problems and developed the vestigial sideband filter for use with television transmitters. This device doubled the horizontal resolution of television pictures in a given bandwidth. Vestigial sideband filters are now an integral part of the Federal Communications Commission's standards for commercial television broadcasting, and vestigial sideband transmission is used in all other countries where television service has been established.

During World War II, Brown worked on the design and development of radio and radar antennas for the military. At the same time, he established many of the basic principles of radio-frequency heating and applied these principles to produce a rapid method of drying penicillin.

Following the war, he turned to ultra-high-frequency propagation and color television. He supervised RCA's field test of ultra-high-frequency television in the Washington area in 1948 and with coworkers published what have become the definitive papers on ultra-high-frequency propagation. After 1948 he was in charge of RCA's color television research and development, and he was one of the leading figures in the lengthy development work that led to the adoption of color television standards in the United States.

Brown majored in electrical engineering at the University of Wisconsin, where he received his B.S. in 1930, his M.S. in 1931, his Ph.D. in 1933, and a professional E.E. degree in 1942. He joined the RCA Manufacturing Company in Camden, NJ, in 1933 as a research engineer and remained there until his transfer to the RCA David Sarnoff Research Center, Princeton, NJ, in 1942. In 1952 he was appointed director of the Systems Research Laboratory of RCA, from which he moved to the position of chief engineer, RCA Commercial Electronic Products Division, in 1957. In 1959 he was appointed vice-president—RCA engineering, and in 1961 vice-president—RCA research and engineering. In 1965 he was elected executive vice-president—RCA research and engineering.

Brown wrote *Theory and Application of Radio-Frequency Heating* (1947).

For background information *see* AN-TENNA ELECTROMAGNETISM; DIRECTION-FINDING EQUIPMENT in the Mc-Graw-Hill Encyclopedia of Science and Technology. ∎

BROWN, HARRISON SCOTT
★ American geochemist

Born Sept. 26, 1917, Sheridan, WY, U.S.A.

Brown became interested in the problems of the origin and evolution of the solar system after World War II. At that time there was no direct measurement of the age of the Earth. The ages of numerous uranium- and thorium-bearing rocks had been determined, from which it was deduced that the Earth must be at least 2×10^9 years old. Measurements of variations in the isotopic composition of lead ores indicated further that the Earth might be 3.3×10^9 years old, but direct measurement seemed impossible. The major difficulty was that although the average isotopic composition of modern terrestrial lead could be determined readily enough, the isotopic composition of "primeval" lead, or lead as it was at the time of the Earth formation, was unknown.

Remelting and weathering of rocks had taken place on too vast a scale on Earth to make it likely that any primeval lead had been safely isolated from uranium and thorium since the time of Earth formation. Brown suggested, however, that perhaps nature had preserved a sample of primeval lead in certain of the extraterrestrial objects which collide with the Earth from time to time and which are called meteorites. He reasoned that lead, having a low oxygen affinity and a high affinity for sulfur, is probably concentrated primarily in the metallic, or "iron," meteorites and in the iron sulfide nodules which occur in such meteorites. By contrast, uranium and thorium have high oxygen affinities and are probably concentrated primarily in the oxide phases of the silicate or "stony" meteorites. Thus lead in iron meteorites would have been safely isolated from uranium and thorium since the time of formation of the solar system. Were that assumption correct, lead in iron meteorites should be "primeval."

Attempts were made to isolate lead from the Canyon Diablo meteorite, and it was soon found that the actual concentration of lead in the meteorite was far lower than had been supposed. Indeed, the concentrations turned out to be so low that the isolated lead was found to consist primarily of lead impurities introduced from

chemicals and the air. This discovery led to the development by Brown and his students of chemical procedures for isolating lead from meteorites in microgram quantities free from contamination. Concomitantly, Mark Inghram at the University of Chicago developed powerful new tools of mass spectrometry, which made possible the precise determination of the isotopic composition of such minute quantities of lead. After many failures, Clair C. Patterson, one of Brown's students, succeeded in isolating contamination-free lead from the Canyon Diablo meteorite. Analysis of the lead by Inghram showed that it indeed possessed an isotopic composition unlike that of any terrestrial lead. Assuming the lead to be primeval, the age of the Earth was calculated to be 4.5×10^9 years. Subsequently, isolation of lead from stony meteorites by Patterson showed them also to be 4.5×10^9 years old, thus proving the original assumption concerning the equality of the age of the Earth and that of meteorites to be correct.

The techniques used in this early work were then applied to a variety of problems in solar system and terrestrial chronology by numerous workers. Brown and his students, Patterson and George Tilton, in collaboration with Inghram and Esper Larson, Jr., were the first to apply the techniques to the determination of the age of an ordinary granite and at the same time to determine the detailed distribution of uranium and lead between the constituent mineral phases. Subsequently, similar techniques were applied to the first precise dating of a sedimentary deposit by using potassium-40 and calcium-40. Brown suggested that it might be possible to extend these concepts and determine the age of the elements themselves by making use of possible extinct radioactive substances such as iodine-129. John Reynolds subsequently found isotopic anomalies in xenon extracted from meteorites, making it possible to establish a maximum interval between the formation of the elements and the formation of the solar system. Brown's interest in meteorites led him and his student Edward Goldberg to develop the neutron activation method of trace element analysis for the determination of gallium, gold, palladium, and rhenium. This work, together with later spectroscopic studies, demonstrated the existence of clear-cut chemical groups of iron meteorites which must have evolved under widely differing physicochemical conditions.

In collaboration with Leon T. Silver, Brown demonstrated that about one-third of the uranium and thorium in a typical granite exists in micromineral phases and interstitially is so loosely bound that it can be washed out of the pulverized rock with dilute acid. They demonstrated that the energy one can get out of granites in this manner is much greater than the energy required for processing, thus in principle placing all granitic rocks on Earth at the disposal of humans as a near-infinite source of energy. The energy releasable in this way from 1 ton (0.9 metric ton) of granite is equivalent to that contained in about 15 tons (13.5 metric tons) of coal. By studying the abundances of noble gases in the Earth's atmosphere, Brown was able to demonstrate that the atmosphere is almost entirely of secondary origin, and that during the early phases of Earth formation the chemical and physical processes involved must have taken place at fairly low temperatures (that is, at temperatures sufficiently low for hydrates of silicate minerals to be fairly stable).

Brown showed that planets can be classified into three groups: class I, those composed primarily of metals and silicates (Mercury, Venus, Earth, and Mars); class II, those composed primarily of methane, ammonia, and water (Uranus and Neptune); and class III, those composed primarily of hydrogen and helium (Jupiter and Saturn). Studies of the compositions of stars suggest that planets in systems associated with other stars can also be classified in this manner.

Son of a livestock broker, Brown began his schooling in Wyoming. Following the death of his father, his mother, who was a teacher of piano and a professional organist, moved to San Francisco, where Brown completed his primary and secondary education. He received his B.S. in chemistry at the University of California at Berkeley in 1938 and his Ph.D. in chemistry at the Johns Hopkins University in 1941. Brown became interested in nuclear physics during his undergraduate days at Berkeley and undertook thesis work in mass spectrometry and the separation of isotopes by gaseous thermal diffusion. With the discovery of nuclear fission in 1939, he devoted his attention to the diffusion properties of uranium hexafluoride. By 1940 he and his professor at Johns Hopkins, Robert Fowler, found themselves with the largest gaseous fluorine generating capacity in the United States. They soon were major suppliers of

uranium tetrafluoride and hexafluoride to the embryo atomic project at Columbia University and elsewhere. In 1942 Brown was asked by G. T. Seaborg to join him at the Metallurgical Laboratories at the University of Chicago to work on the chemistry of plutonium. He started the project's program on transuranic anhydrous halides, then in 1943 moved to the newly created Clinton Laboratories at Oak Ridge, TN, as assistant director of chemistry. In 1946 he joined the staff of the Institute for Nuclear Studies at the University of Chicago and there started his work in geochemistry and cosmochemistry. In 1951 he became professor of geochemistry at the California Institute of Technology. With Trevor Gardner, he wrote the original proposal which gave rise to the creation of the Arms Control and Disarmament Agency within the Federal government in 1961. He became foreign secretary of the National Academy of Sciences in 1962 and professor of science and government at Caltech in 1967. He received the ACS Award in Pure Chemistry in 1952, and was elected to the National Academy of Sciences in 1955.

Brown wrote *Must Destruction Be Our Destiny?* (1946), *The Challenge of Man's Future* (1954), and *The Next Hundred Years* (1957; paper 1963).

For background information *see* ATMOSPHERE, EVOLUTION OF; COSMOGONY; EARTH, AGE OF; LEAD ISOTOPES, GEOCHEMISTRY OF; METEORITE; PLANET in the McGraw-Hill Encyclopedia of Science and Technology. ∎

BROWN, HERBERT CHARLES
★ American chemist
___

Born *May 22, 1912, London, England*

Prior to 1940 the boron hydrides and the organoboranes were laboratory curiosities, not utilized in synthetic work. Together with H. I. Schlesinger of the University of Chicago, Brown developed simple practical methods for the synthesis of diborane and discovered the versatile alkali metal borohydrides, making these materials readily available for organic synthesis. These materials revolutionized the practice of organic reductions. Moreover, the discovery of the rapid quantitative reaction of unsaturated compounds with diborane made the organoboranes readily available for synthetic work. Finally, his investigations of the addition compounds

of trimethylboron and diborane with amines provided a quantitative basis for steric effects in chemical theory. This line of research led in 1979 to Brown's receiving the Nobel Prize in chemistry, shared with Georg Wittig who worked independently.

Diborane is a gas, highly reactive to air and moisture. Prior to the discoveries here described, it was prepared only in small quantities, primarily for study of the unusual bonding evident in these derivatives. Brown and Schlesinger's discovery in 1941 that diborane could readily be synthesized by the reaction of lithium hydride or sodium hydride with boron trihalides [Eq. (1)] made this gas readily available for the first time.

$$6 \, LiH + 2BF_3 \rightarrow B_2H_6 + 6 \, LiF \quad (1)$$

Diborane readily reacts with lithium hydride to produce the borohydride [Eq. (2)].

$$2LiH + B_2H_6 \rightarrow 2LiBH_4 \quad (2)$$

A more direct route to sodium borohydride was then discovered [Eq. (3)].

$$4 \, NaH + B(OCH_3)_3 \xrightarrow{250°} NaBH_4 + 3 \, NaOCH_3 \quad (3)$$

This reaction is the basis of the present industrial method for the manufacture of sodium borohydride. Both diborane and sodium borohydride are excellent reducing agents for organic substances and, together with lithium aluminum hydride, revolutionized the methods used to reduce functional groups [Eq. (4)].

$$RCO_2H \xrightarrow[0°]{B_2H_6} RCH_2OH \quad (4)$$

In 1955 Brown discovered that unsaturated organic compounds can be rapidly and quantitatively converted into organoboranes [Eq. (5)].

$$6\,RCH{=\!=}CH_2 + B_2H_6 \xrightarrow{R_2O} 2\,(RCH_2CH_2)_3B \quad (5)$$

Exploration of the chemical characteristics of these organoboranes led Brown and his students to the discovery of a number of reactions [Eqs. (6)] that cause

$$(RCH_2CH_2)_3B \xrightarrow{RCO_2H} RCH_2CH_3 \quad (6a)$$

$$(RCH_2CH_2)_3B \xrightarrow{NaOH,H_2O_2} RCH_2CH_2OH \quad (6b)$$

$$(RCH_2CH_2)_3B \xrightarrow{H_2NOSO_3H} RCH_2CH_2NH_2 \quad (6c)$$

$$(RCH_2CH_2)_3B \xrightarrow{NaOH,AgNO_3} RCH_2CH_2 \quad (6d)$$
$$.RCH_2CH_2$$

the organoboranes to be of major utility in synthetic chemistry.

Diborane, boron trifluoride, and trimethylboron react with amines to form molecular addition compounds [Eq. (7)].

$$(CH_3)_3N + B(CH_3)_3 \rightarrow (CH_3)_3N{:}B(CH_3)_3 \quad (7)$$

The reaction is reversible at higher temperatures. Consequently, study of the dissociation at several temperatures permits calculation of the free energy, the enthalpy, and the entropy of dissociation. By making a systematic study of the stability of the molecular addition compounds as a function of the steric requirements of the boron component and of the amine component, Brown was able to attain a quantitative estimate of the steric strains accompanying the formation of various types of sterically congested structures. He showed that strains of the same order of magnitude were present in related carbon structures. In this way he was led to propose for the first time that steric effects can assist, as well as hinder, the rates of chemical reactions. This led him to explore the role of steric effects in solvolytic reactions, displacement reactions, and elimination reactions.

At a time when steric hindrance was considered to be "the last refuge of puzzled organic chemists," Brown's studies of molecular addition compounds contributed to the reacceptance of steric effects as a major factor in chemical behavior. His studies on aromatic substitution led

to a quantitative theory based on the new Brown σ^+ constants. His studies on applications of the borohydrides and diborane to organic synthesis have had revolutionary impact on synthetic organic chemistry. Finally, the new borohydride preparation of active hydrogenation catalysts was discovered in collaboration with his son, Charles A. Brown, and this in turn led to the new simplified Brown procedure for laboratory-scale hydrogenations.

Brown is perhaps best known for his explorations of the role of boron in organic chemistry. He discovered that the simplest compound of boron and hydrogen, diborane, adds with remarkable ease to unsaturated organic molecules to give organoboranes [Eq. (8)].

$$\begin{array}{c} C{=}C + H{-}B \longrightarrow \\ H{-}C{-}C{-}B \quad (8) \end{array}$$

With organoboranes now readily available for the first time, Brown undertook to explore their chemistry. This chemistry is proving unusually rich. It is evident that Brown discovered a "new continent" in chemistry, a continent that will take many years of enthusiastic research effort to explore in detail and to exploit for the good of humankind.

From England, Brown was taken to the United States at an early age, and all of his education was in the Chicago schools. He attended Wright Junior Collage (1934–35) and the University of Chicago (B.S., 1936; Ph.D. 1938). Following a year as postdoctorate fellow with Professor M. S. Kharasch, he was appointed to the staff of the University of Chicago with the rank of instructor. In 1943 he went to Wayne University as assistant professor, and in 1947 he went to Purdue as professor. In 1959 he was named the R. B. Wetherill Professor, becoming the R. B. Wetherill Research Professor in 1960, and finally R. B. Wetherill Research Professor Emeritus. Brown was the Harrison Howe Lecturer in 1953, the Centenary Lecturer of the Chemical Society (London) in 1955, and the Baker Lecturer in 1969. He was elected to the National Academy of Sciences in 1957, and the American Academy of Arts and Sciences in 1966, and received an honorary doctorate of Science from the University of Chicago in 1968. He was the recipient of the Nichols Medal for 1959, the Ameri-

can Chemical Society (ACS) Award for Creative Research in Synthetic Organic Chemistry for 1960, the Linus Pauling Medal of the Puget Sound and Oregon Sections of the ACS for 1968, the Medal of Science for 1969, the Roger Adams Medal of the ACS for 1971, the Charles Frederick Chandler Medal of Columbia University for 1973, the Madison Marshall Award of the Northern Alabama Section of the ACS for 1975, and the CCNY Scientific Achievement Award Medal for 1976. In 1977 he was elected honorary fellow of the Chemical Society (London) and foreign fellow of the Indian National Science Academy. In 1978 he was awarded the Elliott Cresson Medal from the Franklin Institute, and was the Ingold Memorial Lecturer and Medalist of the Chemical Society (London).

Brown wrote *Hydroboration* (1962), *Boranes in Organic Chemistry* (1972), *Organic Syntheses via Boranes* (1975), and *The Nonclassical Ion Problem* (1977), as well as more than 700 scientific papers.

For background information *see* BORANE; BORON; HYDROBORATION; STERIC EFFECT in the McGraw-Hill Encyclopedia of Science and Technology. ∎

BROWN, MORTON
★ American mathematician

Born Aug. 12, 1931, New York, NY, U.S.A.

Brown played a principal role in the development of the modern theory of topological manifolds. He was associated with two major developments in this field— the generalized Schönflies theorem and the annulus conjecture. For his proof of the first theorem, he was awarded a share of the Veblen Prize in Geometry by the American Mathematical Society in 1966.

A. Schönfliess achieved a powerful generalization of the Jordan curve theorem by proving that the closed interior of a topological circle embedded in the plane is always the boundary of a two-dimensional disk. This theorem, proved in 1908, was a crucial step in the successful development of the classification theory of two-dimensional manifolds. In a celebrated paper, J. W. Alexander showed in 1923 that Schönfliess's theorem in three-dimensional space is false. He constructed an example, modeled on an idea of L. Antoine, of a topological two-sphere in three-space whose closed interior is not

homeomorphic to a three-dimensional ball. The example, called Alexander's horned sphere (see illustration), has the property that, although it is homeomorphic to a two-sphere, it is locally knotted and as a consequence its closed interior is not a topological three-ball. Although Alexander believed that, without the presence of local knotting, the closed interior of a topological two-sphere is always a topological three-ball, he was able to prove this only in some special cases. A complete proof was finally attained in 1954 by E. Moise and (independently) by R. H. Bing.

For higher dimensions, the generalized Schönfliess theorem takes the following form: Suppose that an $(n-1)$-sphere Σ is embedded in n-space so that, with respect to some neighborhood $N(\Sigma)$, the sphere behaves like a round sphere S^{n-1}; that is, the pair $(N(\Sigma),\Sigma)$ is homeomorphic to the pair $(S^{n-1} \times (-1,1),\ S^{n-1} \times 0)$. Is the closed interior of Σ a topological n-ball? This problem, which already presented considerable difficulty in the case $n = 3$, seemed intractable even for $n = 4$. However, in 1959, B. Mazur showed that the theorem is true for all n, subject to the hypothesis that the embedding of Σ in its neighborhood satisfies one further, anomalous condition. Shortly afterward (1960), Brown, introducing the notion of cellularity, gave a complete, elegant, independent proof which avoided the extra hypothesis that Mazur needed. Thus the generalized Schönfliess theorem was solved. In a later paper (1962) Brown established the complete n-dimensional analog of the Moise-Bing theorem: the closed interior of a locally unknotted (locally flat) $(n-1)$-sphere embedded in n-space is a topological n-ball.

Brown then turned his attention to the so-called annulus conjecture. The problem was this: Suppose that two locally unknotted topological $(n-1)$-spheres are embedded in n-space so that one is in the interior domain of the other. Is the closed space between them homeomorphic to the corresponding region between two concentric round spheres? Although the problem seemed a simple variant of the generalized Schönfliess theorem, it proved to be much deeper. In a series of papers appearing in 1962, Brown and H. Gluck formulated the conjecture and introduced the notions of stable homeomorphism and stable structure. A homeomorphism of euclidean space is stable if it is the composition of a finite sequence of homeomorphisms, each of which is the identity on some nonempty open set. A manifold admits a stable structure if it can be covered with stable charts in much the way differentiable manifolds are covered by smooth charts. Brown and Gluck proved that the annulus conjecture is equivalent to the existence of stable structures on all orientable manifolds, which in turn is equivalent to the conjecture that each orientation-preserving homeomorphism of euclidean space is stable. The latter conjecture became known as the stable homeomorphism conjecture. They showed further that, if the annulus conjecture were false, nontriangulable manifolds would exist. In 1968 R. Kirby made the brilliant observation that the existence of stable structures could be reduced to the study of piecewise linear structures on the n-torus. This, combined with the contemporary work of C. T. C. Wall, W.-C. Hsiang, and J. Shaneson on such structures, led to a complete solution of the annulus conjecture for all dimensions except $n = 4$. That problem still stands.

Brown received his Ph.D. in mathematics in 1958 at the University of Wisconsin. He taught at Wisconsin (1957), the Ohio State University (1957–58), and the University of Michigan (beginning in 1958). He held fellowships from the Office of Naval Research (1958), the National Science Foundation (1960–61), and the Sloan Foundation (1962–63). He held visiting appointments at Cambridge University (1963), the University of California at La Jolla (1967), and the University of Warwick in England (1970).

For background information *see* MANIFOLD (MATHEMATICS); MANIFOLD, SMOOTH; TOPOLOGY in the McGraw-Hill Encyclopedia of Science and Technology. ∎

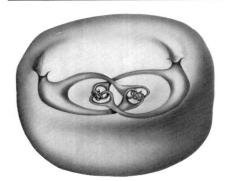

Alexander's horned sphere. (*From J. G. Hocking and G. S. Young, Topology, Addison-Wesley, 1961; reprinted with permission*)

BRUECKNER, KEITH ALLEN
★ American physicist

Born *Mar. 19, 1924, Minneapolis, MN, U.S.A.*

In the late 1940s and early 1950s, experiments carried out with high-energy accelerators made it possible for the first time to determine many details of the interactions between nuclear particles or nucleons (neutrons and protons). The existence and characteristics of the subnuclear particle largely responsible for the nuclear forces, the pi meson, had also been established by this time. In studying the nature of the nuclear forces, Brueckner was led to more general questions concerning the structure of the nucleus, particularly the phenomena of nuclear saturation and the semiempirical model of nuclear motion, the nuclear shell model. He recognized characteristic difficulties in the theories of many-body systems existing at that time and proposed solutions to these problems. His initial steps led to the clarification of several basic problems of nuclear structure and also to the development of the broad-ranging modern theory of the many-body problem, which now is one of the most important fields of mathematical physics. In addition to the application to nuclear structure, this field covers diverse problems in statistical mechanics, solid-state physics, and the theory of liquids and solids. For this work, Brueckner received the Dannie Heineman Prize of the American Physical Society in 1963.

Before the initial operation in 1947 of the first high-energy accelerator, the Berkeley 184-inch (4.67-meter) synchro-cyclotron, information concerning the forces between two nucleons was derived from the interaction of nucleons at low energy and was insufficient to give details of the interaction. During this period, from the early 1930s until the late 1940s, it was assumed, following a suggestion of W. K. Heisenberg in the absence of information to the contrary, that the saturation of nuclear forces leading to the approximately uniform central densities of all large nuclei was due to strong repulsive exchange forces. These would not affect low-energy phenomena, but would become effective at the relatively high energies characteristic of nuclear motion [relative energies as high as 80 megaelectronvolts (MeV)]. By 1950 the Berkeley experiments had shown that this model of nuclear forces was invalid. The rapidly increasing experimental knowledge had by the early 1950s also shown that the nuclear interaction appeared to be strongly repulsive at small distances, so that nucleons upon close encounter acted like hard spheres with a hard-core repulsion at a range of approximately 30 percent of the average nucleus spacing in nuclei. These discoveries could not, within the theoretical methods available at that time, be incorporated into a revised theory of nuclear structure.

The problem of utilizing the experi-

mental results and concurrently developing theoretical understanding of the nucleon-nucleon interaction was further complicated by the independent discovery by M. G. Mayer and J. H. D. Jensen of the highly successful nuclear shell model. The most important feature of the shell model was the assumption that the nucleons moved in independent-particle orbits determined by the shell model potential, which represented the average interaction of the nucleon with the other nuclear particles. For the model to be valid, it appeared to be essential that the very strong short-ranged forces between nucleons not affect their motion. This feature led to several suggestions that, in the dense nuclear medium, the forces were in some way suppressed or averaged out. This view was, however, already contradicted in the early 1950s by high-energy experiments showing marked short-range correlation between nucleons, consistent with the directly measured interactions between nucleon pairs and apparently inconsistent with the shell model. *See* JENSEN, J. HANS D.; MAYER, MARIA GOEPPERT.

In the context of these problems, Brueckner, using the techniques of quantum field theory, first examined the possibility of marked modification in the nuclear medium of the nuclear forces measured in two-nucleon experiments. He came to the conclusion that very small alteration was to be expected and that the forces act at very nearly full strength in the nucleus. He then turned to a direct determination of the nuclear properties, assuming the empirically determined two-nucleon forces to be correct for consideration of nuclear properties. To carry out this evaluation, it was necessary to develop an approximation method suitable for dealing with a large number of particles interacting under conditions where quantum effects were important. Brueckner recognized that existing perturbation methods, in which profound convergence difficulties in dealing with this problem had been known (for 2 decades) to exist, could be readily rearranged into an alternative form. He called this form the linked-cluster expansion, in which formal difficulties were largely removed and successive approximations to the exact answer to the problem could in principle be calculated. This simplification was based on the intuitive argument that if the energy of a many-body system were expanded in powers of the interaction po-

tential, the contributions from separate groups of particles, interacting within each group but not between groups, should contribute separately to the expansion. This simple feature, obscure in the usual approximation methods, was shown by Brueckner to be derivable in the first few orders of perturbation theory. His conjecture that this feature existed in general was later proven by J. Goldstone.

Within this approximation method, Brueckner further introduced a summation of a sequence of interaction terms between nucleon pairs moving in the external field of the remaining nucleons and, within the constraints of the quantum statistics of the nucleons, a further reordering of the perturbation series he termed the reaction-matrix approximation. The formidable mathematical and computational problems presented by these methods were also first solved by Brueckner and his coworkers, who applied the high-speed electronic computer to the evaluation of the basic equations. The numerical results obtained in 1958 by Brueckner and his collaborator, John L. Gammel, for the energy and density of heavy nuclei, using the best empirically derived nucleon-nucleon interactions of that time, were in excellent agreement with the experimental values. These methods have been further elaborated and improved by many other nuclear theorists and applied in alternative forms to the determination of many detailed properties of nuclei. This work continued actively, the latest information on nuclear forces presenting new problems in the quantitative understanding of the nucleus.

Following the initial studies of nuclear properties and of the basic difficulties of the many-body problem, Brueckner proceeded to an examination of the problem of the reconciliation of the nuclear properties as given by the many-body theory and as given by the shell model. He showed that the shell model could be applied literally only for certain low-energy observables of the nuclear motion such as angular momentum, parity, and gross orbital parameters, and that more precise observation of the motion would reveal the more complex correlated motion resulting from the powerful effects of the strong short-range nucleon-nucleon forces, as had already been established by experiment. Further developments of the theory extended to the study of details of the nuclear shell structure, pairing energies, the surface structure of the nucleus, and the scattering interaction of slow nucleons with the nucleus.

In 1968, working as an adviser to the Atomic Energy Commission, Brueckner became interested in the use of very powerful lasers to produce energy by the nuclear fusion reaction, with possible eventual application to commercial power production. At that time this approach had been given only very limited theoretical and experimental attention, primarily in the United States, France, and the Soviet Union. Analyses by Brueckner, which were classified as secret by the Atomic Energy Commission, showed that remarkable possibilities existed for study with lasers that could be built by using the state of the art in laser technology. To pursue these possibilities, Brueckner worked in industry from 1971 to 1974 and in the following years in his academic position at the University of California, San Diego, on the theoretical and experimental aspects of fusion. (This field is now under intensive worldwide study.) Brueckner also directed studies for the United States utility industries on the scientific and engineering feasibility of fusion power systems.

The son of a professor, Brueckner entered the University of Minnesota in 1941 where, after an interruption for service in the U.S. Air Force, he received a B.A. in mathematics in 1945. After a year at Minnesota, he entered the University of California, Berkeley, as a graduate student and received his Ph.D. in physics in 1950. He spent the following year at the Institute for Advanced Study in Princeton, NJ, 1951–55 as assistant and associate professor at Indiana University, 1956 on leave at Brookhaven National Laboratory, and 1956–59 as professor of physics at the University of Pennsylvania. In 1959 he joined the faculty of the new campus of the University of California, San Diego, where he served as chair of the department of physics, dean of letters and science, and dean of graduate studies. He also held in 1961–62, while on leave from the University of California, the position of vice-president and director of research of the Institute for Defense Analysis, Washington. For work on the many-body problem, he was elected in 1969 to the National Academy of Sciences.

For background information *see* NUCLEAR STRUCTURE; NUCLEON in the McGraw-Hill Encyclopedia of Science and Technology. ∎

BRUN, EDMOND ANTOINE
★ French physicist

Born Dec. 31, 1898, Saint-Cannat, Bouches-du-Rhône, France

Throughout his career, which started in 1929 in the modest laboratory of the Lycée de Nice, Brun worked principally in the domain of aerodynamics combined with heat transfer called aerothermodynamics. His thesis, prepared in Paris in the Laboratoire de Physique du Service des Recherches de l'Aéronautique and presented in 1935, dealt with the measurement of the equilibrium temperature which is reached by a perfectly insulating body in uniform translatory motion in a gas. He thus studied the kinetic heating of the flat plate and of the cylinder and presented recovery factor data for both laminar and turbulent flow.

In 1936 Brun pointed out that in the case of constant physical properties, the heat transfer coefficient for high-speed flows is given by the same expression as for low-speed flows, if it is defined in terms of the difference between the actual wall temperature and the adiabatic wall temperature (given by the value of the recovery factor). This result must be established theoretically in the case of laminar flow, but Brun showed experimentally that it is also true in the case of turbulent flow.

In 1937, at the request of the International Air Traffic Association, Brun started studying problems raised by the icing of airplanes. The thermodynamical aspect of the phenomenon led him to define the conditions of anti-icing more precisely. He gave the values of the heating rates necessary either for anti-icing or for deicing of leading edges of wings or of cockpits in terms of the icing conditions; he showed that the most economical conditions of thermal protection were met by a deicer with intermittent electrical heating.

Brun was led, in the study of icing of airplanes, to analyze the conditions of captation of supercooled water droplets by a solid body moving in a cloud at a temperature below 0°C. In 1943 he established, with Marcel Vasseur, the equations of the mechanics of suspensions, and he found a graphical method for drawing the trajectories of particles in suspension in a fluid when the flow field is not uniform. He also gave a method of calculation of anti-icers and applied the equations of the mechanics of suspensions to the study of the characteristics of some dust removers such as cyclones.

The calculation of the convective heat transfer at the nose of a body of revolution, carried out in connection with the problem of icing, served in 1947 as a starting point for the expression of the heat flux density at the nose of a missile during reentry into the atmosphere.

On his nomination as a professor at the Sorbonne in 1942, Brun became head of a laboratory supported by the Centre National de la Recherche Scientifique. He was mainly concerned with studies of heat and mass transfer, especially detailed explorations, both dynamical and thermal, of the boundary layer. This thin layer of fluid exists at the wall of a moving solid, and here are to be found, in the direction perpendicular to the wall, large variations of speed, temperature, and concentration. These rapid variations in the neighborhood of the wall account for both the friction of the fluid on the wall and the convection of heat and of mass from or toward the body. The analogies between these various phenomena led Brun and Gustave Ribaud to establish laws governing heat and mass transfer in good agreement with experiment.

When an insulating body is suddenly put in a gas flow at uniform speed, it heats up progressively until it reaches at each point an equilibrium temperature, which is the adiabatic wall temperature already mentioned. For the study of this unstationary regime, Brun gave a method of measurement of the coefficient of convection in his thesis (1935); this method essentially consists in placing at the surface of the insulating body a small conducting mass flush with the wall and in measuring the beginning of the heating up of this mass. The method, now widely used in accordance with the same unchanged process, is known as the calorimetric method. It was further refined in Brun's laboratory, particularly in the study of supersonic and hypersonic flows.

The study in this laboratory of mass transfer from cylinders and cones at an angle of attack showed the existence of new vortices with axis along the streamlines; it became possible to determine the streamlines by a detailed dynamical exploration of the boundary layer.

Brun's laboratory became an important experimental center for the aerodynamics and thermodynamics of rarefied gases. Flows at high Mach numbers (up to 20) and at low densities (down to 1 micrometer of mercury) can be obtained in wind tunnels. The Second Symposium on Rarefied Gas Dynamics was organized by Brun in Paris in 1961.

Studies of heat and mass transfer in porous media were also carried out and led to practical results on freezing and defreezing of soils, as well as studies of two-phase or n-phase flows in oil reservoirs.

A founder of the International Astronautical Academy, Brun was president of the Société Française d'Astronautique in 1940 and president of the International Astronautical Federation from 1962 to 1964. In 1963 he organized the International Astronautical Congress in Paris. Vice-president of the International Astronautical Academy, he also became president of the Société Française des Thermiciens in 1964. He was a fellow of the Royal Aeronautical Society, London (1958), honorary fellow of the American Institute of Aeronautics and Astronautics (1964), and fellow of the American Astronautical Society (1966). He was elected a foreign associate of the U.S. National Academy of Sciences in 1960. Among the honors he received were the Médaille d'Or de l'Institu Français des Combustibles et de l'Energie in 1961 and the Médaille de la Société des Ingenieurs Civils de France in 1963.

Brun wrote *Les Chaleurs spécifiques* (1940), which received an award from the Académie des Sciences in 1942; *La Convection forcée de la chaleur en régime d'encoulement turbulent,* with Gustave Ribaud (1942; and *Transmission de la chaleur* (1948).

For background information *see* AERO-

THERMODYNAMICS; BOUNDARY-LAYER FLOW; FLUID FLOW PROPERTIES in the McGraw-Hill Encyclopedia of Science and Technology. ∎

BUCHER, WALTER HERMAN
American geologist

Born *Mar. 12, 1889, Akron, OH, U.S.A.*
Died *Feb. 17, 1965, Houston, TX, U.S.A.*

After a lifetime of study on the deformation of the Earth's crust, Bucher set forth a hypothesis to explain the origin and geographic pattern of the great mountain chains on the surface of the Earth. In Bucher's theory, the contraction of the Earth due to cooling and the Earth's gravitation are the dominant orogenic factors.

It is well known to geologists that the Earth's crust is mobile. Simple proof of this is the occurrence of salt-water (marine) fossils in ancient sedimentary rocks now situated high above sea level miles from the nearest ocean. Rock deformation is nowhere more conspicuous than in the orogenic (mountainous) belts where originally flat-lying sedimentary rock layers have been uplifted thousands of feet, tilted, folded, and smashed.

Bucher realized that these orogenic belts yielded to crustal pressure because within them the crust is weaker. The critical question to Bucher was why the volatiles and water vapor rose in only a few long and narrow belts (the sites of mountain chains). An answer was provided

(1939), in part, by Sir Harold Jeffreys, who had studied the occurrence and distribution of deep-seated earthquakes. According to Jeffreys, the depths of these earthquakes are on the same order of magnitude as the most probable depths to which cooling of the Earth can have advanced. In other words, there is a zone between 100 and 700 kilometers within the Earth contracting as cooling takes place, with deep earthquakes being indicative of rock adjustment within that zone. *See* JEFFREYS, SIR HAROLD.

Bucher, seizing upon the data of Jeffreys and others, reasoned that the contractions due to cooling might be sufficiently intense to produce great fractures reaching upward through the crust. These fractures would be ideal conduits for the transfer of heat, water vapor, and volatiles toward the surface.

Based on these assumptions, Bucher advanced his hypothesis in 1956. Postulating an Earth undergoing shrinkage, he visualized the following sequence of events: (1) development of global fractures due to contraction which affected the Earth as a whole; (2) the rise of excess heat, water vapor, and volatiles from deep within the Earth along the fractures; (3) weakening of the crust along the trend of these fractures as viscosity reduction and other alteration of the rocks took place; (4) buckling of the crust in the weakened zones, causing the rise of welts and furrows; (5) partial collapse of the rocks in the welt zone under the influence of gravity after attaining critical height; and (6) production of recumbent or other folds, thrust sheets, and related structures, with gravity continuing to play a major role.

Bucher found highly suggestive evidence to support the concept of global fractures formed in a shrinking Earth by experimenting with models of the Earth. A model was made consisting of a wooden ball 11.25 centimeters in diameter and an outer shell of Plexiglas. A concentric space between the wood and the Plexiglas was filled with Castolite, a plastic that shrinks upon hardening, which represented the Earth's crust. The Plexiglas held the Castolite against the wooden ball.

Shrinkage of the Castolite produced a fracture pattern that strikingly resembled the distribution pattern of mountain chains on the surface of the Earth. For example, one fracture pattern exhibited the hairpin turn created by the West Indies with the Andes–Rocky Mountain Cordillera in the Western Hemisphere.

In order to explain many of the structural details found in the mountainous belts of the Earth and to complete his overall hypothesis, Bucher assigned a major role to the force of gravity. He noted that it was Jeffreys who first (1931) had stated that rocks, if piled high enough, would flatten out under their own weight. This would lead to the spreading and folding of thick sections of rock that had been uplifted within orogenic belts. Virtually all rock types behave as plastics if they are affected by relatively weak but consistent stresses over a very long period of time. Thus, layers of salt and, according to Bucher, even serpentine will flow like glacial ice under gravitational influence. Bucher demonstrated this added characteristic of "solid" rock by using models in which layers of stitching wax, simulating layered sedimentary rocks, were subjected to compression. He was able to duplicate, in this fashion, many of the structural features that are found in Alpine mountain areas.

Although born in Ohio, Bucher and his family moved to Germany during his youth. It was there that he received his education, culminating in a Ph.D. in geology from Heidelberg in 1911. He returned to the United States and joined the faculty at the University of Cincinnati in 1913, becoming chairman of the department of geology and geography at that institution in 1937. He went to Columbia University in New York in 1940, served as chairman of the geology department there from 1950 to 1953, and became professor emeritus in 1956. In that year Bucher became associated with the Humble Oil and Refining Company in Houston, as a consultant in structural geology. It was at that company's research laboratory that many of Bucher's model experiments were conducted with the collaboration of Humble scientists. Bucher was awarded the Bowie Medal of the American Geophysical Union in 1955 and the Penrose Medal of the Geological Society of America in 1960. He was elected to the National Academy of Sciences in 1938.

Bucher wrote *Deformation of the Earth's Crust* (1933; reprinted 1964).

For background information *see* COR-DILLERAN BELT; OROGENY in the McGraw-Hill Encyclopedia of Science and Technology. ∎

BÜCHI, GEORGE HERMANN
★ American chemist

Born Aug. 1, 1921, Baden, Switzerland

Büchi's earliest independent research was devoted to organic photochemistry, a field that received brief attention from Italian chemists prior to World War I but was abandoned shortly thereafter because many of the structural problems created by photochemical transformations were too complex to be solved by using the purely chemical methods then available. Over a period of 10 years Büchi's laboratory announced the discovery of several new photoreactions. Carbonyl compounds were added to olefins and acetylenes; olefins were oxidized by nitrobenzene; [1–3] shifts were observed with β,γ-unsaturated ketones; and olefins were combined with aromatic substrates to produce cyclobutanes.

Long interested in natural products, Büchi then turned to structure elucidation. The structures of the sesquiterpenes patchoulol (in collaboration with J. Dunitz), maaliol, aromadendrene, valerenic acid, calarene, and copaene (with P. de Mayo) were determined. Work on the alkaloids uleine, flavocarpine, and aconitine (with K. Wiesner) led to the accepted structures. A study on the bisindole alkaloid voacamine suggested that the clinically used antitumor alkaloids vinblastine and vincrystine were structurally similar, and this was confirmed in collaboration with K. Biemann, N. Neuss, and M. Gorman.

In 1963 Büchi and G. N. Wogan initi-

ated a research program on mycotoxins present in contaminated foods. The first project was concerned with the structure determination of the aflatoxins, fungal metabolites which had just been isolated from spoiled peanuts and which had been found to be responsible for a mass outbreak of a poultry disease. Aflatoxin B_1, the major metabolite, was shown subsequently to be a potent carcinogen, and its consumption possibly associated with primary liver cancer. A sizable number of other fungi were subsequently examined for new mycotoxins (with A. Demain), and rubratoxins (with J. Z. Gougoutas), tryptoquivalines (with J. Clardy), and malformin C (with Biemann) were isolated and structurally characterized.

Büchi's other work was concerned with multistep total syntheses. The first syntheses of several sesquiterpenes, iboga alkaloids, iridoid glucosides, aflatoxins and their metabolites, neolignans, and the zoanthoxanthins, a group of marine pigments, were accomplished in Büchi's laboratory. Vindoline and catharanthine were prepared by total synthesis and then combined chemically by Pierre Potier to produce the antitumor drug vinblastine.

In 1955 Büchi became a consultant for the Swiss firm Firmenich SA, manufacturers of odoriferous chemicals. In collaboration with M. Stoll and G. Ohloff in Geneva, and with H. Wüest in Cambridge, Büchi synthesized many odor principles, such as damascones, methyl jasmonate, muscone, sinensals, khusimone, and kahweofuran, often by novel chemical methods. In 1957 muscopyridine, a constituent of musk deer glands, was recognized as the first naturally occuring substance containing a bridged aromatic ring. The correct structure of methyl jasmonate, the most important constituent of jasmine oil, was proposed in 1962 (with E. Lederer and E. Demole).

Büchi studied chemistry at the Swiss Federal Institute of Chemistry and received his D.Sc. degree in 1947. As assistant to L. Ruzicka and O. Jeger, he worked on the structures of triterpenes and the synthesis of some of their degradation products. In 1948 he joined M. S. Kharasch at the University of Chicago as a Firestone postdoctoral fellow to work on free-radical reactions. In 1951 he moved to the Massachusetts Institute of Technology, where he became Camille Dreyfus Professor. He received the first Ruzicka Award in 1957, the Ernest Guenther Award in 1958, and the Award for Creative Work in Synthetic Organic Chemistry in 1973. Büchi was elected to the National Academy of Sciences in 1965.

Büchi edited vol. 56 of *Organic Reactions* (1977).

For background information *see* OR-GANIC CHEMICAL SYNTHESIS; PHOTO-CHEMISTRY in the McGraw-Hill Encyclopedia of Science and Technology. ■

BUDDINGTON, ARTHUR FRANCIS
★ American geologist

Born *Nov.29, 1890, Wilmington, DE, U.S.A.*

While studying the base-metal ore deposits in the volcanic rocks of the Cascade Range of Oregon, Buddington found mineral assemblages that included both cherty quartz characteristic of low-temperature formation and tourmaline characteristic of high temperature. Such a combination did not fit into the then current classification for ore deposits. The geological background of these deposits suggested formation at high temperatures and low pressures, and Buddington proposed (1935) the name "xenothermal" for such mineral assemblages. Many ore deposits were subsequently inferred by others to form under these conditions, and the term became widely adopted.

As a result of regional geology studies in the Cascade Range of Oregon, the Coast Ranges of Alaska, and the Adirondack Mountains of New York, Buddington became aware that the granitic masses

or plutons of these different regions had different habits and that the rocks of the three regions represented exposures at successively deeper levels. Subsequently a study of the literature (1959) showed that this relationship was systematic and that the habits of plutons could be correlated with their depth of emplacement.

Regional geologic mapping and petrologic studies in the northern and northwestern Adirondacks of New York State led Buddington to several new interpretations of general significance.

A very extensive banded complex (Diana complex) of metamorphic rocks was found to vary in composition from pyroxene syenite gneiss with thin feldspathic layers very rich in pyroxene, ilmenite, and magnetite, through pyroxene quartz syenite gneiss to hornblende granite gneiss. Buddington showed (1935) that this complex could be satisfactorily interpreted as a metamorphosed, isoclinally overturned folded sheet of differentiated igneous rock. He proposed the term "gravity stratified sheet" to indicate that the variation in composition was the product of fractional crystallization and sorting of crystals in a magma under the influence of gravity.

A study of the great Adirondack anorthosite mass and its bordering rocks led Buddington (1939) to the concept that the rock had formed from a magma intruded into older rocks of sedimentary origin. This was based on the general uniformity of composition, the occurrence of rotated angular inclusions of country rock within the anorthosite, of local garnet and pyroxene aggregates in marble of the wall rock that could be appropriately interpreted as introduced by magmatic solutions, and of sheets of anorthosite isolated within the country rock. At the time the hypothesis of magmatic origin was proposed, the available experimental physicochemical data appeared to preclude a melt of anorthositic composition at any reasonable temperature. Much later (1954, Yoder), however, experimental data showed that H_2O had an exceptionally strong effect both in lowering the melting point of a mixture of diopside and anorthite and in shifting the eutectic ratio toward anorthite. As these two compounds are the major constituents of anorthosite, and the presence of H_2O is reasonable, a probable magmatic origin was supported. Buddington also pointed out that anorthosite in general had two major types of origin, one as crystal accumulates in stratiform sheets and the other as the Adirondack

type, and that the composition of the plagioclase was in general more albitic in the latter as shown by a statistical study of the literature.

The metamorphism of sedimentary rocks is commonly assumed to proceed under conditions such that PH_2O is about equivalent to local pressure at depths of a few miles. Buddington, however, observed (1963) that anhydrous pyroxenic igneous rocks commonly gave rise to equivalent anhydrous pyroxenic gneisses; that hydrous hornblendic igneous rocks commonly yielded hydrous hornblendic gneisses; and that for such orthogneisses, as distinguished from paragneisses, the PH_2O must be considered a variable and not necessarily equal to local pressure.

The use of the compositions of coexistent pairs of titaniferous magnetite and ilmenite as a geologic thermometer stems from the work of Buddington. The history of the idea is interesting as an example of the finding of a significant principle that was completely unanticipated and quite aside from the problem being studied. During World War II Buddington was engaged in exploration for magnetite ore under the auspices of the U.S. Geological Survey. In 1945 an aeromagnetic map of the northern Adirondacks became available and was used successfully in the search for ore.

Buddington in 1949 started a systematic study of the iron-titanium oxide minerals in relation to the normal variations of the magnetic anomalies in general and to certain intense negative magnetic anomalies in particular. He at first thought that the variations in intensity might be due in part to variations in impurities in the magnetite. Magnetite concentrates were made from about 100 different rocks, and all were analyzed for titanium and some for manganese, magnesium, and vanadium. No effective correlation was found between the composition of the magnetite and the magnetic anomalies. This line of attack proved a blind alley. In the course of the work, Buddington realized that the rocks underlying the most intense magnetic anomalies carried titaniferous hematite as the exclusive iron-titanium oxide mineral. His associate, James R. Balsley, then showed that this mineral had an intense remanent magnetization with the north-seeking pole up instead of the south-seeking pole and was the cause of the negative anomaly. Further mineralogic studies and magnetic measurements showed (1958) that where both magnetite and titaniferous hematite occurred in the same rock the resultant magnetic anomaly could be positive, neutral, or negative depending on the ratio of one to the other, the magnetite tending to give a positive anomaly, the titaniferous hematite a negative anomaly. Granite of similar appearance in the field was reflected in part by positive anomalies and in part by negative anomalies. The facies giving a positive anomaly was found to have magnetite and ilmenite, and that giving a negative anomaly almost only ilmenite. It was thus concluded that in this area titaniferous members of the ilmenite-hematite series of minerals uniformly had a negatively oriented remanent magnetism and were responsible for negative anomalies.

Meanwhile Buddington felt guilty for the the work that had gone into analysis of the magnetites, apparently to no good end, and sought to see whether something worthwhile could be salvaged from the data. He explored the possibility that there might be a correlation between the percent of TiO_2 in the magnetite and the temperature at which it formed. To his delight this hypothesis seemed to have possibilities as a geologic thermometer above 600°C, and he published a paper presenting this idea in 1955. He tried to interest several workers in studying experimentally the iron-titanium oxide system, but was unsuccessful until Donald H. Lindsley, one of his former students at Princeton, completed a study at the Geophysical Laboratory. This experimental study showed that extremely small variations in oxygen pressure could cause substantial variations in the amount of TiO_2 dissolved (as Fe_2TiO_4) in magnetite for constant temperature, but did confirm that temperature was a major factor in controlling the percent of titanium compound dissolved in magnetite. The experimental data of Lindsley (1964) showed that the compositions of coexistent magnetite and ilmenite could be used as a thermometer and oxygen barometer between the temperatures of about 550 and 1100°C. Buddington had available some 35 analyzed pairs of titaniferous magnetites and ilmenites from the same host rock, and the application of the experimental data to them yielded temperatures and oxygen pressures consistent with petrologic considerations. The principle promises to be of great value in the interpretation of the conditions of formation of igneous and metamorphic rocks, since the two minerals are present in most such rocks.

A Baptist minister's son, Buddington majored in chemistry and geology at Brown University, where he received the Ph.B. in 1912 and M.Sc. in 1913, and in geology at Princeton, where he received the Ph.D. in 1916. He served successively in the Aviation Section of the Signal Corps and as sergeant first-class in the Chemical Warfare Service during 1918. In 1919–20 he worked on the synthesis of the melilite group of minerals at the Geophysical Laboratory in Washington. From 1920 to 1959 he was professor of geology at Princeton. He spent 45 summer seasons in fieldwork, largely under the auspices of the U.S. Geological Survey or the New York State Geological Survey. Buddington received the Penrose Medal of the Geological Society of America in 1950 and the Roebling Medal of the Mineralogical Society of America in 1956. He was elected to the National Academy of Sciences in 1943.

Buddington wrote *Geology and Mineral Deposits of Southeastern Alaska,* with T. Chapin (1929), *Adirondack Igneous Rocks and Their Metamorphism* (1939), and *Regional Geology of the St. Lawrence County Magnetite District,* with B. F. Leonard (1962).

For background information *see* GEOLOGIC THERMOMETRY; ILMENITE; MAGMA; MAGNETITE; PETROLOGY in the McGraw-Hill Encyclopedia of Science and Technology. ■

BUERGER, MARTIN JULIAN
★ American crystallographer and mineralogist

Born Apr. 8, 1903, Detroit, MI, U.S.A.

Many of the classical fields of science involve crystalline matter in some way, so that some chemists, physicists, mineralogists, metallurgists, and ceramists interested in crystals have been drawn from time to time into the field of crystallography. The attraction of crystallography increased especially after W. H. Bragg and W. L. Bragg showed that the arrangements of atoms in crystals can be determined by x-ray diffraction data. As a graduate student in mineralogy at the Massachusetts Institute of Technology (MIT), Buerger attended the lectures of W. L. Bragg, a visiting lecturer in 1928. He became convinced that an understanding of minerals and their interrelations must be based upon the arrangements of their atoms. *See* BRAGG, SIR (WILLIAM) LAWRENCE.

On receiving his doctorate in 1929, Buerger was appointed assistant professor of mineralogy and petrography at MIT, where he immediately established a small x-ray diffraction laboratory devoted to the study of the crystal structures of minerals. In the next few years he determined the arrangements of atoms in the minerals marcasite, löllingite, arsenopyrite, gudmundite, manganite, and valentinite, when World War II intervened. After the war he solved the structures of cubanite, berthierite, and pectolite. With the assistance of his graduate students, he unraveled the crystal structures of the minerals tourmaline, nepheline, livingstonite, jamesonite, coesite, cahnite, narsarsukite, high chalcocite, rhodizite, bustamite, and rhodonite, as well as the structures of the nonmineral crystals Co_2S_3, diglycine hydrobromide, diglycine hydrochloride, potassium hexatitanate, and terramycin. For their doctoral dissertations his students solved many more structures under his supervision.

During his early contact with x-ray diffraction, Buerger revised some of the experimental apparatus commonly used, including the powder camera. He improved the Weissenberg method and instrumentation by introducing the equi-inclination technique and devised the back-reflection Weissenberg method for obtaining precise values of cell dimensions from single

crystals. He invented the precession method for determining the unit cell and space group of a crystal. These were developments of the 1930s. In 1952 the first counter diffractometer designed especially for measuring the intensities of the diffraction from single crystals was built in Buerger's laboratory, and in 1961 this was converted into the first automated diffractometer.

During the 1930s Fourier series began to be used in crystal structure analysis, the Patterson function was discovered, and their Harker sections pointed out. During World War II Buerger developed the implication theory of interpreting Harker sections, and his results, presented immediately after the war, had an important bearing on the main problem of x-ray crystallography, known as the phase problem. The phase problem was the bottleneck in determining the arrangements of atoms in crystals. Any crystal structure can be revealed by a Fourier inversion of the amplitudes of the diffraction from the crystal. The difficulty is that the amplitudes are complex quantities, that is, each has both a magnitude and a phase. But since there exists no experimental way to measure the phase, the complex amplitudes required for the Fourier inversion are not fully available; thus the crystal structure analyst must solve his problem with only half the required data. But implication theory predicted that, for some symmetries at least, the crystal structures could be found without a knowledge of these phases, and therefore a general solution of crystal structures from experimental data could be devised in spite of the missing phases.

Another barrier found by crystallographers was Friedel's law, which states that the presence or absence of a center of symmetry cannot be determined by x-ray diffraction experiments. This situation has the same origin as the phase problem, and is a consequence of the impossibility of measuring phases. But that this was not wholly true should have been evident when Paul Niggli showed that space groups are characterized by systematic absences (called extinctions) of certain classes of reflections. Buerger contributed to space group classification by the invention of the diffraction symbol, which concentrated all diffraction information in a short list. By tabulating these symbols for all space groups, it was obvious that 58 of the 230 space groups could be unambiguously identified by simple qualitative means. Later, when he presented implication theory, he showed that if quantitative measurement of diffraction intensities were used, all space groups could be identified, except for separating the members of the 11 enantiomorphic pairs. This work (which was confirmed 4 years later in a statistical study by A. J. C. Wilson) succeeded in breaking the blocking effect of Friedel's law.

With the war over, Buerger, like many other crystallographers, turned his attention to the phase problem. Basing his approach on the notion of an image, as suggested by Dorothy Wrinch, he developed the image theory of the Patterson function, discovered the basic image locations theorem, invented image-seeking functions to search the Patterson function for the solution of the crystal structure, and established the basis for the present-day methods of solving crystal structures which make use of the Patterson function. The first structure to be solved by the new theory was that of the orthorhombic mineral berthierite, $FeSb_2S_4$, which in 1950 yielded to the new attack in a few hours.

Although Buerger made significant contributions to the theory of finding the arrangements of atoms in crystals and to the instrumentation used in gathering data for determing these arrangements, he regarded the field of crystal structure analysis chiefly as a necessary step in furnishing data for the explanation of crystal relations and behavior. He contributed to this larger objective in his discovery and explanation of lineage structure (an imperfection which arises during crystal growth) and in his development of general theories of polymorphism and twinning.

The great grandson of Ernst Moritz Buerger, one of the Lutheran clergy who led the Saxon migration to the United States in 1838, Buerger did his undergraduate work in mining engineering at MIT, receiving his B.S. in 1925. He also received his M.S. (1927) and Ph.D. (1929) at MIT, where he remained as a member of the faculty. His early work was in geology. He mapped parts of central Newfoundland in 1928–29 and was a member of the MacMillan Arctic Expedition of 1938. His former students and associates honored him with a Festschrift in the *Zeitschrift für Kristallographie* in 1938 (and again with a Festband in 1973). Buerger received the Day Medal of the Geological Society of America in 1951, the Roebling Medal of the Mineralogical Society of America in 1958 and the Isador Fankuchen Award of the American Crystallographic Association in 1971. He was elected to the National Academy of Sciences in 1953 and to many foreign societies and academies of science. In 1958 he received an honorary doctorate from the University of Bern. Buerger Bay, in the Canadian Arctic, and the mineral buergerite were named in his honor.

On reaching age 65, Buerger, an Institute Professor at MIT from 1956, retired with the title of Institute Professor Emeritus. Although permitted to teach on a half-time basis, he lost his unique laboratory, so he accepted a half-time appointment as Distinguished Professor at the University of Connecticut in the department of geology and the Institute of Materials Science. After 1973 he continued working there with graduate students on a part-time basis as professor emeritus. During this period he was able to advance the understanding of homometric sets by developing the theory of tautoeikonic sets (two different Patterson functions with the same self-image). Some of this work was done at Harvard while he was honorary research associate in the department of geological sciences.

Buerger was coeditor of the *Zeitschrift für Kristallographie* and the *International Tables for Crystallography*. He wrote *X-ray Crystallography* (1942); *Elementary Crystallography* (1956; rev. ed. 1963); *The Powder Method,* with Leonid V. Azaroff (1958); *Vector Space* (1959); *Crystal-Structure Analysis* (1960); *The Precession Method in X-ray Crystallography* (1964); *Contemporary Crystallography* (1970); *Introduction to Crystal Geometry* (1971); and *The Lave Method,* with J. L. Amorós and M. C. de Amorós (1975). He also contributed over 200 articles to journals.

For background information *see* CRYSTAL STRUCTURE; CRYSTALLOGRAPHY; X-RAY CRYSTALLOGRAPHY; X-RAY DIFFRACTION in the McGraw-Hill Encyclopedia of Science and Technology ∎

BULLARD, SIR EDWARD (CRISP)
★ British geophysicist

Born Sept. 21, 1907, Norwich, England

For most of his life Bullard worked on physical problems connected with the Earth, particularly on the geology of the ocean floor and on the origin of the Earth's magnetic field. As a young man, he

worked in E. Rutherford's laboratory on the scattering of slow electrons in gases, but in 1931 difficulty in getting a job caused him to abandon atomic physics and to accept a post in the department of geodesy and geophysics at Cambridge University. There he started work on the measurement of gravity and carried out a gravity survey in East Africa. He also worked on explosion seismology and mapped the thickness of the unconsolidated sediments overlying the Paleozoic basement in eastern England.

In 1937 he was persuaded by Richard Field of Princeton that the major gap in the knowledge of the Earth was an almost complete ignorance of the geology of the oceans. Field introduced Bullard to Maurice Ewing, who had begun the development of seismic methods at sea which subsequently proved so fruitful. Bullard accompanied Ewing on a cruise in 1937 and started similar work in England. In the 2 years remaining before the outbreak of World War II, he and his collaborators measured the thickness of the sediments under the continental shelf south of Ireland. They found that the basement sloped downward to the continental edge, where it was overlain by many thousands of feet of sediments. These results were similar to those obtained by Ewing off the eastern coast of North America. Such sedimentary basins later became a major source of oil. *See* EWING, WILLIAM MAURICE.

In 1939 Bullard left geophysics to work with the British Navy. At first he was in charge of the development of methods for the demagnetization of ships to protect them from magnetic mines. Later he was head of the group responsible for the development of methods of sweeping magnetic and acoustic mines. In 1941 he joined Patrick Blackett, who had established an operations analysis group in the Admiralty. He stayed with this group for the rest of the war, but during 1943–45 his main concern was with the development of the German V weapons, the V2 rocket and the flying bomb, and with the countermeasures to them. *See* BLACKETT, PATRICK MAYNARD STUART.

In 1945 Bullard returned to Cambridge as a reader in geophysics and, with a group of graduate students, renewed work on the problems that had been abandoned in 1939. Substantial progress was made, but in 1948 the difficulties of working in Cambridge seemed so severe that he accepted the post of head of the physics department of the University of Toronto. In 1949 he visited the Scripps Institution of Oceanography in La Jolla, CA, and with Arthur Maxwell, developed a method of measuring the flow of heat through the ocean floor. Several thousand measurements were made in the ensuing years by others, and the results proved illuminating in understanding the mechanism which drives the motions seen at the surface of the Earth.

Before leaving Cambridge, Bullard had become interested in the origin of the Earth's magnetic field, originally stimulated by his work on magnetic mines. While in Canada, he decided to investigate the possibility that the field was produced by a dynamo within the Earth. This had been suggested long before by Sir Joseph Larmor and had been studied further by T. G. Cowling and Walter Elsasser. In 1949 electronic computers were beginning to become available, and Bullard decided to attempt numerical computations which would show that a specific motion of the fluid material in the core of the Earth would act as a dynamo. *See* ELSASSER, WALTER MAURICE.

In 1950, before these calculations were beyond the planning stage, Bullard became director of the National Physical Laboratory in England. There he was occupied mainly with supervising the laboratory, but he also found time to continue his work on both the dynamo theory and the measurement of the flow of heat through the sea floor.

In 1956 Bullard returned to Cambridge, and after a few years resumed his old post as head of the department of geodesy and geophysics, and in 1964 became professor of geophysics. He retired in 1974. This last period in Cambridge saw the rapid development of ideas about continental drift, sea-floor spreading, and the production of new sea floor along the crests of the midocean ridges, which became known as plate tectonics. The staff in Bullard's department, particularly Maurice Hill, D. H. Matthews, and F. Vine, played a large part in these developments. Bullard supported and encouraged the work and, with J. E. Everett and A. G. Smith, wrote a paper showing how surprisingly accurately the continents bordering the Atlantic can be fitted together. This paper came at just the right time to influence waverers, and it played a part in establishing plate tectonics as the generally accepted cause of the development of the oceans.

During this time Bullard spent much of his time on other matters. He chaired the Anglo-American Ballistic Missile Committee, served on many advisory committees concerning the Navy, was involved in disarmament negotiations at Geneva, and was a director of IBM (U.K.).

After retiring from Cambridge in 1974, he moved to the Scripps Institution at La Jolla, where he was a professor and where he had spent parts of many summers. He became interested in the disposal of nuclear waste and also continued his work on the origin of the Earth's magnetic field and on the problems of the sea floor. He presented a course, "The Nature of the Earth," designed primarily for nonscientists.

Bullard was the son of an English brewer. He received the B.A. (1929) and the Ph.D. (1932) degrees from Cambridge. He was elected a fellow of the Royal Society (1941), a foreign associate of the U.S. National Academy of Sciences (1959), and a member of many other societies, including the American Academy of Arts and Sciences (1954) and the American Philosophical Society (1969). He received many medals and awards, including the Agassiz Medal of the National Academy (1965), the Vetlesen Prize (1968), and the Royal Medal of the Royal Society (1975).

For background information *see* CONTINENT FORMATION; GEOMAGNETISM; MARINE GEOLOGY; MARINE SEDIMENTS in the McGraw-Hill Encyclopedia of Science and Technology. ∎

BULLEN, KEITH EDWARD
★ Australian applied mathematician

Born June 29, 1906, Auckland, New Zealand
Died Sept. 23, 1976, Sydney, Australia

Bullen's principal contributions to scientific knowledge arose in the first instance through his mathematical studies of earthquake waves. As an auxiliary to investigating the effect of the Earth's ellipticity of figure on the travel times of earthquake waves, he derived for the first time (1936) reliable values of the density inside the Earth down to a depth of 5000 kilometers and set a lower bound of 12.3 grams per cubic centimeter to the central density. He later refined and extended the original calculations and applied the results to many geophysical and planetary problems.

The work on density carried with it correspondingly reliable determinations of the distributions inside the Earth of pressure, of the principal elastic properties (compressibility and rigidity), and of the gravitational intensity. Bullen was able to infer that the Earth's inner core (of radius about 1200 kilometers) is solid, and he found empirically a connection between compressibility and pressure for materials at pressures of the order of 1,000,000 atmospheres (10^5 megapascals). Relevant parts of the work up to 1950 were incorporated in two Earth models, A and B, which have been much used in geophysics. Bullen also introduced (1940–42) the nomenclature A, B, C, . . . G, which has been widely used for internal layers of the Earth. After 1950, he strengthened the evidence on solidity in the inner core and in 1964 adduced evidence to show that after an initial change from fluidity to solidity at a certain depth inside the core, there is a likely trend back toward fluidity as the depth further increases. He also applied the results to questions of the internal structures of the inner planets Mars, Venus, and Mercury, and proposed a new mechanism concerning the origin of the Moon.

In the original density calculations, Bullen combined data from earthquakes with data from geophysical laboratory experiments and other sources. An important innovation, enabling him to set close bounds to the density values, was the application of a moment of inertia criterion to internal spheres of the Earth. The criterion enabled him (among other things) to show conclusively that there are significant departures from uniform chemical composition (or, alternatively, phase changes) inside the Earth's mantle between crust and core. He evolved a direct method of estimating density gradients in chemically inhomogeneous regions of the Earth's deep interior. His assessment of the accuracy of his results on density, pressure, and elasticity as within 5 percent or less at all depths down to 5000 kilometers was substantiated when long-period fundamental oscillations of the whole Earth were recorded from the Chilean earthquakes of May 1960.

Other contributions include his early work in collaboration with Sir Harold Jeffreys (who was his teacher and great source of inspiration) on seismic travel-time tables, culminating in the Jeffreys-Bullen tables of 1940, which have been since used in preparing the International Seismological Summary. Bullen was responsible also for the tables that give the corrections due to the Earth's ellipticity. He wrote numerous papers on other aspects of theoretical geophysics, especially on seismic-ray theory, and on local seismological problems, for example, in New Zealand. See JEFFREYS, SIR HAROLD.

Of Irish-English parentage (his father's father having come from Trinity College, Dublin, in the 1870s to be headmaster of a Church of England school in Nelson, New Zealand), Bullen obtained master and doctor degrees from the universities of Auckland, Melbourne, and Cambridge (England). He started work as a secondary-school teacher in Auckland, lectured in mathematics at Auckland, Melbourne, and Hull (England), and in 1946 accepted the chair of applied mathematics in the University of Sydney, Australia. Among other honors, Bullen received the William Bowie Medal of the American Geophysical Union in 1961, the Arthur L. Day Medal of the Geological Society of America in 1963, and the Gold Medal of the Royal Astronomical Society in 1974. He was elected a foreign associate of the U.S. National Academy of Sciences in 1961.

Bullen wrote *Theory of Seismology* (1947; 3d ed. 1963), *Seismology* (1954), *Theory of Mechanics* (1949; 8th ed. 1971), and *The Earth's Density* (1975).

For background information *see* EARTH, INTERIOR OF; SEISMOLOGY in the McGraw-Hill Encyclopedia of Science and Technology. ∎

BURCH, CECIL REGINALD
☆ British physicist

Born May 12, 1901, Oxford, England

While working in the research department of Metropolitan-Vickers Company, Manchester, in 1927, Burch carried out a single experiment in vacuum distillation that had peculiarly far-reaching consequences. He was asked to try impregnating with transformer oil, in a very much better vacuum than usual, the pressboard used to insulate transformers. It was hoped that the dielectric strength would be improved in this way. Burch doubted whether this would happen—air is soluble in transformer oil—and, in fact, it did not. Then he was asked to steam-jacket the impregnator. This made nonsense of any attempt to get a really good vacuum, for the vapor pressue of oil is high enough to cause visible clouds of mist to form above a testing tank at less than 100°C. A vacuum would not be obtained until all the oil had distilled away down the pump. How much more interesting, he thought, to do some vacuum distillation of organic materials.

Burch set up a vacuum still analogous to the apparatus with which George de Hevesy had separated the isotopes of mercury. An electrically heated copper tray, 2.5×15 centimeters, 1 centimeter deep, filled with distilland to ½-centimeter depth, was supported inside a sloping water-cooled condensing roof, so that the maximum distance from the liquid surface to condensing roof was about 3 centimeters. This tube was exhausted by a mercury condensation pump—without a tray to freeze out the 1 microbar (dyne/square centimeter) residual vapor pressure of mercury at water-cooling temperature that such a pump cannot remove. The justification for leaving out the cold tray was that the average vapor molecule would have a free path a few centimeters long in the residual mercury vapor, so that a fraction of the order of $1 - 1/e$, or say about two-thirds, of the vapor molecules would pass to the condensing surface without let or hindrance from the mercury vapor. Thus, however low the vapor pressure of the distilland might be, distillation would take place at, say, two-thirds of the rate it would go at in a perfect vacuum. *See* HEVESY, GEORGE DE.

Under these conditions there is no such thing as the "boiling point." Distillation takes place at a rate proportional to the vapor pressure and to the square root of the molecular weight. If vapor molecules do not bounce when they hit the liquid they come from, but are recondensed, vapor is created moving away from the liquid surface with one-fourth of mean molecular velocity. A simple calculation shows that, for a molecular weight of a few hundred, Burch's tray would give about four drops/minute of distillate for 1 microbar vapor pressure. Translated into other terms—1 square yard of evaporating surface would give about 1 ton of distillate per 24 hours at 1 microbar vapor pressure.

If Burch had used a conventional dis-

tilling apparatus in which the vapor had to travel, say, 10 centimeters down a tube 1 centimeter in diameter to reach the condensing surface, the distillation rate would have been about 400 times smaller than with his still, and temperatures of the order of 100°C higher would have been necessary to give distillation at the same rate. So it was reasonable to expect that many organic substances normally regarded as not distillable without decomposition could be distilled unchanged in this still.

Burch started by distilling the oil used in the rotary pump that produced the 10-microbar or so "backing pressure" for the condensation pump. After part had distilled off, it required 120°C to make it distill at four drops/minute; that is, it had at 120°C the same vapor pressure as mercury at room temperature. Clearly, if this oil would stand boiling at a pressure high enough—say 100 microbar—one could reasonably expect an oil condensation pump to work and produce vacuums of perhaps 10^{-3} microbar, with water-cooling only.

And this worked. The first oil condensation pump gave 10^{-3} microbar without difficulty, a pressure low enough for high-power triodes. The undistillable residue at 300°C from petrolatum could be expected to be a suitable sealing grease for the ground joints—and this proved to be the case.

Oil condensation pumps were used immediately by T. E. Allibone in the Cavendish Laboratory to evacuate his 350-kilovolt Lenard tube, and the Cockcroft double rectifiers to feed it. With this apparatus J. D. Cockcroft and E. T. S. Walton achieved the first artificial disintegration not involving the use of radioactive material.

Burch's colleagues F. E. Bancroft, G. Burrows, L. H. J. Phillips, J. H. Ludlow, F. Taylor, his brother F. P. Burch, J. M. Dodds, and others made high-power demountable triodes and tetrodes. The latter, developed by Dodds, were used in the early 5-meter radar stations that played a critical part in the Battle of Britain. *See* COCKCROFT, SIR JOHN (DOUGLAS); WALTON, ERNEST THOMAS SINTON.

Burch measured the ultimate vacuum the pumps would make and got 10^{-4} microbar. Many years later, he communicated to the Royal Society the paper of J. Blears of Metropolitan-Vickers, who

showed that he was wrong: 10^{-3} was right. Burch had, in fact, got 10^{-4}, but he had got it by cleanup, and failed to realize this. (10^{-4} is now got by improvements in the oil.)

Burch found that oils not normally regarded as distillable could be distilled without decomposition—olive oil, arachis oil, and waxes such as beeswax. Carr and Jewel, with one of his stills, found that not only vitamin D but also the very much less volatile vitamin A could be distilled without decomposition.

Unknown to Burch, K. C. D. Hickman at Rochester had been led by a different chain of industrial events to the same idea of using organic fluids—dibutyl phthalate, and later butyl benzyl phthalate—in condensation pumps, and to the same general ideas about the distillation of organic compounds. Hickman created a complete new industry—the concentration of vitamins on a large scale. Meanwhile, E. O. Lawrence used oil condensation pumps to evacuate his cyclotron, and many of the vacuum devices used to produce high-energy particles today are pumped in this way. *See* LAWRENCE, ERNEST ORLANDO.

Later in his career Burch became interested in other areas. For example, he published papers on the reflecting microscope and methods to test it. In 1973 he wrote an article on nonparametric test statistics.

Burch received his B.A. and Ph.D. at Cambridge University, where he was a member of Gonville and Caius College. From 1923 to 1933 he was employed as a physicist in the research department of Metropolitan-Vickers Company in Manchester. He held a Leverhulme fellowship in optics at the Imperial College of Science and Technology in 1933–35. Thereafter he was connected with the H. H. Wills Physics Laboratory of Bristol University, as a research associate (1936–44), fellow (1944–48), and Warren Research Fellow in Physics (after 1948). At Bristol he studied the optics of nonspherical surfaces and built the first Schwarzschild–aplanatic-aspheric reflecting microscope. Elected a fellow of the Royal Society in 1944, he was awarded the society's Rumford Medal in 1954 "in recognition of his distinguished contributions to the technique for the production of high vacua and to the development of the reflecting microscope."

For background information *see* DISTILLATION; VACUUM PUMP in the McGraw-Hill Encyclopedia of Science and Technology. ∎

BURG, ANTON BEHME
★ American chemist

Born Oct. 18, 1904, Dallas City, IL, U.S.A.

During Burg's long career he pioneered in various aspects of inorganic or pseudoorganic chemistry that grew to importance. Basic to his research were the precise high-vacuum methods first elaborated by Alfred Stock, methods to which he added many devices, procedures, and improvements.

For their work Burg and his students used very small quantities of rare and reactive compounds, thus exploring new areas of chemistry—some of which became practical textbook lore. A major purpose was to find new chemical situations requiring new thoughts about the behavior and character of bonding electrons. The initial experiments usually were based upon fairly conventional expectations, but keen observation often brought unexpected results and novel chemistry.

Burg's Ph.D. dissertation (University of Chicago, 1931) was a model of unexpected results: while trying to make pure boron from boron trichloride and hydrogen in an electric arc, he observed in the residual boron chloride a spontaneously flammable component. This led to an efficient new method of synthesis of diborane (B_2H_6)—the first American work on the previously almost unavailable boron hydrides. It was altogether unexpected that such an unstable compound could be made in an electric discharge; only years later was it discovered that the initial product was B_2Cl_4, rapidly seizing H_2 to make $HBCl_2$, and converting finally to BCl_3 and B_2H_6.

From 1931 to 1939 Burg was an instructor at Chicago, developing diborane chemistry more fully and training students in high-vacuum methods and the relevant chemistry, with moral and financial support from H. I. Schlesinger. Since all of the higher polyboranes could be made from diborane, the whole subject became accessible. Emphasis was placed upon the dissociation of diborane to make BH_3 complexes. These complexes were divided sharply into two classes: polar and nonpolar.

The polar type, such as $(CH_3)_3N \cdot BH_3$ and $(CH_3)_2NH \cdot BH_3$, formed very rapidly, had slight volatility, and reacted easily as sources of hydride ion. With a proton on the base atom, such complexes could lose hydrogen to form derivatives of BH_3, a process akin to that occurring when transitory complexes serve as reaction intermediates in organic S_N2 reactions. The conversion of $(CH_3)_2PH \cdot BH_3$ at 150°C to the surprisingly stable and inert dative-bonded ring compound shown in formula (I) had long-term consequences.

$$H_2B \leftarrow P(CH_3)_2$$
$$(CH_3)_2P \qquad BH_2 \qquad (I)$$
$$H_2B \rightarrow P(CH_3)_2$$

Thus the staff of the U.S. Office of Naval Research (ONR) began to think that a heat-resistant plastic might be made from a boron hydride; ONR support ultimately resulted in just such a development, for the polyhedral closo-carboranes $C_2B_nH_{n+2}$ were discovered and inserted into silicone chains to make rubbers suitable for use at −50 to 400°C.

Another important consequence of polar BH_3 complexes was hydroboration. In 1934 Burg tried diborane with acetaldehyde, acetone, and methyl formate, obtaining $(RO)_2BH$ compounds by hydridic reduction. A mechanism was explored by H. C. Brown; it was indicated that $(CH_3)_2CO \cdot BH_3$ at −78° C was formed and was converted to $(CH_3)_2CHOBH_2$, and so on. Brown developed the method and published a book on the subject that was of great value to organic chemistry. *See* BROWN, HERBERT CHARLES.

The first nonpolar BH_3 complex, BH_3CO, came in 1936, when Burg tried to hydroborate CO. In this complex and in analogs such as BH_3PF_3, weak electron-donor bonding by CO or PF_3 is enhanced by the return of B-H bonding electrons to the pi orbitals of C or P; thus the B-H electrons act like the metal *d* electrons in transition-element carbonyls. Such complexes formed slowly, were unusually volatile, and lacked hydridic reactivity. Kinetic studies of the dissociation of BH_3CO and BH_3PF_3 led to a highly dependable value for the energy of dissociation of B_2H_6 to $2BH_3$. Also, BH_3CO and BD_3CO were used in microwave spectroscopic studies which resulted in the discovery that the spin of ^{10}B is 3.

Before Burg's work, students were taught that hydrides of beryllium, magnesium, zinc, and aluminum never could exist. In 1931, however, he found the first evidence of a stable Zn-H bond (understood in 1938 as $HZnBH_4$), thus providing a basis for R. T. Sanderson's discovery (1938) of $Al(BH_4)_3$. This led to a sizable development of hydrides of such metals and to the commercial availability of boron hydrides.

Also during his Chicago period, Burg (with N. V. Thornton) scrambled Freon 12 (Cl_2CF_2) in an electric discharge, deriving products undoubtedly including Cl-C-F polymers at a time (1932) when industrial leaders regarded all such polymers as useless. He also made the first volatile boroxine, shown in formula (II),

$$H_3C-B-O$$
$$O \qquad B-CH_3 \qquad (II)$$
$$H_3C-B-O$$

containing the ring later found to be basic to the structures of borate minerals.

Moving to the University of Southern California in 1939, Burg expanded his research to include unusual donor-acceptor bonding, aprotic ionizing solvents, more fluorine chemistry (for example, in war research, the formation of SF_5Cl and the existence of ONF_3), bonding effects of element–*d* orbitals above the valence shell, and transition-element carbonyl analogs; for example, his student J. C. Dayton (1947) used KCN for the first reversible displacement of CO from $Ni(CO)_4$. Burg became the world leader in the chemistry of CF_3 phosphines, often reversing the rules usually applied to organophosphines and providing strong impetus to the study of the homocyclic polyphosphines (RP)$_n$, and suggesting a new look at the structures of arsenical drugs. His work on new inorganic rings brought him acclaim as an expert on inorganic polymers.

In 1969 Burg received the American Chemical Society (ACS) Award for Distinguished Service in the Advancement of Inorganic Chemistry, having previously received the Tolman Medal from the Southern California Section of the ACS (1962) and the University of Southern California Associates Award for Creative Scholarship (1964–65). Burg was a plenary lecturer at four international meetings (17th Congress of the International Union of Pure and Applied Chemistry, Munich, 1959; Symposium on Boron Chemistry, Chemical Society of London, Liverpool, 1961; International Symposium on Inorganic Polymers, Nottingham, 1961; Robert A. Welch Foundation Conference on Chemical Research, Houston, 1962) and served on three government advisory panels (Office of Naval Research Panel on Inorganic Chemistry, 1948–51; Chemistry Panel for the National Science Foundation, 1956–59; Committee on Inorganic Chemistry for the National Research Council, 1960). He was a fellow and 50-year member of the American Association for the Advancement of Science and was a local leader in the ACS and the American Association of University Professors. He served as head of the chemistry department at the University of Southern California during 1940–50.

For background information *see* BORON; FLUORINE; HYDRIDE; ORGANIC CHEMICAL SYNTHESIS in the McGraw-Hill Encyclopedia of Science and Technology. ∎

BURKITT, DENIS P.

★ Irish surgeon and epidemiologist

Born Feb. 28, 1911, Enniskillen, Ireland

In 1957, while working as a surgeon at Makerere College Medical School in Uganda, Burkitt recognized the similarities in a number of supposedly different tumors in children. He observed that two or more of these tumors developing in certain characteristic sites, such as the jaws orbits, ovaries, kidneys, liver, testicles, and skeleton, were often found coexistent in the same patient. In fact,

careful clinical investigation revealed that the tumors were usually multiple. This observation refuted the existing concept that they were different forms of cancer, and Burkitt was convinced that these clinically different tumors were in fact merely different manifestations of the same tumor process. He then showed that the age distribution of the different tumors was similar. Later epidemiological studies throughout Africa showed that in different situations all the tumors were either common or rare—observations which supported the concept that they were manifestations of a single disease.

This theory was subsequently confirmed by the work of J. N. P. Davies and G. O'Connor, who established the fact that the histological characteristics of the different tumors were identical and that the tumors were composed of lymphoid cells, and later by D. H. Wright, who identified the tumor as a distinct form of lymphoma distinguishable by histological and cytological criteria from other forms.

Burkitt made a detailed study of the distribution of the tumor first by written correspondence and later by extensive personal travel, and related its occurrence to climatic factors of temperature and rainfall, showing that areas in which the tumor was endemic were always warm and wet. A similar relationship between tumor and climate was observed in New Guinea. These observations led to the hypothesis that an insect vector might be responsible for the transmission of the caus-

ative agent, which was postulated to be a virus. Although many animal cancers were by that time known to be virus-induced, no human tumor had as yet been shown to be so caused. The search for such a virus led to the discovery of the now famous Epstein-Barr (EB) virus by the British virologists M. A. Epstein and E. Barr. At a conference held in Paris in January 1963, scientists from many countries met to discuss the nature of the peculiar tumor so commonly observed in tropical Africa. In the absence of general agreement on its pathological nature, they decided that it should be referred to simply as Burkitt's tumor. In time the nondescriptive term "tumor" was with universal agreement changed to the specific histological designation "lymphoma." The EB virus, discovered first in Burkitt's lymphoma, was later shown to be the cause of infectious mononucleosis (glandular fever), and was also found to be closely associated with the commonest cancer affecting men in Southeast Asia, nasopharyngeal cancer. Later it became evident that the distribution of EB virus was ubiquitous and that some cofactor had to be sought to account for the peculiar distribution of the tumor. This distribution was shown to coincide closely with that of holoendemic malaria, a disease that can, in this form, weaken immunological mechanisms including, possibly, those against certain cancers.

In the absence of radiotherapy in Uganda, Burkitt tested the effect of various cytotoxic drugs on the African tumor and found them to be remarkably effective. So sensitive was the tumor to these drugs that a high proportion of patients could be cured. (No other tumor responds to chemotherapy so dramatically.) This high cure rate was found to be partly due to the fact that tumor cells were easily killed and partly to the fact that the patient had mechanisms which could deal with the remaining cells. These observations provided a stimulus to research in leukemia, chemotherapy, and immunological aspects of cancer.

Later Burkitt used a similar approach in mapping the distribution of other forms of cancer.

After he returned to England in 1966, Burkitt was introduced to the work of T. L. Cleave, which suggested that many of the commonest diseases in Western countries were rare in less economically developed countries, and that the refining of carbohydrate foods was a major causative factor. Burkitt, with his extensive contacts in Africa and elsewhere, was able to confirm the disease distribution patterns on which Cleave had based his hypothesis, and provided massive epidemiological evidence in support of the concept that the removal of fiber in the processing of Western foods was a major cause of much disease.

Burkitt, in association with A. R. P. Walker in South Africa, studied the relationship between the amount of stool passed daily, and the time it takes food digesta to traverse the digestive tract, and the frequency of various characteristically Western diseases. He produced epidemiological evidence to suggest that such common diseases as diverticular disease of the colon (following the work of N. S. Painter), appendicitis, hiatus hernia, varicose veins and piles, and large bowel cancer may be in part the result of fiber-depleted diets. In all this work he collaborated closely with his physician friend of former Uganda days, H. C. Trowell.

Burkitt received his M.D. degree from Trinity College (Dublin) in 1935. After 5 years of postgraduate surgical training, he spent 5 years as an army surgeon during World War II and then 20 years as a surgeon in Uganda, working primarily at Makerere College Medical School. He was a member of the External Scientific Staff of the Medical Research Council of England for 12 years.

Burkitt edited *Burkitt's Lymphoma* D. H. Wright (1970) and *Refined Carbohydrate Foods and Disease* with H. C. Trowell (1975).

For background information *see* EPSTEIN-BARR VIRUS; LYMPHOMA; ONCOLOGY in the McGraw-Hill Encyclopedia of Science and Technology. ∎

BURN, JOSHUA HAROLD
★ British pharmacologist

***Born** Mar. 6, 1892, Barnard Castle, Durham, England*

Entering Cambridge University as a student of chemistry, Burn was to find his life's interest after witnessing experimental demonstrations of physiological processes, as conducted by Joseph Barcroft. In 1914 Burn began working under H. H. Dale and further pursued his study of pharmacology. *See* DALE, SIR HENRY (HALLETT).

Having learned from Dale how to perfuse organs removed from the body, he began to study the properties of tyramine, formed by decarboxylization of the amino acid tyrosine. At that time tyramine was considered a vasoconstrictor. Burn soon discovered that this so-called property of constricting blood vessels vanished when tyramine was injected into blood vessels perfused with blood by a pump instead of by the heart. However, in 1930, he found that tyramine's vasoconstrictor effect was restored when adrenaline (epinephrine) was added to the perfusing blood. This led him to prove that tyramine itself had little or no constrictor action but displaced adrenaline from blood vessel walls, and when the adrenaline entered the blood it caused vasoconstriction. In 1958, with M. J. Rand, he showed that this displacement mechanism also acted to release noradrenaline (norepinephrine). He had further demonstrated in 1932 that sympathetic nerve endings in blood vessels could take up adrenaline from the blood. This led in 1958 to his demonstration, again with Rand, that sympathetic nerve endings could take up noradrenaline, as well as liberate noradrenaline when they were stimulated. This finding was the origin of all the research on uptake which was done in the 1960s.

Using E. H. Starling's experimental heart-lung preparation of the dog, along

with E. M. Vaughan Williams and J. M. Walker, Burn began to study the effect of infusing acetylcholine at a slow and steady rate into the atria of the heart. He found that when the atria were briefly stimulated at a frequency of 14 impulses per second during such an infusion, atrial fibrillation was produced which continued until the infusion was stopped. At that point normal atrial rhythm returned. They had found a method of producing atrial fibrillation at will and of maintaining it for as long as desired. It could be started or stopped as often as 10 times in a single experiment. With other colleagues Burn next studied ventricular fibrillation. They found that fibrillation in all cases arose when the refractory period was very short, and when the heart fibers were made to contract asynchronously by a rapid rate of stimulation. They thus showed that fibrillation resulted from fibers stimulating each other. During the course of this work it was also demonstrated that the normal beating heart liberates both acetylcholine and catecholamines. Analyzing the physiologic function of the former, they found that when acetylcholine was not formed, or formed in too small an amount, the transmembrane potential fell to a point where impulses could no longer be propagated. The fall in the potential in the absence of acetylcholine was due to a fall in the permeability of the membrane to potassium ions, so that repolarization became impossible.

A third investigation by Burn concerned the mechanism of the release of noradrenaline from the sympathetic postganglionic fiber. For more than 50 years physiologists believed that the nerve impulses released noradrenaline directly. With Rand, Burn succeeded in establishing the view that the mechanism closely resembled that for the release of catecholamines from the adrenal medulla. The nerve impulse releases acetylcholine, which leaves the fiber. It next acts on the outside of the fiber, rendering it permeable to calcium ions. These ions then enter the fiber and release noradrenaline.

After World War I service in France, Burn did clinical work at Guy's Hospital, London, in 1918–20, then returned to research on biological standardization under H. H. Dale during 1920–25 and received his M.D. in 1925. From 1926 to 1937 he was director of the pharmacological laboratory of the Pharmaceutical Society in London. In 1937 he was appointed professor of pharmacology at Oxford University, a post he held until 1959, when he became emeritus professor of pharmacology. In 1959 he was named visiting professor to Washington University in St. Louis. Elected a fellow of the Royal Society of London in 1942, Burn in 1960 received a Gairdner Foundation Award.

Burn wrote *Biological Standardization* (1937), *Lecture Notes on Pharmacology* (1948; 11th ed. 1971), and *Autonomic Nervous System* (1963; 5th ed. 1975).

For background information *see* ACETYLCHOLINE; EPINEPHRINE; SYMPATHETIC NERVOUS SYSTEM in the McGraw-Hill Encyclopedia of Science and Technology. ∎

BURNET, SIR (FRANK) MACFARLANE
★ Australian immunologist

Born Sept. 3, 1899, Traralgon, Victoria, Australia

When his main work was on the growth of influenza virus strains in chick embryos and on their epidemiological and immunological behavior, Burnet developed the concept that the normal components of the body do not provoke antibody or other immune reactions because, during embryonic life, the body develops a tolerance to any potentially antigenic substance then present. He predicted that tolerance could be established experimentally, and this was achieved a year or two later by a group led by P. B. Medawar. For this development, Burnet and Medawar shared the Nobel Prize in phys-

iology and medicine for 1960. *See* MEDAWAR, PETER BRIAN.

From 1933 onward, Burnet was primarily concerned with the use of the chick embryo in the egg as a means of cultivating and studying viruses. This led to a growing interest in the special character of the embryo by which it seemed to have no power to resist virus infection or to produce antibody against the viruses. Two observations by others brought this interest into definite focus: (1) E. Traub, working at the Rockefeller Institute, had found that a certain virus of mice could infect the young in the uterus without obvious harm. The mice developed normally after birth but carried large amounts of virus in their tissues for the rest of their lives. (2) At the University of Wisconsin, Ray Owen showed in 1946 that twin calves could interchange blood groups through a common placental circulation in the uterus and that they maintained such a mixture of genetically distinct bloods through life.

In both cases the foreign antigen, Traub's lymphocytic choriomeningitis (LCM) virus or the red blood cells of the other calf in Owen's work, would have provoked a typical immune response if it had been introduced for the first time in an adult recipient. This seemed to throw light on the old problem of why, although an animal's cells—red blood cells, for instance—will usually provoke antibodies in other species and sometimes even in other individuals of the same species, they never do so in the animal itself. Obviously, an animal must not destroy its own cells, but the means by which it can recognize the difference between what is its own and what is foreign and therefore to be destroyed is by no means obvious. Most of Burnet's work was at the theoretical level and was dominated throughout by the problem of the recognition of "self" from "not-self."

Early attempts in Burnet's own laboratory to use the chick embryo to show that tolerance could be produced artificially against standard antigens failed, for reasons that can now be understood. Medawar succeeded by applying the technique of skin transplantation rather than by looking for the presence or absence of antibodies. If, to a newborn mouse of strain A, Medawar gave an adequate number of spleen cells from strain B mice, he found that a few weeks later the treated A mouse would retain indefinitely a skin graft of B that would otherwise be rapidly rejected. Beginning in 1957, Burnet's work in

theoretical immunology was dominated by the concept of clonal selection which he developed at that time. This was a quite controversial approach in claiming that antigen had no capacity to induce antibody formation, but rather selected those potential antibody-producing cells whose antibody specificity was such as could react with the antigen. Contact of the antigen with the selected cell stimulated it to proliferate, resulting in a clone of cells, each capable of producing the same specific type of antibody. After 10 years of controversy, clonal selection has remained central to immunological theory and has played a major role in leading experimental immunology to a concentration on genetic and somatic genetic factors.

After his retirement from the directorship of the Hall Institute in 1965, Burnet wrote extensively on theoretical aspects of oncology, immunity, and aging. His most important contribution in this period probably was to suggest the accumulation of genetic errors in somatic cells as the basis of aging. The rate of accumulation of errors is related to the error proneness of the enzyme complexes responsible for controlling deoxyribonucleic acid replication and repair.

Burnet was born in a small Australian country town, a son of the local bank manager. He completed his medical course at Melbourne University in 1923 and spent 2 years at the Lister Institute, London, where he obtained his Ph.D. in bacteriology. He became assistant director of the Walter and Eliza Hall Institute in 1928 and director in early 1944. He was ex officio professor of experimental medicine at Melbourne University. At the experimental level he became best known for his development of methods for virus propagation in chick embryo and for his early work on bacteriophage. Elected to the Royal Society of London in 1942, Burnet received the society's Royal Medal in 1947 and Copley Medal in 1959. In 1954 he was elected a foreign associate of the U.S. National Academy of Sciences. He was knighted in 1951.

Burnet wrote extensively, including three semipopular books: *Natural History of Infectious Diseases* (4th ed. 1972), *Viruses and Man* (2d ed. 1955), *The Integrity of the Body* (1962), and *Endurance of Life* (1978).

For background information *see* IMMUNOLOGICAL TOLERANCE, ACQUIRED in the McGraw-Hill Encyclopedia of Science and Technology. ∎

BURWELL, CHARLES SIDNEY
★ American physician

Born Apr. 10, 1893, Denver, CO, U.S.A.
Died Sept. 3, 1967, Ipswich, MA, U.S.A.

Throughout his career Burwell was involved in the study of blood circulation. In his research he relied on data from tests on living patients, on anatomical peculiarities revealed during surgery, on postmortems, and on tests performed postoperatively (up to 25 years later) on former patients. Beginning at Vanderbilt University and continuing in Boston, he investigated constrictive pericarditis, an uncommon but destructive disease, and the effects of operative treatment upon it. In 1941 he published a report, with Alfred Blalock, on 28 cases of the disease. Pericarditis, an inflammation of the membranous sac enclosing the heart, is constrictive when it interferes with the heart stroke and thus the circulation of the blood. The disorder is amenable to surgery, and both diagnosis and treatment depend upon an understanding of the physiologic abnormalities associated with the disease. *See* BLALOCK, ALFRED.

With his colleagues Burwell used the venous catheter to study chronic constrictive pericarditis in six men, with the result that the importance of constriction on both ventricles was emphasized. Blood flow and pressure were determined under conditions of rest and exercise, before and after operation. The pressure measurements, particularly those in the pulmonary circuit, were of great value to medical practice. Before operation each

patient had a stroke output less than normal. This reduction in stroke volume is the primary dynamic abnormality of constrictive pericarditis. In 1931 F. A. Bainbridge and J. A. Menzies had found the stroke output to be dependent on three factors: myocardial contractility, the work load of the ventricles, and diastolic filling. Burwell and his colleagues found no definite evidence of myocardial contractility, though it is known from postmortems that in constrictive pericarditis myocardial fibers are often atrophic, and that the myocardium itself may be infiltrated by fibrous tissue, presumably a consequence of the original inflammatory process extending from the pericardium. The work load of the ventricles was not estimated because of difficulty in finding a zero point for pressure calculations.

Burwell made detailed studies of diastolic filling, generally held to be influenced by four factors: the diastolic filling pressure, adequacy of the blood available for venous return, the duration of diastole, and the ability of the ventricle to dilate. He found diastolic filling pressure to be high rather than low in the six patients. All six had complete adequacy of blood available for venous return. The duration of the diastole of the left ventricle was not shortened in the four patients in whom adequate preoperative measurements had been made. The ability of the ventricle to dilate sets a limit to the stroke output. Physiologic dilation is a necessary mechanism in the increase of stroke output. Such a dilation implies an increase in fiber length and a resultant increase in the force of contraction. These mechanisms would obviously be impaired by a constricting scar. Burwell emphasized the constancy and severity of this impairment in patients with constrictive pericarditis. Tests indicated that reduced stroke output was the major factor in the disability of this disease, and that the reduced stroke output was due to dilation of the ventricle being limited by the constricting scar. With the six patients he noted that in no case were the circulatory dynamics entirely normal, even when studied months or years after operation. He pointed out that most patients with the disease improved with surgery, but were rarely cured. This was borne out by his critical observations on series of patients over a period of years. In spite of the improved health of many patients after pericardiectomy, it was clear that the simple concept of stroke volume was not the whole story.

Myocardial fibrosis is a diffuse replacement, or invasion, of the myocardium by fibrous connective tissue to such an extent that there is interference with heart action. In 1957 Burwell and E. D. Robin studied the circulatory changes associated with diffuse myocardial fibrosis in 11 patients. They used standard methods of measurement and an innovation of their own—right-heart catheterization. Data were collected on the patients' volume of blood flow. Cardiac outputs varying from 2.0 to 5.3 liters per minute were recorded. The customary derivatives of cardiac output (cardiac index, stroke output, and stroke index) were found to be low, as was the cardiac output itself when related to actual oxygen consumption. Blood pressures in the systemic arteries were within normal limits in all patients. However, every patient showed a definite elevation of pressures in the pulmonary artery and "capillaries," the right atrium and ventricle, and the peripheral veins. Out of nine recorded right-ventricle pulse contours, eight showed a diastolic dip. Data indicated that cardiac failure of myocardial fibrosis was a form of low-output failure. As a working hypothesis, Burwell suggested that low-output failure resulted from two basic physiologic defects—limitation of diastolic filling and impairment of systolic emptying of the heart. The interference with diastolic filling was related to changes in the volume-elasticity characteristics of the fibrotic myocardium.

Burwell's post at the Boston Lying-in Hospital made it possible for him to combine his interests in heart disease and pregnancy. With the help of E. C. Eppinger, J. Metcalf, and D. Strayhorn, he contributed much on the physiology of pregnancy and the influence of heart disease on mother and baby. Again, his procedure was to study a series of patients with heart disease, but under the added load of pregnancy. He demonstrated clearly that most women with heart disease can go safely through pregnancy and pointed out the relation of this fact to the operative treatment of rheumatic, congenital, and various other forms of heart disease.

Raised mostly in Pennsylvania, Burwell graduated from Allegheny College in 1914 and from Harvard Medical School in 1919. He underwent postgraduate training in Boston, Baltimore, and Vienna. When he returned from Europe, he accepted a post at Vanderbilt University under G. Canby Robinson, who was then dean of the medical school. In 1928 he succeeded Robinson as professor of medicine at Vanderbilt and retained that post until 1935, when he became professor of medicine and dean of the faculty of medicine at Harvard. He was appointed director of the medical clinic at the Boston Lying-in Hospital in 1949. Elected to the American Academy of Arts and Sciences in 1939, Burwell received in 1959 the John Phillips Memorial Award of the American College of Physicians.

Burwell wrote *Heart Disease and Pregnancy: Physiology and Management,* with James Metcalfe (1958), covering his work in Boston.

For background information *see* CARDIOVASCULAR SYSTEM (VERTEBRATE); HEART DISORDERS in the McGraw-Hill Encyclopedia of Science and Technology. ∎

BURWELL, ROBERT L., JR.
★ American chemist

Born May 6, 1912, Baltimore, MD, U.S.A.

Most of Burwell's work involved attempts to understand the nature of chemisorption and of chemical reactions catalyzed by surfaces (heterogeneous catalysis).

As a beginning graduate student, after some difficulty in deciding whether to become a physical or an organic chemist, Burwell opted for physical chemistry and worked with H. S. Taylor, one of the major figures in the development of modern heterogeneous catalysis. As a graduate student, Burwell was exposed to the developing area of organic mechanisms, and he became interested in the possibility of extending the concepts of this subject to heterogeneous catalysis. During the interval 1941–58, some of his work was, in fact, in the area of physical organic chemistry and not concerned with heterogeneous catalysis. This background in organic chemistry was unusual in a physical chemist working in heterogeneous catalysis, and it strongly influenced the development of his research activities. *See* TAYLOR, SIR HUGH (STOTT).

In those days, most workers in heterogeneous catalysis were physical chemists. Most of them thought that methane was a rather complicated molecule, that propane was as complicated a molecule as could usefully be investigated, and that the best hope for success in unraveling mechanisms in heterogeneous catalysis lay in the study of reactions of simple molecules such as $H_2 + D_2 = 2HD$. From his exposure to organic mechanisms, Burwell had acquired the view that tests of mechanisms should involve as many different kinds of data as possible and that simple reactions had limited potential for providing a variety of data. The rate of the reaction as a function of the partial pressures of the reactants was the extent to which simple reactions could be studied. If, instead, the isotopic exchange between D_2 and hydrocarbons is studied, the rate of formation of a variety of exchanged species—with cyclopentane, for example, of C_5H_9D, $C_5H_8D_2$, . . . , C_5D_{10}—can be measured. Further, the hydrocarbon can be varied, permitting the study of methylcyclopentane, pentane, bicyclo [2,2,1] heptane, 3,3-dimethylpentane, 3-methylhexane, and adamantane. 3-Methylhexane exists in two mirror-image forms, and information is thus available as to the degree to which isotopic exchange is accompanied by their interconversion (racemization). Burwell was particularly interested in this last item and other stereochemical aspects of catalytic reactions.

In sum, the reactions of simple compounds may be too simple, and the reactions of more complicated molecules may provide a better opportunity for learning about some of the details of the paths by which heterogeneous catalytic processes proceed. Michel Boudart claimed that these views constituted Burwell's paradox: "If you want to obtain simple results in catalysis, better use complicated molecules." But, of course, the idea had novelty only in its application to catalysis. *See* BOUDART, MICHEL.

Heterogeneous catalysis is just a branch of chemistry. However, some of its features require the chemist to be satisfied with a less exact theoretical interpretation than would be acceptable in some other branches of chemistry. Probably the most important of these features is the nonuniformity of catalyst surfaces. In effect, the study of a heterogeneous catalytic reaction is like the study of a reaction catalyzed by a mixture of similar but distinct molecular catalysts. Nevertheless, it is possible to arrive at a number of conclusions about the various adsorbed species which are the intermediates in reactions of hydrocarbons on the surfaces of catalysts—reactions such as the hydrogenation of olefins, acetylenes, and ketones and the hydrogenolysis of cyclopropane. Burwell was one of the main contributors to this development. A rather wide variety of adsorbed hydrocarbon species are needed to accommodate all of these reactions, and considerable consensus arose as to the assignment of particular adsorbed intermediates to particular reactions. Most of these suggested species were later found to have close analogs in organometallic complexes and in homogeneous catalysis by such complexes. Burwell further contributed to the beginning of the discovery of the sets of elementary surface processes which combine in sequence or in parallel to give heterogeneous catalytic reactions.

The other major theme in Burwell's research was inorganic chemistry. He attempted to improve the understanding of the nature of the surface sites which lead to chemisorption and catalysis. His work in this area involved primarily oxide catalysts and, particularly, Cr_2O_3. It had long been considered that surfaces of catalysts were in some way unsaturated. In the 1960s, stimulated by the work of colleagues in his department who were active in developing the field of mechanisms in inorganic chemistry, Burwell applied the ideas of coordinative unsaturation to introduce a more definite concept of the nature of unsaturation at catalytic sites. This concept of coordinatively unsaturated surface sites was widely applied by workers in heterogeneous catalysis. It provided

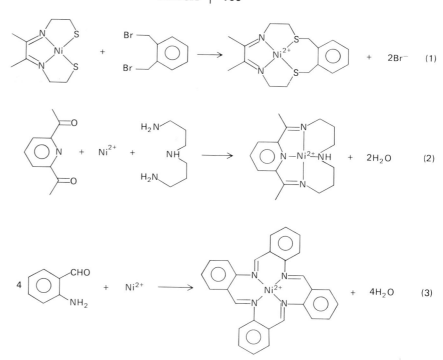

an improved basis for understanding and prediction in the area of the chemical behavior of surfaces in chemisorption and catalysis.

Of Maryland and Virginia ancestry, Burwell received a B.S. at St. John's College, Annapolis, in 1932. Everett S. Wallis was his teacher in freshman chemistry, and a major influence on Burwell's scientific development. Wallis joined the faculty at Princeton in 1929 and, with his assistance, Burwell followed him. He completed work on the doctorate in 1935 and remained as a Procter fellow (postdoctoral) for the succeeding year. After 3 years (1936–39) at Trinity College, Hartford, he was appointed to the faculty of the department of chemistry at Northwestern University, where for a year he worked with V. N. Ipatieff. He chaired the department during 1952–57, and he was appointed Ipatieff Professor of Chemistry in 1970. For his work in chemisorption and heterogeneous catalysis, he received the Kendall Award in Colloid and Surface Chemistry of the American Chemical Society in 1973. Burwell chaired the Division of Physical Chemistry of the American Chemical Society (1958–59), and was president of the Catalysis Society (1973–77) and president-elect (1976–80) of the International Congress on Catalysis.

For background information *see* CATALYSIS in the McGraw-Hill Encyclopedia of Science and Technology. ∎

BUSCH, DARYLE H.
★ American chemist

***Born** Mar. 30, 1928, Carterville, IL, U.S.A.*

The suggestion and demonstration of a coordination template effect opened the field of study of synthetic macrocyclic ligands, species that can encompass a metal ion in a cyclic manner. The only previously known macrocyclic ligands were certain natural products (porphyrins, chlorophylls, vitamin B_{12}) and the pigment phthalocyanine. The occurrence of this unusual type of ligand structure in nature suggested that it afforded some advantages, which were not understood until the synthetic macrocyclic ligands had been studied.

The template hypothesis evolved from two considerations. First, certain organic

groups can still undergo chemical reactions while bound to metal ions (coordinated), and, second, metal ions bind molecules or ions (ligands) to themselves in definite geometric arrangements. Given this geometric organization, reactions that would result in combining these coordinated ligands should produce new ligand molecules whose structures are determined in part by the geometric constraints of the metal ion.

In the mid-1950s Busch sought and

studied organic functional groups that undergo suitable reactions while bound to metal ions. The chemical literature suggested that coordinated mercaptide ions (RS^-) might generally add to electrophiles while bound to metal ions; however, most mercaptide complexes are polymeric. Monomeric structures were developed for the testing of the template model. It was shown that the new complexes undergo the desired reaction and that the sulfur remains bound to the metal ion during the reaction. From this foundation Busch proceeded in 1960–61 to demonstrate the coordination template effect [Eq. (1)].

Simultaneously, other reactions were sought to test the template idea. It became evident that the Schiff base reaction is among the most common organic reactions that occur in the presence of metal ions. Although the mechanistic relationships were not so clear as in the case of metal-bound mercaptides, the many promising reagents and their relatively facile reactions encouraged their early study. Two geometrically distinctive examples of template reactions were soon discovered in this area [Eq. (2) and (3)].

Busch's developments at Ohio State University were paralleled and followed by adventitious discoveries in other laboratories of template reactions leading to complexes of macrocyclic ligands. Beginning in 1962 Busch expanded these studies to produce a variety of novel molecular structures that could be predicted on the basis of the template model. Macrocyclic ligands having from three to eight donor atoms were produced, and an example was found in which two metal ions were contained in a single ring. Busch predicted (1964) that structures could be produced which encapsulate the metal ion in a totally enclosed ligand structure, a prediction that was confirmed several years later in other laboratories. Other investigations demonstrated the template effect in phthalocyanine synthesis and in the total synthesis of vitamin B_{12}. The widely known cyclic polyethers and their complexes and the bicyclic cryptands were developed against this historical background.

The question "What is special about macrocycles as ligands?" was not simple to confront in studies on the natural products because of their highly specialized structures. Much simpler synthetic macrocyclic ligands were more appropriate vehicles for the exploration of this subject. Early studies on the complexes of some of the first synthetic macrocyclic ligands revealed two striking effects. The ligand field strengths were found to be unusually high (as reported by Busch, Plenary Lecturer, International Coordination Chemistry Conference, 1966). Also, synthetic and stereochemical studies showed that macrocyclic complexes are unusually inert toward dissociation of the ligands.

To investigate these effects, Busch designed a family of macrocyclic complexes containing saturated macrocycles having four secondary amine donors and no substituents, with ring sizes varying from 13 to 16 members. The choice of ligands and metal ions was such that the properties of the complexes should correspond to those of the most typical coordination compounds, deviating only in ways that reflected the cyclic structures of the ligands. The ligand field strengths in these complexes showed a strong dependence on ring size, suggesting that the macrocycle acts like a stiff elastic band having a natural radius. The ring either readily accommodates the metal ion or must suffer distortion to accommodate it.

A mathematical strain-energy model was developed to represent the cyclic ligands. The mismatch between the site within the ring and the normal metal-donor distance correlated with the occur-

rence of unusual ligand field strengths. Therefore, strained metal ion sites can be instrumental in determining the extent to which electron density is transmitted from donor atoms to metal ions, a factor that may influence the roles played by metal ions in natural systems.

Other investigators confirmed quantitatively the exceptional inertness toward dissociation of macrocyclic complexes. From the dependence of inertness on ring size, Busch concluded that although macrocyclic complexes are often inert, those complexes in which the fit between metal ion and ring is very good are remarkably inert. The significance to natural products is clear. The tetrafunctional porphyrin ligand accomplishes this immobilization while leaving two additional sites available for other interactions.

The studies on ring size revealed other important relationships. As the ligand field of the planar macrocycle increases, that assignable to the extraplanar ligands decreases. In this way, the extraplanar interaction of metal ions with donors can be controlled by the in-plane macrocycle. The rates at which axial ligands are replaced are controlled by the strain energy of the ring. Therefore, the reactivities at axial sites may be controlled by macrocyclic ligands. Thus, studies on metal complexes with synthetic macrocyclic ligands produced an explanation for their role in nature and revealed important general relationships in coordination chemistry that derive from geometrically constrained systems.

Busch graduated in chemistry from Southern Illinois University in 1951 and attended graduate school at the University of Illinois, where he received the M.S. in 1952 and the Ph.D. in 1954. He served in the U.S. Army from 1946 to 1948. In 1954 he joined the faculty of Ohio State University and advanced to professor in 1963. He served as visiting professor at the University of Florida (1960), the University of California, at Riverside (1968), the University of California at Los Angeles (1975), and Kyushu University (1978). Busch received the American Chemical Society (ACS) Award in Inorganic Chemistry in 1963 and the ACS Award for Distinguished Service to Inorganic Chemistry in 1976.

For background information *see* COORDINATION CHEMISTRY; SCHIFF BASE in the McGraw-Hill Encyclopedia of Science and Technology. ∎

BUSH, VANNEVAR
☆ American electrical engineer

Born *Mar. 11, 1890, Everett, MA, U.S.A.*
Died *June 28, 1974, Belmont, MA, U.S.A.*

As director of the Office of Scientific Research and Development (OSRD) during World War II, Bush was responsible for mobilizing and coordinating the United States scientific war effort, a task that included the development of radar and the atomic bomb. After the war he helped provide the impetus for the Federal government's encouragement of science, especially basic research, and for the institution of agencies to facilitate such encouragement.

In 1940 Bush, then president of the Carnegie Institution in Washington, DC, was appointed chairperson of the National Defense Research Committee (NDRC) by President Franklin Roosevelt. This agency was set up to supplement Army and Navy research work on war devices. Bush brought to the committee his skills as teacher, original researcher, engineer, and administrator. In the same year the Uranium Committee, which had been studying the feasibility of nuclear explosives, was made a subcommittee of the NDRC.

When in 1941 the Office of Scientific Research and Development was established, Bush was appointed its director. This agency was to mobilize the total scientific war effort, to conduct broad research programs, and to advise the President on the status of scientific research and development in connection with defense. During the course of the war, under Bush's direction virtually the entire scientific work force of the United States was at the disposal of the OSRD. The more than 2000 projects to which its scientists were assigned cost more than $300,000,000 directly, and the agency supervised the spending of many hundreds of millions more. The two most massive programs undertaken by the OSRD involved the development of tactical radar and the atomic bomb. The decision to make an all-out effort to produce the bomb was reached in 1941; thereafter, as a member of the Top Policy Group (headed by the U.S. President) and as chair of its Military Policy Committee, Bush shared responsibility for the setting of policy throughout the program, and continued in this work after the task of administration and development had been taken over by the Army in 1943.

In 1944 the President asked Bush to make recommendations as to how the experience gained under the OSRD in mobilizing and directing national scientific efforts might be applied under peacetime conditions. Bush's response was his report *Science, the Endless Frontier* (1945). Drawing on the studies of eminent scientists, engineers, and educators, he made proposals for the consolidation and utilization of scientific skills on a national level. He also urged government support for an unprecedented national effort in basic research. This recommendation was stimulated partly by the realization that, because of the needs of war, basic research had come almost to a standstill in the United States and partly by the fact that new methods of team research, which had been proved effective during the war, and the growing complexity of experimental equipment had made basic research much more costly than before. The proposals embodied in Bush's report led, among other consequences, to the establishment by an act of Congress of the National Science Foundation in 1951.

As an individual, Bush made numerous contributions, mostly in the fields of applied science and engineering. Beginning in 1930 at the Massachusetts Institute of Technology, he and a team from the institute's electrical engineering staff developed the differential analyzer, a device for the machine solution of differential equations, ubiquitous in modern science. Ap-

plicable to such widely diverse fields as atomic physics and acoustics, the machine could handle as many as 18 independent variables simultaneously, and was a forerunner of later analog and digital computing devices. Bush was also responsible for the "Rapid Selector," which he developed in collaboration with Ralph Shaw. This machine was designed to cope with the problem of rapid information retrieval by utilizing microfilm. Using a photoelectric scanner, the machine could recognize a specific item on the film on the basis of a binary visual code, devised by Bush and Shaw, which was printed on the edge of the film. Although the Rapid Selector did not receive wide use, it did much to stimulate interest in the basic problems of information retrieval. Among Bush's other productions were the justifying typewriter, which automatically spaced copy so that both margins were even; the network analyzer, developed in the late 1920s, which could reproduce large electrical networks in miniature and simulate their performance under stress; gaseous conduction devices; and cathode arrangements and coatings for grid-controlled arcs.

Son of a clergyman, Bush received his B.S. and M.S. from Tufts College in 1913. He was granted his D.Eng. simultaneously by Harvard University and the Massachusetts Institute of Technology in 1916. After employment with the General Electric Company in 1913 and the U.S. Navy in 1914, Bush taught at Tufts College from 1914 to 1917. During World War I he did research in submarine detection for the Navy. In 1919 he returned to MIT as associate professor of electric power transmission and became professor in 1923; he was appointed vice-president of the institute and dean of the school of engineering in 1932. Bush was elected president of the Carnegie Institution of Washington in 1938, a position he held until his retirement in 1955. He was chairperson of the National Advisory Committee for Aeronautics in 1938–39. In 1940 he became chair of the National Defense Research Committee, and from 1941 to 1947 directed the OSRD. He was chair of the Joint Research and Development Board of the War and Navy departments in 1946, chair of the Research and Development Board of the National Military Establishment in 1947–48, and later became honorary chair of the Corporation, MIT. Granted many awards and

some two dozen honorary degrees, he received the National Medal of Science in 1964 and the Founders Award of the National Academy of Engineering in 1966.

Bush wrote *Operational Circuit Analysis* (1929), *Endless Horizon* (1946), a collection of papers and addresses, *Modern Arms and Free Men* (1949), *Science is Not Enough* (1967), and *Pieces of the Action* (1970).

For background information *see* ATOMIC BOMB; DIFFERENTIAL ANALYZER; RADAR in the McGraw-Hill Encyclopedia of Science and Technology. ∎

BUSIGNIES, HENRI GASTON
★ American engineer

Born Dec. 29, 1905, Sceaux, France

When Busignies was 21 he invented the Hertzian compass, later known as the airborne radio compass. When tuned to a radio station, the radio compass needle indicates directly on a 360° scale the bearing of the station. This function was achieved first by measuring a ratio of signal amplitude between two fixed-cross receiving loops combined with antennas, and later by comparing the phase of the envelope output signal of a loop rotating at 5 or 10 turns per second with a fixed phase signal generated locally. This was the first continuously rotating directive antenna, later followed by rotating radar antennas.

Shortly thereafter, in 1928, Busignies joined the International Telephone and

Telegraph Corporation (ITT) in Paris and developed some industrial models of the radio compass, as well as ship and land radio direction finders. He then studied wave propagation (at first below 100 megahertz) in such detail that he developed a feel for what happens to an electromagnetic field and its magnetic and electric vectors in any situation, near long and short conductors, metal plates, good or poor conductors, ships, soil, and bodies of water of various conductivities. He calculated reflections and distortions and measured them experimentally. This familiarity helped him considerably in the design of accurate direction finders in the high-frequency range (3–30), which could be used for the detection of radio transmission from tanks, ships, and submarines.

In the meantime the airborne radio compass design was perfected and was ready for application to airline or military aircraft. In 1937 Busignies flew his radio compass on the United Airlines Flight Research Plane across the United States and observed the reflections of the beams of the radio beacons by mountains, and some errors introduced by the loop type of radio beacon transmitters (which were subsequently all replaced by vertical-antenna radio beacons). The mountain effects on the radio signals observed by radio compass were analyzed and described for the first time in a paper published in *Electrical Communication* in 1938. It was shown later that integration of the variations of bearings as a function of airplane displacement decreased error many times. An equivalent effect of error reduction by integration was proposed by the transmission of a wider spectrum, instead of a single frequency or a very limited spectrum. This research became the basis for the analysis of the behavior of various kinds of directive antenna systems to best discriminate between main and reflected waves and to avoid polarization errors. This also resulted in his first suggestions for Doppler-effect direction finders and navigation systems.

A serious problem in all receiving antennas used for high- and medium-frequency direction finders is the reradiation of energy by the conductors connecting the antenna or by the shield used to prevent these conductors from picking up energy directly. This reradiation causes polarization errors, which occur when the wave, without changing its direction of propagation, changes from vertical to horizontal polarization, generally picked up by the feeder conductors or their shields. By placing the feeder cables of antennas at 90° from their orthodox position and then connecting these antennas together or to the receiving equipment through a long rectangle of cables placed horizontally on the ground, the polarization errors were considerably reduced and the requirement for very large ground mats eliminated.

The first phase of World War II found Busignies with more than 10 years of experience in wave propagation and polarization effects, a strong knowledge of the ionosphere E and F layers, and experience in designing radio direction finders up to and including very high frequencies. He then thought that for the high-frequency range (that is, shortwave) the display of the bearing observed should be instantaneous (for instance, on a cathode-ray tube) for two important reasons. First, the variations of polarization and fading could induce changes of signal intensity and bearing which, when observed continuously, would disclose more easily the most nearly correct reading. Second, he realized that in military applications the enemy could decide to transmit extremely short messages to avoid detection. He then designed an instantaneous cathode-ray-tube bearing indicator in which the bearing display shows as a sharp propeller-type pattern on a 360° scale; the eye can integrate and read this display very rapidly. This indicator was available in 1940, and Busignies designed a direction antenna system to use with it in the high-frequency band.

When he joined ITT in the United States in late 1940, Busignies proposed to the U.S. Navy the development of high-frequency direction finders to detect the position of enemy submarines; these finders were superior to any others because of the low polarization error and the instantaneous display. Early in 1941, the Navy responded with a development contract, which resulted in accurate and instantaneous high-frequency direction finders (later called Huff Duff), which were installed throughout the world to detect enemy transmission. The Huff Duff system was credited, together with radar and sonar, with the winning of the battle of the Atlantic in 1942–43. For this work Busignies received the Presidential Certificate of Merit from President Harry Truman in 1945. In the meantime the U.S. Army had asked for a transportable version of the Huff Duff, which became the SCR-291 and SCR-502, used to guide airplanes before loran was available. More than 1500 of these direction finders were used throughout the world. The Huff Duff was installed on aircraft carriers and destroyers and the efficiency of the systems was described in several books and documents.

In France Busignies had also been working on radar problems. He directed the antenna and receiver development of the radar installed to protect the French base of Toulon in the Mediterranean; the system proved successful in 1941. He decided that a considerable improvement of ordinary radar would result from the elimination of the fixed echoes caused by buildings, mountains, stacks, power and other lines, and other reflectors of radio energy, which prevented the observation of airplanes at all distances where these echoes were observed.

Most of the time these fixed radar echoes were much stronger than the echoes from the airplanes and covered large areas. He then invented the moving target indicator (MTI) radar, using a coherent oscillator to produce the radar radio-frequency pulses. In this system, from one pulse to the next the airplane moves in space and the radio frequency changes phase (frequency-shift Doppler effect), while the phase of successive coherent pulses coming from fixed obstacles is the same because of the coherence of radio-frequency pulses. Every other pulse is received and delayed (in a delay line) for the time of a cycle of the recurrence frequency of the radar pulses, and then is opposed to the first pulse. The fixed echoes are eliminated because of the phase coherence, the moving aircraft echoes do not cancel because of the airplane movement, and the aircraft shows up on the radar screen with an improvement of 20–25 decibels with respect to ordinary radar. The MTI radar principle is still in use in airport surveillance and many military radars.

After the war Busignies proposed air navigation systems using radar principles and giving for the first time accurate indications of both distance and direction. A combination of efforts and inventions with the U.S. Navy resulted in the Tacan system, developed at ITT Laboratories under his direction, which became the standard for the United States and the world, and was adopted by all North Atlantic Treaty Organization countries. It became a civil aviation system under the name of Vortac.

In 1959 Busignies proposed synchronous satellites for worldwide communications to the Congressional Committee on Space and Aeronautics. At the time many systems involving lower orbits had been proposed. The synchronous satellites are now used over the Atlantic and Pacific oceans for international communications.

Busignies received a degree in electrical engineering from the Institut Normal Electrotechnique in Paris in 1926. Joining the International Telephone and Telegraph Corporation in Paris in 1928, he moved to the United States in 1941 and became president of ITT's laboratories division in 1958 and vice-president and general technical director of ITT in 1960. He received the Pioneer Award of the Institute of Radio Engineers professional group on aeronautical and navigational electronics, for the invention of the radio compass; the David Sarnoff Award of the Institute of Electrical and Electronic Engineers (1964); the IEEE award in international communication (1969); the Industrial Research Institute Medal (1971); the Armstrong Medal of the Radio Club of America (1975); the IEEE Edison Medal (1977); and two honorary doctorates. In 1966 he was elected to the National Academy of Engineering. Busignies was issued 140 patents.

For background information *see* AIR NAVIGATION; ANTENNA (ELECTROMAGNETISM); COMMUNICATIONS SATELLITE; COMPASS, RADIO; DIRECTION-FINDING EQUIPMENT; NAVIGATION SYSTEMS, ELECTRONIC; RADAR; TACAN; VORTAC in the McGraw-Hill Encyclopedia of Science and Technology. ∎

BUTENANDT, ADOLF
★ German biochemist

Born Mar. 24, 1903, Bremerhaven-Lehe, Germany

Butenandt began his independent scientific work in 1927 as an assistant at the Chemical Institute of the University of Göttingen, where he received his Ph.D. under the direction of Adolf Windaus with a dissertation on the constitution of rotenone, a botanical insecticide. Windaus, the famous researcher on sterols and vitamin D, proposed to his student Butenandt that he undertake the study of the female sex hormone formed in the ovarian follicle; this hormone later received the internationally recognized name of estrone. It had then become possible, through the test developed by Ed-

gar Allen and E. A. Doisy, to detect estrone and to determine it quantitatively by its estrus-inducing effect on the vagina of rodents. *See* DOISY, EDWARD ADELBERT.

In 1929 Butenandt succeeded—independently of Doisy in St. Louis—in obtaining estrone in crystalline form from the urine of pregnant women. This success was made possible by cooperation with Walter Schoeller, the research director of Schering A.G., Berlin, who provided the concentrated extracts from pregnancy urine that Butenandt used as starting material for his work on estrone. Later Schoeller also had concentrates prepared from male urine and pig ovaries, which made it possible for Butenandt to extend his investigations to additional sex hormones: the male gonadic hormone testosterone and the pregnancy hormone progesterone.

In 1931 Butenandt—still in Göttingen—together with K. Tscherning, isolated the first male sex hormone, androsterone. In 1934 Butenandt, with U. Westphal, succeeded in obtaining the first preparation of progesterone in pure form. In the meantime he had assumed the directorship of the Organic Chemical Institute of the Institute of Technology (Technische Hochschule) in Danzig. His work on the constitution of the three sex hormones was carried out during this stay in Danzig. The close relationship of the hormones with each other and their membership in the steroid series were recognized. Progesterone and testosterone

were synthesized, and in 1935 a scheme for degrading cholesterol to the then known steroid hormones was proposed. The scheme was finally proved only decades later in many laboratories throughout the world.

With these results Butenandt reached the first goal he had set at the beginning of his research. It was a fortunate accident that the gonadic hormones proved to be related to cholesterol; this had not been anticipated at the beginning of the work. In this way the considerable experience in the field of sterols that was at hand in Windaus's institute could be utilized. The determination of the constitution of estrone and of the subsequently discovered natural estrogens estriol (G. F. Marrian) and estradiol (E. Schwenck; Doisy) also coincided with the formulation of the valid structural formulas of the sterols and bile acids under the initiative of O. Rosenheim and H. King. Butenandt succeeded for the first time in preparing identical phenanthrene derivatives from the estrogens and the bile acids, so that the chemistry of the steroids and the sex hormones fertilized one another.

In 1936 Max Planck called the young professor from Danzig to the Kaiser Wilhelm Society. Butenandt succeeded Carl Neuberg as director of the Kaiser Wilhelm Institute of Biochemistry in Berlin-Dahlem. The events of World War II and the postwar period led to the removal of the institute to Tübingen (1945–56). It was finally rededicated in 1957 as the Max Planck Institute of Biochemistry in Munich. In Berlin-Dahlem Butenandt brought his investigations of the sex hormones to a close, and with the zoologist Alfred Kühn took up new fields of research, for example, the mode of action of genes and the hormones of insects.

Taking as an example the biosynthesis of the eye pigments of insects as a function of specific genes, Butenandt showed—independently of G. W. Beadle and E. L. Tatum—that individual genes are responsible for the biosynthesis of specific enzymes. It was possible to analyze a chain of genetic activity. The ommochromes, eye pigments of the insects, are formed from tryptophane according to the following scheme: tryptophane → kynurenine → hydroxykynurenine → ommochrome. Each step of the reaction is catalyzed by a specific enzyme, and each enzyme is synthesized as a function of a specific gene. In the ommochromes (xanthommatin, rhodommatin, ommatin D, ommin), representatives of a new class of natural pigments were recognized; they were phenoxazone pigments, which proved to be widely distributed in the animal kingdom. *See* BEADLE, GEORGE WELLS; TATUM, EDWARD LAWRIE.

In 1953 Butenandt, together with Peter Karlson, succeeded in isolating the first crystalline insect hormone, the chrysalis-forming hormone ecdysone, which was recognized through the investigations of Karlson and W. Hoppe as a close relative of the sex hormones, being a derivative of cholesterol. This was again a great surprise. The chemical investigation of the insect hormones was begun in the expectation of discovering new types of substances, but the successful route led the wanderer back, after almost 35 years, to his first area of research and once more showed the great transformability and significance of the sterol skeleton in the realm of hormones. But in another area Butenandt succeeded in achieving access to a new class of substances, the pheromones, with the example of the sex-attractive substance bombykol of the silkworm, *Bombyx mori*. In 1959 Butenandt and E. Hecker were able to report, as the result of 20 years' work, on the isolation of this material from the sacculi laterales, or glands of the hind portion, of the female silkworm. Bombykol was the first representative of this class of substances; it proved to be a hexadecadienol having the structure shown in the formula below. It could also be obtained synthetically.

$$CH_3-(CH_2)_2-CH=CH$$
cis
$$-CH=CH-(CH_2)_8-CH_2OH$$
trans

Butenandt bestowed special love on virus research. The Max Planck Institute for Virus Research in Tübingen was the outgrowth of a center for virus research in Berlin-Dahlem. It became a research center of international significance in the area of molecular biology.

Butenandt studied chemistry and biology at the universities of Marburg and Göttingen from 1921 to 1927, when he received his Ph.D. from the latter university. In 1931 he became privatdozent at the University of Göttingen, and in 1933 associate professor at the Technical Institute of the Free State of Danzig. In 1935 he made an orientation trip to universities in the United States and Canada at the invitation of the Rockefeller Foundation, a visit that was of great value for his later researches. In 1936 Butenandt became director of the Kaiser Wilhelm Institute

of Biochemistry, which after 1949 carried the name of Max Planck Institute of Biochemistry, after the Kaiser Wilhelm Society was renamed the Max Planck Society. In 1936–45 Butenandt was honorary professor at the University of Berlin, in 1945–46 he was professor of physiological chemistry at the University of Tübingen, and in 1956 he became professor of physiological chemistry at the University of Munich. For his work in the field of sex hormones Butenandt received the Nobel Prize in chemistry in 1939. In 1960 he was elected president of the Max Planck Society for the Advancement of Science, succeeding Otto Hahn; he became honorary president of the society in 1972.

For background information *see* CHOLESTEROL; ECDYSONE; ESTROGEN; PHEROMONES; PROGESTERONE; STEROID; TESTOSTERONE in the McGraw-Hill Encyclopedia of Science and Technology. ∎

BUTLER, STUART THOMAS
★ Australian theoretical physicist

***Born** July 4, 1926, Naracoorte, Australia*

Butler is widely known in the field of nuclear physics for his pioneering work in developing an understanding of the mechanism involved in nuclear reactions. His work in the 1950s led to the development of direct nuclear reaction theory and stimulated worldwide accelerator laboratories in experimental programs on nu-

clear reactions. The theory was used to interpret the experimental results, thereby yielding valuable information about nuclear properties. Butler's scientific work also includes contributions to the fields of statistical mechanics and the theory of superconductivity, high-temperature plasma theory, and upper atmospheric behavior.

After graduating in 1947 with a master of science degree from Adelaide University, Butler went to the United Kingdom early in 1949 on an Australian National University traveling scholarship to study nuclear physics at Birmingham University under R. E. Peierls. One of the problems referred to him by Peierls was the interpretation of some recently obtained experimental results on nuclear reactions induced by deuterons obtained by researchers using the cyclotron accelerator at the University of Liverpool. In order to interpret these results, Butler developed a new theory, known as the deuteron stripping theory, applicable to deuteron-induced reactions. On the basis of this theory, he obtained his doctor of philosophy degree by thesis in 1951. A major feature of the deuteron stripping theory was that it pictured the nuclear reaction to proceed in a "direct" manner in which one of the two deuteron particles was stripped off and absorbed by the target nucleus, while the second particle continued its path without being absorbed. This was in contrast to previously accepted notions in which the incident particle, deuteron or otherwise, was envisaged as being totally absorbed by the target nucleus, forming a "compound" nucleus, whose subsequent decay would complete the reaction. *See* PEIERLS, RUDOLF ERNST.

In 1951 Butler accepted an invitation from H. A. Bethe to join the staff of the Laboratory of Nuclear Studies, Cornell University, New York. While at Cornell, and in collaboration with N. Austern and H. W. McManus, he extended the concept of "direct" to apply to most nuclear reactions, not only those involving deuterons. This was postulated in a paper published in 1953, and the concept was confirmed by subsequent agreement of experimental results with the theoretical predictions. Refinement and extensions led to direct nuclear reaction theory.

Butler returned to the Australian National University in 1953, but in 1954 moved to the University of Sydney. He remained on the staff there until 1977, first as reader in physics and from 1959 as professor of theoretical physics. During this period he traveled extensively and spent numerous semesters on leave at various institutions in the United States, including the Institute of Advanced Study, Princeton, NJ; Harvard University; and Cornell University.

During the later 1950s Butler collaborated with J. M. Blatt and M. R. Schaforth at the University of Sydney on various problems involving the theory of statistical mechanics. One aim was to develop a theoretical understanding of the phenomenon of superconductivity. In 1956 they developed a theory which was published under the title "Quasi-Chemical Equilibrium Approach to Superconductivity." In this paper they showed that as a result of correlations between pairs of conduction electrons, a thermodynamic transition will occur in some materials at certain low temperatures below which the material is superconducting. Their proposition that this is the basic mechanism of superconductivity was later verified by N. N. Bogolubov in identifying the equivalence of the quasi-chemical equilibrium theory and the successful model of superconductivity developed independently by J. Bardeen, L. N. Cooper, and J. R. Schrieffer. It was on the basis of this work that Butler was awarded the doctor of science degree by the Australian National University in 1961. *See* BARDEEN, JOHN; BOGOLUBOV, NIKOLAI NIKOLAEVICH; COOPER, LEON N.; SCHRIEFFER, JOHN ROBERT.

During the 1960s Butler's department of theoretical physics at Sydney was highly active and flourished in the fields of nuclear physics, plasma physics, astrophysics, and theory of fundamental particles. His own research ranged widely, with publications on such subjects as the excitations of atmospheric oscillations, energy loss of a fast ion in a plasma, and production of highly excited neutral atoms for injection into plasma devices.

From 1970 onward, Butler turned increasingly toward university administration and science education. He was dean of the Faculty of Science, University of Sydney (1970–73), fellow of the Senate (1970–77), and member of the Finance Committee (1971–77). He was chairperson of the Science Syllabus Committee, Board of Senior School Studies, New South Wales (1966–77). In 1977 he became director of the Australian Atomic Energy Commission Research Establish-

ment, Lucas Heights, New South Wales. In 1966 Butler was awarded the Thomas Rankin Lyle Medal by the Australian Academy of Science for his researches in mathematics and physics, and in 1969 was elected a fellow of the academy. In 1976 the American Physical Society awarded him the T. W. Bonner Prize in Nuclear Physics, given for "recognition and encouragement of outstanding research in nuclear physics."

In addition to numerous scientific articles, Butler published a number of books, including *Nuclear Stripping Reactions* (1956), translated into Russian; *A Modern Introduction to Physics* (vol. 1, 1960; vol. 2, 1961; vol. 3, 1962; reprinted in 6 vols.); and *Uranium on Trial*, with C. N. Watson-Munro and Robert Raymond (1977). Butler was also coauthor or editor of over 20 books on scientific topics for use by senior secondary school students.

For background information *see* NUCLEAR REACTION; PLASMA PHYSICS; SUPERCONDUCTIVITY in the McGraw-Hill Encyclopedia of Science and Technology. ∎

BYERLY, PERRY
★ American geophysicist

Born May 28, 1897, Clarinda, IA, U.S.A.

In 1923 Byerly, then a graduate student in physics at the University of California, entered the field of seismology at the suggestion of professors James B. Macelwane, S.J., and Andrew C. Lawson. He took charge of the university's two seis-

mographic stations at Berkeley and Mount Hamilton in 1925. When he became director emeritus in 1963, there were 20 stations in the network. George D. Louderback was chairperon of the department of geological sciences during the early years of Byerly's tenure and influenced him considerably. Since the state of California supported the stations, Byerly conceived his first duty to be the maintenance of a close watch on northern California earthquakes, both by seismometric instrumentation (epicenters) and by field observations (intensities). The same type of service for southern California was being developed by Harry O. Wood at the California Institute of Technology.

Byerly was concerned that epicenters located in Monterey and San Luis Obispo counties did not lie in the San Andreas Fault zone. In locating these, the east-west control came from the seismograms recorded at Tinemaha and Haiwee (Pasadena network) in the Owens Valley. The Sierran mass lies between. Byerly therefore suspected a delay of P waves under either the San Joaquin Valley or the Sierra Nevada. He established a station at Fresno and was able to show that the delay was under the Sierra Nevada and depended on the length of path under the range. This he interpreted as indicating a low-velocity "root" of the mountains penetrating into the mantle. Such a root had been postulated by Lawson from isostatic considerations. Studying three western United States earthquakes (Montana, Nevada, Texas), Byerly pointed out that the P travel-time curve had an abrupt bend at epicentral distances between 16° and 20°. This led to a continuing discussion as to what velocity distribution exists in the upper mantle, and to the sometimes acrimonious debate as to the possible existence of a low-velocity layer. Byerly also pointed out that the travel-time curves of individual earthquakes are best drawn as a series of straight lines with sharp bends or overlapping at certain critical distances (such as the one between 16° and 20°), and that these distances differ from earthquake to earthquake so that an averaged curve for many shocks loses the sharp discontinuity of slope. This suggests a discretely layered mantle. Such an idea proved unacceptable for many years but is now being considered.

Byerly became interested in the phase of the first motion of the P wave as a function of distance and direction from the source after reading an early paper by

Sommeville. Byerly was the first to introduce a transform which allowed the use of seismograms of distant earthquakes as well as nearby records to compute the nature of the forces at the source of the earthquake from the direction of first motion. A number of his students further developed these methods in their doctoral theses. He also had a continued interest in the use of seismograms to interpret the surface structure of the Earth; and he was the first to study the crustal layering in North America from earthquake records. His treatment of the hinged pendulum seismograph, along with his discussion of the magnitudes of the various terms always neglected, was the first of its kind.

As the only geophysicist in a department of geologists, Byerly relied heavily on discussions with his students. Training students was his greatest pride. He was often called a "philosopher" because of his approach, and he did not feel that there was any finality in the conclusions drawn from scientific observations, such as the interpretations of crustal structures from seismograms.

Byerly moved from Iowa to California when 8 years old. His degrees (A.B., M.A., Ph.D., and LL.D.) were received from the University of California. He was secretary of the Seismological Society of America for 27 years, and later president and honorary member. He served as president of the International Association of Seismology and Physics of the Earth's Interior. He was elected to the National Academy of Sciences in 1946 and to the American Academy of Arts and Sciences in 1960.

For background information *see* EARTHQUAKE; SEISMOLOGY in the Mc-Graw-Hill Encyclopedia of Science and Technology. ∎

BYERS, HORACE ROBERT
★ American meteorologist

***Born** Mar. 12, 1906, Seattle, WA, U.S.A.*

Byers's career illustrates the effectiveness of team research, especially in the years since World War II when large government-sponsored programs were mounted to solve some of the most pressing problems of the Earth's atmosphere. His best-known accomplishment was in exploring the inner workings of thunderstorms through a large project involving

several government agencies from 1945 to 1949.

In a prewar study covering a network of reporting stations, Byers noted a sequence of events with the passage of thunderstorms that gave new clues to how the air circulated and how heat was exchanged within these storms. After the war, when personnel and equipment became available, a major attack on this problem was started jointly by the U.S. Weather Bureau, Air Force, Navy, NACA (predecessor of NASA), and the University of Chicago, all under Byers's direction. By that time instrument flying had reached a stage where it was possible to fly through thunderstorms, and Byers organized flights with up to five airplanes penetrating the storms simultaneously at five different levels. Flown by Air Force pilots and equipped with instruments for a variety of measurements, these planes gave information that, when combined with observations from surface observing networks, radars, balloon soundings, and special equipment, revealed for the first time the true nature of thunderstorm circulations and thermodynamics. The data, collected and analyzed under Byers's direction by such well-known meteorologists as R. R. Braham, Jr., L. J. Battan, R. D. Coons, Harry Moses, Bernice Ackerman, and F. D. White, emphasized the importance of the downdraft. Previous models of thunderstorm circulation had either omitted the downdraft entirely or had granted it only a negligible role in the main con-

vection motions of the storm. The most violent aspects—the heaviest rain, most frequent lightning, strongest and gustiest winds, sharpest temperature drops, and most striking pressure changes—were found by Byers and his team to be associated with the downdraft. The air was shown to be accelerated in its downward plunge by the negative buoyancy caused by cooling in evaporating rain. In a practical sense, the results showed how and under what circumstances flights in thunderstorms can be made. Thunderstorm flying was lifted from the folklore of the ready room to a scientifically based technique. The use of radar for this purpose was demonstrated, while new radar circuitry for this application was being developed by David Atlas in his association with the group. Present-day aircraft radar and the technique of its use evolved from these first steps.

Reassembling some of the leaders of his team and several new scientists and graduate students at the University of Chicago, Byers then turned his attention to the microphysics of convective clouds. He sought to discover how the cloud particles grow to precipitation sizes under a variety of conditions and how the circulation of air and the phase changes of water interact. This work was stimulated by the discoveries of Irving Langmuir, V. J. Schaefer, and Bernard Vonnegut that clouds could be artificially nucleated to increase or produce rainfall. *See* SCHAEFER, VINCENT JOSEPH.

Another aspect studied further was the question of how lightning develops, a question which had not been clearly answered by the thunderstorm project, as had been hoped. With D. R. Fitzgerald, Byers scheduled flights in and around convective clouds with carefully calibrated instrument systems for measuring electrical effects. The data verified the theory that the electricity was generated by the formation of precipitation particles, often in the presence of ice in some form. However, other methods of charge generation continued to be advocated by others.

The team, which included Braham, Battan, Ackerman, and Fitzgerald, was augmented by E. W. Barrett, J. P. Lodge, Guy Goyer, and J. E. McDonald and later by T. R. Hoffer, L. R. Koenig, Motoi Kumai, Ottavio Vittori, Yoshiaki Toba, Ulrich Katz, and others. It devoted its attention to almost every aspect of the microphysics and chemistry of clouds, and the University of Chicago became one of the leading centers of cloud physics study. Again, planes were flown as the principal probing platforms, using unique instruments and sampling devices, while laboratory and theoretical investigations disclosed new properties and characteristics of cloud nucleants, rain, snow, and ice. Numerous discoveries emanated from the Chicago group to establish facts on which cloud science throughout the world has drawn heavily.

During this period Byers also became interested in meteorology in the mesoscale, that scale between roughly 10 and 100 miles (16 and 160 kilometers), in which severe local storms act. He arranged to have Tetsuya Fujita come to Chicago from Japan to lead a subgroup in that study. This project grew into a large undertaking involving also interpretation and study of satellite information. When Byers left Chicago in 1965 to become dean of the college of geosciences at Texas A & M University, the direction of the Cloud Physics Laboratory was assumed by Braham.

Not all of Byers's research and scientific publications were performed in team efforts. As an individual, he achieved and published research results in several areas, ranging from local studies of fogs to thermodynamics of the large circulations of the atmosphere.

Byers received most of his schooling in Berkeley, where he graduated from the University of California (B.S., 1929). He then received a fellowship in meteorology at the Massachusetts Institute of Technology; he studied under C.-G. Rossby for 6 years, with interruptions, receiving an M.S. in 1932 and Sc.D. in 1935. His first permanent position was in the U.S. Weather Bureau in Washington, where he led a group, including Harry Wexler, in the introduction of the new Norwegian methods of weather analysis and forecasting. They also studied the upper air from airplane and radiosonde observations, which were then becoming available in quantity. In 1940 he accepted a position as associate professor at the University of Chicago, and with Rossby helped form a new department of meteorology. He became a full professor in 1944 and succeeded Rossby as chairperson of the department in 1948, holding the post until 1960. He moved to Texas A & M University in 1965 to help that institution build toward excellence in the geosciences. In 1968 he was named vice-president for academic affairs, a post in which he played a leading role in raising the academic standing of Texas A & M University. After reaching retirement age in 1971, he continued for 3 more years as distinguished professor of meteorology, leaving the university in emeritus status in 1974. In 1975 Byers served as a visiting professor at the University of Clermont-Ferrand, France, and subsequently took up permanent residence in Santa Barbara, CA. He continued collaborating in research projects, lecturing, advising, and serving on national scientific committees. Byers was elected to the National Academy of Sciences in 1952. He served as president of the American Meteorological Society in 1952–53; president of the Section of Meteorology, American Geophysical Union, in 1947–49; and president of the International Association of Meteorology and Atmospheric Physics in 1960–63. Honors accorded him included the Robert M. Losey Award, American Institute of Aeronautics and Astronautics; Charles F. Brooks Award and Cleveland Abbe Award, American Meteorological Society; and Award of Merit, Chicago Technical Societies Council.

Byers wrote *General Meteorology* (1937; 4th ed. 1974) and *Elements of Cloud Physics* (1965).

For background information *see* CLOUD PHYSICS; LIGHTNING; THUNDERSTORM in the McGraw-Hill Encyclopedia of Science and Technology. ■

CADY, GEORGE HAMILTON

★ American chemist

Born Jan. 10, 1906, Lawrence, KS, U.S.A.

Cady is noted for his studies of the preparation and properties of the element fluorine and many of its compounds. In the early 1930s he studied the reaction of fluorine gas with water and aqueous solutions of acids and bases. He observed in 1934 that the reaction with nitric acid produced a colorless, explosive, reactive gas, NO_3F. This was the second compound known to contain the O-F bond, the first being OF_2.

Difficulties associated with the electrolytic preparation of fluorine caused Cady to work out details of the KF-HF phase system and to show that the best electrolyte for fluorine production had a composition in the range 1.8–2.0 moles of HF per mole of KF and a temperature in the range 72–100°C. These conditions were later used for industrial production of fluorine.

During 1942–43 Cady and a group of his associates worked in the War Research Division of Columbia University on the development of methods to produce fluorocarbons for use in the gaseous diffusion process to separate isotopes of uranium. It was found that many hydrocarbons could be converted to fluorocarbons of corresponding structure by the action of fluorine diluted by nitrogen when copper turnings coated with silver fluoride were present. By this procedure the first fluorocarbon lubricating oils were obtained.

The process was based upon a method used earlier by L. A. Bigelow and his students at Duke University. This work by Cady and his associates was only a part of the work done on fluorocarbons during the Manhattan Project; there were several other very active groups in the United States and in Great Britian.

Following World War II, much of the research of Cady and his students resulted in the synthesis and characterization of compounds containing the O-F group. Three explosive gaseous compounds of this type were obtained by the reaction of fluorine with acids. Perchloric acid gave ClO_4F. Trifluoroacetic acid and pentafluoropropionic acid gave, respectively, $CF_3C(O)OF$ and $C_2F_5C(O)OF$. By explosive decomposition the latter two compounds gave CO_2 and the fluorocarbons CF_4 and C_2F_6, respectively. A stable fluoroxy compound, CF_3OF, was the first obtained by the reaction of fluorine with methanol. It was soon found, however, that many substances reacted with fluorine to give CF_3OF. For example, carbon monoxide reacted with an excess of fluorine in a hot tube to give CF_3OF together with COF_2 and CF_3OOCF_3. From sulfur trioxide, the gas

$$\begin{array}{c} O \\ FSOF \\ O \end{array}$$

was obtained. Thionyl fluoride, SOF_2, was fluorinated to give F_4SO and F_5SOF. The catalyst consisting of copper turnings or ribbon coated with silver fluoride was useful in these processes.

Compounds containing the O-F group were used in many syntheses. CF_3OF reacted with COF_2 to give the peroxide, CF_3OOCF_3, while $FS(O)_2OF$ reacted with SO_3 in the presence of copper–silver fluoride catalyst to give

$$\begin{array}{c} O \quad O \\ FSOOSF \\ O \quad O \end{array}$$

The latter compound was found to dissociate into SO_3F radical, $S_2O_6F_2 = 2SO_3F$, the degree of dissociation being extensive at 100°C and above. Because of the high reactivity of the fluorosulfate radical, the compound $S_2O_6F_2$ was found to be a very useful reagent for producing both organic and inorganic fluorosulfates. Many chemists made use of the reagent. Some of the interesting new compounds thus obtained were $ClSO_3F$, $BrSO_3F$, $Br(SO_3F)_3$, $I(SO_3F)_3$, ISO_3F, I_3SO_3F, and I_7SO_3F.

During the 1960s the National Aeronautics and Space Administration and other government agencies sponsored an extensive program of research to study fluorine and its high-energy compounds as possible rocket propellants. Cady and his associates were among those engaged in the effort to produce new compounds of possible utility. One of the general lines of effort followed in some of the laboratories was the synthesis of carbon compounds containing the O-F group. This line of research resulted from the earlier discovery of CF_3OF.

As a boy, Cady became interested in chemistry through his father, Hamilton P. Cady, who was professor of chemistry at the University of Kansas. He attended this university and was granted the A.B. and A.M. degrees in 1927 and 1928, respectively. He then attended the University of California at Berkeley and received the Ph.D. degree in chemistry in 1930. His thesis research on some aspects of the chemistry of fluorine and hydrogen fluoride was done under the supervision of Joel H. Hildebrand. During the academic year 1930–31 Cady served as assistant professor at the University of South Dakota. For the next 3 years he was instructor at the Massachusetts Institute of Technology. He then was employed as research chemist for a year by U.S. Rubber Products, Inc., in Passaic, NJ, and for 3 years by the Columbia Chemical Division of the Pittsburgh Plate Glass Company at Barberton, OH. He moved to the University of Washington, Seattle, as assistant professor in 1938 and became associate professor in 1943 and professor in 1947. For the period 1961–63 he was chairperson of the department of chemistry. He retired in 1972 but continued his experimental research. Cady received the American Chemical Society Award for Distinguished Service in the Advancement of Inorganic Chemistry in 1966 and the Fluorine Division of the American Chemical Society Award for Creative Work in Fluorine Chemistry in 1972. He became a member of the American Chemical Society, the American Association for the Advancement of Science, and the Deutsche Akademie der Naturforscher Leopoldina. *See* HILDEBRAND, JOEL HENRY.

For background information *see* FLUORINE; FLUOROCARBON in the McGraw-Hill Encyclopedia of Science and Technology. ∎

CALVIN, MELVIN
★ American chemist

Born Apr. 8, 1911, St. Paul, MN, U.S.A.

For tracing the various steps of the path of carbon in photosynthesis, the most fundamental of all biochemical reactions, Calvin received the 1961 Nobel Prize in chemistry.

Long interested in organic molecular structure and behavior, Calvin turned to the problem of photosynthesis when carbon-14 became readily available after 1945. The basic, initial experiment, performed at the Lawrence Radiation Laboratory of the University of California, Berkeley, in 1948, involved the feeding of radioactive carbon dioxide to a photosynthesizing plant for very short periods of time, followed by a search for the earliest compound or compounds into which that radioactive carbon was incorporated. Calvin and his associates had already gone far toward concentrating the radioactive carbon formed in the first few seconds in photosynthetic tissue (algae and leaves as well) and had a bit of information about the chemistry. They knew that the major compound formed in the early phases was very sticky on an anion exchange resin; that is, it was hard to wash out of an anion exchanger whereas simple carboxylic acids, sulfates, and phosphates would wash out relatively easily. This sticky material required strong acid or strong base to displace it from such an anion exchange column. The idea that it was a carboxylic acid of some sort had already been evolved, but no simple carboxylic acid was as tightly held as this material was.

This gave rise to the idea that perhaps it had more than one holding point on it, that is, more than one anionic center. Now, if it were a carboxylic acid with more than one anionic center, it would presumably be another carboxylic acid or some other anionic center. It seemed unlikely that it might be a di- or polycarboxylic acid, since sugars and citric acid would wash off the column even ahead of this material. Besides, if the CO_2 was entering the carboxyl group, and if two carboxyl groups were put in, it complicated the matter. Therefore the other anionic center that would make it sticky should not be a carboxyl group, and the obvious choice for it was a phosphate.

By that time Calvin already had the information that the material contained phosphorus by virtue of the tracer phosphorus combination with tracer carbon experiments. The simplest point at which carbon could enter into a phosphorylated compound would be a reversal of the oxidation of a phosphorylated pyruvic acid to give a three-carbon compound in which the carboxyl group arose from the CO_2 and the phosphorylated two-carbon piece arose from something resembling acetyl phosphate. The only compound of this general type that had the enormous stability of Calvin's unknown was phosphoglyceric acid, and a few tests soon confirmed that this was indeed what he had.

At the same time, it was clear that if this was the way carbon was getting in, there must be some way of making the two-carbon acceptor from phosphoglyceric acid. Calvin conceived a very simple cycle, which turned out to be wrong but which served as his operating hypothesis for a while. The search over the following years for this two-carbon acceptor that had to be made from the phosphoglyceric acid gave rise to the ultimate solution of the problem, but the beginning was in that moment of recognition that the sticky stuff had to be something with two handles and had to be regeneratable.

The son of Russian immigrant parents, Calvin received his B.S. in chemistry at the Michigan College of Mining and Technology in 1931 and his Ph.D. in chemistry at the University of Minnesota in 1935. After spending 1935–37 at the University of Manchester, England, he joined the faculty of the University of California at Berkeley in 1937 as an instructor, becoming a full professor in 1947 and university professor of chemistry in 1971. In 1946 he was appointed director of the bioorganic chemistry group in the Lawrence Radiation Labatory. This group formed the Laboratory of Chemical Biodynamics in 1960. In 1967 Calvin was appointed associate director of the Lawrence Berkeley Laboratory. In 1971 he was president of the American Chemical Society. He received numerous awards, including the Davy Medal of the Royal Society (1964) and the Priestley medal of the American Chemical Society (1978). Calvin was elected to the National Academy of Sciences in 1954 and the American Academy of Arts and Sciences in 1958.

Calvin wrote *The Theory of Organic Chemistry,* with G. E. K. Branch (1940), *Isotopic Carbon,* with others (1949), *Chemistry of Metal Chelate Compounds,* with Martell (1952), *Path of Carbon in Photosynthesis,* with J. A. Bassham (1957), *Chemical Evolution* (1961; 2d ed. 1969), and *Photosynthesis of Carbon Compounds,* with Bassham (1962).

For background information *see* PHOTOSYNTHESIS in the McGraw-Hill Encyclopedia of Science and Technology. ∎

CAMERON, SIR (GORDON) ROY
★ Anglo-Australian pathologist

Born *June 30, 1899, Echuca, Victoria, Australia*

Died *Oct. 7, 1966, Hadley Wood, Barnet, Herts, England*

Cameron's life work was the experimental analysis of structural and functional upset of the liver caused by prolonged disease of the organ. He adapted and improved methods for excluding the blood supply to the liver and preventing bile outflow, as well as for exposing it to a host of toxic agents for the production of its injury and the study of its repair. From these studies came many investigations by his pupils into the precise mechanics and biochemistry of cellular injury, thereby initiating a new discipline of micropathology. For his contributions in the field of cellular pathology, Cameron received a Royal Medal of the Royal Society of London in 1960.

As a young morbid anatomist concerned with autopsy duties at the Melbourne Hospital, Cameron gained an extensive experience of chronic liver disease, especially the varieties now known to be due to viral infections. Under the influence of his teacher in embryology, he applied embryological interpretations as well as existing histochemical methods to the patterns of liver disease. He soon realized the limitations inherent in such techniques, and after a year's postgraduate study in Germany he settled down at University College Hospital Medical School in London to a long experimental analysis of chronic liver damage, using the above-mentioned methods.

Confronted by the regenerative power of the liver, Cameron soon realized its key position in shaping the finished patterns of liver disease and dimly perceived the idea of "poise," a kind of delicate balance between cell destruction and restoration. Later work with chemical and bacterial agents brought out the importance, in chronic liver upsets, of the duration of injury and its phasing as intermittent or continuous. Investigations with carbon tetrachloride given by various routes were especially rewarding and established a reversible and irreversible stage of liver cirrhosis. Cameron thus was able to enunciate the principle that the time-spacing of the noxious agents decided whether recovery or permanent injury, with fibrosis and true cirrhosis, was to be the outcome. These views were confirmed over the next 26 years with many chemical poisons, bacterial infections, and the parasite *Schistosoma mansoni,* as well as with various forms of biliary obstruction and biliary cirrhosis.

Prewar study of various insecticides and industrial chemical agents led to Cameron's investigations of many potential war gases during World War II. He was the first to work out completely the action of lewisite and allied compounds on animals and introduced the first-aid treatment by means of concentrated H_2O_2. He clarified the pathology of intoxication with mustard gas, nitrogen mustard, phosgene, various selenium salts and particulate selenium, and a host of other agents, including phosphorus. With J. H. Gaddum, he defined the role of the nasal cavities in resisting exposure to toxic gases; they were also responsible for much of the earliest work on nerve gases. Cameron carried the burden of toxicological investigation of DDT on human volunteers and laboratory animals that resulted in its adoption as a safe agent against insect pests in the military services.

From these years devoted to war problems, Cameron realized the value for pathology, especially of the cell, of modern techniques in following the function of organelles. From 1945 onwards he reorganized his department in London with this clear purpose in mind. His team made many contributions to the understanding of injury to mitochrondria, lysosomes, and endoplasmic reticulum.

From Cameron's interest in war-gas pulmonary edema came one of his most original discoveries, with S. N. De of Calcutta— the production of lung edema by inserting an artificial "blanket" of fibrin or blood over the floor of the fourth ventricle of the brain, with resulting stimulation of the outflow of vagal nerve impulses to the circulatory and respiratory systems. This "neurogenic edema" has close parallels in head injuries and apoplexy.

Cameron's breadth of interest was reflected in his well-known studies of inflammation in earthworms and caterpillars, which contrasted invertebrate coordinated host reaction to nonspecific foreign agents with more specific defense mechanisms and peculiar features of repair. He also gave much time to the detailed investigation of regeneration in mammalian tissues such as the alimentary canal lining, the spleen, adipose tissue, and the skin after thermal burning. Despite a varying pattern of research, there was always the underlying challenge of cellular response to abnormal stimulation and injury.

An Australian parson's son whose early life was spent in the bush country, Cameron studied medicine at the University of Melbourne, graduating M.B., B.S. in 1921 and D.Sc. in 1930. He was a junior lecturer in pathology at the university from 1922 to 1925, then deputy director of the Walter and Eliza Hall Institute for Medical Research until 1927. After working with Ludwig Aschoff at Freiburg im Breisgau, Germany, during 1927–28, he settled at University College Hospital Medical School, London, under A. E. Boycott, as Graham Scholar in Pathology, Beit Memorial Fellow, and reader in morbid anatomy. He succeeded Boycott in 1937 as professor and was director of the Graham Research Laboratories from 1945 until his retirement in 1964. He was knighted in 1957.

Cameron wrote *Pathology of the Cell* (1952) and *Biliary Cirrhosis,* with P. C. Hou (1962).

For background information *see* LIVER DISORDERS; LUNG DISORDERS; PATHOLOGY in the McGraw-Hill Encyclopedia of Science and Technology. ■

CAMERON, THOMAS WRIGHT MOIR
★ Canadian parasitologist

Born Apr. 29, 1894, Glasgow, Scotland

Until about 60 years ago, parasites were regarded as a cause of human disease, mainly in the tropics. They were beginning to become suspect as a cause of tropical disease in domestic animals. There was, however, little knowledge of the almost universal distribution of the parasitic worms and still less of their enormous variety. About 50 years ago, after numerous species had been described by F. P. F. Ransom from sheep, Cameron found that they were so common in these animals that it was unusual to find a single animal free from them, even when the sheep were clinically healthy. A little later, he and his colleagues, working under Leiper at the London Zoological Gardens, found a similar situation in wild animals that had died from causes other than parasitic disease. From this date onward, it became obvious that parasitism was a branch of ecology, and that parasitic disease—of enormous importance in both human and veterinary medicine—was essentially due to human interference with the natural, normal ecology of the parasites. Far from being confined to the tropics, parasites were universal in their distribution, occurring as far north as the islands in the Arctic Ocean.

Since then it has been abundantly established that no vertebrate species—and few invertebrates—are free from parasitic worms. It has become equally obvious that most kinds of parasitic worms are confined to restricted species of hosts and that related species of hosts tend to have related species of parasites. Moreover, geologically old species of animals, even if not closely related to each other, often had parasites that were so related. This suggested quite definitely that these hosts had become infected in the distant past, when their internal environments were more generalized and when they congregated together so that the ancestors of the parasites were able to invade the ancestors of the host and evolve parallel with them. In such hosts—for example, the perissodactyls (equines, rhinoceroses) and paenungulates (elephants)—numerous closely related variants of the original stock appeared, testifying to the appearance of many small morphological mutants during this evolutionary development. This was particularly the case with certain roundworms and tapeworms.

There thus appeared a form of parallel evolution that could throw considerable light on the evolution and migration of their hosts. The finding of roundworms in kangaroos related to those in horses and elephants, and in practically no other animals, showed that all these host groups, even if not related to each other, must have been in close association with each other early in their evolution. In the light of the evidence of other sciences—paleontology, paleomagnetism, and so on—this gave strong support to the hypothesis of the close proximity of all the southern continents, including the Antarctic, in the early Tertiary or late Mesozoic and suggested the Antarctic as a diffusion center for South American and Australian animals.

The occurrence of related groups of parasites in related hosts has other consequences. For example, it shows quite conclusively that the New World monkeys evolved, in their early days, in association with the Old World monkeys and that the pinworms and malarial parasites of the Primates were inherited from Mesozoic reptiles. It agrees with the hypothesis that the mammals are polyphyletic and may well have originated from therapsid reptiles in more than one part of the world—for example, Africa and Eurasia.

Cameron entered Glasgow University in 1912 intending to become a chemist, but almost immediately he fell under the influence of the professor of zoology, Graham Kerr, whose ability as a teacher and interest in parasites and human disease caused Cameron to enroll as a medical student. After World War I, in which he served in the Highland Light Infantry and as a pilot in the Royal Flying Corps, Cameron included veterinary medicine in his studies. In 1921 he was appointed to the London School of Tropical Medicine and Seamans Hospital, where he worked until 1929. He moved to Edinburgh in 1929 to teach parasitology at both the medical and veterinary schools and to inaugurate a diploma in tropical veterinary medicine. In 1932 he went to Canada to establish the Institute of Parasitology in McGill University, serving as director until 1964. Thereafter he continued at McGill as professor of parasitology in the department of bacteriology and immunology. He received the Flavelle Medal of the Royal Society of Canada in 1957.

Besides some 200 scientific papers, Cameron wrote *Parasites of Domestic Animals* (1934; 2d ed. 1952), *Parasites of Man in Temperate Climates* (1940; 2d ed. 1946), and *Parasites and Parasitism* (1956).

For background information *see* PARASITOLOGY; PARASITOLOGY, MEDICAL in the McGraw-Hill Encyclopedia of Science and Technology. ■

CARMICHAEL, LEONARD

★ American psychologist and student of animal behavior

Born *Nov. 9, 1898, Philadelphia, PA, U.S.A.*

Died *Sept. 16, 1973, Washington, DC, U.S.A.*

Carmichael developed techniques for the study of the development of behavior in fetal organisms and contributed to the understanding of behavior changes resulting from maturation rather than individual learning. He used electrophysiological techniques in the study of the mechanisms underlying behavior. With an associate he was the first American to record human electroencephalograms and to study their production and interpretation.

Carmichael's early experiments demonstrated that the embryos of the frog *(Rana sylvatica)* and the salamander *(Amblystoma punctatum)* could be reared in a solution of chloretone, in which morphological growth continues but in which bodily movement does not occur. When control animals demonstrated coordinated swimming movements, the experimental animals were placed in water free of the anesthetic. In less than 12 minutes, on the average, animals that had not previously moved were swimming as well as the control animals. This could be interpreted as demonstrating that some complex adaptive behavior depends on the genetic code and a standard environment and not on individual habit formation.

Later Carmichael was able to describe the prenatal development of behavior in a number of mammals. His monograph on the experimental study of the fetal guinea pig traced the origin and development of reflexes and complex patterns of behavior during the total prenatal period. He devised techniques for maintaining mammalian fetal organisms under relatively normal conditions while behavior is studied. He showed that, prior to the onset of responses related to receptor stimulation, muscles can be made to respond to direct stimulation.

Carmichael's study of fetal guinea pigs can be taken as developing facts that are typical of many other mammals as well. Active behavior in the prenatal guinea pig begins in the last hour of the twenty-fifth postinsemination day. Neck flexion and forelimb movements are the first responses noted. This fetus exists during its active prenatal period of about 68 days in a condition much like that of an astronaut in space. It is an essentially weightless organism in its liquid environment. This allows the animal to demonstrate coordinated responses that are not typical immediately after birth, when the newborn organism exists in a gravitational field and in an environment characterized by normal external physical energies.

During fetal life the patterns of behavior released by the stimulation of specific receptor areas remain surprisingly constant. What has been called Carmichael's law states that anatomical behavior mechanisms may be elicited by experimental means at a time prior to that when the normal action of these patterns of behavior is essential in the adaptive life of the organism. He showed the relevance of these observations to an understanding of various psychological processes—for example, perceptual phenomena. He also published research on the postnatal maturation of specific behavior systems, such as the air-writing reflex of falling animals.

Electrophysiological techniques were employed by Carmichael and his associates in the study of the development of responses. For example, they studied the ontogeny of cerebral electrical potentials in the fetal guinea pig. They demonstrated that at 42 postinsemination days the electrical cochlear effect could be recorded. This is the same time in development that the operatively removed guinea pig fetuses first respond to airborne auditory stimuli.

In other behavior studies Carmichael used electrophysiological techniques. He and H. H. Jasper were the first American investigators to record human electroencephalograms. This work, first done in 1934 and published in 1935, confirmed the work of Hans Berger in Germany. He and Jasper also described new electroencephalographic phenomena.

Carmichael adapted an electrical technique for the recording of eye movements to the study of reading and other visual tasks. This method was later used in an elaborate experimental study, conducted jointly with W. F. Dearborn, that led to a book, *Reading and Visual Fatigue* (1947). This study demonstrated that subjects could read continuously for 6 hours from a book or from microfilm without fatigue. Other investigations of Carmichael dealt with certain phenomena of learning in rats and other mammals; motor processes related to handedness and the effect of language on perception; and special problems related to the training of naval aviators.

Carmichael's father was a physician and his mother, before her marriage, was a teacher of psychology. He received his B.S. summa cum laude from Tufts College in 1921 and his Ph.D. from Harvard University in 1924. After teaching at Princeton University from 1924 to 1927 and at Brown University from 1927 to 1936, he was dean and professor of psychology at the University of Rochester from 1936 to 1938. From 1938 to 1952 he was president of Tufts University and director of its Laboratory of Sensory Physiology and Psychology. During World War II he was director of the National Roster of Scientific and Specialized Personnel in Washington; while continuing his duties as president of Tufts, he directed the Roster's 400 workers, who mobilized America's scientists and engineers for the war effort. From 1953 to 1964 he was secretary (administrative head) of the Smithsonian Institution. In 1964 he became vice-president for research exploration of the National Geographic Society. He was president of the American Psychological Association in 1940 and later became president of the International Primatological Society and of the section of Psychology and Animal Behavior of the International Union of Biological Sciences. Carmichael received a number of American and foreign awards. He was elected to the American

Philosophical Society in 1942 and to the National Academy of Sciences in 1943.

Carmichael wrote many papers and was author of *The Making of the Modern Mind* (1956) and *Basic Psychology* (1957). He edited and contributed to *The Manual of Child Psychology* (1946; 3d ed. 1970).

For background information *see* BE-HAVIOR, ONTOGENY OF; ELECTROEN-CEPHALOGRAPHY in the McGraw-Hill Encyclopedia of Science and Technology. ∎

CARTER, HERBERT EDMUND
★ American chemist and biochemist

Born Sept 25, 1910, Mooresville, IN, U.S.A.

Carter's main research activities involved the chemistry and biochemistry of amino acids; the isolation, structure determination, and biological activity of antibiotics; and the isolation, characterization, and structure determination of complex lipids of animals and of plants.

On receiving his Ph.D. in organic chemistry at the University of Illinois in 1933, Carter accepted a position in biochemistry there and undertook synthetic studies on threonine. In the course of this work he developed a number of methods for the synthesis of threonine and other α-amino-β-hydroxy acids (serine, phenylserine, and so forth).

Studies of the chemical properties of α-amino-β-hydroxy acids led to an extensive investigation of α,β-unsaturated azlactones and the discovery that the latter could be readily converted to α-amino-β-thiol acids. These results were directly applicable to later studies on the structure of penicillin, one of whose degradation products, penicillamine, is an α-amino-β-thiol acid.

The amino-hydroxy acid work brought attention to the long-chain base, sphingosine, an essential component of cerebrosides and other lipids of nervous tissue. Thus was initiated a study of the long-chain base-containing lipids of animals and plants. Initial studies led to the establishment of the structure of sphingosine as D-erythro-1,3-dihydroxy-2-amino-*trans*-octadecene-4. Dihydrosphingosine was found also to occur in brain and spinal cord.

World War II interrupted these studies, and for the next 5 years Carter devoted all his efforts to the antibiotic field, serving as executive secretary for the efforts of a group of midwestern pharmaceutical firms. In his own laboratories, studies of the detection of new antibiotics and their isolation, characterization structure, and biological properties were pursued. A number of new antibiotics were discovered, including chloramphenicol (simultaneously with the Parke Davis group), endomycin levomycin, and filipin. Extensive contributions were made to the structure of patulin, streptomycin, streptothricin, viomycin, and filipin. In a study of the antifungal properties of filipin, the very interesting discovery was made that this activity was reversibly inhibited by cholesterol and ergosterol, an observation that has been extended by other workers and provides a tool for study of the biological functions of sterols.

In a study of the antibacterial activity of streptomycin, Carter found that partial reversal was produced by soybean tryptone. A study of the inositol-containing substances of soybean resulted in the totally unexpected discovery of the presence in plant seed lipids of a long-chain base similar to sphingosine. After 1945, therefore, Carter devoted his chief attention to the sphingolipids of plants as well as of animals. Major contributions included the synthesis of sphingosine, determination of the structure of cerebrosides, characterization of the long-chain base from plants (designated as phytosphingosine) as D-ribo-l,3,4-trihydroxyoctadecane, discovery of dehydrophytosphingosine in plant seeds, discovery of cerebrosides derived from phytosphingosine in plants, and discovery and characterization of a novel type of glycolipid – the mono- and digalactosyl-diglycerides in wheat flour.

Carter's major contribution in the plant lipid studies, however, was the discovery of a group of related complex glycolipids for which he coined the general term "phytoglycolipid." These materials consist of an acylated long-chain base joined by a phosphate diester group to inositol-containing oligo- and polysaccharides. Carter elucidated the complete structure of one of these substances (in which the oligosaccharide contains glucosamine, glucuronic acid, mannose, and inositol). For this work he received the American Chemical Society's Nichols Medal in 1965, the American Oil Chemists Society Award in Lipid Chemistry in 1966, the Kenneth A. Spencer Award in 1968, and the Alton E. Bailey Award in 1970.

Carter received his A.B. at DePauw University in 1930 and his Ph.D. in organic chemistry, with Carl S. Marvel, at the University of Illinois in 1933. He moved into the bichemistry division of the chemistry department there, becoming head of the department in 1954. He served as acting dean of the graduate college from 1963 to 1965 and vice-chancellor of academic affairs from 1967 to 1971. From 1971 to 1977 he served the University of Arizona as coordinator of interdisciplinary programs, and from 1977 as head of the department of biochemistry. He was elected to the National Academy of Sciences in 1953 and served on the National Science Board from 1964 to 1976. (chairperson 1970–74).

For backgound information *see* AMINO ACIDS; ANTIBIOTIC; LIPID in the McGraw-Hill Encyclopedia of Science and Technology. ∎

CASERIO, MARJORIE
★ American chemist

Born Feb. 26, 1929, London, England

When a chemical reaction occurs, the chemist's first concern is to identify the reactants and the products. Many times, the matter is given no further thought, but there is more to learn about a reaction than its reactants and products. Caserio's work was concerned with how and why organic reactions occur, or with the elucidation of reaction mechanisms.

While a graduate student in Ernst Berliner's laboratory at Bryn Mawr College Caserio studied the ways in which molecular bromine reacts with aromatic hydrocarbons to produce bromine-containing compounds. Thereafter, she pursued postdoctoral research at the California Institute of Technology in Pasadena with John D. Roberts, and this association led to numerous investigations concerned with the reaction mechanisms of small-ring compounds (derivatives of cyclopropanes and cyclobutanes) and of dicoordinate iodine (iodonium) compounds. During the late 1950s and into the 1960s impressive advances in analytical and instrumental techniques, especially in chromatographic, computational, and spectroscopic techniques, were taking place in the field of chemistry. Thus, Caserio's work with Roberts showed an early appreciation of the application of new instrumental methods such as nuclear magnetic resonance spectroscopy to problems of structure and mechanism in organic chemistry. Also during this period, Roberts and Caserio produced a basic textbook in organic chemistry that had considerable influence on the teaching of the subject in the ensuing decade. The book went a long way toward bringing the theory and practice of modern organic chemistry to the beginning student. It introduced the student to the concepts of organic structure, reactivity, and mechanism, and described important applications of analytical and spectroscopic techniques to organic chemistry. *See* ROBERTS, JOHN D.

In her later work at the Irvine campus of the University of California, Caserio

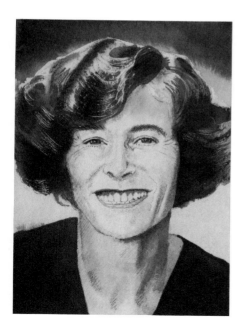

continued research in organic reaction mechanisms. Among her contributions were studies of the reactions of cumulenes (hydrocarbons with contiguous double bonds) with halogens and related compounds. The major result of this work was the determination that electrophilic reagents such as bromine, chlorine, or mercuric salts add to one of the double bonds in a selective manner to produce one major product with a well-defined stereochemistry. Radical substitution reactions of propadiene and propyne were shown to proceed by chain mechanisms involving the same resonance-stabilized radical intermediate from both hydrocarbons.

Caserio also studied the mechanisms of sulfur-containing organic molecules. Sulfur is a remarkable element in that it can display almost any type of chemical behavior, depending on its particular molecular environment. For example, thiosulfonium ions are formed when a disulfide reacts with a powerful alkylating agent. The relatively stable disulfide is transformed into a highly reactive ion that rearranges and reacts rapidly with nucleophiles to cleave carbon-sulfur and sulfur-sulfur bonds. Caserio's work in this area had implications for biological chemistry because of the importance of C-S and S-S bonds in many proteins, coenzymes, and hormones.

The work mentioned hitherto pertained to organic reactions in solution; Caserio's later work, however, dealt with the mechanisms of reactions in the gas phase. When organic ions are formed in the gas phase at low pressures, they are deprived of a coating of solvent molecules. These "naked" ions exhibit behavior and reactivity that differ from those of their solvated counterparts—as the work of Caserio and others in the field showed. She discovered some remarkable rearrangements of gaseous ions that have no analogy in solution. She carried out extensive studies of the mechanisms of acyl transfer reactions, which are among the most important chemical and biochemical reactions known. Although these reactions commonly involve the formation of tetrahedral intermediates in solution, her work showed that they follow a different pathway in the gas phase.

Caserio received her B.Sc. in chemistry from Chelsea College of the University of London in 1950, and her M.A. in chemistry at Bryn Mawr College in Pennsylvania in 1951. After spending a year at the Ful-

mer Research Institute in Stoke Poges in England, she returned to the United States and completed her Ph.D. at Bryn Mawr College in 1956. Subsequently she spent 8 years at Caltech as a postdoctoral fellow (1956–58) and as a senior research fellow (1958–64). In 1965 she joined the chemistry faculty of the newly formed Irvine campus of the University of California.

Caserio wrote *Basic Principles of Organic Chemistry*, with John D. Roberts (1964 2d ed; 1977); *Modern Organic Chemistry*, with Roberts (1967); *Experimental Chemistry* (1967); and *Organic Chemistry, Methane to Macromolecules*, with Roberts and R. Stewart (1971).

For background information *see* NUCLEAR MAGNETIC RESONANCE (NMR); ORGANIC REACTION MECHANISM; SPECTROSCOPY in the McGraw-Hill Encyclopedia of Science and Technology. ∎

CASTAING, RAYMOND
★ French physicist

***Born** Dec. 28, 1921, Monaco*

When a fast electron moves through a solid target, the amount of kinetic energy dE that it loses over a path ds is dependent, as a first approximation, only on its energy E and on the product $\rho \, ds$, where ρ is the local density. The result, as was shown by Castaing, is that the number of deep ionizations that the electron performs in atoms of a given type A, along its whole path in the target, is essentially proportional to the mass concentration of the element A at the bombarded point. The same is true for the total number of x-ray characteristic A photons generated by bombarding a selected point of a sample with a sharp electron beam. This is the principle of electron probe microanalysis, proposed by Castaing and A. Guinier in 1949 and developed by Castaing in his doctoral thesis (Paris, 1951), which presents the principles of quantitative analysis by x-ray emission and describes the first experimental model of the electron probe microanalyzer. The local concentration of any component element A is derived from a comparison between the A characteristic line emitted by the analyzed point under the impingement of the electron probe and that of the same line emitted by a pure sample of A (or by a known compound) bombarded with the same probe. By canceling down all instrumental parameters, this procedure allows absolute measurements.

In his thesis Castaing derived the various "corrections" (absorption of the x-radiation in the target itself, fluorescent radiation excited by the X lines of the heavier elements, and so on) which make it possible to go back from the outcoming raw intensities read on the spectrometer to the initial x-ray emissions arising from direct ionization of the atoms by the primary electrons. The calculation of the self-absorption of the target required a knowledge of the distribution in depth of the characteristic emission; in Castaing's thesis, that self-absorption was derived from a plot of the emerging intensity as a function of the take-off angle of the x-ray beam. In 1955 Castaing and J. Descamps reported the first direct measurement of that depth distribution by a "tracer" technique using thin layers of a neighboring element more or less deeply buried in the target; they applied a similar procedure for estimating the amount of secondary fluorescent radiation excited by the continuous spectrum. Those corrections, together with atomic number corrections developed later, led to absolute elemental analyses whose spatial localization is 1 micrometer, with an accuracy better than 1% and a limit of detection better than 100 parts per million.

Castaing's first work concerned transmission electron microscopy; by using the oxide film replica for visualizing the fine precipitations which occur during the aging of the aluminum alloys, he obtained in 1949 the first micrograph showing the se-

lective nucleation of precipitates on the individual dislocations along a polygonization boundary; he subsequently made visible, by direct observation of thin samples, the very first stages of the precipitation associated with the structural hardening of the light alloys. From that initial work, Castaing had developed a predilection for imagery; a few years later he proposed a new procedure, developed between 1958 and 1962 with his student G. Slodzian, for directly producing distribution images of the various component elements over a wide area of a sample, by combining ion microscopy and mass spectrometry. The secondary ions extracted from the sample by primary ion bombardment are accelerated and focused to form an enlarged image of the sample surface. That global image is the superimposition of the various component images formed by each type of secondary ion; each of the component images carries with it the map of distribution of the corresponding element or isotope over the bombarded area. The secondary ion microscope built by Castaing and Slodzian based on that principle involved a new magnetic filtering device which made possible the isolation of any of the component images without damaging its quality. The spatial resolution of the distribution images is better that 1 micrometer, with a detectability limit better than 1 part per million. In addition, the depth-resolving power of the analysis is very high (a few atomic layers). This instrument has been applied extensively for drawing implantation profiles in semiconductors; it has initiated new research fields, especially in the study of minerals; and it has made possible local isotope analysis. On the other hand, the interpretation of the results in terms of elemental concentrations is not simple, and requires the comparison to standards of similar composition and structure.

The same type of magnetic filtering was applied in 1962 by Castaing and his coworkers L. Henry, A. El Hili, and P. Henoc to energy-filtering of electron microscope images. By isolating, for producing the image, those of the electrons which have undergone a definite energy loss when crossing a thin sample, point analyses may be performed with a spatial resolution of a few angstroms (tenths of a nanometer). Castaing and his coworkers applied this technique to the study of the coherency of the various scattering processes which the fast electrons undergo in crystal lattices, disclosing, for example,

partial coherency in the so-called incoherent thermal scattering associated with phonon excitation or quenching.

Castaing was educated at the Ecole Normale Supérieure in Paris. After serving as a research engineer at the French Office for Aeronautical Research (ONERA) laboratories from 1947 to 1951, he was appointed a lecturer at the University of Toulouse in 1951. He was professor of physics at the University of Paris-Sud (Orsay) from 1959 onward. From 1968 to 1973 he held the position of director general of ONERA. Castaing was awarded the John Price Wetherill Medal of the Franklin Institute in 1960, the Gold Medal of the National Center for Scientific Research (France) in 1975, and the Brinell Medal of the Royal Swedish Academy for Engineering Sciences and the Roebling Medal of the Mineralogical Society of America in 1977. Laureate of the Holweck Prize (Institute of Physics and French Physical Society) in 1966, he was elected to the Deutsche Akademie der Naturforscher Leopoldina in 1968, the French Académie des Sciences in 1977, and the Royal Swedish Academy of Sciences in 1978.

Castaing wrote "Electron Probe Microanalysis" in *Advances in Electronics* (vol. 13, 1960), and "Secondary Ion Microanalysis and Energy-Selecting Electron Microscopy" in *Electron Microscopy in Material Science* (1971).

For background information *see* MICROPROBE, ION; MICROSCOPE, ELECTRON in the McGraw-Hill Encyclopedia of Science and Technology. ∎

CERENKOV, PAVEL ALEXEYEVICH
☆ Soviet physicist

Born July 28, 1904, Voronezh Region, Soviet Russia

Cerenkov was the first to identify correctly the faint blue light emitted in liquids and solids exposed to a source of fast gamma radiation. His studies, conducted during the 1930s, showed that this phenomenon (later known as the Cerenkov effect) was a new kind of radiation, generated when a particle traveling near the speed of light in a vacuum passed through a medium where the speed of light was less than that of the particle. Cerenkov's discovery found employment in the Cerenkov counter, a particle detector whose hypersensitivity made it a crucially valuable laboratory tool. For his work Cerenkov was awarded the Nobel Prize for physics in 1958. He shared the prize with I. M. Frank and I. Y. Tamm, two of his colleagues, who developed a mathematical theory of the radiation. *See* FRANK, ILYA MIKHAILOVICH; TAMM, IGOR YEVGENEVICH.

Cerenkov began his investigations of the effect that now bears his name as a graduate student at the Lebedev Institute at Moscow, where he worked under the direction of academician S. I. Vavilov. The phenomenon had long been known and was assumed to be a luminescence effect such as was often observed in irradiated liquids. To gage the accuracy of this assumption, Cerenkov realized, an entire sequence of sensitive and (above all) qualitative experiments was needed, in order to determine the effect of varying experimental conditions upon the emission of the radiation.

Such experiments were carried on by Cerenkov in a darkened room with nothing more than a weak gamma source and a bottle of test solution. Many of the measurements were made by eye, employing a method of visual photometry used before the advent of the photomultiplier.

One of the first experiments showed that the emission of the radiation was independent of the composition of the irradiated liquid. By using doubly distilled water as a test solution, Cerenkov disposed of the possibility that the radiation stemmed from the fluorescence of minute impurities.

Cerenkov now examined various char-

acteristics of luminescence phenomena, seeking a line along which to organize further experiments. It was insufficient to establish that the new radiation lacked properties seen only in some luminescences—Cerenkov sought to establish that it failed to exhibit a feature common to all luminescent emissions. The feature turned out to be the quenching characteristic. All luminescent emissions (which were due to impurities in solution) could be dimmed without being utterly extinguished, and the dying-out period was longer than 10^{-10} second. It could accordingly be observed.

The next group of experiments was concerned, therefore, with the quenching phenomenon. It was known, for example, that luminescence was quenched by introducing certain substances into the test solution. Painstaking experiments revealed an apparently complete absence of quenching due to additives. The same result was seen when test solutions were heated, another means of quenching luminescence. A variety of additives were used; and to establish the accuracy of these measurements, Cerenkov conducted a parallel series of experiments, under identical conditions but with solutions known to be luminescent. In those, he observed a definite quenching.

Another important fact emerged from these experiments. Luminescent light, which was known to be polarized, could be altered in the direction of its polarization by heating the solution. In contrast, heating had no effect on the polarization of the new radiation. What was more, the direction of polarization was seen to be parallel to the exciting gamma ray, while luminiscent light was always polarized perpendicular to the incoming ray.

Cerenkov suspected that the radiation originated as the incoming gamma radiation, deflected in its passage through the liquid, generated secondary electrons in obedience to the Compton effect. The secondary electrons, he thought, must be the source of the light, rather than the gamma radiation itself. This hypothesis was confirmed in experiments with magnetic poles.

In 1936 Cerenkov performed a series of experiments in which the gamma source was replaced by a source of x-rays. These brought to light the important fact that the radiation was characteristically asymmetrical, being emitted only at a forward angle relative to the direction of the stimulating radiation.

Cerenkov had now determined all the essential properties of the new radiation and proved it to be not a form of luminescence but a new distinct phenomenon. He lacked, however, any convincing theoretical framework into which to fit the new observations. Such a theory was to appear with the advent of Tamm and Frank, who developed a rigorous mathematical explanation of the radiation and tested their ideas in further experiments conducted in conjunction with Cerenkov. The collaboration led, ultimately, to a complete theoretical model of the phenomenon.

For some years the Cerenkov effect was considered an isolated phenomenon with no practical applications. With the development of sensitive photelectric devices, however, which were able to measure the very faint light emitted, an important application of the Cerenkov effect came to be known, namely, the Cerenkov counter. This device became extremely important in experimental physics, since its sensitivity was unrivaled among particle detectors. Cerenkov counters played a significant part in the discovery of the antiproton by Owen Chamberlain and Emilio Segrè in 1956. *See* CHAMBERLAIN, OWEN; SEGRÈ, EMILIO GINO.

Born of peasant parents, Cerenkov graduated in 1928 from Voronezh State University's physicomathematical faculty. In 1930 he was appointed a senior scientific officer at the Lebedev Physical Institute at Moscow. He subsequently became section leader and in 1959 assumed control of the photo-meson processes laboratory. In 1940 Cerenkov was awarded the degree of doctor of physicomathematical sciences; he became a professor of experimental physics in 1959. He was elected a member of the U.S.S.R. Academy of Sciences in 1970.

For background information *see* CERENKOV RADIATION; FLUORESCENCE in the McGraw-Hill Encyclopedia of Science and Technology. ∎

CHADWICK, SIR JAMES
☆ British physicist

Born Oct. 20, 1891, Manchester, England
Died July 24, 1974, Cambridge, England

In 1932 Chadwick established experimentally the existence of the neutron, a particle whose presence in atomic nuclei

he had suspected since 1920. His experiments corroborated the hypothesis that atoms were composed of heavy, uncharged particles as well as of the electrically charged protons and electrons. Chadwick's investigations furnished the first conclusive evidence for such particles, and he was able to give the first determinations of their mass. For this and other contributions to nuclear physics, Chadwick was awarded the 1935 Nobel Prize in physics.

In 1920 the English physicist Ernest Rutherford propounded a neutron theory to help reconcile the numerous contradictions present in the then current knowledge of atomic behavior. Chadwick, adopting this theory, in the early 1920s (as Rutherford's colleague at the Cavendish Laboratory, Cambridge) initiated a long sequence of experiments to detect such a particle: Rutherford had posited one with zero net charge and mass slightly greater than the proton's. Chadwick worked with a variety of experimental arrangements but at first had no success.

In 1930 the German physicists Walther Bothe and Hans Becker, using a stronger radiation source and better detection equipment than had been available to Chadwick (notably the just-invented Geiger-Müller counter) found that the metal beryllium, under bombardment with fast alpha particles, gave off very energetic radiation. This reemitted radiation, while presumed to be some sort of gamma radiation, had several unusual

properties. Especially peculiar was the fact that the reemitted radiation from the beryllium was much more penetrating in the same direction as the bombarding particles than it was in the opposite direction. Chadwick noted that this observation would be difficult to explain unless the reemitted radiation consisted of particles of some sort. Moreover, the very penetrating nature of the radiation led him to suspect that it was made up of neutral particles. *See* BOTHE, WALTHER.

Soon after this, the French physicists Frédéric Joliot and Irène Curie reported that paraffin which had been subjected to the radiation from bombarded beryllium emitted high-energy protons, presumably ejected from the hydrogen nuclei in the wax. Learning of this, Chadwick suspected that here, too, was evidence that neutral particles were present in the beryllium emission.

Chadwick set out to duplicate the Joliot-Curie experiments in his own laboratory. Concentrating upon the character of the high-energy beryllium emission, he directed this radiation onto a variety of experimental materials: hydrogen, nitrogen, argon, air, and others. In each of these substances, the beryllium radiation ejected protons from the substances' atomic nuclei. Now, if the beryllium radiation were some form of gamma photons, the energies of these protons could be readily calculated by means of the well-known Compton effect, which described the interactions of gamma radiation and atomic nuclei. Chadwick made the requisite calculations; the results were completely at variance with the proton energies he had measured experimentally in the laboratory. On the basis, therefore, of the observations of these collisions with atoms, Chadwick concluded that the beryllium radiation was composed of neutral particles of about rest mass 1.005 to 1.008 (the proton rest mass being taken as 1.0).

Having tentatively identified the neutron, it now remained for Chadwick to evince conclusive evidence of its existence. For this purpose, he and his associates at the Cavendish Laboratory began in 1932 a new and extensive series of experiments. One crucial experiment made use of an ionization chamber connected to an amplifier, which was in turn attached to an oscilloscope. Ionizing particles entering the chamber would make the oscilloscope trace fluctuate; the trace was recorded

continually on photographic paper. A source of radiation was constructed from a disk of metal plated with polonium (a powerful alpha emitter) and a disk of pure beryllium, both placed together in an evacuated vessel. With this source stationed at a large distance from the chamber, Chadwick established the rate of oscilloscope deflections as about 7 an hour. When the source was only a few centimeters from the chamber, the rate increased to over 200 an hour. (These deflections were due to atoms of air in the chamber set in motion by the radiation.) The interposition of lead sheets between chamber and source had no effect on the deflection rate, which showed the highly penetrating nature of the radiation. Moreover, replacing the lead sheets with sheets of paraffin doubled the deflection rate. Chadwick ascertained that this doubling was caused by the ejection of protons from the wax, just as in the Joliot-Curie experiment.

All this information, taken together, provided Chadwick with the foundation in fact required to gain widespread acceptance for the neutron hypothesis. The concept quickly gained ground and assumed vital importance in subsequent theoretical advances in nuclear physics; it became, in fact, indispensable for any later theoretical approach to the structure of the atom.

Chadwick majored in physics at Manchester University, graduating in 1911. In 1913 he went to Germany to work in the Reichanstalt, Charlottenburg, under H. Geiger; there he discovered the continuous nature of the energy spectrum of the beta emission of radioactive bodies. During World War I he was interned as a civilian prisoner-of-war. After his return to England he was invited by Rutherford to accompany him to the Cavendish Laboratory, Cambridge, where Rutherford was appointed Cavendish Professor in 1919. Chadwick was elected a fellow of Gonville and Caius College in 1921, and was appointed assistant director of research in the Cavendish Laboratory. During this period in Cambridge he worked in very close collaboration with Rutherford in their efforts to open up the new subject of nuclear physics. In 1935 he left Cambridge to become professor of physics in Liverpool University, where he established a new school of nuclear physics. In the winter of 1939–40 he started what was perhaps the earliest work on the atomic bomb. During the latter part of World War II he was head of the British mission cooperating in the Manhattan Project, and for his services in this work he was awarded in 1946 the Medal for Merit by President Truman. In 1948 he returned to Cambridge as master of Gonville and Caius College, an office that he resigned in 1958. In addition to the Nobel Prize, Chadwick was awarded the Copley Medal of the Royal Society of London in 1950, the Franklin Medal of the Franklin Institute of the State of Pennsylvania in 1951, the Guthrie Medal of the Institute of Physics in 1967, and numerous other honors. He was elected a fellow of the Royal Society in 1927.

Chadwick wrote *Radiations from Radioactive Substances,* with E. Rutherford and C. D. Ellis (1930), and *Radioactivity and Radioactive Substances* (4th ed. 1953).

For background information *see* NEUTRON; NUCLEAR STRUCTURE in the McGraw-Hill Encyclopedia of Science and Technology. ∎

CHADWICK, WALLACE LACY
★ American engineer

Born Dec. 4, 1897, Loring, KS, U.S.A.

Following keen boyhood interest in mountains, water, electricity, and construction Chadwick made a career of designing, building, and managing large electric power projects. First was work in development of the hydroelectric resources of the middle Sierra Nevada in California, followed by design and construction of thermal electric plants, design and construction of the transmission systems to serve these, and the planning and preliminary design for one of the largest nuclear power plants. This work occupied him during some 35 years with Southern California Edison Company. It was interrupted for 6 years—from 1931 to 1937— for work on the design, financing, and construction across the eastern California desert of the 243-mile (389-kilometer) Colorado River Aqueduct of the Metropolitan Water District of Southern California.

The development of water power from the western slope of the central Sierra Nevada Mountains began about 1912. To meet the demand for power in the fast-growing southern California area following World War I, the Southern California Edison Company undertook to divert the South Fork of the San Joaquin River through the 13-mile (20.8-kilometer), 16-foot-diameter (4.8-meter) Florence Lake Tunnel for use by two existing power plants and one new one. Chadwick joined the project early in 1922. After 2 years in the field headquarters engineering office and in the Los Angeles general office, he was sent to the high-altitude Florence Lake project as division field engineer. There he was responsible for the engineering control of the tunnel. This work was followed by field engineering for Florence Lake Multiple Arch Dam and for location of the diversion works for two other streams, Mono and Bear creeks. He then returned to the headquarters engineering office, where he was in charge of office and field engineering, including, in 1927, the construction supervision of the 2420-foot (726-meter) head, 147-megawatt Big Creek 2A project.

Returning to Southern California Edison Company in 1937, after his Colorado River Aqueduct experience, Chadwick directed the design and construction of four additional developments on the Big Creek–San Joaquin project to achieve a total of 690 megawatts in eight plants, using the greatest total head in the world— more than 6200 feet (1860 meters). Included in these works were two large earthfill dams.

Chadwick also became responsible for the Edison Company's engineering and construction, including design and construction of thermal power plants. Before his retirement, Chadwick had directed the design and construction of six large thermal plants totaling 4000 megawatts.

For the thermal plants, Chadwick directed the development of four subaqueous cooling water systems that take water directly from the sea along an exposed seacoast. These systems have operated successfully, even in periods of heavy storm, without sand or fouling interference. Fouling control is unique and is accomplished by periodically reversing the flow in the intake and discharge cooling water conduits. This raises the temperature in the normal intake sufficiently to discourage the growth of fouling organisms.

Chadwick also became interested in control systems that would assist the human operator with many monitoring functions and reduce the chance of equipment damage from operating errors. This work resulted in the development, jointly with Bechtel Corporation and General Electric Company, of the first digital-computer control system to be used for start-up and control of thermal power plants. Chadwick received the Sprague Award of the Instrument Society of America in 1963 for pioneering in this field.

Other departures from traditional thermal plant designs were the extensive use of outdoor construction, use of two of the first universal pressure steam generators, and development of several features for minimizing atmospheric pollution.

When peaceful use of nuclear energy was first considered, Southern California Edison Company built the first nuclear plant to produce electricity commercially. This was the 7.5 megawatt turbine-generator plant associated with the Atomic Energy Commission–Atomics International sodium graphite reactor at Santa Susana. This installation and its subsequent use by Edison for training of engineers in nuclear plant operation was directed by Chadwick. He continued his interest in trying to develop nuclear power on a practical commercial scale and, prior to his retirement, had directed enough of the final design for the 450 megawatt San Onofre reactor plant to facilitate final contracting with Westinghouse and Bechtel Corporation.

A farmer's son, Chadwick received a liberal arts education at the University of Redlands, taking as much engineering as the curriculum allowed. Army service in World War I interfered with graduation, but he continued his education through various extension courses. He was awarded an Honorary D.Eng.S. degree by Redlands in 1965. He joined the Southern California Edison Company in 1922, becoming vice-president in 1951 and retiring in 1962.

For background information *see* ELECTRIC POWER SYSTEMS; WATER SUPPLY ENGINEERING in the McGraw-Hill Encyclopedia of Science and Technology. ■

CHAIN, ERNST BORIS
☆ British biochemist

Born June 19, 1906, Berlin, Germany
Died August 14, 1979, Ireland

With the introduction of sulfonamide in 1939, the medical world was alerted to the possibilities of chemotherapy. A great effort was directed toward isolating, purifying, and manufacturing penicillin, a substance discovered in a mold culture in 1928 by Sir Alexander Fleming. The research group that was particularly instrumental in making this valuable antibiotic available for the treatment of human infectious disease was headed by Howard Florey and Chain. For their achievements in elucidating the chemical structure of penicillin and performing the first clinical trials with this substance, Chain and Florey, together with Fleming, shared the 1945 Nobel Prize in medicine or physiology. *See* FLEMING, SIR ALEXANDER; FLOREY OF ADELAIDE, BARON (HOWARD WALTER FLOREY).

Fleming's discovery of penicillin was accidental. A culture plate on which pathogenic bacteria were growing became contaminated by mold organisms from the air. Fleming noted that as the mold grew, it destroyed bacterial growth; he concluded that a substance produced by the mold was responsible for the bacterial destruction. Since the bacteria were of a type infectious to humans, he pursued this observation, eventually performing tests on animals that showed penicillin (as he named the substance) to be capable of destroying many pathogenic bacteria in living organisms. Fleming also foresaw the possibility of using penicillin to treat human disease but was unable to perform such trials, largely because he was unable to make a sufficient amount of the substance.

In 1931, years after Fleming's discovery, another attempt was made to obtain and purify penicillin, but again without success. The group that performed this work, however, did find that during the purifying process penicillin lost its antibacterial properties.

Fortunately, these findings did not discourage investigation completely, for research on penicillin was once more begun at the Pathological Institute of Oxford University. There Chain and Florey, in 1938, started a systematic investigation of antibacterial substances produced by microorganisms. They began their study with a reinvestigation of Fleming's penicillin because its chemical and biological properties seemed interesting and indicated that it belonged to a new class of antibacterial substances.

First, a method was developed whereby the relative strength of a penicillin-containing broth could be determined by comparing its antibacterial effect (as evidenced on culture plates) with that of a standard penicillin solution 1 cubic centimeter of which was said to contain, by definition, one Oxford unit of penicillin.

Work was next directed toward developing a method of purifying penicillin without destroying its antibacterial effect. The penicillin-producing mold, *Penicillium notatum,* was grown in flasks containing nutritive material and was protected from airborne bacterial or fungal contamination by filters of cotton wool. Since it had previously been found that after 1 week the penicillin content of the broth reached its optimal value, extraction was

begun at this time. In addition, it had been found that free penicillin was an acid, and hence more soluble in certain organic solvents than in water, and that the alkaline salts of penicillin were more soluble in water. By shaking the penicillin broth with acidified ether or amyl acetate (at low temperature to prevent the penicillin from breaking up in water), the Oxford researchers almost completely neutralized its acidity and removed numerous impurities. The purified solution was then evaporated at low temperature, producing a stable, dry form of active substance. Although testing showed that each milligram of this substance contained from 40 to 50 Oxford units of penicillin—and was capable of destroying staphylococci in dilutions of one part per million—the substance was not pure penicillin, 1650 Oxford units.

Through subsequent efforts, Florey and Chain showed (as Fleming had previously done) that penicillin was only slightly toxic and that the presence of blood or pus did not decrease its antibacterial effect. During animal tests they demonstrated 90 percent recovery rates using penicillin on mice that had been infected with gas gangrene bacteria. All of the control (untreated) mice died.

Chain, working primarily with E. P. Abraham, was able to elucidate the chemical structure of crystalline penicillin, finding, in fact, that there were four different penicillins, each differing slightly in their relative elemental constituents. *See* ABRAHAM, EDWARD PENLEY.

Chain's interest in chemistry was early stimulated by visits to the factory and laboratory of his father, a chemist. He received his education at Friedrich-Wilhelm University in Berlin, graduating in 1930. He then specialized in enzyme research in the Charite Hospital in Berlin. Emigrating to England in 1933, he spent 2 years in the school of biochemistry at Cambridge, working on phospholipids under Sir Frederick Gowland Hopkins. In 1935 Chain was invited to Oxford University to the school of pathology. In 1936 he was named demonstrator and lecturer in chemical pathology. After the war, in 1948, Chain was made scientific director of the International Research Center for Chemical Microbiology in Rome. In 1961 he was appointed professor of biochemistry at the Imperial College, University of London, and from 1973 to 1976 he was professor emeritus and senior research fellow there. In 1947 he was made commander of the Legion of Honor (France). His awards included the Paul Ehrlich Prize of the Paul Ehrlich Foundation (1954). He was elected a fellow of the Royal Society (1949), fellow of the Royal Society of Arts (1963), and honorary member of the U.S.S.R. Academy of Sciences (1976).

For background information *see* CHEMOTHERAPY; PENICILLIN in the McGraw-Hill Encyclopedia of Science and Technology. ■

CHAMBERLAIN, OWEN
American physicist

***Born** July 10, 1920, San Francisco, CA, U.S.A.*

For more than 20 years the demonstration of the existence of the antiproton had eluded experimenters. While many doubted that it existed at all, Chamberlain, using the newly built Bevatron particle accelerator, provided physics with a laboratory demonstration of this particle and a brilliant confirmation of physical theory. For this achievement, Chamberlain and his colleague, Emilio Segrè, received the 1959 Nobel Prize in physics. *See* SEGRÈ, EMILIO GINO.

In 1930, P. A. M. Dirac published a paper in which he predicted the existence of particles having masses identical to the masses of the electron, proton, and neutron but having opposite electrical charge.

These particles came to be known as positrons, antiprotons, and antineutrons, respectively. In 1932, while investigating cosmic-ray collisions in the upper atmosphere, C. D. Anderson discovered the existence of the first of these antiparticles, the positron. The production of an antiproton in an analogous manner was estimated to require a considerably higher collision energy, on the order of 6.3×10^9 electronvolts, because of the much greater masses of protons and the still hypothetical antiprotons. Such energies were known to occur in cosmic-ray events, but close observation failed to provide definite evidence of any antiprotons. *See* DIRAC, PAUL ADRIEN MAURICE.

It was not until the completion of the Bevatron particle accelerator at Berkeley, CA, that the creation of a proton-antiproton pair in the laboratory became a possibility. Working with this new 6-billion-electronvolt machine, in the early 1950s Chamberlain, Segrè, and co-workers were able to bombard stationary neutrons with high-energy protons and thus produce the desired antiparticle. The main problem became one of isolation and identification, since there would be large numbers of auxiliary particles produced, mostly mesons. At first it was estimated that only one particle in a million would be an antiproton, but the frequency of occurrence turned out to be somewhat higher, that is, one particle in 30,000.

To identify a particle as an antiproton, it was necessary to know that it had a negative charge and the mass of a proton. Since positive and negative particles are deflected in different directions by a magnetic field, it was easy to separate out all the negatively charged particles produced in the bombardment. To determine the mass, Chamberlain decided to make independent measurements of the velocity and momentum of the negative particles he had separated. Using the fact that the amount of deflection of a negative particle by a given magnetic field is dependent only on the momentum of the particle, he was able to place a shield across the stream of negative particles to select only those in the range of momentum expected for the antiproton. The velocity was then determined by measuring time of flight across a known distance. Thus it was possible to separate the antiprotons from the less massive mesons having the

same momentum by virtue of possessing a higher velocity. During the experiment some 20 particles were identified as being antiprotons. The equipment was then exhaustively tested to be sure that there were no failures in the apparatus and that the observed antiparticles were completely real. They were.

Following the experiment described above, Chamberlain and others carried out related experiments using photographic emulsions to produce visual examples of the annihilation of an antiproton and a proton or neutron, in which these particles die simultaneously.

The son of a radiologist, Chamberlain received his B.S. in physics at Dartmouth in 1941. He interrupted his graduate studies to join the Manhattan Project, where he worked from 1942 to 1945. He received his Ph.D. from the University of Chicago in 1949, having worked under Enrico Fermi. In 1948 he joined the faculty of the University of California at Berkeley and became professor of physics there in 1958. He was elected to the National Academy of Sciences in 1960. *See* FERMI, ENRICO.

For background information *see* ANTIPROTON in the McGraw-Hill Encyclopedia of Science and Technology. ■

CHANCE, BRITTON
★ American biophysicist and physical biochemist

***Born** July 24, 1913, Wilkes-Barre, PA, U.S.A.*

Interested in the measurement of rapid reactions in solutions, Chance perfected, before World War II, new types of flow methods employing oscillographic readout which he termed stopped flow method and accelerated flow method. These sophisticated techniques led to his discovery in 1946–48 of eight of the nine known active or primary enzyme substrate compounds. Following work on radar timing and computing circuits at the Radiation Laboratory at the Massachusetts Institute of Technology from 1941 to 1946, Chance developed sensitive dual-wavelength spectrophotometric and fluorometric methods in order to extend his studies of the mechanism of enzyme action to living cells and tissues, particularly the enzymatic control of the flow of electrons from cellular metabolites to mo-

lecular oxygen. These methods allow the direct recording of the dynamics of intracellular reactions in living tissue.

Between 1936 and 1946 Chance invented a number of devices in the general area of automatic control mechanisms, precision-timing circuits, and analog computers. Some of these inventions applied to automatic ship steering, to circuits for manual and automatic distance measuring by radar, and to computers for solving bombing and navigation problems by radar. At the same time he became interested in sensitive optical methods; in 1940 he published one of the first automatic control systems for stabilizing light intensities in precision spectrophotometry, and in 1942 he applied sophisticated electronic circuitry to the measurement of extremely small changes of light absorption.

Following his development of the stopped flow and accelerated flow methods for measuring rapid reactions in solution, which greatly extended the concentration range of Hartridge and Roughton's flow method and permitted its use for the first time in studying enzyme reactions, Chance turned to the problem of measuring enzymatic reactions in living systems. He first approached this by devising an optical device—the double-beam or dual-wavelength spectrophotometer—suitable for application to living cells and cell particles. This spectrophotometer was found applicable to the study of a number of re-

actions in structured biological systems such as the mitochondrion, cell suspensions (particularly yeast and ascites tumor cells), photosynthetic systems, and strips of tissues. However, the study of enzymatic reactions in tissues with intact blood circulation required the devising of yet another method, namely, reflectance fluorometry, which Chance first developed for the study of reduced pyridine nucleotide components of mitochondria. Later he applied it to a variety of organs—brain, liver, kidney—and skeletal muscle: then he extended it to the study of the flavoprotein component of the tissues.

These sensitive optical techniques were also applied to the study of enzymes in single cells. Chance perfected a microspectrophotometer and a microfluorometer for studying the light absorbency changes in a single large mitochondrion of a spermatid caused by cytochromes or fluorescence changes due to reduced pyridine nucleotide. The sensitivity of these methods was extremely high; roughly 10^6 molecules could be detected.

Finally, Chance developed rapid methods for the study of rapid reactions of living material. A special type of flow apparatus, constituting the regenerative flow method, permitted the observation of millisecond reactions in cell suspensions and elucidated the sequence of reactions in the cytochrome chain in cells and mitochondria. An extension of these rapid methods to the ultrarapid methods came with the first application of laser techniques to flash photolysis in biological systems. This led to the discovery of chlorophyll-cytochrome reaction times in systems containing chlorophyll *a* (green plants) and bacterial chlorophyll.

Chance's use of analog and digital computers in studying biological problems began in the 1940s with the first computer solution of the differential equations for enzyme action. Ultimately, he applied large digital computers to complex problems in metabolic control involving the interaction of glycolysis and respiration.

Although these many techniques developed by Chance were significant advances, the knowledge yielded by his application of them to important biological problems was an even more important contribution. The first such application was the measurement of the kinetic properties of enzyme substrate compounds, particularly those of the iron-containing compounds peroxidase and catalase. This

was the first kinetic study of intermediates in any enzyme system, and led in 1943 to Chance's experimental demonstration of the validity of the 1913 Michaelis-Menton theory of enzyme action. With H. Theorell, he measured the kinetics of intermediates of alcohol dehydrogenase and formulated the current reaction mechanism for this enzyme. His second contribution was the elucidation of the time sequence of reactions in the cytochrome system of cells in intact mitochondria and particles derived therefrom by the rapid-flow method. Chance's third contribution, made with G. R. Williams, was the observation that the oxidation-reduction state of respiratory carriers of mitochondria is controlled not only by the concentration of oxygen but also by the concentration of adenosinediphosphate (ADP) and phosphate. In 1955 Chance turned to the control of metabolism. In particular, he studied the mitochondria as optical indicators of changes of ADP concentration in ascites tumor cells and in the muscle strips, gaining thereby a better understanding of the role of mitochondria in regulation of glucose utilization. This study was extended by the discovery of oscillating properties of enzymatic systems where sustained oscillations were observed to occur over a period of time in cell-free systems due to feedback properties of the glycolytic system. These studies indicated the role of adenine nucleotide in regulating flux of the glycolytic systems. *See* THEORELL, AXEL HUGO TEODOR.

Chance applied photometric techniques to biological problems and achieved the measurement of cell metabolism in living tissue in various physiological states. With C. M. Connelly, A. M. Weber, and F. Jöbsis, he successfully applied the double-beam spectrophotometer to living material (for example, muscle strips) as long as they were blood-free. The reflectance fluorometer now provides a method for working on a tissue with intact circulation. This achievement helped to lay the groundwork for the direct determination of the mode of action of narcotics, hormones, and poisons and the effects of energy demands on the interworkings of the cell.

The son of an engineer, Chance received his B.S. and M.S. at the University of Pennsylvania in 1936 and a Ph.D. in physical chemistry in 1940. Before World War II his research centered on the mechanism of enzyme action, but in 1935–39, while a research student at Cambridge University, he applied his talents to the field of electronics, working on devices of his own invention for the automatic steering of ships. From Cambridge he received both a Ph.D. in biology and physiology and a D.Sci. He returned to the University of Pennsylvania in 1941 as assistant professor of biophysics and acting director of the Johnson Foundation. At the Massachusetts Institute of Technology during the war, he was leader of the Precision Components Group, associate head of the Receiver Components Division, and one of the younger members of the Steering Committee of the Radiation Laboratory. Resuming his investigations into the nature of enzymes after the war, he studied on a Guggenheim Fellowship at the Nobel Institute in Stockholm and at the Molteno Institute in England. He returned to the University of Pennsylvania in 1949 to become professor and chairperson of the department of biophysics and physical biochemistry and to assume the directorship of the Johnson Foundation. In 1976 he was awarded the title of university professor, the highest appointment of the University of Pennsylvania. Chance received the Paul Lewis Award in Enzyme Chemistry in 1950. He was elected to the National Academy of Sciences in 1954. In 1961 he was the first recipient of the William Morlock Award of the Institute of Electrical and Electronics Engineers, for advances in biomedical electronics, and in 1962 he was awarded an honorary doctor of medicine degree by the Karolinska Institute of the University of Stockholm. In 1965 he was the first American recipient of the Genootschaps-Medaille of the Dutch Chemical Society, on the occasion of the 175th anniversary of its founding. He became a foreign fellow of Churchill College, Cambridge, England, in 1966. Also in 1966, he was awarded the highest honor by the Franklin Institute, the Franklin Medal. President Gerald Ford presented him with the National Medal of Science in 1974, the same year he received the Semmelweis Medal.

Chance edited *Energy-Linked Functions of Mitochondria* (1963). He was a coeditor of *Waveforms* (1949; 2d ed. 1964); *Electronic Time Measurements* (1949; 2d ed. 1964); *Rapid Mixing and Sampling Techniques in Biochemistry* (1964); *Control of Energy Metabolism* (1965); the Johnson Foundation Colloquia Series: *Probes and*

Membrane Function (1971), *Probes of Enzymes and Hemoproteins* (1971), *Biological and Biochemical Oscillators* (1973), and *Alcohol and Aldehyde Metabolizing Systems* (vols.1–3, 1974–77); and *Cytochrome Oxidase: Japanese American Seminar on Cytochrome Oxidase* (1979).

For background information *see* CELL, SPECTRAL ANALYSIS OF; ENERGY METABOLISM; ENZYME; SPECTROPHOTOMETRIC ANALYSIS in the McGraw-Hill Encyclopedia of Science and Technology. ∎

CHANDRASEKHAR, SUBRAHMANYAN
Indian-American astrophysicist

Born Oct. 19, 1910, Lahore, India (now Pakistan)

While engaged in the study of stellar evolution and the internal structure of stars, Chandrasekhar developed a theory of white dwarf stars.

The properties of white dwarf stars were discovered by the American astronomer Walter Sydney Adams about 1915. About 1925 the English physicist Ralph Howard Fowler explained the enormous densities of white dwarfs in terms of degenerate matter, that is, matter in which electrons and ionized nuclei are tightly packed under the influence of extreme pressures. And when the English astronomer Arthur Stanley Eddington suggested in 1926 that the conversion of hydrogen into helium was one of the

possible sources of stellar energy, the stage was set for a comprehensive theory of stellar evolution.

Chandrasekhar realized that if a star burned up all of its hydrogen, it would not only be unable to maintain its high rate of energy production but would also begin to progressively contract. As it contracted, he assumed, the star would emit progressively less radiation. Chandrasekhar further assumed that during contraction the mass of the star would remain relatively constant and its density would consequently increase. The process, he reasoned, would cease when a sufficiently high internal pressure was reached to produce the collapse of the central atomic structure. The core would then be composed of degenerate matter and the star would have become a white dwarf.

During the period 1930–36, while working at Trinity College, Cambridge, Chandrasekhar evolved his theory of white dwarfs. Among the predictions of this theory are (1) that the greater the mass of a white dwarf, the smaller will be its radius; (2) that no white dwarf can have a mass greater than about 1.44 times that of the Sun; and (3) that a more massive star must undergo some form of mass reduction, probably through violent explosion, before it can collapse into a white dwarf. Although the small number of white dwarfs known makes it difficult to test the theory by observation, the three predictions enumerated above appear to have been substantiated. When mass is plotted against radius for the known white dwarfs and the main sequence stars, the relation for the white dwarfs agrees with Chandrasekhar's theory and is exactly opposite to that for the main sequence stars. No white dwarf has yet been found with a mass greater than 1.44 solar masses. This figure, called Chandrasekhar's limit, is based on the calculation that the dwarf star contains only elements heavier than hydrogen. Since the theory contends that in a white dwarf all of the hydrogen has been burned up, this observation is therefore a dual confirmation of the theory. The third prediction is still more difficult to prove. However, the Crab Nebula, which is the remains of the supernova of A.D. 1054, has been shown to be a gaseous nebulosity surrounding a white dwarf star. The mass of the gases added to that of the white dwarf exceeds Chandrasekhar's limit. Thus, it can be assumed that the supernova resulted from the blowing off of excess mass by a star with a mass greater than 1.44 times that of the Sun before it collapsed into a white dwarf. Chandrasekhar's theory explains the final stages of stellar evolution, thus contributing to cosmological theory. It is also important in understanding stellar structure. Furthermore, it explains why so few supernovae have been observed, for the masses of the great majority of stars do not exceed Chandrasekhar's limit.

In addition to his theory of white dwarfs, Chandrasekhar made other contributions to astrophysics, among them his studies of the radiative transfer of energy in the atmospheres of stars, of convection on the solar surface, and of polarization of the light from early-type stars. More recent studies dealt with the convective motions of fluids with and without magnetic fields.

Chandrasekhar attended Presidency College, Madras University, in India, receiving his B.A. in 1930. He then went to England to pursue graduate work, receiving his Ph.D. at Cambridge University in 1933. From 1933 to 1937 he remained in England as a fellow of Trinity College, leaving to take a position as research associate at the University of Chicago in the United States. He was appointed assistant professor of astrophysics there in 1938, associate professor in 1942, professor in 1943, and Distinguished Service Professor in 1946. In 1952 he was named Morton D. Hull Distinguished Service Professor of Astrophysics in the departments of astronomy and physics and in the Institute for Nuclear Studies. In that year he also became the managing editor of the *Astrophysical Journal*. He was awarded the Bruce Medal of the Astronomical Society of the Pacific in 1952, the Gold Medal of the Royal Astronomical Society in 1953, the Rumford Medal of the American Academy of Arts and Sciences in 1957, and the Royal Medal of the Royal Society of London in 1962. He was elected to the National Academy of Sciences in 1955.

Chandrasekhar wrote *An Introduction to the Study of Stellar Structure* (1939; reprinted 1957), *Principles of Stellar Dynamics* (1942), *Radiative Transfer* (1950), *Hydrodynamic and Hydromagnetic Stability* (1961), and *Ellipsoidal Figures of Equilibrium* (1969).

For background information *see* STELLAR EVOLUTION; WHITE DWARF STAR in the McGraw-Hill Encyclopedia of Science and Technology. ∎

CHANEY, RALPH WORKS
★ American paleobotanist

Born Aug. 24, 1890, Chicago, IL, U.S.A.
Died Mar. 3, 1971, Berkeley, CA, U.S.A.

In his study of Tertiary forests, Chaney developed a dynamic approach based upon close resemblances between plants of the past and those now living. He considered plant fossils as representatives of the vegetation of their day, in contrast to their study as individual specimens whose structure or phylogeny is the primary concern of many paleobotanists.

Chaney's familiarity with living plants influenced his emphasis on similarities rather than on differences in designating fossil species. But he did not use modern specific names for plants older than Pleistocene, arguing that the incompleteness of their record did not justify assuming that there had been no changes of specific rank since Tertiary time. Firmly believing that taxonomy should be a tool rather than a burden, he set up stratigraphic species where differences in size or other minor characters could be detected in rocks of different ages. In like manner he tended to establish geographic species for similar plants separated by ocean or climatic barriers. Recognition of elements whose fossils had close living equivalents in major areas did much to clarify areal and systematic relationships of fossil plants to each other and to those that have survived in modern forests.

Chaney's collecting procedure required handling of large numbers of specimens, so that variations within designated fossil species could be compared with those of related living plants. A census taken in the field showed which species were abundant near sites of deposition, and perhaps suggested more remote habitats in adjacent uplands for sparsely represented plants.

A standard section was set up in the John Day Basin of eastern Oregon, where abundant and well-preserved fossils occurred in stratigraphic sequence. Successive floras showed differences in composition, and Chaney noted a progressive reduction in size and texture of leaves. This provided a basis for dating the floras of other areas, and for their assignment to the same stage in the Tertiary sequence if they occurred in the same general latitude.

Quantitative appraisal of leaf characters provided a basis for estimating Tertiary climates. Large, thick, camptodrome-veined leaves now characterize the evergreen forests of the tropics, while trees of higher latitudes are largely deciduous, with smaller, thinner leaves, and craspedodrome venation. The change in leaf characters from Lower to Upper Tertiary shows a response to progressive changes toward the cooler and drier climate of the present day.

Chaney pointed out that the temperate Eocene plants of Alaska did not appear in Oregon until Oligocene time, and that subtropical Eocene plants of Oregon have survived only in low latitudes. He suggested the term "geoflora" for groups of plants in mass migration; the Arcto-Tertiary geoflora has maintained itself with only minor changes in composition since the Eocene, during which time its distribution has been shifted from Alaska southward across the United States. The Neotropical-Tertiary geoflora has moved from Washington and Oregon into Mexico and Central America. Recognition of a deciduous conifer, *Metasequoia,* as a fossil by S. Miki in 1941, and its almost contemporary discovery as a living tree by T. Wang in central China, has done much to confirm the concept of geofloras. Chaney had previously predicted that a fossil "redwood" might be discovered, with a deciduous habit suited to occurrence at high latitudes. He visited the natural occurrence of *Metasequoia* in 1948 to determine that its associates were members of the Arcto-Tertiary geoflora, and revised the fossil records of several members of the Taxodiaceae.

Most fossil floras contain plants that lived at low to middle altitudes. Chaney suggested that since the lapse rate corresponds to successively lower temperatures at higher latitudes, an Eocene flora living near sea level in Alaska may have had a counterpart in the mountains of Oregon; its absence or scant representation in the Oregon Eocene was to be expected in view of its remoteness from sites of deposition, but such a montane flora could be reconstructed by studying floras of similar age in deposits to the north. An early elaboration of this concept led to his suggestion that angiosperms may have had their origin at high altitudes during the Jurassic period, although they first appeared in the fossil record in Cretaceous time.

While there has been well-defined latitudinal control of forest distribution during the Tertiary period, Chaney noted significant departures. A given flora lived farther south with increasing distance from the Pacific Coast; it ranged far to the north across ocean basins. Plotting the occurrence of Eocene floras across North America and Eurasia, he showed that lines connecting similar floras (isoflors) followed the paths of modern isotherms and of major forest types. He concluded that the Eocene position of continents and oceans in relation to each other and to the axis of rotation was essentially the same as it is today. This conclusion placed the burden of proof on advocates of continental drift and polar migrations during later geologic time.

A descendant of pioneer Illinois farmers, Chaney majored successively in zoology, botany, and geology at the University of Chicago, where he received his B.S. in geology in 1912 and his Ph.D. in paleontology in 1919. Several years of high school and university teaching (State University of Iowa) preceded his appointment in 1922 as research associate of the Carnegie Institution of Washington; he retired in 1957. From 1930 until 1957, he was also professor of paleontology at the University of California, Berkeley. He carried on field work widely in the Americas and Asia. During World War II he set aside his paleobotanical work to become assistant director of the university's Radiation Laboratory in an administrative capacity. He was elected to the National Academy of Sciences in 1947.

For background information *see* PALEOBOTANY in the McGraw-Hill Encyclopedia of Science and Technology. ∎

CHAPMAN, SYDNEY
★ English mathematician and physicist

Born Jan. 29, 1888, Eccles, Lancashire, England
Died June 16, 1970, Boulder, CO, U.S.A.

During 1912–17 Chapman generalized the accurate kinetic theory of gases given in 1867 by James Maxwell, removing Maxwell's limitation to molecules that repel as the inverse fifth power of the distance. Thus he independently discovered gaseous thermal diffusion (first deduced by D. Enskog in a special case), and with A. T. Dootson (1916) he confirmed it experimentally. Chapman also studied observationally and theoretically the daily variations of the geomagnetic field (from 1913) and magnetic storms (from 1917). This led to, among other things, improved and extended determinations (with A. T. Price) of the electrical conductivity within the Earth. Jointly with V. C. A. Ferraro, Chapman inferred in 1930 that streams of solar plasma would confine the geomagnetic field within a space of order 10 earth radii (verified 30 years afterwards by satellite exploration) and that in this space, the magnetosphere, a ring current would flow (later revealed by J. A. Van Allen's discovery of the radiation belts). With E. H. Vestine he elucidated the electric currents that flow in the polar ionosphere. With S.-I. Akasofu he investigated these currents and those in the magnetosphere and further developed the theory of mag-

netic storms and the aurora. *See* VAN ALLEN, JAMES ALFRED.

Chapman also studied the atmospheres of the Earth and Sun. In 1929 he gave a photochemical theory of atmospheric ozone and inferred that the oxygen in the upper atmosphere, above about 100 kilometers height, would be largely dissociated; this was subsequently confirmed by rocket-borne mass spectrometers. He inferred also that the airglow—the self-luminescence of the atmosphere at night—is mainly energized by the oxygen dissociation energy stored in the atmosphere during the hours of sunlight.

Chapman greatly extended science's knowledge of the lunar tide in the Earth's atmosphere by analysis of long series of meteorological records (barometer, wind, and temperature) and of magnetic data (the latter, to determine the lunisolar daily variations of the magnetic field). He also studied diffusion problems in the lower and upper atmosphere.

While still an undergraduate at Trinity College, Cambridge, Chapman did research in pure mathematics (nonconvergent series and integrals, partly in association with G. H. Hardy) and in gas theory, to which his attention was drawn by J. Larmor. Then he became (co-) chief assistant (with A. S. Eddington) to the Astronomer Royal at Greenwich Observatory (1910–14, 1916–18). There his work included, besides astronomy, the design of a new magnetic observatory to replace the one set up in 1838 by G. B. Airy. This aroused his interest in geomagnetism and its connection with solar phenomena, and led to his analyses of many kinds of geophysical data and to his theoretical researches in these fields. As the solar and lunisolar daily magnetic variations are caused by electric currents in the ionosphere, induced by motions produced thermally and tidally, he investigated the air tides and the ionosphere. Thus he formulated the idealized "Chapman" ionized layer, later much used by radio physicists in studies of radio propagation and other researches. Theoretical work on atmospheric ozone led to his pioneer work on the photochemistry of the upper atmosphere and on the nocturnal emission of light by atoms of oxygen and sodium there.

Thermal diffusion offers a valuable means of studying the fields of force around molecules and provides a method of separating isotopes, made especially convenient after K. Clusius invented the thermal diffusion column. Such isotope separation became nationally and economically important when applied to the separation of the isotopes of uranium, for the development of nuclear energy for bombs and power supply. In 1958 Chapman showed that although thermal diffusion is in general a weak separative agent, it has much greater power in gases that are highly and multiply ionized, as in the solar corona.

Son of a cashier, Chapman took B.Sc. degrees in engineering (1907) and mathematics (1908) at Manchester University, England (M.Sc. 1908, D.Sc. 1912) and the B.A. degree in mathematics (1911) at Cambridge (M.A. 1914). At Greenwich Observatory he worked on astronomy, gas theory, and geophysics. He returned to teach mathematics at Cambridge (1914–16, 1918–19), and later at Manchester (1919–24), Imperial College, London (1924–46), and Queen's College, Oxford (1946–53) as professor of applied mathematics. Visits to the United States as research associate at the department of terrestrial magnetism of the Carnegie Institution of Washington (1935–40), and at the California Institute of Technology (1950–51), led to his long connection with the Geophysical Institute of the University of Alaska (from 1951) and the High Altitude Observatory, Boulder, CO (from 1955). He was president (1953–59) of the central organizing committee for the International Geophysical Year, in which he led the planning of the auroral program. For his theoretical contributions to terrestrial and interplanetary magnetism, the ionosphere, and the aurora borealis, Chapman received the Royal Society's Copley Medal in 1964. In 1965 he received the Hodgkins Medal of the Smithsonian Institute. He was elected a foreign associate of the U.S. National Academy of Sciences in 1946.

Chapman wrote *The Earth's Magnetism* (1936; 2d ed. 1952), *Mathematical Theory of Nonuniform Gases,* with T. G. Cowling (1939; 3d ed. 1970), *Geomagnetism,* with J. Bartels (1940), *IGY: Year of Discovery* (1959), *Solar Plasma, Geomagnetism and Aurora* (1964), *Atmospheric Tides, Thermal and Gravitational,* with R. S. Lindzen (1970), and *Solar-Terrestrial Physics,* with Syun-Ichi Akasofu (1972).

For background information *see* GEOMAGNETISM in the McGraw-Hill Encyclopedia of Science and Technology. ■

CHARGAFF, ERWIN
★ American biochemist

Born Aug. 11, 1905, Austria

Trained as a chemist, Chargaff was attracted early to the application of chemistry to the life sciences; the living cell remained at the center of his scientific interests. He liked to consider his profession as a branch of natural philosophy and himself as a remnant of an extinct species, the naturalist.

Chargaff ranged widely over many fields of chemistry and biochemistry. In the beginning of his career, he concerned himself particularly with the complex lipids of microorganisms and participated in the discovery of unusual fatty acids and waxes in the acid-fast mycobacteria (a group comprising the tubercle bacillus), the diphtheria bacteria, and so on. This led him to more diversified studies of the metabolism and the biological role of tissue lipids and, especially, of the lipid-containing conjugated proteins, the lipoproteins, about which he wrote one of the first reviews. He devoted much effort to investigation of the biochemistry of blood coagulation and to elucidation of the pivotal catalyst in this reaction, the thromboplastic protein. He was among the first to use the radioactive isotope of phosphorus in studies of phospholipid metabolism, and published the first paper on the synthesis of a radioactive organic compound, namely, α-glycerophosphoric acid. Other studies undertaken at about the same time concerned the biological oxidation of hy-

droxyamino acids and of cyclohexitols, such as the inositols.

The great caesura in Chargaff's scientific endeavors occurred in 1944, when O. T. Avery and collaborators showed that the principle active in microbial transformation was a deoxyribonucleic acid (DNA). This discovery made a deep impression of Chargaff, as it was evident to him that this meant that DNA was the principal, or perhaps the sole, operative constituent of the genes. At that time there did not yet exist a biochemistry of heredity. Brought up as he was, in common with his entire generation, with the notion that DNA was an unspecific aggregate of a few "tetranucleotides," a mere coat hanger for the all-important proteins, he concluded, after learning that a DNA could confer new and inheritable properties to a cell, that many different DNA molecules, varying in chemical structure and composition must exist. He set himself the task of testing this proposition. *See* AVERY, OSWALD THEODORE.

By a happy coincidence, at about that time the separation of minute amounts of amino acids by partition chromatography on filter paper had been described as a qualitative procedure, and photoelectric ultraviolet spectrophotometers had become available commercially. Since the nitrogenous constituents of the nucleic acids, the purines and pyrimidines, were distinguished by a very high and characteristic absorption of ultraviolet light, the combination of methods using paper chromatography and ultraviolet absorption made possible for the first time the precise estimation of nucleic acid composition. When DNA preparations of many different cellular species were isolated and studied with respect to their base composition, it became clear that the term "DNA" was a generic one covering a vast multitude of different macromolecules, widely differing in the proportions of their constituents. The tetranucleotide hypothesis was shown to be incorrect; it was demonstrated that DNA was in its composition characteristic of the species, though constant in different organs of the same organism. It became no exaggeration to state that there were at least as many different DNA molecules as there were different species.

When Chargaff reviewed the results on the composition of DNA obtained in his laboratory, a remarkable generalization emerged, which became known as the base-pairing rules in DNA. These state that, despite far-reaching divergences in the proportions of their nitrogenous constituents, all DNA varieties exhibit the following regularities: (1) purines (adenine + guanine) equal pyrimidines (cytosine + thymine); (2) adenine equals thymine; (3) guanine equals cytosine; and (4) 6-amino nucleotides (adenylic + cytidylic acids) equal 6-keto nucleotides (guanylic + thymidylic acids). These relationships, first pointed out in 1950, have had substantial influence on modern biological thought.

As it is not improbable that the primary stucture of DNA, that is, the specific sequence of its nucleotide constituents, carries the biological information often designated as the genetic code, the importance of studies on the nucleotide sequence of the nucleic acids is evident. Much effort was devoted to this problem by Chargaff and his colleagues. The general interests of his laboratory were best described in the title of the Jesup Lectures that he gave in 1959 at Columbia University: "Chemical Aspects of Biological Specificity."

Chargaff was educated in Vienna at the Maximiliansgymnasium and the University of Vienna. He carried out his doctoral research under the direction of Fritz Feigl in Späth's Institute and received the Dr.Phil. in 1928. His second teacher was Rudolph J. Anderson at Yale University, with whom he worked from 1928 to 1930. He was assistant at the University of Berlin in 1930–33, and then spent nearly 2 years in Calmette's laboratory at the Pasteur Institute in Paris. In 1935 he went to Columbia University, where he became professor of biochemistry in 1952. He chaired Columbia's department of biochemistry from 1970 to 1974 and then became professor emeritus. He received the Pasteur Medal in 1949, the Carl Neuberg Medal in 1958, the Charles Léopold Mayer Prize of the French Academy of Sciences in 1963, the H. P. Heineken Prize of the Netherlands Academy of Sciences in 1964, the Bertner Foundation Award in 1965, the Gregor Mendel Medal in 1973, and the National Medal of Science in 1975. He was elected to the American Academy of Arts and Sciences in 1961, to the National Academy of Sciences in 1965, and as a foreign member of the Royal Physiographic Society in Lund in 1959.

Author of more than 300 scientific papers, Chargaff edited, with J. N. Davidson, *The Nucleic Acids* (3 vols., 1955, 1960) and wrote *Essays on Nucleic Acids* (1963).

For background information *see* DEOXYRIBONUCLEIC ACID (DNA); LIPID METABOLISM; NUCLEIC ACID in the McGraw-Hill Encyclopedia of Science and Technology. ■

CHARNEY, JULE GREGORY
★ American meteorologist

Born *Jan. 1, 1917, San Francisco, CA, U.S.A.*

The large-scale weather phenomena in the extratropical zones of the Earth are associated with great migratory waves and vortexes (cyclones) traveling in the belt of prevailing westerly winds. Charney developed a mathematical theory of these disturbances, explaining them as instabilities of a zonal current in which the temperature decreases poleward. His theory led also to a general mathematical characterization of slow motions in a rotating coordinate system, which he applied to a variety of atmospheric and oceanic circulations. In particular, he and his colleagues at the Institute for Advanced Study used it successfully in their pioneering experiments on numerical weather prediction by high-speed computer.

The establishment of an upper-air sounding network in the 1930s permitted for the first time a realistic description of the three-dimensional structure of the atmosphere. The familiar high- and low-pressure areas of the weather map were revealed as but surface manifestations of giant wavelike meanderings of a predominantly zonal flow. These waves were studied by J. Bjerknes, who gave a qualitative explanation for their eastward progression, and by C.-G. Rossby, who derived his well-known formula for their speed of propagation, regarding them as perturbations of a uniform flow of a homogeneous, incompressible atmosphere. Charney was inspired by these works to seek an explanation for the generation of the waves and their three-dimensional structure. He first showed that Bjerknes's treatment could be extended quantitatively to give Rossby's dispersion relationship. He then formulated and solved the problem of wave generation by showing that a zonal flow with a sufficiently strong poleward temperature gradient becomes instable to characteristic perturbation modes having a structure closely resembling the observed wave patterns. *See* BJERKNES, JACOB AALL BONNEVIE; ROSSBY, CARL-GUSTAF ARVID.

In obtaining this solution, Charney encountered the difficulty that a compressible, stratified fluid, held gravitationally to the rotating Earth, can support a variety of wave motions, including acoustic and inertio-gravity waves, which are of no meteorological importance but whose existence seriously complicates the solution of the hydrodynamic equations. He found a method of filtering out these unwanted "noise" motions in the wave problem and later generalized this method to apply to all long-period motions. The generalization was based on the principle that the forces acting on slow motions of a rotating fluid must always be close to equilibrium, that is, must be in a state of quasi-hydrostatic and quasi-geostrophic balance. This principle was incorporated into the hydrodynamic equations by a kind of scale analysis already familiar in the boundary-layer theory of hydrodynamics. The mathematical and physical simplifications thereby introduced had a far-reaching effect on meteorological theory.

In 1947, when J. von Neumann organized a group at the Institute for Advanced Study to attack the problem of numerical weather prediction by means of high-speed electronic computers, difficulties were immediately encountered which could be traced to the inertio-gravitational "noise." Charney had found that these difficulties were automatically overcome by the use of the balance equations. In 1948, on accepting an invitaion from von Neumann to join the group, he initiated a program to integrate the balance equations for a hierarchy of atomspheric models of increasing complexity, hoping in this way to avoid the difficulties attendant on introducing a great many poorly understood factors all at once. Some degree of success was achieved in 1950 with the first numerical prediction of a two-dimensional model flow approximating the actual flow at a mid-level in the atmosphere, and in 1952–53 he obtained the first prediction of cyclogenesis with a three-dimensional model flow. The latter result had two consequences: it tended to confirm Charney's explanation of cyclogenesis, and it interested the United States government in the possibilities of operational numerical prediction. A joint Weather Bureau–Air Force–Navy numerical weather prediction unit was established in 1954 and began operations in 1955. Thereafter, similar units were established in many other countries. See VON NEUMANN, JOHN.

Following the numerical prediction of cyclogenesis, it was natural to study the interactions of the cyclone wave with the zonal flow itself. H. Jeffries, V. Starr, and others had shown that the wave disturbances acted as turbulent eddy elements transferring momentum (against the gradient) to the mean zonal flow. In seeking a mechanism for this phenomenon, Charney proposed the hypothesis that the cyclone waves, in deriving their energy from the unstable zonal flow through release of potential energy associated with the poleward temperature gradient, are also required by the stabilizing effect of horizontal shear to return energy to the flow in kinetic form, and thus maintain it against dissipation by friction. This hypothesis was strikingly confirmed in a numerical experiment carried out by N. Phillips, a member of Charney's group. Phillips introduced a heating function varying uniformly with latitude and a frictional mechanism into the simplest of the three-dimensional models, in consequence of which a broad westerly current with a uniform poleward temperature gradient was generated. As predicted, this current became unstable and developed wave perturbations which transferred kinetic energy back to the current and caused it to

become narrow and intense, as in the observed westerlies. For the first time the principal dynamic elements of the general circulation of the the atmosphere were assembled in a single mathematical model, and the way was opened to a direct numerical attack on the problems of long-range prediction and the dynamic theory of climate. See STARR, VICTOR PAUL.

In other work Charney showed that the principle of balance is quite generally applicable to large-scale atmospheric and oceanic dynamics, and that where simple (geostrophic) balance is violated, a higher-order boundary-layer treatment can often be given. With A. Eliassen, he applied these considerations in treating the layer of surface frictional influence as a boundary layer for the large scale atmospheric and oceanic motions, showing that the quasi-stationary disturbances of the tropospheric westerlies are due largely to topographic deflection. Charney also applied them to the explanation of the Gulf Stream as a western inertial boundary layer, and the Equatorial Undercurrent as a boundary phenomenon produced by the vanishing of the horizontal Coriolis force at the Equator.

In early work Charney had shown that planetary waves are capable of propagating vertically as well as horizontally. In collaboration with P. Drozin, he later showed that topographically and thermally induced waves are trapped aloft by strong westerlies for all but the largest horizontal scales, and by easterlies for all scales.

The tropical cyclone had previously been looked upon as an unbalanced flow with large horizontal and vertical accelerations produced by cumulus convection. Charney and Eliassen found that although the individual cumulus cloud is indeed an unbalanced system, the large-scale flow is balanced, and its growth is due to a cooperative, frictionally controlled interaction between it and the cumulus convection: the clouds supply heat of condensation to the cyclone, and the frictionally induced indraft to the cyclone supplies moisture to the clouds.

In seeking an explanation for the unusually rapid falloff of atmospheric energy with horizontal scale, Charney developed a theory of geostrophic turbulence that accounts for the lack of energy flow from large to small scales and predicts instead that energy flows from small to large horizontal and vertical scales.

Later, Charney worked on biogeophysical feedback mechanisms in relation to drought, showing that under appropriate circumstances a decrease of vegetation can lead to a decrease of rainfall. He also investigated the existence of multiple stable equilibrium states in the atmosphere as a possible explanation for certain weather anomalies.

The son of Russian immigrants, Charney studied at the University of California at Los Angeles, receiving his B.A. in mathematics and physics in 1938, his M.A. in mathematics in 1940, and his Ph.D. in meteorology in 1946. During World War II he assisted in the training of weather officers for the armed services. In 1946 he was awarded a National Research Fellowship, which he spent at the University of Oslo following a 9-month visit with Rossby at the University of Chicago. In 1948 he joined the group in theoretical meteorology at the Institute for Advanced Study in Princeton, NJ, becoming its scientific director and a long-term member of the institute. In 1956 he was appointed professor, and in 1966 Alfred P. Sloan Professor, of meteorology at the Massachusetts Institute of Technology; he was head of the department from 1974 to 1977. He was a Guggenheim fellow at Cambridge University and at the Weizmann Institute of Science in 1972–73, and Symons Lecturer of the Royal Meteorological Society and John von Neumann Lecturer of the Society for Industrial and Applied Mathematics in 1974. He was elected a member of the National Academy of Sciences in 1964, foreign member of the Royal Swedish Academy of Sciences in 1965, and foreign member of the Norwegian Academy of Science in 1971. He received the Meisinger Award (1949) and the Rossby Research Medal (1964) of the American Meteorological Society, the Losey Award of the Institute of Aeronautical Sciences (1957), the Symons Memorial Gold Medal of the Royal Meteorological Society (1961), the Hodgkins Medal of the Smithsonian Institution (1969), the International Meteorological Organization Prize of the World Meteorological Organization (1971), and the Bowie Medal of the American Geophysical Union (1976).

For background information *see* CYCLONE; OCEAN-ATMOSPHERE RELATIONS; WEATHER FORECASTING AND PREDICTION in the McGraw-Hill Encyclopedia of Science and Technology. ∎

CHATT, JOSEPH
★ British chemist

Born Nov. 6, 1914, Horden, England

An interest in chemical bonding to metal atoms led Chatt into the development of many new areas of transition metal chemistry, especially those relevant to the petrochemical industry and nitrogen fixation.

Chatt early acquired his interest in inorganic chemistry, about 1926–28, not knowing that it was an unpopular academic subject. He was introduced to it by his uncle E. L. Burt, who was chief chemist at a steelworks near Newcastle-upon-Tyne, and spent many happy hours in his laboratory. Chatt's interest in inorganic chemistry was heightened when he discovered that his home was adjacent to an area rich in sulfide minerals (Caldbeck Fells), especially ores containing "rare" elements such as molybdenum, tungsten, and tellurium.

Chatt's attraction to physics and chemistry was encouraged by his schoolmasters, and when he entered Cambridge University he was set to become a research scientist. He was rapidly drawn to synthetic organic chemistry, and finally his interests in organic chemistry, chemical bonding, and inorganic chemistry came together in a postgraduate study of the coordination chemistry of palladium(II) complexes with tertiary phosphines and arsines and of the stereochemistry of organo-arsenic(III) compounds under F. G. Mann.

Those years in Cambridge set Chatt on his chosen career, to elucidate some of the outstanding problems of bonding in transition metal chemistry. His postgraduate work (1937–39) gave him an appreciation of the value of tertiary phosphines and arsines in bringing transition metal chemistry into organic solvents, allowing a variety of new reactions with organic and water-sensitive reagents. This led to his early development of organo-transition metal chemistry, but the beginning of his independent work had to await the end of World War II.

At that time the bonding of ligands to metal atoms was considered to result from the donation of a nonbonding pair of electrons (lone pair) from the ligand atom to the positively charged metal ion. This concept was known as the lone pair theory of coordination, but there was a class of ligand, the olefins, which had no lone pair. These ligands were then found in very few complex compounds, such as Zeise's salt, $K[PtCl_3(C_2H_4)]$. The bonding of the olefin to the metal intrigued Chatt because it indicated that the lone pair theory was incomplete. Moreover, if the problem of olefin bonding could be solved, it would point the way to some interesting chemistry.

Chatt soon established that olefins were characteristic of a small class of ligands which attached themselves only to metal ions with filled d-orbitals. Not only had the ligand to donate electrons to the metal to form a σ-type bond as required by the lone pair theory, but the metal had to donate back to the ligand electrons from its d-orbitals to form a type of π-bond. This led to his establishing the nature of the bond between transition metal atoms and olefins and the rationalization of his earlier conceived classification of metal ions into class a or class b according to their bonding characteristics.

These two concepts formed the basis of much of Chatt's life work. It led to his development of ideas concerning the synergic σ-π bonding of olefins and tertiary phosphines to transition metal ions; to a hypothesis to explain the effects of trans ligands on each other, which contributed to a rationalization of the reactivities of metal complexes; and to the rational use of tertiary phosphines to stabilize alkyl, aryl, and hydride complexes of transition metals and to stabilize complexes containing a transition metal ion in the zero oxidation state.

Throughout this work the cis or trans configurations of the coordination complexes were established by dipole moments, leading to data and ideas on the separation of electric charge in coordination compounds. Also, the easy reversible migration of hydrogen from alkyl and aryl groups onto the metal was discovered during attempts to prepare complexes of certain metals in zero oxidation state, as were the first examples of oxidative addition of alkyl halides to transition metal complexes.

Chatt's classic researches in the above areas contributed to the understanding of the mechanisms of catalytic processes used in the rapidly developing petrochemicals industry. He applied the same principles to the discovery and study of the reactions of molecular nitrogen (dinitrogen) in its metal complexes.

This nitrogen work resulted in the discovery of large numbers of new transition metal complexes of dinitrogen, and an appreciation of the circumstances under which dinitrogen becomes attached to a transition metal ion and the circumstances necessary for its subsequent conversion to ammonia by protonation. It led to new ideas concerning the chemical mechanism of biological nitrogen fixation and the production of new types of ligands such as the iminonitrosyl, the thionitrosyl, and various hydrazide anions previously unknown. The salient facets of the mechanism of the reaction of certain organic compounds with ligating dinitrogen to produce organonitrogen compounds were also elucidated. Apart from the advancement of the general understanding of the activation of dinitrogen by ligation, this work had as its aim the production of ammonia, hydrazine, and organonitrogen compounds by mild catalytic reactions directly from dinitrogen.

Chatt graduated from Emmanuel College, Cambridge (B.A., 1937; Ph.D., 1940). After a brief period in the research department of Woolwich Arsenal during World War II, he joined the staff of Peter Spence and Sons Ltd., Widnes, finally becoming chief chemist. In 1946 he became Imperial Chemical Industries Limited (ICI) Research Fellow at the Imperial College of Science and Technology, London, and a year later joined the staff of ICI at their Butterwick (later Akers) Research Laboratories in Welwyn, Hertfordshire, becoming head of the inorganic chemistry department. In 1962 he undertook to establish a research unit of the Agricultural Research Council to study fundamental aspects of nitrogen fixation, which was finally established at the University of Sussex, Brighton, with Chatt as director of the Unit of Nitrogen Fixation and professor in the school of molecular sciences in the university. He was made a commander of the Order of the British Empire in 1978. His many honors and awards included the first Organometallic Chemistry Award of the Chemical Society (1970), the American Chemical Society Award for Distinguished Service to Inorganic Chemistry (1971), an honorary D.Sc. from the University of East Anglia (1974), the Chugaev Commemorative Diploma and Medal of the N. S. Kurnakov Institute of General and Inorganic Chemistry, Soviet Academy of Sciences (1976), and the Chandler Medal of Columbia University, New York (1978). Chatt was elected to the Chemical Society (1937), the Royal Institute of Chemistry (1940), the American Chemical Society (1960), and the Royal Society (1961), and served as chairperson of the Commission on the Nomenclature of Inorganic Chemistry of the International Union of Pure and Applied Chemistry beginning in 1975. His honorary fellowships or memberships included Emmanuel College, Cambridge, the Academia das Ciencias de Lisboa, and the New York Academy of Sciences, all in 1978.

For background information *see* CATALYSIS; COORDINATION CHEMISTRY; NITROGEN FIXATION; ORGANIC CHEMICAL SYNTHESIS; ORGANOMETALLIC COMPOUNDS in the McGraw-Hill Encyclopedia of Science and Technology. ∎

CHEADLE, VERNON IRVIN
★ American botanist

Born Feb. 6, 1910, Salem, SD, U.S.A.

Cheadle's research for the Ph.D. at Harvard University concerned anatomical differences between the monocotyledon families Liliaceae and Amaryllidaceae. These families were thought to differ principally in the position of the ovary in relation to other parts of the flower. The investigation was to determine whether the families could be separated on structural grounds. The research did not settle that problem but led to a wide variety of others. Cheadle chose the xylem (water-conducting tissue) and phloem (food-con-

ducting tissue) for further study because of their importance in the welfare of land plants and their wide range of variability. The literature and thesis research confirmed how scanty was the knowledge of these tissues in the monocotyledons as a whole.

In 1936 Cheadle received a scholarship from Harvard's famous naturalist Thomas Barbour to collect plants in Cuba as a project of the Atkins Institute of the Arnold Arboretum of Harvard University. This provided him with the inital impetus to study phloem and xylem in a broad representation of monocotyledons. Later collecting trips took him over much of the United States and to Australia and South Africa. Research on these collections provided an exposition of evolutionary trends in the structure of conducting cells. Later work on other plants emphasized ultrastructure as revealed by electron microscopy.

Cheadle had given less attention to the phloem, but his early research did make clear, for example, that sieve-tube members (sieve elements) having end walls transversely placed with uniformly distributed pores are specialized, whereas those with oblique end walls and pores not uniformly distributed are primitive. These differences are correlated with differences in the appearance of phloem as seen in transections of vascular bundles in the shoot system. Phloem with primitive sieve-tube members has an irregular appearance because of variations in the diameter of these members; phloem with

specialized sieve-tube members is regular in appearance because of their uniformity of diameter. Evolutionary specialization of sieve-tube members began in the leaves and then occurred successively downward into the roots.

Cheadle's studies of xylem showed that the most evident features of primitive vessel members in the monocotyledons are great length and oblique end walls having many perforations. In contrast, highly evolved vessel members are short and have transversely placed end walls with a single perforation. All variations between these two extremes occur in the monocotyledons as a whole, and may be placed in an evolutionary sequence that seems clearly unidirectional. Study of vessels throughout the plants, in hundreds of species from most families of the monocotyledons, showed that vessels originated from tracheids in the roots and then successively developed upward in the plant. In every organ the vessels originated similarly in the latest-formed metaxylem, then in the earlier-formed metaxylem, and finally in the protoxylem. Specialization of vessel members occurred in the same sequence throughout the plant and within the xylem of each organ. The specializations of xylem in the shoot system are generally correlated with the appearance of the xylem of vascular bundles, as seen in transections of the stems and leaves. For example, the highly specialized bundles in corn have two large vessels, one at each side, separated by smaller cells. The bundles of a lily stem similarly seen have numerous tracheids of nearly uniform size. So clear is this series of developments that, from the study of a stem, one can predict with a high degree of accuracy the limits of specialization elsewhere in the plant. It is physiologically plausible that sieve-tube members specialize first in the leaves and thence downward, whereas the opposite is true of vessel members, for foods are elaborated principally in the leaves and migrate downward in the plant, while water and dissolved salts move into the roots and thence upward to the leaves.

The taxonomic implications of Cheadle's conclusions about tracheary elements have been utilized in discussions of possible relationships within the monocotyledons, and between them and the dicotyledons. Within certain limits, this projection can be done with a high degree of confidence because of the unidirectional evolution of such elements. Thus, present-day species with highly specialized tracheary elements could not have been progenitors of current species that have less specialized, or indeed primitive, tracheary elements. This negation of what otherwise might seem plausible relationships is especially useful. The level of tracheary specialization is much less valuable in determining positive relationships, and in the positive sense is useful only in combination with many other characters.

In 1950 Cheadle began a close association with Professor Katherine Esau at the University of California, Davis (and later at Santa Barbara). He spent a sabbatical year at Davis studying the bark of trees and found this new interest so attractive that he transferred from Rhode Island. A collaboration with Esau on studies of secondary phloem led to a series of papers on comparative structure in a large number of families in the dicotyledons, and on critically detailed analyses of this tissue in Calycanthaceae and *Liriodendron*. The papers clarified many debatable points and also isolated problems for solution. Electron microscopy has greatly increased information on the ultrastructure, ontogeny, and, by inference, functioning of sieve elements and their closely associated parenchyma cells. Development of xylem cells has similarly been studied. Confidence in the recognition of ultrastructural details and in the conclusions derived from the study of them proved to be greatly enhanced by experience gained earlier in the study of variously prepared tissues and cells by light microscopy. Later, Cheadle studied and reported upon vessels in many families of monocotyledons in preparation for a general review and evaluation of vessels as indicators of natural relationships in that large segment of the angiosperms. *See* ESAU, KATHERINE.

Cheadle spent a year at South Dakota State College and then went with his botany professor A. T. Evans to Miami University (Ohio), where he received his A.B. in 1932. He then went to Harvard University, where he earned an M.A. in 1934 and a Ph.D. in biology and botany in 1936. For 16 years he held a variety of positions at the University of Rhode Island (leaving for 2 years to serve in the Navy). In 1952 he became professor and chairperson of the botany department and botanist in the experiment station at the University of California, Davis. In 1962 he became professor of botany and chancellor of the University of California, Santa Barbara. After he retired in 1977,

Cheadle worked on the xylem of the monocotyledons and the phloem of the dicotyledons (with Esau), collections of which, particularly from Australia and South Africa, are probably unrivaled. Elected to the American Academy of Arts and Sciences in 1956, Cheadle received a Merit Award of the Botanical Society of America in 1963.

For background information *see* PHLOEM; XYLEM in the McGraw-Hill Encyclopedia of Science and Technology. ∎

CHERN, SHIING-SHEN
★ American mathematician

Born Oct. 26, 1911, Kashing, Chekiang, China

Chern worked mainly with problems in "differential geometry in the large." Differential geometry in its origin is the study of geometrical problems by the methods of infinitesimal calculus. Later, the field was widened to a theory of manifolds, finite- or infinite-dimensional, with geometrical structures defined on them, such as a Riemannian or Lorentzian metric or a complex analytic structure. The main objective of differential geometry in the large is to study the relationship or interplay between local properties (that is, those pertaining to a neighborhood) and properties of the manifold as a whole (for example, its topological properties).

One of the earliest results in differential geometry in the large is the Gauss-Bonnet formula. For a domain D on a

surface bounded by a curve C, its Euler characteristic $\chi(D)$ can be expressed by the equation below, where K is the

$$2\pi\chi(D) - \sum_i \alpha_i = \iint_D K\, dA + \int_C k_g\, ds$$

Gaussian curvature, k_g the geodesic curvature of C, and α_i the exterior angles at the corners of C. This formula contains as special cases the theorem in elementary geometry that the sum of angles of a triangle is 180° and the theorem that the excess of a spherical triangle is proportional to its area. It also contains the conclusion that the Euler characteristic of a closed orientable surface is $1/2\pi$ times the integral of its Gaussian curvature.

The extension of this result to a high-dimensional space has followed a gradual development, associated with the names of H. Hopf, W. Fenchel, C. Allendoerfer, and A. Weil, among others. After earlier works of Allendoerfer and Weil, Chern gave a proof of the high-dimensional Gauss-Bonnet formula that clarifies in a basic way the concepts involved, namely, the algebraic machinery of curvature and the algebraic topological properties of a fiber space. His work thus opened the way to further results on relations between curvature and the so-called characteristic classes. The latter are the simplest invariants of a fiber space, used to describe its deviation from the special case of a product space.

The characteristic classes so introduced by Chern, later associated with his name, are among the most important invariants of algebraic varieties—that is, loci in an n-dimensional space which are defined by a finite number of polynomial equations. They also constitute an important link between the so-called K cohomology theory of a general topological space and its ordinary cohomology theory. Recent developments have shown the importance of the "Chern character" to various application of topology to geometrical problems.

Other areas in which Chern worked, sometimes with others, include (1) decomposition theorem on harmonic forms of Kahlerian G structures; (2) total curvature of closed submanifolds in euclidean space; (3) uniqueness theorems on submanifolds satisfying geometrical conditions; and (4) kinematic formula in integral geometry.

In Chern's opinion, modern mathematics centers on the theory of high-dimensional manifolds, which are spaces locally indistinguishable from euclidean spaces.

It is because of the high-dimensional phenomena that algebra has been playing a vital role. Analysis has now entered in an essential way, but it is a domain where only the frontiers have been touched.

Chern received his B.S. degree from Nankai University, Tientsin, China, in 1930, and his M.S. degree from Tsing Hua University, Peiping, China, in 1934. He studied in Germany and France and received his D.Sc. degree from the University of Hamburg, Germany, in 1936. From 1937 to 1943 he was professor of mathematics at Tsing Hua University. In 1943 he went to the United States as a member of the Institute for Advanced Study, Princeton, NJ, returning to China in 1946. From 1946 to 1948 he was acting director of the Institute of Mathematics, Academia Sinica, Nanking. He became professor of mathematics at the University of Chicago in 1949 and at the University of California, Berkeley, in 1960. Naturalized a United States citizen in 1961, he was elected the same year to the National Academy of Sciences. In 1976 he received the National Medal of Science.

For background information *see* GEOMETRY, DIFFERENTIAL in the McGraw-Hill Encyclopedia of Science and Technology. ∎

CHEW, GEOFFREY FOUCAR

★ American theoretical physicist

Born June 5, 1924, Washington, DC, U.S.A.

During an extended theoretical investigation of the strong short-range force between nuclear particles (hadrons), Chew and his coworkers were led in 1961 to make the "bootstrap" hypothesis. It proposes that no hadron is elementary, but each is a composite of other hadrons held together by forces arising from the exchange of still other hadrons. This hypothesis abandons the notion of fundamental pointlike constituents of matter, and is correspondingly awkward to formulate within a subnuclear space-time continuum. As an alternative to the traditional space-time basis for nuclear dynamics, Chew and his collaborators employed the analytic matrix of hadron-scattering amplitudes, the so-called S matrix. It was argued that a particular boundary condition on the S matrix, usually described as Regge asymptotic behavior, should be taken as the mathematical definition of

the bootstrap. There subsequently developed sufficient experimental verification of the bootstrap concept and the related Regge boundary condition to make this hypothesis a major subject of research in particle physics.

Chew's initial investigations, starting in 1952, were carried out within the traditional framework that assumed the nucleon and pi meson to be elementary particles that are described by time-dependent wave functions satisfying a Schrödinger equation. Earlier, in 1937, Hideki Yukawa had developed a model which ascribed the force between two nucleons to the exchange of pi mesons. Chew extended Yukawa's reasoning to achieve force between nucleon and pi meson from exchange of nucleons, the strength and character of this new force being controlled by the same parameters that determined the nucleon-nucleon force. Using the theoretically predicted force, Chew was able qualitatively to explain the observed behavior of low-energy pions when scattered by nucleons, including the existence of the famous 1240 megaelectronvolt (MeV), spin 3/2 resonance. In Chew's model this unstable particle is regarded as a pion-nucleon composite held together by nucleon exchange, just as in Yukawa's model the deuteron is a nucleon-nucleon composite held together by pion exchange.

In 1954 Francis Low discovered a new dynamical method, which he and Chew, working together at the University of Illinois, used to reformulate Chew's original

model to avoid explicit reference to a Schrödinger equation. In the new framework the key role was played by the analytic properties of scattering amplitudes as a function of the energies of scattered particles. It turned out to be unnecessary to consider space-time at the subnuclear level.

The Chew-Low model was incomplete in that it treated the nucleon on a nonrelativistic basis, but in 1958 Stanley Mandelstam discovered that relativistic scattering amplitudes are analytic not only in energy but also in angle variables and that the combined analyticity properties have a dynamical content equivalent to that of the Chew-Low model. Chew and Mandelstam, working together at Berkeley, exploited Mandelstam's discovery to develop a detailed set of fully relativistic dynamical equations, the so-called N/D method, that showed how in principle any composite particle might be described in the same spirit as Chew's original model described the 1240-MeV resonance or Yukawa's model described the deuteron. The dynamical equations involved nothing but elements of the scattering matrix and made no reference to a Schrödinger equation or a Hamiltonian. The concept of force appeared as a natural and inevitable consequence of analyticity and Lorentz invariance.

Up to this point Chew had accepted the traditional idea that certain hadrons are elementary and others composite, but the N/D equations made it clear that forces are generated by exchange of any hadrons, whether elementary or composite, stable or unstable. Chew and Mandelstam introduced the term "bootstrap" in 1959 to characterize a model of the rho meson in which this highly unstable particle is regarded as a composite of two pions held together by rho exchange. Such a model does not represent a complete bootstrap because the pions are treated as if elementary, but it was the first model to contain an ingredient of self-generation.

The idea that all hadrons are equally composite and self-generating finally emerged in 1961 in connection with Regge asymptotic behavior. In 1958 Tullio Regge had deduced the asymptotic structure of nonrelativistic scattering amplitudes, and Mandelstam in 1959 pointed out that such asymptotic behavior, if generally valid, would circumvent an apparent mathematical difficulty in the N/D equations when forces arise from exchange of high-spin composite particles.

Working in collaboration, Chew and Steven Frautschi further observed that nuclear reactions at very high energies but with small momentum transfers should be controlled by the so-called Regge trajectories, which also would determine the masses and spins of composite particles—these latter corresponding to discrete points on trajectories. When R. Blankenbecler and M. L. Goldberger suggested that the nucleon might lie on a Regge trajectory, it suddenly became clear to Chew and Frautschi that within the framework of the analytic S matrix there were no known reasons why all hadrons should not lie on trajectories. Such a principle of "nuclear democracy," furthermore, could be formulated quite independently of special models, on which the distinction between elementary and composite particles previously had rested. It was nonetheless reassuring to Chew when he discovered soon afterward, in 1962, that a simple and plausible composite model of the nucleon could in fact be constructed along the same lines as that of the 1240-MeV resonance. Chew's bootstrap model of the nucleon subsequently was generalized by others and applied to a great variety of problems. See GOLDBERGER, MARVIN LEONARD; REGGE, TULLIO.

Chew gained a B.S. in 1944 at George Washington University, worked at Los Alamos during 1944–46 as an assistant to Edward Teller and Enrico Fermi, and then spent 2 years as a graduate student under Fermi at the University of Chicago, receiving his Ph.D. in 1948. After a year's research at Berkeley he was appointed to the University of California teaching staff, but moved to the University of Illinois in 1950, becoming a full professor there in 1955. In 1957 he returned to Berkeley, where he had joint responsibilities in the physics department and Lawrence Radiation Laboratory. He became chairperson of the physics department in 1974. Chew was elected to the National Academy of Sciences (1962) and the American Academy of Arts and Sciences (1965). He received the Hughes Prize of the American Physical Society (1962), the Ernest O. Lawrence Award of the U.S. Atomic Energy Commission (1969), and the Alumni Achievement Award of George Washington University (1973). See FERMI, ENRICO; TELLER, EDWARD.

Chew wrote *The S-Matrix Theory of Strong Interactions* (1961) and *The Analytic S Matrix: A Basis for Nuclear Democracy* (1966).

For background information *see* ELEMENTARY PARTICLE; HADRON; SCATTERING EXPERIMENTS, NUCLEAR in the McGraw-Hill Encyclopedia of Science and Technology. ∎

CHRISTOPHERS, SIR (SAMUEL) RICKARD

★ British malariologist

Born *Nov. 27, 1873, Liverpool, England*
Died *Feb. 19, 1978, Dorset, England*

Christophers became known for his work on malaria and for his studies on the systematics, bionomics, and structure of the mosquito. Among his contributions was his early work (1904) on *Leishmania,* the parasite that causes kala azar, the distribution of which in the body tissues he was the first to describe; for this work he was awarded the Gaspar Medal by the Brazilian government in 1961. He was also the first to describe (1907) the life cycle of *Piroplasma (Babesia canis)* in the tick, on the structure of which arthropod he also made an early study. From 1898, however, to 1960, when he published, after some years' work in Cambridge, his monograph *Aedes aegypti: The Yellow Fever Mosquito,* Christophers worked mainly in connection with malaria in its many varied aspects and in related subjects.

Christophers's earliest work on malaria was with I. W. W. Stephens, when appointed to the Malaria Commission of the Royal Society and Colonial Office to carry out research on malaria and blackwater fever in tropical Africa. This research began shortly after Ronald Ross's discovery of the mosquito cycle and at a time when the prevalence of these diseases in Europeans in Africa had become a matter requiring urgent attention. During some 2 years in central and western Africa, followed by a year in India, they established that in tropical Africa and to a varying extent in India malaria was not, as it seemed, mainly a disease of the visiting or resident European; rather, it was almost universally present in children of the indigenous population, leading to immunity in the adult and infection in the European. Stephens and Christophers had failed to trace the source of infection while investigating cases among European engineers and others living in railway construction camps near Lagos. Later in a small village near Accra they saw a native child suffering from an attack of fever and found

that all the village children, seemingly quite well, but none of the adults, had parasites in their blood. It soon became clear that this was the usual condition to various degrees in tropical Africa and to some extent in India. The percentage of children showing parasites is now known as the endemic index of an area or child parasite rate of a community and is widely used in many ways, for example, as a guide in carrying out measures of protection.

Christophers carried out his researches on malaria mainly in India after entering the Indian Medical Service. Except for a time on first joining the service, when he worked on the kala azar parasite and *Piroplasma* in the tick, Christophers until his retirement from India was almost entirely concerned with problems connected with malaria. Important in his many contributions to prevention of malaria in India were his investigations into malaria conditions in different regions, termed "malaria surveys." He studied the spleen and parasite rate and the systematics, structure, and breeding habits of the Indian species of *Anopheles.* On his retirement from India, Christophers worked on a Leverhulme grant at the London School of Hygiene and Tropical Medicine; he concentrated first on dissociation constants of antimalarial drugs, determining those for the salts of atebrin (atabrine) and quinine, and later (with J. D. Fulton) on respiratory metabolism of *P. knowlesi,* a malarial parasite of monkeys. At Cambridge during and following World War II, he worked on mosquito repellents to protect troops.

Christophers graduated from University College, Liverpool (now Liverpool University), with a M.B. and a Ch.B. He served on the Malaria Commission of the Royal Society of London and the Colonial Office during 1898–1902 and then entered the Indian Medical Service. He was director of the King Institute of Preventive Medicine, Madras, in 1904–08 and was officer in charge of the Central Malaria Bureau in 1910–16. During 1916–19 he was on the Mesopotamian Expeditionary Force and was director of the Kala-azar Commission in 1924–25. Christophers was director of the Central Research Institute at Kasauli in 1925–32, after which he retired from the Indian Medical Service and returned to England, where he was professor of malaria studies at the University of London in 1932–38. Christophers was awarded the Order of the Indian Empire in 1915 and the Order of the British Empire in 1918. He was knighted in 1931.

For background information *see* HAE-MOSPORINA; MALARIA; MOSQUITO; PAR-ASITOLOGY, MEDICAL in the McGraw-Hill Encyclopedia of Science and Technology. ∎

CLARK, JOHN GRAHAME DOUGLAS
★ British prehistorian

Born July 28, 1907, Shortlands, Kent, England

Grahame Clark's interest in the Stone Age dated from his early school days, when he started a collection of flint implements. He enrolled at Cambridge University to prepare for a career in the then hardly recognized field of prehistoric archeology. As an undergraduate, he began with history and passed on to archeology, which at that time was taught in conjuction with anthropology. As a research student, he began by applying comparative typology to artifact assemblages that ostensibly dated from the phase of British prehistory intermediate in age between the Paleolithic and Neolithic. The inadequacies of this approach for defining the Mesolithic, not to mention for refining its chronology, soon became apparent. The example of Scandinavia suggested that the solution lay in refining the stratigraphy of postglacial deposits and then recovering artifacts from an independently estab-

lished sequence. The most important technique employed by the Scandinavians in this work was pollen analysis.

It was fortuitous that while Clark was working on his doctoral dissertation on the Mesolithic Age in Britain at the Museum of Archaeology and Ethnology at Cambridge, Harry Godwin and Margaret Godwin were introducing pollen analysis to Britain in the botany school next door. There was a happy convergence of research interests between Clark and the Godwins. Clark was anxious to use the zonation of first history established by pollen analysis but, in turn, as their classic early paper on barbed bone points from eastern England and the North Sea bed showed, the Godwins were interested in using archeological artifacts as zone fossils. The proximity to Cambridge of a rich sequence of postglacial deposits suggested a combined attack.

The Fenland Research Committee was formed in 1932 by a combination of archeologists, paleobotanists, earth scientists, geographers, zoologists, and geographers with the goal of establishing the development of human settlement in the context of environmental change. The success obtained by the time of its demise as a war casualty was not merely in establishing a sequence for the Fenland but, more importantly, in educating a generation of British scientists in the benefits of interdisciplinary Quaternary research.

The purely chronological importance of this type of work declined as the framework took shape, and decreased even more as radiocarbon dating became established as a more effective tool. On the other hand, the value of pollen analysis, to take only one method, as a means for revealing ecological systems and their history grew with every new application. This in itself was a strong influence in directing Clark's interest toward economic prehistory, in particular toward the ways in which preindustrial communities survived by adapting to, exploiting, and to an increasing degree manipulating and even modifying the ecosystems in which they lived (and indeed of which they formed an integral part). Another influence was his early training. No one brought up as a historian or trained in anthropology could long subscribe to the object fetishism that was threatening to turn archeology into a branch of museology. It was natural for such a person to view artifacts as products designed to serve the activities of life, pri-

marily the activities by which communities obtained their livelihood within ecological systems. From this point of view, archeological data could be interpreted in terms of bioarcheology (a term he coined). One way of demonstrating this was to review the evidence already existing in the archeological record for the main aspects of economic life, as Clark did for prehistoric Europe. Another technique was to undertake the purposeful recovery of systematically acquired data either by the excavation of particular sites, as at Star Carr, or by setting up a project directed toward the elucidation of a particular aspect of economic life, such as that which operated at Cambridge under the direction of Eric Higgs.

Although active in popularizing and stimulating the economic-ecological approach to prehistory, Clark did not subscribe to the doctrine of determinism, whether geographic, economic, social, or specifically Marxist. On the contrary, in his view an ecological approach did not merely include, but positively required, the consideration of cultural factors, including even ideological ones, as contributing to the final determination of choices even at the level of satisfying the most basic biological needs.

Clark obtained his B.A., Ph.D., and Sc.D. at Cambridge. He served in the air photographic intelligence and air history sections during World War II. During his tenure as Disney Professor of Archaeology (1952–74) at Cambridge, he served for two periods as head of the department of archaeology and anthropology. He ended his academic career as master of Peterhouse at Cambridge (1973–80). Clark served as visiting lecturer of professor at Berkeley, Harvard, and Dunedin, New Zealand, and was an associate or honorary member of many academies and learned bodies in Europe and North America. Clark received the Hodgkins Medal from the Smithsonian Institution, the Viking Medal from the Wenner-Gren Foundation, the Drexel Medal from the University of Pennsylvania Museum, and the Gold Medal of the Society of Antiquaries of London.

Clark was founder-editor of the *Proceedings of the Prehistoric Society* (1935–70) and, among other books, wrote *Archaeology and Society* (1939, 1947, 1960, and 1965), *Prehistoric Europe: The Economic Basis* (1952), *Excavations at Star Carr* (1954), *Star Carr: A Case Study in Bioarchaeology* (1972), *Aspects of Prehistory*

(1970), *The Earlier Stone Age Settlement of Scandanavia* (1975), and *World Prehistory* (1961, 1969, and 1977).

For background information *see* ARCHEOLOGY in the McGraw-Hill Encyclopedia of Science and Technology. ∎

CLARK, WILLIAM MANSFIELD
American chemist

Born Aug 17, 1884, Tivoli, NY, U.S.A.
Died Jan. 20, 1964, Baltimore, MD, U.S.A.

While studying the production by bacteria of holes in Swiss cheese, Clark became interested in the effect of hydrogen ion concentration on the media used for growing the bacteria. This led him to develop an expanded series of sulfonphthalein indicators for pH determinations on a quantitative basis.

In his doctoral dissertation in 1884, the Swedish chemist S. A. Arrhenius proposed his theory of ionic dissociation. This led to the concept of the concentration of hydrogen ion as a measure of acidity, and in 1909 the Danish chemist S. P. L. Sørensen introduced the notation of pH as an expression of this concentration. Although acid-base indicators had long been used to determine acidity, at that time the known indicators, such as litmus and phenolphthalein, did not permit an accurate quantitative determination. For this reason, at the beginning of the 20th century the common practice among bacteriologists was to measure the total titratable acidity when determining the acid environment of their cultural media.

Clark realized that a quantitative determination of the hydrogen ion concentration was of greater importance than the titratable acidity in obtaining the proper environment for the growth of bacteria. However, the lack of proper indicators seemed to be an insurmountable obstacle in the path of this goal. In searching for a way around this obstacle, Clark came upon a description of Sørensen's work. Recognizing the applicability of Sørensen's technique, Clark designed his own hydrogen electrode apparatus with which to study acid-base equilibria.

Shortly after beginning his studies with the hydrogen electrode, while working at the dairy division of the U.S. Department of Agriculture, Clark was joined on the project by Herbert A. Lubs. The two began to extend Sørensen's work, and in the course of doing this they developed a series of buffer solutions containing sulfonphthalein dyes that indicated hydrogen ion concentrations from a pH of 1.2 to a pH of 10 in intervals of 0.2 pH. The results of these studies, published in 1917, proved to be invaluable to bacteriologists and chemists, for the indicators gave reasonably accurate measurements without recourse to the delicate and erratic hydrogen electrode.

In 1920, while working in the Hygienic Laboratory of the U.S. Public Health Service, Clark continued his interest in the relationship between bacteriological metabolism and environment by studying oxidation-reduction equilibria in dyes and biological systems. Reactions that occur within a cell and release energy to the organism involve the transfer of electrons from one compound to another within the cell, with corresponding oxidation-reduction potentials that may be measured on a relative basis. The potential measured indicates the direction of the reaction. As the potential decreases in a given medium, the environment changes from one suitable for the growth of aerobic bacteria to one suitable for anaerobic ones. In 1893 the German bacteriologist Paul Ehrlich had arranged different dyes in the order of their ease of reduction by a cell so as to measure the intensity factor in oxidation. However, he had been unable to measure accurately the reducibility of the dyes used. With the improvement of the techniques of physical chemistry, Clark and the German-American chemist Leonor Michaelis did this independently and established a fundamental basis for understanding the reversible oxidation of dyes and biological systems. Although the basis for measuring oxidation potentials still depends on the hydrogen electrode, the difficulty of using it is so great that the dye systems developed by Clark have been widely used by bacteriologists. This method has been most helpful in the exploration of the living cell to determine the mechanism involved in oxidation-reduction equilibria.

Clark received his B.A. (1907) and M.A. (1908) at Williams College and his Ph.D. (1910) at the Johns Hopkins University. From 1910 to 1920 he was a research chemist in the dairy division of the U.S. Department of Agriculture, and from 1920 to 1927 he was professor of chemistry in the Hygiene Laboratory of the U.S. Public Health Service. In 1927 he was appointed DeLamar Professor of Physiological Chemistry at Johns Hopkins. He became DeLamar Professor Emeritus in 1952 but continued at Johns Hopkins as a research professor. Among Clark's numerous scientific honors was the 1957 Passano Foundation Award "for his basic work in the demonstration of the importance of physical methods, particularly in the control of basal metabolism and of oxidation-reduction, to the study of life processes."

Clark wrote *Determination of Hydrogen Ions* (1920; 3d ed. 1928), *Studies on Oxidation-Reduction* (1928), *Topics in Physical Chemistry for Medical Students* (1948; 2d ed. 1952), and *Oxidation-Reduction Potentials of Organic Systems* (1960).

For background information *see* HYDROGEN ELECTRODE; HYDROGEN ION; pH in the McGraw-Hill Encyclopedia of Science and Technology. ∎

CLAUDE, ALBERT
☆ Belgian-American cell biologist

Born Aug. 24, 1898, Longlier, Luxembourg Province, Belgium

Claude went to the United States in 1929 and began his career in scientific research at the Rockefeller University (then the Rockefeller Institute for Medical Research). During his 20-year association with the university his work resulted in numerous major contributions to the understanding of cell structure and function. In recognition of his many achievements, Claude shared the 1974 Nobel Prize for

medicine or physiology with C. de Duve and G. E. Palade.

The success of Claude's cell research is directly attributable to his ability to see the potential in using an electron microscope to view the detailed anatomy of a cell. He also developed centrifugation as a tool for isolating cell components.

During the 5 years after his arrival at Rockefeller University, Claude was engaged in the study of cell-free extracts of tumor cells in an attempt to purify and concentrate the Rous chicken tumor I agent. Utilizing the technique of differential centrifugation, he was able to concentrate it and demonstrated a tumorogenic activity 50 times greater than the original cell extract.

Claude continued to test and improve the general method of cell fractionation over the next 10 years. Working with various kinds of normal cells and tissues, he eventually identified the fraction components with constituents in the intact cell. Moreover, the subcellular fragments continued to function as they would have in their original environment in the cell. In his way he discovered mitochondria and the endoplasmic reticulum. Claude and his coworkers went on to determine the role of these elements in the life of the cell. He clearly demonstrated that the mitochondria were actually the power plants of the cell. In 1946 he concluded his work in this area with the publication of the first detailed account of the basic principles of cell fractionation.

In 1942 Claude had become interested

in electron microscopy as a method for cell research. With Keith R. Porter, he began studying cultured cells and recognized that the network of strands and vesicles was closely linked to the microsomes he had isolated by fractionation.

In 1950 Claude left the United States for Belgium, giving up his research career for laboratory administration. Over the next 20 years he directed the building of a cancer research center at the University of Belgium and then retired to head the Jules Bordet Institute in Brussels. At the institute he returned to research, focusing his attention on the fine structure of cells and tissues.

Claude grew up in Belgium. Partly because of his activities during World War I, he received little formal education. He worked in a steel mill, first as an apprentice and then as a draftsman. When he was 22, he was admitted to the Liège University School of Mining. A year later (1921) he was admitted to the Liège University Medical School, where he received a doctorate in medicine and surgery (1928). He then spent a short period at research institutes in Berlin. Claude went to the United States in 1929 on a government scholarship for overseas study. He was a professor at the Rockefeller Institute (emeritus, 1972) and also at the Université Libre de Bruxelles (from 1948; emeritus, 1969). During 1948–71 he directed the Jules Bordet Institute and the Laboratoire de Biologie Cellulaire et Cancérolgie in Brussels. Thereafter he devoted himself to creating a research laboratory, mainly concerned with cancer, at the Université Libre. He held a double citizenship as a naturalized American (1941) and as a Belgian (by legal process, 1949). In addition to the Nobel Prize, Claude was awarded the Medal of the Belgian Academy of Medicine, the Louisa G. Horowitz Prize of Columbia University (1970), and the Paul Ehrlich and Ludwig Darmstaedter Prize (Frankfurt, 1971). He was a member of the Belgian and French academies of medicine, and an honorary member of the American Academy of Arts and Sciences. Claude received the Grand Cordon of the Order of Léopold II (Belgium) and was made a commander in the Order of the Palmes Académiques (France).

For background information *see* CELL (BIOLOGY) in the McGraw-Hill Encyclopedia of Science and Technology. ∎

CLAUSEN, JENS CHRISTIAN
★ American plant biologist

Born Mar. 11, 1891, N. Eskilstrup, Holbaek County, Denmark
Died Nov. 22, 1969, Palo Alto, CA, U.S.A.

Together with colleagues, Clausen explored the existence of ecological races within species and the hereditary structures that govern the evolution of races, species, and clusters of species within genera. He also clarified the interaction of environment with heredity in the phenotypic expression of the plant. These discoveries have influenced the general thinking about plant breeding, tree breeding, and plant relationships and suggest why certain plant families remain trapped within low, others within high, latitudes.

Charles Darwin in 1859 presented circumstantial evidence that species evolved through natural selection among an immense number of spontaneous variations. In Darwin's time the differences between inherited and noninherited variation were unknown. By 1920 the relative proportion of the two kinds of variability among wild organisms was still unknown, and notions of what constituted a species were primarily based upon speculation.

In the early 1920s three groups of botanists in different countries, unknown to each other, began experiments designed to answer some of these questions. In Sweden Göte Turesson moved plants of presumably the same species but native to seacoasts, inland localities, high altitudes, and low altitudes to an inland sea-level garden near Lund. He found that races from such diverse climates retained their inherited differences in the uniform garden and he named these races ecotypes.

In California Harvey M. Hall of the Carnegie Institution of Washington went a step further, dividing individuals of perennial plants native to contrasting climates across California and transplanting the divisions to experiment plots at different altitudes. In Hall's experiments the environment varied but the heredity of the divided plant remained the same. He found that generally lowland and high-altitude races of a species were unable to survive in each other's habitats. With E. B. Babcock he also intercrossed races and species of the California hayfield tarweeds and studied their genetic differences in a uniform lowland garden.

In Denmark Clausen studied the wild species of the pansy violets from seacoast and inland habitats, sandy and limestone soils. He found that the uncrossed races and species retained their identity in a uniform environment but that they could exchange elements of their heredities by crossings in the wild and in the experiment garden. Through their early papers the three groups of investigators had by 1922 discovered their common interests and begun exchanging notes and visits.

If the species of large genera were systematically intercrossed, Clausen reasoned, one should expect to find species in all stages of evolutionary separation. This he showed to be the case in his 10-year experimental investigation of pansies. He also showed, for the first time, that the differences between species are controlled by inherited genes as are the differences between varieties or races of one species. The genes are carried by the microscopic chromosomes, and in violets the number of chromosomes varies from species to species.

By 1930 Hall, assisted by D. D. Keck and W. M. Hiesey, had established a series of three altitudinal transplant stations. These were located along the 38th parallel from near sea level at Stanford to 4600 feet (1380 meters) on the west side of Sierra Nevada at Mather, and to 10,000 feet (3000 meters) on the east side of Yosemite National Park. The growth season along the 200-mile (320-kilometer) transect ranged from all year near

the coast to only 2 months at the high station. Clausen joined the California group in 1931; Hall died 3 months later.

By direct-transplant experiments at the three-station facility, Clausen, Keck, and Hiesey proved that species of many families were composed of as many as 8 to 11 climatic (ecologic) races across the transect, each race adjusted to the periodicities of the climate where it was native and unadjusted to highly different environments.

By combining crossing and transplant experiments in crossing lowland with high-altitude races, and by dividing parents and first- and second-generation progenies for transplantation, they found that each of the differences that adjusted the parental races to their native zones was controlled not by single genes but by small systems of genes, each gene having a minor but cumulative effect. Moreover, the gene system that regulated the expression of a single trait, as for example petal color or time of flowering, was composed of individual genes that might enhance, counteract, complement, or cover each other's effects. The visible expression depended upon the balance of these interactions and could change with the altitude where the hybrid individual was located.

The genes of the gene systems that regulated the distinguishing traits of each race, they found, were stored within the local races, which thereby served as reservoirs for potential variability that could be combined through crossing and released again in later generations, enriching the variability far beyond what occurs naturally. The genes were interlocked into an arrangement among the chromosomes that ensured relative reproducibility of the racial characteristics during periods of environmental stability but that mobilized potential variability in times of radical changes in the environment, leading to altered selective pressure and evolution.

In crosses between hundreds of species representing many families and kinds of separation, Clausen and his colleagues discovered that many species do not easily fit into existing classificatory systems. Basic to the initial separation was the adjustment to distinct external environments as observed among the climatic races within a species. The next step was the beginning of an inherited internal separation because the genes of the parental species could not be freely interchanged without damage to

the progeny. Finally, species could not be visibly distinguished unless the environmental and genetic separation was accompanied by a morphologically recognizable one, which is the difference the nonexperimenting classifier uses.

It was found that the three modes of evolutionary separation—ecologic, genetic, and morphologic—might proceed simultaneously and gradually through millions of years, or one kind of separation might proceed at a different speed and outrun the others. Groups of species that to a limited extent were able to exchange some of their heredities produced clusters of species (species complexes), such as in oaks or pines, but the experimental work was done with faster-growing herbaceous perennial and annual species.

These new views of the evolutionary processes have changed the prevalent idea that heredity and adjustment to environment are fairly simple; they show that our understanding of the plant kingdom is exceedingly rudimentary. Still largely unexplored are the physiological and biochemical mechanisms that are regulated by the genes and also distinguish races and species.

Son of a farmer and housebuilder, Clausen was taught at home until age 8, then attended the local country school and a private secondary school. At 14 he assumed responsibility for the 15-acre (60,700–square meter) family farm. For some years direct studies in nature guided by master texts substituted for formal schooling. In 1913, at the age of 22, he passed a comprehensive entrance examination for the University of Copenhagen. There he majored in botany with specialties in the systematics of violets under Chresten Raunkiaer and in genetics under Wilhelm Johannsen. In 1921 he received his master's degree in natural sciences and in 1926 his doctorate. From 1921 to 1931 he was research assistant in the new department of genetics at the Royal Agricultural College of Copenhagen headed by Øjvind Winge. In 1931 he joined the staff of the Carnegie Institution of Washington at Stanford, CA. He became an American citizen in 1943 and was elected to the National Academy of Sciences in 1959.

Clausen wrote *Stages in the Evolution of Plant Species* (1951) and, with Keck and Hiesey, four books on the nature of various kinds of species (Carnegie Institution; 1940, 1945, 1948, 1958).

For background information *see* PLANT EVOLUTION; PLANTS, LIFE FORMS OF in the McGraw-Hill Encyclopedia of Science and Technology. ■

CLELAND, RALPH ERSKINE
★ American botanist

Born *Oct. 20, 1892, Le Claire, IA, U.S.A.*

Died *June 11, 1971, Bloomington, IN, U.S.A.*

Most of Cleland's research was devoted to an analysis of the hereditary peculiarities of the evening primrose *(Oenothera)* and the utilization of the facts thus revealed as tools in a study of the evolution of this genus.

Work on *Oenothera* began with Hugo de Vries, who based his mutation theory of evolution largely on this work. *Oenothera* showed, however, certain hereditary anomalies that he was unable to explain. Otto Renner analyzed these peculiarities and found that most oenotheras behave when inbred as though all their genes lie in one chromosome pair, although they possess 14 chromosomes. When outcrossed, however, these genes behave in many hybrids as though they were scattered among different chromosomes. As a result, *Oenothera* shows many genetical anomalies.

The physical basis for these peculiarities remained obscure until Cleland discovered that the chromosomes of most oenotheras also behave peculiarly. In other organisms, corresponding chromosomes from father and mother pair at the forma-

tion of reproductive cells, and the members of each pair separate into different reproductive cells, it being a matter of chance whether the paternal or the maternal chromosome of a pair goes into a particular germ cell. In most oenotheras, however, the 14 chromosomes, instead of forming pairs, become associated end to end to form a closed ring, paternal and maternal chromosomes alternating. Adjacent chromosomes then pass into different germ cells—that is, all paternal chromosomes enter one germ cell, all maternal chromosomes enter another. Thus, linking of all chromosomes into one group causes all genes to be linked in inheritance. This type of chromosome behavior had not been observed before, and is still more widespread in *Oenothera* than in any other organism in which it has been observed.

In hybrids, however, chromosomes are not always linked. It is possible to arrange 14 chromosomes in 15 different ways into closed circles and pairs, and all 15 arrangements have been found. Each hybrid has one of the 15 arrangements. When chromosomes form several groups, instead of being linked into a single group, the genes are no longer all linked in inheritance, and a variety of progeny results. Thus, the linking of all genes into a single group in inbred lines, and their separation into different groups in many hybrids, can be explained on the basis of peculiarities of chromosome behavior.

But why do the chromosomes behave so peculiarly? Following a suggestion of John Belling, it was shown that this has resulted from wholesale exchanges of pairing segments that have occurred between noncorresponding chromosomes in the course of evolution. Each set of seven chromosomes in each race has its own arrangement of pairing segments, which is one of 135,135 possible arrangements. The two sets of chromosomes in a race with a circle of 14 have quite different arrangements; no chromosome of one set has the same two ends as a chromosome in the other set. Thus, numbering the pairing ends, if one set has the arrangement 1·2 3·4 5·6 7·8 9·10 11·12 13·14 and the other set has 2·3 4·5 6·7 8·9 10·11 12·13 14·1, the pairing of like ends will produce a closed circle of 14 instead of paired chromosomes.

That shuffling of pairing ends through exchange has taken place on an extensive scale is shown by two facts: (1) There are 91 possible associations of two pairing ends— 1·2, 1·3, 1·4, etc. All 91 associations have been found in nature. Every end can be,

and has become, associated with every other end. (2) Although only a minute fraction of all oenotheras have been studied, the more than 380 sets of chromosomes whose end arrangements have been fully analyzed by Cleland and his students have revealed over 160 different arrangements. The total number present in nature must be enormous.

It was early observed by Cleland that when two closely related sets of genes were combined into a hybrid, this hybrid tended to have mostly paired chromosomes. On the other hand, relatively unrelated sets when combined produced hybrids with large circles. In other words, similarity in the distribution of pairing segments suggests close relationship, and vice versa.

Following this lead, it proved possible to trace the evolutionary history of the oenotheras in a surprisingly detailed manner. Four and probably five different populations of oenotheras have developed at different periods in geological history. The center of origin has apparently been Central America. Within each population interchanges have occurred as the plants have migrated northward and eastward over the continent. It is possible to trace the migratory pathways in some cases by following the sequence of interchanges as each has occurred in a particular geographical area.

Since, however, the number of possible interchanges is very great, the exchanges that have occurred in one population have usually been quite different from those occurring in another population. For example, when population 1 was invaded by population 2, and crosses occurred, hybrids were occasionally formed in which none of the chromosomes from one population had the same association of ends as any of the chromosomes of the other population. The result was a large circle of chromosomes.

At present, 10 groupings of races may be distinguished, each of which may be considered a species. Six of these have arisen by hybridization between overlapping populations, two are relicts of original populations, one (on the West Coast) has found no population with which it could cross, and one still resides in the center of origin.

In summary, Cleland's work divides itself into three parts: (1) discovery and analysis of the peculiar behavior of the chromosomes in *Oenothera,* and demonstration that this constitutes the physical basis for the unique genetical behavior of the genes; (2) demonstration that circle-formation in *Oenothera* is a result of the extensive shuffling of pairing segments that has been brought about by exchanges of segments between noncorresponding chromosomes; (3) unraveling the story of evolution in *Oenothera* by analyzing the interchanges that have occurred during the migrations of each of a succession of independent populations and showing how these populations have crossed with each other to form the circle-bearing, true-breeding races that now constitute the great bulk of present-day *Oenothera*.

Reared in Philadelphia, Cleland received the A.B. from the University of Pennsylvania in 1915, majoring in classics and history. He received the Ph.D. in botany from the same institution in 1919. Following service overseas during World War I, he taught at Goucher College from 1919 to 1938, then transferred to Indiana University, where he was chairperson of the botany department and later dean of the graduate school. In 1963 he became Distinguished Service Professor of Botany Emeritus. He was elected to the National Academy of Sciences in 1942.

Cleland wrote *Oenothera: Cytogenetics and Evolution* (1971).

For background information *see* CHROMOSOME; PLANT EVOLUTION in the McGraw-Hill Encyclopedia of Science and Technology. ∎

CLEMENCE, GERALD MAURICE
★ American astronomer

Born *Aug. 16, 1908, Springfield, RI, U.S.A.*

Died *Nov. 22, 1974, Providence, RI, U.S.A.*

While studying the motions of the Moon and planets, and the fundamental constants of astronomy, Clemence conceived the idea of measuring time by means of the orbital motions of the Moon and Earth instead of by the rotation of the Earth. This new measure of time was adopted throughout the world in 1956. For it and related work he was awarded the Gold Medal of the Royal Astronomical Society and the James Craig Watson Medal of the National Academy of Sciences, as well as other honors.

It had been suspected for decades, and in 1939 was firmly established, that the Earth's speed of rotation varied in an ir-

regular, unpredictable fashion, such that in the course of a century all the clocks on the Earth would be fast at some times and slow at other times, as compared with uniform time. The size of the error occasionally exceeded 30 seconds, and its statistical behavior indicated that in the course of centuries it would increase to much larger amounts. The cause of the irregularities is not yet fully understood, but is thought to be the interaction between the liquid core of the Earth and the solid mantle.

For many purposes, such irregularities in the measurement of time are of no consequence, so long as all the clocks agree with one another, but in some cases they become important. The values of all physical constants that depend on the time would, in due course, appear to change if the measure of time were not uniform. The velocity of light and the constant of gravitation are important examples.

The motion of the Moon is irregular, like the rotation of the Earth, but with the important difference that the motion of the Moon is precisely calculated by gravitational theory for many centuries in the past and future. The formula giving the position of the Moon at any time may, in principle, be inverted, so as to give the time as a function of the Moon's position; an observation of the Moon's position then yields the time, by substitution in the inverted formula. This was Clemence's basic idea. The Moon, however, is subject to a small acceleration arising from tidal friction between the Moon and the Earth, which is not precisely known; thus it is

not suitable as a standard clock for an indefinite period. For this reason Clemence introduced the position of the Earth in its orbit around the Sun as the primary standard. This latter position is observed less accurately than that of the Moon, and hence is not suitable for measuring time day by day, but only century by century. The Moon, then, may be compared with the second hand of a clock, which interpolates and refines the indication of the hour hand corresponding to the Earth's orbital motion.

The new measure of time is named ephemeris time, and its introduction was accompanied by a new definition of the second. Formerly the second had been defined as the 86,400th part of a day; now it is the fraction 1/31,556,925.9747 of the year.

A farmer's son, Clemence majored in mathematics at Brown University. He went to the U.S. Naval Observatory in Washington in 1930, becoming director of the Nautical Almanac Office in 1945 and scientific director of the observatory in 1958. Retiring in 1963, he went to Yale University, where he became senior research associate and lecturer in astronomy. He was elected to the National Academy of Sciences in 1952.

Clemence wrote *Methods of Celestial Mechanics,* with Dirk Brouwer (1961), and *Spherical Astronomy,* with E. W. Woolard (1966).

For background information *see* EARTH, ROTATION AND ORBITAL MOTION OF; EPHEMERIS TIME; TIME in the McGraw-Hill Encyclopedia of Science and Technology. ∎

CLOOS, HANS
German structural geologist

Born *Nov. 8, 1886, Magdeburg, Germany*
Died *Sept. 26, 1951, Bonn, Germany*

By careful measurement of minor structural details, such as the joints, fractures, and orientation of certain minerals in a rock, Cloos showed how it was possible to reconstruct the manner in which large igneous rock masses moved or flowed into position in the crust of the Earth. He pioneered in the establishment of the branch of geology known as granite tectonics, which is the study of the manner in which rock masses move and the effects of such movement on the components of the rock itself and on surrounding material. Such studies are important in understanding the mode of origin of igneous rocks and related structures and in ascertaining how the crust of the Earth came into its present condition.

Although hundreds of geologists before him had seen these same features in igneous rocks, it remained for Cloos to show how the previously unnoticed details, such as the alignment of platy mica flakes with respect to the contacts of the rocks with surrounding materials, when carefully measured and mapped in detail, could reveal the internal structure of the rock masses. These features are measured in much the same manner as are strike and dip of sedimentary rocks. By examining the maps on which these data have been recorded by means of special symbols, the trained geologist can visualize how the pasty mass of hot magma moved into position in the Earth's crust. Flowing and swirling slowly around and past promontories of hard rock, the viscous magma welled up from some deep-seated source far below the crust of the Earth, pushing aside the rocks previously there and filling crevices created by the great upward pressures exerted on the brittle roof rocks.

Cloos was also one of the first to use true scale models in deciphering the mechanics of faulting. He used soft clays to simulate the behavior of hard rocks undergoing deformation long before the recent development of scale-model theory showed that this was indeed the proper material to use in laboratory models simulating rock behavior. In his later years he extended his investigations from relatively small portions of the crust to the structure and development of the continents, and even probed cautiously the origin of the Earth itself.

Cloos received his doctorate in geology from the University of Freiburg im Breisgau in 1907. From 1909 to 1910 he mapped the Erongo Mountains in South-West Africa. For the next 3 years he worked as a petroleum geologist for the Standard Oil Company in Indonesia. After brief service as a military geologist in France in 1914, he was released from the army because of poor health. He became lecturer in geology at the University of Breslau, where he was appointed to the chair of geology in 1919. In 1925 he went to the University of Bonn as professor of geology. After several trips to the United States he wrote a classic paper on the structural characteristics of the North

American Cordillera. In 1948 he was awarded the Geological Society of America's Penrose Medal.

Cloos wrote *Conversation with the Earth: A Geologist's Autobiography* (1959).

For background information *see* IG-NEOUS ROCKS in the McGraw-Hill Encyclopedia of Science and Technology. ■

CLOUD, PRESTON
★ American geologist and biogeologist

***Born** Sept. 26, 1912, West Upton, MA, U.S.A.*

Cloud is best known for his work on the interactions between early biospheric, atmospheric, and crustal evolution in which he focused on the origin of life, of atmospheric oxygen, of the nucleate cell, and of multicellular animal life (Metazoa). Starting with invertebrate paleontology, marine ecology and paleoecology, and marine sedimentation and geochemistry, he became a principal architect of the modern integrated approach to the study of life processes in geology—a subject he called biogeology. He was first to advance and defend the now-accepted view that Metazoa evolved rapidly and from different ancestors beginning in earliest Paleozoic time (about 6.8×10^8 years ago). He shared in demonstrating the existence of a long pre-metazoan record of microbial life which, linked with geochemistry and sedimentology, tells of the early surface processes on Earth. His model of early Earth history became widely accepted.

His studies of and reports on the capacity of Earth to support continuing industrial growth influenced thought and legislation dealing with this problem. His research in both field and laboratory carried him to all continents except Antarctica.

When Cloud entered science, conventional Earth history dealt almost exclusively with the last 15 percent of the 4.6×10^9 years of geologic time. The succession of the older rocks was uncertain, and the record of life in them was either denied or misunderstood. Age determinations based on radioactivity provided a sequence before the way to a proper history became clear, but Cloud reasoned that interactions among Earth processes had necessarily left a record that only remained to be recognized. Once life appeared on Earth, he hypothesized, surface geochemistry and sedimentation could not have remained the same. The beginning of an oxygenic atmosphere should have left detectable and nearly simultaneous worldwide effects. But oxygen is a biological poison. It could not begin to accumulate until all oxygen sinks were filled and protective enzymes had evolved. It could then accumulate no faster than its by-products could be sequestered by sedimentation or by other means. An eventual balance between oxygen in the atmosphere on the one hand and sedimentation and erosion of carbonaceous deposits on the other was to be expected.

Since no line of inquiry into so fragmentary a record could be definitive, it was necessary to look at all aspects of evolving Earth history simultaneously. Following such a holistic approach, Cloud's research led him to a number of once radical but later widely accepted conclusions: (1) the earliest Paleozoic metazoan record was less an accident of a grossly incomplete geological history than a geologically rapid display of evolutionary opportunism associated with ecological change and the related appearance of new biological modes; (2) the Metazoa descended from more than one pre-metazoan ancestor, probably starting when the atmosphere became sufficiently oxygenic, about 6.8×10^8 years ago; (3) the nucleate cell first appeared between 1.3 and 2×10^9 years ago at still lower oxygen levels; (4) free oxygen first began to accumulate in the atmosphere mainly as a result of biological processes about 2×10^9 years ago; (5) before that time there was an interdependent relationship between the time-restricted banded iron formations and oxygen-producing microbial life; (6) indirect evidence implies that oxygen-producing microbial life was already present at the time of the oldest known sediments, about 3.76×10^9 years ago. Subsequent studies by Cloud and others generally supported these views and provided a broad outline of the first 85 percent of Earth history and a framework within which to coordinate new data.

On completion of undergraduate work at George Washington University in 1938 and graduate work at Yale in 1940, Cloud taught for a year at the Missouri School of Mines. World War II took him to the U.S. Geological Survey (USGS) for work on bauxite and then petroleum, involving geologic mapping and field studies of calcareous rocks. From 1946 to 1948 he taught at Harvard, returning to the USGS in 1948 to study Pacific tropical reefs and islands and to become chief of its Branch of Paleontology and Stratigraphy for 10 years—for which service he received the Rockefeller Public Service Award and the Department of the Interior's Distinguished Service Award and Gold Medal. During that time he also led two marine geology expeditions to the Bahamas and completed a petroleum reconnaissance of northeastern Spain. Between 1959 and 1961 he turned his attention to the role of the USGS in the oceans, eventually securing legislative authorization for such a role and directing efforts to the then neglected continental shelves and coastal zone. From 1961 to 1965 Cloud chaired the department of geology and geophysics at the University of Minnesota, and then became head of the School of Earth Sciences there. During this time his research concentrated on the primitive Earth. Then, in 1965, declining larger administrative roles, he chose to teach at the University of California, first at Los Angeles for 3 years and then at Santa Barbara for 6 years, returning to the USGS in 1974. Also, beginning in 1965, he became deeply involved in the affairs of the National Academy of Science–National Research Council (NAS–NRC), serving tours of duty on the NAS Committee on Science and Public Policy, the council of the NAS and its executive committee, the governing board of NRC, and the NRC Assembly of Mathematical and Physical Sciences, and chairing various studies on resources and environment as well as the NAS Section of Geology. Cloud was elected to the National Academy of Sciences (1961), the American Academy of

Arts and Sciences (1969), and the American Philosophical Society (1973). He was awarded five medals, including the Paleontological Society Medal (1971) and the Penrose Medal (1976) of the Geological Society of America.

In addition to writing papers for scientific journals, Cloud published seven books and scientific monographs. Among them were *Resources and Man* (1969) and *Adventures in Earth History* (1970), both of which he edited and coauthored; and *Cosmos, Earth, and Man* (1978).

For background information *see* ANIMAL EVOLUTION; ATMOSPHERE, EVOLUTION OF; GEOLOGICAL TIME SCALE; LIFE, ORIGIN OF; PALEONTOLOGY in the McGraw-Hill Encyclopedia of Science and Technology. ∎

COCHRAN, WILLIAM
★ British physicist

Born July 30, 1922, Newton Mearns, Scotland

It is impossible to draw a firm dividing line between crystallography and solid-state physics. Cochran worked in this border region, with incursions into topics as separated as biomolecular structures and the theory of ferroelectricity.

Pyrimidines, purines, nucleosides, and nucleotides are molecules occurring as components of nucleic acid. Cochran's work with others at the Cavendish Laboratory during the late 1940s and the early 1950s helped to determine the exact di-

mensions and stereochemistry of some of these comparatively simple molecules by using the techniques of x-ray crystallography; in particular, the work demonstrated the importance of hydrogen bonding for intermolecular associations. In collaboration with F. H. C. Crick, the first conclusive evidence was obtained for the occurrence of a helical molecular structure in nature, that of polymethylglutamate. The principal merit of this work, seen in retrospect, was that it played a part in leading Crick, in association with J. D. Watson, to the discovery of the helical structure of deoxyribonucleic acid (DNA). *See* CRICK, FRANCIS HARRY COMPTON; WATSON, JAMES DEWEY.

The determination of a crystal structure is not a straightforward matter of measurement of x-ray intensities followed by a routine calculation. While the x-ray measurements give the amplitudes of the terms in a Fourier series for the electron density of the crystal, the phase angle to be associated with each term is not directly measurable. This situation is known to crystallographers as the phase problem, and Cochran made a number of contributions to the theory of its solution. Attempts, for the most part unsuccessful, were also made in collaboration with A. S. Douglas to solve the problem in particular instances by using one of the first automatic computers, the EDSAC. Another collaborator from this period, M. M. Woolfson, later successfully continued and much extended the scope of this research.

Discouraged by lack of progress in this direction and feeling that x-ray crystallography was becoming increasingly the preserve of chemists and biologists, Cochran took a year's leave from his lectureship at Cambridge University to work with B. N. Brockhouse at the Chalk River Laboratories of Atomic Energy of Canada. Brockhouse was at that time pioneering the development of neutron spectroscopy as a means of studying the dynamics of atoms in crystals, and hence of interatomic forces. Cochran joined in this work and continued a long-distance collaboration with the Chalk River group over several years. This work led to an improved understanding of interatomic forces in ionic, covalent, and metallic crystals. Cochran developed the theory of the relation between the lattice dynamics of a crystal and its dielectric properties, and in particular applied the theory to treat the phenomenon of ferroelectricity in terms of crystal stability. The predictions made were later confirmed experimentally by R. A. Cowley for ferroelectric crystals having the barium titanate type of structure, and experiments using the technique of neutron spectroscopy led to the conclusion that materials having an even simpler type of crystal structure—for example, germanium telluride—can be ferroelectric.

Son of a Scottish farmer, Cochran graduated in physics from the University of Edinburgh in 1943. He spent 3 more years in Edinburgh as an assistant lecturer in physics, while working as a research student of C. A. Beevers in the department of chemistry. During 1946–64 he worked in the Cavendish Laboratory, apart from two periods of leave in the United States and Canada, and in 1964 returned to Edinburgh as professor of physics. He was elected a fellow of the Royal Society of London in 1962. He was awarded the Guthrie Medal of the Institute of Physics and the Physical Society in 1966 and the Hughes Medal of the Royal Society in 1978 in recognition of his contributions to x-ray crystallography and to lattice dynamics.

Cochran wrote *The Determination of Crystal Structures,* with H. S. Lipson (1966), and *The Dynamics of Atoms in Crystals* (1973).

For background information *see* CRYSTAL STRUCTURE; FERROELECTRICS; X-RAY CRYSTALLOGRAPHY in the McGraw-Hill Encyclopedia of Science and Technology. ∎

COCKCROFT, SIR JOHN (DOUGLAS)
★ British nuclear physicist

Born May 27, 1897, Todmorden, England
Died Sept. 18, 1967, Cambridge, England

While working in the Cavendish Laboratory, Cambridge, whose director was Sir Ernest Rutherford, Cockcroft, together with E. T. S. Walton, conceived the idea of transmuting atomic nuclei of the light elements by using protons accelerated by voltages of up to 500 kilovolts. They were led to this by the theoretical work of George Gamow on the disintegration of elements by alpha particles. The new wave-mechanical theory of penetration of charged particles through nuclear potential barriers showed that protons of com-

paratively modest energies would have a chance of penetrating these barriers. *See* GAMOW, GEORGE; WALTON, ERNEST THOMAS SINTON.

Cockcroft and Walton, therefore, built a steady potential generator for 500 kilovolts using a voltage multiplication circuit. They also built a proton source, injecting protons into a vacuum tube, where they were accelerated by potentials of up to 500 kiloelectronvolts. The high-speed protons emerged from the apparatus and struck targets of lithium, boron, carbon, fluorine, and other elements. Cockcroft and Walton observed that lithium was disintegrated into two alpha particles and boron into three alpha particles, and that other reactions, leading to the emission of alpha particles, took place.

When deuterium became available, Cockcroft and Walton were able to extend their work to the use of deuterons as projectiles, and a wider range of transmutations became possible, particularly those in which protons were emitted.

After the discovery of artificial radioactivity by Frédéric Joliot-Curie, Cockcroft, Walton, and C. W. Gilbert showed that artificial radioactivity could be produced by the bombardment of carbon with protons, leading to the production of nitrogen-13. They compared the energy release in these transmutations in the form of kinetic energy with mass changes in the transmutations and demonstrated that the Einstein equivalence formula $E = mc^2$ accurately accounted for the observed

changes in energy. For their pioneer work on the transmutation of atomic nuclei by artificially accelerated atomic particles, Cockcroft and Walton shared the 1951 Nobel Prize in physics.

The work of Cockcroft and Walton was soon paralleled by the experiments of E. O. Lawrence and his collaborators using the cyclotron as a nuclear accelerator and by the work of R. J. Van de Graaff and collaborators using the Van de Graaff generator as the high-voltage source. As a result, in the period 1932–39, an enormous range of nuclear transmutations was discovered and, in particular, a very large number of radioactive isotopes. A particularly important result of M. L. E. Oliphant and Rutherford was to show that when deuterons bombard deuterium, neutrons and helium-3, or protons and tritium, are produced in great abundance. This proved to be of great practical importance. *See* LAWRENCE, ERNEST ORLANDO; VAN DE GRAAFF, ROBERT JEMISON.

The son of a textile manufacturer, Cockcroft studied mathematics at Manchester University during part of the academic year 1914–15. Returning after the war, he studied electrical engineering at Manchester College of Science and Technology and Metropolitan Vickers Electrical Company. From Manchester he moved to the University of Cambridge in 1922 and studied mathematics for 2 years before joining Rutherford in the Cavendish Laboratory. He worked for a time with P. L. Kapitza on producing magnetic fields of up to 300 kilogauss and in developing a cryogenic laboratory. In the later 1930s he took charge of the Royal Society Mond Laboratory and became Jacksonian Professor of Natural Philosophy in the Cavendish in 1939. At the outbreak of war in 1939, he became an assistant director of research in the Ministry of Supply and was responsible for erecting emergency radar stations to detect low-flying aircraft approaching Scapa Flow and the east coast ports. After this, he became head of the Air Defence Research and Development Establishment at Christchurch and later at Malvern. In April 1944 he moved to Canada to take charge of the Anglo-Canadian Atomic Energy Project, first at Montreal and then at Chalk River. The laboratory built the first two heavy-water reactors in Canada. He became director of the U.K. Atomic Energy Establishment at Harwell in 1946, and was a member of the U.K. Atomic Energy Authority from its foundation in 1954. In 1964 he became master of Churchill College, Cambridge.

For background information *see* NU-CLEAR REACTION; PARTICLE ACCELER-ATOR in the McGraw-Hill Encyclopedia of Science and Technology. ∎

COHEN, PAUL JOSEPH
☆ American mathematician

Born Apr. 2, 1934, Long Branch, NJ, U.S.A.

In 1963 Cohen proved that the continuum hypothesis and the axiom of choice are independent of the other axioms of set theory. This result had profound implications for the foundations of mathematics.

The continuum hypothesis was formulated by G. Cantor in 1878 in the course of his fundamental work on set theory. Cantor defined two sets A and B to have the same cardinality (intuitively, the same number of elements) if there is a one-to-one correspondence between the elements of A and B, and defined a set B to have a larger cardinality than a set A if there is a one-to-one correspondence from A to a subset of B, but no such correspondence from B to A or a subset of A. Cantor proved that the set of real numbers (the continuum) is larger, in this sense, than the set of natural numbers, and that, in general, the power set of any

set A (the set of subsets of A) is larger than A. (The power set of the natural numbers is equivalent to the continuum.)

The question immediately arises: is there an infinite set which is larger than the set of natural numbers but smaller than the continuum? The continuum hypothesis states that no such set exists. The generalized continuum hypothesis states that for any infinite set A there is no set which is larger than A and smaller than the power set of A. The problem of proving or disproving the continuum hypothesis came to occupy a central place in set theory, and it was first in a celebrated list of unsolved problems proposed by D. Hilbert in 1900.

The discovery, about 1900, of paradoxes in Cantor's intuitive theory led E. Zermelo, A. Fraenkel, and others to formulate a collection of axioms for set theory through which they hoped to avoid contradictions. But objections were raised to one of the proposed axioms, the axiom of choice, which states that if A is any collection of nonempty sets, then there exists a set consisting of precisely one element chosen from each of the sets in A. Although many important mathematical results depend on this axiom, some mathematicians questioned the validity of assuming the possibility of such a choice procedure for infinite sets.

In 1938–40 K. Gödel showed that if the collection of Zermelo-Fraenkel axioms minus the axiom of choice, known as restricted set theory, is consistent, then it remains consistent when the axiom of choice and the generalized continuum hypothesis are added simultaneously. In other words, the axiom of choice and the generalized continuum hypothesis do not introduce any contradiction that was not already present among the "safe" axioms of restricted set theory, and therefore they cannot be disproved by restricted set theory. Gödel's proof depended on the method of inner models which had been used to prove the relative consistency of noneuclidean geometries. He constructed, within the framework of restricted set theory, a class of sets L and then showed that the axioms of restricted set theory, the axiom of choice, and the generalized continuum hypothesis could be proved within the realm of L. Intuitively, the sets of the model L are those which can be constructed from the null or empty set by an infinite sequence of several simple operations, and they were

therefore called constructible sets by Gödel. *See* GÖDEL, KURT.

It was left for Cohen to prove that if restricted set theory is consistent, then (1) it remains consistent with the addition of the negation of the axiom of choice, and (2) it remains consistent with the simultaneous addition of the axiom of choice and the negation of the continuum hypothesis. Together with Gödel's result, this shows that (1) the axiom of choice can be neither proved nor disproved from restricted set theory, and (2) the continuum hypothesis and the generalized continuum hypothesis can be neither proved nor disproved by restricted set theory plus the axiom of choice. Just as one can do geometry by assuming either the parallel postulate (euclidean geometry) or some form of its negation (noneuclidean geometry), so one can do mathematics by assuming either the generalized continuum hypothesis (cantorian set theory) or some form of its negation (noncantorian set theory).

In order to derive this result, Cohen, following Gödel, attempted to construct a model in which the axiom of choice or the continuum hypothesis failed. From Gödel's work it was known that a necessary first step was to form a model of restricted set theory which contained at least one nonconstructible element. In 1953 J. C. Shepherdson had shown that an inner model, that is, a model such as Gödel's, consisting of all sets satisfying some condition, cannot qualify for this role. Instead, Cohen started with a countable model M for restricted set theory, added a nonconstructible element a, and then considered the class of sets N generated by all the operations of restricted set theory on M and a. The main problem was to choose a in such a way that (1) a remained nonconstructible, not only in M but also in N, and (2) N, like M, satisfied the axioms of restricted set theory.

The element a thus had to be chosen so that it would disturb M as little as possible. To do this, Cohen used a roundabout procedure which he called forcing. Rather than determine a directly, he listed all the possible propositions concerning a and then determined which should be true. To prevent a from disturbing M, only those properties which were true for almost all sets of M were chosen to be true for a. The element a was thus a generic set which had only those properties it was forced to have in order to be a set.

To construct a model N' in which the continuum hypothesis is false, an infinite number of elements a must be added to M. Although the new elements, which play the role of the real numbers in N', have the cardinality of the natural numbers, they are chosen so as to have a much greater cardinality from the viewpoint of N', so that the continuum hypothesis fails. A model in which the axiom of choice fails, even for countable sets of pairs, can be constructed in a similar manner. In fact, the method of forcing proves quite flexible in constructing a variety of noncantorian models, and has itself acquired great importance in mathematics.

Cohen also made important contributions to analysis, topological groups, the theory of differential equations, and harmonic analysis.

Cohen did undergraduate study at Brooklyn College. He received the M.S. (1954) and Ph.D. (1958) from the University of Chicago. He taught for a year each at the University of Rochester and the Massachusetts Institute of Technology, and spent 2 years at the Institute for Advanced Study before joining the faculty of Stanford University in 1961. He was appointed professor there in 1964. He received the Research Corporation Award (1963), the Bocher Memorial Prize of the American Mathematical Society (1964), the Fields Medal of the International Union of Mathematicians (1966), the National Medal of Science (1967), and the Special Award of the American Nuclear Society (1967). He was elected to the National Academy of Sciences in 1967.

Cohen wrote *Set Theory and the Continuum Hypothesis* (1966).

For background information *see* GEOMETRY, EUCLIDEAN; GEOMETRY, NONEUCLIDEAN; MATHEMATICS; SET THEORY in the McGraw-Hill Encyclopedia of Science and Technology. ∎

COHEN, SEYMOUR STANLEY
★ American biochemist

Born Apr. 30, 1917, New York, NY, U.S.A.

Cohen studied biochemical events in the multiplication of bacterial viruses, or bacteriophages, and of bacteria. Indeed, he was the first to begin a systematic biochemical study of bacteriophage multiplication specifically and of virus-cell inter-

actions generally. In 1947 he demonstrated the extensive alteration in nucleic acid metabolism in cells infected by highly virulent viruses, resulting in the shift of synthesis away from polymeric products characteristic of the host to the types of nucleic acid and protein characteristic of the virus. He also introduced the use of radioactive isotopes into this type of study and by their use proved that viral nucleic acid is made after infection from low-molecular-weight precursors. These initiating studies in cellular pathology produced by viruses stamped certain virus-cell systems as highly favorable materials for the exaggeration of critical and interesting areas of metabolism, such as that of nucleic acid and protein synthesis. This led to the exploitation of these systems by numerous investigators in many directions, of which the discovery of messenger ribonucleic acid (mRNA) is but one example. By the late 1940s Cohen had also studied the nutritional requirements for virus multiplication and showed how certain amino acid analogs can, in preventing protein synthesis, inhibit critical stages in virus synthesis. These early pioneering studies were recognized in awards of the American Society of Microbiology and the American Academy of Pediatrics in 1951 and 1952.

Cohen received his B.S. at the City College of New York in 1936 and then entered Columbia University. After working with Erwin Chargaff, he received his Ph.D. in biochemistry in 1941 for a dissertation on lipoproteins active in

blood coagulation. He began work with viruses almost accidentally, having been appointed a fellow of the National Research Council under a newly established program of the National Foundation for Infantile Paralysis to train workers in virology. He was soon engaged in the isolation, characterization, and degradation of plant viruses in the department of Wendell Stanley at the Rockefeller Institute at Princeton. In this period he observed some curious crystallizations of plant viruses, and he demonstrated for the first time that a ribose nucleic acid, in this instance the nucleic acid of tobacco mosaic virus, is a very large polymer. *See* CHARGAFF, ERWIN; STANLEY, WENDELL MEREDITH.

Shortly after the United States entered World War II, Cohen returned to Columbia University to undertake a purification of the typhus vaccine. The extension of these studies, which demonstrated interesting physical, chemical, and immunological properties of rickettsial components, brought him to the University of Pennsylvania in 1943. The Children's Hospital of Philadelphia, in which his laboratory was situated, placed him in contact with animal virology through Werner and Brigitte Henle and with bacteriophage through Thomas Anderson. At the end of the war he decided to investigate virus-cell interactions, and he explored the possiblities of study of animal viruses in tissue cultures. Believing that animal virology was not yet ready for this type of biochemistry, he began on the phage systems, in collaboration with Anderson. After learning some of the key biological techniques, he began the study of patterns of polymer biosynthesis in infected bacteria.

Despite the initial striking results of this study, it was clear that a knowledge of bacterial physiology would be important in dissecting the biochemical events in phage multiplication. To begin to develop this knowledge, he went to Paris in 1947 and 1948 to work with A. Lwoff and J. Monod at the Pasteur Institute. After returning to the Children's Hospital, Cohen focused on an analysis of possible branch points in sugar metabolism in the host bacterium, *Escherichia coli*, as a possible approach to the redirection of nucleic acid metabolism produced by virus infection. At that time only a single pathway of glucose metabolism, that of anaerobic glycolysis, was believed to be of functional significance. In these studies, Cohen detected, in collaboration with D. B. McNair Scott, the existence of an enzymatic oxidative pathway for the conversion of glucose phosphate to ribose phosphate. He was also the first to use isotopic glucose to determine the relative utilization of sugar by an anaerobic route versus an oxidative pathway. These methods, with some modern improvements, are widely used today. By 1951 he had shown by this approach that virus infection actually affects the balance of these paths. *See* LWOFF, ANDRÉ; MONOD, JACQUES.

In 1952 Cohen began the study of the composition of bacteriophage nucleic acids, in collaboration with G. R. Wyatt. This work led to the detection, isolation, and characterization of the first unique viral component, a previously unknown pyrimidine, 5-hydroxymethylcytosine. This unusual compound, absent from bacterial nucleic acids, pointed to the existence of new types of enzymes in virus-infected cells, that is, of enzymes synthesized in response to infection. In a series of studies of the metabolic origins of the new viral pyrimidine, Cohen and Barner demonstrated that a cell which is unable to synthesize the normal pyrimidine, thymine, acquires this ability after virus infection. In 1957, in collaboration with J. Flaks, he demonstrated the existence of several virus-induced enzymes which are capable of making both of these pyrimidines and whose synthesis is determined by the virus nucleic acid. These studies showed that a virus not only can shift the host's enzymes to synthesis of new polymers but compels the production of new enzymes, of new metabolic machinery to facilitate the production of viral components.

The study of the synthesis of virus-induced enzymes demonstrated numerous controls of such synthesis. The work of Cohen's laboratory showed that production of new types of ribose nucleic acid are essential to the appearance of "early" virus-induced enzymes; the enzymatic basis of the degradation of this nucleic acid was also clarified. Synthesis of early enzymes permitted production of viral deoxyribonucleic acid (DNA), and the synthesis of early enzymes was stopped shortly thereafter, to be followed by synthesis of virus structural proteins. These patterns have been shown to be characteristic of many types of virus infection; the dissection of the molecular mechanisms of these controls of polymer synthesis defines major problems and directions of

work in contemporary virology. The discovery of the new viral pyrimidine and of its metabolic origins were recognized by a medal of the American Association for the Advancement of Science in 1955. In 1967 Cohen presented the Jesup Lectures ("Virus-Induced Enzymes") at Columbia University, and was elected to the National Academy of Sciences.

The study of virus-infected bacteria also led into many apparently peripheral fields. The work on pyrimidine origin led to discovery of some unusual phenomena of cell pathology, such as those of thymineless death and unbalanced growth, which are now studied in many laboratories. An interest in the biosynthesis of thymine and pentose stimulated studies on the metabolism of the spongonucleoside, D-arabinosyl thymine, and Cohen's work on the origin and fate of D-arabinose culminated in work on the mode of action of the chemotherapeutically significant nucleosides, D-arabinosyl cytosine and D-arabinosyl adenine.

In very early work on the characterization of viral nucleic acids Cohen had observed the reaction of the basic antibiotic streptomycin with these polymeric anions. After some 20 years of intermittent study on this problem, his laboratory helped to clarify the mechanism of the lethal action of the streptomycinoid drugs in terms of the production of a complex series of aberrations of nucleic acid metabolism and structure. In the last group of studies his work with A. Raina demonstrated the key role of the cationic polyamines in affecting synthesis of some classes of nucleic acid in bacterial growth. In 1971 he wrote *An Introduction to the Polyamines*. His later studies with the polyamines were diverse, analyzing the effects of these compounds on transfer RNA structure and the interrelations of polyamine synthesis with that of the synthesis of bacterial, plant, and animal viruses.

In 1954 Cohen became professor of biochemistry at the University of Pennsylvania, and in 1957 he was appointed Charles Hayden–American Cancer Society Professor at that university. His numerous experimental interests in virus and cell multiplication and pathology formed the basis for the development of a course in comparative biochemistry that he taught for many years. His teaching explored the problems of the nature and origin of biochemical diversity; he also wrote several essays on problems of bio-

chemical evolution and innovation. In 1963 he became Hartzell Professor and chair of the department of therapeutic research, a post that permitted him to stimulate research efforts in several biochemical areas that he considered to have been neglected. In 1971 Cohen was appointed professor of microbiology at the University of Colorado. Illness in his family led him to return east in 1976, as professor of pharmacological sciences at the State University of New York at Stony Brook. In these various positions, he continued research activities among a relatively small group composed of a few students and postdoctoral fellows. In addition, he developed an active interest in the history of science and wrote several papers on the early history of molecular biology. Cohen and his family spent many summers at the Marine Biological Laboratory at Woods Hole, MA.

For background information *see* BACTERIAL METABOLISM; BACTERIOPHAGE; NUCLEIC ACID; VIRUS in the McGraw-Hill Encyclopedia of Science and Technology. ◼️

COHN, NATHAN
★ American control systems engineer

Born Jan. 2, 1907, Hartford, CT, U.S.A.

Throughout his career, Cohn worked in the fields of measurement and control. He was best known for his engineering achievements in the control of interconnected electric power systems. Many of the generation control techniques currently used in the United States, Canada, and abroad were developed and initially applied by Cohn. In addition, he was an articulate author and lecturer, and many of his papers and his book have served as texts for successive generations of power systems engineers and operators.

In 1938 he was assigned the task of placing into operation, at Indiana and Michigan Electric Company, one of his firm's first frequency-bias controls. It included a retractable bias, based on the concept that unscheduled assistance to a remote area should be time-limited. Despite extensive on-line experimentation, Cohn was unable to achieve stable control results. Concluding that bias assistance needed to be sustained until it was no longer needed, he rebuilt the controller, and excellent operations resulted. All subsequent bias controllers were of the sustained type.

As more control areas were added to the Midwest system, it became increasingly clear to Cohn that the practice of a central frequency-controlling area had major limitations, imposing inequitable and at times impossible regulating burdens on the central area, and causing hunting between areas. He felt that the solution rested in complete decentralization of control. His suggestion that the central frequency-controlling area be eliminated met with little support. But Cohn was persistent. He was confident that the metering and schedule-setting criteria that he had developed would produce the desired results.

The opportunity to test this concept soon arose. Cohn applied it to a new, independent interconnected system encompassing Iowa and portions of Illinois and Missouri. The decentralized technique was applied to all areas of the interconnection early in 1948, and from the outset was a success. The concept was later adopted by other major interconnections, and it remained the standard for interconnected systems control.

In 1951–52 three companies in Missouri and Illinois formed an operating pool and invited Cohn to lay out their control systems, which were to include multistation multiunit regulation for economic dispatch. Cohn devised a new technique that overcame the limitations of the methods for such controls previously available from his company. He developed a generation assignment arrangement that provided a full adjustment range for each generator, and a combination feedforward-feedback reference circuit that made the assignment of each generator independent of the rate at which other generators responded to their assignments. His new system was successful. His arrangement was subsequently applied to dozens of energy control centers, and was later integrated into analog computer and advanced digital computer economic dispatch systems.

In 1956 considerable disagreement among systems control engineers arose regarding the proper magnitude of frequency-bias settings. In response to an invitation to discuss the subject before the Interconnected Systems Group (ISG), Cohn undertook a detailed analysis of bias operation, developing equations to define the quantitative effects of various bias settings. An operating guide for bias settings reflecting Cohn's work was adopted by the ISG, and it remained the accepted industry practice.

In 1961 Cohn devised a control technique for the Pennsylvania–New Jersey–Maryland pool, previously operated as a single area independent of external interconnections, which enabled the pool to tie to the north, west, and south, while retaining hierarchical control execution for overall pool economy by its pool members. A large single interconnection covering most of the United States east of the Rockies, and portions of Canada, was thereby created.

In later years, Cohn worked on unresolved problems related to inadvertent interchange and system time deviation. Early results were reported in 1971 and 1976, and more definitive conclusions were reported in 1978, when Cohn introduced the new concept of inadvertent interchange and time deviation, which was composed of measurable components, each component caused by a specific control area. He suggested that these components would provide, for the first time in the 30 years of decentralized frequency-biased net interchange control, a precise measure of the regulating performance of each control area, and in addition, would permit the use of an independent single-action corrective control technique by each area and the introduction of a dollar penalty-reward system to improve control performance in each area.

Cohn joined the Leeds and Northrup Company of Philadelphia after graduating from the Massachusetts Institute of Technology (MIT) in 1927. His association with Leeds and Northrup continued for 48 years, until his retirement from the position of executive vice-president in 1972 and from the board of directors in 1975. From 1929 to 1955 he served successively as manager of the San Francisco office, the Chicago office, and the West-Central region, returning to Philadelphia in 1955 as manager of market development. In 1958 he was appointed vice-president, technical affairs, responsible for research, development, engineering, and patent activities. In 1961 he was named senior vice-president, technical affairs, and a member of the board of directors, and was appointed executive vice-president in 1968. Throughout his long career with this firm, he maintained an active interest in the electric utility field, contributing to new technology related to problems he encountered or could foresee in interconnected system operations. Throughout his career he participated in activities of the engineering profession and the instrument industry. He served as president of the Scientific Apparatus Makers Association (1969–71), the Instrument Society of America (1963), and the National Electronics Conference (1950), and he chaired the board of managers of the Franklin Institute (1971–75). He served as chairperson of Institute of Electrical and Electronics Engineers (IEEE) committees, and of National Academy of Sciences advisory and survey panels, and was a member of the Massachusetts Institute of Technology visiting committees for libraries (1964– 69) and for philosophy (1972–74). He was active in the affairs of the International Federation of Automatic Control, and served on the board of the Engineers Joint Council. For his work, Cohn was honored with the Lamme Medal of the IEEE (1968), the Wetherill Medal of the Franklin Institute (1968), the Sperry Medal of the Instrument Society of America (1968), membership in the National Academy of Engineering (1969), an honorary doctorate from Rensselaer Polytechnic Institute (1976), honorary membership in the Instrument Society of America (1977), and the Scientific Apparatus Makers Association Award (1978).

For background information *see* CONTROL SYSTEMS; ELECTRIC POWER SYSTEMS in the McGraw-Hill Encyclopedia of Science and Technology. ∎

COHN, WALDO E.
★ American biochemist

***Born** June 28, 1910, San Francisco, CA, U.S.A.*

Cohn's primary contribution was the development of a technique—elution chromatography on ion exchangers—that has proved valuable in the study of nucleic acids, in the separation of a variety of biochemical compounds, and in other areas. Cohn embarked on this work in 1948, when he returned to biochemical research after World War II asisgnments as a radiochemist. He took up a problem that he and A. M. Brues had touched upon in prewar days at Harvard: the metabolic turnover of ribonucleic acid (RNA). After they had demonstrated with the crude chemical techniques then available that RNA is continuously formed and degraded (turned over) even in nongrowing animals whereas deoxyribonucleic acid (DNA), the stuff of chromosomes, is not, the question then posed was: do all the four types of monomers (nucleotides) of RNA turn over at equal rates?

Cohn's approach was to ascertain the rate of radiophosphate incorporation into each mononucleotide component. A necessary element was the separation of each type of mononucleotide from the hydrolysis mixture of the total RNA. However, the only methods available were the imprecise and laborious preparative methods, involving precipitations and crystallizations, used by the previous generation of chemists to isolate and ascertain the

chemical structures of the mononucleotides. A new technique that would permit quantitative separation and isolation of these compounds was essential.

Cohn's previous assignment at the Clinton Laboratories (since 1946, the Oak Ridge National Laboratory) during World War II had been to investigate the radiotoxicity of the fission products, the large number of pure radioactive elements created by the fission of ^{235}U in nuclear reactors. This assignment was based on Cohn's pre- and postdoctoral experience with artificial radioisotopes in biological systems, which began in Berkeley in 1937 with cyclotron products (^{32}P, ^{24}Na, and so on). However, most chemists in the Manhattan Project, as it was known during the war, were engrossed with the problem of extracting the microquantities of plutonium product from the macroquantities of uranium parent and the highly radioactive fission products, and could not undertake the isolation and segregation of each of the many fission products. Hence Cohn and his associates (initially E. R. Tompkins and J. X. Khym, later G. W. Parker and P. C. Tompkins) undertook to isolate the individual fission product species.

Each fission product exists in minute quantities in the mass of uranium, and most emit highly energetic beta and gamma radiations. In addition, many of these are traditionally difficult to separate (such as the rare earths, and Sr and Ba). A procedure was necessary that would be effective at low concentrations (no precipitations) and by remote control (behind protective shielding). No stable carrier could be added because of the projected subsequent biological investigative use. It was decided to explore the possibilities of elution chromatography on synthetic ion-exchange resins. This procedure, which was also being worked on by other Manhattan Project chemists (such as G. E. Boyd, J. A. Swartout, and J. Schubert), could be operated by fluid flow through a column, and therefore seemed a priori to have the mechanical simplicity required. This investigation, guided in part by the biochemist's familiarity with such complexes as calcium citrate, resulted in the important finding that even neighboring rare-earth cations can be separately removed from ion-exchange resin columns in the form of their complexes with polybasic acids (tartrates and citrates). This work led directly to the first isolation of element 61 (promethium) by

Glendenin, Marinsky, and Coryell and to the large-scale production of pure rare-earth compounds by F. H. Spedding and coworkers, as well as to the production of individual fission product radioisotopes for distribution from Oak Ridge, starting in 1946.

The principle involved here—induction of different degrees of electrostatic charge on components of soluble mixtures, leading to different affinities for an ionized solid matrix—was applied by Cohn in 1948 to the mixtures of bases, nucleosides, or nucleotides derived from RNA hydrolysis. As these substances are amphoteric, different electrostatic net charges can be induced by pH control (a necessary component of the rare-earth separations) without the addition of complexing agents—although such were found useful in other situations (as in the use of borate to separate sugars, as in the later work with Khym and L. P. Zill).

The resulting excellent separations of nucleotides, while it settled the original question of a technique for separating the then known four nucleotides of RNA, permitted the discovery (with C. E. Carter) of an isomeric form of each of these four nucleotides, and later (with E. Volkin) led to the discovery of a third hitherto unknown isomeric form of each (the 5'-phosphoric esters of the nucleosides). The establishment of the structures of these compounds (with D. G. Doherty and Khym) raised serious questions as to the then accepted structure of ribonucleic acids (thought to be linked from 2' to 3' by phosphoric residues) and led to the now accepted formulation of RNAs as 3':5'-phosphodiesters (by D. M. Brown and A. R. Todd in 1951)—a structure almost identical to that already known for DNA. This formulation, in turn makes plausible and feasible the present concept of the formation of RNA on DNA templates, a necessary part of the genetic information transfer chain of events, and the hybridization of RNA to DNA.

Besides its value in exploring the chemistry and structure of nucleic acids, elution chromatography on ion exchangers proved of great usefulness in the separations of a large number of biochemically important compounds and led to the discovery of a host of them, especially as a result of the modifications and applications introduced by V. R. Potter and his colleagues. In addition, it finds use in analytical schemes (as in the amino acid ana-lyzer of Stein and Moore), in organic re-action mechanisms, and as a tool for the separation of components of biochemical reactions—the use for which it was origi-nally invented by Cohn. The technique is now in use in the vast majority of bio-chemical and chemical laboratories and in chemical manufacture. Its widespread use and value underlies the American Chemi-cal Society Award in Chromatography and Electrophoresis given to Cohn in 1962.

Susequent work by Cohn was con-cerned more with the structure and chem-istry of nucleic acids and their component nucleotides. He ascertained the structure of pseudouridine, the first and only nu-cleoside known to possess a unique base-ribose bond (C—C instead of C—N). He also devised and developed (with R. P. Singhal) ion-exclusion chromatography for the separation of nucleic acid compo-nents, which made possible or simplified many isolations or analytical procedures in this field.

Another development of Cohn and his associates at Oak Ridge was the produc-tion of radioisotopes other than fission products in reactors (^{14}C, ^{32}P, and so on). He developed the production of ^{32}P by exposure of sulfur to reactor neutrons and its subsequent extraction as phosphoric acid in carrier-free form. At one time in this period his product formed the total United States supply of ^{32}P, and was re-leased via Berkeley, whose cyclotron was completely engaged in uranium bombard-ment for the Oak Ridge plutonium chem-ists. ^{32}P, ^{14}C, and other such radioiso-topes, with a great number of fission-produced radioisotopes, were included in the first catalog of radioisotopes available from Oak Ridge in 1946 (produced by Cohn with R. T. Overman and P. C. Aebersold). Cohn and his associates thus established the still-operating isotope production machinery at Oak Ridge.

Cohn received his B.S. in 1931, M.S. in chemistry in 1932, and Ph.D. in biochem-istry in 1938 under D. M. Greenberg at the University of California, Berkeley. His graduate research involved the use of cyclotron-produced radioisotopes, and was thus among the first investigations in the United States to use these materials as tracers in the uncovering of metabolic and physiological processes. He continued this type of research during his postdoc-toral years at Harvard Medical School (1939–42) before joining the Manhattan

Project and moving to Oak Ridge, where he became a senior biochemist in the Bi-ology Division of the Oak Ridge National Laboratory. He also was part-time direc-tor of the National Academy of Sciences Office of Biochemical Nomenclature, an activity he continued after his retirement from active research in 1975; author or coauthor of over 80 research publications and reviews; an editor of journals and book series in his field; and a consulting editor to various publishers of biomedical compendia. Cohn was named a fellow of the American Academy of Arts and Sci-ences (1962) and of the American Associ-ation for the Advancement of Science (1964), received a Fulbright scholarship (1955) and two Guggenheim fellowships (1955 and 1962), was a visiting professor at the Institut de Biologie in Paris (1963) and the Rockefeller University in New York (1966), and was elected or ap-pointed to various offices in the American Society of Biological Chemists and the American Chemical Society. Cohn also had a long-standing interest in music, both as cellist and as the founder and con-ductor (1944–55) of the Oak Ridge Sym-phony Orchestra, in which he was still playing at the age of 69. He was elected to the Advisory Town Council of Oak Ridge in 1951 and 1953, and served as its chair-person during the latter term.

For background information *see* CHRO-MATOGRAPHY; NUCLEIC ACID; RADIO-ISOTOPE PRODUCTION in the McGraw-Hill Encyclopedia of Science and Tech-nology. ∎

COLE, KENNETH STEWART
★ American biophysicist

Born July 10, 1900, Ithaca, NY, U.S.A.

As a classical physicist, Cole was primar-ily interested in understanding the struc-ture and function of living cell mem-branes in general and of nerve membranes in particular. He and his co-workers largely concentrated on the elec-trical approach to these problems.

Following Hugo Fricke, Cole sharp-ened and extended the analysis of, and did more than anyone else to establish, the now generally accepted principle that all living cell membranes have the electrical capacity of about 1 microfarad per square centimeter to be expected from a dielec-tric a few molecules thick. This principle has been found to hold for membranes

ranging from those of plant cells about a centimeter in diameter, through marine and other egg cells, single nerve and mus-cle fibers, blood cells, yeast, bacteria, mi-tochondria, and pleuropneumonia-like and other single-cell organisms. He later showed, by analog measurements, the low-concentration formulas to apply to up to 100 percent concentrations of regular arrays of cells, such as muscle and epithe-lial cells. It is now generally accepted that the double-layer structure, so widely found by electron microscopy, corre-sponds with this directly measured prop-erty of living cells. There is a dielectric-like loss often associated with this capac-ity, which Cole and his brother, Robert H. Cole, considered in some detail. This characteristic may help ultimately to for-mulate a membrane structure, but it is still a problem of solid-state physics in nonliv-ing systems, often represented as a "Cole-Cole diagram."

Although Cole anticipated the two-fac-tor theories of nerve excitation, he con-tinued the more physical approach. With Howard J. Curtis, he showed that the ca-pacity of a plant cell and a nerve mem-brane remains unchanged during the pas-sage of an impulse, while the membrane conductance increases—thus providing a basic step for subsequent developments. Additional investigations by Cole with others, and many subsequent measure-ments by other workers, established an-other generalization—that physiological function and condition are correlated with the conductance of the membrane, while the capacity is comparatively unaffected.

Cole and Alan L. Hodgkin found the resting membrane conductance of the squid giant axon to be 0.001 mho per square centimeter by means of conventional theory and new experiments. This first reliable value for an animal cell membrane also became an accepted generalization with other forms—usually within an order of magnitude of it—and it showed that the axon conductance increases fortyfold during the passage of a nerve impulse. *See* HODGKIN, SIR ALAN (LLOYD).

Cole and Curtis, independently and simultaneously with Hodgkin and Andrew F. Huxley, made direct internal measurements of the change of membrane potential in the squid axon during activity and confirmed the observation that the action potential is larger than the resting potential. This "overshoot" had been anticipated, has since been generally found in many living forms, and was a key to the present understanding of activity. With Curtis and with Richard F. Baker, Cole further showed the membrane conductance to be a highly nonlinear relation between the electrical potential and current—often since called rectification or anomalous rectification. With Hodgkin, Cole discovered the inductive reactance of a squid axon, and with Baker he localized it in the membrane and carefully measured its properties. This gave a quantitative basis to correlate many oscillatory and repetitive characteristics of nerve. Cole hinted that the rectification and inductive reactance might result from potassium ions, as was later confirmed. He showed an anomalous reactance to be a generally expected phenomenon of nonlinear systems—of which the more recently designated "delayed rectification" is a part. *See* HUXLEY, SIR ANDREW (FIELDING).

Having long recognized the need to simplify the theoretical approach to problems, Cole supported and collaborated with George H. Marmont in his investigation of the squid axon membrane by controlled current flow between large electrodes inside and outside the axon. With the axon no longer able to propagate an impulse, this "space-current clamp" situation—as it was later termed—substantiated much that had been found less directly and added a considerable amount of new, but mostly unpublished, information on the passive and active states of the membrane. Of most importance, however, this work emphasized to Cole the need to bring the explosive response of the membrane under control and recalled to him

the simple mathematical and physical principle that a system which is unstable for a constant value of one variable is usually stable for a constant value of another variable. This led him in 1947 to apply sudden and controlled changes of the membrane potential to the squid axon. The resulting membrane currents showed a transient "negative resistance" behavior, were without any evidence of instability, and were adequate to predict, better than qualitatively, the threshold for excitation, the rise of the action potential, its maximum value and subsequent decline during recovery, and the propagation of such an impulse for an axon in normal function.

These results were not published until 1949, but Cole communicated them to Hodgkin and later discussed them with him in detail in early 1948. With Huxley and Bernard Katz, Hodgkin then started a program based on this new concept of membrane potential control, which they christened the voltage clamp. They improved the technique for its application and confirmed Cole's work. Hodgkin and Huxley then went on to their revolutionary and classic series of papers in 1952 on the ion conductances of the squid axon membrane, and a Nobel Prize in 1963 with J. C. Eccles. *See* ECCLES, SIR JOHN (CAREW); KATZ, SIR BERNARD.

Cole, Henry A. Antosiewicz, and P. Rabinowitz soon undertook the first automatic computer calculations with the Hodgkin and Huxley results to test them and to use them to explain further well-known and accepted experiments on nerve. An error in this work was detected by Cole, and the results were corrected and extended by Richard FitzHugh and Antosiewicz. With Cole's support, FitzHugh continued the analytical and computer investigations of the Hodgkin and Huxley formulations of the squid axon membrane properties.

After making further improvements in the technique, Cole and John W. Moore started again to test and to extend the Hodgkin and Huxley work. They soon began to find, as did others, significant variations from the earlier results. Thus the utility of the voltage clamp concept and the validity of all of the earlier work based on it were called into question. By extensive experimental and theoretical work, and in collaboration with Moore, Robert E. Taylor, FitzHugh, and others, Cole located the imperfections of the technique which were responsible for the anomalies. He then showed that the early experiments and the

Hodgkin and Huxley conclusions based on them were essentially correct.

Cole and his colleagues steadily extended the range and depth of investigations based on the potential control, or voltage clamp, concept. This concept was applied to numerous other excitable membranes by other investigators and by using other techniques—but with the similar and uniquely important results not yet to be obtained by any other approach. It seems certain that the concept will continue for some time to provide the most powerful means of investigating nerve membrane properties, and it may even lead to the ultimate explanation of the nerve impulse.

In another direction Cole, following E. Newton Harvey, devised a new method for measuring the surface force versus the surface area relation in sea urchin eggs. He confirmed Harvey's original observation that the tension is of the order of 0.1 dyne (1 micronewton) per centimeter, but further established that the tension is that to be expected of a solid elastic membrane and is not a capillary or interfacial tension. This discovery led James F. Danielli to do the experiments and formulate the theory suggesting that the living cell membrane is a lipid double layer with protein adsorbed on both sides. Although now more than 40 years old, this is still the most generally acceptable membrane structure theory, and it has also received extensive support from many electron microscope observations.

Other published work of Cole's includes assisting Charles G. Rogers in measuring the heat production of sea urchin eggs before and after fertilization, some electrolyte theory, an irradiation technique and parallax stereoscopy for x-rays, grasshopper egg membrane measurements with Theodore L. Jahn, an artificial membrane note with Robert B. Dean and Curtis, mammalian circulation work with Barry G. King and Enid T. Oppenheimer, an aortic aneurysm surgical procedure, and a number of papers on instrumentation.

Son of a college classics professor and dean, Cole received his A.B. from Oberlin College in 1922 and his Ph.D. in experimental physics from Cornell in 1926. After 3 years of postdoctoral research at Harvard and Leipzig, he became assistant professor of physiology at the College of Physicians and Surgeons, Columbia University. In 1942 he was given the first biomedical appointment in the Metallurgical Laboratory in Chicago, continuing in charge of the Biology Section throughout World War II.

During the war he and the members of the section and a cooperating section that he organized in Oak Ridge, TN, produced much of the foundation for what is now known of the biomedical effects of radiation. After the war Cole became professor of biophysics and physiology at Chicago (1946–49), technical director of the Naval Medical Research Institute (1949–54), organizer and chief of the Laboratory of Biophysics, National Institute of Neurological Diseases and Blindness (1954–66), senior research biophysicist at the National Institutes of Health and professor of biophysics at the University of California, Berkeley (1966–77), and biophysicist emeritus of the National Institutes of Health (1978 onward). Cole received honorary degrees from Oberlin, the University of Chicago, and Uppsala; the Order of the Southern Cross from Brazil (1966); and a National Medal of Science, U.S.A. (1967). He was elected a member of the National Academy of Sciences in 1956, of the American Academy of Arts and Sciences in 1972, a foreign member of the Royal Society, London, in 1972, and an honorary member of the Physiological Society, Cambridge, in 1977. The Annual Cole Award was established in his honor by the Membrane Group of the Biophysical Society in 1974.

Cole wrote *Membranes, Ions, and Impulses* (1968, 1972).

For background information *see* BIO-ELECTRIC MODEL; BIOPOTENTIALS AND ELECTROPHYSIOLOGY; CELL MEMBRANES; MECHANORECEPTORS in the McGraw-Hill Encyclopedia of Science and Technology. ∎

COLLINS, SAMUEL CORNETTE
★ American engineer

***Born** Sept. 28, 1898, Democrat, KY, U.S.A.*

Long active in means for producing and maintaining very low temperatures, Collins concentrated his efforts during World War II on the improvement of apparatus for the manufacture of oxygen. The resultant heat exchangers, expansion machines, and refrigerative cycles were combined in 1946 to form the highly successful helium cryostat, a machine that was orginally intended to provide a cold chamber for low-temperature experiments but is actually used chiefly for liquefying helium for use elsewhere. Its simplicity, reliability, and relatively low cost

have made it an indispensable tool for research.

Liquid helium provides the only known approach to temperatures near absolute zero, and such temperatures are necessary in the study of many of the fundamental properties of matter. Prior to World War II, liquid helium was available in very few places in the world, and there only by the expenditure of much of the investigator's time. There are now about 300 helium cryostats in use in many countries around the globe.

For his invention and further development of the helium cryostat and other cryogenic devices, Collins was awarded the Wetherill Medal of the Franklin Institute in 1951, the Kamerlingh Onnes Gold Medal of the Netherlands Refrigeration Society in 1958, the Rumford Premium of the American Academy of Arts and Sciences in 1965, and the Outstanding Achievement Award of the Cryogenic Engineering Conference also in 1965.

Liquid helium exists over a very narrow temperature range, from $-450.3°F$ $(-267.9°C)$ down to absolute zero, $-459.7°F$ $(-273.2°C)$. Liquid hydrogen, the next coldest liquid, freezes at $-434.3°F$ $(-259.1°C)$. The simplest way to reach very low temperatures is to compel gaseous helium to cool itself by arranging for it to perform external work as it expands against a piston in an engine. This principle of cooling by expansion with the performance of external work was utilized by John Gorrie in the making of artificial ice about 1845, by Georges Claude in the liquefaction of

air about 1900, and by Peter Kapitza in the liquefaction of helium in 1932. *See* KAPITZA, PETER.

In addition to the engine, a compressor and a counterflow heat exchanger are necessary. The compressor returns the pressure of the expanded helium to its original value. The heat of compression is carried away by water or by air. The function of the heat exchanger is to cool the incoming stream of warm compressed helium by transferring heat to the outgoing stream of cold expanded helium. Because of the action of the heat exchanger, the compressed helium arriving at the engine becomes progressively colder until the condensing temperature of helium is attained.

Collin's cycle for helium liquefaction is characterized by the expansion of compressed helium at more than one temperature level. With normal operating pressures the temperature drop across each engine is substantial, and the cold expanded gas provides a thermodynamically ideal coolant for the stream of helium that is to be liquefied. A series of engines spaced at progressively lower temperatures makes possible very high efficiency in the cooling and liquefaction of helium.

Several forms of the expansion engine have proved successful, but the most used one consists of hardened alloy steel cylinders with close-fitting pistons of the same material. There are no piston rings and no lubricant other than the helium gas itself. The motion of the piston is controlled by a long piston rod of relatively small diameter operating in tension. The piston rod passes through the expansion chamber and a sheath tube to the stuffing box, which is at room temperature. The slender piston rod gives the piston a high degree of freedom to move without friction along the axis of the cylinder.

Two types of counterflow heat exchangers of extraordinary effectiveness have evolved from Collins's studies of low-temperature systems. One is used in the helium cryostat. It consists of a closely finned tube some hundreds of feet in length coiled in a helix approximately 8 inches (20.3 centimeters) in diameter and placed in the annulus between two thin-walled stainless steel cylinders. The incoming high-pressure stream flows inside the long tube, and the outgoing low-pressure stream flows in the annulus through the fins and across successive turns of the tube.

The second type of heat exchanger was devised for use in the liquefaction of air and the production of oxygen and nitrogen. Two matched channels alternately bear incoming compressed impure air and outgoing waste gas at low pressure. The impurities, mostly water and carbon dioxide, are condensed on the heat-exchange surfaces during one half-cycle and are evaporated and carried away by the waste gas during the following half-cycle.

A farmer's son, Collins studied agriculture at the University of Tennessee, where he received the B.S. in 1920 and M.S. in 1924. He received his Ph.D. in physical chemistry from the University of North Carolina in 1927. After holding several teaching positions in Tennessee, Collins joined the faculty of the Massachusetts Institute of Technology in 1930, where he remained until his retirement in 1964.

For background information *see* CRYOGENICS; HEAT EXCHANGER; HELIUM, LIQUID in the McGraw-Hill Encyclopedia of Science and Technology. ∎

CONDON, EDWARD UHLER
★ American physicist

Born Mar. 2, 1902, Alamogordo, NM, U.S.A.

Died Mar. 26, 1974, Boulder, CO, U.S.A.

Condon received his Ph.D. at the University of California, Berkeley, in 1926. This was the year in which quantum mechanics was discovered and was beginning to produce revolutionary changes in the understanding of atomic, molecular, and nuclear structure. Condon made research contributions to each of these areas.

In chemical physics he is known for his contributions to the Franck-Condon principle. This represents an extension and quantum-mechanical treatment of some ideas first proposed by James Franck about the changes in nuclear motion in molecules that accompany electronic transitions in molecules. This work led to an interpretation of the intensity distribution in band systems and to the understanding of conditions under which light absorption or electron impact can lead to dissociation of molecules, usually producing fragments with considerable kinetic energy. Predictions of this kind were fully confirmed by mass spectroscopic experiments of Walker Bleakney and of John T. Tate and Wallace Lozier. In atomic physics Condon is known for the basic treatise *The Theory of Atomic Spectra* (1935), which has long been the standard work in the field. He also made numerous research contributions to this field.

In nuclear physics Condon is known for two major contributions. In the fall of 1928, with R. W. Gurney, he developed the barrier leakage or tunneling model for alpha-particle emission by natural radioactive elements, such as radium and uranium. This was the first application of quantum mechanics to a problem in nuclear structure. The same ideas were developed independently at the same time by George Gamow in Göttingen. In 1936–37, working with Gregory Breit and Richard Present, Condon made a detailed analysis of the theory underlying the proton-proton scattering experiments that had just been made by Merle Tuve, Lawrence Hafstad, and Norman Heydenberg at the Carnegie Institution of Washington. This work led to the recognition of the charge independence of the strong interaction forces between nucleons, and therefore to the importance of a variable known as "isotopic spin" for the theory of nuclear structure. In the field of solid-state physics Condon developed ideas about the relation between the contact potential and the photoelectric threshold of semiconductors. These concepts stimulated further experimental research. *See* BREIT, GREGORY; FRANCK, JAMES; GAMOW, GEORGE; HAFSTAD, LAWRENCE RANDOLPH; TUVE, MERLE ANTONY.

In 1948, while director of the National Bureau of Standards, Condon was the subject of a major public attack launched by J. Parnell Thomas, then chairperson of the House Committee on Un-American Activities. Thomas accused him of being "perhaps one of the weakest links in our atomic security." Hearings were promised but never held because soon afterward Congressman Thomas had to serve a term in a Federal penitentiary for taking salary kickbacks from the secretaries in his office. Nevertheless, harassments of this type continued intermittently over a period of 6 years. A brief hearing before a subcommittee of the House Committee on Un-American Activities was held in Chicago by several congressmen from that area just before the elections of 1952. As with all persons engaged in classified research, Condon had been investigated and cleared during World War II. Then he was the subject of unusually extensive investigation in 1948 as a result of Thomas's accusations. These resulted in full clearance by the Department of Commerce and by the Atomic Energy Commission. After Condon went to Corning, another hearing on old charges was held in April 1954, before the Eastern Industrial Personnel Security Board. This resulted in another full clearance. But in October 1954, a few weeks before the election, the clearance was suspended by action of the Secretary of the Navy. As a result, the government excluded Condon's services until the clearance was reinstated in 1966 after another detailed investigation.

Condon took an A.B. in 1924 and a Ph.D. in physics in 1926 at the University of California, Berkeley. His career was marked by a variety of activities outside the field of academic research. Besides teaching in university physics departments, he served during 1937–45 as associate director of research for the Westinghouse Electric Corporation. He was appointed by President Truman in October 1945 as fourth director of the National Bureau of Standards. In October 1951 he became director of research and development for Corning Glass Works, a post he held until the end of 1954. He continued as a research consultant to that company. During World War II he served on the committee to establish the Jet Propulsion Laboratory at the California Institute of Technology and on the S-1 Committee, which established the government atomic bomb project. He also had charge of the Westinghouse microwave radar research program and served as head of the theoretical division of the Lawrence Radiation Laboratory, Berkeley. After the war Condon served as scientific adviser to the Special Senate Committee on Atomic Energy, which drafted the legislation establishing the Atomic Energy Commission. He was a member of the faculty at Princeton University during 1928–37, chairperson of the physics department at Washington University, St. Louis, during 1956–63, and professor of physics of the University of Colorado thereafter. He also served as president of the Colorado Scientific Development Commission by appointment of Governor John A. Love. In November 1966 he undertook the directorship of a study sponsored by the U.S. Air Force on the nature of reports of "unidentified flying objects." The final report of the study (1969) found no evidence that objects or sightings were intelligently guided spacecraft from beyond Earth.

Condon wrote the first book in English on quantum mechanics, *Quantum Mechanics,* with P. M. Morse (1929; paper 1963), and *The Theory of Atomic Spectra,* with G. H. Shortley (1935). With Hugh Odishaw, he edited, and wrote many of the chapters of, *Handbook of Physics* (1958; 2d ed. 1967). Beginning in 1956, he was editor of *Reviews of Modern Physics,* a quarterly journal published by the American Physical Society.

For background information *see* ATOMIC STRUCTURE AND SPECTRA; FRANCK-CONDON PRINCIPLE; MOLECULAR STRUCTURE AND SPECTRA; NUCLEAR STRUCTURE; QUANTUM MECHANICS in the McGraw-Hill Encyclopedia of Science and Technology. ∎

CONSTANCE, LINCOLN
★ American botanist

Born Feb.16, 1909, Eugene, OR, U.S.A.

Constance was one of those who in the mid-20th century attempted to foster the development of a broadly based systematic botany. The goal was the effective utilization of the new comparative data emerging from anatomy-morphology, cytology, genetics, and biochemistry, and their synthesis into a general classification, phylogenetic in orientation, without splintering the field of taxonomy and within the framework of a system not precisely designed to accommodate such information. More or less by accident he

also found himself a spokesperson for a renascent plant taxonomy in his widely cited and influential essays: "The Versatile Taxonomist" (1951), "The Role of Plant Ecology in Biosystematics" (1953), "Plant Taxonomy in an Age of Experiment" (1957), and "Systematic Botany—An Unending Synthesis" (1964). In all of these works he urged that taxonomists should welcome additional comparative information of whatever nature, but that diversity and novelty of data should not seriously alter the general goals of systematics. He also championed the relevance of continuing interest in, and support for, plant taxonomy in an era when the focus of attention was on the physicochemical and subcellular aspects of biology.

In the 1930s and 1940s the San Francisco Bay area was a center of ferment in genetical, ecological, and evolutionary biology, including research on plants. Ernest B. Babcock and G. Ledyard Stebbins were pursuing their critical investigations on the cytology, genetics, and evolution of *Crepis.* T. Harper Goodspeed and Roy Clausen were conducting independent studies of tobacco. Ralph W. Chaney and Herbert L. Mason were exploring the Tertiary history of western floras. The team of Jens C. Clausen, David D. Keck, and William C. Hiesey was carrying out its classical transplant studies at Palo Alto and in the Sierra Nevada, attempting to determine the nature of species. An informal group known as The Biosystematists developed among the biologists located around Berkeley, Stanford, and the Cali-

fornia Academy of Sciences in San Francisco, providing a monthly forum for vigorous debate on such subjects as the proper definition of "species"; the significance of polyploidy; the causes, consequences, and evolutionary role of endemism and isolation; the various factors governing distribution through time and space. These discussions closely paralleled those topics included in Julian Huxley's *The New Systematics* (1940), and although The Biosystematists did not publish a rival volume, these seminars markedly influenced the thinking and subsequent writing and teaching of most of the participants. *See* CHANEY, RALPH WORKS; STEBBINS, GEORGE LEDYARD.

There was considerable doubt that the old taxonomic framework could indeed respond with sufficient flexibility to accommodate all the new information and new concepts that were amassing. The classical "species," cornerstone of all biological classification, was more than ever in danger of being regarded as a mere transitory evolutionary stepping stone or of being transformed into a purely genetically defined category that would no longer be available to the working taxonomist. Clausen, Keck, and Hiesey proposed to correlate the formal taxonomic categories with the Turessonian coenospecies, ecospecies, and ecotypes, which were based on ecological-genetical criteria. Wendell H. Camp proposed that a new science of "biosystematy" be established to replace the now moribund traditional taxonomy. Many taxonomists preferred to close their eyes to the ferment, pretending that it did not concern them and ignoring the data now becoming available. Subsequently, the advocates of "phenetic" taxonomy have attempted to displace "phylogeny" as the philosophical core of any natural system of of classification.

Together with many others, Constance took a liberal view toward the acceptance of new evidence, but a conservative attitude toward the fragmentation of systematic biology, the extravagant claims of successively fashionable subdisciplines, and the proposed abandonment of hard-won knowledge of relationships derived from other data at earlier periods. His own work was mostly monographic and dealt principally with two families of flowering plants, Umbelliferae and Hydrophyllaceae. In his investigations of Umbelliferae he collaborated with Mildred E. Mathias (Hassler), and together they authored most of the manual and flora treatments of American Umbelliferae, as well as a series of comprehensive monographs. With Minosuke Hiroe, he published a revision of *Umbelliferae of Japan* (1958) and, with C. Ritchie Bell, a series of papers embodying a survey of the chromosome numbers of the family. Marion S. Cave joined him in a 20-year survey of chromosome numbers in Hydrophyllaceae, one of the most thorough cytotaxonomic surveys of any family of flowering plants up to that time. His most widely read paper is probably "The Systematics of the Angiosperms" (1955).

Stimulated by a sabbatical trip to South America in 1954 (made possible by a Guggenheim fellowship), Constance became interested in the similarities and differences in the flora and vegetation between the temperate zones of the Northern and Southern hemispheres and the patterns of plant distribution within the Southern Hemisphere. Although he published little on phytogeography, it always fascinated him and profoundly influenced his taxonomic thinking, as shown by his selection of genera for monographic study and by his emphasis on the mapping of distributions. His friendly relations with Latin American botanists greatly assisted his taxonomic work. He was elected a corresponding member of both the Sociedad Argentina de Botánica and the Academia Chilena de Ciencias Naturales, as well as the Société de Biogéographie, Paris. He was exceptionally fortunate in his graduate students, and their cumulative contributions conspicuously outweigh his own.

Son of a lawyer-farmer, Constance graduated from the University of Oregon in biology (A.B., 1930). His early interest in natural history, largely stimulated by his mother as a compensation for the intellectual limitations of rural life, was encouraged by Louis F. Henderson, Albert R. Sweetser, Ethel I. Sanborn, and others. He received an M.A. in 1932 from the University of California, Berkeley, and a Ph.D. in 1934, working under the direction of Willis Linn Jepson, but strongly influenced also by William A. Setchell and his enthusiasm for plant geography. Constance's first teaching position was as an instructor and later an assistant professor at the State College of Washington in 1934–37. He then returned to Berkeley to stay, although he served as visiting lecturer and acting director of the Gray Herbarium of Harvard University in 1948–49. During World War II he held

various positions in the Office of Strategic Services in Washington, DC, including that of geobotanist. For a decade he was heavily involved in university administration at Berkeley, serving as dean of the college of letters and science (1955–62) and vice-chancellor for academic affairs (1962–65). However, he always scrupulously maintained a tie with both undergraduate and graduate teaching and a thin but vital thread of research, and he was thus able to return to the department of botany as professor and director of the University of California Herbarium. In 1970 Constance was elected president of the Botanical Society of America. From 1975 to 1978 he served as president of the California Academy of Sciences, and was designated professor and director emeritus in 1976. In 1978 he was designated dean emeritus of the college of letters and science at Berkeley. Constance was elected a foreign member of the Linnaean Society of London (1970) and of the Swedish Royal Academy of Sciences (1971).

For background information *see* PLANT GEOGRAPHY; PLANT KINGDOM; PLANT TAXONOMY in the McGraw-Hill Encyclopedia of Science and Technology. ∎

COOK, MELVIN A.
★ American chemist

Born Oct. 10, 1911, Swan Creek (Bear Lake), UT, U.S.A.

In April 1947 two shiploads of fertilizer-grade ammonium nitrate exploded and devastated Texas City; in December 1956 the detonation of a 150-pound (67.5-kilogram) charge at Knob Lake mine of Iron Ore Company of Canada (northeastern Quebec), comprising ammonium nitrate, aluminum, and water mixed in a wheelbarrow, was also a news event. Cook, a University of Utah chemist, was intimately involved in both—as expert witness for 26 plaintiffs in the ensuing litigation and as the formulator of the charge, respectively. The two blasts triggered conversion of the commercial explosives industry from powders to slurries, and dangerous high explosives (Nobel's dynamites) to far safer blasting agents: ANFO and slurries. (When an explosive comprises only nonexplosive ingredients and is nondetonable with a #8 commercial blasting cap but detonable with a strong booster, it is classed as a blasting agent. Detonating explosives not fulfilling these

safety requirements are designated Class A explosives.) ANFO constitutes over two-thirds of all commercial explosives today, most of the rest being slurries, with dynamites and other powders rapidly declining.

ANFO, consisting of 94/6 ammonium nitrate (AN) and fuel oil (FO), is the cheapest source of explosive energy in modern technology. Cook's developments helped make it so, especially his cast boosters. Finding that booster efficiency increases sharply with detonation pressure, and then selecting boosters with the highest detonation pressure, he successfully replaced 50-pound (22.5-kilogram) powder boosters with 1-pound (0.45-kilogram) cast boosters, thus contributing greatly to the commercial success and of ANFO as a "do-it-yourself" blasting agent.

Slurries characteristically contain a (thickened and gelled) aqueous oxidizer solution with dispersed excess solid oxidizer (mostly AN) and some soluble or insoluble solid or liquid fuel sensitizer. There are today a variety of slurries differing primarily only as to the sensitizing fuel. Although slurries are orders of magnitude safer than dynamites, those sensitized with high explosives are still Class A explosives (slurry explosives, or SE), while those made with nonexplosive fuels are classed as blasting agents (slurry blasting agents, or SBA).

Cook's first SEs were sensitized with coarse TNT. They were once the ultimate of the industry and are still in use, though rapidly disappearing due to high

cost and an adverse environmental impact of TNT. Up to 250-ton (225-metric-ton) charges of TNT slurry formulated by Cook and his associates were detonated in 1967–68 at nearly a mile (1.6 kilometer) depth in the Pacific Ocean to test recording systems for detecting nuclear explosions. Other commercial Class A slurries are sensitized with methylamine nitrate and nitromethane. Cook's first SBA was the aluminized slurry, even today the most popular in commercial use. Fuel oil slurries (advertised as slurried ANFO), introduced in the early 1960s, became commercially important only after stabilization of atomized fuel oil—aqueous oxidizer emulsions was achieved by Cook and his associates.

Early SEs and SBAs were non-cap-sensitive, requiring Cook's high-pressure cast booster. However, cap-sensitive slurries were also developed by Cook and his associates to function with cap initiation in the same manner as stick dynamites. They are currently being used as boosters for ANFO, SE, and SBA.

Another of Cook's and his associates' pioneering developments was the slurry pump truck, introduced in 1963 at Kaiser Steel's Eagle Mountain (CA) mine. Previously explosives had been cartridged and handloaded into boreholes. Even in the large-diameter boreholes of open-pit mines, loading rates seldom exceeded a ton per worker in an 8-hour shift. By the end of 1964 each of Cook's pump trucks was regularly loading up to 75 tons (67.5 metric tons) per shift. To remain a viable supplier on the Minnesota and Michigan Iron Ranges today, one must have the capability of loading at least 150 tons (135 metric tons) of slurry per shift. Not only did the slurry pump truck permit rapid bulk loading of explosives, but it effected large savings by eliminating costly packaging and by increasing (by more than 35%) the efficiency of the blasting by improving loading densities and borehole coupling.

Slurries are superior in all respects to all other types of commercial explosives, except in "explosives energy per dollar" where they are excelled only by ANFO. Unlike the situation with ANFO and dynamites, however, one may control energy density in bulk slurries over wide ranges, permitting far better engineering of blasts for better economies. Slurries also have excellent water resistance; many dynamites, and especially ANFO, do not. Furthermore, thanks to high water content, slurries are orders of magnitude

safer than dynamites and even safer than ANFO, the least hazardous nonslurry explosive. The great taconite industry of America would likely have been uneconomical without slurries.

From the viewpoint of national defense, Cook's best aluminized slurry was used as the filler for 20-ton (18-metric-ton) bombs for Operation Cloudmaker. (When these bombs were tested over Tonopah, NV, observers for Howard Hughes, then the Atomic Energy Commission's devil's advocate, released a news bulletin that the United States had broken the nuclear test ban treaty.) These tremendous bombs were loaded in about 75 minutes each. Later this powerful filler was used in the "daisy cutter," the highly publicized 15,000-pound (6750-kilogram) bomb used in Vietnam for helicopter landing zone clearance. Cook and his associates loaded these bombs in about 25 minutes each. To load a bomb of this size with TNT would require days and multiple castings.

Born on a farm in northern Utah, Cook majored in physical chemistry at the University of Utah, where he received the B.A. and M.A. degrees in 1933 and 1934, and at Yale University, where he received the Ph.D. (and Loomis Award) in 1937. He worked at Du Pont's Eastern Laboratory (explosives) from 1937 to 1947. Between 1947 and 1970 he was professor of metallurgy and director of the Explosives Research Institute at the University of Utah. He founded IRECO Chemicals in 1958 and served as its president and board chairman until 1972 and 1974, respectively. He then became chairman of Cook Slurry Company. He was an E. V. Murphree Gold Medallist (American Chemical Society) in 1968, Nitro Nobel Gold Medallist (Sweden) in 1969, and Chemical Pioneer Award recipient of the American Institute of Chemists in 1973.

Slurries and their boosters were announced in Cook's *The Science of High Explosives,* American Chemical Society Monograph no. 139 (1958). His book, *The Science of Industrial Explosives,* IRECO Chemicals (1974), discussed them in some detail. Some of Cook's "firsts" in slurry technology are described in the following patents: 2,930,685 (TNT slurries), 3,037,452,3 (cast boosters), 3,121,036 (aluminized slurries), 3,303,738 (pump truck), 3,787,254 (fuel oil slurries), and 4,084,993 (his latest patent, Apr. 18, 1978—dinitrotoluene, or DNT, slurries made by a hot emulsion process). Cook's

Esso (American Chemical Society) Award address (*Industrial and Engineering Chemistry,* pp. 44–55, July 1968) summarizes these developments up to 1968.

For background information *see* EXPLOSION AND EXPLOSIVE in the McGraw-Hill Encyclopedia of Science and Technology. ∎

COON, CARLETON STEVENS
★ American anthropologist

Born June 23, 1904, Wakefield, MA, U.S.A.

Coon worked in three fields: cultural anthropology, prehistoric archeology, and physical anthropology. He not only published in all three but also tried to bring them together into a coherent whole. In this sense he was primarily a historian.

Coon's career in cultural anthropology began with fieldwork in Morocco between 1924 and 1928, culminating in the publication of an ethnography of the Riffian tribes. He continued on this line with a similar study of the north Albanian mountaineers. His *Caravan* (1951) is a synthesis of information about Middle Eastern culture that is used as a text by diplomats and others concerned with that part of the world.

Before World War II Coon collaborated with Eliot D. Chapple in writing *Principles of Anthropology* (1942), in which they attempted to analyze human behavior in terms of patterns of interaction and the requirements of institutions to preserve equilibrium, through the operation of the law of least effort. After the war he simplified and elaborated his ideas about these principles in an appendix to his *A Reader in General Anthropology* (1948).

While thinking about these matters overseas during the war, Coon conceived the idea that humans convert energy derived from outside their organism into social structure at a predictable rate of acceleration, culminating in quanta of energy and global institutions such as have since been achieved. He expressed this idea first in lecture courses, then in an exhibit at the University Museum of the University of Pennsylvania, and finally in his book *The Story of Man* (1954).

Coon's contribution to archeology consisted mainly of excavation of caves in parts of the world previously unexplored in this sense, and discovery of new cultures. In Morocco he found a succession of Aterian phases under the Neolithic in the High Cave of Tangier. In Iran he found in the cave of Bisitun the first Levalloisio-Mousterian industry reported from that country, and in two neighboring caves on the Caspian shore, Belt and Hotu, a sequence of cultures running from the Epipaleolithic through the Mesolithic and Neolithic to the Iron Age. In these caves he also found the bones of what may have been the earliest domestic animals and worked out techniques for distinguishing them from those of wild animals of the same species. In the cave of Kara Kamar in Afghanistan he found an Aurignacian culture older than any in Western Europe, and a Mesolithic over it. In the cave of Jerf Ajla in the Syrian desert he found a transition from Levalloisio-Mousterian to Aurignacian.

In 1967 Coon excavated a cave at Yengema in Sierra Leone which contained a sequence of miniature replicas of a Middle Paleolithic hand-ax industry which overlapped a Neolithic industry. The latter began about 2200 B.C. and lasted until about 1500 B.C., when the cave was flooded and abandoned.

Coon's contribution to physical anthropology—for which he was awarded the Viking Fund Medal in 1952—began in the 1920s and early 1930s, when he measured large series of Moroccans, Albanians, and Arabs of southern Arabia, particularly in Yemen and Hadhramaut. He discovered remains of Pleistocene fossil humans in Morocco in 1939 and 1962 and in Iran in 1949 and 1951. The first two discoveries confirmed the thesis that Bushmen once lived in North Africa. The

1949 discovery was of Neanderthals and the 1951 skeletons were those of modern Caucasoids living near the end of the Pleistocene.

In 1950, in his book *Races,* in which S. M. Garn and J. B. Birdsell also participated, Coon propounded the theory that many of the physical differences between races are results of adaptation to environment. This hypothesis, then received with ridicule, has since been demonstrated many times by physiological research. Coon himself went to southern Chile in 1959 with a team of physiologists who confirmed the superior cold adaptation of the Alakaluf Indians.

In 1962 Coon's *The Origin of Races* appeared, provoking controversy between segregationists and equalitarians although it had nothing to do with race relations in the United States. The publication of that book was the culmination of decades of work in the study of fossil human remains, a task greatly helped by the availability, in the University Museum in Philadelphia, of rubber and plaster molds of many fossil specimens. As a result of these researches Coon came to the conclusion that *Homo sapiens* is divided into five subspecies, and that these same subspecies also existed in his immediate ancestor, *Homo erectus.* The transition from one species to the other involved initial changes in one organ only, the brain. Because each subspecies was physiologically adapted to its environment in other respects, the acquisition of a new gene or genes favoring higher intelligence permitted the existing subspecies to cross the anagentic threshold in concert. Because this mutation possibly arose originally in a single subspecies only, and because the human mating pattern retards gene flow, the transmission of this genetic innovation took time, and the subspecies crossed the threshold at different times. But Coon also stated the possibility that two or more races crossed the *erectus-sapiens* threshold independently. Subsequent work by paleontologists on other mammalian species has confirmed this discovery.

The sequel to *The Origin of Races,* entitled *The Living Races of Man,* appeared in 1965. In it Coon reviewed the racial and cultural history of the races of the world up to the present, and in particular amplified his explanation of the roles of climate and culture in racial differentiation.

In 1949, in an exhibit in the University Museum of Philadelphia, Coon demon-

strated that the use of energy versus time followed a constant slope on a double log chart from the first use of fire to the first nuclear explosion, after which its slope rose steeply. He published this study in 1970 in an article, "Human Evolution and the Avalanche of Culture" (in C. Brooks, ed., *The Changing World and Man*).

Coon's book, *The Hunting Peoples* (1971), showed humans' cultural debts to their preagricultural ancestors.

The son of a Boston importer, Coon attended Phillips Academy at Andover, MA, and Harvard, where he majored in the classics, English, and finally anthropology. He received his B.A. magna cum laude at Harvard in 1925, and his M.A. and Ph.D. in 1928. He did field work for Harvard's Peabody Museum until 1935 and taught at Harvard from 1935 until 1948, except for the war years. During World War II he served in the Office of Strategic Services as a combat major. In 1948 he became curator of ethnology at the University Museum of the University of Pennsylvania, devoting himself principally to fieldwork. He retired in 1963 to his home in West Gloucester, MA. In 1955 Coon was elected to the National Academy of Sciences.

For background information *see* ANTHROPOLOGY, PHYSICAL; ARCHEOLOGY in the McGraw-Hill Encyclopedia of Science and Technology. ∎

COONS, ALBERT HEWETT
★ American physician

Born June 28, 1912, Gloversville, NY, U.S.A.

Died Sept. 30, 1978, Brookline, MA, U.S.A.

Coons originated the concept of using fluorescing antibody molecules for the specific microscopic localization of proteins or polysaccharides. For this achievement he received, among other honors, the 1959 Lasker Award of the American Public Health Association and the 1962 Passano Foundation Award.

Coons and his colleagues, Hugh J. Creech and R. Norman Jones, found that a fluorescent compound could be coupled chemically to antibody without interfering in any way with the interaction between the antibody and its specific antigen. This method has since been employed to identify bacteria in infection, to localize individual animal cells infected

with a virus, to single out cells producing specific antibody, and to localize cells containing a chosen polysaccharide as a structural constituent. All that is needed is a specific antibody solution; the method of labeling the molecules with a fluorochrome has become routine.

It is perhaps necessary to define "specific" as it is used in connection with immunity. Antibodies have areas on their surfaces resembling perfect castings of part of the surface of the antigen molecule that stimulated the making of the antibodies in the first place. Antibody molecules, therefore, fit their specific antigen. Since large molecules, like proteins and polysaccharides, are each relatively unique in their shape and the arrangement of their surface charges, an antibody specific for an area on one of them reacts little if at all with other kinds of molecules. Hence, a labeled antibody behaves like a stain that stains only one material—say, hen's ovalbumin (a molecular species in egg white)—or one kind of bacterial capsule—say, pneumococcus type III.

In 1934 J. R. Marrack produced red antibodies by coupling an antibody solution to a dye-intermediate. The antibodies reacted with bacterial cells of the species against which they had originally been formed and stained them red. This experiment established the principle that antibody molecules could be used as a specific stain. However, the amount of color imparted to a bacterial cell was so faint that it could not be used to localize small amounts of antigen or to identify single

bacterial cells. In 1941 Coons, Creech, and Jones labeled an antibody solution with a fluorescent dye, anthracene, which Creech had been coupling to various proteins. Anthracene is a compound that fluoresces brightly in the blue range when bombarded with ultraviolet light. The anthracene antibody (the antibodies used were directed against pneumococci, the bacteria that cause lobar pneumonia) reacted well with its specific bacteria but not with others and, carrying its label with it, made the specific bacteria brightly fluorescent. Single organisms were easily visible under the fluorescence microscope.

The next step was to select the optimal fluorochrome, one with an emission wavelength not usually encountered in biological material and as brilliantly fluorescent as possible. On both counts fluorescein itself seemed to have the necessary characteristics. Its emission wavelength, at 510 micrometers, was in the yellow-green, an unusual fluorescence color in tissue; and it reemitted 85 percent of the energy it absorbed—that is, it was almost as brightly fluorescent as possible. In the past it had been used to trace the presence of underground rivers and unsuspected connections between water sources. Its coupling to antibody by the same linkage (carbamido-) that Creech had used for anthracene and other compounds completed the first stage in the development of fluorescent antibodies, the use of which has come to be called immunofluorescence.

Fluorescein-labeled antibodies were first used by Coons and his colleagues in 1942 to trace the fate of pneumococci injected into mice. Later, with the principal collaboration of M. H. Kaplan, he extended its use to the distribution after injection of pneumococcal polysaccharide and foreign plasma proteins, and to the detection of animal cells infected with the intracellular parasites mumps virus and typhus rickettsia.

Since these early studies, which were published in 1950, the use of immunofluorescence has slowly spread through biology. A tool forged from two fields, it gives the specificity of immunological reactions to the microscopist and the resolution of the microscope to the immunologist. It is of use to the student of infectious disease because it makes possible rapid specific diagnosis of an increasing number of diseases; indeed, in principle any infectious disease can be diagnosed by this means. Beyond this, immunofluorescence is of use in the study of some of the basic prob-

lems of immunity, such as locating the site of antibody formation and determining the number of cells engaged in the process under various conditions of stimulation. It is also a useful technique for the cytochemist, who can use it to localize various macromolecules such as blood group substances or cell products synthesized for excretion, like enzymes in the cells of the pancreas or albumin and prothrombin in cells of the liver.

In later years Coons concentrated on the study of the cellular aspects of antibody formation and tried, like many immunologists, to fathom the puzzle of specific antibody synthesis.

Coons received his B.A. from Williams College in 1933 and his M.D. from Harvard Medical School in 1937. After clinical training in medicine at the Massachusetts General Hospital and the Thorndike Memorial Laboratory of the Boston City Hospital, he joined the department of bacteriology and immunology at Harvard Medical School in 1940 as a National Research Council fellow. With the exception of World War II, during which he served in the Army Medical Corps in the southwestern Pacific, he remained a member of that department. He was elected to the National Academy of Sciences in 1962.

For background information *see* ANTIBODY; MICROSCOPE, FLUORESCENCE in the McGraw-Hill Encyclopedia of Science and Technology. ∎

COOPER, FRANKLIN SEANEY
★ American physicist and speech scientist

Born Apr. 29, 1908, Robinson, IL, U.S.A.

The nature of spoken language, as revealed by experiments on how speech is produced and perceived, is an area to which Cooper and his colleagues at the Haskins Laboratories made several pioneering contributions beginning in the early 1950s. One contribution was the development of the Pattern Playback as a research tool for investigating speech perception; another was the adaptation of electromyographic methods to the study of speech articulation. Both developments helped to convert research on speech from descriptive studies into a lively and expanding experimental science.

The physical nature of speech, and the effects of noise and distortion on its intelligibility, had been studied extensively during the development of telephony, radio, and sound recording. Thus, by the beginning of the 1940s speech seemed well explored, although there remained some difficulties in characterizing individual speech sounds acoustically. Questions about how speech was perceived and whether or not special modes of perception might be involved had remained unasked. Such neglect is understandable when one considers how easily everyone uses speech and the facility with which it is learned even by the very young.

Cooper and his colleagues had first to recognize that a problem existed and that the perception of speech might somehow be special. Awareness of the problem came from attempts to design an acoustic alphabet, a set of sounds that could be substituted for the letters on a printed page and so be used by the blind to "read" ordinary books. But no useful set of sounds could be found; with the best set, and after much training, the blind listener could read at only 10–15 words per minute. This was scarcely a tenth of the rate at which the blind person listened without effort to the set of sounds called speech. But why should this be so? Surely the explanation was not to be found in an acoustic simplicity or distinctiveness of the speech sounds themselves. Recent work at the Bell Telephone Laboratories had analyzed speech into a three-dimensional picture, the sound spectrogram, in which complexity and nondistictiveness of the speech sounds were notable characteris-

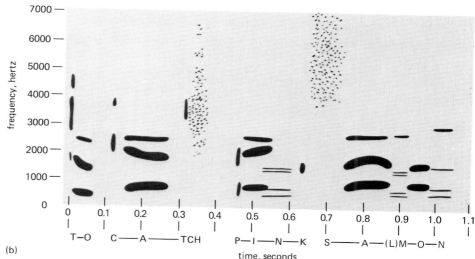

(a)

(b)

Simplification of sound spectrogram. (a) Original spectrogram. (b) Simplified version.

tics. Even the boundaries between words were often unapparent.

Spectograms did, however, show similarities of patterns among words that sounded more or less alike, and this fact prompted a number of descriptive studies; indeed, it launched a new discipline called acoustic phonetics, concerned with relationships between spectrographic patterns and speech sounds. But the wealth of detail in the patterns and the variations usual in speech made unambiguous interpretation difficult.

What was needed, and what Cooper and his colleagues developed, was a way to experiment with the speech patterns and so to find out what elements of the pattern carried the information needed to

hear the speech accurately. The first step was to simplify the spectrograms by making hand-painted "cartoons" of them (see illustration). Then, to test for perceptual adequacy, a mechanooptical device (the Pattern Playback) was built to convert the simplified patterns back into sound. By listening, and then revising and relistening, one could discover the acoustic cues, that is, the essential correspondence, between patterns and speech sounds.

By the end of the 1950s an extensive set of studies by Pierre Delattre, Alvin Liberman, Cooper, and others had identified the principal acoustic cues for the speech sounds of American English, and had extended the experimental study of speech in other directions as well. However, the acoustic cues did not explain, but only hinted at, the nature of spoken language. The systematic relationships among the acoustic cues were not readily interpretable in acoustic terms; rather, they pointed to similarities of articulation. It was as if the listener attended to the speaker's oral gestures rather than the sounds he made.

With this hint that the underlying nature of speech should be sought in the manner of its production, Cooper and his colleagues began to work with x-ray motion pictures of speech. They developed ways to record the speech sounds and then to slow down both picture and sound for careful analyses of the articulatory motions. But what muscular forces caused these motions? Would the relationships between gesture and phonetic structure of the speech be clearer and simpler if one could find out what the muscles were doing? By recording the small electrical signals that muscles generate when they contract, it was possible to study directly the underlying temporospatial patterning of speech production, and indirectly to infer the organization of the neuromotor commands for speech. But before this could be done, Cooper, Katherine Harris, and their colleagues had to adapt the rather crude electromyographic techniques of the early 1960s and develop computer methods for dealing with masses of experimental data.

Some of the simplicities hoped for in starting the research on speech production were found, but, in the main, the nature of speech and the linkage between perception and production remained elusive. Research on speech perception and on the organization of the motor control of speech was continued not only at Haskins Laboratories by Cooper's colleagues, but also in a number of other laboratories worldwide.

Raised on an Illinois farm, Cooper later taught in a one-room rural school. He went on to undergraduate (B.S., 1931) and graduate work in engineering and physics at the University of Illinois. He completed graduate study on the biological effects of electron beams at the Massachusetts Institute of Technology (Ph.D., 1936), then turned to research on gaseous insulation for supervoltage x-ray equipment at the General Electric Research Laboratory. In mid-1939 he left General Electric to found, with Caryl P. Haskins, an interdisciplinary basic science research organization, the Haskins Laboratories.

Managing the operation of these laboratories was Cooper's primary concern until partial retirement in 1975, although with many public-service interludes and overlaps. During World War II, Cooper served under Vannevar Bush as head of the Liaison Office of the Office of Scientific Research and Development, for which he received the Presidential Certificate of Merit in 1948. Postwar, as a scientific consultant to the United Nations, Cooper shared in the effort to bring atomic energy under international control. University relationships included teaching (acoustic phonetics) at Columbia University and the University of Connecticut, advisory roles for New York University and the Massachusetts Institute of Technology, and research affiliation with Yale University. Government services, beginning in 1949, included advisory roles in defense and health research, and, in 1973–74, serving on the Advisory Panel on White House Tapes, U.S. District Court for the District of Columbia. In 1976 Cooper received an honorary doctorate from Yale University and was elected to the National Academy of Engineering. *See* BUSH, VANNEVAR.

For background information *see* SPEECH in the McGraw-Hill Encyclopedia of Science and Technology. ∎

COOPER, GUSTAV ARTHUR

★ American paleontologist and stratigrapher

Born Feb. 9, 1902, College Point, NY, U.S.A.

Cooper started his geological career at Colgate University with the intention of becoming a mineralogist, but the prevalence of fossils on the campus soon turned him from the study of minerals. His work in paleontology was aided by a scholarship from Colgate, permitting him to study for his Ph.D. at Yale University. His master's and doctor's theses were on the stratigraphy of the Hamilton Group of New York from the vicinity of Hamilton, the type area, to Lake Erie.

Although Cooper's studies at Yale led to a dissertation in stratigraphy, his main interest was in paleontology. While at Yale he was selected by Charles Schuchert to assist in a reclassification of the fossil brachiopods. This started Cooper on the main specialty of his career. His work was therefore divided between stratigraphy and paleon-

tology, but the two are complementary.

Cooper's contributions in stratigraphy were the production of the Devonian correlation chart of the National Research Council and assistance in the Ordovician and Permian charts. His Devonian work, preliminary to the Devonian chart, consisted of completion of the Hamilton studies to include all of New York State and a survey of the Middle Devonian of the Midwest. His Hamilton work showed that the north end of the Catskill Mountain mass is of Hamilton age rather than younger, as had previously been thought. In the Devonian investigations in the Midwest, Cooper was joined by A. S. Warthin of Vassar College. This work led to a classification of the Traverse Group of Michigan and realignment of many formations. These studies provided a background for the preparation of the Devonian correlation chart, a comprehensive diagram of the Devonian formations of North America. As chair of the Devonian Committee, Cooper compiled most of the Devonian chart and proposed a new stage terminology and some innovations in age assignment.

Contribution to Ordovician stratigraphy was made not only on the National Research Council chart but on a diagram of Middle Ordovician formations that accompanied the monograph *Chazyan and Related Brachiopods* (1956). In the latter chart the great Ordovician developments in the Appalachians and the West were brought into focus for the first time. It recognized the facies development of the Ordovician, which had been overlooked by Appala-

chian geologists in prior studies, but which had been detailed by Cooper and his colleague B. N. Cooper of Virginia Polytechnic Institute in 1946 in Virginia and by John Rogers in Tennessee. On completing his Ordovician work Cooper devoted much attention to stratigraphic and paleontological studies in the Permian of the Glass Mountains of West Texas. These studies again emphasized facies relationships of the various strata, but rather than innovating they were a perfecting of details.

Cooper's brachiopod work started with Schuchert at Yale and lasted for 2 years, in which two suborders, the Orthida and Pentamerida, were completed. This study emphasized the necessity of using a totality of characters in classification of the brachiopods and indicated the value of brachial valve structures in family classification. The latter theme was again emphasized in a study of the family Triplesiidae with E. O. Ulrich. Cooper published, with Ulrich, *Ozarkian and Canadian Brachiopoda* (1938), a hitherto poorly understood group of brachiopods which existed in Late Cambrian and Early Ordovician time. Although the Ozarkian and Canadian systems have been found unnecessary, the brachiopods of those times are distinctive and characteristic, representing some terminal stocks and some evolving groups. They furnish an evolutionary link between the Cambrian brachiopods and the great brachiopod expansion in the Ordovician. As a sequel to this work and in an effort to establish firmly lines of brachiopod evolution, the monograph mentioned earlier, *Chazyan and Related Brachiopods,* was produced. This covered 163 genera, many of them new, and afforded much new information on Middle Ordovician brachiopod stocks. These brachiopods were also used as the basis for the new stratigraphic scheme of the Middle Ordovician mentioned above.

Another important work on brachiopods was on the extensive superfamily Productidina, prepared with H. M. Muir-Wood of Great Britain. Cooper also published numerous shorter papers on brachiopods of all ages, including those of the modern seas, all having a bearing on classification.

After the Ordovician studies Cooper embarked in earnest on his monumental work dealing with the Permian brachiopods of West Texas. They represent the culmination of many Paleozoic stocks that became extinct at the end of that time. He had been collecting large limestone blocks in the mountain ranges of West Texas since 1939. These were dissolved with acid in the

laboratory to obtain the silicified fossils entombed in them. Approximately 65 tons (58.5 metric tons) of limestone was processed and hundreds of thousands of specimens obtained, not only of brachiopods but of many other groups. The organization and sorting of this vast collection proved a gigantic task. With the help of a grant from the National Science Foundation, R. E. Grant was engaged as a collaborator. More than 200 genera were taken from these rocks. The specimens are so well preserved that new structures have been discovered in them that will help to clarify problems of some of the bizarre forms of brachiopods, such as the *Olhaminida* and the Richthofeniidae, as well as many of the other more usual types. The species number nearly a thousand. This was Cooper's most significant contribution to paleontology. The vast collection alone offered extensive study opportunities for other workers. The first part of the *Permian Brachiopods of West Texas,* which includes all the results of the studies begun in the Glass Mountains in 1939, appeared in 1972. Five additional parts appeared in succeeding years, part 6 being published in 1977.

In February 1972 Cooper retired but remained active through the generosity of the Smithsonian Institution which allotted him office space and other facilities. He devoted himself to the study of living brachiopods, which are found in all of the oceans in surprising diversity. In 1973 he published a study of new species from the Indian Ocean, as well as a study of a collection from many parts of the world made by R/V *Vema* of the Lamont-Doherty Geological Observatory of Columbia University. Two other works on living brachiopods were a study of some deep-sea brachiopods from the abyss off the coast of southern California (1972) and a comprehensive survey of brachiopods from the Caribbean Sea and Gulf of Mexico based on collections made by the University of Miami, Florida (1977). Cooper's most recent work was a study of more Indian Ocean brachiopods and an investigation of the interior details of Mesozoic, Tertiary, and modern Terebratulidae.

After graduating from Colgate University (B.S., 1924), Cooper spent another year at Colgate, in which he laid the groundwork for his future Devonian and brachiopod studies. He received an M.A. from Colgate in 1926 and a Ph.D. from Yale University in 1929, and remained at Yale for 2 years working with Schuchert. He left Yale for the Smithsonian Institution, where he was appointed in 1930 as-

sistant curator in stratigraphic paleontology in the U.S. National Museum, a branch of the Smithsonian. In 1943 he became curator of invertebrate paleontology and paleobotany and in 1956 head curator of the department of geology. In 1963 that department was divided between paleontology and mineralogy, and Cooper became head of a new department of paleobiology. In 1967 he became a senior scientist to devote his full time to research. Cooper was honored by Colgate University in 1953 with a D.Sc. In 1958 he received the Mary Clarke Thompson Medal of the National Academy of Sciences for contributions to paleontology and stratigraphy, and in 1964 the Medal of the Paleontological Society. He served as the society's president in 1956–57.

For background information *see* BRACHIOPODA; DEVONIAN; ORDOVICIAN; PALEONTOLOGY; STRATIGRAPHY in the McGraw-Hill Encyclopedia of Science and Technology. ∎

COOPER, LEON N.
☆ American physicist

Born Feb. 28, 1930, New York, NY, U.S.A.

Cooper worked with J. Bardeen and J. R. Schrieffer to develop a microscopic theory of superconductivity, which they put forth in 1957. For this work, the three were awarded the Nobel Prize in physics in 1972. *See* BARDEEN, JOHN; SCHRIEFFER, JOHN ROBERT.

In 1955 Bardeen invited Cooper, whose earlier training and experience had been in field theory and nuclear physics, to join him and Schrieffer in working out a theory of superconductivity. Since its discovery in 1911, superconductivity—the phenomenon in which many metals and alloys lose all resistance to electric current, completely exclude magnetic flux (the Meissner effect), and display other remarkable properties at temperatures near absolute zero—had been investigated by some of the greatest theoretical physicists. Phenomenological theories describing many of the observed properties were developed, but no theory beginning from the first principles of quantum theory had ever been elaborated.

A first step toward understanding the actual mechanism of superconductivity was the discovery by B. Serin and E. Maxwell in 1950 that, for many superconductors, the transition temperature at which a sample becomes superconducting varies with the isotopic mass of the sample in the same manner as the vibration frequencies of the atoms in the crystal lattice. The existence of the isotope effect indicated that superconductivity might depend in an important way on the interaction of electrons with lattice vibrations.

It was shown by H. Fröhlich, and more generally by Bardeen and D. Pines, that this interaction could lead to an effective attraction between electrons. The manner in which this occurs may be visualized as follows: An electron passing through the lattice will attract the positive ions in the lattice toward itself, inducing a polarization along its path. Since the electron moves much faster than the heavy ions, a narrow trail of positive charge will persist for some time after the electron's passage. If a second electron passes near the positive trail during this period, it will be attracted to it, so that an effective attraction between the electrons is established. If the momenta of both electrons are sufficiently close to the Fermi surface, this attraction may exceed the electrostatic repulsion between the electrons, so that a net attraction is created.

In 1956 Cooper studied the behavior of a many-electron system interacting through such an attraction. For technical reasons, he focused his attention on two electrons at a time, considering that the major effect of the other electrons would be to exclude phase space. According to the Pauli exclusion principle, which speci-

fies that no two electrons can occupy the same quantum state, the other electrons fill the spin and momentum states up to the Fermi surface, and the pair can be assumed to be restricted to energies just above this surface. Cooper showed that, even for an extremely weak interaction, the energy spectrum of such a pair includes a bound state, that is, a state whose energy is separated from all the other states by a finite interval (the binding energy), and whose probability amplitude falls to zero for large distances between the two electrons. In the presence of an attractive interaction, electrons near the Fermi surface could therefore form bound pairs (now known as Cooper pairs), drastically altering the behavior of the system. Furthermore, the binding energies of the pairs could be associated with an energy gap of about 10^{-3} electronvolt. Such a gap had recently been observed in the electronic spectrum of superconductors and was earlier postulated by F. London to be an essential feature of superconductivity. Bardeen had shown how such an energy gap could give rise to the Meissner effect.

However, with the discovery of the possible existence of Cooper pairs, problems still remained. If the binding energy of a pair is set equal to the energy gap, then the uncertainty principle shows that the average separation between electrons in the bound state is on the order of 10^{-6} meter, which is far greater than the spacing between electrons forming pairs, about 10^{-8} meter. Thus, within the volume of a Cooper pair, the centers of about 10^6 other pairs will be found. Thus there are numerous collisions between pairs, which would appear to disrupt the binding of any given pair.

Bardeen, Cooper, and Schrieffer therefore had to construct a wave function involving the cooperative motion of large numbers of particles, in which the Cooper pairs could freely scatter while obeying the exclusion principle. The electron pairs are therefore joined, one to another, in a gigantic quantum state in which the motions of an enormous number of electrons are strictly correlated, so that the exclusion principle is satisfied. Because of the strongly correlated nature of the superconducting state, a localized disturbance, which would normally deflect a single electron and therefore give rise to electric resistance, cannot do so in a superconductor without affecting all the electrons

participating in the superconducting state simultaneously. Although this is not impossible, it is extremely unlikely, so that a collective drift of coherent superconducting electrons, forming a current, is dissipationless.

The Bardeen-Cooper-Schrieffer (BCS) theory not only was successful in explaining all the remarkable properties of superconductors, but also stimulated extensive theoretical and experimental research in superconductivity. One of the most important applications of the BCS theory was its use by B. D. Josephson in 1962 to predict the remarkable phenomena observed in two superconductors separated by a thin normal junction, involving the tunneling through the junction of Cooper pairs. The arguments used by Cooper to show that a pair of electrons in a superconductor have a bound state can be applied equally well to any system of fermions (that is, particles obeying the exclusion principle) with an attractive interaction, and superconductinglike states have thus been postulated in nuclei, in the interior of neutron stars, and in superfluid helium-3. In a paper written in 1958, Cooper, R. L. Mills, and A. M. Sessler discussed the possibility of a superfluid state in helium-3. The discovery in 1972 of such a superfluid state was stimulated by the BCS theory. *See* JOSEPHSON, BRIAN DAVID.

In later years, in addition to his work in theoretical physics, Cooper was actively working in developing a theory of the central nervous system. His particular interest was the means by which neuron modification can lead to the organization of distributed memories and the means by which central nervous system theory can be confronted by experiments on the visual cortex.

Cooper received the A.B. (1951), A.M. (1953), and Ph.D. (1954) from Columbia University. He then spent a year at the Institute for Advanced Study in Princeton, 2 years as a research associate at the University of Illinois, and a year as assistant professor at Ohio State University. In 1958 he joined the faculty of Brown University, where he was Henry Ledyard Goddard University Professor from 1966 to 1974, and became Thomas J. Watson Sr. Professor of Science in 1974. He also became co-director of the Center for Neural Science at Brown University. He received the Comstock Prize (with Schrieffer) of the National Academy of

Sciences (1968), the Award of Excellence of the Graduate Faculties Alumni of Columbia University (1974), the Déscartes Medal of the Academie de Paris, Université René Déscartes (1977), and a number of honorary degrees. He was elected to the National Academy of Sciences in 1975, and became a fellow of the American Physical Society and the American Academy of Arts and Sciences.

Cooper authored *An Introduction to the Meaning and Structure of Physics* (1968), contributed to *The Physicist's Conception of Nature* (1973), and wrote various articles on science and human experience and numerous scientific papers.

For background information *see* HELIUM, LIQUID; NERVOUS SYSTEM (VERTEBRATE); SUPERCONDUCTIVITY in the McGraw-Hill Encyclopedia of Science and Technology. ∎

CORI, CARL FERDINAND
☆ American biochemist

Born Dec. 5, 1896, Prague, Czechoslovakia

The energy necessary for the activities of life is supplied through sugar metabolism in the organism. The processes of this metabolism, therefore, are of extreme importance to the study of life itself. The investigations of Carl Cori and his wife Gerty Radnitz Cori in this problem of carbohydrate metabolism resulted in the discovery of the enzymatic mechanism of glucose-glycogen interconversion and the effects of hormones upon this mechanism. For this achievement they were awarded the 1947 Nobel Prize in physiology or medicine. *See* CORI, GERTY THERESA RADNITZ.

Over a century ago Claude Bernard discovered a starchlike substance he named glycogen. Glycogen consists of large numbers of glucose molecules bonded together and is found mainly in the liver and muscles and, to a slight extent, in skin and other tissues. The sugar content of the blood is effectively constant since, when sugar intake is high, storage of glycogen in the liver is increased, and when the blood sugar level falls below normal, the glycogen of the liver is converted into glucose, which enters the bloodstream. Apparently only the glycogen of the liver can supply blood sugar.

In the early 1930s, then, the Coris faced this challenge: "What are the mechanisms, the chemical reactions, by which glucose is converted into glycogen, and by what means does the reverse process occur?" More than a decade of painstaking effort was needed before an answer was found.

It was known before the Coris began their work that under certain circumstances glucose in living tissues appears to be bound to inorganic phosphate. Closer investigation had demonstrated that the inorganic phosphate was bonded to the sixth carbon atom in the glucose chain, the compound being then designated as glucose-6-phosphate.

After much preliminary work, the Coris were able to show that if ground-up muscle was washed thoroughly with water, the residue could take up free inorganic phosphate, which was found then to be bonded to glucose. In this case, however, the sugar phosphate formed was not glucose-6-phosphate. The new compound, the so-called Cori ester, was found to have the phosphate bonded to the first carbon atom in the glucose chain; it was therefore designated glucose-1-phosphate.

The discovery of the Cori ester proved to be the key that opened the door to an understanding of the glucose-glycogen interconversion. The glucose-1-phosphate could be found only in washed muscle, since washing removed an enzyme from the tissue. This enzyme, now known as phosphoglucomutase, catalyzes the migration of inorganic phosphate between the ends of the sugar-molecule, between the 1 position and the 6 position. In prior work this enzyme was always present, and thus the Cori ester had all been converted to the 6-ester before it could be detected.

After many years of continuous effort, the Coris were able to show that the glucose-glycogen interconversion was actually a three-step process. The first two of these reactions are readily reversible, and each is catalzyed by its own enzyme. Glycogen reversibly reacts with inorganic phosphate and the enzyme phosphorylase to give glucose-1-phosphate. The second step consists of transposition of the phosphate group from the 1 to the 6 position. This reaction is catalyzed by the enzyme phosphoglucomutase, which itself must be activated by the presence of magnesium ions. The third reaction is the hydrolysis of glucose-6-phosphate to glucose, the removal of the phosphate group to convert the ester to the sugar. This final reaction, which is not readily reversible, occurs in the presence of the enzyme phosphatase. The glucose formed in this way is released into the blood, which carries it to the tissues. The reverse process, the conversion of blood glucose to glycogen, requires as its first step the presence of the enzyme hexokinase and adenosinetriphosphate (ATP) to form glucose-6-phosphate.

As a demonstration of the validity of their analysis, the Coris succeeded in synthesizing glycogen in culture from glucose in the presence of hexokinase, ATP, phosphoglucomutase, and phosphorylase. Further, they were able to show that the hexokinase reaction, the interconversion of glucose and glucose-6-phosphate, is promoted by insulin but checked by another hormone in extracts from the anterior lobe of the pituitary gland, the hypophysis. This discovery is of great importance, since it demonstrates that hormones intervene chemically in sugar metabolism, and thus the relation of endocrine function to glucose utilization becomes clearer.

The son of the director of the Marine Biological Station at Trieste, Carl Cori studied at the gymnasium in Trieste and then at the German University of Prague, where he received his M.D. in 1920. He then spent a year at the University of Vienna and a year as assistant in pharmacology at the University of Graz before accepting in 1922 the position of biochemist at the State Institute for the Study of Malignant Diseases in Buffalo, NY. In 1931 he was appointed professor of pharmacology at the Washington University Medical School in St. Louis, where he later became professor of biochemistry. He was elected to the National Academy of Sciences in 1940.

For background information *see* CARBOHYDRATE METABOLISM; GLUCOSE; GLYCOGEN in the McGraw-Hill Encyclopedia of Science and Technology. ∎

CORI, GERTY THERESA RADNITZ
American biochemist

Born Aug. 15, 1896, Prague, Czechoslovakia
Died Oct. 26, 1957, St. Louis, MO, U.S.A.

For their research into the mechanism of carbohydrate metabolism and its relation to certain hormone secretions, Gerty Radnitz Cori and her husband Carl Cori received the 1947 Nobel Prize in physiology or medicine. *See* CORI, CARL FERDINAND.

Gerty Cori also did independent work on hereditable human diseases. Her study of a number of glycogen storage diseases demonstrated that they were intimately related to defects in the molecular structures of certain enzymes or, in some cases, to their total absence.

Gerty Cori received her M.D. from the medical school of the German University of Prague in 1920, then spent 2 years at the Carolinen Children's Hospital. She married Carl Cori in 1920 and in 1922 went with him to the United States. From 1922 to 1931 the Coris worked at the State Institute for the Study of Malignant

Diseases in Buffalo, NY. In 1931 they joined the staff of the Washington University Medical School in St. Louis. In 1947 Gerty Cori was appointed professor of biochemistry there. ∎

CORNER, GEORGE WASHINGTON
★ American medical biologist

Born Dec. 12, 1889, Baltimore, MD, U.S.A.

As a medical student, Corner planned to become a gynecologist, but during his internship he found the problems of human reproduction so fascinating that he devoted himself to laboratory research and medical teaching as anatomist and embryologist.

He became interested in the ovary and especially in the corpus luteum. This is a mass of cells about the size of a cherry that forms for about 2 weeks in each successive monthly cycle of the human female, filling up the emptied Graffian follicle from which the egg cell has been discharged into the oviduct (Fallopian tube). In animals there are as many corpora lutea as young in the litter. When the egg cell is fertilized and develops into an embryo, the corpus luteum does not disappear, but lasts throughout the pregnancy.

Corner began his investigation of the corpus luteum by thorough microscopic study of its cell structure and development, and of its cyclic appearance and disappearance. These studies, made principally on the sow, prepared him for observations on human ovaries and subsequent experimental work on laboratory animals.

About 1910 a European surgeon, Ludwig Fraenkel, showed that this transitory structure was somehow necessary for the attachment of the early embryo in the uterus and for its subsequent development. In very early pregnancy in a rabbit, for example, if the experimenter removes the ovaries or the corpora lutea alone, the embryos do not develop. What happens to them was not known. Two European scientists, the embryologist Paul Ancel and the anatomist Paul Bouin, found in 1912 that the corpus luteum produces some sort of internal secretion that changes the lining of the uterus from an inactive state to one seemingly favorable for receiving and nourishing the embryos. The nature of this internal secretion was also unknown.

Corner, whose training included both surgical methods and a knowledge of early embryology, began in 1928 to follow up these earlier findings. By experiments on rabbits he proved that survival and development of the embryos depend upon the change in the uterus induced by the corpora lutea. If the latter are removed, the progestational change does not occur, and the embryos when they arrive in the uterus fail to survive.

These experiments provided a means of identifying the corpus luteum hormone. Corner and one of his medical students, Willard M. Allen, a competent biochemist, made extracts of sows' ovaries collected at the slaughterhouse. They tested the extracts by injection into spayed rabbits to see whether they would produce changes such as would have been produced by the rabbits' own corpora lutea. The two investigators finally obtained partially purified extracts that brought about the progestational change and maintained pregnancy after removal of the ovaries. Allen, by further purification, prepared a crystalline product now known as progesterone. Expert organic chemists elsewhere later worked out its exact chemical composition and produced it synthetically.

Corner continued his anatomical studies of the ovarian and uterine cycle, and particularly of the menstrual cycle. Since true menstruation occurs only in Primates (humans, apes, and Old World monkeys), Corner organized a small colony of rhesus monkeys, the first in the United States

used for long-term study of the physiology of reproduction. In 35 years of continuous research he worked out the anatomical details of the menstrual cycle and also the physiological processes by which the fluctuating levels of the ovarian hormones (estrogen and progesterone) cause the cyclic menstrual hemorrhage. Corner also contributed to knowledge of early human embryology and the causes of embryonic defects and prenatal abnormalities.

Corner was educated at the Boys' Latin School in Baltimore and at the Johns Hopkins University (A.B., 1909). Following a good training in the Latin classics, he developed in later college years a strong interest in biology and proceeded to study medicine at Johns Hopkins (M.D., 1913). After an internship he was assistant professor of anatomy at the University of California, Berkeley (1915–19); associate professor at Johns Hopkins (1919–23); and professor at the University of Rochester, where he organized and directed the department of anatomy (1923–40). From 1940 to 1955 he was director of the department of embryology of the Carnegie Institution of Washington, at its Baltimore laboratory. In 1958 he received the Passano Foundation Award. He was elected to the National Academy of Sciences in 1940.

Corner wrote *The Hormones in Human Reproduction* (1942; 2d ed. 1947) and *Ourselves Unborn* (1944). *Anatomist at Large* (1955) contains an autobiographical sketch and collected essays. Interested since student days in the history of medicine, Corner also wrote extensively on that subject, producing comprehensive histories of the Rockefeller Institute of New York and the University of Pennsylvania School of Medicine.

For background information *see* OVARY (VERTEBRATE); PROGESTERONE in the McGraw-Hill Encyclopedia of Science and Technology. ∎

CORNFORTH, SIR JOHN (WARCUP)
★ Australian chemist

Born Sept. 7, 1917, Sydney, Australia

Cornforth's major scientific achievement, for which he shared the Nobel Prize with Vladimir Prelog in 1975, was the elucidation of the stereochemistry of a number of enzymic processes, chiefly those involved in the biosynthesis of ster-

ols and terpenoids, such as cholesterol. *See* PRELOG, VLADIMIR.

Cornforth's initial interest in the sterols was in the field of synthesis, in collaboration with Robert Robinson in Oxford. During World War II this work gave way to the more important problem of penicillin. But Cornforth had discovered what was to prove a key reaction for the synthesis of the sterols, and after the war, when he joined the staff of the Medical Research Council, the collaboration with Robinson continued and culminated in 1951 in the first total synthesis, simultaneously with R. B. Woodward, of the nonaromatic steroids. *See* ROBINSON, SIR ROBERT.

Meanwhile, at the National Institute for Medical Research, Cornforth had come into contact with biological scientists, and a particularly fruitful collaboration began with the biochemist George Popják. This collaboration was to last for 20 years; the marriage of the disciplines of chemistry and biochemistry, the availability of radioactive and other isotopes, and the awareness of the potential usefulness of the new physical techniques and improvements in instrumentation which developed after the war led to the devising of ever more subtle experiments.

Cornforth and Popják first demonstrated the pattern of incorporation of the precursor acetic acid into the ring structure of cholesterol biosynthesized in rat liver preparations by using acetic acid labeled with ^{14}C. Later, when mevalonic acid (3,5-dihydroxy-3-methylpentanoic acid)

emerged as the parent substance of steroids and terpenoids, they were able, using mevalonic acid specifically labeled with ^{14}C, to elucidate the mechanism of the molecular rearrangement that takes place when the steroid ring structure is formed by cyclization of the open-chain hydrocarbon squalene and to demonstrate the intermediate stages leading from mevalonic acid to squalene.

Cornforth had always been interested in stereochemistry, and a publication by A. G. Ogston in 1948 fired his imagination. Most molecules, including enzymes, that take part in living processes are asymmetric, and an enzyme catalyzes chemical reactions by binding the reactant molecules (substrates) at a specific site in the enzyme molecule. Not all substrates are asymmetric in the chemical sense, but Ogston explained how an apparently symmetrical molecule appears asymmetric to an enzyme. This could be demonstrated by introducing "hidden" asymmetry into a substrate molecule by replacing one of its atoms by an isotope; the enzyme will accept the "labeled" substrate, and the experimenter can devise ways of finding out what happens to the label.

Cornforth exploited this technique to the full. Mevalonic acid has three methylene groups, and all of these undergo changes in bonding on the way to squalene; each of the six hydrogen atoms in these three groups is stereochemically distinct in the Ogston sense. Cornforth devised ingenious syntheses for labeling each of these hydrogens in turn with deuterium or tritium and equally ingenious methods for determining the fate of the individual hydrogen atoms after the mevalonic acids had been transformed by the enzyme preparations. In the end, he and Popják succeeded in demonstrating stereospecificity for all but one of the enzymic steps then known for squalene biosynthesis. At this point Popják emigrated to America.

The one remaining unsolved enzymic process involved conversion of a terminal methylene group to a methyl group by addition of a proton from the medium; if the methylene group was labeled stereospecifically with two of the isotopes of hydrogen and the third was supplied in the water of incubation, then a stereospecific addition of hydrogen from the water would give a chiral (asymmetric) methyl group. Chiral methyl groups were unknown at the time, as were the means of recognizing them. The solution of the problem grew from a suggestion made by the German biochemist H. Eggerer for an enzymatic assay of chiral acetic acid. Thus a new collaboration began. Cornforth devised a synthesis of the two chiral acetic acids, Eggerer assayed their chirality enzymically, and it was then possible to demonstrate the stereospecificity of the remaining step in squalene biosynthesis. The chiral methyl group was also used to trace the stereochemical consequences of other enzymic processes, such as the cleavage of citrate to acetate by citrate lyase. All proved to be stereospecific.

The techniques developed in the course of this work are now being used to solve a wide range of biosynthetic problems all over the world.

Cornforth always maintained an interest in synthetic organic chemistry. His achievements included a stereoselective synthesis of olefins, a synthesis of oxazoles, N-acetylneuraminic acid, and abscisic acid (a plant hormone formerly known as abscisin II or dormin). His later work, continuing into the late 1970s, was devoted to trying to synthesize an artificial enzyme.

By the time Cornforth married Rita Harradence in 1941, his progressive hearing loss had resulted in complete deafness. His wife, also Australian and an accomplished organic chemist, was his most constant collaborator.

Cornforth graduated in chemistry at the University of Sydney in 1937. He left Australia in 1939 to study with Robinson at Oxford, taking his D.Phil. degree in 1941. He remained in Oxford until 1946, then during the period 1946–62 he was a member of the scientific staff of the National Institute for Medical Research in London. In 1962 he and Popják were appointed codirectors of Shell Research's Milstead Laboratory of Chemical Enzymology at Sittingbourne, Kent; Cornforth became sole director in 1968. During the period with Shell he held visiting professorships at the universities of Warwick (1965–71) and Sussex (1971–75). In 1975 he left Shell to become Royal Society Research Professor at Sussex University. He was elected a fellow of the Royal Society in 1953 and a foreign associate of the U.S. National Academy of Sciences in 1978; he was elected to the Australian Academy of Science in 1977 and to the Royal Netherlands Academy of Arts and Sciences in 1978. He received British, American, and French awards and medals in recognition of his work. He was made a Commander of the British Empire in 1972 and Knight Bachelor in 1977.

For background information see ENZYME; ORGANIC CHEMICAL SYNTHESIS, STEREOCHEMISTRY in the McGraw-Hill Encyclopedia of Science and Technology. ∎

COTTON, FRANK ALBERT
★ American chemist

Born Apr. 9, 1930, Philadelphia, PA, U.S.A.

Most of Cotton's contributions to science were in the area of inorganic chemistry, where his research was characterized by extraordinary versatility in applying a great range of preparative, physical, and theoretical techniques to the discovery and elucidation of new types of compounds, structures, and chemical bonds.

Cotton's most significant contribution was the development of a new kind of non-Wernerian chemistry of the transition metals. Alfred Werner's monumental contribution to chemistry was the concept of the coordination complex, in which metal atoms are surrounded by and interact chemically only with donor molecules or anions, collectively called ligands. There is, however, an extensive and important chemistry of the transition metals in which there are chemical bonds of equal or greater strength between the metal atoms themselves, in addition to the bonds to ligands. In some cases, groups of three or more metal atoms form a cluster. Cotton discovered several of the important kinds of cluster compounds, and was the leading contributor to the elucidation of the bonding in metal atom clusters.

Even more interesting are compounds containing multiple bonds between metal atoms. In 1964 Cotton recognized for the first time the existence in nature of quadruple bonds, that is, bonds in which four electron pairs are shared between two atoms. He subsequently discovered, structurally characterized, and provided theoretical analysis for hundreds of compounds containing such bonds, which until 1963 were not believed to exist. He also discovered the first examples of double and triple bonds between metal atoms and, later, many other examples.

Cotton was one of the first to investigate the stereochemically nonrigid properties of organometallic compounds, and he made most of the basic contributions to the early development of this field. With J. W. Faller and A. Davison, he showed for the first time how nuclear magnetic resonance spectroscopy could be used to determine the mechanisms as well as the rates for the rearrangement processes in fluxional molecules. Cotton was the first to recognize (1966) that the stereochemically nonrigid behavior of a type called carbonyl scrambling is characteristic property of dinuclear and polynuclear metal carbonyl molecules, and his work elucidated nearly all the basic types of scrambling processes recognized today.

Cotton also worked in structural biochemistry. With E. E. Hazen, Jr., he began the high-resolution study of a nuclease of staphylococcal origin in 1964, at a time when only the structures of myglobin and hemoglobin had been obtained, and only at medium resolution. By 1969 a 2.2-angstrom (0.22-nanometer) map of the nuclease had been obtained; the structure became available at 1.5-angstrom (0.15-nanometer) resolution, the optimum resolution obtained for any protein. The implication of the results were broad in respect to the general understanding of protein and enzyme structures. An especially important result was the first recognition of the now generally recognized role played by arginyl residues in enzymes that operate on phosphate-containing substrates. The nuclease structure and the structures of several excellent model compounds provided the first graphic evidence of how arginyl groups interact with phosphates.

Cotton attended Drexel University and received an A. B. from Temple University in 1951 and a Ph.D. from Harvard University in 1955. He rose from instructor (1955) to professor (1961) at the Massachusetts Institute of Technology and in 1972 moved to Texas A&M University, where he became Robert A. Welch Distinguished Professor of Chemistry. He received the American Chemical Society's first Award in Inorganic Chemistry in 1962 and its Award for Distinguished Service in the Advancement of Inorganic Chemistry in 1974. He also received medals and awards from a number of sections of the American Chemical Society, among them, the Baekeland Medal (North Jersey Section) in 1963, the Nichols Medal (New York Section) in 1975, the Harrison Howe Award (Rochester Section) in 1975, the Edgar Fahs Smith Award (Philadelphia Section) in 1976, the Pauling Medal (Puget Sound and Oregon sections) in 1976, the Southwest Regional Award in 1977, and the Kirkwood Medal (New Haven Section and Yale University) in 1978. He also received the Centenary Medal of the Chemical Society of London in 1974 and the Dwyer Medal of the University of South Wales in 1966. He was elected a member of the American Academy of Arts and Sciences in 1962 and of the National Academy of Sciences in 1967. He became a foreign member of the Royal Danish Academy of Sciences and Letters in 1975 and an honorary life member of the New York Academy of Sciences in 1977.

Cotton wrote *Advanced Inorganic Chemistry*, with G. Wilkinson (1962; 2d ed. 1966; 3d ed. 1972); *Chemical Applications of Group Theory* (1963; 2d ed. 1971); a high school–junior college text, *Chemistry: An Investigative Approach*, with L. Lynch (1968; 2d ed. 1973); and *Basic Inorganic Chemistry*, with Wilkinson (1976). The first of these books was translated into eight foreign languages, and the second into four. Cotton founded the annual series *Progress in Inorganic Chemistry* and edited the first 10 volumes, and he edited *Inorganic Syntheses*, vol. 13 (1970), and *Dynamic Nuclear Magnetic Resonance Spectroscopy*, with L. Jackman (1975). His published research papers and technical reviews numbered over 570.

For background information *see*

COORDINATION CHEMISTRY; MOLECULAR STRUCTURE AND SPECTRA; ORGANOMETALLIC COMPOUND; X-RAY CRYSTALLOGRAPHY in the McGraw-Hill Encyclopedia of Science and Technology. ∎

COTTRELL, ALAN HOWARD
★ British metallurgist and physicist

***Born** July 17, 1919, Birmingham, England*

When an opportunity to do basic research came at the end of World War II, Cottrell chose to work on the subject of dislocations in crystals. At that time the idea that metals might owe their strength and ductility to dislocations was already more than 10 years old, but it was still undeveloped and highly speculative, partly because no one then was able to see dislocations in crystals and partly because the mechanical properties of metals seemed too complex to unravel. At about that time N. F. Mott and F. R. N. Nabarro began to tackle the dislocation theory of mechanical properties, and they advanced some important ideas about the influence on the dislocation of foreign atoms situated in fixed positions in crystals. Cottrell then asked the question: what additional effects would appear when these atoms were allowed to move about by solid-state diffusion processes in dislocated crystals? *See* MOTT, SIR NEVILL (FRANCIS).

Cottrell quickly came to the conclusion that under certain circumstances these at-

oms would segregate to the dislocations and would there pin them down, thereby suppressing the ability of the material to deform plastically; and furthermore that this property of plasticity would be restored suddenly, through an avalanche of plastic yielding, if the material were subjected to applied forces strong enough to jerk the dislocations away from their segregated atoms. Mild steel was known to behave just like this, its plasticity being suppressed by aging and restored by overstressing. The possibility that this behavior might be due to pinning of dislocations was greatly strengthened by experimental demonstrations that small numbers of carbon and nitrogen atoms in the metal are in fact responsible for the behavior and that their diffusion kinetics are consistent with the idea that the aging occurs by their migration to dislocations. Cottrell was in this way led to develop, in association with B. A. Bilby, a theory of the yielding and aging of steel. This theory was later elaborated and modified to take account of effects of grain boundaries in polycrystalline metal, of R. E. Peierls and Nabarro's ideas about the natural resistance to motion of dislocations at low temperatures, and of the fact that in fully strain-aged metals the dislocations are often too strongly pinned by foreign atoms to be directly releasable by externally applied forces. *See* PEIERLS, SIR RUDOLF (ERNST).

Cottrell's interest in mobile atoms in crystals led him in 1954 to turn to problems of nuclear radiation damage in solids, which were then becoming important with the development of atomic power. Outstanding among these were the problems of the distortion of uranium fuel rods in nuclear reactors. With R. S. Barnes and A. T. Churchman, Cottrell showed that noble gases can expand into bubbles by capturing lattice vacancies from grain boundaries and that this swelling will be reduced if the bubbles are created in a finely dispersed form, by causing them to nucleate on large numbers of fine alloy precipitates. Cottrell also became interested in the effect of crystal distortion upon the mechanical properties of polycrystalline uranium, and he showed that it produces a special type of viscous flow, called irradiation creep, in the solid metal. This was confirmed experimentally, and metal fuel rods in the British power reactors were redesigned accordingly.

Other interests at that time were radiation damage in graphite and radiation embrittlement of steel. The second of these led Cottrell to consider the fracture of metals from the point of view of dislocation theory. C. Zener, Mott, and A. N. Stroh had already shown how avalanches of dislocations, released by the yield process, can nucleate cleavage cracks in steel at low temperatures. Cottrell and N. J. Petch then independently continued this theory to include the effect of grain size on the ductility of steel. The ductile fracture of metals was shown to be purely a process of plastic deformation. In association with Bilby and K. T. Swinden, Cottrell developed a theory which reconciled the brittleness of thick steel pieces with the ductility of thin pieces, based on the spreading of dislocations into the region ahead of a crack. Later, working with A. Kelly, Cottrell used the analogy between dislocations and cracks to give a description of the atomic structures at the tips of cracks, thereby attempting to explain the basic differences in mechanical properties of various types of crystalline materials, such as diamond, rock salt, gold, and iron. He also considered how brittle nonmetallic solids might be made resistant to fracture by forming them into fiber bundles bonded by plastics or metals.

Cottrell received his B.Sc. in 1939 and his Ph.D. in 1942 from the University of Birmingham. During World War II he was concerned with metallurgical problems, mainly of armor plate. After the war he worked, first as a lecturer and later as professor of physical metallurgy, in the University of Birmingham. In 1955 he moved to the Atomic Energy Research Establishment, Harwell, and in 1958 was appointed Goldsmiths' Professor of Metallurgy at the University of Cambridge, a chair which he held until 1965. He then became chief adviser (studies) to the Secretary of State for Defense. In 1971 he became chief scientific adviser to the British government, resigning in 1974 to become master of Jesus College, Cambridge. He served as vice-chancellor of Cambridge in 1977–79. Cottrell was elected a fellow of the Royal Society of London in 1955 and a foreign member of the American Academy of Arts and Sciences in 1960.

Cottrell wrote *Theoretical Structural Metallurgy* (1948; 2d ed. 1955), *Dislocations and Plastic Flow in Crystals* (1953), *Theory of Crystal Dislocations* (1963; paper 1964), *The Mechanical Properties of Matter* (1964), *An Introduction to Metallurgy* (1967), *Portrait of Nature* (1975), and *Environmental Economics* (1978).

For background information *see* CRYSTAL DEFECTS; METAL, MECHANICAL PROPERTIES OF; RADIATION DAMAGE TO MATERIALS in the McGraw-Hill Encyclopedia of Science and Technology. ∎

COUCH, JOHN NATHANIEL
★ American botanist

Born Oct. 12, 1896, Prince Edward County, VA, U.S.A.

Couch's work is characterized by diversity, which is often the case with a teacher as compared with a full-time research worker, but the main emphasis is on the fungi in their relationship to insects. His first notable contribution was the discovery of bisexual strains in the water mold *Dictyuchus*, which led to the discovery of similar strains in *Achlya* by Coker and A. B. Couch, the subsequent demonstration by J. R. Raper of the hormonal control of sex in *Achlya*, and later the similar demonstration in *Dictyuchus* by Sherwood. *See* RAPER, JOHN ROBERT.

During the summer of 1926 spent in the rainforests of Jamaica, Couch became interested in *Septobasidium*, a fungal genus found on living trees and always associated with scale insects, with resultant damage or even death of the tree. When he started his work on the biology of this genus, two theories had been offered to explain the relationship between fungus and scale insects: that the fungus lives on the excretions of the scale insects, or that the fungus parasitizes and wipes out whole colonies of insects. Couch found that the fungus and scale insects live symbiotically at the expense of the host plant, a perennial relationship depending only upon the life of the tree. The fungus constructs minute "houses" in which the scale insects, protected from their enemies, suck the juices of the host plant, grow, and finally reproduce their young in vast numbers. These young may settle down beneath the same fungus under which they were born and repeat the cycle, or crawl to other fungus-insect colonies, or crawl out and settle down on the clean bark, thereby disseminating the fungus.

In return for a home and protection, a number of the scale insects are parasitized by the fungus. Such insects live longer than the healthy ones but never reproduce. It is from the parasitized insects that the fungus gets its nourishment. The spore-forming period of the fungus reaches its peak in mid-April and dwindles to nothing by the first of June; consequently, the greater number of parasitized insects will be found during late spring and summer, while the reverse is true in fall and winter when no spores are formed. The fungus spore enters the circulatory system of the crawling nymphs and develops slowly in the hemocoele, establishing connection with the parent fungus only after the insect has molted for the last time. Such parasitized insects are finally killed and used up by the fungus. Through this partnership a compound type of organism is formed comparable with lichens but more complex in that a third organism, the living tree, is necessary. Several species of this genus cause damage to economic plants. Couch found that the disease may be controlled by spraying with a combination fungicide and insecticide in mid-spring, when the fungus is sporulating and the first nymphs are crawling.

During World War II mosquito larvae whose coeloms were filled with brown oval bodies were collected from around military camps in southern Georgia and sent to Couch for identification of the "parasites." These turned out to be the resting sporangia of the genus *Coelomomyces*, which belongs in the Blastocladiales. From the material sent him Couch described 11 new species, several of which parasitized and killed some of the most important mosquito species of the Southeast—the first record of this fungus in the Western Hemisphere. He realized that this fungus might be important in the biological control of mosquitoes if it (1) proved to be fatal to mosquitoes, (2) were harmless to other organisms, (3) could be grown in culture or in larvae in large quantities, and (4) produced reproductive bodies which could be dried and mixed with an appropriate carrier for wide dissemination. The first two postulates were satisfied, but attempts to grow *Coelomomyces* in culture have failed. The problem of growing the parasite in larvae has been to get infection. Successful infection experiments have been carried out by others but only by using soild and detritus from a location where infected larvae had been found, and no correlation between egg hatching and sporangial germination was recognized.

Couch and his coworkers found perfect material for study in the local water reservoir at the University of North Carolina: *C. punctatus* in the malarial mosquito, *Anopheles quadrimaculatus*. The mosquito was colonized in the insectary by C. J. Umphlett, and thus a steady supply of eggs and large quantities of infected larvae collected from University Lake were available for use in germination and infection experiments. Couch found that the sporangia would germinate after 48 hours, the same length of time it took for the eggs to hatch; thus there was a remarkable time correlation between sporangial germination and egg hatching. The highest rate of infection occurred when germinating sporangia and hatching eggs were put together in small beakers (150 milliliters) and 24 hours later transferred to large containers in the greenhouse, where such experimentation was carried out. In view of the experience of other workers with soil, experiments were conducted to find out if soil is necessary for infection. Soil from locations where parasitized larvae had been found usually gave a high rate of infection, but this was shown not to be essential.

Several sets of experiments were conducted to find out at what stage in the life of the mosquito infection occurs. Germinating sporangia were put with the first, second, third, and fourth instars, but only with the first did infection occur. To see if the sporangial inoculum could withstand prolonged drying, Couch mixed large numbers of sporangia with wet red clay, molded the clay into pieces the size of yeast cakes, and after drying for 3 months added a cake to a small pan of rainwater. Eggs were added at this time and at intervals of 48 hours for 2 weeks. Infected larvae were recovered from two such experiments.

While examining bits of boiled grass leaves used as bait for aquatic fungi in soil samples from the Philippine Islands, Couch observed sporangia formed on very delicate mycelia with spores arranged in coils. He first suspected a small chytrid, but studies showed that it was an undescribed type of actinomycete with sporangia in which there were motile spores, and hence it was given the name *Actinoplanes*, the actinomycete with planospores. Later studies on the structure and behavior of the spores, the structure and division of the chromatinic bodies, and the chemistry of the cell walls reinforced this conclusion. Isolations from soil samples from many parts of the world showed that these organisms are worldwide in distribution, occuring in practically all soils which contain humus. The greater number of these organisms prefer cellulose or other plant materials, but some were isolated on hair, bits of horn and hoof, and snake skin. The 2000 isolates, most of them incompletely studied, fall into five generic groups based on spore shape and structure and many other characters. Two genera were subsequently added by other workers. The precise role of these organisms in the soil is not known, but they probably assist in the formation of humus. All of the isolates were tested by a pharmaceutical company for possible use as drugs, and a few show promise in the formation of cortisone and antibiotics.

The son of a Baptist minister, Couch attended Trinity College (now Duke University) and earned his A.B. (1919), M.A. (1922), and Ph.D. in botany (1924) from the University of North Carolina. After service in France during World War I, he returned as instructor of botany at the university, where he subsequently became Kenan Professor in 1944 and was head of the department during 1943–59. He acted as consultant for various phases of the National Science Foundation programs in Washington, DC, India, and Japan. Elected to the National Academy of Sciences in 1943, he received a Merit Award of the Botanical Society of America in 1956.

Couch wrote *Gasteromycetes of the Eastern United States and Canada,* with W. C. Coker (1928), and *The Genus Septobasidium* (1938).

For background information *see* ACTINOPLANACEAE; ECOLOGICAL INTERACTIONS; FUNGI; SOIL MICROORGANISMS in the McGraw-Hill Encyclopedia of Science and Technology. ∎

COULSON, CHARLES ALFRED
★ British mathematician and theoretical chemist

Born *Dec. 13, 1910, Dudley, Worcestershire, England*
Died *Jan. 7, 1974, Oxford, England*

Coulson's scientific work was a good illustration of the way in which during the 20th century many branches of science came so close together that they almost merged. He took degree examinations at Cambridge, first in mathematics and then in physics, ending with a Ph.D. in chemistry. The award of a prize fellowship at Trinity College, Cambridge, in 1934 gave him 4 years of complete freedom to do what he wanted; he worked as an experimental bacteriologist to get experience in a kind of scientific inquiry different from the physical sciences.

This overlapping of interests was shown in most of Coulson's scientific work. His best-known studies were in molecular structure, where he was the first person to make calculations of the energy levels of a polyatomic molecule. In 1926 E. Schrödinger's introduction of the wave equation had shown the lines on which this was to be done, as well as the likelihood that chemistry was to become more and more a part of physics. But in 1933 when Coulson set out to calculate the stability of the simplest of all polyatomic molecules, H_3^+, and one of the commonest, methane, CH_4, he found that he had to utilize considerable mathematical techniques even to evaluate some of the necessary integrals.

A similar overlap could be traced in Coulson's work on chemical bonds of fractional order. Ever since the 1860s chemists had talked about single, double, and triple bonds between a pair of atoms. They used the standard symbols, —, ═, and ≡ (for example, H—H, O═O, N≡N for H_2, O_2, N_2). But in many of the most interesting molecules in organic chemistry it was becoming clear, from study of their lengths, that a large number of chemical bonds could not be described in this simple way. Linus Pauling had proposed a certain double-bond character for bonds that were stronger than single but less strong than double bonds. In 1937 Coulson generalized this within the approximation known as the method of molecular orbitals (to which indeed he made many contributions), and was able to define a fractional bond order for bonds intermediate between the integral values. This fractional bond order could be calculated, and properties of the bond and of the molecule as a whole would follow. *See* PAULING, LINUS CARL.

The idea of fractional bonds rationalized a lot of chemical structure and of chemical reactivity. Coulson himself was able to show that an old theory of partial valence due to J. Thiele could be put on a firm basis, and he introduced the idea of free valence.

Some of the most interesting general rules for the electrons in these organic molecules (the pi electrons, as they came to be called) could be found by using the theory of contour integration in a complex plane, thus uniting chemistry and mathematics. Together with his research student G. S. Rushbrooke, Coulson showed that large planar organic molecules can be divided into two main groups with widely differing chemical properties. The first group (for example, benzene and

naphthalene) were called alternants, since the atoms can be divided into two groups, so that no member of one group is adjacent to another member of the same group. The second group of molecules were called nonalternants (for example, azulene). In the ground states of alternant hydrocarbons the charges on all the atoms are equal.

In 1945–50 Coulson and another research student, H. C. Longuet-Higgins, wrote down very general rules showing the changes that will take place all over a molecule if a small change is made in one part of it. Thus the effect of replacing a CH group by a N atom, as in passing from benzene to pyridine, can be predicted easily by the aid of certain polarizability coefficients. The charges on the atoms and the orders of the bonds form a matrix whose behavior is crucial for the full description of a molecule. *See* LONGUET-HIGGINS, HUGH CHRISTOPHER.

It was natural that Coulson's interests should lead him into biochemistry. Together with A. Pullman and B. Pullman and R. Daudel, he started the molecular-orbital discussion of a family of organic molecules that cause tumors (carcinogenic molecules). He later became interested in the theory of drugs, and in the hydrogen-bond forces that hold together the two strands of a deoxyribonucleic acid (DNA) chain or the alpha helix of a polypeptide. In addition, he was one of the best-known writers and speakers on the relation between science and religion.

Coulson spent the years of World War II at Queens College, Dundee, lecturing in mathematics, physics, and chemistry. In 1945 he went to Oxford as the first Imperial Chemical Industries fellow in chemistry, and concurrently as lecturer in mathematics at University College. In 1947 he became Wheatstone Professor of Theoretical Physics at Kings College, London, and in 1952 Rouse Ball Professor of Mathematics at Oxford University and a fellow of Wadham College. He became a fellow of the Royal Society in 1951 and was awarded the Davy Medal of the society in 1970.

Coulson published over 300 scientific papers and the books *Waves* (6th ed. 1955; 8th ed., revised by A. Jeffrey, 1977), *Electricity* (3d rev. ed. 1956), *Valence* (1952; 2d ed. 1961), a *Dictionary of π-Electron Calculations,* with A. Streitwiesser, Jr. (1965), and *The Shape and Structure of Molecules* (1973).

For background information *see* CHEMICAL BINDING; MOLECULAR STRUCTURE AND SPECTRA; VALENCE in the McGraw-Hill Encyclopedia of Science and Technology. ∎

COURANT, RICHARD
★ American mathematician

Born *Jan. 8, 1888, Lublinitz, Germany*
Died *Jan. 27, 1972, New Rochelle, NY, U.S.A.*

From his student days in D. Hilbert's circle in Göttingen, Courant considered mathematics in the context of general scientific endeavor. His doctoral thesis was concerned with the calculus of variations, a subject that aims at determining functions for which given functional expressions attain maximal or minimal or, generally speaking, stationary values. Such variational problems are easily reduced to boundary-value problems for differential equations, but the solution of these equations can present serious difficulties. The foremost instances are the problem of minimal surfaces (to find a surface of least area spanning a prescribed curve in space) and the boundary-value problem of potential theory.

K. F. Gauss and others in the early 19th century tried to dismiss these difficulties with the observation that the problems are equivalent to that of finding the minimum of positive "energy" expressions and that, therefore, the existence of a minimum and hence of the desired solution appears self-evident. This direct procedure, named Dirichlet's principle, served as the fundament on which Bernard Riemann built his geometric theory of functions of a complex variable, one of the central and exciting mathematical achievements of the 19th century. Riemann died before Weierstrass's devastating criticism of the reasoning in Dirichlet's principle became generally known; saving Riemann's theory became a major challenge and stimulus in mathematical analysis. Success was not achieved until 50 years later by Hilbert. His proof of the possibility of a "direct" solution of such variational problems initiated a long and, even now incomplete development of a deep theoretical character, affecting many applications, including numerical methods.

Courant's doctoral dissertation (1910) under Hilbert's sponsorship simplified and modified Hilbert's approach and applied the principle to fundamental problems of geometric function theory; it established general theorems concerning conformal mapping of multiply connected Riemann surfaces of higher genus. Subsequent publications aimed at simplification and extension of Hilbert's theory of Dirichlet's principle; problems of conformal mapping were pursued with a view toward characterizing simple types of "normal" domains on which Riemann domains could be mapped conformally. Other publications emphasizing the viewpoints of variational calculus dealt with aspects of partial differential equations of physics.

Another series of Courant's publications originated from a famous problem of mathematical physics posed by H. A. Lorentz: Vibrating continua, such as a membrane, a plate, or a body of enclosed gas, possess an infinite sequence of eigenfrequencies corresponding to the fundamental tone and the succession of overtones of acoustical systems. For many key questions in physics it is important that approximately or asymptotically (that is, for large frequencies) the distribution of these frequencies depends, for homogeneous media, only on the volume of the vibrating continuous system and not on its shape in detail and that similar facts are true of nonhomogeneous media. The first proof was given by Herman Weyl; soon afterward, Courant disposed of the problem and its ramification by a simple variational method based on the observation that the eigenfrequencies can be defined as successive maximinima of variational problems,

the fundamental frequency being the first. Many other applications of this maximinimum principle were later given by Courant and others.

Yet another of Courant's publications treated the transition by limiting processes from finite difference equations to differential equations. The last of these, written in close collaboration with K. O. Friedrichs and Hans Lewy, though theoretical in its intention, subsequently had a considerable influence on the development of practical numerical methods for the solution of partial differential equations. It showed that in problems of wave propagation and the like the mesh width used for numerical calculations must be subjected to simple restrictions in order to secure convergence or stability. The connection between partial differential equations and "random walk" or stochastic processes also was discussed in this paper.

Other publications dealt with constructive, numerically applicable methods for solving differential equations of physics. Among publications of a later period were a series of papers on minimal surfaces which Courant solved on the basis of Dirichlet's principle; on Plateau's problems of minimal surfaces in given contours; and on the more general problems of J. Douglas, who had led the successful attack on these fascinating classical problems.

Courant was interested in furthering the publication of advanced mathematical textbooks in order to facilitate access to relevant developments in mathematical sciences. He founded a series of such books with the help of his friend Ferdinand Springer, the publisher. This series, continued after Courant's resignation as editor, contains almost 140 volumes.

Courant believed that scientific progress should be presented not merely in specialized papers but also in self-sufficient textbooks and monographs. In several of his works he combined the attitude of research with that of a wider expository scope. An elementary work on calculus, *Differential and Integral Calculus* (2 vols., 1936–37), emphasized the connection of calculus with applications. *What Is Mathematics?*, with H. Robbins (1941), aimed at a not necessarily professional public. With Friedrichs, Courant published *Supersonic Flow and Shock Waves* (1948), the result of research activities during World War II. *Dirichlet's Principle, Conformal Mapping*

and Minimal Surfaces appeared in 1950. The most important of Courant's books is *Methods of Mathematical Physics* (2 vols.; English transl. 1953, 1962), partly rooted in Hilbert's tradition. It appeared in time to be helpful to the evolution of quantum mechanics, mainly within the closely knit circle of young physicists who worked in Göttingen in the 1920s. The second volume, published a decade later in the United States, contained a last chapter written with the cooperation of Friedrichs and stimulated the field of partial differential equations. Most of Courant's books have been translated into various languages.

Courant received his secondary education, largely in the classics, at a gymnasium in Breslau. He studied physics, mathematics, and philosophy briefly in Breslau and Zurich, then under Hilbert in Göttingen, where he received his doctor's degree in 1910. He then became assistant and privatdozent. His scientific development was impeded first by economic hardships, then by military service in the Prussian army, and soon afterward by service in World War I for more than 4 years. After a year in combat he was wounded, and subsequently worked on the development—technical, organizational, and educational—of wireless communications for use in the front lines. This activity brought him into contact with modern electronics in its early stages.

After his discharge from the army in 1918 and a short interlude as a politician, Courant was called in 1919 to the University of Münster as a professor of mathematics, and he returned to Göttingen in 1920 as successor of Felix Klein to develop a center of mathematical sciences. The decisive support of his friends Niels and Harald Bohr and the Rockefeller Foundation and an enlightened Prussian minister of education led to the establishment of the Mathematics Institute and the strengthening of physics and other sciences in Göttingen. In 1933 the National Socialist government moved against Göttingen University, a center of independent liberal tradition. Courant left along with Max Born, James Franck, Emmy Noether, and others. In 1934, after an academic year as a visitor at Cambridge University, he joined the faculty of New York University on the suggestion of Abraham Flexner and helped develop graduate work. Together with K. O.

Friedrichs and with J. J. Stoker, Courant made a systematic attempt at supplementing the more theoretical traditional pursuit of mathematics by drawing applied mathematicians into the program. After a few years of struggle the group at New York University became the nucleus of an increasingly intense effort organized by the Office of Scientific Research and Development (OSRD) under Warren Weaver, and it played a significant role in research arising in the technological war effort. Courant was involved as a member and consultant of the Applied Mathematics Panel of OSRD. *See* BOHR, NIELS HENRIK DAVID; BORN, MAX; FRANCK, JAMES; STOKER, JAMES JOHNSTON.

After the war the NYU group developed into a more stable, largely government-supported Institute of Mathematical Sciences with Courant as director. Supported by the Atomic Energy Commission, one of the first big electronic computers was installed in the institute. A grant by the Alfred P. Sloan Foundation and supplementary grants by the Ford Foundation and the National Science Foundation gave the institute a home (1965), the magnificent Warren Weaver Hall, with excellent facilities for the large staff and more than 500 graduate students, as well as for numerous visitors from many parts of the world. The institute was named after Courant. After his retirement as director and head of department, Courant served on the governing board of the institute, as science adviser of the university, and as scientific consultant to government agencies and primarily to the International Business Machines Corporation.

Courant was elected to the National Academy of Sciences, the American Philosophical Society, the Accademia dei Lincei in Rome, the royal academies of the Netherlands and Denmark, the Academy in Göttingen, and the Academy of Sciences of the Soviet Union. Besides several honorary degrees, he received the Navy Distinguished Public Service Award (1958), the Knight-Commander's Cross and Star of the Order of Merit of the Federal Republic of Germany (1958), and the Award for Distinguished Service to Mathematics from the Mathematical Association of America (1965).

For background information *see* CALCULUS OF VARIATIONS; GROUP THEORY; INTEGRAL TRANSFORM; VIBRATION in the McGraw-Hill Encyclopedia of Science and Technology. ∎

COURNAND, ANDRÉ FREDERIC
★ American physician

Born Sept. 24, 1895, Paris, France

In a fruitful collaboration with Dickinson W. Richards extending over 35 years, Cournand developed a methodology and a body of knowledge basically related to the understanding of cardiocirculatory and pulmonary functions in both normal and diseased human beings. An essential feature of his work involved the safe use, in clinical investigation, of the technique of cardiac catheterization first applied in a human (that is, on himself) by the German surgeon Werner Forssmann in 1929. In 1956 Cournand shared the Nobel Prize in medicine or physiology with Forssmann and Richards for the many contributions in cardiac and pulmonary physiology and pathophysiology derived from this technique. *See* FORSSMANN, WERNER THEODOR OTTO; RICHARDS, DICKINSON WOODRUFF.

In his earliest clinical investigations Cournand studied systematically with new techniques the three main functions of the lungs: ventilation, distribution, and diffusion of respiratory gases. By adding to these techniques catheterization of the right atrium, ventricle, and pulmonary artery in 1941, he made available a complete picture of the transport of respiratory gases between the surrounding atmosphere and the body tissues. With adequate methods and newly devised instrumentation, the output of the heart pump, the blood pressures within its various chambers, and the large vessels issuing from them could be measured accurately.

In the first clinical cardiopulmonary laboratory organized as a result of these developments, Cournand, Richards, and many collaborators trained by them embarked, during World War II, upon a study of the various forms of clinical shock and demonstrated its essential features, namely, a fall in cardiac output, associated with a decreased venous return, and a variable vasomotor response depending on the nature and the extent of circulating fluid lost. More importantly, they proved that in traumatic shock blood replacement is preferable to infusion of plasma. After the war they investigated all forms of cardiac diseases. In congential heart lesions, by directing the catheter through the abnormal pathways and by multiple samplings of blood and pressure recordings, they greatly improved the accuracy of diagnoses of the anatomic defects, the evaluation of their physiological effects, and the success of surgical correction. In acquired heart diseases, various hemodynamic patterns, including cardiac failure, were defined during their evolution; the role of the heart muscle function in valvular lesions and in constrictive pericarditis was evaluated; and the effects of various drugs, in particular digitalis glycosides, were accurately assessed. Among these contributions in cardiology stands out the analysis of the effects of pulmonary disease upon the cardiac function and the pulmonary circulation, which led to physiological methods of prevention and of treatment of pulmonary heart disease.

Maintaining his early interest in pulmonary physiopathology, Cournand studied the effects of pneumonectomy upon the function of the remaining lung and proposed a physiological classification of chronic obstructive diseases of the lungs. He then investigated the problem of conjunction of air and blood in the lungs in a variety of lung diseases by evaluating the alveolar ventilation-perfusion relationships and the diffusion of respiratory gases across the alveolocapillary membrane. Thus he was led to an inquiry into the factors controlling the pulmonary circulation, which resulted in the description of the pressure-flow relationships in pulmonary vessels and the demonstration of their vasomotor controls and of the distribution of that perfusion of the lungs by the local concentration of oxygen in the alveoli.

Cournand received his bachelor's degree in 1913 and in 1914 his diploma in physics, chemistry, and biology from the Sorbonne. After serving in the French army during World War I, he returned to his medical studies, becoming *Interne des Hôpitaux* de Paris in 1925. He was awarded his medical degree in 1930. Cournand then went to the United States and secured a residency in the Tuberculosis Service of the Columbia University Division at Bellevue Hospital in New York, later becoming a visiting physician in this service. From an instructorship, in 1934, at Columbia University College of Physicians and Surgeons, he eventually rose to full professor in 1951. In 1941 Cournand became a naturalized citizen of the United States. He was elected to membership in the National Academy of Sciences in 1958.

For background information *see* CARDIOVASCULAR SYSTEM (VERTEBRATE); HEART (VERTEBRATE) in the McGraw-Hill Encyclopedia of Science and Technology. ∎

COURRIER, ROBERT
★ French endrocrinologist

Born Oct. 6, 1895, Saxon-Sion, Meurthe-et-Moselle, France

Courrier worked chiefly on two subjects: the thyroid and the sex hormones. At the start of his research career (1922–24), he noted that animals that receive large doses of thyroid extract exhibit a thyroid gland that is at rest from the secretory viewpoint. It seemed to him that an equilibrium exists between the activity of the gland and the quantity of its hormone present in the blood, so that if the hormone is administered in excess, the corresponding gland no longer functions. Courrier verified this fact later, with Frédéric Joliot-Curie, by means of radioactivity: the injection of thyroxin opposes the penetration of radioactive iodine into the thyroid, and without iodine the activity of the thyroid stops. Courrier, together with J. Roche, again found this phenomenon by the use of a new thyroid hormone, triiodothyronine.

It is now known that the pituitary gland plays an important role in these endocrine equilibria. Courrier observed, with Joliet-Curie and A. Horeau, that thyroxin, labeled with radioactive iodine, concentrates itself exactly in the pituitary in a selective manner. D. Bovet undertook the study of a new antithyroid, aminothiazole; with Bovet, Joliot-Curie, and Horeau, Courrier confirmed that this antithyroid does not oppose the penetration of iodine into the thyroid, but prevents the synthesis of the iodinated hormone. *See* BOVET, DANIEL.

The scientific activity of Courrier was devoted principally to the field of the sex hormones. He studied the testicle and the ovary. He adduced arguments in favor of the theory of his teacher P. Bouin, who, with his friend P. Ancel, defended the idea that the male hormone is produced, not by the seminiferous tubes, but by the interstitial gland situated between these tubes. Indeed, in certain hibernating mammals the seminiferous tubes can be completely at rest, while the interstitial gland is obviously active; in this case the male hormone is liberated in quantity, as demonstrated by the development of the secondary sexual characteristics. By long treatment of rats with gonadotropic hormones, a collaborator of Courrier, M. Rivière, determined that a tumor of the interstitial gland develops. Courrier studied this tumor with Rivière and R. Colonge; it is easily transplanted from one rat to another and is composed uniquely of interstitial cells. It secretes androgens in abundance, as can be confirmed by grafting it to castrated males.

Courrier took an important part in the first researches on female hormones. He showed that in the guinea pig characteristic modifications appear in the genital apparatus when the first follicles ripen in the ovary. He found in human females the follicular hormone that E. Allen and E. A. Doisy discovered in the sow. He showed the presence of this hormone in human amniotic fluid, and he observed that it can traverse the placenta and the mammary gland and strongly affect the fetus and the newborn (genital crisis). He adduced arguments in favor of the existence of two ovarian hormones at a time when unicism was defended by eminent specialists. He studied the functional relationships that link the two hormones of the ovary (antagonism and synergism). *See* DOISY, EDWARD ADELBERT.

Courrier carried out a detailed analysis of the endocrinology of gestation in an important book published in 1945. In this book is found his unexpected experience wiht experimental extrauterine pregnancy, which normally evolves in the castrated female rabbit, while the removal of the ovaries always involves the interruption of normal uterine pregnancy in this species. When the fetus is in the uterus, the hormones are essential in order to permit this organ to develop and to follow the fetal expansion; but the extrauterine fetus is free of uterine constraint. The uterus is nevertheless indispensable because the fetus can leave from it.

It was in Courrier's laboratory that his collaborators Horeau and J. Jacques carried out the synthesis of a new artificial estrogen derived from an acid named allenolic in honor of E. Allen. Courrier carried out a detailed physiological study on it. He also studied, with his student A. Jost, the first artificial progestive, pregneninolone, synthesized by German chemists. This substance is as progestive as the progesterone of the corpus luteum, but is more androgenic than the latter; this property resulted in adverse effects when the product was utilized in pregnant women, since it traversed the placenta and partially masculinized female fetuses.

Courrier studied science at the University of Nancy and Strasbourg *(Agrégé des facultés de médecine, Docteur ès sciences)*. He was professor of medicine at the University of Algiers during 1926–38 and at the Collège de France during 1938–67. He was one of the members of the Centre National de la Recherche Scientifique from 1957 to 1962 and was awarded the Centre's Gold Medal in 1964. He was elected to the French Academy of Sciences in 1944 and, as a foreign member, to the Royal Society of London in 1953 and the American Academy of Arts and Sciences in 1956.

For background information *see* AN-DROGEN; ENDOCRINE MECHANISMS; ESTROGEN; THYROID GLAND (VERTEBRATE) in the McGraw-Hill Encyclopedia of Science and Technology. ∎

COWAN, GEORGE ARTHUR
★ American radiochemist

Born Feb. 15, 1920, Worcester, MA, U.S.A.

Cowan became best known for his leadership of a group of scientists at Los Alamos which pioneered in the design of experiments that used the intense neutron fluxes generated by nuclear explosions to attack some fundamental problems in nuclear physics and chemistry. This work was recognized by the U.S. Atomic Energy Commission in 1965, when he was selected for an E. O. Lawrence Memorial Award.

In 1932, when James Chadwick first discovered the neutron—a particle with the mass of a proton but zero charge—an exciting era began in nuclear science. The discovery that neutrons induce fission in uranium led in 1942 to the construction of the first fission reactor at Stagg Field in Chicago and, in 1945, to the development of fission weapons. *See* CHADWICK, SIR JAMES.

The deliberate use of neutrons from nuclear explosions for scientific research was first proposed by Cowan in 1955. An initial unique application was in neutron spectroscopy time-of-flight experiments designed to study the fission process in uranium. A sharp pulse of neutrons of mixed energy is produced by an atomic explosion. If these neutrons are transmitted along a pipe, the most energetic arrive first, and the least energetic last. Experiments are performed with monoenergetic neutrons made in this way over the short period of time during which the stretched-out pulse arrives at the end of the pipe.

A phenomenon associated with the high-density neutron gas produced by nuclear explosions is the capture of many neutrons by a single nucleus to make new isotopes. When the target material is as heavy as thorium or uranium, transplutonic elements result. A process of this kind is believed to occur in nature when certain kinds of stars collapse and then explode, creating supernovae which contain a hot neutron gas in their interiors. A similar neutron environment exists in thermonuclear explosions. In the first successful test of such a device, the "Mike" event at the Eniwetok Atoll in 1952, 14 new heavy isotopes were found. The discoveries included two new elements that were named einsteinium and fermium. Starting in 1958, experiments were carried out which led to production of even heavier isotopes by neutron capture. In 1964 the isotope ^{257}Fm was made in this way; it was the heaviest nucleus identified to that time.

The search for new superheavy elements is continuing although the emphasis on production techniques has shifted from neutron capture to heavy-ion reactions. Theoretical models predict that an island of increased nuclear stability exists in the neighborhood of mass 310 and proton number 126 (about 20 elements beyond what is presently known). A number of experimental observations have been made which suggest the existence of such elements in nature, but none has been positively identified. If the existence of superheavy elements in nature is confirmed, new impetus will be given to efforts to reach the elusive island by multiple neutron capture.

Cowan's group also developed relatively inexpensive mass production techniques for the separation of the stable isotopes of carbon, nitrogen, and oxygen which led to a number of innovative uses in the enviromental, agricultural, chemical, and life sciences. An interesting environmental application made possible by inexpensive separated stable isotopes is the synthesis of a form of methane (CH_4) which does not exist to a measurable extent in nature. The synthetic methane is made with heavy carbon (^{13}C) and deuterium (^{2}H) and has a mass of 21 compared with a mass of 16 for the natural variety. Although methane exists in the atmosphere to the extent of 1 to 2 parts per million, modern analytical techniques for distinguishing the mass 21 variety in the presence of 10^{10} to 10^{11} times as much of the mass 16 variety make it possible to tag masses of air with heavy methane and follow their movement over distances of thousands of kilometers. The only alternative way to do this kind of experiment over such long ranges is with radioactive additives at levels which are not considered environmentally acceptable.

Beginning in 1973, Cowan participated in a study of the natural fission reactor discovered in the early 1970s by French scientists in the Republic of Gabon in Africa. The event is commonly referred to as the Oklo phenomenon, after the name of the rich open-pit uranium mine in which it was found. Because the fossil remains of this reactor, including several tons of fission products, have survived almost undisturbed for 2×10^9 years since it ceased to operate, Oklo is of particular interest to scientists concerned with the storage of radioactive wastes generated by modern reactors. As a result of the Oklo studies, it became apparent that the remarkable immobility of many of the fission products was due principally to the extreme immobility of the uranium ore itself, which consists, within the reactor zones, of the mineral uraninite. This observation suggested that incorporation of radioactive reactor products in such a stable mineral matrix might serve as a safe and effective way to store them at a suitable geological site for the very long periods of time required to make them harmless.

Cowan majored in chemistry at Worcester Polytechnic Institute. Upon graduation in 1941, he went to Princeton University, where he became involved in early cyclotron investigations of possible atomic reactor designs. In 1942 he joined the Metallurgical Laboratory at the University of Chicago and contributed to the development of the first chain-reacting pile and the subsequent production of the atomic bomb. In 1946 he participated in Operation Crossroads, the first military tests of nuclear explosives at Bikini Atoll. He completed work for his Sc.D. in chemistry at the Carnegie Institute of

Technology in 1949 and joined the Los Alamos Scientific Laboratory, where he became leader of a division devoted largely to research in physical, inorganic and nuclear chemistry.

For background information *see* NEUTRON; RADIOISOTOPE PRODUCTION; TRANSURANIUM ELEMENTS in the McGraw-Hill Encyclopedia of Science and Technology. ∎

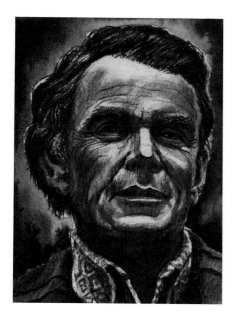

COX, ALLAN
★ American geophysicist and geologist

Born Dec. 17, 1926, Santa Ana, CA, U.S.A.

Cox studied the magnetic memory present in rocks. This memory preserves a record of the magnetic field that existed at the time the rocks were formed. By analyzing the paleomagnetism of rocks formed at different times, he was able to trace past changes of the Earth's magnetic field over very long perods of time.

In his best-known research, Cox, together with his colleagues R. Doell and G. Dalrymple at the U.S. Geological Survey, analyzed the paleomagnetism and radiometric ages of rocks which they had collected from different parts of the world and found that prior to 700,000 years ago the field had pointed south instead of north. Since the reversals were found to occur simultaneously everywhere, the polarity of the entire planetary field must have reversed. By 1966, they, together with I. McDougall, working in Australia, had established a radiometric polarity

time scale for the past 4,500,000 years and had concluded that polarity changes had occurred at an average rate of 5 reversals per million years. They found that the time intervals between successive reversals were highly variable in length, the shortest being less than 50,000 years and the longest greater than 1,000,000 years.

On investigating the statistical structure of these temporal changes, Cox found in 1968 that the timing of polarity reversals is random, and he proposed that the underlying physical process responsible for reversals is stochastic in nature. He pointed out that the timing of polarity reversals is essentially that of a Poisson process in which the probability that an event will occur in a given time increment is independent of the time that has elapsed since the previous event. On the basis of this model, he predicted that a fine structure of very short polarity intervals (less than 50,000 years) would be detected in the course of future refinements of the polarity time scale.

The time scale for magnetic reversals was used by marine geophysicists to explain the linear magnetic anomalies found ubiquitously over ocean basins. The anomalies are produced by bands of volcanic rock on the ocean floor magnetized alternately to the north and to the south and formed by the process of sea-floor spreading away from the mid-oceanic rifts. The radiometric reversal time scale of Cox and his colleagues was used to determine the rate of sea-floor spreading and the age of the ocean floor. The oceanic magnetic anomalies, in turn, provided long, continuous records of changes in the direction and intensity of the Earth's magnetic field. Analyzing these records with R. Blakely in 1972, Cox showed that additional short polarity intervals were present as predicted by the stochastic model for reversals. In subsequent investigations of the statistical structure of polarity changes, Cox and his colleagues Blakely and J. Phillips showed that reversals are generated by a stochastic renewal process of a type that suggests there are no long-term memory effects in the dynamo processes in the Earth's core which generate the Earth's magnetic field.

Cox also used paleomagnetism as a tool for working on other geological and geophysical problems: long-period geomagnetic secular variation, stratigraphic correlation, rotation of microplates along plate boundaries, and the causes of glaciations.

Son of a house painter, Cox attended high school in Santa Ana and then pursued his education through independent reading during 3 years in the merchant marine (1945–48), 3 years of undergraduate chemistry at the University of California at Berkeley (1948-51), and 2 more years of independent reading as a private in the U.S. Army (1951-53). The most important event in his education, and the one that converted him to geology as a career, was a summer job with the U.S. Geological Survey in 1950 as a field assistant to Clyde Wahrhaftig in the Alaska Range. Wahrhaftig had long been intrigued by rock glaciers—moving tongues of rock debris which occupy high valleys in the Alaska Range. Cox's imagination was challenged by these spectacular geomorphic features, and they became the subject of his first research. In a 1959 monograph Wahrhaftig and Cox concluded that the motion of rock glaciers is controlled by ice present in the pore space of the rock debris—that essentially they are dirty glaciers.

Cox received his B.A. (1955), M.A. (1957), and Ph.D. (1959) degrees from the University of California at Berkeley, where he was inspired by the teaching of John Verhoogen and Perry Byerly. From 1959 to 1967 he worked as a geophysicist with the U.S. Geological Survey. In 1968 he joined the faculty at Stanford University, where he was the Cecil and Ida Green Professor of Geophysics. He was elected to the National Academy of Sciences in 1969 and to the American Academy of Arts and Sciences in 1974. He became president of the American Geophysical Union in 1978. He received the Fleming Medal of the American Geophysical Union (1969), the Day Medal of the Geological Society of America (1975), and the Vetlesen Prize (1971). *See* BYERLY, PERRY; VERHOOGEN, JOHN.

For background information *see* GEOMAGNETISM; PALEOMAGNETICS in the McGraw Hill Encyclopedia of Science and Technology. ∎

CRAIG, LYMAN CREIGHTON
★ American biochemist

Born June 12, 1906, Palmyra, IA, U.S.A.
Died July 7, 1974, Glen Rock, NJ, U.S.A.

While carrying out structural studies on alkaloids of ergot, veratrine, and aconite during the 1930s at the Rockefeller Insti-

tute, Craig was impressed by the need for better techniques in separating, isolating, and characterizing pure, single substances. This led him to make the science and technology of separations a major goal in his career. The decision resulted in a long series of papers on micromethods for fractional crystallization, distillation, extraction, and dialysis. The first of these was important in the alkaloid studies, but the fractional extraction method became much more widely used in biochemistry. It included the design of a stepwise extraction train, which permitted up to 1000 simultaneous quantitative extractions to be made. This could be done in such a way that the result could be directly interpreted by the binomial theorem and the normal curve of error. The procedure was called countercurrent distribution, or simply CCD.

A number of techniques were developed to make CCD less tedious. Among them was a method for recovering fragile solutes from dilute solution, the now well-known method of rotary evaporation. The dialysis studies were begun also as a recovery method but soom developed into a major study, potentially as important as the extraction studies. CCD gained acceptance during World War II when it became the tool for documenting the purity of many new synthetic potential antimalarials. It was subsequently used for a similar purpose in the rapidly developing field of the antibiotics, which included the penicillins, bacitracins, polymyxins, tyrocidines, actinomycins, and so forth. It often resolved preparations considered to be pure by other criteria into several components. Many new antibiotics were isolated in pure form for the first time with the technique. CCD proved to be especially useful for separating and characterizing larger solutes which associate strongly, such as the tyrocidines. A method was developed, called the method of partial substitution, for determining the true molecular weight of this type of solute. The procedure, which was based on CCD, was applied to the hormone insulin, and clearly established its true molecular weight as being in the 6000 range, rather than 12,000. In other laboratories a number of hormones were isolated in pure form and characterized for the first time by CCD. These included adrenocorticotropic hormone (ACTH), melatonin, oxytocin, vasopressin, parathyroid hormone, angiotensin, and others. CCD proved to be the best technique for separating the individual transfer ribonucleic acids from the complex mixture of the many different amino acid specific forms.

Craig's interest, with his series of papers on dialysis, began as a modest attempt to improve simple laboratory dialysis. However, he soon realized that, with the appropriate physical arrangement and adjustment of the effective pore size, dialysis through cellophane membranes could be used as a tool of high discrimination for separations, studies of purity, conformation, association, binding, and so on. The approach, which stressed the thinnest film of solution reproducibly realizable against the largest possible membrane surface, included a thin-film countercurrent dialyzer.

Craig began his structural studies when he went to the Rockefeller Institute as an assistant of W. A. Jacobs in 1933. He worked on the chemistry of the alkaloids of ergot, substances which had not previously yielded to chemical investigation. Soon Jacobs and Craig reported the isolation of an unknown amino acid, which they named lysergic acid. Considerably later the dimethyl amide of this acid, now well known as LSD, was prepared at the Sandoz Laboratories in Switzerland and found to have intense psychic properties. During the next few years the major structural features of lysergic acid, as well as those of the alkaloids, were elucidated at Rockefeller Institute. The alkaloids of ergot proved to be cyclic polypeptides of unusual structure, and to be the first members of a much larger group of modified polypeptides elaborated by lower organisms. These included the penicillins, gramicidins, tyrocidines, polymyxins, bacitracins, and others. Craig and his collaborators revealed most of the structural features of the tyrocidines, polymyxins, and bacitracins. CCD played an important role in this work.

In studies with proteins, in collaboration with R. Hill, he found that the CCD method would clearly separate for the first time the two protein chains in hemoglobin in preparative amounts. This made possible a major structural study of hemoglobin. The entire amino acid sequences of the alpha and beta protein chains of human hemoglobin were established by a group of collaborators in Craig's laboratory. Subsequently, in collaboration with N. Hilschmann, he made the first breakthrough in sequence studies with Bence-Jones protein.

The son of a farmer who had served two terms in the Iowa state legislature, Craig, in taking up chemistry, was influenced by his older brother David, who became a well-known rubber chemist and editor of the *Journal of Rubber Chemistry*. Craig received his B.S. in 1928 and his Ph.D. in 1931 from Iowa State University. His original intention was to do research on organic insecticides and study their mechanism of action. He was awarded a postdoctoral National Research Council Fellowship to pursue these studies, and he spent 2 years (1931–33) at the Johns Hopkins University synthesizing analogs of nicotine. Appointed an assistant in the department of chemical pharmacology at the Rockefeller Institute in 1933, he became an associate in 1937, an associate member in 1945, and a member in 1949. He was with the Office of Scientific Research and Development in 1944. Craig received the Albert Lasker Award in Basic Science in 1963 for his work on the CCD method and the Fisher Award in Analytical Chemistry of the American Chemical Society in 1965. He was elected to the National Academy of Sciences in 1950 and became a member of the American Academy of Arts and Sciences in 1961.

For background information *see* DIALYSIS; EXTRACTION; HEMOGLOBIN; POISON in the McGraw-Hill Encyclopedia of Science and Technology. ∎

CRAM, DONALD JAMES
★ American organic chemist

Born Apr. 22, 1919, Chester, VT, U.S.A.

The subject common to Cram's broad research interests was the symmetry properties of organic compounds and their reaction intermediates. His earliest papers dealt with stereochemical evidence for the ethylene phenonium ion, the first of the many bridged carbonium ions discovered in the 1950s and 1960s as intermediates in a variety of carbonium ion molecular rearrangement reactions. In this research the relationships between the three-dimensional (stereochemical) structure of starting material and product were employed to infer the structure of short-lived but discrete reaction intermediates.

Although it was known for almost 100 years that carbanions (compounds containing negatively charged carbon) are one of the most important reaction intermediates in organic reactions, their stereochemical capabilities were not examined until 1955. At that time Cram and his students reported that substitution reactions in which carbanions are intermediates can proceed with either retention, inversion, or complete loss of configuration. After that time they studied the relationships between the stereochemistry of such reactions and the symmetry properties of the anion, the character of the counterion, the properties of the medium, and the mechanism of stabilization of the anion by substituents. Carbanions were discovered

which, although themselves symmetrical, were demonstrated to exist in environments that were asymmetric by virtue of asymmetric solvation or ion pairing. This work was complemented by the investigations of base-catalyzed proton or deuteron transfers in media which are potential deuteron or proton donors. The first intramolecular proton transfer in 1,3- and 1,5-allylic anion rearrangements was discovered, and the phenomenon was demonstrated to be general, performed by enzyme systems and simple basic catalysts alike. Intramolecular proton transfers from the front to the back face of planar carbanions were next observed, and the "conducted tour mechanism for proton conduction along negatively charged, conjugated pi-systems" was announced. This work anticipated 1,3- and 1,5-asymmetric induction during proton transfer reactions and demonstrated the detailed mechanism by which an asymmetric center can be destroyed at one site and generated at a distant site without loss of optical properties.

The early work of A. McKenzie in Great Britain and M. Tiffeneau in France had demonstrated that in conversions of ketones containing an adjacent asymmetric center to secondary or tertiary alcohols the order in which substituents are introduced into a given molecule controls which disastereomer predominates in the product. In 1952 Cram and his students published their celebrated rule of "steric control of asymmetric induction." This rule correlated the configurations of the predominant isomer produced in these reactions with the size and arrangement of the substituents attached to the asymmetric center of the starting ketone. In subsequent studies models for 1,2- and 1,3-asymmetric induction were studied to gain insight into what structural and environmental features produce the high degrees of optical purity found in nature's elaborations of optically active compounds, and the high stereochemical order observed in certain commercial polymerization reactions.

These asymmetric induction studies were addressed to problems of dynamic stereochemistry and the symmetry properties of short-lived organic reaction intermediates. In his invention and study of the paracyclophanes which commenced in 1951, Cram and his coworkers became involved with problems in static stereochemistry. This highly symmetric class of

compound was ideal for examination of transannular electronic and steric effects. Later the simplest member of the class, [2.2] paracyclophane, was found by others to be a monomer for a commercial polymerization by vapor deposition (Union Carbide Plastics Company). Interring activation, deactivation, and directive influences of substituents in electrophilic substitution were examined and interpreted in these systems. Optically active compounds of a new type, which owed their activity to restricted rotation, were prepared, and their optical stability studied. The paracyclophanes were found to exhibit novel electronic spectra when the benzene rings were held within interference radius of one another. They also proved to be exceptionally strong π bases due to transannular electron release.

Starting in 1970, Cram instituted research on the chemistry of complexation. Host compounds with convergent binding sites were designed and synthesized that would provide complementary geometric and electronic relationships to guest compounds with divergent binding sites. This work was inspired by the central role played by structural recognition in complexation in biological processes. Cram and his coworkers synthesized synthetic host compounds which exhibited high chiral recognition in the complexation and reactions of amino acids and their derivatives. A series of compounds were prepared that selectively complexed various metal ions.

A lawyer's son, Cram did his undergraduate work at Rollins College (B.S., 1941). After a year at the University of Nebraska (M.S., 1942), he worked as a research chemist at Merck and Company on penicillin and streptomycin, the first of the natural antibiotics. In 1945 he entered Harvard University as a National Research Council fellow, and obtained his Ph.D. there in 1947. At the University of California at Los Angeles he was an American Chemical Society fellow for a year, was made assistant professor in 1948, and became full professor in 1956. In 1955 he was awarded a Guggenheim fellowship for study at the University of London and the Swiss Federal Institute of Technology (ETH) in Zurich. In 1956 he was visiting professor at the National University of Mexico and in 1958 guest professor at the University of Heidelberg. He was elected to the National Academy of Sciences in 1961, and won the American Chemical Society Award for Creative Work in Synthetic Organic Chemistry in 1965.

Organic Chemistry (1959; 2d ed. 1964), which Cram coauthored with G. S. Hammond, represented the first major departure in organization for a basic textbook on the subject since early in this century; it was translated into eight languages. Cram also wrote *Reaction Mechanism,* with G. S. Hammond and A. Lwowski (1962); *Fundamentals of Carbanion Chemistry* (1965); *Elements of Organic Chemistry,* with J. Richards and G. S. Hammond (1967) and *The Essence of Organic Chemistry* (1978), an elementary organic chemistry textbook which Cram coauthored with his wife, Jane Maxwell Cram, formerly professor of chemistry at Mount Holyoke College.

For background information *see* CARBANION; ORGANIC CHEMISTRY; ORGANIC REACTION MECHANISM; STEREOCHEMISTRY in the McGraw-Hill Encyclopedia of Science and Technology. ∎

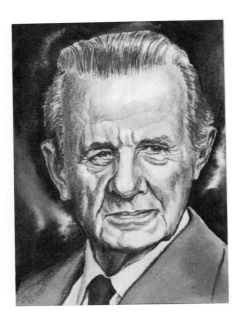

CRAMÉR, HARALD

★ Swedish mathematician and statistician

Born Sept. 25, 1893, Stockholm, Sweden

The earliest investigations of Cramér concerned the analytic theory of numbers. The asymptotic behavior of various arithmetic functions presents unsolved problems of great interest. P. G. L. Dirichlet, G. F. B. Riemann, and their followers had discovered the intimate relations between this type of arithmetic functions and certain analytic functions represented by Dirichlet's series, such as the famous Riemann zeta function. Cramér's main achievement in this field was the proof (1922) of a new type of mean value relations for some of the arithmetic functions concerned. A typical case is the following: Let $r(n)$ denote the number of representations of the positive integer n as the sum of two squares, and consider the summatory function $R(x) = \Sigma r(n)$, the sum being extended to all integers $n \leq x$. It is almost obvious that for large x the function $R(x)$ is asymptotically of the same order of magnitude as πx. Starting from some earlier results by G. H. Hardy, Cramér proved that the mean value integral [notation (1)] tends to a constant limit as

$$x^{-3/2} \int_1^x \left[R(t) - \pi t \right]^2 dt \qquad (1)$$

x tends to infinity. Similar results were obtained in other cases, including functions directly associated with the distribution of prime numbers. The subject has since been extensively pursued by other authors.

About 1925 Cramér turned his research activities to the field of mathematical probability theory. The central limit theorem of this theory asserts that under general conditions the sum of a large number of independent random variables has a probability distribution approximately of the normal (Moivre-Laplace) type. In particular, if $x_1, x_2, \ldots$ are independent random variables, all having the same probability distribution with zero mean and unit variance, the difference [Eq. (2)] tends to zero for every fixed x as n tends to infinity. Here P denotes the probability of the relation between the brackets, while Φ is the standard normal function [Eq. (3)].

$$\Delta_n(x) = P \left\{ \frac{x_1 + \cdots + x_n}{n^{1/2}} \leq x \right\} - \Phi(x) \quad (2)$$

$$\Phi(x) = (2\pi)^{-1/2} \int_{-\infty}^x e^{-t^2/2} dt \qquad (3)$$

It was proved by A. M. Liapounov that $\Delta_n(x)$ is for large n at most of the order of magnitude $n^{-1/2} \log n$. Cramér showed (1928) that under appropriate conditions there exists an asymptotic expansion in powers of $n^{-1/2}$ {Eq. (4)}, where the $A_i(x)$ are independent of n. It follows in particular that $\Delta_n(x)$ is of the order $n^{-1/2}$, which is a best possible result.

$$\Delta_n(x) = A_i(x)n^{-1/2} + A_2(x) n^{-1} + \cdots (4)$$

Later it was shown by A. C. Berry and C. G. Esseen that the last statement is true even under more general conditions than those assumed by Cramér.

The "problem of large deviations" is concerned with the behavior of $\Delta_n(x)$ when x and n both tend to infinity. Cramér obtained (1937) a fundamental theorem giving an asymptotic expansion for this case. He also proved the following theorem conjectured by Paul Lévy. If $\Delta_n(x)$ is for some n identically zero for all x, then every x_i is normally distributed. Both these last-mentioned theorems of Cramér have served as starting points for important work by Y. V. Linnik and other Soviet mathematicians.

In his book *Mathematical Methods of Statistics* (1945), Cramér set forth a treatise of methods of statistical inference, based on rigorous mathematical probability theory. Among the new results contained in the book is a proof of the statement that when an unknown parameter is estimated from a set of statistical data, the precision cannot be improved beyond a certain limit, given by the Cramér-Rao inequality.

Cramér's work on stochastic processes was at first concerned with processes with independent increments. For certain classes of these processes he obtained (1930, 1955) results which are generalizations of classical results associated with the problem of the "gambler's ruin." These results have applications to important practical problems of insurance risk.

For stationary processes he proved (1942) a fundamental theorem on spectral representation. Later he made, in collaboration with M. R. Leadbetter, an extensive study (1962–67) of the properties of the trajectories of these processes, particularly the distribution of the intersections between a trajectory and a given level or curve. As a particular case, an exact form of the extreme value distribution of the trajectories is obtained.

If the variable parameter of a stochastic process is interpreted as time, a process may be called "purely nondeterministic" if the infinitely remote past of the process does not contain any relevant information about its possible future behavior. In the simple particular case when the process is stationary, it is well known that the process admits a representation as the accumulated effect of past "impulses" or "innovations." Cramér showed (1961) that in the general case under mild regularity conditions there exists a similar although somewhat more complicated representation, closely related to the theory of spectral multiplicity of a self-adjoint transformation in Hilbert space.

Cramér came from an old Swedish family, members of which had been judges, teachers, and businesspersons on the island of Gotland. He graduated from the University of Stockholm in 1917, worked for some years as insurance actuary, and from 1929 to 1958 was professor at Stockholm. From 1950 to 1961 he was engaged in university administration, first as president of the University of Stockholm and then as chancellor of the entire Swedish university system. He received honorary degrees from the universities of Princeton (1947), Copenhagen (1950), and Stockholm (1964). He was an honorary member of the International Institute of Statistics and a member of various academies, including the American Academy of Arts and Sciences.

Cramér wrote, in addition to the book already mentioned, *Random Variables and Probability Distributions* (1937; 3d ed. 1970), *The Elements of Probability Theory* (1955), *Stationary and Related Stochastic Processes,* with M. R. Leadbetter (1967), and *Structural and Statistical Problems for a Class of Stochastic Processes* (1971).

For background information *see* NUMBER THEORY; PROBABILITY; STATISTICS; STOCHASTIC PROCESS in the McGraw-Hill Encyclopedia of Science and Technology. ∎

CRANE, HORACE RICHARD
★ American physicist

***Born** Nov. 4, 1907, Turlock, CA, U.S.A.*

Crane began experiments on nuclear reactions and artificial radioactivity produced by accelerated ion beams in the early 1930s, shortly after those processes were discovered. He produced and analyzed for the first time a number of nuclear processes. He helped to validate the neutrino hypothesis by an experiment that showed clearly that, in the beta-decay process, momentum is not conserved by the charged particles. He invented, and built a prototype of, a modified synchrotron called the racetrack, which became the standard design for larger accelerators. He originated a method by which he, and a succession of others in his laboratory, measured, with ever greater precision, the anomaly in the magnetic moment of the free electron. For this work he was awarded the Davisson-Germer

Prize of the American Physical Society in 1967.

Crane also made important contributions to the development of the radio proximity fuse (during World War II), was responsible for advances in biophysics (the unwinding of deoxyribonucleic acid, the basis for helical structure in biological molecules), and performed laboratory experiments pertaining to the reversals of the Earth's magnetic field. In various periods during his research career Crane carried out experiments on the teaching of introductory physics, with results that brought him the Oersted Medal of the American Association of Physics Teachers in 1977.

Crane's introduction to nuclear physics was an example of being in the right place with the right tools at the right time. During the 1920s a 1,000,000-volt, 60-hertz transformer had been installed at the California Institute of Technology (Caltech) for the purpose of testing the insulators that were to be used on the power line from the Hoover Dam to Los Angeles. Charles C. Lauritsen, professor in the physics department, finding the transformer to be available, had undertaken, with some success, to develop an x-ray tube that would withstand that unprecedented voltage (it was about 15 feet or 5 meters long). In 1930 Crane joined the project as a graduate student, and in the following year or so built a variation on the million-volt tube. Then came two momentous pieces of news in rapid succes-

sion: the disintegration of lithium in a beam of accelerated protons by J. D. Cockcroft and E. T. S. Walton, and the artificial production of radioactivity by I. Curie and J. F. Joliot. The conversion of Crane's tube to an accelerator for positive ions instead of electrons was quickly accomplished, and he found himself in possession of a head start in a new field. Such a multitude of nuclear reactions were possible with the 1,000,000-electronvolt beam of protons, deuterons, and helium ions that discoveries came rapidly. Naturally, there was material for a thesis. The "morning-after" research on some of the early discoveries occupied Crane (at the University of Michigan) and Lauritsen (at Caltech) for about 2 decades. *See* COCKCROFT, SIR JOHN (DOUGLAS); LAURITSEN, CHARLES CHRISTIAN; WALTON, ERNEST THOMAS SINTON.

After a year as postdoctoral fellow at Caltech Crane joined the University of Michigan faculty (1935). In the 5 years before World War II intervened, his most interesting research concerned the question of the existence of the neutrino. The fact that energy was "missing" in the radioactive beta-decay process had long been known. The idea that the missing energy might be carried away by another, unseen particle (a neutrino) had been put forward by W. Pauli. An alternate, and earlier, hypothesis was that there was a real uncertainty in energy associated with the creation of the electron in the beta process. Very important additional information would be revealed if the momentum relations in the process could be measured: specifically, the momentum of recoil of the nucleus, and its correlation with that of the electron. There was no clear evidence on that point. Crane, with J. Halpern, a postdoctoral appointee, carried out a series of experiments using a Wilson cloud chamber. These investigations clearly showed the recoil of the nucleus, and in some degree showed that the correlation was what would be expected if an unseen particle were emitted. The difficult part of the experiment was measuring the very small recoil energy of the nucleus. This was achieved by counting the droplets in the small cluster it made in the cloud chamber. *See* PAULI, WOLFGANG.

In 1953 Crane initiated a series of experiments that continued at the University of Michigan through the 1970s. This work concerned the measurement of the anomaly in the magnetic moment of the free electron. Circumstances conspired to create great interest in the problem. The anomaly, which is the small deviation of about one part in a thousand from the classical (Dirac) value, had appeared in spectroscopic studies of hydrogen, and had only recently been explained by the new and at that time somewhat tentative theory of quantum electrodynamics. More precise measurements would be of great importance, especially if they could be carried out on the electron in the free state, not bound in an atom. But the textbooks contained a simple "proof," involving the uncertainty principle, that the observation of the magnetic moment of the electron in the free state would be impossible. Crane found that there was, indeed, a way not only to observe the moment of the free electron but to measure the anomaly in the moment with exceedingly high precision. The idea was at first greeted with skepticism, but it was soon adopted as one of the most sensitive validations of the quantum-electrodynamic theory. The method that Crane devised was, essentially, to trap electrons in a magnetic "bottle" and to measure the difference between the spin precession and the orbital frequencies.

Crane carried out both his undergraduate and his graduate studies at Caltech, receiving the B.S. in 1930 and the Ph.D. in 1934. After an additional year as a research fellow at Caltech, he joined the faculty of the University of Michigan, where, except for short periods during World War II, he continued teaching and research until his retirement in 1978. He became professor in 1946 and university professor in 1972. In addition to the honors mentioned above, he received the Distinguished Alumni Medal from Caltech (1968) and the Distinguished Service Award from the University of Michigan (1957).

Crane was elected Henry Russel Lecturer at the University of Michigan in 1967. He was elected to membership in the National Academy of Sciences in 1966 and to fellowship in the American Academy of Arts and Sciences in 1971. He was president of the American Association of Physics Teachers in 1965, and he chaired the governing board of the American Institute of Physics from 1964 to 1971. He was president of the Midwestern Universities Research Association, a consortium of 15 universities, in 1956–57.

For background information *see* ELEC-TRON SPIN; NEUTRINO; NUCLEAR REACTION; RADIOACTIVITY in the McGraw-Hill Encyclopedia of Science and Technology. ■

CRICK, FRANCIS HARRY COMPTON
☆ English molecular biologist

Born *June 8, 1916, Northampton, England*

Crick and the American biologist James D. Watson in 1953 proposed a model for the deoxyribonucleic acid (DNA) molecule. This model describes the DNA molecule as consisting of two helical chains, each coiled around the same axis. Their hypothesis was based on data obtained from x-ray diffraction studies done by the English physicist Maurice H. F. Wilkins. All of the previous observations of DNA's structure were accounted for by Crick and Watson's 1953 model. *See* WATSON, JAMES DEWEY; WILKINS, MAURICE HUGH FREDERICK.

The Watson-Crick model provided a simple mechanism to explain what had been one of the most baffling problems in biology—the question of how the hereditary material duplicates itself. The model suggested that the two coiled strands that make up the double DNA helix separate, and each then acts as a template to form its complementary DNA strand from nearby molecules. Before very long, the DNA model was also serving as a stimulus for investigations into another related problem—how the genetic material directs the building of enzymes and, through them, the metabolism, growth, and differentiation of the cell.

The determination of the DNA structure has been called the single most important development in biology of the 20th century. For their work with DNA, Crick, Watson, and Wilkins received the 1962 Nobel Prize in medicine or physiology.

During the 70 years following Friedrich Miescher's discovery of DNA in 1869, its biological role remained vague. Those who sought to discover the chemical basis of heredity focused their attention on protein. However, no one ever brought forth a convincing hypothesis as to how protein could produce copies of itself. By 1925 P. A. Levene and others had learned that DNA molecules are built up on nucleotides, molecules composed of a pentose (a five-carbon sugar), a phosphate group, and a nitrogen base. In DNA the sugar of the nucleotides was found to be deoxyribose and the nitrogen base either one of two purines, adenine or guanine, or of two pyrimidines, cytosine or thymine. Leven perceived that the deoxyribose was linked to the base and also to the phosphate group, the latter serving as a link to the next nucleotide in the chain. Levene's chemical approach prevented him from perceiving that natural DNA molecules are giants of the molecular world, with thousands of nucleotides arranged in sequence. This fact, however, was learned before Watson and Crick began their work.

The first decisive evidence that DNA, rather than protein, was the actual carrier of genetic "instructions" was the discovery by O. T. Avery, C. M. MacLeod, and M. McCarty in 1944 that DNA from type III pneumococcus could be incorporated into the genetic makeup of type II pneumococcus. This incorporation results in the transformation of type II pneumococcus into type III pneumococcus. The DNA had brought about a distinct and permanent hereditary change. *See* AVERY, OSWALD THEODORE; McCARTY, MACLYN; MACLEOD, COLIN MUNRO.

The development of paper chromatography in 1944 made it convenient for chemists to separate the components of all sorts of mixtures. Using chromatography, Erwin Chargaff, in the late 1940s, made the provocative discovery that in DNA the number of adenine units was approximately equal to the number of guanine units, and the number of cytosine units was approximately equal to the number of guanine units. Another fruitful suggestion came in 1951 from Linus Pauling and R. B. Corey, who formulated the helical structure of polypeptides and calculated the actual dimensions of the helix. *See* CHARGAFF, ERWIN; PAULING, LINUS CARL.

By 1951 it was known that DNA actually transmitted genetic information in at least some instances and that the DNA molecule was an extremely long polymer of nucleotides. At this point, x-ray diffraction photographs clearly indicated that DNA must be a helix. It was a crucial contribution of Crick and Watson to perceive that the DNA helix was a double one, with two strands coiling around each other. Both helices are right-handed, but the sequence of atoms is in opposite directions, "up" in one chain and "down" in the other.

As conceived by Crick and Watson, the two intertwined strands of the DNA molecule are held together by hydrogen bonds between nitrogen bases. The dimensions and structure of the bases require that a purine of a nucleotide in one strand be bonded to a particular pyrimidine in the other strand. Thus adenine is always found opposite thymine, and cytosine is always bonded to guanine. This confirms the observations of Chargaff as to the equal quantities of adenine and thymine and of cytosine and guanine. The pitch of the helix results in a complete turn every 10 base pairs, and the distance from one pair of bases to the pair above them is 3.4 angstroms (0.34 nanometer).

Crick and Watson thought of the double helix unwinding to achieve replication. As the strands unwound, each would serve as a template (or "mold") for the production of a new strand, with new thymine units guided into position opposite the adenines of the old chain and new guanines guided into position opposite the cytosines, and vice versa. Within a few years reports came in from many experimenters, all of which appeared to confirm the Watson-Crick model and hypothesis of DNA replication.

With fellow workers at Cambridge University, Crick later studied the structure and working of the genetic code— the sequence of the nitrogen bases in DNA that directs the joining of amino acids to build proteins, including enzymes.

The term cistron had already been introduced as signifying the functional unit of the old term gene. Crick used the convenient term codon to indicate the set of bases that codes one amino acid. As a result of experiments at Cambridge with L. Barnett, S. Brenner, and R. J. Watts-Tobin, and consideration of the findings of other workers, Crick was able to state general properties of the genetic code, including the following: (1) It is likely that codons consist of three adjacent bases. (2) Adjacent codons probably do not overlap. (3) The message is read in the correct groups of three by starting at some fixed point, probably one end of the gene. (4) In general, more than one triplet codes each amino acid. (5) It is possible that some triplets may code more than one amino acid—that is, they may be ambiguous. (6) The code is probably much the same in all organisms; and in fact, it may be the same in all organisms.

Some of Crick's evidence for triplet codes came from the study, by his group, of mutations in the A and B cistrons of the *r*II locus of *Escherichia coli* bacteriophage T4.

Crick classified all mutations as plus or minus and assumed that a mutation called plus has an extra base added to the genetic message, and a mutation called minus has a base removed. One or two minus mutations or one or two plus mutations render a gene nonfunctional by putting the message out of phase. However, a minus and a plus mutation not too far separated from each other in the gene makes the gene functional. Also, three plus or three minus mutations would put the message in phase again, making the gene functional from that point on. This corroborated his hypothesis that the genetic message is read off in groups of three bases, starting at one end.

Crick was educated at University College, London (B.Sc., 1937) and at Cambridge University (Ph.D., 1953). He contributed to mine development during World War II. In 1949 he joined the staff of the Medical Research Council Laboratory of Molecular Biology at Cambridge. In 1976 he became Kieckhefer Distinguished Research Professor at the Salk Institute in La Jolla, CA. He received the Warren Triennial Prize of Massachusetts General Hospital (1959), the Lasker Award of the Albert and Mary Lasker Foundation (1960), the Prix Charles Léopold Meyer of the French Academy of

Sciences (1961), the Research Corporation Award (1961), the Gairdner Foundation Award (1962), and the Royal Medal (1972) and the Copley Medal (1975) of the Royal Society. He became a fellow of the Royal Society of London in 1959, and was elected a foreign member of the American Academy of Arts and Sciences (1962), the Royal Irish Academy (1964), the U.S. National Academy of Sciences (1969), the German Academy of Science (1969), and the Royal Society of Canada (1969).

Crick wrote *Of Molecules and Men* (1966).

For background information *see* DEOXYRIBONUCLEIC ACID (DNA); GENE; MUTATION; NUCLEIC ACID in the McGraw-Hill Encyclopedia of Science and Technology. ■

CRISTOL, STANLEY JEROME
★ American chemist

Born June 14, 1916, Chicago, IL, U.S.A.

Cristol's first independent work was concerned with the mechanisms of elimination reactions, and was influenced, on the one hand, by his work with W. G. Young at the University of California at Los Angeles and, on the other, by his work with H. L. Haller on insecticides in which certain theories of insecticidal structure-activity relationships were explored. Cristol and his students, investigating stereochemical influences on reactivity, demonstrated the existence of two mechanisms for bimolecular beta-elimination reactions and the *anti* stereochemical requirement for the normal concerted process. This work led, in turn, to the use, by Cristol's research group, of bridged polycyclic compounds as models of known and rigid geometries for the study of reaction mechanisms not only in elimination reactions, but also in addition and substitution reactions. Stereochemistries of gamma elimination to give cyclopropanes and of 1,4-conjugate eliminations were also studied.

Work with bridged compounds, in particular with bicyclo[2.2.1]heptenes and -heptadienes, with [2.2.2]- and [3.2.1]octadienes and -octatrienes, with [3.2.2.]nonadienes and -nonatrienes, and with their tricyclic isomers, was focused in large part on studies of the nature of the carbocationic (pertaining to a positively charged ion whose charge resides, in part at least, on a carbon atom or a group of carbon atoms) intermediates in electrophilic additions and in unimolecular displacement reactions. The strict geometric requirement for neighboring-group participation was demonstrated, and factors influencing rearrangements were investigated. Cristol's investigations of electrophilic addition mechanisms to olefins, in which he combined deuterium labeling, mass spectrometry, and one of the earliest uses of nuclear magnetic resonance spectroscopy in mechanistic studies, led not only to clarification of how environmental factors affect the choice of mechanism, but also to the first demonstration of a *syn*-concerted mechanism for additions of protic species. Electrophilic additions to bridged cyclopropanes were also investigated, and a variety of stereochemistries observed.

Free-radical addition and displacement reactions were also investigated with bridged compounds. The time-dependent nature of free-radical rearrangements involving unsaturated bonds was demonstrated, and this work, in combination with work on stereochemistry of substitution and addition reactions, showed that homoallylic and cyclopropylcarbinylic radicals have classical structures. These experiments clearly detailed differences between homoconjugated cations, which are often delocalized (that is, are nonclassical) and the corresponding radicals, which are

not delocalized (that is, are classical). In the course of this work a very useful method for conversion of carboxylic acids to alkyl halides was described.

The synthesis in Cristol's group of janusene, a unique hydrocarbon in which two benzene rings are held, by the rigidity of the bridged polycyclic system, almost face to face and very close together, made it possible to study the effects of ring interactions across space, without the complication of ring warping. The area of bridged polycyclic compounds, in which Cristol was one of the pioneers, was utilized by many other research groups not only for mechanistic studies in chemistry and biology, but also for the preparation of commercially valuable, biologically active materials.

The photoisomerization of norbornadienedicarboxylic acid to quadricyclenedicarboxylic acid was (with the exception of a report by G. L. Ciamician a half century earlier, which had been discredited—although it in fact was correct—and largely forgotten) the first describing an intramolecular [2 + 2] photocycloaddition reaction. Whereas Cristol's group emphasized the chemistry of the highly strained and therefore energetic quadricyclene ring skeleton, which contains in its seven-carbon atoms two three-membered rings, a four-membered ring, four five-membered rings, and one six-membered ring, others followed up the photocycloaddition example, and it is now a standard procedure for the construction of highly strained ring systems. The norbornadiene-quadricyclene photoisomerization has become a well-studied system for the conversion of light energy to chemical energy. Cristol also noted the palladium-catalyzed transformation of quadricyclenedicarboxylic acid to the norbornadiene analog, which was apparently the first example of a transition-metal-catalyzed (otherwise symmetry-forbidden) [2 + 2] cycloreversion. The combination of the forward (photochemical) and reverse (catalyzed) reactions was used by others in a model system for solar energy usage.

Photochemistry became a principal focus of Cristol's research group. He discovered that allylic halides can be photoisomerized to cyclopropyl halides, and that many allylic alcohol derivatives suffer photoallylic rearrangements. A number of allylic, homoallylic, benzylic, and homo-

benzylic halides or alcohol derivatives of high nucleofugicity (the measure of how well a nucleofuge, or "leaving group," favors bond heterolysis) were shown to undergo photosolvolyses or photo-Wagner-Meerwein rearrangements in polar solvents. Thus, photoinduced bond heterolysis was demonstrated to be fairly general and complementary to the generally observed homolysis. Cristol and his students described a method for the measurement of lifetimes of triplet reaction intermediates produced by photosensitization, useful down to lifetimes of 1-2 nanoseconds, thus filling a gap in the armamentarium of photochemists and photophysicists.

The son of immigrant parents, Cristol was raised in Chicago and received a B.S. degree in chemistry (1937) at Northwestern University. His graduate training was obtained at the University of California at Los Angeles (M.A., 1939; Ph.D, 1943) in the important school of physical-organic chemistry led by William G. Young and Saul Winstein. This training was of great significance in providing the direction of his studies and those of his students in the then developing field of organic chemical reaction mechanisms. His graduate work was interrupted by a 3-year period in the research laboratories of the Standard Oil Company of California. He was a postdoctoral research associate of Roger Adams at the University of Illinois, after which he joined Haller's group in the U.S. Department of Agriculture. This group was central to the development of organic insecticides and insect repellents in the United States during World War II. In 1946 Cristol joined the chemistry faculty of the University of Colorado, becoming full professor in 1955. He became distinguished professor of chemistry in 1979. In 1972 he was elected to the National Academy of Sciences, and also received the American Chemical Society's James Flack Norris Award in Physical Organic Chemistry. *See* ADAMS, ROGER.

With L. O. Smith, Cristol published *Organic Chemistry* (1966). In addition, he was the author or coauthor of about 200 articles in scientific journals.

For background information *see* KINETICS, CHEMICAL; ORGANIC CHEMICAL SYNTHESIS; PHOTOCHEMISTRY; STEREOCHEMISTRY in the McGraw-Hill Encyclopedia of Science and Technology. ■

DAINTON, SIR FREDERICK (SYDNEY)

★ British physical chemist

___

Born Nov. 11, 1914, Sheffield, Yorkshire, England

Dainton's research centered on the kinetics and mechanisms of reactions in gases and solutions, especially electron and free-radical chemistry, radiation chemistry and photochemistry, and polymerization.

It is correctly taken for granted that the rate of a simple chemical reaction will increase with increasing temperature according to the law of Arrhenius, so that the logarithm of this rate plotted against the reciprocal of the temperature is a straight line of negative slope. Even complex multistage processes such as chain reactions give a straight-line plot, although when some chain reactions are initiated by absorption of light the plot may have a slight positive slope. In 1945, while casting around for new fields with which to restart his research after the war, Dainton accidentally read a publication describing a reaction which seemed totally anomalous in that, whereas the Arrhenius plot fell into one of the two "normal" categories below a particular temperature, gross departures took place at higher temperatures. In all cases the rate of reaction fell off increasingly steeply as the temperature was raised in this region, and became zero at a sharply defined temperature called the ceiling temperature, T_c.

The reaction which displayed this unsuspected phenomenon was the formation of a long-chain molecule containing many thousands of identical units joined end to end. With K. J. Ivin and others, Dainton showed that the phenomenon is a perfectly general one for all addition polymerizations, whether the repeat units are bound together by primary valency bonds or merely by secondary intermolecular forces such as those which exist in crystals. By independent arguments based on either thermodynamics or kinetics, he showed that the ceiling temperature is the equilibrium temperature between the freely translating, rotating polymerizing monomer molecules and the nontranslating, nonexternally rotating, monomeric segment of the big polymer molecule, and is thus defined by $T_c = \Delta H^0/(\Delta S^0 + R \ln [m_1])$, where $[m_1]$ is the monomer concentration, ΔH^0 is the standard increment in enthalpy, ΔS^0 the standard entropy increase accompanying the reaction, and R the universal gas constant.

This equation is identical with the classical Clausius-Clapeyron equation applied to physical aggregation, for example, condensation of a vapor to form a crystal or freezing of a liquid. In both processes the monomer at temperatures below T_c is metastable and can be brought into an active state in which it can add on another monomer by various triggering mechanisms such as light, ionizing radiation, or a catalyst, or in the case of physical aggregation, by a nucleating agent in the supercooled pure vapor or liquid. Once started, the growth process is repeated (the chain is "propagated") until it is adventitiously terminated or $[m_1]$ has dropped to its equilibrium value. The process is thus like the operation of a zip fastener, and the essence of the argument is that the "zipping-up" or propagation reaction is reversible and that at T_c the rates of this and the reverse "depropagation" or "unzipping" reaction are exactly equal and the increments of the thermodynamic quantities for the propagation are identical in magnitude with those for the overall reaction because the polymer molecules are so long. This last assumption was confirmed by direct calorimetric measurement.

The monomer may contain a double bond such as C=C or C=O, or may be a ring compound, and in both cases the bonds may be opened up and the molecules joined end to end. The value of the general theorem is that it enables the polymerizability of compounds to be predicted from the way in which the monomer structure affects the values of ΔH^0 and ΔS^0. For example, as the ring size of cyclic monomers increases, ΔH^0 generally

D

and ΔS^0 often decrease. If both become negative the ceiling temperature was predicted to be replaced by a "floor" temperature, below which the monomer is stable and the polymer metastable, and above which the converse is true. The most striking example of this is liquid sulfur, which on heating to 159°C suddenly becomes very viscous due to the formation of very long chains of sulfur atoms (plastic sulfur).

Dainton was also attracted in 1945 to study the mechanism by which ionizing radiations such as alpha, beta, and gamma rays, fast charged particles from accelerators, can induce chemical change in inanimate or living material; the field is now referred to as radiation chemistry. He made many contributions, but perhaps the most far-reaching was the proof that the electrons ejected from water molecules by this means or by exposing reducing solutes such as ferrous or ferrocyanide ions to light could, despite contrary theoretical predictions, persist for almost a millisecond as a hydrated electron and during that period be considered as a very highly reactive but otherwise normal singly charged anion. The proof of this was established by showing that the relative rates with which the hydrated electron reacted with two solutes, one charged and one uncharged, which competed for it, were affected by the addition of "neutral salts" (electrolytes which took no chemical part in the reaction but merely altered its electrical environment). The same was true in other solvents such as alcohols.

The solvated electron is highly reactive, adding to many solutes at first encounter. This fact made it possible for Dainton to measure the ionic atmosphere relaxation time of the electron and, using the pulse radiolysis technique, to study the actual solvation process, the temperature dependence of microscopic viscosity of glass-forming liquids, electron tunneling, and other properties of wide physicochemical significance. He also carried out many related studies on isotopic electron exchange and redox reactions and, in quite different fields, pioneered the first quantitative understanding of the photochlorination of alkenes and polymerization in aqueous solutions.

The son of a stonemason, Dainton was educated at Oxford and Cambridge, and became professor at Leeds and Oxford. In the 1960s and 1970s he also had many public responsibilities as president of the Faraday Society, the Chemical Society, the Association for Radiation Research, the Library Association, and the Association for Science Education, and as chairperson of many important government bodies, including the Council for Science Policy, the Board of the Research Councils, the National Libraries Committee, the British Library Board, and the National Radiological Protection Board. Dainton was a fellow of the Royal Society (1957) and an honorary fellow of the Royal College of Physicians (1979). He held foreign memberships in the Royal Swedish Society of Science (1968), American Academy of Arts and Sciences (1971), and Academy of Sciences at Göttingen (1974). Recipient of numerous honorary degrees, he was awarded the Tilden Medal of the Chemical Society (1950), the Sylvanus Thomson Medal of the Roentgen Society and Institute of Radiology (1958), the Davy Medal of the Royal Society (1969), and the Faraday Medal of the Chemical Society (1974). He was created knight bachelor in 1971.

Dainton was the author of *Chain Reaction* and coeditor, with P. G. Ashmore and T. M. Sugden, of *Photo-chemistry and Reaction Kinetics*.

For background information *see* CHAIN REACTION, CHEMICAL; PHOTOCHEMISTRY; RADIATION CHEMISTRY in the McGraw-Hill Encyclopedia of Science and Technology. ∎

DALE, SIR HENRY (HALLETT)
★ British pharmacologist and physiologist

Born June 9, 1875, London, England
Died July 22, 1968, Cambridge, England

Working with the parasitic fungus ergot, Dale succeeded in 1914 in isolating the compound acetylcholine, and recognizing its effect, which is similar to that brought about by nerves of the parasympathetic system. The German pharmacologist Otto Loewi showed by experiment in 1921 that nerves do not act directly on the heart, but that the immediate result of nerve stimulation is the freeing of chemical substances that act directly in producing the functional changes in the heart characteristic of nerve action. For their discoveries relating to the chemical transmission of nerve impulses, Dale and Loewi shared the 1936 Nobel Prize for medicine or physiology.

About 1904 Dale's lifelong friend T. R. Elliott had confirmed that adrenaline, which is produced in the medulla of the adrenal glands, produces effects similar to those produced by activity in the sympathetic system. Therefore, he proposed that the result of impulses in the sympathetic nerves is a release of adrenaline at the nerve endings, as the direct cause of the stimulation effect.

In 1914 Dale published his observations on what appeared to be the two distinct types of action of acetylcholine. Through what he termed its "muscarine" action, it reproduced at the periphery all the effects of parasympathetic nerves with a fidelity comparable to that with which adrenaline had been shown to reproduce those of the true sympathetic nerves. These parasympathomimetic effects of acetylcholine were readily abolished by atropine. When they were suppressed, another type of action was revealed. Dale termed this the nicotine action because it closely resembled the action of that alkaloid in its intense stimulant effect on all autonomic ganglion cells and on some voluntary muscle fibers.

From these observations Dale concluded that there was some degree of biochemical similarity between (1) the ganglion cells of the involuntary nervous system and the terminations of the nerve fibers in striated muscle and (2) the mechanism connected with the peripheral terminations of parasympathetic nerves. He also speculated on the possible occur-

rence of acetylcholine in the animal body, and on its physiological significance if it should be found there.

Thus when, in the period 1921–26, Loewi established the characteristics of the peripheral transmission of effects from the autonomic nerves to effector units innervated by them, Dale was in a favorable position to accept Loewi's demonstration and to extend his experiments. In 1929, in collaboration with H. W. Dudley, Dale extracted and identified acetylcholine as a natural constituent of a mammalian organ.

In 1933, working in Dale's laboratory, H. C. Chang and J. H. Gaddum found that sympathetic ganglia are rich in acetylcholine. In the following year W. Feldberg, B. Minz, and H. Tsudzimura observed that the effects of splanchnic nerve stimulation are transmitted to the cells of the suprarenal medulla by the release of acetylcholine at the nerve endings. These medullary cells are morphological analogs of sympathetic ganglion cells. Feldberg, continuing his study in Dale's laboratory, found that this stimulating action of acetylcholine on the suprarenal medulla was one of its nicotine actions. Feldberg, Gaddum, M. Vogt, and G. L. Brown continued this line of experimentation with Dale, and under his direction, to establish the role of acetylcholine as the chemical transmitter of the effects of nerve impulses at ganglionic synapses and at nerve endings on voluntary muscle fibers.

Although Dale came to be recognized mainly as a pharmacologist, this happened by the accident of opportunity rather than by intention. At the time of his training, there were no academic chairs of pharmacology in England or any teaching of it beyond short courses of perfunctory lectures on materia medica. He graduated in 1898 from Trinity College, Cambridge, in physiology and zoology; and the tenure of its Coutts-Trotter studentship enabled him to spend 2 further years, till 1900, in an apprenticeship to research in physiology under the guidance of such eminent investigators as J. N. Langley, W. H. Gaskell, H. K. Anderson, and later, F. G. Hopkins. He then left Cambridge for St. Bartholomew's Hospital, where he spent another 2 years in obtaining the clinical experience required for medical qualification.

By 1902, therefore, Dale had still made no firm decision between medical practice and academic physiology for his main career. The choice, however, seemed then to be almost made for him by the fact that the George Henry Lewes studentship unexpectedly fell vacant. This had been founded by the English novelist George Eliot to provide support for 2 years of research in physiology. It was tenable only by Cambridge graduates and was one of the very few emoluments then available in England for the support of any research in the medical field. Having successfully applied for this studentship, Dale was able to spend most of the next 2 years in the department of physiology of University College, London. This department had a distinguished history, entitling it to be regarded as a cradle, for England, of experimental physiology, for Michael Foster and John Burdon-Sanderson, who were to found the chairs of physiology in Cambridge and, some years later, in Oxford, had both been pupils there of William Sharpey. There, too, Sidney Ringer had discovered the first physiologically balanced saline solution, and Edward Schäfer (later Sir Edward Sharpey-Schäfer), then holding the professorship, had been concerned with the discovery of the potent endocrine principles of the adrenal medulla and the neurohypophysis.

Before Dale's entry there, Schäfer had migrated to Edinburgh, and had been succeeded at University College by Ernest H. Starling, a vigorous and inspiring leader and a devoted champion of research in physiology. In a joint investigation with his brother-in-law, William M. Bayliss, Starling had recently discovered secretin, the chemical messenger for the secretion of the pancreatic juice, and had introduced the term "hormone" to describe its function. He invited Dale to study the histological changes in the pancreas caused by its action; but though this occupied Dale for most of his 2 years as the Lewes student, the results had no novel or lasting significance. Meanwhile, he had arranged to spend the final 4 months of his tenure in widening his research experience by a visit to the Institut für Experimentelle Therapie, in Frankfort am Main, where Paul Ehrlich, its director, was then changing the focus of his activity from his "side-chain" theory of immunity to artificial chemotherapy. Returning then to University College, London, Dale found that the immediate prospect for an academic career in physiology, or in any allied experimental discipline, was exceedingly bleak. He had thoroughly enjoyed his experience in Starling's department, where he had made incidental contacts with many important investigators and a number of stimulating and lasting friendships—including one with Loewi, then making an exploratory visit to physiological centers in London, Cambridge, and Oxford. Dale and Loewi were to maintain these friendly contacts until Loewi died in 1961.

Dale's immediate problem in 1904, however, when he was already 29 years old, was to find an opportunity to use such experience as he had accumulated, and one also to provide such material support as would enable him to marry and to feel settled in a useful career. And, unexpectedly, such an opportunity was soon to be offered, but of a kind and from a quarter which, at that time, were viewed with suspicion by many of conventional opinions in medical and academic circles. Henry Wellcome, who had become the sole proprietor of the pharmaceutical firm of Burroughs Wellcome and Company, wished to find somebody to undertake pharmacological researches in the physiological laboratories which he had established in connection with his business. With Starling's advice and encouragement and after discussion of details with Wellcome himself, Dale accepted this offer, and had no reason to regret having done so. At their first interview Wellcome had expressed a hope that Dale might find it possible "to do something about the pharmacology of ergot." Contrary to Dale's own expectation, his attempts to meet this request, with the help of hints derived from errors and from a remarkable succession of accidental observations, provided openings to researches on sympatholytic alkaloids, on sympathomimetic amines, on histamine and the relation of its activity to the anaphylactic and other "shock" reactions, and, as described above, on acetylcholine.

After 10 years at the Wellcome Laboratories, Dale accepted one of four departmental appointments in the new National Institute for Medical Research, only a month before the outbreak of World War I. His research activities were diverted for more than a decade by more urgent duties, including those concerned with the establishment of international standards and units for such new types of remedy as the endocrines, including the then recently discovered insulin, and the vitamins. Other interests and duties accumulated with his appointment as director of the National Institute and later as president of the Royal Society (1940–45). Association with a series of able colleagues, however, enabled him to take a part in extending the evidence for the chemical transmitter functions of acetylcholine, demonstrated meanwhile by Loewi for the effect of the vagus nerve on the frog's heart, to transmission at ganglionic synapses and at the endings of motor nerve fibers on the "end plates" of voluntary muscle. In addition to the Nobel Prize, Dale received the Royal (1924) and Copley (1937) medals of the Royal Society. He was elected a foreign member of the American Academy of Arts and Sciences in 1927 and of the U.S. National Academy of Sciences in 1940.

For background information *see* ACE-TYLCHOLINE; ERGOT AND ERGOTISM; NERVOUS SYSTEM (VERTEBRATE) in the McGraw-Hill Encyclopedia of Science and Technology. ∎

DALGARNO, ALEXANDER
★ British physicist

Born Jan. 5, 1928, London, England

Dalgarno made important contributions to the theoretical understanding of atomic and molecular processes, especially as they relate to atmospheric and astrophysical phenomena.

After graduating in mathematics in 1948, Dalgarno became interested in applying mathematics to the interpretation of natural phenomena. The field of atomic physics was at that time entering a new phase of development, much of it taking place at University College, London, under the leadership of H. S. W. (later Sir Harrie) Massey, who enhanced the appeal of research in atomic physics to Dalgarno by offering to obtain financial support for him. Dalgarno worked initially under the supervision of R. A. Buckingham on a problem of atomic scattering theory which involved a study of molecular interactions, a subject which was to engage much of his attention in later years and led him into research activities ordinarily belonging to the domain of theoretical chemistry.

In 1951 Dalgarno moved to the Queen's University of Belfast in Northern Ireland, which in a few short years through the guidance of D. R. (later Sir David) Bates achieved a position of eminence in the field of theoretical atomic and molecular physics. In Belfast, Dalgarno worked with a succession of remarkably able graduate students. With them he developed mathematical methods for the solution of the equations of quantum mechanics and applied the methods to the quantitative investigation of an extensive array of atomic and molecular phenomena. His interest in molecular interactions led to a general study of the behavior of atomic and molecular systems in response to small disturbances. The conventional development of such theories involved infinite summations over products of matrix elements which coupled the unperturbed state of the system to all its excited states, including the continuum states. The evaluation of them by summing the individual terms was impracticable, and perturbation theory was regarded as useful mostly as a qualitative or empirical approach. *See* BATES, SIR DAVID (ROBERT).

Working with J. T. Lewis, Dalgarno showed that infinite summations can be transformed into simple integrals, the integrands of which are solutions of inhomogeneous differential equations of a kind that can be solved either by direct integration or by variational methods. Variational methods have general applicability so that the technique introduced by Dalgarno and Lewis converted conventional perturbation theory into a quantitative procedure. It demonstrated that perturbation theory can be formulated so that no infinite summations appear. Such formulations already existed but had been applied only to a restricted class of problems. In collaboration with A. L. Stewart, Dalgarno then studied the response of a system to simultaneous perturbations, and they discovered a simple theorem of considerable utility called the interchange theorem. It demonstrated an equality between different diagonal matrix elements. It was later generalized in collaboration with M. Cohen to off-diagonal elements. The theorem permitted substantial simplifications in certain problems, and it was used widely in analyses of the nuclear charge dependence of a variety of atomic properties.

Although stimulated by time-independent perturbation theory, the summation technique of Dalgarno and Lewis had a wide applicability. The procedures were readily generalized to allow variational calculations of the response to time-dependent perturbations, a development which created practical approaches for the calculation of a wide range of atomic and molecular parameters. In particular indices of refraction, equivalently dynamic polarizabilities could be calculated. The dynamic polarizabilities of the individual atoms could then be incorporated into an expression for the magnitudes of the interactions between atoms of large separations which could be evaluated.

The independent-particle model is a basic approximation in atomic structure. Working with G. A. Victor, Dalgarno combined the time-dependent perturbation procedures with the independent-particle model to obtain a universally applicable approximation for the calculation of response functions. With W. L. Johnson, its generalization to a fully relativistic version was carried through without serious difficulty. The solution of the equations of the resulting relativistic random phase approximation demands considerable technical skill, but it was extensively used by Johnson, C. D. Lin, and P. Shorer in the exploration of relativistic effects at large nuclear charges and in the determination of optically allowed and forbidden transition probabilities.

The summation technique produces moments of the distribution of matrix elements of a given operator. In considering the inverse problem of determining the matrix elements from the moments, efforts focused primarily on empirical trial-and-error methods and met with limited success. Later more sophisticated techniques were applied, particularly by P. Langhoff and W. Reinhardt, and a powerful procedure emerged for the determination of the individual terms.

Dalgarno was interested also in the development and application of the quantal theory of the scattering of atoms and molecules. He worked on the transport properties of gas and on impact excitation, spin change, ionization, charge transfer, and collision-induced absorption. Large fast computers became available, and elaborate mathematical formulations were tractable. With A. M. Arthurs, he took up standard angular momentum theory, familiar in atomic structure, and constructed a scattering theory of the rotational excitation of molecules by particle impact. The formulation appeared at an appropriate point in the evolution of scattering theory, and many numerical studies of rotational excitation and of related processes such as fine-structure excitation were carried out on the basis of the Arthurs-Dalgarno formulation.

Attempts to make quantitative predictions of the efficiency of a particular atomic or molecular collision process are limited by the uncertainties in the interactions between the colliding particles. The long-range part had been treated successfully, but the problem of determining the interaction at small separations remained severe. Efforts to achieve useful accuracy by empirical methods were made, together with C. Bottcher, and a model potential method was developed. Applying it to isolated atoms, Victor and C. Laughlin made it a highly successful procedure, but for atomic interactions further development is necessary.

In molecular spectroscopy Dalgarno's main contribution was probably the identification, in collaboration with G. Herzberg and T. L. Stephens, of the continuous emission spectrum of molecular hydrogen arising from the spontaneous radiative decay of an excited electronic state into the vibrational continuum of the ground electronic state. *See* HERZBERG, GERHARD.

While engaged in mathematical studies of quantum-mechanical applications to atomic and molecular processes, Dalgarno carried out parallel research on the physics and chemistry of the upper atmosphere of the Earth and later of other astrophysical regimes. His interest in the terrestrial atmosphere was stimulated by Bates, the leading authority in the field. After some initial studies of the airglow of the atmosphere suggested by Bates, Dalgarno embarked on an investigation of the thermal balance of the ionosphere, and in association with M. B. McElroy and R. J. Moffett performed calculations to predict the ionic composition and the efficiencies of the heating and cooling mechanisms. This particular study was an early example of a comprehensive approach to problems of atmosphere science which incorporated a detailed description of the atomic, molecular, and radiation processes that occur. In a continuing study of the thermal balance, the identification was made with T. C. Degges of electron impact fine-structure excitation of oxygen as the major cooling mechanism in the ionospheric electron gas. Research was maintained on airglow mechanisms, and the methods developed for the analysis of the terrestrial atmosphere were applied to the other planets.

A detailed knowledge of atomic and molecular processes was useful in the interpretation of more varied circumstances, and Dalgarno turned his attention to questions concerning the interstellar medium. With J. H. Black, he argued that ultraviolet pumping was a significant source of the enhanced rotational population of molecular hydrogen observed in the interstellar gas and that with a suitable analysis the observations could be used to infer the radiation field together with the other characteristics of the interstellar gas. The methods used for the interpretation of measurements of atmospheric composition could be readily transferred to the composition of interstellar clouds, and chemical schemes for the formation of interstellar molecules were proposed. As one consequence, it was pointed out by Black and Dalgarno that the abundances of the interstellar molecules OH and HD provided a direct measure of the galactic cosmic-ray fluxes.

In his researches on natural phenomena, Dalgarno made use of the results of basic quantal calculations to compare and elucidate the role of atomic and molecular processes in a wide range of physical environments occurring in laboratory plasmas, planetary atmospheres, the interstellar medium, and gaseous nebulae.

Dalgarno obtained a Ph.D. degree in theoretical physics at University College, London, in 1951 and joined the faculty of the Queen's University of Belfast in Northern Ireland, where he remained until 1967. He then joined Harvard University as professor of astronomy, later Phillips Professor of Astronomy. He was also on the staff of the Smithsonian Astrophysical Observatory. He served as director of Harvard College Observatory and chairperson of the department of astronomy. Dalgarno was elected a fellow of the Royal Society (1972), and was awarded the Hodgkin's Medal of the Smithsonian Institution (1977).

For background information *see* ATOMIC STRUCTURE AND SPECTRA; INTERSTELLAR MATTER; IONOSPHERE; MOLECULAR STRUCTURE AND SPECTRA; PETURRBATION (QUANTUM MECHANICS); SCATTERING EXPERIMENTS, ATOMIC AND MOLECULAR in the McGraw-Hill Encyclopedia of Science and Technology. ■

DALITZ, RICHARD HENRY

★ British theoretical physicist

***Born** Feb. 28, 1925, Dimboola, Australia*

At Bristol University in 1948 C. F. Powell and his collaborators established the first example of τ^+-meson decay to three pions, $\tau^+ \rightarrow \pi^+ + \pi^+ + \pi^-$, in their studies of cosmic-ray interactions in nuclear emulsion—not much more than a year after this group reported the discovery of the positive pion. Later in 1948 Dalitz became a research assistant at Bristol. The discussion of these discoveries and of other elementary particle processes being investigated at Bristol aroused his interest in these new and rare phenomena and led him to follow closely the development of knowledge of elementary particles in later years. *See* POWELL, CECIL FRANK.

Dalitz's first work, at Cambridge, was a discussion of the properties of internal conversion electron-positron pairs emitted in transitions between nuclear states of zero spin, a process then being investigated for ^{16}O by S. Devons. In 1950 Dalitz's friend D. T. King at Bristol observed that energetic electron pairs occasionally originate very close to the high-energy cosmic-ray stars occurring in nuclear emulsion. In thinking about these pairs, Dalitz realized that internal pair conversion could occur for one of the two photons emitted in the normal decay process $\pi^0 \rightarrow \gamma + \gamma$ for the neutral pion, leading to the visible decay mode, $\pi^0 \rightarrow \gamma + e^+ + e^-$, and he calculated the branching ratio to be about 1.2 percent. Observations of the spatial distribution of such Dalitz pairs, as they are generally termed, were used in the earliest determinations of the lifetime of the π^0-meson.

By 1953 about a dozen examples of τ^+ decay had been reported. Many other K-meson decay processes, including the $\theta^+ \rightarrow \pi^+ + \pi^0$ process, were also becoming established. The τ^+ and θ^+ masses were found to be equal, within appreciable experimental errors; the τ^+ and θ^+ lifetimes were found to have the same order of magnitude. Then Dalitz showed how to analyze the way the total energy is shared between the three pions from τ^+ decay, depending on their total spin J and parity P; it was convenient to represent each decay event by a point on a two-dimensional phase-space plot (often referred to as a Dalitz plot). This analysis depended only on simple physical ideas, on the way the internal angular momenta sum to J and the way the orbital and intrinsic parities combine to give P, and on the role of the centrifugal barriers in controlling the energy dependence of the decay amplitude in certain regions of the phase-space plot. The analysis showed that certain qualitatively striking features would be expected in the Dalitz plot distribution if the spin-parity of the τ^+-meson were such $[P = (-1)^J]$ that angular momentum and parity conservation would permit this particle to decay also through the θ^+ mode. Even the early data on τ^+ decay indicated that these features were not the case, showing that the 3π system from τ^+ decay did not have the same spin and parity as the 2π system from θ^+ decay. But further experiments soon showed that the mass, lifetime, and scattering properties are the same for τ^+- and θ^+-mesons, to a high precision. This dilemma then emboldened T.-D. Lee and C. N. Yang to ask whether there really existed any evidence for parity conservation in weak decay processes, a question which led them to their celebrated proposals for β-decay experiments to seek direct evidence for parity nonconservation in weak interactions. *See* LEE, TSUNG-DAO; YANG, CHEN NING.

By 1957 nuclear emulsion studies had given evidence for many examples of a new nuclear species, the Λ-hypernuclei, consisting of a Λ-hyperon bound to an ordinary nucleus. With B. W. Downs, a postdoctoral visitor at Birmingham University, Dalitz began an extensive study of the systematics of their binding energies and decay properties. Spin-parity values were established quite early for the hypernuclei with mass numbers $A \leq 5$, from analysis of their decay modes. With this information, the observation by M. Block and his collaborators of the process $K^- + {}^4\text{He} \rightarrow \pi^- + {}_\Lambda^4\text{He}$, for K^--mesons coming to rest in helium, directly determined the K-meson parity. These analyses also led to the first knowledge of the low-energy Λ-nucleon interaction, its scattering strength, and its dependence on the total spin. However, the binding-energy data for light Λ-hypernuclei already made clear the necessity of invoking ΛNN three-body forces in these systems. Dalitz's early analysis of the data on the $\Lambda\Lambda$ hypernucleus $_{\Lambda\Lambda}^{6}\text{He}$ gave the first evidence concerning hyperon-hyperon forces, although more elaborate calculations were made subsequently by R. C. Herndon and Y. C. Tang.

In later years this work was extended to heavier Λ-hypernuclei, with spin determinations for $_\Lambda^8\text{Li}$ and $_\Lambda^{12}\text{B}$ (jointly with D. Zieminska), and to the prediction (with A. Gal and J. Soper) of hypernuclear energy-level schemes according to an intermediate-coupling shell model for hypernuclei. With Gal, Dalitz pointed out the possibility of supersymmetric states in hypernuclei, having greater permutation symmetry than is possible for ordinary nuclei of the same mass number, and analyzed the occurrence of strangeness analog states in Λ-hypernuclei, their precise structure, and their excitation in $K^- \rightarrow \pi^-$ reactions, pointing out that the continuous background observed could be accounted for by the quasi-free process $K^- + N \rightarrow \Lambda + \pi^-$, since the Λ-hyperon in nuclear matter is not restricted by the Pauli principle.

At Cornell University, L. Castillejo, F. J. Dyson, and Dalitz discussed in 1955 the general solution of the Chew-Low dispersion theory equation for a special case of meson-nucleon scattering, with the conviction that many solutions must exist corresponding to the possible existence of resonant states (or unstable particles) whose occurrence is due to forces not included in these equations. Such solutions were found, and this CDD ambiguity (so called from the initials of the researchers) has appeared in one form or another in the solutions of all dispersion theoretic schemes. *See* DYSON, FREEMAN JOHN.

At the Enrico Fermi Institute, University of Chicago, with S. F. Tuan, Dalitz developed in 1959 a reaction matrix formalism appropriate for the analysis of data on meson-baryon processes. They applied this to analyze the $\bar{K}N$ interaction when data on the K^--proton processes at low energies became available from hydrogen bubble chamber studies. The strong elastic scattering found in the $\bar{K}N$ state of zero isospin led directly to the prediction of a "Dalitz-Tuan resonance" below the K^--proton threshold, now identified as the π-Σ resonance $\Lambda^*(1405)$.

After 1960 the list of elementary particles increased rapidly with the discovery of many highly unstable particles at higher mass values. This situation suggested to Dalitz that all these particles were actually not "elementary" but composite, representing excited states of an underlying substructure. The evidence that the unitary symmetry SU(3) held well for all these states suggested that the substructure constituents should have special simplicity in this respect, and the triplet of quarks, first proposed by M. Gell-Mann and by G. Zweig, were clearly the logical candidates. Dalitz took this possibility literally and pointed out that the simplest excitations for such a system would be rotational and vibrational excitations, rather than multiquark excitations. In 1967 he pointed out that the newly determined pattern of nucleonic resonances up to mass about 2000 megaelectronvolts corresponded to those patterns expected for the following excitations of the three-quark structure known for the nucleons: (1) the one-quantum excitation ($N=1$), which leads uniquely to a configuration with internal orbital angular momentum $L=1$ and mixed permutation symmetry; (2) a two-quantum rotational excitation ($N=2$) leading to a configuration with $L=2$ and even permutation symmetry; and (3) a two-quantum radial excitation ($N=2$) for which $L=0$ and even permutation symmetry holds, as for the ground-state configuration. *See* GELL-MANN, MURRAY.

In the subsequent decade, these assignments were confirmed, a large fraction of the corresponding strange baryon resonances were established, and the quantitative data on their decay properties received a convincing interpretation within this framework; also, two other configurations predicted to occur for $N=2$ were identified, as well as several of the configurations predicted for $N=3$ and $N=4$. For mesonic resonances, a quite similar situation was predicted, and the many excited nonets predicted for the $N=1$ excitation have all become established, although somewhat later, with indications for further nonets for $N=2$ and $N=3$. A complete elucidation of the dynamics of the higher resonance states has still not been achieved, despite much progress by N. Isgur and G. Karl in the framework of quantum chromodynamics, partly because of uncertainty concerning the proper framework for quantitative calculations of these excitations and partly because of some conflicting experimental data.

Dalitz was educated at Scotch College, Melbourne, where his interest in mathematics was stimulated by a teacher, A. D. Ross. Dalitz graduated in mathematics (B.A., 1944) and physics (B.Sc., 1945) from Melbourne University. He became a research student at Trinity College, Cambridge, as the Aitchison Traveling Scholar of Melbourne University, and received the Ph.D. (theoretical physics) in 1951, after periods at Bristol and Birmingham universities. He was lecturer and later reader in R. E. Peierls's department of mathematical physics at Birmingham, where he was greatly influenced by Dyson's lectures. Dalitz then spent 2 years' leave at Cornell University, working also at Stanford University, the Institute for Advanced Studies, and Brookhaven National Laboratory. In 1956 he joined the Enrico Fermi Institute of Nuclear Studies of the University of Chicago, where he was appointed full professor in 1959. In 1960 he was elected a fellow of the Royal Society, and he was appointed Royal Society Research Professor at Oxford in 1963. He was awarded the Maxwell Medal of the Institute of Physics and the Physical Society in 1966. In 1969 he gave the Bakerian Lecture of the Royal Society, and in 1975 he was awarded the Hughes Medal of the Royal Society for his contributions to elementary particle physics.

For background information *see* COSMIC RAYS; DALITZ PLOT; DISPERSION RELATIONS (ELEMENTARY PARTICLE); ELEMENTARY PARTICLE; MESON; NUCLEAR STRUCTURE; RADIOACTIVITY in the McGraw-Hill Encyclopedia of Science and Technology. ∎

DALLDORF, GILBERT
★ American experimental pathologist

Born Mar. 12, 1900, Davenport, IA, U.S.A.

Following graduate study with Ludwig Aschoff and James Ewing, Dalldorf collaborated for 10 years with Walter H. Eddy in the characterization of vitamin deficiency diseases. The goals were to determine the structural effects of vitamin deprivations and to measure the importance of newly recognized vitamins in terms of human disease. Many of their observations were summarized in a text, *The Avitaminoses* (1937; 3d ed. 1944). Clinical and community surveys were undertaken but failed to establish vitamin deficiencies as currently important causes of disease in the New York area. A good food supply and public education had evidently prevented deficiency diseases, other than those determined by organic defects.

A new and compelling challenge to the medical profession emerged during the 1930s, when epidemics of poliomyelitis grew in size and intensity. Dalldorf established a small experimental poliomyelitis station, initially to test methods of treatment and later to devise a prophylactic. It was discovered that monkeys infected with the choriomeningitis virus withstood experimental infections with virulent polio viruses that otherwise were invariably fatal. This surprising phenomenon was named the sparing effect. That same summer, F. O. MacCallum and G. M. Findlay in Great Britain reported that Rift Valley fever similarly protected monkeys against yellow fever. They called it the interference phenomenon, and that term is now universally used.

Unfortunately the interference phenomenon has not been usefully adapted to current problems in infectious disease, with the possible exception of canine distemper. It was used to good purpose nearly 200 years ago by Thomas Archer, a colonial physician, who discovered that the course of whooping cough, then a serious, debilitating disease, could be aborted by smallpox vaccination. The influence of virus interference is widespread in nature, and its principal mechanism, the formation of an inhibitory protein called interferon, was discovered by A. Isaacs. Eventually this remarkable mechanism may be applied to serve a therapeutic purpose.

Dalldorf's other principal achievement was the discovery of the coxsackieviruses. The stimulus, in this case, was Charles Armstrong's adaptation of a particular strain of polio virus to rodents. Dalldorf undertook to repeat Armstrong's experience and to isolate viruses in mice. No recoveries were made, but an occasional mouse showed minor responses, a little sluggishness, or a slight limp. In such animals close microscopic examination frequently revealed minute but distinctive lesions in the brainstem and spinal cord. Few of the specimens that induced these effects contained polio virus as judged by monkey tests, and the experience suggested that viruses other than poliovirus were involved in the summer epidemics.

In association with Grace M. Sickles, the search for other viruses was expanded and intensified in the Division of Laboratories and Research of the New York State Department of Health. Efforts were made to increase the susceptibility of the mice or to find more suitable rodents. Jeppe Orskov had learned to infect newborn mice with a mouse disease by painting the virus on the dam's nipples, and this finding suggested the use of immature animals as possibly more susceptible hosts of the hypothetical intestinal viruses.

The technique proved to be incredibly successful, and specimens from poliomyelitis patients injected intracerebrally or intraperitoneally into newborn mice were frequently found to harbor viruses of a wholly new variety. They were named coxsackieviruses because they were first found in patients from Coxsackie, NY. They have been often called "polio's cousins" since they resemble polio viruses in so many respects. The Soviets prefer to call one of the many types of coxsackievirus the poliovirus, type 4. Other types were later proved to be responsible for diseases for which etiological agents had not been established. Epidemic pleurodynia, or Bornholm disease, is an example of this group. The coxsackieviruses are ecologically related to the polioviruses, and the suppression of poliomyelitis by vaccination may alter their prevalence and severity in the future.

Immature and embryonic animals had previously served experimentalists in various ways but had not been used in the isolation of viruses. Ludwig Gross quickly applied the method in his studies of mouse leukemia and demonstrated the first leukemia virus. Many mosquito-borne viruses have been identified by means of immature mice, and the technique is widely used at present. The successful use of tissue culture in the propagation of polioviruses was discovered by J. F. Enders, T. H. Weller, and F. C. Robbins in the same year, 1948, that the coxsackieviruses were identified. These two techniques have been invaluable to virologists ever since. *See* ENDERS, JOHN FRANKLIN; ROBBINS, FREDERICK CHAPMAN; WELLER, THOMAS HUCKLE.

Dalldorf received his B.S. from the University of Iowa in 1921 and his M.D. from New York University in 1924. He was pathologist at New York Hospital in 1926–29 and at Grasslands Hospital, New York, during 1929–45. He was on the staff of the New York State Department of Health during 1945–57, and from 1959 worked at the Memorial Walker Laboratory, Sloan-Kettering Institute. He retired in 1967. He received the Fisher Memorial Award of the American Chemical Society (1955), the Distinguished Service Award of the New York University College of Medicine (1956), the Lasker Award of the Albert and Mary Lasker Foundation (1959), and the Medal of the New York Academy of Medicine (1964). He was elected to the National Academy of Sciences in 1955.

In addition to the book mentioned above, Dalldorf wrote *Introduction to Virology* (1955) and edited *Fungi and Fungous Diseases* (1962).

For background information *see* COXSACKIEVIRUS; INTERFERON; POLIOMYELITIS; VIRUS INTERFERENCE; VITAMIN in the McGraw-Hill Encyclopedia of Science and Technology. ∎

DAM, HENRIK
★ Danish biochemist and nutritionist

Born Feb. 21, 1895, Copenhagen, Denmark
Died Apr. 17, 1976, Copenhagen, Denmark

While studying the question of whether chicks can live without dietary cholesterol, Dam noticed that chicks reared on certain artificial diets exhibited a marked bleeding tendency associated with low clotting power of the blood. This condition was not a consequence of the absence of cholesterol from the diet, as the experiments showed that chicks, like many other animals, can synthesize cholesterol. A systematic search for the cause led to the finding of a new fat-soluble vitamin, which in 1935 was termed vitamin K. For this discovery, Dam shared with E. A. Doisy the 1943 Nobel Prize in physiology or medicine. *See* DOISY, EDWARD ADELBERT.

Dam also took part in the investigation of the role played by vitamin K in hemorrhagic diseases in humans. Suitable administration of vitamin K eliminates the risk of fatal bleeding otherwise encountered in surgery on patients with obstructive jaundice. This form of bleeding was shown to be due to insufficient absorption of vitamin K from the intestine in the absence of bile. A bleeding tendency sometimes occurring in children during the first week after birth can be prevented by administration of vitamin K to the infant immediately after birth or by administration of an excess of vitamin K to the mother a suitable time before delivery. This type of bleeding tendency is due to limitation of the passage of vitamin K from mother to fetus. Vitamin K was shown to be unrelated to hereditary hemophilia.

In studies with animals raised on artificial diets, Dam and his associates encountered manifestations of dietary imbalances

due to the combined effect of more than one factor. In chicks, they observed (1937–38) the "exudative diathesis," a condition in which massive amounts of plasma exude from the capillaries. This condition was traced to the lack of vitamin E. K. Schwarz and coworkers and E. L. R. Stokstad and coworkers showed later (1957) that, in addition to the lack of vitamin E, lack of selenium is necessary for the occurrence of exudative diathesis. The "alimentary encephalomalacia" previously described by other investigators and suggested to be caused by lack of vitamin E was shown (1958) by Dam and his associates to be specifically dependent upon dietary fatty acids of the linoleic acid series (as distinguished from the linolenic acid series) concomitantly with absence of vitamin E. A characteristic form of muscular dystrophy in chicks was observed and shown to be caused by lack of vitamin E in combination with low dietary sulfur amino acids.

Other manifestations of vitamin E deficiency in chicks and rats were investigated with respect to their interrelationship to dietary fat and to the role of vitamin E as an antioxidant. A sign of vitamin E deficiency in rats, "depigmentation of incisors," described by other investigators, was shown (1945) by Dam and his associates to depend not simply upon deficiency of vitamin E but also upon the presence and type of fat in the diet. Dam and his associates showed that dietary polyunsaturated fatty acids of the type present in fish oils induce autoxidation of body fat in chicks and rats when vitamin E is lacking. The previously known poor utilization of vitamin A in animals reared on vitamin E–deficient diets was shown to presuppose dietary highly unsaturated fatty acids capable of inducing autoxidation.

In hamsters, Dam and his associates found (1952) that rearing on certain artificial diets induces formation of gallstones. Cholesterol gallstones are formed abundantly when the diet is deficient in polyunsaturated fatty acids and carbohydrate is furnished as an easily absorbable sugar. This condition is unrelated to vitamin E deficiency. Other dietary combinations lead to the formation of amorphous pigmented gallstones. The formation of cholesterol gallstones in hamsters was shown to be associated with low ratios between the concentrations of bile acids and cholesterol and between phospholipids and cholesterol in the bile. These ratios could be raised by giving the carbohydrate in the form of starch and by adding fats rich in polyunsaturated fatty acids to the diet. These investigations led to studies on human bile and to the possibility of changing the composition of the latter, which is usually near the point of saturation with respect to cholesterol.

Dam graduated in chemistry from the Polytechnic Institute of Copenhagen in 1920. From 1923 he was connected with the department of physiology, and from 1928 with the department of biochemistry of the University of Copenhagen. In 1940 he went on a lecture tour to the United States, from where he did not return until 1946. During his stay in the United States, Dam was senior research associate at the University of Rochester (1942–45) and associate member of the Rockefeller Institute for Medical Research in New York (1945–46). In 1941 Dam was appointed professor of biochemistry at the Polytechnic Institute of Copenhagen. From 1956 to 1963 he was also head of the biochemical division of the Danish Fat Research Institute. Dam's work on vitamin K was done primarily in Copenhagen from 1929, the work on vitamin E both in Copenhagen and in the United States from 1937. The gallstone work was done in Copenhagen from 1951.

For background information *see* CHOLESTEROL; GALLSTONES; VITAMIN E; VITAMIN K in the McGraw-Hill Encyclopedia of Science and Technology. ∎

DANCKWERTS, PETER VICTOR

★ British chemical engineer

> **Born** Oct. 14, 1916, Southsea, Hampshire, England

Danckwerts began teaching and research in chemical engineering in 1948, at a time when scientific analysis of the problems of chemical engineering, although recognized to be desirable, had not yet attracted the enormous amount of attention bestowed on it today. In situations where the well-developed disciplines of fluid mechanics and chemical thermodynamics and the laws of conservation could be applied, all was well in principle, although in application mistakes were often made. In many of the typical situations faced by chemical engineers, the models used and the analyses based on them were as crude as children's drawings. This did not matter too much,

perhaps, when the engineering itself was fairly crude, and emphasis was more on making things work than on making them work well. Increasing competition in postwar markets and increasing sophistication in design created a need for more sophisticated concepts on which to base the scientific analysis of chemical engineering problems.

The relationship between a conceptual model and the engineering situation to which it relates is a subtle one. The model must incorporate some of the physical features of the actual situation—enough to predict the way in which the situation will respond to changes in operating conditions. On the other hand, a model which is slavish in detail will be too complicated to be useful. Utility is the criterion of a model for use in engineering analysis; it must lead to results which the designer can use with facility, and should itself be simple enough so that the practical user can return to it and extract new solutions to meet changed circumstances. Finally, the model should have a certain esthetic appeal.

Danckwerts first turned his attention to a classical chemical engineering process—the absorption of a gas by a liquid. Gas absorption is one of the most common processes encountered in the chemical industry. The equipment used for the purpose consists typically of a tower packed with metal or ceramic cylindrical rings. The absorbent liquid trickles down over this extensive surface, and the gas usually passes upward in countercurrent flow. The design and performance of such equipment

is a matter of considerable economic importance. The phenomena occurring in the gas and liquid streams are obviously very complicated, involving convection and diffusion, and in many cases chemical reaction as well. This is not a situation in which it would be constructive to try to make a completely faithful model of the process. Danckwerts proposed a surface-renewal model, in which the liquid at the surface of the descending film is supposed to be replaced piecewise in a random manner by liquid from the interior of the film. During its time of exposure each element of surface is supposed to absorb gas in the same way, as though it were stagnant. The model is reasonably realistic, contains the minimum number of parameters required to fit the facts, and provides an elegant basis for design calculations. It also forms the basis of methods whereby results of relatively simple, laboratory-scale experiments can be used to predict the effects of chemical reactions on rates of absorption in industrial equipment.

Another concept, which proved of considerable value to practicing chemical engineers, was that of the spread of residence times of material flowing in a continuous stream through a plant or process—the typical situation in the modern chemical industry. Usually, some of the material takes a longer time and some a shorter time than the average to pass through the process. This is likely to affect the efficiency of the plant or the acceptability of the product. For instance, if wet material passes through a dryer, some may pass through too quickly and emerge undried, while some may remain too long and become charred. Danckwerts showed how the distribution of residence times about the average can be quantitatively defined, and how it can be measured by simple techniques. He pointed out how the information may be used by plant designers—either in calculating the behavior of a plant if the distribution of residence times is known, or in modifying the design so as to control the distribution and improve the performance. He also pointed out that the extent of mixing on the molecular scale, which could vary in degree within limits set by the residence time distribution, could be an important factor in the performance of chemical reactors. These ideas were widely taken up and developed, and proved useful in many ways.

Danckwerts also contributed ideas to other topics, such as the quantitative study of mixtures and mixing processes and the notion of the scale of scrutiny. He considered that university workers can make valuable contributions to practical technology by devising new concepts and developing new lines of thought—a type of intellectual activity for which they may be better placed than their colleagues in industry, who are usually faced with urgent short-term problems.

Danckwerts received his B.A. from Balliol College, Oxford, in 1939. During World War II he was in the Royal Navy. In 1946 he went as a Commonwealth Fund fellow to the Massachusetts Institute of Technolgy, where he took his S.M. in chemical engineering practice in 1948. He then joined the staff of the newly formed department of chemical engineering at Cambridge University. In 1954 he was appointed deputy director of research and development in the Industrial Group of the Atomic Energy Authority. He was appointed professor of chemical engineering science at Imperial College, London, in 1956. In 1959 he returned to Cambridge as Shell Professor of Chemical Engineering. He retired in 1977 and became emeritus professor. He was elected a fellow of the Royal Society and became a founder fellow of the Fellowship of Engineering, both in 1969, and was elected foreign associate of the U.S. National Academy of Engineers in 1978.

Danckwerts wrote *Gas-Liquid Reactions* (1970).

For background information *see* FLUID MECHANICS; GAS ABSORPTION OPERATIONS; MODEL THEORY in the McGraw-Hill Encyclopedia of Science and Technology. ∎

DANIELS, FARRINGTON
★ American chemist

Born Mar. 8, 1889, Minneapolis, MN, U.S.A.

Died June 23, 1972, Madison, WI, U.S.A.

Daniels's principal researches lay in the field of basic chemical kinetics, but they led him into several related fields that appeared to have possible significance in human affairs. In recognition of his achievements, the American Chemical Society awarded him its Willard Gibbs Medal (1955) and Priestley Medal (1957).

In 1921 Daniels reported quantitative studies on the decomposition of nitrogen pentoxide, a gas-phase chemical reaction that at room temperature follows the first-order rate law with exactness. These researches led to the abandonment of the then current hypothesis that radiation from the containing vessel was a factor in the activation of chemical reactions. The nitrogen pentoxide studies were followed by investigations on the kinetics and decomposition mechanism of all the oxides of nitrogen and other gas reactions. In the thermal decomposition of ethyl bromide, Daniels found that the complete mechanism included the formation of free radicals and wall effects.

The photochemical decomposition of nitrogen pentoxide led to new experimental techniques for the accurate measurements of quantum yields in photochemical reactions. Daniels used these techniques to measure the maximum efficiency of photosynthesis in laboratory algae. A value of about 30 percent was established corresponding to the requirement of eight photons of light for each molecule of carbon dioxide reacting with water. In contrast, ordinary agriculture uses only a few tenths of 1 percent of the annual sunshine in its photosynthesis.

When isotopes became available, Daniels used them as tracers in the elucidation of reaction mechanisms, and in 1937 he calculated the concentration of carbon-13 that might be effected through chemical kinetics. He then carried out experimental measurements of the isotopic concentration in the hydrolysis of urea and other reactions.

In 1940, with N. Gilbert and W. G. Henderson, Daniels applied his knowledge of the chemical kinetics of nitrogen oxides to the fixation of atmospheric nitrogen, using a method proposed by F. G. Cottrell. Air was heated with fuel gas to 2100°C in a pair of pebble bed furnaces of magnesium oxide and then quenched at the rate of 4000°C per second, producing nitric oxide cheaply in concentrations of about 2 percent. The inflowing air was switched from one furnace to the other every few minutes, thus preheating the air, chilling the products rapidly enough to prevent the decomposition of the nitric oxide, and conserving the heat. Silica gel was used for the catalytic oxidation and recovery of nitric oxide. This Wisconsin process produced 40 short tons (36 metric tons) of nitric acid per day, but it was not quite competitive with nitric acid which was produced by the oxidation of ammonia synthesized by the Haber process.

During World War II Daniels was called into the atomic energy program and carried over into this work his experience with high-temperature ceramic furnaces. His design for a peacetime high-temperature gas-cooled nuclear power reactor was implemented in a large program at Oak Ridge, but after 2 years the program was discontinued because of a change in policy emphasis.

After the war Daniels extended his kinetic studies from gases and solutions to solids, starting with the phenomenon of thermoluminescence, which had been observed in quartz vessels exposed to radiations in nuclear reactors. With C. A. Boyd, D. F. Saunders, and others, he studied the thermoluminescence glow curves of many hundreds of natural minerals and laboratory crystals. He pointed out that whereas the laboratory crystals must be activated by exposure to x-rays or gamma rays, the natural minerals are sometimes activated by minute traces of radioactive elements that they contain as impurities.

Daniels extended these studies to researches on glow curves as a tool in geological stratigraphy, to possible age determinations of naturally thermoluminescent minerals, to problems in geochemistry, and even to an exploration of a method for recovering uranium from very low-grade ores at the mine. One practical result was the development of thermoluminescence radiation dosimetry. Using small quantities of lithium fluoride, this dosimeter has come to be important in measuring clinical radiation and in monitoring personnel who are exposed to radiation. Other amplifications of the study of solid reactions led to the use of differential thermal analysis in chemical kinetics and rate measurements of chemical reactions between mixtures of different solid particles.

Disappointed in the cancellation of his wartime project for a nuclear power reactor and impressed with the low efficiency of photosynthesis in agriculture, Daniels turned his attention to the direct use of radiant energy from the Sun. During the 1950s and 1960s, much of his effort was expended in trying to hasten—through lecturing, writing, and research—the direct use of the Sun's energy. In his personal research he emphasized those investigations that might lead to the early use of the solar energy in rural areas of developing countries. In particular, he worked on the development of small, family-size solar stills for desalting sea water, inexpensive focusing collectors of solar radiation, and fuel cells for obtaining electricity from the direct oxidation by air of waste organic material.

Daniels received his B.S. at the University of Minnesota in 1910 and his Ph.D. at Harvard University in 1914. He taught physical chemistry at Worcester Polytechnic Institute from 1914 to 1917. After 1920 he was connected with the University of Wisconsin. In 1945–46 he was director of the Metallurgical Laboratory in Chicago, devoted to research on atomic energy, and was a founder and chair of Argonne National Laboratory. From 1952 until his retirement in 1959 he was the chair of Wisconsin's chemistry department. He was elected to the National Academy of Sciences in 1947.

Daniels was the author or coauthor of over 230 scientific papers and 20 books, including *Physical Chemistry* (2d ed. 1961; 4th ed., with R. A. Alberty, 1975) and *Experimental Physical Chemistry* (7th ed. 1970). His kinetic researches are described in *Chemical Kinetics* (1937) and *Selected Studies in Chemical Kinetics* (1961). He also wrote *Direct Use of the Sun's Energy* (1964).

For background information *see* KINETICS, CHEMICAL; NITROGEN FIXATION; SOLAR ENERGY; THERMOLUMINESCENCE in the McGraw-Hill Encyclopedia of Science and Technology. ∎

DANJON, ANDRÉ LOUIS
★ French astronomer

Born *Apr. 6, 1890, Caen, Calvados, France*
Died *Apr. 21, 1967, Paris, France*

While primarily concerned with the development and improvement of instruments and methods in positional astronomy, Danjon devoted considerable efforts to directing the activities of the Strasbourg Observatory and later the Paris Observatory. At the latter he rebuilt the affiliated Meudon Observatory; created new services, such as the Radio Astronomy Department; and recruited a large number of scientists to work under his direction, increasing the staff from 60 to 350 in 18 years.

Positional astronomy had its beginnings with naked-eye observations in remotest antiquity. The introduction and evolution of early instruments, such as the armillary sphere and the triquetrum, led to increased precision; naked-eye techniques reached their apex with the work of Tycho Brahe. The introduction of the telescope and the subsequent employment of photographic methods raised the accuracy of the discipline to remarkable heights, as evidenced by the compilation of star catalogs of extreme precision.

In his study of the methods of positional astronomy, Danjon concluded that the transit instrument had attained its maximum precision. This led him to investigate new systems of reference, sys-

tems that were simpler and, above all, homogeneous. These studies culminated in the design of a fundamental new instrument, the prismatic 60° astrolabe, which became known as the Danjon astrolabe. The most essential aspects of the instrument are that it is impersonal and coaxial. The optical train includes a double symmetrical Wollaston prism, which is moved linearly by an electric motor with variable speed gearing, and an equilateral glass prism. Both the direct and the reflected star images are seen through the Wollaston prism, the movement of which is adjusted so that the ordinary image of the one and the extraordinary image of the other are seen as approximately stationary and side by side. By periodically making and breaking a circuit through the pen of a choronograph, a series of readings is obtained whose mean corresponds to the time at which the star was at an altitude of 60°. The prototype was built in 1951 at the Paris Observatory, and a final version was completed in 1956. The latter, which has a focal length of 100 centimeters and an aperture of 10 centimeters, can be used to observe stars down to a magnitude of 6.3 with a precision never before achieved in positional astronomy: The mean quadratic error is $0''.17$, and this has been reduced to $0''.10$ at certain sites. The Danjon astrolabe was in operation at more than 30 observatories by the late 1960s and was used in several cooperative projects—for example, in the International Geophysical Year and in the compilation of a fundamental catalog.

Another transit instrument, designed by Danjon while he was at the Strasbourg Observatory, is a reflecting transit instrument whose essential part is a Wollaston reversing prism. The device has an aperture of 6 centimeters, giving a precision of $0''.01$ in star positions. Danjon later built two similar instruments of an improved design at the Paris Observatory.

Early in his career Danjon had been greatly interested in visual photometry. He improved various differential photometers, which could be used to compare stars—day and night—without intermediate artificial stars by superimposing star images rather than by placing them side by side. In 1921 he built a photometer for observations of the lunar eclipse, and the he constructed an Arago-Pickering photometer, with which he made tens of thousands of observations of double stars. Danjon followed this with a double-image photometer, which was used to compare directly the Sun with the Moon, and with a cat's-eye photometer for studying variable stars. The latter had the advantage of also being able to measure the brightness of extended images, for example, of the Moon or of the "Earth light." Through its use Danjon became the first to plot a curve for the brightness of the Earth and to compute the planet's albedo (0.39). Finally, he designed a photometer to be used for the observation of Mercury and Venus, using the Sun as a reference, during the daylight hours. Danjon made more than 30,000 observations between 1937 and 1947, enabling him to calculate an albedo of 0.055 for Mercury and of 0.64 for Venus.

Among the other instruments that he designed were two spectrographs and a half-wave interference micrometer, which is more luminous than the Michelson interferometer and useful for observations of double stars and of Jovian satellites.

In 1958 Danjon became interested in the rotation of the Earth, in which irregularities could be determined by using the fundamental catalog compiled with the aid of the impersonal prismatic 60° astrolabe. Three variations in the rate of rotation must be distinguished: a yearly variation, due probably to atmospheric effects; a latitude variation, determined by S. C. Chandler in 1885; and an empirical irregular variation, representing the difference between universal time and atomic time, which can be represented by a smooth curve whose general trend can vary abruptly. Danjon intuitively deduced that these abrupt transitions were related to solar activity. In December 1958 he published his theory. The paper noted that a sudden increase in the rate of the Earth's rotation coincided with an exceptionally intense solar event which took place on Feb. 23, 1956. Later Danjon was able to relate a new, sudden change in the rotation of the Earth (the length of the day had increased by a little less than a millisecond on July 17, 1959) to an increase in solar activity on July 11, 14, and 16. He documented his calculations with indisputable evidence in *Notes et Informations de l'Observatoire de Paris.*

After studying at the Ecole Normale Supérieure in Paris from 1910 through 1914, Danjon served in the French army until 1919, when he became an astronomer at the Strasbourg Observatory. He obtained the degree of docteur ès sciences in 1928 at Strasbourg. Two years later he was appointed director of the ob-

servatory and in 1931 professor at Strasbourg University. In 1935 Danjon was named dean of the Faculty of Sciences at the university, which was evacuated to Clermont-Ferrand during World War II. He surrendered these posts in 1945 to become director of the Paris Observatory. In 1946 he was appointed a professor at the Sorbonne and in 1954 director of the Institut d'Astrophysique de Paris. He retired from all three posts in 1963. Danjon was elected to the Académie des Sciences in 1948, and he was president of the International Astronomical Union from 1955 to 1958.

Danjon wrote *Lunettes et Telescopes,* with A. Coudon (1935), and *Astronomie Generale* (1952).

For background information *see* AS-TROLABE, PRISMATIC; EARTH, ROTATION AND ORBITAL MOTION OF; PHOTOM-ETER; TRANSIT (ASTRONOMY) in the McGraw-Hill Encyclopedia of Science and Technology. ∎

DANTZIG, GEORGE BERNARD
★ American mathematician

***Born** Nov. 8, 1914, Portland, OR, U.S.A.*

Dantzig's contributions—especially his formulation of linear programs as models for resource allocation and his invention of the simplex method to solve them—were pivotal in the development of mathematical programming from the late 1940s onward. Elected to the National

Academy of Sciences in 1971, and recipient in 1975 of both the National Medal of Science and the John von Neumann Theory Prize, he has been widely regarded as the initiator of, and leading figure in, the revolutionary scientific development of mathematical programming as a powerful method for optimally managing resources in thousands of applications in industry and government.

Mathematical programming is concerned with the problems of minimizing a function, called the objective function, of several variables subject to restrictions on those variables. Many important problems that involve optimal allocation of scarce resources among competing activities, a fundamental problem in economics, can be formulated as mathematical programs.

In 1947 Dantzig discovered that a wide variety of planning problems could be formulated as linear programs, that is, as problems of minimizing a linear function of several nonnegative variables satisfying a system of linear equations. What made this discovery a breakthrough of major scientific and practical importance was that he also found a finite iterative algorithm—the simplex method—for solving such problems, which turned out to be remarkably efficient. That method, probably the most widely used algorithm since the time of its discovery, and its refinements remain the best way to solve nearly all linear programs arising in practice. Fortunately, Dantzig's discovery of linear programming occurred about the same time as the development of the first computers. These simultaneous advances led to an explosion of applications, especially in the industrial sector. Managers were given a powerful and practical method for formulating and comparing extremely large numbers of interdependent alternative courses of action.

Dantzig was a leader in developing applications which exhibited the enormous power of the linear programming approach. Most large firms now use his simplex method for linear programming. A 1972 survey of operations research at the corporate level showed linear programming was used in 19 percent of their projects. Some of the prominent applications are in the petroleum industry (for exploration, blending, production scheduling, and distribution); the iron and steel industry (to evaluate iron ores, explore the addition of coke ovens, and select products); the food processing industry (for shipping from plants to warehouses); paper mills (to reduce trim loss); and the U.S. Department of Energy (to evaluate energy policy alternatives). Several countries use it for economic planning. Linear programming and its generalizations also have had a significant impact on the development of the fields of economics and statistics.

Dantzig contributed significantly to the subsequent development of all major areas of mathematical programming and other parts of operations research. His influence was especially strong in the areas of quadratic programming, complementary pivot theory, nonlinear equations, convex programming, integer programming, stochastic programming, dynamic programming, and game theory. Dantzig recognized early that many problems of practical importance would lead to extremely large linear programs. Consequently, he emphasized the development of techniques for handling large systems by exploiting their special structure, especially the abundance of zero coefficients. The exploitation of special structures has enormous potential in making feasible the solution of very large problems that otherwise would be impossible. He originated with Philip Wolfe the decomposition principle for solving large systems with block-diagonal structure. D. Hirschfeld in 1971 made use of Dantzig's and R. M. Van Slyke's generalized upper bounding method to solve a linear program having 282,468 variables and 50,215 equations on an IBM 370/165 computer in 2½ hours which would have taken 37 years if treated as a matrix without special structure.

The development of linear programming was a principal force leading to the emergence of the mathematical science of decision making as a new discipline, called operations research or management science, in the early 1950s. Linear programming, probably the single most important tool in this field, figures prominently in the more than 30 technical journals devoted to operations research. Most universities offer courses in operations research, nearly all emphasizing linear programming. Each year more than 30,000 students take an introductory course in this field. Many universities have departments of operations research, and operations research also is a major part of most academic programs in business, industrial engineering, and mathematical sciences.

Dantzig earned an A.B. degree in mathematics and physics from the University of Maryland, where his father, Tobias

Dantzig, also a well-known mathematician, taught mathematics; an M.A. in mathematics from the University of Michigan; and a Ph.D. in mathematics from the University of California, Berkeley, in 1946. Subsequently, he received honorary doctorate degrees from Technion, the Israel Institute of Technology; the University of Linköping, Sweden; the University of Maryland; and Yale University.

Dantzig was a junior statistician at the U.S. Bureau of Labor Statistics, 1937–39; chief of the Combat Analysis Branch, Statistical Control, and mathematical adviser at U.S. Air Force Headquarters, 1941–52; research mathematician for the Rand Corporation, 1952–60; and chairperson of the Operations Research Center and professor at the University of California, Berkeley, 1960–66. He became professor of operations research and computer science at Stanford University in 1966. He served as president of two operations research organizations and was a founder of the Mathematical Programming Society, besides holding membership in other groups, including the Institute of Management Science and the Operations Research Society. He was elected a fellow of the Institute of Mathematical Statistics and of the Econometrics Society.

Dantzig was the author of *Linear Programming and Extensions* (1963), which is still a standard reference in the field, and coauthor, with T. Saaty, of *Compact City* (1973), and more than a hundred technical papers contributing to all aspects of mathematical programming and its applications.

For background information *see* LINEAR PROGRAMMING; OPERATIONS RESEARCH in the McGraw-Hill Encyclopedia of Science and Technology. ■

DARLINGTON, CYRIL DEAN
★ British biologist

Born *Dec. 19, 1903, Chorley, Lancashire, England*

Darlington was concerned with showing how the mechanisms of heredity, variation, and reproduction work and how they are adaptively connected in evolution, forming what he described as a genetic system.

After a training in agriculture at Wye College, Darlington went to work in November 1923 under William Bateson at the John Innes Institution. There he was brought face to face with the dilemma of

genetics at that time—the choice between the cytoplasm espoused by Bateson and the chromosomes espoused by his cytologist Frank Newton. Both Bateson and Newton died within 4 years, but not before Newton had given his pupil the idea of using polyploid plants to understand what the chromosomes do at meiosis.

T. H. Morgan, and equally F. A. Janssens, had thought of crossing over between paired chromosomes simply as a matter of recombining their genes. Darlington's first step was to show that it was much more. By way of chiasma formation, it was responsible for association and repulsion, segregation and reduction of the chromosomes—indeed, for the whole succession of events at meiosis. Crossing over was thus the crux of all sexual processes, the prime variable in the character of all sexual populations and species. And, Darlington argued, it had been so from the beginning of evolution (*Recent Advances in Cytology*, 1932; 3d ed. 1965).

This view was long disputed. Its apparent exceptions, however, led to further steps in Darlington's argument. Complex differences, such as occur between the sex chromosomes in animals and plants, arose, he maintained, from the suppression of crossing over between some parts of them. The same was true of the complexes of hybrid species as in *Oenothera*. The size of the gene as a unit of crossing over was thus a function of the similarity of the pairing chromosomes. Hence it depended on the breeding system that brought them together. Again, the ab-

sence of crossing over in one sex (as in male flies) appeared to him as an adaptation acquired in evolution; it had the effect of restricting the amount of recombination in species with a short life cycle (*Evolution of Genetic Systems,* 1939; 2d ed. 1958). Later it became clear that in sexual reproduction with two kinds of germ cell, two forms of meiosis were always differentiated, often giving in effect two tracks in heredity: one created variation by crossing over, the other preserved variation by suppressing crossing over.

While using the chromosomes for the study of evolutionary problems, Darlington maintained that they must always be considered adaptively as physiological agents. The special situation of genes of visible action, such as the centromere, he therefore attempted to relate at the same time to the movements, the activities, and the changing linkage relations of chromosomes.

When interpreting the physiological, mechanical, and evolutionary properties of the chromosomes in such genetic terms, Darlington had two aims. The first was to establish a genetic framework for biology. But a second aim was to establish at the center of this framework rules of chromosome behavior that would fit them into a pattern of chemical structure and activity; the basis of this pattern was successively revealed by T. Caspersson and Jean Brachet, J. D. Watson, F. H. C. Crick, and others. Further, the contrast between genetic particles responsible for nuclear and cytoplasmic heredity, which he related to the primary chemical distinction between deoxyribonucleic and ribonucleic acids, was seen by Darlington as overriding the secondary biological distinctions, whether in the higher organisms or in viruses, between heredity, development, and infection (*Elements of Genetics,* 1949; *Genes, Plants, and People,* with K. Mather, 1950). *See* BRACHET, JEAN LOUIS AUGUSTE; CRICK, FRANCIS HARRY COMPTON; WATSON, JAMES DEWEY.

Darlington began by taking his lead from the then recent work of Janssens and Morgan. His ideas, however, led him farther back, first to August Weismann and then to Francis Galton and Charles Darwin. He claimed to have found an even greater connectedness and a more extreme determinism in evolutionary mechanisms than had his predecessors. This he attributed to the role of breeding systems in controlling variation and exploiting its uncertainty as well as its certainty; and

also to the principle that the heredity of the parent provides so much of the environment of the offspring. This principle, he claimed, reaches its extreme expression in the origin of the flowering plants (angiosperms) and in the evolution of humans.

These new paradoxes suggested to Darlington that the pitfalls besetting the most difficult of all genetic problems, those of human society, might now be avoided. Hence he was led to investigate the reciprocal relations of technical discovery, religious beliefs, and human breeding systems and to foreshadow genetic interpretations of the origin of agriculture, of the evolution of language and of morals, of the structure of society, and indeed of the processes of history in general. These views were expressed in three books: *Genetics of Man* (1964), *The Evolution of Man and Society* (1969), and *The Little Universe of Man* (1978). In them Darlington's genetic arguments began to point in the same direction as the developing opinions of those who see the greatest human responsibility in the relation with the environment, especially in preserving the Earth for posterity. Evolutionary theory had led to an unforeseen convergence.

By 1978, however, the development of molecular and microbial genetics had given the evolution of genetic systems a substantial connectedness that it had lacked in 1932. It became possible to give an account of the action of natural selection working at all the connected levels between units of deoxyribonucleic acid, chromosomes, nuclei, cells, organisms, and species. New and partly contradictory meanings arose in this way for Darwinian assumptions. They exposed the unexpected significance of the passage of variation along two tracks in heredity and its utilization for both the splitting and binding of species. Darlington recommended a diagrammatic rather than an axiomatic approach to this new view of evolution by choice ("A Diagram of Evolution," *Nature,* 1978).

Darlington became director of the John Innes Institution in 1939 and undertook its removal from Merton to Bayfordbury in 1949. In 1953 he was appointed Sherardian Professor of Botany and Keeper of the Botanic Garden at Oxford. He received the Royal Medal of the Royal Society in 1946. With K. R. Lewis, he founded at Oxford the International Chromosome Conference in 1964.

In order to establish the techniques and

applications of chromosome study, Darlington wrote *The Chromosome Atlas of Flowering Plants,* with A. P. Wylie (1956), *Chromosome Botany and the Origins of Cultivated Plants* (1956; 3d ed. 1973), and *The Handling of Chromosomes,* with L. F. La Cour (6th ed. 1973). With R. A. Fisher, he founded and edited the periodical *Heredity* (1947). Darlington wrote also on the reform of university teaching (*Teaching Genetics,* 1963), on the relations of academies and governments with research, on the Vavilov-Lysenko controversy in the Soviet Union (*Conflict of Science and Society,* 1948), and on the history of scientific discovery (*Darwin's Place in History,* 1959).

For background information *see* CHROMOSOME; GENETICS; MEIOSIS; NUCLEIC ACID in the McGraw-Hill Encyclopedia of Science and Technology. ■

DARNELL, JAMES EDWIN, JR.
★ American physician and molecular biologist

Born Sept. 9, 1930, Columbus, MS, U.S.A.

Viruses were described by S. E. Luria as elements of "infectious heredity"; that is, they possess their own genes which, inside the infected cell, use the cell machinery to multiply. Darnell was a leader in the use of viruses that infect human and animal cells to study the mechanisms of gene expression in human cells. The major finding of his work was that animal cells make very long precursor ribonucleic acid (RNA) molecules and then trim them down to functional size. It is suspected that the biochemical steps of cutting and trimming RNA molecules will prove to be important in the control of gene activity in animal cells. His interest in, and first experience with, laboratory science began in medical school, where he worked with Robert J. Glaser and a fellow student, Steven I. Morse, on the participation of group A streptococci in rheumatic fever and on the inability of penicillin to remove all streptococci from rabbits without the concurrent action of white blood cells, an important consideration in the treatment of human streptococcal infections with penicillin. *See* LURIA, SALVADOR EDWARD.

The work with penicillin led Darnell to join the laboratory of Harry Eagle at the National Institutes of Health in Bethesda, MD, where the mechanism of action of penicillin was under study. Darnell finished his internship in internal medicine, but by the time he joined Eagle's group, the whole direction of Eagle's work had been changed by the successful growth of mammalian cells outside the body. Together with Eagle and Leon Levintow, Darnell performed some of the first modern biochemical studies on animal virus growth in the newly developed human cell cultures. With the aid of radioisotopes and a new purification scheme for poliovirus, the time of formation of virus RNA and protein molecules was accurately charted for the first time for any virus other than bacterial viruses. These experiments were the prototypes of others using various animal viruses. *See* EAGLE, HARRY.

Work with poliovirus continued when Darnell established his first independent laboratory at the Massachusetts Institute of Technology (MIT) in 1961. The interest of the group broadened to include the interruption of host cell protein and RNA synthesis caused by virus infection. In order to study cell synthesis before and after virus infection, techniques had to be established to examine the cell structures that were responsible for protein synthesis. Cell messenger RNA (mRNA), the information courier between the DNA library in the cell nucleus and the translation machinery that reads the information contained in mRNA to make protein in the cell cytoplasm, was identified as part of the so-called polyribosomes, collections of many ribosmes that translate into

protein the information contained in one mRNA molecule. Animal cell mRNA was thereby isolated for the first time. During poliovirus infection of cells, and the consequent interruption of cell protein synthesis, the host cell mRNA disappeared from polyribosomes, to be replaced by the virus RNA acting as its own mRNA. This demonstration of the cellular damage caused by a virus strongly encouraged the use of new ideas and techniques in cell and molecular biology in the study of cellular disease processes.

The study of cell RNA that was begun in order to investigate poliovirus RNA had a major impact on Darnell's future scientific career. Poliovirus RNA was thought to be approximately 6000 to 7000 bases long (later, approximately 8000 was shown to be more accurate), and it soon became clear that the cell nucleus contained RNA molecules that were even larger than poliovirus RNA, and larger than the major species of cytoplasmic RNA, the larger ribosomal RNA, which is 5000 bases long. Deciphering the meaning of these large nuclear RNA molecules required more than 15 years of work and constituted the major contribution of Darnell and his associates.

First, it was discovered that the most prominent large nuclear RNA species was cut into specific parts (the individual ribosomal RNA molecules). Later, transfer RNA (tRNA), the other major structural RNA of the cell, was also found to be made by the cutting out of a functional molecule from a larger-size precursor RNA molecule. These were the first demonstrations that cells made a large molecule and later trimmed it to proper functional size. Darnell and his coworkers questioned whether mRNA molecules, like ribosomal RNA and tRNA, might also be carved out of larger precursor RNA molecules. The interest in mRNA manufacture devolved from its role in instructing cells to make different proteins in different amounts in different cells at different times. This controlled inter-play between information storage in nuclear DNA and information retrieval in the form of different mRNAs is the basis of differentiation—the term used to describe how one fertilized cell develops into the multiplicity of different cells that make up whole human or animal bodies.

The research results of 1977–78 finally solved the question of how mRNA is manufactured. Again, work with a virus, this time a DNA virus that used nuclear

(cellular) enzymes to make its mRNA, was the key. Results from the Darnell group indicated that a very long nuclear RNA molecule was the only RNA product copied from the DNA of adenovirus, a common human virus associated with inflammation of the eyes and throat. Two groups of young investigators at MIT (Philip Sharp, Susan Berget, and Clair Moore) and the Cold Spring Harbor Laboratories (Louise Chow, Tom Broker, Richard Gelinas, Richard Roberts, and Dan Klessig) discovered the startling fact that the adenovirus mRNAs in the cytoplasm of infected cells contained sequences from noncontiguous parts of the long nuclear RNA. The surprising conclusion was that, in the manufacture of messenger RNA, not only was the long nuclear molecule cut, but pieces were spliced together again. This cutting and splicing to make mRNA in cell-free extracts was demonstrated in Darnell's lab.

Darnell attended the University of Mississippi (B.A., 1951) and the Washington University School of Medicine (M.D., 1955). He worked in the Laboratory of Cell Biology of the National Institutes of Health (1956–60) and then spent a year at the Institut Pasteur in Paris investigating the repression of bacterial enzyme formation. He was assistant professor and then associate professor of biology at MIT (1961–64). In 1964 Darnell joined the faculty of the Albert Einstein College of Medicine, serving until 1968. In that year he became professor of biological sciences at Columbia University, and in 1971 chairperson of the department. In mid-1974 he joined the faculty of the Rockefeller University. As Vincent Astor Professor there, Darnell and a large group of young sicientists engaged in projects aimed at understanding differentiation. He received the Borden Undergraduate Research Award in 1955, the Career Research Award of the National Cancer Institute in 1962 and 1964, the Career Scientist Award of the Health Research Council of the City of New York in 1965 and 1972, and the Howard Taylor Ricketts Award of the University of Chicago in 1979. In 1973 he became a member of the National Academy of Sciences and the American Academy of Arts and Sciences in recognition of his role in the study of RNA biochemistry in human cells.

Darnell served on the editorial boards of the *Journal of Molecular Biology, Cell, Journal of Cell Biology,* and *Virology.* In addition to publishing more than 125 scientific articles, he coauthored *General Virology* (3d ed. 1977).

For background information *see* ANIMAL VIRUS; GENETICS; MOLECULAR BIOLOGY; RIBONUCLEIC ACID (RNA); RIBOSOMES in the McGraw-Hill Encyclopedia of Science and Technology. ∎

DART, RAYMOND ARTHUR
★ South African anatomist

Born Feb. 4, 1893, Toowong, Brisbane, Queensland, Australia

Dart realized that the fossil brain of a man-ape child that he found in 1924 at Taungs, Republic of South Africa, represented an extinct ape group, which he called *Australopithecus africanus,* or "South African ape." With brains no bigger than those of large gorillas, these apes were more advanced intellectually, lived in caves away from tropical forests, had an erect posture, and pursued a hunting life in the most fierce and bitter mammalian environment ever known. At Makapansgat, 400 miles (640 kilometers) northeast of Taungs, he later identified another site and further specimens of this man-ape and described their predatory behavior and osteodontokeratic (or bone, tooth, and horn) culture by statistical and comparative study of the accompanying faunal remains. For these achievements he received the Viking Medal and Award in Physical Anthropology for 1957.

In *The Descent of Man* (1871), Charles Darwin, who recognized the gorilla and

chimpanzee as humans' nearest relatives, wrote: "It is somewhat more probable that our early progenitors lived on the African continent than elsewhere." However, E. Dubois's discovery of *Pithecanthropus* in Java—and thus in proximity to the gibbon and orangutan of tropical Asia—concentrated the search for human ancestors on the Asiatic continent between World Wars I and II. Darwin and his followers had also expected that humans' progenitors would have developed an appreciably enlarged brain before losing their enlarged canine teeth. The Piltdown *Eoanthropus* discovery of 1912, which was not proved fraudulent until 1953, was officially accepted as supporting this idea. So *Australopithecus* was unacceptable from every current point of view.

The 5-year old infant whose skull Dart found, with its baby teeth still complete and the first adult molars just breaking through, had a brain rivaling that of the largest known gorillas. Furthermore, its face was complete. It differed from chimpanzees and gorillas of similar age in having a vertical forehead instead of eyebrow ridges, a recessed face instead of projecting muzzle and teeth, and vertical front teeth and small incisors and canines instead of fangs. It also resembled humans in the domelike—not flattened—form of brain, the downward-inclined orbits, and the projection of the forebrain backward over the hindbrain or cerebellum.

The expansion of the brain, due to localized growth between the areas for feeling, hearing, and vision, was measurable through the threefold separation of the parallel and lunate brain furrows. The more forward situation of the foramen magnum in the skull base testified to the ape's erectness. Apart from anatomical features, its divergence from living apes was shown by its geological situation in a travertine believed to be of late Tertiary (Pliocene) age; by its southern geographical situation in the temperate zone on the eastern fringe of the Kalahari desert; and by its troglodytic life in a cave amid the bones of the animals he lived on.

In 1937 R. Broom, who had supported Dart's claims from the outset, found adult man-ape remains at Sterkfontein, 30 miles (48 kilometers) west of Johannesburg. During the next 15 years he made repeated discoveries of adult and infant remains of the australopithecine types he called *Plesianthropus* and *Paranthropus.* His monographs gradually removed all doubts of the australopithecines' anatomi-

cal status. Powerful support from Professor (later Sir) Wilfrid Le Gros Clark of Oxford and from Sir Arthur Keith turned the tide. *See* LE GROS CLARK, SIR WILFRID (EDWARD).

The fifth of nine children of a farmer-storekeeper, Dart majored in biology as a foundation scholar in the University of Queensland. He took his B.Sc. in 1913 and his B.Sc. (honors) examination the following year concurrently with beginning medical studies in Sydney University. There he graduated M.B., Ch.M., in 1917 while holding the posts of demonstrator in anatomy and acting vice-principal of St. Andrew's College. After serving overseas in England and France as captain in the Australian Army Medical Corps, he became senior demonstrator in anatomy at University College, London (1919–22), and spent a year (1920–21) in America as one of the first two foreign fellows of the Rockefeller Foundation. Shortly after his return to London as senior lecturer in histology and embryology (1922), he was appointed professor of anatomy in the University of the Witwatersrand. He held that post from 1923 to 1958. From 1926 to 1943 he also served as dean of the Faculty of Medicine.

Dart wrote *Cultural Status of the South African Man-Apes* (1956), *The Osteodontokeratic Culture of Australopithecus promethus* (1957), and, with Denis Craig, *Adventures with the Missing Link* (1959).

For background information *see* FOSSIL MAN in the McGraw-Hill Encyclopedia of Science and Technology. ∎

DARWIN, CHARLES GALTON
British physicist

Born Dec. 19, 1887, Cambridge, England
Died Dec. 31, 1962, Cambridge, England

While investigating the diffraction of x-rays, Darwin developed a method of calculating the intensity of reflection and the shape of the reflection curve. Darwin's theory, discovered independently and about the same time by Ewald in Germany, is known as the dynamical theory of x-ray diffraction. The form of the angular distribution of intensity in the diffraction pattern from a perfect crystal, as originally calculated by Darwin, is known as a Darwin curve.

The discovery of x-rays by Wilhelm

Roentgen in 1895 led to research into their fundamental nature. Arthur Sommerfield, through diffraction experiments with slits and gratings, soon established that these rays are part of the electromagnetic spectrum and that they have a wavelength of about 10^{-9} centimeter. When coupled with an earlier suggestion by William Barlow that interatomic distances are of the order of 10^{-8} centimeter, this led Max von Laue to theorize that if a crystal were an orderly array of atoms, diffraction phenomena would occur that would be characteristic of the crystalline arrangement. In 1912, in collaboration with Friedrich and Knipping, von Laue published a paper indicating that such phenomena do indeed occur. This paper led Darwin, working in collaboration with Henry G. J. Moseley at the University of Manchester, to search for a theory that would better account for the experimental measures of intensity than the simple assumption that each atom scatters radiation as though the others were absent. In July 1913 Darwin and Moseley published a paper that was mostly experimental, measuring the intensities of beams reflected from a crystal by the ionization produced. However, the importance of temperature was realized, and a crude theory of reflection of white radiation was presented.

The following February, Darwin published a paper in which he calculated the intensity of reflection by a crystal, allowing for the effect of temperature and the refractive index of the rays. However,

he showed that the calculated effect was much smaller than that observed if the crystals were perfect. In a paper published 2 months later, the discrepancy was shown not to be caused (as Darwin had at first supposed) by the influence of the waves due to one plane of atoms on the atoms of other planes, though this effect does indeed exist, but to the imperfection of the crystal. In a paper published in 1922, Darwin showed how the theory expressed in these earlier papers justified the method of calculation of atomic scattering from the intensity of crystal reflections used by Sir William Bragg, James, and Bosanquet.

In the 1914 papers Darwin had calculated the efficiency of x-ray reflection by a perfect crystal, showing that over a very short angular range the superficial layers give a complete reflection, and he found that the calculated integrated reflection is far smaller than that observed by him and Moseley. He rightly ascribed the discrepancy to the fact that a crystal is not ideally perfect but is composed of a mosaic of blocks in slightly different orientations. Paradoxically, he found that imperfection increases the intensity of reflection, because the mosaic elements at depths beneath the crystal surface are not robbed of their chance to reflect by more superficial elements, since these are set at slightly different angles. The formulas that Darwin established in these papers were the basis for interpreting subsequent quantitative measurements.

Another significant contribution to theoretical physics was Darwin's use of P. A. M. Dirac's electron theory to derive the explanation of the fine structure of the hydrogen spectrum. In 1927, using as his theme that the electron is to be taken as a wave of two components (like light) and not of one (like sound), Darwin was able to derive two wave equations to fit the hydrogen spectrum. They were unsymmetrical, taking a different form according to the direction of space chosen as the prime axis. Darwin tried to interpret them in terms of a vector, but the vector was arbitrary to some degree. Although this was before Dirac's postulation of the electron with four wave functions, Darwin's solution later proved an approximation to Dirac's. *See* DIRAC, PAUL ADRIEN MAURICE.

In February 1928 Dirac's first paper on his new relativistic electron appeared. Darwin at once recognized its significance and translated Dirac's work from non-

commutative algebra into the ordinary language of differential equations. He also showed that his own two equations were approximations to those derived from Dirac's theory. Then he applied the theory to the problem of the hydrogen atom and determined the energy levels, including their fine structure. In addition, Darwin's paper made the Dirac theory accessible to physicists not yet familiar with the new quantum mechanics, greatly accelerating its general acceptance. Darwin followed this with two papers, one on the magnetic moment of the new electron and the other on its diffraction. In the first paper he analyzed the magnetic field of a moving Dirac electron and showed the relation between the contributions of the current and the intrinsic magnetic moment of the electron. He also examined the relation between the polarization of an electron wave and that of a wave of light. In the second paper Darwin worked out the simplest case of diffraction, namely, that by a line grating exerting periodic electric or magnetic forces, including the polarizing effects if any.

Among the other areas in which Darwin made contributions were classical optics, magnetooptics, and the absorption and scattering of alpha particles. In his later years he was deeply concerned with eugenics.

The grandson of Charles Robert Darwin, the father of the theory of evolution by natural selection, and the eldest son of George Darwin, a prominent astronomer, Charles Galton Darwin studied at Trinity College, Cambridge, and at the University of Manchester, receiving the degrees of M.C., M.A., and Sc.D. After completing his studies at Trinity in 1909, he was appointed a reader in mathematical physics at Manchester, where he worked under the direction of Lord Rutherford. He left this post in 1914 to serve in the army and, following his return to civilian life, in 1919, became a fellow and lecturer at Christ's College, Cambridge. Four years later Darwin was appointed professor of natural philosophy at the University of Edinburgh, a position he retained until 1936, when he returned to Cambridge as master of Christ's College. In 1938 he accepted the directorship of the National Physical Laboratory, a position he held until his retirement in 1949. In 1941–42 Darwin was in charge of the British Central Scientific Office in Washington, DC, set up to improve liaison between the scientific war efforts of Great Britain and the

United States. Among the honors he received was the Royal Medal of the Royal Society of London (1935), of which he was elected a fellow in 1922.

Darwin wrote *The New Conceptions of Matter* (1931) and *The Next Million Years* (1952).

For background information *see* ATOMIC STRUCTURE AND SPECTRA; ELECTRON; QUANTUM THEORY, RELATIVISTIC; X-RAY DIFFRACTION in the McGraw-Hill Encyclopedia of Science and Technology. ∎

DAUSSET, JEAN
★ French biologist and medical scientist

Born Oct. 19, 1916, Toulouse, France

Dausset first became attracted to the biological side of medicine as a result of his time in the resuscitation service during the Tunisian and French campaigns of World War II. Thus, in 1951 he described transfusion reactions caused by dangerous universal donors possessing strong immune anti-A antibodies in their plasma. He demonstrated that these antibodies developed after vaccination by antidiphtheria and antitetanus anatoxins which contained soluble substance A. The systematic testing of donor blood for these antibodies has since helped to avoid such accidents. Dausset introduced a method of exchange transfusion in adults, used particularly in the treatment of septicemia perfringens and cases of renal failure.

Dausset's attention was then attracted by the autoimmune hemolytic anemias. Using as a base the serological characteristics of the corresponding autoantibodies, a classification of these anemias was proposed, and a rare variety due to an acquired polyagglutinability (Tn autoantibody) was described. This work on anemias promoted a natural progression from red cell serology to that of leukocytes and platelets and auto- and alloantibodies. He observed in 1952 a strong leukocyte or platelet agglutination when the sera of polytransfused patients were mixed with these blood elements from other individuals.

This was the turning point, and from that time Dausset's scientific career was entirely devoted to the description of leukocyte or tissue polymorphism. He demonstrated the presence of the antigens of the ABO system on leukocytes and platelets, but his main contribution came in 1958 with the description of the first alloleukocyte antigen, MAC (now called HLA-A2). The MAC (so named after the initials of three nonagglutinated donors) antigen was discovered by a systematic study of many hundreds of sera tested against a panel of normal lymphocytes. Six sera reacted almost identically on the panel. An anti-MAC antibody was developed by purposely transfusing a patient who was MAC-negative with a regular donor who was MAC-positive. In his first publication on this subject, Dausset predicted the possible importance of such leukocyte antigens in human transplantation, in the early days of which he found a correlation between the presence of leukocyte disparities between donor and recipient and the kidney graft function.

In 1965 a systematic study of other antigens was undertaken. In 50 antileukocyte sera, 10 specificities were defined (one being the MAC antigen, three others being independently described by other teams). Analyzing carefully their interrelationships, Dausset concluded that they might be genetically related, and probably belonged to a unique complex system which he proposed to call Hu-1 (now HLA), analogous to the H-2 mouse system. He noticed that out of the 10 specificities three antigens could belong to a second allelic series closely linked in the same complex. These concepts were not universally admitted at the time, but were fully confirmed by family studies carried out in 1967.

In the same year, skin grafts were performed, in collaboration with F. T. Rapaport, which showed that incompatibilities of the few antigens then known were detrimental to the skin's survival—thus demonstrating the predicted role of these antigens in transplantation.

Efforts were then made in three parallel directions. In Dausset's laboratories 32 new specificities of new alleles of the two allelic series of the HLA system were described (some independently by other teams). The HLA-A and B series in Caucasoids were gradually completed. In 1972 Dausset organized the 5th International Workshop on Histocompatibility, when 54 populations of the world were HLA-typed, and the anthropological distribution of the HLA antigen established.

A systematic skin graft program involving precise analysis of the role of these antigens in transplantation was conducted on volunteers which Dausset attracted by his enthusiasm to this endeavor—more than 500 individuals and 200 families were involved. Skin grafts made, with the collaboration of Rapaport, in various genetical situations, with or without preimmunization, gave statistical proof of the prevailing influence of tissue compatibility with respect not only to the HLA system but also to the ABO system. The immunogenetic law of human transplantation was thus established. But this experimental demonstration was more difficult to transpose onto clinical ground. However, Dausset fought tirelessly to convince surgeons of the necessity of HLA donor selection. He first (1966) proposed the organization of an organ exchange network, and he founded France-Transplant.

The first study of the association between HLA antigens and disease was performed by Dausset in 1967, and concerned the possible link between acute lymphocyte leukemia and HLA antigens. In spite of a negative result, this study gave the impetus to thousands of research projects on other diseases, and led to the discovery of several strong or weak connections with diseases such as ankylosing spondylitis, juvenile diabetes, and autoimmune disease, thus opening new avenues to preventive medicine.

Dausset later described two B-lymphocyte antigens, one HLA-independent (Co) and the other HLA-linked (Li). The latter is the first description of a B-lymphocyte HLA-DR determinant, now called DRw5. Reevaluating the skin grafts made 9 years earlier by typing the former recipients and donors for DR led in 1977 to the first demonstration of the beneficial influence of DR compatibility.

Dausset received his M.D. from the University of Paris in 1945; he also graduated from Harvard Medical School, in 1948. He joined the University of Paris Faculty of Medicine as professor of hematology in 1958, and became professor of immunohematology in 1968. The College of France elected him professor of experimental medicine in 1977. He was director of the laboratories of the National Blood Transfusion Center (1946–63), and director of the Research Unit in Immunogenetics of Human Transplantation of the National Institute for Scientific Research (from 1969). In addition to many French awards, Dausset received the Landsteiner Award from the American Association of Blood Banks (1970), the Gairdner Foundation Award (Toronto, 1977), the Robert Koch Prize (1978), and the Wolf Foundation Prize in Medicine (Israel, 1978). He was elected a corresponding member of the Belgian Royal Academy of Medicine in 1969, and a member of the French Academy of Sciences and of the Academy of Medicine, both in 1977, and became an honorary member of the American Academy of Arts and Sciences in 1979. He was made an officer in the Legion of Honor in 1969.

Dausset wrote *Immunohematologie Biologique et Clinique* (1956), and edited several works in collaboration: *Human Transplantation,* with F. Rapaport (1968); *Histocompatibility Testing 1972,* with J. Colombani (1972); and *HLA and Disease,* with A. Svejgaard (1972). He wrote *Histocompatibility,* with G. Snell and S. Nathenson (1976).

For background information *see* BLOOD; IMMUNOLOGY; TRANSPLANTATION BIOLOGY in the McGraw-Hill Encyclopedia of Science and Technology. ∎

DAVIDSON, NORMAN
★ American chemist

Born Apr. 5, 1916, Chicago, IL, U.S.A.

Davidson's earlier research was in areas of physical and inorganic chemistry, but beginning in 1958 his main contributions were in physical-chemical and electron microscopic methods for studying biologically relevant properties of nucleic acids.

In the initial studies in this new field, Davidson and his coworkers showed that the reversible binding of mercuric ion to duplex deoxyribonucleic acid (DNA) was base-composition-dependent, and that centrifugation in a cesium sulfate solvent in the presence of added mercuric or silver ion could be used to separate different components of a DNA mixture that differ in base composition or sequence. Davidson had recognized, from his previous education in inorganic chemistry, that of all the metal ions, silver and mercury have bonding properties that are uniquely suitable for these purposes. These separation methods have been widely used by many investigators, especially for the identification and separation of satellite DNAs in eukaryotic genomes.

Studies by Davidson's coworkers of the kinetics of reassociation of complementary DNA single strands greatly clarified this subject and stimulated its use, by many laboratories, for the measurement of the sequence complexity of the DNA of an organism.

In physical-chemical studies of polymers, one measures a macroscopic average property of many molecules and attempts to deduce from this the characteristics of the individual molecules in the sample. An effective method of directly looking at a sample of nucleic acid molecules in the electron microscope was developed by A. K. Kleinschmidt and his coworkers in 1959. The Davidson group recognized that, in many problems, these methods gave much more precise and convincing determinations of the biologically important properties of a nucleic acid sample than did macroscopic physi-

cal-chemical measurements. Accordingly, from about 1967, one of the major efforts in this group was to develop and apply electron microscopic methods for characterizing nucleic acids. In many cases, the advances contributed by the Davidson group were based on selective chemical or enzymatic modification of particular sequences of nucleic acids so that they could be appropriately labeled and recognized in the electron microscope.

An important early contribution was the development in Davidson's laboratory in Pasadena, and independently at the University of Wisconsin, of the electron microscopic heteroduplex method for mapping those regions on two related nucleic acids which are identical in sequence and those which are different. Heteroduplex analysis was first used in the characterization of the DNA molecules from various bacterial and animal viruses. Later, heteroduplex studies of bacterial F-related plasmids (circular DNA molecules) demonstrated the presence of short elements known as IS sequences and their significance for the special recombination properties of the plasmids. These and other studies not only provided important information about the genes and sequences present on some biologically important molecules, but also provided convincing examples of the power of the technique of heteroduplex analysis.

Davidson then recognized that the now well-established techniques for studying both single-stranded and double-stranded DNA molecules by electron microscopy were not equally effective for the study of ribonucleic acid (RNA) molecules. New methods, including a technique for mapping the polyadenosine stretches that occur at one end of many eukaryotic RNA molecules, were developed. It was thus shown that the high-molecular-weight RNA molecules from mammalian tumor viruses have a common characteristic structure. The transforming (or cancer-inducing) genes and the characteristic envelope genes that determine the host range of RNA tumor viruses were mapped by heteroduplex analysis.

Other contributions included the development of a ferritin-labeling method for mapping transfer RNA genes, a method using the single-strand specific T4 gene 32 protein for specifically labeling single-stranded regions along a nucleic acid molecule, and a method for mapping proteins attached to nucleic acids (see illustration).

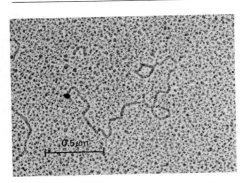

Electron micrograph of an RNA molecule from polio virus. The black dot at one end of the molecule is due to a protein attached to the RNA. The protein has been labeled by a selective chemical procedure to enhance its visibility in the electron microscope. The circle at the other end is another label for identifying 3' poly(A) ends of RNA molecules. (*Micrograph by M. Wu*)

These techniques were first applied to the determination of the distribution of genes on the DNA molecules of bacteria and bacterial viruses. In later years the Davidson group, like many others, turned its attention to the determination of the distribution of genes and related sequences on the DNA molecules of higher organisms. The motivation for this work was to understand the molecular basis for the selective expression of different genes in differentiation and development.

Thus, the overall thrust of Davidson's work was to show how physical-chemical methods, and especially the combination of chemical and enzymatic modification techniques with electron microscopy, can contribute to the understanding of gene organization in the chromosomes of bacteria, viruses, and higher organisms.

The son of a Russian immigrant father and an American-born mother, Davidson received his B.S. in chemistry at the University of Chicago in 1937. He was a Rhodes scholar at the University of Oxford from 1937 to 1939, and then he completed his Ph.D. in inorganic chemistry at the University of Chicago in 1941. During the war he worked on the Plutonium Project on the campus of the University of Chicago. In 1946 he went to the California Institute of Technology as an instructor. He was elected to the National Academy of Sciences in 1960 for his laboratory's work on the development of the shock-wave method for measuring the rates of very fast reactions in the gas phase and for independent development of the flash photolysis method of studying fast reactions.

Davidson was the author of *Statistical Mechanics* (1962).

For background information *see* CHROMOSOME; DEOXYRIBONUCLEIC ACID; MICROSCOPE, ELECTRON; RIBONUCLEIC ACID (RNA) in the McGraw-Hill Encyclopedia of Science and Technology. ∎

DAVIS, HALLOWELL
★ American neurophysiologist

Born Aug. 31, 1896, New York, NY, U.S.A.

Davis was one of the founders of audiology, concerned with hearing and its impairments. He always considered himself a neurophysiologist with a particular interest in the auditory system. In the late 1930s he was one of the pioneers of American electroencephalography, and since 1944 his studies of the effects of noise on humans have had significant military, social, and economic impacts. He rarely worked alone, relying on colleagues for electronic developments, acoustic measurements, microscopic anatomy, statistics, and computer studies. From 1935 onward he divided his efforts evenly between basic research and practical applications, such as the use of the electroencephalogram (EEG) in neurological diagnosis, the military problems of intense sound, the design objectives of hearing aids, speech audiometry, and electric response audiometry.

Davis achieved his eminence through a series of firsts or near-firsts in electrophysiology. In 1926 his experiments with Alexander Forbes and others at Harvard established firmly the "all-or-none" law of nerve conduction and showed that the concept of conduction with a decrement, on which E. D. (later Lord) Adrian's original proof of the law had rested, was erroneous. (G. Kato in Japan did similar experiments and published the same conclusions simultaneously.) In 1933 Davis analyzed the Wever and Bray effect, in which the action potentials from a cat's auditory nerve, when amplified, yielded intelligible speech in a telephone receiver. Davis (and Forbes) doubted Wever and Bray's interpretation. Davis, using concentric electrodes, separated the nerve's action potentials from an unsuspected electrical potential generated in the cochlea. It was this electrical potential that had transduced the high-frequency components of Wever's speech. (Adrian came to the same conclusion virtually simultaneously.) Incidentally, it was the Wever and Bray experiment that led Davis to concentrate on the auditory system.

In 1929 Hans Berger of Jena had described the human EEG in a German psychiatric journal. In 1933 this article somehow came to the attention of Davis and two of his students, A. J. Derbyshire and H. N. Simpson, and all three of them were skeptical of its conclusions. Nevertheless, using the equipment that Davis had assembled for exploring auditory action potentials, Derbyshire and Simpson, with Davis as the subject, became the first observers west of the Atlantic to identify correctly the human cortical 10-per second alpha rhythm. (Characteristically, Adrian also confirmed Berger's results at practically the same time.) Davis, with L. Garceau, then developed an ink-writing oscillograph and a low-frequency amplifier to study the EEG. With it, Davis and colleagues W. G. Lennox and F. A. Gibbs identified the characteristic EEG pattern of petit-mal epilepsy in 1935.

In 1940 Davis was appointed to the newly formed National Defense Research Committee to assess the military potentialities of intense sound and the dangers of noise. Davis and five colleagues, using themselves and later some student volunteers as subjects, ascertained that the only real risk from intense sustained sound was to the ears. Their systematic study of temporary hearing loss following such expo-

sure established for the first time the relations between the duration, frequency, and intensity of the sound and the severity and frequency range of the impairment. Subsequent phases of his work on noise included the hazard of jet engines on the flight deck of aircraft carriers. Noise proved to be far less of a threat to the performance of military duties than had been feared, but the slow erosion of hearing from years of habitual exposure to high-intensity industrial noises was very real. From 1946 to 1966, as a member of numerous committees and panels, Davis played a leading role in establishing safety limits for noise exposure and in creating a formula for the calculation of hearing handicap for purposes of workmen's compensation, and also methods and standards for audiometry.

At the same time Davis continued laboratory studies of the auditory system. In 1943 at Harvard, R. Galambos, assisted by Davis, became the first to record the electrical output of single auditory neural units. The micro electrodes were gross by modern standards, but sufficed for the cell bodies of neurons in the cochlear nucleus of the cat. The input-output relations (tuning curves) obtained were a major advance in auditory physiology. Later (1950) Davis personally introduced intracochlear electrodes in guinea pigs. These enabled him and his collaborators (notably I. Tasaki) at the Central Institute for the Deaf in St. Louis to take the lead in the analysis of electrical and bioacoustic actions of the inner ear (1952), including the discovery of the direct-current response of the organ of Corti (summating potential), and action potentials of single auditory nerve fibers (by Tasaki in 1955). Animal experiments (notably those by D. C. Teas, D. H. Eldredge, and Davis in 1962) laid the foundation for present clinical electrocochleography.

In 1938 Davis's first wife, Pauline, had discovered electric responses evoked by auditory, visual, or electrical stimuli in the records from a few individuals with low-voltage EEGs. These time-locked responses were too small for extensive study until electronic computers could sum a large number of them. In 1958, at Davis's request, his colleague J. R. Cox, Jr., directed the design and construction of a small special-purpose digital computer. With it Davis initiated electric response audiometry, based on the cortical-evoked potentials. This audiometric method works well with cooperative sub-

jects, but not with very young or otherwise uncooperative children. The final solution appears to be to sum many more of the very small electric responses of the brainstem. For them, acoustic stimuli must be carefully tailored, and the best of several different responses must be selected. Davis was a leader in establishing brainstem electric response audiometry as a practical clinical method.

Davis earned his M.D. degree at Harvard in 1922 and turned at once to neurophysiology, spending a year in Cambridge with E. D. Adrian, and then joined the laboratory of Alexander Forbes at Harvard. In 1940 Davis also began serving on the National Defense Research Committee. When the head of the physiology department at Harvard, Walter B. Cannon, retired in 1942, Davis became acting head, but was passed over for the permanent position. Davis came to regard this rejection as fortunate, since it left him free to move, by means of a project on hearing aids at the Harvard Psycho-Acoustic Laboratory, to a position as director of research at the Central Institute for the Deaf in St. Louis in 1946. There Davis received support from the Office of Naval Research (and later from other governmental agencies) to study the auditory system and its impairments. He was later recognized by election to the National Academy of Sciences (1948) and ultimately by the award of a National Medal of Science (1975). Davis served as president of the American Electroencephalographic Society of America (1949–50), of the Acoustical Society of America (1953–54), and of the American Physiological Society (1958). In 1953 he was appointed the first executive secretary of the Committee on Hearing and Bioacoustics (CHABA) of the National Research Council–Armed Forces. He was elected a member of the American Academy of Arts and Sciences and of the American Philosophical Society.

Davis wrote, in addition to review articles and chapters on the auditory system in several handbooks, *Hearing: Its Psychology and Its Physiology,* with S. S. Stevens (1938). A second book which he edited, *Hearing and Deafness* (1946; 4th ed. coedited with S. R. Silverman, 1978), gave form to audiology as a recognized scientific discipline.

For background information *see* AUDIOMETRY; ELECTROENCEPHALOGRAPHY; HEARING (HUMAN); NOISE POLLUTION in the McGraw-Hill Encyclopedia of Science and Technology. ∎

DAVIS, MARTIN DAVID
★ American mathematician and computer scientist

Born *Mar. 8, 1928, New York, NY, U.S.A.*

Davis is best known for his research and expository contributions relating to Hilbert's tenth problem. His much cited *Computability and Unsolvability* (1958), was the first book-length publication in theoretical computer science, and was translated into several languages. Davis was involved in some of the earliest work in automated deduction, an area fundamental to much research in artificial intelligence.

Under the influence of his undergraduate teacher Emil Post, Davis had become deeply interested in the theory of recursive (computable) functions as providing a precise mathematical equivalent of the intuitive notion of what is mechanically calculable. This theory had opened the possibility of finding a theoretical basis for the observed intractability of certain mathematical problems by proving them to be recursively unsolvable, that is, showing that no computational procedure representable by a recursive function exists to solve the problem. An ideal candidate seemed to be the tenth problem in the important list from D. Hilbert's famous address of 1900: the problem asked for a procedure to determine whether or not a given polynomial Diophantine equation possessed a solution in integers. In his doctoral dissertation (1950) Davis was led to compare Diophantine predicates, obtained by regarding certain of the variables in a Diophantine equation as parameters defining the predicate, with recursively enumerable predicates, obtained in the same way from arbitrary recursive conditions. He noted that the recursive unsolvability of Hilbert's tenth problem would be an immediate consequence of the identity of these two notions, and obtained a formal representation for arbitrary recursively enumerable predicates suggestively close to Diophantine form (Davis normal form). His dissertation also initiated the study of hyperarithmetic sets, an area which was to play an important role in later research in mathematical logic.

Davis's first position at the University of Illinois brought him into contact with the ILLIAC group and into involvement with what was in 1951 advanced computational equipment. Davis became convinced not only that recursive functions were important in understanding computation at a theoretical level, but also that A. M. Turing's model of computation as proceeding in simple steps by an automaton capable of moving one square at a time along a linear tape was the appropriate vehicle for bringing them together. His work on universal Turing machines subsequently turned out to have unexpected applications in the theory of degrees of unsolvability of algebraic problems. He gave the first computer implementation of a logical decision procedure at the Institute for Advanced Study in 1954.

Davis began his fruitful collaboration with the logician Hilary Putnam while they were attending the stimulating Institute for Symbolic Logic at Cornell University in the summer of 1957. They decided to investigate the feasibility of using the methods of symbolic logic to automate mathematical deduction and proposed to begin with propositional calculus, the most elementary part of logic. This work led to the much studied Davis-Putnam procedure. But it was in work on Hilbert's tenth problem that Davis and Putnam were able to obtain really exciting results. By beginning with the information in Davis's dissertation and employing methods that had been developed by Julia Robinson, they were able to deduce the identity of recursively enumerable predicates with Diophantine predicates (and thus, as indicated above, the recursive un-

solvability of Hilbert's tenth problem) from two unproved hypotheses in the theory of numbers. When Robinson succeeded in eliminating the need for one of these hypotheses, what remained was to find a single Diophantine equation whose solution had an appropriate rate of growth. Such an equation was in fact eventually found, but only a decade later in an ingenious piece of work by the Soviet mathematician Yuri Matÿacevič, thus finally settling the question.

In the area of automated deduction, the work of Dag Prawitz led Davis to formulate the unification algorithm (as it was later named) and to emphasize its central role. The key fact is that all logical inference can be taken as consisting of appropriate management of basic statements and their negations; this includes locating substitutions of expressions for variables which transform two basic statements into negatives of one another, and manipulation of structures involving these basic statements. Davis was involved in a number of projects devoted to developing, implementing, and testing theorem-proving algorithms based on these ideas.

Davis's work on Diophantine sets after Matÿacevič's decisive contribution centered on problems involving the number of solutions of a Diophantine equation, particularly the degree of unsolvability of such problems. In collaboration with his colleague J. T. Schwartz, Davis worked on the design and logical properties of self-extending automatic proof-checking systems. In still another direction, Davis's interest in the use of so-called nonstandard models of classical mathematical structures led him to develop a book on Abraham Robinson's nonstandard analysis and to apply the special models studied by G. Takeuti to key foundational issues in quantum mechanics.

Davis attended the Bronx High School of Science and the City College of New York. After completing his doctorate (1950) at Princeton University under the direction of Alonzo Church, Davis held numerous academic positions, including a visiting membership at the Institute for Advanced Study in Princeton (1952–54) and faculty positions at the University of California at Davis (1954–55), Ohio State University (1955–56), Rensselaer Polytechnic Institute (1956–59), New York University (1959–60), and Yeshiva University (1960–65). In 1965 he became associated with the Courant Institute of

Mathematical Sciences of New York University. For his work on Hilbert's tenth problem, he was awarded the Steele Prize by the American Mathematical Society and the Chauvenet and Ford prizes by the Mathematical Association of America in 1975.

In addition to the book mentioned, Davis wrote *Lectures on Modern Mathematics* (1967), *First Course in Functional Analysis* (1967), and *Applied Nonstandard Analysis* (1977). He edited the anthology *The Undecidable* (1965).

For background information *see* AUTOMATA THEORY; COMPUTER; LOGIC; NUMBER THEORY in the McGraw-Hill Encyclopedia of Science and Technology. ■

DEACON, GEORGE EDWARD RAVEN
★ British oceanographer

Born Mar. 21, 1906, Leicester, England

After graduating in chemistry at King's College, London, in 1926, Deacon went to the Antarctic as a member of the scientific staff of the Discovery Investigations, a government project aimed at improving the understanding of the migrations, variations in distribution, and fluctuations in populations of the Antarctic whales. The project required detailed study of the breeding and feeding habits of whales and of the factors that influence the distribution of the krill on which the whales feed. His main task was to make a three-dimensional plot of temperature and salinity in the circumpolar Antarctic Ocean; to learn as much as possible about the currents and general circulation of the water; to measure such nutrients as phosphate, nitrate, and silicate that might limit plant growth and general productivity of different areas; and to help in the correlation of the physical and chemical factors with the distribution of whale food and whales.

Deacon wrote a general account of the water masses of the South Atlantic Ocean in 1933, and a similar account of the Southern Ocean—the whole circumpolar ring—in 1937. It is usual in oceanography to regard water movements as geostrophic, which means that the observed density gradients and computed pressure gradients are balanced by the effect of the Earth's rotation. Deacon felt that his geostrophic map, produced in 1937, underestimated the north and south movements. He retained this view when further observations extended the early picture without altering its character. He maintained that the vertical mixing, which amounts to flow across the density surfaces, and the effect of wind stress are sufficiently large in this region to reduce the value of the geostrophic assumptions. In fact, by 1939 he felt that advanced theoretical studies in fluid mechanics and actual measurements of currents at all depths in the Southern Ocean would be needed before much progress could be made. He also believed that a thorough study of the turbulent movements likely to carry the phytoplankton in and out of the near-surface photosynthetic layer would be more interesting than studies of the nutrients, which never seemed to be limiting factors in the Antarctic.

During World War II Deacon worked in naval laboratories on oceanography and underwater acoustics and, toward the end of the war, on sea waves. The team he directed did much to develop wave recorders; they were the first to make a spectrum analysis of sea waves and to show the value of the conception of a wave spectrum. In 1949 the Navy's oceanographic group joined the Discovery Investigations biologists in founding the National Institute of Oceanography, which has done much to advance many aspects of oceanography. It developed methods of measuring deep currents, and Deacon saw these methods put to use during cruises by the USCGS *Glacier* (1975) and the *Discovery* (1979) in the Weddell Sea.

Deacon was awarded the British Polar

Medal in 1942 and the Agassiz Medal of the U.S. National Academy of Sciences in 1962.

For background information *see* OCEANOGRAPHY in the McGraw-Hill Encyclopedia of Science and Technology. ∎

DeBAKEY, MICHAEL ELLIS
★ American surgeon

Born Sept. 7, 1908, Lake Charles, LA, U.S.A.

During the past few decades remarkable developments in cardiovascular surgery have resulted from vigorous research conducted by medical scientists throughout the world. Beginning with the revolutionary work of N. V. Eck, Rudolph Matas, Alexander Jassinowsky, Alexis Carrel, and Charles C. Guthrie more than a half century ago, and continuing with the subsequent outstanding contributions of René Leriche, Robert E. Gross, Alfred Blalock, Clarence Crafoord, Reynaldo Dos Santos, Jean Kunlin, John H. Gibbon, DeBakey, and others, cardiovascular surgery has enjoyed extremely rapid advances. Several developments were primarily responsible for these advances: (1) relatively safe, readily applicable methods of angiography, which permits precise identification of the site, nature, and extent of diseased arterial segments and their effect on the distal arterial circulation; (2) highly successful techniques of vascular surgery, including vascular re-

placements for occluded or diseased segments; and (3) increasingly vigorous research in medical and surgical treatment of previously hopeless diseases. *See* BLALOCK, ALFRED; GIBBON, JOHN H.

Early in his medical career DeBakey recognized the value of technologic development and commercial production of synthetic materials in correcting previously incurable cardiovascular disease. While he was a young medical student doing research in the experimental surgical laboratory at Tulane University, DeBakey devised a pump that would provide continuous flow through a perfusion circuit without causing damage to blood. Widely used for its original purpose, this invention was later to have far more extensive and significant application. Gibbon, working on development of a heart-lung machine in Philadelphia, learned of DeBakey's constant-injection roller pump and, aware of its superiority to other pumps, asked DeBakey to send him a pump for incorporation in the heart-lung machine with which he was experimenting. DeBakey's pump eliminated the need for valves to direct the flow of blood. Previous roller pumps used to move blood through the perfusion circuit had proved unsatisfactory because the rubber tubes compressed by the rollers gradually moved forward as the rollers passed over them. DeBakey eliminated this creeping effect by using a rubber tube with a projecting, flat, rubber flange, which was clamped between the semicircular metal bars. The tube was thus fixed in place, and the rollers did not move forward. DeBakey's pump provided one of the two essential components in the successful development of Gibbon's apparatus, which has become the basic mechanism for the heart-lung machine used throughout the world.

In other pioneering research DeBakey experimented with methods of replacing diseased, obstructed, or otherwise damaged tissues of the vascular system, first by grafting human blood vessels and later by using various synthetic materials for grafts. He found Dacron to be unique among these in producing just the proper amount of tissue attachment without inflammatory reaction. The pseudoendothelium that developed in the lumen simulated the normal blood interface and functioned well indefinitely. Dacron maintained its integrity and did not produce progressive fibrous tissue reaction. With these techniques, DeBakey successfully replaced blood vessels in many parts of the body, including the aorta and smaller vessels that carry blood to the legs and to the brain and various other vital organs.

With increasing experience with angiography in the course of his daily surgical work, DeBakey became aware of the patterns of vascular disease and of its segmental and localized nature. He shifted interest from the cause of arterial disease, which remains obscure and controversial, to the anatomic-pathologic characteristics of the lesion itself and its hemodynamic functional effects. This new approach permitted leaping across the etiologic barrier to effective treatment, which is the ultimate objective of all medical research. On this basis he classified arterial occlusive disease into four major types: (1) lesions affecting the major branches of the aortic arch, (2) lesions affecting the visceral branches of the abdominal aorta, (3) lesions affecting the coronary arteries, and (4) lesions affecting the terminal abdominal aorta and its major branches. The predominant underlying pathologic lesion in all four types is atherosclerosis.

DeBakey began to apply more and more the principles of vascular surgery, namely, excision and graft replacement, endarterectomy, patch graft angioplasty, and bypass operations, in the treatment of all types of aneurysms and occlusive disease of the vascular system, in which restoration of normal circulation was the primary aim. Accordingly, he performed successful surgical treatment for the first time of a number of life-threatening cardiovascular disorders, including the following: resection of an aneurysm of the thoracic aorta (1951); resection with homograft replacement of a fusiform aneurysm of the descending thoracic aorta (1952); thromboendarterectomy of the carotid artery for stroke (1953); resection and homograft replacement of an aneurysm of the distal aortic arch (1954); resection with homograft replacement of a fusiform aneurysm of the thoracoabdominal segment affecting the celiac, superior mesenteric, and renal arteries, with restoration of continuity to all these major visceral branches (1955); resection with homograft replacement of a fusiform aneurysm of the entire ascending aorta with use of cardiopulmonary bypass with the artificial heart-lung apparatus (1956); resection with homograft replacement,

including the innominate and carotid arteries of a fusiform aneurysm involving the entire aortic arch, with use of the artificial heart-lung apparatus (1957); patch graft angioplasty (1958); and aorto-coronary artery bypass with autogenous saphenous vein graft (1964).

In the early 1960s, DeBakey, recognizing the advantages of collaborative efforts by biologic and physical scientists in modern medical research, directed an artificial heart program at Baylor University College of Medicine, in conjunction with Rice University. Because of the complex problems involved in the development of total artificial replacement for the malfunctioning heart, DeBakey and his associates directed their immediate attention to devising a booster pump to be used temporarily in patients with cardiac failure while the damaged heart is recuperating. From his extensive experience with Dacron for artificial arteries, DeBakey conceived the idea of lining his experimental paracorporeal ventricular bypass pump and all its connections with Dacron velour as a blood interface. The velour, which minimizes trauma to the blood, proved to be a key factor in the development of a successful heart assistor. After conclusive evidence was obtained that the device performed satisfactorily in an extensive series of animals, DeBakey became the first, in August 1966, to apply the heart pump successfully in a patient. The patient, previously incapacitated, recovered completely and resumed normal living.

The son of a successful businessman, DeBakey received his early education in southwest Louisiana, his medical education at Tulane University, and his graduate medical education in New Orleans under Alton Ochsner, and in Strasbourg and Heidelberg, where he studied under René Leriche and Martin Kirschner. He received his B.S. in 1930, M.D. in 1932, and M.S. in surgery in 1935 from Tulane. During World War II he became director of the Surgical Consultants Division in the Surgeon General's Office. One of his important contributions while on active duty in this office was his proposal of a systematic followup of veterans with certain medical histories, which subsequently led to the establishment of the Committee on Veterans Medical Problems of the National Research Council and the extensive Medical Research Program by the Veterans Administration. For his war ser-

vices he received the Legion of Merit. After his discharge he returned to Tulane University School of Medicine, where he remained until 1948, when he accepted the chairmanship of surgery at Baylor University College of Medicine. For his contributions to medicine and society, DeBakey received the Hektoen Gold Medal (1954) and the Distinguished Service Award (1959) of the American Medical Association, the Distinguished Service Award (1958) and Leriche Award (1959) of the International Society of Surgery, the Rudolph Matas Award (1954), the Albert Lasker Award for Clinical Research (1963), the first Gold Scalpel Award of the International Cardiology Foundation, the first Max Berg Award of the Berg Foundation, the Drexel Institute Award, the Presidential Medal of Freedom with Distinction, as well as numerous honorary degrees.

DeBakey wrote *The Blood Bank and the Technique and Therapeutics of Transfusions,* with Robert A. Kilduffe (1942); *Christoper's Minor Surgery,* with Alton Ochsner, Sr. (8th ed. 1959); *Battle Casualties: Incidence, Mortality, and Logistic Considerations,* with Gilbert W. Beebe (1952); and *The Living Heart,* with A. M. Gotto, Jr. (1977). For many years he edited *The Year Book of Surgery.* In addition, he wrote more than 1000 articles and chapters of books on surgical and scientific subjects, and served on the editorial boards of more than a dozen national and international scientific publications.

For background information *see* ARTERIOSCLEROSIS; CARDIOVASCULAR SYSTEM DISORDERS; CIRCULATION DISORDERS; HEART DISORDERS; TRANSFUSION in the McGraw-Hill Encyclopedia of Science and Technology. ∎

DE BEER, SIR GAVIN
★ British biologist

> **Born** Nov. 1, 1899, Malden, near London, England
> **Died** June 21, 1972, Alfriston, Sussex, England

Original researches on the segmentation of the head and development of the skull in all groups of vertebrates provided de Beer with abundant material on which to study such general morphological principles as stereometric constancy of topographic relations among blood vessels, nerves, cartilages, and bones; identity of morphological units (two bones in one form homologous with one bone in another); relations of skull to brain; details of evolutionary succession; and bone phylogenetically older than cartilage.

De Beer also investigated afresh the comparative anatomy, development, and histology of the pituitary in all groups of vertebrates, which led to collaboration with L. T. Hogben on the localization of active pituitary principles in different vertebrates. With H. Grüneberg he investigated the action of the gene responsible for dwarfism in mice, which prevents differentiation of eosinophil cells in the anterior pituitary—evidence that these cells secrete growth-promoting hormones, and an example of how genes produce their effects by controlling developmental processes.

Taking up an idea of W. Garstang—that Haeckel's theory of recapitulation was fundamentally unsound—de Beer studied the relations between embryos and ancestors in all groups of animals and some plants, and showed that in many cases adult descendants retained characters of youthful stages of ancestors—the reverse of recapitulation. This principle, paedomorphosis, applies to all cases where a particularly successful and markedly different descendant type evolved from its ancestors (insects, chordates, humans). A consequence of this mode of evolution was that in eventually successful groups the preliminary states of the evolution took place in young stages, unlikely

to have been preserved as fossils because of their soft tissues. This de Beer called "clandestine evolution," not revealed in the fossil record, which explains why precursor stages of such groups (insects, chordates) are poorly represented.

Experiments on removal of neural crest from amphibian embryos were known to result in absence of visceral cartilages, thought to be of mesodermal origin, whereas neural crest is ectodermal. This apparent disregard of the germ-layer theory precipitated a crisis in morphology. The orthodox could only accept it on the view that experimental conditions upset the norms of development. It was therefore necessary to establish the developmental fates of the germ layers without experimental manipulation. Taking advantage of the presence of black pigment in ectoderm and yolk in endoderm, de Beer showed that ectoderm (neural crest) did produce visceral cartilages, odontoblasts, and osteoblasts of dermal bones. He also showed that the enamel organ of teeth could be formed either from stomodaeal ectoderm or gut endoderm, whichever was beneath the odontoblasts. This disproved the germ-layer theory and discredited the classification of tumors based on it.

A complete reinvestigation of the fossil *Archaeopteryx* using ultraviolet and x-rays revealed the sternum, which had eluded discovery for a century (it is flat). Some of the features of *Archaeopteryx* are completely reptilian, others completely avian, whence de Beer propounded the theory of mosaic evolution—piece-by-piece complete conversion from one type to the next—which he also showed in transitional forms between fish, amphibia, reptiles, birds, and mammals.

The reptilian structure of the cerebellum in *Archaeopteryx* and its carinate structure in Ratites enabled de Beer to show that the Ratites certainly evolved from former flying birds. Other features showed that *Archaeopteryx* was incapable of flight (it could only glide) and that it was adapted to climbing trees and perching on branches. This provided proof of the arboreal origin of flight.

De Beer's study of Darwin's Notebooks (previously unpublished) showed that Darwin had independently thought out the principle of natural selection before he read Malthus's *Essay on Population,* from which he derived only the inevitably heavy toll of mortality. Close study of Mendel's paper and of his copies of

Darwin's books showed that Mendel was not opposed to evolution and that he hoped that his discoveries would fill the gaps in Darwin's theories, which they did.

The possibility of using natural science to solve historical problems was applied by de Beer to prehistoric inhabitants of western Europe (genetics of blood groups and hair color); the origin of the Etruscans (blood groups and skull shape); Hannibal's route across the Alps (physiography, meteorology, glaciology, astronomy, pollen analysis); identification of the "Iktin" of classical authors with St. Michael's Mount, Cornwall (C-14, pollen, mineralogy of neolithic axes); Gibbon's illness (pathology, psychology).

Search for and discovery of manuscripts enabled de Beer and T. Graham Brown to reconstruct in detail the first ascent of Mont Blanc in 1786 by M. G. Paccard and to show the speed of ascent from one identified place to another. Other studies on Voltaire, Rousseau, Gibbon, Byron, Shelley, Mme. Roland, and Mme. de Staël, and on relations between British and French men of science while Great Britain and France were at war, established the background of opinion in the 18th century. He also showed that the tables used for converting French Republican Calendar dates to the Gregorian Calendar were wrong.

Son of an English gentleman, de Beer was educated in Paris, at Harrow, and Magdalen College, Oxford. From 1923 to 1938 he was a fellow of Merton College, Oxford. He was professor of embryology at University College, London, from 1945 until 1950, when he became director of the British Museum (Natural History). Knighted in 1954, he received among other scientific honors the Royal Society's Darwin Medal in 1958 "in recognition of his distinguished contributions to evolutionary biology." He served in the Grenadier Guards in both world wars, landing in Normandy in 1944 in charge of psychological warfare.

De Beer published over 300 works, including *Vertebrate Zoology* (1928), *Development of the Vertebrate Skull* (1937), *Embryos and Ancestors* (1940), *Charles Darwin* (1963), and *Atlas of Evolution* (1964).

For background information *see* ANIMAL EVOLUTION; ARCHAEORNITHES; EMBRYOLOGY, EXPERIMENTAL; GERM LAYERS; PITUITARY GLAND (VERTEBRATE) in the McGraw-Hill Encyclopedia of Science and Technology. ∎

DEBYE, PETER JOSEPH WILLIAM
☆ American physical chemist

Born Mar. 24, 1884, Maastricht,
Netherlands
Died Nov. 2, 1966, Ithaca, NY, U.S.A.

For his work on dipole moments and the diffraction of x-rays in gases, Debye was awarded the 1936 Nobel Prize in chemistry. In addition, he collaborated with Ernst Hückel to formulate a theory of the behavior of strong electrolytes that proved superior to the older theory of dissociation proposed by Svante Arrhenius.

It was known from earlier work performed by Debye that the noble gases and diatomic molecules consisting of two equal atoms (for example, N_2, O_2) were nonpolar but that when the atoms were different polarity appeared. The dipole moment measuring this polarity could be determined experimentally from the temperature dependence of the dielectric constant. If the atoms were close to each other in the periodic table, this polarity was small; it became great only in molecules such as HCl. The magnitude of the electric dipole moment, however, was nowhere near as great as would be expected of a molecule consisting of an H ion and a Cl ion held at the supposed nuclear distance. In a triatomic molecule, a linear configuration of the atoms produces no moment (for example CO_2), but a nonlinear arrangement leads to one (for example, H_2O). Debye was able to show that when free molecules are irradiated

with x-rays each molecule produces recognizable interferences with its dispersed radiation. He demonstrated how these patterns could be used to compute the interatomic distances, which enabled chemists to draw molecular configurations to scale.

In 1912 Max von Laue suggested that the wavelength of x-rays and the distance between planes of atoms in a crystal might be of the same order of magnitude. If this were true, the crystal plane could serve as a diffraction grating for x-rays. Sir William Bragg, following this suggestion, passed a beam of x-rays through crystals and detected the characteristic reinforcement and interference bands caused by the diffraction of the beam by successive layers of atoms within the crystals. Knowing the angle of incidence of the x-ray beam at a reinforcement band and the wavelength of the x-rays used, he was able to calculate the distance between successive planes in a crystal and to determine the detailed arrangement of atoms (or ions) within the crystal.

However, an obstacle to the use of the Bragg method was its dependence upon a large, well-formed crystal. In 1916 Debye and P. Scherrer resolved this problem by proving that similar results can be obtained from a powder of the crystalline substance. Since the powder consists of innumerable small crystals oriented in random fashion, there will always be a number in correct orientation to give an x-ray diffraction pattern.

In the Debye-Scherrer method the powdered crystalline substance was pressed into the shape of a small rod approximately 2 millimeters in diameter and 10 millimeters high. This was positioned upright in the center of a light-tight cylindrical camera. The x-ray beam, sharply defined, was led in a horizontal direction into the camera and impinged on the center of the rod. The diffraction pattern from the rod was photographed on two pieces of film, each of which was bent into a half circle to make a continuous lining of the inside wall of the camera. The diffraction pattern produced on the film provided the information necessary for the determination of the crystal structure by the application of Bragg's method. The components of a solid mixture can be rapidly identified by the Debye-Scherrer powder method, since each crystalline substance has its own characteristic spacings between internal crystal planes.

Another major aspect of Debye's work was his study of electrolytes. Arrhenius had stated that electrolytes in water solution dissociated into positively and negatively charged ions. However, he maintained that this separation is not complete, some of the electrolyte remaining undissociated or in molecular form. About 1923 Debye, working with Hückel, believed that electrolytes in solution must be completely ionized since x-ray diffraction studies showed that electrolytes in crystal form, such as sodium chloride, were already completely ionized. He suggested that the apparent incomplete dissociation postulated by Arrhenius could be explained by taking into account the electric interaction between the ions according to Coulomb's law.

Debye supposed that each positive ion was surrounded by an ion atmosphere that was, in the main, negatively charged and that each negative ion was surrounded by an ion atmosphere predominantly positive in charge. The application of an external electric field resulted in a movement of the central ions to oppositely charged electrodes, but the surrounding ion atmospheres tended to impede movement, thus causing a decrease in current conduction and making it appear the electrolyte was not completely ionized. Furthermore, when the central ions began to move to oppositely charged electrodes, a frictional drag set in because some of the solvent molecules moved with the ions. Again ion movement was slowed and current conduction was decreased.

The Debye-Hückel theory developed the mathematics for evaluating the magnitude of the factors of ion atmosphere and ion solvation. The theory extended the work of Arrhenius and provided a new approach to the study of properties of solution.

During the 1940s and 1950s Debye pioneered in the study of polymers. A method of estimating the weight of macromolecules based upon the viscosity of the liquid in which they were dissolved had been worked out by the German chemist Hermann Staudinger. The ultracentrifuge, invented by the Swedish chemist Theodor Svedberg, was also used for weighing macromolecules, but these measurements were not precise for truly giant polymers. Still another method for determining the weight of macromolecules, based on the work of the Dutch chemist Jacobus Henricus Van't Hoff, relied on accurate measurements of osmotic pressures at low concentrations.

In 1944, while working at Cornell University, Debye developed a method, based on the phenomenon that molecules scatter light, for determining these molecular weights with great precision. He found that the increase in turbidity, or light-scattering power, of a solution in which macromolecules had been dissolved is proportional to the number of molecules per cubic centimeter as well as to their molecular weights, whereas in measurements based on the osmotic pressure this dependence on the molecular weight is missing. By combining measurements on the excess turbidity with measurements on the excess refractive index, the molecular weight can be determined absolutely. Later he found that the light scattered by polymer solutions has a higher intensity in the forward than in the backward direction. From this angular dissymmetry the sizes of the polymer molecules can be calculated. Debye also applied the light-scattering technique to the study of micellar solutions and contributed to the theory of micelle stability.

Debye graduated from the University of Aachen in 1905 with a degree in electrical engineering. He received his Ph.D. in 1908 from the University of Munich. After teaching in Zurich (1911–12) and Utrecht (1912–14), he worked, while at Göttingen during World War I, with Scherrer in developing the powder method for studying crystal structure. The Debye-Hückel theory was an outgrowth of his work at Zurich during the years 1919–27. In 1928 he taught at the University of Leipzig, leaving in 1935 to go to the University of Berlin, where he built and became director of the Kaiser Wilhelm Institute of Physics, which he named the Max Planck Institut. With the advent of the Nazi regime, politics began to interfere with his work. He left Germany in 1940 to go to the United States, becoming head of the department of chemistry at Cornell University. In 1950 he became professor emeritus. Debye was honored by the American Chemical Society by the award of its Willard Gibbs Medal (1949), Nichols Award (1961), and Priestley Medal (1963). He was elected a foreign associate of the National Academy of Sciences in 1931 and a member in 1947.

Debye's major papers appear in *Collected Papers of Peter Debye* (1954).

For background information *see* CRYS-TAL STRUCTURE; DIPOLE MOMENT; ELECTROLYTIC CONDUCTANCE; POLYMER; SCATTERING OF ELECTROMAGNETIC RADIATION; X-RAY DIFFRACTION in the McGraw-Hill Encyclopedia of Science and Technology. ∎

DE DUVE, CHRISTIAN RENÉ
★ Belgian-American biochemist and cell biologist

Born Oct. 2, 1917, Thames-Ditton, England

When de Duve was appointed to the chair of physiological chemistry at the Catholic University of Louvain in 1947, his main ambition was to elucidate the mechanism of action of the antidiabetic hormone insulin on liver tissue. At that time even the existence of such an action was doubted by many scientists, but de Duve believed otherwise, and had already been able to bolster his view by proving that the opponents of a hepatic action of insulin had been deluded by the occurrence of the insulin-antagonist glucagon (now known to be a second pancreatic hormone) in the insulin samples used in their experiments.

With a young associate, Géry Hers, and a brilliant medical student, Jacques Berthet, later joined by an increasing band of enthusiasts, de Duve set out first to characterize an enzyme peculiar to liver, glucose-6-phosphatase, which he suspected of interfering with the effect of insulin on isolated liver tissue. When Hers tried to purify this enzyme by isoelectric precipitation, he noted an odd behavior—irreversible, rather than reversible, precipitation at pH 5—which reminded de Duve of a similar observation made on cell particulates by Albert Claude, the famous Belgian-American scientist who, during the 20 years (1929–49) he spent at the Rockefeller Institute for Medical Research in New York, had developed the technique of centrifugal fractionation for the separation of different cell parts. De Duve decided to use this technique to study the subcellular localization of glucose-6-phosphatase. *See* CLAUDE, ALBERT.

The first experiment, carried out on Dec. 16, 1949, was doubly successful. It made glucose-6-phosphatase the first enzyme known to be associated with microsomes, until then an entity of dubious cytological significance. At the same time, it provided de Duve with his first glimpse of lysosomes, in the suitably cryptic form of an enzyme that should have been there but was not: latent acid phosphatase. It was the beginning of a 15-year adventure which made the de Duve laboratory a leading center of cell fractionation methodology and brought about the discovery and characterization of two new subcellular organelles: the lysosomes, tiny "stomachs" in which cells carry out their main digestive processes, and the peroxisomes, sites of multiple oxidative metabolic reactions involving the participation of hydrogen peroxide.

Almost exactly 25 years after this fateful experiment, which completely altered his research career, de Duve stood on the podium in Stockholm, together with Albert Claude and George Palade, Claude's main pupil and follower at the Rockefeller Institute, to receive the 1974 Nobel Prize for physiology or medicine "for their discoveries of the structural and functional organization of the cell." (Ironically, the problem of the mechanism of action of insulin on liver, which provided the original impetus for de Duve's research program, still remains to be elucidated.) *See* PALADE, GEORGE EMIL.

In 1962 de Duve was invited to join the Rockefeller Institute (now Rockefeller University). He is currently Andrew W. Mellon Professor at this institution, but retained his position at the University of Louvain.

Later de Duve became increasingly interested in the medical applications of the "new biology." He has created a new institute for this purpose, the International Institute of Cellular and Molecular Pathology, or ICP, affiliated with the new Louvain medical school in Brussels. At ICP and Rockefeller University he is involved with numerous research groups studying such topics as genetic diseases, arteriosclerosis, polyarthritis and other inflammatory conditions, immune disorders, tropical diseases, leukemia, and cancer, including the development of new drugs to be used against some of these diseases.

De Duve received his formal education at Louvain University, where he graduated as an M.D. in 1941, and subsequently earned the degree of Agrégé de l'Enseignement Supérieur with a thesis on the action of insulin (1945) and an M.Sc. in chemistry (1946). He did postdoctoral work with four Nobel laureates: Hugo Theorell in Stockholm (1946–47) and Carl Cori, Gerty Cori, and Earl Sutherland in St. Louis (1947–48). He received awards and honorary distinctions in a number of countries. He is a member of the main Belgian academies and of the Pontifical Academy of Sciences. He was elected a foreign associate of the U.S. National Academy of Sciences in 1975.

For background information *see* CELL (BIOLOGY); LYSOSOMES in the McGraw-Hill Encyclopedia of Science and Technology. ∎

DEHMELT, HANS
★ American physicist

Born Sept. 9, 1922, Görlitz, Germany

After codiscovering nuclear quadruple resonance in 1949, Dehmelt proposed radio-frequency spectroscopy of stored ions in 1956 and developed techniques for studying atomic particles almost at rest in free space. With his collaborators he applied these techniques to the first spin and hyperfine resonance experiments on free electrons, and the ground states of ^{3}He$^+$, and H$_2$$^+$. In 1976 these efforts culminated in his work on geonium, an individual electron stored in a Penning trap for days (or years), which yielded the most accurate value of the magnetism of an elementary particle to date.

Dehmelt received his graduate education in experimental physics at Göttingen University and the Institute of Hans Kop-

fermann (1946–50). Working with a Thomson parabola mass spectrograph for his master's thesis (under Peter Brix) on the photographic action of 5–17-kiloelectronvolt H$^+$ and H$_2$$^+$ ions exposed him to many phenomena in the field of physics.

A radio amateur since the age of 10, Dehmelt supported himself and his studies in wartorn Germany by reconditioning and bartering radios. This interest also determined the subject of his doctoral dissertation. In 1948 his doctoral adviser, Hubert Krueger, suggested to him a radio-frequency (rf) spectroscopy search in large ionic single crystals for what became known as nuclear quadrupole resonance (NQR). Dehmelt realized that stronger signals could be expected in covalent compounds, such as frozen polycrystalline CH$_3$Cl, for which, moreover, he was able to estimate the transition frequencies from rotational spectra splittings measured by Walter Gordy and his coworkers. NQR was discovered in 1949, and a precise ratio of the ^{35,37}Cl quadrupole moments was measured. NQR is very similar to nuclear magnetic resonance (NMR), and its discovery was in fact prompted by the famous work of E. M. Purcell and of F. Bloch. However, the nuclear precession detected in NQR is not caused by the interaction of the magnetic moment with the field of an expensive magnet but, rather, by the interaction of the nuclear electric quadrupole moment with the less costly crystalline electric field cradling a nucleus. This work was soon extended to

higher frequencies, enabling a study of iodine nuclei and a search for a nuclear electric 16-pole effect. *See* BLOCH, FELIX; PURCELL, EDWARD MILLS.

Dehmelt continued to work at Kopfermann's institute as a Deutsche Forschungs-Gemeinschafts fellow, carrying out NQR studies on Br, Sb, and B isotopes. He also used his superregenerative NQR spectrometer in an unsuccessful search for the hyperfine transition near 460 megahertz in K vapor.

In 1952 he was invited to do postdoctoral work in Gordy's well-known microwave spectroscopy laboratory at Duke University. Collaborating with Gordy and a graduate student, Hugh Robinson, Dehmelt performed NQR studies on Hg, S, Bi, and Ga, and participated in the measurement of the nuclear susceptibility of liquid ^{3}He by W. M. Fairbank and his colleagues. In 1953 he began paramagnetic resonance studies on atomic N and P using a high-pressure carrier gas and a direct-current arc as a dissociator to obtain the first value for the hyperfine-structure (hfs) splitting of atomic P.

In 1955, on the initiative of Edwin Uehling, Dehmelt received an appointment as visiting assistant professor at the University of Washington in Seattle. Setting himself the task of developing rf spectroscopic techniques suitable for the study of atomic particles under conditions approaching the ideal, that is, at rest in free space, Dehmelt turned to trigger techniques similar to those pioneered by I. I. Rabi, Bloch, W. E. Lamb, Jr., Purcell, and A. Kastler, all of which can be reduced to the following scheme: an orienting mechanism acts on an atomic particle, the particle is disoriented by rf resonance, and the disorientation is detected by an analyzing mechanism incorporating an easily observable energetic event. His first variation on this theme, undertaken at the invitation of George Volkoff at the University of British Columbia in 1955, was an unsuccessful attempt to detect, by means of variations of the diode current, magnetic resonance disorientation of metastable Hg ^{3}P$_2$ atoms aligned and analyzed by electron impact in a planar plasma diode. *See* KASTLER, ALFRED; LAMB, WILLIS EUGENE, JR.; RABI, ISIDOR ISAAC.

In Seattle Dehmelt pursued an idea which had occurred to him in Germany, optical absorption monitoring of atomic orientation, applied it successfully to the Hg ^{3}P$_2$ experiment, and also proposed rf

spectroscopy of stored ions in 1956. Noting that unpolarized electron impact near threshold populated not only $m_L = 0$ but also $m_L = \pm 1$ levels of Hg $^3P_2$ via spin exchange, Dehmelt thought that polarized atoms might be used to polarize electrons in a reverse process (polarized alkali atoms had recently become readily available through the optical pumping work of Kastler) which then might be used in the direct measurement of the magnetic moment of free electrons. This old experimental problem, pronounced insoluble by various scientists, had recently been attacked with some success by H. R. Crane and his coworkers in another way. Conditions guaranteeing long atom and electron spin relaxation times were needed in order to have sufficient time to allow back-and-forth spin exchange between electrons and atoms. Here, Dehmelt's high-pressure carrier-buffer gas and optical transmission monitoring techniques led to the first demonstration of sodium spin relaxation times approaching a second. (The corresponding narrow resonances proved to be useful in the development of commercial alkali vapor magnetometers and frequency standards at Varian Associates by Arnold Bloom, Earl Bell, and Martin Packard, in which Dehmelt collaborated.) The first free electron spin resonance was seen in December 1956. The electron spin disorientation occurring on magnetic resonance was transferred to Na atoms, the orientation of which was optically monitored, a randomly oriented sample being less transparent than an oriented one. In 1958 the first value for the magnetic moment excess over unity, as measured on free electrons, and accurate to 4 percent, was published.

The experimental effort next concentrated on the elimination of the buffer gas. Noting that sodium metal is commercially shipped under heavy paraffin oil, Dehmelt demonstrated, in collaboration with Robinson, relaxation times approaching a second for vacuum alkali vapor cells coated with long-chain paraffins. This work led to a search for a small permanent electric dipole in the ground state of alkali atoms (with graduate students Earl Ensberg and Philip Ekstrom); they used atomic-light modulation oscillators and, in 1962, achieved new lower limits.

A new approach was tried in the electron experiment: Electrons stored in a Penning trap were bombarded by a simple Na atomic beam polarized by optical pumping. Monitoring of the electron spin orientation was supposed to be achieved via scattering of the electrons out of the trap via spin-dependent e-Na collisions. Although this experiment was not successful, a similar experiment, on He$^+$ stored in a Paul rf trap, undertaken by Dehmelt and his student Fouad Major in 1962, succeeded. Eventually Dehmelt measured the ^{3}He$^+$ hfs separation in a precision experiment carried out with postdoctoral fellows Norval Fortson and Hans Schuessler using spin-dependent Cs-He$^+$ charge exchange for the He$^+$ orientation monitoring. The e-Na beam experiment was later performed successfully in Germany by G. Graeff, Major, Fortson, and others. The Hg $^3P_2$ idea also provided the model for a magnetic resonance experiment on the simplest of all molecules, H$_2^+$. However, after extended trials with space-charge traps and electron impact, Dehmelt's graduate student Keith Jefferts suggested that photons again might be more effective than electrons. A scheme based on selective photodissociation of H$_2^+$ stored in a Paul rf trap was worked out jointly and proved successful in 1962. Subsequent work by Jefferts at Bell Laboratories and by Charles Richardson and Stephen Menasian in Seattle identified many hfs transitions.

A radically different course was pursued in a free-electron experiment begun in 1962. Coupling the axial motion of the electrons in the parabolic Penning trap to a resonant circuit for the purpose of cooling the electrons, Dehmelt proposed that spin resonance through Majorana flops should result in heating of the electron gas, detectable by the noise increase in the resonant circuit. This led to his development of the bolometric technique, with his graduate student Fred Walls, and to inconclusive attempts by Walls and Talbert Stein to measure the spin-cyclotron-difference frequency. In a parallel experiment on protons stored in a Paul rf trap, Dehmelt's student David Church demonstrated cooling of the proton gas.

Upon reexamination of the Walls-Stein experiment with his postdoctoral assistant David Wineland, Dehmelt, in collaboration with Wineland and Ekstrom, brought to realization a new scheme whose basic feasibility he had pointed out in 1962—the monoelectron oscillator. The axial oscillation of the same individual electron in an approximately 5-volt-deep Penning trap was continuously detected electronically for arbitrary periods (days). In 1973 this achievement opened completely new avenues. The monitoring of the cyclotron orbit radius and spin direction by means of a shallow magnetic bottle superimposed on the Penning trap fields in order to induce related axial frequency shifts was then proposed by Dehmelt and Ekstrom and realized in 1976 by Dehmelt in collaboration with Robert Van Dyck and Ekstrom. Reinforced by a graduate student, Paul Schwinberg, this group achieved the most precise magnetic moment determination to date (early 1979), 4 parts in 10^{11}, by carefully measuring on the same trapped electron almost at rest (geonium) the axial, magnetron, cyclotron, and spin-cyclotron-difference frequencies. Small shifts in the directly observed axial frequency signaled the resonance of the exciting rf fields with the three other electron frequencies.

Extending his zero-Doppler-effect techniques to much higher frequencies, Dehmelt proposed in 1973 laser spectroscopy on an individual Tl$^+$ ion stored in a miniaturized Paul rf trap and refrigerated electronically. Early in 1975 Wineland and Dehmelt proposed to reach much lower temperatures by optical sideband cooling. In sideband cooling, the ion in its parabolic well is irradiated, not at its natural internal frequency, but at a lower vibrational sideband created by the periodic motion in the well. In the excitation process, the ion is forced to make good the energy defect in the exciting quanta from energy stored in the vibrational motion, which is thereby cooled. The effect was demonstrated on geonium in 1976 by Van Dyck and Schwinberg in collaboration with Dehmelt. In this work, magnetron motion temperatures as low as -0.5 K were realized. Optical sideband cooling of Mg$^+$ ions was reported in 1978 by Wineland and Walls in Boulder, CO, using bolometric detection, and by P. E. Toschek's group in Heidelberg using Ba$^+$ and light scattering, Dehmelt collaborating with Toschek.

Dehmelt graduated from the Gymnasium Zum Grauen Kloster, Berlin, in 1940. He served in the German army as a private in 1940–46—until 1943 with antiaircraft batteries near Berlin and in the Soviet Union, barely escaping the Stalingrad debacle. In 1943–44 he studied physics at the Breslau Technical University under an army program. Transferred to a mortar battery, he was taken prisoner by American forces near Bastogne in early 1945. He was released in early 1946 and took up his studies at Göttingen. There he received the Diplom and the Doctor Rer. Nat. degrees in physics in 1948 and 1950. He held postdoctoral appointments at Göttingen in 1950–52 and at Duke University in 1952–55. In 1955 he joined the faculty of the University of Washington, Seattle, becoming assistant professor in 1956, associate professor in 1958, and full professor in 1961. He became an American citizen in 1961. In 1970 he was awarded the Davisson-Germer Prize of the American Physical Society, and in 1978 he was elected to the National Academy of Sciences.

Dehmelt wrote *Radiofrequency Spectroscopy of Stored Ions* (1967; pt. 2 1969).

For background information *see* ATOMIC STRUCTURE AND SPECTRA; MAGNETIC RESONANCE; NUCLEAR MOMENTS in the McGraw-Hill Encyclopedia of Science and Technology. ∎

DELBRÜCK, MAX
☆ American biologist

Born Sept. 4, 1906, Berlin, Germany

At Vanderbilt University in 1946, Delbrück and his coworker, W. T. Bailey, Jr., discovered that bacterial viruses have a sexual mode of reproduction. They were conducting an experiment to learn whether or not different types of bacterial viruses could reproduce in a single bacterial cell. Not only did the subjects of the experiment reproduce, but they also produced offspring reflecting both parental characteristics. Biologists had previously thought that even the one-celled bacterium was asexual and reproduced exclusively by splitting. Nothing was known of the propagation of the virus.

A series of 20th-century investigators (beginning with a Canadian, Felix d'Hérelle, who first discovered bacterial viruses in 1917) studied the organisms in the hope that knowledge about them might have medical application. The Australian microbiologist Macfarland Burnet continued the investigation of the organism that d'Hérelle had called the "bacteriophage." Early in the 1930s Burnet discovered the existence of a great variety of mutant bacteriophages and proved d'Hérelle's idea that viruses accumulate within the body of the host bacterium, only to be liberated suddenly when the bacterium is destroyed. The German researcher Martin Schlesinger—before the invention of the electron microscope in 1941 revealed viruses directly—discovered (1933–34) by indirect means the size and mass of the bacteriophage and, more importantly, that the chemical composition of these organisms resembles that of the substance which carries genetic information, the chromosome. In contrast to these investigators, who were all concerned with the possible medical implications of bacteriophage, another group studied them for any light that they might shed on the mechanism of heredity. Some of this latter group were from the physical sciences, particularly the new quantum physics. Their work would eventually provide the basis for molecular biology. *See* BURNET, SIR (FRANK) MACFARLANE.

Delbrück was a pioneer in this latter group. He was introduced to bacterial viruses in 1937 at the California Institute of Technology by another research fellow, Emory Ellis. Delbrück brought to the study of these viruses his background in theoretical physics at the University of Göttingen and the insights into possible molecular explanations of genetics that he had gathered in discussions with other physicists in Berlin from 1932 to 1937. As Delbrück began his investigations, very little was known of the mechanics of virus propagation. It was known that these viruses are quiescent outside of a bacterium; their activity begins when they find a bacterium to which they may attach themselves. Penetration of the bacterium follows, and the virus begins active reproduction within its host. This is followed by destruction of the cell walls of the bacterium as the new viruses burst forth.

Burnet had previously demonstrated that the great variety of bacteriophages can be divided into groups of related ones. Related strains were shown by Delbrück and Bailey to have the ability to reproduce at the same time in a bacterium. In an experiment intended to produce offspring from each of two different types of viruses, the observers were startled to find not only viruses related to the two parent types, but two new types representing two different combinations of the characteristics of the two parent viruses.

Delbrück and Bailey realized that this meant that the two parent viruses had exchanged some type of genetic material. Apparently the simple bacterial viruses shared the ability of higher organisms to evolve through mutations, selection, and recombination in response to hostile environmental conditions and thus avoid extinction. This discovery opened the way for subsequent investigations into the exact biochemical nature of the genetic process by which these organisms transmit their characteristics.

In the early 1950s Delbrück turned his attention to other aspects of molecular biology, especially to signal handling in sensory physiology. His experimental object for this work was the fungus *Phycomyces*, whose single-celled sporangiophore is capable of an astonishing variety of signal handling, of which light signals, producing phototropism, show the most spectacular features. These light responses were shown (1975) to be mediated by a photoreceptor containing riboflavin as the light-absorbing component.

Delbrück received his Ph.D. in physics at the University of Göttingen in 1930. From 1931 to 1932 he was a Rockefeller Foundation fellow in physics in Copenhagen and Zurich, from 1932 to 1937 an assistant at the Kaiser Wilhelm Institut für Chemie in Berlin, and from 1937 to 1939 a Rockefeller Foundation fellow again, this time in biology at the California Institute of Technology. Thereafter he went to Vanderbilt University as an instructor in physics, remaining until 1947 when he became professor of biology at Caltech. Elected to the National Academy of Sciences in 1949, he received its Kimber Genetics Award in 1965, and the Nobel Prize in physiology or medicine in 1969 (together with A. D. Hershey and S. E. Luria).

For background information *see* BACTERIOPHAGE; MOLECULAR BIOLOGY; VIRUS in the McGraw-Hill Encyclopedia of Science and Technology. ∎

DELIGNE, PIERRE
☆ Belgian mathematician

Born Oct. 3, 1944, Brussels, Belgium

Much of Deligne's early work was in algebraic geometry and was carried out in collaboration with A. Grothendieck. Whereas Grothendieck was involved in completely reworking the field of algebraic geometry into a powerful structure in which each concept was treated with the greatest possible degree of generality, Deligne was keener on finding key ideas that suddenly clarified a problem or an entire area.

Deligne's most important result was his proof in 1973 of a conjecture put forth by A. Weil in 1949. Weil's conjecture was concerned with a set of one or more polynomial equations in several unknowns. In general, these equations have the form $f_1(x,y,z, \ldots) = 0$, $f_2(x,y,z, \ldots) = 0$, $\ldots$, where $f_1, f_2, \ldots$, are polynomials which are assumed to have integer coefficients. One can consider various types of solutions to these equations. On the one hand, if the unknowns x, y, z, $\ldots$, are complex numbers, then the solutions form a continuum or manifold, known as an algebraic variety, whose topological properties have been studied extensively. On the other hand, if the unknowns belong to the finite field with p^r elements, where p is a prime number and r is any positive integer, then there is a finite number of solutions, denoted N_{p^r}.

Weil's conjecture sets up a connection between the geometry of the continuum of complex solutions and the arithmetic solutions in the finite field. Very roughly, it states that for each prime p there exist complex numbers x_{ij} such that, for each r, Eq. (1) is satisfied. Here n is the dimension of the space of complex solutions X, and the B_j are the Betti numbers of this space. Furthermore, the absolute values of the numbers x_{ij} are given by Eq. (2).

$$N_{p^r} = \sum_{j=1}^{n} (-1)^j \sum_{i=1}^{B_j} x_{ij}{}^r \quad (1)$$

$$|x_{ij}| = p^{j/2} \quad (2)$$

(To obtain a precise statement of the conjecture, one must modify both the manifold X and the procedure for counting solutions in finite fields, and exclude certain primes p.)

Grothendieck verified Eq. (1) in 1965, but Eq. (2) was more difficult, and remained for Deligne to prove. His proof employed both a new cohomology theory, known as étale cohomology, developed by Grothendieck, M. Artin, and J. L. Verdier, which yielded the numbers x_{ij} in a natural way, and work done in 1939 by R. Rankin on an analogous conjecture of S. Ramanujan. Deligne had already shown in 1968 that Weil's conjecture implied Ramanujan's. Deligne's proof of Weil's conjecture not only was of great importance in its own right but also led to the proof of other important results in algebraic geometry and number theory.

After 1973 Deligne's interests shifted somewhat from geometry to number theory. He made several important contributions to problems associated with the program of R. P. Langlands to elucidate the relationship between the manner in which the numbers x_{ij} mentioned above vary with p and the theory of automorphic forms.

At the age of 14 Deligne began to sudy N. Bourbaki's *Elements of Mathematics*, furnished by his teacher M. J. Nijs, and thus acquired some of the fundamentals of modern mathematics while still in high school. He studied at the Free University of Brussels, where his development was assisted by the group theorist J. Tits. In 1965–66 he was a foreign resident at the École Normale Supérieure in Paris, where he was strongly influenced by Grothendieck and J.-P. Serre, and in 1967–68 he did research at the Fonds National de la Recherche Scientifique (FNRS) in Brussels. In 1967 he became a guest at the Institut des Hautes Études Scientifiques (European Institute for Advanced Study) at Buressur-Yvette near Paris, and in 1970 he became a permanent professor there. In 1968 he received the doctor of science degree from the Free University of Brussels and was appointed a professor there. He received the François Deruyts Prize of the Royal Academy of Belgium (1974), the Henri Poincaré Gold Medal of the French Academy of Sciences (1974), the De Leeuw Damry Bourlart Prize of the FNRS (1975), and the Fields Medal of the International Congress of Mathematicians (1978). He was elected a foreign associate of the French Academy of Sciences (1978) and a foreign honorary member of the American Academy of Arts and Sciences (1978).

For background information *see* NUMBER THEORY; POLYNOMIAL SYSTEMS OF EQUATIONS in the McGraw-Hill Encyclopedia of Science and Technology. ∎

DE LUCA, LUIGI M.
★ American biochemist

Born Feb. 25, 1941, Maglie (Lecce), Italy

In the early 1960s, while still a student at the University of Pavia (Italy), De Luca became interested in the role of vitamin A in controlling the growth of tissues. At that time, the function of retinaldehyde (vitamin A aldehyde) as the chromophore of rhodopsin had been amply documented by G. Wald, and R. A. Morton and their collaborators. De Luca's attention was attracted by the work of George Wolf, who had found that deficiency of vitamin A decreased the sulfation of sugar polymers, known as mucopolysaccharides.

After completing his doctoral research, under the supervision of Alessandro Castellani, on the nature of the linkage between the carbohydrate and the protein moieties of protein-polysaccharide complexes from several sources, De Luca joined Wolf's group at the Massachusetts Institute of Technology (MIT) in 1965. He found that vitamin A was indeed a fascinating substance and that much was known about the effects of its deficiency on epithelial tissues. In experiments with rats, some of these tissues, such as those of the respiratory tract, lost their usual morphology of mucociliary epithelia and were replaced by a layer of keratin-producing cells. The visual and the reproductive functions were also defective in the

vitamin A–depleted rats. This enormous range of effects made it very difficult to define target tissues and specificity of responses to vitamin A deficiency. The production of mucus appeared to be perhaps the most responsive parameter of vitamin A action in epitheliel tissues, at least as far as could be judged from histochemical studies conducted in collaboration with Paul Newberne, also of MIT. On the basis of such histochemical studies, De Luca and Wolf decided to investigate the biosynthesis of glycoproteins of the rat intestinal epithelium, and they found that a specific glycoprotein was under the direct control of vitamin A for its biosynthesis. Conversely, administration of vitamin A to depleted rats restored this biosynthetic activity and the number of mucous cells to normal levels. An antiserum was raised against the specific vitamin A–dependent glycoprotein, and permitted its localization exclusively in goblet cells in a variety of epithelial tissues of the body, including the respiratory tract and the conjunctiva. A series of experiments on the incorporation of radioactively labeled monosaccharide mannose into liver glycoproteins showed a decrease of 95 percent in vitamin A–deficient animals. Conversely, administration of excessive doses of vitamin A caused an increase of 610 percent in such biosynthetic activity. Similar work in other tissues suggested that the most profound and general biochemical effect of vitamin A was indeed at the level of controlling the biosynthesis of glycoproteins. But the question still remained as to how vitamin A controlled such events.

By the late 1960s it was known that glycosyl transferases, the enzymes which synthesize the saccharide chains of glycoproteins, are hydrophobic molecules located in the lipid bilayer of the membrane. From work in microorganisms it was recognized that the biosynthesis of bacterial polysaccharides involved, in addition to the glycosyl-transferase enzymes, the hydrophobic lipid called undecaprenol, a compound containing 11 isoprenoid units. Undecaprenol was phosphorylated by a specific enzyme to undecaprenol phosphate, which functioned in bacterial membranes as a carrier of monosaccharides from their activated form, the sugar nucleotides, to specific polysaccharidic acceptors.

In 1969 De Luca and Wolf considered the possibility that, inasmuch as vitamin A (retinol) is a tetraprenoid derivative, it may serve a function in glycoprotein biosynthesis in mammalian tissues that is analogous to the carrier function of undecaprenol phosphate in the biosynthesis of bacterial polysaccharides. The working hypothesis is simply stated as follows: retinol → retinylphosphate → retinylphosphate sugar → glycoproteins.

Although initially not overenthusiastic about the idea, mainly because ideas on the systemic function of vitamin A had not withstood the test of time, Wolf was very generous in supporting De Luca with his resources, which included many weekends shared at the bench. In 1970 De Luca and Wolf reported that rat liver membranes synthesize retinylphosphatemannose.

That same year, Luis Leloir and his group reported that a glucosyl derivative of another polyisoprenoid, dolichylphosphate, was also synthesized in mammalian tissues. The dolichols had been discovered by Morton's group at Liverpool, and it was not long before Frank Hemming, a codiscoverer of the dolichols, reported he had also found a mannosyl derivative of dolichylphosphate. Leloir received the Nobel Prize in chemistry in 1970.

Obviously the burden was on De Luca and Wolf to show that two biosynthetic systems exist in mammalian membranes, one using retinol and the other dolichol. The alternative—that they had been dealing with an artifact—was also considered very carefully, since vitamin A is easily amenable to oxidations and most of their preliminary data were based on the incorporation of radioactivity from radioactive vitamin A into the mannolipid. With the

assistance of Gloria Rosso, it eventually became clear that, in fact, two different mannolipids were synthesized by the rat liver.

In 1971 De Luca joined a group that had been organized at the National Cancer Institute (NCI) by Umberto Saffiotti to study preventive mechanisms in chemical carcinogenesis, particularly in the respiratory tract. Working with Michael B. Sporn, he continued to pursue the idea of the involvement of vitamin A in glycoprotein biosynthesis. The progress of the work was substantially facilitated by the chemical synthesis of retinylphosphate. De Luca, with Jacques Frot-Coutaz, Robert Barr, and Carol Jones, found that the intestinal mucosa and liver of rats and hamsters synthesize the phosphorylated vitamin A and that retinylphosphate functions as an acceptor of the monosaccharide mannose in mammalian membranes in animals and in laboratory-cultured tissues.

A new chromatographic procedure, developed with Wlodzimierz Sasak, permitted the separation of retinylphosphate mannose from dolichylphosphate mannose in one relatively easy chromatographic step. This fast technique made it possible to conclude that most epithelial tissues contain retinylphosphatemannose and dolichylphosphatemannose as normal constituents of the membrane bilayer. Although work was still in progress in this area, as of early 1979 it appeared that the two mannolipids serve as donors of mannose to distinct glycoprotein acceptors.

In 1973, De Luca set up the Differentiation Control Section of the NCI Lung Cancer Branch, which became part of the NCI Laboratory of Experimental Pathology under Saffiotti. Mechanisms of chemical carcinogenesis and its control were the main subjects of investigation.

Work with Sergio Adamo and Irene Akalovsky demonstrated that vitamin A has the ability to modify the adhesive properties and morphology of neoplastically transformed mouse fibroblasts in culture to resemble a "normal" phenotype. These morphological observations correlate with biochemical changes at the level of the biosynthesis of a mannose-containing glycoprotein of molecular weight 180,000. This system of retinoid-induced adhesion is a useful preliminary screen for vitamin A activity of a variety of vitamin A compounds, collectively named retinoids. It seems that only retinoids with vitamin A activity in other systems increase the adhesive properties of cultured transformed fibroblasts. With Pangala V. Bhat, De Luca's group found that retinoic acid, a compound which has partial vitamin A activity in animals and activity in increasing adhesion, is reduced to a retinollike metabolite, which follows the same path of phosphorylation and mannosylation as retinol.

Interestingly, Bhat found that 3T-12 cells contain a new enzyme activity. This new enzyme removed water from vitamin A, yielding anhydroretinol, an inactive hydrocarbon. This enzyme activity is present in normal mouse dermal fibroblasts, although in a much smaller concentration than in transformed fibroblasts. Epithelial cells do not seem to have this retinol dehydratase activity.

The biological manifestations of the action of vitamin A may well be the result of its function as a carrier of specific glycosyl residues for the biosynthesis of specific glycoproteins. The function and topology of glycoprotein products in different tissues may be responsible for the tissue-specific manifestation of vitamin A function or for its absence in depleted tissues. From the work on adhesion of transformed cells, De Luca and his coworkers felt that the role of vitamin A in controlling the expression of the transformed state may be mediated by the action of the vitamin on glycoprotein biosynthesis. This work on basic mechanisms of membrane biochemistry was expected to contribute to the understanding of key mechanisms of control of the expression of the transformed phenotype.

De Luca received the *Maturità Classica* (1959) from the Collegio Capece of Maglie, Italy, and the doctorate in organic chemistry (1964) from the Institute of Biological Chemistry of the University of Pavia. He served as director of the Clinical Laboratory at the Institute of Phthisiology, Ospedale Maggiore, Milan, in 1964–65. He then served as research associate (1965–69) and instructor (1969–71) in the department of nutrition and food science at MIT. In 1971 he joined the staff of the National Institutes of Health, serving as research chemist at NCI (1971–73), chief of the Differentiation Control Section of the Lung Cancer Branch, (1973–75), and chief of the Differentiation Control Section of the Laboratory of Experimental Pathology (beginning in 1975). De Luca received the Mead-Johnson Award of the American Institute of Nutrition (1978). He was a

member of the American Association for the Advancement of Science, the Society for Complex Carbohydrates, the American Institute for Nutrition, the American Society of Biological Chemists, the American Chemical Society, the Federation of American Scientists, and the American Society of Cell Biologists.

De Luca was the author or coauthor of many research publications. In addition, he contributed to *Mammalian Cell Membranes,* vol. 3, (1977); *Vitamins and Hormones* (1977); and *Fat-Soluble Vitamins* (1978).

For background information *see* CARCINOGENESIS; VITAMIN A in the McGraw-Hill Encyclopedia of Science and Technology. ∎

DEMEREC, MILISLAV
★ American geneticist

Born Jan. 11, 1895, Kostajnica, Yugoslavia
Died Apr. 12, 1966, Laurel Hollow, NY, U.S.A.

From its beginning in 1920, Demerec's research was directed toward a better understanding of the mechanisms of heredity—the nature of genes, their structure and function, and their spontaneous and induced mutability. His earliest work was concerned with the genes responsible for various chlorophyll deficiencies in maize, but he soon turned to investigations of unstable genes in the annual larkspur (*Delphinium ajacis*) and the fruit flies (*Drosophila virilis* and *D. melanogaster*).

These studies were developed to include the previously obscure field of biological control of mutability. Demerec discovered that some genes differed in mutation rate at different stages of the life cycle, in different tissues of an organism, or in different genetic lines; that certain regulator genes could modify the mutation rates of unstable genes; and that other genes possessed a high degree of stability. His results provided conclusive evidence that a gene was a unit structure, rather than one made up of two or more components whose assortment could account for the observed reverse mutability of unstable genes (as was proposed by a then current hypothesis).

In *Drosophila* a deficiency (absence) of one gene is often lethal to the organism. By means of an intricate technique, Demerec succeeded in showing that such a condition was frequently "cell-lethal," so that even a small island of cells within the body of a fly could not survive if a certain gene was missing. Thus it was demonstrated that genes play a very important role in individual cells of higher organisms.

In 1927 H. J. Muller discovered that ionizing and ultraviolet radiations induced changes in genes and chromosomes; and in 1933 E. Heitz and H. Bauer, as well as T. S. Painter, found that chromosomes of *Drosophila* salivary gland cells were very large and displayed conspicuous bands that could be correlated with gene loci. Utilizing these disclosures, Demerec extended his studies of induced mutations and of the relation between mutational changes and chromosomal breaks. His experiments showed that lethal events were often due to deletion of chromosomal segments. Moreover, when chromosomes were broken, a portion of one might become attached to a certain region of the same or another chromosome, and the functioning of genes located near the attachment point—sometimes many genes—might be suppressed. This finding further confirmed the view that a gene's function depends not only on its structure but also on its surroundings.

As the research progressed, it became evident that more sensitive methods were necessary to deal with events (such as mutations, deletions, chromosomal rearrangements) that occurred so rarely. Since genetic studies, as a rule, depend on statistical evaluations of frequency of the events being observed, large numbers of individuals are required for significant results. In

1943, therefore, Demerec turned to work with bacteria (*Escherichia coli* and *Salmonella typhimurium*), where experiments involving billions of individuals could easily be carried out. He was among the first of many to utilize bacteria in genetical research. His studies of alleles (different mutant forms of the same gene) revealed recombination between them, thus showing that a gene locus was not an ultimate genetic unit, as had been generally assumed, but comprised a section of chromosome within which mutational changes, occurring at different sublocations, gave rise to different allelic mutants. Other analyses, made with *Salmonella,* showed that its genes were not distributed at random along the chromosome, as might be expected from the results of genetic studies of higher organisms. In this bacterial species, at least, genes affecting related functions were frequently clustered together. Work carried on in several laboratories has since indicated that these clusters form units of operation ("operons").

During World War II Demerec employed radiation techniques to induce mutations in the mold *Penicillium*, selecting those mutants that were most efficient producers of penicillin. One of the selected strains proved to be such a high yielder of the antibiotic that it immediately replaced those then being used in commercial production. Subsequent adaptations of the principle demonstrated in that work contributed greatly to the rapid development of the antibiotics industry. A few years later, Demerec proved for the first time that genetic mechanisms were responsible for bacterial resistance to antibiotics, and his research revealed two important principles to be followed in antibiotics therapy. The initial doses of these drugs should be large enough to prevent the occurrence of "second-step" (highly) resistant bacterial mutants; and the drugs should be used in combination rather than singly, since a mutant that is resistant to one antibiotic has a very small chance of being resistant to another one also.

Demerec graduated from the College of Agriculture, Krizevci, Yugoslavia, in 1916 and held a position as adjunct at the Krizevci Experiment Station until 1919, when he went to the United States to study at Cornell University. He received the Ph.D. degree in genetics from Cornell in 1923, working under Professor R. A. Emerson. In 1923 he joined the staff of the department of genetics, Carnegie Institution of Washington, at Cold Spring Harbor, NY, as a resident investigator. He was appointed assistant director in 1936, acting director in 1942, and director in 1943. In 1941 he also became director of the neighboring biological laboratory of the Long Island Biological Association. When in 1960 he retired from both these positions, he joined the research staff of Brookhaven National Laboratory, Upton, NY, as a senior staff member, continuing his program of research in bacterial genetics. Elected to the National Academy of Sciences in 1946, Demerec received the Academy's Kimber Genetics Award in 1962.

Demerec published some 200 articles in scientific journals, and served as editor of *Advances in Genetics* (9 vols., 1947–58), *Biology of Drosophila* (1950), *Cold Spring Harbor Symposia on Quantitative Biology* (17 vols., 1941–60), and *Drosophila Information Service* (33 vols., 1934–60).

For background information *see* BACTERIAL GENETICS; CHROMOSOME; DRUG RESISTANCE; GENE; GENETICS; OPERON in the McGraw-Hill Encyclopedia of Science and Technology. ∎

DENISSE, JEAN-FRANÇOIS
★ French astronomer

Born *May 16, 1915, Saint-Quentin, Aisne, France*

Trained as a physicist, Denisse took an interest in radio-astronomical research when the pioneering discoveries of G. Reber and J. S. Hey became known in France shortly after World War II. The opening of this new spectral range for the study of cosmic bodies led to major discoveries in all branches of astronomy. Denisse's main contribution in the field was the exploitation of this new tool for a better understanding of the Sun and of its various forms of activity and their relation with terrestrial effects in the upper atmosphere, together with basic theoretical studies aimed at a better knowledge of radio-wave generation and behavior in the extensive astrophysical plasmas.

Denisse's first research work was devoted to the study (1947) of solar waves radiated in the range of decimetric wavelengths. No high-resolution observations were available at that time, but from statistical studies it was possible to show that part of this radiation comes from the extended chromospheric plasma (the quiet component), and that another component, slowly varying, is related to sunspots. Theoretical study of the quiet component led to the construction of a model determining variations with height of the electronic density and temperature in the chromospheric layers of the Sun. The varying component was shown being radiated by hot coronal condensations of gas located above the sunspots and embedded in their magnetic fields extending high into the solar atmosphere.

Denisse and M. R. Kundu later noticed a close correlation between these short-wave solar emissions and the degree of ionization of the terrestrial E layer, and they attributed this ionization to the x-ray bremsstrahlung emission of the hot solar condensations. That the solar condensations are also strong sources of x-rays was later directly demonstrated by space-borne x-ray detectors.

In 1953 Denisse was appointed to the Paris Observatory to lead a group of radio astronomers, including among others E. J. Blum, J. L. Steinberg, and A. Boischot. A few years later, this group, with the development of the Radio Astronomy Center at Nançay, became one of the most active in the field. It was clear at that time that the most original contribution of radio astronomy to knowledge of the universe, and of the Sun in particular, was its ability to detect by their radio emission the invisible particles accelerated in cosmic plasmas to high energy from the thermal equilibrium of the ambient gases observed optically. Several powerful instruments (interferometers) were specially devised at Nançay to study the solar radio emissions on metric wavelengths, where these solar particles were likely to be best observed. This work led in particular to the discovery of a new type of radio emission (the type IV burst), which was identified with synchrotron radiation of relativistic electrons in the coronal magnetic fields. This result was the first direct evidence of acceleration of particles during the process of solar flares, and brought about a direct access to the major problem of natural acceleration of particles in the cosmic plasmas.

Acceleration of high-energy particles by the Sun (as revealed by the type IV burst) proved to be extremely significant, notably in relation to most forms of perturbations induced by solar activity in the terrestrial upper atmosphere. Denisse and his collaborators (P. Simon and M. Pick) made notable contributions to the explanation of the various aspects of solar terrestrial relationships. The arrival in the vicinity of the Earth of solar protons with energy in the range of tens of millions of electronvolts produces strong ionization and absorption of radio waves in the upper atmosphere above the polar regions; these "polar cap absorptions" were shown to be strongly correlated with the type IV bursts, and this finding demonstrated that protons as well as electrons were readily accelerated during the process of a solar flare. It was shown along the same line that the velocity and strength of the interplanetary shock waves that produce the geomagnetic storms are directly related to the energy developed in the type IV burst.

Interested in the various interpretations that can be given to the multiple aspects of solar radio emissions, Denisse carried out theoretical investigations on the excitation and propagation of waves in plasma. In collaboration with J. L. Delcroix, he wrote a monograph on the subject, *Théorie des ondes dans les plasmas* (1958).

Son of a painter, Denisse graduated from the Ecole Normale Supérieure in Paris with a degree in physical science in 1942. He was in French West Africa to the end of World War II. After several years as research assistant under Y. Rocard and at the National Bureau of Standards in Washington, DC., and as associate professor at the University of Dakar, Denisse went to the Paris Observatory in 1953. He was appointed director of the Radio Astronomy Station at Nançay in 1955 and director of the Paris

Observatory in 1963. He was a member of the advisory council to the French government for scientific and technical research from 1963 to 1967. Elected a member of the French Academy of Science (1967), he was director of the Institut National d'Astronomie et de Géophysique (1967–70) and head of the Centre National des Etudes Spatiale (1967–73). He subsequently headed the Mission de la Recherche at the Ministry of the Universities and chaired the Commission de la Recherche for the preparation of the VIIth Plan.

For background information *see* PLASMA PHYSICS; RADIO ASTRONOMY; SUN in the McGraw-Hill Encyclopedia of Science and Technology. ∎

DENT, CHARLES ENRIQUE
★ British chemist and physician

Born Aug. 25, 1911, Burgos, Spain
Died Sept. 19, 1976, London, England

The discovery in 1944 by A. J. P. Martin and R. L. M. Synge of paper chromatography for the identification of amino acids in protein hydrolysates was applied by Dent to the analysis of more complex material, such as biological fluids. It was realized that this relatively simple semiquantitative method required only minor modifications to make it a new general method of chemistry, potentially applicable to any type of chemical substance and, when combined with specific detecting reagents, of remarkable specificity

and sensitivity. *See* MARTIN, ARCHER JOHN PORTER; SYNGE, RICHARD LAURENCE MILLINGTON.

After toying with sugars, inorganic salts, purines, and other compounds, Dent concentrated his efforts on opening up the new world of chemistry revealed in the amino acid chromatograms of normal and pathological body fluids. When he had mapped the behavior of known amino acids, it became clear that many unknown amino acids were also present (shown by unidentifiable spots in the chromatograms). Improved chemical and chromatographic methods were devised for the isolation of pure substances from urine. β-Aminoisobutyric acid was an early substance isolated and identified from urine by his collaborators. Soon after, porphobilinogen was isolated in pure crystalline form for the first time by Roland G. Westall. Cystinuria and acute necrosis of the liver, then the only known amino acid disorders, were studied. Dent, with G. Alan Rose's help, suggested that cystinuria was a disorder of renal tubular function, a theory as yet unchallenged. Cystinuria and cystinosis were shown to be different diseases.

Dent early developed methods of random testing for metabolic disorders, various chemical and chromatographic methods being routinely applied to body fluids of patients with disorders of unknown origin. New amino acid diseases were identified with frequency by his research team—among them various forms of "Fanconi syndrome," Hartnup disease, argininosuccinic aciduria, and homocystinuria. Many similar diseases were later independently discovered by workers trained by his team. The fact that so many of these diseases are associated with mental deficiency led to his permanent interest in that subject. Treatment was attempted in all such cases, the most spectacularly successful being the care of a child with maple syrup urine disease.

The original patients with Fanconi syndrome and other disorders of renal tubular dysfunction frequently suffered from rickets (osteomalacia), a metabolic bone disease. Dent's studies of the various forms of metabolic bone diseases were further stimulated by a short visit to Fuller Albright's department at the Massachusetts General Hospital (during the tenure of a Rockefeller medical fellowship in G. H. Whipple's department at the University of Rochester), and by the appearance in 1948 of the classic textbook of Albright and E. C. Reifenstein. In 1951 his own hospital (University College Hospital, London) provided him with beds and laboratories for patients with metabolic disorders; he also had facilities for outpatient clinics. This opportunity served to channel his interests, for patients with disorders of calcium, vitamin D, and bone metabolism were far commoner than those with amino acid disorders. One line of research involved a further study of renal tubular function in these patients. Another scrutinized the cause and treatment of osteomalacia, and of hyperparathyroidism secondary to other systemic diseases, such as renal glomerular failure and the group of malabsorption syndromes. Further study was directed toward improving the accuracy of diagnosis of primary hyperparathyroidism and with the associated problem of the differential diagnosis of hypercalcemia. The cortisone test was devised and was shown to distinguish hypercalcemia of primary hyperparathyroidism from that due to nearly all other causes. A chemical method for determining ionized calcium in plasma was devised by Rose and was found to be most useful in detecting marginally raised hypercalcemia. Evidence accumulated later indicated that some cases of apparent primary hyperparathyroidism arise as a consequence of prolonged secondary hyperparathyroidism, and that this situation may be fairly common. The term "tertiary hyperparathyroidism" came into use to describe this condition. *See* WHIPPLE, GEORGE HOYT.

The problem of renal stone formation was of continuing interest from the time of Dent's early cystinuria studies. Cystine stones were shown to be capable of prevention, or of dissolution when already present, by strict adherence to a planned, high-fluid intake. A new cause of stone formation, xanthinuria, was discovered and defined. Calcium-containing stones were also studied, with special respect paid to those due to "idiopathic hypercalcuria." For the latter a treatment with low calcium intake was developed with promising results.

Most of the inborn errors of amino acid metabolism were shown to be hereditary, as well as many of the disorders of renal tubular dysfunction. Diseases such as fibrogenesis imperfecta ossium, osteopetrosis, metaphyseal dysostosis, primary hyperoxaluria, idiopathic osteoporosis, hypohyperparathyroidism, hypophosphatasia, sarcoidosis, and the various malabsorption syndromes were also investigated.

After a year as a clerk in the Midland Bank Ltd. and a year as a chemical technician, Dent took his B.Sc. (1931) in chemistry at Imperial College, London. He took his Ph.D. (1933) in organic chemistry, the subject being the structure and properties of copper phthalocyanine—later marketed as Monastral blue. After working in Imperial Chemical Industries (Dyestuffs Group), he began to study medicine at University College, London, in 1937. In September 1939 he joined the British Expeditionary Force. He saw service in France, during which he was besieged for a week in Arras and was evacuated at Dunkirk. He returned in June 1940 to his medical studies, but in November he volunteered to join the British Censorship (Scientific Department), and for 2 years he sought enemy messages in secret writing in the mail passing through Bermuda. In 1942 he gave evidence in New York at the first trial of Nazi spies captured by this means. He qualified in medicine in 1944 and later joined the Medical Unit, University College Hospital, London, where he began to work on disorders of amino acid metabolism produced by dietary means. Soon afterward he was sent to the recently captured concentration camp at Belsen to study the treatment of starvation by amino acid mixtures. After the war he remained attached to University College Hospital, London. Elected a fellow of the Royal Society of London in 1962, Dent received a Gairdner Foundation Award in 1965. He was given an honorary M.D. by the University of Louvain in 1966.

For background information *see* AMINO ACIDS; CHROMATOGRAPHY; METABOLIC DISORDERS in the McGraw-Hill Encyclopedia of Science and Technology. ∎

DETHIER, VINCENT GASTON
★ American biologist

***Born** Feb. 20, 1915, Boston, MA, U.S.A.*

Interested in the neural basis of behavior, Dethier employed insects as experimental animals. He became recognized primarily for his studies of the host plant relationship of plant-feeding caterpillars and his investigations of the chemical senses of insects. Dethier's other major contributions lie in the field of comparative psychology, where he studied the mech-

anisms of hunger and satiation in insects —in particular, the blowfly—and the application of the concept of motivation to these animals.

The ability of caterpillars to discriminate among species of plants and to restrict their feeding to certain species presented a unique opportunity to analyze behavior at a time when the study of animal behavior, especially that of invertebrates, was still more descriptive than analytical. Dethier was the first to prove that feeding preference by caterpillars is mediated by olfactory and gustatory stimuli produced by host plants. He proposed that the critical stimuli are token stimuli, principally components of essential oils, not absolutely associated with nutritional values.

Refined analytical techniques, such as gas chromatography, for detecting and characterizing relevant plant chemicals had not been developed at that time. Nonetheless, it was clear that further understanding of feeding behavior depended upon a knowledge of the physiology of the chemical senses. Accordingly, the locus of the chemical senses of caterpillars was sought by means of ablation experiments. When the organs were identified, their neuroanatomy was described. Attempts were made in 1937 to record action potentials from these receptors, but recording and amplifying instruments then available were unequal to the task.

Dethier turned his attention to a study of the evolutionary development of host

plant relationships and feeding preferences. He investigated in detail the relation between swallowtail larvae and their host plants, the chemistry of these plants, and the role of the chemicals in regulating feeding preferences. This work led to a theory which, by relating known facts of animal geography and population genetics to facts of feeding behavior, attempted to explain origins and contemporary changes of restricted feeding habits.

After a 4-year interruption by World War II, Dethier returned to the study of the chemical senses of insects. He chose as an experimental animal the black blowfly. This study led to a long series of investigations of the chemical senses of insects that constitute Dethier's most significant contribution to sensory physiology. At that time no insect chemoreceptor had been identified with absolute certainty. By exploiting D. E. Minnich's observation that flies extended their proboscis when sugar was applied to the feet or mouthparts, Dethier was able to identify the chemoreceptors behaviorally. During the next 10 years the neuroanatomy of the receptors was elucidated and the stimulating efficiency of more than 400 compounds assessed. From these and other studies emerged a hypothesis that the fly possesses single-neuron receptors mediating acceptance and other single-neuron receptors mediating rejection. Organic compounds that act on rejection (so-called salt receptors) were presumed to operate in a two-phase system—water and lipid. It was subsequently demonstrated that electrolytes are perceived by the salt receptor, and that nonpolar organic compounds act as narcotics on the acceptance receptors.

Parallel studies conducted by Dethier on the olfactory receptors formed the basis for a hypothesis describing the nature of the receptor-transducing mechanism. As a result of these coordinated behavioral and histological studies, a body of knowledge was built that made the fly chemoreceptive system one of the best known in the animal kingdom. The work presented physiologists with the unique opportunity of isolating a single chemoreceptive neuron whose activities could be studied at both the behavioral and the molecular level. It paved the way for elaborate electrophysiological analyses that were subsequently developed by E. S. Hodgson, K. D. Roeder, and J. Y. Lettvin at Tufts University, H. Morita and his associates at Kyushu University, and by Dethier's students M. L. Wolbarsht and D. R. Evans at the Johns Hopkins University. *See* ROEDER, KENNETH DAVID.

The background was also laid for studies of the regulation of food and water intake. In collaboration with Dietrich Bodenstein, Dethier developed techniques in microsurgery that led to the discovery that ingestion is under direct oral sensory control and that satiation occurs as a result of inhibitory feedback from the foregut. Thus, for the blowfly a relatively complete understanding of feeding regulation was developed. The mechanism of thirst was also elucidated.

The fact that feeding could be satisfactorily explained without invoking central nervous system feeding centers of the sort known in vertebrate animals raised the question of whether or not the fly, and insects in general, behave in a manner that is qualitatively different from that of vertebrates. These considerations led Dethier to challenge the idea that higher animals exhibit forms of behavior (such as motivation) qualitatively different from the behavior of lower organisms. He held that a disciplined anthropomorphism is essential to inquiry if one is ever to find out whether there is truly a dichotomy in animal behavior. These ideas stimulated an intensive investigation into the whole question of motivation and learning in insects. Some of the results were the demonstration and analysis of central excitatory and inhibitory states in flies, confirmation of the dual role of sense organs as sources of specific information and generators of generalized excitation, and illustration of the importance of attention and arousal systems to the behavior of insects.

Son of a Belgian musician, Dethier was educated in the public schools of Boston. He went to Harvard, receiving his A.B. in 1936, A.M. in 1937, and Ph.D. in 1939. During World War II he served with the Army Air Corps in the African–Middle East theater, rising to the rank of major. After the war he held professorships at Ohio State University and the Johns Hopkins University. He spent a year at the London School of Hygiene and Tropical Medicine as a Fulbright scholar, half a year in the Belgian Congo as a special fellow of the Belgian American Educational Foundation, and a year at the Landbouwhogeschool te Wageningen, Netherlands, as a

Guggenheim fellow. From 1958 to 1967 he was a professor of zoology and psychology at the University of Pennsylvania and a member of the Institute of Neurological Sciences of the School of Medicine; later he became professor of biology at Princeton University. He retired from Princeton in 1975, and became Gilbert L. Woodside Professor of Zoology at the University of Massachusetts in Amherst. He was elected to the American Academy of Arts and Sciences in 1961, the National Academy of Sciences in 1965, the Royal Society of Arts (London) in 1972, and the Explorers Club (New York) in 1977.

Dethier's ideas concerning the interrelations of insects and the numerous chemical stimuli in their lives were formulated in *Chemical Insect Atttractants and Repellents* (1947), which became the basic reference for studies in this field. He also wrote *Animal Behavior,* with E. Stellar (1961; 2d ed. 1964), *To Know a Fly* (1963), and *The Physiology of Insect Senses* (1963). *The Hungry Fly* (1976) is a complete review of all existing work on the behavior and physiology of feeding in flies.

For background information *see* CHEMORECEPTION; INSECT PHYSIOLOGY; SENSE ORGAN in the McGraw-Hill Encyclopedia of Science and Technology. ■

DEUTSCH, MARTIN
★ American physicist

Born Jan. 29, 1917, Vienna, Austria

Deutsch and his students observed in 1950 that the rate at which positrons are annihilated by electrons when passing through a gas depends strongly on the chemical nature of the gas and can be modified by a magnetic field. The same factors were observed to affect the energy distribution of the gamma rays resulting from the annihilation. The energy involved in the annihilation process is 10^5 times larger than that of chemical interactions and 10^9 times larger than that of magnetic interactions. Therefore Deutsch concluded that the annihilation must occur from a relatively stable electron-positron system and that it is the dynamics of this system that is affected by the weak perturbations.

Positronium is the bound system of electron and positron, closely analogous

to the hydrogen atom. Some of its properties had been predicted theoretically. The interaction between the particles depends on the relative orientation of their spins, so that the dynamically most stable state (ground state) of positronium is split into two energetically slightly different states (fine structure). The state with opposed spins (parapositronium) transforms spontaneously into two gamma rays of equal energy with a mean life of about 10^{-10} second. The state with parallel spins (ortho-positronium) has a 10^3 times longer lifetime and results in the emission of three gamma rays of variable energy. The presence of a magnetic field or collisions with certain types of molecules can cause reorientation of the particle spins, modifying the relative probability of the two annihilation modes. The quantitative experimental results showed that the proposed stable system is indeed positronium with the theoretically expected properties.

Deutsch and his coworkers immediately performed a precision measurement of the energy difference between the ortho and para states. The importance of this measurement lay in the fact that positronium is the only available system involving only electromagetic interactions. All ordinary atoms have properties depending to some degree on the structure of the nucleus. The quantum theory of electromagnetic interactions had been radically recast to interpret the precision measurement of the hydrogen fine struc-

ture by W. E. Lamb and R. C. Retherford in 1947. The fine structure of positronium provided a second powerful confirmation of the new theory. *See* LAMB, WILLIS EUGENE, JR.

Despite the nonnuclear character of positronium, Deutsch had been led to his investigation through a series of studies of nuclear processes. In the late 1930s, when he was a student of R. D. Evans at the Massachusetts Institute of Technology (MIT), many artificial radioactive nuclei were first becoming available. Together with A. Roberts and others, he planned a program to develop methods of nuclear spectroscopy that would illuminate the nature of nuclear energy states through the study of radioactive decay processes. World War II soon scattered the original group, but he maintained some continuity of the program in connection with his work on the fission process in Los Alamos, and he resumed his work at MIT at the end of the war. In a steady development, which lasted almost a quarter of a century, the program produced some of the earliest, reasonably complete studies of radioactive decay schemes by the systematic application of coincidence methods and use of a high-luminosity magnetic spectrometer developed for this purpose. It yielded the first valid measurements of angular correlations of radioactive radiations and their polarization, the first application of scintillation counters to nuclear physics, and some of the earliest measurement of submicrosecond nuclear lifetimes. Many of these methods became standard procedures, developed further and refined by others. It was familiarity with the relevant techniques that led Deutsch to study the annihilation of positrons when the development of quantum electrodynamics in the late 1940s focused interest on this process. After studying positronium, he extended his experiments to annihilation at high energies and applied this method to obtain the first determination of the spin orientation of positrons in beta decay, when this problem became of great importance in connection with the reformulation of beta decay theory in 1957.

In 1960 Deutsch shifted his work to high-energy elementary-particle physics. He extended his interest in nuclear beta decay to the study of other weak interactions, particularly the decay of charged and neutral *K*-mesons. Continuing also in the field of gamma-ray interactions, he

and his collaborators performed some of the earliest experiments on the scattering of high-energy photons by protons and on the production of neutral pi mesons by gamma rays.

Deutsch received a B.S. (1937) and a Ph.D. in physics (1941) at MIT, where he remained as a member of the faculty, becoming professor of physics in 1953. He was elected to the American Academy of Arts and Sciences in 1953 and to the National Academy of Sciences in 1958.

For background information *see* POSITRONIUM; RADIOACTIVITY in the McGraw-Hill Encyclopedia of Science and Technology. ■

DICKE, ROBERT HENRY
★ American physicist

Born *May 6, 1916, St. Louis, MO, U.S.A.*

Dicke's scientific career can be divided into three periods.

(1) Beginning in 1956, Dicke was concerned with cosmological, gravitational, and relativistic problems. Together with his colleagues R. Krotkov and P. G. Roll, he showed with an accuracy of 1 part in 10^{11} that the gravitational accelerations of heavy and light elements are equal. With C. Brans, a graduate student, Dicke investigated a new relativistic theory of gravitation called the scalar-tensor theory. He also showed the relation of this theory to general relativity, Einstein's theory of gravitation.

To provide a test for general relativity, Dicke and his colleague H. M. Goldenberg measured the oblateness of the Sun during the summer of 1966. These measurements indicated that the Sun is oblate enough to account for 8% of the excess perihelion rotation of Mercury's orbit. If these measurements and the observations of Mercury's orbit are accurate and have been properly interpreted, they are in agreement with the scalar-tensor theory but not with Einstein's theory of gravitation. Dicke also investigated a number of possible astrophysical and geophysical implications of the scalar-tensor theory.

In 1964 with his colleagues P. J. E. Peebles, Roll, and D. T. Wilkinson, Dicke reactivated an old idea of G. Gamow and R. A. Alpher, that the universe might have expanded out of a hot fireball. Thermal radiation from this fireball should still remain in the universe as microwaves. The radiation was first observed by Arno A. Penzias and Robert W. Wilson of the Bell Telephone Laboratories, and was confirmed by Roll and Wilkinson of the Princeton group.

(2) In 1941, after completing his graduate work, Dicke joined the Radiation Laboratory at the Massachusetts Institute of Technology to help with the development of microwave radar. Many of his 54 patents involve radar inventions. These include monopulse radar, coherent pulse radar, chirp radar, and a number of microwave components, including the "magic tee" and the balanced mixer. Among his nonradar inventions are the switched microwave radiometer (1944), the heart of most radio telescopes. The radiometer employed a "lock-in amplifier," a common ingredient in most of his subsequent experiments. He also held the basic patent for the mirrored laser. Invented in 1956, a model of this coherent generator of infrared radiation was never constructed.

(3) In 1946 Dicke joined the faculty of Princeton University, and for 10 years his research was concerned with atomic physics, particularly various fundamental radiation processes. He developed the theory of collision reduction of Doppler-broadened lines, including both the coated wall and the buffer gas techniques. The techniques, involving both a buffering gas and glass walls coated with silane, were first used in 1954 by his student J. P. Wittke to make what was at the time the highest-precision measurement of the hy-

perfine splitting of the ground state of atomic hydrogen. It was also used in 1955 by his student E. B. D. Lambe to make the first high-precision measurement of the electron *g* factor. In this connection Lambe introduced the use of Teflon as a buffering wall material. In 1955 Dicke's student P. L. Bender introduced the use of the buffer gas technique in optical pumping. Earlier his student Bruce Hawkins had carried out one of the first two successful optical pumping experiments. This experiment overlapped, and was independent of, Alfred Kastler's experiment, the one first completed. Using optical pumping with the buffer gas technique and the buffer gas narrowing of magnetic dipole transitions, Dicke's colleague T. R. Carver first investigated the rubidium hyperfine transition with the expectation that this combination of techniques would make a good atomic clock. This technique, almost unmodified, led to one of the principal commercially important atomic clocks. *See* KASTLER, ALFRED.

The first quantum theory of the coherent emission of electromagnetic radiation was published by Dicke in 1953. He showed that for an assemblage of atoms there exists strongly radiating quantum-mechanical states, which he called superradiant, and that a compact system of atoms, initially excited, would spontaneously make transitions to these energy states. The operation of a laser can be described in terms of transitions between these states.

Dicke received an A.B. from Princeton University in 1939, a Ph.D. from the University of Rochester in 1941, and an honorary D.Sc. from the University of Edinburgh in 1972. He was elected to the American Academy of Arts and Sciences in 1963 and was a recipient in 1967 of the academy's Rumford Prize. He was elected to the National Academy of Sciences in 1967 and received its Comstock Prize in 1973. He was elected to the American Philosophical Society in 1978. He received the National Medal of Science in 1971, the Exceptional Scientific Achievement Medal of NASA in 1973, and the Cresson Medal of the Franklin Institute in 1974.

Dicke wrote *Principles of Microwave Circuits,* with C. G. Montgomery and E. M. Purcell (1948); *Introduction to Quantum Mechanics,* with J. P. Wittke (1960); and *The Theoretical Significance of Experimental Relativity* (1964).

For background information *see* ATOMIC CLOCK; LASER; MICROWAVE; OPTICAL PUMPING; RADAR; RELATIVITY in the McGraw-Hill Encyclopedia of Science and Technology. ■

DIELS, OTTO PAUL HERMANN
German chemist

Born *Jan. 23, 1876, Hamburg, Germany*
Died *Mar. 7, 1954, Kiel, Germany*

While studying the reactions of conjugated dienes (organic compounds containing two double bonds separated by one single bond), Diels and his associate Kurt Alder developed a general organic reaction called diene synthesis. Now known as the Diels-Alder reaction, diene synthesis promotes the production of highly stable six-membered ring structures and has made possible great advances in chemical technology. For their achievements Diels and Alder shared the Nobel Prize in chemistry in 1950. *See* ALDER, KURT.

It had long been known that molecules containing bonds were exceptionally reactive. In addition, such molecules tend to attach to one another to form long-chain polymers. Diels found that when the temperature of a quantity of a diene, such as butadiene or isoprene, was increased for a period of time, the physical and chemical properties of the compound were altered considerably. On analysis, he discovered that more complex compounds were formed without the need of any outside reagent as a catalyst or participant. His experiments in comparing the activity of a number of dienes with compounds not containing a pair of double bonds showed that the presence of two double bonds was necessary if the rather effortless linking with further chemical components was to take place.

The conditions required for the linkage are so mild, and the basic dienes are so plentiful, that Diels felt a great number of naturally occurring large and complex organic compounds probably are synthesized in this manner. He felt this was especially true within organisms where the necessary temperature regulations can and do take place.

A difficulty in determining what linkages were occurring lay in identifying the orientation of the joining molecules. Early experiments showed cyclopentadiene would polymerize on heating to form a polymer-homologous chain. Thorough analysis of the stereochemical properties of the components of the chain showed that each linkage resulted in another five-membered ring formation. Hence the polymerization must occur in all dimensions and cannot occur at each and every double bond but only where another cyclopentane can be formed.

Diels and Alder, who had been working at the University of Kiel, first published reports of their findings in 1928. They showed that the diene synthesis was a union of two unsaturated partners, a diene and a philodiene. The diene is the carrier of a system of conjugated double bonds; the philodiene must carry at least one double bond. The adduct is always a six-membered ring with the reaction taking place in the 1:4 positions, as shown by the accompanying general equation.

Since the publication of the Diels-Alder reaction, the principles of diene synthesis have enabled scientists to analyze many organic compounds and to artificially reproduce them. Compound synthesis from dienes resulted in the production of a number of drugs and medicines that had not previously been analyzed. One such compound exhibited properties similar to vitamin K; ensuing research indicated that a number of vitamins and hormones may be produced in living organisms by similar diene synthesis. Butadiene combined with styrene leads to synthetic rubber; plastics and

rubberlike materials are produced in similar ways.

Diels was noted also for his research with saturated fats and fatty acids. While performing experiments on cholesterol, he discovered the use of selenium as an agent to remove hydrogen from the saturated organic molecule. This method of dehydrogenation led to the production of polyunsaturated oils that are commonly marketed. The technique also contributed to further research in sterol chemistry.

The properties of carbon and oxygen were known, and the ways in which they combine were established, but a synthesis experiment performed by Diels in 1906 produced a carbon oxide composed of three atoms of carbon and two of oxygen. The resultant unique gas, named carbon suboxide, has a penetrating odor and an irritating effect on the eyes. Such variations in "known" properties of elements and compound formation contribute to chemical knowledge even though the product is itself of no great value.

The son of a professor at the University of Berlin, Diels was educated there, receiving his Ph.D. in 1899 under the direction of Emil Fischer. He was immediately appointed an assistant at the university's Institute of Chemistry, becoming a professor in 1906 and head of the department in 1913. Diels became a professor at the University of Berlin in 1915. In 1916 he became a professor at the University of Kiel and director of its Institute of Chemistry. He retired in 1945.

For background information *see* DIELS-ALDER REACTION; DIENE in the McGraw-Hill Encyclopedia of Science and Technology. ∎

DIETZ, ROBERT S.
★ American geologist

Born Sept. 14, 1914, Westfield, NJ, U.S.A.

Dietz's chief work was in the field of marine geology, in which he contributed to the study of continental margins, actualistic geosynclinal theory, deep-sea bathymetry, submarine canyon surveys, marine sedimentation, and geotectonics. As an early advocate of the theory of continental drift, Dietz suggested in 1961 that new ocean floor was being generated by crustal divergence along the mid-ocean rifts; he coined the term sea floor spreading to describe this phenomenon. He wrote extensively about plate tectonics, especially regarding the fitting of continental margins, cross-rifted ocean basins, and the breakup and dispersion of Pangaea. He was also interested in the study of meteorite craters and ancient terrestrial impact scars, and identified many examples, but perhaps most significantly the Sudbury Basin, the source of most of the world's nickel.

In the field of marine geology, Dietz first described the value of manganese nodules as potential ores of copper, nickel, and cobalt. With F. P. Shepard and K. O. Emery, he discovered and described the submarine phosphorites off California. Dietz first equated continental rise prisms with eugeoclines, and continental terrace wedges with miogeoclines. He also showed that the shelf break was cut by low Pleistocene sea levels and that it was not due to deposition at the wave base. At the Navy Electronics Laboratory, he led a group of scientists on oceanographic expeditions that revealed much new information on the Pacific Basin. In 1951 he led an oceanographic cruise during which Cretaceous fossils were dredged from the tops of mid-Pacific flat-topped seamounts (guyots). The age of these fossils was determined to be about 100,000,000 years, rather than Precambrian as thought. He mapped the moat and arch structure around the Hawaiian Islands. With H. W. Menard, he first described the Gulf of Alaska region and discovered the great submarine scarp off Cape Mendocino and identified it as the prototype of a new class of geotectonic structures, called fracture zones, which were subsequently found to occur worldwide. As an oceanographer, Dietz first showed that oceanic slicks were contaminant monolayers of phytoplanktonic oil and that the acoustic deep-scattering layers were distributed worldwide and were associated with myctophid fishes, euphausiids, and sergestid shrimps. *See* SHEPARD, FRANCIS PARKER.

During his student days at the University of Illinois, Dietz became interested in the Kentland structure in Indiana as a possible meteorite impact scar, a bizarre idea which was subsequently verified. Although his 1939 proposal to write a Ph.D. dissertation at the University of Illinois on earth and lunar impact craters was rejected, he retained, as a somewhat frustrated astrogeologist, a lifelong secondary interest in meteorite craters and ancient impact scars on Earth, which he termed astroblemes. He used a type of shock fracturing, called shatter coning, to identify such structures, of which more than 100 were discovered on Earth. Among the many impact sites to which he applied this criterion were the Ries and Steinheim basins in Germany (1958), the Vredefort Ring in South Africa (1961), and the Sudbury Basin in Canada (1962). He also identified Elgygytgyn Crater (1976) in Siberia as the world's largest modern meteorite crater, and he suggested that it is the possible source of the Australasian tektite field.

During 1953, while a Fulbright fellow at the University of Tokyo, Dietz studied the trans-Pacific transmission of underwater sound from the Myojin volcanic eruption, which caused an undersea explosion on Sept. 23, 1952, that blew up the *Kaiyo*

Maru, an oceanographic research ship, with the loss of all hands. He also described the regional submarine geology of the northwest Pacific Basin and named the Emperor Seamounts, deriving the names from semimythical Japanese emperors and empresses. This study convinced him that trenches were subduction zones and that a mobilistic model of the Earth, involving continental drift, was needed.

While with the Office of Naval Research in London (1954–58), Dietz initiated the collaboration of the U.S. Navy with Jacques Piccard on the development and use of the bathyscaphe *Trieste* for ultra deep diving. This led in 1961 to a 7-mile (11-kilometer) descent by Piccard and Lt. Don Walsh into the Challenger Deep, the world's deepest depression. Piccard and Dietz published a documentary account of the *Trieste* and this event in the book *Seven Miles Down*.

Son of a civil engineer, Dietz received his Ph.D. in 1941 from the University of Illinois, where he came under the inspiring tutelage of Francis P. Shepard. During World War II he served in the U.S. Army Air Force as a pilot, attaining the rank of lieutenant colonel. From 1946 to 1973 Dietz was a civilian scientist with the U.S. Navy, serving with the Navy Electronics Laboratory and the Office of Naval Research. As his first assignment, he was placed in charge of oceanographic research on Admiral Richard E. Byrd's last Antarctic expedition (Operation Highjump, 1946–47). In 1963 Dietz joined the U.S. Coast and Geodetic Survey (later incorporated into the National Oceanic and Atmospheric Administration). In 1977 he became professor of geology at Arizona State University. Dietz received the Gold Medal of the U.S. Department of Commerce for oceanographic research (1971), the Walter H. Bucher Medal of the American Geophysical Union for original contributions to the basic knowledge of the Earth's crust (1971), the Alexander von Humboldt Award of West Germany for geologic studies (1978), and the Francis P. Shepard Medal of the Society of Economic Geologists and Paleontologists for marine geologic research (1979).

For background information *see* CONTINENT FORMATION; MARINE GEOLOGY; METEORITE; PLATE TECTONICS in the McGraw-Hill Encyclopedia of Science and Technology. ∎

DIEUDONNÉ, JEAN
★ French mathematician

Born July 1, 1906, Lille, France

As the result of collaboration on the preparation of N. Bourbaki's *Eléments de mathématique* (which began publication in 1939), Dieudonné was led to work on research problems in several aspects of topology and algebra.

In 1937, simultaneously with, and independently of, S. Bochner, Dieudonné introduced the concept of continuous partition of unity. If a real continuous function f is given on a normal space X, and if (U_i) is a locally finite covering of X by open subsets, the partition of unity allows one to write f as a sum

$$\sum_i f_i$$

in which each f_i is continuous, but is 0 outside U_i; if X is a differentiable manifold and f is differentiable, f_i can be taken as differentiable. This result became a tool that was useful in all aspects of topology and differential geometry, making it possible to localize problems without introducing discontinuities. *See* BOCHNER, SALOMON.

In 1944 Dieudonné defined and studied a new class of topological spaces which he called paracompact spaces. These are normal spaces in which any open covering can be refined in an open covering which is locally finite (any point has a neighborhood which meets only finitely many sets of the covering). This property is very useful in all questions related to algebraic topology, for it makes it possible to apply the definition of Čech cohomology. Furthermore, most usual spaces are paracompact. Dieudonné proved that separable metrizable spaces are paracompact, and A. H. Stone extended this result to all metrizable spaces.

In 1942 Dieudonné initiated a general study of the concept of duality in locally convex spaces, following the more specific theories developed by E. Helly, H. Hahn, and S. Banach for normed spaces, and by G. Köthe and O. Toeplitz for sequence spaces. In 1949 Dieudonné and L. Schwartz published a paper in which they showed that many results obtained by Schwartz for spaces of distributions were special cases of theorems applying to the duality of general Fréchet spaces or inductive limits of increasing sequences of Fréchet spaces. These results were the starting point of many studies on duality and its applications to functional analysis, among which the papers of A. Grothendieck were the most outstanding and influential.

Beginning in 1943, Dieudonné wrote numerous papers on the theory of classical groups (general linear groups, symplectic groups, orthogonal and unitary groups). Until 1937 the theory was confined almost entirely to cases in which the ground field was the field of real or complex numbers or a finite field. In 1937 E. Witt provided a general theory for quadratic forms over a completely arbitrary field K. This enabled Dieudonné to extend the results of C. Jordan and E. Dickson (for groups over a finite field) to classical groups over general (and even noncommutative) fields. In particular, for a linear group $GL(n,K)$ over a noncommutative field K, it is still possible to define, for a square invertible matrix X with elements in K, a determinant which has many properties of the classical determinants but which takes its values, not in the multiplicative group K^* of elements $\neq 0$ of K, but in the quotient group K^*/C, where C is the group of commutators of K^*; the kernel of the homomorphism $X \mapsto \det(X)$ is a normal subgroup $SL(n,K)$, which, as in the case of a commutative field K, is simple over its center.

Furthermore, in the theory of orthogonal and unitary groups, Dieudonné discovered that there are two very different cases, depending on whether isotropic vectors (that is, vectors other than 0 for which the quadratic or hermitian form vanishes) exist. When there are such vectors, the structure of the group obeys general laws independent of the field K, whereas if no such vectors exist, the structure of the group may be very different, according to the nature of K.

After 1952 most of Dieudonné's research focused on the theory of formal Lie groups, which is an algebraization of the classical Lie theory. When one considers only the local Lie groups, such an n-dimensional group may be regarded as being defined by n analytic function $z_j = \varphi_j(x_1, \ldots, x_n, y_1, \ldots, y_n)$, where $1 \leq j \leq n$, which give the local coordinates of the point $z = xy$ in the group, as expressed by the local coordinates $x_j(1 \leq j \leq n)$ of x and $y_j(1 \leq j \leq n)$ of y, in a neighborhood of the neutral element of the group. The theory of formal groups consists of substituting in that definition the formal power series for the convergent power series φ_j; the result that the group axioms impose algebraic conditions on the coefficients of the φ_j which do not depend on the convergence of the series permits the coefficients to be taken in an arbitrary commutative field K instead of the real or complex field. Dieudonné developed the theory for the case when K is an algebraically closed field of characteristic $p > 0$; for formal commutative groups, it is possible, to a large extent, to reduce the theory to the study of special types of modules over a noncommutative ring of formal power series over the ring of Witt vectors over K. This approach was applied to many problems of algebraic geometry over such fields K, and was generalized by others to formal groups defined over rings more general than K.

Dieudonné attended high school in Lille and Paris and was a student at the École Normale Supérieure in Paris from 1924 to 1927; in 1931 he obtained his doctor's degree with a dissertation on holomorphic functions of one complex variable, written under the direction of P. Montel. He taught in many universities in France and other countries. In 1968 he was elected to the French Academy of Sciences.

Dieudonné published 18 books, including the 9-volume *Treatise on Analysis* (as of 1978, 8 vols. had appeared in French, and 6 vols. in English).

For background information *see* ALGEBRA, ABSTRACT; ALGEBRA, LINEAR; DETERMINANT; GEOMETRY, DIFFERENTIAL; GROUP THEORY; MANIFOLD, SMOOTH; MATRIX THEORY; TOPOLOGY in the McGraw-Hill Encyclopedia of Science and Technology. ∎

DIRAC, PAUL ADRIEN MAURICE
☆ British mathematician

Born Aug. 8, 1902, Bristol, England

In 1928 Dirac developed an abstract mathematical theory to describe the properties of the electron. Given only the particle's charge and mass, he was able to derive the electron's spin, magnetic moment, and other quantitative aspects of its behavior. This equation was the first to account rigorously for observed properties of the electron. One of its consequences was the prediction of a particle, then unknown, identical to the electron but with positive electric charge. C. D. Anderson's discovery of the positron in 1932 gave experimental confirmation of this consequence of Dirac's theory. For his accomplishment, Dirac shared with Erwin Schrödinger the 1933 Nobel Prize in physics.

In 1925 S. A. Goudsmit and G. E. Uhlenbeck, in attempting to account for anomalies in x-ray spectra, introduced the hypothesis that an electron spun about its own axis. Although it disposed of the spectroscopic inconsistencies, the new model of the atom brought difficulties of a theoretical nature, since nothing in current theory required the electron to spin.

It thus became necessary to transform the spinning-electron hypothesis from an ad hoc assumption to a theoretically explicable fundamental of quantum theory. *See* GOUDSMIT, SAMUEL ABRAHAM.

First to make assault on the problem were Wolfgang Pauli and C. G. Darwin. Both their efforts, however, suffered from a multiplicity of assumptions unjustified except for the need to introduce them into an equation describing the electron's spin. It therefore remained for Dirac to propose a new and more satisfactory approach. *See* DARWIN, CHARLES GALTON; PAULI, WOLFGANG.

In classical relativistic mechanics the energy equation of a particle was written as in Eq. (1),

$$\frac{W^2}{c^2} - p_r^2 - m^2c^2 = 0 \qquad (1)$$

where W represented the particles's kinetic energy; p_r ($r = 1, 2, 3$) its momentum; m its mass; and c the speed of light. From this, the quantum-mechanical wave equation was derived by replacing W and p_r by operators (2),

$$ih\frac{\partial}{\partial t}, \; -ih\frac{\partial}{\partial x_r} \qquad (2)$$

and causing the left-hand side to operate on a wave function ψ. This gave Eq. (3).

$$\left[\frac{W^2}{c^2} - p_r^2 - m^2c^2\right]\psi = 0 \qquad (3)$$

This of course gave rise to squared operators $\partial^2/\partial t^2$. Dirac's reasoning led him to regard this matter as being the crucial difficulty, since, in general, quantum mechanics required energy equations to be linear in $\partial/\partial t$ or W. He therefore sought to replace Eq. (3) with an equivalent one which, however, would be linear in W and thus also would contain only the linear operator $\partial/\partial t$.

To do this, Dirac factored the left-hand side of Eq. (3) into two new equations, both linear in W. Either of these, when set equal to 0, became an energy equation of the sort required [Eq. (4)].

$$\left[\frac{W}{c} - \alpha_r p_r - \alpha_0 mc\right]\psi = 0 \qquad (4)$$

Having shown that the two factors were equivalent, Dirac discarded one and was left with Eq. (4).

Here, the α's were new variables, operating on ψ, which had initially been introduced in order to obtain a wave equation linear in W. Since the α's can be represented by four-dimensional matrices involving only constants, Dirac concluded that they should refer to some inner property of the electron. He proceeded to demonstrate that the property involved was precisely the electron's spin.

Dirac now modified Eq. (4) so as to represent the energy of an electron in the presence of an electromagnetic field. The resultant equation gave the electron a magnetic moment of one Bohr magneton. It further stated that the orbital angular momentum was not sufficient to uphold the conservation of angular momentum of an electron moving in a central field. Dirac showed that the conservation of angular momentum was restored by supposing the electron to have an additional spin angular momentum of $\frac{1}{2}h$. He went on to show how his equation accounted for the behavior of the electron in H atoms and the anomalous spectra which had first suggested the idea of a spinning electron. Other experimental verification quickly followed.

Dirac noted that his equation for the electron gave two possible kinds of solution, which seemed to represent a positive or negative kinetic energy for the electron respectively. The solutions yielding a negative kinetic energy seemed impossible to interpret except in terms of a particle identical to the electron in mass but with reversed electric charge and other properties.

To make the interpretation definite, Dirac supposed that in the universe as ordinarily observed, all the negative-energy states of electrons are occupied, with one electron in each. The exclusion principle of Pauli then prevents a second electron from going into one of these states, so that a positive-energy electron cannot jump into a negative-energy state. However, it may happen that a negative-energy state is unoccupied and appears as a hole among the occupied ones. Such a hole is to be interpreted as a positron.

An ordinary or positive-energy electron may jump into the hole and fill it up. Then both the electron and the hole disappear. This is interpreted as the electron and positron annihilating one another. Their energy will be emitted in the form of chargeless photons. Dirac also predicted that the opposite reaction could occur: that two photons could interact to form an electron-positron pair. Both these predictions, little more than speculation at the time they were advanced, were directly confirmed by experiment not long afterward.

In addition to the discovery of the positron, Dirac's theory led eventually to the discovery of the antiproton and the other antiparticles, whose existence was a sign that there were indeed realms of antimatter, which would be highly reactive with ordinary matter, the juxtaposition of the two leading immediately to mutual annihilation. Dirac's theory, then, marked the beginning of the investigation of antimatter that was essential to later developments in particle physics.

Dirac received his B.Sc. from Bristol University in 1921 and his Ph.D. from the University of Cambridge in 1926. He embarked on extensive travel, including stints as visiting lecturer at the University of Wisconsin and University of Michigan (1929) and Princeton University (1931). He then returned to Cambridge where, in 1932, he became Lucasian Professor of Mathematics. During 1947–48 and again in 1958–59 he was a member of the Institute for Advanced Studies, Princeton, NJ. He retired from Cambridge in 1969, and in 1971 he became professor of physics at Florida State University. He was awarded the Royal Medal (1939) and the Copley Medal (1952) of the Royal Society of London. He was elected a fellow of the Royal Society in 1930 and a foreign associate of the U.S. National Academy of Sciences in 1949. In 1973 he was appointed to the Order of Merit.

Dirac wrote *Principles of Quantum Mechanics* (1930; 4th ed. 1958), *Lectures on Quantum Mechanics* (1966), *The Development of Quantum Theory* (1971), *Spinors in Hilbert Space* (1974), and *General Theory of Relativity* (1975).

For background information *see* ANTIMATTER; ELECTRON; POSITRON; QUANTUM THEORY, RELATIVISTIC in the McGraw-Hill Encyclopedia of Science and Technology. ∎

DITCHBURN, ROBERT WILLIAM
★ British physicist

Born Jan. 14, 1903, Lancashire, England

Ditchburn made contributions to ultraviolet spectroscopy, vision, and solid-state physics. The absorption of radiation in ultraviolet light leading to the photoionization of atoms and molecules is important

in relation to the balance of radiation and the formation of ionized layers in the terrestrial atmosphere; to the corresponding processes in the outer layers of the Sun and other stars; and to the interpretation of measurements on plasmas—especially the high-temperature plasmas involved in experiments on controlled thermonuclear fusion. Ditchburn worked in this field from 1925 onward and, with his colleagues, was responsible for development of techniques for vacuum ultraviolet absorption spectroscopy and for detailed experiments on photoionization in many elements (including the alkali and alkaline earth metals) and some molecules. Measurements were also made on the optical properties of solids in the visible and ultraviolet regions.

As a result of observations during 1939–45 on performance of naval personnel using optical instruments, Ditchburn was led to investigate the effect of small eye movements in visual perception. These movements remained even when good subjects believed that they were fixating accurately on a well-defined target. Eye movements caused the retinal image to move to-and-fro in an irregular way across the mosaic of retinal receptors. An optical system was devised that allowed the movements of the eye to control movements of a target, so that its image remained fixed on the retina despite rotation of the eye or translation of the head (stabilized retinal image). It was found that when this apparatus was well adjusted, the target disappeared in a few

seconds. It was afterward seen intermittently and with a hazy appearance like an afterimage. In extreme conditions the whole field went black. These observations showed that movements of the retinal image were essential for normal visual perception.

In normal vision the movement of boundaries (between light and dark areas in the retinal image) across the receptor mosaic causes fluctuations of illumination and produces on-off signals in appropriate fibers of the optic nerve. With the stabilized image, these on-off signals are lost; each part of the retina suffers local adaptation, and only very weak signals remain. In this situation the visual perceptual system receives information that is both inadequate and outside normal visual experience. The "interpretation" of this information causes parts of targets to be seen clearly, whereas others are not seen at all; "false" interpretations occur, leading to the subject's "seeing" features that are not present in the target. The effects on color discrimination are most interesting.

Experiments on the stabilized image were carried out independently by L. A. Riggs and coworkers in the United States and by L. Yarbus in the Soviet Union. The results obtained by the different groups were in general agreement. Much of the work on stabilized images may be understood in terms of concepts stated by W. H. Marshall and S. A. Talbot in 1942. *See* RIGGS, LORRIN ANDREWS.

Son of a schoolmaster, Ditchburn graduated with a B.Sc. from Liverpool University in 1922, the year in which he entered Trinity College, Cambridge (senior scholar, 1923; Isaac Newton Scholar, 1924–25). He was a research pupil of J. J. Thomson during 1924–28. He received an M.A. and a Ph.D. at Cambridge, and became a fellow at Trinity College, Dublin, and professor of experimental philosophy (1929–46).

Ditchburn worked in the British Admiralty in 1942–45, and was professor of physics at Reading University during 1946–68. Ditchburn was active in promoting the extension of the university in the direction of technology and engineering. He successfully advocated the establishment of a department of applied physical science and chaired the department during its first year (1965–66). It subsequently developed into two departments, engineering and cybernetics. Recipient in 1959 of the Thomas Young Award of the Physical Society of London,

Ditchburn was elected a fellow of the Royal Society of London in 1962. After his retirement from the university chair, he acted as a consultant, chiefly to the diamond industry. He worked to establish a research organization for the gem aspect of the industry.

Ditchburn wrote *Light* (3d ed. 1976) and *Eye-Movements and Visual Perception* (1973).

For background information *see* SPECTROSCOPY; VISION in the McGraw-Hill Encyclopedia of Science and Technology. ∎

DJERASSI, CARL
★ American chemist

Born Oct. 29, 1923, Vienna, Austria

Djerassi's chemical work started with synthetic medicinals but shortly thereafter extended to steroids and eventually to other natural products, such as terpenoids, alkaloids, and antibiotics. Studies in the steroid field and subsequent work on structure elucidation of complex natural products were greatly dependent on the use of physical methods, and in this context Djerassi performed basic research on such physical tools. He developed optical rotatory dispersion and, at a later date, circular dichroism as standard tools of organic chemistry. His contributions to the use of mass spectrometry in structural and mechanistic organic chemistry were noteworthy. In the development of each of these techniques, steroids were used initially as model compounds and, if one common thread can be discerned throughout the fabric of his scientific contributions, it was his use of steroids for biological, synthetic, physical, and mechanistic purposes.

Before entering graduate school, Djerassi was involved in research on antihistamines, and was a co-inventor of tripelennamine (Pyribenzamine, one of the first clinically efficacious antihistamines, and still widely used in medicine). After completing his graduate studies, he continued his interest in the development of medicinal agents with his principal emphasis on steroids. Particularly productive were the years he spent at Syntex, S.A., in Mexico City. There, in association with his collaborators, he initiated a novel, industrially feasible synthesis of the female sex hormones estrone and estradiol; the first synthesis of cortisone from plant raw materials (diosgenin from yams and hecogenin from sisal); the development of the first oral contraceptive agent (norethisterone; formula I); and development of the powerful anti-inflammatory agents paramethasone acetate (Haldrone), flurandrenolone acetonide (Cordran), and fluocinolone acetonide (Synalar; formula II). As of the

![Chemical structure of norethisterone with OH, CH₃, C≡CH groups](I)

(I)

![Chemical structure of fluocinolone acetonide with CH₂OH, C=O, O-CH₃, F groups](II)

(II)

late 1970s, norethisterone and fluocinolone acetonide were still among the most widely used contraceptives and topical corticosteroids in medicine.

Djerassi's first stay in Mexico (1949–52) was responsible for his interest in tropical plants. Upon his return to the United States he commenced a systematic chemical study of the constituents of such plants, especially of cacti. Giant cacti from

Mexico and Central and South America proved to be a rich source of pentacyclic triterpenoids, and the structures of 20 new triterpenes were established over the course of a half dozen years. Other terpenoids whose constitution was elucidated during that time were iresin (a novel sesquiterpene representing a "missing link" in terpene biogenesis) and cafestol (a pentacyclic diterpene from coffee). These chemical studies of giant cacti also resulted in the isolation of some new cactus alkaloids, which turned his attention to the general field of alkaloid chemistry, notably of indole alkaloids from South American Apocynaceae species. Over a 10-year period ending in the mid-1960s, well over 50 new alkaloids were isolated and their structures established by his research group. Much of this work was aided by the use of physical methods, such as mass spectrometry, as discussed below.

Another area of natural products chemistry investigated by Djerassi and his students was that of macrolide antibiotics, which include a number of clinically important representatives (for example, erythromycin and nystatin). At the time that this work was undertaken, the structure of none of the macrolides was as yet known. In 1956 Djerassi and J. A. Zderic announced the first complete structure of a macrolide antibiotic, namely, methymycin (formula III). Subsequently, Djerassi

![Chemical structure of methymycin with (CH₃)₂N, CH₃, HO, OH, C₂H₅CH-C-CH=CH-CO-CH-CH₂-CH-CH-CHCH₃, C=O groups](III)

(III)

and his colleagues were occupied with the chemistry of neomethymycin and erythromycin. They also investigated the important antifungal agents filipin and nystatin.

In 1953 Djerassi and his students started their systematic studies on optical rotatory dispersion, which ultimately led to the wide use that this method and the closely related method of circular dichroism now enjoy in organic chemistry. Optical rotatory dispersion (the variation of optical rotatory power with wavelength) is a phenomenon which was known since the last century but which, for all practical purposes, remained unused by organic chemists. For the 20-year period prior to

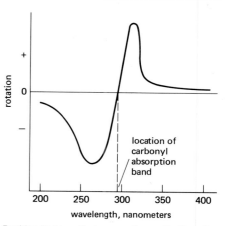

Positive Cotton effect curve of an optically active ketone.

1953, less than a half dozen articles were concerned with organic chemical applications of optical rotatory dispersion; but since the publication of Djerassi's book *Optical Rotatory Disperson: Applications to Organic Chemistry* (1960), several thousand papers have appeared dealing with organic and biochemical applications of optical rotatory dispersion and circular dichroism. His initial work concentrated on steroids and especially on steroid ketones, since the carbonyl chromophore exhibits maximal absorption in a convenient spectral range (about 290 nanometers with relatively low extinction, which permits measurement of the optical rotation through the region of the absorption band. The resulting curve (see the illustration), called a Cotton effect curve, was shown to be diagnostic—in terms of both shape and sign—with a particular optically active environment of the carbonyl group. Subsequent studies with many hundreds of model ketones showed that the Cotton effect curve could be employed for assignments of absolute configuration and for determination of the conformation of organic molecules. Thus, the absolute configurations of many natural products were established for the first time by this method. In fact, it was through the use of optical rotatory dispersion that Djerassi and his collaborators first demonstrated the existence of the "nonsteroidal" absolute configuration in terpenoids, such as cafestol and iresin. In 1963 K. Wellman, E. Bunnenberg, and Djerassi introduced the technique of measuring circular dichroism at low temperatures (down to the boiling point of liquid nitrogen), thus offering an additional approach for examining the subtle problems of conformational and rotational mobility.

Early in 1961 Djerassi and his associates at Stanford University started a series of investigations on the use of mass spectrometry in structural organic chemistry. The potential of this method in the natural products field had already been indicated a few years earlier by E. Stenhagen and R. Ryhage in Sweden, by R. I. Reed and J. Beynon in Britain, and by K. Biemann in the United States, but it soon became obvious that intelligent and extensive use of this tool would have to be based on a detailed knowledge of the fragmentation behavior of organic molecules after electron bombardment. A systematic study was undertaken at Stanford University of model compounds (frequently steroids) possessing a single functional group in order to determine how such a functionality affects the electron impact–induced fragmentation behavior of the molecule. The interplay of several such functionalities in one molecule was examined, with isotopic labeling and high-resolution mass spectrometry playing important roles. This work, performed since the early 1960s and covered in about 250 articles and 4 books, showed that many standard organic chemical concepts from solution chemistry, especially as far as relative stability of carbonium ions and free radicals was concerned, could also be applied to interpretation and even prediction of fragmentation behavior of organic molecules after electron bombardment.

Partly as a result of the work that Djerassi and his colleagues carried out in this area, mass spectrometry has become one of the two most widely used physical tools in organic chemistry. In an attempt to examine the computer-aided interpretation of organic mass spectra, Djerassi together with the research groups of J. Lederberg (department of genetics) and E. Feigenbaum (department of computer science) undertook a major collaborative program on the use of computer "artificial intelligence" techniques in organic chemistry. This work, notably through the contributions of their younger collaborators, D. H. Smith, B. Buchanan, J. Nourse, and R. Carhart, led to a series of programs that not only permitted the extensive use of computers for the interpretation of organic mass spectra but led in a much wider sense to the use of interactive computer

programs for structure elucidation of organic molecules using various physical as well as chemical constraints. This collaborative work extended over a period of 10 years and found numerous practical applications by natural products chemists.

Djerassi's earlier work on chiroptical methods, such as circular dichroism and optical rotatory dispersion, led, beginning in the late 1960s, to another series of investigations dealing with possible applications of magnetic circular dichroism (Faraday effect) in organic chemistry and biochemistry. This work, performed principally in collaboration with E. Bunnenberg, R. Linder, and G. Barth, was published in well over 50 papers and led to a number of practical and theoretical conclusions, the latter in collaboration with A. Moscowitz and L. Seamans of the University of Minnesota. Aside from certain analytical applications such as a very convenient method of determining tryptophan in intact proteins and of detecting minute quantities of porphyrins in human body liquids such as urine, magnetic circular dichroism was particularly useful for a variety of spectroscopic problems, notably among metal loenzymes, porphyrins, and carbonyl compounds.

Finally, in continuation of Djerassi's interest in the steroid field, from 1970 onward his group carried out a series of investigations on the steroid constituents of lower marine animals, such as sponges, soft corals, and sea cucumbers. This work led to the isolation, structure determination, and in a number of instances synthesis of a wide variety of sterols with unique side chains which have not had any counterpart among terrestrial plants or animals. This work was greatly aided by Djerassi's early studies on the mass spectrometry of sterols, because in many instances the structure elucidation was carried out through the use of combined gas chromatography–mass spectrometry coupled with one or two additional physical measurements, such as nuclear magnetic resonance spectroscopy. Djerassi's group also examined the biosynthesis of these unusual sterols and especially their biological role, which is probably a functional one involving membrane stabilization.

Djerassi graduated summa cum laude from Kenyon College (A.B., 1942). After a year as research chemist at Ciba Pharmaceutical Company, Summit, NJ, he entered the University of Wisconsin, where he received his Ph.D. in organic chemistry in 1945. He returned to Ciba and re-

mained there until 1949, when he became associate director of chemical research at Syntex, S.A., in Mexico City. During 1957–60, while on academic leave of absence, he was research vice-president of Syntex. From 1952 to 1959 he was associate professor and then professor of chemistry at Wayne State University; in 1959 he moved to Stanford University as professor of chemistry. Concurrently he also held various positions at Syntex until 1972, including that of president of Syntex Research (1968–72). Since 1968 he also held the position of president of Zoecon Corporation, which he helped found and which is dedicated to the development of new types of "biorational" insect control agents based on insect hormones, sex attractants, and such. Recipient of nine honorary doctorates, Djerassi was a member of the National Academy of Sciences, the American Academy of Arts and Sciences, the Royal Swedish Academy of Sciences, and the German Leopoldina Academy. The American Chemical Society honored him with its Award in Pure Chemistry, Baekeland Medal, Fritzsche Award, and Award for Creative Invention. He was also the recipient of the Freedman Foundation Patent Award of the American Institute of Chemists, the Chemical Pioneer Award of the American Institute of Chemists, the National Medal of Science, the Perkin Medal of the Society of Chemical Industry, and the first Wolf Prize in Chemistry. In 1978 he was inducted into the National Inventors Hall of Fame.

Djerassi was the author or coauthor of over 900 scientific articles. In addition to four books on mass spectrometry, he wrote *Optical Rotatory Dispersion: Applications to Organic Chemistry* (1960) and *The Politics of Contraception* (1979) and edited *Steroid Reactions* (1963).

For background information *see* COTTON EFFECT; MASS SPECTROMETRY; ROTATORY DISPERSION; STEROL in the McGraw-Hill Encyclopedia of Science and Technology. ∎

DOBZHANSKY, THEODOSIUS
★ American biologist

Born *Jan. 25, 1900, Nemirov, Russia*
Died *Dec. 18, 1975, Davis, CA, U.S.A.*

The work of T. H. Morgan and his school on the genetics of vinegar flies, *Drosophila,* elucidated some of the mechanisms of heredity and variation in living beings. Dobzhansky's research in this field added greatly to knowledge of how these mechanisms operate, not only in laboratory experiments but also in natural populations.

The genetic diversity found in *Drosophila* in nature was proved by Dobzhansky to be very great. The idea, entertained by some classical geneticists, that natural populations consisted mostly of genetically similar "normal" or "wild-type" individuals, with a minority of aberrant or mutant specimens, had to be abandoned. It is likely that no two individuals in *Drosophila,* or in humans, or in any sexually reproducing and outbreeding species, ever have identical genetic endowments (identical twins excepted). Only a fraction of this genetic diversity is apparent on casual inspection. Most of it is concealed in heterozygous condition.

Dobzhansky used special genetic techniques available in *Drosophila* to show that most apparently normal and healthy individuals are heterozygous for one or more genes, or gene complexes, that are lethal, semilethal, debilitating in various degrees, diminishing the fertility or sterilizing, or causing various kinds of physiological or structural changes in the body. The magnitude of this "genetic load" is not uniform in different species or in different populations of the same species. And contrary to what one might expect, Dobzhansky's experiments with *Drosophila* showed that biologically more successful and versatile species tend to have greater, not smaller, genetic loads than

the less successful ones. This is intelligible, because there are several biologically disparate components in the genetic diversity. Some harmful genetic variants arise from time to time by mutation and persist for one or several generations until eliminated by natural selection. Other variants are balanced and are maintained by natural selection. The balancing selection may be due to a hybrid vigor, heterosis, produced in heterozygous condition; it may also be due to diversifying natural selection, when different variants fit different ecological niches, extending opportunities for living; other forms of balancing selection are also known.

Dobzhansky set up experiments to observe the operation of natural selection in *Drosophila* populations directly. In some of these populations cyclic genetic changes occur at different seasons, year after year. Since 1940, long-range genetic changes have also been observed in a species of *Drosophila* in California and in parts of adjacent states. What causes these latter changes is as yet uncertain; contamination of the natural habitats of the flies by traces of insecticides is a possibility. Some of the seasonal changes have also been reproduced in laboratory experiments, and a rough measure of the magnitude of the natural selection involved has been obtained. This helps to elucidate the origin of genetic differences between local populations and races of certain *Drosophila* species.

The findings made in *Drosophila* by Dobzhansky and others obviously cannot be "extrapolated" to humans. Genetic processes in human populations are influenced by cultural factors that have no close analogs in *Drosophila*. Nevertheless, humans are a biological species, subject to some general biological regularities. Understanding of human evolution, historical and current, is a challenging problem. Here the work of a biologist impinges on matters anthropological, medical, sociological, and philosophical.

Son of a high school teacher, Dobzhansky majored in zoology at the University of Kiev, Russia, graduating in 1921. He taught zoology and genetics as an assistant (lecturer) in Kiev and Leningrad. In 1927 he went as a fellow of the International Education Board (Rockefeller Foundation) to work with T. H. Morgan at Columbia University and the California Institute of Technology. Returning to Columbia University in 1940, he was a professor there until 1962, when

he joined the Rockefeller University. He was a visiting professor in Brazil, Chile, and Australia and did biological research in these and other countries. Dobzhansky received the National Academy of Sciences' Kimber Genetics Award in 1958. In 1964 he was awarded the National Medal of Science, and in 1973 he received the Franklin Medal from the Franklin Institute.

Dobzhansky wrote *Genetics and the Origin of Species* (1937; 3d ed. 1951), *Heredity, Race, and Society,* with L. C. Dunn (1937; 3d ed. 1952), *Principles of Genetics,* with L. C. Dunn (1950), *Evolution, Genetics, and Man* (1955), *The Biological Basis of Human Freedom* (1956), *Radiation, Genetics, and Man,* with B. Wallace (1959), *Mankind Evolving* (1963), *Heredity and the Nature of Man* (1964), *Biology of Ultimate Concern* (1967), *Genetics of the Evolutionary Process* (1970), *Genetic Diversity and Human Equality* (1973), and some 350 papers in various scientific periodicals.

For background information *see* GENETICS; HETEROSIS; HUMAN GENETICS in the McGraw-Hill Encyclopedia of Science and Technology. ∎

DOELL, RICHARD RAYMAN
★ American geophysicist

Born June 28, 1923, Oakland, CA, U.S.A.

The most useful contribution to science made by Doell, working closely with his colleagues Allan Cox and Brent Dalrymple, was the set of experiments utilizing paleomagnetic and potassium-argon radiometric studies that established the theory of reversals of the geomagnetic field and delineated the more recent chronology of these reversals. This contribution was a key piece of research leading to the discovery of sea-floor spreading and the resulting plate tectonic revolution in Earth science thought. For this contribution, Doell was a corecipient of the Vetlesen Prize in 1971. *See* COX, ALLAN.

Doell's first interest in Earth science was engendered in 1948 while working with a seismic oil exploration crew in California, and later in the Middle East. Among Doell's doctoral research studies was a series of experiments on "blue" sandstones of Miocene age from northern California. These studies enabled him to suggest a new method for rocks to

obtain a remanent magnetization—through postdepositional recrystallization of magnetic minerals. He named this process crystallization remanent magnetization.

In early 1959, after having set up paleomagnetic laboratories at Berkeley, Toronto, and the Massachusetts Institute of Technology, Doell again accepted the challenge of building such a laboratory; but this time it was in cooperation with Cox and as project chief of a full-time research facility. The Rock Magnetics Laboratory of the U.S. Geological Survey was soon in operation, and one of the immediate goals of Doell and Cox was to establish the validity of the paleomagnetic method within the American geological profession. Doell soon traveled to the Hawaiian Islands to collect from lavas erupted and magnetized in historical times—when the magnetic field was known from direct measurements—as well as from older rocks; and thus began a series of collections spanning several years and thousands of samples from these islands. The studies on historically erupted lavas gave many insights into the accuracy with which lava flows depict ancient magnetic fields by means of their remanent magnetization.

Other subjects that early interested Doell and Cox were the possibility that the Earth's magnetic field had repeatedly reversed its polarity, and the degree to which local magnetic fields differ from the overall "dipole" field configuration. The latter phenomenon is known as secular variation. These two subjects occupied the bulk of Doell's research efforts and involved collections of rocks not only from the Hawaiian Islands but also from California, New Mexico, Iceland, and France.

The reversal experiment was an interesting one. Rocks with reversed magnetic polarity had been recognized for many years, but it was uncertain whether they had been magnetized in reversed magnetic fields. There were theoretical reasons why volcanic rocks might become magnetized exactly opposite to the magnetic field direction they cooled in—and indeed one such rock had been discovered in 1958. However, there were reasons to believe that many, if not most, reverse rocks reflected reversed magnetic fields. Clearly, students of Earth magnetism wanted an answer to this interesting question. The experiment was basically a simple one: since self-reversal was the result of a chemistry different from that of normal rocks, and field reversal was a time-dependent property of the geomagnetic field, all that was needed was to collect rocks of varying chemistry and to measure their polarity and age. There were two possibilities: (1) If it turned out that normally and reversely magnetized rocks were randomly distributed with time but not by type, then self-reversal could be expected to be the main cause for reversals. (2) On the other hand, if all rocks of a given age possessed the same polarity, no matter what their type might be, then field reversal would be strongly suspected. It was not difficult, in the early 1960s, to measure magnetic properties of rocks. However, to determine ages of young volcanic rocks with sufficient accuracy for this experiment was a formidable problem indeed. The Rock Magnetics Laboratory was very fortunate to get the services of Dalrymple, who had just obtained his doctorate working with the developers of the potassium-argon method for dating young volcanic rocks, namely G. Curtiss and J. Everenden. Thus the laboratory was able to apply this new and very appropriate method to the reversal question. The resulting studies soon established the second of the possibilities outlined above and delineated a rather aperiodic history of reversals of the geomagnetic field during the last few million years. This same time sequence was soon recognized spatially in the linear magnetic anomalies associated with mid-ocean rises, leading to the establishment of the theory of sea-floor spreading and subsequently to the concept of plate tectonics—a concept that has revolutionized geoscience thought.

In the late 1960s Doell became interested in "geosocial problems," especially those concerned with modern society's increasing use of limited resources. In 1970 he left the Rock Magnetics Laboratory and spent a year at the University of Wisconsin studying environmental and resource subjects. Upon his return to the Geological Survey, he concerned himself primarily with work in these fields. He was also active during this period on many National Research Council and National Academy of Sciences boards and committees working on resource problems of national interest.

Doell's early university studies in mathematics at the University of California, Los Angeles (1940–42), were interrupted by World War II, when he served in the Army infantry. After working at seismic oil exploration for 2 years, he returned to academic work, obtaining the Ph.D. degree at the University of California, Berkeley, in 1955. He then took a lectureship position at the University of Toronto, and a year later he joined the geology faculty at the Massachusetts Institute of Technology. After 3 years he joined the U.S. Geological Survey as a research geophysicist. Doell was elected to the National Academy of Sciences in 1971. In addition, he was a member or fellow, and sometimes officer, of several national and foreign professional geoscience societies. In 1977 he accepted an opportunity for early retirement from the Geological Survey in order to pursue a strong interest in offshore sailing vessels.

For background information *see* DAT-ING METHODS; PALEOMAGNETICS; ROCK MAGNETISM in the McGraw-Hill Encyclopedia of Science and Technology. ∎

DOISY, EDWARD ADELBERT
★ American biochemist

***Born** Nov. 13,1893, Hume, IL, U.S.A.*

Doisy's principal scientific contributions were the isolation of pure crystalline compounds of importance to the well-being of humans.

In collaboration with a biologist, Edgar Allen, Doisy undertook a study of ovarian factors that regulate the sex cycle of rats and mice. Armed with Allen's method of assay, he continued experiments on the nature of the active principles for 12 years (1922–34), isolating the first crystalline steroidal hormone, estrone, in 1929. Subsequently, he isolated two other related products, estriol and estradiol-17β; about 10 milligrams of the latter was obtained from 4 tons of sow ovaries. Administrations of each one of these compounds in microgram quantities to ovariectomized rats or mice caused an estrual response in the animal. These compounds or closely related derivatives have been extensively used in the treatment of diseases of women.

In 1936 Doisy turned to the elucidation of a hemorrhagic condition of chickens that had been discovered in 1929 by Henrik Dam. After 3 years of intensive effort, he and his associates had isolated two pure compounds, vitamin K_1 from a plant source and vitamin K_2 from a mixed culture of microorganisms. With the two compounds at hand the structures were determined. Both contained 2-methyl-1,4-naphthoquinone but differed significantly in the hydrocarbon radical attached at carbon atom 3. Vitamin K_1 was synthesized, thereby verifying the postulated structure. These compounds have been very effective in restoring the clotting time of blood to normal in patients suffering from obstructive jaundice. For this achievement Doisy and Dam shared the 1943 Nobel Prize for medicine or physiology. *See* DAM, HENRIK.

During World War II Doisy's investiga-

tions were diverted to the study of antibiotics. Although a good therapeutic product was not obtained, one of the earliest reports on antibacterial effects (Bouchard, 1889) was clarified by the isolation of four active crystalline compounds from *Bacillus pyocyaneous*. Subsequently, one of those engaged in this work completed the study on constitution by synthesizing three of the compounds.

After the introduction of labeling with radioactive carbon, Doisy undertook studies on the metabolism of hormones and bile acids. The most significant aspect of these investigations was the discovery of four new metabolites that were hitherto unknown bile acids. The constitutions of these acids were postulated from the results of degradation and the postulations verified by synthesis.

Doisy was fortunate in being the son of parents who, although they had little formal education, revered education and encouraged him to attend college. He received his A.B. in 1914 and his M.S. in 1916 from the University of Illinois. He enrolled in the Division of Medical Sciences of Harvard University in 1915, but completion of his education was delayed by 2 years of service in World War I, and he did not receive his Ph.D. until 1920. From 1919 to 1923 he served successively as instructor, associate, and associate professor of biochemistry in Washington University School of Medicine, St. Louis. In 1923 he was appointed to the chair of biochemistry at St. Louis University School of Medicine. He was named distinguished service professor in 1951. He was elected to the National Academy of Sciences in 1938.

For background information *see* BILE ACID; ESTROGEN; VITAMIN K in the McGraw-Hill Encyclopedia of Science and Technology. ∎

DOMAGK, GERHARD
German biochemist

Born Oct. 30, 1895, Lagow, Brandenburg, Germany
Died Apr. 24, 1964, Burberg, Württemburg-Baden, Germany

While investigating the potential therapeutic effect of various chemical compounds, a study that entailed the screening of many very different agents, Domagk discovered the first synthetic antimicrobial of broad clinical usefulness, sulfonamido-

crysoidin. In recognition of the importance of this breakthrough, Domagk was awarded the 1939 Nobel Prize for medicine or physiology.

Modern chemotherapy began about 1910, when Paul Ehrlich, a German biochemist, developed a specific chemical agent to combat a specific disease. Ehrlich had experimented for years with various chemical compounds to try to find a cure for the trypanosomes and, in 1907, formulated his 606th compound, dihydroxydiamino-arsenobenzene-dihydrobenzene (now also known as arsphenamine, 606, and Ehrlich 606). This proved of little value in treating the trypanosomes and was discarded, but 3 years later it was discovered to be effective in the treatment of syphilis. His announcement in 1910 of the successful therapeutic application of the chemical, which he called Salversan, triggered a search for other chemotherapeutic agents. However, except for the synthesis of the antimalarials plasmoquine and Atebrin, progress was negligible.

Domagk began his search for chemotherapeutic agents while on the staff of I. G. Farbenindustrie at Wuppertal-Elberfeld. His method was to first study the chemicals in culture to find their effect upon the several microbic genera; then to find the doses that were tolerated by laboratory animals; and finally, if it seemed warranted, their effect upon the infections, natural or experimental, of humans.

For several years this work yielded no clear leads, but at the end of 1932 a surprising result was obtained when a red azo dye combined with a sulfonamide radical—commercially marketed by I. G. Farbenindustrie under the trade name Prontosil Rubrum—was under investigation. Although preliminary tests with it had shown little bacterial activity while in the test tube, it seemed to have some protective power against streptococcal infections in the mouse. Furthermore, its toxicity was also low for mice.

In view of these findings it seemed worthwhile to repeat the mouse protection test with 26 animals and a test culture of hemolytic streptococci, which was always fatal when injected into the peritoneum. Fourteen mice were kept as controls and died within 4 days, most of them on the second day. The remaining 12 were treated with a single dose of the red dye 1.5 hours after the streptococcal injection. All remained in good condition during the 7 days they were under observation.

Three years elapsed before this striking result was reported in 1935. The reason why publication was delayed is unclear. However, during this period Domagk's daughter was infected by streptococci following the prick of a needle. The girl was near death until Domagk in desperation injected her with large quantities of Prontosil Rubrum, thus effecting a near miraculous recovery in his daughter.

Domagk's discovery opened an immense field for therapeutic advance. Not only was it immediately seized upon to treat the many previously fatal infections of hemolytic streptococci, but it also prompted an immediate inquiry in many laboratories as to whether Prontosil Rubrum or substances related to it could exert a similar effect upon human diseases caused by bacteria quite different from hemolytic streptococci. In England it was quickly found that cerebrospinal meningitis, pneumonia, and gonorrhea were but three of the diseases that could be brought under control through its use. Laboratory work also brought new understanding of the means by which the drug achieved its results, showing that the sulfonamide radical was dissociated in living subjects and that this was responsible for the antibacterial effects. As a result, more powerful antibacterials, such as sulfanilamide, sulfapyridine, and sulfathiazole, were introduced.

During World War II Domagk was chiefly concerned with the chemotherapeutic approach to tuberculosis. In 1944, when the antibiotics were becoming available, the most promising line of attack seemed to be by streptomycin, which had been discovered by Selman A. Waksman in the United States. Other approaches, such as the use of p-aminosalicylic acid, were also taken. Domagk, however, had tried using sulfonamide derivatives. Only sulfathiazole and sulfathiadiazole seemed to offer any sort of hope, and this effect appeared to come from the thiazole rather than from the SO group. He therefore synthesized aminothiazole and aminothiadiazole, and in 1946 Domagk reported success with the thiosemicarbazones. However, extended clinical trials later showed that these had a hepatic toxicity that precluded their general use. Furthermore, the almost simultaneous discovery of another antituberculosis drug, isonicotinic acid hydrazide, which did not have this failing, made use of the thiosemicarbazones unnecessary. *See* WAKSMAN, SELMAN ABRAHAM.

During the last few years of his active life, Domagk became increasingly interested in the problem of cancer. He hoped that a substance might be found that would be effectively cytostatic for tumor cells, that is, would destroy them without destroying the host. However, he achieved no striking success in this research.

Domagk began his studies at the University of Kiel shortly before World War I. Although his education was interrupted by military service, he returned to Kiel at the conclusion of the conflict, and was awarded his medical degree in 1921. After serving for short periods as an assistant at Kiel and then at the University of Greifswald, he joined the staff of I. G. Farbenindustrie. In 1927 he was appointed director of research in experimental pathology and bacteriology, and continued in this post for the remainder of his active career. For political reasons Domagk was forced to decline the Nobel Prize when it was awarded to him in 1939. However, in 1947, he was presented with the Nobel Medal, although the prize money had reverted to the foundation so he was unable to benefit from it. Domagk also received many other honors, among them the Paul Ehrlich Gold Medal and the Cameron Medal of the University of Edinburgh. In 1959 he was elected a fellow of the Royal Society of London.

For background information *see* ANTIMICROBIAL AGENTS; CHEMOTHERAPY; ISONICOTINIC ACID HYDRAZIDE; SULFA DRUGS; THIOSEMICARBAZONE in the McGraw-Hill Encyclopedia of Science and Technology. ∎

DONNAY, JOSEPH DÉSIRÉ HUBERT
☆ American crystallographer and mineralogist

Born June 6, 1902, Grandville, Belgium

In 1931, in connection with the description of a triclinic mineral, A. F. Rogers of Stanford University wrote: "From these five measured angles . . . the geometrical constants were calculated by spherical trigonometry"; and noted: "I am indebted to my assistant, Dr. J. D. H. Donnay, for a careful checking of the computations." Years later Donnay published a book entitled *Spherical Trigonometry after the Cesàro Method.* His work always emphasized rigor. A number of his early papers dealt with form birefringence and spherulite optics, subjects neglected by nearly all American teachers of crystal optics. Donnay began this work at Stanford with H. W. Morse in 1930. Major papers appeared in 1932 and 1936, but even in later years Donnay pursued the subject with his wife, Gabrielle Donnay, in work on the bastnaesite-vaterite series (1961) and on the water content of spherulitic vaterite (1967).

Donnay's studies on the law of Bravais continued those of E. Mallard, G. Friedel, and H. Ungemach. His work led to the first generalization, with David Harker, in 1937, showing that in some cases the space group of a crystal is clearly indicated by the morphology, and to an extension of this generalization, with Gabrielle Donnay, in 1961. The results were not readily accepted. The distinction drawn as early as 1933 between the Haüy-Bravais (or morphological) lattice and the x-ray (or structural) lattice was considered to be nonsense by some scientists. However, the idea that different properties have different symmetries was subsequently accepted.

Donnay began the compilation of *Crystal Data* in 1943. His idea was to determine crystalline species from their cell dimensions. In the first edition, published in 1954 as Memoir no. 60 of the Geological Society of America and containing determinative tables for about 6000 substances, the Delaunay cell was adopted. In the second edition, covering 13,000 substances, and published in 1963 as Monograph No. 5 of the American Crystallographic Association, the reduced cell was adopted. Donnay and his coworkers introduced it into the *International Tables for X-ray Crystallography* in the reprinting of vol. 1 (pages 530–535) in 1969. (Ten years earlier Donnay and Gabrielle Donnay had contributed a 50-page section on geometrical crystallography to vol. 2 of the *Tables*.) The third edition of *Crystal Data,* covering over 24,000 substances in two volumes, was published by the National Bureau of Standards in 1973. This book alone would be enough to make Donnay known among crystallographers throughout the world.

Twins and other crystalline intergrowths (epitactic, syntactic, and topotactic) repeatedly engaged Donnay's attention. In this realm he applied the ideas of C. Friedel to albite twinning and to many other cases. Later, with H. Curien, he was concerned with the symbolization of the symmetry of the complete twin, which involved the use of color point groups. Shubnikov groups were applied to the description of magnetic structures for which Donnay and Gabrielle Donnay tabulated all of the possibilities for one tetragonal point group.

The concept of lattice complex, due to P. Niggli, was elaborated by Carl Hermann. Donnay joined a group of Hermann's followers, headed by E. Hellner, to complete this work, which was published by the National Bureau of Standards in 1973 as Monograph no. 134 under the title *Space Groups and Lattice Complexes.*

When Donnay accepted the Roebling Medal of the Mineralogical Society of America (1971), he said: "I still think a scientist should investigate the questions that haunt him, not those that might be forced upon him by official guidelines. And so I say to you, young researchers: Take an interest in as many fields as you can, help as many people as you can, but select your own problems. Enjoy your work. Never get discouraged. Money is getting scarce? What of it? 'The passion for truth dulls acquisitiveness.' . . . Besides, austerity weeds out the operators! Your greatest reward will always be the bliss of solving your problem and seeing the pieces of the puzzle fall harmoniously into place. This reward no one can ever take from you."

In 1970 Donnay entered a new phase of his career, and Canadian mineralogy was enriched, when the family moved to Montreal to enable Gabrielle Donnay to become professor of crystallography at McGill University. To make this possible, he arranged to commute between Montreal and Baltimore for the first year so that he could complete his commitment to Johns Hopkins University as professor of mineralogy and crystallography. In later years he was a guest professor at the University of Montreal and a research associate at McGill University. He emphasized the importance of optical mineralogy and crystal morphology and their relationship to crystal structure, decrying the lack of interest presently shown in these important subjects. Strongly committed to the use of precise, elegant English and French, he also applied his talents in assisting the editors of the *Canadian Mineralogist.* Soon after arriving in Montreal, Donnay and his wife founded Krystallos, an interdisciplinary organization of crystallographers.

Donnay received his early schooling in Belgium and graduated as *Ingénieur civil des Mines* from the University of Liège in 1925. He received his Ph.D. from Stanford University in 1929. His career as a university professor was varied. He spent most of the years between 1931 and 1972 at the Johns Hopkins University. He also held appointments at Stanford, Laval, Liège, Harvard, Utah, the U.S. Naval Postgraduate School, the Sorbonne, Marburg, Montreal, and McGill. His list of research appointments was also extensive, and included the Hercules Powder Company, the Auburn Research Foundation, the Brookhaven National Laboratory, the Geophysical Laboratory in Washington, and the National Bureau of Standards. He received the medal of the University of Liège (1959), the Roebling Medal of the Mineralogical Society of America (1971), and the Queen's Silver Jubilee Medal (1977).

Among Donnay's works were 100 abstracts, 148 papers, 36 books or chapters in books, 38 reviews, and numerous computer programs, memorials, presentations, and translations.

For background information *see* CRYSTAL STRUCTURE; MINERALOGY in the McGraw-Hill Encyclopedia of Science and Technology. ∎

DONNELL, LLOYD HAMILTON
★ American mechanicist

***Born** May 20, 1895, Kents Hill, ME, U.S.A.*

In 1930 Theodore von Kármán was building up the Guggenheim Aeronautical Laboratory of the California Institute of Technology. Aerodynamics research was already well developed, and he was looking for someone to head aeronautical structures research. Donnell, then working under Stephen Timoshenko at the University of Michigan, had already published several papers in this area; his doctoral thesis on longitudinal wave transmission became a classic in its field, and included the first published solutions for elastic-plastic wave transmission. With Timoshenko's recommendation he went to the California Institute of Technology and started a career-long study of the basics of shell theory and buckling problems (however, this specialization left time for study of other fields of solid mechanics also). *See* VON KÁRMÁN, THEODORE.

Shell theory—the study of the stresses and displacements, under any loading or motion, of thin shells of any shape (such as airplane fuselage and wing coverings and rocket or satellite casings, including flat plates as a special case)—is one of the most complex subjects of mechanics. While at the institute, Donnell set up a structures laboratory for which he designed special machines for testing shells under various loadings, and made many tests with his associates. He also developed a number of theories, including the first wholly successful theory for the buckling of thin cylindrical shells under torsion. This required the development of a new, simplified theory of thin cylindrical shells. It was the first "shallow shell" theory (meaning applicable to shells, portions of which between nodes have deviations from flatness which are small compared to their widths) as well as the first "uncoupled" theory (meaning that relations are derived between the loads and the deflections alone, with supplementary relations connecting the other two displacements in the plane of the surface with the deflection). This simplified theory, applicable to any loading, was developed in 1933 and has been used throughout the world; it is now known as the Donnell equations.

In 1933 Donnell went to Goodyear Zeppelin Corporation, where he was in charge of structures, and in 1939 he moved to the Illinois Institute of Technology, where he remained until his retirement in 1960. His work in shell theory during these years included solutions for buckling of thin cylindrical shells under the other basic loading conditions, axial compression and external pressure (or internal vacuum). Axial compression had been a focus of controversy since 1911, when an adequate classical analysis, that is, one assuming small deflections and perfect initial shape, was published by R. Lorenz. Unfortunately, tests gave widely different results from those predicted by this theory, and in 1934 Donnell made the first attempt to explain this discrepancy by considering large deflection effects and initial defects. This attempt was unsatisfactory because of excessive simplifications required at the time to permit a solution, and the limitation of the study to failures initiated by yielding. However, the paper contained the development of a practical theory for thin cylinders which includes the effects of both large deflections and initial defects, and which has

been used by practically all subsequent investigators.

In 1941 Karman and H. S. Tsien studied this case by using Donnell's theory for large deflection effects without any simplification but ignoring initial defects; their analysis was further refined by D. M. A. Leggett and R. P. N. Jones and later by B. O. Almroth. This analysis showed a strikingly sharp drop-off of resistance after buckling, but the peak resistance was still the same as that found by Lorenz. Many attempts were made to explain the still-existing discrepancy with tests, until in 1950 Donnell and C. C. Wan showed that the explanation lay in the great sensitivity of this case to the initial defects which are present in even the most carefully made cylinders, a conclusion which later became generally accepted. In 1956 and 1958 Donnell applied these methods to the case of buckling under external pressure and showed that the much smaller discrepancy between tests and the classical analysis (made in 1914 by R. von Mises) could be similarly explained.

Donnell then devoted himself to expanding his earlier work on thin circular cylindrical shells in order to develop at least a basic theory for thin shells of any shape and loading. Such general theories have been developed by using tensor mathematics, but solutions in this form are not applicable to numerical problems. Donnell found, in 1962, that in spite of the complexity of the problem it is not difficult to develop exact (within the limitation to thin shells) relations between the displacements of a point on the middle surface of a general shell and the strains (and therefore the stresses) at any point in the shell wall by using ordinary number mathematics. These relations are not direct, as they involve intermediate quantities which cannot be eliminated in the general case, but it was shown that it is not impractical to use such indirect relations in numerical problems. In 1965 Donnell showed that these relations can be greatly simplified without introducing significant error. In his book *Beams, Plates and Shells* (1976) he extended these general relations between displacements and strains to equilibrium conditions and thus developed a complete theory of general shells, essentially exact for thin shells, and showed how this general theory can be greatly simplified when applied to particular types of shells.

Donnell received his B.S. in mechanical

engineering (1915) and his Ph.D. in mechanics (1930) from the University of Michigan. After several early positions in engineering he joined the staff of the University of Michigan, first as instructor and later as assistant professor of mechanics. From 1930 to 1933 he was a research fellow in charge of the aerostructures laboratory at the California Institute of Technology. He was in charge of stress analysis and structural research at Goodyear Zeppelin Corporation in 1933–39. Donnell then moved to the Illinois Institute of Technology, where he served as associate professor and professor of mechanical engineering (1939–62) and as acting chairperson of the mechanics department (1952–53). He became professor emeritus in 1962. He was in charge of structures development at Chance Vought Aircraft from 1942 to 1944, and was senior research scientist at the Institute of Science and Technology of the University of Michigan in 1960–61. Donnell was the recipient of the Worcester Reed Warner Medal of the American Society of Mechanical Engineers (1960), the Sesquicentennial Award of the University of Michigan (1967), the Von Kármán Medal of the American Society of Civil Engineers (1968), and the ASME Medal of the American Society of Mechanical Engineers (1969).

For background information *see* MECHANICS in the McGraw-Hill Encyclopedia of Science and Technology. ■

DOOB, JOSEPH LEO
★ American mathematician

Born Feb. 27, 1910, Cincinnati, OH, U.S.A.

In mathematical probability theory—that is, in the mathematical model of probability—what corresponds to a real event is a set of points in some space. (For example, in the rather trivial model for tossing a coin once, the mathematical model has two points, say H and T, one identified with heads and the other with tails. The set containing the single point H corresponds to the event that the tossed coin comes up heads.) Events have probabilities. In the model this means that certain subsets of the space are assigned numbers. The function of sets so defined is a measure, and the well-developed theory of measure is now available. Probability concepts in the model are defined as suggested by the background of the real context and the mathematical context. Thus a random variable, empirically a number produced by some probabilistic phenomenon, is defined mathematically as a function on the probability space, and its expected value is defined mathematically as the integral of that function with respect to the given probability measure.

This subsuming of the basic concepts of probability theory to those of measure theory had been set up formally by A. N. Kolmogorov in 1933. In accordance with this approach, a stochastic process—that is, a process proceeding in accordance with probabilistic laws—has as its counterpart in the mathematical model a family $\{x(t,.), t \epsilon T\}$ of random variables. Here for each t in the index set T (usually identified with a set of numbers, as suggested by the idea that t represents time) $x(t,.)$ is a random variable, with value $x(t, \omega)$ at the point ω of the probability space. A complete experiment gives a value to each random variable of the process. Mathematically this means that ω is chosen and t is allowed to vary to obtain the function $x(., \omega)$ defined on T. This function is called a sample function of the stochastic process (or sometimes a sample sequence if T is countably infinite or finite). In most applications the joint distributions of finite sets of the random variables are given—that is, if $t_1, \ldots, t_n$ are in T, the joint distribution of $x(t_1,.), \ldots, x(t_n,.)$ is given. Natural problems are to

find the distributions of other functions and to analyze the properties of the sample functions. Effective work on such problems had been proceeding since the 17th century, and it was not clear in the 1930s that the measure-theoretic approach would radically transform the subject. Some mathematicians thought that measure theory would only furnish the necessary but disagreeable rigor and that interesting results would not be inspired by the technical background.

In a series of papers beginning in 1935 Doob investigated various parts of probability theory, ranging from the continuity properties of sample functions to the mathematical version of the concept of a fair game. In each case the point was both to obtain mathematical results and to demonstrate the intrinsically necessary role of measure theory. Of course, much other probability research tended in the same direction, but the tendency was somewhat more obvious in Doob's work, at least in the 1930s. Mathematical probability is both duller and more productive as a result of his efforts.

Two examples will give some idea of both aspects of his work. Let the set T above be the real line, and consider the following problem: What are the probabilities that the sample functions of a given stochastic process are everywhere positive, everywhere continuous? Such questions, involving the character of the sample functions at a continuum of points are inevitable, but are also unanswerable in terms of the given distributions of the random variables, as described above. In fact, the desired probabilities are not determined by these given distributions by using the usual measure-theoretic rules of calculation. It was necessary to modify the allowable procedures to obtain a new context in which such probabilities could be calculated. As a second example, consider the notion of a fair game. One definition of "fair" that seems not unreasonable is that a game is fair to a gambler if his expected fortune after a play is what he had before. This definition can be put into abstract mathematical form to define a certain type of stochastic process (a martingale). Doob developed many of the basic concepts of martingale theory, which has wide applications in pure mathematics (derivation, ergodic theory, potential theory, Markov process theory) and in applied mathematics (information theory, statistics).

Doob majored in mathematics at Har-

vard University, where he received his B.A. (1930), M.A. (1931), and Ph.D. (1932). He taught at the University of Illinois from 1935. In 1957 he was elected to the National Academy of Sciences, in 1965 to the American Academy of Arts and Sciences, and in 1975 to the French Académie des Sciences.

Doob wrote *Stochastic Processes* (1953).

For background information *see* PROBABILITY; STOCHASTIC PROCESS in the McGraw-Hill Encyclopedia of Science and Technology. ∎

DOUGLAS, DONALD WILLS
☆ American aeronautical engineer

***Born** Apr. 6, 1892, Brooklyn, NY, U.S.A.*

In 1920, when he was not yet 30 and had assets totaling only $600, Douglas started his own airplane manufacturing venture. The small company eventually became one of the giants of the aircraft industry, designing and building transports that played key roles in world air transportation.

Douglas's first contract was to build a plane for a Los Angeles sportsman who wished to fly across the continent nonstop. The plane that Douglas designed and built was a two-place wood and fabric biplane called the *Cloudster*. Although engine trouble forced abandonment of the transcontinental flight in Texas, the *Cloudster* was a milestone in aircraft design: it was the first airplane ever to airlift a useful load equal to its own weight. Later, the same basic design was utilized to build the U.S. Navy's first torpedo bomber.

World recognition of Douglas's design integrity came with the first flight around the world. U.S. Army pilots, flying Douglas World Cruisers, began their historic journey in March 1924. They returned 6 months later to Clover Field, Santa Monica, CA, where the flight had begun. They had covered 27,553 miles (44,360 kilometers) in 15 days, 11 hours, 7 minutes actual flying time.

Notable in early Douglas history was the development of the DC-3–type transport in 1935. That twin-engine airliner revolutionized passenger air travel by establishing new standards of safety, speed, comfort, and dependability. It is generally credited with having made commercial aviation economically feasible. The basic DC-3 design was adapted for military use during World War II; the adaptation, the C-47 military transport, was used in every theater of war and by all Allied Powers. Nearly 11,000 DC-3–type transports were built.

Another noteworthy Douglas development was the B-19 experimental bomber, until 1948 the largest land-based aircraft built. Conceived as a flying laboratory to prove design details of huge aircraft, the B-19 was first flown on June 27, 1941. Its wingspan was 212 feet (64.7 meters) and its fuselage length was 132 feet (40.3 meters). The B-19 is credited by the U.S. Air Force with paving the way for design and construction of the wartime B-29 and its successor, the B-50 bomber. Until late in 1946 it was used to test new engines, propellers, hydraulic and electrical equipment, and other new devices for large aircraft.

Next in order of development was the DC-4 transport. This four-engined airliner, designed originally for commercial use, was in 1942, before the first aircraft was completed, transformed on the production line into the C-54 military transport. The C-54 proved the practicability of transoceanic service by land-based aircraft by establishing a record of 40,000 Pacific and 30,500 Atlantic crossings in military service.

In 1946 the DC-6 evolved from the DC-4 and established new standards of comfort, speed, and dependability in air travel. In 1951 later versions of the same basic transport were introduced under the designations DC-6A for cargo and DC-6B for deluxe passenger service.

Douglas Aircraft then produced the DC-7, which established itself as the world's fastest piston-powered commercial transport. Retaining the general external configuration of the DC-6 series, the DC-7 had a longer fuselage with increased cabin capacity. It was ultimately expanded through several larger and more powerful versions, ending with the DC-7C.

In 1955 Douglas decided to proceed with manufacture of the DC-8 jet transport. The first flight of the airplane took place May 30, 1958, and it first went into airline service on Sept. 18, 1959.

The short-to-medium-range DC-9 was the next plane in the Douglas line of commercial aircraft. It was first flown in 1965 and entered airline service the same year.

Post-World War II military aircraft engineered and produced by Douglas Aircraft include the Navy AD-Skyraider series, the twin-jet F3D Skyknight, the A3D Skywarrior twin-jet attack plane, the A4D Skyhawk, the F4D Skyray, the F5D Skylancer, the RB-66 Destroyer Air Force bombers, the C-124 Globemaster II, military versions of the DC-6A Liftmaster, and the C-133A and C-133B cargo transports.

Under Douglas's direction his company engaged in development and production of guided missiles for the Army, Navy, and Air Force beginning in 1940. Among these were several models of the Nike ground-to-air missile; the Honest John ground-to-ground missile; and the Sparrow air-to-air series.

Douglas Aircraft was also a leader in the field of space penetration, providing the basic boost that thrust many scientific satellites into orbit. The reliable Douglas Thor, in a variety of modifications, was the first stage in launch vehicles for such satellites as *Explorer 1, Pioneer 5,* the Discoverer series, *Explorer 6,* Transit, Echo, *Courier 1B,* high-altitude nuclear devices, the orbiting solar observatory, Telstar, and the world's first international satellite, the S-51.

Douglas Aircraft also provided leadership in the programs for exploration of lunar areas and outer space. It was assigned development of the S-IV and S-IVB upper stages of the Saturn rocket, the booster vehicle in the Apollo programs. In 1965 Douglas was awarded the contract for manufacture of the first manned orbiting laboratory (MOL) by the U.S. Air Force.

The son of a bank official, Douglas at-

tended the U.S. Naval Academy at Annapolis (1909–12) and the Massachusetts Institute of Technology, where he received a B.S. in aeronautical engineering in 1914. He became consultant to the Connecticut Aircraft Company in 1915 and chief engineer for the Glenn L. Martin Company the same year. After serving a year during World War I as chief civilian aeronautical engineer for the U.S. Signal Corps, he returned to the Martin Company as chief engineer and designed the first Martin bomber. In 1920 he founded the Douglas Company, which became the Douglas Aircraft Company in 1928. He served as president of this company until 1957, when he became chairperson of the board and chief executive officer. In 1967 Douglas Aircraft Company merged with McDonnell Aircraft Corporation to form McDonnell Douglas Corporation, and Douglas became honorary chairperson of its board of directors.

For background information *see* AERO-NAUTICAL ENGINEERING in the McGraw-Hill Encyclopedia of Science and Technology. ∎

DOUGLAS, ROBERT JOHN WILSON
★ Canadian geologist

Born Aug. 3, 1920, Southampton, Ontario, Canada

The structures of the Rocky Mountains and Foothills of southern Alberta were thought for many years to be analogous to those of well-known mountain belts, such as the Swiss Alps, in which nappes developed from recumbent folds, or the Scottish Highlands, which originated as imbrications cut by low-angle sole faults. Douglas contended that the mechanics of low-angle overthrusting as set forth by John L. Rich in 1934 were fundamental to the interpretation of Foothills structures. In the decade after 1945, when his investigations started, Douglas further developed the theory and its economic implications in exploration for oil and gas in the Foothills. According to Rich, a low-angle thrust may originate in stratified rocks without prior folding as a fracture that follows, for considerable distance, close to the bedding in zones of easy gliding, such as shale, and cuts across intervening brittle strata at an angle. As a result of displacement, folds are produced in the overthrust mass, and the initial anticlinal and synclinal warps in the thrust plane may be accentuated. The shales serve to reduce frictional resistance and the force required to produce displacement.

In the southern Rocky Mountains and Foothills several scattered initial breaks were postulated by Douglas, the more westerly fractures originating first, low within the Palaeozoic and Proterozoic successions. These fractures were subsequently extended, preferentially following the bedding, upward through the Mesozoic and Tertiary strata to the surface and laterally in both directions along the strike. As the initial breaks grew, new ones formed, and eventually the extensions of the various thrusts interlocked and merged, or subsidiary connecting faults formed between them. Tear faults arose along the locus of the initial transverse cutoff of the strata by the thrust. Great lateral displacements were accomplished by the riding out of little deformed sheets of rock, the lower zones of gliding being brought into juxtaposition with higher zones. Concomitantly with displacement, the initial folds were induced, and subsequently drag folds developed with décollement at the thrust plane. Splays from the initial thrust plane, sigmoidal in cross section, asymptotically merged both downward with the thrust and upward with earlier-formed thrusts so that a succession of thin fault slices or imbrications was produced. These are considered to have been formed in succession from east to west within the overthrust mass, the easternmost slices being detached and overridden by the main overthrust mass along the newly formed splay.

Where associated with folds, most

faults occur on the less steeply dipping or back limb of the anticline, dipping subparallel to the strata, and may have undergone steepening through collapse of the core of the fold, the concave character of fault plane imparting rotation to the strata even to the extent of overturning. Displacement on a new fault in footwall strata of a fault can bring about, as a result of the formation of an induced anticline, a superimposed anticline in both the hanging wall strata and the fault plane itself, the formation of another fault on the back limb of this anticline, and the cessation of displacement on the folded portion of the first-formed fault. The sequence of faulting and of the folding of strata and fault planes is considered by Douglas to be the result of a continuous, self-perpetuating process, but not all geologists agree; some think superimposed folds and folded faults are the result of two stages of deformation: formation of several fault slices and subsequent folding of them as a group.

Douglas's studies of the stratigraphy of the Mississippian established the present standard of succession and nomenclature, as well as the correlation between the outcrop and the subsurface extension of the system in southern Alberta. His studies on the petrography and classification of the carbonate rocks and their insoluble residues were some of the first undertaken, and formed the basis for conclusions regarding their mode of origin, environment of deposition, temporal equivalence of facies, and formation of cyclical alternations. He envisaged shallow, warm, clear seas with widespread shoals where the bulk of the rock-forming organisms, echinoderms, flourished and their calcareous remains accumulated to be subjected to the sorting processes of waves and currents. The shoals were interspersed with shallow-water banks where oolites formed and aragonite mud precipitated from waters saturated in calcium carbonate. Near shore, sandbars and beaches were formed of quartz, dolomite, and calcite drived from the erosion of older carbonate rocks and, together with the banks, produced conditions where influx of normal sea water was restricted and precipitation of gypsum and anhydrite took place. He also concluded that dolomitization was a secondary process but nearly contemporaneous with the deposition of the altered limestones, and was effected on a volume-for-volume basis so that the porosity present in the dolomites, which form some of the principal

reservoirs for oil and gas, was inherited from the original limestone.

In 1963 Douglas, with three collaborators, prepared a synthesis of the geology of northern Canada pertinent to the assessment of the petroleum potential of the northernmost sedimentary basins. The study included restorations of the three-dimensional form of gross rock facies and their tectonic environment. Douglas's contribution was based on data obtained in 1957 in the course of a helicopter-assisted study of the Interior Platform and Mackenzie Fold Belt in the Northwest Territories by specialists in stratigraphy, paleontology, and structural and Pleistocene geology from the Geological Survey of Canada. The investigation, for which he was officer in charge and in which he engaged in mapping, established the geological framework in 100,000 square miles (2.59×10^5 square kilometers) of a frontier region of hitherto unknown geology. The structural style of the Mackenzie Fold Belt is distinctively different from other broadly arcuate mountain systems of the world, and is attributed by Douglas to the occurrence of several sets of fractures or faults in the thick Proterozoic strata and crystalline basement underlying the relatively thin veneer of Paleozoic and Mesozoic strata that during deformation were activated as reverse, tear and thrust faults wherever preferentially oriented.

In the compilation of the 1969 edition of the Geological Map of Canada, Douglas used four basic geological parameters—age, facies, structure, and metamorphism—to establish and depict the significant features of the various geological provinces and subprovinces of Canada, aspects that cannot be conveyed by designating only the age of the stratified rocks and the lithology of the intrusive igneous rocks, as is customarily shown on conventional geological compilations. This established a clearer understanding of the character, form, and extent of the various geological subprovinces or crustal blocks that compose the three Phanerozoic mountain systems in Canada—the Appalachian, Cordilleran, and Inuitian orogens—and has assisted in the interpretation of the less well understood constituent geological elements of the more deeply eroded Precambrian orogenic belts of the Canadian Shield. He concluded that large parts of the Shield were the basement or sialic crust upon which younger assemblages of supracrustal rocks accumulated, now preserved only as remnants or in adjacent subprovinces. Douglas also contended that rocks are given a geological age according to two different standards—either a depositional age or an orogenic age—which led him to question the significance of isotopic age determinations, especially with respect to dating the time of intrusion of igneous rocks in polymetamorphic terranes.

Douglas was scientific editor of the fifth edition of *Geology and Economic Minerals of Canada*, a representation of selected factual data and interpretations of the geology, tectonics, and metallogeny of the 17 geological provinces of Canada. The folio accompanying the book contains maps showing the geology, tectonics, glacial features, physiography, mineral deposits, magnetic anomalies and gravity; and four geotectonic correlation charts which are an innovation that reduces to visual form the sequence of rocks and tectonic events that ultimately produced the geology of each local sector as it is known today. Douglas treated individual geological provinces, and especially their subprovinces or constituent crustal blocks, as being identified by certain unifying attributes that arise from the geological environments in which the rocks originally accumulated, and from the tectonic events that subsequently affected them. In considering the geology of the underwater regions, Douglas recognized that, unique among the nations of the world, Canada embraces within the extremities of its land areas large regions of enclosed marine waters beneath which the geology is akin to that on shore. Although considered offshore, these regions are different from the geologically new deposits of the continental shelves which rim the continental mass at its junction with oceanic crust, and which alone are comparable to the continental shelves of other maritime nations. This distinction is reflected in the exercise of Canada's sovereign rights for the exploitation of the natural resources of the continental shelves.

In the *National Atlas of Canada*, Douglas presented three maps—Geology, Geological Provinces, and Tectonics, the last reflecting his concept of lithotectonic assemblages. All rocks are the product of their geotectonic environment, and by studying the character of younger assemblages and their tectonic environment it may be possible to deduce what the tectonic environments may have been for

other, incomplete and less well known assemblages, especially those of Precambrian age. In comparing Phanerozoic, Proterozoic, and Archean tectonic styles, Douglas and his coauthor, R. A. Price, concluded that continental cratons occured in all geological eras, including the late Archean, decreasing in size and increasing in mobility with age. The mobile belts exhibit increased mobility and greater interaction between lithosphere plates with age, as reflected in the thickness of supracrustal rocks preserved, the relative amount of the magmatic components, and the breadth of sialic crust involved. The degree of cratonization increases with the older orogenic belts, and also the extent of engulfment of cratonic regions in the thermal, metamorphic, and plutonic regimes associated with the orogenies.

Douglas received his early education at Hawkesbury, Ontario, where his father was principal of the high school. He attended Queen's University, graduating in 1942 with a B.Sc. and the Manley B. Baker Scholarship. From 1943 to 1945 he served in the Royal Canadian Air Force. He received his Ph.D. from Columbia University in 1950. Douglas joined the staff of the Geological Survey of Canada in 1947, becoming head of the Geology of Fuels Section in 1957, chief of the Regional Geology Division in 1964, and principal research scientist in 1966. He was elected a fellow of the Royal Society of Canada in 1959 and was awarded the Willet G. Miller Medal by the society in 1965. In 1976 he received the Logan Medal from the Geological Association of Canada.

For background information *see* FAULT AND FAULT STRUCTURES; FOLD AND FOLD SYSTEMS; PETROLEUM GEOLOGY; SEDIMENTATION (GEOLOGY); STRATIGRAPHY; TECTONIC PATTERNS in the McGraw-Hill Encyclopedia of Science and Technology. ∎

DRAGSTEDT, LESTER REYNOLD
★ American surgeon and physiologist

Born Oct. 2, 1893, Anaconda, MT, U.S.A.
Died July 16, 1975, Rapid City, MI, U.S.A.

When Dragstedt began his work in 1916 as an assistant in the department of physiology at the University of Chicago

under A. J. Carlson, he attempted to demonstrate the significance of acid gastric juice in producing ulcers in the stomach duodenum. This problem continued to engage his attention throughout his career.

Dragstedt became an instructor in pharmacology at the State University of Iowa in 1917 and subsequently assistant professor of physiology. During this period, with his brother Carl, he found that dogs could survive the complete removal of the duodenum, thus indicating that the organ does not produce an internal secretion necessary for life as was previously believed. Allen Whipple cited this work as the stimulus for the development of his operation for the radical surgical treatment of carcinoma of the pancreas.

After a year of military service in World War I, Dragstedt returned to the University of Chicago to complete his work for a Ph.D. in physiology (1920) and then went to Rush Medical College for an M.D. (1921). In 1921 he became assistant professor of physiology at the University of Chicago and in 1923 professor of physiology and chairman of the department of physiology and pharmacology at Northwestern University Medical School. During this period he found that dogs from which the thyroid and parathyroid glands had been completely removed could be kept alive indefinitely and free from parathyroid tetany if placed on a diet of bread, milk, and lactose. Prior to this work it was commonly believed that removal of the parathyroid glands was inevitably fatal. De Noel Paton was chiefly re-

sponsible for the view that parathyroid tetany was due to intoxication with guanidine, a waste product of protein metabolism, and that it was the function of the parathyroid glands to detoxify or eliminate this substance. Dragstedt harmonized his findings with this view by suggesting that the toxic agents responsible for parathyroid tetany are produced in the intestinal tract by bacterial proteolysis and that his diet prevents their production by changing the intestinal flora and substituting bacterial fermentation for putrefaction. When Hanson and Collip later isolated the hormone of the parathyroids and demonstrated its relation to calcium metabolism, Dragstedt was chagrined at his attempt to explain his own experiments on the basis of Paton's ideas.

In 1925 D. B. Phemister was appointed chairman of the department of surgery at the University of Chicago. He persuaded Dragstedt to give up his post at Northwestern, secure additional clinical training in Vienna and Budapest, and join him in developing a university department, inspired by the threefold ideal of research, teaching, and surgical practice. It was at the University of Chicago that Dragstedt developed the concept that peptic ulcers are caused by an increase in the corrosive properties of the gastric content rather than a decrease in the resistance of a local area of the mucosa to the digestant action of gastric juice. He found by experiments on dogs that pure gastric juice such as may be secured from Pavlov pouches is an exceedingly corrosive fluid and can digest away the normal mucosa of the stomach or intestines and produce chronic, progressive peptic ulcers. In sharp contrast, the normal gastric content, which is a mixture of gastric juice and food, is relatively innocuous. Organs such as the kidney and spleen were not digested if implanted into defects produced in the stomach wall and exposed to gastric digestion for prolonged periods. He theorized that normally the stomach does not digest itself because food, which is the usual stimulus for gastric secretion, buffers and reduces its corrosive properties. Should gastric secretion be stimulated by agencies other than food, however, or if a hypersecretion of gastric juice should occur, the gastric content might well approach the acid and pepsin concentration of pure gastric juice and so produce and maintain a chronic, progressive peptic ulcer.

Henning and Norpoth discovered that duodenal ulcer patients usually secrete abnormally large amounts of gastric juice in the fasting empty stomach at night. When Varco, Code, and Wangensteen found that a similar secretion of gastric juice induced in animals by histamine would regularly produce duodenal ulcers, it seemed probable that this was also the cause of these ulcers in humans. The clinical impression that duodenal ulcers tend to occur in people subjected to long-continued anxiety, tension, and mental strain prompted Dragstedt to the view that the fasting hypersecretion in these patients might be of nervous origin and led to his introduction of vagotomy in the surgical treatment of duodenal ulcers in 1942. In succeeding years gastric vagotomy combined with gastroenterostomy or pyloroplasty was widely adopted and largely replaced the more hazardous operation of gastric resection in the treatment of this disease.

Although Dragstedt and his associates also treated gastric ulcers successfully by vagotomy and gastroenterostomy in 1943, this procedure suffered from the objection that failure to resect the stomach would be unfortunate should the diagnosis prove incorrect and the lesion prove to be a cancer. In the intervening years the sharp decline in the incidence of gastric cancer and the increasing reliability of diagnosis by biopsy of the lesion at the time of surgery have brought about a return to favor of vagotomy and gastroenterostomy in the treatment of gastric ulcers. Many surgeons believe that this operation leads to earlier recognition of gastric cancers masquerading as benign ulcers. Meanwhile, Dragstedt and E. R. Woodward continued their experimental studies on the physiology of the gastric antrum and secured conclusive evidence supporting Edkin's hypothesis that the stimulation of gastric secretion by food in the stomach is brought about by a hormone, gastrin, released into the bloodstream from the mucosa of the pyloric antrum. These experiments also led to the view that gastric ulcers are usually caused by a hypersecretion of gastric juice of hormonal or gastrin origin due to stasis of food in the stomach from pyloric stenosis or gastric atony.

When Phemister retired as chairperson of the department of surgery at the University of Chicago in 1949, Dragstedt became chairperson and Thomas D. Janes Distinguished Service Professor of Surgery. He left in 1959 to become research professor of surgery at the University of Florida, where Woodward, his former student and colleague, was professor of surgery and department head. There the two men continued their collaboration in surgical and physiological research and teaching. Dragstedt received the Distinguished Service Medal of the American Medical Association (1963), the Bigelow Gold Medal of the Boston Surgical Society (1964), the Samuel D. Gross Prize of the Philadelphia Academy of Surgery (1964), the Julius Friedenwald Medal of the American Gastroenterological Society (1964), the Silver (1945) and Gold (1953) medals of the American Medical Association for original investigation, and the Swedish Royal Order of the North Star (1967). An honorary fellow of the Royal College of Surgeons of England, the Royal College of Physicians and Surgeons of Canada, and the Swedish Surgical Society, he was elected to the National Academy of Sciences in 1950.

For background information *see* DIGESTIVE SYSTEM (VERTEBRATE); PARATHYROID GLAND (VERTEBRATE); PEPTIC ULCER in the McGraw-Hill Encyclopedia of Science and Technology. ∎

DRAPER, CHARLES STARK
☆ American aeronautical engineer

Born Oct. 2, 1901, Windsor, MO, U.S.A.

Attacking a succession of challenging research and engineering projects, Draper and his associates at the Massachusetts Institute of Technology (MIT) Instrumentation Laboratory provided the United

States with new and advanced weapon technologies. Draper's early studies in aircraft instrumentation led to inquiries into navigational and guidance systems, from which emerged a variety of instruments for sensing, measuring, and controlling physical properties, featuring significant advances in the design and use of gyroscopes. Application of these results helped yield advanced fire-control and gun-director systems during World War II. Subsequently, the MIT group under Draper addressed the problem of inertial navigation and guidance for ships, submarines, aircraft, and missiles. The highly reliable Polaris inertial guidance system, of vast importance to the security posture of the United States, grew from the energies of the MIT Instrumentation Laboratory. Eventually, Draper's group designed the navigational systems for the Apollo crewed expedition to the Moon.

Perhaps no weapon more purely bears the Draper hallmark than the Mark 14 gunsight which, along with the Mark 15 sight, also engineered under Draper, was used to direct the antiaircraft batteries of virtually every U.S. Navy vessel of World War II. The Navy's problem in 1941 was to protect surface vessels from the threat of close-in hostile air attack. One difficulty was smoothing out erratic tracking data to permit computer operation based on human sighting. As late as 1938 it had been held that it was impossible to stabilize effectively such rates for computer prediction. Draper met the problem with "damping"–using rotors immersed in a viscous fluid. His earlier development of rate-measuring gyros of high precision permitted use of these as automatic computers whose output offset the observer's line of sighting an amount corresponding to the correct angle of gun lead. Corrections for range, wind, and ballistics entered the system semiautomatically. The system pointed the way for a host of similar wartime sighting and tracking instruments. Draper defied prevailing methods, vastly simplifying the sight, by using deck coordinates as reference axes, rejecting the need for gyro-stabilized references. The resulting cross-roll errors proved unimportant.

Vastly more sophisticated was Draper's later work in inertial navigation and guidance systems. Inertial instrument systems are fully self-contained and require no external information such as that from radio signals or celestial bodies. In designing the inertial reference stabilizing system, Draper applied the MIT-developed single-degree-of-freedom gyro of the 1940s, floated in a viscous fluid and equipped with microsyn sensors to measure angular displacements. Accelerometers to measure forces resulting from motions in inertial space became improved with the pendulous gyro accelerometer, where acceleration forces are made to induce measurable precession of a gyro mounted on the stabilized reference. Cumulative displacement of the gyro represents accumulated acceleration, or velocity. This value can then be further integrated by electrical circuits to yield distance, or position. By 1954 the MIT Instrumentation Laboratory had completed the first ship's inertial navigation system (SINS). Thus by the mid-1950s the elements of a ballistic missile inertial guidance system existed. Indeed, the short time of flight of missiles permitted easement in the stringent rate of drift requirements of the earlier ship's navigation system. The 1956 contract of the Draper group with the Navy Special Projects Office for development of the Polaris inertial guidance system was quickly fulfilled, a product of the line of development begun 3 decades earlier in Draper's investigations of simple flight gyros.

Draper studied at the University of Missouri and at Stanford University, receiving the B.A. degree in psychology from the latter in 1922. His decision to enroll in electrochemistry at MIT later that year constituted the turning point in his life, leading to a continuing and distinguished association with that institution. A series of fellowships and research appointments furthered his early studies and investigations at MIT. He earned the B.S. degree in electrochemical engineering in 1926, the M.S. in 1928, and the Sc.D. in physics in 1938. He attained the faculty rank of assistant professor in aeronautical engineering in 1935, rising to the rank of full professor in 1939, and served as chairperson of the aeronautical engineering department from 1951 to 1966. He was director of the MIT Instrumentation Laboratory from 1940 to 1969. He was president of the laboratory, now renamed the Charles Stark Draper Laboratory, in 1971–73, and senior scientist there after 1973. Draper's contributions to the United States' defense posture and to the space program were acknowledged by many awards from the Navy and Air Force and NASA; his yet more numerous awards from professional societies included the Holley Medal of the American Society of Mechanical Engineers (1957), the Sylvanus Albert Reed Award (1945) and the Louis W. Hill Space Transportation Award (1962) of the Institute of the Aeronautical Sciences, the William Proctor Prize of the Scientific Research Society of America (1959), the Daniel Guggenheim Medal of the United Engineering Trusts (1967), and the Rufus Oldenburger Medal of the American Society of Mechanical Engineers (1971). In 1964 Draper was awarded the National Medal of Science, and in 1970 the Founders Medal of the National Academy of Engineering. He was elected to the National Academy of Sciences (1957), and the National Academy of Engineering (1965).

Draper wrote *Inertial Guidance*, with Walter Wrigley and John Hovorka (1960), and *Instrument Engineering*, with Walter McKay and Sidney Lees (3 vols., 1952, 1953, 1955).

For background information *see* GUIDED MISSILE; GYROSCOPE; INERTIAL GUIDANCE SYSTEM in the McGraw-Hill Encyclopedia of Science and Technology. ∎

DRICKAMER, HARRY GEORGE
★ American chemist

Born Nov. 19, 1918, Cleveland, OH, U.S.A.

Drickamer's principal area of research was concerned with the use of high pressure to investigate the electronic structure of solids. In his laboratory, techniques were developed to measure optical absorption and luminescence, electrical resistance, Mössbauer resonance, and x-ray diffraction, to pressures of several hundred thousand atmospheres (1 atmosphere = 10^5 pascals).

For the study of electronic phenomena in solids the basic effect of pressure is to reduce interatomic or intermolecular distance and thus to increase overlap of electronic orbitals. Since different types of orbitals have different radial extents or orbital shapes (diffuseness), they will be perturbed in varying degrees by this change of overlap. The information obtained from a study of these perturbations can conveniently be considered in three ways: one can characterize electronic states, electronic excitations, or molecular conformations; one can perform critical tests of theories; and under some circumstances, one can observe an electronic transition to a new ground state which has different physical or chemical properties.

Examples of characterization include the following: (1) The effect of pressure on the optical absorption measuring the gap between the valence band and conduction band in silicon, germanium, and such III-IV and II-VI compounds as GaAs, GaSb, and ZnS gives detailed information on the band structure. (2) Changes in absorption and emission peak location and shape with pressure for localized excitations in organic and inorganic materials provide a characterization of the ground and excited electronic states. (3) Mössbauer resonance studies of changes in isomer shift, quadrupole splitting, and magnetic field in iron compounds are very useful in establishing the effect of pressure on the type of chemical bonding and magnetic properties. (4) The effects of pressure on luminescent efficiency, peak location, and polarization for a series of proteins can demonstrate the stepwise character of pressure-induced denaturation.

Some of the earliest and most basic tests of ligand field theory as applied to transition-metal complexes were obtained from high-pressure optical studies. The measured changes in ligand field strength and interelectronic repulsion (Racah) parameters clearly illustrate the possibilities and limitations of the theory.

The radiationless (resonant) transfer of excitation energy from one luminescent center to another is basic to applications ranging from fluorescent lighting to photosynthesis. The process depends critically on the overlap of sensitizer (donor) emission and activator (acceptor) absorption peaks. These peaks can be shifted in a controlled and clearly established way with pressure, which thus provides a very clearcut test of the theory.

The efficiency of fluorescence of a phosphor depends on the relative probability of radiative emission versus nonradiative return to the ground state via internal conversion. These probabilities depend on the shapes of the potential energy wells, their relative displacement along the configuration coordinate of interest, and their displacement in energy. Since these parameters can be varied in a controlled and measurable way with pressure, one can directly test theories of fluorescent efficiency.

Resistance anomalies associated with electronic transitions were observed in alkali, alkaline-earth, and rare-earth metals. Cesium, rubidium, and possibly potassium become transition metals at high pressure. Calcium, strontium, and ytterbium exhibit metal-to-semiconductor transitions at high pressure.

Insulator-metal transitions with a variety of characteristics were observed. Transitions with no discontinuities in structure or resistance occur in iodine, in several crystals involving large organic molecules such as pentacene, and in the thallous halides. Transitions involving discontinuities in resistance and changes in structure occur in silicon, germanium, and many III-V and II-VI compounds.

An extensive series of studies involving both Mössbauer resonance and optical absorption revealed a rich variety of electronic transitions in iron compounds. These include both (reversible) high spin–to–low spin and low spin–to–high spin transitions, which depend on the nature of the ligand and its binding to the iron. The reversible reduction of Fe(III) to Fe(II) was observed in a wide variety of compounds. Intensive collaboration with C. P. Slichter resulted in considerable progress in explaining these and related electronic transitions.

A large decrease in excitation energy with pressure was observed in many aromatic organic molecules. In some cases this is sufficient to permit thermal occupation of the excited state at high pressure and consequent chemical reactivity of a new sort. Similarly, the decrease in donor-acceptor excitation energy with pressure in a large variety of charge-transfer complexes results in thermal occupation of the excited state and a series of new reactions. A study of the behavior of iodine-pyrene and iodine-perylene complexes demonstrated the existence of hydrocarbon dimers and tetramers with structures entirely unlike any previously reported.

In photochromic compounds an optically excited electron decays to a new metastable ground state which involves a change of chemical conformation. High-pressure studies on bianthrones, spiropyrans, and anils demonstrated that pressure can change the relative energies of the stable and metastable states sufficiently to permit thermal occupation of the metastable state, that is, piezochromism replaces photochromism at high pressure.

Drickamer received his B.S., M.S., and Ph.D. at the University of Michigan in 1941, 1942, and 1946, respectively. During 1942–45 he worked as a research engineer at Pan American Refinery Corporation in Texas City. He moved to the University of Illinois in 1946, becoming professor of physical chemistry and chemical engineering in 1953 and a member of the Center for Advanced Study in 1963. His awards include the Colburn Award (1947), the Alpha Chi Sigma Award (1967), and the Walker Award (1972) of the American Institute of Chemical Engineers; the Ipatieff Prize (1956) and the Langmuir Chemical Physics Prize (1974) of the American Chemical Society; the Buckley Solid State Physics Award (1967) of the American Physical Society; the Bendix Research Prize (1968) of the American Society for Engineering Education; the first P. W. Bridgman Award (1977) of the International Association for High Pressure Research and Technology; and the Michelson-Morley Award (1978) of Case-Western Reserve University. He was elected a member of the National Academy of Sciences in 1965, a fellow of the American Academy of Arts and Sciences in 1970, and a member of the National Academy of Engineering in 1979.

For background information *see* BAND THEORY OF SOLIDS; HIGH-PRESSURE

PHENOMENA; HIGH-PRESSURE PROCESSES; LUMINESCENCE in the McGraw-Hill Encyclopedia of Science and Technology. ∎

DRUCKER, DANIEL CHARLES
★ American engineer and researcher in applied mechanics

Born June 3, 1918, New York, NY, U.S.A.

In the late 1930s photoelasticity in three dimensions emerged as the only available technique for the determination of stress in the interior of complex bodies under load. However, experimental techniques and an underlying theoretical base for observing and interpreting the optical fringe patterns were in their infancy. Under the tutelage of R. D. Mindlin, Drucker studied the effect on birefringence of the rotation of the axes of principal stress along the path of the light beam. He developed an understanding of the effect, a simple and useful correction factor that could be applied for photoelastic stress analysis, and several experimental techniques for the production and use of fringes in transmitted light and in scattered light. His early ambition to become a design engineer was gradually transformed into a goal of abstracting the essence of problems in the simplest permissible general form in order to uncover fundamental new concepts basic to effective engineering teaching and innovative interrelated theoretical and experimental engineering research.

With H. Tachau, Drucker found a simple criterion for designing wire rope to protect it against fatigue failure that correlated all of the extensive experimental data then available. Later, the classification of materials and structures according to their degree of stability (known as Drucker's postulate) led to a general but simple approach to very broad classes of stress-strain relations for metals and alloys, as well as to general theorems for the analysis and design of engineering structures in the important range of relatively small displacement. The plastic limit theorems developed with H. J. Greenberg and W. Prager combined simplicity and general elegance in forms directly useful to the designer. With time, the focus of Drucker's research was increasingly in the direction of mechanical engineering. Studies on wear, machining, brittle fracture (with C. Mylonas and J. R. Rice), and the American Society of Mechanical Engineers (ASME) pressure vessel code (with R. T. Shield) were intermixed with the establishment of codes and specifications for civil engineering structures and the application of plasticity theory to soils, rocks, concrete, and polymeric materials. His attention turned also to research on materials at the level of the optical and electron microscopes. He predicted, before they were observed, that extremely small precipitates, rather than the grain size itself, were responsible for the flow strength of steel and aluminum alloys, and he explained some of the interesting properties of pearlitic versus spheroidized steels and of sintered carbides.

The son of a civil engineer, Drucker received the B.S. in 1937, C.E. in 1938, and Ph.D. in 1940 from Columbia University. He went to Cornell University in 1940 as an instructor, became supervisor of mechanics of solids at Armour Research Foundation, spent a brief period in the U.S. Army Air Corps, and returned to academic life as assistant professor at the Illinois Institute of Technology. Next came 21 years at Brown University, during which time he chaired the Division of Engineering for 6 years and the Physical Sciences Council for 2 years. He then spent 5 years as L. Herbert Ballou University Professor at Brown before going to the University of Illinois at Urbana-Champaign as dean of the college of engineering in 1968. Drucker received a Guggenheim Fellowship in 1960; the Von

Kármán Medal of the American Society of Civil Engineers (ASCE) in 1966; the Max M. Frocht Award of the Society for Experimental Stress Analysis (SESA) and the Lamme Award of the American Society for Engineering Education (ASEE), both in 1967; and the Egleston Medal of the Engineering Alumni Association of Columbia University in 1978. He was selected as Marburg Lecturer by the American Society for Testing and Materials in 1966, as W. M. Murray Lecturer by SESA in 1967, and as Raymond R. Tucker Memorial Lecturer by Washington University in 1978. He was elected to membership in the American Academy of Arts and Sciences in 1955 and to the National Academy of Engineering in 1967. He gave unstintingly of his time to professional and technical societies and to the community, serving as technical editor of the *Journal of Applied Mechanics* of ASME (1956–68), as president of ASME, of SESA, of the American Society of Mechanics, and of the Providence section and of the New England Council of ASCE, as first vice-president and chairperson of the Engineering College Council of ASEE, as chairperson of the U.S. National Committee on Theoretical and Applied Mechanics, as a member of the General Committee of the International Council of Scientific Unions (ICSU), and as a member of numerous other committees.

For background information *see* METALS, MECHANICAL PROPERTIES OF; PHOTOELASTICITY; STRESS AND STRAIN in the McGraw-Hill Encyclopedia of Science and Technology. ∎

DRYDEN, HUGH LATIMER
American physicist and aeronautical engineer

Born July 2, 1898, Pocomoke City, MD, U.S.A.
Died Dec. 2, 1965, Washington, DC, U.S.A.

A specialist in aerodynamics, Dryden gained international recognition for his fundamental work on air turbulence and boundary-layer control. Later, while directing the guided missile program of the National Bureau of Standards, he led the development of the first operational radar homing missile, the Bat.

During the late 1920s it was discovered

that the findings on the same airship model tested in different wind tunnels varied by as much as 100 percent. Dryden, working at the National Bureau of Standards, undertook an investigation to determine the cause of the variation. He found that the airflow in the wind tunnels had turbulence and that the amount of turbulence varied in wind tunnels of different design. To measure the amount of turbulence, Dryden and his associates developed the hot-wire anemometer. In this device a change in resistance and a drop in voltage across a hot platinum wire result from variations in air speed. By using the anemometer to measure airflow in different wind tunnels, Dryden was able to show that a variation in turbulence of 1 percent was sufficient to cause a 100 percent variation in airship test results. He also found that he could increase the turbulence of a wind tunnel by introducing a wire screen of fine and coarse mesh, and—based on his findings—he and his associates were able to design wind tunnels of very low turbulence.

Dryden then extended his research to include the effects of turbulence on airships and airplane wings. For any object in motion, the air at the surface is at rest with respect to the object, while the air a short distance away is moving at high speed relative to the object. The interface between these two airflows is called the boundary layer. He discovered that the turbulence most affected the flow that was very close to the surfaces of the models.

His investigations of turbulence and the mechanics of the boundary layer led to improved design in airplanes and in predictions of their performance.

Late in 1940 the National Defense Research Committee began an investigation of a winged bomb that would automatically seek out a target and guide itself to it. Early in 1942 the National Bureau of Standards was asked to take over the aerodynamic and servomechanism (control) development of the weapon, and Dryden was appointed to take charge of the project.

Two basic types of radar homing missile were considered. One was a glider bomb with a radar receiver tuned to an enemy transmitter on which the bomb could home in. The other, also a glide bomb, contained both a transmitter and a receiver; the transmitter emitted short pulses of high intensity, and the missile was guided by the returning echoes from the target. Dryden's group investigated both types of missile. The receiver-containing missile, called the Pelican, was constructed first and tested in December 1942. However, the results were unsatisfactory, and a decision was made to concentrate on the second type, called the Bat. Flight tests started in May 1944, and the weapon proved effective. The Bat was put into production and used against Japanese shipping in the Okinawa campaign, thus becoming the first automatic guided missile to be used in combat.

Dryden's investigations covered many areas of aerodynamics in addition to wind-tunnel turbulence and boundary-layer flow. He pioneered studies of the effect of wind pressure on structures and on the streamlining of automobiles. He directed the National Bureau of Standards research on jet propulsion and on acoustic fuses. A sports enthusiast, he even studied—in collaboration with Lyman J. Briggs—the coefficient of restitution and the spin of a baseball and the aerodynamic considerations in throwing a curve ball. Near the end of World War II, as deputy scientific director of the Army Air Force Scientific Advisory Group, which was headed by Theodore von Kármán, he toured Germany to investigate German scientific progress during the war years; in this capacity he was a contributor to *Toward New Horizons,* a report intended to channel military scientific research in the following decade. *See* VON KÁRMÁN, THEODORE.

Dryden studied at the Johns Hopkins University (A.B., 1916; A.M., 1918; Ph.D., 1919). He joined the National Bureau of Standards in 1918 as a laboratory assistant. Two years later he was appointed chief of the Aerodynamic Section, and in 1934 he was named chief of the Mechanics and Sound Division. Dryden served in the latter capacity until 1946, when he was appointed associate director of the bureau. In 1947 he left to join the National Advisory Committee for Aeronautics as director of aeronautical research, and in 1950 he was named director of the committee. In 1958 Dryden was a member of the President's advisory committee whose recommendations resulted in the establishment of the National Aeronautics and Space Administration, of which he became deputy administrator, a position he retained until his death. He received many awards in recognition of both his scientific efforts and his contributions to the United States, among them the Sylvanus Albert Reed Medal of the Institute of Aeronautical Sciences (for his work on boundary-layer phenomena), the Presidential Certificate of Merit (for his work on the Bat missile), the Medal of Freedom (for advising the U.S. Air Force on future research and development), the Langley Medal, and the von Kármán, Hill, and Goddard awards.

For background information *see* AERODYNAMICS; BOUNDARY-LAYER FLOW; GUIDED MISSILE; MISSILE GUIDANCE SYSTEMS; TURBULENT FLOW; WIND TUNNEL in the McGraw-Hill Encyclopedia of Science and Technology. ∎

DUBININ, MIKHAIL MIKHAILOVICH
★ Soviet physicochemist

Born Jan. 1, 1901, Moscow, Russia

Dubinin's scientific interests were primarily in porous structures of solids and related adsorption and capillary phenomena.

Most adsorbents and catalysts are porous bodies. Their pore sizes may range from near-molecule to magnitudes observable visually with slight magnification. Active carbons—porous carbonaceous absorbents—encompass all pore sizes from several angstroms to millions of angstroms (10 angstroms=1 nanometer). Detailed study of the porous structure of ac-

tive carbons using combined methods (sorption, forcing mercury into pores, small angle x-ray analysis, electron microscopy, and so on) revealed polymodal pore distribution according to effective radii, that is, the presence in active carbons of different pore varieties: macropores, transitional pores, and micropores. The established different mechanisms of adsorption and capillary phenomena in these pores served as a physical basis for their classification and its extension to adsorbents of different chemical nature.

The largest pores, macropores (effective radii $r > 200-300$ nanometers, surface area S several square meters per gram), act as transport pores in most adsorption processes. In transitional pores ($300-200 > r > 1.5-1.6$ nanometers; $S = 30-500$ square meters per gram) there occurs mono- and polymolecular adsorption of vapors, that is, formation of successive adsorption layers. At high relative pressures transitional pores undergo volume filling by the capillary condensation mechanism. The lower limit of effective pore radii corresponds to the limit of applicability of Kelvin's equation. Macropores and transitional pores are filled by mercury forced into them. The smallest pores, micropores ($r < 1.5-1.6$ nanometers), are characterized by volume filling in adsorption of gases and vapors. Adsorption in micropores differs radically from layer-by-layer adsorption in larger pore varieties, and is described by the de-

veloped theory of volume filling of micropores, especially when the dispersion component of the adsorption interaction is the deciding factor. The macroscopic concept of surface area loses its physical meaning for micropores.

The principal theoretical investigations based on extensive experimental data involved the creation of the theory of gas and vapor adsorption in micropores. The main proposition of the theory is the temperature invariance of the characteristic curve expressing the dependence of the differential molar work of adsorption, that is, the variation in free energy, on the degree of filling of the adsorption space. In cooperation with L. V. Radushkevich, Dubinin substantiated the two-constant equation of the characteristic adsorption curve. Characteristic curves for different vapors are affine, the affinity coefficient being determined by the physical constants of the vapors adsorbed. With B. P. Bering and V. V. Serpinsky, Dubinin developed the thermodynamics of the volume filling of pores: transitional pores due to capillary condensation and micropores due to adsorption. This made it possible to show that the invariance of characteristic curves is a sufficiently good approximation in observing the thermodynamic criterion of the applicability of the theory. Thus, possessing a minimum of experimental information, such as one absorption isotherm, it is easy to determine the two main constants of the absorption equation: the limiting volume of the absorption space (micropore volume) and the constant associated with the pore sizes. Using these constants, one can calculate to a good approximation absorption equilibria and thermodynamic functions (heat and entropy of adsorption) for different vapors over a wide range of temperatures and equilibrium pressures. Subsequently, Bering and Serpinsky of the laboratory headed by Dubinin suggested a new, more universal version of the theory of volume filling of micropores applicable to a wider range of adsorbents, including zeolites, and to a still wider region of fillings of the adsorption space.

On the basis of physically substantiated concepts of adsorbent pore varieties, the most rational classification of porous adsorbents and catalysts into macroporous, transitional-pore, and microporous ones was suggested. In addition to the indicated pure structural types of adsorbents, one frequently encounters adsorbents of

mixed structural types containing two or all three pore varieties. For this general case, methods for calculating the parameters of the structure of all pore varieties with the use of digital computers were developed (in cooperation with J. S. Lezin). On the basis of experimental data it was established, among other things, that a number of adsorbents, for example, some active carbons and fine-pore silica gels, possess more complex porous structures reduceable to the presence in the adsorbent of two independent microporous structures with different micropore sizes within the general effective radii range from 0.6 to 1.4 nanometers. These conclusions from adsorption measurements were directly confirmed by small-angle x-ray analysis.

Ways of controlling the development of different pore varieties in the course of synthesis of adsorbents and of modifying the chemical nature of their skeletons were elaborated. For nonspecific adsorption of gases and vapors by microporous adsorbents, a quantitative description of adsorption equilibria was given as a function of the parameters of the microporous structure of the adsorbents and the physical properties of the adsorbates. The features of filling of the adsorption space of micropores were studied on examples of microporous crystals: synthetic zeolites, whose micropore volumes were calculated from x-ray data. The secondary porous structures of molded zeolites were studied comprehensively by combined methods.

Dubinin graduated from the chemistry department of the Moscow Higher Technical School in 1921. He served on the staff of the school from 1922 to 1941, advancing from assistant to associate professor and in 1933 to professor. He was awarded a degree of doctor of chemical sciences in 1936 and in 1943 was elected a member of the U.S.S.R. Academy of Sciences. In 1946 he became head of the Department of Sorption on Processes at the Institute of Physical Chemistry of the U.S.S.R. Academy of Sciences. He was chairperson of the Chemical Sciences Section in 1948–57 and a member of the presidium of the academy in 1948–62. Dubinin won the U.S.S.R. State Prize in 1942 and 1950.

For background information *see* ACTIVATED CARBON; ADSORPTION; MOLECULAR SIEVE in the McGraw-Hill Encyclopedia of Science and Technology. ■

DUBOS, RENÉ JULES
★ American microbiologist

Born Feb. 20, 1901, Saint Brice, France

Although his early training was in the agricultural sciences, Dubos devoted most of his professional life to the experimental study of microbial diseases and to the analysis of the environmental and social factors that affect human well-being.

Dubo's Ph.D. thesis (Rutgers University, 1927) dealt with the decomposition of cellulose by soil microorganisms under various physiological conditions. While seemingly unrelated to medicine, this study helped Dubos to develop an awareness of the wide range of potential activities of microbial life and of the profound influence that the environment exerts on biological processes. This awareness was reflected in the different phases of his subsequent career.

In 1930, while associated with the Hospital of the Rockefeller Institute, Dubos isolated from a soil bacterium an enzyme capable of hydrolyzing the capsular polysaccharide of type III pneumococcus, a cause of lobar pneumonia in humans. As the capsular polysaccharide normally protects pneumococci against the defense mechanisms of the host, the enzyme proved to have therapeutic effectiveness against pneumococcal infections in various animal species.

Dubos observed that the bacterial polysaccharidase was highly specific for the pneumococcus polysaccharide and was produced only when the soil bacterium was compelled to use it, or a closely related substance, as a source of energy. These findings constituted the first extensive documentation of the phenomenon of induced production of enzyme. Furthermore, it led Dubos to develop techniques for the production of other induced bacterial enzymes specific for creatine and creatinine. By virtue of their specificity, the bacterial enzymes proved useful in the study of the metabolism of these substances.

The demonstration that the bacterial polysaccharidase isolated in 1930 had a therapeutic effect against pneumococcal infection encouraged Dubos to search for other anti-infectious substances in soil microorganisms. In 1939 he reported the isolation from a soil bacterium of a product, "tyrothricin," that proved effective in the treatment of certain bacterial infections in animals and humans; he later showed that tyrothricin was a mixture of two complex antibacterial polypeptides: gramicidin and tyrocidine. Although tyrothricin and the two peptides of which it was made proved too toxic for large-scale use, they are of historical interest because they were the first "antibiotics" manufactured commercially and used in the practice of veterinary and human medicine.

After working on problems of war medicine during World War II, Dubos turned his attention to tuberculosis, developing new methods for the cultivation of tubercle bacilli, for the production of experimental tuberculosis in mice, and for the study of Bacillus Calmette-Guérin (BCG) vaccination. More importantly, however, the work on tuberculosis gave him the opportunity to investigate the influence of hereditary, nutritional, physiological, and social factors on susceptibility to infection. From then on, most of his investigative work was focused on the study of the environmental agencies that play a role in resistance to disease—not only to tuberculosis but also to other infectious processes, and to various noninfectious stresses.

During subsequent years, concern with the effects of the environment on growth and health led to the recognition in Dubos's laboratory that the indigenous microbial flora, in particular the flora of the gastrointestinal tract, profoundly influences the rate of growth of the host, its ultimate size, its efficiency in food utilization, and its resistance to many forms of stress.

The studies of the indigenous flora also revealed that while certain of its microbial species are of course deleterious to the host, others are absolutely essential for physiological well-being. In fact, it appears that each animal species, including humans, requires association with a certain specialized microbial flora in order to achieve normal development and function. Dubos showed, furthermore, that the microbial environment to which the host is exposed during early life determines to a very large extent the composition of the indigenous flora. Many microbial species acquired at that time persist throughout the life-span and condition many important physiological and immunological characteristics. Indeed, many traits—such as body size or resistance to infection—that had been thought to be genetically determined are in reality the expression of such very early influences.

It will be apparent from the preceding account that Dubos's scientific research followed an ecological approach; health and disease were analyzed as manifestations of the interplay between the host, the environment, and the microbial pathogens (or other stressful agents). Through his interest in the influence of the total environment, Dubos became involved in the sociomedical problems of the underprivileged communities as well as in problems created by economic affluence in industrialized countries. In particular, he emphasized the part played by early influences, that is, the environmental factors that impinge on the developing organism during the prenatal and early postnatal period. These early influences can exert an effect on biological and mental characteristics throughout the life-span, an effect that may extend even to subsequent generations. The study of these influences constitutes a science that Dubos termed biological Freudianism. From about 1968, Dubos became increasingly involved in theoretical and practical problems bearing on environmental quality and on the future of technological societies.

The more bacteriological aspects of this ecological attitude were presented by Dubos in four books: *The Bacterial Cell* (1945), *Biochemical Determinants of Microbial Diseases* (1954), *The Unseen World* (1962), and *Bacterial and Mycotic Infections of Man* (4th ed. 1965). Concern with the effects of environmental and social forces on human welfare was expressed in a number of other books on subjects ranging from the history of science to social philosophy: *Louis Pasteur: Free Lance of Science* (1950; 2d ed., 1976), *The White Plague: Tuberculosis, Man, and Society* (1952), *Pasteur and Modern Science* (1960), *Dreams of Reason: Science and Utopias* (1961), and *The Torch of Life: Continuity in Living Experience* (1962). In a later book, *Man Adapting* (1965), Dubos analyzed the biological and social mechanisms through which individual human beings and human societies become adapted to different kinds of environments, and he discussed the relevance of this adaptability to the science and practice of medicine. Other books included *Man, Medicine and Environment* (1968), *So Human an Animal* (1968), *Reason Awake: Science for Man* (1970), *Only One Earth,* with Barbara Ward (1972), *A God Within* (1972), *Beast or Angel: Choices That Make Us Human* and *Of Human Diversity* (1974), and *The Professor, the Institute and DNA: Oswald T. Avery and His Scientific Achievements* (1976).

Dubos was born into a very modest family and received his early education in a small French village. After graduating from the Institut National Agronomique in Paris, he worked for 2 years at the International Institute of Agriculture in Rome. He emigrated to the United States in 1924 and became an American citizen in 1938. Except for 2 years as professor of comparative pathology and tropical medicine at Harvard University (1942–44), he spent his entire professional life at the Rockefeller Institute in New York. He became professor emeritus in 1971. Among his many national and international awards were the John Phillips Memorial Award of the American College of Physicians (1940), the Lasker Award of the American Public Health Association (1948), the Trudeau Medal of the National Tuberculosis Association 1951), the Passano Foundation Award (1960), the American Medical Association's Scientific Achievement Award (1964), the Arches of Science Award of the Pacific Science Center (1966), the Harold Terry Clark Award (1970), the Prix International of the Institut de la Vie (1972), the Forsythia Award of the Brooklyn Botanic Garden (1974), the Washburn Award of the Boston Museum of Science (1974), the Cullum Geographical Medal (1975), the Tyler Ecology Award (1976), and the Walter Penfield Award of the Vanier Institute of Ottawa (1979).

For background information *see* BACTERIAL ENZYME; BACTERIOLOGY, MEDICAL in the McGraw-Hill Encyclopedia of Science and Technology. ∎

DUCKWORTH, HENRY EDMISON
★ Canadian physicist

Born Nov. 1, 1915, Brandon, Manitoba, Canada

By determining atomic masses with high precision, Duckworth provided evidence for sudden changes in nuclear stability that correspond to the completion of nuclear shells or to the onset of nuclear distortion. These determinations were made with specially constructed mass spectrometers of exceptionally high resolving power.

The fact that mass spectrometers could provide useful information concerning nuclear binding energies was demonstrated first by F. W. Aston at Cambridge in 1927. In the next decade this work was extended by A. J. Dempster at Chicago, K. T. Bainbridge at Harvard, and J. Mattauch in Vienna, who provided an overall, albeit approximate, view of the manner in which the nuclear binding energy varies with increasing atomic mass. Duckworth was a student of Dempster's during 1940–42, and realized that detailed information concerning nuclear structure, and of a unique sort, could be obtained with a mass spectrometer, provided the precision could be improved sufficiently. This led after World War II to the construction

and utilization by Duckworth and his associates of a series of improved mass spectrometers, culminating in 1962 in an instrument whose resolving power exceeded a quarter million.

The first result of this work was the discovery in 1949 that the binding energy per nucleon displays a large and sudden decline at or near $A = 90$. This was immediately attributed to the closure of the $N = 50$ shell, in accordance with concurrent speculations concerning the existence of nuclear shell structure, and atomic mass evidence for other alleged shells or subshells was then sought. Definitive evidence was found for the $Z = 28$, $Z = 50$, and $N = 82$ shells, and useful information was given concerning the magnitudes of these effects. Also, a study was made in 1953 with B. G. Hogg of the mass region $140 \leq A$ in the hope of discovering evidence for nuclear subshells among the rare-earth elements. Although no localized effects were observed, a broad region of extra stability was identified which did not appear to be explicable on the basis of nuclear shells or the underlying theory based on the independent particle model. It was to clarify this matter that the very large instrument, completed in 1962, was begun. In the meantime, in 1957 A. O. C. Nier and W. H. Johnson at Minnesota confirmed the existence of the region of extra stability above $A = 140$ and identified it with the $N = 90$ configuration.

The very high resolving power of the new mass spectrometer made it possible to determine directly the energy with which the last two neutrons in a nucleus are bound, rather than, as previously, the average binding energy per nucleon. As a result, local effects were greatly magnified, and the picture in the neighborhood of $N = 90$ emerged with unexpected clarity. Up to and including $N = 88$, the nucleus is described to a good approximation by the single-particle theory, and also to a fair approximation beyond $N = 92$. But the four neutrons $N = 89, 90, 91,$ and 92 display an extra stability which can be reasonably associated with the nuclear distortion now known to exist in the rare-earth region. Thus, as far as nuclear distortion involving neutrons is concerned, it begins very suddenly at $N = 88$, it involves four neutrons principally (and perhaps only), and the magnitude of the effect can be estimated to good accuracy from the mass spectrometric data.

Duckworth and his associates utilized

their data to predict the energies released in various nuclear transmutations. These predictions proved accurate to a few kilovolts of energy, and they corrected significant errors that had been made in the study of nuclear reactions and radioactive decays. A by-product of the group's work was the discovery in 1949 of the rare stable isotope of platinum at mass number 190.

Only child of a minister of the United Church of Canada, Duckworth graduated from the University of Manitoba with a B.A. in 1935 and a B.Sc. in 1936. Following 3 years of secondary and junior college teaching, he enrolled at the University of Chicago, where he obtained his Ph.D. in physics in 1942. After 3 years of war research with the National Research Council of Canada, he was on the staff at the University of Manitoba (1945–46), Wesleyan University (1946–51), and McMaster University (1951–65). In 1965 he became vice-president of the University of Manitoba and in 1971 president of the University of Winnipeg. Elected to the Royal Society of Canada in 1954, he was awarded the Medal of the Canadian Association of Physicists in 1964 and the Tory Medal of the Royal Society of Canada in 1965; he was appointed Officer of the Order of Canada in 1976.

Duckworth wrote *Mass Spectroscopy* (1958), *Electricity and Magnetism* (1960; rev. ed. 1966), and *Little Men in the Unseen World* (1963) and edited the *Proceedings of the International Conference on Atomic Masses* (1960).

For background information *see* ATOMIC STRUCTURE AND SPECTRA; BINDING ENERGY, NUCLEAR; MASS SPECTROMETRY; NUCLEAR STRUCTURE in the McGraw-Hill Encyclopedia of Science and Technology. ∎

DULBECCO, RENATO
☆ American virologist

Born Feb. 22, 1914, Catanzaro, Italy

Dulbecco developed a basic procedure used in studying animal virus. He used this to study the genetics of viruses and how animal virus interacts with the host-cell. He then turned to cancer-producing viruses, demonstrating the interactions of the genetic materials of the virus and of the host cells in the development of cancer. For this work he shared the Nobel Prize for medicine or physiology in 1975

with Howard Temin and David Baltimore. *See* BALTIMORE, DAVID; TEMIN, HOWARD M.

After early work in Italy Dulbecco came to the United States in 1947 to work in Salvador Luria's laboratory at the University of Indiana. Luria's group was involved in research on bacteriophage, a virus that infects bacteria. Bacteriophage, or phage, had been known since 1915, and by the late 1940s the techniques used in researching it had become more refined. Dulbecco left Indiana in 1949 for the California Institute of Technology, where he applied phage methodology to the study of animal virus. He soon developed a bioassay for western equine encephalitis virus, a ribonucleic acid (RNA) virus. In this procedure, plaques, clear areas formed by lysis or dissolution of the host cell, represent a colony of virus in a plate culture. The plaque technique is used to count the virus and isolate genetically pure stocks, among other purposes.

At the California Institute of Technology Dulbecco began a 20-year collaboration with Marguerite Vogt. Their studies with poliovirus are considered to have contributed to the development of a polio vaccine.

Dulbecco then focused his attention on tumor viruses because of his interest in cancer and because they would provide an opportunity to learn more about cell regulatory mechanisms. Some of Dulbecco's group began to work with Rous sarcoma virus, which causes tumors in chickens. In

the late 1950s the main effort of the group was focused on polyoma virus, a newly discovered tumor virus, and later on simian virus 40 (SV40). They developed a bioassay for polyoma virus by showing that, depending on the type of animal cell, the virus either infects it and multiplies until the cell is killed, or enters the cell, does not multiply, and induces a cancerlike state in which the cell continues to grow and divide. The change from the normal to cancerlike state was called transformation. The Dulbecco group demonstrated that transformation was the direct result of viral deoxyribonucleic acid (DNA) being integrated into host-cell DNA, remaining there as a provirus, being transcribed into messenger RNA, and controlling the host genetic mechanism. As a result, the transformed cell reproduces a clonal line that does not follow the controlled growth pattern of the normal or nontransformed cell, but rather is in a continual state of multiplication. In the normal cell there is a feedback mechanism between the cell membrane and the nucleus that halts cell multiplication if the cell is encroaching upon other types of tissues or if the architectural requirements of the particular cell tissue have been met. This mechanism appears to be inoperative in the transformed cell. They also showed that injection of transformed cells into an appropriate host animal causes a tumor to develop.

Dulbecco received his M.D. from the University of Torino in 1936 and was involved in research and teaching there. In 1947 he emigrated to the United States to work at the University of Indiana for 2 years. He then became an associate professor and professor at the California Institute of Technology, leaving in 1963 to become a senior research fellow at the Salk Institute for Biological Studies. In 1972 he joined the staff of the Imperial Cancer Research Fund in London, where he later became deputy director of research. In addition to the Nobel Prize, Dulbecco received many honors and awards, including the Albert and Mary Lasker Award in 1964, the Howard Taylor Ricketts Award in 1965, and the Selman A. Waksman Award in microbiology in 1974. He was a member of the National Academy of Sciences and a foreign member of the Royal Society (London) and the Accademia dei Lincei (Italy).

For background information *see* ANIMAL VIRUS; BACTERIOPHAGE in the McGraw-Hill Encyclopedia of Science and Technology. ∎

DUNBAR, CARL OWEN
★ American geologist

Born Jan. 1, 1891, Hallowell, KS, U.S.A.

Dunbar was an American pioneer in the study of the Fusulinacea, a prolific group of large foraminifera that was an important rock maker in late Paleozoic time and is one of the most widely used means of dating and correlating the rock formations of that time.

About 1920 J. W. Beede, who had done extensive fieldwork in the Upper Carboniferous rocks of the Mid-Continent region, ventured the prophecy that when the evolutionary history of the fusulines was known they could be used to identify faunal zones not over 100 feet (30 meters) thick. With this stimulus, Dunbar began a comprehensive study of these fossils, of which only a few species and two genera had at that time been described from America. This proceeded in two stages: the first was to establish their stratigraphic succession, and the second to determine the progressive modifications of shell features that would reveal their evolutionary history. Six summers of fieldwork while serving as paleontologist for the Geological Survey of Nebraska afforded the opportunity to secure large collections of fusulines from every known fossiliferous stratigraphic level in the Pennsylvanian System in Nebraska and adjacent states. With their chronology established, the biologic study was begun.

Because these quite complex shells could be studied only in thin sections, it was necessary, as the first step, to cut some thousands of carefully oriented slices and grind them to transparent thinness. It was then possible to examine in turn each of the shell structures, measuring their sizes and other characteristics at successive levels in the stratigraphic sequence. Evolutionary trends were thereby established and important changes dated. In 1927 Dunbar and G. E. Condra published the first volume devoted to the study of American fusulines.

The opportunity to extend the study upward into the Permian System came in 1926, when large collections made by Robert E. King in the Permian Basin of West Texas and New Mexico were turned over to Dunbar for study. The stratigraphic succession had been carefully worked out by the brothers Robert and Philip King, Simultaneously, John W. Skinner of the Humble Petroleum Company was beginning a study of the same faunas. Dunbar and Skinner decided to collaborate, and in 1937 published *The Permian Fusulinidae of Texas*.

From 1925 to 1928 Lloyd G. Henbest was engaged by the Illinois Geological Survey in making systematic collections of the fusulines from every fossiliferous level in the coal measures of that state, and in the fall of 1928 he went to Yale to study with Dunbar. Together they spent part of a summer in the field reviewing the stratigraphy and making additional collections. This project resulted in Bulletin 67 of the Illinois Geological Survey, *Pennsylvanian Fusulinidae of Illinois* (1942), by Dunbar and Henbest.

These three volumes, plus many shorter articles in technical journals, established numerous genera and species and demonstrated progressive evolutionary trends that could be used to date the rocks and correlate formations in other regions.

Dunbar grew up on a wheat ranch in Kansas, received his undergraduate training at the University of Kansas (A.B., 1913) and graduate training in geology at Yale (Ph.D., 1917). After 2 years at the University of Minnesota he joined the Yale faculty in 1920 as assistant professor of historical geology and assistant curator of invertebrate paleontology in the Peabody Museum of Natural History. Several years of teaching large undergraduate classes widened his interest in synthesizing the history of the Earth and led to his collaboration with Charles Schuchert on the third and fourth editions (1933, 1941) of the latter's *Textbook of Historical Geol-*

ogy, and subsequently to three editions of his own *Historical Geology* (1949; 1960; 3d ed., with Karl M. Waage, 1969). In 1930 Dunbar was promoted to professor of paleontology and stratigraphy. From 1942 until his retirement in 1959 he served also as director of the Peabody Museum of Natural History. In 1959 Dunbar received the Hayden Medal of the Philadelphia Academy of Sciences. He was elected to the National Academy of Sciences in 1944.

Besides the books already mentioned, Dunbar wrote *Principles of Stratigraphy,* with John Rodgers (1957), and *The Earth* (1966).

For background information *see* FORAMINIFERA; FUSULINACEA in the McGraw-Hill Encyclopedia of Science and Technology. ∎

DUNHAM, SIR KINGSLEY (CHARLES)
★ British geologist

Born Jan. 2, 1910, Sturminster Newton, England

In 1930 Dunham had the good fortune to become Arthur Holmes's first graduate student after that inspired researcher's appointment to the chair of geology in the University of Durham. Holmes introduced him to the northern English Pennines, where the widespread ore deposits offered interesting genetic problems. This district was to become the focus of Dunham's investigation of the causes of natural concentration of minerals for the next

50 years, taking him to every continent and to most countries. Initial work disclosed a systematic zonal disposition of the minerals in the lead-zinc-copper-fluorine-barium deposits of the Pennines, pointing by analogy with the zoned veins of Cornubia to a possible association with a granitic intrusive concealed beneath the gently domed Carboniferous host rocks. *See* HOLMES, ARTHUR.

Three years at Harvard as a Commonwealth Fund (now Harkness) Fellow enabled Dunham to explore the association of mineralization with high-level granitic stocks in one of its classic areas, the southwestern United States. Here his field study of the Organ Mountains of New Mexico—suggested by Waldemar Lindgren of the Massachusetts Institute of Technology, a leading exponent of the relationship since the early years of the 20th century—was accompanied by studies in the laboratories of L. C. Graton and Esper S. Larsen, Jr., at Harvard. Returning to England in 1935, Dunham became an officer of the Geological Survey of Great Britain and was assigned to undertake, in collaboration with William Colin Campbell Rose, a detailed survey of the once important hematite mining field of Furness and South Cumberland. This work, although disappointing in that it did not disclose large additional resources, was stimulating in the clear picture of stratigraphic control of introduced ores that it provided.

The onset of World War II saw the research completed but not published. Dunham was sent back to the Pennines to assist and stimulate the production of needed minerals. The records of more than 250 years of mining by four companies in the area became available to him, giving remarkably clear evidence—when assessed in the light of underground mapping—of the tectonic, stratigraphical, and geochemical factors controlling the emplacement and size of some hundreds of ore shoots. In particular, distribution of fluids from a small number of feeding centers through laterally extensive channels determined by the coincidence of refracted fractures with hard, brittle stratigraphic units in the cyclothemic country rock was indicated. The enigma of a granitic source remained.

Dunham was appointed head of the Petrographical Department of the Geological Survey after the war, involving him in a wide variety of researches, including the mineralogy of the newly discovered potash deposits in Yorkshire, the petrography of the chamosite–siderite ores of the Lias, the elucidation of the titanium-bearing banded gabbros of Carrock Fell, and the survey of the plateau lavas of North Skye. In 1950 he returned to Durham to become professor and head of the department of geology. The many problems remaining in the Pennines could again be pursued; this was done with the collaboration of able graduate students and research assistants, all now well-known geologists. Particular mention must be made of M. H. P. Bott and D. Masson-Smith, whose gravimetric survey showed a regional negative Bouguer anomaly remarkably coincident with the regional zonal pattern of the Pennine mineralization, the form of which strongly indicated a concealed granite.

The Department of Scientific and Industrial Research provided substantial funds to enable a deep borehole to be drilled at one of the focal points, a step unusual at the time for what had to be regarded as a largely academic project. The boring fully justified the geophysical prediction by proving granite underneath the Carboniferous, but the speculation that the granite might be the direct source of the mineralizing fluids was disproved since its age turned out to be pre-Carboniferous. Dunham was now forced to consider alternatives to the juvenile hydrothermal hypothesis, and was already beginning to espouse deep hypersaline brines of connate or membrane-filtered origin as the principal agents of low-temperature epigenetic mineralization, when controversy with C. F. Davidson and a conference organized by C. H. Behre, Jr., at United Nations headquarters in New York provided further good reasons to move in that direction. It cannot yet be proved that these fluids, widespread in the Earth's crust down to the greatest depths yet penetrated, are also the main agents for introducing minerals into veins at shallow depths, but it is certain that they can no longer be ignored in the total problem of mineral concentration.

In 1967 Dunham returned to London as director of the Institute of Geological Sciences, newly formed under the Natural Environment Research Council by the incorporation of the Geological Survey, Overseas Surveys, and the Geological Museum. His 9 years as director saw the establishment of the institute in an international context and its closer integration with the needs of government departments, coupled with a threefold increase in staff. His visits to foreign and commonwealth countries, begun during his academic days, became more frequent, providing many opportunities to widen the scope of the researches influenced by him. His later research interests included the general problems of mineral and fuel supply for the world.

Dunham's father, estate agent to landed proprietors including the Duke of Westminster, although he had no interest in geology, named him after the noted amateur geologist Charles Kingsley, whose fictional writings and staunch Protestantism he admired. He received his B.Sc. in 1930 and his Ph.D. in 1933 from Durham, and his S.D. in 1935 from Harvard.

Dunham's work was recognized by his knighthood in 1972 and by the award of the Royal Medal of the Royal Society, the two gold medals of the Institution of Mining and Metallurgy, and the Bigsby, Murchison, and Wollaston medals of the Geological Society of London. He was elected a fellow of the Royal Society in 1955 and was its foreign secretary and a vice-president from 1971 to 1976. He was president of the Yorkshire Geological Society, the Institution of Mining and Metallurgy, the Geological Society of London, the British Association for the Advancement of Science, and the International Union of Geological Sciences. He launched the UNESCO/International Union of Geological Sciences International Geological Correlation project, involving 65 member states, and was chairman of its board for its first 4 years. He was elected a corresponding foreign member of the Sustrian Academy of Sciences and was British member of the Council of the International Institute for Applied Systems Analysis at Schloss Laxenburg for its first 5 years.

Dunham's works include *The Geology of the Organ Mountains, New Mexico* (1936); volume 1 of the *Geology of the Northern Pennine Orefield* (1948), *Fluorspar* (1952), *Geology of Moor House*, with G. A. L. Johnson (1963); *Geology of Northern Skye*, with F. W. Anderson (1966); and *Geology and Hematite Deposits of South Cumbria*, with W. C. C. Rose (1977).

For background information *see* MINERALOGY; PETROLOGY in the McGraw-Hill Encyclopedia of Science and Technology. ∎

DUNN, LESLIE CLARENCE
★ American geneticist

Born Nov. 2, 1893, Buffalo, NY, U.S.A.
Died Mar. 19, 1974, North Tarryton, NY, U.S.A.

As a student, Dunn was impressed by the ease with which hereditary endowment (the genotype) can be analyzed into its transmission components (genes) by simple breeding experiments or by observations of gene frequencies in populations. He carried out many such analyses in chickens and in laboratory mice, and his interest was especially attracted by genes with drastic or abnormal effects. His analyses led to questions as to how different genes produce their different effects during the development of the individual. Several genes, some with lethal effects, were studied by examining early embryos, first in the chicken and later in the mouse. From this work the idea emerged that genes produce their effects by controlling the rates of specific processes in early development.

Discovery that the same kinds of abnormalities as those due to gene differences, such as absence of tail or disproportionate dwarfism, could occur in birds of normal genotype led to the recognition that environmental or accidental changes in early development can simulate the kinds of changes produced by gene differences. The use of simulation as a tool to explore causal relations in development was begun, but was chiefly exploited by W. Landauer in his studies of chemical teratology. In the laboratory mouse, Dunn's analyses of quantitative or intergrading differences in hair color and especially in localized absence of hair pigments (white spotting) showed that such differences can be resolved into components due to many genes, each with small effects interacting in complex ways.

A problem which occupied Dunn for many years was provided by the discovery in the mouse of a series of hereditary changes in one region of one linkage group (chromosome). The hereditary changes involved (1) early processes in the organization of the embryo, some of them providing examples of the origin of very early disturbances and abnormalities, such as absence of tail, limbs, and other parts, constituting the earliest effects of lethal genes in mammals; (2) the ratio in which some genes were transmitted to offspring through the sperm, certain lethal genes going from male carriers to over 90 percent of the progeny instead of the normal 50 percent; (3) effects on the probability of recombination of genes in this chromosome region through crossing-over exchange; and (4) effects on the fertility of males bearing certain combinations of such genes, varying from complete sterility to nearly normal. Interest in this chromosome region increased when it was discovered that its variant genes, generally lethals, are present in most natural populations of house mice in North America and elsewhere. It was shown that these genes are retained in the populations in spite of their lethal effects by an evolutionary force different from, and opposed to, natural selection; this force was called transmission ratio advantage. Studies of the population dynamics of this striking polymorphism indicated that it was probably fluctuating—the genes involved being propelled through the populations by high sperm transmission ratios and migrations and being subject to local extinction by random processes in small breeding groups. A rather novel type of flux equilibrium was suggested. An attempt was thus made in this case to bring into relation the structure of a region of the genetic material and its function in development and evolution.

At Dartmouth College (A.B. 1915) Dunn was attracted to the new field of genetics through the influence of John H. Gerould. He went in 1915 to the Bussey Institution of Harvard University, where he was a student and assistant of William E. Castle. His graduate work was interrupted in 1917–19 by war service as a lieutenant of infantry. On return from France he completed his doctoral research on linkage in mice and rats, took his Sc.D. at Harvard in 1920, and joined the staff of the Storrs Agricultural Experiment Station in Connecticut as a geneticist. In 1928 Dunn became professor of zoology at Columbia University, serving until 1962, when he became emeritus professor with a research laboratory at Nevis Biological Station, Irvington, NY. While at Columbia he was visiting professor or lecturer at Oslo, Berlin, London, and Harvard universities and the New School in New York City. He carried out research in human genetics in Rome. He was elected to the National Academy of Sciences and to the American Philosophical Society, both in 1943, and to the American Academy of Arts and Sciences in 1950.

Dunn wrote *Principles of Genetics,* with E. W. Sinnott (1925; 5th ed., with T. Dobzhansky, 1958); *Heredity and Variation* (1932); *Heredity, Race and Society,* with T. Dobzhansky (1946; rev. ed. 1952); *Race and Biology* (reprint 1965); *Heredity and Evolution in Human Populations* (1958; 2d ed. 1965); and *A Short History of Genetics* (1965). He also wrote some 250 articles in scientific periodicals and encyclopedias. He was editor of *Genetics, The American Naturalist,* and *Genetics in the 20th Century.*

For background information *see* CHROMOSOME; GENE ACTION; LETHAL GENE; POLYMORPHISM (GENETICS) in the McGraw-Hill Encyclopedia of Science and Technology. ■

DU VIGNEAUD, VINCENT
★ American biochemist

Born May 18, 1901, Chicago, IL, U.S.A.
Died Dec. 11, 1978, Scarsdale, NY, U.S.A.

For the first synthesis of a polypeptide hormone, oxytocin, and for his work on other biologically important sulfur compounds, du Vigneaud was awarded the Nobel Prize for chemistry in 1955.

Du Vigneaud approached the study of the posterior pituitary hormones, oxytocin and vasopressin, with a background of knowledge and experience in the area of organic sulfur compounds. He and his associates at Cornell University Medical College first isolated these hormones in highly purified form from the glands. They then proceeded to determine the nature of the hormones and found them to be polypeptides containing eight amino acid residues, the sulfur being present as cystine. On the basis of various degradative studies, they postulated cyclic disulfide octapeptide amide structures for both of these highly active compounds and then tested the correctness of their postulates by synthesizing the compounds so designated and comparing the synthetic compounds with the natural products. The synthesis of oxytocin was accomplished in 1953 by building up the amino acid chain and finally closing the ring through formation of a bond between the two sulfur atoms; the synthetic polypeptide was found to be identical in physical, chemical, and biological properties with the natural hormone. Du Vigneaud and his associates also synthesized both lysine-vasopressin and arginine-vasopressin, the pressor-antidiuretic hormones found respectively in hog and beef posterior pituitary glands.

Synthetic oxytocin was tested in human patients in the Lying-in Hospital of the New York Hospital–Cornell Medical Center through the collaboration of Gordon Douglas, professor of obstetrics and gynecology, and his associates. The synthetic was found to be as effective in the induction of labor as the purified natural oxytocin. When the synthetic compound

and natural oxytocin were tested for milk-ejecting activity, they were again found indistinguishable in effectiveness. Thus it was demonstrated that one and the same molecule possesses these two important biological activities.

The synthesis of these posterior pituitary hormones also provided the first opportunity to study the relationship of structure to biological activity of a polypeptide hormone by the total synthesis and biological study of analogs incorporating various structural modifications. Through such studies with oxytocin and the vasopressins insight has been gained as to the structural requirements for the exhibition of the various biological activities of these hormones.

Almost all of du Vigneaud's researches involved sulfur-containing compounds of diverse types—the vitamin biotin; the antibiotic penicillin; the protein hormone insulin; and the sulfur-containing amino acids methionine, homocystine, cystathionine, and cystine. His researches on the posterior pituitary hormones were thus a natural outgrowth of an interest in sulfur compounds dating from 1925, when he showed that the disulfide present in insulin could be accounted for as the amino acid cystine—the same amino acid that he was later to find in the posterior pituitary hormones.

Du Vigneaud received his B.S. in 1923 and his M.S. in 1924 under C. S. Marvel at the University of Illinois. In 1924–25 he was assistant biochemist to W. G. Karr at the Philadelphia General Hospital and was on the staff of the Graduate School of Medicine of the University of Pennsylvania. The University of Rochester conferred the Ph.D. degree upon him in 1927. His thesis work was carried out under John R. Murlin at the school of medicine. As a National Research Council fellow, du Vigneaud worked with John J. Abel at the Johns Hopkins University Medical School, with Max Bergmann at the Kaiser Wilhelm Institute in Dresden, with George Barger at the University of Edinburgh Medical School, and with Charles R. Harington at the University College Hospital Medical School in London. Returning to the United States, he joined the physiological chemistry staff under W. C. Rose at the University of Illinois, and in 1932 became head of the department of biochemistry at George Washington University School of Medicine. Du Vigneaud was appointed professor and head of the de-

partment of biochemistry at Cornell University Medical College in 1938. He was elected to the National Academy of Sciences in 1944.

Du Vigneaud wrote *A Trail of Research in Sulfur Chemistry and Metabolism and Related Fields* (1952).

For background information *see* HORMONE, NEUROHYPOPHYSIS in the McGraw-Hill Encyclopedia of Science and Technology. ∎

DYER, ROLLA EUGENE
☆ American physician

Born Nov. 4, 1886, Delaware County, OH, U.S.A.
Died June 2, 1971, Atlanta, GA, U.S.A.

Dyer discovered the agent of murine typhus in the common rat flea (*Xenopsylla cheopis*) and showed that this flea transmits the disease from rats to humans.

Epidemic typhus is a rickettsial disease transmitted in nature only by lice that feed exclusively on human blood. In 1922 K. F. Maxcy began to see evidence of another kind of typhus and to challenge the old notion of "no lice, no typhus." He noted that in the southern United States there had been cases of typhus unassociated with lice and that persons handling foodstuffs risked contracting the disease apparently from an animal reservoir other than a human. He suggested the rat and the mouse as the most likely reservoirs and some blood-sucking arthropod that fed both on rodents and humans as the most likely vector.

Carrying on where Maxcy left off, Dyer set out to find the reservoir and vector of what had become known as "endemic typhus," to distinguish it from the louse-borne type. His opportunity came when in 1930 several cases of typhus broke out in rat-infested houses near food-handling firms in Baltimore, MD. Dyer and his associates, L. F. Badger and A. S. Rumreich, combed rat fleas out of rats they trapped in these houses. Dyer now assumed that the rat was the reservoir of endemic typhus and that the flea was the vector of the disease. He reasoned that he could test the hypothesis only by isolating a strain of typhus rickettsia from the rat flea and comparing it with a strain isolated from a human case.

Dyer and his associates ground up the fleas in saline solution and injected the resulting emulsion into guinea pigs. The pigs got typhus. Dyer and his associates repeated these experiments and achieved the same results with fleas from rats trapped at a house in Savannah, GA, where there had been two cases of typhus. They also found that the strains of rickettsiae recovered from fleas taken from the Baltimore and Savannah rats were clinically identical with a strain Maxcy isolated from a human case of typhus in Wilmington, NC, in 1928. Finally, in 1931, Dyer and his associates experimentally transmitted the rickettsiae from rats to rats by fleas. They therefore established that endemic typhus is, in fact, a variety of typhus not transmitted by lice parasitic on humans. In 1932 H. Mooser renamed the disease "murine typhus."

Dyer also did pioneer work on scarlet fever, Rocky Mountain spotted fever, and Q fever. In 1928 his studies resulted in a world standard unit for scarlet fever antitoxin. In 1931 he helped determine that Rocky Mountain spotted fever is endemic in the eastern United States. In 1939 he showed that a supposedly new tick-borne disease in the United States was actually the same as Australian Q fever.

Director of the National Institute of Health, U.S. Public Health Service, during World War II, Dyer channeled the resources of the organization into the war effort. Under his leadership, the institute produced a yellow fever vaccine and developed a typhus vaccine for the Armed Forces, carried out fundamental research in blood substitutes and in aviation medi-

cine, conducted toxicological studies on new explosives and synthetic substances, and synthesized and clinically tested antimalarial drugs. After the war Dyer's efforts led to the recognition of the chronic diseases as a major public health problem. He directed the expansion of the National Institute of Health into one of the world's leading institutions for research in virtually all diseases of humans. Under him, it became the National Institutes of Health (NIH) in 1948. He organized the NIH Division of Research Grants and Fellowships. The work of this division in allocating Federal financial assistance to public and private nonprofit scientific institutions greatly expanded the nation's medical research.

The son of a clergyman, Dyer received a B.A. degree from Kenyon College, Gambier, OH, in 1907 and an M.D. from the University of Texas in 1915. He completed his internship at Philadelphia General Hospital in 1916, when he was commissioned a medical officer in the U.S. Public Health Service. Until 1920 he engaged in various field activities, including control of bubonic plague and research in pellagra. In 1921 he became a staff member of the Hygienic Laboratory (renamed the National Institute of Health in 1930). He served as assistant director from 1922 to 1942 and concurrently from 1936 to 1942 as chief of the institute's Division of Infectious Diseases (a predecessor of the present National Institute of Allergy and Infectious Diseases). He was director, with the rank of assistant surgeon general, from 1942 to 1950. From 1950 (when he retired from the U.S. Public Health Service) to 1957, he was director of research of the Robert Winship Memorial Clinic of Emory University, Atlanta, GA. In 1948 Dyer received the Lasker Award of the American Public Health Association for his work on rickettsial diseases and for his service to the nation as director of NIH. His many other awards include the Sedgwick Memorial Medal of the American Public Health Association, the Walter Reed Medal of the American Society of Tropical Medicine, and the James D. Bruce Memorial Medal of the American College of Physicians. In his honor, the R. E. Dyer Lectureship, awarded annually to an American who has made an outstanding contribution to knowledge in some field of biomedical research, was established at NIH in 1950.

For background information *see* TYPHUS FEVER, EPIDEMIC; TYPHUS FEVER, MURINE (FLEA-BORNE) in the McGraw-Hill Encyclopedia of Science and Technology. ∎

DYSON, FREEMAN JOHN
★ American theoretical physicist

Born Dec. 15, 1923, Crowthorne, England

Dyson belonged to the class of physicists who solve problems rather than create new theories. He looked for problems in various branches of physics where a thorough mathematical analysis might lead to a useful clarification of ideas. He never worked at the same problem for more than 2 or 3 years. His main contributions were in the fields of quantum electrodynamics (1948), ferromagnetism (1955), field theory (1958), statistical mechanics (1961), the stability of matter (1966), optical telescopes (1973), and phase transitions (1976). Only quantum electrodynamics and the stability of matter will be discussed here.

Quantum electrodynamics is a theory invented about 1930 by Werner Heisenberg, Wolfgang Pauli, P. A. M. Dirac, and Enrico Fermi to describe the processes of atomic physics and electromagnetic radiation in a unified way. The theory was from the beginning enormously successful in accounting for the electric and magnetic properties of atoms, the emission and absorption of light, the creation and annihilation of electron-positron pairs, and a whole gamut of other phenomena observed in nature. The theory covers the central territory of physics, including all the familiar processes of heat, light, electricity, and chemistry; it excludes only the submicroscopic world of nuclear physics on the one hand and the astronomical world of gravitation on the other. *See* DIRAC, PAUL ADRIEN MAURICE; FERMI, ENRICO; PAULI, WOLFGANG.

In the late 1930s it was found that quantum electrodynamics, in spite of its overwhelming successes, was mathematically inconsistent. To certain reasonable questions, it gave unreasonable or absurd answers. In particular, it never was able to predict how much the energy levels of an atom would be affected by the existence of electromagnetic radiation. During the 1930s these difficulties were disturbing only to theoreticians, because the experiments were then not accurate enough to detect any of the effects for which the theory gave ambiguous answers. However, in 1946 a far more exact measurement of the energy of the hydrogen atom, made by W. E. Lamb and R. C. Retherford at Columbia University, put the theory to a decisive test. Either the theory had to explain the new observations, or it had to be discarded.

Under the pressure of the Columbia experiments, first H. A. Bethe and then Julian Schwinger, Sin-Itiro Tomonaga, and R. P. Feynman succeeded in forcing the theory to speak plainly. They were

able, without changing the theory in any essential way, to extract from it definite values for the quantities that had been measured. In all cases the theoretical and experimental numbers agreed. It was at this happy moment in 1948 that Dyson arrived on the scene. His contribution was to tidy up and systematize the newly invented techniques of calculation. Bethe, Schwinger, Tomonaga, and Feynman had used different methods, each adapted to a special situation. Dyson was able to develop these methods into a general scheme, to show that they were all consistent with one another, and to formulate uniform rules of calculation applicable to all experimental situations. The main result of Dyson's work was to show that the mathematical ambiguities inherent in quantum electrodynamics would arise only when one tried to calculate unobservable quantities. He proved that for every measurable quantity the theory would give an unambiguous and finite value. In this way the theory was preserved as a working tool, although its basic mathematical inconsistency was not cured. It has survived triumphantly all the experimental tests made subsequently. *See* BETHE, HANS ALBRECHT; FEYNMAN, RICHARD PHILLIPS; SCHWINGER, JULIAN SEYMOUR; TOMONAGA, SIN-ITIRO.

Dyson's work on the stability of matter was done in collaboration with Andrew Lenard. They gave the first mathematical proof that the electric forces between electrons and protons in ordinary matter cannot release an indefinite amount of en-

ergy; that is, the energy available in electric forces is strictly limited to a fixed amount in each atom. They also proved that matter would be unstable if the electrons did not satisfy the Pauli exclusion principle, which forbids two electrons to occupy the same quantum state. Thus the exclusion principle is both necessary and sufficient to ensure the stability of matter. This mathematical theorem perhaps explains why all particles in nature that are electrically charged and lack nuclear interactions are found to obey the exclusion principle.

Dyson was educated as a mathematician at the University of Cambridge. During World War II he was at the headquarters of the Royal Air Force Bomber Command doing operations research. After the war he went to Cornell University to study physics with Bethe and Feynman, and in 1951 he became a professor there. In 1953 he moved to the Institute for Advanced Study, Princeton, NJ. Beside working on problems of pure physics, he helped to design the Triga reactor (1956) and the Orion spaceship (1959) at General Atomic in San Diego. He was elected to the Royal Society of London in 1952, the American Academy of Arts and Sciences in 1958, and the U.S. National Academy of Sciences in 1964.

For background information *see* EXCLUSION PRINCIPLE; NUCLEAR STRUCTURE; QUANTUM ELECTRODYNAMICS in the McGraw-Hill Encyclopedia of Science and Technology. ■

EAGLE, HARRY
★ American medical scientist

Born July 13, 1905, New York, NY, U.S.A.

During a long research career Eagle worked in a number of areas. In his early studies in immunology and the serology of syphilis (1930–48) he demonstrated the mutual multivalence of diphtheria toxin and antitoxin and proved that the fixation of a component of complement to the red blood cell surface was an essential preliminary to hemolysis. There followed the finding that the seemingly paradoxical Wasserman and precipitation tests for syphilis, employing normal tissue lipids as "antigen," were strictly analogous to classical specific agglutination, precipitation, and complement-fixation reactions; and he devised a flocculation test for syphilis which gained currency in the early 1930s. His book *Laboratory Diagnosis of Syphilis* (1937) emphasized the theoretical and practical aspects of these tests. He further demonstrated the presence in syphilitic sera of antibodies to treponemata, and the immunologic relationships between cultured and pathogenic strains. The nutritional requirements for the growth of the Reiter strain were described in detail.

Beginning in 1935 Eagle demonstrated that the conversion of prothrombin to thrombin was a proteolytic reaction which could be carried out by trypsin as well as by certain proteolytic snake venoms. The conversion of fibrinogen to fibrin by thrombin was similarly described as a proteolytic reaction which could be carried out by papain and snake venoms.

Beginning in 1938, in collaboration with George O. Doak, Harry G. Steinman, and Leon B. Friedman, Eagle synthesized a large series of phenylarsenoxides and examined them for therapeutic efficacy in syphilis. By 1941 a number of compounds had been identified which seemed to merit clinical trial; but these studies were aborted with the development of penicillin. One of these compounds, *p*-arsenosophenylbutyric acid, proved to be an extraordinarily active trypanocidal agent; during World War II, therapeutic trials were initiated in a number of areas in Africa in which trypanosomiasis was endemic. The drug confirmed the laboratory findings with *Treponema equiperdum* and was effective in the treatment of early human trypanosomiasis, when organisms are in the blood and in the lymph nodes. Disappointingly, it proved to be essentially inactive in the late form of the disease, when central nervous system involvement occurs. Growing out of these studies was the demonstration that 2, 3-dimercaptoethanol (BAL), originally developed for the topical treatment of burns caused by arsenical war gases (lewisite), could be incorporated in an oily menstruum, suitable for systemic injection, which was effective in the treatment of acute arsenic poisoning. It later proved effective also in the treatment of acute mercurial and lead poisoning.

As a natural outgrowth of the chemotherapy studies, Eagle carried out (1944–55) a series of studies on antibiotics and their mode of action. The renal clearance of penicillin was described. Differences in the therapeutic effectiveness of various molecular species of penicillin were defined, as were their varying degrees of binding and inactivation by serum proteins. The therapeutic efficacy of penicillin was shown to be simply and directly related to the total time for which the drug remained at levels effective for the specific organism, regardless of the dosage and frequency of injection; too long an interval between injections permitted an interim remultiplication of the organisms, after their recovery from the effects of the drug. The extraordinary effectiveness of penicillin as a prophylactic agent and in the treatment of early stages of experimental infections contrasted sharply with its relative lack of efficacy in the later stages of experimental infections, when the organisms were multiplying only slowly. Penicillin was shown to bind to receptor sites on the surface of bacteria; and

E

the widely varying susceptibility of organisms of different species was shown to be related to differences in that binding affinity. At the lethal concentration, whether 0.01 or 100 micrograms per milliliter, all species studied were found to have bound essentially equivalent amounts of penicillin, on the order of 2000 molecules per organism, a finding confirmed many years later by J. L. Strominger in his classical studies on the inhibitory effects of penicillin on cell wall synthesis.

Beginning in 1955, Eagle's interests were directed to the culture of animal cells. He showed that the minimal essential requirements for the growth of animal cells consisted of 13 amino acids, 8 vitamins, 6 ionic species, glucose, and an unidentified factor or factors present in serum protein (dialyzed serum). This minimal essential medium sufficed for the growth in both monolayer and suspension of a wide variety of normal and malignant cells. (The identification of the many factors supplied by serum protein was in the process of being resolved in the late 1970s in a number of laboratories.) In collaboration with George Foley, Eagle proposed that the toxicity of drugs in cell culture be used as a screen for potential antitumor agents; this approach was used on a large scale by the Cancer Chemotherapy National Service Center. A series of papers dealt with various physiological aspects of cells growing in culture: the nutritional activity of vitamin cofactors and of small peptides, the high rate of protein turnover in cultured cells, the utilization of various precursors for the biosynthesis of nucleic acid bases, and differences in the metabolic utilization of various carbohydrates which could be substituted for glucose. Attention was called to a series of population-dependent requirements by various cell lines for materials (for example, asparagine, aspartic acid, cystine, glutamine, inositol, pyruvate, and serine) which the cells could in fact synthesize, but which at low population densities were lost to the medium in amounts which exceeded the biosynthetic capacity of the cells. The critical importance of the size of the amino acid pool for protein synthesis was described; and a number of studies explored the population-dependent inhibition of growth in crowded cultures of normal cells. Eagle emphasized the importance of the pH of the environment for the growth of mammalian cells, an obvious but neglected ele-

ment in the techniques of cell culture, in a series of papers in 1970.

Eagle received his M.D. degree at the Johns Hopkins University in 1927. He was a member of the faculties of the Johns Hopkins Medical School (medicine) and the University of Pennsylvania Medical School (microbiology) before he rejoined the Johns Hopkins faculty in 1936 as a member of the U.S. Public Health Service. In that capacity he was successively director of the Laboratory of Experimental Therapeutics at the Johns Hopkins School of Hygiene (1936–46), scientific director of the National Cancer Institute (1946–48), and director of the Laboratory for Cell Biology in the National Institute for Allergy and Infectious Diseases (1948–61). In 1961 he resigned from the Public Health Service to join the factulty of the Albert Einstein College of Medicine, first as chairperson of the department of cell biology and subsequently as head of the Division of Biology and director of the Cancer Center. He then served as university professor and associate dean for scientific affairs, and remained head of the Cancer Center. Eagle's diversified research interests were reflected in his active participation in a number of professional societies, including the American Society of Biological Chemists, the American Association of Immunologists, the American Society for Pharmacology and Experimental Therapeutics, the Society for Clinical Investigation, and the American Association for Cancer Research. He was elected member of the American Academy of Arts and Sciences (1960) and the National Academy of Sciences (1963).

For background information *see* BLOOD; CULTURE, TISSUE; PENICILLIN; SYPHILIS in the McGraw-Hill Encyclopedia of Science and Technology. ∎

ECCLES, SIR JOHN (CAREW)
★ Australian physiologist

***Born** Jan. 27, 1903, Melbourne, Australia*

Eccles solved the problem of how brief electrical messages or nerve impulses act across the zones of close contact between nerve cells. For this achievement he received the 1963 Nobel Prize in physiology or medicine.

A. L. Hodgkin and A. F. Huxley, who

shared this Nobel Prize with Eccles, had shown how the nerve impulse was generated by the movements of ions such as sodium and potassium across the membrane surrounding nerve fibers. Their work was done largely on the giant nerve fibers of the squid, which offer singular advantages for precise quantitative studies of electrical potentials and of ion movements. In this way, they were able to elaborate one of the most elegant and satisfying theories in biology and to convert it into mathematical terms. Their theory had great success in predicting the behavior of nerve fibers under a wide variety of experimental conditions. *See* HODGKIN, SIR ALAN (LLOYD); HUXLEY, SIR ANDREW (FIELDING).

Nerve impulses provide the means of communication within the single units or nerve cells that compose the nervous system. Largely on account of the investigations of the great Spanish histologist S. Ramón y Cajal, it was recognized that nerve cells must communicate with each other not by direct transmission of nerve impulses but by a complex transmission process of another kind that occurs across the regions of intimate contact called synapses. It was also recognized that this synaptic communication between nerve cells was of two kinds: in one kind, the receiving cell was excited to discharge an impulse or message; in the other, there was depression or inhibition of the actions of excitatory synapses.

In 1952 Eccles and his colleagues at the Australian National University inserted

extremely fine glass tubes (about 1/50,000 inch or about 500 nanometers across) filled with conducting salt solutions into nerve cells and so gained a privileged view of the synaptic actions of the other nerve cells upon the one under examination. They were able to show that the excitatory actions were due to removal of electrical charges from the surface of the nerve cell, whereas the inhibitory synapses increased this electrical charge. This latter fact was singled out for mention by the Nobel Committee as a special example of the ionic properties of the surface membrane that Hodgkin and Huxley had done so much to clarify.

Subsequent work enabled Eccles and his colleagues to define with precision the ionic mechanism normally responsible for the increase in charge on the nerve cell membrane and the consequent inhibition of this cell. The increase in charge, they found, was due to the opening up of very fine pores or holes on the membrane of the order of about 1/10,000 millionth of an inch (about 3 picometers) in diameter. This size allowed the passage of small ions with their surrounding water molecules such as chloride and potassium, but obstructed the movement across the membrane of the larger ions such as sodium with its surround of water molecules. This theory was tested by a wide variety of ions in many laboratories and was shown to be an essentially correct account of the mode of operation of this fundamental nerve action. The excitatory synapses differ in that they cause the membrane of the cell to have rather larger pores—in fact, at least twice the size—so that sodium ions pass through very readily.

Beginning in 1963, Eccles investigated the neuronal mechanisms at higher levels of the mammalian central nervous system, always seeking to discover the synaptic excitatory and inhibitory actions. He had already proposed the important generalization that nerve cells have either excitatory or inhibitory actions at all of their contacts with other cells, none being ambivalent. These investigations were carried out initially on the dorsal column nuclei, the thalamus, and the hippocampus. During 1963–67 the mode of operation of the exquisite neural machinery of the cerebellum was solved, and the functions of the two input pathways and the five cell types were identified. Following that success, Eccles concentrated on the mode of operation of the input and output path-

ways from the cerebellum (1967–75), which opened up many complicated and extensive problems yet to be solved. Later he became immersed in the study of the cerebral cortex and in the related philosophical problems dealing with the nature of the conscious self in all its manifestations and with its interaction with the brain in special regions of the neocortex. This work was presented in four books and in a number of lectures.

The son of a teacher, Eccles graduated M.B., B.S. at the University of Melbourne in 1925. He was Victorian Rhodes scholar in 1925 and at Oxford studied for the Final Honours School in the Natural Sciences in 1927 and for his D.Phil. in 1929. He was a fellow of Exeter College, Oxford, from 1927 to 1934, and then was a fellow of Magdalen College, Oxford, from 1934 to 1937. In 1937 he returned to Australia and for 7 years directed the Research Institute at Sydney Hospital. From 1944 to 1951 he was professor of physiology at the University of Otago Medical School, Dunedin, New Zealand, and from 1952 to 1966 at the Australian National University at Canberra. In 1966–68 he was a member of the Institute for Biomedical Research in Chicago, and in 1968–75 he was distinguished professor of physiology at the State University of New York at Buffalo. He was elected a foreign member of the Max Planck Institute for Biophysical Chemistry at Göttingen. Eccles was elected a fellow of the Royal Society in 1941 and received the Royal Medal. He was president of the Australian Academy of Science from 1957 to 1961. In 1958 he was made a Knight Bachelor in the Order of the British Empire.

Eccles wrote *The Neurophysiological Basis of Mind: The Principles of Neurophysiology* (1953); *The Physiology of Nerve Cells* (1957); *The Physiology of Synapses* (1964); *The Cerebellum as a Neuronal Machine,* with J. Szentágothai and M. Ito (1967); *The Inhibitory Pathways of the Central Nervous System* (1969); *Facing Reality: Philosophical Adventures by a Brain Scientist* (1970); *The Understanding of the Brain* (1973); *The Self and Its Brain,* with K. R. Popper (1977); *The Molecular Neurobiology of the Mammalian Brain,* with P. L. McGeer and E. G. McGeer (1978); *The Human Mystery* (1979); and *Sherrington: His Life and Thought,* with W. C. Gibson (1979).

For background information *see* BIO-

ELECTRIC MODEL; SYNAPTIC TRANSMISSION in the McGraw-Hill Encyclopedia of Science and Technology. ■

ECKART, CARL
★ American physicist and geophysicist

Born May 4, 1902, St. Louis, MO, U.S.A.
Died Oct. 23, 1973, La Jolla, CA, U.S.A.

Eckart had the good fortune to be a first-year graduate student in the laboratory of Arthur H. Compton at the time (1923) of the latter's discovery of the change of wavelength of x-rays on scattering by electrons. With G. E. M. Jauncey, Eckart showed that there would be no measurable change of wavelength on reflection from crystals, since the momentum of the photon would be transferred to an entire atom or possibly to the entire lattice. Ten years later, during the investigation of discrepancies in the values of the fundamental constants, he returned to a related problem, the reflection of x-rays from ruled gratings.

In 1924–25 Eckart worked on apparent discrepancies between the theory of excitation and ionization and certain phenomena in low-voltage electric arcs. He explained some of these by demonstrating experimentally that the phenomenon was due to oscillations generated by the arc itself. With Karl T. Compton, he showed that other discrepancies were due to the electromotive force generated by differences in the concentration of free electrons in various parts of the arc plasma.

In 1925 Eckart proposed to investigate the de Broglie wave theory of quantum effects, and was awarded a National Research fellowship for this project. Temporarily diverted by W. Heisenberg's publication of matrix mechanics, he later showed the identity of this with Erwin Schrödinger's wave mechanics. During the 1930s he worked on various quantum theoretical problems, including the development of group theoretical methods for their solution. The numerical calculation of screening constants and the theoretical justification of approximations for molecular problems also occupied his attention. In 1940 he began developing a synthesis of classical continuum mechanics and thermodynamics, publishing a series of papers under the title of "Irreversible Thermodynamics." *See* BROGLIE, PRINCE LOUIS DE.

During World War II Eckart led a project on underwater sound, which made him aware of the hydrodynamic and thermodynamic problems of the oceans, as well as of the stochastic problems of three-dimensional acoustics. A series of papers on the latter was published in 1953. His studies on the effects of thermal stratification in the atmosphere and oceans were summarized in book form in 1960. Thereafter he contributed to the transformation theory of the hydrodynamic equations.

Eckart received his B.S. (1922) and M.S. (1923) at Washington University and his Ph.D. in physics (1925) at Princeton University. A National Research Council and Guggenheim fellow from 1925 to 1928, he joined the physics department of the University of Chicago in 1928. During World War II he was assistant director and later director of the Division of War Research of the University of California, and in 1946 he joined the faculty of that university as professor, serving as director of the Marine Physics Laboratory, University of California, San Diego (1946–52), and of the Scripps Institution of Oceanography (1948–65). From 1965 to 1967 he was vice-chancellor for academic affairs at the University of California, San Diego. Elected to the National Academy of Sciences in 1953 and to the American Academy of Arts and Sciences in 1959, Eckart was awarded the National Academy's Agassiz Medal in 1966 for his contributions to oceanography; he re-

ceived the American Geophysical Union's William Bowie Medal in 1972.

Eckart wrote *Hydrodynamics of Oceans and Atmospheres* (1960).

For background information *see* QUANTUM MECHANICS; THERMODYNAMIC PROCESSES; UNDERWATER SOUND in the McGraw-Hill Encyclopedia of Science and Technology. ∎

ECKERT, JOHN PRESPER
☆ American engineer

***Born** Apr. 9, 1919, Philadelphia, PA, U.S.A.*

During World War II it was realized in the U.S. War Department that the artillery firing tables for many American guns were useless in the terrain of North Africa. Firing tables were also required for the newly developed armament employed in aircraft. New tables for these and many other purposes had to be computed as rapidly as possible. To carry out this assignment, many hundreds of persons were employed by the Army to operate mechanical calculating machines, but the job seemed endless despite the urgent need. In an attempt to speed up the task, the Army also used punched-card accounting machines and two differential analyzers.

At the Moore School of Engineering at the University of Pennsylvania, a much faster method of completing the project was considered by Eckert, then a 24-year-

old graduate engineer, and John W. Mauchly, an associate professor of electrical engineering. Eckert worked on speeding up and improving the accuracy of the differential analyzer at the university. This device was speeded up 10 times, and its accuracy increased by a factor of 10. Because it was clear that further improvements with the differential analyzer would not be successful Eckert and Mauchly considered a number of ways to overcome the limitations of this device and the desk calculator.

In the course of the work with the differential analyzer, several hundred vacuum tubes were incorporated in the machine. Both Eckert and Mauchly had independently built electronic counter circuits, and this, in addition to the electronic experience with the differential analyzer, impressed them with the future potential of electronics for computing. They thought the next step might be to build an electronic integrator by simply adding or-integrating long strings of pulses with vacuum tubes. It was realized, however, that long trains of pulses to represent numbers would be inefficient, and it was decided to make an arithmetic calculator with the information in coded form as it passed from one unit to another, and to add and perform other arithmetic operations in coded form as well. Finally, it was agreed to proceed with a general-purpose digital computer so that problems other than ballistic firing tables could be studied.

A proposal giving details of the plan was presented to the U.S. Army's Ordnance Department, and this eventually resulted in a contract to build a general-purpose digital machine. Later, in 1946, the world's first electronic computer, containing over 18,000 vacuum tubes, over 10,000 capacitors, and 70,000 resistors, was completed. It was christened ENIAC (electronic numerical integrator and computer). Eckert was chief engineer and Mauchly a consultant in the project, which, considering the final achievement, represented a small investment in time and resources. An average of 40 persons was employed in the undertaking. Of these, only a dozen were engineers or scientists. ENIAC had more than 500,000 hand-soldered connections and consumed over 150 kilowatts of power—as much as a typical broadcasting station. The ENIAC equipment weighed 30 tons (27 metric tons) and filled a 30 × 50 foot (9 × 15 meter) room.

ENIAC was the prototype from which

most, other modern computers have evolved. It embodied almost all the concepts and components of today's high-speed digital computers. Its circuit design incorporated elements that become standard in computers, such as the gate (logical "and" element), the buffer (logical "or" element), and flip-flops. These were used as logic and as high-speed storage and control devices. It even had buffered and overlapped input and output, a feature not found in many later electronic computers. ENIAC could discriminate the sign of a number, compare quantities, add, subtract, multiply, divide, and extract square roots. Its accumulators combined the functions of an adding and storage unit. Central read-only memory (ROM) units, called function tables, were used. These were also subsequently used as part of the program control system. There were three function tables with a total storage of several hundred words, the exact number depending on word length. Storage was localized within many of the functioning accumulator units of the computer. Programming panels associated with the accumulators and the other panels of the machine provided a decentralized program control system, along with the master programmer panel and the centralized control possible with the three function tables, and could control the program path and provide for transfer of control and use of stored program control data. In addition to its cycling unit, 20 accumulators, and the master programmer, ENIAC included an initiating unit, a high-speed multiplier, a combined divider–square root unit, and switch-controlled function tables. To make the electronics in the machine simple and reliable, vacuum tubes were employed very conservatively and in a relatively few basic circuit combinations. The success of the project was due in large part to the careful design and calculation of the circuits, which were used in such a way as to allow for the wide manufacturing variations and the considerable deterioration of the electronic parts available at that time. ENIAC was put to work at the U.S. Army's Aberdeen Proving Ground in Maryland in August 1947, where it solved many of the trajectory problems of the atomic cannon, computed ballistics tables, and eventually was used in weather predictions, the hydrogen bomb calculations, cosmic-ray investigation, and wind tunnel design.

In 1948 Eckert became a partner in the newly formed Eckert-Mauchly Computer Corporation. By 1949 a second electronic machine, BINAC (binary automatic computer), was produced that was faster and more economical to operate than ENIAC. Instead of punched cards, BINAC used magnetic tape to store information. Many electronic tubes were replaced with germanium diodes, enabling a great reduction in size and an increase in speed. Eckert's idea of using internal storage for all of the program control was used in this machine, although he had proposed it for the EDVAC (electronic discrete variable computer) while still at the University of Pennsylvania. Remington Rand, Inc. (now Sperry Rand Corporation) acquired the Eckert-Mauchly Computer Corporation in 1950.

The third computer, following BINAC, was UNIVAC I (universal automatic computer), the first computer designed to handle business data. Its ability to deal with numbers and descriptive material made it especially attractive for commercial use. It was the first commercial computer with a stored program and built-in automatic checking circuits, and incorporated many other innovations in the field. With the completion of UNIVAC I, electronic data processing moved into high gear. The computer had developed from a laboratory curiosity to a highly practical device with a multitude of applications.

Eckert attended the University of Pennsylvania, where he graduated from the Moore School in 1941 with a B.S. in electrical engineering and obtained his M.S. in 1943. In 1964 he received an honorary D.Sc. in engineering from the university; his earlier graduate work on this degree had been interrupted by his work on ENIAC. Prior to becoming a vice-president of UNIVAC in 1955, he served successively as director of research, director of commercial engineering, and executive assistant to the general manager. Eckert was later technical adviser to the president of the UNIVAC Division. He was awarded the Horace N. Potts Medal by the Franklin Institute in 1949, and in that same year he was made a fellow of the Institute of Electrical and Electronic Engineers. In 1961 he and Mauchly received the John Scott Medal for "adding to the comfort, welfare, and happiness of mankind." This award was followed by receipt of the National Association of Manufacturers' Medal of Modern Pioneers in Creative Industry. In 1966 Eckert was the joint recipient with

Mauchly of the Harry Goode Memorial Award for "contributions to and pioneering efforts in automatic computing." In 1969 Eckert was awarded the National Medal of Science by President Lyndon Johnson. He was corecipient with Mauchly in 1973 of the Philadelphia Award for outstanding service to the Philadelphia community through their invention of ENIAC. During 1948-66 Eckert was granted 85 patents by the U.S. Patent Office. Many other patents issued since that time were for numerous electronic inventions, ranging from a supersonic method of deflecting a light beam to a complete computing system.

For background information *see* COMPUTER; DIFFERENTIAL ANALYZER; DIGITAL COMPUTER in the McGraw-Hill Encyclopedia of Science and Technology. ∎

EDELMAN, GERALD MAURICE
American biochemist

***Born** July 1, 1929, New York, NY, U.S.A.*

After completing his medical education and training, Edelman decided on a career in biochemistry and joined Henry Kunkel's laboratory at the Rockefeller University. His doctoral dissertation in 1960 was on structural studies of human immunoglobulins (gamma globulin, Ig). Gamma globulin is the part of the serum protein that contains antibody—the organism's response to foreign protein or polysaccharides. The body's antigen-antibody system is one of its defenses against infectious disease. In 1972 Edelman shared the Nobel Prize in medicine with Rodney Porter for chemical characterization of antibody. *See* PORTER, RODNEY ROBERT.

When Edelman became involved in antibody research, he joined a growing number of scientists working on the problem in the United States and in Europe. Because the IgG antibody is a large (molecular weight approximately 150,000) heterogeneous molecule, it presented enormous problems for structural analysis. If the molecule could be broken into smaller pieces that still retained their ability to combine with antigen, analysis of the molecular structure would be simpler. Porter and his colleagues in England had published several years earlier the results of their studies of antibody using proteolytic enzymes such as pepsin and papain to hydrolyze rabbit antibody. Porter proposed a one-polypeptide-chain model for antibody. Edelman and M. D. Poulik reported in 1961 on their fractionation studies of two classes of human immunoglobulin, IgG and IgM. The method they used to break the antibody into smaller pieces was to reduce the disulfide bonds and pull them apart with urea. These fractions had a molecular weight of approximately 20,000 and were quite different from those obtained by Porter. Edelman concluded from the reduction in molecular weight (as compared with the weight of the whole antibody) that IgG and IgM had more than one polypeptide chain that Porter theorized. He further determined that there were two types of chains—light and heavy.

When Edelman's results were reported, Porter's group tried to equate the pieces obtained from both types of antibody fractionation. As a result of these studies, Porter proposed the four-chain model for antibody—a heavy- and light-chain pair combined with a heavy- and light-chain pair.

Although the size of antibody fragments was now in a more manageable size range for structural analysis, the chemical heterogeneity still presented a problem for determination of their structure. The heterogeneity also raised questions about the mechanism of antibody specificities. Did they begin and end with the conformational differences assumed to exist in the polypeptide chains? Or were the specificities the result of structural differences in the molecule?

Fortunately it had been known that patients with multiple myelomas had homogeneous serum proteins that were like normal immunoglobulin. Myeloma serum proteins were fractionated, and the polypeptide chains were analyzed by starch-gel electrophoresis. The data confirmed the homogeneous character of the chains. Myeloma patients also secreted Bence-Jones proteins in their urine. Edelman suggested that the Bence-Jones proteins were polypeptide chains formed in response to the tumor and were not being included in the serum protein, for they were excreted in urine in large quantities. Confirmation of this idea was obtained by experiments which further showed that Bence-Jones proteins were similar to light chains found in normal immunoglobulin.

Edelman, B. Benacerraf, and others in the group began to prepare special antibodies by fractionating the antigen-antibody complex with free hapten, which is a partial antigen. These incomplete antigens can inhibit and often react visibly with antibodies formed from complete antigen, but cannot of themselves engender formation of antibody. The polypeptide chains of these special antibodies, analyzed by starch-gel electrophoresis, showed sharp patterns that were different for different antibodies, while analysis of normal immunoglobulin with the same technique showed diffuse patterns. This indicated that antibodies formed in response to different antigens possessed differences in their primary structure that accounted for their specificity. Classes of immunoglobulins have appeared during evolution, and an analysis of their polypeptide chains showed that while the light chains in each class were similar, the structures of the heavy chains differed from class to class, and it appears that this difference in structure confers on each class its specificity. *See* BENACERRAF, BARUJ.

In 1965 Edelman and his associates began their studies to determine the structure of human myeloma protein because it is far more homogeneous than an antibody. They elucidated the primary structure in 1969 and applied their results to antibody. Edelman theorized from their data that the antibody molecule is folded into aggregations of compact domains, each having a homologous variable (V) region or constant (C) region. Edelman's solution of the molecular structure of IgG has aided in analyzing the molecular basis for the immunological response.

Edelman's research effort then turned to the cellular mechanism involved in immune responses and to the converse-immune tolerance. He and his group began to work with lectins, plant proteins that, like an antigen, stimulate lymphocytes (white blood cells). He selected a lectin, concanavalin A (con A), and changed its structure to see what effect the change had on the lymphocyte's activities. The changes that took place showed the potential of lectins as a tool to study lymphocyte activity. The next step in the study of the immune system was to break up the lymphocytes to determine the specificity of the receptors on the cell surface. Results of these researches shed some light on the T and B cells of the thymus and other lymphoid organs, and their receptors.

Edelman's continued line of research was concerned with the general problem of the mechanisms of cellular recognition and interaction.

Edelman received a bachelor's degree from Ursinus College in Pennsylvania in 1950 and completed his medical education in 1954 at the University of Pennsylvania Medical School. He fulfilled the requirements for a Ph.D. at the Rockefeller University in 1960 and remained there as a faculty member. He was promoted to professor in 1966 and became Vincent Astor Distinguished Professor in 1970. Edelman published widely on his antibody research. In addition to the Nobel Prize in 1972, he received other prizes and awards, including the Eli Lilly Award in biological chemistry in 1965 and the Albert Einstein Commemorative Award in 1975.

For background information *see* ANTIBODY; ANTIGEN; IMMUNOGLOBULIN in the McGraw-Hill Encyclopedia of Science and Technology. ∎

EDGERTON, HAROLD EUGENE
☆ American electrical engineer

Born Apr. 6, 1903, Fremont, NE, U.S.A.

Edgerton developed the electronic flash lamp and pioneered its use in stroboscopic and high-speed photography. In later years he designed underwater cameras, and sonar equipment for geological and archeological exploration beneath the ocean floor.

Edgerton's interest in electrical machinery was initiated when he was working summers at the Nebraska Light and Power Company (Aurora, NE) while still in high school. At that time, technicians had no way of examining rapidly rotating or vibrating components of generators and other machinery, and could often only guess at the cause of troubles that arose. It occurred to Edgerton, when he was a graduate student, that one could photograph a moving component by flashing a brilliant light at intervals in synchronism with its rotation or vibration period, thus making it appear stationary.

In 1928 this idea led Edgerton to begin work on the electronic flash lamp, a device in which electrical discharges would produce light flashes of extremely short duration and high intensity, either singly or at controllable intervals. To store the energy required to produce the necessary peak power, Edgerton and his associates started with mercury-filled flash lamps. They developed circuitry which enabled them to control the intervals between the flashes, as well as the intensity and duration (as short as 1 microsecond).

Edgerton's devices, announced in 1931, were quickly recognized by the National Geographic Society, which used them to make stop-motion photographs of bats and hummingbirds in flight. Although engineers almost immediately began using his stroboscope to examine machinery in motion, Edgerton felt that his invention was not sufficiently appreciated, and he therefore began holding demonstrations for scientists, industrialists, and the general public, and inter-

ested the photographer G. Mili in his work. Edgerton's photograph of the splash of a milk drop (1938) and Mili's stop-motion photographs of dancers and athletes brought worldwide attention to stroboscopic photography, and it soon became a basic tool in science and industry. Over the years, Edgerton's distinctive single- and multiple-exposure stop-motion photographs of such subjects as birds, athletes, shattering light bulbs, and bullets piercing apples and slicing playing cards continued to receive wide dissemination.

The electronic flash lamp also revolutionized high-speed motion picture photography. Edgerton developed a camera in which a flash lamp was synchronized to flash for each frame of film by means of an electrical contactor driven by the sprocket moving the film. This made possible uniform motion of the film at speeds as high as 6000 frames per second.

During World War II Edgerton and his associates adapted stroboscopic photography to nighttime aerial reconnaissance. In the early 1950s Edgerton designed a camera for photographing nuclear explosions, whose intense light makes conventional cameras useless. The camera had a shutter, triggered by circuitry similar to that of the electronic flash lamp, which allowed light to pass through it for a period as short as 1 microsecond.

In 1958 Edgerton perfected a method of photographing shock waves generated by rockets and aircraft in flight. In this technique, light from an electronic flash lamp is reflected from a Scotchlite screen and is refracted by shock waves, causing shadows on the film.

Beginning in 1953, Edgerton became involved in underwater exploration. He designed watertight cameras with electronic flash lamps, capable of operating in the deepest parts of the ocean, and worked with J.-Y. Cousteau in explorations of the sea floor. He also assisted with cameras and lighting equipment for the bathyscaphes *FNRS III*, *Trieste*, and *Archimede*. To position his underwater camera, Edgerton attached to it a pinger, a device resembling the electronic flash lamp but emitting sound instead of light. Sound waves emitted from the pinger and reflected from the ocean floor indicated the distance of the camera from the bottom.

Observing that the pinger's sound pulses often penetrated the ocean floor, Edgerton began to use it for seismic

probes beneath the bottom in shallow water, and built another device, the boomer, to probe beneath the ocean floor in deeper water. Previously, since ordinary sonar does not penetrate the ocean floor, explosive blasts had been required for these investigations. The boomer generated short pulses of sound—8 megawatts for 0.5 millisecond—which could penetrate the sediment and all but the hardest rock beneath the bottom. The sonic echoes were recorded on an instrument which generated a seismic profile, a vertical cross section of the layers of sediment and rock. The device was used for geological investigations of such formations as the Puerto Rico Trench, and for underwater archeological explorations and for location of submerged objects such as shipwrecks.

Edgerton received his B.S. from the University of Nebraska in 1925, and spent a year at the machine-testing laboratory of General Electric Company before beginning graduate study at the Massachusetts Institute of Technology (MIT), where he obtained his M.S. in 1927 and D.Sc. in 1931. In 1927 he also joined the staff of the electrical engineering department at MIT as a research assistant, and remained there for the rest of his career, attaining the rank of professor in 1948. He became institute professor emeritus in 1966. In 1934 Edgerton entered into partnership with K. J. Germeshausen and H. Grier. In 1947 the partnership was incorporated as Edgerton, Germeshausen and Grier Inc., later changing its name to EG&G Inc. The firm became a major element in the world's electronics industry. Edgerton received numerous awards, including the Medal of the Royal Photographic Society of London (1936), the Modern Pioneers Award of the National Association of Manufacturers (1940), the Potts Medal (1941) and the Albert A. Michelson Medal (1969) of the Franklin Institute, the U.S. Medal of Freedom (1946), the U.S. Camera Achievement Gold Medal of U.S. Camera Magazine (1951), the E. I. du Pont Gold Medal of the Society of Motion Picture and Television Engineers (1962), the Morris E. Leeds Award of the Institute of Electrical and Electronics Engineers (1965), the David Richardson Medal of the Optical Society of America (1968), the John Oliver La Gorce Gold Medal of the National Geographic Society (1968), the Holley Medal of the American Society of Mechanical Engineers (1973), and the

National Medal of Science (1973). He was elected to numerous societies and academies, including the American Academy of Arts and Sciences (1956), the National Academy of Sciences (1964), and the National Academy of Engineering (1966).

Edgerton was an author of over 140 technical articles. He wrote *Flash! Seeing the Unseen by Ultra High-Speed Photography*, with J. R. Killian, Jr. (1939; 2d ed. 1954), which was revised as *Moments of Vision* (1979); and *Electronic Flash, Strobe* (1970; paper 1979).

For background information *see* SONAR; STROBOSCOPIC PHOTOGRAPHY; UNDERWATER PHOTOGRAPHY in the McGraw-Hill Encyclopedia of Science and Technology. ∎

EDLUND, MILTON CARL
★ American physicist

Born Dec. 13, 1924, Jamestown, NY, U.S.A.

While designing the nuclear reactor at Indian Point, NY, Edlund conceived the spectral shift control principle, an improved method for controlling reactors. For his work in reactor development, he received the U.S. Atomic Energy Commission's E. O. Lawrence Award in 1965.

During work on the first round of pressurized-water reactors, it became clear that their performance could be substantially improved by eliminating the use of neutron-absorbing control rods for the reactivity shim required to offset burnup of fuel and buildup of fission products. Control rods reduced fuel utilization by absorbing neutrons that could otherwise by absorbed in fertile material; they distorted the power distribution in the reactor core, thus limiting the maximum power capability of a given core and primary coolant system.

By using as moderator a mixture of heavy and light water, the proportions of which could be changed as the reactor was operated, Edlund effected a substantial improvement in both neutron economy and power. The reactivity of the close-packed lattices typical of pressurized-water reactor cores can be changed by the addition of heavy water, primarily because heavy water is not as effective a moderator as light water. The slowing-down power of light water is seven times greater than that of heavy water, and thus the resonance neutron flux and resonance absorptions are increased by the addition of heavy water. Since the ratio of the effective absorption cross sections of fertile material to fuel is larger in the resonance energy region than at thermal energies, the addition of heavy water to the moderator decreases reactivity. Thus, by shifting the neutron spectrum toward the resonance region by having a high concentration of D_2O at the beginning of operation with a new core, the fertile material acts as a control rod—except that the neutrons that would normally be lost to the fuel cycle are now producing new fuel.

The principle of spectral shift control was confirmed by an extensive series of critical and exponential experiments performed at the Babcock and Wilcox Company's Critical Experiment Laboratory in Lynchburg, VA, under contract to the U.S. Atomic Energy Commission.

Among Edlund's later contributions were the invention and preliminary design of fuel assemblies for use in light-water reactors, as a result of which near-breeding of nuclear fuel can be achieved. These assemblies made it possible to reduce significantly the requirements for both uranium ore and enrichment capacity. This work was supported by the Electric Power Research Institute, Palo Alto, CA, and the U.S. Department of Energy.

Edlund majored in mathematics and physics at the University of Michigan, where he received his B.S. and M.S. in 1948 and his Ph.D. in nuclear science and engineering in 1966. He did additional graduate work at the University of Tennessee and Princeton University. Starting work at the Oak Ridge National Laboratory in 1948 as a mathematical physicist, he became deeply interested in neutron diffusion and the design of nuclear fission chain reactors. Within a short time he had collected and organized the major theoretical work done at the various laboratories of the Manhattan Project during World War II. This led to his coauthorship, with Samuel Glasstone, of the first authoritative textbook on nuclear reactor theory, *The Elements of Nuclear Reactor Theory* (1951). During this period he also taught reactor theory at the Oak Ridge School of Reactor Technology and contributed to several reactor development projects, including the aqueous homogeneous reactor and the aircraft nuclear propulsion projects. In 1955 Edlund joined the Babcock and Wilcox Company, where he was successively manager of physics and mathematics, manager of development, and assistant division manager of the company's atomic energy division, and where he was in charge of the nuclear design and development of the Indian Point and the NS *Savannah* reactors. In 1966 Edlund became professor of nuclear engineering at the University of Michigan. He was a planning consultant to the Atomic Energy Commission in 1967–68, and cofounder and executive vice-president of the Nuclear Assurance Corporation, Atlanta, GA, in 1968–70. Subsequently he returned to academia as chairperson of the nuclear engineering department of the Virginia Polytechnic Institute and State University. In 1974 he became the first director of the University Center for Energy Research. In 1977 he returned to teaching and research. He was elected to the National Academy of Engineering in 1976.

For background information *see* REACTOR, NUCLEAR in the McGraw-Hill Encyclopedia of Science and Technology. ∎

EDSALL, JOHN TILESTON
★ American biochemist

Born Nov. 3, 1902, Philadelphia, PA, U.S.A.

Edsall's scientific research was concerned with the structure and function of proteins. As a medical student at Harvard in 1924, he undertook research on the physiology of muscle with A. C. Redfield. Edsall continued work on the biochemistry of muscle as a student in Cambridge in 1924–26 in the department headed by Frederick Hopkins. On his return to Harvard Medical School, Edsall began the study of the muscle protein myosin from beef muscle in the laboratory of Edwin J. Cohn, a leader in the study of the physical chemistry of proteins. In 1928 Alexander von Muralt came from Switzerland to spend 2 years in the laboratory. He discovered that Edsall's myosin (actomyosin) preparations showed intense birefringence when subjected to mild shearing stress in flow. This led to a joint research by von Muralt and Edsall in which they demonstrated that actomyosin is a highly elongated structure, readily oriented in a velocity gradient, and that it is primarily responsible for the well-known birefringence of the muscle fiber. They were led to infer that actomyosin plays a fundamental role in the process of contraction in muscle—a hypothesis that was abundantly confirmed by later work.

During the 1930s Cohn, Edsall, Jeffries Wyman, J. P. Greenstein, T. L. McMeekin, and others undertook a comprehensive study of the physical chemistry of amino acids and peptides and the relation of their properties to those characteristic of the much larger protein molecules found in nature. Earlier, E. Q. Adams in the United States and Niels Bjerrum in Denmark had demonstrated that amino acids, even when electrically neutral, are dipoles of very high electric moment; compared to most organic compounds, amino acids have very high melting points, which are best explained by interactions between electri-

cally charged groups in the crystal lattice. The ionization constants of amino acids in solution also point to the type of structure known as a dipolar ion (zwitterion). For instance, the true formula for glycine, the simplest of the amino acids, should be written $^+H_3N \cdot CH_2 \cdot COO^-$ rather than $H_2N \cdot CH_2 \cdot COOH$. The group at Harvard realized the implications of this structure for other properties of amino acids, peptides, and proteins. Wyman demonstrated that the dielectric constants of their solutions are extraordinarily high, surpassing those of all other compounds. J. L. Oncley, who joined the laboratory in 1936, made important dielectric constant studies on proteins. Moreover, these molecules, with two widely separated centers of charge, exert powerful electrostatic forces on neighboring molecules, including those of the surrounding solvent. The apparent molal volumes and heat capacities of amino acids and peptides in water are also smaller than those of most organic molecules because of electrostriction of the solvent.

Edsall studied the vibrational structure of these compounds by Raman spectroscopy in aqueous solution. He showed that amino, carboxyl, and other ionizable groups show characteristic vibrational frequencies which are markedly different for the ionized and un-ionized form of each of these groups. By means of such spectra, therefore, it was possible to identify the state of ionization of various groups in amino acid and peptide molecules and to show the simultaneous presence of positive and negative charges in different portions of the molecule.

The dipolar ion structure of amino acids and peptides also profoundly influences their solubility. Like most inorganic salts, the amino acids in general are far more soluble in water than in organic solvents; glycine, for example, is about 2500 times more soluble in water than in ethanol. Cohn, McMeekin, and Edsall showed that such relative solubility values can be systematically correlated with the structure of the molecule. The presence of electric charges favors solubility in water and other media of high dielectric constant, whereas nonpolar side chains favor solubility in media of low dielectric constant. Quantitative rules relating the structure of the solute to its relative solubility in water and in organic solvents were formulated on this basis. George Scatchard and John G. Kirkwood, who were both in the chemistry department at

the Massachusetts Institute of Technology, collaborated closely with the workers at Harvard Medical School in this work. They developed an important extension of the Debye-Hückel theory of interionic attraction to describe quantitatively the interactions of these dipolar ions with ions and with other dipolar ions. *See* SCATCHARD, GEORGE.

About 1940 Cohn, Edsall, Oncley, and their associates returned to intensive studies on proteins, which were greatly accelerated and expanded by the urgent practical need for blood plasma, and the proteins derived from it, in World War II. With strong support from the Office of Scientific Research and Development, Cohn instituted a very large program for fractionation of human blood plasma proteins to obtain purified serum albumin, gamma globulin, fibrinogen, thrombin, and other products needed for clinical use. Selective precipitation with ethanol at low temperature with suitable variation of pH and ionic strength permitted the large-scale separation in purified form of all these and other proteins. Cohn was the major director of this program, which came to include a large number of scientific workers, as well as many clinicians who were involved in the testing of the resulting products. Apart from their practical significance, these studies led to a great increase in the knowledge of blood plasma and to the separation of various proteins of great scientific interest which had not been characterized before, such as the alpha and beta lipoproteins and the iron-binding protein, transferrin. Edsall's major concern during these years was the study of proteins involved in blood clotting, especially fibrinogen, prothrombin, and thrombin.

After 1945 Edsall concentrated on basic studies of the physical chemistry of proteins, especially blood proteins. He made extensive use of light-scattering measurements to determine the size and shape of protein molecules and the nature of their interactions with one another and with smaller ions and molecules. After the death of Cohn in 1953, Edsall moved to the Biological Laboratories of Harvard University in Cambridge, where he continued this work and also greatly extended his studies on the Raman spectroscopy of amino acids, peptides, and related molecules. He also studied the binding of metallic ions to amino acids and peptides.

From 1959 Edsall devoted his research primarily to the enzyme carbonic anhydrase, from red blood cells; this enzyme molecule which contains an atom of zinc as an essential constituent, catalyzes the hydration of carbon dioxide and the dehydration of carbonic acid, and is of fundamental importance for the transport of carbon dioxide in the blood. E. E. Rickli in Edsall's laboratory soon demonstrated that human red blood cells contain at least two distinct enzymes, both having carbonic anhydrase activity; independent work in two other laboratories also demonstrated the same fact by different techniques, and a third minor enzyme was discovered as well. Subsequent researches in Edsall's laboratory were devoted to the further characterization of the conditions governing the activity of these enzymes and a study of their unusual physical properties, particularly their optical rotation and rotatory dispersion, which demonstrate strong interactions between the aromatic amino acid residues and the main framework of the molecule. His students, including B. H. Gibbons, S. L. Bradbury, P. L. Whitney, and R. G. Khalifah, did important work on the kinetics and chemical modification of these enzymes.

From 1970 on, Edsall worked extensively on the history of biochemistry and molecular biology. He served as chair of a committee of the American Academy of Arts and Sciences that deals with this subject. From 1975 to 1979 he was director (with Whitfield J. Bell, Jr.) of the Survey of Sources for the History of Biochemistry and Molecular Biology, which gathered autobiographical material from several hundred scientists in this area, both American and foreign. The Survey also actively promoted the collection and preservation of important correspondence, notebooks, and other unpublished materials of important scientists, in suitable archives.

Edsall received his A.B. in 1923 and his M.D. in 1928 from Harvard University, where he was an instructor in biochemical sciences in 1928–32 and then professor of biochemistry. He was a member of the U.S. National Commission for UNESCO during 1950–56. He was elected to the American Academy of Arts and Sciences in 1937, to the National Academy of Sciences in 1951, and to the American Philosophical Society in 1955. He received the Passano Foundation Award in 1966 and the Willard Gibbs Medal of the American Chemical Society in 1972.

In 1943 Edsall became coeditor of *Ad-*

vances in Protein Chemistry, a serial review publication, of which 32 volumes were published as of 1978. From 1958 through 1967 he was editor in chief of the *Journal of Biological Chemistry.* He wrote *Proteins, Amino Acids, and Peptides,* with Edwin J. Cohn (1943), and *Biophysical Chemistry,* with Jeffries Wyman (vol. 1, 1958).

For background information *see* AMINO ACID; BLOOD; PROTEIN in the McGraw-Hill Encyclopedia of Science and Technology. ∎

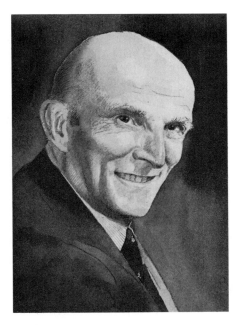

EDWARDS, SIR GEORGE
English aeronautical engineer

Born July 9, 1908, Highams Park, Essex, England

Edwards directed the design of numerous military and civilian aircraft, many of which represented important advances.

Between 1945 and 1953, as chief designer at Vickers-Armstrongs Limited, he was head of the design team responsible for the Viking, the Valetta, the Varsity, the Viscount, and the Valiant bomber. Between 1953 and 1960, as managing director of Vickers-Armstrongs, he continued to be responsible for the Vanguard, VC 10, and TSR 2. In 1961, as executive director of British Aircraft Corporation and overall technical leader of the aircraft design teams, Edwards initiated the BAC One-Eleven short-haul jet airliner, the first joint product of the corporation. He played a prominent part in the negotiations with Aerospatiale of France which

led in 1962 to the Concorde supersonic airliner, and he subsequently played a continuing and leading role in its vast program. He later had a prominent part in developing the Anglo-French Jaguar tactical support and advanced trainer aircraft, and the Anglo-German-Italian Panavia Tornado MRCA (multi-role combat aircraft). At the time of his retirement in 1975, British Aircraft Corporation factories, with a workforce of 35,000, were engaged in working on an extensive series of advanced civil and military aircraft, and missile and space hardware programs.

Edwards attended South West Essex Technical College and the University of London, from which he received the B.Sc. degree in engineering in 1935. During 1928–35 he gained general engineering and civil engineering experience. He joined the design staff of Vickers-Armstrongs in 1935 and was appointed experimental manager there in 1940. He served on its board of directors from 1955 to 1960. He was executive director, aircraft, of British Aircraft Corporation from 1960, shortly after its founding, until 1972, and chairperson from 1963 until 1975. He served as president of the Royal Aeronautical Society in 1957–58 and vice-president of the Royal Society of Arts in 1958–61. In 1966 he was installed as pro-chancellor of the University of Surrey. He received the George Taylor Gold Medal of the Royal Aeronautical Society (1948), the British Gold Medal for Aeronautics of the Royal Aeronautical Society (1952), the Daniel Guggenheim Gold Medal of the Society of Automotive Engineers (1959), the Air League Founders Medal (1969), the Albert Gold Medal of the Royal Society of Arts (1972), and the Silver Jubilee Medal of the Institute of Sheet Metal Engineering (1974). He was made a commander of the Order of the British Empire (1952), a knight (1957), and a member of the Order of Merit (1971). He received honorary degrees from Southampton University (1962), Salford University (1967), Cranfield Institute of Technology (1970), London University (1970), Bristol University (1973), The City University (1975), University of Stirling (1979), and University of Surrey (1979). He was elected an honorary fellow of the American Institute of Aeronautics and Astronautics (1959), and the Royal Aeronautical Society (1960), a fellow of the Royal Society of London (1968), and an honorary fellow of the Institution of Mechanical Engineers (1976).

He was made pro-chancellor emeritus of the University of Surrey in 1979.

For background information *see* AERONAUTICAL ENGINEERING; AIRFRAME; AIRPLANE in the McGraw-Hill Encyclopedia of Science and Technology. ∎

EIGEN, MANFRED
☆ German chemist

Born May 9, 1927, Bochum, Germany

Eigen and his colleagues devised a battery of approaches to the study of high-speed chemical reactions, collectively known as relaxation techniques. These methods, together with the flash photolysis approach developed by the British chemists R. G. W. Norrish and George Porter, provided the basis for the rapid expansion of understanding of different types of fast reactions that began about 1950. Eigen, Norrish, and Porter shared the 1967 Nobel Prize in chemistry. *See* NORRISH, RONALD GEORGE WREYFORD; PORTER, GEORGE.

Prior to the 1950s, because of the limitations of methods available for the investigation of very fast reactions, such as those employing flame-front, shock-tube, or fast mixing techniques, the lower limit of observable reaction time was in the tens of milliseconds. Flash photolysis, which came into use about 1949, proved to be a great advance and brought the limit of reaction measurements to below a millisecond. This approach, however, was found to be most fruitful in dealing with reactions of highly excited chemical states far from any equilibrium point. Eigen announced in 1954 the first of a series of methods for producing and measuring high-speed reactions in states relatively close to equilibrium, thus opening up many fields of chemistry to direct observation for the first time.

All the relaxation techniques devised by Eigen proceed by upsetting the balance of a chemical system near equilibrium; measurements are made as the system "relaxes" to a new equilibrium state. The reactants to be studied are commonly dissolved in an electrically conductive solution. The perturbation could be either single or periodic, according to the particular technique, and could take the form of a brief electrical pulse or an abrupt change in temperature, hydrostatic pressure, or electrical field intensity. Measurements were made either spectrophotometrically or conductometrically.

Eigen's own investigations employing relaxation techniques include the following: highly accurate measurements of ionic dissociation and recombination in pure liquid water (1955, with DeMaeyer); studies of diffusion-controlled protolytic reactions in aqueous solutions (1955, with Schoen); a paper introducing the widely useful Joule heating-temperature jump technique (1959, with Czerlinski); the elucidation of the discrete reaction steps causing sound absorption in 2-2 electrolyte solutions (with Tamm, 1962); investigations of the kinetics of keto-enol tautomerism (with Ilgenfritz and Kruse, 1965).

Eigen turned his attention in the 1960s to the application of relaxation techniques to the complex chemical events of molecular biology. Relaxation techniques have yielded important results in fields as diverse as radiation chemistry, enzyme-catalyzed reactions, and transformation mechanisms of polynucleotides.

Later, Eigen became interested in questions about the origin of life. He and his colleagues endeavored to develop a theory of self-organization and to test some predictions of the theory by test-tube experiments using enzymic and nucleic acid systems isolated from phages and bacteria.

Eigen received early training in physics and chemistry at the University of Göttingen and after service in World War II obtained a doctorate in natural science there in 1951. After a year (1951–52) as an assistant at the university's Institute for Physical Chemistry, he joined the staff of the Max Planck Institute for Physical Chemistry, Göttingen, in 1953. He became the institute's director in 1964 and thereafter its chairperson. He was elected a foreign honorary member of the American Academy of Arts and Sciences in 1964; the U.S. National Academy of Sciences in 1966; the Royal Danish Academy of Sciences in 1971; the Royal Society, London, in 1973; and the U.S.S.R. Academy of Sciences in 1976. In addition to the Nobel Prize, Eigen was the recipient of the Otto Hahn Prize for Chemistry and Physics (1962), the Linus Pauling Medal of the American Chemical Society (1967), the Keilin Medal of the Biochemical Society of Great Britain (1969), the Order pour le Mérite (1973), the Faraday Medal of the Chemical Society, London (1977), and many other international awards.

For background information *see* FAST CHEMICAL REACTIONS in the McGraw-Hill Encyclopedia of Science and Technology. ∎

ELKIND, MORTIMER MURRAY
★ American biophysicist

Born Oct. 25, 1922, New York, NY, U.S.A.

Why is radiation (particulate and electromagnetic) lethal to living matter? Where in a cell are the lethal effects of radiation registered? Can cells tolerate some degree of radiation damage and, if so, can they repair such damage? These and other questions stimulated Elkind's imagination when he turned from pure physics to biology in 1953.

Effects of solar radiation aside, interest in radiobiology in the present-day sense started in 1895 with W. Roentgen's discovery of x-rays. From the outset, biological and physical scientists inquired how matter is affected by radiation. It soon became apparent, even from these early observations, that radiation is an efficient producer of major biological effects. Cell viability and growth, for example, can be suppressed by the deposition of an amount of radiant energy sufficient to raise the average temperature of a cell by only a fraction of a degree. Indeed, animals exposed to quite moderate doses of 500 to 1000 rad (5 to 10 gray) can be killed with essentially no attendant increases in their body temperatures due to the exposure. Facts such as these, plus the discrete and random nature of radiation, led in the 1920s to the complementary concepts of hits and targets. According to these ideas, small doses of radiation produce dramatic effects—in cells, for example—because relatively large amounts of energy are absorbed in local areas (the hits) in sites or structures (the targets) whose integrity is essential for coordinated function. As a physicist, Elkind was attracted to these ideas since they include the elegant feature of permitting the derivation of simple mathematical relationships between cause and effect.

Starting in 1953 with studies of the lethal effects of x-rays and alpha particles in yeast cells, Elkind soon became aware of the practical limitations of formal hit-target theory. While some inactivation schemes could be shown to fit a given set of data better than others, survival curve analysis alone lacked the elements of uniqueness needed for the unambiguous specification of target number or target size. Moreover, this approach usually gave little insight into where and what the targets are.

To extract more biological information from survival measurements, Elkind turned first to experiments involving ultraviolet light and x-rays, and later to studies of radiation damage repair. Since the 254-nanometer line from a low-pressure mercury discharge is absorbed preferentially in nucleic acids, sequential exposures involving x-rays and ultraviolet light yield insights into effects produced in these critical molecules. However, Elkind's most significant contributions came from his studies of damage repair. In ad-

dition to their bearing on the mechanism of damage registration, as well as repair, these studies were important because they were performed with mammalian cells and consequently had a greater relevance to effects in humans than might be expected from experiments with microorganisms.

By the late 1950s the pioneering work of T. T. Puck and his associates had brought the art of the culturing of mammalian cells to the point where single-cell experiments could be performed with a quantitation equivalent to that available with bacteria and yeasts. This so impressed Elkind that he dropped microorganisms in favor of mammalian cells in spite of the greater costs involved and the considerably longer cycle times from the beginning to the end of each experiment. Not only did he change his experimental format, but at this juncture Elkind also altered his thinking about hit-target concepts by deciding to pursue their more general rather than specific implications. *See* PUCK, THEODORE THOMAS.

In 1956 Puck and Philip Marcus published the first single-cell survival curve determined with mammalian cells. They used a line of cells derived originally from a human cervical carcinoma. In a general way this curve had features typical of survival curves measured with bacteria and yeasts. One feature of particular interest to Elkind, however, was the fact that the curve had a threshold. In the region of small doses the curve became progressively steeper. This characteristic meant that damage had to be accumulated for a lethal effect to be registered. From this it followed that, regardless of the particular target structure involved, a surviving cell is a sublethally damaged cell and, hence, a surviving cell may repair such damage. Elkind next devised a test for the repair of sublethal damage. The test was quite specific and yet simple since it consisted only of a second dose of radiation. If sublethal damage is repaired in time after a first dose, this can be demonstrated by irradiating surviving cells a second time to see if between the doses they have resumed a capacity for sublethal damage. If sublethal damage is repaired, the net survival after dose fractionation should be higher than that for the same total dose given as one exposure. This indeed was what Elkind and his associates observed, as well as a number of other features later shown to be due to other important properties of mammalian cells.

The initial recovery experiments of Elkind and his associates were published in 1959. They have been confirmed in microorganisms, plant cells, many types of cultured mammalian cells, and normal and malignant mammalian cells grown and assayed in animal bodies. Elkind developed theoretical extensions of his results to the radiation responses of normal and malignant tissues; his predictions have been borne out many times in the observations of others.

Elkind did his undergraduate work in mechanical engineering at the Cooper Union School of Engineering, New York, where he received a B.M.E. in 1943. Following service as a naval officer during World War II, he returned to engineering in 1946. In 1949 he was awarded a master's degree in mechanical engineering from the Brooklyn Polytechnic Institute, and then he continued his graduate study at the Massachusetts Institute of Technology, where he was awarded an M.S. in electrical engineering in 1951 and a Ph.D. in physics in 1953. He then spent 9 months at the Donner Laboratory, University of California, Berkeley, where he was first introduced to biological work. In 1954 he joined the National Cancer Institute, Bethesda, MD, where he pursued biophysical research for 15 years. In 1969 he started a 4-year period as a senior scientist at the Brookhaven National Laboratory, Upton, NY, although for the latter 2 years of this period he was a guest scientist in the Medical Research Council's Experimental Radiopathology Unit at Hammersmith Hospital, London. Returning to the United States in 1973, Elkind became a senior biophysicist at the Argonne National Laboratory, in Illinois. In 1974 he also became a professor of radiology at the University of Chicago. He received the E. O. Lawrence Award from the U.S. Atomic Energy Commission in 1967, the Superior Service Award from the Department of Health, Education, and Welfare in 1969, the L. H. Gray Award from the International Commission on Radiation Units and Measurements in 1977, and the E. W. Bertner Award from the M. D. Anderson Hospital and Tumor Institute in 1979. Elkind was a special fellow of the National Cancer Institute from 1971 to 1973.

For background information *see* RADIATION BIOLOGY; RADIATION CYTOLOGY; RADIATION INJURY (BIOLOGY) in the McGraw-Hill Encyclopedia of Science and Technology. ∎

ELSASSER, WALTER MAURICE
☆ American geophysicist

Born Mar. 20, 1904, Mannheim, Germany

Elsasser's studies of the makeup and movement of the Earth's core led to his formulation of the "dynamo" theory of the permanent terrestrial magnetic field. According to this model, the presence of a magnetic field H_1 in the core will result in motion of matter V_1 perpendicular to the field, which in turn will give rise to a field H_2 producing motion V_2, and so on in self-sustaining action. For this and other work, Elsasser was awarded the Bowie Medal of the American Geophysical Union in 1959.

The origin of the Earth's permanent magnetic field has been a prime question in the study of geophysical phenomena. In the past, efforts to account for the presence of the "permanent" field included explanations based on (1) the supposed ferromagnetism of the Earth's interior and (2) circulation of electrical currents in the interior. The second explanation divided again into (*a*) production of electrons by circulating matter impinging on crossed thermal gradients in the magnetic field, and (*b*) a dynamo hypothesis, such as the one outlined above. Neither theory, however, was elaborated to the point of constituting a plausible model; each suffered from severe internal contradictions.

Elsasser assumed that if the Earth's metallic core were in convective motion, it might obey the same laws of cosmic magnetohydrodynamics that govern, for example, the ionized gases in the Sun's magnetic field. He first attacked the phenomenon of the secular variation, reasoning that any theory of the permanent field would also have to explain this slight, cumulative change in the field. Assuming the core to be in thermally induced convection, Elsasser's formulation of the magnetohydrodynamics of a spherical conductor furnished quantitative results in agreement with the observed secular variation. However, it was still necessary to account for the self-sustaining nature of the permanent field.

While Elsasser was conducting these researches, evidence emerged for the concept of the coexistence of toroidal and poloidal modes in the Earth's magnetic field. Using this information, he contributed to the development of a model of the Earth as represented by an assembly of concentric spheres, in mutual electrical contact and rotating relative to each other. In this model, the magnetic field is amplified by the nonuniform rotation as magnetic torques are transmitted outward from the core to the surface.

It still remained to furnish an explanation of the regularity of the permanent field; the dynamo model thus far would not necessarily produce a field even partially regular. It appeared that there must be some force that regulated and ordered the amplification effect of the magnetic field, relative to the axis of rotation of the core. Elsasser's theory called for the formation of eddies near the boundary layers of the revolving spheres, very similar to the major perturbations of the atmosphere. His studies of atmospheric circulation prepared him for the conclusion that the same force could be instrumental in ordering both varieties of eddy—namely, the Coriolis effect, the force producing a deflection toward the center of a rotating mass.

Elsasser's dynamo model represented the Earth's permanent field as initially quite weak, building up very gradually to its present strength. It provided a full explanation of the permanence of the field and the presence of the secular variation. Moreover, it has led subsequent investigators to an explanation of observed fluctuations in the Earth's rate of rotation. His work has been subsequently independently confirmed and elaborated upon by H. Takeuchi, E. C. Bullard, and others. *See* BULLARD, SIR EDWARD (CRISP).

After early work in nuclear physics, Elsasser took up atmospheric studies and devised a graphic method of calculating spontaneous emission of infrared by various gases in the atmosphere. He did research in magnetohydrodynamics and terrestrial magnetism. His book, *The Physical Foundation of Biology* (1958), is an inductive investigation of the relationship between the biological sciences and the quantum-mechanical concepts of theoretical physics.

Elsasser took his Ph.D. in physics in 1927 at Göttingen and subsequently taught at Frankfurt and the Sorbonne. In 1936 he went to the California Institute of Technology, becoming an American citizen in 1940. After taking part in war work and industrial research, he was professor of physics at the University of Pennsylvania from 1947 to 1950 and at the University of Utah from 1950 to 1958. Then he became professor of theoretical physics at the Scripps Institution of Oceanography and the University of California at La Jolla. In 1962 he was named professor of geophysics at Princeton University. Elsasser was research professor at the University of Maryland from 1968 until his retirement in 1974, at which time he joined the Johns Hopkins University as an adjunct professor. He was elected to the National Academy of Sciences in 1957.

In addition to work already mentioned, Elsasser wrote two more books and numbers of scientific papers on the relation of biology to physics.

For background information *see* GEOMAGNETISM; MAGNETOHYDRODYNAMICS in the McGraw-Hill Encyclopedia of Science and Technology. ∎

ELVEHJEM, CONRAD ARNOLD
American biochemist

Born May 27, 1901, McFarland, WI, U.S.A.
Died July 27, 1962, Madison, WI, U.S.A.

Elvehjem is best known for his identification, in 1937, of nicotinic acid as the factor in the vitamin B complex necessary in the cure and prevention of canine black tongue. Joseph Goldberger and his associates had previously demonstrated that the factor in liver that cured black tongue in dogs also cured human pellagra, both diseases being characterized by skin, gastrointestinal, and neurologic symptoms. Elvehjem's contribution in identifying this compound was therefore of great importance in the prevention and treatment

of human pellagra, which was common in tropical and subtropical countries.

By the 1930s the principal vitamins, A, B, C, and D, had been discovered and their role in nutrition evaluated. Goldberger had proven that pellagra was caused by a vitamin deficiency but had assumed that a deficiency of vitamin B_2 (riboflavin) was the immediate cause. However, this assumption was open to considerable doubt as liver extract in which the B_2 vitamin had been destroyed still displayed excellent therapeutic effects on pellagra. Moreover, by 1933 several German investigators had isolated riboflavin, but it proved ineffective against pellagra.

Elvehjem set out to determine which factor in liver extract was potent against pellagra. Goldberger had developed a special diet for dogs that produced the disease black tongue, a canine pellagra. Using this diet, Elvehjem produced black tongue among his laboratory dogs. He used these dogs to test the efficacy of various liver extracts in curing the condition. By using a variety of organic solvents, adsorbents, and eluting agents, he constantly purified and concentrated his extracts until he produced a white crystalline material that proved to be nicotinic acid. This substance was first prepared in 1867 by C. Huber by the oxidation of the alkaloid nicotine. In 1912 nicotinic acid was isolated from yeast by C. Funk and from rice bran by U. Suzuki during their attempts to find the antiberiberi factor. They noted that it had no

beneficial effect on beriberi but did not suspect that they had actually isolated a vitamin capable of curing a different deficiency disease.

After Elvehjem isolated nicotinic acid, he tried a 30-milligram dose of it on one of the dogs suffering from black tongue. The acid worked almost like magic in its rapid cure of the dog. Within a year Thomas Spies had tried the acid on a human pellagra victim with equal success.

Further study has shown that the human body is able to synthesize some nicotinic acid from tryptophan, an amino acid found in milk and eggs. However, as the quantity of the vitamin produced from this source is insufficient for good health, some nicotinic acid (niacin) must be supplied in the diet. Fortunately, it is widely distributed in foods such as meat, fish, and some cereals. It is now known that pellagra patients do not always recover completely when treated only with nicotinic acid. Other components of the vitamin B complex must be administered, probably due to the fact that a diet sufficiently deficient in nicotinic acid to cause pellagra would also be deficient in other factors of the vitamin B complex. This bears out Elvehjem's recommendation that human vitamin needs should be obtained from natural foods if possible. These natural vitamins are generally cheaper, more palatable, and in better balance with other factors when taken in this form. The occurrence of pellagra in the United States has been greatly decreased by enriching white flour with niacin.

A major part of Elvehjem's research work was concerned with studies of metabolism. Beginning in 1928, in collaboration with Hart, Steenbock, and Waddell, he studied anemia produced in rats fed solely on a diet of milk, a food that contains little iron. The addition of soluble iron compounds to their diet had no effect until ashes obtained from the calcining of lettuce, liver, and corn were added. Then the anemia disappeared. The utilization of the iron was found to depend on the slight trace of copper in the ash, without which iron could not be utilized in the rat's metabolism to form the essential hemoglobin. This interest in the effect of traces of elements led to subsequent investigations of manganese, zinc, cobalt, selenium, boron, and cadmium. Like vitamins, these trace elements perform their work as parts of essential enzymes.

Elvehjem attended the University of Wisconsin, where he received his B.S. in 1923, his M.S. in 1924, and his Ph.D. in 1927. He remained at Wisconsin as a member of the faculty, becoming head of the biochemistry department in 1944, dean of the graduate school in 1946, and president of the university in 1958. Elvehjem received the Willard Gibbs Medal of the American Chemical Society in 1943, the Osborne and Mendel Award of the American Institute of Nutrition in 1950, and the Lasker Award of the American Public Health Association in 1952.

For background information *see* NIACIN; NICOTINIC ACID in the McGraw-Hill Encyclopedia of Science and Technology. ∎

EMELÉUS, HARRY JULIUS
★ British chemist

Born June 22, 1903, London, England

In the period following World War I, it appeared to many that preparative inorganic chemistry had come to a standstill in Britian. Eméleus was one of a small group of researchers who helped to reestablish a flourishing tradition, both by his own research and, in later years, through those who had been associated with him as students.

Eméleus received his early training at the Imperial College of Science and Technology in London, where, after graduation, he completed his research for the Ph.D. degree under the supervision of H. B. Baker. In Baker's laboratory all the research students were encouraged to develop projects of their own devising. Facilities were rather poor, and all were expected to do their own glassblowing. It was in this setting that Emeléus did his early work on the low-temperature oxidation of phosphorus, arsenic, sulfur, and ether.

In 1927 Emeléus spent a year in the laboratory of A. Stock at the Technische Hochschule, Karlsruhe, where he worked with E. Pohland on the chemistry of decaborane. This proved to be a turning point in that it provided an opportunity to learn the preparative techniques that had been developed to a high state of perfection in Stock's laboratory. Emeléus was appointed to the staff at Imperial College in 1931, following a period of 2 years in the laboratory of H. S. Taylor at Princeton as a Commonwealth Fund fellow. This interlude provided an opportunity to study photochemistry, and the following years at Imperial College were devoted to preparative work linked to some extent with physicochemical studies, particularly on the kinetics of gaseous reactions, and the study of critical explosion limits in, for example, the silicon hydrides. *See* TAYLOR, SIR HUGH (STOTT).

Emeléus's interest in fluorine chemistry dated from the period 1939–43, when, in association with H. V. A. Briscoe, he directed a small group at Imperial College that was charged with the task of preparing and examining for toxicity a wide range of little-known nonmetallic fluorides, including chlorine trifluoride, bromine trifluoride, and iodine pentafluoride. He continued this work when he moved to Cambridge in 1945 (in 1970 he retired from the chair of inorganic chemistry at Cambridge). Bromine trifluoride and iodine pentafluoride were shown to behave as typical solvent systems and, on the basis of the postulated ionization modes ($2BrF_3 \rightleftharpoons BrF_2^+ + BrF_4^-$; $2IF_5 \rightleftharpoons IF_4^+ + IF_6^-$), it was possible to prepare new series of "acids" and "bases" (for example, BrF_2SbF_6, $KBrF_4$, IF_4SbF_6, KIF_6) containing the cations and anions believed to be associated with the pure solvents. The detailed study of the fluorinating reactions of these interhalogen compounds had a further important consequence when it was shown that reaction between iodine pentafluoride and carbon tetraiodide gave the new compound trifluoroiodomethane, CF_3I. This provided a key to

the preparation of a new group of fluoroorganometallic compounds.

Reaction with mercury, for example, gave the mercurial CF_3HgI, from which the bis mercurial was readily prepared. Similarly, reaction with phosphorus, arsenic, antimony, sulfur, and selenium led to simple fluoroalkyls of these elements and also, indirectly, or through further reactions of such intermediates as $(CF_3)_2PI$, to a wide range of other compounds. This field was subsequently greatly extended by former students from the Cambridge school and in other schools of fluorine chemistry, and it remained an active area of inorganic research. Emeléus and his students extended the work on fluorine chemistry to perfluoroalkyl nitrogen compounds, preparing inorganic derivatives, such as those of sulfur and selenium. This rich field offered numerous opportunities for investigation. With the advance of modern spectroscopic techniques, structural studies of many of the new compounds took their place alongside the preparative work. The approach adopted throughout was, however, that of an experimentalist with a highly developed instinct, rather than that of a logical theoretician.

Emeléus was elected a fellow of the Royal Society in 1946 and was awarded its Davy Medal in 1962. He also received the Lavoisier Medal of the French Chemical Society and the Stock Medal of the Gesellschaft Deutscher Chemiker.

A large number of publications by Emeléus and his students and associates appeared in chemical journals. With J. S. Anderson, he wrote *Modern Aspects of Inorganic Chemistry* (1938).

For background information *see* FLUORINE; ORGANOMETALLIC COMPOUNDS in the McGraw-Hill Encyclopedia of Science and Technology. ■

EMMETT, PAUL HUGH
★ American chemist

Born Sept. 22, 1900, Portland, OR, U.S.A.

The early 1920s saw a turning point in the field of catalysis. During the 90 years since the coining of the word by J. J. Berzelius, attention had been directed mostly to developing and perfecting industrial catalytic processes, and relatively little attention had been given to the elucidation

of the basic catalytic mechanisms. In the 1920s, however, the work of such leaders as Irving Langmuir, Hugh Taylor, and Eric Rideal directed attention toward the fundamental aspects of catalysis and surface chemistry in general. The book by Taylor and Rideal, combined with the book on organic catalysis by Paul Sabatier, afforded a rich and inspirational survey of the field and constituted a major influence on the work of Emmett as he entered the graduate school of the California Institute of Technology in 1922. The other influence that directed his career toward the study of surface chemistry was the contact with A. F. Benton, a former student of Taylor. Emmett worked under Benton for 2 of his 3 years of graduate work and from him received valuable laboratory training and a lasting interest in the fields of adsorption and catalysis. *See* RIDEAL, SIR ERIC (KEIGHTLEY); TAYLOR, SIR HUGH (STOTT).

After a year of teaching at Oregon State College in 1925–26, Emmett accepted a position at the Fixed Nitrogen Research Laboratory in Washington, DC, because it promised an opportunity to pursue his new interest in catalysis. Circumstances served to plunge him into full responsibility and freedom in planning his career, for the inception of the synthetic ammonia industry in 1926 soon removed most of the skilled catalytic personnel to industrial jobs, and left Emmett in charge of his own program by 1927. Basically, the 11 years he spent at the laboratory helped Emmett to focus his attention on the field of catalysis. His work there was centered upon trying to elucidate the mechanism of reactions important to the field of nitrogen fixation. It included a study of catalysts for ammonia synthesis and for the water-gas conversion reaction.

Perhaps foremost among the useful findings of Emmett's work on ammonia catalysts was the development of a method for measuring the surface areas of porous catalysts and of finely divided solids. The need for such a method arose from the desirability of finding some explanation for the differences in activity among the iron catalysts. The clue to the method was provided by a paper by Benton suggesting it might be possible to select an adsorption isotherm for nitrogen at −195°C, a point corresponding to a monolayer of adsorbed gas. In the early 1930s Emmett organized a program to explore the possibility of measuring the surface areas of catalysts by the physical adsorption of gases near their boiling points. With the assistance of Stephen Brunauer, a large number of adsorption isotherms were measured on iron catalysts and interpreted by the point B method in terms of monolayers of adsorbed gas. This research led directly to the calculation of absolute surface areas. About this time Edward Teller and Brunauer worked out a mathematical approach to the interpretation of the shapes of the adsorption isotherms. This work, published as a collaborative paper by Brunauer, Emmett, and Teller and applied to the experimental work, promptly became known as the BET method for measuring surface areas. It is still an internationally used and approved method for obtaining the surface areas of finely divided or porous solids. The program of research leading to this method for measuring surface areas was probably the best known of all of Emmett's scientific activities. *See* TELLER, EDWARD.

The remaining work on iron catalysts involved chemisorption measurements for nitrogen and hydrogen on iron catalysts, phase studies of the solid iron-nitrogen compounds, and some measurements on the kinetics of ammonia synthesis. These studies combined to give a picture of the ammonia synthesis that is still fundamentally accepted. The "slow step" that is observed under usual synthesis conditions appears to reflect the rate of chemisorption of nitrogen by the promoted iron catalysts. However, the exact details of the synthesis are still undetermined and will probably be worked out in the years to come.

The other work Emmett and his group carried out at the Fixed Nitrogen Research Laboratory was directed toward the elucidation of the mechanism of the water-gas conversion reaction over iron oxide and cobalt catalysts. The group eventually centered its efforts on the measurement of a number of gas-solid equilibria in the interaction of hydrogen–water vapor mixtures with $Fe-Fe_3O_4$, $Fe-FeO$, $FeO-Fe_3O_4$, $Co-CoO$, and $SnO-SnO_2$. This work led to the first application of the thermal diffusion theory of David Enskog and of Sydney Chapman to actual gas-solid equilibria and succeeded in explaining the 40 percent discrepancy that was encountered in the results of workers attempting to study the interaction of hydrogen–water vapor mixtures with the iron–iron oxide systems. It also

led to a reliable value for the equilibrium constant pertaining to the water-gas conversion reaction. All of the experimental work on these metal oxide systems was carried out by Floyd Shultz. *See* CHAPMAN, SYDNEY.

In 1937 Emmett moved on to head the department of chemical engineering at the Johns Hopkins University, where a combination of teaching and research on the application and development of the surface area measuring procedures occupied his attention. In 1943 he joined the Manhattan Project and served under Harold Urey as chief of the chemical division concerned with the production and study of the chemical properties of the diffusion barrier, used later in the Oak Ridge diffusion plant for separating the isotopes of uranium. Emmett encouraged the continuation of the fluorocarbon research program of W. T. Miller that later proved so important in producing products contributing to the successful operation of the diffusion plant. *See* UREY, HAROLD CLAYTON.

In early 1945 Emmett was appointed a senior fellow to direct a group on basic catalytic research at the Mellon Institute under the sponsorship of the Gulf Oil Company. They made use of newly available radioactive and nonradioactive isotopes to explore the nature of some of the catalysts and catalytic processes of potential value to the petroleum industry. In particular, Emmett studied the exchange of the hydrogen atoms of hydrocarbons with the deuterium content of deuterated silica-alumina catalysts, with R. Haldeman; the measurement of the adsorption of isobutane on silica-alumina catalysts by using radioactive isobutane, with Donald MacIver; and the mechanism of the Fischer-Tropsch synthesis of hydrocarbons over cobalt and iron catalysts by using tracers containing radioactive carbon, with J. T. Kummer, Thomas DeWitt, H. Podgurski, and W. Spencer. The Fischer-Tropsch work also led to a series of gas-solid equilibrium systems important to this hydrocarbon synthesis. These included a study of the equilibration of hydrogen-methane mixtures with $Fe-Fe_2C$, $Fe-Fe_3C$, $Ni-Ni_3C$, $Co-Co_2C$, carbon, $Mo-Mo_2C$, and $MoC-Mo_2C$. This work was done with the assistance of Luther Browning. Other studies involved adsorption measurements with L. Joyner and with R. Zabor and R. T. Davis. These were all directed toward the use of physical adsorption in measuring surface areas

or the study of chemisorption on pertinent catalysts.

In 1955 Emmett was appointed W. R. Grace Professor of Chemistry at the Johns Hopkins University. The research efforts of his numerous students and postdoctorate assistants from that time were devoted to studying, with the help of radioactive hydrocarbons as tracers, the catalytic cracking of hydrocarbons over silica-alumina catalysts, and to the study of the catalytic properties of nickel-copper, nickel-iron, and iron catalysts in catalytic hydrogenation. In this latter endeavor he and his students were trying to obtain experimental data relative to the electronic factor in catalysis, as proposed by D. A. Dowden and others. The metal alloys were studied both as reduced from the oxides and prepared as thin films. Alloy films were prepared by M. K Gharpurey and by John Campbell by successive deposition of nickel and copper and homogenization of the two elements into an alloy by heating. During the first years of this period, the assistance of R. J. Kokes should be especially acknowledged. Earlier he had been instrumental in suggesting and helping to develop a microcatalytic-chromatographic technique for studying rapidly the qualitative and quantitative behavior of various catalyst systems.

Emmett received his early training at Oregon State College, from which he obtained a B.S. in chemical engineering in 1922. He studied for 3 years for a Ph.D. at the California Institute of Technology. During this period he came under the inspiring influence of A. A. Noyes, R. C. Tolman, and R. A. Millikan. His honors included the Kendall Award of the American Chemical Society in Colloid Chemistry in 1958, the Pittsburgh Award of the American Chemical Society in 1953, the award of the degree of doctor honoris causa by the University of Lyon, France in 1964, and the election to the Consejo Superior in Spain in 1964. He was elected to the National Academy of Sciences in 1955.

Emmett published about 150 technical papers and edited *Catalysis* (7 vols., 1954). He was a coauthor of *Catalysis Then and Now* (1965).

For background information *see* ADSORPTION; AMMONIA; CATALYSIS; FISCHER-TROPSCH PROCESS; NITROGEN FIXATION; PARTICLE SIZE ANALYSIS in the McGraw-Hill Encyclopedia of Science and Technology. ∎

EMMONS, HOWARD WILSON
★ American mechanical engineer

Born *Aug. 30, 1912, Morristown, NJ, U.S.A.*

As Emmons progressed through high school and college, his interests were divided about equally among chemistry, vibrations and applied mechanics of machines, and fluid mechanics and heat transfer. On graduation from college in the depths of the Depression, he accepted the only opening available, instructor in a mechanical engineering thermodynamics laboratory, and thus fluid mechanics and heat transfer was "selected" as his lifework. Although a considerable range of phenomena occupied his attention through the years, three items stand out as his most important contributions:

1. Spot transition from laminar to turbulent flow: At low velocity a fluid flowing along a surface does so very smoothly. At high velocity the flow becomes very turbulent. Emmons was interested in how this change occurs. Both theory and experiment concurred in the instability of the laminar flow, which developed internal waves (the Tollmein-Schlicting waves) which presumably grew to become turbulent.

In 1948 Emmons built a piece of apparatus to demonstrate other flow phenomena in the flow of a thin layer of water down a sloped glass plate. Odd-shaped irregularities occurred on the surface of the water. Varous visitors were asked about these moving turbulent spots, but no one had any ideas as to what they were. Em-

mons soon concluded that he was encountering a formerly unreported process by which the smooth laminar flow was converted to turbulence.

This same process was important in rocket heat transfer, so Emmons spent several months developing a probability theory of spot origin and growth as a model of the transition process. As is often the case, this new observation of the transition process led to new experiments, mostly by others, to verify the initial observation and then to clarify the details of the phenomena. The crowning step would be the ability to predict the entire sequence of phenomena from the first principles of physics. Unfortunately, this process is so complex that no comprehensive theory has yet become possible.

2. Compressor stall in rotating machinery: When a fan or axial-flow jet engine air compressor discharges into a region of too high pressure, it is unable to continue to pump air and fails in catastrophic fashion. It was usually assumed that the fluid stopped moving forward throughout the whole rotating wheel in a time-periodic fashion. During some internal compressor measurements using then-new instruments (hot wire anemometer), Emmons discovered that the flow through the compressor wheels during initial stall operation was indeed reversed periodically, but not at a period related to the overall flow oscillations, and not in synchronism with the wheel speed. Further analysis of the experimental results showed that the flow through the machine was spatially nonuniform, with the reverse-flow regions rotating around the wheel at a speed unrelated to that of the wheel. Further work both in Emmons's laboratory and many other laboratories greatly clarified the nature, number, and speed of the flow-separated regions.

It is now clear that in a multistage compressor the possible instabilities can be either time or spatially periodic, or both. This knowledge makes it possible to design better rotating machines, because the engineer knows the general nature of the stall and where to look for the trouble. However, like all flow separation processes, the exact quantitative nature of the performance failure cannot be predicted because of its complexity. Such prediction will probably have to wait until the computing capacity available to engineers has increased by several orders of magnitude.

3. Computer fire code: Each of the above discoveries began with research

which developed a considerable store of what was currently known in an important area, so that a chance observation could be recognized as new and significant. The third contribution, under development as of 1979, is a preplanned effort to put fire safety engineering on the same quantitative type of foundation which underlies, for example, structural analysis or electronic circuit design. At present, fire safety design is accomplished largely by handbook empirical rules with scant or no scientific basis. Yet much knowledge has accumulated about the various parts of a fire, ignition, burning rates, hot gas plume, formation of a hot ceiling layer, and so on, to make possible a quantitative prediction of fire growth.

Only the existence of the modern computer makes possible so extensive a problem as the prediction of the growth of fire in a multistory building. However, with such a computer program under development, the growth of fire in a single room has already been successfully calculated, and the future success of a new, more quantitative, and scientifically well-founded fire safety engineering seems assured.

Emmons received the M.E. (1933) and M.S. (1935) degrees from the Stevens Institute of Technology and the Sc.D. (1938) from Harvard University. He joined the Westinghouse Steam Turbine Division in 1937, and became assistant professor at the University of Pennsylvania in 1939. In 1940 he joined the faculty of Harvard University, where he became Gordon McKay Professor of Mechanical Engineering in 1952. He was also a consultant to Army Ordnance (1942–56), where he participated in the design of a large supersonic wind tunnel, and to Pratt and Whitney Aircraft (1940–60), where he did research on aircraft engine superchargers. He served on numerous committees, including the Fire Research Committee of the National Research Council/National Academy of Sciences (1956–72), of which he was chairperson in 1967–70. He was also chairperson of the National Bureau of Standards Fire Panel 490 (1971–76). He was elected to the National Academy of Engineering (1965) and the National Academy of Sciences (1966), and was made an honorary member of the American Society of Mechanical Engineers (1978). His awards included the Egerton Gold Medal of the International Combustion Symposium (1968), the 100th Anniversary Medal of the Stevens Institute of Technology

(1970), and the Timoshenko Medal of the American Society of Mechanical Engineers (1971). He received an honorary doctor of science degree from the Stevens Institute of Technology in 1963.

Emmons edited volume 3 of *High Speed Aerodynamics and Jet Propulsion* (1958).

For background information *see* COMPRESSOR; FIRE TECHNOLOGY; FLUID-FLOW PROPERTIES; TURBOJET in the McGraw-Hill Encyclopedia of Science and Technology. ∎

ENDERS, JOHN FRANKLIN
☆ American microbiologist

***Born** Feb. 10, 1897, West Hartford, CT, U.S.A.*

For their discovery of the capacity of the poliomyelitis virus to grow in test-tube cultures of various tissues, Enders, F. C. Robbins, and T. H. Weller were awarded the 1954 Nobel Prize in physiology or medicine. *See* ROBBINS, FREDERICK CHAPMAN; WELLER, THOMAS HUCKLE.

In the 1870s the German bacteriologist Robert Koch established the techniques of cultivating bacteria in test tubes. Culture techniques enabled bacteriologists to isolate disease-causing bacteria, study them, and devise effective remedies. Such techniques, however, were not successful for the cultivation of viruses. Viruses could live and develop only in living cells, not in the lifeless culture media of test tubes. For this reason virus research was

seriously hampered. With direct experimentation ruled out, virologists had to inoculate living animals with the virus to be studied and then observe the animal's reaction. This inferential procedure was time-consuming and inaccurate, and it was impossible to use on the scale needed to control epidemics.

Early in the 20th century the French-American biologist Alexis Carrel developed the technique of growing animal tissues in the test tube. The necessity of preventing contamination of the cultures by microorganisms made Carrel's technique extremely complicated. Nevertheless, tissue culture promised to become a valuable tool for virologists. At his laboratory for research in infectious diseases at the Children's Hospital, Boston, Enders, together with Weller and Robbins, took up in 1947 a study of the potentialities of tissue culture for the propagation of viruses. They soon demonstrated that it was possible to grow mumps virus in a simple suspended cell culture consisting of fragments of chick amniotic membrane nourished with a balanced salt solution and ox serum ultrafiltrate.

In 1948 Enders and his coworkers turned to the poliomyelitis virus. It was then generally believed that the poliomyelitis virus could live only in nerve cells; because nerve tissue is the most specialized and difficult to cultivate, prospects for successful experimentation with the polio virus were not bright. Enders, however, along with other scientists, doubted that the poliovirus was strictly neurotropic; if so, how could one account for the enormous quantities of the virus observed in the feces of polio patients? In their first experiment, Enders, Robbins, and Weller introduced the poliovirus in the form of an infected suspension of mouse brain into a culture of human embryonic skin and muscle tissue. These cultures were handled in the same manner as in the experiments with mumps virus. When mice were inoculated with fluid removed from the original cultures, it became apparent that the virus had multiplied. When the fluid was introduced into the brains of monkeys, paralysis of the legs typical of polio ensued. These experiments proved that the poliovirus was not neurotropic. Enders and his coworkers soon grew the virus in a variety of human embryonic tissues, including intestine, liver, kidney, adrenal, brain, heart, spleen, and lung.

A factor limiting the value of these experiments was that viral multiplication in the culture could be demonstrated only by inoculating experimental animals. However, phenomena indicating viral multiplication were soon discovered in the tissue-culture system itself. Tissues originally infected with the virus strain showed widespread cellular degeneration, while uninoculated tissues in the same culture remained in excellent condition. This direct evidence of viral multiplication was substantiated by indirect evidence: decline in the metabolic rate of tissues infected with virus as expressed by a progressive reduction of acid formation. In investigating these phenomena, Enders and his associates found that the addition of type-specific antiserum to the suspended cell culture before the virus was introduced protected the tissue cells from the destructive effect of the virus. Thus not only had they found a prompt and efficient way of proving viral multiplication, but by demonstrating the inhibitory effect of homologous antiserum they showed that it was possible to determine in culture the antigenic type of poliomyelitis virus.

Enders, Weller, and Robbins found later that they were not dependent on embryonic tissues for their cultures. Tissues secured from operations on children and adults served just as well. All tissues except bone and cartilage proved suitable. Finally, by successfully isolating the polio virus from various specimens directly in tissue cultures, they established the tissue-culture technique on a par with the bacteria culture.

By means of the tissue-culture technique, Enders and T. C. Pebbles in 1954 isolated the measles virus, which previously had not been grown consistently under laboratory conditions. This finding laid the basis for the development by Enders, Samuel Katz, and Milano Milovanovic of an attenuated live measles virus vaccine that is now widely used in the United States either in its original form or after further attenuation, which was accomplished by Anton Schwarz.

A banker's son, Enders served as a pilot in World War I before receiving his B.A. from Yale in 1919. For a time he engaged in the real estate business, then did graduate work in English at Harvard before switching to bacteriology and immunology. He received his Ph.D. from Harvard in 1930, remaining there as a member of the faculty. In 1946 he established a laboratory for research in infectious diseases at the Children's Medical Center in Boston. In 1956 he became Higgins University Professor at Harvard. He was elected to the National Academy of Sciences in 1953.

For background information see CULTURE, TISSUE; POLIOMYELITIS in the McGraw-Hill Encyclopedia of Science and Technology. ∎

ENGELHARDT, WLADIMIR ALEKSANDROVITCH
★ Soviet biochemist

Born Dec. 4, 1894, Moscow, Russia

Engelhardt's research was concerned principally with the study of biochemical processes associated with transformations of energy, such as cellular respiration, its mutual interrelations with fermentation, and the molecular basis of muscular contraction.

Transformations of energy are among the basic phenomena of life and are involved in nearly all biological functions. The transformations are of two kinds: free energy of a chemical reaction into other types of chemical energy, and the further transformation of chemical energy into mechanical, osmotic, electrical, or other kinds of energy. Examples of these processes, which are important for the functioning of living matter, are the conversion of the energy of exergonic reactions of biological compounds into the potential energy of certain phosphorous com-

pounds, and the utilization of this potential energy for the performance of work during the contraction of muscle. A key role belongs to adenosinetriphosphate (ATP), which serves as the store and universal source of driving force for innumerable metabolic processes.

When Engelhardt started his work in this field, it was known, from the work of O. Meyerhof and K. Lohmann and of J. Parnas, that ATP is formed during glycolytic (fermentative) breakdown of sugar and that its hydrolytic splitting is accompanied by liberation of a considerable amount of energy. In other words, the energy of glycolysis (fermentation) is transformed into the potential energy of labile phosphate bonds of ATP. Engelhardt demonstrated that ATP also can be formed during cellular respiration. Nucleated red blood cells possess an intense oxidative metabolism (respiration) and a high content of ATP. Engelhardt found that if these cells are depleted of ATP by anaerobic incubation, an excess of oxygen respiration sets in and there is a rapid resynthesis of ATP from its split products, almost reaching the initial level. Thus the process of oxidative phosphorylation was discovered. An attempt was also made to determine the quantitative relationship between O_2 consumption above the normal level during the period of synthesis of ATP, and the amount of ATP synthesized. A value of phosphorus/oxygen equal to about 1 was found. Later determinations by others using more efficient systems showed that the yield may often be higher by a factor of about 2, but the order of magnitude determined by Engelhardt was fairly accurate in terms of the rather crude methods then available. These findings led researchers to regard ATP as the common storing form for the energy of the two fundamental exergonic processes of cellular metabolism, fermentation and respiration.

From Pasteur's time, scientists knew of the existence of an antagonistic interaction between aerobic and anaerobic metabolism, namely, the suppression of fermentation by respiration. Engelhardt proposed a plausible chemical interpretation of the basic mechanism of this "Pasteur effect." The hexose monophosphate stage appeared to be the crucial point at which the fate of the hexose molecule is determined. If it is phosphorylated to hexose diphosphate by transfer of a second phosphate from ATP, it enters the

fermentative pathway. The enzyme catalyzing this transphosphorylation was found to be particularly sensitive to oxidative conditions. Presumably, under aerobic conditions in the cell it becomes inactivated, fermentation is suppressed, and the metabolism of the sugar molecule is shunted over to the respiratory pathway; that is, instead of being phosphorylated, the first carbon atom of the hexose monophosphate becomes oxidized, and the molecule is metabolized along the respiratory route.

In muscle the ATP, generated glycolytically or by oxidative phosphorylation, was regarded in the late 1930s as the immediate source of energy for muscular contraction. Nothing was known about the intimate mechanism that connects the source of energy with myosin, the contractile substance of muscle and its main protein. Engelhardt, in collaboration with his wife, M. N. Liubimova, discovered that the mechanism is the myosin itself, which possesses the enzymatic property to split ATP and thus to liberate the energy stored in its labile, energy-rich phosphate bond. The interrelation between energy source and contractile substance was shown to be that of enzyme and substrate. Myosin could duly be designated as a functional enzyme, which when exerting its catalytic activity carries out a definite physiological function.

The demonstration of the enzymatic (ATP-ase) properties of myosin was followed by the equally important observation that the relations between ATP and myosin are reciprocal. In experiments on artificially prepared myosin threads, it was shown that ATP alters their mechanical properties. These changes appear to be intimately connected with contraction and relaxation, the phases of muscular activity. In turn, the myosin, acting as an enzyme, liberates from ATP the energy necessary for the performance of work. These findings formed the basis of what has been designated as the mechanochemistry of muscular contraction. The subsequent discovery, by F. B. Straub in Hungary, of the second muscle protein, actin, which is closely associated with myosin, brought new details in this field. Later investigations by others on a large variety of subjects (such as spermatozoa, cilia of unicellular organisms, and protoplasma flow) showed that similar fundamental principles apparently hold true for biological motility in general.

Engelhardt graduated from Moscow

University in 1919. After 2 years in military service as head of a hospital during the civil war, he joined the Biochemical Institute in Moscow. From 1929 to 1956 he held professorships in biochemistry at the universities of Kazan, Leningrad, and Moscow. From 1935 he worked at the Institute of Biochemistry, Moscow, until his appointment in 1959 as director of the newly organized Institute of Molecular Biology of the U.S.S.R. Academy of Sciences in Moscow. Engelhardt was elected to the U.S.S.R. Academy of Sciences in 1946, and he became a foreign member of the American Academy of Arts and Sciences in 1961.

For background information *see* ADENOSINETRIPHOSPHATE (ATP); CARBOHYDRATE METABOLISM; MUSCLE (BIOPHYSICS) in the McGraw-Hill Encyclopedia of Science and Technology. ∎

ERLANGER, JOSEPH
American physician and physiologist

Born Jan. 5, 1874, San Francisco, CA, U.S.A.

Died Dec. 5, 1965, St. Louis, MO, U.S.A.

While engaged in neurophysiologic research, Erlanger, in collaboration with Herbert Gasser, adapted the cathode-ray oscillograph for studying the passage of impulses through single nerve fibers. Erlanger and Gasser were able, through their new methods, to demonstrate many significant properties of nerve fibers and the transmission of nerve impulses. For their discoveries, which became the foundation for future work in neurophysiology, they received the 1944 Nobel Prize in physiology or medicine. *See* GASSER, HERBERT SPENCER.

The successful collaboration between Erlanger and Gasser began in the early 1900s when Gasser was a student of Erlanger's at the University of Wisconsin. The association that led to their Nobel Prize researches took place at Washington University in St. Louis, where both were on the faculty of the medical school. There, beginning in 1921, they undertook a systematic study of the transmission of nerve impulses.

By stimulating an isolated nerve fiber, a "picture" of the passage of the electrical impulse through the fiber can be obtained on an oscilloscope. Since the action potential of nervous tissue (the electrical manifestation of the nerve impulse) is of extremely short duration, Erlanger felt that, with the instruments then in use, the details of the nerve impulse configuration had never been accurately recorded. By utilizing a highly sensitive cathode-ray oscillograph, coupled with a special amplifier, he and Gasser were able to record nerve impulses with greater accuracy than had previously been achieved. But it was not until 1932, when an improved amplification device became available, that the fine details of nerve transmission were revealed.

Utilizing nerve fibers from the phalangeal nerve or a spinal root of the frog—and the improved amplification device coupled to the cathode-ray oscillograph—Erlanger demonstrated an instability in the reactivity of the nerve fiber. He attributed this to independent variations in the excitabilities of the individual nerve fibers. To determine the reasons for the variable excitabilities, he exposed the nerve fibers to different conditions that were known to affect their reactivity. Anode and cathode polarization, which respectively decrease and increase nerve excitability, did not have any consistent effect on the variations. Cold, however, which lowers nerve excitability, increased the range of variations by as much as 50 percent. Strychnine, of all the conditions and agents tested, had the greatest effect: applied to the nerve fibers in a concentration of 1:100,000, it caused a fourfold increase in the range of excitability fluctuations.

Although he made many investigations on variations in nerve fiber excitability, Erlanger was unable to discover the actual mechanism by which these variations were produced.

Some of Erlanger's most fruitful researches aimed to determine the manner of nerve impulse transmission. One earlier view held that the action potential, as it passes each locus of a nerve fiber, stimulates the next locus, and so on. In effect, the propagation of the excitation acted as an electrical restimulation. (This became known as the local-circuit hypothesis of nerve impulse propagation.) An alternate theory proposed that nerve impulse conduction was due to some propagated chemical reaction. Later it was suggested that a combination of the two theories might account for the phenomenon: a substance called acetycholine is released upon stimulation of a nerve and acts to break down the resistance of the nerve membrane, thereby allowing the impulse to pass to the next nerve locus, where the process is repeated.

Erlanger's experiments elucidated the role of the action potential in nerve impulse propagation. He also performed tests that provided evidence to support the local-circuit hypothesis of nerve impulse propagation.

In addition to his experimental work in neurophysiology, Erlanger made valuable contributions to knowledge of circulatory physiology. For example, he developed a device which recorded blood pressure and with which he was able to study the effects of pulse pressure on human kidney secretion.

Erlanger received his B.S. in chemistry at the University of California in 1895 and his M.D. at the Johns Hopkins University in 1899. He remained at Johns Hopkins until 1906, becoming successively an assistant in the department of physiology, instructor, associate, and associate professor. In 1906 he became professor of physiology at the University of Wisconsin Medical School, and in 1910 he was named professor of physiology at the Medical School of Washington University in St. Louis. He retired in 1946. He was elected to the National Academy of Sciences in 1922.

For background information *see* ACETYLCHOLINE; BIOPOTENTIALS AND ELECTROPHYSIOLOGY in the McGraw-Hill Encyclopedia of Science and Technology. ∎

ERNST, WALLACE GARY
★ American geochemist and geologist

Born Dec. 14, 1931, St. Louis, MO, U.S.A.

Ernst's chief scientific contributions involved the stability relations, crystal chemistry, and occurrence of rock-forming silicates; the field geology and plate tectonic settings of high-pressure metamorphic terranes in the Circumpacific and Alpine mountain belts; and the petrogenesis of oceanic crust and underlying mantle sections.

Ernst began his research career with experimental studies of the phase equilibrium relations of clinoamphiboles and related minerals under controlled conditions of temperature, aqueous fluid pressure, and oxidation state at the Geophysical Laboratory of the Carnegie Institution of Washington, DC, in 1956, then moved to the University of California, Los Angeles. This program of experimental, x-ray, and Mössbauer mineralogic investigations extended over a 15-year period, but gradually gave way to integrated field mapping and petrologic and microprobe chemical studies of glaucophane schists and allied lithologies in western California, southwestern Japan, southeastern Alaska, central Chile, eastern Taiwan, and the western Alps. Application of the unifying theory of plate tectonics showed that such high-pressure belts of recrystallized rock mark the now exhumed sites of ancient oceanic trenches adjacent to accreting continental margins.

Ernst postulated that these blueschist terranes mark the suture between pairs of convergent lithospheric plates. The complete assemblage of rock types in this structurally imbricated environment includes the latest topics of his petrochemical, rare-earth element, and mineralogic work—namely, oceanic crust and uppermost mantle underpinnings (the so-called ophiolite suite). The structural regimes of these occurrences testify to the near-surface (that is, crustal) low-angle thrust faulting characteristic of inclined seismic shear zones.

Ernst received his formal education at Carleton College (B.A., 1953), the University of Minnesota (M.S., 1955), and the Johns Hopkins University (Ph.D., 1959), all degrees being in geology. From his research position at the Carnegie Institution of Washington, he went to the University of California, Los Angeles, and served as an assistant professor (1960–63), associate professor (1963–68), and then professor of geology and geophysics. He held joint appointment to the department of earth and space sciences and the Institute of Geophysics and Space Physics at that institution. He chaired the department of geology during the period 1970–74, and subsequently chaired the department of earth and space sciences. His awards included a Fulbright Research Scholarship to the University of Tokyo (1963), a Crosby Visiting Professorship at the Massachusetts Institute of Technology (1968), the Mineralogical Society of America Award (1969), a National Science Foundation Senior Postdoctoral Fellowship to the University of Basel (1970), and a Guggenheim Memorial Fellowship to the Swiss Federal Institute of Zürich (1975). He was elected a member of the National Academy of Sciences (1974) and also became a member of the American Geophysical Union, the Geological Society of America, the Geochemical Society, and the Mineralogical Society of America.

Ernst wrote more than 70 scientific journal articles. He authored or edited seven books and research monographs: *Amphiboles, Crystal Chemistry, Phase Relations and Occurrence* (1968); *Earth Materials* (1969); *Comparative Study of Low-Grade Metamorphism in the California Coast Ranges and the Outer Metamorphic Belt of Japan,* with Y. Seki, H. Onuki, and M. C. Gilbert (1970); *Metamorphism and Plate Tectonic Regimes* (1975); *Subduction Zone Metamorphism* (1975); *Petrologic*

Phase Equilibria (1976); and *The Geotectonic Development of California* (in press).

For background information *see* META-MORPHISM; TECTONIC PATTERNS in the McGraw-Hill Encyclopedia of Science and Technology. ∎

ESAKI, LEO
★ Japanese physicist

Born Mar. 12, 1925, Osaka, Japan

Esaki's pioneering studies on *p-n* junctions made of heavily doped (having large impurity concentrations) germanium and silicon resulted in the discovery of the tunnel, or Esaki, diode in 1957. This discovery, published in 1958, opened a new field of research on tunneling in semiconductors. The method quickly became very important in solid-state physics because of its simplicity in principle and the high sensitivity of tunneling to many finer details. Since the diode exhibited a hitherto unseen negative resistance, its practical application for high-speed circuits was soon realized. For his achievement, Esaki was awarded the Nobel Prize in physics in 1973.

The idea of quantum tunneling of a particle through an energy barrier was introduced as early as 1927 in the explanation of field ionization of atoms and the interpretation of field emission of electrons from surfaces. It was also used in the following year to explain alpha-particle emission. According to classical mechanics, a particle arriving at a potential barrier is reflected at the point where its potential energy equals its original kinetic energy. However, in quantum mechanics, electrons and other particles are considered as waves, and these waves may penetrate into the "forbidden" region. In consequence, the particle may travel through the barrier even though it does not have sufficient energy to surmount it. This is called tunneling.

In classical mechanics the probability of tunneling is zero; in quantum mechanics it decreases exponentially as the length of the forbidden path increases. The first theory of barrier-layer rectification, developed in 1932 independently by A. H Wilson, L. Nordheim, and J. Frenkel and A. Joffe, was based on the quantum-mechanical tunneling effect. This theory was accepted for a number of years until physicists realized that it predicted rectification in the wrong direction. The ordinary rectifier has a barrier width far greater than 100 angstroms (10 nanometers)— much too thick for any tunneling current. Tunneling between bands in a dielectric (insulator) was first proposed in 1934 by C. Zener. His idea was applied in 1951 to explain the reverse breakdown of the germanium *p-n* junction diode, the so-called Zener breakdown, but this interpretation later turned out to be not necessarily correct. Thus, as late as the middle 1950s, no one had yet been able to clearly identify a tunneling current in a *p-n* junction.

In 1957, while he was a member of a small research group at the Sony Corporation, Tokyo, Esaki decided to look into the tunneling effect in germanium *p-n* junctions. The major initial requirement was to make the junction extremely narrow so that the probability of tunneling would become large enough to permit a measurable current flow across the junction. This required heavy impurity doping of the semiconductor, since the junction width is inversely proportional to the square root of impurity concentration. The first result of this work was the successful operation of a backward diode, so-called because it had a polarity opposite to that of the ordinary diode. Esaki was pleased to obtain this situation because of its excellent qualitative agreement with the 1932 quantum-mechanical rectification theory.

One day, while testing one of the more heavily doped diodes, Esaki noticed some fuzziness in the current-voltage character-

istic in the forward direction. A measurement at liquid-nitrogen temperatures showed a significant anomaly. Then he realized that because of the energy-band structure of the semiconductor the diode should have a negative resistance region if a large tunneling current was made possible in the forward direction. Esaki quickly proceeded to make still more heavily doped diodes with junctions only 100 angstroms wide and found the expected negative resistance. Thus the tunnel diode was born. Its value as a fast-switching or high-frequency-amplifying electronic device was recognized in 1958, and widespread research began on electron tunneling in junctions. Study of tunneling in semi- and superconductors has proved to be a powerful tool in solid-state physics.

An architect's son, Esaki majored in physics at the University of Tokyo, where he received his M.S. in 1947 and his Ph.D. on the tunneling study in 1959. In 1956 he went to work for the Sony Corporation while continuing to work on his thesis at the university. He went to the United States in 1960 to join the International Business Machines (IBM) Corporation. He became engaged in research at the IBM Thomas J. Watson Research Center, Yorktown Heights, NY, in 1960; his major field was semiconductor physics. In 1965 he became an IBM fellow. Among his later interests was research on a man-made semiconductor superlattice to seek predicted quantum-mechanical effects. His honors included the Nishina Memorial Award, the Asahi Press Award, the Morris N. Liebmann Memorial Prize, the Stuart Ballantine Medal, and the Japan Academy Award in 1965. He held honorary degrees from Doshisha School, Japan, and the Universidad Politecnica de Madrid, Spain. He was named a director of IBM-Japan, Ltd., a board member of the Yamada Science Foundation, and a guest editorial writer for the Yomiuri Press. He was chosen for the Order of Culture by the Japanese government in 1974. Esaki was elected a fellow of the American Academy of Arts and Sciences in 1974, a member of the Japan Academy in 1975, a foreign associate of the U.S. National Academy of Sciences in 1976, and a foreign associate of the U.S. National Academy of Engineering in 1977.

For background information *see* QUANTUM MECHANICS; TUNNEL DIODE in the McGraw-Hill Encyclopedia of Science and Technology. ∎

ESAU, KATHERINE
★ American botanist

Born *Apr. 3, 1898, Ekaterinoslav, Russia*

Esau's initial interest centered on the histological and cytological effects of viruses on plants as seen with the light microscope. When electron microscopy became available, a correlation between the pathological changes in plants and the distribution of virus particles in host tissues and cells became possible. Since knowledge of normal anatomy was a prerequisite for the interpretation of pathological changes, Esau developed a comprehensive research program on the anatomy of higher plants.

Esau began her work on viruses as a member of the experiment station staff of the Spreckels Sugar Company in California. There she was concerned with developing sugarbeet strains resistant to the virus disease called curly top. In 1928 this work was transferred to the Davis campus of the University of California, where gradually the histological aspects of plant virus diseases became dominant in Esau's research; and since the curly top virus was a distinctly phloem-limited disease agent, the phloem—the food-conducting tissue of plants—was singled out for major attention in her research in plant anatomy.

The occurrence of specialized relationships between viruses and plants became evident soon after research on plant viruses began. Some viruses were found to be more easily transmitted from plant to plant than others, and the differences were reflected in their more or less specific relationships to insects serving as vectors in virus transmission. Concomitantly, variations in the feeding habits of the insects with regard to the type of tissue they selected for obtaining food became known. Viruses exemplifying the more specialized relationships were frequently those that, in order to infect the plant, had to be placed into the phloem by an insect that utilized that tissue in feeding.

Esau's contributions to plant science can be divided into three areas: (1) With regard to virus-plant relationships, the recognition of a distinction between primary and secondary abnormalities in the host made it possible to judge whether a virus selectively invades a specific tissue. Evidence was obtained that a virus may initiate the degenerative process next to the first sieve element to mature in a given organ, a phenomenon indicating virus transport in that food conduit. Esau's application of ultrastructural research methods (with collaborators) confirmed the concepts of specialization of certain viruses in their relationship to plant tissues and also revealed the hitherto unrecognized variation in the association of viruses with cell organelles. Viruses were shown to be present in plasmodesmata, apparently in transit between cells. The concept of long-distance transport of the virus in phloem with the food was correlated with the detection of virus particles in the food conduit and in the channels interconnecting the conduits. In some viral infections, the site of virus formation could be visualized by the localization of virus-related vesicles enclosing networks resembling those of nucleic acids. (2) In the work on structure of healthy plants, Esau made considerable progress in clarifying the ontogenetic history of the primary vascular tissues and their distinction from the secondary tissues. These studies led to an appreciation of the fundamental differences in the patterns of initiation of the first xylem and the first phloem in the various organs of the plant and a new understanding of the relationship between leaf development and vascularization. This work stimulated other investigators to carry out similar studies and served to establish one of the bases for experimental research on differentiation in plants. (3) Esau's research on the phloem tissue led to a clarification of the developmental

features of the tissue, especially those of the main conducting cell, the sieve element. This research broadened into comparative studies of phloem structure as seen with the light and electron microscopes, and led to a better understanding of the functional relation between the specialized sieve element and the associated, less specialized parenchyma cells. Esau's work was influential in promoting phloem research in the United States.

Esau received her initial education, including a year of college, in Russia. In 1919 she and her parents left for Germany, where she continued in college, graduating in 1922. In the same year the family migrated to the United States. After several years of employment, Esau entered the University of California as a graduate student and obtained the Ph.D. in botany at Berkeley in 1931. She taught and conducted her research at the University of California at Davis until 1963. She was transferred to the Santa Barbara campus of the university in 1963 and became emeritus professor in 1975. Through support from the National Science Foundation, she was able to continue research after 1965. Esau was elected to the American Academy of Arts and Sciences (1949), the National Academy of Sciences (1957), the American Philosophical Society (1964), and the Swedish Royal Academy of Sciences (1971).

Esau wrote *Plant Anatomy* (1953; 2d ed. 1965), *Anatomy of Seed Plants* (1960; 2d ed. 1977), *Vascular Differentiation in Plants* (1965), *Plants, Viruses, and Insects* (1968), and *The Phloem* (1969).

For background information *see* PHLOEM; PLANT ANATOMY; PLANT VIRUS in the McGraw-Hill Encyclopedia of Science and Technology. ∎

ESHELBY, JOHN DOUGLAS
★ British physicist and materials scientist

Born Dec. 21, 1916, Puddington, Cheshire, England

It was the chance realization that some inconclusive calculations on dielectric loss could be salvaged and used to treat dislocation-induced mechanical damping in metals that first led Eshelby to study the theory of elasticity, the application of which to lattice defects and macroscopic imperfections in solids was to form the major part of his work.

After prewar experimental work on soft x-rays and ferromagnetism, Eshelby decided, on returning to academic life after World War II, to become a theoretician. As a member of N. F. Mott's school of solid-state physics at the University of Bristol, he helped to set up some of the theoretical apparatus that was needed before dislocation theory could be employed in solving practical problems in materials technology. He developed a method of applying anisotropic elasticity theory to dislocations; this method, later corrected and extended in collaboration with W. Thornton Read and W. Shockley, and further improved by A. N. Stroh and others, became widely used. He devised a general formula for the force (in the sense in which the word is used in the theory of defects) that acts on a lattice defect in a stress field. With F. C. Frank and F. R. N. Nabarro, he worked out the theory of dislocation pileups, which played an important role in the theories of work hardening and fracture. *See* MOTT, SIR NEVILL (FRANCIS); SHOCKLEY, WILLIAM.

While at the University of Illinois, Eshelby, at the suggestion of F. Seitz, established the relationship between the change in dimensions and the apparent change in x-ray lattice parameter which a crystal undergoes when it contains lattice vacancies or other point defects. This relationship was used to find the variation of vacancy concentration with temperature, and hence deduce the energy of formation of a vacancy, by making simultaneous

measurements of size and x-ray lattice parameter. He also contributed to the study of crystal whiskers, showing that, rather surprisingly, a screw dislocation in a whisker is stable (strictly, metastable) against displacement away from the whisker axis, and that it produces a macroscopic twist of the whisker as a whole. The existence of this so-called Eshelby twist was confirmed experimentally. *See* SEITZ, FREDERICK.

At the University of Birmingham, Eshelby continued his work on dislocations and point defects. In an excursion outside elasticity, he developed, with A. B. Lidiard, C. W. A. Newey, and P. L. Pratt, a theory which predicted that variations in temperature and impurity content change the electrical charge on the dislocations in an ionic crystal, and so lead to changes in its mechanical properties. Although it was criticized in detail, this theory served to stimulate experimental and theoretical work by others. Eshelby also devised a simple and intuitive method for finding the stresses associated with inclusions and inhomogeneities in solids (for example, martensite plates, precipitates, cavities, cracks) with the help of a succession of imaginary cutting, straining, and welding operations. Because of its unorthodox approach, the method was at first looked at askance by some applied mathematicians, but it finally became popular and was applied to problems in the theory of solids, materials technology, and geophysics. Later, in B. A. Bilby's department of the theory of materials at the University of Sheffield, the method was adapted by Eshelby and his colleagues to deal with viscous inclusions, and it was applied to certain problems that arise in the study of tectonics and the homogenization of glass. He also turned his attention to fracture mechanics, a major interest of the department, devising methods for obtaining the elastic field near the tip of an arbitrarily moving antiplane crack and calculating the rate of flow of energy into a moving crack. Returning to an earlier interest, he also studied various applications of the energy-momentum tensor concept to continuum mechanics.

Although he was primarily concerned with the theory of elasticity, both linear and nonlinear, Eshelby made a point of drawing into its service ideas from areas of mathematics and physics not commonly connected with continuum mechanics. Examples were the exploitation

of the equivalence between the positions of piled-up dislocations and the zeros of the classical orthogonal polynomials; recognition of the connection between the force on an elastic singularity and the energy-momentum tensor which the theory of fields prescribes for an elastic continuum; and use of techniques borrowed from electrodynamics and quantum field theory to handle the motion of dislocations, kinks, and cracks.

The son of an army officer, Eshelby received his B.Sc. (1937) and Ph.D. (1950) in physics from the University of Bristol, where, after serving in the Royal Air Force during World War II, he worked in various capacities until, after a spell at the University of Illinois, he joined the faculty of the University of Birmingham. After 10 years as a lecturer in the department of metallurgy at Birmingham, interrupted by a visit to the Technische Hochschule and the Max Planck Institute, Stuttgart, Germany, he moved to the Cavendish Laboratory, Cambridge, for 2 years. In 1966 he went to the University of Sheffield, where in 1971 he was appointed to a personal chair in the Department of the Theory of Materials. He was elected a fellow of the Royal Society of London in 1974, and in 1977 received the Timoshenko Medal of the American Society of Mechanical Engineers.

For background information *see* CRYSTAL DEFECTS; ELASTICITY; PLASTIC DEFORMATION OF METAL; WHISKERS, CRYSTAL in the McGraw-Hill Encyclopedia of Science and Technology. ∎

ESSEN, LOUIS
★ British physicist

Born Sept. 6, 1908, Nottingham, England

Essen joined the National Physical Laboratory (NPL) in 1929 and worked with D. W. Dye, who was engaged in his fundamental investigation on tuning forks and quartz oscillators. Together they designed a tuning fork clock good enough to reveal the variations in standard pendulum clocks. After Dye's death in 1932, Essen continued the work on quartz standards. He worked in the field of frequency and time standards throughout his career and applied them to a number of interesting problems.

The Essen quartz ring clock was made

in 1938 and for many years was widely used as an observatory time standard. During 1940–45 he worked on urgent measurement problems at high radio and microwave frequencies such as the design and testing of radio-frequency cables. He developed a number of measuring instruments, including cavity resonator wavemeters. The resonant frequencies of these wavemeters depend in a simple way on their dimensions and the electromagnetic constant c, or the velocity of light. It became obvious to him that the measurement of dimensions and resonant frequency would constitute a simple and accurate way of determining the value of c. Essen's first measurement of the velocity of light, carried out with A. C. Gordon-Smith in 1946, gave the value $299,792 \pm 3$ kilometers per second, and was thus 16 km/s higher than the accepted value. With an improved cavity resonator he obtained in 1950 the value $299,792.5 \pm 1$ km/s. In later years more accurate values were obtained in the United States and United Kingdom by measuring the wavelength and frequency of a laser. The value internationally adopted in 1975 was $299,792.458$ km/s. Essen realized that the new techniques would enable the value of c to be used as a standard for distance measurement, which could be reduced to the measurement of the travel time of a pulse of light or radio waves. The measurements in air would require an accurate value of its refractive index. With K. D. Froome, he designed a cavity reso-

nator method of measurement and obtained the values still generally accepted for modern geodetic surveying. Essen continued to be responsible for frequency standards at the NPL, and during visits to the United States in 1948 and 1953 he became very interested in the proposal, which had been made originally by I. I. Rabi, to use a hyperfine spectral line as a standard of time and frequency. *See* RABI, ISIDOR ISAAC.

The atomic-beam technique, which Essen discussed at Columbia University, the Massachusetts Institute of Technology, and the National Bureau of Standards, was quite new to him, but it was clear that his experiences with time measurement, quartz clocks, and microwave measurements would all be valuable in the development of an atomic standard. He started work at the NPL with J. V. L. Parry, and in 1955 their first atomic cesium standard was in operation. It was immediately obvious that since the accuracy was so much greater than any astronomical unit, it was necessary to define an atomic unit for the purpose of furthering the investigation. Any new unit must, of course, be related to the old one in order to secure continuity of measurement; Essen and Parry therefore adopted a provisional unit equal to the mean solar second at that time. The mean solar second was known to vary, and an experiment was undertaken, together with the U.S. Naval Observatory, to relate the atomic unit with the second of ephemeris time. The measurements, which were extended over a period of 3 years to reduce the effect of the rather large errors in the astronomical measurements, gave a value of $9,192,631,770 \pm 20$ hertz for the frequency of cesium, and this has been used to define a unit of atomic time since 1958 with the full accuracy of atomic clocks.

The initial work by Essen and Parry led to the construction of a second model accurate to 1 part in 10^{12}. Similar cesium standards have now been constructed at a number of national standards laboratories, and a commercial standard of comparable accuracy and more convenient size is made in the United States.

The unit of time differs from those of length and mass in that it can be made available throughout the world by means of radio transmissions. In the United Kingdom standard frequency transmissions are made from the Rugby Post Office station on behalf of the NPL. Essen

pointed out in 1954 the advantages of using very-low-frequency transmissions, and two Rugby transmissions on 60 and 16 kilohertz were widely used for the study of the propagation of radio waves. From 1955 onward, the frequencies were expressed in terms of the atomic unit provisionally adopted, making it immediately available over a wide area. The transmissions were used for the first international comparison of atomic standards between the United Kingdom and the United States.

During the course of his work Essen carried out two very precise experiments concerned with the relativity theory. In the first, with G. A. Tomlinson in 1937, the frequencies of two quartz oscillators were compared as one was rotated. The second experiment, carried out in 1955, was a fairly close analogy to the Michelson-Morley experiment, using radio waves instead of light waves. A simple experiment gave a null result with a much higher precision than that originally achieved. Essen was much intrigued by the controversy concerning certain aspects of relativity theory, and his experience in the precise measurements of time and velocity led him to examine closely the thought experiments in Einstein's papers. He published a detailed criticism of the theory in which it is pointed out that the thought experiments contained implicit assumptions which contradicted the initial assumptions.

Essen gained a B.Sc. in physics (1928), Ph.D. (1941), and D.Sc. (1948) from London University. He was elected a fellow of the Royal Society of London in 1960, and received several awards and gold medals for his work on the velocity of light and time measurement, including the Charles Vernon Boys Prize from the Physical Society in 1957 and the A. S. Popov Gold Medal from the U.S.S.R. Academy of Sciences in 1959. He became a deputy chief scientific officer at the National Physical Laboratory in 1960. He was a member of the Institution of Electrical Engineers, serving on a number of its committees, and he was also active in the International Union for Scientific Radio, of which he was president of Commission 1.

For background information *see* ATOMIC CLOCK; FREQUENCY MEASUREMENT; LIGHT; QUARTZ CLOCK; RELATIVITY; TIME in the McGraw-Hill Encyclopedia of Science and Technology. ■

ESTES, WILLIAM KAYE
★ American psychologist

Born June 17, 1919, Minneapolis, MN, U.S.A.

Fears and anxieties develop through a learning process, and yet these emotional states involve such widespread and persisting disturbances of behavior that they cannot be explained on the basis of simple Pavlovian conditioning by stimulus substitution. Estes began studying this problem while still an undergraduate, working with B. F. Skinner, the innovator of methods for the analysis of behavior. They developed an experimental technique to elucidate the way in which a stimulus that precedes a painful or traumatic event, however brief that event may be, develops the capacity to suppress the normal activity of the organism over relatively long periods of time. *See* SKINNER, BURRHUS FREDERIC.

The method for establishing a conditioned emotional response (CER), refined and extended by other investigators, has been widely applied for such purposes as analyzing effects of tranquilizing drugs, electroconvulsive shock, and various types of brain lesions. In Estes's own work, understanding of the CER set the stage for a major series of experiments analyzing the ways in which punishment affects behavior. In the classical psychological theories of reward and punishment, notably that of Edward L. Thorndike, it was assumed that a response which leads to reward is directly and automatically strengthened (that is, becomes more likely to recur under similar circumstances). However, the mode of operation of punishment long remained a controversial issue. Other learning theorists, and indeed Thorndike himself at different times, held on the one hand that punishment simply reduces the strength of the punished response, and on the other hand that punishment exerts its effects by instigating competing behaviors (such as withdrawal) which conflict with the punished response.

Estes's investigations adduced a number of new lines of evidence supporting a modified conflict theory, the primary mechanism being the establishment of a CER to cues which precede punishment. In one experiment, for example, he showed that effects of punishment on a simple instrumental response in the rat can be counteracted if conditions are arranged so that the CER undergoes experimental extinction (unlearning); in another he showed that effects of punishment can be closely mimicked if the stimuli which normally lead to a given response are associated with a punishing stimulus (such as electric shock) even during a period when the response is physically prevented from occurring.

Theoretical problems that arose in analyzing the mechanisms of punishment, and later in similar analyses of other learning processes, tended increasingly to require mathematical as well as experimental methods for solution. Estes, influenced by the work of the behavior theorist Clark L. Hull, became interested in the possibility of progressing toward a general mathematical theory of learning. Drawing on a variety of mathematical models and techniques, some suggested by analogies between certain aspects of associative learning and multimolecular chemical reactions, and some by modern developments in probability theory and stochastic processes, Estes formulated a statistical theory of elementary learning processes. The theory, set forth in a series of papers between 1950 and 1955, took the form of a small set of basic concepts and axioms, together with methods of derivation which permitted generation of descriptive mathematical models for specific learning situations.

During the subsequent decade Estes and a growing number of students and colleagues tested consequences of the theory for numerous experimental phenomena, including verbal learning and memory, probability learning, competitive and cooperative interactions between individuals in minimal social situations, tachistoscopic perception, signal detection by human observers, and choice behavior.

One of the most widely applied theoretical results produced by this work was the probability matching theorem, which states that under certain conditions an individual's probability of predicting an uncertain event (such as the fall of a die) will come with repeated experiences to approximate the true probability of the event.

These contributions to the methods and concepts of learning theory were recognized by the Distinguished Scientific Contribution Award of the American Psychological Association in 1962 and the Warren Medal of the Society of Experimental Psychologists in 1963.

Estes's inclinations turned toward science at an early age under the influence of his father, George D. Estes, a man of broad scholarly interests. He received his B.A. from the University of Minnesota in 1940 and his Ph.D. in psychology in 1943. He served in the armed forces from 1944 to 1946, first in an Air Force Gunnery Research Unit and then as a medical administrative officer in the Asiatic-Pacific theater.

Estes joined the faculty of Indiana University in 1946 and reached the rank of professor in 1955 and research professor of psychology in 1960. He moved to Stanford University as a professor of psychology in 1962, then to Rockefeller University as professor and head of the Laboratory of Mathematical Psychology in 1968. He was elected to the National Academy of Sciences in 1963.

Estes wrote *An Experimental Study of Punishment* (1944) and *Modern Learning Theory,* with S. Koch and others (1954). He was coeditor of *Studies in Mathematical Learning Theory,* with R. R. Bush (1959), editor and coauthor of *Handbook of Learning and Cognitive Processes* (1975–78), and coauthor of *Stimulus Sampling Theory,* with E. D. Neimark (1967). He edited the *Journal of Comparative and Physiological Psychology* (1962–68) and the *Psychological Review* (1977–).

For background information *see* LEARNING THEORIES; PROBLEM SOLVING (PSYCHOLOGY) in the McGraw-Hill Encyclopedia of Science and Technology. ∎

EUGSTER, HANS PETER
★ Swiss-American geologist and geochemist

Born Nov. 19, 1925, Landquart, Switzerland

Eugster contributed to a wide range of problems in chemical geology. His development of oxygen buffers for controlling redox reactions at elevated pressures and temperatures is best known. In collaboration with his students, he extended buffering techniques to reactions with carbon, fluorine, nitrogen, and sulfur species, as well as acids, bases, and metal chlorides in supercritical aqueous fluids. This led to a quantitative understanding of the role of fluids and solutions in mineral formations within the Earth's crust and mantle. Beginning with a study of the Eocene Green River Formation of Wyoming, he evaluated, in collaboration with L. A. Hardie and B. F. Jones, the hydrologic, chemical, and sedimentological processes leading to evaporite formation in continental and marine basins.

Educated in his native Switzerland as a field petrologist, Eugster went to the United States to study experimental petrology and the recently developed techniques of mineral synthesis under high water pressures. After synthesizing the micas muscovite, $KAl_3Si_3O_{10}(OH)_2$, and phlogopite, $KMg_3AlSi_3O_{10}(OH)_2$, with H. S. Yoder, he turned in 1956 to the iron biotite annite, $KFe_3AlSi_3O_{10}(OH)_2$, but the standard techniques yielded oxidized minerals instead, such as magnetite,

Fe_3O_4. Suspecting hydrogen loss to be the cause, he placed the starting materials in a sealed platinum tube, with the platinum acting as an osmotic membrane, and surrounded that tube with zinc + HCl as a hydrogen generator. This assembly was protected by a gold tube, which in turn was placed in the autoclave. The first experiment was successful and produced annite. In order to control the hydrogen fugacity quantitatively, Eugster replaced the zinc of the buffer with pairs of iron oxides or other metal + metal oxide pairs having a fixed oxygen fugacity, and replaced the HCl with H_2O. Hydrogen diffusion through the platinum tube proved to be sufficiently fast for effective control of f_{O_2} (fugacity of oxygen) down to temperatures as low as 400°C. These oxygen buffers were thereafter used extensively. *See* YODER, HATTEN SCHUYLER, JR.

Their first application, with D. R. Wones, was concerned with the stability of biotites and solid-solution models. The graphite buffer (1965, with B. M. French) and the methane buffer (1967, with G. B. Skippen) extended gas compositions to the system C-O-H and permitted the calibration of the most important reactions which occur during the metamorphism of impure limestones. In 1969 Eugster, with J. L. Munoz, added fluorine species, and in 1973, with J. D. Frantz, he calibrated the Ag + AgCl buffer, the first buffer to control the fugacity of an acid species at elevated pressure and temperature. Other acid-base buffers were concerned with HBr, HI, and H_2S, and the way was open to study supercritical aqueous fluids as solutions.

In a series of publications with Frantz, W. D. Gunter, and I-Ming Chou, Eugster defined the solubilities of the minerals talc, serpentine, forsterite, magnetite, hematite, wollastonite, diopside, tremolite, muscovite, phlogopite, and clinochlore. With I-Ming Chou, he developed the hydrogen sensor (1977), which permitted the inplace measurement of f_{H_2} (fugacity of hydrogen) at elevated pressure and temperature. The buffering experiments had a profound effect on the thinking of field petrologists, who had long been cognizant of the importance of fluids and volatile constituents for the growth of minerals. The experiments emphasized the role the minerals play in controlling (or buffering) the composition of fluids in nature. In fact, mineral assemblages can often be used to deduce the important fugacities

which existed at the time the minerals formed.

In 1958, while reviewing a manuscript by C. Milton on the authigenic minerals of the Green River Formation, Eugster was struck by the applicability of chemical thermodynamics to sedimentary deposits. The effort to acccount for the presence of trona, $NaHCO_3 \cdot Na_2CO_3 \cdot 2H_2O$, and other strange minerals led Eugster to a study of mineral equilibria in the Green River Formation and in Searles Lake (with G. I. Smith) and to an extended involvement (1966–73) with Lake Magadi, a trona-producing lake in the Rift Valley of Kenya, Africa. While there, Eugster discovered two new minerals, magadiite and kenyaite, and an inorganic process for depositing bedded chert which he applied to Precambrian bedded iron formations. The importance of the sedimentological aspects for evaporite formation became evident during Eugster's field study of the Miocene marine evaporites of Sicily (1969) with L. A. Hardie, a study which emphasized the shallowness of the Messinian environment. This concept was later confirmed and extended to the whole Mediterranean by K. Hsu, based on deep-sea drilling.

Sedimentological studies of the Green River Formation in 1971 revealed abundant evidence for the shallowness of Eocene Lake Gosiute and led to the formulation, with R. C. Surdam, of the playa-lake model, which visualized a central lake surrounded by wide mud flats. Oil shales and evaporites were considered lake facies, and most of the carbonate production was placed on the mud flats and the surrounding alluvial fans. This model received considerable attention, pro and con, and sparked interest in closed-basin geochemistry and sedimentology. Eugster's subsequent work was concerned with playas of the high Andes of Bolivia, with the Great Salt Lake of Utah, and with the general principles of the chemical evolution of continental waters.

Eugster obtained his professional training at the Swiss Federal Institute of Technology in Zurich, where he received a degree in geological engineering in 1948 and a Dr.Sc. degree in 1951 under Paul Niggli, one of the world's foremost petrologists and mineralogists. After a year as a postdoctoral fellow with L. H. Ahrens at the Massachusetts Institute of Technology, he joined the Geophysical Labora-

tory in Washington, DC (1952). In 1958 he became associate professor, and in 1960 professor of geology, at the Johns Hopkins University. For many years he was also associated with the U.S. Geological Survey, with the University of Wyoming, and with the Swiss Institute of Technology. In an effort to combine experimental studies with fieldwork, he traveled and worked in many parts of the world. Eugster was elected to the National Academy of Sciences and the American Academy of Arts and Sciences in 1972, and he received the Arthur L. Day Medal of the Geological Society of America in 1971 and the V. M. Goldschmidt Medal of the Geochemical Society in 1976. In 1974 he was a Fairchild visiting scholar at the California Institute of Technology.

For background information *see* HIGH-PRESSURE PHENOMENA; MINERALOGY; SEDIMENTATION (GEOLOGY) in the McGraw-Hill Encyclopedia of Science and Technology. ∎

EULER, ULF SVANTE VON
★ Swedish physiologist and pharmacologist

Born Feb. 7, 1905, Stockholm, Sweden

With the aid of a Rockefeller Fellowship, Euler, after finishing his medical studies in Stockholm, went to London in 1930 for postgraduate work under H. H. Dale at the National Institute for Medical

Research at Hampstead. During studies aimed at demonstrating acetylcholine in the gastrointestinal tract, he observed that extracts of rabbit intestine caused contraction of the isolated rabbit jejunum, which was atropine-resistant, and not explainable by any of the then known biologically active compounds of natural origin. In collaboration with J. H. Gaddum, it was shown that the extracts also lowered the rabbit blood pressure and that a principle with similar actions was present in the brain. The active substance became known as substance P (from "preparation"). After his return to Stockholm, Euler found that the active substance had the properties of a peptide. This was the first of several peptides which subsequently have been found to occur in the intestine as well as in the brain. Some years later, in 1961, Euler in collaboration with F. Lishajko showed that substance P is bound to subcellular particles in peripheral nerves such as vagus or splenic nerves. This finding suggested that substance P is of neurohormonal character, possibly serving as a modulator of nerve action, if not as a transmitter, as proposed by F. Lembeck for primary sensory neurons. The high concentration of substance P in the intestine suggests that it is of importance for the atropine-fast motility of the intestine. See DALE, SIR HENRY (HALLETT).

Euler's further studies on the biological actions of extracts of various organs revealed that male accessory genital glands contained, in addition to an adrenalinelike principle, also some blood-pressure-lowering material. This led to the discovery of a new highly active principle, present in the vesicular gland of sheep and in human and sheep seminal fluid. In 1935 he showed that it had the properties of a lipidic acid, apparently unsaturated, which he named prostaglandin. A related substance found in extracts of monkey seminal vesicle was named vesiglandin. The presence of large amounts of prostaglandin in human and sheep seminal fluid suggested that it played some part in reproduction, further supported by its presence in the ovary.

Purified prostaglandin preparations stimulated smooth muscle in various organs, especially intestine and uterus. The action on the uterus later became the basis for the use of prostaglandins to induce labor or abortion.

In the course of experiments involving extraction with lipid solvents, Euler observed that extraction of urine with ether yielded a material with nicotinelike action. After isolating it as picrate, he could identify it as piperidine (1942), probably the first "alkaloid" to be extracted from normal urine from humans and animals.

Extracts of various organs obtained by fluid extraction with ether showed that the ether had an adrenalinelike action. This was the beginning of a series of experiments showing large amounts of this active principle in sympathetic nerves, which raised the question of the nature of the "adrenergic" neurotransmitter, generally held to be adrenaline. Biological assay of the purified extracts, combined with chemical tests, enabled Euler to identify the active substance as noradrenaline (1946–48).

Utilizing improved methods for purification, especially adsorption on alumina, as developed by F. H. Shaw, Euler studied the distribution of noradrenaline in different organs. The results indicated that the noradrenaline content of an organ or vascular tissue was a measure of its supply with adrenergic nerves. Section and subsequent degeneration of a postsynaptic sympathetic nerve such as the splenic nerve caused a disappearance of the noradrenaline content of the organ, followed by reappearance after regeneration.

Euler also developed a technique for measuring the catecholamine content in urine which provided a convenient method for obtaining information about the degree of activity of the sympathoadrenal system. Differential estimation of adrenaline and noradrenaline by biological or chemical assay of the extracts yielded further information in that most of the adrenaline derived from the adrenal medulla whereas the noradrenaline mainly originated from the adrenergic nerves. Erect posture and physical work were found to be associated with increased activity of the vasoconstrictor nerves, while mental stress, caused by apprehension or fear, went with an increased urinary excretion of adrenaline from the adrenal medulla.

In some cases the urine analysis for catecholamine had a diagnostic value. Thus Euler showed, with A. Engel, a large increase in urinary catecholamine output in phaeochromocytoma, which could be successfully treated by surgery.

After having established that noradrenaline serves as neurotransmitter in the sympathetic system, Euler turned to the problem of storage and release of the noradrenaline from the adrenergic nerve endings. Following the discovery by H. Blaschko, N. A. Hillarp, and collaborators that the catecholamines in the adrenal medulla were bound to subcellular granules, Euler and Hillarp showed that this was also the case in the adrenergic nerves (1956). The granules accumulated in the terminal parts of the nerve fiber, from which the transmitter was released by nerve stimuli.

In collaboration with Lishajko, Euler elaborated methods to isolate the noradrenaline granules from splenic nerves, allowing a study of their properties as regards release, uptake, and storage of noradrenaline. The experiments showed that the noradrenaline was firmly bound to the granules at low temperature, while higher temperatures of the incubation medium caused an accelerated release. Isolated nerve granules incorporated catecholamines from the incubation medium, an effect which was greatly enhanced by addition of adenosinetriphosphate (ATP). Euler and Lishajko further showed that this uptake could be annulled by various metabolic inhibitors, in particular uncouplers of oxidative phosphorylation. Although the mechanism underlying uptake and release of noradrenaline from the granules is still largely unknown, it appears conceivable that the noradrenaline, after local synthesis, binds to a highly temperature-dependent complex.

Other studies concerned the regulation of respiration and circulation (with C. Heymans), experimental hypertension (with E. Braun-Menendez), and pulmonary circulation (with G. Liljestrand). The studies on pulmonary circulation led to the observation of an automatic regulation mechanism for the distribution of pulmonary blood flow, depending on the oxygen content of the respiratory air.

Many drugs were shown to affect uptake and release, particularly reserpine and a variety of psychotropic drugs, which seemed to inactivate these processes even in low concentrations, presumably by interfering with the complex formation.

Euler's father was a biochemist and Nobel laureate in chemistry in 1929. His mother was a specialist in diatome research and daughter of P. T. Cleve, professor of chemistry in Uppsala and discoverer of the elements holmium and thulium. After medical studies at the Karolinska Institute (1922–30) and studies abroad, Euler was assistant professor in pharmacology and physiology at the institute until 1939, when he became professor of physiology; he retired from that position in 1971. He received the Gairdner Prize (1961), the Jahre Award (1965), the Stouffer Prize (1967), the Nobel Prize in medicine and physiology (1970), and the F. Cuenca Villoro Award (1973). He was elected a foreign member of the Leopoldina Academy (1962), the Philosophical Society (1971), the American Academy of Arts and Sciences (1972), the National Academy of Sciences (1972), and the Royal Society (1973).

Euler published a monograph, *Noradrenaline* (1956) and, with R. Eliasson *Prostaglandins* (1968).

For background information *see* HORMONE, ADRENAL MEDULLA; NEUROPHYSIOLOGY; SYMPATHETIC NERVOUS SYSTEM in the McGraw-Hill Encyclopedia of Science and Technology. ∎

EVANS, GRIFFITH CONRAD
★ American mathematician

Born May 11, 1887, Boston, MA, U.S.A.
Died Dec. 8, 1973, Walnut Creek, CA, U.S.A.

Evans worked in the fields of integral and functional equations, harmonic functions, and potential theory.

In second-order partial differential equations, the second-order derivatives often require conditions not essential for the problem. Thus, for example, in 1916 Evans replaced second-order partial differential expressions by integral expressions over variable domains of first-order terms, deriving a corresponding Green's theorem, and so forth.

In 1906 Maxime Bôcher proved that if $u(x,y)$ is of class C^1 and the relation $\int_s (du/dn)ds = 0$ is satisfied for all circles in a bounded domain Ω, then u is of class $C\infty$ and satisfies Laplace's equation $\nabla^2 u = 0$. A corresponding problem is Poisson's equation $\nabla^2 u = f(x,y)$.

This equation implies a similar generalization, for which Evans in 1919 introduced the concept of mass as a completely (infinitely) additive function of point sets $f(e)$. The statement of the problem and a particular solution become

$$\int_s D_n u\, ds = F(s)$$

$$u_0(M) = \frac{1}{2\pi} \int_\Omega \log \frac{1}{MP}\, df(e_p)$$

valid for closed curves s that intersect a certain set E of two-dimensional measure >0 at most in a one-dimensional set of measure >0; $D_n u$ is the normal component of the vector $D_h u$, defined except on E as the limit, when the area $\sigma \to 0$ as in a Lebesgue derivative, of $(1/\sigma)\int_s u\, dh'$, where $\angle hh' = \pi/2$, and s is the boundary of σ; $F(s)$ is the Volterra function of curves corresponding to $f(e)$. A change in the order of integration of this last relation produces the solution.

With the use of this concept of mass, H. E. Bray and Evans (1923) gave necessary and sufficient conditions for correspondingly generalized forms of the Poisson integral for the circle and the sphere. In 1929 Evans and E. R. C. Miles solved Dirichlet and Neumann boundary value problems of new types, on smooth surfaces. Here the functions to be determined are functions of curves, solutions of Lebesgue-Stieltjes integral equations, with attention to the critical values 1 and -1 in the Poincaré-Robin equations.

The answer to a crucial question about the nature of boundary points, regular for the Dirichlet boundary value problem, is O. D. Kellogg's conjecture of 1926, known as Kellogg's lemma: if F is a bounded set of positive capacity, it contains a regular boundary point. Kellogg died before finding a proof of its validity. That Evans succeeded, in 1933, was a result of the use of completely additive set functions. He followed this note with an extensive memoir in 1935 on potentials of positive masses.

In 1936 Evans proved the following theorem: Let F be a bounded closed set in space with exterior domain D, s the interior boundary of D, and $u(M)$ harmonic in D; let M in $D \to Q$, Q in s. Then $u(M) \to +\infty$ for every Q if, and only if, capacity $s = 0$. The necessity part of Evans's theorem he had proved in the above cited memoir. The sufficiency is obtained by examining the energy of the generated potential function in terms of transfinite diameter.

Given a simple closed curve s in space, itself of zero capacity—for example, consisting of a finite number of "regular" arcs—Evans proved (1940) that among the surfaces with boundary s there is one, S, of minimum capacity. In fact, the Euler condition is the same as saying that the desired function $V(M)$ can be prolonged across S to form a double-valued function, harmonic in the whole space, with S the unique branch surface and s the branch curve. That the capacity is a strict minimum derives from a comparison of energy integrals. Generalizations of such problems were the subject of publication in 1951 and 1961, the second with consideration of two branch curves, each of order 1, the total space consisting of infinity subspaces.

Evans studied mathematics, physics, and philosophy at Harvard University, where he received his B.A. in 1907 and his Ph.D. in 1910. After 2 years in Europe with V. Volterra, except for a summer with Max Planck, he taught from 1912 to 1934 at the Rice Institute and from 1934 to 1955 at the University of California, Berkeley, becoming emeritus in 1954. With a strong philosophical interest in the relation of mathematics to "reality," he was able to successfully apply his scientific-mathematical knowledge in both world wars. He also wrote extensively in economics, using mostly, but not entirely, elementary mathematics. Beginning in 1924, he and his students initiated theories of dynamical economics, in contrast to those of moving equilibria, by using time derivatives and functionals over time intervals, in economic relations. In *Mathematical Introduction to Economics* (1930), he gave a systematic exposition of this subject, and incidentally showed by examples how small is the change from cycle to crisis. He was elected to the National Academy of Sciences in 1933.

For background information *see* CALCULUS, DIFFERENTIAL AND INTEGRAL;

SPHERICAL HARMONICS in the McGraw-Hill Encyclopedia of Science and Technology. ∎

EWING, WILLIAM MAURICE
☆ American geophysicist

Born May 12, 1906, Lockney, TX, U.S.A.
Died May 4, 1974, Galveston, TX, U.S.A.

For his fundamental contributions to general geophysics, including seismology, geodesy, oceanography, and submarine geology, Ewing received the Day Medal of the Geological Society of America (1949), the Agassiz (1955) and Carty (1963) medals of the National Academy of Sciences, the Vetlesen Prize (1960), the Gold Medal of the Royal Astronomical Society (1964), the National Medal of Science (1973), and other medals and awards.

In the late 1920s Ewing spent the summers employed by geophysical prospecting companies. During the early 1930s he engaged in academic research in geophysical exploration. After 1935 his interests extended to applications of all of the major methods of exploration to problems concerning the oceanic crust of the Earth and the transition from continental to oceanic crust at continental margins. This was an environment where little geophysical work had been attempted. Hence methods and instruments had to be devised as needed. Before the end of the decade Ewing had made remarkable progress in his study of the "Emerged and Submerged Atlantic Coastal Plain." The most valuable contribution of this study came from his newly developed seismic method of refraction shooting at sea. He also made gravity measurements with F. A. Vening Meinesz's pendulum method. This work resulted in a series of papers that revealed the great thickness of sedimentary rocks on and near the continental boundary and the great vertical movements that must have been associated with their deposition. *See* VENING MEINESZ, FELIX ANDRIES.

Ewing spent much of World War II working at the Woods Hole Oceanographic Institution on the propagation of sound in the sea and on photography of shipwrecks. Although these investigations were, to a large extent, for defense purposes, this work led to the SOFAR sound transmission system, a utilization of the sound channel in the ocean that formed the basis for subsequent extensive applications. This war work provided bases for Ewing's postwar work at Columbia University's Lamont Geological Observatory, an establishment that he was instrumental in forming and of which he became director at its founding in 1949. Small to begin with, Lamont (now Lamont-Doherty) Geological Observatory has become perhaps the most comprehensive geological and geophysical research unit in the world. The work at Lamont in its early days had three dominant aspects. First, there was the geophysical and geological work at sea: it was in 1949 that Ewing made the first determination of the crustal thickness of the ocean floor, and eventually the Lamont team established the system of marine geophysical measurement that is used in many other laboratories. Second, there was the development of a powerful group of earthquake seismologists, theoretical and experimental, who built a seismological observatory on the grounds of Lamont and a worldwide network of similar seismograph stations. Third, an active program of radio and isotope geology was established for measuring the ages of marine samples. Ewing's main interest in the field of seismology was the study of surface waves as a method of gaining more information concerning the crustal and mantle rocks of the Earth, particularly the water-covered part. He identified the T-phase from earthquakes as sound waves propagated in the ocean water. His other interests included paleoclimatology, micropaleontology, and radiochemical age determinations.

In marine research, Ewing's name is particularly associated with turbidity currents, abyssal plains, mid-ocean ridges, and crustal thicknesses. This phase of his career began with cruises of the *Atlantis* to the Mid-Atlantic Ridge in 1947 and 1948, during which many of the instruments which came into wide use were devised. By means of seismic reflections, gravity measurements, photographs, long sediment cores, and dredge hauls from the bottom, Ewing and his fellow Columbia oceanographers showed the ocean floor to be as various a structure as the land surface with rugged mountains, exposed basaltic rocks, flat-topped plateaus (guyots), pebble-strewn regions, and extremely flat plains; a deep gorge within the Mid-Atlantic Ridge was also found. In 1952 Ewing took sediment cores and soundings that showed that the Hudson Canyon had been carved out by turbulent undersea flows of mud and sediment, which was deposited further seaward to form the abyssal plain. In 1956 he showed that the Mid-Atlantic Ridge followed the known belt of seismic activity and continued around Africa into the Indian Ocean and around Antarctica into the Pacific, forming a world-girdling undersea mountain system. Later, from many crossings, he showed that there was a fault or chasm from 8 to 30 miles (12.8 to 48 kilometers) wide in the crest of the Mid-Atlantic Ridge, and interpreted this to be evidence that the process that formed the ridge and rift was still active.

Ewing's controversial theory of ice ages stimulated study in the field of paleoclimatology. Periodic ice ages had traditionally been thought to occur at times when, for some obscure reason, the Earth became cooler than normal. During the 1950s Ewing and his group found evidence in deep-sea sediments suggesting that ice ages result from changes in oceanic circulation. He offered the hypothesis that when the Arctic Ocean is free of ice cover it serves as a source of water vapor, which is deposited on Siberia and Canada as snow. As the snow accumulates, it forms a barrier that also increases precipitation from winds from the south. Temperatures drop, glaciers move down from the north, sea level falls, and eventually the Arctic Ocean freezes over. Once that happens, the source of snow is choked off, the glaciers retreat, and temperatures rise until, as now, the glaciers are mostly gone from the lowlands (though still lingering on Antarctica and Greenland) while the Arctic Ocean remains frozen over. If warming continues to the point where the Arctic ice melts, the Arctic Ocean will then contribute water vapor to the polar atmosphere and the cycle will begin again.

Beginning in 1960, Ewing organized seven worldwide cruises of the research vessels *Vema* and *Robert D. Conrad* for the primary purpose of systematically mapping stratification and thickness of sediment cover in the world ocean, and sampling the oldest sediments available. An ingenious inventor of instruments, Ewing developed improved echo sounders, magnetometers, bathythermographs, sediment coring apparatus, sediment temperature probes, and an underwater camera that permitted oceanographers for the first time to see what life there was in the ocean depths. Because of the great pressures and the absence of light below a few thousand feet, oceanographers had thought that little marine life existed there. Ewing's photographs proved the presence of marine life, sometimes strikingly different from any known earlier, and gave valuable information about other surface features of the ocean floor, such as burrows, tracks and trails, outcrops, current ripples, and manganese nodules.

Research of this type requires the teamwork of many scientists, and all of these developments were characterized by collaboration with others, usually his former students.

Ewing received his B.A. (1926), M.A. (1927), and Ph.D. (1931) in physics at the Rice Institute in Houston. He was an instructor in physics at the University of Pittsburgh (1929–30) and an instructor and assistant professor of physics at Lehigh University (1930–40). In 1940 he was named associate professor of geology at Lehigh, but he spent much of the next 4 years on leave of absence at the Woods Hole Oceanographic Institution. In 1944 he was appointed associate professor of geology at Columbia University, becoming a full professor in 1947. In 1949 he was appointed director of Columbia's Lamont Geological Observatory, and in 1959 was named Higgins Professor of Geology. He was elected to the National Academy of Sciences in 1948.

Ewing wrote *Propagation of Sound in the Ocean,* with J. L. Worzel and C. Pekeris (1948), *Elastic Waves in Layered Media,* with Frank Press and W. Jardetsky

(1957), and *The Floors of the Oceans: I. The North Atlantic,* with B. C. Heezen and M. Tharp (1959), and a large number of papers and chapters in books.

For background information *see* GEODESY; MARINE GEOLOGY; OCEANOGRAPHY; PALEOCLIMATOLOGY; SEISMOLOGY; TURBIDITY CURRENT in the McGraw-Hill Encyclopedia of Science and Technology. ∎

EYRING, HENRY
★ American chemist

***Born** Feb. 20, 1901, Colonia Juarez, Chihuahua, Mexico*

Eyring pioneered in the application of quantum and statistical mechanics to chemistry and developed the theory of absolute reaction rates and the significant structure theory of liquids. Absolute reaction rate theory provides a basis for treating all chemical reactions. The theory of liquids provides the basis of a quantitative formulation of the thermodynamic properties of liquids and, together with rate theory, provides a similar basis for transport properties. Eyring also developed theories of optical activity, mass spectrography, the addition of dipoles and bond lengths in flexible high polymers, and bioluminescence. For his contributions to theoretical chemistry, Eyring was awarded the American Chemical Society's Gilbert Newton Lewis Medal in 1963.

Quantum mechanics, by providing a theory for calculating the interactions between atoms and molecules, makes it pos-

sible to calculate the energy of any configuration of atoms. If this energy is plotted "vertically," and if appropriate interatomic distances are chosen in such a way as to specify the atomic configuration, the resulting multidimensional surface is called the potential surface in configuration space. The low regions of this surface correspond to compounds, and a reaction may be described as the passage of a point from one minimum through the saddle point into a neighboring valley. Fritz London, in 1928, called attention to the possibility of constructing such surfaces and gave approximate formulas for simple three- and four-atom systems.

In 1929 and 1930 Eyring and Michael Polanyi calculated the potential surface for three hydrogen atoms. Subsequently, Eyring with his collaborators extended the quantum-mechanical calculations to many atoms and constructed surfaces for a wide variety of molecular systems. In the meantime, E. P. Wigner and Pelzer, using the Eyring-Polanyi surface, calculated the rate of reaction (1). *See* WIGNER, EUGENE PAUL.

$$H + H_2 \text{ (para)} \rightarrow H_2 \text{ (ortho)} + H \quad (1)$$

In 1935 Eyring formulated the general rate expression: A system at the saddle point, the activated complex, is like any other molecule in all of its degrees of freedom except for the reaction coordinate, that is, the coordinate normal to the potential barrier. The activated complex is next assumed to be in equilibrium with the reactants. Using the theory of small vibrations to calculate the normal modes, one can arrive at the explicit expression for the specific rate of reaction (2).

$$k' = \kappa \frac{kT}{h} e^{-\Delta G^{\ddagger}/RT} \quad (2)$$

Here $\Delta G^{\ddagger}$ is the work required to assemble the activated complex from reactants. Transmission coefficient κ is ordinarily near unity and is the factor that corrects for quantum-mechanical effects and any departure from equilibrium. The symbols k, R, h, and T are the Boltzmann constant, gas constant, Planck's constant, and absolute temperature, respectively.

Now, to pass on to the theory of liquids: Removing a molecule from a condensed phase to the vapor state, leaving a vacancy, involves breaking all the bonds holding the molecule, whereas to vaporize a molecule without leaving a vacancy involves breaking only half the bonds. It follows that the creation of a vacancy costs the same energy as the vaporization of a molecule. If an isolated vacancy is formed in a solid, it is locked in and provides only a positional degeneracy. At the melting point enough vacancies go into a liquid, acting cooperatively, to mobilize the vacancies, giving them gaslike properties.

The result is that the liquid contains a mixture of gas- and solidlike degrees of freedom. This model leads to an expression for the Helmholtz free energy of the liquid in agreement with the experiment. For simple liquids all parameters are calculable from the models. For complicated liquids the appropriate model may be selected by comparing calculated and observed thermodynamic properties much as structure can be determined in x-ray analysis.

Absolute rate theory has been applied successfully to all types of problems. Modern developments are concerned with explicit calculations of the transmission coefficient κ. Liquid theory is also widely applicable and has been successful in calculating the properties of ordinary liquids, molten metals, molten salts, and water.

Born in northern Mexico, Eyring rode the range with his father until the Mexican revolution forced the American colonists to leave in 1912. After a year in El Paso the family moved to Arizona. Eyring attended the University of Arizona, where he obtained a B.S. in mining engineering (1923) and an M.S. in metallurgy (1924). He obtained his Ph.D. in chemistry at the University of California, Berkeley, in 1927; taught for 2 years at the University of Wisconsin, where he collaborated with Farrington Daniels, spent a year at Fritz Haber's laboratory in Berlin working with Polanyi; returned to Berkeley for a year as lecturer; and for 15 years (1931–46) was on the faculty of Princeton University. In 1946 he became dean of the graduate school and professor of chemistry and metallurgy at the University of Utah. He retired as dean in 1966 and was named Distinguished Professor of Chemistry. Later research activities, with some 20 collaborators, were concerned with corrosion, the oxygen electrode, high explosives, molecular structure and drug design, anesthesia, reaction rates, and liquid structure. Eyring's

contributions were recognized by 15 honorary doctorates and over 20 distinguished awards. He was elected to the National Academy of Sciences in 1945. *See* DANIELS, FARRINGTON.

Eyring published over 600 scientific papers and coauthored nine books: *The Theory of Rate Processes* (1941), *Quantum Chemistry* (1944), *The Kinetic Basis of Molecular Biology* (1954), *Modern Chemical Kinetics* (1963), *Statistical Mechanics and Dynamics* (1964), *Significant Liquid Structures* (1969), *The Theory of Optical Activity* (1971), *The Theory of Rate Processes in Biology and Medicine* (1974), and *Deformation Kinetics* (1975). He was the editor of *Annual Reviews of Physical Chemistry* (1956–75), of 15 volumes of *Physical Chemistry: An Advanced Treatise*, with Henderson and Jost, and 4 volumes of *Theoretical Chemistry: Advances and Perspectives*, with Henderson.

For background information *see* LIQUID; QUANTUM MECHANICS in the McGraw-Hill Encyclopedia of Science and Technology. ∎

FADDEEV, LUDWIG DMITRIEVITCH
★ Soviet mathematician

Born Mar. 10, 1934, Leningrad, Soviet Union

Faddeev's scientific views owe much to the influence of the St. Petersburg– Leningrad mathematical school, whose prominent representatives in mathematical physics were M. V. Ostrogradsky, A. M. Lyapunov, V. A. Steklov, and in later decades, V. A. Fock. Characteristic of the school was its interest in concrete problems, important for applications both in physics and in pure mathematics, and presenting considerable theoretical difficulties.

Faddeev's first publications were concerned with scattering theory, one of the central topics in quantum mechanics. An intensive study of scattering processes, started as soon as quantum mechanics came into being, provided a basis for its statistical interpretation. The work of K. O. Friedrichs made it clear that an adequate mathematics for scattering theory was perturbation theory of continuous spectra of operators. Along these lines, a detailed theory of two-particle scattering was developed in the 1950s. Still, the many-particle problem was impeded by fundamental difficulties stemming from the existence of many scattering channels. The physical importance of the problem stimulated numerous palliative methods of approximate solution, K. M. Watson's method of multiple scattering being the best known. All these methods assumed that the interaction between the particles

was small and therefore could not account for multichannel scattering processes and bound states for many-particle systems. The difficulties were overcome by Faddeev. In 1963, in his paper "Mathematical Problems of Quantum Scattering Theory for a System of Three Particles," he developed a complete theory of multichannel scattering for three-particle systems. His method, later called the method of Faddeev's equations, and its generalizations to many-particle systems constitute the main tool of multichannel scattering theory. *See* FRIEDRICHS, KURT OTTO.

Another branch of scattering theory that constantly drew Faddeev's attention was the so-called inverse problem. He considered it to be one of the most intriguing topics in modern mathematical physics. Physically speaking, the problem is to reconstruct the interactions between the particles from their scattering data. The one-dimensional case was thoroughly investigated in the 1950s in both physical and mathematical aspects. With regard to the many-dimensional system, a uniqueness theorem proved by Faddeev in his first publication (1956) remained for a long time the only rigorous mathematical solution. In 1965 Faddeev returned to the subject and constructed many-dimensional analogs of Jost functions which are special solutions of the Schrödinger equation and which play a central role in the study of the inverse problem. This provided a key to the whole problem. By 1972 Faddeev completed the theory and obtained a full solution of the many-dimensional problem.

Many-particle scattering theory naturally led Faddeev to quantum field theory, which poses the most difficult many-particle problems. His first publication on this subject indicated an approach, later realized by his pupils, to a rigorous scattering theory for some models in quantum field theory.

Mathematical methods of quantum scattering theory proved very useful in quite another branch of pure mathematics. In 1967 Faddeev published a paper in which he applied the above methods to the spectral theory of automorphic functions. This work brought about a new insight into A. Selberg's theory and strongly stimulated investigation of some of its ramifications.

Nonetheless, Faddeev's main concern at the time was the problem of quantization, that is, the connection between classical and quantum physics. Generally, it is

F

stated as the correspondence principle of N. Bohr. In nonrelativistic quantum mechanics, the problem is of a philosophic nature and related to the logical foundations. In relativistic quantum field theory, which is far from its final form, it should not be disregarded even by the most pragmatic theorist. The problem was first treated in general terms by P. A. M. Dirac. He gave particular attention to quantizing classical systems with singular Lagrangians. Among them are all gauge-invariant fields such as gravitational and Yang-Mills fields. The nonlinear character of their phase space and, in the case of the gravitational field, the lack of relativistic invariance caused serious difficulties in his approach. Faddeev realized that a breakthrough was possible if, instead of canonical quantization, the Feynman integral was used. This elegant mathematical concept was introduced by R. P. Feynman in his famous work on quantum electrodynamics. Despite its lucidity and efficiency, the integral had long been considered to be a kind of museum piece. Having performed a systematic study of functional integration, Faddeev and his pupil V. N. Popov succeeded in constructing a consistent perturbation theory for the quantum theory of gauge fields. See BOHR, NIELS HENRIK DAVID; DIRAC, PAUL ADRIAN MAURICE; FEYNMAN, RICHARD PHILLIPS.

The concept of gauge field and its generally accepted physical relevance renewed the idea of the geometrical formulation of physics, which goes back to N. I. Lobachevsky and G. F. B. Riemann. Physical space is seen as a fiber bundle, with the space-time manifold as a base and the gauge group as a structure group, the gauge field being an infinitesimal connection. Faddeev was one of the first to advocate this geometrical idea of unification in elementary particle physics. At a conference on mathematical physics held in Moscow in 1972, he put forward a "geometrical manifesto" on the relationship of differential geometry and physics.

In the late 1960s a group of American scientists, including M. D. Kruskal, C. S. Gardner, R. M. Miura, J. M. Greene, and P. D. Lax, invented a method for solving some nonlinear evolution equations, which was later called the inverse scattering method. Faddeev took an active part in the formulation and development of this method. In a joint paper he and V. E. Zakharov were the first to show that the infinite-dimensional systems treated by

the method were completely integrable in the sense of Hamiltonian dynamics. It is noteworthy that this work united Faddeev's early interests: the inverse scattering problem for the one-dimensional Schrödinger operator, trace identities, and the Hamiltonian formalism. A subsequent study of various nonlinear equations which he carried out with his pupils was aimed at nontrivial models in classical field theory, the sine-Gordon equation being a well-known instance. The rich particle spectrum of the latter brought to life Einstein's old dream of a correspondence between elementary particles and some special solutions of classical field equations (in the inverse scattering method they are called solitons). Using functional integration, Faddeev developed a quantum theory of solitons. Later he and his pupils obtained an answer to the intriguing question concerning the relationship between a classical system and its quantum analog with regard to complete integrability, thus constructing a self-consistent quantum version of the inverse method.

The son of D. K. Faddeev, a well-known mathematician, Faddeev received his education at Leningrad University, from which he graduated in 1956. In 1969 he became a professor at Leningrad. In 1976 he became deputy director of the Steklov Mathematical Institute of the Academy of Sciences, responsible for its Leningrad branch. In 1976 he was elected a member of the Academy of Sciences of the U.S.S.R., and in 1979 a foreign honorary member of the American Academy of Arts and Sciences. Faddeev received the U.S.S.R. State Prize in 1971 and the Dannie Heineman Prize in Mathematical Physics of the American Physical Society in 1975.

For background information *see* FIBER BUNDLE; GEOMETRY, DIFFERENTIAL; QUANTUM FIELD THEORY; QUANTUM MECHANICS in the McGraw-Hill Encyclopedia of Science and Technology. ∎

FAGET, MAXIME ALLAN

★ American engineer and spacecraft designer

Born Aug. 26, 1921, Stann Creek, British Honduras

Faget spent his career in service to the United States government. During World War II he was assigned to submarine ser-

vice in the Pacific. Upon leaving the Navy in 1946, he became employed by the National Advisory Committee for Aeronautics (NACA) and continued after it was reorganized as the National Aeronautics and Space Administration (NASA). His first assignment with NACA was with the Pilotless Aircraft Research Division (PARD) at the Langley Laboratory in Hampton, VA. The work carried out at PARD was in the forefront of high-speed aerodynamic research. Surplus military rockets were used to propel research vehicles to test conditions not obtainable in wind tunnels. In the early years of PARD, tests were primarily directed toward obtaining data at transonic speeds. Later, when transonic wind tunnels became perfected, the emphasis at PARD moved to higher-speed flight, with much of the effort carried out in support of the United States' ballistic missile program. Here the primary concern was survival of the warhead during the extreme heating that occurs during atmospheric entry. Five-stage research vehicles launched from Wallops Island, VA, provided heating data at speeds in excess of 15,000 feet (4575 meters) per second. During this time Faget was assigned as the NACA consultant to the Polaris Missile Special Task Group. In that role he proposed a superior aerodynamic shape for the nose cone, resulting in a significant weight reduction.

Faget's career at PARD focused on research on supersonic inlets, ramjets, transonic drag, boundary-layer phenomena, and aerodynamic heating. He was an in-

novator and spent as much time on finding new ways to use the rocket-powered test vehicles as he did on pure research. By 1949 he had designed and developed a small (6-inch or 15-centimeter diameter) supersonic ramjet and a test vehicle that mounted two of these ramjets on its horizontal tail. When boosted to supersonic speed by a rocket, these ramjets accelerated the test vehicle and operated in flight at a higher altitude (65,000 feet or 19.8 kilometers) and a greater speed ($M = 3.1$) than attained by any previous air-breathing engine.

During the early 1950s NACA began a series of analytical and sizing studies directed toward the proposal of a new rocket-powered research airplane that would fly much faster than existing machines. Faget's contributions to these studies were in the areas of propulsion system definition, weight analysis, and performance prediction. These studies led to the construction of the X-15, which subsequently flew at $M = 6.7$. However, before the X-15 made its first flight, the Soviet Union launched the first artificial satellite and the space era was born.

Although NASA did not become an official entity until October 1958, NACA started planning its space program early in 1958. The development of the Scout launch vehicle was started, based on preliminary design studies carried out under Faget's supervision. The Scout, which became NASA's lowest-cost launch vehicle, was still in service more than 20 years later.

The first crewed space program undertaken by NASA was Project Mercury. Faget conceived its major design features and the basic flight development program. He conceived the idea of using a contour couch to support the human body during periods of launch and reentry acceleration. The form-fitting couch sucessfully protected human test subjects on a centrifuge for periods of up to 1 minute at 20 g. He also came up with the idea of using a tractor rocket to provide the spacecraft and crew with a means of escape when conditions leading to a catastrophic failure of the launch are detected. Many design features of both the Gemini and Apollo spacecraft are derivations of Faget's original basic concepts.

When NASA organized the Manned Spacecraft Center in Houston, Faget was appointed director of engineering and development. In this position he influenced the major design aspects of all crewed

spacecraft built by the United States. Even before the first astronaut landed on the Moon, Faget had organized a design team to study the feasibility of a completely recoverable spacecraft. These studies were preliminary to the space shuttle program.

Faget's father, Guy H. Faget, pioneered in the use of sulfones to cure leprosy. His great-grandfather, Jean Charles Faget, is credited with the discovery of the "Faget sign," a symptom that facilitated the early diagnosis and epidemic control of yellow fever. Maxime Faget received a B.S. degree in mechanical engineering from Louisiana State University in 1943. He was elected a member of the National Academy of Engineering and the International Academy of Astronautics, and received major awards from the American Institute of Aeronautics and Astronautics, International Astronautical Foundation, American Astronautical Society, American Society of Mechanical Engineers, Institute of Electrical and Electronics Engineers, Instrument Society of America, and NASA. Louisiana State University and the University of Pittsburgh awarded him honorary doctorates of engineering. He wrote *Manned Space Flight* (1965) and coauthored *Manned Spacecraft: Engineering Design and Operations,* with P. E. Purser and N. F. Smith (1964).

For background information *see* AERO-DYNAMICS; MANNED SPACE FLIGHT; ROCKET ENGINE in the McGraw-Hill Encyclopedia of Science and Technology. ∎

FARBER, SIDNEY
American pathologist and medical scientist

Born Sept. 30, 1903, Buffalo, NY, U.S.A.
Died Mar. 30, 1973, Boston, MA, U.S.A.

As a medical student in 1923, Farber became a disciple of S. B. Wolbach, professor of pathology at Harvard Medical School. Trained by this great general pathologist, he specialized in pediatric pathology. Farber's subsequent lectures and demonstrations reflected the transition of pathology from static anatomic and histologic statements to dynamic descriptions of the biological changes occurring during the course of human disease.

In 1929 Farber became instructor in pathology at Harvard Medical School and

the first full-time pathologist at the (Boston) Children's Hospital. His early lectures on the history and application of the autopsy to medicine, as well as his book, *The Postmortem Examination*, are classics. The long list of classic descriptions of pediatric disease appearing from his department included cystic fibrosis as a systemic disease; human infection with Eastern equine encephalitis virus; hyaline membrane disease and sudden death syndrome in the newborn; and transposition of the great vessels, which contributed immensely to the development of pediatric cardiac surgery.

Farber's interest in pediatric disease was not limited to biology and pathology, but encompassed patient care and treatment as well—he was the kind of physician-pathologist who went "upstairs" to the wards and clinics rather than waiting for the patient to come "downstairs" to pathology. He often expressed concern that so little was being done in those early days for the child with disseminated neoplastic disease, especially the leukemias, although much was already being done for the child with a tumor amenable to surgical extirpation. His early studies on acute leukemia, probably undertaken because of his refusal to accept the debilitating feeling of hopelessness and the consequent lack of real therapeutic effort then typically occasioned by this diagnosis, led him into an area of research wherein he made perhaps his greatest contributions.

Shortly after World War II Farber undertook studies on "folic acid" (pteroylglutamic acid) and its conjugates, synthe-

sized by Y. Subba-Row at Lederle Laboratories. Farber observed an "acceleration phenomenon" in the bone marrows and viscera of children with acute leukemia who had been treated with these agents. He ventured a prediction that an "antagonist" to folic acid might be useful in the treatment of acute leukemia, and asked Subba-Row for such an agent, who soon provided a series of potential antagonists, including aminopterin (4-aminopterolyglutamic acid) in November 1947. The results of the evaluation of this agent were reported in 1948, describing the induction of complete remissions in children with acute leukemia treated with it. This medical milestone, opening new vistas of research and clinical study, clearly marked Farber as the father of the modern era of chemotherapy of neoplastic disease.

The new directions of investigation opened by these studies required additional staff and facilities. Thus in 1947 Farber conceived, and with two lifelong associates, William S. Koster and George E. Foley, organized the Children's Cancer Research Foundation. This world-famous institution, better known as the "Jimmy Fund," was the first to be devoted solely to the study, care, and treatment of children with neoplastic disease. His pioneering studies and those of his staff at the foundation led to the development of philosophy, precepts, and methods which have led to dramatic changes in the care and treatment of patients with neoplastic disease in institutions throughout the world. He conceived and implemented "total care," the mobilization of all medical and social resources to assist not only the patient with neoplastic disease, but the stricken family as well. Directly or indirectly, because of his work, remarkable advances were made in the treatment of Wilms' tumor, rhabdomyosarcoma, osteogenic sarcoma, Ewing's tumor, Hodgkin's disease, lymphoma, and acute leukemia—indeed, there is now free discussion of the cure of acute leukemia in children.

In 1971 Farber initiated the Charles A. Dana Cancer Center to extend the services of his foundation to adult patients. Shortly after his death in 1973, his foundation was designated a comprehensive cancer center by the National Cancer Institute. The foundation was renamed the Sidney Farber Cancer Institute, and now consists of three buildings: the original "Jimmy Fund" Building, the Michael D. Redstone Laboratories, and the Charles A. Dana Cancer Center.

Farber's participation in health and biomedical affairs at the national level spanned more than 20 years, during which he served as an articulate spokesman and medical statesman for the health and biomedical community. In addition to participating in various study sections of the National Institutes of Health, Food and Drug Administration, and the Armed Forces Institute of Pathology, he served on the National Advisory Cancer Council, National Advisory Health Council, Panel on Cancer of the President's Comission on Heart Disease, Cancer and Stroke, and National Panel of Consultants on the Conquest of Cancer, among others. In 1955 he participated in organization of the Cancer Chemotherapy National Committee and served for 7 years as its first chairperson. This committee implemented the organization of the Cancer Chemotherapy National Service Center. His service in voluntary health agencies was equally all-encompassing, especially in those concerned with pediatric or neoplastic disease. He was president of seven scientific societies, including the American Cancer Society.

Farber graduated from the University of Buffalo (B.S., 1923) and from Harvard Medical School (M.D., 1927). In 1929 he became instructor in pathology at Harvard and pathologist at the Children's Hospital in Boston. He became chairperson of the Staff Planning Committee and of the Division of Laboratories and Research at the Children's Hospital in 1946, and pathologist in chief in 1949. His Harvard professorship came in 1948, and in 1967 he became the first incumbent of the S. B. Wolbach Chair in Pathology at Harvard Medical School. In 1964 he became chairperson of the staff, responsible for the planning and policies of the Children's Hospital Medical Center. His concept of an Institute of Pediatric Pathology took form as the Pediatric Research Building, enabling the grouping of scientific and medical resources. He received nine honorary degrees from American and European universities and more than 20 humanitarian and scientific awards in cancer research, biomedical research, patient care, therapeutics, and chemotherapy, including the Lasker Award.

Farber was author or coauthor of more than 270 publications on pediatric disease and cancer research, including chapters in 12 books. He wrote *The Postmortem Examination* (1937).

For background information *see* CHEMOTHERAPY; LEUKEMIA in the McGraw-Hill Encyclopedia of Science and Technology. ∎

FEFFERMAN, CHARLES LOUIS
☆ American mathematician

Born Apr. 18, 1949, Washington, DC, U.S.A.

Fefferman worked in several areas of analysis, including Fourier analysis, partial differential equations, and the theory of functions of several complex variables.

In the area of Fourier analysis, some of Fefferman's major results concerned convergence properties of Fourier series of periodic functions of two variables. These Fourier series were found to behave quite differently from series associated with functions of one variable. The Fourier series of a function $f(x,y)$ of period 2π in x and y has the form (1), where m and n run

$$\sum_m \sum_n a_{mn} e^{i(mx+ny)} \qquad (1)$$

over all the integers. To examine its convergence, one can study the convergence of the trigonometric polynomials $p_{MN}(x,y)$, defined by Eq. (2), as M and N

$$p_{MN}(x,y) = \sum_{|m| \leqslant M} \sum_{|n| \leqslant N} a_{mn} e^{i(mx+ny)} \qquad (2)$$

approach infinity. Fefferman showed that,

contrary to what might have been expected, there are rather simple continuous functions for which the p_{MN} do not have to converge almost everywhere even if the ratios M/N and N/M are bounded. Remarkably, the polynomials do converge almost everywhere for the case $M = N$. Fefferman also arrived at a surprising result concerning the trigonometric polynomials $p_R(x,y)$ obtained by summing the Fourier series (1) over integer pairs satisfying $m^2 + n^2 < R$. It had long been known that if f is an L^2 function (that is, a function which, when squared, is integrable), then the p_R converge to f in the space of L^2 functions, but Fefferman proved that the corresponding statement is false for L^p functions (that is, functions which, when raised to the pth power, are integrable) for $1 < p < \infty$ and $p \neq 2$.

In proving these results, Fefferman made use of results obtained many years previously in the study of a geometric problem known as Kekeya's needle problem: what is the smallest area of a plane region in which a line segment of unit length can be continuously moved so that it returns to its original position after turning through 360°? In 1928 A. S. Besicovitch showed that a region of arbitrarily small area would suffice. Fefferman's use of this result exemplified his practice of using work done in different branches of mathematics to attack problems on a broad front. *See* BESICOVITCH, ABRAM SAMOILOVITCH.

Another of Fefferman's results concerned functions of bounded mean oscillation (BMO functions), and the Hardy spaces H^p. The latter are spaces consisting of L^p functions of period 2π which are boundary values of functions that are analytic inside the unit disk. The Hardy spaces are Banach spaces, as are the L^p spaces, and it has long been known that for $p > 1$ the dual space of L^p is L^q and the dual space of H^p is H^q, where $q = p/(p - 1)$. The dual space of L^1 is the space L^∞ of all bounded, measurable functions, but the properties of the dual space of H^1 remained unknown until they were investigated by Fefferman. In 1971 he showed that the elements of this space are the same as the BMO functions, introduced in 1961 by F. John in studies motivated by elasticity theory. In John's work the BMO functions were used to represent derivatives of displacements, and while they can be unbounded they are large only on relatively small sets.

In the area of partial differential equations, R. Beals and Fefferman obtained decisive results in 1973 concerning the local solvability of nondegenerate linear partial differential equations, completing earlier work of L. Nirenberg and F. Trèves.

In the theory of functions of several complex variables, Fefferman proved in 1974 that a biholomorphic mapping that takes one strictly pseudoconvex region with a smooth boundary into another will also be smooth up to the boundary. This theorem was extremely difficult to prove, and was previously worked on unsuccessfully by several mathematicians. The difficulty arose from the fact that, in contrast to the situation for one complex variable, simply connected regions in two or more complex variables are generally not biholomorphically equivalent and are, in fact, quite "rigid" under biholomorphic mappings. This rigidity makes methods used for one complex variable inapplicable.

In 1976, in related work, Fefferman constructed an indefinite metric (or Lorentz metric) on $d\Omega \times S_1$, the product of the boundary $d\Omega$ of a strictly pseudoconvex domain in several complex variables and the unit circle S_1, that changes by only a factor under biholomorphic transformations. The projections of the null geodesics for this metric (or light rays, in the terminology of relativity theory) form a set of invariant curves on $d\Omega$, known as chains, which had been discovered previously by completely different methods, and play roughly the same role as do geodesics in differential geometry.

A child prodigy, Fefferman entered college at the age of 14. He received his B.S. from the University of Maryland in 1966 and his Ph.D. from Princeton University in 1969. After another year at Princeton as an instructor, he went to the University of Chicago where, in 1971, he became the youngest full professor at a United States college. In 1974 he returned to Princeton. He received the Salem Prize, administered through the University of Paris (1971), the Alan T. Waterman Award of the National Science Foundation (1976), and the Fields Medal of the International Congress of Mathematicians (1978). He was elected to the American Academy of Arts and Sciences in 1972.

For background information *see* COMPLEX NUMBERS AND COMPLEX VARIABLES; DIFFERENTIAL EQUATION; FOUR-

IER SERIES AND INTEGRALS in the McGraw-Hill Encyclopedia of Science and Technology. ∎

FEIT, WALTER
★ American mathematician

Born Oct. 26, 1930, Vienna, Austria

From his days in graduate school, Feit was intrigued by questions about the structure of finite simple groups and, especially, about the connection between such questions and the theory of characters and modular representations. After a dormant period of several decades, progress was again being made in this area, primarily because of the work of R. Brauer, which had a strong influence on Feit. *See* BRAUER, RICHARD.

Feit's first application of characters to group theory involved the study of Zassenhaus groups. A Zassenhaus group G is a doubly transitive permutation group on a set of n letters such that no element of $G - \{1\}$ fixes three or more letters. The groups $PGL_2(q)$ and $PSL_2(q)$ acting on the projective line are the prototypes of Zassenhaus groups. For these groups, $q = n - 1$ is a prime power. Feit showed that if G is a Zassenhaus group which is not a Frobenius group (that is, $G_{ab} \neq <1>$, where G_{ab} is the group of all elements fixing the two letters a and b), then $n - 1 = p^k$ for some prime p. Furthermore, G contains a subgroup G_0 of index at most 2 such that $G_0 \simeq PSL_2(p^k)$, unless the normalizer of a Sylow p group satisfies some special conditions. Later, N. Ito showed that if $p \neq 2$, the latter possibility cannot occur. If $p = 2$, the situation is more complicated; M. Suzuki was able to complete the classification of Zassenhaus groups only after he had discovered a new class of finite simple groups and characterized them in terms of involutions.

Feit's work on Zassenhaus groups was based on the ideas of coherent sets of characters, a concept which generalized the idea of exceptional characters introduced by Brauer and Suzuki. Before it was possible to apply this idea, it was necessary to show that the Frobenius kernel of a Frobenius group is nilpotent. This had been accomplished by J. G. Thompson in his dissertation when he introduced highly original purely group-theoretic methods. The results on Zassenhaus groups provided evidence that the combination of these purely group-theoretic methods with character theory could be very powerful. This evidence was reinforced when Feit, in a joint paper with M. Hall, Jr., and Thompson, generalized an older result of Suzuki and proved that a group of odd order in which every element $x \neq 1$ has a nilpotent centralizer is solvable. *See* THOMPSON, JOHN GRIGGS.

It had been observed in the 19th century that all known noncyclic simple groups had even order. At the turn of the century, W. Burnside had explicitly conjectured that this was true for noncyclic simple groups in general or, equivalently, that every group of odd order is solvable. This assumption was proved in a joint paper by Feit and Thompson in 1963. The proof was much more complicated than had been anticipated, and it required some arguments about generators and relations in addition to the expected mixture of purely group-theoretic results and character theory.

Beginning in the mid-1960s, Feit worked on various aspects of group theory and on the theory of modular representations. In characterizing Conway's groups, he carried out some work on integral representations.

Feit was brought up in England. After going to the United States in 1946, he spent a term in high school before attending the University of Chicago. He received his Ph.D. in 1954 from the University of Michigan. In 1953 he took a position as instructor at Cornell University, where he remained until 1964. This stay was interrupted by Army service (1955–57) and by leaves to the Institute for Advanced Study (1958–59), University of Chicago (1960–61), and Harvard University (1963–64). In 1964 he accepted a position at Yale. Feit and Thompson received the Cole Prize of the American Mathematical Society in 1964 for their proof of the solvability of groups of odd order. In 1977 Feit was elected to the National Academy of Sciences.

For background information *see* GROUP THEORY in the McGraw-Hill Encyclopedia of Science and Technology. ∎

FELL, DAME HONOR (BRIDGET)
★ British cell biologist

Born May 22, 1900, Filey, Yorkshire, England

Fell concentrated her researches on the reactions of differentiated tissues isolated from the body and cultivated in the laboratory by the organ culture method. By this technique, largely developed at the Strangeways Laboratory, the normal structure and many of the physiological functions of tissues are maintained and early embryonic material continues to grow and develop, in culture.

For some years Fell's work was related to developmental mechanics, with special reference to skeletogenesis. Though deprived of their normal association with muscles, nerves, blood vessels, and adjacent bones, skeletal rudiments from early chick embryos continued to develop in culture. Not only did the histological structure differentiate, but the isolated rudiments acquired much of their normal shape. The early stages of joint formation took place in culture in the isolated limb blastema. It was possible to perform very delicate surgery on these explants and thereby identify some of the factors concerned in early joint formation.

Tissues isolated in organ culture, when treated with certain vitamins and hormones, were found to undergo morphological changes similar to those produced by the same agents in the intact animal. For example, it is well known that when animals are given too much vitamin A, severe changes appear in their skeleton: their cartilage loses some of its intercellular material, and rarefaction of the bone leads to spontaneous fractures. In collaboration with Sir Edward Mellanby, Fell studied the effect of excess vitamin A, added to the culture medium, on explanted limb bones from fetal mice near term. They were astonished to observe that the intercellular material of both cartilage and bone disappeared in a few days under the influence of the vitamin, though the cells appeared healthy and divided actively. Embryonic chick cartilage behaved in a similar way. In animals suffering from vitamin A deficiency, certain mucous epithelia, such as tracheal epithelium, became transformed into squamous, keratinizing tissue resembling the epidermis. Fell and Mellanby were able to produce the opposite effect in organ cultures of embryonic chicken skin exposed to excess amounts of vitamin A. The epidermis of the controls formed a squamous, keratinizing epithelium in culture, but the epidermis of vitamin A-treated explants acquired a cubical or columnar structure, many of the cells becoming ciliated and mucus being profusely secreted. The effect was reversible in normal medium.

The fact that these and many other responses to biologically active agents could be produced in a culture system from which the complex systemic reactions of the body were excluded suggested that organ cultures would be ideal for biochemical study of vitamins and hormones. It was not until after World War II, however, that rapid development of microchemistry and simple fluid media made such a biochemical approach possible and thus enormously increased the value of organ culture as a research method. The technique was thereafter applied to a very wide range of physiological problems.

Fell had long wished to identify the biochemical mechanism responsible for rapid dissolution of intercellular material in skeletal explants exposed to excess of vitamin A. She had noticed that tissue growing on a plasma-embryo extract clot in the presence of vitamin A always liquefied the clot much more than did controls on normal medium. This liquefying power indicated that vitamin A was increasing the proteolytic activity of the tissues, and she suspected that a cathepsin might be involved. Her biochemist colleague, John Dingle, suggested that vitamin A affected the membranes of the lysosomes (cytoplasmic organelles that C. R. de Duve had shown to be associated with a wide range of acid hydrolases, including a protease). Dingle demonstrated that his hypothesis was correct by experiments on subcellular fractions, where vitamin A liberated the enzymes from the isolated lysosomes of rat liver; this effect had a high degree of molecular specificity. In cultures of embryonic cartilage, Fell, Dingle, and Lucy found that vitamin A greatly increased both synthesis and release into the culture medium of the lysosomal acid protease. This enzyme digested the protein moiety of the protein-mucopolysaccharide complex of the cartilage matrix and thus liberated chondroitin sulfate. *See* DE DUVE, CHRISTIAN RENÉ.

The enormous advantage of being able to examine not only the tissue but also its humoral environment was emphasized by these enzymic studies and by observations on the synthesis and release of certain intercellular components. Fell and Dingle found that cartilaginous explants, exposed to hypervitaminosis A, may synthesize almost as much hexosamine and hydroxyproline as their untreated controls do, but a much greater proportion of these substances is released into the medium than is retained in the tissues by incorporation into intercellular material.

Fell's work with R. R. A. Coombs and Dingle demonstrated that complement-sufficient antiserum also causes breakdown of embryonic bone and cartilage matrix. This process, which is reversible, is accompanied by much-increased synthesis and release of lysosomal enzymes; a nonlysosomal enzyme, lactic acid dehydrogenase, was found to be unaffected.

In 1970 Fell turned her attention from embryonic to postfetal tissues. In the hope of shedding light on the pathogenesis of arthritis, she and her coworkers studied the influence of various factors on the breakdown of pig articular cartilage in organ culture. Fell and R. W. Jubb found that synovial tissue caused breakdown of cartilage (1) by a direct action on the matrix, for which contact between the two tissues was required, and (2) by an indirect action mediated through the chondrocytes, for which contact was not necessary. The addition to the medium of complement-sufficient antiserum to pig erythrocytes enhanced the direct action of the synovial tissue on cartilage; it caused the disruption of cartilage associated with subchondral marrow, but had virtually no effect on pure cartilage, for immunoglobulins cannot penetrate the intact matrix (with M. E. J. Barratt, A. R. Poole, and others). That chondrocytes can degrade their own matrix was shown by cultivating pure cartilage in medium containing excess amounts of retinol (vitamin A; with Dingle, Barratt, Jubb, and others).

Fell was a graduate (B.Sc., 1922) of Edinburgh University, where she took her Ph.D. in 1923 and D.Sc. in 1930. She became assistant to T. S. P. Strangeways at the Cambridge Research Hospital, later renamed the Strangeways Research Laboratory. In 1928, a year after Strangeways's death, she was put in temporary charge of the laboratory and in 1929 was appointed director. For many years she was also a member of the Royal Society's research staff. In 1970 she retired from the directorship of the Strangeways Research Laboratory and thereafter worked in the immunology division of the department of pathology of Cambridge University. She became a fellow of the Royal Society in 1952 and a Dame Commander of the Order of the British Empire in 1963. She received the Prix Charles-Leopold Mayer of the Academie des Sciences de l'Institut de France in 1965.

For background information *see* CULTURE, TISSUE; CYTOCHEMISTRY; VITAMIN A in the McGraw-Hill Encyclopedia of Science and Technology. ∎

FELLER, WILLIAM
★ American mathematician

Born *July 7, 1906, Zagreb, Yugoslavia*
Died *Jan. 14, 1970, Princeton, NJ, U.S.A.*

Although he worked in several fields, Feller became best known for his contributions to probability theory, starting in 1934. At that time it was not clear whether probability was a mathematical discipline or merely a source of inspiration and problems. Feller tried to develop an appropriate analytical framework for probability and at the same time to build probabilistic models for biological, physical, and statistical phenomena. He showed that the traditional method of considering only expectations (averages) could obscure the dominant effect of chance fluctuations. Widely accepted views concerning the operation of "laws of large numbers" were shown to be without rational foundation. For example, a "fair game" can be grossly unfair in the sense that the accumulated gain may tend (in probability) to infinity. Similarly, it is a myth that prolonged observations on one specimen reflect the typical averages in a large population. Indeed, an individual coin is likely to be "maladjusted" in the sense that for long periods the accumulated number of heads will remain either excessively large or excessively small. The nature of chance fluctuations, Feller concluded, did not agree with preconceived notions, and their analysis required a new framework.

Feller's main work may be summarized under three headings:

1. Limit theorems: Feller widened the scope of limit theorems describing chance fluctuations, and clarified the role of infinite expectations. Outstanding was his discovery of the true form of the so-called law of the iterated logarithm, but his early work on the central limit theorem had a

greater effect. In modern language, this theorem refers to sums $S_n = X_1 + \cdots + X_n$ of many independent random variables ("observations"). Viewed on an appropriate scale, such sums are likely to be subject to a normal distribution. This is the law of errors discovered by Abraham Demoivre and P. S. de Laplace, and elaborated by K. F. Gauss and many later mathematicians. To obtain an appropriate scale, these authors considered the reduced variable $(S_n - a_n)/b_n$, where a_n denotes the expectation and b_n^2 the variance of S_n. Feller showed that the problem must be modified by permitting arbitrary scale parameters a_n and b_n and found the most general conditions for the normal limit. The possibility of a purely analytic approach attracted wide attention. Indeed, from a modern point of view a result published simultaneously by P. Lévy is trivially equivalent to one of Feller's theorems, but Lévy's probabilistic conditions were then believed not expressible in analytic terms.

2. Markov processes: The probabilistic counterpart to classical mechanics treats chance-dependent processes in which the past history bears no influence on the future development. Basic equations for such processes were derived by A. N. Kolmogorov in 1931, but it was not clear whether they were compatible or whether there existed solutions satisfying the starting conditions. In 1936 Feller found an affirmative answer based on an improved version of the basic model (eliminating the assumption of finite expectations). The highly disturbing discovery of the basic nonuniqueness of solutions led to further research resulting ultimately in a theory of boundaries. Feller introduced the notion of adjoint semigroups and used it for a general theory of Markov processes. He elucidated the nature of various operators associated with such processes and developed a theory of lateral conditions with ramifications outside probability theory. These studies led to a generalized form for differential operators that has many applications. Feller also promoted the use of Markov processes in other fields.

3. Methodology: Much of Feller's energy was spent on improving and unifying methods. He showed the power of the renewal method and introduced the notion of recurrent events. These endeavors culminated in his book *An Introduction to Probability Theory and Its Applications*, vol. 1 (1950; 3d ed. 1968), which intro-

duced a new style and attitude. Older texts centered on games of chance and combinatorics; the only applications of Markov chains in the mathematical literature were to card shuffling and literary word counts. By contrast, Feller's book contained a huge collection of examples and problems explaining new applications of probability theory. To illustrate probabilistic thinking without the burden of extraneous analytical tools, the first volume was limited to discrete sample spaces. Because of this device the book was accessible to nonspecialists, and it became instrumental in establishing probability in college curricula and in several fields of applications. Even specialists had not been aware that so elementary a framework could contain rich material, and the book contributed to the present resurrection of combinatorial methods. The popularity of the book was probably due to the fact that it did not aim at a particular market or audience, but was written for an intelligent uninitiated reader. The second volume appeared in 1966 (2d ed. 1971).

Feller received his M.S. from the University of Zagreb in 1925 and his Ph.D. from Göttingen in 1926. He served at the universities of Göttingen and Kiel (1926–33) and then in Stockholm as consultant to statisticians, biologists, and economists. He went to the United States in 1939 as executive editor of the newly founded *Mathematical Reviews*. From 1945 to 1950 he served as professor of mathematics at Cornell University and then as Eugene Higgins Professor of Mathematics at Princeton University. He was elected to the National Academy of Sciences in 1960. He was posthumously awarded the 1969 National Medal of Science.

For background information *see* PROBABILITY in the McGraw-Hill Encyclopedia of Science and Technology. ∎

FENN, WALLACE OSGOOD
★ American physiologist

Born Aug. 27, 1893, Lanesboro, MA, U.S.A.
Died Sept. 21, 1971, Rochester, NY, U.S.A.

As an undergraduate at Harvard, Fenn originally planned to become a forester, but accepted instead a graduate fellowship in plant physiology. His thesis work in-

volved chiefly colloid chemistry and problems of salt antagonism. During World War I he was assigned from the infantry to work with L. J. Henderson at Harvard and was later commissioned and made camp nutrition officer at Camp Dodge, IA. In 1919 he received his Ph.D. and accepted a position as instructor in applied physiology at the Harvard Medical School. He worked with C. K. Drinker on the phagocytosis of solid particles and found that leukocytes ingest carbon particles more readily than quartz, a fact pertinent to problems of silicosis in the lung; the results were analyzed theoretically in terms of surface tension relations. Then, in 1922, as a traveling fellow from the Rockefeller Institute for Medical Research, he began work with A. V. Hill, first in Manchester and later in London, on the heat production of muscles. He discovered that muscles automatically mobilize an extra amount of energy equal to the work they perform when they contract and lift a load. This relation between work and heat has since become an important concept in muscle physiology.

After 2 years in England, Fenn returned to become professor of physiology and chairman of the department in the new School of Medicine and Dentistry at the University of Rochester. He continued his work on muscles, making some further measurements of heat production and observing the rate of oxygen consumption by muscle under different conditions. From high-speed motion pictures of sprint runners, Fenn measured the work done in the to-and-fro movements

of the arms and legs, and the work of the body against gravity and wind resistance. He found that the total work of a runner was all that could be expected from the amount of oxygen he used. This meant that very little work could have been done against any viscous resistance in the muscles themselves. Fenn proposed, therefore, that speed of running is not limited by the viscosity of the muscles themselves, but rather by the time required to mobilize extra energy for the work required. In isolated muscles he further supported this idea by measuring the speed of shortening of muscles lifting different loads. The resulting force-velocity curve was thus shown not to be linear, as demanded by the viscosity theory. At this time Fenn also devised a differential volumeter of sufficient sensitivity to demonstrate clearly that nerves consume more oxygen when they are stimulated to conduct nerve impulses than when they are merely resting.

Fenn next turned to his original interest, the biological effects of electrolytes, and began some of the pioneer work on the movement of potassium between cells and their surroundings. He found that the cells usually are freely permeable to potassium, which tends to move toward the phase which shows the greater increase in acidity. A part of the buffering capacity of the body depends, therefore, on the free movements of potassium in and out of cells. When radioactive potassium first became available, he and his collaborators studied the distribution of injected potassium among the various tissues of the body. The research showed definitely that red blood corpuscles, like other cells of the body, are slowly permeable to potassium, although for most purposes they had always been regarded as permeable only to anions. Perhaps the most important of these studies was the demonstration that, when muscles are stimulated, they lose potassium in exchange for an equivalent amount of sodium. This interchange of electrolytes has since been shown by others to represent the fundamental mechanism involved in the conduction of a nerve impulse. By careful analysis of rat livers Fenn showed that the deposition of glycogen in the liver is always accompanied by the deposition of a fixed amount of water and potassium. Under the influence of epinephrine, either injected intravenously or liberated from the adrenal glands under the influence of inhaled

carbon dioxide, he showed that both potassium and glucose escape from the liver into the bloodstream.

During World War II Fenn offered his services for the study of pressure breathing, which had been suggested by the Air Force to enable aviators to obtain adequate oxygen at an altitude somewhat higher than was possible breathing 100% oxygen at ambient pressure. This work was carried on with H. Rahn and A. B. Otis and a crew of conscientious objectors assigned to the laboratory. Because of the advent of the pressurized cabin soon afterward, the practical value of this study for aviation was not as great as for clinical medicine in general, where it opened up many new avenues of investigation importantly affecting clinical physiology of the chest and lungs. In particular, Fenn and his collaborators were responsible for rediscovering forgotten data concerning the pressure-volume diagrams of the chest and lungs and for expanding these data in different directions. Another important aspect of this work was the development of the oxygen–carbon dioxide diagram of the respiratory gases, by means of which predictions could easily be made of the composition of the air in the lung alveoli under different ambient pressures with different mixtures of inhaled gases.

Fenn continued to work in the field of respiratory physiology, having become concerned chiefly with oxygen poisoning and inert gas narcosis. In experiments with fruit flies he found a striking synergism between high pressures of oxygen and inert gases. In extending this study to bacteria, he found that a culture of *Streptococcus faecalis* increases in total volume in proportion to the amount of lactic acid which is formed. Presumably because of this, the growth of these organisms is inhibited appropriately by an increase in hydrostatic pressure, as well as by oxygen and inert gases at sufficient partial pressures.

Fenn received his A.B. (1914), M.A. (1916), and Ph.D. in plant physiology (1919) from Harvard University. After working in England during 1922–24, he joined the faculty of the University of Rochester; he resigned as chairperson of the physiology department in 1959, after 35 years. In 1961 he was appointed Distinguished University Professor of Physiology. Between 1962 and 1965 he served as the first director of the Space Science Center of the university. Besides several honorary degrees, he received the Modern

Medicine Distinguished Achievement Award in 1965, the Antonio Feltrinelli International Prize of the Accademia Internazionale dei Lincei of Rome in 1964, and the Research Achievement Award of the American Heart Association in 1967. He was elected to the National Academy of Sciences in 1943, the American Philosophical Society in 1946, and the American Academy of Arts and Sciences in 1948.

Fenn wrote *History of the American Physiological Society: The Third Quarter Century* (1963), as well as some 200 scientific papers.

For background information *see* ION EXCHANGE; MUSCLE (BIOPHYSICS); RESPIRATION, EXTERNAL in the McGraw-Hill Encyclopedia of Science and Technology. ∎

FERMI, ENRICO
American physicist

Born Sept. 29, 1901, Rome, Italy
Died Nov. 28, 1954, Chicago, IL, U.S.A.

When Fermi found that neutrons shot into the nucleus of an atom could induce artificial radioactivity, he began a systematic study of the effect of neutron bombardment on each of the elements. His success in producing artificial radioactivity and in analyzing the decay products won for him the 1938 Nobel Prize in physics.

The alpha particle had previously been established as an agent that could induce nuclear transformations. In 1919 Ernest Rutherford had shot an alpha particle directly into a nitrogen nucleus, thus causing the emission of a proton that left behind a stable oxygen isotope. In a similar experiment in 1934 Frédéric and Irène Joliot-Curie shot an alpha particle into an aluminum nucleus, causing the emission of a proton that left behind a phosphorus isotope. Although phosphorus is normally a stable element, the isotope thus produced was radioactive.

When Fermi learned that radioactivity in the light element aluminum could be induced by alpha-particle bombardment, he considered the possibility of inducing artificial radioactivity in the heavier elements. He recognized that the chief obstacle was the fact that the heavier the nucleus the larger its positive charge, and the larger its positive charge the stronger it repels the positively charged alpha particle. As an alternative projectile, Fermi thought of the neutron, a particle discovered by James Chadwick only 2 years before. Since the neutron bore no charge at all, the positive charge of even the heaviest nucleus would provide no protection from such a projectile. With a number of collaborators Fermi set out to test the effect of neutron bombardment on all the elements he could obtain. Within a few months he found that among the 63 elements he had been able to investigate there were 37 that showed easily detectable artificial radioactivity. *See* CHADWICK, SIR JAMES.

Many of these new radioactive elements decayed by emitting beta particles, with the result that the daughter element lay nearer the end of the periodic table than the parent element. This fact led Fermi to bombard uranium, the last element then listed on the periodic table, in the hope of producing a transuranium element. In June 1934 he described the result of this experiment as a "rather complex phenomenon" since the decay curves showed three well-defined half-lives and at least two others. (This complexity arose because he had produced not only the desired transuranium element but also the first atomic fission, a process that was not identified until 5 years later.) By the following month Fermi and his colleagues had found that if neutrons were first slowed down by collisions with the protons of paraffin, water, or some other hydrogen-rich material, these neutrons might be as much as 100 times more effective in producing radioactivity than a fast neutron. The 1938 Nobel Prize committee cited Fermi "for his discovery of new radioactive elements produced by neutron irradiation, and for the discovery of nuclear reactions brought about by slow neutrons."

Fermi had made his first major contribution to physics in 1926, almost a decade before he began his work with neutrons. S. N. Bose and Albert Einstein, in applying statistical mechanics to a "gas" of photons, had succeeded in deriving Planck's blackbody radiation equation by assuming that the individual members of certain sets of photons were indistinguishable. However, photons could pass through one another and in this sense occupy the same space at the same time. The possible locations of electrons are severely restricted, the limitations being set forth in the exclusion principle of Wolfgang Pauli. Fermi recognized the implications of this principle and proposed an alternative statistical mechanics to account for the behavior of a "gas" of electrons. (P. A. M. Dirac independently derived the same theory, which is now called Fermi-Dirac statistical mechanics.) All indistinguishable particles (photons, electrons, neutrons, and others) obey either Bose-Einstein or Fermi-Dirac statistical mechanics. *See* DIRAC, PAUL ADRIEN MAURICE; PAULI, WOLFGANG.

Fermi's second major contribution was made in 1933, when he solved the beta-decay problem. If an element undergoes alpha decay, all the alpha particles are emitted with the same energy; if an element undergoes beta decay, the beta particles emitted exhibit energies that vary from zero up to a maximum value characteristic of the element. Pauli suggested that this apparent violation of the principles of conservation of energy and conservation of momentum could be explained by assuming that there was emitted with the electron another, up to that time undetected, particle whose properties were exactly those needed to preserve those principles. On the basis of this suggestion, Fermi constructed a beta-decay theory analogous to photon-emission theory. He said that just as an atom changes from a high-energy state to a low-energy state by emitting a photon, so a neutron (the high-energy state) changes to a proton (the low-energy state) by emitting both an electron (which is the beta particle) and a neutrino (which is needed to preserve the energy and momentum).

Another major contribution, following his investigations of neutron bombardment, was Fermi's work on the design and construction of the first nuclear reactor. He saw in the discovery of nuclear fission, announced in 1939, an important possibility. Since the uranium nucleus is characterized by a neutron-to-proton ratio of about 2.6 while the fission products have a ratio of about 2.5, each fission must produce, in addition to the energy released, a number of free neutrons. If a condition could be achieved in which more than one of the new neutrons struck another uranium nucleus and induced fission, then a chain of reactions would result and a continuous flow of energy would be obtained. To achieve this condition, Fermi helped design and construct the first nuclear reactor, a lattice of graphite and uranium built in a squash court under the stands of the unused University of Chicago stadium. A plaque placed near this point reads: "On December 2, 1942, man achieved here the first self-sustaining chain reaction and thereby initiated the controlled release of nuclear energy." This event marked the beginning of the atomic era.

Fermi was awarded a doctor's degree in physics at the University of Pisa in 1922, after which he studied with Max Born at Göttingen and with Paul Ehrenfest at Leiden. While a lecturer at the University of Florence, he published the theoretical papers that first demonstrated his abilities. At the age of 25 he won a position as professor of physics at the University of Rome, where his experimental work was begun (1926–38). In 1930, when he taught in the summer session of the University of Michigan, he began a series of visits to the United States, and after receiving the Nobel Prize he made his home in the United States, becoming an American citizen in 1944. He worked successively at Columbia University, where he began the design of the nuclear reactor; at the University of Chicago, where he completed the construction of this reactor; and at Los Alamos, where he contributed to the design of the first atomic bomb. In 1946 he returned to the University of Chicago as a member of an institute that, in 1955, the year after his death, was renamed the Enrico Fermi Institute for Nuclear Studies. A new element artificially produced that same year, of atomic number 100, was named fermium in his honor.

Fermi wrote *Thermodynamics* (1937), *Nuclear Theory* (rev. ed. 1950), and *Elementary Particles* (1951). A set of lecture outlines in his own handwriting has been reproduced as *Notes on Quantum Mechanics* (1961).

For background information *see* FERMI-DIRAC STATISTICS; NEUTRINO; NEUTRON; REACTOR, NUCLEAR in the McGraw-Hill Encyclopedia of Science and Technology. ■

FERNÁNDEZ-MORÁN, HUMBERTO
★ American physician and biophysicist

Born Feb. 18, 1924, Maracaibo, Venezuela

Fernández-Morán was a prototype of the modern Latin American scientist. A "man for all seasons" by virtue of his origin and education, he was a representative of his country's multifaceted intellect, and was proud of his nation's rich history and confident in its potential.

Fernández-Morán was a physician, biophysicist, neurologist, cell biologist, and, most of all, electron microscopist. Hans Selye, a highly creative physician and original thinker, dedicated his book *In Vivo* to Fernández-Morán as a "token of my great admiration for his work on the finest particles of life."

Fernández-Morán's pioneering studies led to new ways of looking at the brain, permitting direct visualization of its molecular structure; the development of new tools for exploring the finest structure of matter, actually permitting molecular chemistry by sectioning; and new areas of thought and research in the domain of low-temperature electron microscopy.

Fernández-Morán's greatest influences were his father, who instilled in him a deep interest in and devotion to the origins and language of his native Venezuela; Simón Bolívar, the great South American liberator and visionary; and his education, largely through private tutors. These factors contributed in large measure to his Renaissance approach to science.

At the age of 15 Fernández-Morán entered the University of Munich as one of the youngest students in the history of that institution. He studied under C. Carathéodory; F. Knoop, Nobel laureate and biochemist; and K. von Frisch, Nobel laureate, zoologist, and pioneer of studies of insect behavior. His experiences in Germany during the war developed in him a keen sensitivity to human suffering. *See* FRISCH, KARL VON.

After his M.D. degree was revalidated at the University of Caracas in 1945, Fernández-Morán's awareness of the misery of tropical disease and hunger and the viruses carried by tropical insects, as well as his interest in the brain and the central nervous system, led him to specialize in neurology and neuropathology at George Washington University in Washington, DC. Yet it was his meeting with Albert Einstein in 1945 at Princeton University that helped him to decide his future; he was inspired by the true humility of this great human being, who gave him the leitmotiv of physics applied to medicine.

Shortly thereafter Fernández-Morán began his lifelong investigation of the brain, as a research fellow at the Nobel Institute of Physics in Stockholm, Sweden. Under the direction of Nobel laureate Karl Manne Siegbahn, he developed one of his most significant contributions to electron microscopy, the diamond knife. The diamond knife enabled electron microscopists to look directly at molecules in biological tissues. Its cutting edge, about 20–50 angstroms thick, is so sharp that it can slice macromolecules, including deoxyribonucleic acid (DNA). *See* SIEGBAHN, KARL MANNE GEORGE.

During his residency under the neurosurgeon Herbert Olivecrona, and while continuing work on his master's degree in cell biology and doctoral studies in biophysics, Fernández-Morán was a practicing physician who was moved by the deaths caused by malignant brain tumors in spite of surgical endeavors, and he turned to basic research to learn more about these tumors. Electron microscopy

was the detour, and the indirect strategy, which led to his work on the nerve fiber.

Fernández-Morán's elucidation of the general submicroscopic organization of the nerve myelin sheath can be regarded as the cornerstone of membrane ultrastructural research. Using the knowledge gained from work with polarized optics and x-ray diffraction, he became the first person, in 1950, to employ the electron microscope, to view the regular, concentric liquid crystalline arrangement of the myelin sheath and photoreceptor layers. This was a pioneering step in the understanding of the fine structure of the nervous system. The discovery of the paracrystalline structure had great implications because it proved that the major constituent of the brain is invested with exquisite regularity and elaborate, coherent, and meaningful design. Moreover, as Fernández-Morán postulated, in 1966: "There is increasing evidence that biological membrane systems may have many properties in common with semiconductors. It may therefore be of interest to reconsider as a working hypothesis suggestive of new experimental approaches our earlier speculations on certain specific crystalline properties such as piezoelectric effects, semiconductor properties or equivalent phenomena which may be associated with the fluid-crystalline nature of myelin and related lamellar systems. In connection with correlated studies on basic mechanisms of electroencephalography, I had previously discussed the hypothetical possibility that myelin and other paracrystalline nerve membrane systems might function as generators or specific amplifiers of coherent electromagnetic radiation, mainly in the infrared or UHF range between 1 and about 10 microns wavelength. Similar hypothetical mechanisms involving far-infrared quanta, and coherent phenomena in the transfer of biological information on the macro- and supramolecular level are now being considered by J. Polonsky in the scope of molecular exciton theory and quantum electronics."

Fernández-Morán's approach in his research was to conduct his work systematically under optimal conditions, using the unique properties of the material involved. In searching for a cutting instrument, he selected the hardest material known, the diamond. And in working with biological systems, in order to arrest biological activity and yet preserve the structure by leaving the water composition intact, he turned to a wide variety of controlled physical and chemical treatments, including the freezing of nerve sections and liquid-helium low-temperature fixation and embedding techniques.

Fernández-Morán returned to Venezuela in 1954, planning to fashion a career that would combine medicine, biology, and the education of the scientists that Latin America needed. He developed a center for research in neurology and brain physiology which ultimately cost $50,000,000 and became a magnet for researchers from all over the world. The Venezuelan Institute of Neurological and Brain Research (IVNIC) was chartered in 1954. There he continued his studies on the submicroscopic structure of nerve fibers and on the improvement of the resolving power of the electron microscope, and was the first to use liquid helium in biomedical studies in the South American continent. In this unique submicroscopic laboratory polarized light receptors embodied in the fine structure of the insect eye were discovered, and Erwin Mueller first examined atoms cooled to liquid-helium temperatures in his field-ion microscope. *See* MUELLER, ERWIN W.

In 1958, after 4 years of pioneering studies, during which time he also served as Minister of Education, Fernández-Morán left Venezuela and went to the Massachusetts Institute of Technology (MIT) and the Massachusetts General Hospital, where his colleagues included Francis O. Schmitt and William Sweet. In Boston he organized the Mixter Laboratory for Electron Microscopy, where the multienzyme pyruvate dehydrogenase complex isolated by Lester Reed was elucidated by correlated electron microscopic and biochemical studies. This work and its subsequent extension remained a bench mark of its class. At the same time, in extensive collaboration with the eminent biochemist David Green of the University of Wisconsin, Fernández-Morán began to work on the mitochondria, beginning at MIT and continuing at the University of Chicago (1959–66). *See* SCHMITT, FRANCIS OTTO.

Until this time, mitochondrial structural analysis had revealed membranes, but their structures did not correlate with their complex biochemical functions. Fernández-Morán discovered the hitherto unseen and unexpected elements in the inner membrane of mitochondria isolated from heart muscle by Green, the tripartite elementary particles, and provided the first direct visualization of how enzymes are arranged in the membrane. The concept of the tripartite molecular repeating unit of mitochondrial structure and function became generally accepted, and the unit was believed to be the prototype of a class of functional particles or macromolecular assemblies found in association with membranes generally.

During 1963–74, at the University of Chicago, Fernández-Morán created a multimillion-dollar laboratory and assembled a staff of scientists and students that pushed high-resolution electron microscopy to its limit. It was a world center for learning not merely the morphology of electron microscopy but also its chemical and physical correlates as a biochemical tool. With his colleagues, Fernández-Morán worked to develop the full potential of the electron microscope, while teaching a multidisciplinary course as the A. N. Pritzker Professor of Biophysics.

At the same time he began a detailed description of the hemocyanin molecules with Ernest van Bruggen, and work dealing with the direct visualization of DNA readout through ribonucleic acid (RNA) polymerase with Samuel Weiss. With his low-temperature ultramicrotome, Fernández-Morán initiated molecular sectioning of DNA, a promising new field. In 1961, with Samuel Collins, he developed and tested the first superfluid liquid-helium closed-cycle system applied to electron optics. With this superfluid helium, and with new types of superconductive alloys, Fernández-Morán was able to build and test the first electron microscopes with superconducting lenses. Between 1965 and 1974 he built the high-resolution Collins closed-cycle superfluid helium system coupled to high-resolution electron microscopy. *See* COLLINS, SAMUEL CORNETTE.

This led to a number of new discoveries, including the elucidation of the atomic structure and behavior of thin layers in superconducting intercalated layers, and the visualization through cryoelectron microscopy of phenomena exhibited at temperatures of only 1–2 degrees above absolute zero at ultrahigh vacuums, and at high magnetic fields. Fernández-Morán continued his work with high-resolution electron microscopy and electron diffraction at cryogenic temperatures through the 1970s.

Fernández-Morán earned the B.A. at Shulgemeinde Wickersdorf (Germany, 1939) and the M.D. at the University of Munich (1945). He was a fellow in neurology and neuropathology at George Washington University and an intern at the George Washington University Hospital (1945–46). He spent the next few years in Stockholm, where he was a resident at the Neurosurgical Clinic (1946–48), research fellow at the Nobel Institute for Physics (1947–49), and research fellow at the Institute for Cell Research and Genetics at the Karolinska Institute (1948–51). He earned the M.S. (1951) in cell biology and the Ph.D. (1952) in biophysics at the University of Stockholm. He served as professor and chairperson of the department of biophysics of the University of Caracas (1951–58) and director of IVNIC. He then became associate biophysicist of the neurological service of the Massachusetts General Hospital (1958–62). During this period he also was a visiting lecturer in the department of biology at MIT and research associate in neuropathology at Harvard University. In 1962 he joined the faculty of the University of Chicago as professor of biophysics, subsequently being named A. N. Pritzker Professor of Biophysics in the Division of Biological Sciences in the medical school. He was made Knight of the Polar Star by the King of Sweden in 1952. He received the Claude Bernard Medal from the University of Montreal and the John Scott Award from the city of Philadelphia for the invention of the diamond knife, both in 1967. He received the highest award granted to a Latin American scholar for outstanding achievement, the Venezuelan Medalla Andres Bello, in 1973. He was a member of the Venezuelan Academy of Sciences and a fellow of the American Academy of Arts and Sciences.

Fernández-Morán was the author of *The Submicroscopic Organization of Vertebrate Nerve Fibers* (1952), *The Submicroscopic Organization of the Internode Portion of Vertebrate Myelinated Nerve Fibers* (1953), and *Studies of the Submicroscopic Organization of the Thalamus* (1955), and of 150 scientific papers, monographs, and books in medicine, molecular biology, electron microscopy, and other fields.

For background information *see* MICROSCOPE, ELECTRON; MITOCHONDRIA; MYELIN; SUPERCONDUCTIVITY in the McGraw-Hill Encyclopedia of Science and Technology. ∎

FERRY, JOHN DOUGLASS
★ American chemist

Born May 4, 1912, Dawson, Yukon Territory, Canada

Ferry's work on viscoelasticity and other aspects of the dynamics of macromolecules concerned a wide range of polymeric materials, including dilute and concentrated solutions, rubbery and hard glassy polymers, and biomacromolecules such as proteins and nucleic acids. The theme underlying his research was the relationship of the modes of molecular motion to mechanical and other physical properties.

When a polymeric material is subjected to small oscillating deformations, the work of deformation is partly stored and recovered and partly dissipated as heat; such behavior is called viscoelastic. The material properties (moduli or compliances) which describe the energy storage and dissipation depend in a complicated manner on the frequency of oscillation as well as on temperature, pressure, concentration, and other variables. The principle that, within certain ranges, the molecular motions correspond to a spectrum of relaxation times all of which have the same dependence on external variables makes it possible to combine data at different frequencies and temperatures, for example, and to construct a temperature-dependence function and a frequency-dependence function over a greatly expanded range without making assumptions concerning the form of either. Ferry and his associates exploited this principle to obtain accurate data for the frequency and temperature dependences of viscoelastic properties over wide ranges for several dozen polymers and their concentrated solutions. (Others used the principle to describe stress relaxation and creep data, which are related to oscillatory behavior by the theory of linear viscoelasticity.)

With M. L. Williams and R. F. Landel, Ferry showed that the temperature dependence could be described by a universal function (the WLF equation) and that it could be related to the average free volume in the material, which determines the local frictional resistance to motion of short segments of a polymer molecule. Ferry and his associates also showed that the concept of fractional free volume, while remaining somewhat vaguely defined, serves also to interpret the dependence of relaxation times on pressure, concentration of a diluent or plasticizer, molecular weight, and material history following an abrupt temperature change. The temperature dependence function was applied widely to many mechanical and other physical properties, including viscosity, diffusion, dielectric dispersion, friction, and rupture processes, all of which are influenced by the rates of local motions.

In describing the time or frequency dependence of viscoelastic properties, it is necessary to distinguish several characteristic zones of characteristic behavior. In the so-called transition zone, the modulus (a measure of stiffness) changes with decreasing time or increasing frequency from a magnitude corresponding to a soft rubber to that corresponding to a hard glass. The range of time or frequency in which this change occurs is governed by the local frictional resistance to motion of short segments. Ferry and his associates showed that in certain homologous series of polymers with related chemical structures this resistance can again be related to the fractional free volume.

At longer times or lower frequencies, the viscoelastic properties in the so-called terminal zone reflect molecular motions over much larger ranges which appear to be impeded by topological restraints. These restraints are usually interpreted as being due to rather widely spaced molecular entanglements (though more recently as being due to obstacles which constrain each molecule as though it were in a tube); viscoelastic measurements at lower frequencies enabled Ferry and his associates, as well as other investigators, to estimate the distance between effective entanglement points (equivalent to the diameter of a constraining tube) for many different polymers. When cross-links are introduced chemically to form a three-dimensional network structure, the entanglements persist and affect both equilibrium elasticity and viscoelastic properties. The effects depend critically on the extent to which the entanglements are trapped by the cross-links and become incapable of subsequent topological rearrangement. In a series of experiments, Ferry introduced cross-links in strained polymers at a low temperature at which the molecules were essentially immobilized. Subsequently, such a material seeks a state of ease in which the network strands between cross-links and those between trapped entanglements exert forces in opposite directions. The properties of networks of this type probably provide the most direct evidence of entanglement restraints.

Detailed molecular theories for polymer dynamics are confined to the behavior of isolated molecules, as treated by P. E. Rouse, Jr., B. H. Zimm, and others, and can be compared only with difficult experimental measurements in dilute solution extrapolated to zero concentration. During a period of 30 years, Ferry and his associates pushed viscoelastic measurements to progressively lower concentration ranges, and finally Ferry, with J. L. Schrag, obtained the infinite-dilution properties for a wide variety of molecular types. At low and intermediate frequencies, the viscoelastic properties reflect long-range motions which can be described by the bead-spring model of Rouse and Zimm; they are sensitive to molecular topology such as branching but independent of detailed chemical structure. At high frequencies, just the opposite is true: the long-range topology and the molecular weight are irrelevant, but the viscoelastic properties depend on detailed chemical structure.

Among Ferry's other investigations were studies on the diffusion of small foreign molecules in polymer systems, which also provided information on the motions of polymer molecules; slow relaxation mechanisms in polymer networks; and the mechanism of polymerization of fibrinogen.

The son of a mining engineer, Ferry received his A.B. (1932) and Ph.D. (1935) degrees in chemistry at Stanford University. From 1938 to 1941 he was a member of the Society of Fellows at Harvard University, and from 1941 to 1945 he contributed to wartime research on antifouling paint at the Woods Hole Oceanographic Institution and on medical products from human plasma at the Harvard Medical School. He joined the faculty of the University of Wisconsin in 1946 and was appointed full professor of chemistry in 1947. From 1959 to 1967 he was chairman of the department of chemistry. He was elected to the National Academy of Sciences in 1959. Ferry's work was recognized by a number of medals and awards, including the Bingham Medal of the Society of Rheology (1953) and the Colwyn Medal of the Institution of the Rubber Industry (United Kingdom; 1972).

Ferry wrote *Viscoelastic Properties of Polymers* (1961; 2d ed. 1970).

For background information *see* FLUID, NON-NEWTONIAN; RHEOLOGY in the McGraw-Hill Encyclopedia of Science and Technology. ∎

FESHBACH, HERMAN
★ American theoretical nuclear physicist

Born Feb. 2, 1917, New York, NY, U.S.A.

It was largely because of a superb high school teacher, Irving Mosbacher, that Feshbach became interested in physics. Mosbacher would invite a few students to his home on Friday night to listen to music, play chess, and discuss physics. In college Feshbach had the good fortune to work with Mark Zemansky and to enjoy the friendship of J. Schwinger, M. Hamermesh, E. Gerjuoy, and J. Weinberg. He then went on to study with P. M. Morse and to collaborate with him, with V. F. Weisskopf, and with A. K. Kerman. *See* MORSE, PHILIP MCCORD; SCHWINGER, JULIAN SEYMOUR; WEISSKOPF, VICTOR FREDERICK.

From the beginning Feshbach was interested in two areas of research, nuclear physics (and nuclear forces) and the mathematical methods of physics. His interest in the latter led him to research in the acoustics of rooms, and he developed a theory of boundary perturbations in which the effect of deviations in the

boundary shape or boundary conditions from those for which exact solutions are available was considered. Some of the first applications to acoustic problems of the Wiener-Hopf method were made with A. E. Heins. Feshbach's most important accomplishment in this area was the book with Morse, *Methods of Theoretical Physics* (1953).

At the same time, Feshbach was very concerned with the problems of nuclear physics. Research into the problems of nuclear forces as they manifest themselves in the two- and three-body nuclear problems led to papers with Schwinger on the properties of the deuteron and on low-energy two-body phenomena, with W. Rarita and W. Pease on the properties of the triton, and with E. Lomon on the boundary condition of nuclear forces. In the last-named study, the totality of the two-body data available was considered by using the predictions of the field theory of nuclear forces to describe those forces for interparticle separation greater than one-half of the pion Compton wavelength. A boundary condition on the wave function at this point was used to describe the system for smaller values of the interparticle distance. This theory was justified by using dispersion theory. In later attempts to describe the nucleon-nucleon interaction by Vinh Mau, the boundary condition assumption was found to be required empirically.

Another area of endeavor, in which Feshbach continued to work, was nuclear reactions. His collaboration with Weiss-

kopf led to the paper with C. Porter in which the optical model description of relatively low-energy nuclear reactions was formulated, derived, and applied to the measurements of neutron scattering by nuclei. When first obtained, these data presented a problem because the energy and target dependence deviated strongly from the predictions of the statistical theory of nuclear reactions. The optical model, which resolved this problem, was essentially an extension of the shell model concept to scattering phenomena.

The statistical theory still had its use. In 1952 Feshbach, together with W. Hauser, applied it to the description of processes in which the residual nucleus was left in discrete levels. The angular distribution and energy dependence were predicted in terms of quantities which could be calculated directly in terms of quantities obtainable from the optical model. When the residual nucleus was left in a highly excited state so that the excitation of many levels had to be considered, the results obtained were identical with the evaporation theory of Weisskopf.

It was in responding to a question raised by Weisskopf—"Is there a Kramers-Kronig relation for nuclear reactions?"—that Feshbach developed his theory of nuclear reactions. This theory provided a description of nuclear reactions in which both the prompt direct processes and the time-delayed resonances were simultaneously developed in a uniform manner. At the same time, the problem of satisfying the Pauli exclusion principle was solved, a better derivation of the optical model together with its relation to the statistical model was provided, and the theory was extended to include processes involving gamma rays.

The existence of an anomaly in the *s*-wave neutron strength function in the region of nuclei with mass numbers near 115 led to the formulation of the concept of the doorway state in a paper published in 1962 with B. Block. This theory postulated the existence of a state through which the system had to pass before the complexity of the compound nuclear state could be developed. A statistical theory of doorway states was formulated in order to explain the behavior of the neutron strength function. But it was also noted that when a doorway state is isolated the reaction will exhibit a resonance and thus provide an explanation of intermediate structure in the energy dependence of cross sections. This consequence was further developed in a definitive paper written with Kerman and R. Lemmer, and the relation to various examples of giant resonances and intermediate structure such as the giant dipole resonance and the isobar analog resonance was described.

The concept of doorway states was extended to include secondary, tertiary, and other such states, to explain the strong deviations from the predictions of the statistical theory of nuclear reactions which were uncovered in the 1970s. Starting with the ideas developed by J. Griffin, a theory of statistical multistep direct and compound reactions was proposed with Kerman and S. Koonin. This theory has a wide applicability, the ordinary statistical theory and direct reactions appearing as limits. The cascade theory appears as a high-energy limit, while a diffusion approximation results if small momentum changes are assumed to be dominant at each step.

In later years experiments were performed using energetic beams of protons and heavy ions in the gigaelectronvolt-per-nucleon range. Feshbach was interested in the development of an accurate multiple scattering approximation which could be used to interpret these experiments. A coupled channel approach was derived with A. Gal and J. Hüfner and used to interpret high-energy proton-nucleus scattering to obtain the neutron density inside nuclei. In the case of relativistic heavy ions, there is a nuclear analog of projectile fragmentation by means of the target's "fringing" field of force acting on the projectile.

Feshbach graduated from the City College of New York in 1937, being awarded the Ward Medal in Physics. His graduate work was done at the Massachusetts Institute of Technology. He was appointed an instructor there in 1941 and became director of its Center for Theoretical Physics in 1967, head of the department of physics in 1973, and Cecil and Ida Green Professor of Physics in 1976. He chaired the Division of Nuclear Physics of the American Physical Society, chaired its Panel of Public Affairs, and was elected to serve as president from February 1980 for a year. He received its Bonner Prize in 1973. Feshbach was elected to the National Academy of Sciences in 1969.

Besides the book mentioned, Feshbach published *Theoretical Nuclear Physics,* with A. deShalit (vol. 1, 1974).

For background information *see* DISPERSION RELATIONS; NUCLEAR REACTION; NUCLEAR RESONANCES, GIANT; NUCLEAR STRUCTURE in the McGraw-Hill Encyclopedia of Science and Technology. ■

FESSARD, ALFRED EUGÈNE
★ French neurophysiologist and psychophysiologist

Born Apr. 28, 1900, Paris, France

Fessard began his scientific career around 1925 and during the prewar period became known as one of the French pioneers in modern electrophysiology and elementary neurophysiology. At this time he was mainly occupied in showing that autorhythmic states of activity are a general occurrence in isolated excitable preparations such as nerve or muscle fibers, certain plant cells, stretch receptors, and ganglion cells when these are treated with different physical or chemical agents.

As a pupil of the great French psychologist Henri Piéron, Fessard became interested in problems of psychophysiology and did research in the fields of sensation—visual, auditory, and tactile—and on voluntary movement in humans. When the electroencephalographic technique was made available, he unified his interests by trying to correlate certain mental activities with electroencephalogram rhythms. It was he, in fact, who first introduced this technique to French medical circles, a merit later recognized when he was elected to the Académie Nationale de Médecine in 1961. He is mainly known for his discovery that the blocking reaction of the alpha rhythm may be conditioned, a property which has since been widely exploited by others.

The field of research in which Fessard worked most persistently was the physiology of the electrogenic organs known to exist in certain species of fish. He first worked with the torpedo fish and demonstrated the marked impedance drop in its electric organ at the time of discharge. Also, by nerve degeneration experiments he confirmed the old and puzzling observation that this organ has no electrical excitability of its own. With W. Feldberg he demonstrated the cholinergic nature of nerve-organ transmission of excitation, and with B. C. Abbott and X. Aubert he discovered in 1958 the initial cooling that accompanies the discharge and precedes the metabolic phase during which exothermic recovery reactions take place.

Fessard left to his collaborators, D. Albe-Fessard (his wife) and T. Szabo, the task of analyzing the electrogenic properties of electric organs of other fishes, such as rays, *Astroscopus,* mormyrids, *Gymnarchus,* and *Electrophorus.* His own interests were oriented around the then unsolved problem of the central control of discharges. First in the brain stem of the torpedo fish he disclosed the locus of origin of the rhythmic command. Similar pacemaker sites were gradually discovered in the central nervous system of other fishes, such as *Electrophorus* (in Brazil, with A. Couceiro), rays, mormyrids, and *Gymnarchus* (with Szabo). A striking unity in the organization of the central nervous control, as opposed to the great morphological diversity of the electric organs themselves, was thus revealed. When a sensory mechanism for object location was found by H. W. Lissmann and K. Machin (1958) in the electric fish, the problem of specific electroreceptors was posed. It was Szabo who discovered the autorhythmic activity of the cutaneous electroreceptors in the African electric fishes mormyrids and *Gymnarchus* (1961). Fessard and he studied the coding characteristics that give the informational content, representing the surrounding field intensity, to messages emitted by the electroreceptors. The manner in which the repetitive discharges of the electric organ are involved in the functioning of the electroreceptors was also demonstrated.

Together with his wife, a professor at the Paris Faculté des Sciences, Fessard sponsored the training of many young French workers and foreign fellows in the fields of electrophysiology and brain research. This group made many contributions concerning central nervous system activity at diverse levels, from single ganglion cells of *Aplysia* to the brains of pigeons, rats, cats, and monkeys. Implanted macro- or microelectrodes in chronic preparations were used to investigate nervous correlates of controlled manifestations in behavior. Fessard devoted most of his efforts to writing syntheses of the results of work from his laboratories. Here he expressed his own views on theoretical problems related to brain activity, such as those of transmission of information, integration, conditioning, and memory.

Fessard graduated from the Sorbonne in 1925 and received his D.Sc. there in 1936. He spent a year in England at the Cambridge Physiological Laboratory in 1936–37 as a Rockefeller fellow. After several years as associate director at H. Piéron's laboratory, he obtained means from the Centre National de la Recherche Scientifique to create an institute, now called Centre d'Études de Physiologie Nerveuse, of which he became director in 1947. He continued to hold this post after being appointed chairperson in general neurophysiology at the Collège de France in 1949. He retired from both positions in 1971. In 1958 he played a major role in founding the International Brain Research Organization. A member of the French Académie des Sciences and of the Académie Nationale de Médecine, he was elected a foreign member of the Brazilian Academy of Sciences, foreign honorary member of the American Academy of Arts and Sciences, honorary life member of the New York Academy of Sciences, and honorary member of the Physiological Society of Great Britain. He was an officer of the Légion d'Honneur and commander of the Ordre National du Mérite.

Apart from a general article entitled "Les Organes électriques" (in *Traité de Zoologie* by P. P. Grassé, 1958), titles of some of Fessard's main contributions to symposiums indicate the trend of his later scientific interests: "Mechanisms of Nervous Integration and Conscious Experience" (1954), "Corrélations neurophysiologiques de la formation des réflexes conditionnés," with H. Gastaut (1958), "Le conditionnement considéré à l'échelle du neurone" (1960), "The Role of Neuronal Networks in Sensory Communications within the Brain" (1961), "Thalamic Integrations and Their Consequences at the Telencephalic Level," with D. Albe-Fessard (1963).

For background information *see* ELECTRIC ORGAN (BIOLOGY); ELECTROENCEPHALOGRAPHY; NERVOUS SYSTEM (VERTEBRATE); NEUROPHYSIOLOGY in the McGraw-Hill Encyclopedia of Science and Technology. ∎

FEYNMAN, RICHARD PHILLIPS
American physicist

***Born** May 11, 1918, New York, NY, U.S.A.*

In 1948, Feynman introduced a theory designed to remove certain difficulties that had arisen in the study of the interaction among electrons, positrons, and radiation. This hypothesis proved to be a turning point in the development of modern quantum electrodynamics. For his achievement, Feynman was awarded the 1965 Nobel Prize in physics, which he shared with the American physicist Julian S. Schwinger and the Japanese physicist Sin-itiro Tomonaga, both of whom had independently developed theories similar to Feynman's. *See* SCHWINGER, JULIAN SEYMOUR; TOMONAGA, SIN-ITIRO.

Quantum electrodynamics emerged in the late 1920s, in large part out of the fundamental work of the physicists P. A. M. Dirac, Werner Heisenberg, Wolfgang Pauli, and Enrico Fermi. The initial version of the theory was based on the direct application of quantum mechanics to classical electrodynamic theory. It described the interaction of radiation, positrons, and electrons and appeared to give an accurate picture of the processes involved. Problems of a quantitative nature, however, quickly developed. Moreover, measurements of the fine structure of the hydrogen spectrum, obtained shortly after World War II by W. E. Lamb, Jr., and R. E. Retherford, demonstrated clearly that the observed energy levels of the hydrogen atom were not those predicted by the theory of Dirac and others. For these reasons many physicists during the 1930s and 1940s sought a solution to the dilemma in radical departures from the original theory, convinced that the latter must be either fundamentally altered or dispensed with entirely. *See* DIRAC, PAUL ADRIEN MAURICE; FERMI, ENRICO; LAMB, WILLIS EUGENE, JR.; PAULI, WOLFGANG.

During the early and middle 1940s Feynman worked on this problem at Princeton University. Among the difficulties of the original theory had been the occurrence of "divergent integrals": When measurements involving these terms were pressed beyond first-degree accuracy, infinite or meaningless answers resulted. The result of Feynman's mathematical approach was to show that the perplexing infinite terms could be put into a form that would be invariant under the Lorentz transformations. Feynman was able to demonstrate the feasibility of a program of "renormalization" of the electron mass and charge, aimed at eliminating the infinite terms from all actual calculations. In this process the formerly used values were replaced with new ones that would always have immediate significance in measurements of electron charge and mass. These new values made the measurement of electron properties completely finite and unambiguous. Feynman's approach, while not removing the "divergence difficulties," in fact eliminated them from any possible calculation of observable quantities. Part of the value of the new hypothesis was that it did not require the physical basis of the original electrodynamic theory to be abandoned.

An indirect product of Feynman's work on this problem was the "Feynman diagram," a graphical representation of the progress of an electrodynamic interaction that showed intermediate states as well as initial and final ones. This device considerably simplified the analysis of quantum-electrodynamic problems.

Feynman and Schwinger, who had

worked independently of one another, announced their results at about the same time. Tomonaga's work, much of which had been completed by 1943, also began to be known in the United States in English translation about 1948. All three had arrived at the same conclusions via different mathematical routes. Their results were immediately subjected to experimental testing that tended to substantiate their claims to provide accurate and unambiguous quantitative calculations.

Acceptance of the Feynman-Schwinger-Tomonaga theory led to a reconstruction of the fundamentals of quantum electrodynamics, which was accompanied by a great advance in the accuracy with which the behavior of the electron could be computed. In one experiment a value was obtained for the magnetic moment of the electron accurate to within 1 part in 10,000,000.

Besides his work in quantum electrodynamics, Feynman provided the atomic basis of the theory of liquid helium II that had been developed by the Russian physicist L. D. Landau. Feynman was also jointly responsible, with the American physicist Murray Gell-Mann, for an important and influential theory of β-decay. *See* GELL-MANN, MURRAY; LANDAU, LEV DAVYDOVICH.

Feynman received his B.S. at the Massachusetts Institute of Technology in 1939 and his Ph.D. at Princeton University in 1942. During World War II he worked at Los Alamos on the atomic bomb, returning to academic life in 1945 as an associate professor of theoretical physics at Cornell University. In 1950 he became professor of theoretical physics at the California Institute of Technology. In addition to the Nobel Prize, Feynman in 1954 received the Albert Einstein Award. He was elected to the National Academy of Sciences in 1954.

Feynman wrote *Quantum Electrodynamics* (1961), *Theory of Fundamental Processes* (1961), *Feynman Lectures on Physics* (3 vols., 1963–64), *Character of Physical Law* (1965), *Quantum Mechanics and Path Integrals,* with A. R. Hibbs (1966), *Photon-Hadron Interactions* (1972), and *Statistical Mechanics* (1972).

For background information *see* QUANTUM ELECTRODYNAMICS; QUANTUM FIELD THEORY; QUANTUM THEORY, RELATIVISTIC; SCATTERING MATRIX in the McGraw-Hill Encyclopedia of Science and Technology. ∎

FIELDS, PAUL R.
★ American chemist

Born Feb. 4, 1919, Chicago, IL, U.S.A.

Fields's primary interest was the study of the nuclear and chemical properties of the transuranium elements. His interest in these elements began when he joined the Metallurgical Laboratory at the University of Chicago in 1943. Initially, he worked on the chemical properties of neptunium using isotope 239, a beta emitter with 2.3-day half-life. He later helped isolate weighable amounts of ^{237}Np, an alpha-emitting isotope with a very long half-life which has been used for most chemical studies of this element. He contributed to the early development of ion exchange as a technique for separating uranium and plutonium from fission products. For several years he studied the properties of plutonium isotopes with masses greater than 239, produced by irradiating ^{238}U and ^{239}Pu with neutrons in the Hanford and Chalk River reactors. In the late 1940s these were the highest-neutron-flux reactors available.

When the materials testing reactor (MTR) was nearing completion in 1951, Fields and his associates prepared for an irradiation program in this reactor using ^{239}Pu as the starting material. The reactor was expected to have a tenfold-higher flux than the earlier reactors, and for the production of elements above plutonium this factor was expected to have a profound effect on the rates of formation. At that time, the heaviest element known was cal-

ifornium, element 98. To produce the next-heavier element, 99, would require the capture of 14 successive neutrons by ^{239}Pu to eventually form ^{253}Es, the first isotope of element 99 expected to be produced in a nuclear reactor. Thus, to a first approximation, the yield of ^{253}Es would vary as the fourteenth power of the neutron flux. Thus, in the MTR the yield of element 99 should be increased by a factor of 10^{14} compared with earlier reactors. With this exciting prospect in mind, ^{239}Pu samples were fabricated and inserted into the MTR early in 1952 with the intention of removing samples 6 months, 1 year, and 1.5 years after irradiation to look for new isotopes of plutonium, americium, and curium, known elements, as well as to look for new elements. Since the probability of neutron capture for the very-heavy-mass isotopes of the known transplutonium elements was unknown, it was not possible to predict accurately how rapidly new elements might form during irradiation.

While the plutonium samples were in the reactor, and before a single sample had been removed for examination, the first thermonuclear test device was detonated by the United States in November 1952. Samples from the detonation were returned and examined at Los Alamos Scientific Laboratory (LASL) and Argonne National Laboratory (ANL). When a new, very heavy isotope of plutonium, ^{246}Pu, was identified in the debris, it was apparent that an enormous neutron flux had been generated by the device. Since the formation of elements of very high atomic number is so strongly dependent on neutron flux, an immediate search was instituted for transplutonium elements at LASL, ANL, and the Radiation Laboratory, University of California, Berkeley. Within a year, two new elements, 99 and 100, had been discovered, and the neutron-rich isotopes of elements 94, 95, 96, 97, and 98 were identified and characterized.

The amounts of material isolated from the debris of the thermonuclear explosion were so minute that they could be measured in terms of numbers of atoms, for example, 10^5 atoms of ^{254}Cf. In order to obtain larger samples of transplutonium elements, some of the irradiated plutonium samples were removed from the MTR and examined. The neutron-rich isotopes of curium and californium were observed in the early irradiated samples, and later samples yielded relatively large amounts of elements 99 and 100. Using the long-lived isotopes of curium (96), berkelium (97), californium (98), einsteinium (99), and fermium (100), Fields and his coworkers studied the chemical properties, electronic structure, and nuclear structure of these elements and their isotopes—some for the first time.

In the early 1960s Fields utilized nuclear techniques to study the chemistry of radon to complement the investigations of xenon and krypton chemistry. He prepared radon fluoride and studied its stability and relative reactivity as compared with xenon fluorides.

Fields majored in chemistry at the University of Chicago, where he received his B.S. in 1941. He joined the Tennessee Valley Authority in 1941 and worked until 1943 on developing a process for producing aluminum from clay. From 1943 to 1945 he worked at the Metallurgical Laboratory, University of Chicago, on the wartime nuclear project to extract plutonium from irradiated uranium. He spent a year, 1945-46, with Standard Oil Company (Indiana) on the oxidation of organic compounds, and then returned in 1946 to nuclear research at Argonne National Laboratory, successor to the Metallurgical Laboratory. Later he became director of the Chemistry Division at Argonne. Fields received the 1970 American Society Award for Nuclear Applications in Chemistry.

For background information *see* NUCLEAR CHEMISTRY; TRANSURANIUM ELEMENTS in the McGraw-Hill Encyclopedia of Science and Technology. ■

FIESER, LOUIS FREDERICK
★ American chemist

Born Apr. 7, 1899, Columbus, OH, U.S.A.
Died July 25, 1977, Cambridge, MA, U.S.A.

A plantinum electrode introduced into a solution of quinone and hydroquinone [reaction (1)] at a fixed hydrogen ion concentration acquires an electric potential, which can be measured by making connection through a conducting liquid to a hydrogen electrode as reference half-cell.

The electrode potential E of the organic half-cell is dependent on the concentration of quinone, hydroquinone, and hydrogen ions in accordance with the

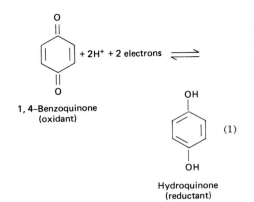

1,4-Benzoquinone (oxidant)

Hydroquinone (reductant)

(1)

equation below. The quantity E_0 is the normal potential characteristic of a particular quinone-hydroquinone system, and it

$$E^{25°} = E_0 + 0.05912 \log (H^+)$$

$$+ 0.02956 \log \frac{(quinone)}{(hydroquinone)}$$

is defined as the potential of the half-cell when the hydrogen-ion concentration is unity and the concentration of oxidant is equal to that of reductant. For 1,4-benzoquinone, $E_0^{25} = 0.699$ volt. Extending his research for the doctorate at Harvard under James B. Conant, Fieser prepared many known and new quinones, measured the potentials, and correlated the results. *m*-Directing, electron-attracting groups such as NO_2, CN, $COAr$, CO_2H, and SO_3H, as well as halogens, raise the potential of the parent quinone, whereas a potential-lowering effect is exerted by electron-releasing groups NH_2, $N(CH_3)_2$, OH, OCH_3, CH_3, $NHCOCH_3$, and $OCOCH_3$.

A reinvestigation of the work by Russian and German groups on the reaction of the silver salt of hydroxynaphthoquinone with alkyl halides showed both groups to have been in error, and established [reaction (2)] that the hydroxy compound and its salt are α-naphthoquinones (I_a, II_a) but that alkylation produces the α-ether (III) by displacement and the β-ether (IV) by 1,4-addition.

Several pairs of pure α- and β-ethers were prepared and characterized with the finding that the β-ethers such as (IV) are higher in normal potential than the α-ethers (III) by 0.080 volt. Fieser inferred (1928) that a solution of the free hydroxyquinone contains no more than about 0.2 percent of the less stable tautomeric form (Iβ). The more elaborate tautomerism of 4-amino-1,2-naphthoquinone was studied in 1934 with his coworker and wife, Mary.

Alkylation of the silver salt (IIα) with an allylic halide gave, in addition to the two oxygen-ethers, an acidic product shown to be the result of carbon alkylation. With this novel reaction available, Fieser was able to achieve (1927) the first synthesis of the natural quinone pigment lapachol [reaction (3)] and so received the plaudits of Samuel C. Hooker, who in 1889 had discovered lapachol as a yellow pigment in the grain of bethabara wood. Lapachol has an isoprenoid side chain, and the alkylating agent for Fieser's synthesis was prepared by the 1,4-addition of hydrogen bromide to isoprene.

In 1929 Fieser and Emma M. Dietz at Bryn Mawr described a highly improved method for the synthesis of 1,2,5,6-dibenzanthracene [reaction (4)]. In 1930 Kennaway at the Royal Cancer Institute in London reported that this hydrocarbon has the power to induce cancerous growth in mice; it was the first known pure carcinogen. When Wieland and Dane (1933) effected [reaction (5)] the chemical degradation of the bile acid derivative (V) to methylcholanthrene (VI), the British group noted the structural similarity to 1,2,5,6-dibenzanthracene, prepared and tested the new hydrocarbon, and found it to be the most potent known carcinogen. Fieser and A. M. Seligman 1935 found [reaction (6)] the Fieser-Dietz synthesis to work well with the ketone (IX) and so, by synthesis, made methylcholanthrene abundantly available for biological experimentation. With the collaboration of Seligman, E. B. Hershberg, M. S. Newman, and others, work on the synthesis of carcinogens was continued by Fieser until World War II; in recognition of this work Fieser received the Judd Prize for cancer research from Memorial Hospital (1941).

Work during 1929–39 by H. Dam, P. Karrer, E. A. Doisy, and others on the isolation from alfalfa of the antihemorrhagic principle, vitamin K_1, as a yellow oil suggested to Fieser that the substance may be a naphthoquinone, and possibly related to lapachol but with a larger isoprenoid side chain and no hydroxyl group. Bioassays of synthetic model compounds and study of their absorption spectra supported the idea, and in a communication in 1939 Fieser suggested that vitamin K_1 is either 2-methyl-3-phytyl-1,4-naphthoquinone (XII) or the 2-ethyl compound. 2-Methyl-1,4-naphthohydroquinone (X) proved to be a better starting material for synthesis [reaction (7)] than the quinone, and condensation with phytol in dioxane in the presence of oxalic acid gave a mixture containing considerable substituted hydroquinone (XI). The unchanged hydroquinone (X) was removed by extraction from ether with dilute alkaline hydrosulfite, and the more lipophilic phytyl-substituted hydroquinone was separated from the ether residue as a waxy white solid by digestion with petroleum ether and centrifugation. Oxidation of the white sludge in ether with silver oxide and evaporation gave pure 2-methyl-3-phytyl-1,4-naphthoquinone as a yellow oil. The synthetic material corresponded to natural vitamin K_1 in antihemorrhagic potency and absorption spectrum, and on reductive acetylation the substance gave a crystalline hydroquinone diacetate (melting point 59°C), as reported by Doisy for the K_1 derivative.

Complete identification required only a mixed melting point determination and, when Doisy declined to cooperate until he had completed his own degradative study of structure, Fieser decided to apply what he had learned about the vitamin by its synthesis for the isolation of a comparison sample. A 5.3-gram portion of a 3–5 percent alfalfa K_1 concentrate was reduced and put through the extraction and precipitation procedures worked out for the synthetic substance, and in a few hours 60 milligrams of pure vitamin K_1 was isolated. This quantity sufficed for analysis, color test, bioassay, determination of the spectrum, and for the preparation, analysis, and mixed melting point determination with the synthetic hydroquinone diacetate, which showed no depression. Finally, the

$$
\text{(X)} \quad + \quad \text{Phytol}
$$

$$
\xrightarrow{\text{(COOH)}_2} \quad \text{(XI)}
$$

$$
\xrightarrow{\text{Ag}_2\text{O}} \quad \text{(XII) Vitamin K}_1 \tag{7}
$$

2-ethyl compound was synthesized and found devoid of vitamin K activity. Thus a program of synthetic research, independent of any work on the natural product itself, established that vitamin K_1 is 2-methyl - 3 - phytyl - 1,4 - naphthoquinone. Fieser's synthesis, protected by a patent assigned to Research Corporation, provided a practical method for the manufacture of a vitamin factor which soon found significant uses in therapy. The amounts of vitamin K_1 present in green plants are much too small for use in therapy. *See* DAM, HENRIK; DOISY, EDWARD ADELBERT.

Fieser received his A.B. in 1920 from Williams College and his Ph.D. in chemistry in 1924 from Harvard University. In 1924–25 he did postdoctoral research in Frankfurt, Germany, and Oxford, England. He was a professor of chemistry at Bryn Mawr College in 1925–30, and then he joined the staff at Harvard, where he became Sheldon Emery Professor of Organic Chemistry in 1939. During World War II he developed napalm and other incendiaries and directed a large research group in exploiting the clue that lapachol derivatives possess antimalarial activity. This latter work was resumed at the time of the war in Vietnam, and new lapachol-like drugs of promise still await full evaluation. Among the awards received by Fieser were the Manufacturing Chemists' Association Award for teaching (1959), the Norris Award for teaching (1959), and the ACS Award in Chemical Education (1967). He was elected to the National Academy of Sciences in 1940.

Fieser published about 340 research papers, 40 of which were based on his own experiments. He wrote *Organic Experiments* (2d ed. 1964; 3d ed. with Kenneth L. Williamson, 1975) and *The Scientific Method: A Personal Account of Unusual Projects in War and in Peace* (1964). He and his wife were coauthors of *Organic Chemistry* (3d ed. 1956), *Steroids* (4th ed. 1959), *Introduction to Organic Chemistry* (1957), *Basic Organic Chemistry* (1959), *Style Guide for Chemists* (1960), *Advanced Organic Chemistry* (1961), *Topics in Organic Chemistry* (1963), *Current Topics in Organic Chemistry* (1963), and *Reagents for Organic Synthesis* (6 vols., 1967–1977).

For background information *see* ONCOLOGY; QUINONE; VITAMIN K in the McGraw-Hill Encyclopedia of Science and Technology. ∎

FIESER, MARY PETERS
★ American organic chemist

Born *May 27, 1909, Atchison, KS, U.S.A.*

Fieser became interested in organic chemistry while still an undergraduate student. In association with her husband and colleague, Louis F. Fieser, she made contributions to the investigation of quinones and steroids and to the development of textbooks on organic chemistry. *See* FIESER, LOUIS FREDERICK.

When the Fiesers began their work in

the field of quinones, the subject seemed to be of only theoretical interest. The later realization of the importance of quinones in biological processes during the early 1940s added to the excitement of research in this field. The investigations of the Fiesers included preparing new and known quinones, measuring the potentials by using a combination of a platinum electrode and a reference hydrogen electrode, and using these techniques to study the tautomerism of 4-amino-1,2-naphthoquinone.

When the steroids began generating wide interest because of their physiological functions, Mary and Louis Fieser began research in this field, and together they published papers concerning their research.

The Fiesers were coauthors of a noted series of books in the field of organic chemistry, beginning with *Organic Chemistry* in 1946. This text represented a departure from the European models in that it included a large amount of material that conveyed the varied interesting aspects of the field, including applications to medicine and technology. This text was ultimately translated into 15 languages.

In 1959, after about 10 years of research, the Fiesers published a monograph on steroids, just prior to the discovery of the medical uses of cortisone. In 1967 they published the first volume of a series, *Reagents for Organic Synthesis,* and subsequently published six more volumes (vol. 7 in 1978). This series is a source of information concerning new reagents for

synthesis. As new syntheses became more sophisticated, new reagents, including novel inorganic chemicals as well as organometallic reagents, were introduced at an extremely rapid rate.

Fieser entered Bryn Mawr College in 1926, intending to pursue premedical studies. Her first course in chemistry sparked her interest, and organic chemistry became a lifelong career. She attended Radcliffe for a year of graduate study. For her contributions to books and articles in the field of organic chemistry, Fieser received an honorary D.Sc. from Smith in 1969. At Harvard University, she was an honorary research associate in chemistry. In 1971 she received the Garvon Medal of the American Chemical Society.

For background information *see* OR-GANIC CHEMICAL SYNTHESIS; ORGANIC CHEMISTRY; QUINONE; STEROID in the McGraw-Hill Encyclopedia of Science and Technology. ■

FISCHER, ERNST OTTO
German chemist

Born Nov. 10, 1918, Munich, Germany

Fischer pioneered in the field of organometallic chemistry. In 1973 he was awarded the Nobel Prize for chemistry in recognition of his work in the preparation and structural determination of "sandwich" complexes of organic and metallic atoms. He shared the prize with Geoffrey Wilkinson for simultaneous and independent studies of these compounds. *See* WILKINSON, SIR GEOFFREY.

The first report of Fischer's work was in 1951. At that time he described the preparation of dicyclopentadienyliron, a highly stable organometallic compound. Its extraordinary chemical and thermal stability intrigued Fischer, and he continued with his experimental investigations to determine the structure and explain the properties of this compound. The structure was identified by x-ray crystallography. Fischer published the results of these studies in 1952, describing a π-complexed sandwich structure. Since the compound was also noted to have high aromatic reactivity, it was subsequently named ferrocene.

Fischer's work continued in the metallocene area after this breakthrough, and he went on to make a number of other original contributions. Shortly after the ferrocene structure determination he prepared similar sandwich derivatives of cyclopentadienyl and indenyl ligands with other transition metals. Based on his views concerning the nature of π-bonded cyclopentadienyl complexes, he predicted that the compound dibenzenechromium(0) could exist. This theory received considerable criticism since it was known that both the chromium atom and the two benzene molecules of the sandwich were neutral. However, with the assistance of Walter Hafner, he was successful in proving his theory by developing a high-yield synthesis of the molecule.

New contributions followed in rapid succession. Fischer was responsible for the development of the chemistry of transition-metal complexes of arenes, carbocyclic molecules, and mono-, di-, and oligoolefins. He prepared the first carbene–transition-metal complex (1964) and the first carbyne-transition-metal complex (1973), thereby developing new classes of compounds.

Fischer established himself and remained as a forerunner in transition-metal–organic chemistry. This work had a significant influence on the fields of inorganic, organic, and theoretical chemistry and has set the pace for the fast-moving developments in his field in laboratories around the world. The Inorganic Chemistry Laboratory of Technische Hochschule (now Technische Universität) in Munich, under Fischer's direction, became a leading center for organometallic chemistry research.

The son of Karl T. Fischer, a physics professor at the Technical University of Munich, Fischer studied chemistry and natural science there. His studies were interrupted by World War II, during which he served for almost 6 years in the German army. After the war he returned to the Technical University of Munich and received his Ph.D. in 1952. He continued his career there, becoming assistant professor (1954) and later full professor (1959) of chemistry at the University of Munich. In 1964 he was appointed director of the Technical University's Institute for Inorganic Chemistry. He authored many technical publications, and was the recipient of the Chemistry Prize of the Academy of Sciences at Göttingen (1957) and the Alfred Stock Memorial Prize from the Society of German Chemists (1959). Fischer was elected to the Bavarian Academy of Sciences in 1964.

For background *see* ORGANOMETALLIC COMPOUNDS in the McGraw-Hill Encyclopedia of Science and Technology. ■

FISHER, SIR RONALD (AYLMER)
English geneticist and statistician

Born Feb. 17, 1890, East Finchley, Middlesex, England
Died July 29, 1962, Adelaide, Australia

From his early studies in genetics and evolution Fisher was awakened to the need for precise statistical methods to interpret quantitative data. For his contributions to the theory and application of statistics for making quantitative a vast field of biology, he was awarded the Royal Society's Copley Medal in 1955.

Karl Pearson established the first body of knowledge that could be called statistics and founded the first statistical journal, *Biometrika*. His outstanding achievement was the χ^2 test (chi-square test) in which χ^2 represented the probability of any sample value being obtained from a population with a known mean and variance (distribution about the mean). For a particular sample, χ^2 was found by formula (1),

$$x^2 = \sum \frac{(O - E)^2}{E} \qquad (1)$$

where E is the expected class frequency and O the observed frequency. The corresponding probability was then found in a table of χ^2 values. For example, a low probability could be used as evidence that an experimental treatment was associated with samples differing from the parent population. The test was accurate if large samples were used.

As a rule, limitations of time and funds restricted researchers to small samples in the testing of biological material. The inherent variability of the material thus introduced great uncertainty into their results. Fisher saw that if only the feature of randomization were incorporated into experimental designs, then statistical machinery could provide the needed quantitative assessments of accuracy. Nonrandom, or systematic, design consisted of distributing individuals receiving different treatments over an experimental area according to a preconceived plan. For example, for three treatments (A,B,C,), a common design was that shown in notation (2). Though such a design sought to elimi-

```
┌─────────┐ ┌─────────┐ ┌─────────┐
│ A  B  C │ │ A  B  C │ │ A  B  C │
└─────────┘ └─────────┘ └─────────┘
                                    (2)
```

nate environmental inhomogeneity, a gradient of environmental condition that existed, let us say, from left to right, would affect treatment A to a greater extent than the others. In agricultural field experiments it had been found that gradients of soil conditions were of universal occurrence and existed over very short distances. Systematic designs were powerless to overcome or measure their effects. Fisher showed that if treatment positions were assigned randomly, the laws of chance would allow statistics to provide unbiased quantitative estimates of the error due both to environmental conditions and to the variability of the material being tested. In addition, a probability statement, in the form of a percentage

figure, could be attached to the error estimate. For example, a statement that an error is at the 5 percent level of significance would mean that the results could be trusted to include the true figure 95 out of 100 times.

One of the most generally applicable of the procedures Fisher supplied for the testing of variance of small samples from a population is the F ratio. This method was found to be important because it utilized the entire population of the experiment. Fisher's analyses first determined the pooled variance ($S_p{}^2$) obtained from the entire population. Second, an estimate of the variance of the means for each category of the population ($S_M{}^2$) was computed. These two quantities may be tested to see if there is a significant difference between them by forming the F ratio, $S_p{}^2/S_M{}^2$. The hypothesis of equal means is rejected if the F ratio obtained exceeds the critical value of the F table.

Among Fisher's other outstanding contributions to mathematical statistics were his solution for the exact distribution of the correlation coefficient (r), the concepts of consistent, efficient, and sufficient statistics, and the maximum likelihood solution, which was a formula for finding these statistics. Fisher's theoretical work on inductive inference laid the foundation for advances in statistics.

The other major phase of Fisher's work was in genetics. An important achievement was his demonstration of mendelian inheritance in certain examples of continuous inheritance that were thought to be nonmendelian in nature, such as those in human relatives. Also notable is his theory of the evolution of dominance, which has become a cornerstone of the theory that selection and not mutation is the directing force in evolution. It had occurred to Fisher that if all known mutations were recessive, then selection of advantageous mutations could not be the mechanism of evolution. Mutations were rare events. If they were recessive, they would most certainly be eliminated from the population before they had a chance to attain the homozygous state and express themselves phenotypically. Fisher was struck by the claim that crosses between fancy breeds of domestic poultry had shown the mutant and not the wild type to be dominant in a number of cases. He hypothesized that over the centuries human selection had resulted in the evolution of dominance. He assumed that mutations had occurred, not wholly reces-

sive, which were deemed desirable by the breeders as curious novelties. These heterozygotes would be selected and bred in favor of the others. In future generations selection would always favor the mutants that showed the greatest amount of influence over the dominant, and the recessive would evolve into a strong but incomplete dominant (that is, its homozygous effect would be distinguishable from its heterozygous effect).

Fisher then proposed that if he were to interbreed the domestic poultry with wild jungle fowl, the mutations would show the history of their development and would be neither recessive nor dominant, but intermediate or semidominant. Fisher believed that crossing the mutants to other domestic breeds would give inconclusive results because they very likely possessed other mutations for the gene in question or for related genes. The recessive was held to have developed its dominance over the dominant gene of the wild ancestors that came out of the forest to cover the domestic hens.

Choosing a single stock for each of seven mutations, Fisher crossed each with wild fowl, backcrossing and inbreeding alternate generations in order to have the mutation contrasted against a great amount of wild germ plasm. After the fifth generation the heterozygotes were interbred in order to obtain homozygotes. With the possible exception of rose comb, none of the factors showed complete dominance. Fisher considered his results good evidence that the raw materials of progressive evolutionary adaptation were recessive mutations that, at first not wholly recessive, were selected for their minute advantages. Once established, selection favored those recessives that showed themselves to be increasingly less recessive or more dominant. This afforded an explanation as to why advantageous genes were dominants. Likewise, harmful mutations, at first not wholly recessive, would be selected against and would evolve toward a complete recessive condition.

Fisher attended Gonville and Caius College, Cambridge. From 1913 to 1915 he worked as a statistician for the Mercantile and General Investment Company, and from 1915 to 1919 he taught in the public schools. In 1919 he was chosen to work in the statistical department at Rothamsted Experimental Station, Harpenden. He left in 1933 to become Galton Professor of Eugenics at University College, London, leaving only upon his election to the Arthur Balfour Chair of Genetics at Cambridge University. In 1957 he retired, though he remained at Cambridge until his successor was appointed in 1959. For the last years of his life Fisher worked as a researcher for the Commonwealth Scientific and Industrial Research Organization (CSIRO) in Adelaide, Australia. Fisher became a fellow of the Royal Society in 1929. He was knighted in 1952.

Fisher wrote *Statistical Methods for Research Workers* (1925; 13th ed. 1958); *The Genetical Theory of Natural Selection* (1938; 2d ed. 1958); *The Design of Experiments* 1935; 7th ed. 1960); and *Statistical Tables for Biological, Agricultural, and Medical Research,* with F. Yates (1938; 6th ed. 1963).

For background information *see* GENETICS; MUTATION; STATISTICS in the McGraw-Hill Encyclopedia of Science and Technology. ∎

FITCH, VAL LOGSDON
★ American physicist

Born Mar 10, 1923, Merriman, NE, U.S.A.

By the late 1940s a clear distinction had been established between the strongly interacting π-meson, which is largely responsible for nuclear forces, and the weakly interacting μ-meson. Today it is known that the μ-meson is identical to the electron except that it is 207 times heavier, a "heavy brother" of the electron. In the early 1950s the weakness with which the μ-meson interacts with nuclear matter suggested a number of unique experi-

ments. Among these was a proposal that the μ-meson could be an important probe of the electrical properties of the nucleus. The μ-meson, in coming to rest in matter, is eventually trapped in one of the outer Bohr orbits about a nucleus, and thereupon proceeds to cascade down through the various atomic orbits to the lowest state. The μ-mesonic atom differs in one important respect from the conventional electronic atom. Because of the greater mass of the μ-meson, its Bohr orbit has a radius 207 times smaller than the corresponding electron orbit. Indeed, in the case of lead, the lowest level has an associated orbit so small that the μ-meson spends more than 50 percent of its time inside the nucleus. This nuclear penetration causes the energy levels to be substantially modified. For example, the transition energy between the two lowest atomic levels in lead is 18 megaelectronvolts (MeV) if the lead nucleus is a point charge. With the nucleus extended to a radius of 8.4×10^{-13} centimeter, thought to be the proper value in 1952, the transition energy computes to be 4.5 MeV. Fitch and L. J. Rainwater, working at the Nevis cyclotron at Columbia University, set about to study these radiations. They were the first to observe the spectral lines from these rather curious atoms. They discovered, in the case of lead nuclei, the K line is not at 4.5 MeV, as had been predicted, but rather at 6 MeV. Indeed, this result was so unexpected that they were unsuccessful in initial attempts to see the radiation because the spectrometer at first was not set to extend to 6 MeV. *See* RAINWATER, LEO JAMES.

The immediate conclusion from these observations turned out to be correct, that is, the radius of the lead nucleus was very substantially smaller than had been determined previously by a variety of methods. All the other nuclei studied showed the smaller radii. Shortly afterward, the smaller nuclear radius was confirmed by the electron-scattering experiments of Robert Hofstadter and his coworkers at Stanford. The other older methods of determining nuclear radii have been refined and corrected to give consistent results. One of the spectacular features of the μ-mesonic atom is that the μ-meson, before it finally interacts with the nucleus, traverses about 1 meter of nuclear matter—and nuclear matter has a density 10^{13} times that of water! *See* HOFSTADTER, ROBERT.

After the studies of μ-mesonic atoms

Fitch turned his attention to the newly discovered K-mesons (mesons with slightly more than half the mass of the proton) and contributed to the so-called $\tau\theta$ puzzle. This puzzle led T.-D. Lee and C. N. Yang to suggest the violation of parity in the weak interactions. *See* LEE, TSUNG-DAO; YANG, CHEN NING.

The neutral K-mesons have always presented a fascinating picture. It was known in the early 1950s that the neutral K, the K^0, decays to π^+ and π^-. It was also known that the antiparticle, the $\bar{K}^0$, decays the same way. If one sees in a detector the π^+- and π^--mesons, one describes the decay, in the tradition of quantum mechanics, as having orginated from a linear combination of the two particle states, that is, either a $K^0 + \bar{K}^0$ or $K^0 - \bar{K}^0$. Which is it? The $\pi^+\pi^-$ system is even under the combined operations of charge conjugation and parity, CP. If one defines $|\bar{K}^0 \geq CP\ |K^0>$, then it is the first combination, $K^0+\bar{K}^0 = K_1{}^0$, that decays to $\pi^+\pi^-$. The second combination, $K_2{}^0 = K^0 - \bar{K}^0$, exists, but it cannot decay to π^+ and π^- if the interaction responsible for the decay of the particles is invariant under CP. Both the $K_1{}^0$ and the $K_2{}^0$ were found to exist as early as 1957. In 1964 Fitch and his collaborators, J. H. Christenson, J. W. Cronin, and R. Turlay, discovered that the $K_2{}^0$ also does decay to the $\pi^+\pi^-$-mesons. It happens very rarely, 1/250,000 times as fast as the $K_1{}^0$ decays to $\pi^+\pi^-$. But it definitely does happen, and it means that CP is violated in the decay— that the universe is not completely symmetric under the combined operations of charge conjugation and parity.

This observation has important implications, particularly in view of a theorem which is at the core of all modern field theories, the CPT theorem. On the basis of special relativity it is possible to show that all interactions must be symmetrical under the combined operations of charge conjugation C, parity P, and time reversal T. With the violation of CP the CPT theorem requires a violation of time reversal invariance to correct the wronged. Detailed experiments done on the neutral K-mesons show that, indeed, T-reversed invariance is violated while CPT remains inviolate. Physicists are now preoccupied with the relation between the microscopic time violation observed in K-decay thermodynamics and cosmology. Does time violation have some connection, for example, with the fact that the universe is composed largely of matter (as opposed to mixtures of matter-antimatter)? It is interesting to observe that the studies of the K-meson have led to the overthrow of major symmetry principles—parity in 1957 and now charge conjugation parity.

Fitch had an early interest in chemistry. He was first exposed to physics when, in the U.S. Army, he was sent to Los Alamos, NM, during World War II to work on the atomic bomb project. He participated in the initial bomb test at Alamogordo in July 1945. He received his bachelor's degree in electrical engineering from McGill University in 1948 and a Ph.D. in physics from Columbia University in 1954. He became a professor of physics at Princeton University in 1960, and later the Cyrus Fogg Brackett Professor of Physics. In 1966 he was elected to the National Academy of Sciences and the American Academy of Arts and Sciences.

For background information *see* INTERACTIONS, WEAK NUCLEAR; MESON; RELATIVITY; SCATTERING EXPERIMENTS, NUCLEAR in the McGraw-Hill Encyclopedia of Science and Technology. ■

FITZ-JAMES, PHILIP CHESTER
★ Canadian microbiologist

***Born** Nov. 26, 1920, Vancouver, British Columbia, Canada*

The resting, heat- and chemical-resistant bacterial spore has fascinated microbiologists since the initial studies (published in 1877) of Ferdinand Cohn on *Bacillus subtilis* and of his student Robert Koch on *B.*

anthrax. This resting state in the life cycle of certain members of the genera *Bacillus* and *Clostridium* has been the object of much study as a physiological entity. Until about 1950, however, when Fitz-James began his studies on the bacterial spore, little was known of the exact structure and chemical nature of this completely resting cell. During the following 10 years, not only the general composition and structure of bacterial spores were described, but also their requirements for germination and their mode of formation. Moreover, the localization of chemical components in their special layers of the spore was partly elucidated. By combining morphological (light and electron microscopy) and biochemical analyses, Fitz-James made a leading contribution to this work.

Fitz-James and his student Elizabeth Young found that spore formation is essentially a peculiar form of division, involving first a membrane folding at the cell end which encloses approximately half of the cell's deoxyribonucleic acid (DNA). In the resulting double-membrane forespore, the internal and external orientations of the cell membrane are preserved so that an outer zone now separates the original cell (sporangium) from the spore protoplast. In the space between the forespore membranes a layer (the cortex), originally described by Fitz-James's colleague C. F. Robinow, appears. The formation of the spore coat or coats commences and appears outside the outer membrane of the forming spore. By the use of mutants blocked at various stages of spore formation and by the use of antibiotics inhibiting cell wall and protein synthesis, the nature of much of this spore formation was worked out.

In 1953 Fitz-James was invited by C. L. Hannay to assist in a joint study of the characteristics of parasporal crystals, which form along with the spores in certain insect-pathogenic species of the *B. cereus* group. Later, Fitz-James and Young made initial biochemical and structural studies on the formation of these fascinating protein crystals in sporulating bacilli.

In 1955 Fitz-James became a morphological collaborator with Sol Spiegelman and Arthur Aronson and contributed to their studies on the isolation of nuclear bodies from bacterial protoplasts. Fitz-James continued to study the synthesis of cell components in growing protoplasts with both morphological and chemical methods. Later, by using protoplasting techniques, the dependence of sporulat-

ing cells on an intact cell wall was shown. Following Alexander Rich's demonstration of polysomes in red blood cells, Fitz-James used protoplasts to isolate polyribosomes from *B. megaterium*. The growing protoplast system was shown to be ideal for the study of the action of a number of membrane-active antibiotics and fat-soluble vitamins.

In 1962 a collaboration with Ronald Hancock demonstrated the failure of penicillin to inhibit the growing protoplast. At the same time, by comparing the effects of penicillin on cells growing in a variety of stabilizing media, Fitz-James and Hancock described the accumulation of what appeared to be open strands of cell wall at the growing sites of wall synthesis in dividing bacilli. From the work of J. L. Strominger and J. T. Park, it became apparent that these uncross-linked monomer strands of mucopeptide. Thus, the initial lesion of penicillin action was sharply demonstrated by using the electron microscope.

With the application of modern methods of fixation and embedding, Fitz-James, along with many other electron microscopists, encountered the peculiar membranous organelles in the growing and sporulating cells of the bacilli. His name for this organelle, the mesosome, is now commonly accepted. Subsequent studies by Fitz-James and others were directed toward the isolation and characterization of these organelles. A confusing array of membrane functions were localized by these earlier efforts. It now appears from morphological, immunological, and autolytic studies by others that the highly complex and vesicle-filled mesosomes develop rapidly in bacterial cells in early stages of fixation (or preparation) from perturbation at sensitive membrane pockets (the basic mesosome) by a phospholipase degradation of phospholipid leading to the formation of diglyceride-rich vesicles within a membrane pocket.

The characterization of a peculiar cross-striated strand initially observed on the outer surface of the plasma membrane of *B. megaterium* occupied the research efforts of Fitz-James and his assistant Doryth Loewy in the early 1970s. These fascinating structures were best seen in negative-stained smears in the electron microscope. They were found on the membranes of all *Bacillus* species examined and some *Clostridia*. These polymers, anchored at one end to the membrane and in transit to the cell wall, are found in great length in the lysing walls in some filamentous *Bacilli*. This appearance suggested the name monorails. Although initial studies of impure preparations indicated these might be uncross-linked strands of peptidoglycan, analysis of more purified preparations showed that they are membrane teichoic acids which ultimately become part of the cell wall. From this study, a procedure for the preparation of structurally intact teichoic acid by nonchemical extraction was developed.

Working in collaboration with Aronson of Purdue University, Fitz-James was involved in an extensive study of the synthesis of spore coat protein and its assembly into coat layers. Out of this came studies of the role of spore coats in germination, coat-localized enzymes, and the interrelationship of coat and parasporal inclusion (protein crystal) synthesis. This necessitated the isolation of "crystal minus," "crystal only," and "coatless" mutants of *Bacillus* species and led both Fitz-James and Aronson to an interest in the plasmid control or modification of sporulation and inclusion body formation.

Son of a wood-products engineer of Anglo-Scot origin and an Irish mother of the Dublin Shaws, Fitz-James grew up in a land abounding in biology. As a teen-ager, he made hobbies of bird banding and taxidermy. He also kept 10 beehives and tended a large garden. His early training at the University of British Columbia was in agricultural microbiology (B.S.A., 1943); on graduation he went to the Banting and Best Department of Medical Research at the University of Toronto to assist organic chemist Fergus MacDonald in the operation of a penicillin pilot plant. At Toronto he took an M.S.A. in physiology and biochemistry (1945) and then entered medicine at the University of Western Ontario (M.D., 1949). After a year's internship in Vancouver, he enrolled for a Ph.D. (awarded in 1953) at Western, where under the combined guidance of R. J. Rossiter in biochemistry and R. G. E. Murray and Robinow in microbiology he began his studies of the bacterial spore. He was awarded the Royal Society of Canada's Harrison Prize in 1963 and the Canadian Society of Microbiologists Award in 1977. *See* MURRAY, ROBERT GEORGE EVERITT; ROSSITER, ROGER JAMES.

For background information *see* BACILLACEAE; BACTERIAL ENDOSPORES in the McGraw-Hill Encyclopedia of Science and Technology. ∎

FIXMAN, MARSHALL
★ American physical chemist

Born Sept. 21, 1930, St. Louis, MO, U.S.A.

Fixman was a theorist who worked primarily on the statistical mechanics of fluids and solutions, and especially on polymer theory. His first effort in theory, concerning dilute polymer solutions, took place while he was a graduate student at the Massachusetts Institute of Technology. If chainlike polymers are long enough, they are capable of curving back to their starting points, and so the beginning of the chain interferes with the freedom of the end to select a spatial position randomly. P. J. Flory had first shown that this interference causes an expansion of the chain, and Fixman's contribution was to exploit the resemblance of this expansion to the expansion of a gas. The dimensions of the polymer chain, like the pressure of a gas, can be expanded in powers of the spatial density of repeating units.

Experimental determination of polymer dimensions is usually obtained from the scattering of light by chains in dilute solution. Although the basic theory of light scattering from pure liquids had been worked out by Albert Einstein on the basis of fluctuations in the refractive index, the difficulty of measuring absolute scattering intensities had caused some concern regarding the correctness of the theory. Fixman therefore took up the problem of constructing a molecular theory. This had been attempted before, usually with the conclusion that the refractive index was a nonlocal property of matter and therefore could not be considered to fluctuate independently from one volume element to another, as had been assumed by Einstein. Fixman, however, accepted the local nature of the refractive index as a working hypothesis, and showed that this could be true only if the amplitudes of the electric field and its induced polarization, the relative values of which are controlled by the refractive index, fluctuated together in such a way as to cancel out their nonlocal parts. Calculation on this basis confirmed Einstein's theory. A quite similar problem arose in the transport theory of concentrated solutions of colloids or polymers. Each polymer molecule moving through a solution perturbs the solvent flow field at a great distance, and so the stress and velocity fields have nonlocal contributions. However, these were found to drop out of the calculation of relative magnitudes, which was used to determine the viscosity coefficient.

This interest in nonlocal phenomena led next to the dynamical theory of liquids and solutions near the critical point, where large-scale fluctuations of density or concentration occur because the solution is near a limit of stability of a homogeneous phase. Experiments had pointed to the possibility of singularities in transport coefficients such as the viscosity and thermal conductivity, and the problem was to understand how large spontaneous fluctuations could give rise to anomalous transport properties. A coupling was found in nonlinear terms in the equations of fluid motion. For example, a nonuniform velocity field imposed on a medium that is inhomogeneous because of concentration fluctuations will distort the fluctuations, and will increase the amount of energy dissipated during their relaxation back to the uniform state. This increase in dissipation shows up in the experiment as an anomalous viscosity. A considerable body of theory, known as mode-mode coupling theory, grew out of this method of analysis.

Fixman's work on polymers, initiated and carried out under the frequent guidance of his former thesis adviser, W. H. Stockmayer, continued. The theory of polymer motion, important to the dielectric and mechanical properties of plastics, was the major focus in later years. To aid in the development of models and physical insight, Fixman carried out a computer simulation of polymer motion. The theoretically challenging aspect of this work was to incorporate constraints on the motion of one part of the chain that result from its connection to the remainder of the polymer. Analytical study of the constraining forces made it possible to simulate the motion of chains with rigid bond lengths and (adjacent) bond angles. The only source of conformational rearrangements is hindered rotation about bond axes. A surprising result of these simulations was the relatively small polymeric effect on the rate of internal rearrangements. This had often been inferred from experiments on polymers, but it was not apparent that the experimental results were consistent with a simple dynamical model.

Fixman received his bachelor's degree from Washington University in St. Louis in 1950, and his doctorate from the Massachusetts Institute of Technology in 1954. After a year of advanced study with J. G. Kirkwood at Yale University, and 2 years in the U.S. Army, Fixman entered his first academic position, in the chemistry department at Harvard University. He was at Harvard during 1956–59, at the Mellon Institute in Pittsburgh during 1959–61, at the University of Oregon during 1961–65, and in the chemistry department of Yale University during 1965–79. He then joined the chemistry and physics departments of Colorado State University in Fort Collins. He received the American Chemistry Society Award in Pure Chemistry in 1964 and was elected to the National Academy of Sciences in 1973.

For background information *see* POLYMER PROPERTIES; POLYMERIZATION; STATISTICAL MECHANICS in the McGraw-Hill Encyclopedia of Science and Technology. ■

FLEMING, SIR ALEXANDER
Scottish bacteriologist

Born Aug. 6, 1881, Lochfield, Ayrshire, Scotland
Died Mar. 11, 1955, London, England

In 1928, while experimenting with bacteria of the staphylococcus group, Fleming noticed on a culture plate, which had been contaminated by mold, a clear, bacteria-free ring around the mold growth. Further experimentation showed that a substance in the mold culture itself prevented the growth of the bacteria. Since the mold organism was of the *Penicillium* group, Fleming named the antibacterial substance it contained "penicillin." For this discovery he received, together with H. W. Florey and E. B. Chain, the 1945 Nobel Prize in physiology or medicine. *See* CHAIN, ERNST BORIS; FLOREY OF ADELAIDE, BARON (HOWARD WALTER FLOREY).

The observation that one species of microorganism is capable of producing substances that destroy another was first made in 1877 by Louis Pasteur and Jules François Joubert. They noted that when a culture of anthrax bacilli was exposed to bacteria from the air, the former were destroyed. Although Pasteur realized the significance of this phenomenon in relation to the treatment of infectious diseases, and certain later investigators made similar observations on the antagonistic or inhibitory properties of bacteria, Fleming's work on penicillin marked the beginning of the practical application of these observations.

Fleming himself claimed that although he was well aware of the phenomenon of bacterial antagonisms, and had even discovered another antibacterial substance—lysozome—before penicillin, his discovery of penicillin began as a chance observation. The culture techniques used in his work with lysozome (an antibacterial substance in human tears and saliva), however, were applicable to his later penicillin experimentation.

The age of antibiotics began, in effect,

when a culture of staphylococci was accidentally contaminated by exposure to mold organisms in the air. As the mold organisms grew on the culture plate, around each mold colony a translucent area developed, indicating that the staphylococci were being lysed, or destroyed. Because the bacteria undergoing lysis were of a type infectious to humans, Fleming decided to pursue this chance occurrence. He isolated the mold organism in pure culture and identified it as *Penicillium notatum,* a mold originally isolated from rotting hyssop (an aromatic plant native to Europe). The pure culture was grown on another plate at room temperature and, after 4 or 5 days, was streaked radially with several infectious bacterial cultures. Some of the bacteria grew up to the mold, but others were inhibited from growing in a region several centimeters from the mold colony. Thus the antibacterial substance in the mold destroyed some bacteria but not others. Fleming made comparative studies with mold cultures other than *Penicillium,* but the same bacterial destruction did not occur. *Penicillium notatum* was exceptional.

Next, the *Penicillium* was grown in a fluid medium and the fluid was tested to see whether the antibacterial substance occurred in it. It did, and when a variety of pathogenic bacteria were streaked on an agar culture plate containing a trough of the mold fluid, their growth was strongly inhibited. By noting which bacteria were sensitive to the mold fluid (actually crude penicillin), it became possible to isolate organisms such as the whooping cough and influenza bacteria, which normally occur in the human respiratory tract and are insensitive to penicillin.

Further experiments elucidated more fully the remarkable properties of penicillin. It not only inhibited the growth of human pathogens, it actually destroyed a number of them. When diluted 1000 times, the culture fluid still retained its antibacterial properties. Unlike earlier antiseptic agents (phenol, for example) with which Fleming had worked, penicillin exerted its inhibitory effect on bacteria without destroying human white blood cells (leukocytes, which are the body's natural defense against pathogenic organisms). Carrying this latter observation further, Fleming injected penicillin into animals and found it to be nontoxic. Although realizing that penicillin had decided therapeutic potential, Fleming was unable to pursue such investigations because of the essentially unstable nature of the substance, which prevented accumulation of an amount sufficient for extensive testing. He also realized that before such work could be undertaken the active antibiotic substance would have to be concentrated and some of the crude culture fluid removed.

Fleming published the results of his penicillin experiments in 1929 and at that time suggested its possible therapeutic applications. His suggestion was largely neglected until about 1939, when the introduction of sulfonamide alerted the medical world to the promise of chemotherapy. Obtaining a sample of Fleming's culture strain of *Penicillium notatum,* Florey and Chain succeeded in concentrating and purifying the active substance, penicillin, and instituted clinical trials that eventually demonstrated its phenomenal antibiotic effect in humans.

Fleming was educated in Scotland and London, qualifying with distinction in 1906 for his medical degree from St. Mary's Medical School, London. He lectured there until 1914, served in the Army Medical Corps during World War I, and returned to St. Mary's in 1918. In 1928 he was elected professor of the school and in 1948 emeritus professor of bacteriology, University of London. In 1943 Fleming was elected a fellow of the Royal Society; he was knighted in 1944.

For background information *see* ANTIBIOTIC; LYSOZYME; PENICILLIN in the McGraw-Hill Encyclopedia of Science and Technology. ∎

FLOREY OF ADELAIDE, BARON (HOWARD WALTER FLOREY)
☆ Australian pathologist

Born *Sept. 24, 1898, Adelaide, Australia*
Died *Feb. 22, 1968, Oxford, England*

While working on the properties of antibacterial substances, Florey and his collaborators at Oxford succeeded in extracting and purifying penicillin, an antibacterial of mold origin that had been discovered by Alexander Fleming in 1928. They demonstrated its protective and curative effects in animals, and Florey conducted the first trials in which penicillin was used to treat human infectious disease. For their contributions, Florey and his collaborator Ernst Chain shared, with Fleming, the 1945 Nobel Prize in

physiology or medicine. *See* CHAIN, ERNST BORIS; FLEMING, SIR ALEXANDER.

It might reasonably be thought that advances in medicine would depend on the study of sick people, but this is not necessarily so. The investigation of an invalid at the bedside and in the laboratory may reveal much about a disease and the way it affects the patient, but it often fails to show what went wrong in the first place so that illness resulted, or why that person was attacked. A different approach is to study the normal body functions and, building on this, to study how such functions may become deranged.

Florey believed that this was a useful, and might be a very profitable, way of investigating disease. When he was first appointed to a chair of pathology, all his research experience had been as a physiologist, and this became the basis for his new work. For example, his interest in the small blood and lymph vessels led naturally to a study of the part played by these structures in inflammation and to other aspects of the inflammatory reaction. He was interested also in the secretions of mucous membranes, and he investigated their role in protecting the stomach and duodenum from ulceration and in helping to prevent bacterial invasion of the respiratory and gastrointestinal tracts. Thus, his attention was drawn to a substance, lysozyme, which was known to be present in human saliva and other bodily secretions and which could dissolve certain bacteria. Following this up with his colleagues, he found that

for centuries natural substances had been described as acting against harmful bacteria. These included extracts of plants—of the wallflower, for example—and products of fungi and of bacteria themselves. Working with Chain, Florey chose, in 1939, three such products for investigation; one of them was penicillin, the product of a green mold, or fungus.

The name "penicillin" had been given by Fleming to a crude broth on which the fungus *Penicillium notatum* had grown. Under Florey, the group of workers at Oxford soon made the first steps toward concentrating and purifying the active substance in the mold broth. Although their first products were crude, they were sufficiently concentrated to make possible certain crucial tests in mice and other laboratory animals. These tests showed that penicillin injected into the body could save the life of an animal that had been given a fatal dose of bacteria some hours before—and without doing the animal any harm. In other words, penicillin had a marked "differential toxicity"; when administered in concentrations that were harmless to the body tissues, penicillin was still capable of destroying harmful bacteria.

With great labor, enough penicillin was made in the laboratory to treat a few patients—those with serious infections who had not responded to other treatments. It became clear that in humans, as in animals, penicillin could save lives and eliminate certain virulent bacteria from the body. Subsequently, with his colleagues, Florey investigated numerous other antibiotics, contributing substantially to knowledge of these substances and their modes of action.

With the advent of antibiotics, many serious bacterial diseases came under control and Florey turned his attention to another common disease, atherosclerosis, a disease of the blood vessels that gives rise to coronary thrombosis and cerebral "stroke." Florey began by studying normal blood vessels, choosing those aspects of their form and function that might throw light on the origins of the disease. Among other contributions, Florey and his colleagues discovered that the domestic pig develops atherosclerosis similar to that of humans, thus offering scope for the experimental investigation of the human disease.

Florey qualified in medicine at Adelaide University in 1921. He then went to Oxford as a Rhodes Scholar, where he took a first-class degree in physiology in 1924 and began research under Sir Charles Sherrington. He took his Ph.D. at Cambridge in 1927, having studied in the United States on a Rockefeller traveling fellowship during 1925–26. He was appointed professor of pathology at Sheffield in 1931 and at Oxford in 1935. On retiring from his chair in 1962 he became provost of the Queen's College, Oxford. Florey served on the Medical Research Council and other official bodies. He became a fellow of the Royal Society in 1941 and president in 1960. In 1963 he was elected a foreign associate of the U.S. National Academy of Sciences. For his services to medicine he was knighted in 1944 and received a life peerage and the Order of Merit in 1965.

For background information *see* ARTER-IOSCLEROSIS; LYSOZYME; PENICILLIN in the McGraw-Hill Encyclopedia of Science and Technology. ∎

FLORY, PAUL JOHN
★ American chemist

Born June 19, 1910, Sterling, IL, U.S.A.

After completing his university studies in 1934, Flory was employed by the Du Pont Company, where he was assigned to the pioneering research group headed by Wallace H. Carothers. There he became interested in polymers. The fact that typical members of this class of substances such as cellulose, rubber, and the family of proteins vital to living organisms, not to mention the myriads of synthetic polymers that are now widely used as fibers, films, rubbers, and plastics, consist of very large molecules had been established only a few years earlier by Hermann Staudinger, Carothers, and their contemporaries. *See* STAUDINGER, HERMANN.

The macromolecules composing polymers generally are made up of hundreds of thousands of units joined one to another by chemical bonds to form very long chains. Each unit is comparable in size and in the number of atoms it contains to a molecule such as benzene, a simple sugar, or any of the many chemical compounds amenable to the traditional techniques of the chemist, in particular, distillation and crystallization. Although much too small to be seen with the microscope, polymer molecules are hundreds to many thousands of times larger than the molecules that have engaged the interests of most chemists.

In the 1930s the investigation of polymers presented both a challenge and an opportunity to explore a virgin area. In this setting, a small number of scientists, Flory among them, sensitive to the possibilities and importance of extending the purview of science to encompass polymers, undertook the quest for a set of principles that would comprehend the properties and behavior of this broad class of substances.

Flory first confronted the fact that polymers violate one of the main precepts of chemical dogma. Unlike a traditional chemical compound consisting of one unique kind of molecule, a polymer usually consists of a broad spectrum of molecules differing in the lengths of their chains, and sometimes in finer details of chemical structure as well. Flory hit upon the idea of treating the molecular composition of polymers statistically. The difficulties posed by their molecular complexity could thus be circumvented. Recognizing that the chemical reactions leading to the formation of polymer molecules must conform to the laws of probability, he succeeded in deriving mathematical expressions to represent the distributions of chain lengths in various linear polymers. The distribution of most common occurrence is a simple exponential function of the chain length, called by mathematicians the negative binomial distribution. Statistically deduced molecular distributions have gained widespread acceptance and serve as guidelines in the analysis of constitution and behavior of many polymers.

Comprehension of nonlinear polymers containing branched or cross-linked units presented greater difficulties. These units, usually present in minority, are joined to three, four, or more other units. They introduce points of branching like forks in a road. Hence, they impart a ramified pattern of structure. Starch, some of the proteins, vulcanized rubber, and thermosetting resins afford examples of nonlinear polymers. Often, as in vulcanized rubber, branching and cross-linking in this manner proliferate the chemical structure to the extent that it becomes a giant network embracing all, or nearly all, of the polymer.

Flory developed a theory which explains the phenomenon of gelation in nonlinear polymers, whereby a soluble, viscous polymer fluid is transformed to a network which is an insoluble and elastic body. The incipient emergence of the network and the properties associated with it is manifested in a sharply defined gel point. The theory also accounts for partitioning of the material between soluble sol and insoluble gel, and for the amounts of variously branched molecular species in the sol. This theory has far-reaching applications. It gives an accurate account of gelation in polymers made up of long-chain molecules that undergo cross-linking or that can otherwise be converted to network structures.

The theory of nonlinear polymers has precedents in the mathematical theory of gambling games, an ancient subject. It finds partial analogies in chain reactions, chemical or nuclear, culminating in explosions. The formation of a benign network in a polymer is the analog of this catastrophic event. It occurs, however, without wreaking havoc in the laboratory—or on humankind.

Soon after he pioneered the theory of nonlinear polymers and gelation, Flory turned his attention to rubber elasticity, a characteristic property of polymer networks. This subject commanded his active interest from the early 1940s onward.

The configuration in space of a linear polymer chain is a recurrent theme in Flory's researches. He devoted his main efforts to this subject, commencing in 1964. His *Statistical Mechanics of Chain Molecules* (1969) is an outgrowth of these investigations.

In 1974 Flory received the Nobel Prize in chemistry "for his fundamental achievements, both theoretical and experimental, in the physical chemistry of macromolecules." Specifically cited was his work on the properties of solutions of polymers. He developed the concept of the so-called Flory temperature, at which, in a given solvent, the spatial form of the macromolecule is unaffected by the balance of forces between two parts of a chain when in contact, on the one hand, and the intermolecular forces operating between polymer and solvent on the other. Intrinsic characteristics of the polymer molecule can be determined from measurements conducted on solutions at the Flory temperature.

The son of a clergyman-educator, Flory graduated from Manchester College in Indiana in 1931. He received his Ph.D. in physical chemistry from Ohio State University in 1934. Except for 2 years (1938–40) as a research associate at the University of Cincinnati, Flory held industrial research positions (Du Pont, Exxon, and Goodyear) during the succeeding 14 years. In 1948 he was invited to Cornell University to deliver the Baker Lectures, and then to remain there as professor of chemistry. In 1957 he moved to the Mellon Institute in Pittsburgh, where he served as executive director of research. In 1961 he joined the faculty of the department of chemistry of Stanford University, becoming J. G. Jackson–C. J. Wood Professor in 1966 and emeritus in 1975. He was elected to the National Academy of Sciences in 1953.

Flory authored *Principles of Polymer Chemistry* (1953) and *Statistical Mechanics of Chain Molecules* (1969).

For background information *see* POLYMER PROPERTIES in the McGraw-Hill Encyclopedia of Science and Technology. ∎

FOLKERS, KARL AUGUST
★ American chemist

Born *Sept. 1, 1906, Decatur, IL, U.S.A.*

Folkers's principal contributions to chemical research were in the field of therapeutic agents, particularly vitamins and antibiotics.

At the research laboratories of Merck and Company, Inc., beginning in 1934, Folkers concentrated on the chemistry of morphine alkaloids, *Erythrina* alkaloids, curare, vitamin B_6, pantothenic acid, biotin, penicillin, streptomycin, vitamin B_{12}, and corticotropin B. Later he studied inhibitors of virus multiplication and participated in the discovery of mevalonic acid, the isolation and structural determination of novobiocin, and the structural determination and synthesis of members of the coenzyme Q group. His research on coenzyme Q was extended to biological studies on sperm motility, animal nutri-

tion, and an exploration of coenzyme Q in human medicine.

Folkers's studies on the substance that later became known as vitamin B_{12} were begun in 1938. Ten years later he and his research group at the Merck Sharp and Dohme Research Laboratories isolated a red crystalline compound, vitamin B_{12}, that proved to be active in the treatment of patients with pernicious anemia.

In the field of antibiotics, Folkers's research group published nearly 50 papers on the isolation, synthesis, and structural elucidation of antibiotics in the streptomycin series, and on penicillin, neomycin, subtilin, grisein, oxamycin, and novobiocin.

Folkers pioneered in the study of the *Erythrina* alkaloid family. He and his coworkers published many papers on the isolation and characterization of such members of this family as erythroidine, erythramine, erythraline, erythratine, erysodine, erysopine, erysovine, and erysonine.

The discovery of mevalonic acid by Folkers and his coworkers was of major scientific importance. This compound was recognized as a key and fundamental substance in the biosynthesis of a wide range of very important natural products, including steroids, carotenoids, and terpenes.

Folkers received a B.S. in chemistry from the University of Illinois in 1928 and a Ph.D. in organic chemistry, under Homer Adkins, at the University of Wisconsin in 1931. His research concerned

the reactions of aldehydes and of esters over oxide catalysts, and later the catalytic hydrogenation of esters to alcohols under elevated temperatures and pressures. From 1931 to 1934 he was a postdoctorate research fellow in organic chemistry with Treat B. Johnson at Yale University. His research at Yale was on the synthesis, mechanism of formation, and reactions of certain pyrimidine derivatives.

In 1934 Folkers joined the Laboratory of Pure Research of Merck and Company, Inc., Rahway, NJ. He became assistant director of research in 1938, director of the organic and biochemical research department in 1945, associate director of the research and development division in 1951, director of organic and biological chemical research in 1953, executive director of fundamental research in 1956, and vice-president for exploratory research in 1962. In 1963 he became president of the Stanford Research Institute, Menlo Park, CA. Also in 1963 he received courtesy appointments as professor of chemistry at Stanford University and lecturer in vitamin chemistry at the University of California, Berkeley. In 1968 he became professor of chemistry and director of the Institute for Biomedical Research at the University of Texas. Among his numerous honors are the Perkin Medal of the Society of Chemical Industry (1960), the Van Meter Prize of the American Thyroid Association (1969), and the Research Achievement Award of the Academy of Pharmaceutical Sciences (1974). He was elected to the National Academy of Sciences in 1948.

Folkers and Arthur F. Wagner wrote *Vitamins and Coenzymes* (1964).

For background information *see* ANTIBIOTIC; COENZYME; VITAMIN; VITAMIN B_{12} in the McGraw-Hill Encyclopedia of Science and Technology. ∎

FORBUSH, SCOTT ELLSWORTH
★ American geophysicist

Born *Apr. 10, 1904, Hudson, OH, U.S.A.*

The contributions made by Forbush to geophysical knowledge resulted principally from his statistical investigations of time variations of cosmic-ray intensity and their relation to geomagnetic phenomena. For these researches the Institute of Physics and the Physical Society (London) awarded him the Sir Charles Chree Medal

and Prize in 1961. In 1965 he received the John A. Fleming Award of the American Geophysical Union.

Forbush started investigating cosmic-ray intensity variations in 1937, shortly after the first worldwide network of continuously recording cosmic-ray ionization chambers commenced operation. Maintenance and operation of these identical instruments at Godhaven (Greenland), Cheltenham (United States), Mexico City (Mexico), Huancayo (Peru), and Christchurch (New Zealand) were effected through the unselfish cooperation of the governments of these countries in a program sponsored by the Carnegie Institution of Washington.

In 1937 Forbush discovered the worldwide decrease in cosmic-ray intensity associated with some magnetic storms— now called the Forbush effect. When this effect was observed, the variation of cosmic-ray intensity during the magnetic storm was sufficiently similar to that of the geomagnetic field from the equatorial ring current (ERC) to suggest that it results from the influence of the magnetic field of the ERC on cosmic-ray trajectories. That this was not the cause was demonstrated in 1959 from results obtained by John Simpson and colleagues at the University of Chicago, using detectors in the *Explorer 6* satellite. Their results showed that the magnitude of the cosmic-ray intensity decrease is essentially the same out to distances of 7.5 earth radii (47,835 kilometers), and thus was not due to the ERC but rather to the fact that in-

side the plasma cloud, coming from the Sun, the intensity is reduced by the effect of magnetic fields carried within the clouds.

In 1946 Forbush discovered the solar flare effect, or increase of cosmic-ray intensity due to protons ejected by the Sun in some large chromospheric eruptions. The solar flare event of Nov. 19, 1949, was recorded by Carnegie ionization chambers at Climax, CO, Cheltenham, MD, and Huancayo. From this increase of about 200 percent at Climax (11,000 feet, or 3.36 kilometers, altitude), 45 percent at Cheltenham (near sea level), and undetectable at Huancayo (11,000 feet altitude at the geomagnetic equator), Forbush, M. Schein, and T. B. Stinchcomb showed that it is due principally to the nucleonic component generated in the atmosphere by relatively low-energy primaries. They consequently predicted that an increase at least 10 times greater would have been registered by a nucleonic detector. During this event N. Adams observed an increase of 550 percent in a neutron detector at Manchester, England, but thought it was due to instrumental troubles until he saw the predictions of Forbush, Schein, and Stinchcomb.

Forbush also established the solar cycle variation in cosmic-ray intensity from ionization chamber data over many years. This decrease of about 4 percent at sunspot maximum relative to that at sunspot minimum was later also found to be several times greater in neutron monitors.

Other investigations by Forbush included rigorous statistical analysis of the sidereal diurnal variation of cosmic-ray intensity, which was found too small to be statistically significant in contrast to the significant solar diurnal variation. He also investigated the solar diurnal variation, using ionization chamber data from three stations covering the period 1937–74. Using the deviations of yearly means of the diurnal variation from the average for 25 years, he avoided the uncertainties of atmospheric effects that have troubled many investigators. On the basis of rigorous statistical procedures, he reliably demonstrated the remarkable agreement between the diurnal variation at Cheltenham, Christchurch, and Huancayo. The annual mean total diurnal anisotropy derived from data at these stations from 1937–74, with temperature effect thoroughly eliminated, was shown to result from the sum of two independent components. One has its maximum in the

asymptotic direction 128° east of the Sun with amplitude varying (about zero) with a "period" of two sunspot cycles and with zeroes in 1958 and 1971 coincident with changes in the Sun's north polar magnetic field. The other component has its maximum in the direction 90° east of the Sun, and is correlated with geomagnetic activity as derived from the magnetic field of the ERC.

Forbush also made the first comprehensive observations of magnetic field variations arising from the equatorial electrojet current system. These observations, made during the International Geophysical Year, included continuous registration at five locations and a survey along the west coast of South America from the Equator to about latitude 20°S. Forbush was the first to reliably determine the absolute field from the equatorial ring current, and showed that even on magnetically quiet days the annual mean ring current varies with the solar cycle, being more intense near the maxima of solar activity. He showed that the ERC vanishes only on a few quiet days near the minima of solar activity. While a visiting professor under J. A. Van Allen at the University of Iowa, he investigated, with D. Venkatesan and G. Pizzella, the temporal variations in the density of electrons trapped in the Van Allen radiation belt. *See* VAN ALLEN, JAMES ALFRED.

Forbush received his B.Sc. in physics from the Case School of Applied Science in 1925 and, after two quarters as a graduate student instructor in the physics department at Ohio State University, he joined the National Bureau of Standards. In 1927 he joined the staff of the Carnegie Institution of Washington, Department of Terrestrial Magnetism, and spent 2 years at its Huancayo Magnetic Observatory. He served on the staff of the department's ill-fated, nonmagnetic research ship, the *Carnegie*. He said he owed his life to having been asleep in his cabin when an explosion occurred on Nov. 19, 1929, in the afterpart of the *Carnegie*, while it was anchored a mile from shore in Apia, Samoa. The ship burned and sank. Forbush later returned to Huancayo as observer in charge, and in 1931 was granted a year's leave of absence for graduate study in physics and mathematics at the Johns Hopkins University. He did additional graduate study at George Washington University, the National Bureau of Standards, and the Department of Agriculture. During the war years Forbush was head of a mathematical analysis section at the Naval Ordnance Laboratory, and also worked in operations research in the Navy Department. In 1957 he became head of the section of analytical and statistical geophysics at the Department of Terrestrial Magnetism. He was elected to the National Academy of Sciences in 1962. In 1959 he was made an honorary professor of the University of San Marcos, Lima, Peru, the oldest university in the Western Hemisphere. In 1962 the Case Institute of Technology granted him an honorary doctorate.

Forbush wrote *The Equatorial Electrojet in Peru,* with Mateo Casaverde (1961).

For background information *see* COSMIC RAYS; GEOMAGNETISM; SUN in the McGraw-Hill Encyclopedia of Science and Technology. ∎

FORD, EDMUND BRISCO
★ British geneticist

***Born** Apr. 23, 1901, Papcastle, Cumberland, England*

For his contributions to the genetical theory of evolution by natural selection, particularly in natural populations, Ford received in 1954 the Darwin Medal of the Royal Society of London.

From 1923 to 1926 Ford collaborated with Julian Huxley in work on *Gammarus chevreuxi* (Amphipoda), a brackish-water crustacean. They were the first to show that genes control the time of onset and rate of development of processes in the

body. That concept, foreshadowed by R. Goldschmidt, is an important one in physiology and in evolution, especially that of humans. *See* HUXLEY, SIR JULIAN (SORELL).

In 1923 Ford also began collaborating with R. A. Fisher, who in 1927 envisaged the selective modification of the effects of genes in natural conditions. This was followed by the publication of Fisher's *Theory of Dominance* (1928). In view of these developments, Ford expanded the experimental study of adaptation and evolution in wild populations that he had already begun. He did so by identifying certain conditions in which these processes occur rapidly and subjecting them to combined ecological investigations in the field, including the quantitative analysis of populations, and genetic experiments in the laboratory. This technique he named ecological genetics. In 1928 he planned a book on this subject, to be written after about 25 years of research. The work, in fact, took over 30 years, and the volume thus contemplated, *Ecological Genetics,* was published in 1964. *See* FISHER, SIR RONALD (AYLMER).

Meanwhile, in 1930, Ford suggested the marking, release, and recapture of specimens as a means of estimating the numbers of animals in wild populations. This proposal and the paper by F. C. Lincoln initiating that technique were in press at the same time, but Lincoln's work, which moreover had already undergone a practical test, appeared first. The method, initially crude, was subsequently refined and developed mathematically by Fisher. Ford and W. H. Dowdeswell then applied it to the Lepidoptera (moths and butterflies) and were the first to use it so as to estimate survival rates in nature.

In 1939 Ford began work on the moth *Panaxia dominula.* This showed the importance of selection compared with random drift and provided the most extensive quantitative study of an animal population ever carried out in natural conditions. He was also responsible for the early analysis of industrial melanism, which was subsequently investigated far more thoroughly by H. B. D. Kettlewell. Ford also further developed Fisher's interpretation of Batesian mimicry, which was later the subject of outstanding researches by C. A. Clarke and P. M. Sheppard, using the techniques of ecological genetics.

Ford was the first to demonstrate experimentally (1940) the evolution of

dominance and recessiveness in wild material, working on the moth *Abraxas grossulariata.* He later extended this study to other species, providing a proof that dominance of the same unifactorial character can be built up by dissimilar adjustments of the gene complex in isolated populations.

At this time also Ford carried out a large-scale investigation of the chemistry of pigments in the Lepidoptera, with reference to classification. By this means he obtained new and independent evidence for the validity of taxonomic groups in that order.

In 1946 Ford and Dowdeswell began an experimental study of evolution using a polygenic character in the butterfly *Maniola jurtina.* In the course of that work, later much extended by others, it proved possible to detect and analyze evolution in progress and to measure selection pressures for advantageous qualities in nature.

In 1940 Ford had provided a precise definition of genetic polymorphism, demonstrating the condition to be a distinct form of variation—one that spreads by favorable selection when "transient" and is maintained by contending advantages and disadvantages in equilibrium when "balanced." It tends to bind populations together, instead of potentially splitting them as do all other forms of variation. He then showed that the human blood groups are balanced polymorphisms (1942) and deduced that they must be associated with liability to specific diseases (1945), a prediction that was fully substantiated from 1953 onward.

Beginning in 1952, the Nuffield Foundation provided grants to assist in maintaining laboratories of ecological genetics at Oxford. Work on that subject showed that selection for advantageous qualities in wild populations is 30 to 40 times more powerful than had previously been supposed—a consideration that affected fundamentally the general concept of evolution.

Ford received the degrees of M.A. and D.Sc. at Oxford University, of which he was a prizeman and medallist. He was a distinguished fellow and dean of All Souls College, the first scientist to be elected there since the 17th century. He was a professor of ecological genetics and director of the genetics laboratory at Oxford. Ford held the degree of Hon. D.Sc. at Liverpool and was an academician of Finland and a medallist of Helsinki University. He was a fellow of the Royal Society and an honorary fellow of the Royal College of Physicians and of Wadham College.

In addition to many scientific and some archeological articles, Ford wrote *Mendelism and Evolution* (1931; 8th ed. 1965), *The Study of Heredity* (1938; 2d ed. 1950), *Genetics for Medical Students* (1942; 7th ed. 1973), *Butterflies* (1945; 4th ed. 1977; Fontana ed. 1975), *Moths* (1955; 4th ed. 1977), *Ecological Genetics* (1964; 4th ed. 1975, transl. into French, Polish, and Italian), *Genetic Polymorphism* (1965), and *Genetics and Adaptation* (1976).

For background information *see* ANIMAL EVOLUTION; GENETICS; POLYMORPHISM (GENETICS); POPULATION GENETICS in the McGraw-Hill Encyclopedia of Science and Technology. ∎

FORRESTER, JAY WRIGHT

★ American electrical engineer and management expert

Born July 14, 1918, Anselmo, NE, U.S.A.

The invention of the random-access magnetic core memory for digital computers and the development of "system dynamics" as a way to analyze the behavior of social systems marked the evolution of Forrester's career from electrical engineer to professor of industrial management. His work in computers resulted in 1949 in the information storage method used in nearly all digital computers for several decades. Twelve years later, his

book *Industrial Dynamics* proposed a new way to understand the growth and stability of socioeconomic systems.

During the late 1940s, when the first digital computers were being developed, each exploratory machine reflected the nature and shortcomings of the information storage system around which it was built. The available storage devices were slow, expensive, or unreliable. Forrester was then director of the Digital Computer Laboratory at the Massachusetts Institute of Technology (MIT). His group was developing a digital computer to process air defense information and to generate instructions to defense weapons. For such computer applications, speed and reliability beyond that of any existing information storage device were essential. While many techniques would store information, the missing element of a successful system was a low-cost, reliable way to select the stored binary digit of information at speeds of a few microseconds. Previous storage devices had stored information in linear sequence, as along a magnetic wire, where selection was made by moving the wire; or storage was in a two-dimensional array, as on the face of a vacuum tube, where selection was accomplished by scanning with an electron beam.

Forrester undertook to create a reliable storage system with a selection system capable of locating storage cells within a three-dimensional array. To do so would require a storage cell sensitive to a coincidence of signals on each of the coordinate axes. He first devised a selection and storage system using the nonlinear characteristics of a glow discharge in a vacuum, but this was not pursued because of its inherent low reliability. In 1949, still searching for a reliable nonlinear electronic cell, Forrester noticed the extremely rectangular hysteresis loops of magnetic materials that had been developed for magnetic amplifiers. Pressed by the need for a better storage system in the computer he was building, he undertook to use a magnetic cell as both the switching and storage element in a memory system. This led to the coincident-current magnetic memory, in which a memory cell in a three-dimensional array is unaffected by selecting currents on one or two coordinates but does respond to receive or read out information when it experiences proper selecting currents on all three coordinate axes.

In the field of management, Forrester built on his early training in servomechanisms and his later work in digital comput-

ers for the control of military operations to develop the system dynamics approach for analyzing the growth and stability of industrial organizations. The central philosophy of system dynamics was based on the ideas of feedback control as first developed by engineers and mathematicians for application to the control of physical systems. His study of decision making during the introduction of computers to military control had shown him the similarity between "policy" in a human organization and the "transfer function" of an engineering device. It thus became possible to formulate mathematical models of the information flows and policy structure of an organization. Such models, however, were far too complex for mathematical solution. Moving away from the mathematical methods then conventional in the social sciences, Forrester emphasized instead the empirical and experimental approaches of engineering by applying computer simulation as a way to determine the implications of the complex models. System dynamics opened the way for designing policies to enhance the desirable characteristics of social organizations. Its methods are being followed for policy design in a number of industrial organizations and are being taught in numerous universities.

Forrester's subsequent work was involved with directing the development of the System Dynamics National Model. The model is a comprehensive representation of the economy with 15 production sectors, labor mobility, a banking system, Federal Reserve, government operations, and demographic sectors. It is designed to evaluate national policies related to inflation, unemployment, energy, balanced trade, and monetary fiscal actions.

From his home on a Nebraska cattle ranch, Forrester went to the University of Nebraska to study electrical engineering (B.S., 1939). Graduate study in the same field at MIT (M.S., 1945) led to a series of staff and faculty positions there. As a research assistant he was in the group led by Gordon S. Brown, who founded the MIT Servomechanisms Laboratory for the development of feedback control systems during World War II. From 1945 to 1952 Forrester started and was director of the Digital Computer Laboratory, which built Whirlwind I, one of the first general-purpose digital computers. From 1952 to 1956 he was head of the digital computer division of the Lincoln Laboratory, where the Semiautomatic Ground Environment (SAGE) system for air defense was designed for installation throughout the continental United States. In 1956 he became professor of management at the Alfred P. Sloan School of Management at MIT.

Forrester wrote *Industrial Dynamics* (1961), *Principles of Systems* (1968), *Urban Dynamics* (1969), and *World Dynamics* (1971), and the *Collected Papers* was published in 1975.

For background information *see* DIGITAL COMPUTER; STORAGE DEVICES in the McGraw-Hill Encyclopedia of Science and Technology. ∎

FORSSMANN, WERNER THEODOR OTTO
☆ German physician

Born Aug. 29, 1904, Berlin, Germany
Died June 1, 1979, Schopfheim (Black Forest), West Germany

While engaged in research on the heart, Forssmann developed a method for visualization of the right side of the heart by passing a catheter through a vein into his own right atrium, then photographing the heart by x-ray. This daring experiment made possible many findings in the field of cardiology and paved the way for the use of angiocardiograph. For his pioneering work Forssmann received the 1956 Nobel Prize in medicine or physiology, which he shared with D. W. Richards and A. F. Cournand. *See* COURNAND, ANDRÉ FREDERIC; RICHARDS, DICKINSON WOODRUFF.

The earliest work on determining blood pressure within the living heart was performed by two French investigators, Auguste Chauveau and Etienne Marey, in 1861. They led manometers from the neck vessels into both compartments of the right heart, and into the left, of an experimental animal and thus recorded pressure changes. In 1912 three German physicians, Unger, Bleichröder, and Loeb, were investigating puerperal sepsis ("childbed fever"). In an attempt to bring a suitable chemotherapeutic agent to the part of the body where it would be most effective, they inserted ureteral catheters into arteries in the leg and pushed them upward to the estimated height of the abdominal aorta, then injected the drug. Although no x-ray verifications of catheter placement were carried out, these early intraarterial probings caused no ill effects.

Forssmann began his work on cardiac catheterization in 1929. To prove that the methods that Chauveau and Marey had employed on animals were applicable to humans, he inserted a narrow catheter into a cubital vein in his own arm, passed it onward into the right atrium, and then had an x-ray examination made to visualize the catheter in his heart. This achievement opened the way to study of pathologic changes in the circulatory system and to x-ray study of the right side of the heart and the pulmonary vessels. Again experimenting on himself, Forssmann twice injected contrast medium directly into his own heart so that x-ray pictures could be made.

During this same period, Forssmann conducted his first experiments in angiocardiography. He inserted catheters into the heart of a living dog, then examined them in position with x-ray. He also demonstrated that it was possible, once a catheter had been placed in the right auricle, to pass it diagonally from the upper to the lower vena cava, thus permitting the collection of blood samples from the liver.

Forssmann's work did not bear immediate fruit, in part because of the technical requirements for further investigations; progress in cardiology had to wait, for example, upon the development of modern anesthetic techniques and antibiotics. Another cause, however, was the extreme criticisms to which Forssmann was subjected because of the presumably dangerous nature of his experiments. Deterred from further cardiographic research, he turned to urology, in which field he gained distinction.

Forssmann studied medicine at the University of Berlin, from which he received his degree in 1929. He became chief of the surgical clinic of the City Hospital in Dresden-Friedrichstadt and at Robert Koch Hospital in Berlin. In 1958 he was named chief of the Surgical Division of the Evangelical Hospital in Düsseldorf. He retired in 1970. He was awarded the Leibniz Medal of the Berlin Academy of Sciences (1954) and the Gold Medal of the Society of Surgical Medicine of Ferrara (1968).

Forssmann wrote *Experiments on Myself: Memoirs of a Surgeon in Germany* (English transl. 1975).

For background information *see* RADIOLOGY in the McGraw-Hill Encyclopedia of Science and Technology. ∎

FOSTER, JOHN STUART, JR.
☆ American physicist

Born Sept. 18, 1922, New Haven, CT, U.S.A.

Foster's main contributions were in the application of nuclear explosives to military and peaceful uses. Although he became best known for a breakthrough in the development of small, or tactical, nuclear weapons, the long-range potential of his work may find its best application to large-scale earthmoving and other nonmilitary engineering projects employing nuclear explosives. For his "unique contributions, demanding unusual imagination and technical skill, to the development of atomic weapons." President

Dwight Eisenhower bestowed on him the Atomic Energy Commission's E. O. Lawrence Memorial Award in 1960.

Much of Foster's novel applied research was motivated by problems associated with the relative inflexibility and inefficiency of early nuclear explosives. To achieve a nuclear explosion, it is necessary to bring together rapidly two or more fragments of fissionable material to form a mass of critical size. Under these conditions, an explosive chain reaction can take place. The first nuclear weapons had a minimum yield equal in explosive force to about 20,000 tons of TNT (8.4×10^{13} joules). They were relatively large and cumbersome, with consequent limitations on modes of delivery and flexibility of application. The yields were not efficient relative to the amount of fissionable material used. It was militarily desirable to achieve flexibility by obtaining varied yields, both much smaller and larger than the nominal 20 kilotons; by improving the yield relative to fissionable materials used; and by building devices of lighter weight and smaller size.

Foster's breakthrough in new concepts was facilitated by his development at the Lawrence Radiation Laboratory, Livermore, CA, of the computational and experimental tools necessary to design nuclear explosives in detail. In the course of this research, Foster elaborated upon these and other advanced calculations, and was responsible for significant progress in hydrodynamics, the science of the behavior of matter at very high pressures.

Foster's subsequent leadership in the development of thermonuclear explosives with reduced fission yields ("clean" nuclear explosives) was made possible in part by his earlier work and was motivated by a need for devices for the Plowshare Program. The Plowshare Program, which originated at Livermore, proposed to use the great power of nuclear explosives for projects that were otherwise beyond human power or were uneconomical by conventional means. Examples are large-scale excavation for canals and other earthmoving projects and new techniques for recovery of natural gas, petroleum, and mineral resources. Plowshare required devices that yielded a minimum fallout of fission fragments and therefore left little residual radiation. Early thermonuclear devices yielded an explosive force generated about half from the igniting fission explosive and half from fusion material.

Foster pioneered the development of improved devices, and this line of research resulted in a hundredfold reduction in the amount of fallout from a given explosive yield.

Foster was also a pioneer in the development of Command and Control, a system for retaining central control over a nuclear weapon independent of its location.

In earlier research, Foster developed the first large-scale ion pump for the rapid achievement of improved high vacuums. He applied this device in a Van de Graaff accelerator, in a high-intensity linear accelerator, and in some of the early research in Project Sherwood, the United States program of research in controlled thermonuclear reactions. Subsequent advances in ion-pump technology made the device extremely important in Sherwood machines.

The son of a prominent research physicist, Foster took his B.S. in physics at McGill University in 1948. He received his Ph.D. in 1952 at the University of California, Berkeley. His undergraduate studies were interrupted by World War II, during which he worked at Harvard on the development of radar countermeasures and in the European theater on the implementation of countermeasures to enemy radar. He was in the original cadre of young scientists who formed the staff of the Lawrence Radiation Laboratory at Livermore in 1952. Initially, he was a group leader in research on controlled thermonuclear reactions, entering upon nuclear weapons development in 1953. He became an associate director of the laboratory in 1958, and was appointed director of the Lawrence Radiation Laboratory, Livermore, in 1961. In 1965 he was appointed director of defense research and engineering for the U.S. Department of Defense, where he served in both Democratic and Republican administrations until 1973. In September 1973 Foster joined TRW Inc., first as vice-president of energy research and development, and from January 1976 as vice-president and general manager of the TRW Energy Systems Group. In addition to the E. O. Lawrence Award, Foster received the H. H. Arnold Trophy of the Air Force Association (1971), the Defense Department's Distinguished Public Service Medal (1969), the James Forrestal Memorial Award of the National Security Industries Association (1969), the Crowell

Medal of the Cleveland Chapter, American Defense Preparedness Association (1972), and the award of the Western Electronics Manufacturers Association (now called the American Electronics Association; 1973), and the Knight Commander's Cross (Badge and Star) of the Order of Merit of the Federal Republic of Germany (1974). He was also a commander in the French Legion of Honor (1973). Foster was elected to the National Academy of Engineering in 1969.

For background information *see* NUCLEAR EXPLOSION in the McGraw-Hill Encyclopedia of Science and Technology. ∎

FOWLER, WILLIAM ALFRED
☆ American physicist

Born *Aug. 9, 1911, Pittsburgh, PA, U.S.A.*

Fowler made fundamental contributions to the understanding of nuclear reactions which generate the energy of stars and synthesize the elements of the universe.

Fowler began his research work as a graduate student, under C. C. Lauritsen, the head of the W. K. Kellogg Radiation Laboratory at the California Institute of Technology, in experiments in which light elements ranging from lithium through fluorine were bombarded with protons and deuterons. After completing his doctoral dissertation on radioactive nuclides produced in these bombardments, he continued these experiments with Lauritsen and others. During World War II, Fowler, Lauritsen, and other Kellogg researchers worked on proximity fuses, rocket ordnance, and atomic weapons. After the war they returned to nuclear physics research, making a comprehensive study of the excited states of all the light nuclei. See LAURITSEN, CHARLES CHRISTIAN.

In 1946 Fowler and his colleagues began an experimental study of nuclear reactions thought to take place in stars, encouraged by the astronomers I. S. Bowen and J. L. Greenstein. Measurements were made of cross sections of reactions in the carbon-nitrogen cycle and the proton-proton chain, which convert hydrogen into helium. The cross sections at stellar energies are extremely small, making it impossible to measure them directly, and it was therefore necessary to carry out detailed measurements at the lowest possible energies and extrapolate downward from these measurements to stellar energies. See BOWEN, IRA SPRAGUE; GREENSTEIN, JESSE LEONARD.

In the 1950s Fowler and his coworkers turned their attention to helium burning, the conversion of helium into heavier elements in late stages of stellar evolution. A process in which three helium-4 nuclei combine to form a carbon-12 nucleus was studied theoretically by E. E. Salpeter in 1952 and by F. Hoyle in 1954. Hoyle pointed out that in order for this process to take place carbon-12 must have an excited state in resonance with the interaction of a helium-4 nucleus with the ground state of unstable beryllium-8. In 1956 Fowler participated in demonstrating the existence of this state, with the predicted energy, spin, parity, and decay modes. See HOYLE, SIR FRED; SALPETER, EDWIN ERNEST.

The helium-burning process formed a crucial link in a comprehensive theory, developed in 1955–57 by E. M. Burbidge, G. R. Burbidge, Fowler, and Hoyle, which described the synthesis of all naturally occurring nuclear species by means of nuclear reactions in stars. Starting from a galaxy formed from pure hydrogen, the theory envisions a series of processes, taking place in successive generations of stars, which produced the presently observed abundances of elements and nuclides. The interiors of stars which condense from hydrogen are heated by gravitational contraction, re-

sulting in a sequence of processes at successively higher temperatures. First the proton-proton chain converts hydrogen into helium, then helium-4 is converted to carbon-12, and then even-even nuclei up to calcium-40, as well as a group of nuclei around iron-56, are synthesized.

As stars evolve, some of the transmuted material is returned to interstellar space, either gradually, as with the Sun, or suddenly, as in novae and supernovae, and eventually incorporated into other stars. These second-and later-generation stars may convert hydrogen to helium through catalytic processes, such as the carbon-nitrogen cycle, which produce additional isotopes of elements ranging from carbon through sodium.

Elements heavier than iron cannot be produced by charged-particle processes and are instead formed in the slow (s) and rapid (r) neutron capture processes. The reaction of neon-21 with alpha particles was shown to be an effective neutron source for the s-process in late stages of second generation stars. Evidence for the r-process was adduced from the fact that the exponential decay in luminosity of type I supernovae matches the decay of the isotope californium-254 and the fact that a similar process occurs in hydrogen bomb explosions.

The solar system represents at least a third generation, its elements generated in stars long extinct.

Throughout the 1960s and into the 1970s Fowler worked out details of all the processes of stellar nucleosynthesis and also investigated nucleosynthesis in places other than stars. In 1963 Hoyle and Fowler suggested that from time to time bodies of gas at the centers of galaxies might condense into stars containing as much as 10^8 solar masses, and that the gravitational collapse of the cores of such supermassive stars might generate huge explosions, resulting in radio galaxies. They suggested that such explosions, rather then supernovae, might be the chief site of the r-process. Fowler also suggested that quasars might be supermassive stars. In 1967 Hoyle and Fowler suggested that the large red shifts of quasars might be of gravitational rather than cosmological origin and that quasars might supply the "missing mass" needed to "close" the universe.

The most serious shortcoming of the theory of stellar nucleosynthesis was its failure to account for the abundances of deuterium, helium-4, and the isotopes of

lithium, beryllium, and boron (except perhaps lithium-7). In 1966 R. V. Waggoner, Fowler, and Hoyle calculated the production of the lightest nuclides in the "big bang" origin of the universe, and in 1970 H. Reeves, Fowler, and Hoyle showed that lithium, beryllium, and boron are produced by the action of galactic cosmic rays on interstellar matter. These two sources appeared sufficient to account for the abundances of the light nuclides. Among these nuclides, deuterium was of particular interest, since it appeared to have originated entirely in the big bang. Assuming this to be the case, its abundance indicated that the universal mass density was too small to close the universe. However, in 1973 Hoyle and Fowler showed that deuterium could also be formed by shock waves injecting energetic helium nuclei into clouds of hydrogen gas.

In the late 1960s and 1970s much of Fowler's attention was devoted to the complex thermonuclear reactions which occur at temperatures above 10^9 K, particularly silicon burning. His work involved both measurements of reaction cross sections and numerical analysis, using advanced computers, to apply the laboratory data gathered by many physicists to astrophysical conditions. He was also involved in calculating the flux of solar neutrinos, and subsequently attempted to explain (along with many other physicists) why the flux measured by R. Davis, Jr., and his colleagues was much smaller than the theoretically calculated values.

Fowler received the bachelor of engineering physics degree (1933) from Ohio State University and the Ph.D. (1936) from the California Institute of Technology, where he was subsequently research fellow, assistant professor (1939), associate professor (1942), professor (1946), and first Institute Professor of Physics (1970). He held visiting positions at a number of other institutions, including Guggenheim fellowships at Cambridge University in 1954–55 and 1961–62. In 1951–52 he served as scientific director of Project Vista for the Department of Defense. He served as a member of the National Science Board of the National Science Foundation (NSF; 1968–74) and of a number of other advisory boards for the government. In 1977 he was appointed chairperson of the Nuclear Science Advisory Committee (NUSAC) to the Department of Energy and NSF. He received the Naval Ordnance Development Award (1945), the Presidential Medal for Merit (1948), the Lamme Medal of Ohio State University (1952), the Liège Medal of the University of Liège (1955), the California Co-Scientist of the Year Award (1958) by the California Museum of Science and Industry, the Barnard Medal for Meritorius Service to Science (1965) and the G. Unger Vetlesen Prize (1973) of Columbia University, the Apollo Achievement Award of the National Aeronautics and Space Administration (1969), the Tom W. Bonner Prize of the American Physical Society (1970) the National Medal of Science (1974), and the Eddington Medal of the Royal Astronomical Society (1978), and the Bruce Gold Medal of the Astronomical Society of the Pacific (1979). He was elected to the National Academy of Sciences (1956), the Amercian Philosophical Society (1962), the American Academy of Arts and Sciences (1965), and a number of other honorary societies. He was president of the American Physical Society in 1976.

Fowler wrote more than 180 articles. Two articles that he coauthored with Hoyle were published as *Nucleosynthesis in Massive Stars and Supernovae* (1965). His Jayne Lectures for the American Philosophical Society in 1965 were published as *Nuclear Astrophysics* (1967).

For background information *see* COSMOLOGY; ELEMENTS AND NUCLIDES, ORIGIN OF; NUCLEAR REACTION; STELLAR EVOLUTION; SUPERMASSIVE STARS in the McGraw-Hill Encyclopedia of Science and Technology. ∎

FRAENKEL-CONRAT, HEINZ L.

★ American biochemist

Born July 29, 1910, Breslau, Germany

Fraenkel-Conrat's research focused on the relationship between chemical structure and biological activity with regard to the macromolecular components of living systems. The achievement for which he is noted was the disassembly of tobacco mosaic virus into noninfectious protein and almost noninfectious nucleic acid, and the reconstitution of fully infective virus from these components. This led to the discovery of the intrinsic genetic activity of ribonucleic acid and opened up a fruitful field of research. For these contributions, Fraenkel-Conrat was honored by a Lasker

Award and the first California Scientist of the Year Award in 1958.

After receiving his Ph.D. in biochemistry at Edinburgh for studies on ergot alkaloids and thiamine under G. Barger and A. R. Todd, Fraenkel-Conrat joined M. Bergmann's group at the Rockefeller Institute for Medical Research in New York. In studying the specificity of proteolytic enzymes, particularly papain, he found, contrary to expectation, that these enzymes were able to form peptide bonds, the equilibrium being shifted toward synthesis by insolubilizing substituents (benzoyl and anilid groups). In a subsequent year at the Instituto Butantan at São Paulo, Brazil, he collaborated with his brother-in-law, K. H. Slotta, in the study of the proteinaceous components of snake venoms, separating various enzymatic activities and obtaining a crystalline and physicochemically apparently homogeneous protein that showed both the neurotoxic and the hemolytic activities of rattlesnake venom, crotoxin.

In 1938 Fraenkel-Conrat joined H. M. Evans's Institute of Experimental Biology at the Berkeley campus of the University of California. There he purified several hormones of the anterior pituitary, particularly the follicle-stimulating and thyrotropic hormones. The effect of changes in structure on hormonal activity was studied with the lactogenic and other hormones. He pursued similar studies for over 10 years, in good part at the Western Regional Research Laboratory of the U.S. Department of Agriculture, in collabora-

tion with H. S. Olcott and others. Methods for selective modification of protein groups, such as amino, carboxyl, thiol, disulfide, and phenolic, were developed and applied to many biologically active proteins, and the effects of such treatments on the ability of these proteins to function were recorded. Several of the methods then developed proved of value when applied a decade later to proteins of known structure.

Methods for protein structure analysis (end groups, amino-acid sequences) were applied by Fraenkel-Conrat to viruses, particularly the plentiful and stable tobacco mosaic virus, beginning in 1952, when he joined the virus laboratory of the University of California, headed by W. M. Stanley. This work, carried out in collaboration with a team of investigators, yielded the complete amino acid sequence of this protein chain of 158 amino acid residues, the biggest protein of known structure, in 1960. *See* STANLEY, WENDELL MEREDITH.

The isolation of the viral protein in native form, and the concurrent isolation of native viral ribonucleic acid (RNA) by separate methods, led to experimental attempts to recombine the two to regenerate virus particles. It became clear that the tendency of the two components to combine was a function of the integrity of structure and shape of the above protein subunit. If the RNA chain molecule was also intact, then fully infective virus formed spontaneously under suitable conditions in a process akin to the crystallization of a coordination complex.

Studies of the significance of the reconstitution reaction led to the discovery that viral RNA itself was infective and genetically fully competent. But quantitatively the RNA was very inefficient, largely owing to its susceptibility to nucleases. The coating of the RNA by the protein potentiated its infectivity a thousandfold. In collaboration with B. Singer (now his wife) and a number of students and colleagues, Fraenkel-Conrat elaborated methods for stabilizing the RNA and for the study of its structure, end groups, nucleotide sequences, and chemical modification. Several of the chemical modifications of RNA produced biologically distinct mutants; the study of the protein of these mutants gave important clues to the nature of the genetic code. A certain type of alteration of the RNA led frequently to certain exchanges of amino acids in the protein, and these data could be correlated with the identification of coding triplets of nucleotides, as elaborated by M. W. Nirenberg and others in cell-free amino acid incorporating systems from *Escherichia coli. See* NIRENBERG, MARSHALL WARREN.

From 1968 onward, Fraenkel-Conrat's research on viruses centered on the modes of translation and replication of viral RNAs, in part aiming at an understanding of the interrelation of a singly noninfectious satellite virus to its helper virus. It became evident from these studies that healthy plants carry an RNA replicating capability: enzymes whose prime role has not yet been established. It appears probable that viral RNAs are replicated by these host enzymes.

Another active line of research in this period was a return to the study of crotoxin, the quite singular neurotoxin of the Brazilian rattlesnake. It appears that this toxin represents a complex of two unrelated proteins, one of which is phospholipase A-active and shows indirect hemolytic activity, but only the complex is highly neurotoxic. Since this neurotoxicity shows aspects of both pre- and postsynaptic function, it is of considerable interest to neurobiologists. Studies were begun with this neurotoxin in several laboratories, in part in collaboration with Fraenkel-Conrat's laboratory.

Fraenkel-Conrat, son of the famed gynecologist Ludwig Fraenkel (discoverer of the function of the corpus luteum), received his preparation for a research career by going through the medical curriculum at Munich, Vienna, Geneva, and Breslau, where he received his M.D. in 1934. He received a Ph.D. in biochemistry at Edinburgh in 1936. In 1958 he became professor of virology and later of molecular biology at the University of California, Berkeley. He was a member of the National Academy of Sciences, the American Academy of Arts and Sciences, and several professional societies.

Fraenkel-Conrat wrote *Design and Function at the Threshold of Life: The Viruses* (1962) and *The Chemistry and Biology of Viruses* (1968; translated into German and greatly updated in 1973). He edited *Molecular Basis of Virology* (1968). He began editing, together with Dr. R. R. Wagner, and contributing to, *Comprehensive Virology,* appearing in about 20 volumes from 1973 to about 1983.

For background information *see* PROTEIN; RIBONUCLEIC ACID (RNA); VIRUS in the McGraw-Hill Encyclopedia of Science and Technology. ∎

FRANCIS, THOMAS, JR.
★ American epidemiologist

> ***Born*** *July 15, 1900, Gas City, IN, U.S.A.*
> ***Died*** *Oct. 1, 1969, Ann Arbor, MI, U.S.A.*

Francis's studies centered on problems of infectious disease, especially pneumonia, influenza, and poliomyelitis. For his contributions in these areas he received, among other honors, the 1947 Lasker Award of the American Public Health Association, the 1953 Bruce Medal in Preventive Medicine of the American College of Physicians, and, posthumously, the 1970 Jessie Stevenson Kovalenko Medal of the National Academy of Sciences.

Investigations of the immunologic reactions of pneumonia patients to type-specific polysaccharides of the pneumococcus, carried out in the 1920s by Francis and W. S. Tillett at the Hospital of the Rockefeller Institute, revealed characteristic wheal and erythema cutaneous reactions that subsequently proved to be a valuable guide to serum treatment. It was then demonstrated that these polysaccharides were of themselves able to induce antibodies and immunity in humans. This caused a revolution in immunologic theory, which then held that only proteins could function as antigens. Tillett and Francis also described the pneumococcus C reaction, used in clinical medicine as an indicator of pathologic conditions. *See* TILLETT, WILLIAM SMITH.

In 1934, during a search for a viral precursor of the bacterial invasion of lobar pneumonia, Francis isolated human influenza virus, the first to confirm the 1933 report of W. Smith, C. H. Andrewes, and P. P. Laidlaw in England. This led to establishment of the virus in mice and tissue culture and to the first description, with T. P. Magill, of the extensive serologic variations among strains of the type A virus. In 1940 Francis identified influenza virus, type B, and its earlier epidemic prevalences. In 1950 he and his associates established influenza C as an epidemic disease. In 1943 a polyvalent vaccine that Francis had developed was shown by well-controlled studies of the Commission on Influenza of the Army Epidemiology Board, of which he was director, to be highly effective against influenza A in military personnel and, in 1945, against influenza B.

Despite the demonstrable diversity of influenza viruses, Francis and his colleagues demonstrated that these viruses contain numerous antigens in common. The effort, then, is to compound a vaccine of multiple strains or antigens that cover the entire range. The different major variants are considered to be rearrangements of antigens, among which previously suppressed ones may reemerge as dominant antigens of apparently new pandemic viruses. When the general population becomes thoroughly immunized by a prevalent variant, the pressure upon the virus for selective variation increases. Thus cyclic recurrences of major antigens were postulated and such was observed in the Asian strains of 1957 and subsequent years, which present the pandemic antigen of the 1890s. This interpretation is based upon the doctrine of original antigenic sin propounded by Francis, F. M. Davenport, and A. V. Hennessy. According to that doctrine, the first childhood infection by influenza virus leaves the imprint of the dominant antigen of that strain on the antibody of the individual; this is enhanced by subsequent experiences with other strains so as to be characteristic of that age group throughout its later life. Hence the history of influenza virus strains is written in the serum antibody pattern of different age groups of the population. Persons first exposed in the 1890 pandemic period had antibodies to the 1957 strain; persons first exposed in the 1918–22 pandemic period have their characteristic antibody to the swine influenza virus described by R. E. Shope. Desirable vaccine would fill the gaps in immunity of the population to potential oncoming strains.

At the University of Michigan, Francis

undertook studies in the epidemiology and immunology of poliomyelitis to determine the mode of entrance and spread of that virus in a community. In 1954 he was asked by the National Foundation for Infantile Paralysis to conduct the large-scale evaluation of the inactivated poliomyelitis vaccine developed by Jonas Salk. The test comprised some 1,800,000 children in 44 states. A major component of the study was carried out as a strictly controlled double blind experiment—the largest of its kind. The vaccine was shown to be safe and effective and resulted in the remarkable decline of the disease.

In 1955 Francis served as chairman of a visiting committee that drew up the plan adopted by the National Research Council for the studies of the Atomic Bomb Casualty Commission in Japan. In later years he and his colleagues engaged in a study of a total community in Michigan, seeking to detect the causative factors, genetic or environmental, of arteriosclerotic heart disease and related disorders with the hope of developing preventive measures.

Francis graduated from Allegheny College (B.S., 1921) and Yale Medical School (M.D., 1925), proceeding through a residency in internal medicine and an instructorship at Yale. In 1925 he went to the Hospital of the Rockefeller Institute on the Clinical Pneumonia Service under Rufus Cole and in the laboratory of O. T. Avery. In 1936 he joined the staff of the International Health Division of the Rockefeller Foundation to pursue influenza researches. He went to New York University College of Medicine in 1938 as professor and chairman of the department of bacteriology and attending physician at Bellevue and Willard Parker hospitals. In 1941 he became professor of epidemiology and chair of the department in the University of Michigan School of Public Health and professor of epidemiology in the University of Michigan Medical School. He was elected to the National Academy of Sciences in 1948. See AVERY, OSWALD THEODORE.

Francis wrote extensively on basic immunological phenomena, the pathogenesis of infectious disease, and immunity to viral infections. He edited *Diagnostic Procedures for Viral and Rickettsial Diseases* (1948; 2d ed. 1956).

For background information see EPIDEMIOLOGY; IMMUNOLOGY; INFLUENZA; POLIOMYELITIS; VACCINATION in the McGraw-Hill Encyclopedia of Science and Technology. ∎

FRANCK, JAMES
American physicist

Born Aug. 26, 1882, Hamburg, Germany
Died May 21, 1964, Göttingen, Germany

While engaged in a quantitative study of elastic collisions between electrons and atoms, Franck and the German physicist Gustav Hertz formulated the concept of excitation potentials, gave experimental support to Niels Bohr's concept of the quantized atom, and provided a method for determining the value of Planck's constant. In recognition of their work, Franck and Hertz shared the 1925 Nobel Prize in physics (awarded in 1926). See BOHR, NIELS HENRIK DAVID.

The concept of the nuclear atom was developed by Ernest Rutherford during the first decade of the 20th century. In 1900 Max Planck had derived the basis for quantum theory, as well as an equation relating the energy of a quantum to its frequency multiplied by a proportionality constant, which is now known as Planck's constant, h. In 1913 Bohr combined Rutherford's atom with Planck's quantum theory to propose an atom whose electrons occupy discrete energy levels surrounding the nucleus. His theory was greeted with skepticism, however, since for certain aspects classical laws still had to be applied simultaneously with quantum postulates with which they were in contradiction.

In 1912, working at the University of Berlin, Franck and Hertz began to study the effects of the impact between an electron and an atom. By 1913 they had devised a classic experiment: Atoms of mercury vapor were bombarded with electrons, whose energy was controlled by an accelerating voltage. As the voltage was increased slowly, a point was reached at which resonance occurred. Energy was then transferred to the atoms and the gas glowed. As a result of the experiment, in 1914 Franck and Hertz were able to announce three results: (1) Collisions of electrons with mercury atoms are perfectly elastic for electron energies up to 4.9 electronvolts. (2) Above this limit, energy is transferred to the atom, but always in quanta of 4.9 electronvolts, while any excess is retained as kinetic energy. (3) Inelastic collisions lead to the emission of light of the resonance line 2537 A of mercury, and this line only—the energy loss of the electron is equal to the quantum energy $h\nu$ of this line.

Franck and Hertz realized the importance of their discovery, which demonstrated the quantized energy transfer from kinetic to electromagnetic energy. Einstein's interpretation of the photoelectric effect had implied the quantized conversion of electromagnetic energy into kinetic and potential energy, but it was based on scanty experimental evidence. Far more clearly and directly than the photoelectric effect, the experiments of Franck and Hertz proved the reality of the energy quanta postulated by Planck and provided a new method to measure Planck's constant. Furthermore, the results gave experimental support to Bohr's theory of the quantized atom, which had been published some 6 months before, for they demonstrated that an atom can take up internal energy only in such discrete amounts as to transform it from one stationary state to another.

In 1925, while at the University of Göttingen, Franck published a paper dealing with the elementary processes of photochemical reactions. In this he drew upon the work of three previously unconnected sources: (1) Heinrich Lenz, in his theory of band spectra, had pointed out that the correspondence principle leads to a connection between the coupling strength of oscillatory and electronic motion, and the change of vibrational energy. (2) Franck and Max Born had separated clearly the electronic motion and that of the nuclei. (3) Mecke had observed a long series of vibrational transitions with markedly decreasing spacings in the spectrum of iodine. Utilizing these, Franck arrived at a clear, graphic statement of the connection between electron transition and the motion of nuclei. Later E. U. Condon's quantum-mechanical treatment added rigor and quantitative information to what is now known as the Franck-Condon principle. *See* BORN, MAX; CONDON, EDWARD UHLER.

Having established many of the basic relationships determining the interaction between simple molecules and light quanta, in 1933 Franck became interested in the fundamental photochemical process in nature, photosynthesis. He hoped at first that application of quantitative, physical experimentation to this process would clarify its most puzzling aspect, the mechanism by which a large portion of the energy of several quanta of visible light is converted into chemical energy. He carried out a large number of experimental investigations, particularly on the fluorescence of chlorophyll in the living cell. Franck found that a very high intensity of illumination brought the yield of fluorescence of chlorophyll in living cells to about twice the level observed in weak light.

These and similar findings led Franck to develop a biochemical and a biophysical model of photosynthesis. The biochemical model deals with the transformations involved in the conversion of carbon dioxide into carbohydrates. The biophysical model is concerned with the primary photochemical act in which light is converted into chemical energy.

During Franck's half-century of productive work, he investigated many phenomena, not all of which were related exclusively to physics. Among the many areas to which he made significant contributions were the formation and dissociation of molecules, the polarization of fluorescent light, and the development of the atomic bomb. While involved in the last-named project, Franck chaired a committee of scientists considering the social and political implications of employing the atomic bomb. Their conclusions, which were submitted to the Secretary of War in 1945, have become known as the Franck Report. The report urges the United States government to consider the use of the bomb as a fateful political decision and not merely as a matter of military tactics, to consider the danger of beginning a nuclear arms race, and to demonstrate the weapon in an uninhabited area so as not to take human life.

The son of a banker, Franck pursued

his studies at the University of Heidelberg and the University of Berlin (Dr.Phil., 1906). He became an instructor at Berlin, and in 1916 was made an assistant professor and in 1918 an associate professor. He spent a year in the German army at the beginning of World War I. From 1917 to 1921 Franck was the head of a section at the Kaiser Wilhelm Institut für Physikalische Chemie, later called the Max Planck Institut. In 1921, however, he accepted the offer of a chair of experimental physics at the University of Göttingen. He remained at this post until 1933 when, in protest against Adolf Hitler's anti-Semitic policies, he resigned and left Germany. After spending more than a year in Denmark doing research at the University of Copenhagen, he moved to the United States and accepted a professorship at the Johns Hopkins University in 1935. Three years later he was appointed professor of physical chemistry at the University of Chicago, where he later worked on the Metallurgical Project—which was part of the atomic bomb project—during World War II. Franck became professor emeritus in 1949. In addition to his Nobel Prize, Franck received many honors, among them the Rumford Medal of the American Academy of Arts and Sciences in 1955 and the Max Planck Medal of the German Physical Society in 1951. He was a foreign member of the Royal Society of London and a member of the U.S. National Academy of Sciences.

Franck wrote *Anregung von Quantensprüngen durch Stösse* (1926) and *Photosynthesis in Plants* (1949).

For background information *see* ATOMIC STRUCTURE AND SPECTRA; FRANCK-CONDON PRINCIPLE; MOLECULAR STRUCTURE AND SPECTRA; PHOTOSYNTHESIS in the McGraw-Hill Encyclopedia of Science and Technology. ■

FRANK, ILYA MIKHAILOVICH
☆ Soviet physicist

Born *Oct. 23, 1908, Leningrad, U.S.S.R.*

Frank, together with I. Y. Tamm, developed the theoretical interpretation of the so-called Cerenkov radiation. For this achievement he shared with Tamm and P. A. Cerenkov the 1958 Nobel Prize for physics. *See* CERENKOV, PAVEL ALEXEYEVICH; TAMM, IGOR YEVGENEVICH.

The son of a professor of mathematics, Frank graduated in 1930 from the Moscow State University, where he studied physics. The next year, he joined the staff of the State Optical Institute in Leningrad. In 1934 he became a scientific officer at the Lebedev Physical Institute of the U.S.S.R. Academy of Sciences. There, in 1941, he took charge of the Atomic Nucleus Laboratory. He also assumed the directorship, in 1957, of the Neutron Laboratory of the Joint Institute of Nuclear Investigations. Frank attained the degree of doctor of physicomathematical sciences in 1935; in 1944 he became a professor on the faculty of the Moscow State University. He was elected a member of the U.S.S.R. Academy of Sciences in 1968. ■

FREED, KARL F.
★ American theoretical chemist

Born *Sept. 25, 1942, New York, NY, U.S.A.*

For his theoretical contributions to the understanding of molecular structure and the problem of electron correlation, the behavior of polymers, nonradiative decay processes in polyatomic molecules, and electronic states in disordered materials, Freed received the Marlow Medal Award for 1973 from the Faraday Division of the Chemical Society of London. For contributions in theoretical chemistry, particularly the analysis of radiationless processes and photochemical reactions and of

the properties of concentrated polymer solutions, he received the 1976 American Chemical Society Award in Pure Chemistry, sponsored by Alpha Chi Sigma Fraternity.

Freed studied the diverse molecular processes associated with photochemistry, the conversion of light energy into chemical energy. In recognition of the need for studying the individual primary steps in photochemistry, he began his investigations by a consideration of these primary events in isolated gas-phase molecules and, in particular, of the photophysical processes whereby various forms of molecular energy, electronic, vibrational, and rotational, become interconverted. Considerable difficulties had previously been encountered with understanding how this energy interconversion could occur in an isolated molecule, and Freed provided an explanation of this observed behavior in terms of the concept of practical irreversibility due to the finite time scales of experiments. Freed and his coworkers developed a theory on the variation of rates of interconversion of electronic to vibrational energy of the particular vibrations which are initially excited in an isolated molecule.

Freed's investigations then naturally turned to a consideration of the effect of intermolecular collisions on these relaxation processes. He and his coworkers demonstrated how the combined effects of the dependence of electronic relaxation rates on vibrational energy and the collisional changes in this vibrational en-

ergy served to provide an understanding of the pressure dependence of the relaxation and luminescence properties of large molecules in both singlet states and the long-lived triplet states which are produced by electronic relaxation from the singlets. In small molecules, Freed explained the previously perplexing observations of strong collision-induced transitions between the singlet and triplet states. His research also dealt with the analogous processes of the interconversion of energy between the different vibrations in large molecules. This natural progression of interests led Freed to investigate these molecular relaxation processes in condensed systems. He and his coworkers provided theoretical descriptions of the reorientation and migration of atoms in crystalline solids, a description of vibrational relaxation processes in liquids, and an analysis of how vibrationally excited small molecules in rare gas matrices first convert their vibrational energy into molecular rotational energy, which is subsequently converted into lattice vibrational energy.

In parallel, Freed and his coworkers also developed theories on the primary steps of photochemistry, in particular, on molecular decomposition processes in polyatomic molecules. Their research focused on the prediction of how the available energy is partitioned among the electronic, vibrational, rotational, and translational degrees of freedom of the decomposition products and how these distributions depend on the manner in which the molecule is initially energized. An important guiding principle in this work was the fact that the natural vibrational motions for a stable, bound molecular state differ markedly from those for an electronic state of a dissociating molecule, and that this change in natural motions can have an important bearing on the energy partitioning of the fragments. The theory had reduced the multidimensional character of the mathematical description of the problem to a one-dimensional representation which could simply be visualized pictorially. The theory provided simple guidelines to understanding when the fragments would be vibrationally and rotationally excited and when there should be large isotopic effects in the decomposition process.

Freed had an early interest in theories of chemical bonding in molecules. These theories had fragmented into the often contradictory extremes of semiempirical

theories, which utilize experimental information as their basis, and the ab initio theories, which utilize large digital computers to deduce the nature of chemical bonding directly from the laws of motion for the constituent electrons. Freed's research aimed to provide a bridge between the ab initio and semiempirical theories, and demonstrated how a new generalized formulation could be obtained on the basis of the laws of the motion of electrons in molecules. This new theory was shown to have a structure which is very similar to that utilized on an intuitive basis by the semiempirical theories. With this new approach it became possible to perform numerical calculations with digital computers to test the various approximations and assumptions that were present in semiempirical theories of bonding, as well as to provide new ab initio methods.

Freed and his coworkers developed theories to describe the behavior of polymer solutions in terms of the properties of the constituent units of the polymer molecule. Theories of the rheology of polymer solutions had been available only in the extreme limiting case of infinite dilution (essentially a single polymer molecule in solution), very low frequencies of motion, and zero shear rate (essentially a stationary solution). The work of Freed and his coworkers considered the treatment of the flow and frictional properties of polymer solutions in the regime of nonzero concentrations, where previous theories were hampered by the presence of divergent integrals. The new theory provided a simple understanding of the physical origin of these divergences as well as a description of concentration dependences which could be compared with experiments and used as a guide for prediction about systems not studied.

The son of immigrants, Freed received his B.S. in chemical engineering at Columbia University in 1963 and his A.M. in physics and Ph.D. in chemical physics from Harvard University in 1965 and 1967, respectively. After spending 1967–68 as a NATO postdoctoral fellow in the department of theoretical physics at the University of Manchester, England, he joined the faculty of the University of Chicago in 1968 as an assistant professor, becoming a full professor in 1976.

For background information *see* CHEMICAL BINDING; PHOTOCHEMISTRY; POLYMER PROPERTIES in the McGraw-Hill Encyclopedia of Science and Technology. ∎

FREEMAN, JOAN MAIE
★ British physicist

Born *Jan. 7, 1918, Perth, Western Australia*

Freeman's major scientific work, starting in the early 1960s, was concerned with the experimental study of nuclear beta decays of a particular type, known as superallowed Fermi transitions, and the use of very accurate measurements on these decays to further the basic understanding of the weak interaction. For this work Freeman shared with R. J. Blin-Stoyle the 1976 Rutherford Medal of the British Institute of Physics.

Although the phenomenon of beta radioactivity had first been observed before the turn of the century, more than 50 years elapsed before the fundamental nature of the process began to be considered. With the continuing discoveries of new types of "elementary" particles, for example, the muon (heavy electron), the pion (mediator of strong interactions), and particles characterized by strangeness, it became evident that these also decayed in a manner similar to that of nucleons in nuclear beta decay, the rates of these processes being much slower than those controlled by the strong (nuclear) forces. The concept of a distinct type of fundamental force, which was called the weak interaction, emerged, the physical world being visualized as operating through four fundamental interactions: the electromagnetic, gravitational, strong, and weak. But questions had to be posed: Was there, in fact, one basic weak interaction

responsible for all the observed particle decays? Were the various interaction strengths, expressed as coupling constants for these processes, related to a basic constant g which was characteristic of a universal weak interaction? It was this concept of universality which Freeman set out to test by measuring the intrinsic decay rates for a number of nuclear beta decays, from which the coupling constants could be derived for comparison with each other, and with the coupling constant for muon decay.

The beta decays chosen for study were superallowed Fermi transitions, each taking place between a pair of zero-spin nuclei virtually identical in nuclear structure apart from the interchange of a neutron for a proton. For such a decay an explicit relation, largely independent of unknown nuclear structure details, exists between the weak-interaction coupling constant g_{β_V} (V indicating the vector character of a Fermi decay) and the ft value, a quantity determined by the total energy release and half-life for the decay. Freeman, with her colleagues at the Atomic Energy Research Establishment, Harwell, used nuclear reaction techniques on an electrostatic (tandem) accelerator to obtain very accurate values for the energy release and half-life for a number of superallowed-Fermi-decaying nuclei in the mass range 14 to 54. In most cases, a target containing nuclei representing the stable daughter-product of the decay was bombarded by protons, with gradually increasing energy, until a threshold was reached at which the production of the parent nucleus plus a neutron became energetically possible. An absolute calibration of this threshold energy provided a measure of the corresponding energy release for the beta decay. For measurement of the half-lives (which were mostly of the order of a second), the radioactive nuclei were produced at a proton energy above the (p,n) threshold, and their decay was followed repeatedly over many half-lives. Using considerable care and thoroughness, the Freeman group succeeded in obtaining experimental values for the various coupling constants with accuracies approaching one part in a thousand.

The coupling-constant values agreed with one another to within a few parts per thousand. This was in itself an important result, giving support to the basic conserved vector current hypothesis which was closely associated with the principle of universality. A further significant ob-

servation was that the coupling constants, $g_{\beta V}$, differed by over 2 percent from the coupling constant, g_μ, for muon decay, determined from the muon mass and half-life. This discrepancy, an apparent challenge to universality, received a possible explanation through a theory put forward by N. Cabibbo (1963), who extended the principle of universality to include decays of particles with strangeness. According to this theory, $g_{\beta V} = g_\mu \cos \theta_c$, θ_c being a parameter known as the Cabibbo angle, while, for the decay of particles in which strangeness was not conserved, the coupling constant was $g_\mu \sin \theta_c$. The nuclear beta decay data gave a value for θ_c which was reasonably consistent with that inferred from strange-particle decay data. Thus universality, in the Cabibbo sense, was well supported.

Freeman continued her work, increasing the range and accuracy of her measurements, while Blin-Stoyle collaborated closely with her on the theoretical interpretation. In 1970 they showed, in a joint paper, that the experimental data provided a value for a small but significant electromagnetic radiative correction to the beta-decay rates. This correction had been expressed theoretically in terms of the mass of the hypothetical intermediate vector boson, supposed to mediate the weak interaction, together with the mean charge of the proposed quark constituents of protons and neutrons. Thus, indirectly, the nuclear beta-decay data gave some information on these as yet unobserved fundamental particles.

Freeman gained her physics honors B.Sc. (1939) and M.Sc. (1941) degrees at the University of Sydney. From 1941 to 1946 she engaged in radar research and development at the Radiophysics Laboratory of the Commonwealth Scientific and Industrial Research Organization (Australia). Later in 1946, she went to the Cavendish Laboratory, Cambridge, where she took her Ph.D. degree in nuclear physics in 1949, and continued her research for a further 2 years. In 1951 she joined the Nuclear Physics Division of the Atomic Energy Research Establishment at Harwell. Her early interest there was the study of inelastic neutron scattering from light and medium-weight nuclei. After a sabbatical period (1958–59) at the Massachusetts Institute of Technology, she returned to head the group based on the Harwell tandem accelerator, and soon afterward initiated the beta-decay studies. She was made a fellow of the Institute of

Physics in 1976 and of the American Physical Society in 1977.

For background information *see* INTERACTIONS, FUNDAMENTAL; INTERACTIONS, WEAK NUCLEAR; RADIOACTIVITY in the McGraw-Hill Encyclopedia of Science and Technology. ■

FREISER, HENRY
★ American chemist

Born Aug. 27, 1920, New York, NY, U.S.A.

Ion-selective electrodes represent one of the most exciting developments in modern electroanalytical chemistry. Freiser and his students at the University of Arizona became interested in such electrodes primarily because of the promise the electrodes showed for revealing information about solvent extraction equilibria and, possibly, kinetics. The group soon became fascinated with the work in developing electrochemical ion sensors.

Freiser and his students had been studying the extraction behavior of a number of ion-pair compounds (so named because the bonding of the charged species was fundamentally electrostatic, rather than covalent) involving higher-molecular-weight quaternary ammonium salts (R_4NX, where R is an alkyl group of four or more carbon atoms). They decided to try basing ion-selective electrodes on systems using such salts. With tricaprylylmethylammonium chloride

(Aliquat 336S) dissolved in decanol, a series of solutions (liquid membrane exchangers) was prepared by placing the decanol phase in contact with successive portions of a saturated aqueous sodium salt of an anion of interest until the chloride ion was entirely replaced by the anion. In this manner, practical working electrodes were developed for ClO_4^-, NO_3^-, halides, and CNS^-, as well as for a number of organic anions, including those of amino acids, sulfonates, and common carboxylates. Freiser's group was able to describe definitively the close correlation between ion-pair extraction equilibria and electrode selectivity, and had hopes of returning soon to its original intention of using electrodes as a novel means of studying many solvent extraction processes.

Two Japanese scientists, H. Hirata and K. Date, decided in 1970 to paste the Cu_2S on the Cu metal by first preparing a thick slurry of finely divided Cu_2S in a solution of polyvinyl chloride (PVC) in cyclohexanone and then embedding a Cu wire in the disk-shaped mass. The resulting device functioned very well as a sulfide electrode.

Freiser's research team tried to make an electrode by coating a Pt wire attached to the central conductor of a coaxial cable with a mixture of the PVC solution and an aliquat salt in decanol and allowing the film to air-dry for 3 to 4 hours. The remaining exposed wire was then wrapped in Parafilm to prevent shorting. The coated wire electrodes prepared in this manner gave potential responses to changes in anion activities immediately upon being immersed in solution. Best results were obtained, however, after an initial conditioning, accomplished by soaking the electrode for about 15 minutes in a 0.1-molar solution of the appropriate sodium salt. Electrodes stored in air when not in use exhibited lifetimes greater than 6 months. Just before reuse, they were soaked for 5 minutes in a 0.1-molar solution.

In general, coated wire electrodes are freer from interference than conventional ion-selective electrodes are. The advantages of the coated wire electrodes over the conventional barrel types are several: Coated wire electrodes are much smaller; and it is possible, using a hair-thin metal conductor and a very fine polymer coating, to carry out intracellular ion sensing. Coated wire electrodes are inexpensive and exceptionally simple to prepare.

Using a nitrate-selective coated wire electrode, Freiser and his coworkers found that they could rapidly, conveniently, and reliably carry out the determination of the atmospheric pollutant NO_x. This approach was subsequently used in determining nitrates in atmospheric particulate matter.

An application of coated wire electrodes to the fields of clinical and oceanographic analysis is illustrated by the K^+-responsive electrode, which permits the determination of potassium in whole blood, whereas flame photometry requires prior spinning off of the platelets. The method is also convenient for determining K in sea water.

The absence of an internal reference solution in the coated wire electrodes presents a puzzle to the orthodox electroanalytical chemist. In an attempt to learn why the reference solution is apparently not necessary, and to find answers to other questions about the functioning of the coated wire electrode, Freiser's team decided to study the electrical conductivity of the polymeric coatings. They prepared compositions of a number of quaternary salts dissolved in a variety of polymeric matrices: polyethylene, polystyrene, Nylon 66, polymethylmethacrylate, and epoxy resin cast in thin disks. The results produced surprises as well as answers. The most unusual feature of the conductivity of the polymer-dispersed salts is its unusually high positive temperature coefficient. These materials compare favorably with commercially available inorganic semiconductor thermistors, which exhibit a 4–6-percent change in conductivity per degree Celsius, which is equivalent to the behavior of polyethylene or polystyrene compositions. Epoxy formulations produce an increase of about 50 percent conductivity for each increase in degree Celsius.

The results of the Freiser team's studies of the variation of conductivity of the films from ambient to 2×10^8 pascals (2000 atmospheres) clearly showed a range of activation volumes (32–37 cubic centimeters per mole for Aliquat-chloride in PVC) that unequivocally demonstrated an ionic rather than electronic charge-conduction mechanism. The large activation energies of the process that are observed are somehow associated with the effect of extremely high viscosities on ionic mobilities. Investigations into the mechanism as well as the applications of these interesting electrochemical sensors continued at the University of Arizona.

Freiser received his B.S. degree from the City College of New York (1941) and his M.S. and Ph.D. degrees from Duke University (1942 and 1944, respectively). In 1944–45 he chaired the department of physical and analytical chemistry at North Dakota State College. He spent a year (1945–46) as a research fellow at the Mellon Institute of Industrial Research, leaving to become associate professor at the University of Pittsburgh. In 1958 he joined the faculty of the University of Arizona, serving as professor and as head of the chemistry department (1958–68). Freiser was a visiting professor at the University of California at Los Angeles (1968), at Kyoto University (1972), and at the California Institute of Technology at Pasadena (1979). He received an honorary professorship from the Universidad Autonoma de Guadlajara in 1970. He was elected a member of the American Chemical Society, the American Society for Testing Materials, and the Chemical Society of London. A member of the National Research Council, he served on the Committee on Analytical Chemistry (1972–75) and was a staff officer of the Panel on Platinum Group Metals (1974–77). In 1978 he received the Fisher Award in Analytical Chemistry from the American Chemical Society.

For background information *see* ELECTROCHEMISTRY; ELECTRODE in the McGraw-Hill Encyclopedia of Science and Technology. ■

FRENCH, CHARLES STACY

★ American plant physiologist

Born Dec. 13, 1907, Lowell, MA, U.S.A.

French had the good luck, as a college sophomore in 1928, to hear lectures on photosynthesis by Robert Emerson, who had just returned to Harvard after several years with Otto Warburg in Berlin. Deducing the nature of the photosynthetic process from simple but precise measurements of such phenomena as light absorption, gas exchange, and growth rate of photosynthetic cells under various controlled conditions was fascinating to French. He learned from Emerson that in such experimental work an interest in the development of techniques, mechanical contraptions, and application of the sim-

pler principles of chemistry and physics to biological problems can lead to significant discoveries. *See* WARBURG, OTTO HEINRICH.

As a graduate student in general physiology at Harvard under W. J. Crozier, French participated in the Chlorella Club, a student discussion group led by William Arnold that included Pei-Sung Tang, Caryl Haskins, and Henry Kohn. With Tang and Kohn, he studied *Chlorella* respiration as influenced by temperature and oxygen pressure. He heard about photosynthetic bacteria from Albert Navez. After the *Chlorella* work he went in 1934 to the Hopkins Marine Station in California to learn from Cornelis B. Van Niel how to grow photosynthetic bacteria and study their metabolism. A postdoctoral year with Emerson at the California Institute of Technology was followed by a year in Berlin with Warburg. The action spectrum and efficiency of bacterial photosynthesis were measured. This led French to a comparative study of the absorption spectra of different photosynthetic bacteria, which he carried out at the Harvard Medical School's biochemistry department as a teaching fellow under Baird Hastings. Similar work on bacteria had been going on in the biophysical research group under Wassink at Utrecht. Thereafter the work of that group, later led by Jan B. Thomas, and French's interests in photosynthetic pigments remained closely associated. *See* HASTINGS, ALBERT BAIRD; VAN NIEL, CORNELIS BERNARDUS.

As an assistant to James Franck at Chicago, French worked on the time course of chlorophyll fluorescence in leaves and on photooxidation in leaves free of carbon dioxide. He learned to make reliable physical measurements from Foster Rieke, Hans Gaffron, and Robert Livingston, other members of Franck's group. *See* FRANCK, JAMES.

The difference between two contrasting philosophies of experimental investigation became clear during this work on fluorescence. One approach to the understanding of a phenomenon is to devise a theoretical scheme to correlate the known facts, and then to plan a few critical experiments to support the postulates of the theory. In simple enough systems with well-understood variables, the "theory first" philosophy may be useful. However, in complex and poorly understood systems, such as photosynthesis, French preferred the opposite philosophy, first developing a knowledge of the phenomenon by systematic measurements under very different conditions, and then letting the theory develop on a broad basis of experimental experience.

A casual visit to Chicago by Mortimer Anson of the Rockefeller Institute led to collaborative experiments on oxygen evolution from chloroplasts, an effect that Anson had recently heard about when visiting Robert Hill in Cambridge. At Anson's suggestion this effect was named the Hill reaction, a designation later used by all but Hill himself. Studies of the Hill reaction were continued at the botany department of the University of Minnesota, where French taught plant physiology. There, in collaboration with A. Stanley Holt, he found that various dyes could be reduced by illuminated chloroplasts. He started a long-continued but only partially successful attempt to concentrate the photochemically active components of chloroplasts.

Later, with Harold Milner and others at the Carnegie Institution, French continued the chloroplast fractionation experiments for several years, using his dye-reduction method for the activity measurements of the fractions. To disintegrate chloroplasts for this work, he made a needle-valve homogenizer, which thereafter was widely used for breaking bacteria. With Violet Koski Young, French measured the fluorescence spectra of photosynthetic pigments and confirmed the idea of energy transfer from accessory pigments to chlorophyll as a part of photosynthesis in live cells. To aid in the interpretation of fluorescence spectra and other data, a graphical computer called a curve analyzer was built. A recording fluorescence spectrophotometer, a derivative spectrophotometer, an automatic spectrophotometer for recording action spectra of photosynthesis, and several monochromators and platinum electrode assemblies for photosynthesis measurements were also constructed. With the derivative spectrophotometer the existence of several forms of chlorophyll in many different plants was confirmed, and a new form of chlorophyll absorbing at 695 nanometers was discovered.

French's later work with Jeanette S. Brown on the computer deconvolution of low-temperature absorption spectra of chlorophyll in various algae and leaf chloroplasts showed the universal presence of specific forms of chlorophyll *a* complexes with absorption maxima at 662, 670, 677, and 684 nanometers. Most plants also were found to contain small amounts of chlorophyll forms with longer wavelength maxima in the 693–710-nanometer region.

The chemical nature and method of participation of various plant pigments in photosynthesis were French's main concerns. These problems were approached in many different ways, ranging from studies of isolated pigments to kinetic studies of photosynthesis in whole plants. He worked on measurements of fluorescence, absorption, and action spectra of the individual forms of chlorophyll and of other pigments, so that their participation in photosynthesis could be understood in a quantitative sense. After retiring in 1973, French worked on the measurement and interpretation of action spectra for some of the partial reactions of photosynthesis, using a balanced photostationary-state method instead of rate measurements.

Son of a New England doctor, French graduated from Harvard University with a B.S. in 1930 and a Ph.D. in 1934. He worked a year with Emerson in California and a year with Warburg in Berlin. Two years as Austin teaching fellow at Harvard Medical School were followed by 3 years as an assistant to Franck at the University of Chicago. From 1941 to 1947 he taught plant physiology at the University of Minnesota. He became director of the department of plant biology at the Carnegie Institution of Washington at Stanford University in 1947. He was elected to the National Academy of Sciences and the American Academy of Arts and Sciences in 1963 and to the Deutsche Akademie der Naturforscher Leopoldina in 1965. In 1974 he received an honorary doctorate from the University of Göteborg.

For background information *see* BACTERIAL PHOTOSYNTHESIS; CHLOROPHYLL; PHOTOSYNTHESIS in the McGraw-Hill Encyclopedia of Science and Technology. ∎

FREUDENBERG, KARL JOHANN
★ German chemist

Born Jan. 29, 1886, Weinheim, Baden, Germany

As a student of Emil Fischer, Freudenberg acquainted himself with the bifunctional linkage of hydrobenzoic acids. After taking his doctorate (1910), he worked another 3 years with Fischer and studied galloylgallic acid, as well as gallotannins. The acyl group migration and transesterification through methanol in the presence of diazomethane were observed.

After world War I the work on tannins was continued—for example, on hamamelitannin, from which a new branched hexose was isolated with the help of tannase. Chlorogenic acid was elucidated. Catechin was assigned to flavonoids; its constitution and the steric relationship with epicatechin were established. The tetramethyl catechin undergoes a pinacol rearrangement without racemization. This was explained through a phenonium ion mechanism (1927). The self-condensation of catechin to tannins was clarified. It was shown, at the same time as by Roux, that quebrachotannin is the condensation product of a trihydroxyflavandiol. The proanthocyanidins, as a broad group of natural tannins, were opened up; they are dimeric flavonoids.

In Freudenberg's stereochemistry research the configurational system of the α-hydroxy acids was extended through chemical transformations. The tertiary carbon atom of dihydroshikimic acid, as well as that of the methylethylpropylmethane obtained from it, was related to glucose through the implication of cis-trans isomerism on the ring system of the acid. From this point on, in filling up some gaps, the absolute configuration of citronellal, of camphor, and of the entire terpene system was established through chemical transformations. By making use of the rule of shift (displacement rule), which was discovered during the hydrogenation of mandelic acid, the lactone-, amide-, and phenylhydrazide rules of Hudson were corrected, and the amino-, azido-, and halogeno-fatty acids were sterically related to α-hydroxy acids. It could then be predicted when the Walden inversion would take place and when not; also, the basis for the theoretical interpretation of the results later obtained by others was laid. As the validity of Tschugajeff's optical rule of distance was shown to be the same for steric changes as for chemical ones (1931), the van't Hoff law of superposition could be corrected. By using the displacement rule, the absolute configuration of the catechin and pinoresinol group as well as that of glucosamin was determined (1931). The presence of a clear relationship between cellulose and its oligosaccharides was shown. A result of the collaboration with Werner Kuhn was the explanation, by Kuhn, of the rule of shift through the measurement of the Cotton effect in the ultraviolet region.

In his work on cellulose and starch, Freudenberg found, by the acetolysis of cellulose, that two-thirds of all the glucose units pass through the biose stage (1921). This was explained through chains of uniformly linked units, as in cellobiose, and was shown to be in accordance with the x-ray diagrams. Staudinger and Haworth after a few years came to the same conclusion. The rotation and the rate of hydrolysis of cellulose and its oligosaccharides are also in accordance with this. The synthesis of methylated cellotriose confirms the uniformity of both glucoside bonds. 2,3,6-*O*-methylglucose anhydride-1,4 was synthesized and found to be monomolecular (according to K. Hess, it should have been methyl cellulose). A crystalline "glucosan" of Hess is composed of 15—30 units. Cellulose, completely methylated in cold and obtained in good yields, has no end groups, and is degraded to 2,3,6-trimethylglucose in formic acid with 1% acetyl chloride at 20°C. In 1928 Freudenberg established the first valid formula of the molecular constitution of cellulose. In thoroughly methylated starch the branching was found at the sixth position. Schardinger's dextrins from starch are cyclooligosaccharides, and were supplemented through the discovery of cyclooctaamylose. The dark-colored addition product of cyclohexaamylose with iodine was identified as a clathrate compound. Its similarity with the iodine-starch complex, also a clathrate, led to the conception of a helix with tubelike hollow spaces for a part of the starch molecule (1938).

Working on mono- and oligosaccharides from 1921, Freudenberg clarified the structure of the acetone compounds of simple sugars, thus permitting the syntheses of disaccharides and trisaccharides, among them that of sophorose, laminaribiose, cellobiose, and 5-β-glucosidoglucose. Supernumerary acetohalogenosugars and acetylated glucosides led to the discovery of cyclic acetates. The 6-deoxyhexose system was extended. The hydrogenolysis of benzylidene and arylsulfonic acid compounds was achieved.

In his amino sugars and protein studies, Freudenberg hydrolyzed blood group A substance and found D-galactose, D-acetylglucosamine, and amino acids, among them L-threonine. Insulin, inactivated by various methods, was partly reactivated. From the behavior of insulin toward cysteine it was inferred in 1935 that the former is composed of at least two parallel protein chains which are joined together through SS bridges in the form of ladder rungs. In 1941 sugars and amino sugars were separated by using exchangers; furthermore, sugars were separated from amino acids, as well as acidic, neutral, and basic amino acids from each other.

Freudenberg started work on lignin in 1922 to find if it, like cellulose, possesses a definite order. Lignin is a phenolic body rich in ethereal oxygen (1926), and even in wood has a refractive index of an aromatic substance (1929). It is not an artifact of carbohydrates. Along with Klason and others, Freudenberg assumed and then proved that spruce lignin is an oxidation product of coniferyl, *p*-coumaryl, and sinapinyl alcohols. Its oxidation to vanillin and vanillin derivatives was increased to more than 40% of the theoretically possible amount. The oxidation of methylated lignin yields about 30 substances, mostly methoxybenzoic acids. Enzymatic dehydrogenation of a suitable mixture of the *p*-hydroxycinnamyl alcohols gave artificial lignin that yielded the same acids on degradation (1950). Through dehydrogenation of coniferyl alcohol, about 30 oligolignols were isolated, which rendered information about the mechanism of formation and constitution of lignin. The intermediate products are quinone methides, to which water, phenols, or sugars are added. In this way phenols are formed again, which after dehydrogenation react further. The bonding to the polysaccharides is simultaneously explained. Schematic formula of spruce lignin explains all recorded information, and also a great amount of other information which was not considered at the time of its presentation. Of importance are the irregular sequence of units, which appear in various forms, and of isolated benzylaryl ether bonds, which are easily hydrolyzed to give oligolignols to a small extent.

In 1914 Freudenberg became privatdozent at the University of Kiel, with a 4-year leave for military service. He spent 1920—21 at the University of Munich and 1921–22 at the University of Freiburg as professor extraordinarius. During 1922–26 he was professor ordinarius of chemistry in Karlsruhe and during 1926–56 at Heidelberg. He then became director of a state research institute.

Freudenberg wrote *Die Chemie der natürlichen Gerbstoffe* (1920) and *Tannin, Cellulose, Lignin* (1933), and edited *Stereochemie* (1933). With Hans Plieninger, he wrote *Organische Chemie* (13th ed. 1977), and with A. C. Neish, *Constitution and Biosynthesis of Lignin* (1968).

For background information *see* AMINO SUGAR; CELLULOSE; INSULIN; MONOSACCHARIDE; OLIGOSACCHARIDE; STARCH; STEREOCHEMISTRY; TANNIN in the McGraw-Hill Encyclopedia of Science and Technology. ∎

FREY-WYSSLING, ALBERT FRIEDRICH
★ Swiss botanist

Born Nov. 8, 1900, Küsnacht-Zurich, Switzerland

After World War I, research fellows in biology were still divided into two opposing camps: the "histomorphologists" and the "physiological chemists" (biochemists). The chemists called the histologists "stamp collectors," while the latter thought of their chemical colleagues as poor biologists because they analyzed awful mixtures of different cell constituents, whimsical breis, and structureless homogenates.

Frey-Wyssling recognized that this dispute arose from the fact that cytologists worked in the domain of microscopic dimensions but chemists in that of amicroscopic dimensions. He concluded that in the submicroscopic domain, which covers the dimensions of macromolecules with their characteristic shape and chemical behavior, morphology and chemistry would meet. He hoped to reestablish an undivided biology by research in this neglected field, so he undertook what he later called submicroscopic morphology (1938). He reactivated biological research with the polarizing microscope, which had been neglected in this century after a brilliant start at the Swiss Federal Institute of Technology (ETH) in Zurich by his early predecessors, C. W. Nägeli, the first molecular biologist, and C. Cramer. In addition to the classical notion of intrinsic anisotropy, the concept of form anisotropy, developed after 1915 by H. Ambronn at the University of Jena, was introduced. This effect reveals fibrillar or lamellar systems whose periodicity lies below the resolution power of the light microscope (1926). The application of the relevant methods showed that plant cell walls consist of rodlike fibrils (then called micellar strands) embedded in an amorphous mass (now called matrix). The arrangement of the rodlets varies so that different textures of the same submicroscopic structure can be distinguished (fiber texture, helical texture, tubular texture, and so on). In starch granules a similar structure of spherically arranged rodlets was found, while the cuticular layer of epidermal cells and chloroplasts proved to have a submicroscopic lamellar structure.

These optical studies, based on effects of birefringence and dichroism, were supported by the x-ray analysis of the same or similar biological objects (W. T. Astbury, *Fundamentals of Fibre Structure*, 1933). The x-ray diffraction method permitted a more quantitative evaluation of the invisible structural elements. By staining plant fibers with colloidal gold and silver particles of about 100-angstrom (10-nanometer) diameter, Frey-Wyssling could show that the bast fibers must consist of microfibrils with about 250-angstrom (25-nanometer) diameter which are subdivided into much smaller elementary fibrils with the order of 50-angstrom (5-nanometer) diameter (1937).

In applying these indirect methods, an elaborate insight into submicroscopic morphology was gained (1938). When, in 1940, the electron microscope became a tool for biological research, the derived submicroscopic structures, now termed ultrastructures, could be imaged directly. The lamellar structure of chloroplasts, retinal rods, and the myelin sheath of nerves, as well as the fibrillar patterns of cell walls, connective tissue, muscles, and so forth, became evident. In this way the general concept of submicroscopic structures gained by indirect methods was corroborated.

Frey-Wyssling, together with K. Mühlethaler, utilized electron microscopy from the start. With the aid of the freeze-etching method developed at the ETH by H. Moor, researchers hoped to help solve the multiple problems concerning the function of the numerous types of organelles revealed by the electron microscope in the cytoplasm (1965).

Whereas before 1940 only a few scientists were involved in submicroscopic research, the electron microscope mobilized a whole army of histologists, cytologists, bacteriologists, virologists, and so on, who considered submicroscopic morphology no longer an adequate term for their ambitions. This humble science thus became a highly diversified technical branch of biology with such proud titles as biophysics, and molecular biology.

Son of a college teacher, Frey-Wyssling was trained at the ETH. He majored in biology (diploma of natural sciences, 1923) and obtained a Ph.D. in 1924. In 1925 he studied optics with Ambronn at the University of Jena and in the following year, plant physiology with M. Molliard at the Sorbonne in Paris. In 1927 at the ETH he qualified in general botany, and in 1928–32 he was plant physiologist to the Rubber Experiment Station AVROS in Medan (Sumatra, Indonesia). He then returned to the ETH as a lecturer, and was appointed full professor in the department of general botany and plant physiology in 1938. He became head of this department, and in 1948 established the electron microscopy laboratory as a third research laboratory, in addition to those on histochemistry and plant physiology. In 1957–61 he was rector of the ETH.

Frey-Wyssling wrote *Das Polarisationsmikroskop*, with H. Ambronn (1926); *Die Stoffausscheidung der höheren Pflanzen* (1935); *Submikroskopische Morphologie des Protoplasmas und seiner Derivate* (1938); *Submicroscopic Morphology of Protoplasm* (1948; 2d ed. 1953); *Submikroskopische Struktur des Cytoplasmas* (1955); *Macromolecules in Cell Structure* (1957); *Die pflanzliche Zellwand* (1959); and *Ultrastructural Plant Cytology*, with K. Mühlethaler (1965).

For background information *see* CYTOLOGY; MICROSCOPE, ELECTRON; MOLECULAR BIOLOGY in the McGraw-Hill Encyclopedia of Science and Technology. ∎

FRIEDLANDER, GERHART

★ American nuclear chemist

Born July 28, 1916, Munich, Germany

W‌hen the Brookhaven National Laboratory's cosmotron, the first accelerator capable of producing particle beams in the gigaelectronvolt (GeV) energy range,

came into operation in 1952, it was justifiably hailed as an important new tool for elementary particle physics. However, few scientists expected it to be of much interest for studies of nuclear reactions in complex nuclei because, with bombarding particles whose kinetic energies exceed the total binding energies of nuclei, one might expect nuclei to be broken up into their constituent neutrons and protons. Friedlander and his collaborators were able to show that, contrary to such predictions, protons in the GeV energy range produce a rich variety of nuclear reactions. For his extensive work on the systematic study and interpretation of these reactions, Friedlander received the American Chemical Society's Award for Nuclear Applications in Chemistry in 1967.

In the years following World War II, reactions between various nuclei and protons of energies up to a few hundred million electronvolts were extensively studied in a number of laboratories possessing synchrocyclotrons. Two principal types of reactions were recognized: spallation reactions, in which a number of nucleons (a term meaning neutrons and protons) or small nucleon aggregates, such as deuterons and alpha particles, are emitted (spalled off), leaving behind a single major residual nucleus; and fission reactions, in which the nucleus splits into two (or possibly more) fragments of comparable mass.

When Friedlander and his coworkers extended nuclear reaction studies into the GeV range, they found that spallation and fission reactions continued to be important, but they soon observed phenomena

that led them to postulate a third class of reactions, which they termed fragmentation. The first evidence came from the observation that large quantities of light nuclei with mass numbers between 10 and 40 are formed when protons in the GeV range interact with heavy-element targets. The onset of these reactions was found to be in the neighborhood of 0.5 GeV, and as the bombarding energy is increased above that value, their probabilities increase steeply. The Brookhaven chemists postulated that the light fragments result from processes in which local energy deposition in a region of the target nucleus leads to breakup of the nucleus before the energy can be distributed throughout the nucleus. This would be a mechanism distinctly different from that believed to be operative in spallation and fission. These are described as two-step processes in which a fast step consisting of a cascade of nucleon-nucleon collisions and lasting on the order of 10^{-22} second leads to excited intermediate nuclei, and these in turn deexcite on a slower time scale (10^{-15} to 10^{-20} second) by particle emission or fission. Confirmatory evidence for the idea that fragmentation reactions cannot be described as two-step processes came from work of some of Friedlander's Brookhaven colleagues on the angular distribution of ^{24}Na fragments produced from bismuth by 3-GeV protons.

The exact nature of fragmentation reactions is still not completely clear. Friedlander and his coworkers proposed that the partners of the light fragments may be found among the neutron-deficient isotopes of much heavier elements. This suggestion originally came from the observation that the excitation functions (formation probabilities as a function of bombarding energy) for the production of neutron-deficient species in the barium region from heavy-element bombardments have the same shape as those for light-fragment production. The hypothesis that these neutron-deficient products are formed in processes distinctly different from those leading to the (generally neutron-excess) fission products was further strengthened by a set of experiments carried out by Friedlander, L. Friedman, B. Gordon, and L. Yaffe. In this mass-spectrometric and radio-chemical study of cesium and barium isotopes formed from uranium by protons of various energies, it was shown that above about 0.5 GeV the isobaric yield distribution—that is, the distribution of primary yields of different products at a given mass number—is double-peaked with a valley near beta stability. The products on the neutron-deficient and neutron-excess side of beta stability were also shown to have quite different momentum properties. Subsequent, more detailed investigations by other workers have borne out that the light fragments have partners among the neutron-deficient products in the fission region, but more complex processes, with three fragments, are also indicated.

Friedlander's experimental studies of fragmentation and other high-energy reactions were complemented by his interest in attempts to calculate the behavior of nuclei under high-energy bombardment on the basis of simple models. Only those reactions describable by the two-step mechanism lent themselves to this approach, but here, and particularly for spallation reactions, the calculations, carried out by Monte Carlo methods on high-speed computers, were quite successful in reproducing a large body of experimental data. Some of the special features of reactions at GeV energies not found at lower energies could be correlated with the production and subsequent interactions of pi mesons in nuclei. One of the major aims of the numerical calculations is to test, and hopefully to improve, the models and assumptions used through comparison of the computed results with experimental data.

Later, Friedlander turned his attention to solar neutrino research. In particular, he was active in devising an experiment for the detection of low-energy neutrinos from the Sun, those coming from the primary proton-proton fusion reaction. It was planned that this experiment would use about 50 metric tons of gallium in a deep mine (to provide shielding from cosmic rays) as a detector and would involve the detection and measurement of a few atoms of radioactive ^{71}Ge formed by neutrino capture in ^{71}Ga. The importance of this very difficult and expensive experiment lay in the fact that its results would decide whether astrophysical theories of stellar evolution require serious revision or whether neutrinos produced in the Sun do not reach the Earth. One of these two classes of modifications of existing knowledge was indicated by the results of the previously performed experiment of Raymond Davis and collaborators with a ^{37}Cl detector for solar neutrinos. This experiment, which was sensitive to high-energy neutrinos only, indicated a flux only one-third of that predicted by theory, but the calculated flux of these high-energy neutrinos (mainly from ^{8}B formed in a very small branch of the thermonuclear reaction cycle) was very sensitive to details of the solar model, whereas the flux of low-energy proton-proton neutrinos was not expected to be sensitive.

Friedlander majored in chemistry at the University of California, Berkeley, earning his B.S. in 1939. He continued there as a graduate student under Glenn T. Seaborg and received his Ph.D. in 1942. After a year's teaching at the University of Idaho, he joined the Los Alamos Laboratory in 1943, remaining there until 1946. For the next 2 years he worked at the General Electric Company's Research Laboratory in Schenectady, and in 1948 became a member of the staff of Brookhaven National Laboratory. In 1952 he became a senior chemist there, and from 1968 to 1977 he chaired the chemistry department. In 1978–79 he was at the University of Mainz, Germany, as recipient of an Alexander von Humboldt Award. *See* SEABORG, GLENN THEODORE.

Associate editor of the *Annual Review of Nuclear Science,* Friedlander wrote *Introduction to Radiochemistry,* with J. W. Kennedy (1949), and *Nuclear and Radiochemistry,* with J. W. Kennedy and J. M. Miller (1955; 2d ed. 1964).

For background information *see* NEUTRINO; NUCLEAR REACTION; RADIOCHEMISTRY in the McGraw-Hill Encyclopedia of Science and Technology. ■

FRIEDMAN, HERBERT
☆ American astrophysicist

Born *June 21, 1916, New York, NY, U.S.A.*

Beginning in 1949 with captured German V-2 rockets that had been brought to White Sands, NM, after World War II, Friedman pioneered in the development of rocket and satellite astronomy. Experiments conducted under his direction detected and studied x-ray and ultraviolet radiations from the Sun, produced the first astronomical photographs made in x-ray wavelengths, discovered the hydrogen corona around the Earth, and measured x-ray and ultraviolet radiations from certain stars. For his achievements, Friedman received the U.S. Navy's Distinguished Scientific Achievement Award in 1962, the Presidential Medal for Distinguished Federal Service in 1964, the Eddington

Medal of the Royal Astronomical Society, also in 1964, the National Medal of Science in 1968, and the Michelson Medal of the Franklin Institute in 1972.

The advantages of making observations from space, above the interference of the Earth's atmosphere, have been long appreciated by astronomers. The Earth's atmosphere absorbs all radiation with wavelengths shorter than 2850 angstroms (285 nanometers), as well as several other regions of the electromagnetic spectrum. Only in outer space could gamma- and x-radiation, which give evidence of ultra-high-energy events, be detected, and the x-ray and ultraviolet spectra of the Sun and stars be measured.

Friedman and his colleagues at the U.S. Naval Research Laboratory were faced with many problems unknown to ground-based astronomers. The rocket astronomer relies on the same two instruments—the telescope and the spectrograph—but they must be designed to function in a vehicle in erratic motion. The instruments must be compact, since the observatory payload of the rockets is extremely limited; they must be able to withstand accelerations amounting to several hundred times that of gravity; and the exposed film must be recoverable or the measurements must be radioed to a ground receiver while the rocket is aloft. Early efforts to obtain spectrograms of the Sun met with so many problems that the spectrograph was supplemented by sensitive detectors, such as Geiger counters and ionization chambers tuned to narrow bands of wavelengths.

The Sun was the first celestial object to be studied by rocket astronomy. Friedman directed the rocket astronomy program to study the solar x-ray spectrum (below 100 angstroms, or 10 nanometers) and in 1949 obtained the first scientific proof that x-rays emanate from the Sun. Later he directed many studies of the Sun for more than a full sunspot cycle.

Friedman directed the earliest attempts to study solar flares in 1956. A Rockoon, a small solid-propellant rocket carried aloft to 80,000 feet (24,400 meters) on a Skyhook balloon, was launched each day from a ship in the Pacific Ocean. When a flare was detected optically or was indirectly indicated by a short-wave radio fade-out, the rocket was fired by radio command. In 10 tries the emission of only one small flare was measured, but this was sufficient to clearly reveal that the energy, radiated as x-rays, represents a major portion of the total energy output of a solar flare and is entirely adequate to explain the accompanying ionospheric disturbances, such as short-wave radio fade-out.

Friedman continued to study the nature and effects of solar flares in 1957 as director of Project Sunflare, the opening event of the International Geophysical Year. By then, two-stage, rail-launched, solid-propellant rockets capable of carrying a 50-pound (22.5-kilogram) payload to about 150 miles (240 kilometers) had become available. Instrumented rockets were kept in constant readiness and launched by push button when a flare was observed. With this approach, a number of measurements of x-ray and ultraviolet emissions were obtained during solar flares.

During the total solar eclipse of Oct. 12, 1958, Friedman supervised a rocket experiment carried out from the deck of the USS *Point Defiance* near the Danger Islands in the South Pacific. As the Moon crossed the face of the Sun, six solid-propellant rockets were launched in sequence to take turns measuring the x-ray and ultraviolet emission coming from the uneclipsed portions of the Sun. The experiments provided the first proof that x-radiation comes from the Sun's corona, or outer atmosphere, and that ultraviolet radiation comes from its chromosphere, or inner atmosphere.

The first x-ray photograph of the Sun was obtained on Apr. 19, 1960. A simple pinhole camera in an Aerobee-Hi rocket was mounted on a pointing control to aim it continuously at the Sun. The camera was 6 inches (15 centimeters) long with a

pinhole 0.005 inch (0.13 millimeter) in diameter covered with an aluminized plastic film to exclude visible and ultraviolet light. This combination transmitted the x-ray spectrum below 50 angstroms (5 nanometers).

In addition to his solar observations, Friedman began to survey the Galaxy for x-ray sources. The first evidence for an extra–solar system source of x-rays was obtained in 1956. In 1963 two discrete galactic x-ray sources, *Sco X-1* and *Tau X-2*, were located to within 1°. *Tau X-2* was positively identified with the Crab Nebula by observing its lunar occultation in 1964. By 1965 a catalog of some 30 discrete sources had been accumulated, including distant galaxies. In 1968 x-ray pulsations were observed from the neutron star remnant of the Crab Supernova. With the launch of *HEAO-1* in August 1977, Friedman and his colleagues began a full sky survey which promised to produce a catalog of more than a thousand galactic and extragalactic x-ray sources.

The son of an art dealer, Friedman graduated from Brooklyn College in 1936. He received a Ph.D. in physics in 1940 from the Johns Hopkins University, where he remained for a year as a physics instructor. He then joined the staff of the Metallurgy Division at the U.S. Naval Research Laboratory. He was named supervisor of the Electron Optics Branch in 1942. In 1958 he was appointed superintendent of the Atmosphere and Astrophysics Division and in 1962 chief scientist at the laboratory's E. O. Hulburt Center for Space Research. He was elected to the National Academy of Sciences in 1960.

For background information *see* ROCKET ASTRONOMY; SUN; X-RAY ASTRONOMY in the McGraw-Hill Encyclopedia of Science and Technology. ∎

FRIEDMANN, HERBERT
★ American zoologist and ornithologist

Born Apr. 22, 1900, New York, NY, U.S.A.

From the beginning of his career, Friedmann was interested in the evolutionary and ethological problems associated with reproductive parasitism, especially in birds. With extensive field experience with parasitic birds in the Americas and Africa, supplemented with wide reading and correspondence with collectors and observers the world over, he made this special aspect of avian biology almost a personal field. He also dealt with the taxonomy of birds of all parts of the world.

In 1950, while in South Africa studying a group of parasitic birds known as honey guides, he investigated their peculiar, symbiotic "guiding" behavior. One of their species was long known to guide humans to wild bees' nests. Previously it had been assumed that the birds fed on the honey and bee larvae and eggs, but Friedmann found that the primary interest of the birds was in the beeswax.

This discovery led to a prolonged study of the mechanism of wax digestion, as waxes were then considered indigestible and, hence, nonnutritious to animals. In the birds' intestinal tracts Friedmann found a wax-breaking bacterium, which he isolated and described as *Micrococcus cerolyticus*. This microbe was found on the wild bee comb, from which the birds acquired it when eating the comb. Its wax-breaking effect was discovered to be far greater in the presence of an avian cofactor than by itself, and it was found that this cofactor was added in the upper end of the small intestine. Beeswax passing through the alimentary tract of the honey guides lost more than half of its lipid content, which was absorbed as nutriment by the birds. The wax also underwent very marked changes in its saponification number, indicating that it was broken down into simpler fatty acids, which made it possible for the birds to utilize it.

From the start of the work on wax digestion, Friedmann realized that any organism, chemical, or process that could break down wax might conceivably be of interest in tuberculosis therapy. The tubercle bacillus has a waxy impregnation that protects it from the counter effects of the body and from medication. Anything that could break down this waxy protection might render the tubercle bacillus more readily susceptible to treatment. He found that the *Micrococcus* from the honey guides had a marked effect on the metabolism of the tubercle bacillus, suggesting that the results might be applicable to tuberculosis therapy.

Friedmann was also interested in the emergence of objective "natural history" out of the mysticism and allegorical attitude of the Middle Ages. For material he turned to works of art of medieval and Renaissance times. He published numerous studies of symbolic content and usage of various animal forms, in an effort to learn what they meant to the people at the time and to appraise the growth of knowledge of the animals themselves. Because the only interest in animals was an ecclesiatical one in the allegorical meanings, scholars of the time paid little attention to the animals as such. It required a profound mental reorientation to alter this approach, and until then the advance of observational biology was not possible. Friedmann's papers contributed to a historical survey of the transition from the logic of allegory to that of natural science.

After graduating with a B.S. from the College of the City of New York in 1920, Friedmann went to Cornell University, where he obtained a Ph.D. in ornithology in 1923. For the next 3 years he held a National Research Council postdoctoral fellowship at Harvard, but much of the time was spent in the field, in Argentina in 1923–24 and in Africa in 1924–25. Because of his interest in taxonomy, Friedmann gravitated from university teaching to museum research and curating as a professional career. Thus, after teaching at Cornell, Virginia, Brown, and Amherst, he left the campus for the museum in 1929, when he was appointed curator of birds in the U.S. National Museum, Smithsonian Institution, Washington, DC. There he remained as head curator of zoology until 1961, when he retired to accept the directorship of the Los Angeles County Museum of Natural History. He also accepted nominal appointments as professor of zoology in residence at the University of California at Los Angeles and at the University of Southern California. He retired from all these positions in 1970.

Friedmann's work on avian brood parasitism earned him the Leidy Medal of the Academy of Natural Sciences of Philadelphia in 1955, the Elliot Medal of the National Academy of Sciences in 1959, and the Brewster Medal of the American Ornithologists Union in 1964. He was elected to the National Academy of Sciences in 1962.

Friedmann published about 400 works, including the following books and monographs: *The Cowbirds* (1929); *Birds Collected by the Childs Frick Expedition to Ethiopia and Kenya* (2 vols., 1930, 1937); *Ornithology of Tropical East Africa*, with A. Loveridge (1937); *Birds of North and Middle America* (3 vols., 1941, 1950); *The Symbolic Goldfinch* (1946); *Parasitic Cuckoos of Africa* (1949); *Distributional Check List of Birds of Mexico*, with others (2 vols., paper, 1950, 1957); *The Honey-Guides* (1955); *Check-list of North American Birds*, with others (5th ed. 1957); *The Parasitic Weaverbirds* (1960); and *Host Relations of the Parasitic Cowbirds* (1963).

For background information *see* ECOLOGIC INTERACTIONS in the McGraw-Hill Encyclopedia of Science and Technology. ∎

FRIEDRICHS, KURT OTTO
★ American mathematician

Born Sept. 28, 1901, Kiel, Germany

During his education at various German universities, Friedrichs's interests were primarily in mathematics, but also in physics and philosophy. His interest in philosophy made him concentrate his work just as much on points of view as on proofs.

Friedrichs's attitude toward mathematics was strongly influenced by mathematicians Hermann Weyl, Richard Courant, and John von Neumann, and by working closely with Hans Lewy and J. J. Stoker. Mainly, Friedrichs worked in the theory of partial differential equations, especially those representing the laws of physics and engineering science. He alternated periods of working on more applied problems with periods of work on problems of a purely mathematical character. *See* COURANT, RICHARD; STOKER, JAMES JOHNSTON; VON NEUMANN, JOHN.

Friedrichs's early work was primarily concerned with existence theorems. During this period he collaborated with Lewy and Courant by using finite differences for the existence theory of hyperbolic equations of the first order. One of the points that emerged is that one cannot replace a hyperbolic-differential equation by a difference equation in an arbitrary manner and expect that the solutions of the latter will approach those of the first. The ratio of the time difference to the space difference must be sufficiently small. However, the ability to compute at that time was so limited that it was not until the advent of the modern computer that this observation (made by Lewy) came to have much more practical importance than the existence theorems.

In 1929 von Neumann had introduced the modern geometric theory of operators in Hilbert space. Friedrichs was the first to apply it to partial differential operators. He showed how to solve the initial-value problem for linear hyperbolic equations by using energy integrals. He later showed how to apply this method to elliptic equations. In this work Lebesgue theory played no role; the underlying Hilbert spaces were defined by completion of spaces of smooth functions. Operators were defined by completion (strong extension) or by adjointness (weak extension); the identity of these two extensions is one of the fundamental results, proved with the aid of so-called mollifiers. These methods are rather simple and direct; they preceded the development of the theory of distributions of Laurent Schwartz as applied to partial differential equations.

Following Rellich's discovery that, for an operator with only a discrete spectrum, the spectrum is moved smoothly by specified smooth perturbations, Friedrichs investigated the same problem for an operator with continuous spectrum. He found that, again under appropriate conditions, the spectrum is unchanged. But it is also possible for the spectrum to change drastically. The theory of these perturbations lies behind the theory of scattering, as Friedrichs showed in 1948. Later the pair of operators he had introduced turned out to be identical with the forward- and backward-wave operators which formed the basis for subsequent development.

Early in 1937 Friedrichs resigned his professorship in the Institute of Technology in Brunswick and emigrated to the United States since, for political and personal reasons, he found it intolerable to remain in Germany.

Perhaps the most significant work in the years after 1937 was on a class of equations that Friedrichs introduced and called symmetric hyperbolic linear differential equations. These are systems of first order; the symmetry involved is that of the matrix of the coefficients of the differentiated terms. Friedrichs proved the existence of the solution of the initial-value problem. Again, the treatment was based on general operator theory and again used mollifiers. The equations have two striking properties: the eigenvectors associated with the matrix need not be distinct, and the initial data need not have infinitely many derivatives but only a finite number. It is this class of equations to which essentially all nondegenerate equations of motion can be reduced. Later he extended this theory to accretive equations, in which it is irrelevant whether the systems are elliptic or hyperbolic. In a note written in 1970, with P. D. Lax, and in a later paper, Friedrichs showed that general systems of conservation equations which possess a convex extension can be reduced to symmetric hyperbolic systems.

In the field of elasticity, his most significant work, done with Stoker, was on the boundary problem of the buckled plate with large deflections. This nonlinear problem concerned a circular plate subject to uniform compressive forces acting on the edge. If these forces are increased beyond a certain value, the plate will buckle. The problem was to investigate what happens to the plate when the compressive forces are increased further. This was done by hand-computing and took many months. One surprising feature was that eventually the radial stress at and near the center of the plates becomes a tensile one. This computational result was verified by asymptotic analysis and, some years later, even experimentally.

Friedrichs published additional papers connected with plate theory. One of them, of a purely mathematical character, concerns Korn's inequality, which is needed in the theory of elastic plates with free boundaries. In another paper the peculiar boundary conditions one may impose at the edge of a plate with a free boundary were derived by an asymptotic analysis, with R. F. Dressler.

During World War II, Friedrichs resumed his interest in fluid dynamics, begun in Aachen in 1927, where he had been assistant to Theodore von Kármán. He concentrated on problems of flow past airfoils, shock waves, and combustion. Although he made many contributions to theory in these areas, the most important achievement was the book *Supersonic Flow and Shock Waves*, written with Courant (1947), on compressible fluid flow and shock waves. Their object was to make accessible the extremely complicated physical phenomena involved and to establish a firmer mathematical footing. The book is still widely used by mathematically minded aerodynamicists. He also analyzed the mathematical aspects of deflagrations and detonations. He showed that a boundary-layer type of argument, which he had introduced earlier in airfoil theory, would explain why certain types of detonations (weak) and deflagrations (strong) would not occur. Later he showed that the Lundquist equations which govern magnetofluid dynamics could be written as a symmetric hyperbolic system (1954) and, still later, that the same was true in the relativistic case. *See* VON KÁRMÁN, THEODORE.

Since his early years in Göttingen Friedrichs retained an active interest in quantum mechanics. In a series of five papers on quantum theory of fields he attempted to put this theory on a sound mathematical basis and made some particular observations, among them that there are different, nonequivalent, realizations of the basic field operators. These five papers reappeared in the book *Mathematical Aspects of the Quantum Theory of Fields* (1953). A somewhat different approach to this theory is presented in the book *Perturbation of Spectra in Hilbert Space* (1965; 2d ed. 1967). In 1979 in the paper "On the Notion of State in Quantum Mechanics," he showed that the future values of unobserved observables are determined in terms of their unobserved initial values, thus in some sense validating causality.

Friedrichs attended a realgymnasium in Düsseldorf from 1911 to 1920. He then became a student at various universities, in particular the University of Göttingen, where he received the Ph.D. in 1925. His scientific career in Germany was spent at Göttingen (1925–27), Aachen (1927–29), and Brunswick (1930–37). In 1937 he joined the faculty of New York University, beginning as visiting professor and later serving as Distinguished Professor. During the year 1966–67 he was director of the Courant Institute of New York University. In 1974 he became professor emeritus. In 1954 Friedrichs gave the Josiah Willard Gibbs Lecture of the American Mathematical Society, "Asymptotic Phenomena in Mathematical Physics." He was elected a member of the U.S. National Academy of Sciences (1959) and received its Applied Mathematics and Numerical Analysis Award (1972). He was also elected a fellow of the American Academy of Arts and Sciences (1958), and a corresponding member of the academies of Göttingen, Braunschweig, and Munich. He received honorary doctorates at the Technische Hochschule at Aachen (1970) and at Uppsala University (1977). In 1977 he was awarded the National Medal of Science in Washington, D.C.

For background information *see* DIF-FERENTIAL EQUATION; ELASTICITY; FLUID DYNAMICS; OPERATOR THEORY; SHOCK WAVE in the McGraw-Hill Encyclopedia of Science and Technology. ∎

FRISCH, KARL VON
★ German biologist

Born Nov. 20, 1886, Vienna, Austria

In his early work Frisch concentrated largely on comparative physiology, which had just begun to flourish. Later he became a co-originator of modern behavioral research. Both fields are often closely linked in his publications.

Frisch's doctoral thesis (Vienna, 1910) explained the influence of the sympathetic nerve ganglia during color changes in fish and traced the course of the nerve strands involved in the process. In his subsequent work, he studied the ability of fish to adapt not only to the relative brightness but also to the color of the ground. The prevailing opinion at the

time was that fish and all other invertebrates are totally color-blind. Frisch, through his experiments, disproved this theory. He demonstrated that this adaptability to the bottom is determined by its color quality.

That insects should be totally color-blind was improbable from a biological viewpoint because the colors of flowers only make sense as signals to blossom-seeking insects. Frisch was able to prove color awareness in honeybees. After conditioning them to a particular color by giving them sugar water, they succeeded in finding this same color (without food) in the midst of a chessboardlike arrangement of different shades of gray. Through conditioning them to flower scents and other odors, he was able to clarify the effectiveness of the sense of smell and its many-sided biological significance in the life of the honeybee.

Frisch's methods of conditioning proved to be successful also with other animals. Many researchers considered fish to be deaf because they did not react to sounds and because their inner ear does not have a cochlea. Frisch was able to produce clear reactions when he made the sound signal biologically significant by preceding it with a food offering. In many species of fish a good ability to distinguish between different tone levels and an acute sense of hearing could be demonstrated. Through operations on the ears of fish, he located the area of sound perception and thus proved genuine hearing capability.

By chance, Frisch discovered a biologically significant phenomenon in fish: The slightest injury to their skin—for example, as inflicted by the teeth of a predatory fish—causes certain glands to release an alarm substance which sends other members of the species as well as those of related species into quick flight and induces continued and heightened vigilance.

During the experiments of conditioning bees to colors and scents, feeding was interrupted periodically in order to avoid an overcrowding of the feeder by the insects. It was remarkable how quickly the swarm returned when food was offered again. This led Frisch to investigating communication among bees. A suitable test hive and a method of color-coding individual insects brought about the discovery of their dance language. Bees which have found a source of food in the vicinity of the hive communicate this to others by means of a circular dance on the surface of the honeycomb. The scent residue on the

body of the dancer tells the others clearly what type of blossom they have to look for in their food gathering. The liveliness and duration of the dance indicate the quantity and sweetness of the nectar. In the case of more distant food sources, the waggle dance also communicates the location of the goal. Its distance is expressed symbolically by the duration of the linear part of the dance figure: the duration increases proportionately with the increase in distance to the goal, and the dance phase is sharply accented by a waggling of the tail and a simultaneous humming sound.

The direction of the goal is indicated on a horizontal dance surface (such as the landing board of the hive) by a tail-waggling run whose direction maintains the same relationship to the angle of the sun as prevailed earlier during the searching bee's flight to the food source. Inside the dark hive and on a vertical honeycomb surface, the angle of the sun is transposed by the dancer into the angle to gravity, whereby the direction toward the top of the honeycomb takes the place of the direction toward the sun. When leaving the hive, the other bees transpose the gravity angle back to the angle to the sun. On horizontal honeycombs the dances are disoriented when the bees cannot see the sky. They are immediately corrected as soon as the dancers see the sun or even just a piece of blue sky. This led Frisch to the discovery that bees are able to perceive the polarization of the light of the blue sky whose angle of oscillation has a fixed relationship to the position of the sun. It turned out that this ability to determine the position of the sun is quite common among arthropods and is of the greatest importance to their spatial orientation. The analysis of the direction of the light-wave oscillation is carried out by a microstructure inside certain sensory cells within the eye. The precise mechanism of this process is still not entirely understood.

Frisch conditioned a group of bees to a food source which was located in a certain direction. He then moved the hive to a completely different and, to the bees, unknown surrounding. They still sought the food source in the same direction to which they had been conditioned. The bees were able to orient themselves by the position of the sun because of their extraordinary sense of time and their awareness of the daily course of the sun.

Frisch comes from a Viennese family of

scientists and physicians. He studied medicine for several semesters, then turned to zoology in Vienna and in Munich, where he became assistant to Richard Hertwig at the Zoological Institute in 1910. In 1921 he was appointed full professor and director of the Zoological Institute of the University of Rostock, moved to Breslau in 1923, and back to Munich in 1925 as successor to Hertwig. There, with the help of the Rockefeller Foundation, he built the new Zoological Institute in 1932. During World War II it suffered almost complete destruction. In 1946 Frisch was called to Graz (Austria) but he returned to Munich in 1950, where the institute meanwhile had been rebuilt. He became professor emeritus in 1958 but continued experimental research at the institute for several years. Frisch received honorary doctorates from the Technical University of Zurich and the universities of Bern, Graz, Tübingen, Rostock, and Harvard. He became a member and honorary member of numerous academic and scientific societies. He was awarded the Order "Pour le Mérite" for Arts and Sciences, the Kalinga Prize, the Balzan Prize for Biology, the Nobel Prize for medicine or physiology in 1973, and many more distinctions.

In his books Frisch tried to be intelligible to the layman and to representatives from other scientific disciplines alike. They include *Aus dem Leben der Bienen* (The Life of the Bee), 1927, 9th ed. 1977; *The Dancing Bees,* 1954; *Du und das Leben* (You and Life), 1936, 19th ed. 1974; *Bees,* 1950, 2d ed. 1971; *Erinnerungen eines Biologen,* 1957, 3d ed. 1973 (transl. as *A Biologist Remembers,* 1967); *Tanzsprache und Orientierung der Bienen,* 1965 (transl. as *The Dance Language and Orientation of Bees,* 1967); *Tiere als Baumeister,* 1974 (transl. as *Animal Architecture,* 1974); and approximately 120 papers.

For background information *see* BEE; SOCIAL INSECTS in the McGraw-Hill Encyclopedia of Science and Technology. ∎

FRUTON, JOSEPH STEWART

★ American biochemist

***Born** May 14, 1912, Czestochowa, Poland*

Fruton's principal research activities were on the chemistry of amino acids and peptides, the chemical mechanisms in the catalytic action of proteolytic enzymes, and the enzymic synthesis of peptide bonds. During World War II he worked on the chemistry of war gases, notably mustard gas and the nitrogen mustards.

On receiving his Ph.D. in 1934, Fruton joined the laboratory of Max Bergmann at the Rockefeller Institute and undertook the study of the specificity of enzymes that cleave proteins to small fragments. The best-known enzyme of this class is pepsin, which was obtained in crystalline form by J. H. Northrop in 1930; a few years later Northrop's colleague M. Kunitz crystallized two other digestive proteinases, trypsin and chymotrypsin. At that time some biochemists believed that enzymes such as pepsin effect a physical deaggregation of small peptides thought to be associated by noncovalent bonds to form macromolecular proteins. In beginning the study of pepsin, trypsin, and chymotrypsin, Fruton assumed that this view was incorrect, and that these enzymes were peptidases, that is, they catalyze the hydrolysis of peptide bonds between the amino acid units of peptide chains. He further assumed that the action of a given proteinase on a peptide bond depends on the specific nature of the amino acid units joined by that bond. As there are about 20 different kinds of amino acid units in protein chains, the choice of the units preferred by an enzyme such as pepsin was uncertain. *See* NORTHROP, JOHN HOWARD.

Fruton decided to be guided by the re-

sults of experiments in which each enzyme was allowed to act on a series of proteins of widely different amino acid composition. From the relative extent of fragmentation, he formulated the working hypothesis that pepsin and chymotrypsin preferentially cleave bonds involving aromatic amino acids (phenylalanine, tyrosine), and that trypsin prefers to act at bonds involving basic amino acids (arginine, lysine). The hypothesis was tested during 1937–39 by synthesizing appropriate small peptides of known structure and by subjecting them to the action of crystalline pepsin, trypsin, and chymotrypsin. In large part, the working hypothesis was fruitful, and synthetic substrates became available with chemical structures that could be varied systematically, thus permitting a start toward the definition of the specificity of these proteinases. This approach was actively continued after World War II by Fruton and in several other laboratories, notably those of H. Neurath and of C. Niemann. Furthermore, during the postwar period the knowledge of the specificity of the proteinases, in particular that of trypsin, proved to be valuable for the controlled degradation of proteins in the determination of the sequence of the amino acid units in the peptide chains of proteins. *See* NEURATH, HANS.

The success in finding synthetic substrates for the crystalline digestive proteinases led Fruton to initiate studies during 1938–41 on the specificity of other protein-cleaving enzymes, especially those found in animal tissues. The use of suitable peptide substrates permitted the differentiation, purification, and characterization of individual components of the multienzyme complex which includes the intracellular proteolytic enzymes of animal tissues. In addition, the application of this approach to the specificity and mode of action of several plant proteinases (papain, ficin) served as the starting point for later fruitful investigations, especially by E. L. Smith.

During 1949–52 Fruton showed that several proteolytic enzymes catalyze attack of a sensitive bond not only by water, to cause hydrolysis, but also by the amino group of a suitable amino acid derivative to form a new peptide bond. Such transfer reactions, termed transpeptidation or transamidation reactions, are effected by most members of this class of enzymes; exceptional efficiency in this regard is exhibited, however, by some enzymes (for example, dipeptidyl transferase) present in animal tissues characterized by active protein biosynthesis. Fruton's later work included the study of the polymerization by such enzymes of amino acid units to form well-defined peptides. It subsequently became clear that transpeptidation plays an important role in a variety of physiological processes, such as the intracellular synthesis of proteins and blood coagulation. The demonstration that proteinases, such as chymotrypsin or papain, catalyze transpeptidation reactions also focused attention on the chemical mechanism of catalysis by these and related enzymes, and led to the hypothesis that an acyl-enzyme intermediate is involved in the hydrolytic cleavage of suitable substrates. This hypothesis received extensive support, and was greatly extended through the studies of numerous workers, notably J. M. Sturtevant and M. L. Bender.

During the 1960s Fruton gave renewed attention to the chemical mechanism of pepsin catalysis through the development of new synthetic substrates for this enzyme, the study of the kinetics of pepsin action, and the selective chemical modification of pepsin by diazo compounds. These studies led to significant progress in the elucidation of the intimate mechanism of pepsin action, and also to the elaboration of the general concept of the secondary specificity of enzymes that act on polymeric substrates. Thus, in additon to the primary specificity of proteinases, discovered during the 1930s, the secondary specificity is an expression of enzyme-substrate interactions at a distance from the site of catalytic attack on a sensitive bond. Because these secondary interactions, in many cases, caused large enhancements in catalytic efficiency, without extensive apparent change in the tightness of substrate binding, Fruton proposed that the active site of pepsin is a flexible structure. At the time this hypothesis was offered, it was widely believed on the basis of x-ray crystallographic studies of enzymes that their active sites are relatively rigid, but subsequent work in several laboratories showed this view to be incorrect. In his own work on the flexibility of active sites, Fruton used fluorescence methods. Specific peptide substrates were labeled with groups whose fluorescence changes markedly with alterations in their environment, and the course of binding of substrate to enzyme and of substrate cleavage was followed spectrophotometrically by fast kinetic (stopped-flow) techniques. Subsequently, Fruton extended this approach to demonstrate the flexibility of the active sites of other proteinases (papain, thermolysin).

From the beginning, Fruton's work depended heavily on the laboratory synthesis of peptides of known structure and the use of these compounds as models for the study of the behavior of the more complex proteins. For this reason the chemistry of amino acids and peptides received continuous attention, and considerable effort was devoted to the improvement of the art of peptide synthesis. In particular, research was conducted from time to time on the synthesis of peptides presenting special problems encountered with certain amino acids, such as serine, methionine, and tryptophan.

From his student days, Fruton had been interested in the history of science, and in the late 1960s he began to devote much effort to the study of the emergence, after 1800, of biochemistry from the interplay of chemistry and biology. This led to his book *Molecules and Life* (1972), for which he received in 1973 the Pfizer Award of the History of Science Society, and for which he was designated Sarton Lecturer in 1976.

Fruton received his B.A. in 1931 and his Ph.D. in biochemistry under H. T. Clarke in 1934 at Columbia University. He was on the staff of the Rockefeller Institute for Medical Research from 1934 to 1945, when he moved to Yale University as associate professor of physiological chemistry. He was professor of biochemistry from 1950 to 1957, Eugene Higgins Professor of Biochemistry from 1957, head of the department of biochemistry from 1951 to 1967, and director of the Division of Science from 1959 to 1962. In 1944 he received the Lilly Award in Biological Chemistry of the American Chemical Society. He was elected to the National Academy of Sciences in 1952 and to the American Philosophical Society in 1967. The Rockefeller University conferred upon him an honarary D.Sc. in 1976.

In addition to the book mentioned, Fruton wrote *General Biochemistry,* with S. Simmonds (1953; 2d ed. 1958).

For background information *see* AMINO ACID; ENZYME; PROTEIN in the McGraw-Hill Encyclopedia of Science and Technology. ∎

FUBINI, SERGIO PIERO
★ Italian theoretical physicist

Born Dec. 31, 1928, Turin, Italy

Up to about 1961, Fubini made a number of contributions to the field theory of strong interactions, to dispersion relations, and to the theory of pion photoproduction and electroproduction phenomena. He introduced, in collaboration with M. Cini, an important method of approximating scattering amplitudes in the Mandelstam representation. This became an important tool for the study of pion-nucleon scattering. At the same time, the application of variational methods to the theory of the scattering matrix led Cini and him to introduce the Padé approximation technique in problems of field theory.

It was in 1961 that Fubini, in collaboration with D. Amati and A. Stanghellini, carried out his work on the multiperipheral model and on related questions concerning Regge poles and Regge cuts. The importance of the multiperipheral model is easily measured by the role which it has played since the late 1960s not only as one of the most interesting attempts at describing general inelastic collisions, but also as a sort of theoretical laboratory for investigating a large number of purely theoretical problems. The connections of the model with the vast domain of Regge theory (including, in the model, the existence of cuts in addition to poles in the angular momentum plane) has turned out to have many far-reaching consequences. Studies of the multiperipheral problem have enabled physicists to determine for the first time the scaling properties of strong interaction amplitudes. In particular, such studies have shown that the natural scale for soft hadronic processes is related to the logarithm of the center-of-mass energy.

Fubini also played an important part in the formulation and investigation of current algebra. He contributed much to this general method of strong interaction theory and introduced, together with G. Furlan, an important technical tool, the so-called infinite momentum frame. Two important results are the Fubini-Furlan-Rossetti sum rule for photoproduction of pions and the general Dashen–Gell-Mann–Fubini sum rule relating the scattering amplitude to electromagnetic and weak form factors.

Fubini and his collaborators opened yet another line of research in strong interaction theory, based on the concept that certain dispersion relations are superconvergent (that is, have a very rapid convergence of the dispersion integrals), a fact which implies strong constraints on physical parameters. This line of work introduced theoreticians into the wide field of finite-energy sum rules relating low-energy and high-energy parameters. Very rapidly this method became the basis of numerous investigations by many people. It is now a completely classical technique of strong interaction physics.

Another major contribution made by Fubini concerns the general theory of dual-resonance models (or generalized Veneziano models). In well-known papers written with G. Veneziano, he studied the factorization properties of such models and established the high multiplicity of states which they imply. In addition, he introduced an appropriate operator formalism which soon became a fundamental tool in all investigations on dual-resonance models.

Later work concerned Yang-Mills theory, which plays a central role in the theory of strong interactions. The meron solution (a classical solution of the equations of chromodynamics) obtained in collaboration with V. De Alfaro and Furlan seems to offer hope of understanding the fundamental problem of quark confinement.

Fubini received his *laurea in fisica* from the University of Turin in 1950. From 1950 to 1952 he was instructor at the Politecnico di Torino and from 1952 to

1957 assistant professor at the University of Turin. He was a senior physicist in the theory division of the European Commission for Nuclear Research (CERN) from 1957 until 1965. Fubini was professor of physics at the University of Padua from 1960 until 1962, when he was appointed professor of physics at the University of Turin. During 1968–73 he was professor of physics at the Massachusetts Institute of Technology. He returned to CERN in 1973 and became a member of its directorate (in charge of theoretical physics) in 1974. Fubini received the Dannie Heineman Prize for Mathematical Physics from the American Physical Society in 1967. He was a fellow of the American Academy of Arts and Sciences (1969).

Fubini wrote *Currents in Hadron Physics*, with V. De Alfaro, G. Furlan, and C. Rossetti (1973).

For background information *see* CURRENT ALGEBRA; DISPERSION RELATIONS (ELEMENTARY PARTICLE); ELEMENTARY PARTICLE; REGGE POLE in the McGraw-Hill Encyclopedia of Science and Technology. ∎

FULLER, DUDLEY DEAN
★ American educator and engineer

Born Feb. 8, 1913, Woodhaven, NY, U.S.A.

Active in research, teaching, and consulting, Fuller evolved and developed new concepts concerned with the application of fluid mechanics to the lubrication of a broad spectrum of fluid-film bearings in machines and machine components.

In 1947 Fuller published the first articles dealing with an externally pressurized concept for establishing fluid films between contacting bearing surfaces, which he named hydrostatic lubrication. This designation was subsequently used worldwide.

The hydrostatic bearing can be used to provide friction approaching zero, film stiffness approaching infinity, and almost any reasonable film thickness, and it can also introduce controlled damping into the system.

In the late 1950s Fuller carried out early research in the field of gas lubrication of bearings and contributed to the demonstration of the many special benefits that can accrue from the use of gas. One of these benefits was the elimination of conventional lubricants that could contaminate the process system or the chemical environment. Gas lubricants also provide a high-temperature capability far exceeding that of other lubricants or bearings. Friction can also be so low as to be negligible.

After 1957 Fuller was active in coordinating research in gas-bearing lubrication through quarterly meetings sponsored by the Office of Naval Research. The attendance at these meetings was international in scope and remained an ongoing activity, highly successful in coordinating widespread research, development, and design activity in this field. In 1967, the tenth anniversary of the program, Fuller received a special citation from the Office of Naval Research for his efforts.

In the late 1960s Fuller initiated research in the field of compliant-surface, fluid-film bearings, both hydrostatic and hydrodynamic. The concept was widely applied and was developed by many organizations and research laboratories. Many advantages were derived from the use of these bearings. Machining tolerances were greatly reduced in comparison with those required for rigid-surface bearings. Indeed, large-diameter bearings (measured in feet) became practical, whereas before the use of these bearings, they were not. Side flow is reduced with compliant-surface bearings, and consequently the feed rate of lubricant can be dramatically reduced with no loss in performance; indeed, these bearings permit operation at speeds much below those of rigid-surface fluid-film bearings while maintaining separation of the bearing surfaces, thus avoiding touching, wear, abrasion, and noise.

Fuller attended the City College of New York (B.M.E., 1941) and Columbia University (M.S., 1946); he taught at Columbia from 1943 onward. He was the founder and first president (1946–47) of the New York Section of the American Society of Lubrication Engineers (ASLE). In 1957 he became principal investigator of the Gas Bearing Research Program at the Franklin Institute. He was director of the Cooperative Journal Bearing Research Project of the ASLE, which made an extensive literature survey on journal bearing lubrication producing finally a report (*Journal Bearings*, 1958) on journal bearing design based on the most important references. In 1959 Fuller chaired the First International Gas Bearing Symposium in Washington, D.C. He received a number of awards for work in his field, including the Mayo D. Hersey Award in Tribology from the American Society of Mechanical Engineers (1971) and the Tribology Gold Medal from the International Tribology Council, Institution of Mechanical Engineers, (1978). He was appointed Stevens Professor of Mechanical Engineering at Columbia University (1972) and received the Great Teacher Award from the Society of Older Graduates at Columbia (1977).

Fuller was the author of *Theory and Practice of Lubrication for Engineers* (1956), available in four languages.

For background information *see* BEARING, ANTIFRICTION; LUBRICATION in the McGraw-Hill Encyclopedia of Science and Technology. ■

FUOSS, RAYMOND MATTHEW
★ American chemist

Born Sept. 28, 1905, Bellwood, PA, U.S.A.

The response evoked by application of an electric field to a chemical system depends on the molecular structure of the system; therefore, the field serves as a research probe for exploring the system. Electrolytic solutions contain ions, which are atoms or molecules carrying electrostatic charges; an electric field superposes a component of motion in the field direction on the thermal motion of the ions; this component is measured as an electrical conductance. The magnitude of the conductance depends on the concentration of ions, on their charges, and on their mobilities. Polar dielectrics contain no free charges, but their molecules are electrically asymmetric and experience a torque in an electric field; the resulting orientation superposed on the thermal motion is measured as a dielectric constant (and a dielectric loss in the dispersion range of frequency). Both the translatory motion of ions and the rotatory motion of dipoles depend on the structure of solute and solvent molecules and on their mutual interactions. Experimental determination of electrical properties and their theoretical interpretation in terms of molecular parameters form the general research field in which Fuoss was active from 1930 on. The systems studied included solutions of electrolytes in solvents ranging from nonpolar to highly polar, polymers (especially polar compounds), and polyelectrolytes.

When Fuoss began investigation of dilute solutions at Brown University with C. A. Kraus in 1930, the conductance of aqueous solutions had been studied since the time of Michael Faraday and Friedrich Kohlrausch; the pattern for strong electrolytes was familiar, and the limiting behavior for extremely dilute solutions was quantitatively predictable by the Debye-Hückel-Onsager theory. Weak electrolytes, on the other hand, conformed fairly well to the behavior predicted by the Ar-

rhenius theory of incomplete dissociation. Some information was available for nonaqueous systems, especially work by Kraus on solutions in liquid ammonia and by Paul Walden on a variety of organic solvents. However, no overall pattern for solvents in general was discernible. Salts that were typical strong electrolytes in water showed conductance curves in ammonia that closely resembled those for moderately weak electrolytes in water. In the organic solvents, both minima and maxima in the conductance curves had been observed, in contrast to the uniform curves characteristic of most aqueous solutions. The general impression was that the shape of the conductance curve was something quite specific for a given solute-solvent combination. By using a mixture of polar and nonpolar solvents, such as water with dioxane or benzene with ethylene chloride, Fuoss was able to trace the continuous transition from the water pattern to the benzene pattern. Theoretical analysis showed that the controlling parameter is the dielectric constant of the solvent. In solvents of high dielectric constant, the curves are concave-up and approach linearity in square root of concentration at low concentrations. As the dielectric constant is decreased, electrostatic attraction stabilizes pairs of oppositely charged ions, as N. Bjerrum suggested in 1926 for multivalent ions in water, and the Arrhenius-type curve becomes dominant. At still lower dielectric constants, clusters containing three, four, and more ions become stable; the triple ions account for the appearance of the minima in the conductance curves, and the shift in the location of the minimum with dielectric constant is given a satisfactory theoretical explanation. In 1935 Fuoss received the American Chemical Society Award "in recognition of his important research contributions which, for the first time, provide a comprehensive theory of electrolytic solutions applicable to all solvent media and to all electrolytes."

Also in 1935 an investigation of the electrical properties of polar polymers was started at the research laboratory of the General Electric Company in Schenectady. At that time a certain amount of engineering data was available: It was known that some plastics and elastomers had low dielectric constants, and others had relatively high values; some showed negligible electrical losses, and others were very lossy. The electrical properties were known to be sensitive to temperature and to change with frequency, but no comprehensive correlations between electrical properties and structure were known. Measured values varied from sample to sample. Therefore, it was necessary to develop research methods that would give reproducible results so that one could say that a given composition of matter would have a certain dielectric constant and loss factor at a given temperature and frequency. Elimination of surface effects and control of ionic content were the key problems. Once these problems were solved, it became possible to collect meaningful data on the electrical properties of various plasticizer-polymer compositions. Theoretical analysis of the results showed that the dielectric response of polar polymers was describable in terms of a distribution of relaxation times corresponding to the response of segments of different lengths in the polymer chain. Whether the dipole was attached directly to the chain, as in polyvinyl chloride, or coupled flexibly, as in polyvinyl chloroacetate, for example, had a predictable effect on dielectric relaxation. The shift of the dispersion region was correlated theoretically with temperature and plasticizer content. Location of the dispersion region was found to be controlled not only by plasticizer concentration but also by the shape and size of the plasticizer molecule. About 65 research papers on polar polymers and on electrolytic solutions had been published when World War II interrupted fundamental research.

In 1945 Fucoss was invited to Yale as Sterling Professor of Chemistry, and there continued research on the properties of electrochemical systems. Electrolytes and polymers were combined into a new type of synthetic molecule, the polyelectrolyte. A typical example is quaternized polyvinyl pyridine, a normal random-coil polymer, which in solution exhibits all the familiar properties of this class of compounds. On addition of alkyl halide, the pyridine nitrogens are converted to positively charged ions, whereas the halogen atom of the alkyl halide becomes a halide ion. The product differs in one fundamental way from a quaternary salt of low molecular weight, such as quaternized monomeric pyridine: the cationic sites are covalently bonded to the polymeric chain and can never diffuse apart on dilution as can the ions of ordinary salts. This restriction has a pro-

found effect on the electrical properties of solutions of the polyelectrolyte; furthermore, the presence of the fixed charges on the polymer chain completely modifies the polymeric properties. The reduced viscosity increases on dilution, as does the ratio of osmotic pressure to concentration.

For neutral polymers the effect is just the opposite. Light scattering is markedly reduced by quaternization. The solutions behave conductimetrically like weak electrolytes (although monomeric quaternary salts are typical strong electrolytes) and show a remarkably large Wien effect (increase of conductance with field strength). All of the unusual properties can be masked by the addition of an excess of simple electrolyte. These effects can be explained in terms of a molecular model in which mobile counter ions are distributed both to the volume of solvent between polymer molecules and to the volume of the polymer coils. With increasing dilution, more counter ions diffuse away from the polymer; the polymer then expands because of increased electrostatic repulsion between uncompensated charges on the coil. The expansion in turn produces the higher viscosity. The increase in osmotic pressure ratio on dilution is due to dissociation of counter ions from the polyelectrolyte, which tends toward a cylindrical structure as the solution is diluted. Addition of simple electrolyte provides an excess of charges of both signs that screen the counter ions and the polymeric ions. Analogs of naturally occurring biochemical substances were synthesized by Fuoss; copolymers of acrylic acid and basic amine monomers gave polyelectrolytes which showed a characteristic isoelectric point.

The interaction of ions with each other and with solvent molecules was also a continuing field of interest for Fuoss. Studies of the conductance of a wide variety of electrolytes in mixtures of polar and nonpolar solvents led to a series of theoretical papers published between 1953 and 1978. The earlier theories were based on the primitive model proposed by P. J. W. Debye and E. Hückel in 1923: rigid charged spheres of diameter a in a continuum which is described electrostatically by the dielectric constant of the solvent, and hydrodynamically by its viscosity. Ions which are large compared with solvent molecules were adequately represented by this model: the logarithm of the association constant was found to be a linear function of the reciprocal of the dielectric constant, and the values of a de-

rived from the slope of the log $K-1/D$ plots agreed with the values calculated from the limiting conductance by the Stokes equation. In solvents of high dielectric constant, the conductance curves usually lie above the limiting target. By integration of the 1932 Onsager-Fuoss equation with boundary conditions appropriate to the primitive model, this behavior was shown to be the consequence of the finite size of the ions. The theory (1953) gave a theoretical explanation of conductance data for the alkali halides in dioxane-water mixtures up to concentrations of the order of 0.01 normal in water.

This theoretical work was completed just before electronic computers became available. Consequently, mathematical approximations had to be made in order to simplify the equations to forms which could be handled by a human computer. In 1967 a number of these approximations were dropped, and the explicit functions resulting from the integration were programmed for machine calculation. The result was a theory of conductance of symmetrical electrolytes which reproduced observed data up to about 0.1 normal in water. This is the upper limit of concentrations to which the model on which the theory was based could be expected to be valid (long-range interactions between unpaired ions and short-range pairwise interactions). At higher concentrations, interaction between ion pairs and single ions (three-ion clusters) begin to contribute significantly to the conductance function.

Further experimental work on simple electrolytes whose ions were comparable in volume to the volume of the solvent molecules showed that the primitive model was an oversimplification, adequate only for large ions as a limiting case (much as the point-mass model is adequate for the derivation of the limiting equation of state $pV=RT$ for gases at low pressure). For salts like potassium iodide in mixed solvents, the log $K-1/D$ plots were curved instead of linear. For the primitive model, the association constant calculated for the Coulomb interaction between two oppositely charged spheres in a dielectric continuum was of the form $K=F(a,D)$; that is, for a given electrolyte (a fixed), the same value of K should be found in chemically different solvents which have the same dielectric constant. Many violations of this isodielectric rule were found, giving experimental proof that the primitive model was insufficiently realistic as a starting point for a general theory of conductance. A more realistic model, which would consider other short-range interionic effects in addition to those resulting from electrostatic attraction and hard-core repulsion, as well as short-range ion-solvent interactions (dielectric saturation, particulate structure, and so on), was needed. A diffusion-controlled equilibrium between unpaired and paired ions was postulated, paired ions being defined as those for which the center-to-center distance is less than R, the diameter of the Gurney cosphere. Classical continuum theory could then be used to compute the long-range interaction between unpaired ions. Paired ions were divided into two categories: those which had one or more solvent molecules between them, and those which had one ion of opposite charge as a nearest neighbor. The latter act like electrical dipoles, contributing only to charging current, not to transport current. A second equilibrium between solvent-separated pairs and contact pairs was also postulated, this equilibrium controlled by short-range forces of attraction and repulsion. Using this model, Fuoss derived a conductance function which reproduced experimental observations; furthermore, the pairing constant was found to depend on dielectric constant, on the distance R, and on E_s, the difference in energy between a pair of ions at the distance R and at contact. Since both R and E_s are system-specific parameters, they are in general different for different solvents. Consequently, the 1978 theory does not imply the isodielectric rule or the linearity of log $K-1/D$ plots; it is therefore a general theory for the conductance of symmetrical electrolytes.

After graduating from Harvard (Sc.B., 1925), Fuoss spent an academic year at the University of Munich, where he worked with Heinrich Wieland, Kasimir Fajans, and Erich Lange. After several years as chemical consultant, he entered the graduate school of Brown University in 1930 and received the Ph.D. in 1932. He was appointed research instructor at Brown in 1932 and later assistant professor for research. On leave of absence as International Research fellow in 1933–34, he worked with Debye in Leipzig and R. H. Fowler in Cambridge. In 1936 he joined the research staff of the General Electric Company, where most of his work on polar polymers was done. In 1945 he was appointed Sterling Professor

of Chemistry at Yale. During leaves from Yale, Fuoss was visiting professor at the University of Alexandria (1951), the Weizmann Institute of Science (1951 and 1961), the Hebrew University (Jerusalem, 1957), the University of Rome (1958 and 1978), the Technical Institute of Ankara (1963), the University of Paris (1965), and the Rockefeller University (1969–74). He became emeritus professor at Yale in 1974. He was elected to the National Academy of Sciences in 1951 and to the American Academy of Arts and Sciences in 1958.

Fuoss published about 270 research papers, most of them on the electrical properties of chemical systems. He wrote *La Conducibilita Elettrolitica,* with F. Accascina (1958).

For background information *see* DIELECTRICS; ELECTROLYTIC CONDUCTANCE; POLYMER PROPERTIES in the McGraw-Hill Encyclopedia of Science and Technology. ∎

FURUKAWA, JUNJI
★ Japanese chemist

Born Dec. 18, 1912, Osaka, Japan

A new chemistry of polymerization was opened by the success of K. Ziegler and G. Natta in isotactic polymerization of α-olefins by catalysts composed of titanium compound and alkyl aluminum compound. In the next step, interest turned to the polymerization of 1,3-diolefin to give the polymer of cis, trans, or 1,2 structure,

and the polymerization of two kinds of monomers to give the copolymer of block or sequentially alternating structure. Furukawa contributed a great deal to elucidating the mechanism of this type of polymerization. *See* NATTA, GIULIO; ZIEGLER, KARL.

By 1956, *cis*-1,4-polyisoprene, that is, the synthetic "natural" rubber, had already been prepared by several investigators using an ordinary Ziegler-Natta catalyst, but *cis*-1,4-polybutadiene had not yet been synthesized. Furukawa and his coworker found excellent catalysts composed of nickel compounds for cis-1,4 polymerization of butadiene, and the method was industrialized in various countries. Elucidation of the mechanism of cis polymerization is not always easy because the mode of polymerization is changeable by the addition of a cocatalyst to give *cis-, trans-,* or 1,2- and sometimes *cis-trans*-1:1-polybutadiene. Furukawa proposed a mechanism involving the intermediate complex linked with not only the polymer terminal but also the double bond of the second unit—the so-called back-biting coordination, which facilitates the cis polymerization. The cocatalyst disturbs the back-biting coordination to give trans and 1,2 polymer. This hypothesis seems to be helpful in exploring new catalysts.

Furukawa achieved the alternating copolymerization of diolefin and olefin by finding the modified transition metal catalyst having the suitable coordination number. Butadiene is in general more easily coordinated bidentately on the catalyst, but this action is prohibited when the catalyst is linked with the butadiene polymer unit forming a π-allylic terminal and leaving an insufficient number of vacant sites. In this way, the sequential regulation in copolymerization became applicable for various diolefins and olefins. The copolymer of butadiene and propylene thus prepared is a useful synthetic rubber, since it is highly alternating and exhibits good orientation of the molecular chain when the rubber is stretched. As a result, it shows excellent tensile properties, just like natural rubber.

Oligomerization is a kind of polymerization yielding exclusively a dimer or trimer of definite structure. Furukawa made contributions to this field. He found that various kinds of butadiene dimers are exclusively produced with nickel catalyst modified by the addition of protic substances of controlled amount and strength. Acid reacts with zero-valent nickel to form a hydridonickel as a reaction intermediate, and its stability modified by acid plays an important role in the determination of the mode of oligomerization. By this concept, the mechanism of oligomerization became more easily understandable.

The regular polymerizations exemplified above are governed by two important factors; one is the effect of the polymer terminal or second terminal unit, and the other is the effect of the catalyst on the polymerization. Accordingly, there are two types of statistics for the regular polymerizations. Furukawa proposed the statistics for the latter case applicable to isotactic polymerizations, where the catalyst is composed of two sites, the *d*-selective site and *l*-selective site, and is referred to as an enantiomorphic catalyst.

For example, the crystalline polymer prepared from *d,l*-propylene oxide by the catalyst prepared from dialkyl zinc and alcohol is an equibinary mixture of *d*- and *l*-polymer capable of being resolved to the optically active polymer antipodes. Asymmetric polymerization of *d,l*-propylene oxides was carried out successfully by the use of an asymmetric catalyst to give an optically active polymer, leaving an optically active antipode monomer. The statistical relation between optical activity and stereoregularity in asymmetric polymerization and enantiomorphic polymerization was elucidated.

Furukawa graduated from Kyoto University in 1936 and was appointed assistant and then assistant professor at that university. He devoted himself to research on synthetic rubber. During the World War II he oversaw manufacture of synthetic rubber from butadiene and methyl vinyl ketone, both of which were prepared from acetylene. After the war he was appointed professor at Kyoto University to teach synthetic chemistry, especially polymer synthesis. In 1976 he retired from Kyoto University and became professor at the Science University of Tokyo and the Aichi Institute of Technology. He was a visiting professor in the United States and Germany. He was elected a member of the Academy of Science in the German Democratic Republic.

For background information *see* ASYMMETRIC SYNTHESIS; COORDINATION CHEMISTRY; STEREOSPECIFIC CATALYST in the McGraw-Hill Encyclopedia of Science and Technology. ∎

FUSON, REYNOLD CLAYTON
★ American organic chemist

Born June 1, 1895, Wakefield, IL, U.S.A.

Reactions of the carbonyl group of aldehydes and ketones generally are hindered by the attached radicals, which may present a problem when the compounds are to be used in synthesis. Fuson had the idea of turning this drawback to advantage by introducing excessive hindrance deliberately to find out what might happen when normal behavior of the carbonyl group is not possible.

Early experiments carried out by him and his students involved aromatic ketones in which the carbonyl group was hedged about by methyl groups in ortho positions of the ring. Mesityl and duryl radicals were found to inhibit or greatly retard most of the reactions typical of carbonyl compounds. Failure of the reactions to proceed was linked with the inability of the carbonyl group to lie in the plane of the aromatic ring of the obstructing radicals. Ortho-disubstituted ketones were prepared by Kadesh, however, in which the carbonyl group must lie in the plane of the ring. The situation is achieved by making the carbonyl group a part of a five- or six-membered ring. Thus, in 4,7-dimethyl-α-indanone (I) and 5,8-dimethyl-α-tetralone (II), the *o*-methylene groups may be supposed to have an effect similar to that of a methyl group. The carbonyl group, constrained to lie in the plane of the bicyclic system, is not hindered. In 6,9-dimethylbenzosuberone (III), on the

other hand, the seven-membered ring is sufficiently flexible to allow the carbonyl group to be twisted out of the plane of the aromatic ring. The behavior of the suberone, unlike that of the indanone and tetralone, is very similar to that of acetomesitylene (Fig. 1).

$$MesC = O \xrightarrow{C_6H_5MgBr} MesC = O \quad -C_6H_5$$

Fig. 1. Reaction of acetomesitylene.

If the carbonyl group of an aryl ketone is sufficiently shackled by its neighbors to be unable to react in the 1,2 manner, the ketone may react as if the electron deficit of the carbonyl carbon atom has been transferred to the ring, that is, the benzene ring may behave as if it has double bonds. This type of reaction was called by its discoverers Kohler and Nygaard "unlocking the benzene ring." Deliberate blocking of the carbonyl group with radicals of the mesityl type made it possible to study the unlocking reaction; *o*-alkylation or *o*-arylation of the benzene ring was accomplished. Phenylation of mesityl phenyl ketone, for example, occurred to the extent of 18 percent (M. D. Armstrong, S. B. Speck).

At this point new life was put into the study by the discovery that certain Grignard reagents, notably benzyl- and *t*-butylmagnesium chloride, are very much more effective in this type of attack than are reagents such as methyl, ethyl, and phenyl. This difference in reactivity was pointed out by Kharasch and Weinhouse, and later led to the discovery that Grignard reagents can be added to fulvenes

(I)

(II)

(III)

(H. A. DeWald). The more powerful reagents differed from the others also in showing a preference for the para position. *sec*-Butylmagnesium bromide, for instance, converted duryl phenyl ketone (Fig. 2) to *p-sec*-butylphenyl duryl ketone in a yield of 63 percent (R. Tull). The addition products are, of course, dihydrobenzenoid compounds, and can be aromatized by admitting air to the reaction vessel before the mixture is worked up.

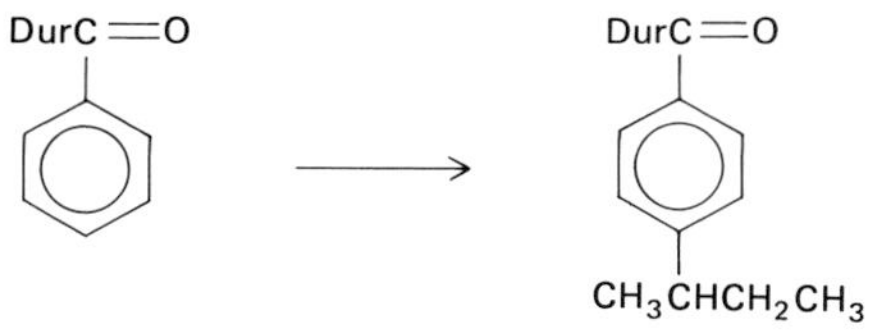

Fig. 2. Reaction of duryl phenyl ketone.

An early example of the use of steric hindrance to interrupt a reaction sequence is the demonstration that the haloform reaction (Fig. 3) is stopped at the trihalomethyl ketone stage. Acetomesitylene and sodium hypobromite, for example, give mesityl tribromomethyl ketone in a yield of 89 percent (J. T. Walker). The base responsible for the cleavage is prevented by the *o*-methyl radicals from reaching the carbonyl group.

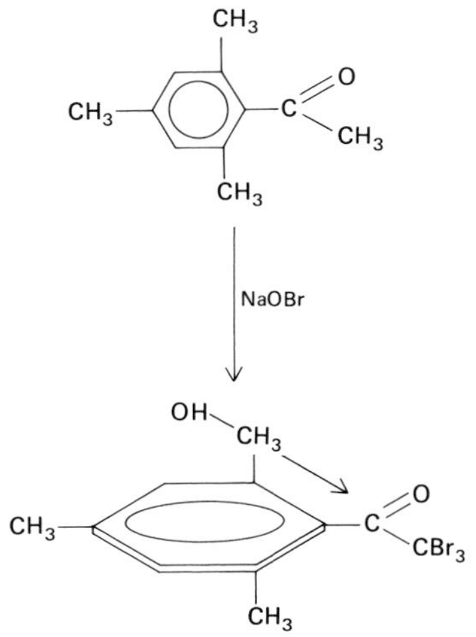

Fig. 3. Haloform reaction.

Another example of the interruption of a reaction sequence was encountered in the synthesis of aldehydes and ketones by way of the corresponding enols (Fig. 4). If

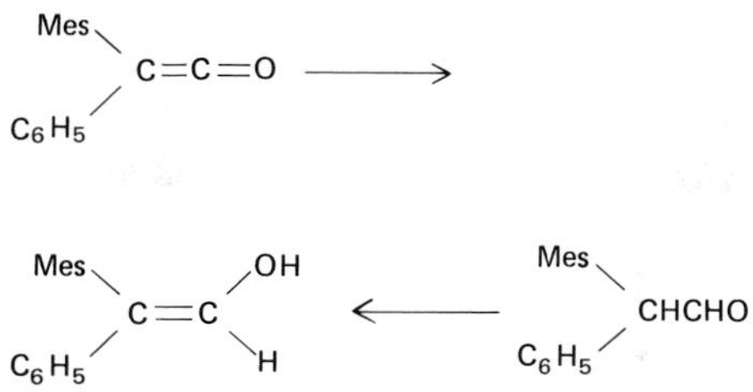

Fig. 4. Enol formation.

the enol is sufficiently engulfed by the surrounding parts, it fails to ketonize. An example is the vinyl alcohol obtained by reduction of mesitylphenylketene. The reduction is accomplished with cyclohexylmagnesium chloride in 80 percent yield (R. E. Foster, W. J. Shenk, Jr., E. W. Maynert). The corresponding aldehyde rearranged to the enol when heated at 150°C or when treated with alkali (T. L. Tan).

Hydrogenation of benzils (Fig. 5) to form the corresponding benzoins is halted at the enediol stage by hindrance. An example is the enediol from hexaethylbenzil (J. W. Corse, C. H. McKeever).

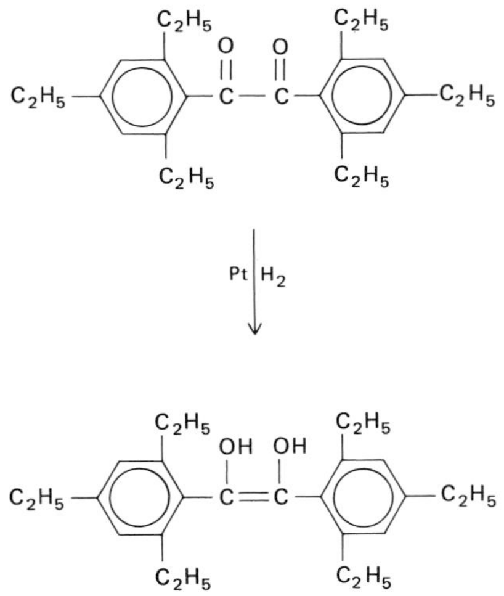

Fig. 5. Hydrogenation of benzils.

The keto phenolates produced by the action of Grignard reagents on hindered *o*- and *p*-hydroxy ketones show still another way in which steric hindrance diverts a reaction from its normal course. The results obtained with them can be interpreted by assuming that they react as keto enolates. It is as if the imprisoned ketone group eludes its pickets and emerges at an unblocked position on the ring, now a cyclohexadienone. That is, the molecule behaves as if the —O⁻ and >C=O functions have been interchanged. If it is assumed that the anion is free, its behavior, in the case of 2-hydroxy-1-mesitoylnaphthalene, for example, would then be that corresponding to resonance structure II rather than resonance structure I (Fig. 6).

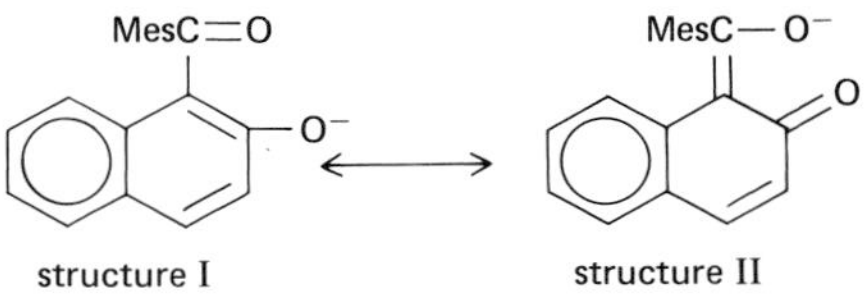

Fig. 6. Resonance structures I and II.

The reaction of *t*-butylmagnesium chloride may be formulated as a 1,4-addition (Fig. 7); the yield of dihydro compound amounts to 91 percent (F. T. Fang).

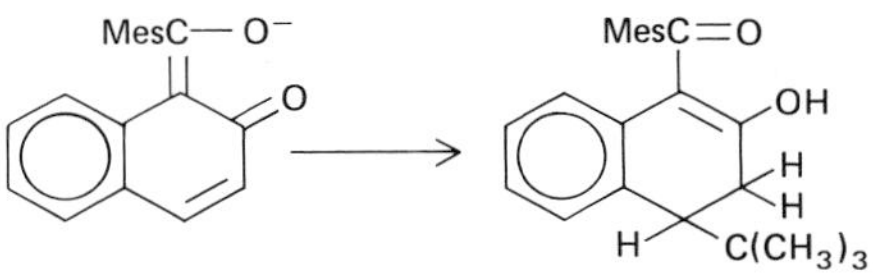

Fig. 7. l,4-Addition reaction.

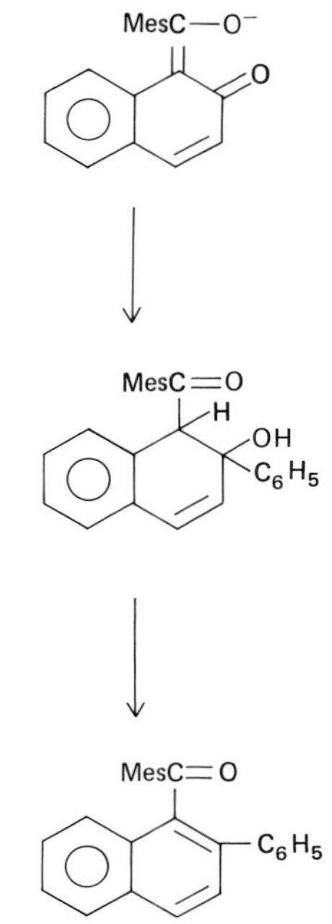

Fig. 8. l,2-Addition reaction.

Reaction with the phenyl reagent would appear to be 1,2-addition (Fig. 8) followed in the work-up procedure by loss of the elements of water.

Fuson received his A.B. From the University of Montana in 1920, his M.A. from the University of California at Berkeley in 1921, and his Ph.D. from the University of Minnesota in 1924. He was a National Research fellow for 2 years and an instructor for 1 year at Harvard University. He became a professor of chemistry at the University of Illinois in 1927. He was elected to the National Academy of Sciences in 1944 and received the Nichols Medal in 1953.

Besides some 300 papers in chemical journals, Fuson wrote *Reactions of Organic Compounds* (1962) and *Systematic Identification of Organic Compounds,* with R. L. Shriner and D. Y. Curtin (5th ed. 1964).

For background information *see* CARBON; GRIGNARD REACTION; ORGANIC REACTION MECHANISM in the McGraw-Hill Encyclopedia of Science and Technology. ∎

GABOR, DENNIS
★ British physicist

Born June 5, 1900, Budapest, Hungary
Died Feb. 8, 1979, London, England

In 1947, when Gabor was working in the Research Laboratory of the British Thomson-Houston Company in Rugby, England, he was very interested in the electron microscope. This wonderful instrument had at that time produced a hundredfold improvement on the resolving power of the best light microscopes, and yet it was disappointing because it had stopped short of resolving atomic lattices. The de Broglie wavelength of fast electrons, about 0.05 ångström (0.005 nanometer), was short enough, but the optics was imperfect. The best electron objective which one could make may be compared in optical perfection to a raindrop rather than to a microscope objective, and through the theoretical work of O. Scherzer it was known that it could never be perfected. The theoretical limit at that time was estimated at 4 ångströms (0.4 nanometer), just about twice what was needed to resolve atomic lattices, while the practical limit stood at about 12 ångströms (1.2 nanometers). These limits resulted from the necessity of restricting the aperture of the electron lenses to about 0.005 radian, at which angle the spherical aberration error is about equal to the diffraction error. If one doubles this aperture so that the diffraction error is halved, the spherical aberration error is increased eight times, and the image is hopelessly blurred.

After he pondered this problem for a long time, a solution suddenly dawned on

Gabor. Why not take a bad electron picture, but one which contains the *whole* information, and correct it by optical means? It had been clear to him for some time that this could be done, if at all, only with coherent electron beams, with electron waves which have a definite phase. But an ordinary photograph loses the phase completely and records only the intensities. The reason why the phase is lost is that there is nothing to compare it with. This led him to the idea of adding a standard to it, a "coherent background"; the interference of the object wave and of the coherent background or "reference wave" will then produce interference fringes. There will be maxima wherever the phases of the two waves were identical. Let us make a hard positive record, so that it transmits only at the maxima, and illuminate it with the reference source alone. Now the phases are of course right for the reference source A, but since at the slits the phases are identical, they must be right also for B; therefore the wave of B must also appear, *reconstructed.*

A little mathematics soon showed that the principle was right, and for more than one object point, for any complicated object. This encouraged Gabor to complete his scheme of electron microscopy by reconstructed wavefronts and to propose a two-stage process: The electron microscope was to produce the interference figure between the object beam and the coherent background, that is to say, the nondiffracted part of the illuminating beam. This interference pattern he called a "hologram", from the Greek *holos*, "the whole," because it contained the whole information. **The** hologram was then reconstructed with light, in an optical system which corrected the aberrations of electron optics.

In order to demonstrate the principle, Gabor carried out some experiments. They were by no means easy, since the best compromise between coherence and intensity was offered by the high-pressure mercury lamp, which had a coherence length of only 0.1 millimeter, enough for about 200 fringes. In order to achieve spatial coherence, he had to illuminate, with one mercury line, a pinhole of 3 micrometers diameter, with exposures of a few minutes, on the most sensitive emulsion then available. The small coherence length made it necessary to arrange everything in one axis; this is now called "in-line" holography, and it was the only way

possible at that time. The result was far from perfect. Apart from the random disturbances caused by *schlieren,* there was a systematic defect in the pictures, due to the fact that there were *two* images instead of one.

Subsequently, the superior coherence of laser light got rid of this disturbance, but Gabor was confident long before the invention of the laser that he could eliminate the second image and thereby make it possible to see atoms with the electron microscope. His method utilized the very defect of electron lenses, the spherical aberration, to defeat the second image.

Gabor published the principle of his invention and the results of his initial experiments in *Nature* (1948), *Proceedings of the Royal Society* (1949), and *Proceedings of the Physical Society* (1951).

Gabor was Emeritus Professor of Applied Electron Physics in the University of London, Commander of the Most Excellent Order of the British Empire, Nobel Laureate in Physics, and Fellow of the Royal Society. He obtained his first degree and doctorate in the Technical University of Berlin; subsequently the University of London awarded him the degree of Doctor of Science. Honorary doctorates were conferred on him by the universities of Southampton, Delft, Surrey, Bridgeport, the City, Columbia (New York), and London; he was also the recipient of many other international distinctions.

Gabor's publications included *The Electron Microscope* (1946); *Electronic Inventions and Their Impact on Civilization* (1959); *Inventing the Future* (1963); *Innovations, Scientific, Technological and Social* (1970); *Holography, 1948–1971* (Nobel Lecture, Dec. 11, 1971); *The Mature Society* (1972); *Beyond the Age of Waste* (1978); and about 100 scientific papers.

For background information *see* HO-LOGRAPHY; MICROSCOPE, ELECTRON in the McGraw-Hill Encyclopedia of Science and Technology. ∎

GAJDUSEK, D. CARLETON
☆ American pediatrician and virologist

> ***Born** Sept. 9, 1923, Yonkers, NY, U.S.A.*

Although Gajdusek began his career as a pediatrician and physical chemist in the mid-1940s, his wide-ranging interests brought him also into the fields of neurology and virology. After contributions to geographic medicine and acute virus disease and autoimmune disease research in the 1940s and early 1950s, he returned to his prime interest in ethropediatrics. He discovered the etiology of kuru in New Guinea and the mode of transmission of this chronic degenerative neurological disease from one human to another. It was the first evidence that this type of disease could be caused by a "slow" virus that may take as much as 5 to 30 years before it shows the effect of its growth and multiplication.

For his studies of kuru and other such neurological diseases and of the new group of unconventional viruses which cause them, Gajdusek shared the 1976 Nobel Prize in medicine or physiology with Baruch S. Blumberg.

Gajdusek visited New Guinea repeatedly for various medical investigations while he was on a postdoctoral fellowship at the Walter and Eliza Hull Institute in Melbourne, Australia. A public health doctor in New Guinea, Vincent Zigas, called his attention to a neurological disease known to the native people as kuru, which killed approximately 1 percent of the populations that practiced cannibalism as part of a funeral rite for close relatives. Gajdusek and Zigas launched a wide-ranging quest for the cause of kuru which kept them in the field with the New Guinea peoples who are its victims for much of the next decade. Gajdusek and Zigas's first attempts to isolate an infectious agent in 1957 were unsuccessful, using conventional animal inoculation and chick embryo and tissue culture techniques.

W. Hadlow, an American veterinary neuropathologist working in Compton, England, on scrapie, a viral disease in sheep, was struck by the similarity in the pathologies of scrapie and kuru. He suggested the possibility that kuru, like scrapie, was caused by a virus with a very long incubation period. In 1963 Gajdusek and his collaborator C. J. Gibbs, Jr., succeeded in transmitting kuru first to chimpanzees, then to New World monkeys, and finally to Old World monkeys and to minks and ferrets. The highest concentration of the virus was found in the brain tissue.

Gajdusek's group's work with kuru suggested the possibility that other chronic degenerative diseases of humans were caused by a group of viruses whose chemical and biological characteristics set them apart from other animal viruses. Gajdusek referred to them as unconventional viruses because (1) a long length of time (incubation period) elapsed between infection and the outbreak of the disease, (2) they do not produce an inflammatory or specific immune response, (3) they are resistant to ultraviolet or ionizing radiation, and (4) they are resistant to many chemicals such as formaldehyde and to enzyme degradation by proteases and nucleases.

Gajdusek and his group turned their attention to a presenile dementia called Creutzfeldt-Jakob disease (CJD), which has a pathology similar to kuru and is found all over the world. They isolated a virus similar in behavior to kuru virus, and were able to transmit the disease by inoculation of diseased brain tissue to chimpanzees, New and Old World monkeys, and the domestic cat, and confirmed the subsequent transmissions, by other workers in the United States and Japan, of some strains of the virus to guinea pigs and mice and rats. There are cases of CJD which have apparently resulted from a corneal transplant, from the use of implanted silver stereotactic electrodes in the preparation of epilepsy patients for neurosurgery, and from other types of instrument contamination in neurosurgery, but these iatrogenic ac-

cidents account for no more than 5 percent of the cases of CJD.

Other chronic diseases of humans such as Parkinson's disease, multiple sclerosis, amyotrophic lateral sclerosis, Alzheimer's disease, and Huntington's disease were studied to determine whether they had a slow-virus etiology. Unfortunately, transmission of these diseases to subhuman primates was unsuccessful, and no virus was isolated from any of the disease tissues. Gajdusek's team continued their investigations of these disorders into neuroendocrinology and other biochemical and immunological areas.

After the viral nature of kuru and CJD were established, Gajdusek's group turned to study the group of unconventional viruses to elucidate their molecular composition and configuration and to discover why they behave so differently from other viruses.

Gajdusek, a graduate of the University of Rochester, earned an M.D. at Harvard Medical School and did his pediatric specialty training at Columbia University, Harvard, and Cincinnati. After a series of postdoctoral fellowships in physical chemistry, virology, and immunology that took him to the California Institute of Technology and back to Harvard, to the Institut Pasteur in Iran, and the Hull Institute in Melbourne, he began to work at the National Institutes of Health as chief of the Section for the Study of Child Growth, Development and Behavior and Disease Patterns in Primitive Cultures, which has evolved into the dual laboratory of Slow, Latent and Temperate Infections and of Central Nervous Systems Studies in the National Institute of Neurological and Communicative Disorders and Strokes.

Gajdusek wrote many reports for research journals describing his results, and he was the author and editor of numerous monographs. In addition to the Nobel Prize, he was honored with the Mead-Johnson Award by the American Academy of Pediatrics in 1963 and the Lucien Dautrebaud Prize in Pathophysiology (Belgium) in 1976. He was a member of the National Academy of Sciences, the American Academy of Arts and Sciences, the American Philosophical Society, and other national scientific organizations.

For background information *see* VIRUS INFECTION, LATENT, PERSISTENT, SLOW in the McGraw-Hill Encyclopedia of Science and Technology. ∎

GALAMBOS, ROBERT
★ American psychologist

Born Apr. 20, 1914, OH, U.S.A.

Galambos, a physiological psychologist, was concerned with brain research. His experiments with bats, performed in collaboration with D. R. Griffin, yielded his doctoral thesis (1941), which described the essential mechanisms these animals use to avoid obstacles as they fly about in total darkness. An Italian priest named Spallanzani knew in 1794 that normal bats with ears plugged fly awkwardly and smash into obstacles, and later experimenters suspected that sound emission and reception were the crucial factors in the skillful obstacle avoidance of bats. However, Galambos and Griffin were the first to record the ultrasonic cries that flying bats emit; they clearly demonstrated the correlation between successful avoidance and the emission of these cries, described the special features of bat ears that enable them to hear sounds that humans cannot, and on the basis of these facts announced the theory that bats use the echoes of their high-pitched cries to locate and avoid the objects before them.

Galambos next studied the behavior of single nerve cells in the cat brain (1942). Using the then new microelectrodes which permit electrical recordings from one brain cell at a time and working with Hallowell Davis, he systematically explored the cochlear nucleus, the first auditory relay nucleus in the cat brain. There are about 80,000 nerve cells there, any one of which is likely to be found discharging itself a dozen or so times per second, even though no sound strikes the cat's ear. In response to sounds, such a cell reacts to some–not all–tones a cat can hear: one cell may respond to the low notes and another the high notes of the piano, and so which cells out of the available thousands respond seems to determine what pitch will be experienced. The stimulated cell reacts, furthermore, by discharging either faster or slower than its base-line rate, so that each heard tone creates a unique pattern of excited and inhibited cells. These patterns, finally, are characteristically different for the same tone when soft as opposed to loud; thus the excitation-inhibition pattern is fundamental for the loudness experience as well. This same basic plan of nerve action was subsequently shown by other experimenters to hold for the cells involved in the sensations of touch and vision. *See* DAVIS, HALLOWELL.

Besides pitch and loudness, human auditory experience includes the ability to locate where a sound comes from when heard with both ears (binaural localization). It is easy to show that a bat or a human with one ear plugged localizes sounds poorly; hence, the separate messages originating in the two ears must mix and interact in the brain to make normal localization possible. Using the microelectrode technique once more, Galambos and his collaborators uncovered the place where this mixing first occurs in the cat brain (the accessory nucleus of the superior olive) and showed that when sounds to the two ears are given first simultaneously, then separated by as little as 100 microseconds in time, nerve cells there detect the difference (1958).

Auditory attention and learning are two further problems Galambos studied in the laboratory. Sounds tend to be unheard unless one pays attention; this means the brain can admit sounds selectively, analyzing some and not others at a given moment or allowing a particular sound to enter at one time and not at another. Galambos studied a system of nerve fibers known to leave the brain and terminate in the ear and showed that activity in these feedback fibers makes the ear less sensitive to sounds (1956). However, he was not able to demonstrate convincingly that these fibers act during the listening process. As for learning, the simple fact that one recalls at will the notes of a favorite song illustrates the remarkable capacity of brains to store a series of auditory signals and retrieve them later as memories. Galambos investigated this biological equivalent of the tape recorder by examining the brain waves of cats and monkeys before and after they learned various tasks for which sounds were important cues. For instance, he and his collaborators placed wires deep in the brains by surgery, kept the animals in the laboratory as pets for months, and recorded their brain waves in response to click sounds day after day. Brain waves turned out to be large when an animal heard a sound for the first time, progressively smaller with its monotonous repetition hour after hour, and large once more when the experimenter fed the animal at the time of the clicks, in the way Pavlov rang a bell to signal the arrival of food for dogs. In these simple learning experiments sound-evoked activity appeared in regions of the brain previously thought to be uninvolved in the hearing process (1961).

Galambos pointed out in a theoretical paper (1962) the need for more information on the activities of glial cells in the brain. These cells, which outnumber by 10 to 1 the nerve cells in the human-type brain, may help make brains function as they do by collaborating and cooperating with the nerve cells in ways still unknown. Galambos's later research (1967) included attempts to prepare an antibody specific for glial cells with the ultimate aim of changing brain function by injecting such antibody into behaving animals.

Galambos attended Oberlin College (A.B., 1935; M.A., 1936); he took graduate degrees at Harvard (Ph.D., 1941) and the University of Rochester (M.D., 1946). After teaching anatomy briefly at the Emory University School of Medicine in 1946, he worked with S. S. Stevens at the Harvard Psychoacoustic Laboratory until joining the Walter Reed Army Institute of Research in Washington, DC, where he served as chief of the department of neurophysiology. In 1962 he became Eugene Higgins Professor of Psychology and Physiology at Yale University. He was elected to the American Academy of Arts and Sciences in 1958 and to the National Academy of Sciences in 1961. He was also a member of the American Physiological Society, and the Acoustical Society of America. Galambos wrote *Nerves and Muscles* (paper, 1962) in the "Science Study Series" for high school students.

For background information *see* BAT; HEARING; NERVOUS SYSTEM (VERTEBRATE); PHONORECEPTION in the McGraw-Hill Encyclopedia of Science and Technology. ■

GALSTON, ARTHUR W.
★ American botanist

Born Apr. 21, 1920, New York, NY, U.S.A.

Galston's work focused on light and hormones as controlling influences in plant development. His doctoral thesis, completed in 1943, showed that 2, 3, 5-triiodobenzoic acid (TIBA), a synthetic inhibitor of the transport of the growth hormone indoleacetic acid (IAA), greatly increases the number of flower buds and thus of harvestable pods in photoperiodically induced soybeans. This discovery led others to exploit TIBA commercially for increased soybean yield. Galston's observation that higher levels of TIBA could cause leaf abscission influenced research in the development of chemical defoliants. This connection later led him to express concern about the military use of defoliants in Vietnam.

Trained as an undergraduate at Cornell University and as a graduate student at the University of Illinois, Galston received his main research stimulus from 9 years of association with James Bonner and Frits Went at the California Institute of Technology. There, in 1943–44, he in-

vestigated with Bonner the biochemistry of growth and rubber formation in guayule, a Mexican shrub developed for natural rubber production during the early years of World War II. He isolated and identified *trans*-cinnamic acid, a natural antiauxin, as the growth inhibitor excreted by guayule roots. *See* BONNER, JAMES FREDERICK; WENT, FRITS WARMOLT.

Returning to Caltech after several years in the U.S. Navy, where he served for a while as agriculture officer for the military government on Okinawa, Galston began investigations into the mechanism of light action in dark-grown plants. In 1949 he discovered the riboflavin-sensitized photooxidation of IAA and the photoactivation of flavoprotein enzymes, and suggested that riboflavin, not the generally accepted carotene, is the photoreceptor pigment for phototropism.

In 1950–51, as a Guggenheim fellow in the laboratory of Hugo Theorell in Stockholm, Galston isolated crystalline plant catalase from spinach leaves. This directed his interest toward hydroperoxidase enzymes in plants, and led him to a series of studies on IAA oxidase, an enzyme that destroys the plant growth hormone. He helped clarify its distribution, peroxidase nature, light-regulated inhibitor, isozymal compexity, and inducible nature. *See* THEORELL, AXEL HUGO TEODOR.

At the time of his move to Yale University, in 1955, Galston became involved in physiological investigations on phytochrome, a recently discovered pigment that regulates both the photoperiodic control of flowering and the change from the dark-grown (etiolated) growth habit to the more familiar green plant morphology. With W. S. Hillman, he showed that phytochrome controls IAA oxidase activity through regulation of the synthesis of cofactors and inhibitors of the enzyme. With M. Furuya and B. Stowe, he identified these cofactors and inhibitors as conjugates of the flavonoids kaempferol and quercitin, respectively; and with W. Bottomley and H. Smith he studied their relationship to light-induced bud growth. Later studies on phytochrome emphasized its rapid action in regulating leaflet movement in the leguminous plants *Albizzia* and *Samanea*, and its interaction with circadian rhythms in photoperiodic timing mechanisms. With R. L. Satter, he showed that both light and rhythms control leaf movement through regulation of potassium and chloride flux from one group of motor cells in the pulvinus to the other and, with R. H. Racusen, that the transmembrane potentials of the motor cells change in response to light and rhythmic signals. These investigations strengthened the view, advanced by S. B. Hendricks and H. A. Borthwick, that phytochrome and rhythms act on membrane systems. His interest in plant movements also led to a series of studies with M. J. Jaffe on the mechanism of the rapid curling of pea tendrils in response to mechanical stimuli.

In the 1970s Galston's interest in plant cell physiology led him to investigate protoplasts (naked cells without walls). In some species, single protoplasts cultured on artificial media can regenerate entire plants. Aware that protoplasts held promise for plant improvement through somatic fusion and introduction of exogenous genetic information, he attempted to cultivate leaf protoplasts of cereals, the most important food plants. With R. K. Sawhney and A. Altman, he found that polyamines greatly improve stability, vigor, and macromolecular synthesis in oat protoplasts. Further investigations led to the discovery that the naturally occurring polyamines are effective in preventing leaf senescence in many plants, and that they may serve as regulators of many important biochemical processes in plants.

Galston's interest in the ecological and public health implications of the massive military use of herbicides in Vietnam led him to visit the Far East in 1971. He and E. Signer of the Massachusetts Institute of Technology were the first American scientists to enter the People's Republic of China. Interviews with Premiers Chou En-lai, Norodom Sihanouk, and Pham Van Dong led him to develop programs of international exchange, lectures, and scientific aid to China and Indochina, which he continued to visit frequently. Concern with the public health implications of the dioxin impurities in the herbicide 2, 4, 5-T led him to frequent writing and speaking activity on this subject.

The son of Jewish immigrants, Galston entered Cornell University's College of Agriculture in 1936 to prepare for study in veterinary medicine, but switched to botany under the influence of a teacher, L. C. Petry. He received the B.A. at Cornell (1940), and the M.A. (1942) and the Ph.D. (1943) from the University of Illi-

nois, where he was further influenced by H. J. Fuller, a botanist, and H. E. Carter, a biochemist. After military service and a decade at Caltech, he went to Yale in 1955, subsequently becoming Eaton Professor of Botany. Galston received the Merit Award of the Botanical Society of America in 1970. He served as president of the Botanical Society of America, the American Society of Plant Physiologists, and the Society for Social Responsibility in Science.

Galston's interest in both teaching and public education was reflected in his books *Principles of Plant Physiology*, with J. Bonner (1952); *The Life of the Green Plant* (1960); *Control Mechanisms in Plant Development*, with P. J. Davies (1970); and *Daily Life in People's China* (1973). He also wrote numerous articles for the lay public in *Natural History* magazine and other periodicals.

For background information *see* PLANT GROWTH; PLANT HORMONES; PLANT PHYSIOLOGY in the McGraw-Hill Encyclopedia of Science and Technology. ■

GAMOW, GEORGE
★ American physicist

Born Mar. 4, 1904, Odessa, Russia
Died Aug. 19, 1969, Boulder, CO, U.S.A.

Gamow made significant theoretical contributions to nuclear physics, astronomy, and biology. He also became well known as a popularizer of science,

winning for his achievements in this area the 1956 Kalinga Prize of the United Nations Educational, Scientific, and Cultural Organization.

In his schooldays Gamow became very interested in astronomy, examining the starry sky through a little telescope that his father gave him on his thirteenth birthday. He decided then to become a scientist and began his study of mathematics, physics, and astronomy.

After graduation from the University of Leningrad in 1928, Gamow attended summer school in Göttingen and decided to see if the newly formulated quantum theory, so successful in explaining the structure of the atom, could also be applied to the atomic nucleus. Through research he was able to explain the then mysterious phenomenon of natural radioactivity as well as the experiments of Lord Rutherford on the induced transformation of light elements. On the basis of this research, Gamow received his Ph.D. from the University of Leningrad in 1928.

Later, in Copenhagen, when he told Niels Bohr of his work, Bohr offered him a year at the Institute of Theoretical Physics on a stipend from the Royal Danish Academy. There Gamow proposed a hypothesis that atomic nuclei can be treated as little droplets of so-called "nuclear fluid." These views led ultimately to the present theory of nuclear fission and fusion. *See* BOHR, NIELS HENRIK DAVID.

At this period Gamow also collaborated with F. Houtermans and R. Atkinson in attempts to apply his formula for calculating the rate of induced nuclear transformations to the so-called thermonuclear reaction in the interior of the Sun and other stars. This formula, originally applied only to astronomical topics, was later successfully used for designing H-bombs, as well as for studying the possibility of controlled thermonuclear reactions.

Gamow spent a year working with Lord Rutherford at Cambridge, a second year in Copenhagen, and later became a professor at the University of Leningrad (1931–33). While attending the International Solvay Congress in Brussels, he was invited to lecture at the University of Michigan. He sailed to the United States, eventually obtaining a professorship at the George Washington University, Washington, DC (1933–55). During the early years in Washington he collaborated with Edward

Teller on the theory of beta decay, and formulated the so-called Gamow-Teller selection rule for beta emission. *See* TELLER, EDWARD.

While Gamow was in Washington, he developed the theory of the internal structure of red giant stars. With Mario Schoenberg he developed the theory of the so-called Urca process and, with Ralph Alpher, the theory of the origin of chemical elements by the process of successive neutron capture.

In 1954 Gamow developed an interest in biological phenomena and published papers on the information storage and transfer in a living cell. In these papers he proposed the "genetic code," an idea later completely confirmed by experimental studies in laboratories.

In 1956 Gamow joined the faculty of the University of Colorado. He was elected to the Royal Danish Academy of Sciences in 1950 and the U.S. National Academy of Sciences in 1953. In 1965 he was elected an overseas fellow of Churchill College, University of Cambridge.

Among Gamow's many books are *The Constitution of Atomic Nuclei and Radioactivity* (1931), *Structure of Atomic Nuclei and Nuclear Transformations* (1937), and *Theory of Atomic Nucleus and Nuclear Energy Sources,* with C. Critchfield (1949). Gamow's papers and correspondence are being collected by the Library of Congress.

For background information *see* NUCLEAR STRUCTURE; SELECTION RULES (PHYSICS) in the McGraw-Hill Encyclopedia of Science and Technology. ■

GASSER, HERBERT SPENCER

★ American neurophysiologist and physician

> **Born** July 5, 1888, Platteville, WI, U.S.A.
>
> **Died** May 11, 1963, New York, NY, U.S.A.

While experimenting on the electrophysiology of mammalian nerves, Gasser, in collaboration with Joseph Erlanger, demonstrated that nerve impulses are transmitted at different velocities depending on the thickness of the nerve fibers along which they pass. This work, for which Gasser and Erlanger shared the 1944 Nobel Prize in physiology or medicine, has led to great advances in understanding the mechanism of pain and reflex action. *See* ERLANGER, JOSEPH.

The first truly significant discovery in neurophysiology was made during the mid-19th century by Emil Du Bois-Reymond, a German physiologist, who demonstrated that the nerve impulse was an electronegative wave propagated along a nerve. Later the speed of propagation was successfully measured by Herman Helmholtz. Early in the 20th century an English biologist, Edward Adrian, observed that nerve impulses are discharged by sense organs and neurons (nerve cells) in bursts, like machine-gun fire.

The work that actually paved the way for Gasser and Erlanger was an assumption made in 1907 by Gustaf Göthlin, a Swedish physiologist. Extrapolating from a formula for electrical cable conduction, Göthlin hypothesized that the velocity of nerve impulses is more rapid along thick nerve fibers than along thin ones. His assumption was correlated with the observed fact that the diameters of fibers in a nerve stem differ in cross section. Although indirect supporting evidence for Göthlin's hypothesis was offered by the French physiologist Louis Lapicque, it remained for Gasser and Erlanger to prove it conclusively.

The early neurophysiologic researches of Gasser and Erlanger (their actual collaboration dates from 1916, when Gasser joined Erlanger at Washington University in St. Louis) were hampered by the insensitivity of existing physical instruments. In 1921, however, an extremely sensitive cathode-ray oscilloscope became available, which, coupled with an improved

amplification device, enabled the accurate recording of the electrical manifestations of nerve impulses.

Early in their work on isolated mammalian nerve fibers, Gasser and Erlanger recognized that they would have to simulate, as closely as possible, the natural environment of nerve fibers in the living body. Utilizing an existing technique, the nerves were examined in a 5 percent carbon dioxide in oxygen atmosphere saturated with water vapor and maintained at normal body temperature. When a comparison was made of the recorded electrical activity of isolated nerve fibers using this technique and of nerve fibers in the body, the observed correlation gave assurance that the artificial environment was satisfactory.

In their oscillographic recordings of electrical impulses passing through isolated nerve fibers, the investigators noted the following sequence of events: an initial and rapid negative deviation in electric potential (the spike), a relatively long period of ascending then descending potential (the actual stage of transmission), followed by a sequence of low potential changes (the after-potential), the latter consisting of first a negative and then a positive deviation. In measuring the potential cycles of different nerve fibers, three distinct patterns seemed to emerge, based on duration of spikes and after-potentials. These constant patterns indicated that there were three main groups of nerve fibers, which were designated A, B, and C. Spike durations in A group fibers were 0.45 millisecond, about 1.2 ms in those of the B group, and 2.0 ms in the C group. After-potentials also varied distinctively in each group as did the velocities of conduction. In the A group conduction velocities ranged from 115 meters per second to 10 mps; in the B group from 15 to 3 mps; in the C group from slightly over 2 to 0.6 mps. Returning to Göthlin's hypothesis, Gasser and Erlanger concluded that an approximately linear relationship existed between fiber diameter and velocity of nerve impulse conduction.

As a result of this discovery, it became possible to demonstrate the distribution of the three groups of fibers throughout the nervous system and to elucidate the highly complex problem of nerve impulse transmission. In addition, Gasser and Erlanger contributed information on the essential differences between sensory and motor nerves and demonstrated how pain is perceived and how muscle is caused to move. Their researches constituted an entirely new synthesis of neurophysiology on which future discoveries would be based.

Gasser received his A.B. (1910) and A.M. (1911) degrees from the University of Wisconsin, where he first encountered Erlanger. He received an M.D. from Johns Hopkins University in 1915, returned to Wisconsin for a year of research in pharmacology, and in 1916 went to Washington University in St. Louis, there beginning his collaboration with Erlanger. He was named professor of pharmacology in 1921. Gasser studied in Europe from 1923 to 1925 and then returned to St. Louis until 1931, when he became professor of physiology at Cornell University Medical College in New York City. From 1935 to 1953 Gasser was director of the Rockefeller Institute for Medical Research.

For background information *see* NEUROPHYSIOLOGY in the McGraw-Hill Encyclopedia of Science and Technology. ■

GAUDIN, ANTOINE MARC
★ American mineral engineer

***Born** Aug. 8, 1900, Smyrna, Turkey*
***Died** Aug. 23, 1974, Boston, MA, U.S.A.*

When Gaudin began his researches in the field of mineral engineering, it was not even called by any engineering name. He gave the field scientific cohesion by insisting on the relationship that must exist between the microscopic properties of minerals and their macroscopic properties (in which humans are practically interested).

Gaudin's work, which spanned almost a half century, elucidated the flotation process of mineral separation to the point that this once obscure method of mineral concentration is now clearly the major process in mineral engineering. He showed that flotation depends on the crystal structure of the surface of every mineral particle. This surficial crystal structure, in turn, depends upon the ability of the substratum to adsorb selectively upon itself in the proper orientation one or another of the ions in the surrounding bath.

When the mineral surface adsorbs hydrocarbon-bearing ions, with their hydrocarbon ends away from the mineral, it becomes indifferent to the fluid medium surrounding it, instead of being highly water-avid as usual. The result is that the surface sticks to the gas of an air bubble, with the consequent flotation of the particle attached to air. Conversely, if the mineral surface adsorbs instead a non-hydrocarbon-bearing ion or a hydrocarbon-bearing ion which also has several water-avid spots, it becomes "glued" to the water and sinks instead of floating. Combination of these effects on different minerals associated in an ore results in mineral A floating and mineral B sinking, which is the practical result sought by the technician. Improvements in the separation can result from changes in the proportions of reagents used, from the place and the sequence of their addition, from varying the fineness of grinding of the ore, from variations in the proportions of solids to water in the ore pulp, from the design of the flotation cell, and from the extent of the aeration used. All of these factors give wide scope to the technical skill of the operator.

Gaudin spent much effort in the detailed study of ores under the microscope. Many an ore contains 10 to 20 different mineral species, the nature of which must be known, as well as the structural and textural relationship between these minerals. Some ores are so coarsely associated that fracture to 5 millimeters permits very considerable liberation of the minerals from mutual attachment. In other cases even fracture to 5 micrometers (a size a thousand times smaller in diameter and a billion times smaller in volume) will not do. These facts may all be revealed by pa-tient quantitative study under the microscope, petrographic or metallurgical, as the case requires. Gaudin's interest in these aspects of ores led to development of a technique called selective iridescent filming, which permits easy differentiation between solids that normally appear similar. It also led to a study of the dry synthesis of sulfide minerals, as a step to their understanding.

Among other problems to which Gaudin turned his attention was the size distribution of fragments produced by breaking, crushing, or grinding. Rather than accept a product as having a fragmentation resulting capriciously from the crushing tool used, he saw fragmentation as the result of a statistical process following laws worthy of being worked out. He and his former student Reinhardt Schuhmann, Jr., developed a widely used equation to describe the size distribution of a fragmented homogeneous rock. This work was further developed jointly with other students, particularly with Risto Hukki and with Thomas P. Meloy.

Gaudin also worked extensively with uranium ores, for which he and his associates developed the leading extraction process. This requires dissolving the uranium with a solvent (for example, aqueous sulfuric acid in oxidizing environment) from the residue and purifying the liquor by use of ion-exchange resins or by use of solvent extraction. This purification by ion-exchange resins uses the resins to remove selectively the uranium from solution until the liquor becomes barren, at which time it is discarded. The resin, when fully loaded with uranium, is contacted with an eluting liquor that reverses the process, taking the purified uranium in solution, from which it can be precipitated by changing the pH (for example, by adding ammonia). The process can be automated entirely. Where purification is by solvent extraction, the solvent is in the form of droplets, which otherwise behave exactly as an ion-exchanging resin.

For this development Gaudin received from his colleagues in the mining and metallurgical fields the Robert H. Richards Award in 1957. He was also the Sir Julius Wernher Memorial Lecturer of the Institution of Mining and Metallurgy of London, for which occasion he was given the honor of using Faraday's lecture room at the Royal Society.

Gaudin took a B.S. at the University of Paris in 1917 and an E.M. at Columbia University in 1921. In 1924–26 he was a lecturer in mining at Columbia, in 1926–29 an associate professor at the University of Utah, and in 1929–39 a research professor at the Montana School of Mines, which granted him the Sc.D. in 1941. He became Richards Professor at the Massachusetts Institute of Technology in 1939. A founding member of the National Academy of Engineering, he was elected to the American Academy of Arts and Sciences in 1956.

Gaudin wrote *Flotation* (2d ed. 1957) and *Principles of Mineral Dressing* (1939), as well as about 150 papers, some with coauthors.

For background information *see* FLOTATION; METAL AND MINERAL PROCESSING; MINERALOGY in the McGraw-Hill Encyclopedia of Science and Technology. ■

GAYDON, ALFRED GORDON
★ British physicist

Born Sept. 26, 1911, London, England

As an experimental spectroscopist, Gaydon applied molecular spectroscopy to a number of fields, including the determination of dissociation energies, study of flame chemistry and structure, measurement of gas temperature, and interpretation of shock-tube phenomena. In 1960 he was awarded the Rumford Medal of the Royal Society for his work on molecular spectra, and also the Bernard Lewis Gold Medal of the Combustion Institute for his researches on flame spectroscopy.

Sir Norman Lockyer, an early pioneer in spectroscopy and astronomy, had founded an astrophysics department at the Royal College of Science at the end of the 19th century, and this attracted other distinguished workers, including the 2d Lord Rayleigh and Alfred Fowler, who did valuable work on the excitation and analysis of spectra. Gaydon's early interest in astronomy led him to join this group, under Fowler, in 1932.

Early work on the spectra of afterglows of electric discharges and on the analysis of spectra of diatomic hybrides gave Gaydon an initial training in molecular spectroscopy. One of his early papers, with R. W. B. Pearse, on a wave-mechanical treatment of the intensity distribution of RbH, pioneered the more refined methods of calculating vibrational intensity distributions which are now in use. Other papers described previously unknown types of electronic transitions $^2\triangle-^2\triangle$ in NiH and $^7\Pi-^7\Sigma$ in MnH. With H. P. Broida, Gaydon was the first to find a laboratory source of the night-sky spectrum of O_2. In 1971, with R. E. Smith, he observed for the first time the band spectrum of TiH; later Yerle found these bands in M-type stars.

Detailed analysis of the spectrum of a molecule gives information about its energy levels and can be used to derive the energy of dissociation to free atoms. In some cases, convergence of vibrational energy levels to the dissociation limit is observed, while in other cases the approximate limit may be determined by a Birge-Sponer extrapolation. Another very accurate way is by observation of a predissociation limit beyond which the spectrum lines become diffuse. About 1934–37 the dissociation energies of N_2 and CO (the latter especially important because it was related to the heat of sublimation of carbon) were determined from predissociations, and the low values so obtained were widely accepted for a number of years, despite disagreement with the values from Birge-Sponer extrapolations and independent thermochemical observations. Gaydon realized this difficulty and noted that acceptance of the low values involved violation of the rule that the potential energy curves of electronic states of the same symmetry must not cross (noncrossing rule). A critical examination of all data led him to reinterpret the predissociations by assuming a different type of coupling of the angular momenta in the molecule; this led to precise but much higher values

of the dissociation energies. After some initial controversy, these higher values were definitely established by further experimental work and received general acceptance. Gaydon then made a systematic study of the dissociation energies of all known diatomic molecules for which spectroscopic data were available.

Gaydon's interest in flame spectroscopy was aroused by early observation of the afterglow of CO_2, the spectrum of which resembled that of a flame, and direct work on flames greatly increased knowledge of the chemical and physical processes which occur. His spectroscopic studies included flames at very low pressure; chilled flames; preheated flames; the development of a nitric oxide test to detect atomic oxygen; the effect of adding halogenated inhibitors; flames supported by free atoms from a discharge; flames supported by fluorine; and the use of deuterium as tracer to follow chemical processes. He has also made temperature measurements by spectroscopic methods and showed the occurrence of abnormalities in the reaction zone.

The development of the shock tube as a tool for high-temperature research gave Gaydon a further opportunity to exploit spectroscopic techniques, and he studied pyrolysis, detonation, ignition, and rates of dissociation and of vibrational relaxation of molecules. With colleagues he developed the spectrum-line reversal method of temperature measurement so that it could be used to follow rapid processes behind shock waves.

Gaydon graduated in physics in 1932 at Imperial College, London, did 2 years' research with A. Fowler, and then joined the British Cotton Industry Research Association. In 1936, while distilling an ether, he was involved in an explosion that cost him an eye and injured his sight, but in 1937 he returned to Imperial College to resume spectroscopic research. In 1939 he transferred to the chemical technology department with Sir Alfred Egerton. He obtained his London Ph.D. in 1937 and his D.SC. in 1941. He was elected to the Royal Society of London in 1953. He was Warren Research Fellow of the Royal Society (1945–74) and professor of molecular spectroscopy in the University of London (1961–73).

Gaydon wrote *Identification of Molecular Spectra*, with R. W. B. Pearse (1940; 4th ed. 1976), *Spectroscopy and Combustion Theory* (1942; 2d ed. 1948), *Dissociation Energies* (1947; 3d ed. 1963), *Flames,*

Their Structure, Radiation and Temperature, with H. G. Wolfhard (1953; 4th ed. 1978), *The Spectroscopy of Flames* (1957; 2d ed. 1974), and *The Shock Tube in High-temperature Chemical Physics,* with I. R. Hurle (1963).

For background information *see* SPECTROSCOPY in the McGraw-Hill Encyclopedia of Science and Technology. ■

GEIJER, PER
★ Swedish geologist

***Born** May 7, 1886, Stockholm, Sweden*
***Died** Apr. 18, 1976*

Ore deposits in two provinces of the Precambrian in Sweden and the general geology of these provinces were the chief subjects of Geijer's studies. His first published work (1910) was a monograph on the important magnetite deposits and the associated volcanics at Kiruna in northernmost Sweden. Two hypotheses, both implying a close genetic connection with the volcanics, had been proposed to explain the origin of these ores. One hypothesis proposed that they were formed magmatically, the other that they were the products of fumarolic action at the surface—what was later called an exhalative sedimentary process. The chief argument for the latter interpretation was the fact that the porphyry forming the footwall of the ore bodies contains, as vesicle fillings and the like, mineral aggregates closely related to the ores. Geijer's results confirmed the magmatic hypothesis, mainly

through the study of details in the ores. The vesicle fillings of the porphyry were shown to be local concentrations in the solidifying rock and not the products of later fumarolic activity. However, the noted similarities led Geijer to the conclusion that volatiles had played an important role in the separation of the ores from the parent magma, and also in the determination of their further development.

Geijer continued to work on these problems with detailed studies on other deposits in the same province and with visits to genetically related deposits in Missouri (1913) and in Chile (1928), compiling observations that brought out the significant features of the type. The magmatic interpretation is supported by the much later discovery of similar ores as lava flows in northern Chile (C. F. Park, Jr. and others) and the role of volatiles in the differentiation process by experimental work (R. Fischer).

A widespread but generally lean copper mineralization in the same part of Sweden was shown by Geijer to be associated with a regional scapolitization, which in turn was found to be connected with the intrusion of the Lina granite. From characteristic textural features of this granite, which forms a number of batholiths and stocks in northernmost Sweden and northern Finland, Geijer concluded that all these granite bodies stem from one vast reservoir of homogeneous magma, which in the depth underlay the region.

In the ore-bearing region of central Sweden, Geijer began (1914) the study of the renowned copper and pyrite mine at Falun and related deposits. He found that the metasomatic process by which these ores were formed had also greatly affected the siliceous volcanics around the ore bodies, and that this latter process implied the formation of such magnesian minerals as cordierite and anthophyllite. Independently and earlier, P. Eskola, from his studies on the genetically analogous Orijärvi deposit in Finland, had reached the same conclusion, which he presented in an excellent monograph; the mineralization was regarded as related to a granite intrusion. Geijer evolved this concept further and found that the sulfide mineralization in the whole region had occurred during the Svecofennian orogeny and the concomitant intrusion of the earliest group of Svecofennian granites. He pointed out (1916), from comparisons with younger mountain chains,

that the emplacement of such granites was largely controlled by the fold structures of the invaded supracrustal rocks, and he also concluded that it took place while folding was still proceeding—what was later called synkinematic intrusion. He followed up these studies in a series of later works, up to 1965. The amount of magnesium introduced metasomatically was found to be enormous in some districts, as at Riddarhyttan, and comparable to what was recorded in other countries as accompanying the introduction of sulfides of lead and zinc in carbonate rocks. Fractionation of the ore-forming solutions was also studied, illustrated by certain characteristic combinations of sulfides of the various metals and the alteration products in the wall rock, and by local, pyrometasomatically formed concentrations of cerium minerals belonging to the same epoch of mineralization. The regional distribution of the latter, rare minerals was regarded by Geijer as an indication that the mineralizing solutions might largely have risen in advance of the granite invasion.

Geijer also investigated many districts with iron ores in the same region, such as Norberg, Stråssa, and Stripa. Among pyrometasomatic deposits, formed during the same epoch as the sulfide ores, he found several occurrences with ludwigite and other borates, always accompanied by a pronouncedly magnesian skarn. His studies of quartz-banded ores contributed to the understanding of this much discussed type. Some arguments for an interpretation through an exhalative sedimentary process as far as local conditions were concerned were the regular association with rhyolitic volcanics, and the rare but significant occurrence of nonsulfidic lead in a manganiferous variety. Jointly with N. H. Magnusson, Geijer produced (1944) a survey of all iron ore deposits of the region and their geological setting.

Geijer entered Uppsala University in 1904 and received his doctorate there in 1910. He was dozent, Stockholm University, in 1910–25; geologist, Geological Survey of Sweden, during 1914–31; professor of mineralogy and geology, Royal Technological Institute, Stockholm, in 1931–41; and director, Geological Survey of Sweden, in 1942–51. After retirement he did research work in the Mineralogical Department, Swedish Museum of Natural History, in Stockholm. Geijer was elected to the Royal Swedish Academy of Science in 1939 and, as a foreign associate, to the

U.S. National Academy of Sciences in 1958. The mineral perite, $PbBiO_2Cl$, was named after him.

For background information *see* MAGMA; MINERALOGY; PETROLOGY in the McGraw-Hill Encyclopedia of Science and Technology. ∎

GELFAND, IZRAIL MOISEEVICH
★ Soviet mathematician and biologist

Born Sept. 2, 1913, Krasnye Okny, Russia

Gelfand's main work dealt with functional analysis and exerted a substantial influence in shaping many basic trends of scientific studies. He developed the theory of commutative normed rings. A normed ring is a set for whose elements the operations of addition, multiplication by a number, and multiplication have been determined, and for each element y a definite norm has been determined—the nonnegative number $\| y \|$. For example, the set $C(a,b)$ of all continuous functions $f(x)$ over the segment $[a,b]$ is a normed ring. The operations in this set are determined as usual operations on functions, and the norm is determined by the formula in Eq. (1).

$$\| f \| = \max_{a \le x \le b} | f(x) | \qquad (1)$$

The concept of the maximal ideal, which was introduced by Gelfand, is central in this theory. His approach cast new light on many sections of the classical analysis. The well-known theorem by

Norbert Wiener, "If a function $f(x)$ decomposes into an absolutely convergent Fourier series and nowhere vanishes, then $1/f(x)$ has the same properties," is a simple consequence of the developed general theory. The ring operations and the norm exist also in the set of all continuous linear operators in the Hilbert space. Besides that, there is in this set an involution—a transition from the operator A to the operator A^* which is conjugate with it. In 1942 Gelfand and M. A. Naimark proved that any noncommutative normed ring with an involution can be realized as a ring of linear operators in the Hilbert space. This work was continued by Gelfand and Naimark in subsequent investigations which dealt with the theory of infinite-dimensional representations of continuous groups. *See* WIENER, NORBERT.

The representation T of group G is a mapping of its elements $g \rightarrow T(g)$ in a ring of linear operators which satisfies the relationship in Eq. (2).

$$T(g_1 g_2) = T(g_1)T(g_2) \qquad (2)$$

This relationship is a far-ranging generalization of the functional equation shown as Eq. (3); which is satisfied by the expo-

$$\varphi (x + y) = \varphi(x)\varphi(y) \qquad (3)$$

nential function $\varphi (x) = \exp (ax)$. The problems of harmonic analysis on groups are closely related to the theory of representations. An analog of the decomposition of the functions into Fourier series and integrals is the decomposition of the functions on the group into series and integrals by functions which belong to irreducible representations.

The theory of representations for compact groups (an example of which can be served by the group of rotations of a three-dimensional space) was studied in detail by I. Schur, G. Frobenius, E. Cartan, H. Weyl, and others. In this case, all the irreducible representations of the group are finite-dimensional. For noncompact groups, for example, for a group of Lorentz transformations of the four-dimensional space-time, the situation seemed in comparably more complicated, and even the very statements of the basic problems were not clear.

In a series of works by Gelfand and his coworkers, studies were made of infinite-dimensional representations of classical groups, and harmonic analysis on noncompact groups. The representations of the groups gave a mathematical apparatus which made it possible to utilize the sym-

metry of the object during its mathematical study (for example, to utilize in the study of the Schrödinger equation the symmetry of the Coulomb field of the atomic nucleus or the symmetry of the atom with respect to the rearrangements of the electrons). These works by Gelfand and his coworkers were used widely by physicists in attempts to develop a theory of the symmetry of elementary particles.

The theory of generalized functions occupied a large place in the studies by Gelfand. His interest was greatly stimulated by his previous works on the theory of infinite-dimensional representations, in which these functions were essentially utilized in an implicit form. Following the appearance of the works by L. Schwarz, Gelfand and his students and colleagues performed the universal development of an apparatus of generalized functions after carrying out, in particular, a harmonic analysis of rapidly growing functions; they also studied the applications to the theory of differential equations, and they laid the geometric bases of integral transformations.

The work by Gelfand and his school made a great contribution to the theory of the solution of the inverse Sturm-Liouville problem, which has diverse physical applications. A number of works by Gelfand dealt with computational mathematics, in which he proposed a simple, stable algorithm for the numerical solution of the boundary-value problems for differential equations.

The development of integral geometry, begun by Gelfand in the 1960s, was connected with the theory of unitary representations of semi-simple Lie groups. The simplest problem of integral geometry is how to find the function $f(x)$ if only the values of its integral over hyperplanes are given. This problem is connected with the Fourier integral. Gelfand and M. Graev proved that the problem of finding a formula similar to Plancherel's is actually the problem of reconstructing a function on a group from the given values of its integrals over orispheres (that is, trajectories of the maximal unipotent group and of its conjugates). A number of works by Gelfand and others were connnected with the integration of functions over hyperplanes of codimension greater than 1.

Beginning in 1968, Gelfand became interested in studying the cohomology of infinite Lie algebras. Although the subject itself was classical, nothing had been known about it before. Gelfand and D. B. Fuchs succeeded in calculating the co-homology of the Lie algebras of formal and smooth vector fields. This so-called Gelfand-Fuchs cohomology had important applications in differential geometry (especially in foliation theory) and in algebraic topology.

In 1958 Gelfand became interested in biology and physiology. In his first study, with M. L. Tsetlin, he analyzed the propagation of impulses in excitable tissues. This work had important applications in modeling the pathological regimes in the heart muscle with the help of continuously excitable media.

Most of Gelfand's physiological works were concerned with neurophysiology or with motion control problems. The ideas of Gelfand and Tsetlin regarding synergies and the multilevel control system (when the higher level changes the character of interactions and connections of the elements of the lower level, that is, nonindividual control) stimulated a number of experimental works concerning the mechanisms in the human body which maintain it in a stable vertical position, physiological tremor, and the simplest voluntary motions.

Gelfand and his colleagues made a detailed study of the connections between the various levels of the nervous system and of the signals transmitted in it during the natural rhythmic motions of animals, that is, locomotion and scratching. The activity of neurons of descending and ascending tracts of the spinal cord, as well as that of interneurons and motoneurons, was recorded while these motions were occurring. It was shown that when rhythmic motions take place, some tracts of the spinal cord transmit signals containing information on the activity of the various muscles to the higher regions of the nervous system, and the other tracts (the ventral spinocerebellar tract, for example) transmit the signals about what is taking place in the spinal cord itself. The signals of the second type remain practically unchanged even when all the afferent fibers leading to the spinal cord are cut (and if the animal keeps moving after the operation).

Beginning about 1963 Gelfand, together with Vasiliev and others, worked in cell biology. The main direction of their research was the comparative study of the interactions of cultured normal and neoplastic cells with their environment. In particular, Gelfand and his colleagues

studied the cell reactions responsible for cell shape alterations and cell attachment to various surfaces. Several basic morphogenetic reactions responsible for these changes were revealed and investigated, among them, the pseudopodial attachment reaction and the stabilization reaction. It was shown that only the surface of a pseudopod can form attachments to other surfaces. Stabilization is the process regulating distribution of pseudopodia in various parts of the cell surface. Because of stabilization, the cell is able to extend pseudopodia only in one direction and thus to perform oriented movement. It was found that microtubules are responsible for stabilization. The research also indicated that neoplastic cells in cultures are deficient in pseudopodial attachment reactions and that the deficiency of these reactions is responsible for many manifestations of pathological behavior of these cells.

After completing his secondary education, Gelfand was admitted to postgraduate studies at Moscow University at the age of 19 without attending the usual 5-year university course. He obtained his first degree in mathematics (Candidate of Sciences) after completing postgraduate work in 1935, and his second degree in mathematics (Doctor of Sciences) in 1940 for his study of the theory of normed rings. Beginning in 1932 he taught at Moscow University, where he became assistant professor in 1935 and full professor in 1943. He later became head of the Laboratory of Mathematical Methods in Biology at Moscow State University. He became an associate member of the Academy of Sciences of the U.S.S.R. in 1953. Gelfand was also elected a foreign member of the Royal Society of London (1977), the U.S. National Academy of Sciences (1970), the American Academy of Arts and Sciences (1964), the Academie des Sciences (France, 1976), the Royal Swedish Academy of Sciences (1974), and the Royal Irish Society (1970). He was elected doctor honoris causa at Oxford University (1973), Harvard University (1976), Pierre et Marie Curie University (Paris VI, 1975), University of Paris (VII, 1975), and Uppsala University (1977). He was elected an honorary member of the London Mathematical Society (1967), and of the Moscow Mathematical Society (1971). Gelfand was awarded the Wolf Prize in Mathematics by the Wolf Foundation, Israel, in 1978.

For background information see CELL (BIOLOGY); GROUP THEORY; LIE GROUP; NEUROPHYSIOLOGY; RING THEORY in the McGraw-Hill Encyclopedia of Science and Technology. ∎

GELL-MANN, MURRAY
☆ American physicist

Born Sept. 15, 1929, New York, NY, U.S.A.

For his contributions and discoveries concerning the classification of elementary particles and their interactions, Gell-Mann was awarded the 1969 Nobel Prize in physics.

In 1953 Gell-Mann proposed that certain sub-atomic particles possessed an invariant quality, which he called strangeness, that was conserved in strong and electromagnetic interactions, but not in weak interactions. This law of conservation of strangeness, first enunciated by him, explained a number of peculiarities in the behavior of the short-lived, heavy, artifically produced strange particles. The notion of conservation of strangeness was essential to later symmetry schemes for classification of strongly interacting particles, including the SU(3) symmetry brought forward in 1961 by Gell-Mann himself.

Shortly after 1950, physicists began to notice anomalous tracks in cloud chambers, which were best explained by supposing that an unknown neutral particle had decayed into two charged particles.

With further study of these events, it became evident that at least two sorts of neutral particle were being detected. One, about as massive as a nucleon, was called the Λ⁰ (lambda-zero); the other, considerably lighter, came to be known as the K^0 (K-zero). Very soon, the list of hitherto unknown particles was extended to include the Σ (sigma) in charged and neutral form; the Ξ⁻ (xi-minus); and two charged K particles, positive and negative. These particles came to be called, collectively, the strange particles, because of several peculiarities that they exhibited. They appeared very frequently in cloud chambers, so that their creation had to be attributed to the rapid strong process, with a time scale in the order of about 10^{-23} second. According to theory, therefore, their preferred modes of decay ought to be some variety of strong interaction. However, not only did strange particles not decay in this fashion, but they did not even decay through electromagnetic interaction (time scale about 10^{-13} second); instead, they decayed through the very much slower and less probable weak interactions (time scale about 10^{-9} second).

To explain the anomalously long lifetimes of the strange particles (ranging from 10^{-8} to 10^{-10} second), the theory of associated production was presently advanced. It stated that the strong forces responsible for the strange particles could only act to create them in batches of two or more at a time. It was shown that if strange particles thus produced immediately moved apart, their separate decay modes via the strong interactions would always prove to require more energy than had gone into their formation as a pair. This explained how strange particles, forbidden to decay separately by the strong interaction, survived long enough to disintegrate ultimately via the weak processes. The idea of associated production, while helpful in this regard, remained an empirical idea and was not very satisfactory from a theoretical standpoint.

The concept of isotopic spin was a mathematical device used to express the fact that protons and neutrons exhibited charge independence; all the possible strong interactions between them were equal in force, and they were distinguished only by charge. The isotopic-spin values of $+\frac{1}{2}$ for the proton and $-\frac{1}{2}$ for the neutron were adopted; together they were said to form the charge doublet of the nucleon, with two possible charges,

+1 or 0, and thus a charge center at $+\frac{1}{2}$. (The antiproton and antineutron made up another doublet with charge center at $-\frac{1}{2}$, and so on for all the antiparticles.)

The notion of charge multiplets (a general term for doublets, triplets, and so forth) was shown to apply to all particles that conserved isotopic spin in strong interactions. Accordingly, since the pions fitted this description, they were considered a triplet of positive, neutral, and negative states; isotopic spins $+1, 0, -1$; and a charge center at 0.

It seemed natural to apply this terminology to the newly discovered strange particles in the hope of imposing some order on their rather unruly behavior. Since they obeyed the strong interaction and might be hypothesized to exhibit charge independence, the heavy Λ, Σ, and Ξ were tentatively placed in doublets like the nucleon, which they resembled in mass. The lighter K seemed to belong to a triplet like the pion. The rule seemed to be: baryons in doublets, mesons in triplets.

Gell-Mann, contemplating this arrangement, began to suspect that there was no particular reason why this need be the case. In fact, he suspected that if the strange particles could be shown to depart from this scheme of things, the manner of their incongruity would itself be a significant clue to their behavior.

First of all, then, what were the possible varieties of multiplets? Triplets, clearly, could have a charge center at 0; doublets, at either $-\frac{1}{2}$ or $+\frac{1}{2}$; singlets (multiplets with one member only) at 0. Gell-Mann now tabulated the heavy strange particles, assigning each to a tentative multiplet and measuring the charge center of that multiplet according to its displacement from the reference mark ($+\frac{1}{2}$) of the charge center of nucleon doublet. The Λ⁰ he assigned to the possible singlet; and, since its charge center was at 0, it seemed displaced by a matter of $-\frac{1}{2}$. Supposing this displacement to be an intrinsic quality of the particles, Gell-Mann began to think of it as a quantum number. (For reasons of arithmetical convenience, strangeness is measured as twice the displacement; thus, the Λ⁰ had strangeness -1. Strangeness of antiparticles was measured according to the displacement from the charge center of the antinucleon doublet, which was $-\frac{1}{2}$; thus, the strangeness of the $\overline{\Lambda}^0$, with charge center at 0, was $+\frac{1}{2}$.)

Another possibility was a baryon triplet centered at 0, with a displacement of $-\frac{1}{2}$ and thus a strangeness of -1. The Σ might

fit here; it did seem to comprise a charge multiplet of positive, negative, and neutral particles. Finally, there was the possibility of a doublet with a charge center at $-\frac{1}{2}$ and therefore a strangeness of -2. Such a pair would contain a neutral and a negative particle. Mann suggested that the Ξ⁻ was the required negative particle and that there should exist a Ξ⁰ to complete the doublet. (The subsequent experimental detection of this particle formed a striking confirmation of the notion of strangeness.)

Continuing his tabulation, Gell-Mann went on to classify the K particles by placing them in doublets: the $\overline{K}^0$ and K^+ in one, with a charge center at $+\frac{1}{2}$; and the K^0 and K^- in another, with a charge center at $-\frac{1}{2}$. Using the charge center of the pion triplet (0) as a reference mark, Gell-Mann assigned the K doublets strangeness of, respectively, $+1$ and -1.

Gell-Mann was now able to show that strangeness was conserved in all strong interactions; that is, the total strangeness on each side of any strong event must be equal. If this were so, it would immediately provide a theoretical basis for the doctrine of associated production. In an equation with ordinary particles (total strangeness $= 0$) on one side of the reaction, any strange particles on the other side must be produced at least two at a time, so that the resulting strangenesses would add to a net value also of 0.

Gell-Mann was also able to equate strangeness with the isotopic-spin component I_z in explaining how the strange particles avoided decay via the electromagnetic processes, which he also proved must obey conservation of strangeness. The crucial item here was that isolated strange particles were forbidden to decay into ordinary particles, since then the conservation of strangeness would once more be violated. Thus he explained how the strange particles survived long enough to fall into the domain of the weak interaction, for which the conservation of strangeness (like parity) failed.

Using the strangeness formulations (which were proposed independently by the Japanese physicist Kazuhiko Nishijima), Gell-Mann successfully gave detailed predictions of numerous decay events of strange particles, as well as prophesying the existence of the Ξ⁰ as mentioned above.

In 1961 Gell-Mann announced a new system of unified classification of strongly interacting particles, which he called the eightfold way. In this scheme, the varied strange particles, and others, are expressed as recurrences of a few ground states. Confirmation was forthcoming almost at once from experiment; the Ω^- (omega-minus) particle, which had been predicted by the eightfold way, was found in 1964.

Gell-Mann received his B.S. at Yale in 1948 and his Ph.D. at the Massachusetts Institute of Technology in 1951. He then became, briefly, a member of the Institute for Advanced Study (1952) and an instructor and later associate professor at the University of Chicago (1952–54). In 1954 he moved to the California Institute of Technology, where he became professor of physics in 1956 and R.A. Millikan Professor of Theoretical Physics in 1967. He served on the President's Scientific Advisory Committee from 1972 to 1975. He received the Dannie Heineman Prize of the American Physical Society (1959), the Ernest O. Lawrence Award of the Atomic Energy Commission (1966), the Franklin Medal of the Franklin Institute (1967), the John J. Carty Medal of the National Academy of Sciences (1968), and the Research Corporation Award (1969). He was elected to the National Academy of Sciences (1960), and the American Academy of Arts and Sciences (1964).

Gell-Mann wrote *The Eightfold Way*, with Y. Ne'eman (1964), and *Broken Scale Variance and the Light Cone*, with K. Wilson (1971).

For background information *see* BARYON; ELEMENTARY PARTICLE; INTERACTIONS, WEAK NUCLEAR; ISOTOPIC SPIN; MESON; STRANGE PARTICLE in the McGraw-Hill Encyclopedia of Science and Technology. ■

GERARD, RALPH WALDO
★ American physiologist

Born Oct. 7, 1900, Chicago, IL, U.S.A.
Died Feb. 17, 1974, Newport Beach, CA, U.S.A.

A long career in analysis and research carried Gerard from chemistry, through electrophysiology and medicine, to the general examination of the brain and behavior, and ultimately to computer use in education.

Gerard's first contribution to neural science was the demonstration—partly with A. V. Hill and partly with O. Meyerhoff, who had made comparable studies on far more energetic muscle cells—of a minute increase in metabolism of nerve cells when carrying messages. Both the heat produced and oxygen used were so small that new instruments were required to measure them, yet this work proved nerve activity to be a normal kind of body activity. Indeed, although the nerve impulse passes in a thousandth of a second, the chemical and physical changes that this tiny "explosion" sets up continue for minutes or hours and involve changes in ions and compounds, in electric circuits and flow, and in the ability of nerve to respond further.

To relate metabolism with activity, fine electrical measures were needed, and a capillary electrode was developed that could be inserted into single muscle, nerve, and other cells for more precise analysis. This technique was used by J. C. Eccles and A. L. Hodgkin in the studies for which they shared a Nobel Prize in 1963. *See* ECCLES, SIR JOHN (CAREW); HODGKIN, SIR ALAN (LLOYD).

In further neural studies Gerard poked electrodes into the brain and thus revealed that incoming visual, auditory, tactile, and other sensory messages reach many regions of the cerebrum and cerebellum previously thought to have no such inputs. This neural activity also requires metabolic energy and is associated with an increased blood supply to the active regions. A small brain, like the frog's, can receive enough oxygen by diffusion and can continue vigorous activity—even show electrical convulsions under drug

treatment—when removed from the body. The frog brain also carries waves of activity across a complete section by a newly recognized type of electrical mechanism.

The relation of nerve cell to fiber also interested Gerard, since the fiber, though receiving its own nourishment, degenerates when separated from the cell. Gerard developed evidence that enzymes move from the cell down the fiber; this movement was later shown by P. A. Weiss to involve flow of the whole protoplasm. Such flow is related to the regeneration of a new fiber in peripheral nerve. Regeneration was long believed impossible in the central nervous system, but Gerard and others proved this important capacity to be present under favorable conditions. *See* WEISS, PAUL ALFRED.

Such studies stimulated Gerard's interest in normal and disturbed brain functioning. He related learning and remembering to physiological and biochemical changes in appropriate brain regions and showed them to require considerable time to become "fixed"—a time that could be increased or shortened by various means, including drugs. On the abnormal side, he conducted an extensive study of the biological and psychosocial attributes of hospitalized schizophrenic and other patients; this work revealed a number of distinguishable subtypes of this psychosis.

Behavior and learning studies led Gerard to give more formal attention to education and to the application of modern computer and related technology in this field. This endeavor capped his lifelong interest in teaching science to laymen as well as to university students, and he early experimented with the laboratory research project method and with the animation of theoretical models in instructional films.

Given much attention by an intellectual father, Gerard entered the University of Chicago at 14, receiving there the B.S. in 1919, Ph.D. in 1921, and M.D. in 1924. He served as professor of physiology at two medical schools along the way. After an internship in Los Angeles and study in London and Berlin, Gerard was a professor of physiology at Chicago for about 25 years. He then was professor and director of laboratories in the Neuropsychiatric Institute, University of Illinois, and in the department of psychiatry and the Mental Health Research Institute, University of Michigan. He became dean of the graduate division and director of special studies at the University of California, Irvine, in 1966. Recipient of several honorary degrees, in 1955 Gerard was elected to both the American Academy of Arts and Sciences and the National Academy of Sciences.

Gerard wrote *Unresting Cells* (1940; 2d ed. 1949; paper 1961); *Body Functions* (1941); *Mirror to Physiology* (1958). He edited *Methods in Medical Research* (vol. 3, 1950); *Food for Life* (1952; paper 1965); *Concepts of Biology,* with Russell B. Stevens (1958); *Psychopharmacology: Problems in Evaluation,* with J. O. Cole (1959); *Information Processing in the Nervous System,* with Jan W. Duyff (1963); and *Computers and Education,* with J. G. Miller (1967).

For background information *see* MEMORY; NERVOUS SYSTEM (VERTEBRATE) in the McGraw-Hill Encyclopedia of Science and Technology. ∎

GHIORSO, ALBERT
★ American nuclear scientist

Born July 15, 1915, Vallejo, CA, U.S.A.

Ghiorso had a most unusual career as a nuclear scientist, taking part in the discovery of 12 new chemical elements (as of 1978). In 1942 he joined the research staff at the famous wartime Metallurgical Laboratory at the University of Chicago to work under Glenn T. Seaborg for the Manhattan Project. Ghiorso's work involved maintenance and design of the complex instrumentation to make the nuclear mea-

surements for research into the new chemical processes needed for the atomic bomb program. His formal training was as an electrical engineer, but his new responsibilities perforce were in the fields of nuclear chemistry and physics, when he was introduced to the fascinating world of the transuranium elements. *See* SEABORG, GLENN THEODORE.

By late 1943 Seaborg felt that his team had its principal tasks under control, and decided to devote some time to trying to identify elements of atomic number higher than 94 (plutonium). Accordingly, he organized a small exploratory group and invited Ghiorso to join them. At that time the available nuclear tools were very primitive; consequently, the search method utilized the techniques of nuclear chemistry. Careful chemical separations were made on the basis of assumed chemical properties to isolate new element fractions from plutonium bombarded in cyclotrons and neutron reactors, and these fractions were then examined for unusual alpha-particle radioactivity. For the analysis of the final products Ghiorso refined a high-geometry technique using mica absorbers to measure the range of the observed alpha particles. After many failures elements 96 (curium) and 95 (americium) were discovered (and named) in July and October 1944, respectively. It subsequently became possible to make much larger quantities of these elements in nuclear reactors.

When Seaborg transferred back to the University of California in 1946 he took some of his team, including Ghiorso, with him, and the process of element building continued. To make elements 97 (berkelium) and 98 (californium) required helium ion bombardments of extremely hazardous quantitites of americium and curium followed by rapid chemical isolation of new elements whose chemical properties had to be predicted accurately. Again, these tasks were principally chemical, with the leader in these exhausting efforts being S. G. Thompson. The final analyses had to have higher sensitivity and resolution in order to distinguish the new alpha emitters from other activities, and for this purpose Ghiorso developed a 48-channel pulse-height analyzer to identify the short-lived elements with rapidity and certainty, and by early 1950 two more elements had been added to the periodic system. *See* THOMPSON, STANLEY GERALD.

The addition of the next two elements

was quite extraordinary. In November 1952 the first large-scale themonuclear explosion was set off in the South Pacific. The Argonne and Los Alamos laboratories soon found that as many as six neutrons had been added instantaneously to ^{238}U atoms, by the intense neutron flux in the test device, to form ^{244}U atoms which then beta-decayed to ^{244}Np which in turn decayed to ^{244}Pu. When Ghiorso heard of this phenomenon, he made a few naive assumptions (which turned out to be essentially correct) and calculated that it might be possible to find traces of neutron-heavy elements up to atomic number 100. He persuaded Thompson to isolate a transcalifornium fraction from an intensely radioactive airborne filter paper on which had been collected a bit of the explosive debris. Within a few days of this effort Ghiorso and Thompson knew that they had succeeded in finding yet another new element, 99 (einsteinium), for the same 48-channel analyzer showed a new alpha emitter in the transcalifornium fraction. The discovery of element 100 (fermium) followed about a month later in January 1953, when about 100 atoms were chemically isolated and identified from a much larger sample of fallout collected from the coral of an adjacent island. Within a year it was found that larger accessible quantities of these elements could be manufactured in reactors by neutron bombardments of curium over a long period of time.

The conventional tools of nuclear chemistry were unequal to the task of discovering the next elements because their half-lives were too short. Ghiorso decided to take advantage of the feeble recoil kick that occurs when a cyclotron projectile hits a target atom. A very thin target was used that allowed the newly transmuted atoms to leave the target material, thus enormously simplifying the chemical procedures so that the highly radioactive target was left intact and only the catcher foil needed to be dissolved. With a single-atom-at-a-time production rate, element 101 (mendelevium) was discovered in February 1955 by helium ion bombardment of ^{253}Es only a few years after that same isotope had been discovered in the test thermonuclear explosion known as "Mike."

Of necessity the next elements had to be fashioned by bombardment with particles heavier than helium since there were no suitable targets of higher atomic number than einsteinium. The heavy-ion linear accelerator (HILAC) had been constructed by 1957 with this in mind, and it was soon put to the test. Ghiorso and his colleagues evolved increasingly complicated instrumental techniques to identify with certainty rare alpha emitters. Instead of using chemistry to determine the atomic number, methods were devised to genetically relate one alpha emitter to another known one and thus build up a network of stepping stones to ever-higher atomic numbers. Elements 102 (nobelium), 103 (lawrencium), 104 (rutherfordium), 105 (hahnium), and 106 (unnamed as yet) were carefully characterized by their alpha-particle radiations. The discoveries of these elements were disputed by Soviet experimenters, who brought forth substitute candidates which decayed by spontaneous fission; however, their claims have been highly criticized as being nonspecific and ambiguous, since there is no known way of differentiating one fission event from another without chemical means.

In 1964 Ghiorso and two of his co-workers invented a highly advanced type of accelerator, which they called Ommitron, having a synchrotron accelerating ring and a storage ring. It was designed to accelerate all of the available elements of the periodic system from hydrogen to uranium, from low to high energies. Unfortunately, because of the war in Vietnam, funding was unavailable, and Ghiorso had to settle for improving the HILAC to make it into SuperHILAC, completed in 1971. To satisfy a promise he had made to biomedical researchers to provide high-energy heavy ions, Ghiorso invented the highly successful BevaLac, wherein the heavy-ion beam from the SuperHILAC is injected into the Bevatron, conveniently located a few hundred feet away.

In addition to his work with the dozen new elements, Ghiorso participated in the discovery of most of the nuclides in the heavy end of the isotope chart and played an important role in the development of the nuclear systematics of the region. He and his colleagues also used the Super-HILAC to determine whether there exists a hypothetical "island of stability" of superheavy elements in the region of 114 protons and 184 neutrons.

Ghiorso received a B.S. degree in electrical engineering in 1937 from the University of California, Berkeley. He worked until 1942 with a small firm, Cyclotron Specialties Company, designing, building, and testing various types of radio equipment; he built the first commercial Geiger counting systems for the Radiation Laboratory at Berkeley. During World War II he was associated with the Metallurgical Laboratory, University of Chicago. In 1946 he became a research associate at the renamed Lawrence Berkeley Laboratory. In 1966 he was awarded an honorary doctorate from Gustavus Adolphus College in Minnesota, and in 1973 received the American Chemical Society Nuclear Applications Award.

For background information *see* TRANSURANIUM ELEMENTS in the McGraw-Hill Encyclopedia of Science and Technology. ∎

GIAEVER, IVAR
★ American physicist

Born Apr. 5, 1929, Bergen, Norway

Giaever started his career in physics by studying the current flow between two metals separated by an extremely thin insulating film. For sufficiently thin films, almost all of the current flow would be due to a quantum-mechanical process known as electron tunneling. Giaever realized, and showed experimentally, that it was possible to get large amounts of information about the electron density of states of superconductors from the current-voltage characteristics obtained in an electron tunneling experiment. For this discovery he shared in the Nobel Prize for physics in 1973.

According to classical mechanics, when two regions of space are separated by a potential barrier, a particle can pass between them only if it has sufficient energy to surmount the barrier. Almost from the very beginning of quantum mechanics, it was realized that this was not a necessary condition; a particle with insufficient energy to surmount the barrier may pass from one region to another by going through the barrier. This process had been termed tunneling. Early theoretical calculations of electron transport between two metals separated by a thin insulating layer were made by S. Sommerfeld and H. A. Bethe; R. Holm later extended the calculations and furnished the first experimental evidence for the effect. *See* BETHE, HANS ALBRECHT.

J. C. Fisher and Giaever made a detailed study of electron tunneling through thin aluminum oxide films separating two layers of aluminum. At that time, the very successful theory of superconductivity by John Bardeen, L. N. Cooper, and J. R. Schrieffer had been formulated. The critical part in this theory is that an energy gap appears in the electron density of states when a metal is taken from its normal into its superconducting state. Giaever guessed that this change in the electron density of states should be reflected in the current-voltage characteristic in an electron tunneling experiment. This turned out to be true. The current-voltage characteristic for a tunneling experiment between two metals in the normal state is linear at low voltages; between one metal in the normal state and one metal in the superconducting state it is highly nonlinear; and between two metals in the superconducting state even a negative resistance may appear in the current-voltage characteristic. The experiment was soon repeated and extended in other laboratories in the United States and abroad. In 1962 B. D. Josephson predicted an interesting new tunneling effect which was verified shortly afterward. These experiments had a large scientific impact and advanced knowledge about both superconductors and ordinary metals. Practical devices based upon the effect and capable of measuring very small magnetic fields and currents have been devised. In the late 1970s devices based upon these tunneling experiments were being considered for possible use in large computers. *See* BARDEEN, JOHN; COOPER, LEON N.; JOSEPHSON, BRIAN DAVID; SCHRIEFFER, JOHN ROBERT. ∎

In 1969 Giaever spent a year in Cambridge, England, on a Guggenheim Fellowship and thereafter he spent most of his efforts on research in biophysics. His major interest was the interaction of proteins with solid surfaces. Based upon this research, he developed a simple visual test for use in immunology which has potential clinical use.

Giaever also turned his attention toward tissue culture research to attempt to study the interaction of mamalian cells with solid surfaces.

Giaever graduated as a mechanical engineer at the Norwegian Institute of Technology in Trodheim. He then served his compulsory year in the Norwegian army and afterward worked for a year as a patent examiner in the Norwegian government's patent office. In 1954 he migrated to Canada, where after working a short time as an architect's aide he joined the Canadian General Electric's Test Program, Peterborough, Ontario. In 1956 he went to the United States, where he attended an advanced engineering program at the General Electric Company, Schenectady, N.Y. In 1958 he became a research staff member in metallurgy and ceramics at the General Electric Research Laboratory. At the same time he started attending night classes in the physics department at Rensselaer Polytechnic Institute, Troy, NY, and received his Ph.D. there in 1964. He received the Oliver E. Buckley Prize of the American Physical Society in 1965 and the V. K. Zworykin Award of the National Academy of Engineering in 1974.

For background information *see* SUPERCONDUCTIVITY; TUNNEL JUNCTION in the McGraw-Hill Encyclopedia of Science and Technology. ∎

GIAUQUE, WILLIAM FRANCIS
☆ American chemist

> **Born** May 12, 1895, Niagara Falls, Ontario, Canada

While doing undergraduate research on the measurement of entropy at low temperatures under G. E. Gibson at the University of California, Berkeley, Giauque became interested in what has become known as the third law of thermodynamics. Following graduation, he continued work under Gibson on a doctoral thesis which showed experimentally that glycerine glass, which is an example of a system with molecular disorder, retained a large excess of entropy above that of crystalline glycerine at limiting low temperatures. After joining the faculty of the College of Chemistry in 1922, he continued low-temperature research, and his participation in the development of the cryogenic facilities at Berkeley afforded him a means to prove the third law of thermodynamics to be a fundamental law of nature, to determine accurately the entropy at temperatures approximating absolute zero of a large number of substances, and to accurately calculate chemical equilibria. For his work in the field of chemical thermodynamics, particularly on the behavior of substances at extremely low temperatures, Giauque was awarded the 1949 Nobel Prize in chemistry.

In 1906 the German chemist W. H. Nernst announced the Nernst heat theorem, which—after clarification and considerable limitation, such as the exclusion of disordered systems, by Max Planck (1911) and by G. N. Lewis and G. E. Gibson (1920)—was proposed as the third law of thermodynamics. This law associates zero entropy with the perfect crystalline (that is, the perfectly ordered) state at the absolute zero of temperature. Employing what has become known as statistical thermodynamics, Giauque used the actual energy levels of gas molecules, obtainable from the then newly developing work on band spectra of gases, in an attempt to learn and verify the rules of quantum statistics. This was done by comparing the entropies so calculated with experimental entropy values obtained from

low-temperature heat capacity measurements on the liquid and solid phases of the condensed gases, and the assumed correctness of the third law of thermodynamics. A large number of repetitions of this procedure using various gases, with close experimental agreements, served to establish the validity of both statistical thermodynamic calculations and the third law of thermodynamics.

Having provided a sound basis for these closely related methods, Giauque and his students proceeded to use observed molecular data for statistical calculations on gases, and calorimetric observations for third-law calculation on condensed phases, to tabulate the free energy and other thermodynamic properties of pure substances ranging from 0° absolute to extremely high temperatures. The general acceptance and use of these methods have created very extensive tabulations, which now provide a major source of chemical thermodynamic data. This work also led to the discovery of a few examples, such as CO, NO, and NNO, where lack of discrimination between the somewhat similar ends of these molecules caused them to crystallize with "frozen-in" molecular disorder. Such cases were shown not to approach zero entropy at the absolute zero of temperature by calculable amounts, and they illustrate the requirement that zero entropy applies only to perfect molecular order.

In 1910 the Dutch physicist Heike Kamerlingh Onnes managed to produce a temperature of 0.8° absolute by evaporative cooling of liquid helium, whose normal boiling point is about 4°, by using a large battery of vacuum pumps. Temperatures of 0.4° absolute have been produced by a similar technique, utilizing the synthetically produced helium-3 isotope, but this appears to be about the limit of this method.

Giauque's work on the magnetic cooling method of producing very low temperatures had its origin in calculations in which he considered the effect of magnetic fields on various thermodynamic properties, including entropy. Since the heat capacities of substances ordinarily become very small at temperatures in the vicinity of 10° absolute, it had long been assumed that essentially all of the entropy was eliminated from substances at these low temperatures. However, in 1924, on the basis of magnetic susceptibility measurements made on gadolinium sulfate octahydrate at the temperature of liquid helium by Kamerlingh Onnes, Giauque was able to calculate that a large amount of entropy was removed from the substance when a magnetic field was applied. Giauque reasoned that under normal conditions the atomic magnets within a substance have no regular arrangement, which corresponds to the presence of entropy. He assumed that when a magnetic field of sufficient strength is applied to a paramagnetic substance, such as gadolinium sulfate, the atomic magnets line up with the field and entropy is removed. Since the removal of entropy is accompanied by the evolution of heat, Giauque reasoned that he could use this technique to produce a lowering of temperature. He further reasoned that if he could adiabatically demagnetize the material while causing it to do work, he could lower the temperature still more to a temperature approximating absolute zero. Since no thermometer was calibrated at temperatures below those already achieved, the problem was not only to produce extremely low temperatures by the magnetic cooling method but also to determine the temperature reached.

By 1933 Giauque and his associates had constructed the necessary apparatus. A paramagnetic substance, enclosed in a jacket filled with helium gas to conduct heat, was placed within the coil of a solenoid magnet. The apparatus within the coil was immersed in liquid helium. When an electric current was passed through the coils of the solenoid, the atomic magnets began to orient themselves with the magnetic field. The heat given off as the entropy was removed was conducted by the helium gas to the liquid helium, some of which proceeded to boil off. When the magnetization of the paramagnetic substance was complete, the helium gas was evacuated from the jacket to insulate the material against the flow of heat. The electric current was then turned off and, as the magnetic field decreased, the paramagnetic material did work at the expense of molecular energy by contributing to the current in the surrounding circuits. In this way the paramagnetic material was further cooled.

To determine the temperature of the material, a measuring coil, immersed in liquid helium, had been placed around the cylindrical sample. As the experiment progressed, it became increasingly difficult for an alternating electric current to pass through the measuring coil as the magnetic susceptibility of the paramagnetic substance increased. This effect made possible the quantitative determination of the magnetic susceptibility of the sample. From early results on several gadolinium compounds, with relatively small magnetic fields, Giauque and his student D. P. MacDougall were able to calculate the temperature, which was about 0.1° absolute, since the magnetic susceptibility increases approximately proportionally to the decrease in temperature. However, with the later development of this technique and the availability of high magnetic fields, temperatures of the order of a thousandth of a degree absolute may be attained. Also, by means of appropriate measurements, the temperatures may be calculated by means of rigorous thermodynamic equations. One of the valuable contributions to temperature measurement in this region was Giauque's discovery of the properties of the amorphous carbon resistance thermometer. The extremely large negative temperature coefficient of the electrical resistance of amorphous carbon at very low temperatures enables temperature measurements of great precision in the presence of magnetic fields.

Among Giauque's other significant contributions was his discovery in 1929, with his student H. L. Johnston that atmospheric oxygen contains small amounts of isotopes of atomic weights 17 and 18, as well as the more common isotope of atomic weight 16. This not only disclosed that chemists and physicists were unknowingly using different atomic weight scales, it provided a basis for computing the difference between the chemical and physical atomic weight scales (which was not eliminated until the present scale on carbon-12 was adopted in 1961) and also provided scientists with an isotope tracer, oxygen-18, with which respiration and photosynthesis mechanisms could be studied. The isotope work on oxygen also proved experimentally that molecules retain one-half quantum unit of zero point vibrational energy in their lowest energy states, as had been predicted on a somewhat mystical basis by Planck early in the century. Thus a still too common uninformed statement, that motions cease at 0° absolute, is false, as had long been evident in terms of elctron motions in atoms that could hardly be expected to cease at any temperature.

Giauque majored in chemistry but included a heavy program of engineering courses at the University of California at Berkeley, where he received his B.S. with highest honors in 1920 and his Ph.D. in chemistry, with a minor in physics, in 1922. He became an instructor in the College of Chemistry of the university in 1922, rising to professor in 1934. From 1939 to 1944 he organized and led a group at Berkeley that worked for the United States government on problems of the design and construction of mobile units for the production of liquid oxygen. After 1944 he continued his low-temperature researches with increased emphasis on high-field magnet design and magnetothermodynamic measurements. He was elected to the National Academy of Sciences in 1936.

For background information *see* CRYOGENICS; LOW-TEMPERATURE THERMOMETRY; THERMODYNAMICS, CHEMICAL in the McGraw-Hill Encyclopedia of Science and Technology. ∎

GIBBON, JOHN H., JR.
American surgeon

Born Sept. 29, 1903, Philadelphia, PA, U.S.A.
Died Feb. 5, 1973, Philadelphia, PA, U.S.A.

Gibbon's most important contribution to medical science was the development of the heart-lung machine. The idea of developing a heart-lung machine came to him in October 1930, while, as a young surgical research fellow at the Massachusetts General Hospital in Boston, he sat at the bedside of a patient dying from a massive pulmonary embolism. The thought occurred and recurred to him, during a long night's vigil, that if there were some apparatus that could take over temporarily the functions of the heart and lungs, it would be possible for a surgeon to stop the blood from entering the patient's heart, open up the major vessels, remove the clot in the pulmonary artery, and possibly save the life of the patient. But at that time this was only a dream; there was no such apparatus.

To perform open operations on the heart, it was necessary to develop an apparatus which could take over the functions of both sides of the heart, which is really two pumping systems. One side receives blood returning from the body and pumps it out through the lungs; the second receives blood returning from the lungs and pumps it out into the general circulation.

Initial laboratory studies on a heart-lung machine were carried out at the Massachusetts General Hospital in 1934-35. Cats were the experimental animals of choice at that time. Occasionally the supply of cats ran short at the laboratory, and Gibbon would prowl around Beacon Hill at night with a can of salmon to entice one or two of the many stray cats. His willing assistant in the laboratory was Maly Hopkinson (whom he married), a technician for Edward D. Churchill, then professor of surgery at the Harvard Medical School, which had a research laboratory at the Massachusetts General Hospital.

Gibbon's first report of this work at the 1937 meeting of the American Association for Thoracic Surgery brought forth only one discusser, who said "Shades of Jules Verne!" Gibbon returned to his native Philadelphia after the second year in Boston, where the earliest work on a heart-lung machine had begun, and set up his project in the Harrison Department of Surgical Research at the University of Pennsylvania Medical School. This work was interrupted in 1942 by World War II, in which he served long and illustriously in the South Pacific area.

Back in Philadelphia after the war, Gibbon moved to Jefferson Medical College as professor of surgery and head of a newly created department of surgical research. In 1947 his work was given very substantial impetus when Thomas Watson, the head of International Business Machines, became personally interested in the project and made available to Gibbon the vast technological expertise of IBM.

There were many problems to be solved. Gibbon had to devise a means of taking the blood from the body of the experimental animal, oxygenating the blood and removing the carbon dioxide, and returning the blood to the animal without damaging the fragile red blood cells or introducing bubbles of oxygen into the animal's circulation. He always felt that such an application had to be proved safe in the laboratory before it could be considered for clinical use.

The need for large amounts of blood for the laboratory culture experiments was solved by collecting blood at the local abbatoir. Later, blood was obtained from donor cats to prime the apparatus before connecting it to the cat's own circulation in the animal experiments. The most desirable method of effecting gas exchange was explored by many different techniques. The most difficult problem throughout the early work was the introduction of sufficient oxygen to meet the needs of the experimental animal. Initially the blood was exposed to oxygen on the inner surface of a large revolving cylinder: it was introduced at the top of the cylinder, tangentially in the direction of the revolutions, and was collected in a stationary cup at the bottom; it was then pumped back into the animal's arteries. Gibbon also experimented with the use of some of the elaborate condensing chambers used in commercial chemistry, but discarded these methods as too damaging to the red cells. He finally found that blood flowing down, over a vertical screen lining the cylinder, developed a turbulent flow which exposed more of the red cells to the adjacent atmosphere than the laminar flow.

A pump which was highly efficient caused a great deal of hemolysis. The use of a DeBakey pump, a roller pump, so set that the walls of the blood tubing did not meet, was not as efficient but was far less traumatic to the red cells. If there was a narrowing in the blood circuit, it caused a jet effect distal to the point of narrowing. Any jet effect caused hemolysis. Some work was done on creating a pulsatile flow, but later it was found to be unnecessary in the cats and dogs used for these experiments.

Once the problems of oxygenation and hemolysis were largely controlled, laboratory perfusions were begun by using dogs and creating artificial defects in their hearts, which were repaired by using the heart-lung machine. Here hypothermia, acidosis, and appropriate blood flow had to be addressed. Gibbon had set a goal of 10 consecutive, successful 1-hour perfusions in dogs before attempting clinical application. Only after that had been achieved was he willing to use the apparatus clinically with a human patient. At this point, he found that the coronary blood flow was far greater than anyone appreciated, and the loss of blood from the coronary vein could exsanguinate the patient. Direct aspiration of the blood from the right atrium back into the extracorporeal circulation corrected this problem, although excessive suction could cause hemolysis.

Gibbon finally performed the first successful open-heart operation, using the heart-lung machine, on a patient in May 1953, when he repaired an interatrial defect in the heart of a 19-year-old girl. This historic operation, the first successful one using such a machine, opened up the field of open-heart surgery throughout the world.

Gibbon made many other contributions. With his wife, he established the anoxic time that the brain of cats would tolerate. With John Healy, he spelled out the intrapericardial anatomy of the heart during the infancy of cardiac surgery. Gibbon and his coworkers demonstrated that respiratory acidosis could be prevented by providing adequate pulmonary ventilation. They developed the Jefferson ventilator, an intermittent positive- and negative-pressure device which showed that adequate ventilation could be accomplished without interfering with cardiac output by maintaining a low mean endotracheal pressure.

As a fifth generation of doctors in his family, Gibbon graduated from Princeton University in 1923 and received his M.D. degree at Jefferson Medical College in 1927. He interned at Pennsylvania Hospital in Philadelphia and then took a year of training (1929–30) at the Massachusetts General Hospital in Surgical Research, under the direction of Churchill. He married his research assistant, Maly Hopkinson, in 1931, and they resided and worked in Philadelphia until 1934-35, when they returned to Boston and began the earliest studies on the development of the heart-lung machine. From 1936 to 1942 Gibbon continued work at the Harrison Department of Surgical Research at the Pennsylvania University Medical School under the direction of I. S. Ravdin. After war service, Gibbon returned to Jefferson Medical College as professor of surgery and head of surgical research. In 1956 he was made the Samuel D. Gross Professor and chairperson of the department of surgery. His many awards included the Distinguished Service Award of the International Society of Surgery (1959), Gairdner Award of the Foundation International, Toronto (1960), Distinguished Service Award of the Pennsylvania Medical Society (1962), Research Achievement Award of the American Heart Association (1965), Albert Lasker Medical Research Award, New York (1968), and Dickinson Award of the University of Pittsburgh (1972). Gibbon received honorary degrees from many universities, and delivered many honorary lectures. He was made an honorary fellow of the Royal College of Surgery of England (1959) and an honorary member of the Society of Thoracic Surgery of Great Britain and Ireland (1961).

Author of over a hundred papers published in various surgical journals, Gibbon edited *Surgery of the Chest* (1950). ∎

GIBBS, WILLIAM FRANCIS

☆ American naval architect and marine engineer

Born Aug. 24, 1886, Philadelphia, PA, U.S.A.

Died Sept. 6, 1967, New York, NY, U.S.A.

Designing safer, more efficient, and faster ships for American commercial and naval fleets was Gibbs's purpose throughout his career. His advanced ship design concepts and techniques and his judicious use of materials are exemplified in the *SS United States,* which set new speed records in transatlantic passenger service in 1952. This record-shattering crossing was made at an average speed for the round voyage of 35.05 knots (18 meters per second). Thus 3.71 knots (1.9 meters per second) were clipped off the previous record made by the *Queen Mary* 17 years before.

The *United States* incorporated supership design concepts formulated by Gibbs in the previous quarter-century and was built to rigid naval specifications to permit its speedy conversion to a troop transport. Welded construction was employed to reduce weight, and extensive use was made of aluminum alloys as shipbuilding materials. Increased compartmentation was incorporated in the design for maximum practicable safety and survival after collison or war damage. The ship propulsion power plant, well protected from underwater damage, was designed to achieve high efficiency and economy. The ship is capable of long voyages at high speed without refueling. Only fireproof furniture and decorative fabrics were used, and the only wood on board was in the butchers' chopping blocks and the pianos.

Gibbs's other major contributions include the development of lightweight, compact, high-pressure, high-temperature marine power plants of improved efficiency and economy, advance-design feed systems and heat balances, and high-speed gearing.

Gibbs devoted more than 40 years to the advocacy of superships. In 1922, at the government's request, he and his brother, Frederic H. Gibbs, organized Gibbs Brothers, Inc., to supervise the reconditioning of the SS *Leviathan,* SS *Republic,* and several American Merchant Line vessels. In 1929 the firm's name became Gibbs and Cox, Inc. In 1924 Gibbs designed and supervised construction of the SS *Malolo,* the fastest liner of its time built in America. The ship was unique because of extensive watertight compartmentation, which enabled it to survive a severe

collision that occurred during its trials. In 1937 he designed the SS *America,* at the time the largest and fastest merchant vessel built in the United States.

Beginning in 1933, in cooperation with the Navy, his firm undertook the design and engineering of destroyers for the U.S. Navy. As a result, there was developed high-pressure, high-temperature steam turbine machinery of exceptional efficiency that was later adopted for the Navy's battleships, aircraft carriers, cruisers, and destroyers. Before the United States' entry into World War II, the firm developed the working drawings for light cruisers, icebreakers, and Army transports. During the war it continued with the preparation of working plans and procurement of materials, apparatus, and equipment for cruisers, aircraft carriers, destroyers, escort vessels, landing craft, and mine sweepers. By the end of the war, the firm had procured materials valued in excess of $2,000,000,000 and had directed the preparation of working plans of more than 60 percent of all ships of major size, except battleships and submarines, constructed in American shipyards and Navy yards during the war. Between 5000 and 6000 ships of major size had been built to working plans produced by Gibb's firm. It was under Gibbs's leadership that the Liberty Ship program and other World War II multiple-shipbuilding programs first became practicable.

During World War II Gibbs served as controller of shipbuilding, War Production Board, and later as chairman, Combined Shipbuilding Committee (Standardization of Design) of the Combined Chiefs of Staff. He was special assistant to the director, Office of War Mobilization, and representative of the Office of War Mobilization on the Procurement Review Board of the Navy.

After the war, Gibbs and Cox, with the cooperation of the Navy, continued the design and preparation of working plans for various types of naval vessels, including the most modern guided-missile destroyers and frigates. In addition, numerous commercial projects were undertaken by the firm.

Gibbs attended Harvard University from 1906 to 1910; in 1913 he received M.A. and LL.B. degrees from Columbia University. Among the many science awards he received during his career was the 1953 Franklin Medal of the Franklin Institute of the State of Pennsylvania. He was elected to the National Academy of Sciences in 1949 and to the National Academy of Engineering in 1965.

For background information *see* SHIP DESIGN; SHIP POWERING AND STEERING in the McGraw-Hill Encyclopedia of Science and Technology. ∎

GILLULY, JAMES
☆ American geologist

Born June 24, 1896, Seattle, WA, U.S.A.

Prior to the mid-20th century, it was widely believed by geologists that mountain-making episodes (orogenies) had occurred at more or less regular intervals throughout the physical history of the Earth. According to this theory, long periods of quiescence, millions of years in duration, were punctuated by relatively short intervals of great crustal mobility, which produced both present and past mountain ranges. In 1949 Gilluly challenged this classic concept. He argued that orogenic activity, while perhaps not continuous, took place little by little rather than as one great "spasm." Further, he doubted that the crustal unrest evident today was any different from that of the past.

Invoking a major premise in geology that "the present is the key to the past," Gilluly cited evidence from California to show that movements of the Earth's crust took place in small "bits." He noted that the northwestern part of the Baldwin Hills in California was rising at the rate of 3 feet (0.9 meter) per century, as determined by precise leveling, and that the country between San Bernardino and Victorville across the pass in the Mojave Desert was arching upward at a rate of 20 inches (51 centimeters) per century. He also pointed out that during the 1933 earthquake at Long Beach a 4-mile (6.4-kilometer) area east of Long Beach was uplifted a full 7 inches (18 centimeters). Given the countless centuries of geologic time, Gilluly argued, these apparently trivial rates of rise were quite sufficient to account for any mountains on Earth and even to make a Mount Everest in only 2,000,000 years.

Gilluly marshaled evidence from the Earth's rock record to support his theory. The record of sediments formed during the Cretaceous Period in the United States (the time of the greatest development of the dinosaurs), he noted, indicated that repeated small uplifts took place rather than one or two major uplifts. At that time, the Nevada-Idaho region was being uplifted, and acted as a source of sediments that were eroded and carried far to the east. Gilluly calculated that nearly 10^6 cubic miles (4,096,000 cubic kilometers) of rock had been eroded away in the Nevada-Idaho region and that this would necessitate a vertical uplift and resulting denudation of about 3 miles (4.8 kilometers) in the source area.

If this uplift had taken place all at once, such a great spasm of the Earth's crust should be reflected in the sediments resulting from the erosion of lofty mountains. The sediments would be very coarse, containing boulders and other large pieces in the lower part of the sediment layers. As the source area was worn down, streams and other eastward-flowing currents would transport and deposit finer and finer particles. The Cretaceous sediments, therefore should show an upward progression of finer and finer sediment, according to the classic theory. On the contrary, Gilluly pointed to the abundant field evidence from the western states showing that the Cretaceous sediments are remarkably uniform in particle size. He concluded that erosion must have kept pace with numerous small uplifts in the Cretaceous source area, thus preventing any marked deviation in sediment character.

Gilluly also became well known for his work on thrust faults and the economic geology of copper deposits.

Gilluly received his B.S. from the University of Washington in 1920 and his Ph.D. from Yale University in 1926. He joined the U.S. Geological Survey in 1921, becoming a senior geologist in 1936, principal geologist in 1943, and chief of the general geology branch in 1954. He later served as chief of the fuels branch. Gilluly received the Penrose Medal of the Geological Society of America in 1958. He was elected to the National Academy of Sciences in 1947.

Gilluly wrote *Principles of Geology*, with A. C. Waters and A. O. Woodward (1959; 4th ed. 1975).

For background information *see* OROGENY in the McGraw-Hill Encyclopedia of Science and Technology. ∎

GILRUTH, ROBERT ROWE
★ American aeronautical and space engineer

Born Oct. 8, 1913, Nashwauk, MN, U.S.A.

Gilruth's principal engineering achievements were associated with the design and operation of high-speed flight vehicles, including the aircraft of World War II, the supersonic aircraft and guided missiles of the postwar period, and the space vehicles that carried American astronauts into orbit and to the lunar surface. In these activities he played the role of scientist, engineer, and manager of complex national programs.

Although Gilruth's work covered activities in many fields of flight, in retrospect they seem almost to have been selected to equip him for leadership in the manned space program. His early work, when associated with the National Advisory Committee for Aeronautics (NACA) at Langley Field, VA, included research in aircraft stability and control characteristics and their relation to human abilities and the preferences of pilots. His close association with test pilots and his own participation in the test flight programs gave him an insight into the man-machine relations that were to be so important in the spacecraft designs nearly 20 years later. His work in this field, which was published in 1941, brought him national and international recognition.

In 1943 Gilruth became technical head of flight research projects at NACA, but continued to pursue his individual research as well. He pioneered the development of techniques for exploring the aerodynamics of wings and controls at transonic flight speeds—which the wind tunnels of the day could not study because of the choking phenomena of closed-throat tunnels. One such technique used carefully shaped airplanelike models, equipped with telemeters to measure drag and pressure distribution. These models were dropped from high altitude by bomber aircraft and programmed to accelerate through the speed of sound before they impacted the earth. The first measurements of drag rise and other aerodynamic parameters for bodies accelerating through the speed of sound were obtained from these studies. For more detailed studies of wing and control characteristics, Gilruth invented the wing flow technique, which utilized the transonic flow region above the wing of a diving airplane for force tests of small wings and control surfaces mounted in this flow. This means of research was widely used in both free flight and wind tunnels (transonic bump technique) in the late 1940s and prior to the invention of the slotted-throat wind tunnel. It was particularly important in the design of the wings for the X-1 research airplane, which was the first to break the sound barrier, and later in showing the need for all-movable horizontal tails for all airplanes designed to fly through the speed of sound.

The advent of rocket power, the jet engine, and the guided missiles in the later war years gave great impetus to aeronautical research at higher and higher speeds. In 1945 Gilruth was put in charge of building a new research missile range at Wallops Island, VA, and of developing and directing its research program. The Wallops Island work utilized telemetry, radars, rocket motors, and all kinds of pyrotechnic devices, and came face to face with the problems of flight at extremely high speeds and under actual conditions. These new regimes of flight attracted a group of highly competent and inventive young engineers and scientists who became skilled in solving problems ranging from those of transonic and supersonic flight to those of the ballistic missile a few years later. The know-how generated in these efforts was, of course, directly applicable to space flight, and it was here that Gilruth created the team of young engineers and scientists that were to pioneer with him the manned space flight programs after the National Aeronautics and Space Administration (NASA) was formed.

When *Sputnik* was launched in October 1957, Gilruth was no longer at Wallops Island, but was an assistant director of the NACA Langley Laboratory. In the following year he was given the task of recommending the future course of NACA in the light of the space developments. In 1958 he went to Washington, DC, and under the guidance of H. L. Dryden, the director of NACA, he and others from NACA pulled together a new program and budget for a new space agency. They also defended their budget before Congress. In October 1958, when NASA was founded, it utilized the old NACA as a nucleus, and other groups, such as the Vanguard group of the Naval Research Laboratory, the Redstone group under Wernher von Braun, and the Jet Propulsion Laboratory under W. H. Pickering, were added. *See* DRYDEN, HUGH LATIMER; PICKERING, WILLIAM HAYWARD.

In October 1958 Gilruth was appointed head of the new NASA man-in-space program which was to be named Project Mercury. His group, the Space Task Group, had developed a concept utilizing a blunt reentry body with ablative heat shield and refractory metal afterbody, a pressure shell of titanium to contain the breathing oxygen, reaction control rockets for attitude control, retro-rockets to initiate reentry, parachute landing on the water, and the Atlas system for boost to orbit and for guidance. The final additions to the concept were the supine couch which allowed the astronaut to withstand accelerations up to 20 *g*, if required, and the escape tower in case of launch failure.

This novel but elegant solution to the manned satellite was so sound and efficient that it was to be used also for the lunar program, Apollo. The first astronauts were selected in 1959, and after several unmanned and animal flights, astronaut A. B. Shepard flew in a suborbital flight in May 1961–a few weeks after the Soviets' Y. A. Gagarin had flown in orbit. As a result of these activities, the Soviets' early success, and the world reaction, President John F. Kennedy, with advice of space experts, as well as his close political advisers, launched the United States on a lunar landing program to be completed in the 1960s.

In November 1961 Gilruth took his Space Task Group to Houston, TX, where they built and staffed the new Manned Spacecraft Center (now the Lyndon B. Johnson Space Center). They completed Project Mercury with four orbital flights, and to pave the way for Apollo they developed and flew a two-man spacecraft, Project Gemini, to study the problems of long-duration flight at zero gravity, rendezvous and docking, controlled reentry, and extravehicular activity, and most importantly, to provide space flight training and experience for the astronauts and the mission control specialists. The basic concepts of the lunar program were defined during this period of intense activity in flight operations, physical relocation of staff, and the building of new facilities. Critical technical decisions were required very early in the program, as were definitions of roles and missions between the NASA centers concerned. This was a most demanding and difficult time for Gilruth and his staff. However, during the first year of Apollo, all major decisions had been agreed upon and a master plan was created so sound that it needed no significant change as it went forward to completion.

The Apollo flights to the Moon commenced in December 1968 with a three-man flight around the Moon on Christmas. The lunar landing came in July 1969, and was followed over a period of 3 years by five more landings of ever-increasing capability, which included the reaching of more interesting sites on the Moon, increased mobility of astronauts, and more sophisticated instruments and techniques. The last landing occurred in December 1972.

Gilruth's parents were both schoolteachers. All his life he was interested in flying machines, and he was a student in one of the first classes in aeronautical engineering at the University of Minnesota, where he received his B.S. in 1935 and his M.S. in aeronautical engineering in 1936. Gilruth went to work with NACA in 1937. He retired as director of the Manned Spacecraft Center in 1972. His work was recognized by many honors, including the Presidential Medal for Distinguished Service (1962), the Robert H. Goddard Trophy of the American Rocket Society (1962), the Louis W. Hill Space Transportation Award of the American Institute of Aeronautics and Astronautics (1962), the Spirit of St. Louis Medal (1964), the Medal of the American Society of Mechanical Engineers (1970), and the International Astronautics Award of the Guggenheim Foundation (1966). He was elected to membership in the National Academy of Engineering (1968) and the National Academy of Sciences (1974).

For background information *see* AERODYNAMICS; AIRCRAFT TESTING; MANNED SPACE FLIGHT; TRANSONIC FLIGHT in the McGraw-Hill Encyclopedia of Science and Technology. ■

GINZTON, EDWARD LEONARD
★ American electronics engineer

Born Dec. 27, 1915, Ekaterinoslawsk, Russia

A major step in making the generation of the klystron tube of microwaves practical was the invention at Stanford University in 1937. This invention, by Russell and Sigurd Varian, demonstrated that a stream of electrons could be made to generate radio-frequency currents by the principle of velocity modulation of the electron stream. It was soon evident that this invention was destined to play an important role in making practical utilization of a vast new portion of the radio-frequency spectrum. Before much could be done, however, the characteristics of the klystron had to be understood and measured. Yet in this new region of the electromagnetic spectrum, methods of measurement had not yet been developed and such commonplace and important quantities as wavelength, frequency, power, and impedance could only be guessed with the aid of the most rudimentary experiments.

While still a graduate student at Stanford, Ginzton was asked by the Varian brothers and William W. Hansen to work in the physics department to help explore the characteristics of the klystron and the range of its usefulness, as well as to develop methods of microwave measurements. While a member of the now famous Stanford team of Russell and Sigurd Varian, David Webster, Hansen, and John Woodyard, Ginzton demonstrated the usefulness of the klystron as an amplifier and superheterodyne receiver and in master oscillator power amplifier chains. He also helped develop methods of measuring power, wavelength, and other significant parameters.

World War II made the microwave field important overnight. The Stanford group transferred to the larger laboratories of the Sperry Gyroscope Company in New York, where their work was continued on an expanded and accelerated scale. Study of military applications for the klystron resulted in the development of such important applications as Doppler radar, pulsed radar, and microwave communications. Twice during the war Ginzton traveled to Great Britain to exchange information with members of British research establishments concerning the progress of the klystron research and related system development. While visiting the EMI Laboratories in 1944, he found that British research demonstrated the usefulness of the klystron for pulsed applications and that peak power of several kilowatts could be obtained. He realized immediately that still larger power could be obtained from the klystron and that only the effects of relativity would limit the voltage at which a klystron could work. This realization stimulated his ideas about the possible usefulness of the klystron at very high power and caused him to think about various new approaches to research in the microwave field.

After the war Ginzton returned to Stanford as a member of the physics faculty and continued his work in the microwave field. He chose three closely related avenues of research: continuation of the development of methods of microwave measurements; development of the klystron with the intent of obtaining millions of watts of pulsed power; and application of such klystrons to the development of large electron accelerators for use in high-energy physics research.

In the first of these, Ginzton continued to work for many years, gradually attaining a satisfactory understanding of the various classes of physical phenomena basic to a satisfactory system of microwave measurements. Parallel with his research in this field, he taught graduate courses on microwave measurements, and the notes from his lectures eventually led to publication of a textbook on the subject.

The second avenue of research led to what is probably the outstanding accomplishment in Ginzton's career, the demonstration of the high-power klystron. Working closely with his colleague Marvin Chodorow, Ginzton decided that the idea of generating very high power could best be demonstrated by making one large extrapolation from the work of the British instead of the more conventional step-by-step increase of knowledge and experience. Ginzton and Chodorow decided to test the feasibility of building a klystron for the generation of pulse power at the level of about 25 megawatts at a wavelength of 10 centimeters. In this original investigation in the field of such unusually high power, many new and basic problems were encountered which had to be solved before a successful design could be established. Among the most important of these were: (1) the basic klystron theory had to be extended into the range of relativistic velocities; (2) the theory of magnetic focusing of the cylindrical electron beams had to be developed; (3) the practicality of obtaining emission from oxide cathodes at voltages approximating 500,000 volts had to be explored experimentally; (4) the voltage breakdown phenomena at microwave frequencies had to be understood; (5) methods of generating short pulses at about

100,000 volts and 1000 amperes had to be developed, together with requisite gap switches; (6) pulse transformers, stepping up voltages to 500,000-volt level, had to be developed. As it turned out, none of these problems proved to be very difficult, and the first tube designed on paper operated successfully in 1949 after 2 years of work. For his work in this field, Ginzton was awarded the Morris Liebmann Memorial Prize in 1957.

Along with the klystron development, Hansen developed the theory of the linear electron accelerator and demonstrated its validity on a small-scale machine. Hansen then proposed the construction of a billion-volt accelerator and sketched the design for a 220-foot (67-meter) machine to be powered by 22 of the high-power klystrons mentioned above. Unfortunately, Hansen died before this project was barely started, and it became Ginzton's responsibility to complete this work. He supervised a small staff of coworkers and graduate students, and the machine was completed in 1952. Perhaps the greatest demonstration of the usefulness of this accelerator was its use by Robert Hofstadter in measuring the size and charge distribution of a number of nuclei—the work for which Hofstadter was awarded the 1961 Nobel Prize in physics. *See* HOFSTADTER, ROBERT.

With the completion of the billion-volt machine, it was clear that smaller machines of the same variety could be used to generate x-rays and electrons for cancer therapy. With Henry Kaplan, Ginzton designed and supervised the construction of a 6-megaelectronvolt (MeV) linear electron accelerator. This experimental machine was installed at the Stanford University department of radiology in 1955 and was used in pioneering research in the treatment of cancer. This work proved significant enough so that more than 500 such machines are now to be found in several parts of the world for use in routine treatment of cancer.

The success of the billion-volt linear accelerator showed that the usefulness of high-energy electrons for research on elementary particles would be greater at even higher energies and that there were no fundamental reasons to limit the construction of a much larger machine. With Ginzton as the director of a new project, a group of Stanford physicists and engineers began to study the practicality, usefulness, and costs of a machine several miles in length. These studies resulted in a report entitled "Project M," which was submitted to the United States government in 1957. It described a 2-mile (3.2-kilometer) accelerator which would be capable of generating up to 50 billion electronvolts (BeV) and which could provide enormous intensities for research in high-energy particle physics. Under Ginzton's supervision, the preliminary design of this machine was finished, and the project received congressional approval in 1961. The 2-mile accelerator was completed in 1966 and is being used for research as the highest-energy electron accelerator in the world. For his contributions toward development of the linear accelerator, Ginzton was awarded the Medal of Honor of the Institute of Electrical and Electronics Engineers (IEEE) in 1969.

In 1948 Ginzton became deeply involved with the formation of Varian Associates. Just prior to the congressional approval of the 2-mile accelerator, he was asked to become board chairman. With approval of the project assured, Ginzton chose to continue with his work at Varian and left the Stanford project. This company is the principal manufacturer of high-power klystrons, linear electron accelerators, nuclear magnetic resonance spectrometers, electronic vacuum pumps, and other devices which formerly were subjects of theoretical and experimental research in the physics laboratories of Stanford and other universities.

Ginzton received his B.S. (1936) and M.S. (1937) at the University of California at Berkeley. He obtained his E.E. (1938) and Ph.D. (1940) under F. E. Terman at Stanford. He returned to Stanford after the World War II to join its faculty, remaining there as professor of applied physics and electrical engineering until 1961. He was also the director of the Microwave Laboratory from 1949 to 1961. One of the founders of Varian Associates, in 1959 he was appointed chairman of the board, was president from 1964 to 1968, and served as chief executive officer from 1959 to 1972. He was elected to the National Academy of Engineering in 1965, the National Academy of Sciences in 1966, and the American Academy of Arts and Sciences in 1971. During 1971–74 Ginzton acted as a chairperson of the National Academy of Sciences Committee on Motor Vehicle Emissions, and from 1975 was chairperson of the Academy Committee on Nuclear and Alternative Energy Systems. In 1971–72 he served as a member of the board of directors of IEEE; from 1972 to 1978 he was a member of the Lawrence Berkeley Laboratory Scientific and Educational Advisory Committee; he was chair of the advisory board of the school of engineering of Stanford University from 1968 to 1970. From 1968 to 1974 he was co-chairperson of the Stanford Mid-Peninsula Urban Coalition, and a member of the board of directors of the Mid-Peninsula Housing Development Corporation from 1970 onward. He served as a member of the board of directors of Stanford University Hospital from 1975, and a member of the Stanford University Board of Trustees from 1977. In 1974 he received the California Manufacturers Association's award as the California Manufacturer of the Year. *See* TERMAN, FREDERICK EMMONS.

Ginzton wrote *Microwave Measurements* (1957) and numerous articles in technical journals. Approximately 40 patents were issued in his name for inventions in the fields of microwave measurements, microwave tubes, and other electronic devices.

For background information *see* KLYSTRON; MICROWAVE TUBE; PARTICLE ACCELERATOR in the McGraw-Hill Encyclopedia of Science and Technology. ∎

GLASER, DONALD ARTHUR

☆ American physicist and molecular biologist

Born Sept. 21, 1926, Cleveland, OH, U.S.A.

Glaser invented the bubble chamber, a device for detecting the paths of high-energy atomic particles. It has yielded much new data unobtainable in other ways and has given precise pictorial information about high-energy particles and phenomena, such as masses, lifetimes, and decay modes. In 1960 Glaser was awarded the Nobel Prize in physics for his invention.

The cloud chamber, invented by C. T. R. Wilson in 1927, marked the beginning of precise visual investigation of the interaction of atomic particles. This device contained a supersaturated gas in a state of expansion; ionizing radiation traversing the chamber condensed the gas along its path to form droplets of liquid. It could detect particles with energies ranging up to several million electronvolts. However, both it and the nuclear emulsion

were severely limited for investigation of the high-energy (several billion electron-volts) particles whose production was becoming practicable upon the completion of the giant particle accelerators in the early 1950s.

Glaser, engaged in work on the strange particles produced in high-energy cosmic-ray collisions, recognized the need for a high-energy detector. Elaborations of the nuclear emulsion or the Wilson chamber (whose low-density contents permitted relatively few particle collisions), he reasoned, would prove cumbersome and impractical. He sought a high-density, large-volume medium in which to observe the trails of fast particles. Studying the properties of liquids and solids that might be useful, Glaser became intrigued with the instability of superheated liquids. If the surface tension of such a liquid could be drastically reduced and the vapor pressure simultaneously raised, ionizing radiation passing through the liquid should induce the formation of bubbles along the paths of the particles. Such a reversal of the Wilson-chamber effect—formation of gas bubbles in a liquid, rather than of liquid droplets in a gas—would fulfill the conditions he sought and would also have a conveniently short piston-evacuation cycle. (Large Wilson chambers took up to one-half hour per cycle.)

At the University of Michigan, Glaser began by showing that ionizing radiation would produce boiling in a superheated liquid. In an initial experiment, diethyl ether (chosen for practical reasons) was superheated under pressure to 140°C (normal boiling point 36°C) and exposed to fast gamma radiation. The liquid boiled instantly. Glaser then wished to see if he could make accurate tracts of ionizing particles. He made small glass bubble chambers, in different shapes, each containing a few cubic centimeters of superheated diethyl ether. A hand-operated mechanism simultaneously expanded the chamber (thus lowering the pressure) and operated a high-speed movie camera. The resulting films showed that well-defined bubble tracks were indeed produced by bombardment of fast particles.

Glaser saw indications that other liquids would yield much more accurate data, the most likely theoretically being liquid hydrogen, superheated to about 27 K. In 1953, at the University of Chicago, he constructed the first liquid-hydrogen bubble chamber. For larger chambers and very low temperatures, glass containers had to be abandoned. But he suspected that ordinary structural materials could be used, even though joints and scratches on the inner walls of such a "dirty" chamber would instantly induce boiling. By expanding the chamber extremely rapidly, the liquid in the center of the chamber could be kept superheated long enough to be sensitive to fast particles. This proved to be correct. Construction began immediately on different-size bubble chambers, equipped with powerful deflecting electromagnets and filled with liquid hydrogen, xenon, propane, and other media.

When used in conjunction with particle accelerators, bubble chambers could be made to react only during the actual emission of particles, thus reducing the problem of background radiation. The short cycling rate and large volume proved to be very convenient, and the use of the bubble chamber quickly spread. Glaser's work, together with independent research by J. K. Wood, L. W. Alvarez, and others, has produced large masses of new data about high-energy reactions and has led to the discovery of several new elementary particles. *See* ALVAREZ, LUIS WALTER.

From 1964 onward, Glaser was engaged in research on molecular biology. Among his subjects were bacterial evolution, control of biological cell growth, automatic identification of bacterial species, and automation of cell biology in order to study growth of somatic cells and effects of carcinogens, mutagens, and teratogens.

Son of a businessman, Glaser received his B.S. in physics and mathematics at the Case Institute of Technology in 1946, and his Ph.D. in the same subjects at the California Institute of Technology in 1950. In 1949 he began teaching physics at the University of Michigan and became a professor of physics there in 1957. In 1959 he took the post of professor of physics at the University of California, Berkeley, and in 1964 became professor of physics and molecular biology there. He was elected to the National Academy of Sciences in 1962.

For background information *see* BUBBLE CHAMBER; CLOUD CHAMBER in the McGraw-Hill Encyclopedia of Science and Technology. ∎

GÖDEL, KURT
American logician and philosopher

Born *Apr. 28, 1906, Brno, Czechoslovakia*
Died *Jan. 14, 1978, Princeton, NJ, U.S.A.*

In 1924 Gödel went to Vienna to study physics at the university. His interest in precision led him from physics to mathematics and to mathematical logic. After making fundamental contributions to logic, he turned his attention to philosophy when he was about 40. A scientific fruit of his interest in Immanuel Kant's theory of space and time was his rotating-universe model for general relativity. He thought deeply on the philosophy of mathematics and on general philosophy. Parts of these reflections have been published and are highly influential, at least among logicians.

It was probably a unique occurrence in the history of science that a single individual settled all the basic problems of a whole area shortly after they had been pulled together and posed in public. At the 1928 International Congress of Mathematicians in Bologna, D. Hilbert listed four central open problems on the foundations of mathematics. The first problem is the consistency of analysis, which Hilbert considered to be essentially solved. The second problem is to extend the consistency proof to functions of real variables and even higher types; in particular, the consistency question of the axiom of choice was mentioned. The third problem is the question of the completeness of formal systems of number theory and analysis. The fourth problem is the completeness of first-order logic. All these problems were answered in a surprisingly definite manner by Gödel within the next few years.

Gödel finished his college education in the spring of 1929. Shortly afterward, he proved the completeness of first-order logic and presented the result as his doctoral dissertation. Therein a positive solution to Hilbert's fourth problem is given. In the summer of 1930 Gödel began to study the problem of proving the consistency of analysis. His approach led to a paradoxical situation from which he arrived at his famous first theorem of incompleteness: every formal system of number theory or analysis or set theory, if consistent, is incomplete. In particular, he introduced a general method by which, given a formal system S adequate to developing number theory, one can construct a statement A in S such that A is not decidable in S (that is, neither A nor its negation is a theorem of S). This of course gives a negative solution to Hilbert's third problem.

Soon afterward, in the autumn of 1930, Gödel obtained, as an extension of the first theorem, his second theorem of incompleteness: if a formal system adequate to number theory is consistent, the statement of its consistency can be expressed by a sentence of the system but cannot be proved in the system. This yields negative solutions to Hilbert's first and second problems as originally understood by Hilbert. Hilbert believed not only that there are consistency proofs in both cases, but also that the proofs would be of an elementary character and, therefore, could

certainly be carried out in the system to be proved consistent. Gödel's second theorem shows that there cannot be consistency proofs satisfying Hilbert's "finitist" requirement. Consequently, the whole program of searching for consistency proofs was turned into something much less definite and decisive. The special part of Hilbert's second problem which deals with the axiom of choice was also settled by Gödel, in 1935. By that time Gödel had obtained his model of set theory in terms of constructible sets and verified that the axioms of set theory hold in the model. Hence, if the other axioms of set theory are consistent, adding the axiom of choice does not destroy consistency.

Gödel's response to Hilbert was not limited to settling all four problems publicized by Hilbert in 1928. In 1925 Hilbert announced the outline of what he took to be a proof of Georg Cantor's famous continuum hypothesis, proposed in 1878. It is clear now that Hilbert's outline cannot be completed to get a proof of the continuum hypothesis. Gödel was, however, able to use the constructible sets to obtain a proof of the (relative) consistency of the continuum hypothesis. In 1938 Gödel demonstrated that the generalized continuum hypothesis holds in his model of set theory consisting of the constructible sets. Hence, if the usual axioms of set theory are consistent, then they remain consistent when one adds the assertion that the cardinal number of the continuum is the next cardinal number after that of the set of integers, or more generally, that the cardinal number of the set of all subsets of a set B is the next cardinal number after that of B itself.

Such is the drama of Gödel the logician's response to the great mathematician Hilbert. Gödel's work in philosophy cannot be summarized so easily, and much of it remains unpublished. Some of his philosophical views are reported with his approval in Hao Wang's *From Mathematics to Philosophy* (1974).

Gödel received the Ph.D. from the University of Vienna in 1930 and was privatdozent there from 1933 to 1938. He was a visitor at the Institute for Advanced Study, Princeton, NJ, in 1933–34 and in the autumn of 1935, and he became a member of the institute in 1938, a permanent member in 1947, and a professor in 1953. He retired in 1976. He received the Albert Einstein Award of the Lewis and Rosa Strauss Memorial Fund (1951),

the National Medal of Science (1975), and honorary degrees from Yale University (1951), Harvard University (1952), Amherst College (1967), and the Rockefeller University (1972). He was elected a fellow of the American Academy of Arts and Sciences and the National Academy of Sciences (1955), and a foreign fellow of the Royal Society of London (1968) and the British Academy (1972).

Gödel wrote a monograph, *The Consistency of the Continuum Hypothesis* (1940; 2d ed. 1951; 3d ed. 1966). Several of his papers are widely anthologized; in particular, an English translation of his famous 1931 paper appears as a separate book, *On Formally Undecidable Propositions* (1962; transl. by B. Meltzer).

For background information *see* LOGIC; MATHEMATICS; RELATIVITY; SET THEORY in the McGraw-Hill Encyclopedia of Science and Technology. ■

GODWIN, SIR HARRY

★ British botanist and Quaternary scientist

Born May 9, 1901, Rotherham, England

Godwin explored those scientific problems that call for knowledge of the natural environment and the disciplines of both botany and geology. In the 1920s he began investigations into the successional changes in fen vegetation and the controlling mechanisms of the hydrosere. From this study Godwin came to realize the anthropogenic character of many types of fen vegetation and proposed the concept of deflected succession, which proved to be applicable to a wide range of ecological situations. Subsequently he extended his studies to raised mosses and the natural evolution of topogenous mire and fen to ombrogenous *Sphagnum* bog. By the time he and his wife began to investigate British vegetational history by pollen analysis, they could draw upon a substantial knowledge of the ecological situations recorded in peat and lake deposits, particularly in the East Anglian Fenland basin, where they first concentrated their efforts and where their research was reinforced by the work of archeologists, geologists, geographers, and biologists of the Fenland Research Committee active in the 1930s. The coordination of the results of all these disciplines was assured by pollen analysis and the identification of macroscopic plant fossils. The stratigraphy and postglacial history of the Fenland basin were made clear as a result, especially as they reflected the intermittent progress and relaxation of marine invasion. At the classic site, Shippea Hill, no less than four archeological horizons were correlated with the stratigraphic sequence.

Meanwhile, the potentialities and limitations of pollen analysis came under review, and as analyses were extended over a wider area, a tentative zonation scheme was proposed for England and Wales, keyed to the Irish and Scandinavian systems. It proved a useful quasi-chronological basis for the division of postglacial time. From 1935 Godwin conducted investigations, parallel to those in the Fenland basin, in the derelict raised bogs of the Somerset Levels, where a profusion of archeological discoveries were coordinated by means of frequent pollen diagrams and were related to a consistent stratigraphic sequence of peat types. In the course of this work, many prehistoric wooden trackways were excavated and described, one series from the late Bronze Age and the other from the Neolithic, an attribution fully confirmed afterward by radiocarbon dating. At Star Carr in eastern Yorkshire, extensive stratigraphic and pollen analyses of the former lake deposits provided detailed information on the hunter-fisher Mesolithic people. Star Carr proved to be the classic site for this culture in western Europe.

In the course of his studies, Godwin accumulated a large index catalog to all identifications of higher plants referable to known stages of Quaternary history in Britain. This compilation was found to provide the first factual basis for an objective history of the British flora. It became possible for the first time to dispense with the idea that the last glaciation swept the British Isles clear of flora and fauna. The history of the country from the treeless tundra of the Weichselian glaciation was traced from the tentative advances of woodland in the late-glacial period, to the blanketing by mixed oak forest that lasted through the postglacial thermal maximum, and on to Neolithic and subsequent disforestation and replacement of continuous woodland by communities initiated and maintained by plant and animal husbandry.

By 1948 the University of Cambridge had established a subdepartment of Quaternary research, and many able research workers exploited diverse fields of Quaternary study under Godwin's direction. In particular, the interglacial periods proved exceedingly rewarding, and the sequence of East Anglian glaciations was substantially resolved by combined biological stratigraphic studies. Similar methods revealed at many places in the British Isles the triple stratigraphic sequence of the late-glacial Allerød oscillation, and pollen analyses, together with fruit and seed analyses, permitted a clear characterization of the vegetation and, indirectly, of the climate. Other and older Weichselian deposits were likewise described, thus providing a clear picure of vegetational conditions in southern England through the last glaciation. Meanwhile, a radiocarbon dating laboratory, established in the subdepartment in 1953, made it possible to confirm the identification of the late-glacial zones and to establish their synchroneity with the Allerød interstadial on the European mainland. The major postglacial pollen zones were also dated, as were the main horizons of the Fenland basin and Somerset Levels, the various manifestations of the Mesolithic and early Neolithic cultures in Britain, and many prehistoric structures and occupation levels of different ages. It was also possible to begin the resolution of the complex interaction of eustatic and isostatic effects upon relative changes in the level of the land and sea in the British Isles. The major restoration of water to the oceans, as the ice of the last glaciation melted, caused a worldwide rise in the sea level of 100 meters or more; this was very rapid during the Boreal period (roughly 7600–5500 B.C.), effectively filling the North Sea basin and inhibiting further dry-land invasion of plants and animals from the continental mainland. It appears that during its concluding stages, about 6000–3000 B.C., the so-called Neolithic raised beach of northern Britain was formed, as pollen analyses had already suggested.

Godwin spent his entire academic career in the University of Cambridge, where in 1919 he entered as an open scholar of Clare College, of which he became a fellow in 1925. Successive teaching offices from 1923 onward led to the directorship of the subdepartment of Quaternary research in 1948 and the professorship of botany in 1960. He was elected to the Royal Society in 1945 and gave the Croonian Lecture in 1960. He received the Gold Medal of the Linnean Society of London in 1966. He was knighted in 1970.

Godwin wrote *History of the British Flora* (1956; 2d ed. 1975) and *Fenland: Its Ancient Past and Uncertain Future* (1978). He served as joint editor of the *New Phytologist* and of the *Journal of Ecology*.

For background information *see* FOSSIL SEEDS AND FRUITS; GLACIAL EPOCH; PALEOBOTANY; PALYNOLOGY in the McGraw-Hill Encyclopedia of Science and Technology. ■

GOGUEL, JEAN

★ French geologist and geophysicist

Born Jan. 2, 1908, Paris, France

The son of Maurice Goguel, the historian of the origins of Christianity, Jean Goguel studied at the Ecole Polytechnique, where he received a solid mathematical and physical backgound, and at the School of Mines of Paris, where he was the student of Pierre Termier. Entering the Geologic Map Service, where he remained throughout his career and eventually became director, he was assigned to map surveying in the sedimentary regions of the southern French Alps. This led him to study all aspects of regional geology, including stratigraphy and even paleontology. These regional studies subsequently extended to other parts of the French Alps and to other regions of France, enabling him to devote a small book to the geology of France. He also carried out numerous trips abroad.

In these regional studies Goguel interested himself principally in tectonics, and he quickly realized that beyond the study of cartography and classical geometrics it was necessary to take up the mechanical study of tectonic deformations. He devoted an important memoir to this subject in 1942, and he continued thereafter to pursue the subject in depth. From the viewpoint of theoretical mechanics, he showed that the only schematics that can give satisfactory results are those of plasticity; the deformation does not begin to manifest itself until the stress exceeds a certain threshold level. His experiments on the deformation of rocks showed him the necessity of distinguishing different modes of evolution of rocks, all of which manifest themselves by a global deformation but obey completely different laws. Thus, the rapid deformations achieved in the laboratory are brought about by twinning or by mutual displacements of grains, while the slow deformations in nature are brought about essentially by recrystallization and diffusion.

These considerations, when applied to the genesis of mountains taken as a whole, permit a better understanding of the influence of the different natures of rocks and the role of different kinds of geologic folds. They lead, if not to a determination of the form of the folds, at least to an estimation of the total energy absorbed. When applied to the details of the deformations, they permit an interpretation of multiple particularities that provides information on the mode of deformation and the properties of different rocks. In

particular, the relation between schistosity and stress was shown (with a maximum pressure perpendicular to the schistosity). In 1965 Goguel proposed a new interpretation of the schistosity of crystallophylic rocks by means of a selection among the crystalline grains according to their orientation relative to the mechanical stress. Their solubility is in fact modified by their elastic strain and increases proportionally to the elastic energy stored per unit volume; the orientations for which this energy is minimum should be preferred. The detailed calculations based on the elastic coefficients for the principal minerals give results for their orientation that are, on the whole, in conformity with observation.

The systematic application of mechanical and physical considerations in the realm of geology led Goguel in other directions. On the one hand, he was frequently called upon for studies in civil engineering and construction of dams, tunnels, and so on. In the field of rock mechanics, he studied large rock falls and pointed out the part played, on some occasions, by vaporization of water (caused by the heat produced by friction) in making gliding on bedding planes much easier. On the other hand, he undertook various aspects of geophysics, both prospecting (he was president of the European Association of Exploration Geophysicists) and fundamental. He devoted numerous publications to gravimetry (including an account of the entire subject), from the scale of the prospector to that of the Earth as a whole. In particular, he undertook to develop the idea of isostasy of the schematic models of geodesists and showed that it is compatible with all of the irregularities of the Earth's crust that geology suggests, including variations of elasticity or mechanical resistance.

Goguel also devoted a great deal of attention to geothermy, as early as 1953. In order to undertake analysis of the conditions for exploitation of geothermal energy, he analyzed the behavior of water in a heated porous terrane and specified the condition under which thermal convection can appear. He attempted to interpret the temperature distributions that can result thereby and calculated the energy available in the sudden vaporization of a superheated moist terrane as a function of the porosity and temperature; the high value of this energy explains phreatic explosions. He was later involved in the exploitation of geothermal energy which, in

France, implies the use of low-energy sites for central heating. His book on the subject was translated into English (*Geothermics,* 1976).

Goguel was chief editor of the volume devoted to the Earth in the *Pleiad Encyclopedia;* this volume combined geophysics and geology (later expanded to one volume on geophysics and two on geology). In his *Tectonics* (English transl. 1962) he sought to evolve a method of studying the deformation phenomenon of the solid Earth. He also wrote *L'Homme dans l'univers* (1947). Goguel was elected a foreign member of the American Academy of Arts and Sciences in 1958 and of the National Academy of Sciences in 1973. He was a foreign honorary member of the Geological Society of America and the Geological Society of London.

For background information *see* OROGENY; ROCK MECHANICS; TECTONOPHYSICS in the McGraw-Hill Encyclopedia of Science and Technology. ∎

GOLDBERGER, MARVIN LEONARD
★ American theoretical physicist

Born Oct. 22, 1922, Chicago, IL, U.S.A.

For his development of dispersion theory, Goldberger received the American Physical Society's Dannie Heineman Prize in 1961. This theory is concerned with the relation between the real and imaginary parts of scattering amplitudes and is a generalization of much earlier work by H. Kramers and R. Kronig.

Goldberger's work in this area began in 1953 in collaboration with Murray Gell-Mann; the fundamental paper on the subject was published with Gell-Mann and W. Thirring. Later Goldberger greatly simplified this work and generalized it from the original electromagnetic case to apply to massive projectiles. The theory played a fundamental role in the analysis of pion-nucleon scattering experiments. The general technique was developed by Goldberger and his collaborators and by many others and was applied to a host of problems involving strong and weak interactions. Indeed, dispersion theory has become a basic part of theoretical physics. See GELL-MANN, MURRAY.

Goldberger began his career in physics on the wartime Manhattan (atomic bomb) Project in 1944. While then concerned primarily with problems of reactor design, he also worked with F. Seitz on the theory of neutron diffraction in crystals, a phenomenon now widely employed in the study of the structure of matter. In 1948 he turned to high-energy and elementary-particle physics. Under the supervision of Enrico Fermi, he developed a theory of high-energy nuclear reactions based on the Monte Carlo method of following the trajectory of a particle through a nucleus in detail and predicting the energy and angular distribution of all emerging particles. This work is the basis of almost all theoretical discussions relating to shielding of high-energy accelerators as well as to many discussions of high-energy nuclear reactions in heavy nuclei. See FERMI, ENRICO; SEITZ, FREDERICK.

In the next few years, in collaboration with G. F. Chew, Goldberger worked on the theory of nucleon-nucleon scattering and on the impulse approximation, a technique for describing the high-energy interactions between nucleons and complex nuclei. In 1952 he and Gell-Mann presented a general theory of collision processes that has been very widely employed. See CHEW, GEOFFREY FOUCAR.

The work on dispersion theory occupied Goldberger from 1953 to 1961. In 1961, in connection with a study of the theory of complex angular momenta begun by T. Regge, Goldberger and R. Blankenbecler suggested that "elementary" particles such as the nucleon should be regarded as composite, lying on so-called Regge trajectories. This view is now very popular. Goldberger and Gell-Mann pointed out in 1962 that the distinction between conventional field theory and the idea of composite "elementary" particles was not at all clear and that there may well be no difference in the various points of view. See REGGE, TULLIO.

The possibility of utilizing the intensity correlation techniques of R. Hanbury Brown and R. Twiss in connection with x-rays and particle beams was suggested in 1963 by Goldberger, H. W. Lewis, and K. Watson. They showed that in principle the famous phase problem of x-ray structure analysis could now be solved. This could have great practical consequences, since the structure of complex molecules of interest in biology could be readily determined. Goldberger and Watson explored a number of problems in connection with the quantum theory of measurement pointed up by this work. See HANBURY BROWN, ROBERT.

Goldberger did his undergraduate work in physics at the Carnegie Institute of Technology, receiving his B.S. in 1943. He received his Ph.D. at the University of Chicago in 1948. He was a research associate at the University of California and at the Massachusetts Institute of Technology before joining the faculty of the University of Chicago in 1950. In 1957 he was appointed Eugene Higgins Professor of Theoretical Physics at Princeton University. In 1970 he became chairperson of the department of physics, a position he held until 1976. In 1977 he was named Joseph Henry Professor of Physics. In mid-1978 he became president of the California Institute of Technology. He was elected to the National Academy of Sciences in 1963 and the American Academy of Arts and Sciences in 1965.

Goldberger wrote *Collision Theory*, with W. Watson (1964).

For background information *see* ELEMENTARY PARTICLE; NEUTRON DIFFRACTION; SCATTERING EXPERIMENTS, NUCLEAR in the McGraw-Hill Encyclopedia of Science and Technology. ∎

GOLDHABER, MAURICE
★ American physicist

***Born** Apr. 18, 1911, Lemberg, Austria*

Goldhaber started his research in nuclear physics at Cambridge University's Cavendish Laboratory, then under the direction of Ernest Rutherford. Goldhaber, collaborating with James Chadwick, discovered (1934) the nuclear photoelectric effect, the first example being the disintegration of the deuteron by gamma rays from a radiothorium source. These gamma rays of well-known energy produce photoprotons and photoneutrons from deuterium. The energy of these particles can be measured, and thus the binding energy of the deuteron as well as the mass of the neutron can be obtained. Convincing evidence was obtained that the neutron is heavier than the proton, and it was concluded that a free neutron should be able to decay spontaneously by beta-ray activity into a proton. Decaying "elementary" particles are now known to be a very general phenomenon. With x-rays of higher energy, which became available later through the development of high-energy electron machines, all nuclei can be photodisintegrated so that copious sources of neutrons as well as of radioactive isotopes can be produced. The photodisintegration of deuterons also plays an important role in the neutron economy of nuclear reactors in which heavy water is used as a moderator. See CHADWICK, SIR JAMES.

After the discovery of slow neutrons by E. Fermi and his collaborators, Chadwick and Goldhaber established (1934–35) the disintegration of the light elements lithium, boron, and nitrogen by slow neutrons. These reactions have taken on particular importance: $^6Li + n \rightarrow {}^4He + {}^3H$ is the reaction by which tritium is produced, and in turn tritium is the best source of ^3He, to which it decays. The reaction $^{10}B + n \rightarrow {}^7Li + {}^4He$ is one of the stan-

dard methods of detecting slow neutrons. The reaction $^{14}N + n \rightarrow {}^{14}C + p$, first established (1936) in detail by W. E. Burcham and Goldhaber, is the most important source of ^{14}C, both in nature and in artificial production. In 1935 H. J. Taylor and Goldhaber, using emulsions impregnated with lithium or boron, showed the usefulness of nuclear emulsions for the studies of nuclear reactions taking place right inside the emulsion. The further development of these emulsions by C. F. Powell and G. Occhialini led to the detection of pi mesons. Goldhaber and G. H. Briggs made (1937) the first systematic study of slow neutron scattering in the majority of elements, and the cross sections they found were very useful later in the development of the first reactors. See FERMI, ENRICO; POWELL, CECIL FRANK.

In 1938 Goldhaber joined the faculty of the University of Illinois, where he and his wife, Gertrude Scharff-Goldhaber, showed that beta rays are identical with atomic electrons. If they were not identical, beta rays could fall into the K shell, giving x-rays, but this cannot happen to identical particles because of the Pauli principle. Together with a number of students, they made further contributions to the understanding of slow neutrons. In 1940 J. W. Coltman and Goldhaber showed that beryllium has a sufficiently low cross section for slow neutrons to be a useful neutron moderator in reactors. They voluntarily kept this fact a secret during World War II and did not publish it until after the war. In 1946 A. A. Yalow and Goldhaber found the first example of a slow neutron resonance in which scattering was more important than absorption.

In 1950 Goldhaber joined Brookhaven National Laboratory, where he specialized in the study of nuclear isomers and fundamental particles. Isomers are nuclei which do not differ in either their proton number or their neutron number, but possess a different internal structure and lifetime. Systematics of nuclear-level energies and spins and transition probabilities between nuclear levels were studied with E. der Mateosian, R. D. Hill, A. W. Sunyar, and Scharff-Goldhaber. K. T. Bainbridge, Goldhaber, and E. Wilson showed (1951) that the lifetime of an isomer is affected in a measurable way by its chemical state. In 1957 Goldhaber, L. Grodzins, and Sunyar established the fact that the elusive neutrino has a left-handed spin. They were able to show this by finding

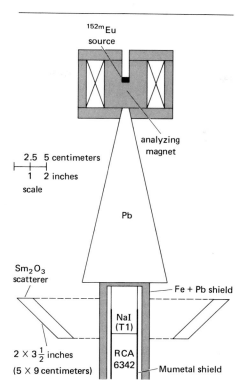

^{152m}Eu source

analyzing magnet

2.5 5 centimeters
1 2 inches
scale

Pb

Sm_2O_3 scatterer

Fe + Pb shield

NaI (T1)

$2 \times 3\frac{1}{2}$ inches
(5 × 9 centimeters)

RCA 6342

Mumetal shield

Experimental arrangement for analyzing the circular polarization of resonant-scattered gamma rays. The weight of the Sm_2O_3 scatterer is 1850 grams.

a K-electron–capturing nuclide (^{152m}Eu) in which neutrinos are emitted of approximately equal energy to that of a successive gamma ray. When emitted opposite to the neutrino, the gamma ray has in this case the same helicity (handedness) as the neutrino and the correct energy to be resonant-scattered by the daughter product (^{152}Sm). By measuring the helicity of the gamma ray with the help of an analyzing magnet as absorber (see illustration), they were able to determine the neutrino helicity. This ended a long chapter of controversy in beta-ray research. The same authors also showed that beta rays produce circularly polarized x-rays. In 1966 der Mateosian and Goldhaber developed a new technique for searching for double beta decay by using a scintillating crystal of enriched $^{40}CaF_2$. By this means they obtained improved lower limits for this process.

In 1954 Goldhaber, in collaboration with F. Reines and C. L. Cowan, made the first measurement of a lower limit for the proton lifetime.

Among Goldhaber's theoretical contributions were an early suggestion of a single-particle model of nuclear transformations

(1934); the Goldhaber-Teller model (1948) of photointeractions in nuclei (giant dipole resonance); the role of mixed configurations in nuclei, with A. de-Shalit (1953); a compound hypothesis of hyperons (1953, 1956); a review of the theory of electromagnetic transitions in nuclei, with J. Weneser (1955); decay modes of a ($k^0 + \bar{k}^0$) system, with T.-D. Lee and C. N. Yang (1958); and a discussion of tests of conservation laws for elementary particles, with G. Feinberg (1959). In 1965 Goldhaber invented the Ne bubble chamber, a useful research tool. See LEE, TSUNG-DAO; YANG, CHEN NING.

Goldhaber was educated at the University of Berlin and Cambridge University, where he received his Ph.D. in 1936. He was Charles Kingsley Bye fellow of Magdalene College, Cambridge, for 2 years before going to the United States in 1938. He was assistant professor of physics at the University of Illinois in 1938–45, and professor in 1945–50. In 1950 he became a senior scientist at Brookhaven National Laboratory, chairperson of the physics department in 1960, director in 1961, and Associated Universities Incorporated Distinguished Scientist in 1973. In 1971 Goldhaber received the Tom W. Bonner Prize in Nuclear Physics. He was elected to the National Academy of Sciences in 1958.

For background information see BUBBLE CHAMBER; ELEMENTARY PARTICLE; EXCLUSION PRINCIPLE; FISSION, NUCLEAR; NUCLEAR REACTION in the McGraw-Hill Encyclopedia of Science and Technology. ■

GOLDMARK, PETER CARL
★ American scientist

Born Dec. 2, 1906, Budapest, Hungary
Died Dec. 7, 1977, Rye, NY, U.S.A.

The many aspects of handling information—aural and visual—occupied Goldmark's mind since 1929, when he built a simple television receiver with a postage stamp–size screen while he was a student at the University of Vienna. His work had a profound influence in at least two major areas which blossomed into giant industries: color television and the microgroove long-playing record. The first practical color television system was developed at CBS Laboratories under his direction, and the first color broadcast in history was transmitted from CBS's experimental

transmitter in New York in August 1940. Although his field-sequential system did not lead to the current standards of commercial color television broadcasting, it nevertheless found wide acceptance in closed-circuit medical, teaching, and industrial applications, because the modern field-sequential color camera is much smaller, lighter, and simpler to operate and maintain than the broadcast-standard models.

During World War II Goldmark was responsible for many military developments in the fields of electronic countermeasures and reconnaissance. In 1948 he and his associates at CBS Laboratories developed the long-playing record, which compressed the equivalent of six 78-rpm phonograph records into a single disk.

This compression and retrieval of information by phonographic, photographic, or any other graphic record was Goldmark's special field of endeavor, with the highest possible density at the highest possible resolution his aim. One of the results of his thinking was the Lunar Orbiter's dazzling photographs of the lunar surface, which were transmitted to the Earth with astonishing detail, even though they were taken from an average altitude of 29 miles (46.4 kilometers) above the Moon, some 238,000 miles (380,800 kilometers) from the Earth. An extremely bright, small, flying spot of light scanned the photographic film in three ways ("zone scanning") aboard the spacecraft line by line, so that the fluctuations in light, as it passed through the negative,

were translated into electrical impulses for transmission to the ground recording system on Earth.

That small, intense spot of light, emitted by a special line-scan tube aboard the Orbiter, became feasible only after a number of major technical problems were overcome. Because of the high intensity of the beam, the phosphor on the anode burned away quickly. Goldmark and his associates solved the problem by building a rotating anode—a phosphor-coated metal drum which revolved rapidly in the path of the beam so that the coating could cool off before the same area on the anode was struck again. Another serious obstacle arose because the bearings on the revolving drum froze quickly when the then available lubricants boiled away in the high vacuum of the electron tube. Thus, a new type of lubricant had to be developed, one which would withstand not only the vacuum but also the extreme temperature changes encountered in space. Goldmark developed a metallic solid lubricant which extended the life of the bearings beyond that of the Lunar Orbiter missions.

Goldmark also played an active part in practically all of the work of CBS Laboratories. He contributed to such varied developments as special electron tubes, audio and acoustical systems, magnetic recording, and data storage and display.

One of the most complex systems developed under his supervision was a computer-tape-driven, ultra-high-speed photocomposing system called the Linotron. It could produce electronically page-by-page composition at the rate of 1000 characters per second with high graphic arts quality.

One of Goldmark's great concerns was education, not only that of children but also that of adults and even of fellow scientists. Since he considered teaching in its broadest sense as one aspect of information handling, he felt that machines must also help teachers, instructors, and other communicators in amassing, storing, and reading out the increasingly vast amounts of information resulting from the rapid advances in many fields of science. Educational technology was the subject of much of his effort in later years, with a number of his systems approaching completion during the 1960s.

One such system, which was destined to play an important part in the establishment of a new educational art form, was Electronic Video Recording (EVR). Developed by Goldmark and his associates at CBS Laboratories, EVR represented a

significant step in the application of television to education by making it possible for the first time to show on conventional television sets, in the home or classroom, prerecorded programming from motion picture film and video tape at low cost. The EVR system combined optics and electron physics to transfer any film or video taped programming to special unperforated thin film (or optical tape) stored in a small cartridge. The cartridge would be inserted into a player attached to the antenna terminals of a television receiver and automatically played on a single television screen or several as the teacher desired. EVR provided the teacher with the advantage of adapting film from anywhere in the world to the lessons each day. The teacher could show the same film as many times as desired or could reproduce it in either black and white or color.

To develop EVR, Goldmark and his associates had to overcome a series of difficult technological problems relating to film miniaturization. Before EVR the miniaturization of individual frames of film was technically unfeasible, because there was no method of projecting enough light through a miniaturized film to make it readable on a screen. Another major difficulty overcome by EVR technology involved showing for the first time both animated film and stills on the same optical tape. Thus, animation could be followed by an important document, which could be "frozen" on the television screen for class study.

Goldmark studied at the universities of Vienna and Berlin, receiving his B.Sc. (1930) and Ph.D. in physics (1931) from the former. He went to the United States in 1933, and joined CBS in New York in 1936 as chief engineer of its newly formed television research department. In 1950 he became vice-president in charge of engineering, and in 1954 was named president of CBS Laboratories, a division of the Columbia Broadcasting System. He served as visiting professor for medical electronics at the University of Pennsylvania Medical School. In 1954 Goldmark was awarded the Television Broadcasters Association Medal for his pioneering work in color television. From the Institute of Electrical and Electronics Engineers he received both the Morris Liebmann Memorial Prize for electronic research (1946) and the Vladimir K. Zworykin Television Prize (1961). He was elected to the National Academy of

Engineering in 1966, and was awarded the 1976 National Medal of Science.

Goldmark received many patents in the fields of visual and audio communications, and wrote numerous papers in these fields.

For background information *see* COLOR TELEVISION; DISK RECORDING; TELEVISION CAMERA TUBE; TELEVISION SCANNING in the McGraw-Hill Encyclopedia of Science and Technology ■

GOLDSMITH, JULIAN ROYCE
★ American geochemist

Born Feb. 26, 1918, Chicago, IL, U.S.A.

The chemistry of silicates and related substances, especially at high temperatures and high pressures, has for the most part been neglected by chemists. Chemistry as a science developed out of the study of mineralogy and geology, but in the area of inorganic chemistry it drifted away from the consideration of the materials of the Earth. In the early years of the 20th century, the Geophysical Laboratory of the Carnegie Institution of Washington began an intensive investigation of systems involving silicates, with particular emphasis on high-temperature crystal-liquid equilibria. The Geophysical Laboratory, staffed largely with scientists whose main interest was petrology and geology, operated almost alone in this field until shortly before World War II. In 1936 N. L. Bowen, who had been a pioneer in modern petrology at the Geophysical Laboratory and whose work greatly in-

creased understanding of the evolution of igneous rocks, joined the faculty of the University of Chicago and set up a high-temperature laboratory. After the war a number of universities developed areas of what can be called modern experimental geochemistry, for the most part in the departments of geology or Earth science. *See* BOWEN, NORMAN LEVI.

Goldsmith was a student of Bowen, and his early work dealt with heterogeneous phase equilibria in silicate systems at elevated temperatures. The feldspar family of minerals is perhaps the most important mineral group in the Earth's crust, and in working with some of the feldspar-liquid (melt) equilibrium relations, Goldsmith grew to realize that many of the relationships observed in the natural minerals in rocks were not being adequately explained by the laboratory work on high-temperature equilibria, important as this work was in connection with some of the problems of differentiation and genesis of igneous rocks. At the time, little or no active investigation of the role of order-disorder relations had been carried out in mineral structures, although in 1931 T. F. W. Barth and E. Posnjak had applied the variate atom equipoint concept to spinels. Also, in 1934 Barth had suggested that microcline, a triclinic potassium feldspar, might have an ordered array of Si and Al atoms, whereas the monoclinic modifications, such as sanidine or orthoclase, might be disordered with respect to Al and Si. All modifications have the same composition, $KAlSi_3O_8$. Goldsmith synthesized a series of feldspars ($KAlSi_3O_8$, $NaAlSi_3O_8$, and the $NaAlSi_3O_8$-$CaAl_2Si_2O_8$ solid-solution series, or plagioclase feldspars) in which the aluminum was replaced by gallium, or the silicon was replaced by germanium, or both. This heavier-element substitution was done to produce a larger difference in x-ray scattering power between the Al and Si sites in the crystals, for Al and Si are adjacent elements in the periodic table and, having similar x-ray scattering factors, cannot readily be differentiated in a crystal structure analysis. Although useful structural interpretations were obtained (largely in conjunction with F. Laves), the full exploitation of this line of investigation was seriously hampered by the fact that the low-temperature (and as is now known, the ordered) modifications of the feldspars cannot be synthesized, although there is no difficulty with the high-temperature (dis-

ordered) forms. This condition held true for the gallium and germanium feldspars as well as for the "normal" Al and Si counterparts.

It also became apparent that even in nature the high-temperature modifications (particularly $KAlSi_3O_8$) almost universally developed even at low temperatures and inverted to the low-temperature or stable modifications in the solid state only over some period of geologic time. In many cases, the high-temperature state has persisted, a clear indication of the failure of equilibrium. Failure to achieve equilibrium is also shown by the common presence of compositionally zoned plagioclase feldspars in igneous rocks, and Goldsmith pointed out the particular difficulty in the case of plagioclase: The solid-state diffusion necessary to produce a homogeneous equilibrium composition requires breaking the very strong aluminum-oxygen and silicon-oxygen bonds concurrently with the migration of Na and Ca in the structure, for the Na-Ca ratio is dependent upon the Al-Si ratio in the crystal. Equilibrium in this case becomes exceedingly difficult, even at temperatures close to the melting point.

These and similar observations led Goldsmith into consideration of the relationship between crystal structure and what might be called ease of crystallization, or more generally between structural details and heterogeneous and homogeneous equilibria. In 1955 he received the Mineralogical Society of America Award for contributions to the understanding of the equilibrium relations and genesis of the feldspar group of minerals.

By this time Goldsmith was well into a series of laboratory investigations on the rhombohedral carbonates, using both natural and synthetic materials. These compounds are important in sedimentary and metamorphic petrology, and much of this work was done in collaboration with D. L. Graf. At elevated temperatures the carbonates are difficult to deal with because thermal decomposition becomes a factor, and much of the work must be done in high-pressure apparatus at elevated CO_2 pressures. The complex relations of both pressure and temperature in controlling the decomposition as well as the composition of solid solutions in systems such as $CaCO_3$-$MgCO_3$ and $CaCO_3$-$MnCO_3$ were elucidated, and the practicality of using the $MgCO_3$ content of calcite in geologic thermometry was demonstrated. The underlying factor is that increasing amounts of Mg become soluble in the calcite ($CaCO_3$) structure with the increasing temperature.

The compound dolomite, $CaMg(CO_3)_2$, loomed important in this work, and equilibrium order-disorder relations between Ca and Mg were shown to exist at high temperatures. Dolomite is also a mineral that has not been synthesized at low temperatures (below approximately 200°C). Although it is an exceedingly common mineral, and many large rock units are almost pure dolomite, it is almost always observed to be a secondary, or replacement, mineral. It is but rarely formed as a primary precipitate in carbonate sediments, even though it is now known to be the stable carbonate in equilibrium with sea water. This enigma, often referred to as the dolomite problem, is largely explained by the fact that the ordered array of Ca and Mg atoms is attained only with great difficulty at low temperatures, where crystallization may be rapid but where diffusion is very slow. Furthermore, poorly ordered or nonstoichiometric dolomite-like phases (called protodolomite) may persist metastably over geologic time.

Later Goldsmith was involved in a series of studies carried out at pressures up to 35 kilobars (3.5 gigapascals), collaborating in part with R. C. Newton. Advantage was taken of the observation that reaction rates in certain systems containing water, even in trace amounts, are accelerated enormously at pressures greater than 10 kilobars (1 gigapascal). The solid-solubility *equilibrium* relations in the alkali feldspar system ($NaAlSi_3O_8$-$KAlSi_3O_8$) were elucidated, as was the pressure effect on the equilibrium. The hitherto unknown stability relations of the scapolite group of minerals, which are silicates that contain Cl^-, SO_4^{--}, and or CO_3^{--} in their structure, were also worked out. These little-understood compounds proved to be high-temperature high-pressure phases, and may act as the principal storehouse for C and S in the lower crust of the Earth. The use of high pressure to speed up oxygen isotope exchange between water and various minerals in previously intractable systems was also proved feasible. This work, in collaboration with R. N. Clayton, provided fractionation factors of the stable oxygen isotopes as a function of temperature and was of significance to geothermometry.

Goldsmith received his A.B. (1940) and Ph.D. (1947) from the University of Chicago. From 1942 to 1946 he was a research chemist at the Corning Glass Works. He joined the faculty of the University of Chicago in 1947 and served as associate dean of the division of the physical sciences from 1960 to 1971. He was head of the department of the geophysical sciences from 1963 to 1971, and became Charles E. Merriam Distinguished Service Professor in 1969. Elected to the American Academy of Arts and Sciences in 1963, he was appointed by President Johnson to the National Science Board in 1964, and served as president of the Geochemical Society in 1966, of the Mineralogical Society in 1970–71, and of the Geological Society of America in 1974–75.

For background information *see* CARBONATE MINERALS; DOLOMITE; HIGH-PRESSURE PHENOMENA; SILICATE PHASE EQUILIBRIA in the McGraw-Hill Encyclopedia of Science and Technology. ∎

GOLDSTEIN, HERBERT
★ American physicist

***Born** June 26, 1922, New York, NY, U.S.A.*

For his contributions to the development of reactor science, particularly in shielding against nuclear radiation, Goldstein received in 1962 the E. O. Lawrence Memorial Award of the U.S. Atomic Energy Commission.

One of the obstacles to the peaceful development of nuclear energy lies in the vast quantity of nuclear radiation released from an operating reactor. Much of this radiation is easily attenuated or is harmless (for example, the neutrinos), but the high-energy photon and neutron components require massive shielding. The first reactor shields in the days of the Manhattan Project in World War II had to be designed on the basis of scanty empirical data. After the war, however, it was realized that the development of economic nuclear power, as well as the success of applications where space and weight are at a premium (as in space propulsion), required a detailed and accurate knowledge of how photons and neutrons are attenuated through thick layers of shields. The fundamental equation describing the penetration of such neutral particles in matter is a linearized form of the same Boltzmann transport equation that forms the basis of the kinetic theory of gases. Initial attempts at solving the Boltzmann equation for shielding concentrated on the photon part of the problem, because the basic interactions of the photons with individual atoms and their constituents are simpler and better known than the interactions of the neutrons. Even so, the resulting photon transport equation seemed much too complicated for solution, and great effort was expended in devising simple approximations to the interaction processes leading to soluble equations. The extent and direction of the errors introduced by the approximations were largely unknown, and the results obtained were shrouded in uncertainty.

Entering the field in 1950 as a staff member of Nuclear Development Associates, Goldstein decided to apply the then emerging digital computer in large-scale numerical computations toward solving the Boltzmann equation without introducing physical approximations. Of the numerical techniques then known, he felt that the moments method developed by L. V. Spencer and U. Fano of the National Bureau of Standards gave the best promise of leading to the needed results. With the support of the Atomic Energy Commission, he embarked on an extensive program, in collaboration with the National Bureau of Standards, to apply the moments method to the computation of photon attenuation in simple shields. The fruits of the program were published in 1954, in collaboration with J. Ernest

Wilkins, Jr., in the report "Calculations of the Penetration of Gamma Rays." The penetration of photons from 0.25 to 10 megaelectronvolts in energy were computed for a variety of materials ranging from water to uranium and for thicknesses up to 20 mean-free-path lengths. From the wide range of results obtained, a qualitative physical picture of attenuation mechanisms in thick shields was derived, enabling one to understand the errors introduced by earlier approximate treatments. The computations quickly found extensive applications in a variety of fields besides reactor shielding, including radiation medical therapy, irradiation sterilization of foods and other materials, and the design of fallout shelters.

Turning next to the neutron problem, Goldstein and his collaborators successfully applied the moments method to calculate the penetration of neutrons from fission in common moderators and shield materials such as light and heavy water, beryllium, graphite, lithium hydride, and so on. One by-product of the moments method is a very precise value for the mean square distance a neutron travels in slowing down to very low energies. This quantity plays an important role in one of the historic methods of reactor design. Goldstein's calculations of this mean square distance for water differed drastically from an apparently well-established experimental value. It was, moreover, possible to show that uncertainties in the basic nuclear data or in the calculational method did not cause significant error in the theoretical value. Goldstein was able, on the other hand, to point to some possible sources of error in the experiments that had been overlooked. Subsequently measurements confirmed the theoretical prediction.

One of the greatest sources of uncertainties in the calculation of neutron penetration in shields lies in the basic cross-section data needed for the computations. To build up an adequate picture of how neutrons interact with a particular type of nucleus requires sifting and evaluating hundreds of diverse pieces of experimental and theoretical evidence. An often difficult and time-consuming part of this task is collecting these pieces of evidence out of a widespread and rapidly proliferating literature. Starting in 1956, Goldstein devised a computer-based system, called CINDA (Computer Index Neutron Data), for keeping track in a systematic and continuous fashion of the literature on neutron cross-sections. Operation of the system has since become an international cooperative venture with the assistance of governmental laboratories and of scientists in almost all countries involved in nuclear research.

Son of a teacher, Goldstein graduated from the College of the City of New York in 1940. He received a Ph.D. from the Massachusetts Institute of Technology (MIT) in 1943. During World War II he worked in the microwave radar field in the MIT Radiation Laboratory. In 1946 he was appointed instructor in the department of physics, Harvard University, and he joined Nuclear Development Associates in 1950. In 1961 he became professor of nuclear science and engineering at Columbia University. He was elected a member of the American Physical Society.

Goldstein wrote *Classical Mechanics* (1950) and *Fundamental Aspects of Reactor Shielding* (1959).

For background information *see* BOLTZMANN STATISTICS; RADIOACTIVITY; REACTOR, NUCLEAR in the McGraw-Hill Encyclopedia of Science and Technology. ∎

GOMER, ROBERT
★ American chemical physicist

Born Mar. 24, 1924, Vienna, Austria

For his contributions to the study of adsorption of atoms and molecules on metal surfaces, both experimentally and theoretically, Gomer received the American Chemical Society Award in Surface or Colloid Chemistry (the Kendall Award) in 1975.

In 1950 Gomer became interested in the field-emission microscope, invented by 1937 by E. W. Mueller. This consists of a very sharply etched metal wire, or tip, 100 nanometers in radius at its apex, surrounded by a fluorescent screen. When a moderate negative voltage is applied to the tip with the bulb evacuated, electrons are emitted by tunneling through the field-deformed potential barrier at its surface even at very low temperature. Since they follow the divergent lines of electrical force from the tip, a highly magnified (about 10^6 times) image or emission map of the surface is projected onto the screen. Emission is sensitive to the nature of the surface itself and also to adsorbed atoms or molecules, since even 1/100 of a single atomic layer of adsorbate, that is, 10^{13} atoms, modifies the emission properties enough to become noticeable. Gomer was enchanted by the simplicity and potential applications of this device, which he developed into a quantitative tool for the study of adsorption, desorption, and surface diffusion. He immersed a field-emission microscope in liquid helium; since the vapor pressure of all gases except helium and hydrogen is negligibly low at the boiling point of helium, $-269°C$ or 4.2 K, this automatically established an ultrahigh vacuum within the device. Even more importantly, at 4.2 K molecules hitting the inside wall of the microscope bulb stuck on impact. This made it possible to place a gas source to one side of the tip to cover only the portion directly "seeing" the gas source. On heating the tip, the migration of gas over the originally bare portions could be observed visually because of the resultant changes in the emission pattern. The high magnification made it possible to follow rates of migration as low as 10 nanometers per minute. This work provided the first data on the diffusion behavior of simple adsorbates such as hydrogen, oxygen, and similar atoms on metal surfaces. This knowledge is important for the understanding of all surface processes involving such adsorbates. Much of this work was carried out in the 1950s. *See* MUELLER, ERWIN W.

Much later, Gomer returned to the problem of surface diffusion and, again using the field-emission microscope, devised a method capable of determining diffusion on a single crystal plane of the emitter. A small portion of the electron beam, corresponding to emission from a region about 10 nanometers in radius, was allowed to pass into a collector. By suitable adjustments, the particular portion of the tip so examined could be varied at will. The emitter was then uniformly covered with adsorbate and heated until the latter became mobile. Small statistical fluctuations in the number of adsorbate particles in the probed region occurred and gave rise to corresponding fluctuations in the emission current, which were measured. These fluctuations built up and decayed with a characteristic relaxation time related to the surface diffusion coefficient of the adsorbate. By measuring the so-called time correlation function of the current fluctuations, it was then possible to find the diffusion coefficient; by varying temperature, activation energies could also be obtained.

Following his early work in field emission, Gomer became interested in the related phenomenon of field ionization, and with M. Inghram demonstrated in 1954 that it was the basis of the field-ion microscope, which had also been invented by Mueller. Field ionization refers to the tunneling of electrons from atoms or molecules under the action of very high electric fields. Inghram and Gomer realized that this constituted a much gentler method of ionization than the customary method of electron bombardment and would lead to less fragmentation. Field ionization is now widely used in analytical mass spectrometry. Shortly thereafter, Gomer became interested in field desorption, that is, the removal of adsorbates as ions by very high positive electric fields, and formulated a theory of this process.

Gomer's interest in field emission and field ionization led him to investigate these phenomena in insulating liquids with his student, B. Halpern. They were able to verify that these phenomena occurred in liquids, and to explain them quantitatively. This work provided the first detailed explanation of electrical breakdown in such liquids.

In 1963 Gomer and his collaborator, D. Menzel, became interested in the desorption of neutral and ionic particles from adsorbate-covered metal surfaces by electron impact. They worked out a theory, almost simultaneously with but independently of P. Redhead in Canada, which predicted very much smaller cross sections than for comparable electron impact events in the gas phase, and were able to demonstrate this experimentally. Their reasoning was that the large number of electrons in a metal would be able to "heal" bonds broken by the initial excitation, so that an excited particle had a relatively poor chance of escaping from the surface without being recaptured. Since a lighter particle moves away from the surface more rapidly than a heavier one, they argued that the escape probability for the former would be exponentially greater. This isotope effect has since been confirmed in many cases. Since the details of the escape process hinge delicately on the position and bonding of the adsorbate, electron impact desorption provides a sensitive probe of adsorption states. The phenomenon is also of considerable importance as an unwanted side reaction on the walls of fusion reactors.

In 1975, in the course of teaching a chemistry course, Gomer encountered the often made statement that it is impossible to measure absolutely the potential of half-cells, because of the fact that introduction of an electrode into the medium sets up a counter half-cell, thus vitiating any attempts at measurement. He realized that it was possible to measure the potential difference between the surface of an aqueous solution and an electrode above the surface, but not in physical contact with it, by means of a vibrating-capacitor method, so that the half-cell electromotive force could be determined to within the difference in electrical potential between the bulk of the aqueous solution and its surface. He and a student, G. Tryson, carried out this measurement. The interpretation of such potential-difference measurements in terms of half-cell electromotive forces (emf's) had also been noted by the Italian electrochemist S. Trasatti, although Gomer and Tryson did not become aware of this until after publication of their work. Gomer also devised a simple method of estimating the potential difference between the interior and the surface of the solution, which utilized the fact that this potential would be partially screened by ions and so would vary with the concentration of (otherwise inert) electrolyte. It turned out that the surface of water is negative by 50 millivolts relative to the bulk. Thus it was possible to obtain absolute half-cell emf's and through these the free energies of solvation of single ions, thereby solving an electrochemical problem of long standing.

Gomer left Austria with his parents shortly after the Anschluss in 1938. He received part of his education in Scotland, and went to the United States in 1940. He received a B.A. degree in chemistry from Pomona College in 1944, spent the following 2 years in the U.S. Army, and received his Ph.D. from the University of Rochester in 1949. He joined the University of Chicago in 1950 as an instructor and eventually became professor of chemistry (1958) and director of the James Franck Institue (1977) there. He was elected to membership in the Leopoldina Academy of Sciences.

Gomer edited with C. S. Smith, *Structure and Properties of Solid Surfaces* (1952), wrote *Field Emission and Field Ionization* (1960), and edited *Interactions on Metals Surfaces* (1975).

For background information *see* ADSORPTION; ELECTRODE POTENTIAL; FIELD EMISSION; FIELD-EMISSION MICROSCOPY in the McGraw-Hill Encyclopedia of Science and Technology. ∎

GOOD, ROBERT A.
☆ American physician and immunobiologist

Born May 21, 1922, Crosby, MN, U.S.A.

Good spent more than 3 decades (1940–73) of his career at the University of Minnesota. From this base he contributed significantly to the understanding of the mechanisms of immunity, discovered the role of the thymus in the development of the immune response, analyzed development of immunity function in ontogenetic and phylogenetic perspective, and introduced the principles of cellular engineering.

A main thrust of Good's early researches was in the area of immunodeficiency diseases in humans. During the course of his comprehensive studies, Good described, for the first time, a number of diseases and syndromes of primary immunodeficiency and introduced and defined the two-component concept of immunity. He analyzed and defined the immunological deficiencies in Hodgkin's disease, leukemias, and lymphomas and myelomas; defined *Pneumocystis carinii* infections and their association with human immunodeficiency diseases; discovered and defined the immunodeficiency associated with ataxiatelangiectasia, thymoma, and the Wiskott-Aldrich syndromes.

Good demonstrated the high incidence of mesenchymal and rheumatoid diseases and autoimmunity in patients with immunodeficiencies and discovered the association of autoimmunity with experimental immunodeficiencies in animals. He introduced and amplified the concepts of forbidden antigens and immunodeficiency as a basis of autoimmunity. From his linking of autoimmunity and immunodeficiency to aging, he proceeded in later work to explore the relationship between deficient immunologic function and nutritional deprivation, analyzing the influence of nutrition on development and maintenance of immunological function, on malignancy, and on the waning of immunological vigor with aging and prolongation of life. He made major contributions to understanding of kidney disease, vascular injury, and rheumatic and hematologic disorders.

With H. Gewurz, Good defined and introduced to clinical medicine the concept of profiles of complement perturbation in human disease. He described the association of complement component deficiencies with infectious vascular, renal, and mesenchymal diseases. In this context, he specifically analyzed and defined C1r, C1q, C2, and C1 esterase inhibitor deficiencies. He contributed to the analysis of the role of complement in many biological phenomena, for example, immunological tolerance, immune response, allograft rejections, and vascular injury. He developed and trained more than 75 professors of pediatrics, medicine, microbiology, pathology, surgery, and biology.

The discoverer of the role of the thymus in developmental immunobiology, Good showed that the thymus is essential to the development of full humoral immunological vigor and for cell-mediated immunity. He demonstrated that the thymus must act in two ways to differentiate and to maintain or expand the T-cell population through hormones it produces to differentiate human stem cells to T lymphocytes and different stages of functional T lymphocytes.

Chief among Good's accomplishments was his introduction of the concept of cellular engineering. He performed the first marrow transplant to correct an inborn error of metabolism—severe combined immunodeficiency. He was also the first to perform a successful marrow transplant to correct aregenerative anemia and pancytopenia. With his Danish colleagues, he carried out the first successful marrow transplant to correct immunodeficiency with marrow from an uncle donor matched at the HLA-D locus and completely mismatched at the HL-A determinants; and he was the first to transplant marrow from a donor matched from a pool of donors in the general population in a successful effort to correct severe combined immunodeficiency.

A native of Minnesota, Good attended the University of Minnesota, where he received his B.A. (1944), M.B. (1946), and M.D. and Ph.D. (1947) degrees. He began his career at the university as a teaching assistant in the department of anatomy (1944). He interned in pediatrics and moved from instructor in pediatrics (1950) to professor (1954). In 1962 he became professor of microbiology, and in 1970 professor and head of the department of pathology. He was elected Regents' Professor of Pediatrics and Microbiology in 1969. He spent a year (1949–50) at the Rockefeller Institute as visiting investigator and assistant physician to the hospital. In 1973 he became president and director of the Sloan-Kettering Institute for Cancer Research in New York City. In addition to his institute positions, Good was professor of medicine and pediatrics at Cornell University Medical College; attending pediatrician at both New York and Memorial hospitals; director and professor of pathology of the Sloan-Kettering Division,

Graduate School of Medical Sciences, Cornell University; adjunct professor and visiting physician at Rockefeller University; and director of research of Memorial Sloan-Kettering Cancer Center, and Memorial Hospital. In 1970 Good was cited in the Albert D. Lasker Medical Research Award for his many contributions to medicine. In 1978 the regents of the University of Minnesota conferred on him the Outstanding Achievement Award for internationally respected leadership in the fields of immunology, pediatrics, pathology, medicine, and cancer research. His many other honors include the Gairdner, Borden, Parke-Davis, Ricketts, Mead-Johnson, Theobald Smith, Squibb, and Golden Plate awards; the Lila Gruber Memorial Award for Cancer Research, and the Cancer Research Institute's Cancer Immunology Award. He was awarded numerous honorary degrees, including the universities of Chicago and Uppsala. Good served for a year on the President's Cancer Panel, the group that spurred the development of the "Conquest of Cancer" program. He was a member of the National Academy of Sciences, the American Academy of Arts and Sciences, the American Association of Immunologists, the American Association of Pathologists, the American Pediatric Society, and the Harvey Society, among numerous other professional associations in several disciplines.

Good's publications, numbering more than 1300 scientific articles and 23 books, reflect his broad interests and activities and his collaborative efforts with other scientists. He served on the editorial boards of numerous journals.

For background information *see* IMMUNITY; THYMUS GLAND (VERTEBRATE) in the McGraw-Hill Encyclopedia of Science and Technology. ∎

GOODPASTURE, ERNEST WILLIAM
American pathologist

Born Oct. 17, 1886, Montgomery County, TN, U.S.A.
Died Sept. 20, 1960, Nashville, TN, U.S.A.

Viruses, unlike bacteria, require living tissues for survival and propagation. This was a great obstacle to scientific study of viruses in laboratories until Goodpasture found, in 1931, that fertile chick eggs offered an inexpensive and sterile environ-

ment for the luxuriant growth of the virus of fowlpox. Nearly all the later practical advances in the control of virus diseases of humans and animals sprang from this single discovery, since it paved the way for large-scale production of vaccine against diseases such as smallpox, yellow fever, influenza, and typhus. Wartime use of his technique made possible the production of vaccines for use with all troops sent overseas. For his achievement Goodpasture received, among other honors, the Passano Foundation Award in 1946 and the Kovalenko Medal of the National Academy of Sciences in 1958.

In order to produce a vaccine for large-scale use, a virologist must have an abundant source of live viruses. Before the 1930s, there were only two virus vaccines in use: one against smallpox, the other against rabies. Jenner had utilized the cow for the development of the first, and Pasteur had found it possible to grow the viruses causing rabies by infecting rabbits. Though Karl Landsteiner had infected the rhesus monkey with poliomyelitis in 1908 and the Maitlands had cultivated cowpox virus in a flask containing chicken kidney, there was no acceptable method for the mass production of viruses until the work of Woodruff and Goodpasture on the chorioallantoic membrane of the chick embryo.

The membrane had been used by a number of investigators for the study of the growth of various implanted tissues. F. P. Rous and J. B. Murphy were the first to use this technique for the study of tumors in 1911, and Danchakoff used the method to grow embryonic chick tissues in 1916. Subsequent research using this technique involved experiments with auto- and heteroplastic grafts, as well as auto- and heterogeneous tumors. Only two previous reports of the production of experimental infection using this technique were reported prior to the 1931 report from Vanderbilt University: Rous and Murphy grew virus of Rous sarcoma, and Askanazy reported the production of tuberculous chicks by infection of fertile eggs in 1923.

Goodpasture, professor of pathology at the Vanderbilt University School of Medicine, was interested in pathogenesis, the development of disease, and was, therefore, interested in producing sufficient virus for study. He had been engaged in the study of fowlpox, or sorehead, as it was called by farmers. Though several methods for obtaining sterile virus were known and employed, he found a new method for the propagation of fowlpox virus, free from contaminants, that could provide sufficient quantity for immunological experiments.

To secure sterile fowlpox virus for inoculation of chick embryos, feathers were plucked from the head of a chick 1–2 weeks old, and virus was inoculated at three points, 1 centimeter apart, to permit the development of separate nodules that could be removed by one stroke of the knife. Since nodules of more than 7 days' development were likely to be invaded by pyogenic bacteria, the chick was sacrificed 6–7 days after inoculation. The head was bathed with a 95 percent alcohol solution and permitted to dry. A nodule was cut off at a level deep enough to obtain infected cores of most of the follicles. The severed nodule was placed, epithelial surface down, on a sterile glass slide, while the infected cores were forced out of the follicles from the cut surface. The pieces were washed twice with sterile Tyrode's solution and stored at 4°C in a small amount of the same solution. One piece was tested and, if no bacterial growth was apparent within 24 hours, the remaining virus was made into a suspension for inoculation by grinding with a few drops of Tyrode's solution.

The technique for opening the eggs, improved upon in later experiments, involved candling the eggs to outline the position of the chorioallantoic membrane in order to ensure that the window would be cut directly over it. The surface of the egg shell was coated with a thin layer of melted paraffin over an area somewhat larger than the proposed window to prevent infection from pieces of shell. After the shell was removed, the shell membrane was also coated with paraffin of low melting point so that this membrane might be torn with a sharp-pointed instrument on three sides of the window, exposing the chorioallantoic membrane.

Inoculation was done by pricking the membrane and applying a drop of uncontaminated virus suspension. In order to watch the effects of the virus, a glass cover slip was substituted for the original shell and fixed in position with a petrolatum-paraffin ring. Embryos at various stages of development were used, with those from 10–15 days giving the best results.

Fowlpox infection of the chorioallantoic membrane occurred in every case where the embryo survived for at least 4 days. Three tests were used to prove infection: (1) Tissue, removed with sterile precautions and inoculated into scarified epithelium of adult hens, produced massive fowlpox lesions. (2) Smears of the lesion, stained by Morosow's method, showed Borrel bodies, the etiological agent of the disease, present in large numbers. (3) Histological sections of the tissue showed the typical picture of the fowlpox lesion.

Inoculation, as a method of cultivating virus, gave larger quantities of uncontaminated virus than any other means previously used. The fact that the virus was free of antigens not directly associated with the disease made the technique especially useful in immunological experiments and opened the way for the development of vaccines to protect people from diseases where no protection had previously existed.

The successful infection of the chorioallantoic membrane of chick embryos with fowlpox virus led Goodpasture to investigate the effect of the inoculation of other viruses upon this tissue. He and his coworkers at Vanderbilt were able to show that the viruses of vaccinia and of herpes simplex, which causes cold sores and fever blisters, infect the membrane in spite of the fact that vaccinia is only slightly pathogenic for adult fowls, and that repeated attempts to infect adult and young chickens with the virus of herpes simplex had failed. This emphasized the value of the embryonic cells in virus development and led to the preparation of antismallpox vaccine that could be used for human immunization.

Goodpasture graduated from Vanderbilt University in 1907 and taught for a year before entering medical school at the Johns Hopkins University. After graduation in 1912, he stayed on as a research fellow and instructor until 1915. He taught at the Harvard Medical School from 1915 to 1922 and was director of the Singer Memorial Research Laboratory in Pennsylvania from 1922 to 1924. In 1924 he was appointed professor of pathology at Vanderbilt University Medical School, serving as dean from 1945 to 1950 and retiring in 1955.

For background information *see* CULTURE, EMBRYONATED EGG; CULTURE, TISSUE; VACCINATION; VIRUS in the McGraw-Hill Encyclopedia of Science and Technology. ■

GORTER, CORNELIS JACOBUS
★ Dutch physicist

Born *Aug. 14,1907, Utrecht, Netherlands*

Gorter was a pupil of the school of low-temperature physicists founded at the University of Leiden by H. Kamerlingh Onnes, who liquefied helium in 1908 and discovered superconductivity in 1911. Gorter's main fields of research were magnetism and superconductivity. Having started by studying paramagnetism in salts of the iron group and of the rare earths, he soon met with the problem of the mechanisms which orient the ionic magnetic moments into the direction of an external magnetic field. One such mechanism is the interaction between the magnetic moments and the heat motion of the crystalline lattice in which they are placed. Another mechanism, pointed out by I. Waller, is the interaction between different magnetic moments. The first mechanism should lead to a relaxation time which increases rapidly upon decreasing the temperature, while the second should give a relaxation time which hardly depends on temperature. By introducing radio-frequency magnetic fields and studying the heat dissipation as well as the high-frequency susceptibility as a function of frequency, external magnetic field, and temperature, Gorter discovered and studied both relaxation processes. He then tried to observe the absorption frequency of radio power corresponding to transitions between the different possible orientations of the magnetic moments with respect to the constant external field. But his repeated attempts thus to observe nuclear magnetic resonance due to nuclear magnetic moments, and, at higher frequencies, electron spin resonance remained unsuccessful, since the investigated substances were too pure and the microwave equipment was too simple, respectively. Later these resonances were discovered in the United States by I. I. Rabi, F. Bloch, and E. M. Purcell, and in the Soviet Union by E. Zavoisky. Magnetic resonances became important tools in physics and chemistry and have several practical applications. *See* BLOCH, FELIX; PURCELL, EDWARD MILLS; RABI, ISIDOR ISAAC.

A second group of magnetic researches was aimed at orienting atomic nuclei which possess a magnetic moment and then studying the anisotropy of their properties. Though the original suggestion, made in 1934, concerned orienting them in a large external field at extremely low temperatures, it was later pointed out that the interaction between the electrons in a paramagnetic ion and its nucleus must lead to considerable orienting at temperatures not quite so low.

The latter suggestion was independently made by M. E. Rose. Oriented nuclei, in fact, made possible the study of anisotropy of nuclear properties such as radioactive emissions, nuclear reactions, and scattering of other nuclei.

Gorter's third field of research in magnetism was antiferromagnetism, consisting in the formation of crystalline sublattices in a solid; these sublattices differ in the direction and sometimes in the magnitude of their magnetizations. In cooperation with N. J. Poulis and others, various properties were analyzed, including antiferromagnetic resonance of hydrated copper chloride, which is antiferromagnetic below a Néel temperature of 4.3 K.

Kamerlingh Onnes had found that superconductivity is disturbed upon application of a magnetic field which surpasses a critical field. This critical field is of the order of a few hundred oersteds near the absolute zero of temperature and gradually goes to zero when the transition temperature of the superconductor is approached. In 1933 Gorter gave a simple thermodynamical explanation of this. As a consequence of the surface currents induced just below the surface of the sample, its Gibbs free energy is raised proportionally to the square of the external magnetic field. As soon as this Gibbs free energy becomes equal to that of the non-superconductive normal metal, the sample passes into that normal state. In part of this work Gorter cooperated with H. B. G. Casimir, with whom he also introduced a so-called order parameter, describing a degree of superconductivity.

The discovery by W. J. de Haas and J. Voogd that in some alloys superconductivity persists up to much higher fields than should be expected from the thermodynamical argument was attributed by Gorter to the formation of a mixed structure of thin superconducting regions into which the magnetic field may partially penetrate so that the rise of the Gibbs free energy is much slower. In the 1950s these early suggestions, as well as those of F. London on the slight penetration of magnetic fields below the surface of a superconducting region, were transposed into an image on a quantum-mechanical basis by the Moscow school of L. D. Landau, V. L. Ginsburg, and A. A. Abrikosov. In that image the order parameter has the character of a wave function and thus is not a real but a complex quantity. This condition permits the introduction of a rigorous model of the "mixed" structure, which may occur under certain conditions. If, moreover, the metal contains local inhomogeneities of the right character, the mixed structure can stand up to magnetic fields of the order of 100,000 oersteds and even then can carry considerable magnetic current. This finding is now used in superconducting magnets which can produce high magnetic fields without continuously converting precious electric energy into heat. American scientists, including J. E. Kunzler and B. T. Matthias, pioneered in finding the right metal compounds. Nowadays one can buy "superconducting" coils with safety devices or the materials to prepare such a coil or coil system. *See* LANDAU, LEV DAVYDOVICH; MATTHIAS, BERND TEO.

As director of the Kamerlingh Onnes Laboratory, Gorter added to magnetism and superconductivity research on the quantum fluid helium in cooperation with K. W. Taconis, H. C. Kramers, and R. de Bruyn Ouboter. In the framework of the two-fluid model he introduced a nonlinear mutual fraction between the normal fluid and superfluid (with J. H. Mellink). He reinitiated the research in metallophysics (with A. N. Gerritsen and G. J. van den Berg) and optics (C. Vlam). In 1938 Gorter published a qualitative explanation of the Senftleben effect for oxygen. Since 1962 the molecular physics group (J. J. M. Beenakker and H. F. P. Knaap) gave much attention to this effect for other rotating molecules (Senftleben-Beenakker effect) in order to study nonspherical molecules.

Son of a government official, Gorter studied in Leiden from 1924 to 1932 under W. J. de Haas and P. Ehrenfest. After occupying positions in Haarlem and the University of Groningen, he was appointed in 1940 as P. Zeeman's successor at the University of Amsterdam. In 1946 he returned to Leiden as director of the Kamerlingh Onnes Laboratory. In addition, he served in national scientific positions, such as president of the Foundation for Fundamental Research on Matter during 1955–60 and president of the Royal Netherlands Academy of Sciences and Letters during 1960–66. He was vice-president of the International Union of Pure and Applied Physics during 1946–51 and 1960–66, chairman of its commission on very low temperature, and president of the technical board of the International Institute of Refrigeration. Awarded seven honorary degrees, Gorter received the F. London Award for research in low-temperature physics in 1966. He was elected a foreign member

of the American Academy of Arts and Sciences in 1952, a foreign research associate of the U.S. National Academy of Sciences in 1967, and a foreign member of the American Philosophical Society (Philadelphia) in 1970. He was corresponding member of the Swedish, Belgian, Finnish, and French (1974) academies of science. For many years (1956–76) he was a member of the scientific committee of the Conseils de Physique Solvay. An extended illness was the reason for his retirement in 1973 as a professor of physics at the University of Leiden and as (scientific) director of the Kamerlingh Onnes Laboratory.

Besides his thesis, *Paramagnetische Eigenschaften von Salzen* (1932), Gorter wrote *Paramagnetic Relaxation* (1947) and edited six volumes of *Progress in Low Temperature Physics* (1955–70).

For background information *see* ANTIFERROMAGNETISM: MAGNETIC RESONANCE; SUPERCONDUCTIVITY in the McGraw-Hill Encyclopedia of Science of Technology. ■

GOUDSMIT, SAMUEL ABRAHAM
★ American physicist

Born July 11, 1901, The Hague, Netherlands
Died Dec. 4, 1978, Reno, NV, U.S.A.

In 1925, while a student at the University of Leiden, Goudsmit, together with his fellow student George E. Uhlenbeck,

discovered that all electrons spin about an axis. It was soon recognized that spin is a property not only of electrons but also of protons, neutrons, and most other elementary particles, a property as fundamental as mass and charge. For this discovery, Goudsmit and Uhlenbeck received Research Corporation Awards in 1953, Max Planck Medals in 1964, and U. S. National Medals of Science in 1976. They were made Commanders in the Royal Netherlands Order of Orange-Nassau in 1977.

Goudsmit had specialized in the structure of atomic spectra and had already published a number of papers on this subject. On Uhlenbeck's return to Leiden in the summer of 1925 after several years in Rome, it was Goudsmit's task to bring his colleague up to date on the advances resulting from Niels Bohr's ideas on atomic structure. In Rome, Uhlenbeck had been in contact primarily with older subjects in theoretical physics. Their differences in training and background proved to be extremely fruitful for their discussions, and several useful new ideas resulted, of which the electron spin was the most significant. *See* BOHR, NIELS HENRIK DAVID.

Goudsmit and Uhlenbeck were aware that the number of spectral lines observed for any atom was always twice as many as that predicted by Bohr's atomic model. The splitting of these lines when the light source was placed in a magnetic field did not agree at all with expectations. Wolfgang Pauli had shown that each electron orbit in an atom had to be characterized by four numbers rather than the three—corresponding to the three dimensions of space—that one would have expected to be sufficient. Assuming that electrons were not merely charged points but were spinning particles, Goudsmit and Uhlenbeck found that these difficulties and many others could be fully explained. A spinning electric charge is also a magnet, and the magnetism of each electron accounted for the unexplained magnetic properties of atoms. *See* PAULI, WOLFGANG.

The idea of spin turned out to be far more significant than its original discoverers could have foreseen. It led in 1928 to a fundamental change in the mathematical structure of quantum mechanics by P. A. M. Dirac, who showed that the spin of elementary particles could be considered a relativistic effect. Modern quantum theory, moreover, showed that the picture of an electron as a tiny spinning sphere could not be taken literally. Abstract mathematical relations replaced the primitive models of atoms and particles, although these models were still very useful in descriptive discussion. *See* DIRAC, PAUL ADRIEN MAURICE.

Goudsmit was born in The Hague, where his mother had a millinery shop and his father was a wholesale dealer in bathroom fixtures. He studied theoretical physics, and Egyptology as a sideline, at the University of Leiden and did experimental research at the University of Amsterdam. He received his Ph.D. from Leiden in 1927 shortly before going to the University of Michigan, where he taught until 1941. During World War II (1941–45) he worked first on radar at the Massachusetts Institute of Technology and in England and then in 1944 became head of a secret intelligence group that moved with the advancing armies to investigate the German atomic bomb project. For this work he received the Medal of Freedom from the U.S. Department of Defense and was appointed an honorary officer in the Order of the British Empire (OBE). In 1948 Goudsmit joined the physics staff of Brookhaven National Laboratory. He was elected to the National Academy of Sciences in 1947.

Goudsmit wrote *The Structure of Line Spectra,* with Linus Pauling (1930), *Atomic Energy States,* with R. F. Bacher (1932), and an account of his war experiences, *Alsos* (1947).

For background information *see* QUANTUM MECHANICS; SPIN (QUANTUM MECHANICS) in the McGraw-Hill Encyclopedia of Science and Technology. ■

GOWANS, JAMES LEARMONTH
★ British medical scientist

Born May 7, 1924, Sheffield, England

Gowans was responsible for elucidating the life history and function of lymphocytes. In the early 1950s lymphocytes were recognized as cells which normally circulated in the blood, which were a major component of normal lymphoid tissue, and which accumulated in tissues undergoing a variety of pathological changes. Their function was unknown. H. W. Florey, the professor of pathology in Oxford, drew the attention of Gowans to the lymphocyte problem in 1953 and suggested that he

might try and solve "the mystery of the disappearing lymphocytes." Briefly, it was known that the output of lymphocytes from the major lymphatic ducts was sufficient to replace all the lymphocytes circulating in the blood several times daily. Large numbers of lymphocytes must therefore be leaving the circulation each day for an unknown destination, and the current view was that they might migrate into the bone marrow where they provided the precursors from which other blood cells were generated. This view proved to be incorrect. In experiments in rats, involving the transfusion and recovery of radioactive-labeled lymphocytes, Gowans showed that the rapid turnover of the blood lymphocytes was more apparent than real. Lymphocytes which enter the blood from the lymphatics migrate from the blood back into the lymphatics and reappear once more in the blood. The demonstration of lymphocyte recirculation reconciled the long lifespan enjoyed by most lymphocytes with the observation that they turned over rapidly in the blood. Subsequent work showed that the main anatomical site of lymphocyte recirculation lies in the lymph nodes and that the migration from blood into the nodes occurs across the high-walled endothelium of a specialized set of venules which lie deep in the lymph node cortex.

Studies on the function of lymphocytes were much influenced by the brilliant work of P. B. Medawar and R. E. Billingham on the immunology of tissue transplantation. By exploiting their discoveries Gowans was able to show that

the small lymphocytes could interact with foreign tissue antigens and initiate graft-against-host reactions and that the interaction with antigen caused lymphocytes to enlarge, divide, and give rise to a progeny of new lymphocytes. Subsequent work showed that lymphocytes could also initiate antibody responses against conventional antigens and that the interaction led to the formation from lymphocytes of antibody-secreting plasma cells. Thus, the generalization emerged that a major function of lymphocytes was to initiate immune responses; antigen induced cell division and differentiation which gave rise to the effector lymphocytes of cellular immunity or to the plasma cells of humoral immunity. It was also shown that recirculating lymphocytes carried the property of immunological memory. *See* MEDAWAR, PETER BRIAN.

A contemporary worker, J. F. A. P. Miller, who had discovered the crucial role of the thymus in the development of lymphoid tissue, later found that the predicted functional heterogeneity of lymphocytes had its basis in the existence of two distinct populations of cells: B lymphocytes which give rise to antibody-secreting cells, and T lymphocytes which are responsible for cell-mediated immunity and for collaborative interactions with B lymphocytes. Gowans and Miller helped to lay the foundations of the subject of cellular immunology.

Gowans and his colleagues showed that both B and T lymphocytes recirculate through the lymph nodes but that they come to occupy quite distinct regions within lymphoid organs known as the B and T areas. A separate migration pathway was also identified by which circulating lymphocytes, originating in the gastrointestinal lymphoid tissue, migrate into the wall of the small intestine and give rise to the plasma cells responsible for local intestinal immunity.

Gowans qualified in medicine at Kings College Hospital, London, in 1947. He then studied physiology at Oxford University and went on to take a D.Phil. under Florey in the Sir William Dunn School of Pathology, Oxford, in which all his subsequent scientific work was carried out. He held a Royal Society Research Professorship from 1962 to 1977 and directed the Medical Research Council's Cellular Immunology Unit. In 1977 he left the laboratory to become secretary of the Medical Research Council in London. He received a Gairdner Foundation Award in 1968 and shared the Paul Ehrlich–Ludwig Darmstaedter Prize with Miller in 1974.

For background information *see* IMMUNOLOGY, CELLULAR in the McGraw-Hill Encyclopedia of Science and Technology. ■

GRAHAM, CLARENCE HENRY
★ American psychophysiologist

Born Jan. 6, 1906, Worcester, MA, U.S.A.
Died July 25, 1971, New York, NY, U.S.A.

In the course of his studies on vision and visual perception, Graham heard of a young student at Barnard College who seemed to have normal vision in one eye and color-blind vision in the other. Such a subject, referred to as unilaterally color-blind, is very rare. Although about 10 such subjects have been studied effectively in the last 100 years, technical methods and equipment have not been such as to make possible a proper classification of most cases. In addition, the fact that the subjects could not be observed for sufficient periods of time precluded extensive analyses of most cases. Analysis of unilateral cases of color blindness is of great importance to color theory because it is only in the case of the unilaterally color-blind person that researchers can learn what colors the color-blind person sees. The usual color-blind person, color-blind in both eyes, never sees color in the way a normal person does and hence

cannot tell in terms of normal color vision what he views in his color-blind eye (although he early learns to give correct color names to factors other than color—for example, the intensities or relative positions of traffic lights rather than their hues).

Graham decided to study the basic visual discriminations and sensitivities in each eye of the subject. For this purpose, he made the following determinations in each of her eyes: the least energies of lights of pure spectral color that could be seen; the least difference in wavelength that could be seen as a difference in color; the manner in which pure colors of the spectrum entered into a color match involving a reference set of three pure colors—red, green, and blue—called primaries. In addition, other tests were made: the matching of a color seen in the color-blind eye by one seen in the normal eye; and the least rate of alternation of light and dark (flicker) required to give the appearance of steady light for different colors. Observations were also made by the usual screening color-plate and instrument tests for color blindness. The work was done in the psychology laboratory of Columbia University in collaboration with Yun Hsia from 1954 to 1957.

Three major types of color-blind individuals constitute a class called dichromats—that is, persons who confuse pure colors with a mixture of two primaries. Persons in one of the subclasses, protanopes, are mainly insensitive in the red; those in another group, tritanopes, are mainly insensitive in the blue. An important third subclass, deuteranopes, has been described as showing normal sensitivity in the green linked with a fusion mechanism whereby reds and greens are always seen as yellow. This latter mechanism is not attributed to loss of green receptors but rather to the subject's inability to distinguish red and green.

Graham found, first, that the subject's normal eye functioned in all respects like that of a normal person. However, her color-blind eye showed a number of differences from normal. The so-called luminosity determinations indicated much greater energy requirements for just seeing lights from the violet to the orange than for the normal eye; reds required the same energy as for the normal eye. Thus the subject showed a luminosity loss in the violet-to-orange range. Only two primaries, blue and red, were required to match any pure color of the spectrum.

These results were similar to those for the usual deuteranope except for a minor atypical result in the blue. The results on hue discrimination showed that the subject required much greater wavelength changes to see a difference in color than are required by normal subjects. Again the results were similar to those obtained with the usual deuteranope except for a small variation in the blue. On the binocular matching of colors, the results were especially important, for they showed that the subject saw in the color-blind eye all colors in the violet, blue, and blue-green range of the spectrum as corresponding to a single blue of 470 nanometers in the normal eye. She saw in the color-blind eye all colors in the green, yellow, orange, and red ranges as a yellow of 570 nanometers in the normal eye. Thus her color-blind eye saw two colors, yellow and blue.

Finally, the subject required considerably higher energies just to see minimum light in the spectrum over the wavelength range from violet to orange. This luminosity loss was very considerable. The seeing of yellow by deuteranopes has been accounted for by an idea ascribed mainly to A. Fick, according to whom characteristic sensitivities in red and green receptors (hence their absorption properties) become similar but with no change in central brain connections. Thus reds and greens are absorbed indiscriminately by both types of receptors, but their excitations stimulate red and green centers and thus give rise to the yellow mixture of red and green. This conclusion is in accord with the "fusion" idea. However, the fact of luminosity loss in Graham's subject shows that not only does the Fick-fusion type of process take place but some loss of receptors, most likely the green, must also be posited to account for the luminosity deficit seen in this case and probably in deuteranopes generally.

Graham, son of a metalworker, majored in psychology at Clark University, Worcester, MA, where he received his A.B. in 1927 and his Ph.D. in 1930. He was successively at Temple University, the Johnson Foundation for Medical Physics of the University of Pennsylvania, Clark University, and Brown University until 1945. During World War II he was a member of the Applied Psychology Panel of the National Defense Research Committee. In 1945 he went to Columbia University as professor of psychology. Graham received the Warren Medal of the Society of Experimental Psychologists in 1941 and the Tillyer Award of the Optical Society of America in 1963. He was elected to the National Academy of Sciences in 1946.

Graham edited, and wrote many of the chapters in, *Vision and Visual Perception* (1965).

For background information *see* COLOR VISION in the McGraw-Hill Encyclopedia of Science and Technology. ∎

GRANIT, RAGNAR ARTHUR
★ Swedish physiologist

Born Oct. 30, 1900, Helsinge, Finland

Granit is best known for his work in vision and in the field of motor control by muscular afferents; for the former he received the 1967 Nobel Prize in medicine or physiology. During his medical studies he became interested in the psychophysics of vision but soon concluded that a physiological approach was needed. E. D. Adrian had demonstrated the value of this approach in pioneer work with the eye of the conger eel. Granit's leading idea was that since the retina had been shown by S. Ramón y Cajal to be a nervous center, it should be studied as such. He acquired the necessary background during 2 years in Sir Charles Sherrington's laboratory in Oxford. The idea was first tested psychophysically by the flicker method during 2 years at the Johnson Foundation, University of Pennsylvania. The so-called Granit-Harper law of summation was thus established.

Granit began electrophysiological work by developing his well-known analysis of the components of the electroretinogram in 1932. The question of whether light could inhibit, as well as elicit, impulses in the optic nerve seemed fundamental at the time. In 1934 he produced evidence for inhibition, and this fact is today a cornerstone in visual physiology. Also unknown was the relation between amount of rhodopsin (visual purple) and retinal sensitivity. Granit, with T. Holmberg and M. Zewi, studied this quantitatively. It was further shown that intensities of spectral green which failed to bleach rhodopsin caused very large reductions of retinal sensitivity. The explanation may lie in the later discovery, by K. O. Donner and T. Reuter, of a strong feedback inhibition of sensitivity by small quantities of the photoproducts called metarhodopsins.

Thomas Young's conception of three types of fiber in the optic nerve for the three fundamental colors had been interpreted psychophysically by S. Hecht on the theory of three types of receptors (cones) with almost wholly overlapping spectral distributions of sensitivity. Granit's first tests with the electroretinogram in 1937 clearly indicated greater spectral differentiation. A microelectrode technique developed by Granit and G. Svaetichin in 1939 was the first ever used for sensory work. The technique soon showed that some optic nerve fibers (the dominators) responded to the whole spectrum, while others, being narrow-banded "modulators," were color-specific and occurred with slightly varying location within three main regions of the spectrum. This work was extended to a large number of species with variable cone populations. Finally, selective adaptation was used to isolate in a mammal (cat) the three basic spectral sensitivity curves for red, green, and blue. Other researchers have since demonstrated, in training experiments, color sensitivity in the cat. Granit concluded this phase of activity with a summary of his color work in his Thomas Young Oration in 1945, and he covered the whole of retinal electrophysiology in *Sensory Mechanisms of the Retina* in 1947.

Granit next turned to the length meters and tension meters in the muscles known as muscle spindles and tendon organs, respectively. The spindles are extremely complex organs with a motor innervation by special fibers, the gamma fibers, whose capacity for making spindles discharge had been demonstrated in his laboratory

by L. Leksell. Granit found that sites in the brain and the cerebellum which excite or inhibit the muscles' motor or alpha neurons had parallel actions on the gamma motoneurons. The concept of the gamma loop through the length-measuring spindles, serving as a second motor system, was then developed experimentally, and it led to a differentiation of alpha and gamma rigidities in neuropathology. The concept of linked alpha and gamma action and its significance was elaborated. Breakdown of this linkage was observed after cerebellar ablation, and this was held to explain the clinical symptoms of dysmetria. Expanding this work to a circuit analysis of the components of the alpha and gamma reflex arcs, Granit differentiated tonic from phasic motoneurons; he studied, by extra- and intracellular recording, the effects of tendon organs and muscle spindles on motoneurons, the role of inhibition, including recurrent or feedback inhibition through fibers which return to the motoneurons from the outgoing axons, and so on. He maintained throughout this experimentation strong emphasis on the organizational aspects and the principles of motor control by the muscles' sense organs. In particular, the spindles were defined as sensory-motor end organs, at the same time measuring and controlling motor action. Finally, feeling the need for precise information on impulse frequency as an instrument of communication, Granit set out to establish by intra- and extracellular recording the rules by which excitation and inhibition balance out quantitatively at the membrane of single cells. He chose motoneurons as his prototype.

Granit graduated from the Swedish Normal-lyceum, Helsinki, in 1919, took Mag.Phil. and M.D. degrees at the University of Helsinki, and served there as professor of physiology during 1935–40. He was invited to a personal research chair in neurophysiology at the Royal Caroline Institute of Stockholm in 1940. In 1945 the Caroline Institute approved a building program for the Medical Nobel Institute, which was to be provided with three departments, one to be devoted to neurophysiology with Granit as director. A special chair of neurophysiology was erected for him by the Swedish government for this purpose. In 1945 Granit delivered the Thomas Young Oration of the Physical Society, London, and in 1960 he was elected a foreign member of the Royal Society of London. In 1967 he gave the Sherrington Lecture of the Royal Society of Medicine, London; in 1972 the Sherrington Lecture of the University of Liverpool; and in 1975 the Hughlings Jackson Lecture of McGill University. He was appointed resident scholar of the Fogarty International Center, Bethesda, MD, for 1971–72 and 1974. Granit was elected a foreign member of the National Academy of Sciences, Washington, and of the Accademia dei Lincei, Rome. He was awarded the Donders, Purkinje, Retzius, and Sherrington medals and seven honorary degrees.

Granit wrote *Sensory Mechanisms of the Retina* (1947; 2d ed. 1963). He delivered the Silliman Lectures at Yale University in 1954, published as *Receptors and Sensory Perception: A Discussion of Aims, Means and Results of Electrophysiological Research into the Process of Reception* (1955). In 1965 Granit organized Nobel Symposium I for the Nobel Foundation. He edited the proceedings under the subtitle *Muscular Afferents and Motor Control* (1966). For the series "British Men of Science" he wrote *Charles Scott Sherrington: An Appraisal* (1966). Other books are *The Basis of Motor Control* (1970) and *The Purposive Brain* (1977). In the Swedish language he published a collection of essays on the scientific life, *Ung Mans Väg till Minerva* (1941; 2d ed. 1958).

For background information *see* COLOR VISION; EYE (VERTEBRATE); MOTOR SYSTEMS; PSYCHOPHYSICAL METHODS in the McGraw-Hill Encyclopedia of Science and Technology. ∎

GRAY, HARRY
★ American chemist

Born *Nov. 14, 1935, Woodburn, KY, U.S.A.*

Gray's early interest in transition metal compounds led him to investigate their electronic structures after he joined the chemistry faculty of Columbia University in 1961. His training at Northwestern University with Fred Basolo and Ralph Pearson and later at Copenhagen University with Carl Ballhausen allowed him to interpret the visible and ultraviolet absorptions of compounds containing metal-to-carbon bonds. In 1963 Gray was able to explain why molecules containing nickel, palladium, platinum, rhodium, and iridium bonded to four other groups in a planar ar-

rangement absorb near-ultraviolet light so strongly, and in 1969 he interpreted for the first time the intense near-ultraviolet absorptions of compounds containing two metal atoms directly bonded together. Both investigations played a major role in laying the foundation for his later work in solar energy conversion. *See* BASOLO, FRED; PEARSON, RALPH GOTTFRID.

In the 1960s during frequent visits to the Rockefeller University, Gray became interested in the role of transition metal ions in living systems. With Harvey Schugar, he investigated the nature of tripositive iron ions in aqueous solutions, and he used the results of this work in interpreting the structures of several iron-containing proteins. At the California Institute of Technology in the late 1960s and early 1970s, he started a major study of the pathways by which electrons are transferred in iron and copper proteins. At about the same time, he became interested in photochemistry, and with George Hammond and Mark Wrighton, he elucidated the ways in which transition metal compounds react when raised to high energy levels by irradiation with visible and ultraviolet light. *See* HAMMOND, GEORGE SIMMS.

Gray's work on the electron transfer reactions of metalloproteins and his interests in photochemistry led him in the mid-1970s to try experiments in the area of solar energy conversion. Utilizing his knowledge of the electronic energy levels of metal complexes, he, Kent Mann, and

Nate Lewis began to investigate the photochemistry of molecules in which two rhodium atoms are held together by isocyanide (NC) groups at the ends of carbon chains. As it turned out, these molecules were able both to trap the energy in sunlight and to perform the necessary catalytic steps to store this energy by transferring electrons to protons in water to make hydrogen gas.

In 1977 the first solar energy storage reaction involving hydrogen production in homogeneous solutions was discovered by Gray and his coworkers. The photocatalyst was a blue rhodium compound, called rhodium bridge, which was shown in work in the next 2 years to contain four rhodium atoms in its light-active form. The four-rhodium molecule split apart when it absorbed sunlight, and one two-rhodium fragment carried the two electrons needed to reduce two protons to one diatomic hydrogen molecule. Further work by Gray and his coworkers in 1979 suggested several ways of improving the quantum efficiencies of solar energy storage reactions of this type.

Gray received his B.S. in chemistry at Western Kentucky University in 1957 and his Ph.D. at Northwestern University in 1960. The following year he was a National Science Foundation postdoctoral fellow at the University of Copenhagen, where he collaborated with Ballhausen on studies of the electronic structures of metal complexes. From Copenhagen he went to Columbia University, where he became a full professor in 1965. In 1966 he was appointed professor of chemistry at the California Institute of Technology. For his work Gray received two American Chemical Society awards, in Pure Chemistry (1970) and Inorganic Chemistry (1978). He was elected to the National Academy of Sciences in 1971.

Gray wrote *Electrons and Chemical Bonding* (1964); *Molecular Orbital Theory*, with C. J. Ballhausen (1964); *Ligand Substitution Processes*, with C. H. Langford (1966); *Basic Principles of Chemistry*, with G. P. Haight (1967); *Chemical Dynamics*, with J. B. Dence and G. S. Hammond (1968); *Chemical Principles*, with R. E. Dickerson and Haight (1970, 1974); *Models in Chemical Science*, with Hammond, J. Osteryoung, and T. H. Crawford (1971); *Project Acac: An Experimental Investigation in Synthesis and Structure*, with J. G. Swanson and Crawford (1972); and *Chemical Bonds* (1973).

For background information *see* BIO-INORGANIC CHEMISTRY; PHOTOCHEMISTRY; TRANSITION ELEMENTS in the McGraw-Hill Encyclopedia of Science and Technology. ■

GREEN, DAVID EZRA
★ American biochemist

Born Aug. 5, 1910, New York, NY, U.S.A.

Green's training at New York University aroused in him an intense interest in the mechanisms of biological oxidations. Then at Cambridge University he was part of the group that laid the foundations of modern enzymology. Five oxidative enzymes were discovered and characterized during that period, notably α-glycerophosphate and β-hydroxybutyrate dehydrogenases. He was among the first to undertake the large-scale isolation of enzymes with functional groups, and he characterized a series of enzymes containing respectively flavin (for example, aldehyde and xanthine oxidases) and thiamine (yeast carboxylase) as prosthetic groups. His book *Mechanisms of Biological Oxidations* (1939) provides an account of the developments in oxidative enzymes in which he and other members of the Cambridge group took part. In addition to his isolation studies, Green was the first to demonstrate and analyze coenzyme-linked reactions between dehydrogenase systems, and he pioneered in the reconstitution of sequential reactions cat-alyzed by multiple enzymes linked via carriers.

At Harvard and Columbia medical schools, Green extended his large-scale isolation studies to flavoprotein enzymes (L-amino acid oxidase, glycine oxidase), thiaminoprotein enzymes (pyruvate keto-lase), and pyridoxal-containing enzymes (transaminases). A polyglutamyl deriva-tive of *p*-aminobenzoate (later identified as a fragment of folic acid) was isolated and characterized.

In 1945 Green became engaged in the isolation of the pyruvate dehydrogenase system of animal tissues and found it im-possible to separate the dehydrogenase from a large group of accompanying en-zymes catalyzing the citric cycle, terminal electron transfer, and oxidative phos-phorylation. He concluded from this non-separability that the pyruvate dehydro-genase is an integral part of an organized particulate system. This system, called the cyclophorase system, was conceived of as a single, complete operational unit. For some 5 years a lively controversy raged over the cyclophorase concept. With the discovery in 1950 (V. R. Potter, W. C. Schneider, A. L. Lehninger, and E. Ken-nedy) that the mitochondrion could be identified as the physical housing of the cyclophorase system, the notion of orga-nized, structured enzyme systems became firmly established in biochemical thought. *See* KENNEDY, EUGENE PATRICK; LEHN-INGER, ALBERT LESTER; POTTER, VAN RENSSELAER.

At the University of Wisconsin, Green formed a research group, uniquely equipped for large-scale isolation and study of particulate systems—a constantly changing group of postdoctoral fellows who stayed for periods of 1–5 years. In quick succession there came the isolation of the α-ketoglutarate and pyruvate dehy-drogenating complexes; the isolation of the kinase systems for activation of ace-tate, succinate, and acetoacetate via acyl CoA formation; the large-scale isolation of purified coenzyme A; and finally the reconstruction of the entire fatty acid sequence from the isolated component enzymes and intermediates. Systems re-search was the specialty of the institute group during 1948–55, culminating in the isolation and characterization of the fatty acid–synthesizing system. The require-ment for CO_2 by this system was rational-ized in terms of a biotin-catalyzed carbox-ylation of acetyl CoA to malonyl CoA.

All of this set the stage for the system-atic fragmentation and degradation of the mitochondrion, which started in 1955. The mitochondrion was comminuted into submitochondrial particles, the particles into complexes, and the complexes into the component catalytic proteins. This breakdown led to the concept of the elec-tron transfer chain as a composite of four separable complexes. As a by-product, these fragmentation studies initiated the discovery and chemical characterization of coenzyme Q, and the recognition of nonheme iron and copper as integral oxi-dation-reduction components of the elec-tron transfer chain. Coenzyme Q and cy-tochrome *c* were shown to be mobile components linking the various com-plexes. In addition to the catalytic com-ponents of the chain and of the other mitochondrial systems, Green and his colleagues discovered a set of organizing proteins, such as structural protein, which were intrinsic parts of all mitochondrial systems.

The role of lipid in mitochondrial func-tion was then systematically probed. Mi-tochondrial lipid was shown to be predom-inantly phospholipid (>90 percent) and to be bonded hydrophobically to protein. The essentiality of phospholipid for the electron transfer process was conclusively demonstrated. The predominantly hydro-phobic character of lipid-protein binding in the mitochondrion was the critical ob-servation that eventually led to a reexami-nation and rejection of the Danielli-Dav-son model of membrane structure and to a definition of membrane systems in terms of nesting lipoprotein repeating units. The ultrastructural study of the mitochon-drion, initiated in 1960–61 by H. Fernan-dez-Moran and Green, revealed the pres-ence of tripartite repeating units in the inner membrane, and it soon became evi-dent that repeating units are the hallmarks of all membranes. *See* FERNÁNDEZ-MORÁN, HUMBERTO.

The delineation of the ultrastructural picture and the definition of membrane systems led rapidly to a spate of related de-velopments: the demonstration of lipid as the determinant of membrane formation by restriction of binding modalities and the demonstration of reconstitution of the chain as a membrane phenomenon (all the complexes in the same membrane).

In 1975 Green developed the paired moving-charge model of energy coupling based on the principle that coupling is always direct and involves electrostatic interaction between moving charges in each of two closely associated reaction centers. These principles were shown to apply to the electron transfer complexes of the mitochondrial electron transfer chain, each of which was found to be resolvable into a set of proteins concerned with electron transfer (ETC) and a set of proteins concerned with ion transfer (ITC). These resolutions opened the door to the systematic isolation and identification of the functional subunits in both the ETC and ITC centers of each electron transfer complex. The electron transfer complexes were the first energy-coupling systems to be systematically analyzed by controlled disassembly and reconstitution. These studies were suggestive of a similar molecular strategy for all energy-coupling systems.

At New York University, Green received a B.Sc. in 1930 and an A.M. in 1932. In the latter year he joined the department of biochemistry at Cambridge University, where he received a Ph.D. in 1934 under Malcolm Dixon. Remaining at Cambridge until 1940, he then moved to the Harvard Medical School (1940–41) and the Columbia University Medical School (1941–48). In 1948 he went to the University of Wisconsin to inaugurate the Institute for Enzyme Research.

Recipient of the American Chemical Society Award in Enzyme Chemistry in 1946, Green was elected to the American Academy of Arts and Sciences in 1960 and the National Academy of Sciences in 1962.

Besides the book mentioned above, Green wrote *Molecular Insights into the Living Process*, with R. Goldberger (1967).

For background information *see* BIOLOGICAL OXIDATION; ENZYME; LIPID; MITOCHONDRIA in the McGraw-Hill Encyclopedia of Science and Technology. ∎

GREENSTEIN, JESSE LEONARD
★ American astronomer

Born Oct. 15, 1909, New York, NY, U.S.A.

New ideas and techniques have shifted emphasis from the classical astronomy of gravitation to the modern astrophysics of atoms and nuclei, stellar evolution, high-energy particles in magnetic fields, and matter at high density (though perhaps there is a trend back to gravitation again).

Greenstein pioneered in opening a variety of such new subjects, combining observational discoveries with theoretical interpretations. Much of his earlier work involved spectroscopic investigation of the atmospheres of stars. Later he turned to the structure and composition of the degenerate stars. He also took part in the discovery of the interstellar magnetic field in the galaxy. He was a leader in the development of radio astronomy in the United States and in the discovery and interpretation of the quasistellar radio sources, or quasars.

In the 1930s the great variety of stellar spectra was recognized to have been caused by differences in the temperatures and pressures in stellar atmospheres. To a first approximation, all stars seemed to have the same composition, even though certain stars were "peculiar." It was supposed that all chemical elements and isotopes had a common origin at the "beginning" of time; except for hydrogen and helium, this is no longer acceptable.

Greenstein made his first spectroscopic investigations of peculiar stars by searching for stellar-atmosphere effects that might explain anomalous spectra. By 1948 the understanding of nuclear reactions showed how energy sources in stars involved nuclear transmutations. Could effects of fusion reactions be studied as abundance changes at the surfaces of stars? The major source of stellar energy is successive capture of three hydrogen atoms by an initial single proton, producing a helium atom. Are there stars rich in

helium? In still another process, the carbon-nitrogen cycle, ^{12}C captures four successive protons and produces ^{13}C and ^{14}N as well as ^4He. Can stars abnormally rich in ^{13}C or ^{14}N be found? How is ^{13}C synthesized; what is the significance of carbon-rich stars?

In spectroscopic abundance determinations, high resolution is required, and the most interesting stars are often faint. Using the spectrographs at the McDonald Observatory, and later the Mount Wilson and Palomar Observatories (now the Hale Observatories), Greenstein developed the theoretical method of differential-curve-of-growth analysis, permitting comparison of normal stars or the Sun with peculiar stars, that bypassed many difficulties. He initiated a program of spectroscopic data collection that was closely linked with a parallel growth of new ideas in nuclear astrophysics. These studies led to the view that nuclear reactions in stars produced most of the chemical elements and isotopes from hydrogen. The atoms in the Earth were synthesized in many different, long-dead stars. Peculiar evolutionary histories lead to stars rich in helium or carbon. One star was found in which there was more ^3He than ^4He. In the oldest stars, heavy elements are only 1 percent as abundant as in the Sun. Greenstein independently suggested the neutron-producing reaction in red giant stars required for the production of heavier elements. Subsequently, explosive nucleosyntheses during stellar catastrophes have added another source of isotopes requiring proton-addition processes. For this, gravitational collapse is the driving force.

Beginning with his Ph.D. thesis on interstellar dust in 1937, Greenstein studied the nature of the interstellar medium. With Leverett Davis, he developed the idea that space was pervaded by dominantly regular magnetic fields, near 10^{-5} to 10^{-6} gauss, which aligned nonspherical, rapidly spinning, paramagnetic dust grains and produced interstellar polarization of light. The rapid growth of radio astronomy resulted in 1964 in his discovery, with colleagues, of the quasi-stellar radio sources, the most luminous—and enigmatic—objects in the universe. With Maarten Schmidt, he proposed a detailed physical model for their size, mass, temperature, luminosity, magnetic field, and high-energy particle content. The nature of the quasars is still moot, but it is now generally assumed that a massive black hole is present within a galaxy and that gravitational infall is the energy source.

At one extreme of astronomical size and brightness are the white dwarfs, stars no larger than the Earth but nearly as massive as the Sun. Their significance as the final stage of evolution led Greenstein to a series of discoveries concerning their spectra. In collaboration with Olin Eggen, he greatly multiplied the quantitative information on the size, temperature, motion, and composition of these faint objects. By 1978 he had discovered some 500 degenerates and studied their temperatures and radii. He noted the existence of unidentifiable spectral features in stars with intense magnetic fields, as well as the strange dichotomy of their atmospheres. Some are essentially pure hydrogen, others pure helium; in the latter he discovered the nucleosynthetic tracer element carbon. He confirmed the Einstein gravitational red shift by velocity measurements of members of clusters or binary star systems. A major evolutionary problem is raised by the cooling rates of some of these stars, which lack nuclear energy sources. Problems arising from the missing stages of evolution between red giant and white dwarf have led to the first detailed spectroscopy of such stars from space.

The growth of Federal support of astronomy and research in space led Greenstein to a growing involvement with science planning. He headed the study of astronomy in the 1970s for the National Academy of Sciences, producing a committee report which has guided the National Science Foundation and National Aeronautic and Space Administration in major new facility construction. He chaired the board of directors of the Association of Universities for Research in Astronomy (1974–77), which operates the national observatories at Kitt Peak (Arizona) and Cerro Tololo (Chile).

Greenstein studied at Harvard, receiving his A.B. in 1929 and his Ph.D. in 1937. After 2 years as National Research Council fellow, he taught at the University of Chicago, doing research at the Yerkes Observatory, until 1948. During World War II he designed specialized optical instruments, afterward retaining connections with related defense reconnaissance problems and serving on numerous government advisory committees. In 1948 he joined the faculty of the Califor-

nia Institute of Technology, initiating its Graduate School of Astrophysics. He was executive officer for astronomy during 1948–1972 and chairman of the faculty in 1965. In 1948, also, he joined the Mount Wilson and Palomar Observatories. He became the Lee DuBridge Professor of Astrophysics in 1971. He was elected to the National Academy of Sciences in 1957 and the American Philosophical Society; he was awarded the gold medals of the Royal Astronomical Society and the Astronomical Society of the Pacific, and NASA's Distinguished Public Service Medal.

Author of about 350 technical papers, Greenstein edited several books, notably *Stellar Atmospheres* (1960).

For background information *see* Astrophysics; Radio astronomy; Star in the McGraw-Hill Encyclopedia of Science and Technology. ∎

GROSS, LUDWIK
★ American physician and oncologist

Born Sept. 11, 1904, Cracow, Poland

In spite of the early transmission of leukemia in chickens at the turn of the century by V. Ellermann and O. Bang in Copenhagen, all subsequent attempts to transmit leukemia in mice by filtered extracts prepared from leukemic mouse organs failed consistently. As a result, leukemia in mice, and in mammals in general, was considered to be a genetic

disease, unrelated to viruses. However, in 1951 Gross unexpectedly demonstrated for the first time that leukemia in mice is caused by a filterable virus. This demonstration was based on experimental transmission of mouse leukemia by inoculation of filtered extracts prepared from leukemic mouse organs. The success of this experiment was due to the fact that newborn mice of a susceptible, but essentially leukemia-free, inbred line were employed for inoculation. The mouse leukemia virus induced leukemia not only in mice but also in rats, and could be passed serially in both species. Gross also demonstrated that radiation-induced leukemia in mice is caused by a virus which could be isolated from leukemic mouse organs and passed serially in newborn mice. He also showed that the mouse leukemia virus is present in normal healthy embryos of mice of certain inbred lines, such as Ak or C58, which have a high incidence of spontaneous leukemia. Cell-free extracts prepared from such embryos induced leukemia following inoculation into newborn mice.

Prompted by observations of familial occurrence of tumors and leukemia in several animal species and in humans, and also on the basis of results of his experiments on mouse leukemia, Gross suggested, as a working hypothesis, that malignant tumors and leukemia are caused by oncogenic viruses, transmitted from one generation to another. Gross coined the term "vertical transmission" to describe this form of transmission of oncogenic viruses. According to this concept, oncogenic viruses are harmless in most instances, but may become activated by a variety of trigger factors; these activating factors may be internal, of hormonal or metabolic origin, or they may be external, such as carcinogenic chemicals or ionizing radiation. Once activated, the oncogenic viruses become pathogenic and cause the development of tumors or leukemia in their carrier hosts. On the basis of this hypothesis, one could regard the development of tumors or leukemia as a result of an activation, frequently accidental, of a previously latent virus carried by the host since birth. According to this concept, the law of obligate communicability, established for all common communicable diseases, would also apply to viruses causing malignant tumors or leukemias. Each case of cancer or leukemia could thus be traced to another case of neoplastic disease; however, consecutive cases of tumors or leukemia could be separated by one or several generations, making attempts to trace their epidemiology extremely difficult, particularly in hosts having a relatively long life-span.

In the course of experiments on cell-free transmission of mouse leukemia, Gross noticed that some of the leukemic filtrates induced parotid and other salivary gland carcinomas and sarcomas instead of leukemia. He demonstrated that these tumors were caused by a smaller, relatively heat-resistant virus. This virus was later designated polyoma virus by S. E. Stewart and B. Eddy, who observed a considerable increase in the oncogenic potential of this virus following serial passage on mouse embryo cells in tissue culture.

The isolation of the mouse leukemia virus following introduction of the newborn mouse for bioassay experiments, the demonstration of natural transmission of this virus through the embryos, and the unexpected isolation of the polyoma virus stimulated general interest in viral etiology of cancer. These initial observations were soon followed by other investigations in which newborn animals of other species, such as rats, hamsters, and cats, were used for similar bioassay studies. Within the short span of 20 years a variety of tumors and leukemias in several animal species were found to be caused by filterable viruses. Gradually, the concept of viral etiology of cancer and leukemia gained sufficient impetus to represent one of the principal approaches in the research effort directed toward the conquest of neoplastic diseases.

In his experiments on immunization against cancer, carried out on mice of the C3H inbred line with a methylcholanthrene-induced sarcoma, Gross demonstrated that this tumor, consisting of genetically the same cells as those of its host, was uniformly fatal when inoculated subcutaneously. However, when very small doses of tumor cells were inoculated intradermally, they induced intracutaneous tumors which in some animals regressed spontaneously. Mice which recovered from such tumors were immune to reinoculation of the same tumor cells. This experiment demonstrated for the first time that cancer cells have specific antigens which differentiate them from normal cells and can elicit a cancer-destructive immune response. This observation was of fundamental importance in the development of modern studies on cancer immunology.

Gross received his M.D. degree in 1929 at the Iagellon University in Cracow. After internship and residency at the St. Lazar Hospital in Cracow, he worked between 1932 and 1939, (with some interruptions) on experimental cancer immunity at the Pasteur Institute in Paris. In 1940, after the outbreak of the war, he emigrated to the United States, where he continued his studies on cancer immunity at the Institute for Medical Research at the Christ Hospital in Cincinnati until 1943, when he joined the Medical Corps of the U.S. Army. He remained in the Army until 1946. Toward the end of the war he was sent by the Army, as a captain, to the Bronx Veterans Administration Hospital, where he organized a small cancer research laboratory in 1945. At first, this laboratory consisted of only a single room, but Gross was able to expand it gradually into a cancer research unit of which he became the head. Gross served simultaneously as a consultant (1953–1956) and later as an associate scientist (1957–1960) at the Sloan-Kettering Memorial Center in New York City. In 1971 he received an appointment as research professor of medicine at the Mount Sinai School of Medicine of the City University of New York, which is affiliated with the Bronx Veterans Administration Hospital. Gross continued working actively beyond the usual retirement age at the Veterans Administration Hospital as a "distinguished physician." Among the prizes and honors which Gross received were the R. R. de Villiers Foundation (Leukemia Society) Award for Leukemia Research (1953), the Walker Prize of the Royal College of Surgeons of England in London (1961), the Pasteur Silver Medal of the Pasteur Institute in Paris (1962), the World Health Organization United Nations Prize for Cancer Research (1962), the Bertner Foundation Award (1963), the Special Virus Cancer Program Award of the National Cancer Institute (1972), the Albert Lasker Basic Medical Research Award (1974), the principal 1978 Paul Ehrlich–Ludwig Darmstaedter Prize in Frankfurt, and the Griffuel Prize in Paris (1978). In 1973 Gross was elected to the National Academy of Sciences. In recognition of his scientific accomplishments, he received the French Legion of Honor (1977).

Gross published over 200 scientific papers on cancer and leukemia; his monograph *Oncogenic Viruses* (2d ed. 1970) is considered a standard reference book in cancer research laboratories. He also published, in his early years, two books in Po-lish, written for the general public, on medicine and medical discoveries.

For background information *see* ANIMAL VIRUS; LEUKEMIA; ONCOLOGY in the McGraw-Hill Encyclopedia of Science and Technology. ∎

GUILFORD, JOY PAUL
★ American psychologist

Born Mar. 7, 1897, Marquette, NE, U.S.A.

A man of many interests in his general field, Guilford was most productive in the area of psychological measurement. His output was in the form of invention or improvement of methods (psychophysical, scaling, and testing) and of application of those methods to psychological problems. His book *Psychometric Methods* (1936; 2d ed. 1954) brought together and systematized such procedures, including factor analysis, all of which were given basic, quantitative theory.

In psychophysics Guilford proposed a power law to the effect that stimulus changes ΔS, which give equal increments on a psychological variable, are proportional to the nth power of the absolute quantity ϕ on the stimulus variable at which the increment occurs. This relationship was designed to replace the Weber law, which is the special case in which $n = 1.0$. To replace the Fechner logarithmic psychophysical law, relating psychological quantity to physical quantity, he proposed another power law, which states that a measured psychological quantity ψ is proportional to a corresponding physical-stimulus quantity ϕ to some power β. Later, S. S. Stevens demonstrated that this law applies to a number of perceptual variables, the exponent varying to suit the circumstances. The power law of psychophysics thus became known as Stevens' law.

Guilford made a number of novel applications of scaling methods to the measurement of subjective experiences, such as preferences or values, particularly affective values of colors, sounds, odor, and of some of their combinations. He demonstrated the possibility of deriving quantitative relationships between degrees of preference and variables describing appearances of colors (hue, value, and chroma of the Munsell scale) or properties of sounds (pitch, loudness). He proposed a field of "psychodynamics" for this kind of investigation, which was later pursued imaginatively by Gösta Ekman and others in Sweden.

Guilford's greatest contributions, however, were in the field of testing, particularly in connection with intelligence. From his student days he seriously doubted the validity of the doctrine that intelligence is one global ability, a single variable along which individuals differ in a linear fashion. He was also keenly aware of the lack of basic psychological theory needed to support testing operations.

Utilizing the multiple-factor methods developed in the United States by L. L. Thurstone and applied by him in some preliminary investigations, Guilford and others demonstrated additional distinct intellectual abilities. When the number of abilities approached 40, Guilford developed a comprehensive and systematic theory of the intellectual abilities, known as the structure of intellect (SI), which took on a stable form in 1958 and was extended in 1977.

The theory is represented by a three-dimensional, rectangular model with 150 cubic cells, each representing a different ability. One dimension of the model represents five discrete kinds of "operation": cognition (knowing, recognizing, and understanding), memory (committing information to storage), divergent production (generating logical alternatives), convergent production (generating logically necessary conclusions), and evaluation (deciding truth values or relative values of alternatives). A second dimension of the SI model represents five large "content"

categories of information: visual, auditory, symbolic (signs, for example, letters or numbers), semantic ("imageless thoughts"), and behavioral (psychological events, mental states). The third dimension of the model has six kinds of "products": units, classes, relations, systems, transformations, and implications. The six kinds of products constitute a psychologic or an empirically derived logic, with some clear parallels in modern formal logic. Multiplying the five content categories by the six product categories yields 30 basic categories of information, a psychoepistemology, also empirically derived. Any one ability in the SI model is clearly defined by its unique combination of operation, content, and product categories (for example, cognition of semantic systems, which would mean the ability to grasp in thought the organizations or structures).

By analogy to the chemists' periodic table, which led to the discovery of new elements, the SI model has successfully predicted abilities to be demonstrated, and now the number yet to be isolated is in a small minority. Even more significant is the general psychological theory that was deduced from the SI model and its basic concepts. The type of psychology generated is well described as "informational-operational." It conceives of an organism psychologically as a processor of information, by analogy to a modern computer rather than to the behaviorists' oversimplified "touch-and-go," stimulus-response mechanism. Complex psychological activities, such as problem solving and creative production, can now be accounted for in terms of operational models by utilizing SI concepts.

The SI model revealed many aspects of intellectual functioning that are not touched by traditional intelligence scales, large portions of which are devoted to cognition abilities, which essentially tell how well the long-term memory storage is stocked with semantic information. Very seriously neglected had been the productive-thinking and evaluative categories, with little to indicate potential for problem solving and creative performance. SI conceptions are having some impact upon education in its goals, curricula, and teaching and examining procedures. A promoting agency is the International Society for Intelligence Education.

Guilford received his A.B. (1922) and A.M. (1924) at the University of Nebraska and his Ph.D. (1927) at Cornell University. He taught at various universi-

ties—Illinois, Kansas, Nebraska, Northwestern, and Southern California. During World War II he served as aviation psychologist in the Army Air Force, directing various research units, with the terminal rank of colonel; he received the Legion of Merit Award for this work. Other recognitions included the American Psychological Association's Walter V. Bingham Lectureship (1959), Distinguished Scientific Contribution Award (1964), the first Richardson Creativity Award (1966) the Edward Lee Thorndike Award (1975), the Creative Education Founders Award (1970), and the Educational Testing Service Award (1974), besides several honorary degrees. He was elected to the National Academy of Sciences in 1954.

In addition to the book mentioned, Guilford wrote *Fundamental Statistics in Psychology and Education* (1942; 6th ed. 1978), *General Psychology* (1939; 2d ed. 1952), *Personality* (1959), *The Nature of Human Intelligence* (1967), *The Analysis of Intelligence* (1971), *Way beyond the IQ* (1977), and *Cognitive Psychology with a Frame of Reference* (1979).

For background information *see* INTELLIGENCE; PSYCHOLOGY, PHYSIOLOGICAL AND EXPERIMENTAL; PSYCHOPHYSICAL METHODS in the McGraw-Hill Encyclopedia of Science and Technology. ∎

GUILLEMIN, ERNST ADOLPH
★ American electrical engineer

***Born** May 8, 1898, Milwaukee, WI, U.S.A.*

The teaching of electrical engineering subjects, in particular electrical network theory, was of primary interest to Guillemin and led to his research, both theoretical and practical. Early in his teaching career he had a deep interest in the importance of providing students with information of a lasting basic character rather than the currently popular applicational topics, which provided momentary interest but did not enhance the ability to solve new problems by unconventional means. Thus, much of his time and energy was spent in curriculum revision activities, which proved to be an uphill struggle against deeply entrenched conservatism during the decade preceding World War II.

The relatively small group of electrical engineering faculty at the Massachusetts Institute of Technology (MIT) who were interested in bringing about these curric-

ulum revisions were all specializing in communication subjects, including electronic circuit theory. This circumstance was rather natural, since the majority of problems in this area were far from having reached a status of conventionality, and hence they required much basic thinking to provide acceptable solutions. The faculty working in these areas were compelled to use much more flexible methods of attack, so the basic scientific approach was part of their way of life. The advent of the war and the establishment of the Radiation Laboratory at MIT marked the turning point in these efforts. Because of the predominance of conventionality in the training of electrical engineers up to this point, the Radiation Laboratory had to look for the majority of its staff to physicists, both theoretical and experimental, notwithstanding that the task was eminently of an engineering nature.

In the postwar years emphasis on basic science in the engineering curriculum suddenly became popular, and the pendulum swung too far in the opposite direction. Several attempts have been made to settle down at some compromise point, but have been unsuccessful because of a feeling that stagnation must be avoided at all costs. Everything must be changed, whether for better or for worse.

Fortunately in the field of circuit theory the postwar attitude created an opportunity to make some sweeping changes reaching down to the sophomore or "first-course" level. Here it was felt that the treatment of circuit theory should limit its considerations to lumped, linear, passive, and bilateral elements, since these form an essential and indispensable background for the more difficult circuit problems dealing with active, nonbilateral, and nonlinear elements.

Linear circuit theory is linear system theory, regardless of whether that system is electrical, mechanical, acoustical, or a combination of these. Even problems in economics and business procedures, or any others in which the controlling relations are linear, may be included in this broad class. All of the theory of classical dynamics is applicable here, as is the theory of linear algebra and of functions of a complex variable, with its collateral overlap in potential theory and conformal mapping. Last but not least is the pertinence of combinatorial topology, through which the properties of circuits dealing with invariance to changes in geometrical form or topological structure, as well as questions relating to the introduction and transformation of variables, can be studied effectively. Linear system theory, together with the collateral branches of physics and mathematics upon which it rests, is indeed the essential foundation. Without it no engineer can get beyond the conventional tasks which have been learned by rote; with linear system theory an engineer can adapt and devise and thus create methods of solution where none existed before.

The mention of Fourier or Laplace theory in the above summary of linear system theory content is studiously avoided. Fourier representation is a mathematical trick, dealing with the subject of how one constructs arbitrary functions out of sinusoids. The given function emerges as the result of an interference of sinusoidal components, and hence is also referred to as an interference pattern. One can build the same interference pattern out of sinusoids with steady amplitudes, or out of sinusoids with exponentially growing or decaying amplitudes, or out of endless mixtures of these; and there are all sorts of rules as to what can and what cannot be built in this way and what restrictions must be placed upon the mixtures, and so forth. This is Fourier theory. It has no relation to circuit theory, but when Fourier theory is applied to the problem of computing network response, some additional restrictions and rules enter the picture. It is important to be able to distinguish between conditions imposed by Fourier theory and those imposed by circuit theory. In the ususal presentation of this topic, especially in the simplified curriculum presented in an introductory circuits subject, these restrictions become rather confused. The student who does not have a classical background in circuit theory cannot possibly salvage anything useful from such a presentation. Fourier and Laplace theory are tremendously useful aids in the practical application of circuit theory, but their introduction into the curriculum should not come until an adequate understanding of classical network theory has been achieved.

Guillemin's research activities were concerned with a wide variety of network analysis and synthesis problems. Among these was the synthesis of a network for the generation of essentially rectangular pulses for radar applications during World War II. This work was later extended to consider pulses of arbitrary shape. A related problem was the design of a network to produce loran pulses. Here the conventional procedure involved an oscillator to generate the carrier, means for its amplitude modulation, a filter to eliminate interference from the resulting spectrum, and a matching network to adapt the filter output to a given antenna. These four operations were combined into a single pulse-generating network excited by the discharge of a condenser, resulting in greatly increased overall efficiency and reduced size and weight of the total apparatus. These and numerous other problems were solved through formulating an approach aimed as directly as possible at the desired functional result, and avoiding existing conventional approaches, whereever this seemed wise.

Guillemin received his B.S. in electrical engineering from the University of Wisconsin in 1922, his S.M. from MIT in 1924, and his Ph.D. in physics and mathematics from the University of Munich in 1926. He returned to MIT as an instructor in electrical engineering and there spent his entire career, as an assistant professor from 1928 to 1936, associate professor from 1936 to 1944, and full professor thereafter. He was appointed to the Edwin Sibly Webster Chair in 1960 and retired in 1963. In 1948 he was awarded the President's Certificate of Merit for his contributions to the war effort as consultant to the Radiation Laboratory. In 1961 he was awarded the Medal of Honor of the Institute of Radio Engineers, and in

1962 he received the Medal in Electrical Engineering Education from the American Institute of Electrical Engineers. He was a fellow of the Institute of Electrical and Electronic Engineers, the American Academy of Arts and Sciences, and the Royal Society of Arts.

Guillemin wrote *Communication Networks* (2 vols., 1931, 1935), *The Mathematics of Circuit Analysis* (1949), *Introductory Circuit Theory* (1953), *Synthesis of Passive Networks* (1957), and *Theory of Linear Physical Systems* (1963).

For background information *see* CIRCUIT, ELECTRIC; COMMUNICATIONS, ELECTRICAL; ELECTRICAL ENGINEERING; NETWORK THEORY, ELECTRICAL in the McGraw-Hill Encyclopedia of Science and Technology. ∎

GUILLEMIN, ROGER
☆ American endocrinologist

Born Jan. 11, 1924, Dijon, France

Guillemin's research dealt with the hypothalamic hormones that control the secretions of the anterior pituitary gland; the structure and activity of the hypothalamic polypeptide hormones; the design and synthesis of antagonists of the luteinizing-hormone releasing factor as a new approach to fertility control; the isolation of somatostatin, leading to major contributions in the field of diabetes; and the isolation and synthesis of endorphins, possibly a new type of transmitter in the brain. For his work Guillemin was honored in 1977 with the Nobel Prize in medicine and the National Medal of Science, presented by the President of the United States.

Although Guillemin's early medical studies in France were clinically oriented, he developed an interest in endocrinology and hoped someday to work in a laboratory. The way was opened to him when he met Hans Selye, lecturing in Paris on the alarm reaction and the endocrinology of the general adaptation syndrome. A few months later he was working in Selye's newly created Institute of Medicine and Surgery at the University of Montreal. In one year he completed some experimental work on desoxycorticosterone-induced hypertension in bilaterally nephrectomized rats; this constituted his thesis leading to his M.D. degree from Lyon. Spending 3 more years at Selye's institute, Guillemin learned experimental endocrinology in a remarkable program conducted jointly by McGill and Montreal universities.

At the Baylor University College of Medicine in Houston, Guillemin started his research on the physiological mechanisms involved in the control of the secretions of the pituitary gland. Using methods of tissue culture, he showed that the control of the functions of the pituitary gland involved information coming from the hypothalamus of the brain, not in the form of nerve impulses but as some kind of humoral factor(s). In order to charactere these then unknown hypothalamic substances, he realized that enormous quantities of brain tissue had to be made available in view of the infinitesimal amounts of the substances in each brain fragment. Over the following few years he organized the collection of more than 5,000,000 sheep brains and handled in the laboratory more than 45 metric tons of brain tissues.

After 7 years of effort, in 1968, Guillemin and Burgus isolated 1 milligram of the first of the hypothalamic hormones, thyrotropin-releasing factor (TRF), an unusual molecule which regulates the function of the thyroid gland through its effects on the pituitary. TRF was characterized in 1969 by mass spectroscopy. The hormone has been synthesized in large quantities and is now widely used throughout the world in studies and diagnosis of a variety of thyroid diseases.

The following year, at the Salk Institute in San Diego, another hypothalamic factor, luteinizing-hormone releasing factor (LRF), was isolated and synthesized. LRF controls the reproductive functions of both males and females. It is also widely used in clinical medicine dealing with various problems of infertility. The synthesis of special analogs of LRF started at the Salk Institute is leading to a new approach for contraceptive medications.

In 1972 Guillemin and his colleagues isolated and synthesized a third brain factor, somatostatin, which regulates the secretion of growth hormone from the pituitary gland and also of insulin and glucagon from the pancreas. Somatostatin, both in laboratory and clinical studies, has already proved to be of major significance in fundamental studies demonstrating the role of glucagon in juvenile diabetes. Somatostatin, or more likely one of its novel analogs, in conjunction with reduced doses of insulin represents a novel approach to the treatment of juvenile diabetes. Somatostatin has been shown to be made by several types of cells in the body, outside of the brain. It appears to be a key regulatory substance in several physiological systems, from the central nervous system to the gastrointestinal tract and pancreas.

Guillemin also isolated from the hypothalamus and from the hypophysis new peptides called endorphins which acted like opiates in a series of tests. The molecular structures of three endorphins were determined, and compounds synthesized, by Guillemin and his collaborators. Availability of these substances in large quantity, and many analogs, permitted the study of their physiology in the brain as well as of their pharmacological actions. Early results led to the hypothesis that the endorphins may be involved in the etiology of mental illnesses.

Guillemin attended the public schools and lycée in Dijon. He served in the French underground during World War II. Entering medical school in Dijon in 1943, he received the M.D. degree from the school of medicine in Lyon in 1949. He went to Canada for postgraduate work at McGill University and the University of Montreal, where in 1953 he was awarded a Ph.D. degree in physiology and experimental medicine. In that year he moved to the Baylor College of Medicine, where he remained until 1970 (except for a return to France in 1960–63) teaching fundamental endocrinology as a professor of physiology. Then he went to the Salk Institute to establish the Laboratories for Neuroendocrinology.

Guillemin served for 11 years on several advisory groups (Study Sections) of the National Institutes of Health and as a member of the Council of the American Endocrine Society from 1969 to 1973. He was elected a member of the National Academy of Sciences in 1974 and of the American Academy of Arts and Sciences in 1976. In addition to the awards mentioned at the outset, he received many other honors and honorary degrees and delivered a number of memorial lectures.

For background information *see* ENDOCRINE MECHANISMS; PITUITARY GLAND (VERTEBRATE) in the McGraw-Hill Encyclopedia of Science and Technology. ∎

GUTOWSKY, HERBERT SANDER
★ American chemist

Born Nov. 8, 1919, Bridgman, MI, U.S.A.

In 1977 Gutowsky was awarded the National Medal of Science by President Jimmy Carter "in recognition of pioneering studies in the field of nuclear magnetic resonance spectroscopy." On the occasion of his receiving the 1974 Award of the International Society for Magnetic Resonance, it was stated that "today when one examines the vast literature of nuclear magnetic resonance in biology, biochemistry, and chemistry, one finds that Gutowsky was either a co-discoverer or a principal developer of nearly every essential concept employed."

Gutowsky's interest in nuclear magnetic resonance (NMR) began in late 1947 when he was a graduate student studying molecular structure and spectroscopy at Harvard under George Kistiakowsky. At that time there was considerable controversy as to whether the structure of diborane was H_3BBH_3 (like ethane) or $H_2BH_2BH_2$ (like ethylene). Gutowsky's interest in the problem led to a collaborative effort with physicists G. E. Pake and E. M. Purcell to resolve the issue by what is now known as broadline NMR. *See* KISTIAKOWSKY, GEORGE BOGDAN.

Two years earlier Purcell had invented a radio-frequency NMR method for observing changes in the orientation of the proton's magnetic moment with respect to a large magnetic field applied to an ordinary bulk sample. In 1947 Pake was completing a study of the broad doublet absorption line shape of the protons in solid gypsum ($CaSO_4 \cdot 2H_2O$), produced by the direct magnetic interactions between the closely spaced pairs of protons in each water molecule. For diborane, it was thought that these magnetic dipole-dipole interactions might give a line shape for the solid that would differentiate between the two structures.

The broad (approximately 12 gauss or 0.0012 tesla) proton line shape which was found was not readily interpretable, so Gutowsky proposed comparing the proton line shape of diborane with those of ethane (CH_3CH_3) and ethylene ($CH_2 = CH_2$), all in the solid phase at approximately 95 K. The results of this approach supported the ethylene-type structure for diborane. Totally unanticipated, however, was the narrowness of the proton absorption in ethane, which was determined by the inhomogeneities in the applied magnetic field (then approximately 0.5 gauss or 0.0005 tesla).

It was known that dipolar interactions are "averaged out" by the fast translational or rotational motions of atoms in liquids and gases, giving very narrow absorption lines, but this result was unexpected for solids. It was even more surprising to find the same narrow line at approximately 95 K in disilane (SiH_3SiH_3), which melts at 141 K compared with 101 K for ethane. These results led the group to explore in more detail the dependence of the dipolar broadening in solids on the mobility of the ions or molecules composing the solid. Line width and line shape were found to be sensitive indicators of the nature and rates of restricted rotational motions of groups, and were particularly useful in characterizing phase transitions.

After this initiation into NMR, Gutowsky joined the faculty at the University of Illinois at Urbana-Champaign. By the time his first homemade NMR apparatus was in operation there in late 1949, the chemical shift had been discovered. The electrons about a nucleus shield it to varying degrees from a magnetic field, depending on the chemical environment. This gives rise to so-called chemical shifts in the positions of the corresponding resonance lines. The magnitude of the shifts is proportional to the nuclear charge, the range being about 1 part in 10^5 for protons and about 1 percent for lead.

To the physicists, who were interested in nuclear structure and wanted precise magnetic moments to test their theories, the chemical shifts were a nuisance, because it is difficult to correct for them very accurately. However, Gutowsky viewed the complexity of chemical shifts as a challenging opportunity to learn more about molecular structure. First he studied the proton and fluorine shifts in simple liquid binary compound such as H_nM and MF_n and found general correlations between bond type and chemical shift. Fluorine shifts are particularly simple, being proportional to the ionic character of the M-F bond. He improved the apparatus so that it could resolve the small shifts between protons in more complex molecules. With this apparatus, he established a characterization chart for the NMR of protons in a wide range of functional groups. Some overlap was found in chemical shifts, but there was enough spread that resonance positions and intensities could be used to provide ready identification of the structural units containing the protons. A report of this work at a meeting of the American Chemical Society in Chicago in August 1953 encouraged Varian Associates to develop the commercial high-resolution spectrometers that have become so important to chemical research.

In the course of his early chemical shift studies, Gutowsky discovered and characterized a new type of intramolecular magnetic interaction, the indirect spin-spin coupling of nuclei via the bonding electrons. He also found that the splittings produced by this type of interaction were not observed in all cases where they might be expected. He attributed their absence to the effects of chemical exchange, predicting and later verifying that such exchange averaging could be used to measure reaction rates in the 10^{-2} to 10^{-4} per second range, which were too fast for conventional techniques.

Gutowsky graduated with a degree in chemistry from Indiana University in 1940. His graduate studies at Berkeley were interrupted by service in the armed forces from 1941 to 1945. He then returned to Berkeley, completing his M.S. in 1946. He received his Ph.D. from Harvard in 1948. Gutowsky joined the faculty at the University of Illinois in the fall of 1948, where he remained. In 1967 he was made head of the department of chemistry and chemical engineering (now the school of chemical sciences). Gutowsky was elected to the National Academy of Sciences in 1960.

For background information *see* NUCLEAR MAGNETIC RESONANCE (NMR) in the McGraw-Hill Encyclopedia of Science and Technology. ∎

GYORGY, PAUL
American biochemist
and physician

Born Apr. 7, 1893, Nagyoard, Hungary
Died Mar. 1, 1976, Morristown, NJ, U.S.A.

Trained as a biochemist and physician and devoted to human service, Gyorgy became one of the world's foremost scientists. In the record of his research accomplishments, special contributions are recognized in relation to vitamins A and D and their effect on child health; the benefits of breast feeding in infancy; and the multiple nature of the vitamin B group, including biotin, and the isolation of vitamin B_6. The return to breast feeding among many mothers today may be attributed largely to the classical research conducted by Gyorgy and his students.

Gyorgy achieved worldwide recognition in research, particularly in association with R. Kuhn and T. Wagner-Jauregg at the University of Heidelberg. They succeeded in isolating vitamin B_2 and made extensive studies of its occurrence and functions in living organisms, including humans. Additional studies included experimental work with plant life such as yeasts and bacteria, and animals, both rats and cattle.

Parallel with the vitamin studies, there was marked success in research pertaining to protection of infants against infections, by feeding breast milk instead of cows' milk. This concern led to intensive studies of the nutritional characteristics of the respective milk microorganisms.

After several years devoted to research in England, Gyorgy traveled to the United States and settled in Cleveland. During this period he continued his research, including work on nutrients designated initially as vitamins 3, 4, and 5. He also had a major role in isolating and elucidating the functions of vitamin B_6. In 1964 an international symposium on vitamin B_6 was held in Gyorgy's honor.

During a large part of his service at the University of Pennsylvania, where he went in 1944, Gyorgy had a very competent associate in the research laboratory, Catherine Rose, who had good administrative ability in addition to an excellent capacity for research. A former graduate student, R. M. Tomarelli, was helpful in relations with the chemical and pharmaceutical industries.

As a teacher, Gyorgy was highly regarded for his enthusiasm, discipline, and personal interest in his students—an interest which continued through the years as he followed with pride and pleasure the lives of men and women he had trained. He had a phenomenal memory. His knowledge of the literature in his field was the envy of many fellow scientists.

Son of a physician, Gyorgy received the degree of Doctor of Medicine from the University of Budapest in 1915. He then joined Ernest Moro at the University of Heidelberg, working in research and teaching, then later serving as professor of pediatrics (1927–33). In 1933 he was appointed research fellow at Cambridge University. Leaving England in 1935, he became assistant professor of pediatrics at Western Reserve University in Cleveland. He served as associate pediatrician at the University Hospital there (1937–44). Gyorgy joined the faculty of the School of Medicine of the University of Pennsylvania in 1944 as associate research professor, becoming professor of pediatrics in 1946 and emeritus professor of pediatrics in 1958. In addition, he served as chief of pediatrics at Philadelphia General Hospital (1957–63). Among the major scientific societies related to nutrition and pediatrics, Gyorgy was active in those affiliated with the United Nations, particularly UNICEF, WHO, and FAO, and the major national organizations related to child health and nutrition, including the American Institute of Nutrition and the American Medical Association. He served as chairperson of the Executive Committee of the Washington meeting of the International Union of Nutrition Sciences, and continued through his lifetime to serve in the worldwide program of the organization.

Gyorgy was recognized for his contributions by national and international honors. Among them were the Borden Award of both the American Institute of Nutrition (1951) and the American Academy of Pediatrics (1954); the Goldberger Award of the American Medical Society (1957); and the Osborne and Mendel Award of the American Institute of Nutrition (1958). He received an honorary doctorate from the University of Heidelberg (1958); a Paul Gyorgy Fellowship from the American Medical Association (1958); Institute of Nutrition (1958). a Mickle Fellowship from the University of Toronto (1962); a Howland Award from the American Pediatric Society (1968); a Faculty Award from the University of Wisconsin (1972); a Paul Gyorgy Award–LaLeche League International Award (1964); and the National Medal of Science for 1975, presented by President Jimmy Carter to Mrs. Gyorgy on behalf of her deceased husband.

For background information *see* NUTRITION; RIBOFLAVIN; VITAMIN B_6 in the McGraw-Hill Encyclopedia of Science and Technology. ∎